WHERE to SKI
AND Snowboard 2008

Published in Great Britain by
NortonWood Publishing
The Old Forge
Norton St Philip
Bath BA2 7LW
United Kingdom

tel 01373 835208
e-mail w12@wtss.co.uk

Editors Chris Gill and Dave Watts
Assistant editors Mandy Crook,
Wendy-Jane King, Rebecca Miles,
Sheila Reid, Catherine Weakley
Pacific editor Bronwen Gora
Parks/boarding Les Seddon-Brown
Contributors Chris Allan,
Minty Clinch, Alan Coulson,
Nicky Holford, James Hooke,
Eric Jackson, Tim Perry, Ian Porter,
Adam Ruck, Helena Wiesner,
Fraser Wilkin

Advertising managers
Sam Palmer, Dave Ashmore

Design by Val Fox
Production by Guide Editors
Contents photos generally
by Snowpix.com / Chris Gill
Production manager Ian Stratford
Proofreaders Sally Vince,
Robin Campbell
Printed and bound in Italy
by LegoPrint SpA

10 9 8 7 6 5 4 3 2 1

ISBN-10:   0–9536371–9–0
ISBN-13:   978–0–9536371–9–5

A CIP catalogue entry for this book is
available from the British Library.

Book trade sales are handled by
Portfolio Books Ltd
Unit 5, Perivale Industrial Park
Horsenden Lane South
Greenford UB6 7RL
tel 020 8997 9000
fax 020 8997 9097
e-mail sales@portfoliobooks.com

**Individual copies of the book can be
bought by calling: 01373 835208**

**You can buy the book online at
amazon.co.uk by using a link from our
website at www.wtss.co.uk**

This edition published 2007
Copyright (text and illustrations)
© Chris Gill and Dave Watts 2007

The right of Chris Gill and Dave Watts
to be identified as Authors of this
Work has been asserted by them in
accordance with the Copyright,
Design and Patents Act 1988.

WHERE *to* SKI AND Snowboard 2008

The 1,000 Best Winter Sports Resorts in the World

Edited by
Chris Gill
and
Dave Watts

NortonWood

That's just the start of it – here's the heart of it ...

fascinates YOU.

Sartori & Thaler Marketing Services GmbH

Stubai Facts

- Stubai Glacier – Austria's largest glacier area
- Absolutely snow-guaranteed from October until May
- Family-friendly: children under 10 ride the cablecars free of charge
- Child care at Ski Club Micky Maus
- Family hotels
- 2 Flights from London to Innsbruck daily.
- Easily reachable - just 20 minutes transfer from Innsbruck Airport to your hotel
- Winter diversity: 4 ski areas, 147 km of ski runs, 67 km of sledding runs, 130 km of cross country ski trails

Stubai Package

- 7 overnights with breakfast
- 6-day Stubaital Super Ski Pass
- free ski bus in the Stubaital

from **£ 265,00**

Tourist Board Stubai Tyrol
Dorf 3 | 6167 Neustift | Austria
Tel. +43 5018810 | Fax +43 501881-199
info@stubai.at | **www.stubai.at**

Contents 2

Resort chapters

9

About this book

It's simply the best

Where to Ski and Snowboard is the best guide to winter sports resorts that you can buy. Here's why:

- With every new edition we aim to take a step forward. This year, we have **new chapters** on areas in Italy and Switzerland (including an almost unheard of valley with charming, unspoiled resorts and some great slopes), and ten more resort chapters have been upgraded to get enlarged, annotated piste maps.

- By making the most of technology we are able to publish at the right time while going to press very late by conventional book publishing standards – so we can include the late-breaking news that makes the book **up to date for the season ahead**. We were still feeding in news from French resorts in late July. When we started *Where to Ski and Snowboard* in the early 1990s, we went to press in June; this year, it's 2 August, only a month ahead of publication day.

- We work hard to make our information **reader-friendly**, with clearly structured text, comparative ratings and no-nonsense verdicts for the main aspects of each resort.

- We don't hesitate to express **critical views**. We learned our craft at Consumers' Association, where Chris became editor of *Holiday Which?* magazine and Dave became editor of *Which?* itself – so a consumerist attitude comes naturally to us.

- Our resort chapters give an **unrivalled level of detail** – including scale plans of each major resort, so that you get a clear idea of size – and all the facts you need.

- The book benefits enormously from the **hundreds of reports** that readers send in on the resorts they visit. (Every year, the 100 best reports are rewarded by a free copy of the book, and many of our best regular reporters get a free week's lift pass; prove your worth by sending us useful reports, and you too could ski for free.)

- We use **colour printing** fully – we include not only piste maps for every major resort but also scores of photographs, carefully chosen so that you can see for yourself what the resorts are like.

Our ability to keep on investing in *Where to Ski and Snowboard* is largely due to the support of our advertisers – many of whom have been with us since the first edition in 1994. We are grateful for that support, and hope you will in turn support our advertisers. It also helps if you tell them that you saw their ads in these pages: we know from book trade statistics that we outsell rival books by a huge margin, but advertisers can't be reminded of the fact too often.

We are absolutely committed to helping you, our readers, to make an informed choice; and we're confident that you'll find this edition the best yet. Enjoy your skiing and riding this season.

Chris Gill and Dave Watts
Norton St Philip, 2 August 2007

GET YOUR MONEY BACK
when you book a holiday

You can reclaim the price of Where to Ski and Snowboard when you book a winter sports holiday for the 2007/08 or 2008/09 seasons. All you have to do is book the holiday through the specialist ski travel agency Ski Solutions.

Ski Solutions is Britain's original and leading ski travel agency. You can buy whatever kind of holiday you want through them.

Ski Solutions sells the package holidays offered by all the bonded tour operators in Britain (apart from the very few who are direct-sell only). And if that isn't enough choice, they can tailor-make a holiday, based on any form of travel and any kind of accommodation. No one is better placed to find you what you want than Ski Solutions.

Making a claim
Claiming your refund could not be easier. When you make your definite booking, tell Ski Solutions that you want to take up this offer and claim the refund. They will deduct the price of the book from your bill.

Phone Ski Solutions on
020 7471 7700

Get next year's edition free
by reporting on your holiday

There are too many resorts for us to visit them all every year, and too many hotels, bars and mountain restaurants for us to see. So we are very keen to encourage more readers to send in reports on their holiday experiences. As usual, we'll be giving 100 copies of the next edition to the writers of the best reports.

There are five main kinds of feedback we need:

- what you particularly **liked and disliked** about the resort
- what aspects of the resort came as a **surprise** to you
- your suggestions for **other changes to our evaluation** of the resort – changes we should make to the ratings, verdicts, descriptions etc
- your experience of **queues** and other weaknesses in the lift system, and the **ski school** and associated childcare arrangements (take care to name the school)
- your feedback on **individual facilities** in the resort – the hotels, bars, restaurants (including mountain restaurants), nightspots, equipment shops, sports facilities etc.

You can send your reports to us in two main ways. In order of preference, they are:

- by e-mail to: reports@wtss.co.uk (don't forget to give us your postal address)
- word-processed and printed on paper.

We're also aiming to develop better reporting facilities on our website – www.wtss.co.uk.

Consistently helpful reporters are invited to become 'resort observers', which means that when possible we'll arrange free lift passes in your holiday resorts, in exchange for detailed reports on those resorts.

Our postal address is:
Where to Ski and Snowboard, FREEPOST SN815,
The Old Forge, Norton St Philip, Bath BA2 7ZZ

The editorial

The editors have their say

THE SNOW IS GETTING LATER

It wasn't a good year for snow in Europe, let's face it. But the sensational stories in the media about lack of snow didn't paint a true picture. We had the best powder of our whole season in France, in February, despite a pretty thorough sampling of what Canada had to offer. We had excellent piste skiing in France and Switzerland in March, too. Down the page, there's a balanced review of the season.

But the start of the season in the Alps is a problem. If we were booking a ski holiday in Europe, we'd go for March. The snow seems to be arriving later now than it once did; you can no longer be sure of good snow at Christmas and New Year, even in the highest resorts. And the first half of January has been dodgy in parts of the Alps in some recent seasons (including last season). By March, you can hope that snow will accumulate. An example: Zermatt's Triftji-Stockhorn free-ride area never opens early, but last season it didn't open until mid-March.

Last season's poor snow also emphasised the importance of snowmaking – very noticeable in the reports we got from readers. From the Sella Ronda area in Italy: 'Snowmaking is everywhere and highly effective – there had been no real snow for a month but the piste coverage was impressive'; 'nearly 100 per cent of the area was open'. From Grindelwald in Switzerland: 'virtually no snow below 1400m'; 'a long weekend where we did not ski as there was insufficient snow – just a few bare runs were open'.

A LOOK BACK AT THE 2006/07 SEASON

We have again asked our tame snowfall expert, Fraser Wilkin, to review the last season. Here is his report.

Not since the infamous snow droughts of the late 1980s and early 1990s have conditions in the Alps caused such a stir. The winter of 2006/07 will rightly be judged a poor one – it was, after all, one of the warmest winters in living memory – but snow conditions were not as bad as the media suggested, particularly at higher altitudes. Low resorts had a tough time, but it's worth remembering that low Austrian resorts had one of their best ever seasons the previous year.

Autumn was the warmest since records began, and it stayed mild into December, with many resorts struggling over the festive season and into January – again, the warmest since records began. Still, there was enjoyable skiing to be had. Towards the end of January a colder interlude brought some welcome snow, particularly for the southern Alps. February was changeable but mild, with Atlantic storms bringing rain, not snow, to the lower slopes. Many resorts still struggled below 1500m/4,920ft, but conditions improved higher up, and by the end of the month snow depths above 2000m/6,560ft were close to the seasonal average. March continued in much the same vein. April often brings heavy snowfalls, but this year it was the warmest, driest and sunniest on record (just as in Britain). In the whole month, Courchevel recorded just one day of snow.

In North America, fortunes were very mixed. There were below-average falls across much of the southern and south-western Rockies, including Utah. Most of Colorado had an average season overall.

Western Canada enjoyed the best conditions, with early snowfalls at or near record levels in many areas. Warm spells affected the snow, but overall Whistler had 40 per cent more than its average snowfall.

SNOW PART III: MORE GUARANTEES, PLEASE

Most 'snow guarantees' are pretty worthless. Insurance policies, for example, may give you £15 or £20 a day if you are unable to ski because of lack of snow – and that's usually if 80 per cent or 90 per cent of the pistes are closed. Last summer, Crystal operated an eye-catching 50 per cent money back guarantee: for December and January holidays booked before 31 July, closure of more than half your resort's lifts and pistes because of lack of snow will trigger a 50 per cent refund of your money. That's what we call a guarantee.

A RECORD LUNCH?

As regular readers will have deduced, we like good lunches on the mountain; but we are models of abstinence compared with some readers. Keith Wild – a diligent assessor of resort bars and mountain restaurants wherever he goes – reported this year on a meal that set a record for lengthy lunching that we don't expect to beat: 'The food was excellent, view breathtaking and the hospitality and service first-class; on our last day we got there at 1.30pm and left in the dark at 6pm.' Good job it wasn't really a mountain restaurant but a hotel near the foot of the slopes. Well done, Keith – a free copy of this edition is winging its way to you as soon as it comes off the presses. Fellow serious lunchers may wish to note that we've added special 'Editors' choice' recommendations to the 'Mountain restaurants' sections of selected resorts this year.

PERSISTENT PISTE MAP PROBLEMS

The piste map of the SkiWelt – Austria's biggest linked area of lifts and slopes, about 15km/9 miles across – has long been an object of derision in these offices. For large parts of this large area, we have found it literally useless. So our corporate heart leapt when we heard that the SkiWelt was having its map redrawn. We had no doubt the lift company would be breaking the thing down into half a dozen maps showing different sectors in detail. Like the Portes du Soleil and the Trois Vallées, say, or any self-respecting American resort.

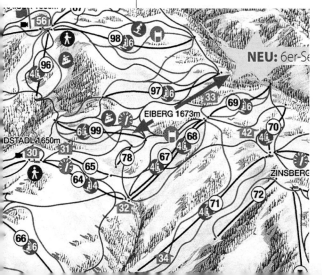

Well, we were being a tad optimistic. The map is hugely improved; you now can, with care, find your way around the areas at the 'back' of the map – the eastern end of the SkiWelt – where in the past you were left floundering. But the one-view-covers-all approach still prevails, and the result is still in parts difficult to use. Our favourite bit is reproduced here. Study it for a while and you will be able to deduce that lift 99 goes up from left to right, and that lift 70 rises as you follow it down the page (despite the symbol on it, which suggests the contrary).

KÄRNTEN carinthia

| Carinthia – Austria's sunny south. |

Ski amadé

Live action in Austria's

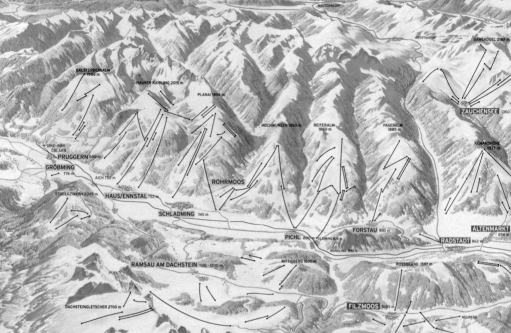

Not only **huge,** but also **hugely attractive**

greatest **ski paradise!**

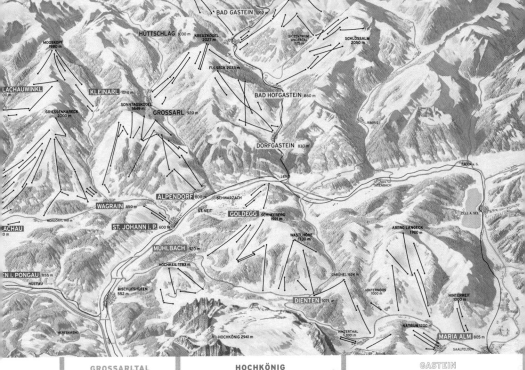

| EBEN | **GROSSARLTAL**
Tel. +43 (0) 6414/281
info@grossarltal.info | **HOCHKÖNIG**
Tel. +43 (0) 6216/2020 2727
region@hochkoenig.at | **GASTEIN**
Tel. +43 (0) 6432/3393-101
amade@gastein.com |

Hugely attractive for …

… everyone who can't get enough of endless slopes, inviting ski chalets, **value-for-money packages** and the unique feeling of live action. Each of the five ski regions in the alliance is fantastic in itself - together they provide the added value so typical of Ski amadé. And with only one ticket you can join in the live action! In no other alpine region will you find such a wide range of facilities within such a small area. And access is so easy – there are **plenty of budget flights into Salzburg,** and **transfer is only an hour** – you'll get to spend more time on the slopes. Information on package deals, snow reports and live cams at:

AUSTRIA'S SKI PARADISE

1 TICKET FOR:

- **860KM OF RUNS**
  (280km blue, 483km red
  and 97km black)

- **270 LIFTS**

- PISTES **UP TO 2,700m**

- **120 PISTE GROOMING MACHINES**

- **75% OF PISTES
  WITH SNOW-MAKING**

www.skiamade.co.uk

Why do these people think that we need to keep in view the slopes above Hopfgarten when we are skiing the slopes of Eiberg, 6km/4 miles away? Our guess is that they think size matters: 'We have a big area – it needs a big map to show just how big it is.' Wrong. It needs lots of little maps to show us how to get around.

A MUCH BETTER PISTE MAP IDEA
At Copper Mountain in Colorado we were delighted to ride a couple of lifts that have a piste map built in to the safety bar – shown at the bottom of the page. This is a great idea, because you can plan your route while travelling, without taking off your gloves and getting your map ruined by snow or wind. Other resorts, please follow suit.

FINDING YOUR WAY
The GPS (Global Positioning System) is entirely miraculous, but one of the minor miracles it involves is the fact that extremely affordable GPS sets can include data on Continental as well as British roads. So they're as useful for getting to your resort as for getting to that business meeting in Gloucester. But there are one or two snags, as we found using a Garmin satnav device in the French Alps last winter.

On many occasions, we found the GPS sending us down narrow lanes we wouldn't have dreamed of tackling without it. We soon learned that it was worth sticking with the route – you'd emerge on to a main road in due course. But on one such occasion the lane got narrower and rougher as we ventured deeper into the forest, and eventually turned into a rough, unsurfaced cart track. We stopped and checked the Michelin atlas, to find that we were way off-piste – the atlas showed the most minor of minor roads coming to an end a couple of kilometres behind us. We decided to carry on, and eventually our cart track joined a proper road – so all was well. But we were left wondering where Garmin gets its data.

More seriously, you need to know that some satnav systems are not aware that mountain passes can be snowbound and closed for the whole winter. We heard of one couple bound for Val d'Isère who followed their satnav directions through the Mont Blanc tunnel into Italy, expecting to turn right at La Thuile to go over the Petit St Bernard pass back into France. Sadly, the road is a piste in winter. They had to head back through the tunnel (which is not cheap) and drive round via Megève and Albertville – arriving in Val many hours later than planned. You have been warned.

CALLED TO THE BAR
It's 6pm on a March evening in Val d'Isère. Three of us have just gathered in the cosily beamed first-floor bar of the hotel Blizzard for a post-shopping drink; we're comfortably installed in low armchairs. I catch the eye of the very efficient waiter who has just deposited a round of beers with the bunch of Swedes happily chatting around the next low table. Within a minute, we're sipping beautifully scented Chignin Bergeron.

Another minute later, I'm wondering: why don't we talk about places like this in *Where to Ski and Snowboard*? I can't explain it; but somehow, dear reader, both we and you have largely overlooked hotel bars

Ski + Spa

In chilean`s mountains white means freedom

when swapping notes. Despite the fact that many grown-ups are happier lounging comfortably in relative peace than fighting for attention at the bar of some throbbing sports cafe-cum-disco.

Obviously, we need to do something about this. You'll find a smattering of hotel bar recommendations in this edition. For the next one, we'd like to hear much more from you on civilised hotel bars where it's possible to converse without shouting and buy drinks without budging from your sofa. Usual address: reports@wtss.co.uk.

TIME TO GET FIT

Your editors have developed diverging attitudes to fitness. Chris remains a firm believer in getting fit for skiing by ... well, by skiing. This works, but only if you take it very gently at first; if you overcook it on day one, as Chris did in Canada last season, you can damage both your thighs and your confidence. Dave, much to Chris's irritation, has decided to become a gym enthusiast, working out two or three times a week from September onwards. Dave is now very tempted by the Skier's Edge training machine, which improves your ski technique as well as your fitness (sounds a good plan, Dave); and it saves time too, as you don't have to travel to the gym to use it if you have one in your spare room or garage.

COLLISION COURSE

We've been warning for years about the danger of pistes becoming more crowded, and the resulting increased danger of collisions. We also detect an increasing tendency for people to ski too fast, and out of control – and readers seem to be reporting more incidents. From the Three Valleys area alone, we had two scary reports this year. One of our regular reporters acquired a complex fracture of the shoulder that needed a major operation when she was knocked over on an almost deserted blue piste by a petite British female in her 40s. Another reporter was standing watching his children when he was taken out by a British lad: 'He was flying, and I didn't know what had hit me; witnesses said he wasn't even looking.' Some North American resorts have 'speed patrols' who slow people down – and confiscate lift passes in extreme cases. Some European resorts have played with that concept. But we'd like to see it become much more widespread.

'The Big Mountain RPM' with slope simulator, demonstrated by Graham Bell

no wonder people keep coming back

- 185 km pistes
- 56 lift facilities
- 36 ski huts and après-ski bars
- Host of the FIS Ski World Cup 05/06.01.2008
- Family-friendly
- Snow secure from December to April with ski mountains up to 8000 ft. in height

- First accredited Alpine Wellness Holiday destination in Switzerland
- 1 hour drive from Berne airport
- Direct flights to Berne airport from Birmingham, London City, London Gatwick, London Stansted, Manchester, Southampton

(subject to schedule changes)

Further information: **www.adelboden.ch**

Adelboden
Frutigen

Adelboden Tourismus, Dorfstrasse 23, 3715 Adelboden, Switzerland
Tel. +41 (0)33 673 80 80, Fax +41 (0)33 673 80 92, info@adelboden.ch

Berner Oberland

AND ANOTHER GOOD IDEA FROM NORTH AMERICA
Sometimes, it seems that all the good ideas come from North American resorts. Take a look at the picture of the information board on the left, taken in Panorama, Canada. It is packed with information on the conditions you are going to find on expert runs in the resort. Brilliant.

NO BARGAIN FOR BEGINNERS
When you start skiing or boarding, you don't need many lifts, and you don't need to ride them many times. (When your editors learned to snowboard, a decade or so ago, we spent two days riding the same slow chair-lift.) So beginners shouldn't expect to pay for a full lift pass. In some resorts, though, it's inescapable. In Ischgl, for example, the nursery slopes are at the mid-mountain lift junction of Idalp, reached by gondolas – and there are no special deals for beginners. So to learn to ski you have to buy a £130 pass. Ridiculous.

At the other extreme, there are lots of resorts where there are nursery slopes at village level served by free lifts. But this is apparently very unusual in Austria: according to its tourist office, Kitzbühel is alone in making all its valley-level beginner lifts free.

All of which we plan to look at more carefully for the next edition, so that beginners will be able to see clearly what costs they face. We know already that it's a bit of a minefield: some 'free' lifts are ones meant for pedestrians rather than beginners, and then you come across weird things like the policy of Les Arcs, which makes some free only at weekends. Reports on this topic welcome.

PHOTO FINISH
Last year we again invited readers to submit resort pictures for publication in the book, and offered 'some sort of prize' for the best. Many thanks to all who sent in contributions. This year the prize goes to David Maxwell-Lees, who has pics published in the Alpbach, Arinsal, Ellmau and Söll chapters, and wins a sailing day on a splendid yacht in the Solent provided by our associated enterprise Yacht Ventures, worth £145. The others with pictures published in this edition are Eddie Baines (Kitzbühel), Ewan Barr (Bad Gastein), Tanya Booth (Vail), Tom Broadbent (Saalbach), Jill Cook (St Anton), Roy Cunningham (Ischgl), Michael Marlais (Lech) and Simon Medley (Davos). If you'd like to see your photos in print, send the best ones to photos@wtss.co.uk. There will again be a prize for the best ones.

OUR ANNUAL AWARDS
Two years back we introduced annual awards to recognise the most important new resort developments. Here are this year's winners.

Best European Resort Development 2007 – St Anton
The gondola that was installed last season to Galzig, with three times the capacity of the cable-car it replaced, has made the morning exit from St Anton a positive pleasure.

Best North American Resort Development 2007 – Revelstoke
This season, the town of Revelstoke in British Columbia becomes a proper ski resort, and if all goes according to plan, within a couple of years it will become the new star of North American skiing. There's more in our introduction to Western Canada on page 664.

WWWhat's up?

What we're planning at www.wtss.co.uk

by **Chris Gill**

Where to Ski has always been internet-savvy. Since 1995, a year after the book's first publication, we've licensed the content for use on websites run by other people – airlines, travel agents, credit card companies, publishers. We've always made full use of the internet to streamline production of the book, shuttling chapters endlessly between the editors, designers and printers in different locations (the printers usually being overseas). These days, the database that underlies both the book content and the production process is hosted remotely, at a mysterious location in southern England, and accessed over the net.

Since 1997 we've had a website of our own, too. We set it up on a shoestring, and for many years invested neither time nor money in it; in the dotcom boom years we had our hands full licensing our stuff to others, and in the years following the dotcom crash we, like everyone else, were extremely cautious about the future of the medium. But a couple of years ago, with broadband internet access at last becoming the norm in British households, we recognised that the time had come to start making serious use of the web, and we had a new site built with various bells and whistles.

Now, we're about to take the next step. This featurette is designed to keep you up to date on our plans. If you haven't visited the site, please do, and let us know what you think. And while you're at it, register for our excellent newsletter, so that we can keep you up to date.

Our current site does a decent job of giving readers several key things you can't get out of the book – an interactive resort shortlist-builder; up-to-date news from resorts and the travel trade; a forum where you can exchange ideas with other readers and with us; and a simple system for posting your own resort reviews and reading those of other site visitors. What we now want to do is develop all of those facilities to state-of-the-art standard, and add others that will make the site an essential port of call. Our current plans are set out over the page.

www.wtss.co.uk – the home page ↓

If you are on our email list, you'll be aware that we also now send out excellent email newsletters trailing news stories on the site, and giving links to other items of current interest – lively exchanges on the forum, for example. The newsletter is free, and signing up to receive it couldn't be easier: there's a button on the home page of the website – click on that, enter your email address and hit the submit button.

WHERE TO SKI AND SNOWBOARD WEBSITE MK III

Here are the features we are working on.

Interactive resort shortlist-builder We'll develop this to cover a broader range of resort characteristics, and a broader range of resorts.

News We think we're doing this fairly well, but we want to add more news from the UK travel trade.

Snow Any serious winter sports site needs snow reports, so we'll be adding them as winter approaches. We're planning on having snow forecast information, too. We're also looking at having a system for readers to file snow reports while they are on holiday in the resorts.

Photographs We have a big archive of informative pictures from past editions that could be helpful to readers, so we'll put them up.

Forum Our existing one is now quite active; but we plan to make it easier and more rewarding to use.

Blogs We aren't natural bloggers, but we see the attraction of having reports posted from resorts when we're checking them out – so we've resolved to keep a constant flow of editorial blogs next winter.

Resort reviews What we're planning here is to make the online review system the main channel for conveying resort reports to us.

Hotel/chalet/restaurant reviews Ideally, we'd like to create a system for these more detailed reviews, too – so that readers can see other readers' reviews of individual restaurants etc.

Resort tips wiki We've had requests for a place to leave tips about particular resorts (lifts to avoid etc); a wiki (a reader-edited, continually growing document) could be the solution.

Reference information We plan to include in the site all the reference information that exists in the book, but with hotlinks where appropriate – so you'll be able to get from our resort pages to the sites of relevant tour operators, hotels, ski schools etc.

Holiday offers We know many of our advertisers are keen to be able to sell through the site, so we'll be adding that facility (including news of last-minute bargains).

LOOKING BACK TO 1997

We launched our first website in our third edition, in 1997. We felt it necessary, at the time, to explain how it all worked – the internet, the web, hyperlinks, email, modems and Internet Service Providers. It all seems a long time ago.

One thing we foresaw in 1997 was that 'the web will become a major channel for carrying out all sorts of transactions – such as booking holidays'.

www.wtss.co.uk – the resort shortlist-builder interface (and, on the right, an early example of our email newsletter) ↓

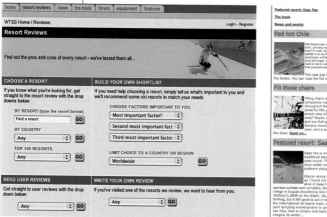

What's new?

New lifts and other major developments in top resorts

In this chapter we summarise major developments in ski resorts last season and those planned for 2007/08. Each major resort chapter has a 'News' panel near the start; you'll find many more news items in those panels. If you want to keep up to date with resort developments in the run-up to the season, go to our website at www.wtss.co.uk and sign up for our email newsletters; you'll also find a constant flow of news on the opening page of the site, and an archive of past items.

ANDORRA

SOLDEU'S FIRST 5-STAR HOTEL
Last season the 5-star Sport Hotel Hermitage opened with a huge new spa. And a new six-pack from the resort cut queues for the gondola.

AUSTRIA

BAD GASTEIN'S NEW RUN
Last season a second gondola was built above Grossarl. For 2007/08 a new red run is planned from Schlossalm to Angertal.

ELLMAU IMPROVEMENT
In 2006/07 the Tanzboden drag-lift below Hartkaiser and Brandstadl was upgraded to a six-pack, improving the connection to Scheffau.

QUICKER LINK TO NORDPARK FROM CENTRAL INNSBRUCK
A new funicular will run this season from the centre of Innsbruck to the cable-car from Hungerburg to Seegrube.

BIGGER, BETTER GONDOLA FOR ISCHGL
For 2007/08 the Fimbabahn gondola is to be upgraded, with heated eight-seat cabins and a total capacity of 2,800 people per hour.

KITZBÜHEL BOTTLENECK REMOVED
An eight-seater chair will replace the old double to Steinbergkogel this season, transforming the Ehrenbachgraben lift bottleneck. Last season a triple here and the Haglalm T-bar at Resterhöhe were replaced by six-packs. Bichlalm has reopened marked ski routes for snowcat-skiing.

MORE AHORN IMPROVEMENTS AT MAYRHOFEN
This year sees the replacement of two T-bars on the Ahorn beginner area by a fast eight-person chair. Access to this sector was transformed in 2006 by a new 160-person cable-car – Austria's biggest.

SERIOUS UPGRADES FOR OBERGURGL
For 2007/08 a two-stage gondola will replace the Gaisberg double chair and the two chairs above it – the double Nederlift and the long single chair to Hohe Mut. A second new gondola will replace the old Schermerspitz double chair at Hochgurgl.

SAALBACH'S IMPROVED LINKS
Last season the link from Schattberg Ost to Schattberg Est became an eight-seat gondola. And there was a new six-pack at Schönleiten.

SCHLADMING LINKS IMPROVED
In 2006/07 a gondola opened at the base of Planai and Hochwurzen, replacing two old chair-lifts linking the two sectors at low level.

SKI SOLUTIONS

Britain's original and largest specialist ski travel agency

- the first and only place you need to call to book your ski holiday

Call SKI SOLUTIONS first, rather than ringing round lots of tour operators - it's an instant short cut to your ideal ski holiday. Start the snowball rolling by giving us a rough idea of what you're looking for:

- *How many in your party?*
- *Are there any children? What ages?*
- *What levels of skier?*
- *Traditional or modern resort?*
- *Which departure airport?*
- *What standard of accommodation?*

Our experienced staff will gently "cross-examine" you to reveal any personal preferences. We will then research a shortlist of suitable holidays and e-mail you with accommodation descriptions, pictures and prices for both hotels and chalets alike.

Or, if you are looking for the ideal chalet for your party, visit our chalet-search service at www.skisolutions.com. Here you will be able to browse through hundreds of chalets in Europe and

North America, compile a shortlist and, if you like, e-mail this to your group. Once you've made your final selection, contact us by e-mail or phone.

We save you time, effort and money by costing each option exactly, taking into account all the various supplements and discounts. (We spend our lives immersed in brochures, so we are experts on the small print.) Without any obligation on your part, we can "hold" the holidays that interest you for a couple of days, while you make up your mind.

After further discussions with you we will then book the holiday of your choice. The price of the holiday will be exactly as in the brochure: our service is absolutely FREE.

Between us, the 25 staff of SKI SOLUTIONS have skied over 100 resorts on both sides of the Atlantic and we have a first-hand up-to-date knowledge of the hotels, chalets and apartments offered by most of the operators in these places.

St Anton's jumbo celebration

Last season, St Anton's 70th, a smart new jumbo gondola replaced the first stage of the queue-prone cable-car to Galzig.

Stubai glacier improvements

T-bars on the glacier will be replaced by a fast six-pack this season.

An eight and a six at Zell am See

For 2007/08 a new eight-person gondola will start next to the cable-car from Schmittental and end at the same place as the gondola up from Schüttdorf, cutting queues to get up the mountain. A new six-pack with covers will replace the Breiteckbahn triple.

FRANCE

Alpe-d'Huez quad

The slow Louvets double chair to Auris-en-Oisans was replaced by a fast quad chair last season.

Key lift replaced at Les Arcs

For 2007/08 a six-pack replaces the slow Plan Bois chair-lift – a key lift on the way from Vallandry to Arc 1800.

Six-packs at Avoriaz

A six-pack will replace the triple Combe du Machon chair to Hauts-Forts this season. Last year a major bottleneck on the way to Châtel was eliminated by the Chaux Fleurie chair becoming a six-pack.

Chondola, quad for La Clusaz

For 2007/08 a new chondola will replace the cable-car in the Etale area, carrying over five times as many people per hour. A quad chair will replace the old double to the top, and new runs back to the village will be built.

Piste-side 4-Star at Courchevel 1650

Courchevel 1650 will get its first 4-star hotel, the Manali, right on the piste, this season.

Platieres relief for Flaine

For 2007/08 a new six-pack will go from the bottom of the resort to the middle of the main slopes above Flaine, relieving pressure on the Platières gondola.

Megeve: six-pack on Mont Joux

A six-pack will replace a slow chair and a drag-lift back towards Mont Joux from the St-Nicolas-de-Véroce direction.

Six-pack at Les Menuires

For 2007/08 a new six-pack is planned, to the top of Roc des 3 Marches. This will replace the old slow Allamands chair, speeding the journey to Méribel and Courchevel.

Meribel's Tougnete upgrade

A six-pack with covers will replace the second stage of the Tougnète gondola this season.

La Plagne drags go

The Charmettes and Bouclet drag-lifts from La Roche to Aime-la-Plagne were replaced by a six-pack in 2006/07.

Puy-St-Vincent's fast chair

A new fast chair-lift will go from the La Balme blue to the Lauzes drag-lifts this season.

What's new?

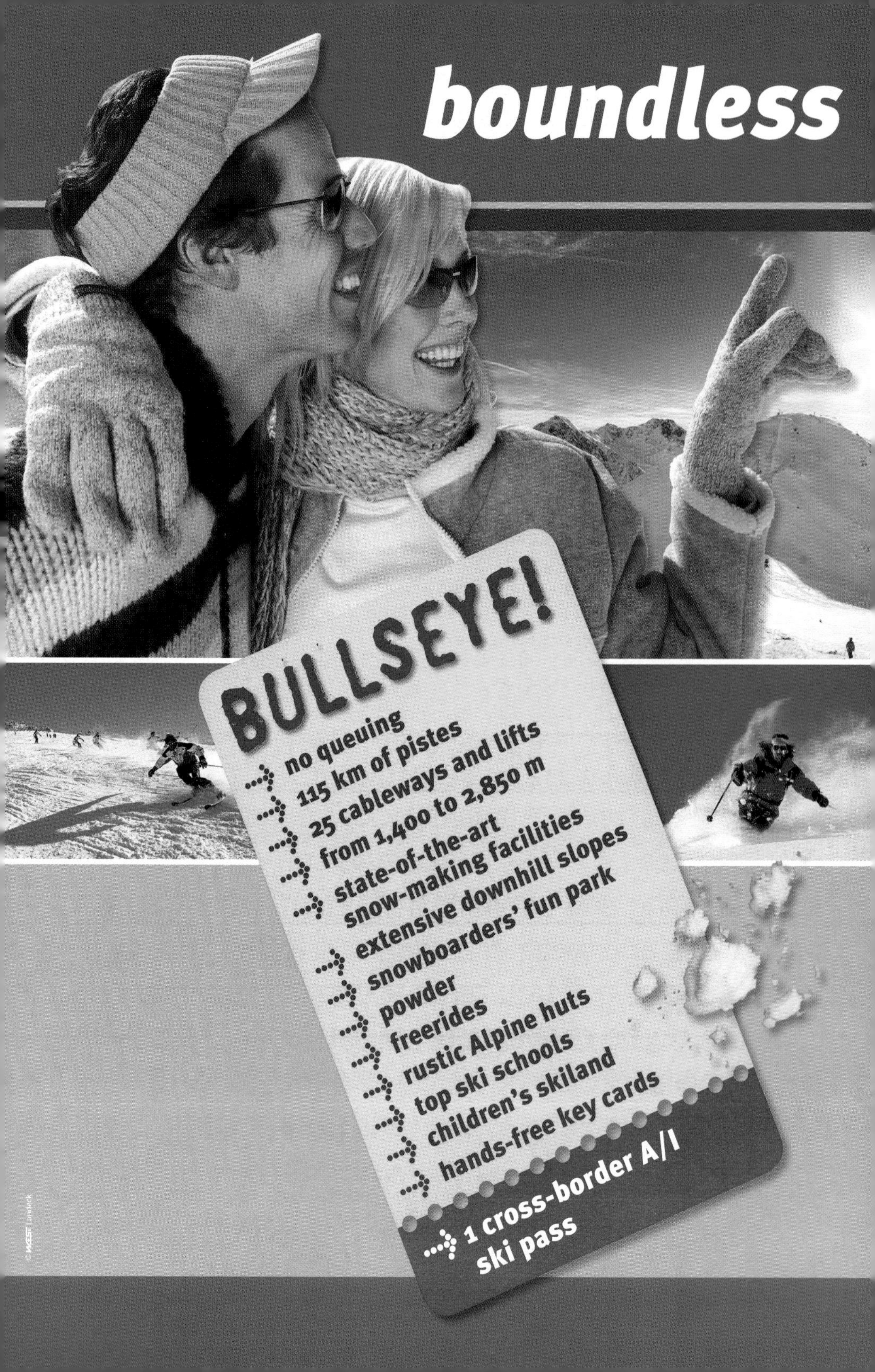
boundless
BULLSEYE!
no queuing
115 km of pistes
25 cableways and lifts
from 1,400 to 2,850 m
state-of-the-art
snow-making facilities
extensive downhill slopes
snowboarders' fun park
powder
freerides
rustic Alpine huts
top ski schools
children's skiland
hands-free key cards
1 cross-border A/I
ski pass
© WEST Landeck

winter

RESCHENPASS

Skiparadies

Fewer drags at Serre-Chevalier

For 2007/08 a new six-pack replaces the Combes 1 and 2 drag-lifts above Chantemerle, but starting much lower down at Serre-Ratier.

Les Sybelles less tricky

In La Toussuire a new six-pack is planned this season to replace a tricky drag-lift from the resort to Tête de Bellard.

Tignes gets a grip

For 2007/08 the Brévières chair-lift up to Les Boisses is to be upgraded to a fixed-grip quad. Last season the two Palafour triple chairs were replaced by a six-pack.

Val d'Isere's fast chair

A new fast chair was built above the Le Fornet cable-car last season.

Valmorel's quad

For 2007/08 the Buffle chair at St-François will become a quad.

New gondolas for Val Thorens

Eight-seat gondolas will replace the Cairn and Caron gondolas (from the resort to the Cîme de Caron cable-car) this season.

Italy

Eight-seater for Bormio

The Isolaccia chair-lift at Valdidentro will be replaced by an eight-seat gondola for 2007/08.

Cervinia: multiple improvements

Five new lifts opened last season: a quad on the nursery slopes, a six-pack up to Plan Torrette and a six-pack and two quads in the Valtournenche sector, speeding up the way back from there.

Courmayeur's better gondolas

Last season there was a new gondola from Dolonne to Plan Checrouit (the gondola there was renovated) and a six-pack replacement for the Pra Neyron chair.

New gondola for Madonna

A new eight-seat gondola is being built this season from the centre of Madonna to the top of the Cinque Laghi area.

Monterosa: less off-piste

The ancient Punta Indren cable-car in Alagna is being taken out of service. Lots of fabulous off-piste will be accessible only by climbing or heli-lifts until its replacement is built from Passo Salati.

Selva/Val Gardena speeds up

The slow double Sole chair above Plan de Gralba will be replaced by a fast quad this season. Last season fast quads replaced the Sotsaslonch drag in the same area and the Sochers lift at Ciampinoi.

Switzerland

Freer movement at Adelboden

For 2007/08 a fast quad with covers is to replace the triple chair from Geils to Lavey, removing a major bottleneck.

Sector links improve at Crans-Montana
Links between the main sectors will be improved by a six-pack to replace the Nationale chair from the mid-station of the Violettes gondola this season, almost doubling the capacity of the existing lift.

Upgrade at Grindelwald's Kleine Scheidegg
For 2007/08 a six-pack will replace the Honegg drag.

St Moritz's revamped 5-Star
The 5-star Carlton Hotel is due to reopen this season in all-suite form, with a new wellness centre.

Verbier: new gondola at La Tzoumaz
For 2007/08 an eight-person gondola is planned to replace the existing one from La Tzoumaz on the back of Savoleyres.

Zermatt retires cable-cars, adds fast quad
This season the old cable-cars from Gornergrat to Hohtälli and from Hohtälli to Stockhorn will be decommissioned and replaced by a T-bar from Triftji to Stockhorn. A fast quad will replace the double chair from Findeln to Sunnegga. A gondola from Furi to Riffelberg, opened last season, means you can go from Klein Matterhorn to other sectors without going through town.

UNITED STATES

CALIFORNIA

Heavenly's Olympic speed
For 2007/08 the slow Olympic chair on the Nevada slopes is due to be upgraded to a fast quad. Six new trails are planned.

Mammoth six-pack
For 2007/08 the 38-year-old Chair 9 will be replaced by a six-pack.

Squaw Valley upgrade
For 2007/08 the Shirley Lake fast quad (the resort's busiest chair-lift) will be replaced by a six-pack.

COLORADO

A-Basin's expansion
A new fixed-grip quad will open in Arapahoe Basin this season, expanding the skiable terrain by 80 per cent and adding 34 runs.

Breckenridge peak access
Last season access to Peak 8 was improved by the opening of the Breckconnect gondola.

Diamonds at Copper Mountain
For 2007/08 a new gladed area – with single- and double-black diamond trails – is planned above the East Village.

Elk Camp developments at Snowmass
A new beginner area with three lifts will open at Elk Camp this season – now reached by an eight-person gondola from Base Village.

Steamboat: six into three will go
The Christie Express six-pack will replace three chairs in the Headwall beginner area at the base for 2007/08.

Fast quads for Two Elk at Vail
For 2007/08 the slow Highline and Sourdough chairs going up towards Two Elk are due to become fast quads.

Winter Park: quicker up to Parsenn Bowl
This season the slow Timberline double, which serves Parsenn Bowl,

is to be replaced by a six-pack, the Panoramic Express, cutting the queues here for the highest lift-served terrain. Last season the Eagle Wind triple was built on the back side of the Bowl.

UTAH

DEER VALLEY'S FAST LADY

For 2007/08 there will be a new fast quad, the Lady Morgan Express, for the Empire Canyon area. A new 200-acre gladed area with eight new runs (ranging from beginner to expert) will be added there.

REST OF THE WEST

DAKOTA TRIPLE FOR BIG SKY

For 2007/08 a triple chair-lift is planned to serve the 212 acres of Dakota Territory, which opened on Lone Mountain last season. This will also access other runs on Lone Mountain's south face, making the tiny cable-car less of a bottleneck.

STOPGAP AT JACKSON HOLE

A temporary double chair-lift, East Ridge, has been installed to access the summit of Rendezvous until a new cable-car is up and running.

CANADA

BIG WHITE GHOST

The Snow Ghost Express, parallel to the Ridge Rocket chair, opened for 2006/07.

STAY UP AT SUN PEAKS

The new fixed-grip Elevation quad chair, opened last season, allows repeated skiing of more runs without returning to the lower slopes.

WHISTLER'S WAIT

Whistler's two mountains are due to be connected by a spectacular gondola, but not until 2008.

FINLAND

GONDOLA FOR YLLAS

At Ylläs, Finland's second gondola (the first is in Levi) is expected to run from the Iso-Ylläs (Ylläsjärvi) base up to Ylläskammi this season.

NORWAY

GEILO IMPROVEMENTS

At Geilo, snowmaking is due to be increased for 2007/08, and the terrain-parks are being upgraded.

HEMSEDAL UPGRADES

A new skier services centre beside the children's area is due for completion in December 2008. Snowmaking is to be increased, along with two more runs and further floodlights for night-skiing.

SWEDEN

SÄLEN'S EIGHT-SEATER

For 2007/08 in the Sälen area a new eight-seat chair will replace a quad and a new blue run will be built.

BULGARIA

BANSKO IMPROVEMENTS

A fast quad will replace the drag-lift below the mid-station this season. The two red runs here will get snowmaking.

Heli-skiing

Fresh tracks, deserted slopes, no lift queues ... bliss!

by **Dave Watts**

With the recent move to wider skis, more and more of us have been getting the taste for off-piste adventure. The ultimate off-piste adventure is to enjoy run after run of virgin powder snow. And that can be achieved by using the ultimate ski lift – a helicopter. You don't have to be an expert to enjoy heli-skiing; big fat skis help you to float through the powder and make the ultimate adventure something a good, fit intermediate skier or rider can experience. There's nothing quite like the feeling at the point when you've been dropped on a remote mountain summit, the chopper has flown away, and you are left – with just your small group – in the silence and majesty of the mountains.

In Europe heli-skiing is severely limited – choppers are banned from dropping skiers at the tops of mountains in France, for example (though strangely, they can pick you up at the end of off-piste runs and bring you home) – and it is not common elsewhere. Areas where we have enjoyed Alpine heli-skiing include Zermatt in Switzerland, the Monterosa region of Italy and La Thuile in Italy – see those chapters for short descriptions of some of the runs. Heli-skiing is also possible in places such as Courmayeur in Italy, Lech in Austria and Verbier in Switzerland. You normally get just one flight and drop, and your guide takes you down one long run, which might take up to a couple of hours. You do it for the splendid isolation of being the only people around as much as for the powder snow.

HEAD FOR CANADA

Western Canada is the world capital of heli-skiing – there are tens of companies offering heli-skiing or heli-boarding by the day or in multi-day packages. Heli-skiing by the day might typically be three drops and runs at a cost of around £350 – maybe with extra runs available at extra cost (£40 each, say). The day starts with a thorough safety briefing and a period practising using an avalanche transceiver – safety equipment and the rental of extra-wide skis specially designed for heli-skiing are normally included in the price. We've had great days out with both RK Heliski (based in Panorama) and Whistler Heli-skiing; and both take a lot of first-time heli-skiers.

Multi-day heli-skiing packages normally include meals and accommodation in a lodge – run by the heli-skiing operation and with facilities such as a sauna, a hot-tub and a massage therapist. This creates a great atmosphere of camaraderie. We've done these packages a few times, most recently last winter with Great Canadian, which has a lodge just 40 minutes from Kicking Horse. It is a personal, small-scale operation, with groups of just four skiers and a guide per helicopter and a maximum of 24 guests in the lodge – compared with 11 skiers, a guide and 44 guests with CMH, a much larger-scale operation that we've also been with. Both experiences were wonderful: being picked up by a chopper from the door of the lodge, whisked into a snowy wilderness and dropped at the top of an isolated peak, with virgin snow everywhere you look, is just amazing. You follow your guide, making your own fresh tracks, for maybe 700m/2,300ft vertical, find the helicopter waiting for you in another isolated spot and get whisked to the top of another run of virgin powder. Typically, you might get 10 to 15 runs in a day and, say, between 4,000m/13,120ft and 10,000m/32,810ft vertical. If it's sunny weather, you're likely to be above the tree line and among the glaciers. If it's snowing, you're likely to be among the trees for better

visibility. It's rare for the weather to be so bad that you can't ski at all. Prices vary between companies and over the season, but you should expect to pay from around £1,200 for a two- or three-day package and from around £3,000 for a week. A guaranteed minimum vertical is included in the price, and extra is typically charged at £40 to £50 per 1,000m/3,280ft (though Great Canadian has no extra charge); you get a rebate if you are not able to do the guaranteed vertical (eg because of weather), and you don't have to ski extra vertical if you choose not to.

Heli-packages are offered by tour operators such as Canadian specialist Frontier Ski and (new for 2007/08) Mark Warner.

DAVE WATTS

← As soon as you finish one run in perfect Canadian powder, you're whisked up to another

Jobs in the mountains

Is it time to do that season on snow you hanker for?

by **Wendy King**

You enjoy the holidays, but they're not enough. You pine for the pistes on your return, drool over the latest snowy webcam shots and are getting to think that maybe it's time to ditch the daily grind back home and seek out the ultimate winter tonic: a season in the mountains. After all, your chalet host and resort rep seemed to be having a wonderful time, so why shouldn't you? Good question.

Every winter, seasonal workers head for ski resorts in Europe and North America expecting to have a great time on the slopes, with a little work thrown in to pay for it. Having persuaded a first-time season-worker to confess all, we have tried to outline answers to some of the questions you might ask.

IS IT ONLY FOR YOUNG SINGLES?
The work generally attracts the 18-35 age group – many are gap-year students. But anyone in a position to take the time out, or willing to rearrange their lives to pursue their dream, can find something suitable. Even if you are in serious employment, you might be able to negotiate a sabbatical. You don't need to go alone either. Some employers seek couples to run their chalets (Silver Ski, for example).

FIRST STEPS?
Start by reflecting on what type of work you enjoy, what specialist skills you possess and where you would like to be based. When on holiday, chat to those already employed in the resort to find out what their jobs involve. Your host/rep may be able to put you in touch with their employer – and working for an outfit you were happy to travel with has a certain logic.

WHAT'S THE TIMETABLE?
Recruitment generally takes place between July and October, though many businesses look for a second intake in November to fill remaining vacancies. Apply early, though, if you want to pick and choose, and have some preparation time. You'll normally head out to the resort in early December. But you don't have to do a full season: some employers need cover during peak weeks, such as school holidays, or when vacancies arise due to staff drop-out, illness or injury. School specialists such as PGL and TOPS have part-time placements for reps and instructors.

WHAT JOBS CAN I DO?
Many vacancies are for chalet hosts or for tour operator resort representatives. But there are other possibilities. Hotels and other resort businesses need staff for administration and reception roles. Most companies need maintenance people. Plongeurs (or 'washers-up' to you and me) usually work late shifts, so often get a lot of time on the mountain, as do bar staff – but you'll need to sleep sometime.

WHERE CAN I WORK?
Matching the type of job you want with where you want to go could be tricky. If you are hoping for chalet work, then the major French

resorts are the obvious starting point. Verbier in Switzerland has chalets galore. But Austrian and North American resorts are generally better suited to hotel, leisure or rep work. In North America one company usually runs the whole resort infrastructure – lifts, ski school, kindergarten, ski shops – so it can be simpler to look for casual work, especially if you plan to head out independently.

TOUR OP OR NOT?

You will need to decide whether you want a 'packaged' job with a tour operator, or to look for a job with a resort business.

Heading out independently means you have to find both accommodation and employment in the resort, and sort out such things as your lift pass and insurance. It is wise to have enough savings to support your adventure should the search end fruitlessly. Some returning seasonnaires like the flexibility it can bring, but for first-timers a tour operator package has clear attractions.

You could apply to tour operators directly. Major companies generally have the most vacancies to fill and will appeal if you aren't fussy over destination or want a broader choice of job. Smaller businesses can offer a more individual and personal approach.

There are also web-based agencies, whose sites are a great source of information and advice. This market has grown rapidly since 2000, when the first ski recruitment site with online CV registration started. Signing up to the database is usually free; although a couple charge a small fee. Some mediate between you and employers.

BUNAC (British Universities North America Club) is an excellent starting point if you fancy the States or Canada, although its scope is considerably wider than that.

WHAT ABOUT QUALIFICATIONS AND TRAINING?

Previous experience and/or relevant qualifications will almost certainly be required in some form. Some posts necessitate a formal qualification: an NNEB certificate to work with children, for example. Instructors must also be certified. There are ways you can obtain the bare necessities, though. Natives, for example, runs a four-day cookery workshop and there are online food hygiene courses.

Even if you don't need or get skills training, there is likely to be training designed to impart company standards in certain areas, whether in hygiene or customer service. Most courses are held just before the season begins.

DO I NEED TO SPEAK THE LINGO?

Foreign language skills are helpful, but essential only for resort reps. Of course, being able to communicate effectively will make settling into resort life easier and help you to establish a better rapport with the locals. If you are hoping to improve your foreign languages, make sure you go to a resort where English doesn't dominate. In a resort like Val d'Isère, there may be more English-speakers than French-speakers.

WHAT WILL I EARN?

You don't take a job in the mountains for the money. Tour operators who are providing your accommodation, season lift pass and insurance are likely to pay £50 to £60 a week (which some employers pay on a monthly basis – if that bothers you, it's best to ask at the interview).

DOES THE DREAM MATCH REALITY?

Seasonal work is tough, but reports suggest 30-40 per cent of workers return for more. You will be expected to juggle early starts and late nights over a six-day week. Key factors in survival seem to be development of a sensible routine, and maintaining the right attitude – keeping your expectations realistic. Go expecting a full-on party and not much work, and you are likely to be disappointed. Go with an open mind, a strong work ethic and the determination to enjoy the experience, and you are likely to end the season planning the next. Mid-season is crunch time, when the novelty is over and there is little scope for rest and play. This period generally sees the highest drop-out rate. For more feedback from those who know, take a look at the Natives website.

Last word goes to our first-timer: 'Better than I thought it would be. Waking up in the mountains and walking to work in knee-deep snow are things I will never forget.'

Jobs in the mountains

41

Gap year courses

How to qualify as a ski or snowboard instructor

by **Rebecca Miles**

Growing numbers of 18-year-olds, career-breakers and even early retirees are going on gap year instructor courses. Many want to become instructors. But many simply want to spend 10 weeks on the slopes and feel they've had a good time and achieved something, as well as improving their skiing or snowboarding by the end of it. We've looked at what's on offer and what it qualifies you to do.

Ski Le Gap was the first company to offer gap year instructor courses to the British in 1994. But now there are lots of course providers and there has been a burst of new companies, particularly since 2002.

Previously it took years to qualify as an instructor, slowly working your way through the levels. Now, if you've got the cash, you can get the first stage in the bag in a season. And there's the catch – courses cost in the region of £6,500. But that's not putting people off.

Last season, around 1,000 Brits took instructor exams as part of a gap course with the British (BASI), Canadian (CSIA) or New Zealand (NZSI) governing bodies, the three most popular for UK gappers. Course directors estimate that between 25 and 50 per cent of their pupils go on to work in the snowsports industry – the rest return to their job, make a career change or go to university. Tom Saxlund, a director of New Generation, said 'Our gappers really like skiing, want to improve and want to devote more time to doing it.' Matt Cooke, New Gen's marketing manager, added, 'We really welcome those who want to make a career of it – it's great for us as we get the pick of the best up-and-coming instructors.'

On most courses, around two-thirds of pupils will be either pre- or immediately post-university; the other third will be made up of late-20s to 60-somethings – taking sabbaticals, giving themselves an early retirement present, or taking the opportunity to change their career, thanks to, say, a redundancy payment. On the gap course run by BASI in Nendaz, Switzerland in 2005/06, for example, there was a 50-year-old doctor taking a sabbatical and a 61-year-old early retiree, alongside four 18-year-olds. One of the 18-year-olds on New Gen's course in Courchevel in 2006/07 plans to make a career out of instructing. Lara Crisp, having not particularly enjoyed school, found it 'a relief to be around like-minded people', and she'd 'never learnt as much nor enjoyed learning as much' as when she was training. She's planning early season race training in November and will then work towards the next BASI level.

Course providers are often very proud to state that there is no maximum age to join their course; as long as you are fit and able, you'll find a place. Youngsters have to wait until they are over 16. And some also offer much shorter courses (eg four weeks), which typically include three weeks of intensive training and the week-long BASI Alpine Instructor level 1 course and exam (see below).

WHAT DO YOU DO AFTERWARDS?
How easy is it to work as an instructor after having done a gap year course? The snowsports instruction industry is a political minefield and, despite valiant efforts by BASI and others to make it possible for Brits to work in, say, France, it's just not that easy.

Thirty-seven countries are members of the International Ski Instructors Association (ISIA), a political body that recognises national qualifications and sets minimum standards that must be met for its members to be accredited. The theory is that if you have an ISIA qualification, then you can teach in any of the ISIA member countries. In practice, this isn't possible because some countries specify further qualifications to reach the top level within their governing body. So, for example, to be a fully qualified ski instructor in France, you do need to pass the notorious speed test.

BASI has a four-level system starting at instructor (two levels) and progressing to ski teacher ISIA and then international ski teacher diploma. If you pass at the end of a 10-week course, you qualify as a BASI Alpine Instructor level 2 (formerly BASI 3). This entitles you to teach in the UK, Canada, USA, Germany, Austria, Italy, Andorra, Spain, eastern Europe, Australia and New Zealand. For some countries you will need a work visa, but in New Zealand, for example, it is fairly easy for a Brit to get a temporary working visa. The 10-week course also includes the BASI Alpine Instructor level 1 (formerly BASI trainee): this is done over the first week, includes first aid and child protection modules, and concludes with an exam. Once you've successfully completed the level 1 course, you can teach on UK dry slopes.

The Canadian system has four levels, 1 being the lowest, 4 the highest. On a gap year course, you could expect to pass level 1 and some people reach level 2. With level 1, you would be able to teach beginners, with level 2, up to blue runs. With a level 1 you can teach in Canada, USA, New Zealand, Australia and South America. To teach in most European countries, you would need to be level 4.

New Zealand also has four stages. On a typical gap year course, you would work towards the first two: the certificate in ski or snowboard instruction (CSI), which allows you to teach advanced beginners, and stage 1, which allows you to teach advanced intermediates. A CSI certificate entitles you to teach in New Zealand; stage 1 broadens your choice to include USA, Canada, Australia, Japan, Andorra, Switzerland, Austria and Italy.

HOW MUCH DOES IT COST?
The average 10-week gap year instructor course is £6,500, which includes full-time tuition (the norm is five days a week), accommodation (the norm is with five or six evening meals a week, but it may be self-catering) and lift pass for the season. Lunches aren't usually included and spending money of around £100 a week is recommended. It's worth checking that all your exam fees and necessary modules are included – with New Gen they are. Gap year courses typically start in January and go through to March.

Smart apartments

The transformation of French self-catering holidays

by **Dave Watts**

Apartment holidays used to be the budget option for most people – shoehorn six people into a studio advertised for six and you'd have a cheap, but not very comfortable time. Now things have changed, particularly in France, home of the cramped apartment: smart apartments are increasingly available where you have room to swing several cats. Some even have comfortable furniture to relax in, and a pool, sauna, steam room and gym to add to the pampering. Sure, the budget option still exists, but now you can have a comfortable apartment holiday with all the other advantages that it brings (see below). For each Alpine resort in the book we've looked for smart apartments to recommend. And on page 46 is a table summarising some of what's on offer and in which resorts.

I've been taking my annual ski holiday with my wife and a couple of friends in apartments ever since 1992. That's because we value the freedom an apartment gives you. You don't have to stick to meal times (and meals) dictated by the hotel or chalet staff; you can slob around in whatever clothes you want; you can go out and come back in whenever you choose. And, crucially, you are free to have a big lunch up the mountain without worrying about having to eat a huge meal – which your chalet staff or hotel will have prepared for you – in the evening; if you lack the appetite for a full meal in the evening, you can buy snacks such as oysters, smoked salmon, paté and local cheeses along with a good bottle of wine or two from the supermarket. If you are hungry, you can go out to a restaurant to eat. Staying in an apartment doesn't mean having to cook big meals or wash up – not for us anyway.

When we started this apartment lark, we couldn't find the sort of thing we were looking for in tour operators' brochures – all the apartments were of the cram-'em-in-and-make-it-cheap variety. So we ended up booking independently, through agents in resorts and direct with apartment owners. But it was hard work doing the research – especially as it was before the internet took off.

Now, at least in France – the country that used to have the smallest, most sordid apartments – a few tour operators (notably those advertising in this chapter) offer some really smart and spacious places. The French smart apartment concept was kick-

ERNA LOW

If you want sofas you can sink into, make this clear to the tour operator before you book ➔

↑ Many of the new smart apartment buildings have pools, hot-tubs, saunas, steam rooms and gyms

ERNA LOW

started by apartments built by or opened in the Montagnettes and MGM names. Now they've been joined by other brands, such as Lagrange Prestige and Intrawest. Many properties constructed by MGM are now operated by other companies, such as CGH.

What can you expect in one of the places we feature in our table? First, you get more space than in your average French apartment – but not as much as you'd get as standard in North America. (Note that we haven't put any Canadian or US apartments in our table because, in our experience, they are nearly all smart.) You still need to check the space is enough to meet your expectations – I reckon an apartment for four adults needs to be at least 50m² – and check whether the number it's advertised for involves anyone sleeping in the living room, in bunk beds or on a mezzanine, which might not suit you. You might also be disappointed by the amount of hanging and storage space, especially for wet ski gear and storing suitcases. Second, you get a modern design with smartish furniture (but we're

Smart apartments

45

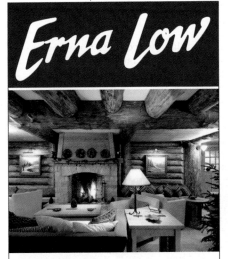

sometimes disappointed by the lack of really comfy sofas and easy chairs you can sink into and relax – often because sofas are designed as sofa beds and are more comfortable to sleep in than sit on). Third, many new smart apartments now include leisure facilities such as a pool, sauna, steam room and gym (but check whether there will be a charge for using these, and if so, how much). Fourth, a lot of them also have comfortable reception areas with comfy furniture and log fires. Personally, we think this is a bit of a waste of space; we'd prefer more space and more comfortable furniture in the living rooms. Fifth, many new apartments come with dishwashers; but separate kitchens are relatively rare – most new places that we've seen have small open-plan kitchen areas forming part of the living room.

You'll gather from the above that these places aren't perfect. We'd prefer to stay in a smart North American condo with loads of space, comfortable furniture and a private hot-tub on your own balcony. But smart apartments in Europe are a vast improvement on what was on offer ten years ago. And if you quiz the tour operator you are booking through, and tell them what you want and don't want, they will point you towards the best places for you – the tour operators advertising in this chapter don't pretend everything is perfect and they don't want dissatisfied clients.

SMART APARTMENTS MENTIONED IN THE CHAPTERS

Alpe-d'Huez	**Oz-en-Oisans:** Chalet des Neiges
Les Arcs	Arc 1950, Chalet des Neiges, Chalet Altitude, Alpages de Chantal
	Peisey-Vallandry: L'Orée des Cimes
Chamonix	Balcons du Savoy, Ginabelle
	Les Houches: Le Hameau de Pierre Blanche
Courchevel	Chalets les Montagnettes, Chalets du Forum
Les Deux-Alpes	Cortina, Alpina Lodge
Flaine	**Les Carroz:** Les Fermes du Soleil
Megève	Chateau & Residence Megève
Les Menuires	Residence Montalys, Chalets les Montagnettes, Les Alpages, Chalets du Soleil, Les Chalets de l'Adonis
Méribel	Les Fermes de Méribel
Morzine	L'Aiglon
La Plagne	Chalets les Montagnettes, Les Hauts Bois, Pelvoux, Les Granges du Soleil
	Montalbert: Chalets de Montalbert, Les Granges
	Les Coches: Les Chalets de Wengen
	Champagny-en-Vanoise: Les Alpages de Champagny
Puy-St-Vincent	Gentianes
La Rosière	Cîmes Blanche, Balcons
Samoëns	Fermes de Samoëns, Chalet la Ferme des Fontany
Serre-Chevalier	Hameau du Rocher Blanche
Ste-Foy-Tarentaise	See resort chapter, page 380
St-Martin	Les Chalets du Gypse, Les Chalets de St-Martin
Les Sybelles	**La Toussuire:** Les Hauts de Comborciere
Tignes	L'Ecrin des Neiges, Residence Village Montana, Ferme du Val-Claret, Chalets d'Hercule
	Tignes-Les-Brévières: Le Belvedere
Val d'Isère	Chalets du Jardin Alpin, Chalets du Laisinant
Val Thorens	Too many to list – see resort chapter, page 422

Luxury chalets

The ultimate ski holiday?

by **Chris Gill**

The catered chalet concept (explained for the benefit of newcomers in the panel below) goes from strength to strength, with ever-expanding programmes from the established operators and ever-increasing numbers of competitors. So, not surprisingly, in compiling this annual review of the top of the market – chalets that rival good hotels for comfort and quality of cuisine – we've found more choice than ever: more companies offering more chalets in more resorts. But there is no immediate threat to the ruling trio of Méribel·and Val d'Isère in France, and Verbier in Switzerland.

You can find isolated luxury chalets in all sorts of places, from Austria to Aspen, but the breed in general is still not widespread: most are concentrated in the more upmarket French mega-resorts. We have for years harboured plans to run a website to help you find chalets to meet your needs, but haven't found the time. Meanwhile, of course, quite a few effective sites have been set up by travel agents; those run by Alpine Answers (www.alpineanswers.co.uk/chalets) and Ski Solutions (www.skisolutions.com/chalets) are the most valuable ones I've found.

The greatest concentration is found in **Méribel**. Long-time local specialist Meriski, more than any other operator, illustrates the transformation of the chalet business over the last two decades. In the 1980s it was a run-of-the-mill operation, but then it successfully repositioned itself upmarket. It hasn't all been plain sailing for the company, which has changed hands a couple of times recently, but it still has a wide range of impressively comfortable chalets.

Descent International now has an enviable portfolio of properties in the secluded Brames area of the resort, including the famously luxurious chalet Brames, with a two-storey living room and a glorious view up the valley towards Mont Vallon.

THE EVOLUTION OF THE CHALET HOLIDAY

The catered chalet holiday is a uniquely British idea. Tour operators install their own cooks and housekeepers in private chalets that they take over for the season. They package accommodation in these chalets with travel from the UK, normally offering half-board. Dinner is a no-choice affair at a communal table, including wine unlimited in quantity but often severely limited in quality. You can either book a whole chalet (the smallest typically sleep six or eight) or book space in a larger chalet that you share with whoever else turns up.

In the early days of the chalet, in the 1960s and 1970s, the catered chalet business didn't do luxury. Taking a chalet holiday meant roughing it in creaky old buildings, putting up with spartan furniture and paper-thin walls, and with six or more people sharing a bathroom. And the chalet girl – always a girl, back then – was often straight out of college or finishing school, and more intent on having a fun season on the slopes than preparing gourmet meals.

It was only in the late 1980s that one or two companies realised that people would pay a lot more for comfortable and stylish accommodation, good food and wine, and a little bit of personal service – just enough to make the customer feel the staff are there to do something other than have a good time. The new formula worked, probably better than anyone would have expected.

Luxury chalets

Purple Ski has impressive places in every part of the resort, including the lovely Iamato in Village and the piste-side Kouneli, being revamped this summer. Several of Total's properties here deserve to be included in the luxury category, particularly chalet Phoebe. Ski Olympic takes a big step into the luxury market this year with the acquisition of the 24-bed Parc Alpin, formerly run as a boutique hotel. Alpine Action has five smart-looking chalets, most with saunas and hot-tubs; best is the well-positioned 14-bed chalet de Launey. Crystal Finest has two properties here, including the contemporary-style Neige with outdoor hot-tub.

VIP has eight impressive chalets, including Indiana Lodge – right on the slopes, with great views over the resort – and Kublai Lodge – with Indonesian artefacts, steam room, gym and cinema. Flexiski now has the 10-bed Leonardo, down near Dick's Tea Bar.

A degree of luxury can be combined with economy by staying down the hill in Les Allues (on the gondola up from Brides-les-Bains). Ski Blanc has six properties here, including the 16-bed Vieille Scierie, with hot-tub.

Courchevel is well established as the smartest resort in France, and now has a growing number of smart chalets on the UK package market. The resort is at the heart of the Supertravel programme; it has 11 desirable properties here – some apartments but some proper chalets including the firm's 'flagship' Montana. Kaluma has two swanky properties. Flexiski has the cute little eight-bed chalet Chinchilla in the exclusive Hameau du Cospillot. The 10-bed Hermine, nearby, is now in the Descent portfolio. Scott Dunn Ski's properties include one of its two 'flagship' chalets, Aurea – complete with dinky swimming pool. Crystal Finest has four chalets or catered apartments here, plus a chalet-hotel. New this year in 1850 is the central, piste-side apartment chalet Nano. Total's portfolio includes some smart, modern places up in the Jardin Alpin area. In 1650, Le Ski's range continues to slide upmarket with six new properties this year, all with hot-tub.

La Tania, not far away on the road towards Méribel, has developed quite a range of comfortable chalet properties, including the best of the Ski Amis range, the 14-bed Balkiss. Ski Power and Le Ski have some neat-looking properties with en suite bedrooms and the usual trimmings here.

Curiously, **Val Thorens** doesn't have much to offer in the way of chalets, but Total has had a neat one built, offered in two units with 12 and 18 beds.

Val d'Isère is the great rival to Méribel in the French chalet business. The local specialist, YSE, doesn't operate at the very top of the market, but the company's ancient Mountain Lodges are old favourites, offering no picture windows but atmospheric and comfortable living rooms, with stone walls and ample leather sofas. The newly built Chalet des Pistes is their top 'real' chalet, part of a small cluster in a great on-slope location at La Daille. Scott Dunn's impressive portfolio here is dominated by the 12-bed Eagle's Nest – an extraordinary place, with an indoor jet-stream pool.

The grand enclave of four modern chalets at the southern extremity of the resort – Bergerie, Mistral, Lafitenia and Le Chardon – have passed into the hands of Le Chardon Mountain Lodges. Descent's portfolio now includes the chalet du Crêt, a renovated farmhouse well known to many Brits in its previous incarnation as a restaurant. Not far away in Le Crêt are two very attractive places

recently added to the Le Ski programme – La Bouclia and La Pierre de Complia.

VIP has some very smart places, including 12 spacious, stylish chalet-apartments in Aspen Lodge on the main street – a novel concept in chalets, with a reception desk, lounge area and coffee bar. Their 200-year-old Farmhouse, by the church, is something else – a beautifully converted, er, farmhouse. Sister company Snowline has several properties, though the best are apartments. Crystal Finest's programme includes a smart, central recent development of three chalet units, sharing a lower-ground-floor wellness area. Total has several properties, including smart ones out in Le Legettaz.

Luxury places in next-door **Tignes** are thin on the ground. Total has some of the best properties here, including some striking modern places with pool and outdoor hot-tub. Crystal has a modern chalet in a slope-side position, divided into two units, Emile and Isabella.

The other great French mega-area, Paradiski, offers lots of chalets in **La Plagne** and growing numbers at **Peisey-Vallandry**, on the Les Arcs side of the cable-car link from La Plagne. Few deserve a mention here; start with the Ski Amis and Ski Beat brochures.

The small-but-growing resort of **Ste-Foy** contains a growing selection of luxury places offered by Gite de Sainte Foy and Première Neige, which has now added the revamped chalet Yellowstone to its impressive chalets Emma and Bouquetin.

Chamonix isn't known for luxury chalets, but Flexiski has a gem in the wood-built eight-bed chalet Bornian, with a particularly welcoming beamed living room. It's a walk out of town, but enjoys great views. Locally based Collineige has secured an enviable range of very individual properties. Total has the very civilised chalet Blaitère.

Morzine is known mainly for cheap-and-cheerful properties, but Snowline has an impressive cluster of 'town house' properties right in the centre. Up at **Les Gets,** seductively converted farmhouses are not hard to find. Descent has the Ferme de Moudon, as seen on Channel 4's programme *Grand Designs Abroad*: a chic interior in a 17th-century chalet. There is the Ferme de Montagne – a beautifully renovated old chalet with eight rooms, with wood and stone everywhere. It operates as a small hotel rather than a tour-operator-managed catered chalet, with lots of services and great attention to detail. Total has the impressive-looking Ferme du Lavay, among others.

In Switzerland, **Verbier** is the chalet capital, and Ski Verbier's portfolio includes several glorious properties. This year the firm has added the swanky Septième Ciel – high on the Savoleyres side of the resort – at the top of its range alongside the recently built Attelas, Sorojasa and Cheyenne. Ski Verbier also has more modest places including several apartments for smaller parties. Crystal Finest has three properties here, including the very stylish top-floor Sophia. Descent still has the absolutely central and very impressive chalet Goodwood.

Zermatt, curiously, has never been a great chalet resort. Scott Dunn has long been the main source, but its offerings are all in apartments. I'm not convinced about the antique furnishings of Descent's chalet Zen, but its facilities and position are excellent. VIP now has two apartment-based chalets here – the very central Haus Glacier and radically modern Haus Bor.

Total's handful of properties here includes the Génépy, stylishly created within a lovely old wooden building. The firm is having two smart new little chalets built for the coming season – apparently with Matterhorn views. Crystal Finest has two apartments here; one is Victoria, a hip designer penthouse up in the Hof area, reached by elevator through the rock.

Elsewhere in Switzerland, Descent's chalet Eugenia in **Klosters** is a fabulous place – even the bathrooms are remarkable. Possibly even more remarkable is the company's palatial Chesa Albertini in hotel-dominated **St Moritz** – 'more a mansion than a chalet', as they say, and with 1000m^2 of floor space they are not exaggerating.

In Austria, luxury chalets are curiously rare. In **St Anton**, Flexiski's absolutely central Amalien Haus got a bit of a makeover in 2006, with slick new bathrooms – and the public areas are now much more inviting. Descent is adding the dramatically modern chalet Katharina, and Kaluma will be offering the new chalet Montfort this season. Supertravel has the minimalist Chiara, plus several more traditional places. Scott Dunn is adding four units in the same building this year, all done up in modern style. Crystal Finest has four properties in its programme, ranging from an apartment for 8 to the modern Tirolerhaus for about 30. Total has properties both here and over the hill in **Lech**.

Luxury chalets

51

Luxury hotels

For the perfect indulgent break – and more

by **Chris Gill** | **Our chapters on luxury catered chalets and luxury apartments came about for the same sort of reason: in each case, we wanted to draw attention to a new, improved breed of accommodation. Chalets improved hugely in quality in the late 1980s. Self-catering in France took a similarly major step up in the 1990s. No such spur has led to the introduction of this chapter: luxury hotels are nothing new. If there is a trigger to the addition of this chapter it is that short holidays are on the increase – and for short holidays, hotels are the obvious form of accommodation.**

For many of us, of course, hotels are also the ultimate form of luxury. They may not offer the privacy of your own chalet or apartment, but in other respects – service, food, facilities – they take some beating.

No one who has an appetite for luxurious ski hotels (and an inclination towards letting a tour operator make the arrangements) should fail to get hold of a copy of the Inghams Ski Luxury brochure, containing scores of difficult-to-resist places in North America and the Alps (plus the unprecedented Kempinski Grand Arena in Bansko, Bulgaria). Of course, it's not a definitive guide – Inghams wouldn't pretend it is – but it contains many excellent spots.

If you like to be guided by star ratings when comparing hotels, remember that the French don't do five stars, but top off their range with the 4-star luxe category.

PERSONAL FAVOURITES

I'm sure I'm not alone in finding that luxury all too often goes hand in hand with formality – which results in places that instead of being deeply welcoming are actually a bit impersonal. Happily, there are plenty of places that avoid this trap.

Interestingly, many of them are in Italy. One of my favourites is the Rosa Alpina, in San Cassiano, just off the Sella Ronda circuit in the Dolomites – a great combination of relaxed ambience, well-furnished rooms and superb food (it now has two Michelin stars for its serious restaurant). Not far away is the similarly welcoming Fanes. At the other (western) end of the Italian mountains, in the Monterosa area, the Breithorn is a beautifully furnished, welcoming place – all wooden beams and panelling – with a choice of excellent restaurants, formal and less formal. All of these places are represented by the UK operator Ski 2.

There are some resorts where luxury hotels are virtually the norm. Switzerland, in many eyes the spiritual home of the luxury hotel, boasts astonishing concentrations of 4-star and 5-star places in some resorts. For me, you can keep the glitz of St Moritz. I'll settle for the Alpina in Klosters, the exceptionally welcoming Ferienart in Saas Fee, and the peaceful Chalet d'Adrien in Verbier. Of course, you can't ignore Zermatt; but I'm not wowed by its hotels, with the exception of the impeccable Riffelalp, isolated halfway up the mountain (with evening trains so that you can dine and dance in the village).

In Austria, luxury generally comes with a softening rustic edge. Lech and neighbouring Zürs are the leaders. They offer an exceptional six 5-star places – the Almhof Schneider, Arlberg and

Post in Lech, and the Lorunser, Thurnhers Alpenhof and Zürserhof in Zürs (recommended by Mr Editor Watts). There is a particularly handsome range of 4-star options, some of which advertise in our Lech chapter (Zürs is covered in the Lech chapter). St Anton, over the hill, does not offer the same range of swanky places, but again we have a couple of impressive 4-star advertisers. Other Austrian favourites include the Bär above Ellmau and the Central in Sölden – not only central but clearly the best in town.

In France, Courchevel has lots of extremely swanky places, including some of the most expensive in the Alps. Most leave me cold, but I like the Mélézin and Bellecôte – and the Chabichou has the attraction of a famous restaurant. Megève, where the old money still goes, excels in the rustic chic that seems to elude Courchevel – places like the Chalet du Mont d'Arbois, Fer à Cheval and Ferme Hôtel Duvillard come close to perfection. In Méribel, the Grand-Coeur and Altiport vie for editorial affections. In Val d'Isère the Barmes de l'Ours is very compelling, with skiing more or less from the door, although the more central Christiania and Blizzard have attractions. In Val Thorens my favourite is the Fitz Roy, which has an excellent central position on the snow.

Not surprisingly, North America has its share of deeply comfortable lodgings. In Aspen, I'll take the Little Nell or the historic Jerome. At Deer Valley in Utah, Stein Eriksen Lodge is the place to go. It's tempting to avoid chains, but they sometimes deliver. The new Four Seasons in Jackson Hole takes some beating for careful design location and excellent service. In Whistler, the Fairmont Chateau Whistler has the edge – whereas at Lake Louise another Chateau has to take second place to the perfectly relaxing Post hotel.

Family holidays

by **Chris Gill**

Regular readers will know that my personal stock of fresh things to tell you about family winter sports holidays has dwindled as the junior Gills have drifted towards adulthood. When I can, I find someone else to provide the insights. This year, I had a cunning plan based on student poverty. I reckoned that by mid-July, elder child Alex, 19, completing his first year at uni, would be approaching destitution and therefore desperate to earn a few bob. He would obviously be prepared to knock out 2,000 words of reflection on his experiences of family skiing holidays with me, Val (his mum) and Laura (his kid sister). Sadly, I was wrong. At the vital time in the book's production process I stumbled to the breakfast table to find a scribbled note: 'Just popped out to Cornwall with Miles, Anna & co. See you Friday. Love, Alex.' Ah, well; at least he's doing something energetic. (Surfing, that is.) So it's all down to me, as usual.

Actually, it didn't take me long to come up with another cunning plan. You've had the benefit of my advice on family holidays in eight past editions, the advice of daughter Laura once and the advice of other readers once. This year, the advice comes from the coalface: the tour operators who take hundreds, even thousands of British families to the Alps every year. (Incidentally, if all goes according to plan, all ten of those previous family features will be made available on our website over the coming months.)

I put some standard questions to some of our friends in the business, and I've attempted to make some sense out of their responses. Sorry, let me put that another way: I've woven their answers together in a crystal-clear guide to success on family ski holidays. Before I go any further, I should explain that I put this chapter together in the height of summer when many people in the ski business were away on holiday – including my contacts at Esprit Holidays and Mark Warner, the two firms with which the Gill family travelled most often when the little ones were little. Maybe they and other industry experts will be persuaded to have their say on our website, come the autumn.

The advice that follows comes from Lisa Dance of Family Ski Company, Prue Johnson of Crystal and Christine van Zadelhoff of Ski Amis. I asked them for guidance on choosing your resort and choosing your accommodation, and for advice on other keys to success in organising a family holiday. And I asked them to think about children of different ages.

CHOOSING A RESORT

The first thing I've learned – a bit late in the day, you may say – is that with babies on board you have to think about altitude. 'Infants almost invariably have some difficulty with high resorts in terms of altitude sickness in various degrees, and a lower resort will be much easier for infants to adapt to,' says Christine. Lisa agrees, but points out that you don't have to ski at low altitude to sleep at low altitude: 'Reberty is at 2000m/6,560ft, and we don't recommend it for children under one year old. But lowish villages such as Ardent or Les Coches have access to high slopes.'

With altitude taken care of, the next thing you need to focus on, not surprisingly, is childcare arrangements. 'If parents want to ski together on holiday then they will need to choose a resort that offers childcare for their infants/toddlers,' says Prue – reminding us, in the process, that parents could, instead, share parenting responsibilities and ski only part of the time. I realise this may be a bit unrealistic; when we took our tinies to the Alps even my wife Val, the world's least enthusiastic skier, was mysteriously keen to spend her days on the slopes rather than back at the chalet. Strange.

So what should you look for in childcare? Christine suggests you look for 'crèche facilities with a range of activities – imaginative activity programmes to introduce the children to snow – and, of course, English-speaking carers'. Given the extensive childcare operations their firms offer, it's not surprising that Lisa and Prue see the role of the tour operator as central here. 'Operators like Crystal offer a large number of resorts with their own crèches and children's clubs,' says Prue, 'run by experienced, qualified and CRB-checked staff and run to strict adult-child ratios.'

As children get slightly older, other aspects of the resort start to come into play. 'For older toddlers,' says Christine, 'look for specially designed snow-garden areas where they can safely be introduced to skiing.'

For a family with children of school age, or at least pre-school age, the focus moves from crèche arrangements to the ski school. As the children become more mobile, Lisa suggests you look for 'small family-friendly villages with easy access to ski school'. And the ski school itself is important. 'For a start,' says Prue, 'establish the minimum age for tuition – in some resorts child tuition doesn't start until the age of seven or even higher, but in others children can ski from as young as three.' Then, do they offer half-day or full-day tuition? 'If half-day,' says Prue, 'you may need a childcare facility (with your tour operator, the ski school or a resort facility) for the other half of the day if your child isn't of the ability to free ski with you.' Prue has a list of questions

for you to check off: 'Does the ski school offer lunchtime supervision or will you have to collect your child for lunch each day? Do the adult and child ski school times match up? Do they offer an indoor facility for young children who may need time inside to warm up or play and have a break from skiing during their lesson?'

CHOOSING ACCOMMODATION

Both Lisa and Christine emphasise the merits of sharing a chalet with other families, especially when taking babies. 'Accommodation designed for families is likely to have other like-minded people with children,' says Christine, 'and the childcare burden can be shared without any hassle from other guests if an infant is difficult.'

Lisa stresses: 'Chalets give flexibility and a homely feel, and are usually safe and secure. Hotels can be rather impersonal, with dining rooms often a long way from bedrooms – so it can be difficult to listen out for children.' Prue points out that the facilities provided for infants/toddlers can vary. 'Do they provide cots (and will a cot fit in the room available)? Do they provide baby kits with bottle warmers, sterilisers, potties, changing mats, high chairs, etc? If so, you don't have to take so much with you.'

For school-age children, who will be trooping off to the ski school and ski lifts in the morning, proximity to those facilities becomes paramount. Prue paints a vivid picture: 'As soon as you make that first walk, in ski boots, with children in ski boots, carrying skis, sticks, gloves, helmets, goggles, etc for everyone, you'll appreciate the wisdom of choosing accommodation that is only a couple of minutes' walk (rather than a long walk or ski-bus-ride) from the ski school meeting point. If the meeting point is also close to the main

ski lifts, you can all make the most of each day on the piste.' Another option is to choose accommodation that offers a shuttle-bus service (rather than public ski-bus) to the ski school meeting point and main lifts.

KEY ADVICE

Those issues apart, what key advice did my experts have to offer? 'If you can, take the grandparents with you,' says Christine. 'The infant is familiar with them and unlikely to be disrupted.' And if using resort childcare facilities, she says: 'Introduce the child to foreign accents before the holiday.'

Lisa rightly makes the point that it's your holiday too, and that you shouldn't lose sight of what you want out of the resort and your accommodation. 'Of course you want to know that your children will be well looked after,' she says, 'but you don't have to miss out on top-notch skiing.'

Prue has some advice on judging what you should expect of your child. 'If taking your child skiing or snowboarding for the first time, think first about your child's character. One four-year-old may love to join ski school, make new friends and spend the whole day falling about in the snow. Another may hate it and may be better enjoying a kids' club for another year or two before they start skiing. Far better not to force the issue: wait until the child is ready to go to ski school rather than insist they'll love it and have them hate skiing from the word go. If possible, let your child give it a go in the UK (ideally on snow in an indoor ski centre, but if necessary on a dry slope) to see how they get on before you go.'

New gear for 2008

Innovations mean better performance and comfort

by **Dave Watts**

Skis keep on getting wider and more versatile – and high-performance, female-specific models are helping women to outperform men. Boots are becoming comfier and more responsive, to help get the best performance out of the wider sidecuts of the latest skis. And there are exciting new developments with both ski and snowboard bindings.

Versatility is the name of the game with the top skis for 2008. For years skis have been getting shorter and fatter, giving better performance in return for less effort. Now they've got about as short as they can get without losing performance. But they are still getting fatter – a lot fatter. And these days fat means versatile.

Four years ago the ski of choice for Dion Taylor, managing director of Britain's leading ski and snowboard gear retailer Snow+Rock, was the Rossignol Bandit B2. This was 76mm at the waist and widely regarded as the best all-round ski on the market. Now his ski of choice is the Volkl Mantra, an astonishing 25 per cent wider at 96mm. His wife used to be a World Cup racer and skied on 63mm wide slalom skis; her favourites now are the K2 Nancy, an even more astonishing 50 per cent wider at 95mm. Dion Taylor says, 'The great thing about these new wide skis is all-terrain versatility. They float fantastically in powder and work as well on-piste as off.'

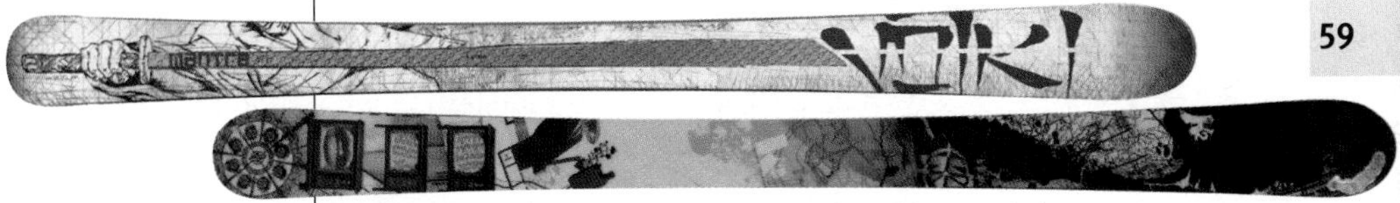

↑ Volkl Mantra
 K2 Nancy

GREAT NEW SKIS FOR 2008

Last March I went on a week-long test of all the new skis for the 2007/08 season, organised by the Snowsports Industries of Great Britain (a trade body of ski distributors and retailers). Out of 625 skis from 15 different manufacturers, there wasn't a poor ski to be seen.

Of the free-ride skis, I loved the K2 Apache Recon, Salomon X-Wing Tornado and Rossignol B83 aimed at the more advanced and expert skier. The Head Monster iM 78, Volkl AC30 and, a little down the ability (and price) bracket, the K2 Apache Raider and Salomon X-Wing 10 all came out of the test with flying colours too. All these are in the region of 75mm to 85mm wide under the boot. Of the fatter skis that Dion Taylor prefers, as well as the Volkl Mantra, the Dynastar Legend Pro Rider, K2 Coomba, Rossignol B100 Quad and Salomon Sandstorm came out well in the test – these are all over 90mm wide at the waist and the Coomba is 102mm.

Twin-tip skis (where the tails as well as the tips curve upwards) are

growing in popularity. The concept was invented to allow freestylers to make jumps in the terrain-park, half-pipe or just off natural hits in the snow, and land or take off backwards (aka 'fakie'). But now many younger skiers ('mainly 15 to 35', says Snow+Rock) are buying them as their main or only pair of skis because they work on- or off-piste just as well as many 'normal' free-ride skis – in addition to being good for jumps and tricks and having graphics that look cool and funky. The Head JO Pro, Scott Punisher, Salomon Dumont and Volkl Wall are likely best-sellers.

FLICK THAT SWITCH

With on-piste skis, the most interesting innovation for 2008 is the brand new Volkl Power Switch system, fitted on their top-of-the-range Tigershark model. The skis come with an easy-to-flick switch – flick the power on and two carbon rods built into each ski stiffen and enable the ski to react more quickly and precisely to aggressive skiing. Flick the switch to 'off' and the ski becomes more flexible and better suited to easy cruising. So you can adjust the ski to suit your mood or energy level during the day. This follows last year's introduction of Rossignol's Mutix system. This was fitted to its top-of-the-range Radical R11 ski last year, with a choice of using long or short arms that you attach to the ski both in front and behind the bindings; you get both sets and can interchange them as you like. The idea is that the short arms make the ski lively and quick to turn, and the long arms give the ski extra power and stability at speed and make it ideal for fast cruising and long GS turns. This year the design has been modified to make them easier to fit and remove, and the concept has been extended to the Zenith Z11 model (and its women's equivalent, the Attraxion 11) with stiff power arms (for more response, grip and stability) and regular arms (for more vibration absorption and easier cruising).

↑
K2 Apache Recon
Salomon X-Wing
 Tornado
Head Monster iM78
Volkl AC30
Dynastar Pro Rider
K2 Coomba
Rossignol B100 Quad
Salomon X-Wing
 Sandstorm
Head JO Pro
Scott Punisher
Salomon Aero-X
Head Xenon Xi9.0
Atomic Metron 10
Fischer RX8 Fire FTi
Volkl Tigershark

As well as these innovative skis, there are lots of other good skis aimed at those who want to ski primarily on-piste. Skis to look at include the Atomic Metron 10, Fischer RX6 Fire, Head Xenon Xi9, K2 Apache Crossfire and Salomon Aero X. And Snow+Rock has a bargain package aimed at first-time buyers: Head Xenon Xi3.5 skis and bindings, Head Edge 7.8 ski boots, poles and a bag for £279 – a saving of over £100.

WOMEN'S SKIS: A RAPIDLY GROWING MARKET

Nearly every manufacturer now produces a range of skis designed specifically for women (from novice to expert), taking account of their different physical make-up to men. In general, women tend to be lighter and less powerful; so manufacturers give their women's skis a different construction, and they design the flex and shape specifically for women. All this makes for skis that are easier to turn.

In the ski test, almost a quarter of the skis were made specifically for women. And our women testers found that, compared with the unisex equivalent, nearly all the skis they tried worked very well for them. These included the K2 T:Nine, Volkl Attiva, Salomon Jewel and Instinct, Dynastar Exclusive, Nordica Olympia, Fischer Vision, Atomic Balanze and Rossignol Attraxion and Bandit Women ranges. There are even special women's twin-tip skis such as the Atomic She Devil, K2 MissDemeanor, Rossignol Scratch Girl FS, Salomon Temptress and Volkl Pearl.

BOOTS GET LIGHTER, MORE CONVENIENT AND COMFIER

Ski boots are your most important purchase. Set aside enough time for a boot fitter to find the right pair for you and fit them properly. This will enhance your skiing pleasure and performance, as well as comfort. The main

↑ Atomic Hawx 110

development with boots recently has been to make them fit your feet better by all sorts of shaping improvements. The use of different, softer plastics in key areas of the boot gives a better fit and makes it easier to get it on and off. Boots have also become much lighter and more dynamically flexible, making it easier to flex the boot to adapt to terrain and control your skis.

Almost all boots today have heat-mouldable liners to mirror your foot for comfort as well as performance; and improvements in boot design have allowed these thermal liners to become thinner, giving greater power and control between foot and ski. Always use footbeds in your boots, especially custom-built footbeds made to the shape of your particular feet. These will support and distribute pressure evenly under the whole foot, improving comfort and control and reducing muscle cramps and foot fatigue. For ultimate performance, consider personalising your boots with a custom-fit liner from Zipfit or from Conform'able, with foam injection. Boots can be fitted with a Booster strap, which makes the flex more progressive, and gives a closer fit and better transmission from foot to ski.

Atomic is making big news in the boot market this year with its revolutionary new Hawx range of boots. Up until now, ski boots have locked your forefoot in the boot, but the Hawx boots allow it to flex in combination with the shell underfoot, leading to more comfort and performance. This is made possible by a new 'elastic i-flex zone' which absorbs vibrations; the visible signs of that are distinctive 'gills' at the side of the forefoot area of the boots. Salomon also has a new improved range of boots this year.

OTHER BIG NEWS ....

Up until now it has been difficult to find bindings to suit the adventurous powder-seeker who wants to skin uphill on fat skis in search of untracked powder and then rip it up coming down. Now Marker has come up with its new Duke binding – which is a free-ride/touring binding that will fit fat skis and that works superbly as a normal downhill ski binding too. It can be set from DIN 6 to DIN 16 and will work well even with race boots on skis such as the K2 Coomba and Volkl Mantra. Another big innovation of interest to off-piste enthusiasts concerns the ABS pack, which incorporates two airbags that you can inflate if you are caught in an avalanche – the idea is that they (and you) stay on the surface and do not get buried. You can now buy this with a backpack harness and use the size of pack that suits you on that particular day – a small one if you're just out for the day, a bigger one if you are touring overnight or longer.

Helmets are now recommended for safety, whether you are on- or off-piste. One brand that Snow+Rock is particularly recommending this year is Sweet – 'F1 technology for skiing at an affordable price,' says Dion Taylor, Snow+Rock's MD. 'It's a low-profile helmet that looks good and is of carbon thermo-plastic monocoque construction.'

Marker Duke
↓

↑ ABS Vario 30

Sweet Trooper ↓

K2 Auto ↓

SNOWBOARD GEAR

This season sees some great innovations in the snowboard world, especially with bindings. Often overlooked, your bindings are an important part of your set-up. Burton has come up with some kit that is really pushing snowboard technology to the next level. The new EST system allows you to adjust your stance more quickly and is easier and smoother to ride. Working in conjunction with the EST Burton boards, the binding has only two screws, which are done up either side of your boots on the outside of the binding chassis. This allows you to strap into your binding first, shuffle around on the board to find your perfect stance, then quickly fasten up and you're away. As well as being so easy to adjust and fasten, they provide great dampening, which has to be felt to be believed. As the binding chassis effectively has no base plate, it allows a truer flex beneath your feet for an extra feel and more control.

Flow is introducing a new range of bindings this season. Continuing on the success of the NXT series, it has made its chassis lighter and more slender, providing a better boot-to-binding fit. The I-straps allow a greater degree of flexibility, whilst maintaining that amazing foot hold and response that Flow is known for. K2 has also upped its game, and has made a binding called the 'Auto'. By running a cable through the binding chassis from the ankle strap to the toe strap, you now only need to do up one strap. Once the toe strap is initially set up, all you do is tighten the ankle strap and it in turn tightens the toe strap as well. This makes for a convenient, hassle-free way of getting in and out of your bindings.

On the snowboard front Burton has developed its EST boards, which you'll find on the Jeremy Jones and brand new X8 models. This introduces a new system requiring only four bolts, and offering unlimited stance options and easier adjustability and convenience on the hill. The boards also come with special base plates, enabling you to ride any Burton binding on them. But for the ultimate ride they are best combined with the EST bindings. At the high end, the T6 has been improved again. Utilising a dampening technology, the T6 incorporates a rubber film on the top sheet that absorbs vibration, creating the smoothest ride imaginable and meaning you get less fatigued so you can ride for longer. New from Ride this year is the Concept UL, one of the lightest boards on the market, which incorporates a scratch-resistant top sheet so your board stays in top condition. K2 has also introduced lighter cores, mixing a blend of woodcore and honeycomb construction to provide the classic feel of a woodcore board but shedding more weight for a more agile ride.

Arbor continues to produce boards utilising eco-friendly materials that not only set it apart from all other board companies but also provide a high level of performance.

The popularity of freestyle boards is on the increase, as more people are learning new tricks, or are buying second boards for messing around the pistes on. Boards like the K2 WWW allow you to have more stability when carving around the piste

25 year anniversary

Burton Jeremy Jones
K2 WWW
Ride Concept UL (top and base)
Arbor Element 58
Burton X8
↘

because of a longer effective edge, riding like a much longer board, but because you ride it 5cm shorter than your normal length, you can manoeuvre it with ease. So it is a good board for developing your skills in the shortest time possible. Forum has been at the forefront of freestyle progression for years. Boards such as the Stomper and its best-selling Destroyer are perfect for riders who use the whole mountain like a playground to jump off everything in sight.

Snowboard boots are the most important purchase you'll make, so when buying a complete set-up this is the best place to start. Once you have the correct boots, you can then choose a pair of bindings that complement them and enhance control and comfort. Salomon give us their 10th Boot, which marks the 10th edition of their limited edition boots. Using the finest Italian leather available to come up with one of the most stylish and comfortable boots to date, these spare no expense. Vans is introducing a new boot called the Cirro, which uses two Boa dials for the most customised fit yet. This means you can alter the fit of the lower and upper boot separately, to get the perfect flex and ultimate heel hold. Boots also seem to be getting shorter in overall length, meaning that bigger-footed riders can now fit more comfortably on narrower boards without having to worry about their toes dragging in the snow. Salomon's F-boot series and Burton's SL-10s reduce boot length by one whole size.

WHY BUY IN THE UK

Prices in the UK are competitive with Europe and the range of choice available in the UK is far better. Shops in the mountains often tend to stock mainly local brands (eg French brands in France, Austrian or German in Austria). What's more, if you do find the product cheaper elsewhere in Europe, Snow+Rock offers a price pledge on all products to give you the confidence to buy in the UK. It also offers a number of other exclusive guarantees to give you peace of mind to purchase in England, such as a comfort guarantee on all ski boots and a ski suitability and breakage guarantee.

A home in the snow

More and more of us are buying properties in the Alps

by **Dave Watts**

Buying a place in a ski resort has been many people's ambition for years. And now more and more of us are doing just that. Despite restrictions on new building in many parts of the Alps and restrictions on foreigners buying property in parts of Switzerland and Austria, there are still plenty of attractive new developments on offer, as well as resale properties. So where should you look? What can you expect to pay? And what are the pitfalls?

Most people see the idea of a place in the snow as a mixture of pleasure and investment. They hope to use the place themselves for a few weeks each year and let it out for some of rest of the time. While you can expect to pay well over £1 million for a nice chalet in top resorts such as Val d'Isère and Megève, you can find decent-sized apartments in France, Switzerland and Austria for £200,000 to £300,000 or less. And in Bulgaria, half as much goes a long way.

So what should you look for when buying a home in the snow? First, you need to decide whether you want somewhere just for the skiing or whether you want a place in a resort that is attractive in the summer as well. Many French resorts developed after the 1950s can be deadly dull in summer, whereas resorts such as Morzine or Chamonix are as busy in summer as in winter. Second, if you want the place primarily for skiing and snowboarding, you will want reliable snow. And with global warming likely to continue, that means going for somewhere with access to high, snow-sure slopes. Third, if you intend to use the place yourself frequently, you will probably want somewhere within a couple of hours of an easily accessible airport. Fourth, make sure you understand the legal and taxation aspects – buying and running costs, all types of taxes and any resale restrictions. It is highly advisable to get professional advice on these. Fifth, make sure you understand any arrangements that you may be offered for 'sale and leaseback' or 'guaranteed return' from renting it out – these can vary enormously and are particularly common in France where you can save VAT on the purchase price in some circumstances. Sixth, if you are intending to rent the property out yourself, don't overestimate the income you will get from it.

You also need to decide whether you want to buy a new or a resale property. Building restrictions in many areas of the Alps have severely curtailed the number of new properties. But more and more old buildings are now being converted into high-quality apartments.

65

INTRAWEST / ERNA LOW

Intrawest is now building its second major Alpine development, Flaine Montsoleil – for more details, see the Flaine chapter →

↑ Villars in Switzerland is very popular with second-home owners who want to spend lengthy periods rather than just the odd week there

PURE INTERNATIONAL

You'll soon be able to access Serre-Chevalier's extensive slopes from 'loft-style' apartments being built in a 19th-century silk mill ↗

SNOWPIX.COM / CHRIS GILL

FRANCE – STILL THE MOST POPULAR PLACE TO BUY

Most British buyers still head for France. One reason for this is that second-home ownership by foreigners is banned or severely restricted in many parts of Austria and Switzerland. One of the most successful new French developments in the last few years has been Arc 1950, a brand new, ski-in/ski-out, traffic-free village in the Les Arcs ski area, designed and built by Canadian company Intrawest. That development has now been sold out, and Intrawest has started selling properties in two new Alpine developments. See the Flaine chapter for details of the Montsoleil development there. Intrawest is also building Edenarc 1800 on a crest above Arc 1800. The design of this will be quite a contrast to the old-world feel of Arc 1950; it will be 'modern and contemporary, with clean lines, using glass, native woods and natural stone'. There will be an aqua-relaxation area with hot-tubs and pools, and a fitness area with panoramic windows.

These Intrawest developments are available through Erna Low Property. Bertie Sanderson, their director of marketing, says, 'We are very proud to be able to sell these unique developments as well as many other exciting new properties in the Alps.' One of the most exciting is a project by property developer SPACE to convert a former silk mill built in the mid-19th century into around 250 'loft-style' apartments (see back cover). The development, called La Schappe, is just below the beautiful medieval walled part of Briançon (aka Serre-Chevalier 1200), which has its own gondola into the Serre-Chevalier ski area. La Schappe will also have a 4-star hotel with a spa, a panoramic restaurant, a museum and a traditional covered market. Prices are expected to range from £100,000 upwards.

Sanderson also recommends the 4-star Aiguille Rouge apartments, right by the gondola into the Balme ski area at Vallorcine in the Chamonix valley, starting at £165,000. In the old village of Tignes-Les-Brévières, part of the Tignes-Val d'Isère ski area, the second phase of a smart development is now on the market – apartments starting at around £250,000 with underground parking, a 24-hour reception, and spa facilities. Chamrousse, near Grenoble, is where Jean-Claude Killy won the Olympic men's downhill in 1968. It's a functional family resort with almost 80km/50 miles of pistes – one-bed apartments start at around £110,000 and four-bed chalets at £220,000. As well as these and other properties, Erna Low has some businesses, such as bars, restaurants and hotels, for sale.

Zigi Davenport of the Alpine Apartments Agency says the Portes du Soleil area and other relatively low resorts are still popular 'despite the talk of global warming'; she offers a large selection of apartments.

CONTACTS

Erna Low Property
020 7590 1624
www.ernalowproperty.
co.uk

Investors in Property
020 8905 5511
www.investorsin
property.com

**Alpine Apartments
Agency**
01554 388234
www.alpineapart
mentsagency.com

Pure International
020 7331 4500
www.pureintl.com

Barrasford and Bird
01566 782624
www.barrasfordand
bird.co.uk

SWITZERLAND AND AUSTRIA OFFER GOOD VALUE FOR MONEY

Simon Malster of Investors in Property now concentrates on Switzerland and Austria because 'there are some great properties available, and they are much better value for money than in France'.

Because so many foreigners have been applying for the limited number of permits available for non-residents to buy property in Switzerland and because waiting lists have grown, some cantons, including the Valais, have imposed moratoriums on sales to foreigners. But as Malster says: 'Some parts of the Valais are not affected by this. Part of Les Collons (linked to the Verbier ski area) is not covered, for example.' Malster is keen on Les Collons because 'it is high (1800m/5,910ft), with some lovely uncrowded ski pistes and wonderful views of the mountains, including the Matterhorn'. A new traditional-style four-bed chalet there costs around £460,000. Malster also likes the unspoiled and little-known resorts of Val d'Anniviers (see our new chapter on this area on page 541). He has apartments in St Luc starting at £175,000 for two bedrooms. Pure International also likes this valley and has properties in Grimentz starting at £263,000. Both Investors in Property and Pure have places in the traditional resort of Villars (very close to Geneva airport). Malster says: 'Villars is in the canton of Vaud, so not affected by the Valais moratorium, though there are rumours that it may impose restrictions soon.' He says that properties here have seen dramatic price rises recently and are popular with people who live in their second home for several months a year, not just the odd week. Malster has a piste-side development here with spa facilities, starting at £565,000.

Malster also says: 'The Valais moratorium will end in January 2008 unless it is renewed. And the Swiss government has announced that the present system of foreigner purchase permits will be phased out by 2010.'

Paul Sidebottom of Alpine Switzerland sells Swiss properties and recommends three developments in the ski and spa resort of Leukerbad and a large, luxurious development with pool and spa in Saas-Fee that is still awaiting planning approval.

There are restrictions on buying in Austria (foreigners can't buy in the Tirol, for example). But there are lots of properties available around Salzburg, within easy driving distance of many big-name resorts (see the feature box on Ski Amadé on page 126, for example). Investors in Property has chalets in St Margareth, St Martin and Rauris, all within an hour of Salzburg. The first two are also near Obertauern, and Rauris is near Zell am See and Kaprun; detached chalets start at under £200,000. Investors in Property is also selling apartments on the golf course near Bad Gastein.

OTHER POPULAR COUNTRIES TO BUY IN

If rock-bottom prices are your priority, look at Bulgaria. Bulgarian specialist Barrasford and Bird is selling studios in Pamporovo for around £30,000 and in Bansko for £46,000, with two- or three-bed apartments costing £120,000.

Or consider North America – a surprising number of people are willing to buy that far away for the atmosphere and, in the west at least, the high-quality snow. Both Erna Low and Pure International have a variety of properties in and near Tremblant (like Arc 1950 etc, an Intrawest-developed resort) and further west. Pure, for example, has a 1908 school (and grounds) in Fernie that has been transformed into two- and three-bed apartments; starting price £299,000.

Corporate ski trips

A great way to motivate your staff and clients

Most companies choose to get groups of staff or clients together out of the office occasionally for a whole variety of reasons. Team building, rewarding performance, bonding with clients, problem solving, communicating key messages and planning future strategy are just a few. Getting together in another boring UK hotel can seem a bit tedious – but getting together in a splendid ski resort environment most certainly is not. That's why more and more firms are doing just that.

The mountain environment is one that has lots of advantages for corporate events. The perceived status of ski resorts is high – whoever you invite will be in no doubt that they are being given a treat (as will their friends and business colleagues). And the clear fresh air, the sun and the snowy, dramatic mountain scenery have a huge and immediate impact on people arriving from the European lowlands and their dreary winters. There is a great sense of fun and liberation, and people are happy to cast inhibitions aside and let their hair down. And a winter sports break need not appeal just to skiers. Helena Kania went on a team-building weekend to Morzine organised by her company, Cable & Wireless, and told us, 'I didn't set foot on skis or board but just loved the fresh air, sunshine, views, walks and meeting up with the others in mountain restaurants. And we all got on much better when we got back to work after sharing a great experience.'

by **Dave Watts**

HOW LONG FOR AND WHAT'S THE COST?

Corporate trips of a few days are the norm – Thursday to Sunday, say. But you can have two full, action-packed days in the Alps by leaving on Friday after work and returning late on Sunday night – arriving back at work on Monday morning refreshed, invigorated and remotivated. Some companies take over a cluster of chalets for a week or two and have different groups moving in and out, staying for a variety of durations. Others hire helicopters for airport transfers and go for just one night. The cost can be a lot less than you'd think and, indeed, less than some of the alternatives, because UK hotel and restaurant costs are relatively high.

HOW BIG A GROUP?

In principle, your group can be any size you like; but with really small groups, be aware that the social success of the trip is going to depend on how the individuals mesh.

Charlie Paddock of The Corporate Ski Company says that the groups they work with vary in number from 15 to several hundred but that generally the average size is between 30 and 50. For the last two years Momentum Ski has organised trips to Courmayeur for Google. 'Last season there were 1,500 people, possibly the biggest Alpine event ever organised by a tour operator,' says Momentum MD Amin Momen. 'The delegates flew in from 24 international airports on scheduled flights and private charters, and every minute of their programme and stay was coordinated by one of Momentum's multilingual staff. The Alps provide inspirational natural surroundings and an immense variety of activities is possible – the perfect incentive or thank you from the management.'

SWISS INTERNATIONAL CITY SKI CHAMPIONSHIPS

The City Ski Championships have been organised by Momentum Ski and held annually in Courmayeur in Italy's Aosta valley since 2000. Among their attractions is the array of former skiing and sporting stars who turn up. British downhill stars of the 1980s and 90s Konrad Bartelski and Graham Bell are regulars. They were joined in 2007 by Olympic athlete Colin Jackson and racing driver Damon Hill – both are expected back this season, along with other sporting legends. Around 200 skiers from 40 City firms take part in the event.

The Saturday GS race is the main event but only part of the attraction of this weekend. Three other races are held on the Friday: the Accenture parallel slalom (a relay race with four in each team), the Radar Trap (speed skiing) and a boarder-cross. On the Friday evening there's a welcome drinks party, dinner at various restaurants and late-night drinks in the Bar Roma; on the Saturday, there's a race-side buffet sponsored by Cheviot, a Mumm champagne reception in the evening, followed by a gala presentation dinner and then ... clubbing till dawn. On Sunday the hard core either take advantage of Courmayeur's off-piste terrain on the Toula Glacier or heli-ski; others just enjoy Momentum's complimentary Bloody Marys at Christiania's on the slopes.

The 2008 event, from 13 to 16 March, promises to be better than ever. Konrad Bartelski will again be running the Snow+Rock pre-race ski clinics, which are really popular with the competitors, and Graham Bell and Matt Chilton from the BBC will be doing the commentary. For more details contact Momentum on 020 7371 9111 or City Championships on 020 7863 8813 – or see www.cityskichampionships.com. The City Ski Championships are part of the City Championships Calendar.

WHERE TO GO AND WHAT KIND OF ACCOMMODATION?

How easy it is to settle on a resort for a corporate trip depends hugely on the nature of your project. If it's a group spread around the world that you want to get together, you could consider North American resorts as well as the Alps. But if the group is UK or European based, the Alps would be best. Because corporate trips tend to be short, you'll want to keep the travel time to the minimum so that it doesn't dominate the proceedings. Transfer times from airports to resorts generally range from one to four hours, and you'll probably want to operate at the lower end of that range if you can. On the other hand, you may want your choice of resort to carry a message to your 'delegates'. Choosing Courchevel or St Moritz is effectively saying, 'No expense spared – nothing but the best for you.'

Whatever you do, choose a resort with a good snow record and/or extensive snowmaking. You don't want to invite people on a skiing break to find that there's no snow. Avoid early season for the same reason. A March trip to a high resort will mean good snow, and it should mean strong sunshine, too. Don't get hung up on size – with only a couple of days to spend on the slopes, almost any resort has plenty of terrain, especially with good local guides to help you make the most of it. It's likely that not everyone in the group will want

Some of the City Ski Championships competitors after the end of the 2007 race
↓

to go skiing or boarding, so you may want to choose a resort that has good walks available and maybe lots of other activities that can be organised, such as snow-shoeing, dog-sledding, snowmobiling, skating, curling, tobogganing, ballooning, flights in planes or helicopters or luxuriating in a spa enjoying treatments and massages.

As for accommodation, if it's a dozen or so people travelling out together for a relaxed couple of days, a swanky chalet might work well: see the 'Luxury chalets' chapter on page 47 to get an idea of what's available.

Ingrid Watts of Flexiski says: 'A short transfer time is usually a high priority for our clients. If they want to stay in a hotel, we might suggest Chamonix, Megève or Verbier; if they want the more intimate feel of a chalet, then Méribel or St Anton might be the answer.'

If you are getting a large group together and need good conference facilities, finding the right resort and accommodation, meeting rooms and support services can be a real headache, and it's in dealing with this sort of challenge that the services of a tour operator or event management company will really pay off. If you put them in charge of the whole event, you can make them responsible for staying within budget, including on-the-spot costs, as well as the basic accommodation and travel costs.

Charlie Paddock of The Corporate Ski Company says: 'We operate in over 40 ski resorts worldwide; however, many of our groups go to Switzerland and Austria because of the excellent flight access and wider choice of 4- and 5-star hotels, which tend to be more accommodating for short stay and weekend corporate groups. Since the Winter Olympics were held in Turin in 2006, Italy has also become more accessible to corporate groups on a budget, due to a

Corporate ski trips

wide range of more affordable places to stay.' And Laura Newton of Ski Verbier says: 'We deal with a large number of corporate groups who are looking to exploit the joys of a 100-minute transfer time from Geneva to Verbier, combined with world-class skiing and a very lively nightlife. Our two boutique hotels (15 rooms each) cater perfectly for groups that want a property exclusively to themselves, combining chalet-style accommodation with a five-star service. Our flexible booking policy is imperative for corporate groups who enjoy long weekends and midweek breaks.'

ORGANISING THE DAYS AND EVENINGS

This is another area where the services of a tour operator or event management company will really pay off. You'll need to make sure everyone is equipped with suitable clothing, equipment and lift passes. You'll also want to organise tuition or guiding specially for your group. Make sure you have enough instructors/guides so that you can form groups of equal ability. You'll also want to ensure that activities for non-skiers are carefully choreographed, so that people do what they want to do and have their time filled (or have time off to relax if that's what they want). Lunch in a mountain restaurant can be an opportunity to get your group together, and if you choose a restaurant near the top of a lift that pedestrians can use, everyone will be able to get there easily. Another possibility, in good weather, is a swanky picnic, with plenty of champagne buried in the snow.

You might want to think about a race for delegates, though bear in mind that this won't appeal to the complete beginners in the group. Other forms of competition, such as on-snow treasure hunts, could be used to include non-skiers too. You might want to make these team events (eg relay races) to build relationships.

Then there are the evenings to consider. They are a time when all the group can be brought together, so it's important to think about how you're going to use those opportunities to best effect. You can create social events that reinforce your message – perhaps taking over a whole bar or a mountain restaurant, for example. In the right resort, dinner in a mountain restaurant could be followed by toboggan runs or torchlit descents on skis.

Simon Brown of Ski 2, whose corporate groups normally go to Champoluc in the Monterosa region of Italy, says: 'Most of our groups are office jollies organised for bonding purposes and we'll lay on anything they want – maybe ski instructors for beginners and heli-skiing for the good skiers, a night out at Milan's San Siro stadium to watch the soccer, a trip to the Casino in Chamonix, an evening having dinner in an old restaurant up the mountain reached by snowcat. Anything's possible.'

Weekend breaks

Three days on the slopes can feel as good as a week

A weekend away with just one day off work can give you three great days on the slopes, leaving you with the feeling of having been away for ages and returning to work refreshed.

Short-break ski trips have become much more popular in the last few years, partly because of the growth of budget airlines. Given that travel to and from ski resorts is prone to hassle, going for two or three days on the slopes rather than the usual six may seem an unattractive prospect. But we're converts: a quick fix of the white stuff really does seem almost as good as a week.

The classic weekend destination is Chamonix, which has slopes suitable for all types of weather and snow conditions, abundant hotels and a short transfer from Geneva. But we've done successful weekend trips to all sorts of places: Zell am See in Austria, with skiing on the glacier at Kaprun; Val d'Isère (at the time of the Premier Neige races) and Courchevel in France; Saas-Fee, Engelberg and Verbier in Switzerland; in Italy, Courmayeur and Aosta (skiing Cervinia, Monterosa and Pila on successive days).

We've met many other weekend converts in the process, including people who rent apartments for the season and go out whenever it suits them, and others who book up 12 or so weekend flights well in advance and decide on the resort when they know where the best snow is.

The key to making the most of your time is to catch late flights each way (or a very early flight out, allowing you to be on the slopes by lunch time) – so it helps if you live near a suitable airport. With the growth of budget airlines, there's a big choice of regional and destination airports to use, as well as the major airports favoured by longer-established airlines. From our bases in the west and east of England, we routinely use flights from Bristol and Stansted, in particular.

We've had excellently timed Ryanair flights to and from Salzburg and Pisa from Stansted, as well as EasyJet to Geneva from Luton, for example. At the other extreme of the price range, of course, you could fly in your own private jet, with the whole itinerary tailored to meet your needs.

We don't recommend flying to Munich if you are travelling out on a Friday or back on a Sunday – the queues on the motorway can be horrendous, as the whole of Munich seems to go weekend skiing, and the airport is on the far side of the city from the Alps. Similarly, allow plenty of time if you are driving back to Lyon airport on a Sunday evening – we encountered very heavy traffic after leaving Courchevel in what we had thought was good time.

GETTING TO THE RESORT

Booking a rental car or transfer in advance is usually cheaper than arranging one after you arrive. Taxis can be ridiculously expensive compared with the cost of renting a car. For example, you would expect to pay over £200 each way between Geneva airport and Courchevel by taxi if you book locally – but renting a small car for the weekend would be much less than the one-way taxi price. In our experience, train and bus times between airports and resorts are more suitable for weekly visitors than for weekenders looking for maximum time on the slopes. Airport transfer companies (see our chapter on Flying to the Alps) are worth trying; but you might waste valuable time waiting around if you go for a shared transfer.

PACKAGE DEALS

Using a tour operator or travel agent specialising in weekend trips, such as one of those advertising in this chapter, makes sense if you don't want the hassle of making your own arrangements. They know the best resorts to go to, can arrange transfers or car hire and have special deals with hotels. Some arrange special weekend courses (eg with off-piste guides or even heli-skiing) and can arrange groups of similar standard for you to ski with. And local tour operator reps and contacts can save you valuable time arranging lift passes (beware of big queues on Saturday and Sunday mornings) and equipment hire, and advise on local restaurants and other facilities.

CHOOSING A RESORT

Many people think they should go for a resort within a short drive of their arrival airport. But by definition, resorts close to major airports are close to large numbers of people poised to hit the slopes on fine weekends, which can mean queues for the lifts, crowds on the slopes and competition for hotel beds. These days, most resorts are within striking distance of a major airport, and an hour's extra transfer time is not really that much if it gets you to quieter slopes.

Resorts within an hour or so of Geneva include Chamonix, St-Gervais, Megève and Les Contamines (all in the Mont Blanc area and sharing an area lift pass), Flaine and La Clusaz in France, and Villars and Les Diablerets in Switzerland. Verbier and Crans-Montana in Switzerland are a bit further, as are the Three Valleys and other Tarentaise resorts – Val d'Isère can be reached in under three hours now – and Morzine and the Portes du Soleil resorts in France.

Flying to Zürich opens up lots of other possibilities. Flims, Davos and Klosters are the nearest big resorts, and Engelberg and Andermatt are within easy reach. St Anton and Lech in Austria are within striking distance – though Friedrichshafen in Germany is closer. Salzburg is handy for most of the eastern Austrian resorts.

In Italy, Courmayeur is a popular weekend destination and is easily accessible from Geneva through the Mont Blanc tunnel. Resorts such as Champoluc, Sauze d'Oulx and Sestriere are easily accessible from Milan or Turin. Ryanair's Verona flights put you very near the Sella Ronda resorts and Cortina d'Ampezzo, and Bergamo is convenient for Trentino resorts such as Madonna di Campiglio.

Unless you are booking at short notice we would suggest avoiding low resorts where snow may be unreliable and very high resorts where the skiing is entirely above the tree line – this rules out places such as Tignes, Val Thorens, Obergurgl and Cervinia. Another important consideration is that hotels in many resorts will often refuse weekend bookings except in very low season (eg early Jan or late March). More summer-oriented resorts, which generally have accommodation spare in winter, are worth considering – such as Chamonix, Morzine, Engelberg, Villars and Mürren.

WHAT ABOUT PRICE?

The cost can vary enormously. Unless you manage to find bargain flights, a weekend will obviously cost more per day than a full week. In general, through a good specialist tour operator you can expect to pay from around £350 a head for flights, car hire and a double room in a 3-star hotel or B&B for three nights, assuming two people sharing. With lift passes and meals you could be looking at around £500. For a 4-star hotel add another £100 or so.

MIDWEEK BREAKS

If you can get away midweek, there are many advantages. Flights (especially on budget airlines) should be cheaper, and possibly accommodation, too. And resorts that get busy at weekends, such as Verbier and Courmayeur, can be very quiet midweek in low season.

Flying to the snow

Flights and transfers for independent travellers

by **Rebecca Miles**

Most Brits going to the Alps go by plane; that's been the case since skiing became a mass-market activity in the 1960s. But most of us have traditionally travelled on one-week packages, using charter flights. What has changed in the last decade is that a growing number of us travel independently by air, often going for non-standard periods, paying bargain fares and arranging our own resort transfers.

This change in our travelling habits has been brought about by budget airlines operating scheduled services. The key player was EasyJet, which started cheap scheduled flights to the Alps in the mid-1990s. EasyJet and other major budget airlines have added more routes as well as more flights, while more minor airlines have entered the market. The budget flight business is clearly here to stay.

ONLINE BOOKING

Most budget airlines expect you to make your booking online. The web addresses of the airlines we list are given in the reference section at the back of the book, and will also be found as links on our own website at www.wtss.co.uk.

78

AIRLINES FOR THE ALPS

Budget airlines operate from most UK airports other than pricey Heathrow. Our map shows the arrival airports dotted around the Alps. There isn't so much scope here as in other parts of the Continent for budget airlines to use budget airports, but there are one or two unfamiliar names on the map. You can see from the map which arrival airports are likely to work for your chosen resort. We're concentrating on the Alps, but budget airlines can also get you to the Pyrenees, the Massif Central and the Sierra Nevada.

EasyJet still has by far the biggest range of flights to the key Alpine destination airport of Geneva – from eight provincial departure airports around the UK. The airline serves nine Alpine airports from the London area. For those living south of London, the fact that it operates several routes from Gatwick will be important.

Ryanair has a lot of flights from Stansted (and a couple from Luton) to a number of useful airports, including places such as Friedrichshafen – which you may not have heard of but which is handy for St Anton and eastern Switzerland.

Flybe serves Geneva and Chambéry from several airports (including Exeter, Southampton, Birmingham and Norwich), and Berne, Salzburg, Nice and Milan from one or two.

Bmibaby has flights from Cardiff, Manchester, Birmingham and Nottingham to Geneva and from Birmingham to Nice.

Jet2.com is based at Manchester and Leeds/Bradford (and has a limited number of flights from some other places), with flights to airports including Geneva, Chambéry, Salzburg, Milan and Venice.

Thomsonfly goes to Grenoble, Geneva, Salzburg and Venice from several provincial airports.

Don't overlook foreign national airlines – Air France, Alitalia, Austrian, Lufthansa – which fly between Heathrow (and sometimes major regional airports such as Birmingham and Manchester) and major home-country airports. They are increasingly competitive.

Swiss International Air Lines operates several flights a day from Birmingham and Manchester to Zürich, and from Heathrow and London City to Zürich and Geneva. And **British Airways** goes to lots of relevant airports from a variety of UK airports.

TRAVEL TIPS

How low can you go? Budget airline fares vary according to demand, and in general the cheapest flights are for midweek, early or late in the day, booked months in advance, or at the last minute – as a flight fills up, the fares go up; if it looks like the flight might not sell out, the fares go down again. You can pay less than £40 return if you time it right. We made trips last winter for which the cost of carrying skis and boots was much the same as the basic fares we paid.

Flexibility Although the budget airlines won't normally give you a refund if you decide not to travel, most will now allow you to change the flight time or route, or the name of the passenger – but at a cost of perhaps £15 each way for each change plus, maybe, the difference between the current cost of the new flight and the price you originally paid. Check when you book, because the rules change.

Baggage Airline policies on baggage vary, fees can mount up and are liable to change – so it's important to check. As we go to press, EasyJet allows hold baggage of 20kg per person – one bag is free, but additional bags cost extra. Ryanair has a mean baggage allowance of 15kg and every piece of checked luggage has to be paid for. Excess baggage is generally charged at £5/kg to £6/kg per flight. Both these airlines charge £15 or more per flight to carry skis and boots. Major national airlines treat skis as part of your general baggage. Swiss carries one pair of skis or a snowboard free. BA allows one bag (of up to 23kg) free; additional bags cost £42 (when pre-paid online), but a pair of skis or a snowboard is carried free.

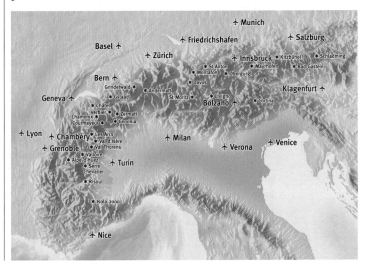

DON'T FORGET CHARTER FLIGHTS

We've been concentrating here on scheduled services, which allow a wide choice of travel arrangements. Charter flights – where a tour operator (or group of operators) takes over a plane for package holiday purposes – are sometimes sold on a seat-only basis; you can find out about these, as well as scheduled flight options, by spending hours on the internet. Charter flights can allow you to use airports not served by scheduled services.

GETTING TO THE RESORT

It's all very well getting a cheap flight, but how do you get from the airport to the resort and back? Renting a car is one option and can be cost-effective if you are going only for a few days or if there are three or four of you, but watch out for hidden extra costs. Or there are public transport options.

Arriving into Switzerland is a dream – both Zürich and Geneva airports have railway stations from which most Swiss and many western Austrian resorts can be reached (perhaps with a bus link at the other end). Swiss Railways (www.sbb.ch/en) has an excellent site for planning and booking journeys. It might be cheaper to get a special rail pass than a simple return ticket – contact the Swiss Travel Centre (www.stc.co.uk) for more information on these.

In Austria, Salzburg airport is 20 minutes from the railway station by regular public bus; resorts such as Zell am See, Kitzbühel and Bad Gastein can all easily be reached by train. From Innsbruck airport, buses run every 15 minutes to the main train and bus stations, from where St Anton, Seefeld and Mayrhofen can all easily be reached. See www.oebb.at/en for train information.

Reaching French resorts by public transport from airports is slightly trickier. Trains are not that regular and you might be better off on a bus. Altibus (www.altibus.com) operates from Chambéry, Lyon and Geneva airports to many resorts in the northern half of the French Alps. A return ticket from Lyon airport to Méribel is around £90, for example. Reservations are strongly advised.

In Italy there is a Terravision bus service (www.lowcostcoach.com) to a few Dolomite resorts from Verona or Bergamo airports.

There is a growing number of private companies operating transfers, mainly in eight-seat minibuses. In most cases, you can either book a seat on a shared transfer (and potentially have to wait around for other flights to land) or reserve the whole minibus.

AlpineCab (www.alpinecab.com) operates from Geneva, Chambéry and Lyon (and Grenoble and St-Etienne with prior arrangement) to 38 resorts, including Cervinia in Italy. Airport Transfer Service (www.a-t-s.net) runs from key airports in Switzerland, France and Austria to almost every resort in those countries. The Cool Bus Co (www.thecoolbus.co.uk) operates from Geneva, Grenoble, Lyon and Chambéry to all resorts in the Tarentaise and the Three Valleys. Alp-line (www.alp-line.com) runs from Geneva, Lyon, Chambéry, Grenoble and Turin airports to a host of destinations. Skihoppa (www.skihoppa.com) operates from over 40 airports to hundreds of resorts (they also offer heli-transfer options, costing from about £250 per person one way – expensive, but your transfer time will be about 20 minutes). A few other companies that have more limited minibus services (mostly specialising in Chamonix or the Three Valleys) are listed in the directory at the back of the book.

Drive to the Alps

And ski where you please

by **Chris Allan**

More and more people from Britain are doing what the French, the Germans and the Dutch have done for years, and driving to their Alpine resorts. It has various advantages, even for those going on a pretty standard week in the Alps. For many people, it's just less hassle than checking in at dawn for a flight from Gatwick, and less tedious than sitting around waiting for a delayed charter plane that's stuck in Majorca. For families (especially those going self-catering), it simplifies the job of moving half the contents of your house to the Alps. If there are four or five people in your party, the cost can be low. (These days, how it compares to travelling by air depends, of course, on what bargains are on offer from budget airlines.)

If you fancy something a bit more adventurous, taking a car opens up the exciting possibility of touring around several resorts in one trip, and even making up your plans as you go.

Cross-Channel ferries are faster and more pleasant than ever, with the possibility of a seriously good lunch on short crossings as an alternative to the quicker shuttle-trains through the tunnel. And the motorway networks in north-eastern France and on the approaches to the Alps have improved immensely in the last decade. You can now get to most resorts easily in a day from south-east England, in some cases using motorways virtually all the way.

For us, the freedom factor is the key. If the snow is bad in your resort, if the lift queues are horrendous, or if the resort you've plumped for turns out to be a let-down, you don't have to grin and bear it – if you have a car, you can try somewhere else (provided of course that you haven't already invested in a weekly lift pass).

Another plus-point is that you can extend the standard six-day holiday – spending a full day on the slopes on the final Saturday, then driving for a few hours before stopping for the night means you won't find Sunday's journey too demanding, and you may even have time for a traditional French Sunday lunch.

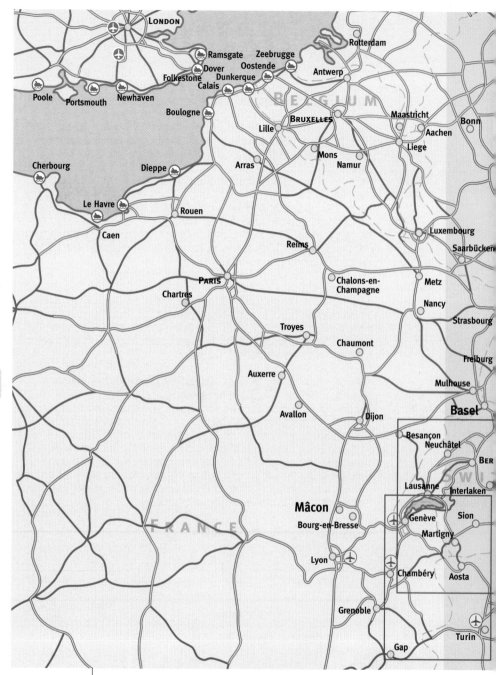

This map should help you plan your route to the Alps. All the main routes from the Channel and all the routes up into the mountains funnel through (or close to) three 'gateways', picked out on the map in larger type – Mâcon, Basel and Ulm. Decide which gateway suits your destination, and pick a route to it. Occasionally, using different Channel ports will lead you to use different gateways.

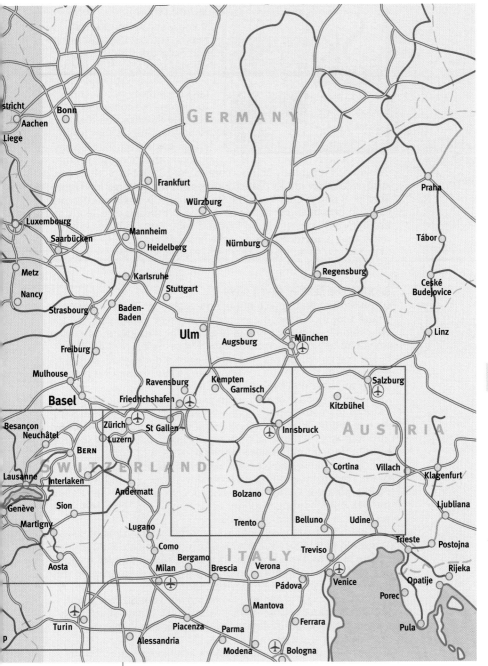

The boxes on the map correspond to the areas covered by the more detailed maps at the start of the main country sections of the book:
Austria page 120
France page 240
Italy page 424
Switzerland page 490

AS YOU LIKE IT

If you fancy visiting several resorts, you can use one as a base and make day trips to others when it suits you. This way, you can still take advantage of package holiday prices. The key to success is to go for a base that offers easy road access to other resorts. Our suggestions for France are in a separate chapter. A good choice in Austria is the Tirol east of Innsbruck. Söll is a convenient base for exploring resorts such as Alpbach and Kitzbühel. Further east in Salzburgerland there are lots of possibilities – and the Ski Amadé lift pass described in our Austrian introduction means you can exploit them conveniently and economically. Western Austria is not ideal for this sort of holiday – many resorts are tucked away at the head of long valleys – but from St Anton you could make day trips to Ischgl and Serfaus, as well as nearby Lech and Zürs.

AROUND THE ALPS IN SEVEN DAYS

If you want to see as much of the Alps as possible, consider making a Grand Tour by car, moving every day or two to a different resort and enjoying the complete freedom of going where you want, when you want. Out of high season there's no need to book accommodation before you go, so you can decide at the last minute which part of the Alps and which countries to visit – going where the snow is best, unless you have other special requirements.

A touring holiday doesn't mean you'll be spending more time on the road than on the piste – provided you plan your route carefully. An hour's drive after the lifts have shut is all it need take. It does eat into your après-ski time, of course; you have to be prepared to trade beers in the bar for fruit juice in the car.

Italy is far more suitable for tourers than day-trippers, provided you're prepared to put up with some slow drives on winding passes. For example, you could start in Livigno, drive to Bormio and then to the Dolomites, visiting Madonna di Campiglio and Selva, and finish your Italian expedition in Cortina.

Eastern Switzerland also offers a very attractive touring holiday. You could start in Davos/Klosters, take in Lenzerheide and Arosa and end up in Flims. With a little extra driving, you could even include St Moritz. Or tack Disentis, Sedrun and snowy Andermatt on to the end, leaving a short drive to Zürich airport.

There's no need to confine yourself to one country. You could imitate the famous Haute-Route by starting in Argentière in France and ending up in Switzerland's Saas-Fee, taking in Verbier and Zermatt along the way.

The major thing that you have to watch out for with a touring holiday is the cost of accommodation. Checking into a resort hotel for a night or two doesn't come cheap, and can be a bit of a rip-off. You can save money by staying down the valley – and you don't necessarily have to drive up to the slopes in the morning: some valley towns are linked by lifts. For example, you can take a funicular from Bourg-St-Maurice up to Les Arcs; a gondola links Brides-les-Bains to Méribel.

BRITAIN'S BEST SELLING SNOWSPORTS MAGAZINE

DAILY MAIL
SKI
& SNOWBOARD
YOUR COMPLETE GUIDE TO THE SLOPES

WIN A £2000 HOLIDAY
PLUS MORE THAN £2000 OF TECHNICAL KIT

GEAR
BEST ON TEST PISTE SKIS

GEEK PLEASING GADGETS

STATE OF THE ART BOARD BOOTS

EYE-CATCHING BASE LAYERS

CELEBS ON THEIR ARSE
Robin Williams
Buzz Aldrin
Alec Baldwin
Lyle Lovett
Robert F Kennedy Jr
Kelsey Grammer

Real slope stars Lasse Kjus and Chris Davenport

SPREAD YOUR WINGS
> Fabulous resorts we bet you don't know about

POW WOW!
Get to grips with the fresh stuff

SLAP YOUR LEDERHOSEN
Why Austria turns us on

SUPERNANNY
Essential guide to family holidays

Published monthly from October to March, *DMS&S* has everything you need for an action-packed winter season:

■ Resort reviews
■ Gear tests
■ Technique tips
■ Holiday offers
■ Amazing pics
■ Plus loads more

FREE CAMELBAK WORTH £32*

SUBSCRIBE NOW!

Subscribe to the UK's best selling snowsports magazine *Daily Mail Ski & Snowboard* and receive a slimline Camelbak Snobowl hydration pack, worth £32, free.

Subscribe today for £44 and enjoy two season's worth of the latest news and info, delivered straight to your door.

Visit www.subcription.co.uk/dmski/sko7 or call 01858 438831 and quote sko7

* Offer applies to Direct Debit payments only, subject to availability

Drive to the French Alps

To make the most of them

by **Chris Gill**

If you've read the preceding chapter, you'll have gathered that we are keen on driving to the Alps in general. But we're particularly keen on driving to the French Alps. The drive is a relatively short one, whereas many of the transfers to major French resorts from Geneva airport are relatively long. And the route from the Channel is through France rather than Germany, which for Francophiles like us means it's a pleasant prospect rather than a vaguely off-putting one.

TRAVEL TIME

The French Alps are the number-one destination for British car-borne skiers. The journey time is surprisingly short, at least if you are starting from south-east England. From Calais, for example, you can comfortably cover the 900km/560 miles to Chamonix in about nine hours plus stops – with the exception of the final few miles, the whole journey is on motorways. And except on peak weekends the traffic is relatively light, if you steer clear of Paris.

With some exceptions in the southern Alps, all the resorts of the French Alps are within a day's driving range, provided you cross the Channel early in the day (or overnight). Weekend traffic jams used to make the journey from Albertville to the Tarentaise resorts (from the Trois Vallées to Val d'Isère) a nightmare for drivers and coach passengers alike; thanks to road improvements for the 1992 Olympics these are nowhere near as serious as in the past, though the volume of traffic has built up over the last decade, and on peak-season Saturdays you can again encounter serious queues around Moûtiers. There are traffic lights placed well away from the town, to keep the queues and associated pollution away from Moûtier's tightly enclosed setting.

DAY-TRIP BASES

As we explained in the previous chapter, a car opens up different kinds of holiday for the adventurous holidaymaker. Day tripping from a base resort, for example.

In the southern French Alps, Serre-Chevalier and Montgenèvre are ideal bases for day tripping. They are within easy reach of one another, and Montgenèvre is at one end of the Milky Way lift network, which includes Sauze d'Oulx and Sestriere in Italy – you can drive on to these resorts, or reach them by lift and piste. On the French side of the border, a few miles south, Puy-St-Vincent is an underrated resort that is well worth a visit for a day – as is Risoul, a little further south. The major resorts of Alpe-d'Huez and Les Deux-Alpes are also within range, as is the cult off-piste resort of La Grave. Getting to them involves crossing a high pass, but it's a major route and is kept open pretty reliably.

The Chamonix valley is an ideal destination for the dedicated day tripper. The Mont-Blanc lift pass covers Chamonix, Les Contamines, Megève and others. Flaine and its satellites are fairly accessible – and so are Verbier in Switzerland, if the intervening passes are open, and Courmayeur in Italy, via the Mont Blanc tunnel. You could stay in a valley town such as Cluses, to escape resort prices – but Chamonix itself is not an expensive town.

UNBEATABLE!

* **Great value fares**

* **Award-winning vessels**

* **Up to 24 sailings per day**

* **The newest fleet on the Channel**

* **Easy access to main European destinations**

* **Motorists only – no coach parties or foot passengers**

**Book online or call
0870 870 10 20**

norfolkline.com
DOVER - DUNKERQUE FERRIES

Norfolkline Terms and Conditions apply. £4 administration fee applies to telephone bookings.

MOVING ON

A look at the map on the facing page shows that a different approach will pay dividends in the Tarentaise region of France. Practically all the resorts here – from Valmorel to Val d'Isère – are found at the end of long winding roads up from the main valley. You could visit them all from a base such as Aime, but it would be pretty hard work. If instead you stayed in a series of different resorts for a day or two each, moving on from one to the next in the early evening, you could have the trip of a lifetime. There's a new deal for lift-pass extensions in the Tarentaise region this year: you can buy daily extensions to a weekly pass for 10 euros; but it's no more economical than buying day passes.

GETTING THERE

There are three 'gateways' to the different regions of the French Alps. For the northern Alps – Chamonix valley, Portes du Soleil, Flaine and neighbours – you want to head for Geneva. If coming from Calais or another short-crossing port, you no longer have to tangle with the busy A6 from Paris via Beaune to Mâcon and Lyon. The relatively new A39 autoroute south from Dijon means you can head for Bourg-en-Bresse, well east of Mâcon.

For the central Alps – the mega-resorts of the Tarentaise, from Valmorel to Val d'Isère, and the Maurienne valley – you want to head for Chambéry. For the southern Alps – Alpe-d'Huez, Les Deux-Alpes, Serre-Chevalier – you want to head for Grenoble. And for either of these gateways you first of all head for Mâcon and turn left at Lyon.

If you are taking a short Channel crossing, there are plenty of characterful towns for an overnight stop between the Channel and Dijon – Arras, St-Quentin, Laon, Troyes, Reims. All have plenty of choice of budget hotels, some of them in central locations where you can easily enjoy the facilities of the town, others on bleak estates on the outskirts.

From the more westerly Channel ports of Le Havre or Caen, your route to Geneva or Mâcon sounds dead simple: take the A13 to Paris then the A6 south. But you have to get through or around Paris in the process. The most direct way around the city is the notorious périphérique – a hectic, multi-lane, urban motorway close to the centre, with exits every few hundred yards and traffic that is either worryingly fast-moving or jammed solid. If the périphérique is jammed it takes ages. The more reliable alternative is to take a series of motorways and dual carriageways through the south-west fringes of Greater Paris. The route is not well signed, so it's a great help to have a competent navigator.

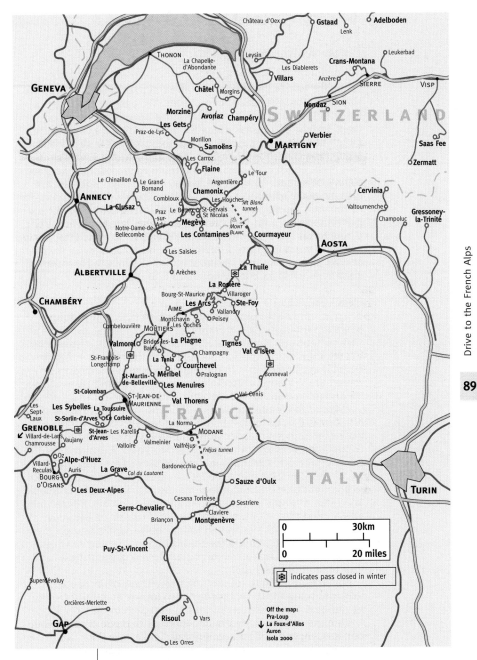

Pick the right gateway – Geneva, Chambéry or Grenoble – and you can hardly go wrong. The approach to Serre-Chevalier and Montgenèvre involves the 2060m/6,760ft Col du Lauteret; but the road is a major one and is kept clear of snow or reopened quickly after a fall. Crossing the French-Swiss border between Chamonix and Verbier involves two closure-prone passes – the Montets and the Forclaz. When necessary, one-way traffic runs beside the tracks through the rail tunnel beneath the passes.

Let the train take the strain

Taking the train to the Alps will doubtless become more popular as we start to wrestle with our carbon footprints. The opening of a faster rail link from London to the Channel tunnel this winter will help. In any event, travelling by train is one of the most restful ways to get to the Alps. It can also be a great way to get more time on the slopes without taking more time off work. You can leave on Friday night, arriving in your resort on Saturday morning, and return on the following Saturday night, arriving back home on the Sunday – eight days' skiing for five days out of the office.

The most popular train destination, with several different direct and indirect services, is the Tarentaise valley in France – resorts from Val d'Isère to Val Thorens. But you can travel by train to many other resorts. And many traditional resorts, especially in Switzerland, are on the rail network and are therefore reachable without resorting to buses. How many times you'll have to change trains is another matter.

DIRECT SERVICES TO THE FRENCH ALPS

Eurostar – the fast passenger service through the Channel tunnel direct to various stations in France and Belgium – is at last about to start operating on a new dedicated line from London, starting from the revamped St Pancras station. As a result, journey times will be cut by "at least 20 minutes". To the regret of those of us who can get trains in to Waterloo, Eurostar services from there will cease when the switch happens in mid-November 2007.

Eurostar offers direct services to the Alps – you disembark at Moûtiers (for buses to the Three Valleys resorts), Aime (bus to La Plagne) or Bourg-St-Maurice (funicular to Les Arcs, buses to Val d'Isère/Tignes). There are overnight services outward on Fridays (28 December to 21 March) and back on Saturdays (5 January to 29 March). These get you to Bourg at 6.30am, and leave at 10.15pm, so you can ski on both Saturdays, getting back to London on Sunday at 7.15am. Daytime services run outward on Saturdays (22 December to 5 April); for most of the season the return is also on Saturdays (29 December to 29 March) – so you get only the standard six days on the slopes; but there are then two additional Sunday services (6 and 13 April). Daytime services get you to Bourg at 6.20pm, and back to London at 4.10pm.

Standard return tickets cost from £179. There are no special sleeping arrangements on overnight services – you just doze (or not) in your seat. For £269 you can get a Leisure Select ticket which gets you a bigger seat pitch, meals, and drinks with meals. Seats can also be booked as part of a package holiday.

INDIRECT SERVICES TO THE FRENCH ALPS

There is an overnight Snowtrain sleeper service from Paris Gare du Nord, specially for UK passengers arriving there on Friday afternoon Eurostar services. It has the traditional bar/disco carriage, just like the old service from Calais. There are couchettes (simple flat beds) to sleep on. Last season this service stopped at Chambéry and Albertville as well as Moûtiers, Aime and Bourg-St-Maurice. The return service leaves the Alps on Saturday evening, arriving in Paris early on Sunday morning. Last season this service ran from 19 January until 6 April, and cost from £219 return.

These services aside, the French rail network can get you to Chamonix, or to Chambéry or Grenoble for onward buses to more southerly resorts. And of course you can get to the stations for Tarentaise resorts on regular services on weekdays. If you have the time and energy to seek out the cheapest fares, assembling your own itinerary can save money. Bear in mind that changing trains in Lille is likely to be less hassle than in Paris, where you normally have to cross the city to change services. But going via Paris opens up the possibility of using overnight sleeper services (not just the special Snowtrain one).

SERVICES TO OTHER COUNTRIES

Lots of resorts in Switzerland are on the rail network, making rail travel particularly attractive. There are several useful services from Paris, going to both western and eastern Switzerland. In Austria, quite a few resorts are valley towns, again on the rail network. Getting there from the UK currently entails quite a complex itinerary, though. There are trains from Paris to Bardonecchia in Italy, close to Sauze d'Oulx and neighbours.

PUTTING YOUR CAR ON A TRAIN

Sadly, French Railways no longer runs suitable motorail services that you can put your car on overnight and wake up in the Alps. But Deutsche Bahn does. Its services from northern Germany (eg Düsseldorf) to Austria (Salzburg, Innsbruck, Villach) and northern Italy (Bolzano) are most likely to be of interest to UK-based drivers.

Choosing your resort

Get it right first time

Most people get to go skiing or boarding only once or twice a year, so choosing the right resort is crucially important. Chamonix, Châtel and Courchevel are all French resorts, but they are as similar as chalk and Camembert. Start to consider resorts in other countries – Alpbach in Austria, say, or Zermatt in Switzerland – and the differences become even more pronounced. For the benefit of readers with relatively narrow experience of different resorts, here is some advice on how to use our information to best effect.

Lots of factors need to be taken into account when making your choice. The weight you attach to each of them depends on your own personal preferences, and on the make-up of the group you are going on holiday with. Starting on page 101 you'll find 21 shortlists of resorts which we rate as outstanding in various key respects.

Minor resorts and regions not widely known in the UK are described in short chapters of two or three pages. Major resorts get more detail, and more pages. Each resort chapter is organised in the same way. This short introduction takes you through the structure and explains what you will find under each heading we use.

GETTING A FEEL FOR THE PLACE

We start each chapter with a two-line verdict, in which we aim to sum up the resort in a few words. If you like the sound of it, you might want to go next to our Costs rating, in the margin. These ratings, ranging from ① to ①②③④⑤⑥ , reflect the total cost of a week's holiday from Britain, including a typical package of flights plus half-board accommodation, a lift pass and meals and drinks on the spot. Three coins means on the low side of average, four means on the high side. Then, in the 'Ratings' section, we rate each resort from 12 points of view – the more stars the better. (All these star ratings are brought together in one chart, which follows this chapter, so that you can easily track down resorts that might suit you.) Still looking at the information in the margin, in most chapters we have a 'News' section; this is likely to be of most use and interest in resorts you already know from past visits.

For major resorts, the next things to look at are our lists of the main good and bad points about the resort and its slopes, picked out with ➕ and ➖. These lists are followed by a summary in **bold type**, in which we've aimed to weigh up the pros and cons, coming off the fence and giving our view of who might like the resort.

You'll know by now whether this is, for example, a high, hideous, convenient, purpose-built resort with superb, snow-sure, challenging slopes but absolutely no nightlife; or a pretty, traditional village with gentle wooded slopes, ideal for beginners if only it had some decent snow.

THE RESORT

Resorts vary enormously in character and charm. At the extremes of the range are the handful of really hideous modern apartment-block resorts thrown up in France in the 1960s, and the captivating old traffic-free mountain villages of which Switzerland has an unfair number. But it isn't simply a question of old versus new. Some purpose-built places can have a much friendlier feel than some long-established resorts with big blocky buildings. Some places can be remarkably strung out, whereas others are surprisingly compact; our village plans are drawn to a standard scale, to help you gauge this. The landscape can have an important impact – whether the resort is at the bottom of a shady valley or on a sunny shelf with panoramic views. Some places are working towns as well as ski resorts. Some are full of bars, discos and shops; others are peaceful backwaters. Traffic may choke the streets; or the village may be traffic-free.

THE MOUNTAINS

The slopes Some mountains and lift networks are vast and complex, while others are much smaller and lacking variety.

Terrain-parks We summarise here the specially prepared fun-parks and other terrain features most resorts now arrange for freestylers.

Snow reliability This is a crucial factor for many people, and one that varies enormously. In some resorts you don't have to worry at all about a lack of snow, while others (including some very big names) are notorious for treating their paying guests to ice, mud and slush. Whether a resort is likely to have decent snow on its slopes normally depends on the height, the direction most of the slopes face (north good, south bad), its snow record and how much snowmaking it has.

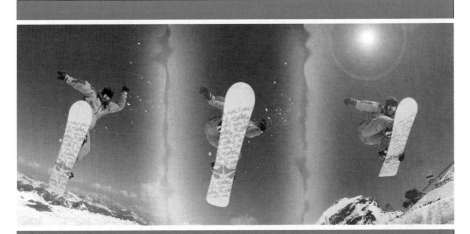

But bear in mind that in the Alps high resorts tend to have rocky terrain, where the runs will need more snow than those on the pasture land of lower resorts. Many resorts have increased their snowmaking capacity in recent years; in the Key facts section we list the latest amount they claim to have, and comment on it in the snow reliability text.

For experts, intermediates, beginners Most (though not all) resorts have something to offer beginners, but relatively few will keep an expert happy for a week's holiday. As for intermediates, whether a resort will suit you really depends on your standard and inclinations.

For cross-country We don't pretend that this is a guide for avid cross-country skiers. But we do try to help.

Queues Monster queues are largely a thing of the past, but it still pays to avoid the resorts with the worst queues, especially in high season. Crowding on the pistes is more of a worry in many resorts, and we mention problems of this kind under this heading. On our piste maps, note that we mark with a chair symbol only fast chairs; travelling at two or three times the speed of old-fashioned chairs, these lifts offer short ride times, and shift large numbers of people per hour. Lifts not marked with a symbol are slow chairs or drag-lifts.

Mountain restaurants If you like a decent lunch, beware: some resorts offer miserable restaurants and food (eg many resorts in America). Some people regard a prolonged mid-day stop as a waste of valuable skiing time, as well as valuable spending money, of course.

Schools and guides This is an area where we rely heavily on readers' reports of their own or their friends' experiences.

Facilities for children Again, to be of real help we need first-hand reports from people whose children have actually used the facilities.

STAYING THERE

How to go The basic choice is between catered chalets, hotels and self-catering accommodation. Some resorts have few hotels or few chalets. Note that we now have feature chapters on notably good hotels, as well as chalets and apartments.

Eating out The range of restaurants varies widely. Even some big resorts, such as Les Arcs, may have little choice because most of the visitors stay in their apartments. Most American resorts offer lots of choice.

Après-ski Tastes and styles vary enormously. Most resorts have pleasant places in which to have an immediate post-skiing beer or hot chocolate. Some then go dead. Others have noisy bars and discos until the early hours.

Off the slopes This is largely aimed at assessing how suitable a resort is for someone who doesn't intend to use the slopes, such as a non-skiing spouse.

Staying up the mountain/down the valley If there are interesting options for staying in isolation on the slopes above the resort village, or in valley towns below it, we pick them out in this section.

Resort ratings at a glance

AUSTRIA

	ALPBACH	BAD GASTEIN	BAD KLEIN-KIRCHHEIM	ELLMAU	HINTERTUX	HOCHKÖNIG	ISCHGL	KITZBÜHEL
Page	127	129	132	135	138	144	151	158
Fast lifts	**	**	**	**	***	**	*****	***
Snow	**	***	***	**	*****	***	****	**
Extent	*	****	**	****	***	***	****	***
Expert	*	***	**	*	***	**	***	***
Intermediate	**	****	***	****	***	****	****	***
Beginner	****	**	**	****	**	***	**	**
Convenience	**	**	***	***	**	**	***	**
Queues	***	***	****	****	***	****	****	**
Restaurants‡	***	****	***	**	**	***	****	****
Scenery	***	***	***	***	***	***	***	***
Resort charm	*****	***	***	***	***	***	****	****
Off-slope	***	****	***	***	*	***	***	*****

	LECH	MAYRHOFEN	NAUDERS	OBERGURGL	OBERTAUERN	SAALBACH-HINTERGLEMM	SCHLADMING	SÖLDEN
Page	165	175	183	185	190	192	199	203
Fast lifts	****	***	***	*****	*****	****	****	*****
Snow	****	***	****	*****	****	**	****	*****
Extent	****	***	**	**	**	***	***	***
Expert	****	**	***	**	***	**	**	***
Intermediate	****	***	****	***	****	****	****	****
Beginner	****	**	**	****	****	***	***	**
Convenience	***	*	**	****	****	****	***	**
Queues	****	*	****	*****	****	***	****	***
Restaurants‡	***	***	***	**	****	****	****	***
Scenery	***	***	***	***	***	***	***	***
Resort charm	****	***	****	****	**	****	***	**
Off-slope	***	****	***	**	**	**	****	**

	SÖLL	ST ANTON	ST JOHANN IN TIROL	STUBAI VALLEY	WESTENDORF	WILD-SCHÖNAU	ZELL AM SEE	
Page	206	213	225	227	229	231	235	
Fast lifts	**	***	**	***	**	**	***	
Snow	**	****	**	*****	**	**	**	
Extent	****	****	*	***	*	*	**	
Expert	*	*****	*	***	**	*	**	
Intermediate	****	***	***	***	***	**	***	
Beginner	***	*	****	**	***	***	***	
Convenience	**	***	***	**	***	***	**	
Queues	***	**	****	***	****	***	**	
Restaurants‡	**	***	****	**	***	**	***	
Scenery	***	***	***	****	***	***	***	
Resort charm	***	****	***	****	****	***	***	
Off-slope	**	**	****	***	**	**	****	

Note: Andorra appears on the last page of the chapter   ‡ Refers to mountain restaurants only

FRANCE

Resort ratings at a glance

96

	ALPE-D'HUEZ	LES ARCS	AVORIAZ	CHAMONIX	CHATEL	LA CLUSAZ	LES CONTAMINES	COURCHEVEL
Page	245	255	265	269	279	284	286	288
Fast lifts	**	***	***	***	**	**	**	****
Snow	****	****	***	****	**	**	****	****
Extent	****	***	*****	***	*****	***	***	*****
Expert	****	*****	***	*****	***	***	***	****
Intermediate	****	****	****	**	****	****	****	*****
Beginner	*****	****	****	*	***	****	**	****
Convenience	****	****	*****	*	**	***	**	****
Queues	****	***	***	**	***	***	***	****
Restaurants‡	****	***	****	**	***	****	****	****
Scenery	****	***	***	*****	****	***	****	***
Resort charm	*	*	**	****	***	****	***	**
Off-slope	****	*	*	*****	**	***	**	***

	LES DEUX-ALPES	FLAINE	LES GETS	LA GRAVE	MEGEVE	LES MENUIRES	MERIBEL	MONTGENEVRE
Page	300	306	313	315	317	324	326	337
Fast lifts	**	**	**	***	**	***	****	*
Snow	****	****	**	***	**	****	***	****
Extent	***	****	***	*	*****	*****	*****	****
Expert	****	****	***	*****	**	****	****	**
Intermediate	**	*****	****	*	****	*****	*****	****
Beginner	***	*****	****	*	***	***	****	*****
Convenience	***	*****	***	***	**	*****	***	****
Queues	**	***	***	****	****	****	****	****
Restaurants‡	**	**	***	**	****	***	***	**
Scenery	****	****	***	****	*****	***	***	***
Resort charm	**	*	****	***	****	*	***	***
Off-slope	**	*	***	*	****	*	***	*

	MORZINE	LA PLAGNE	PUY-ST-VINCENT	RISOUL	LA ROSIERE	SAMOENS	SERRE-CHEVALIER	STE-FOY
Page	341	350	360	362	365	368	370	378
Fast lifts	**	**	**	*	**	**	**	**
Snow	**	****	***	***	***	***	***	***
Extent	*****	****	**	***	***	****	****	*
Expert	***	****	***	**	**	****	***	****
Intermediate	****	*****	***	****	***	*****	****	***
Beginner	***	****	***	****	*****	**	****	**
Convenience	**	*****	*****	****	***	*	***	***
Queues	***	***	***	****	***	****	***	*****
Restaurants‡	***	****	***	***	*	**	***	**
Scenery	***	****	****	***	***	****	***	***
Resort charm	***	*	**	**	***	****	****	***
Off-slope	***	*	*	*	*	***	**	*

	ST-MARTIN-DE-BELLEVILLE	LES SYBELLES	LA TANIA	TIGNES	VAL D'ISERE	VALMOREL	VAL THORENS	
Page	381	384	389	393	404	414	416	
Fast lifts	***	*	****	***	****	*	****	
Snow	***	***	***	*****	*****	**	*****	
Extent	*****	*****	*****	*****	*****	***	*****	
Expert	****	**	****	*****	*****	**	****	
Intermediate	*****	***	*****	*****	*****	****	*****	
Beginner	**	****	***	**	***	*****	****	
Convenience	***	***	****	****	***	*****	*****	
Queues	****	****	****	****	****	***	***	
Restaurants‡	****	**	****	***	***	**	****	
Scenery	***	***	***	***	***	***	***	
Resort charm	****	*/****	***	**	***	****	**	
Off-slope	*	**	*	*	**	**	**	

	BORMIO	CERVINIA	CORTINA D'AMPEZZO	COURMAYEUR	LIVIGNO	MADONNA DI CAMPIGLIO	MONTEROSA SKI	PASSO TONALE
Page	428	430	436	441	446	450	452	456
Fast lifts	***	****	**	***	***	****	***	****
Snow	***	*****	***	****	****	***	****	****
Extent	**	***	***	**	**	***	***	**
Expert	*	*	**	***	**	**	****	*
Intermediate	***	****	***	****	***	****	****	***
Beginner	**	*****	*****	**	****	****	**	*****
Convenience	***	***	*	*	**	***	***	***
Queues	***	***	****	***	****	****	****	****
Restaurants‡	****	***	****	****	***	***	**	**
Scenery	***	****	*****	****	***	****	****	***
Resort charm	****	**	****	****	***	***	***	*
Off-slope	****	*	*****	***	**	***	*	*

	SAUZE D'OULX	SELLA RONDA	SELVA	SESTRIERE	LA THUILE			
Page	458	463	470	477	483			
Fast lifts	***	***	***	***	**			
Snow	**	****	****	****	****			
Extent	****	*****	*****	****	***			
Expert	**	**	**	***	**			
Intermediate	****	*****	*****	****	****			
Beginner	**	****	***	***	****			
Convenience	**	***	***	***	***			
Queues	***	***	***	***	****			
Restaurants‡	***	****	****	**	*			
Scenery	***	*****	*****	***	***			
Resort charm	**	***	***	*	***			
Off-slope	*	***	***	*	**			

‡ Refers to mountain restaurants only

SWITZERLAND

Resort ratings at a glance

	ADELBODEN	ANDERMATT	AROSA	CHAMPERY	CRANS-MONTANA	DAVOS		
Page	498	500	503	506	508	510		
Fast lifts	***	**	***	**	***	***		
Snow	***	****	***	**	**	****		
Extent	***	*	**	*****	***	*****		
Expert	**	****	**	***	**	****		
Intermediate	***	**	***	****	****	*****		
Beginner	****	*	****	**	***	**		
Convenience	**	***	**	*	**	**		
Queues	***	**	****	****	***	***		
Restaurants‡	***	*	***	***	***	***		
Scenery	****	***	***	****	****	****		
Resort charm	****	****	**	****	**	**		
Off-slope	****	**	****	***	****	*****		

	GRINDEL-WALD	KLOSTERS	LAAX	MÜRREN	SAAS-FEE	ST MORITZ		
Page	517	521	523	525	529	534		
Fast lifts	****	***	****	****	****	****		
Snow	**	****	***	***	*****	****		
Extent	***	*****	****	*	**	*****		
Expert	**	****	***	***	***	****		
Intermediate	****	*****	*****	***	****	****		
Beginner	***	***	****	**	*****	**		
Convenience	**	**	***	***	***	*		
Queues	**	**	****	***	***	**		
Restaurants‡	***	***	***	**	***	****		
Scenery	*****	****	***	*****	****	****		
Resort charm	****	****	***	*****	*****	*		
Off-slope	****	****	***	***	****	*****		

	VAL D'ANNIVIERS	VERBIER	VILLARS	WENGEN	ZERMATT			
Page	541	544	556	558	563			
Fast lifts	**	**	***	****	*****			
Snow	****	***	**	**	****			
Extent	**	*****	***	***	****			
Expert	****	*****	**	**	*****			
Intermediate	***	***	***	****	****			
Beginner	***	**	****	***	*			
Convenience	**	**	***	***	*			
Queues	****	***	***	***	***			
Restaurants‡	**	***	***	****	*****			
Scenery	****	****	***	*****	*****			
Resort charm	*****	***	****	*****	*****			
Off-slope	*	***	****	****	****			

USA

	CALIFORNIA		SQUAW VALLEY	COLORADO	BEAVER CREEK	BRECKEN-RIDGE	COPPER MOUNTAIN	KEYSTONE
	HEAVENLY	MAMMOTH		ASPEN				
Page	579	584	589	592	599	601	606	608
Fast lifts	***	****	***	***	*****	****	**	****
Snow	****	****	****	*****	*****	*****	*****	*****
Extent	***	***	***	****	**	**	**	**
Expert	***	****	****	*****	****	****	****	***
Intermediate	****	****	**	*****	****	****	****	****
Beginner	****	****	****	*****	*****	****	****	****
Convenience	*	**	****	**	****	***	****	**
Queues	****	****	****	****	*****	****	****	****
Restaurants‡	*	*	*	***	**	**	*	***
Scenery	****	***	***	***	***	***	***	***
Resort charm	*	**	***	****	**	***	**	**
Off-slope	**	*	*	****	***	***	*	**

	SNOWMASS	STEAMBOAT	TELLURIDE	VAIL	WINTER PARK	UTAH ALTA	THE CANYONS	DEER VALLEY
Page	610	612	615	617	624	629	631	633
Fast lifts	***	***	*****	****	***	***	***	****
Snow	*****	****	****	*****	*****	*****	****	****
Extent	****	***	**	****	***	***	***	**
Expert	*****	***	****	****	****	*****	****	***
Intermediate	*****	****	***	*****	****	***	****	****
Beginner	*****	*****	*****	***	*****	***	**	****
Convenience	****	***	****	***	***	****	****	****
Queues	****	****	*****	**	****	***	****	****
Restaurants‡	***	***	*	**	***	**	***	****
Scenery	****	***	****	***	***	***	***	***
Resort charm	**	**	****	***	**	**	**	***
Off-slope	***	**	**	***	*	*	**	**

	PARK CITY	SNOWBIRD	REST OF THE WEST BIG SKY	JACKSON HOLE	NEW ENGLAND KILLINGTON	STOWE
Page	635	640	643	648	654	658
Fast lifts	***	***	***	**	**	***
Snow	****	*****	*****	****	***	***
Extent	***	***	****	***	**	*
Expert	****	*****	****	*****	***	***
Intermediate	****	***	****	**	***	****
Beginner	****	**	*****	***	****	****
Convenience	**	*****	****	***	*	*
Queues	****	***	*****	***	****	****
Restaurants‡	**	*	*	*	*	**
Scenery	***	***	***	***	***	***
Resort charm	***	*	*	***	*	****
Off-slope	***	*	**	***	*	*

‡ Refers to mountain restaurants only

99

Resort ratings at a glance

100

	WESTERN CANADA BANFF	BIG WHITE	FERNIE	KICKING HORSE	LAKE LOUISE	PANORAMA	SUN PEAKS	WHISTLER
Page	665	672	675	680	682	687	689	692
Fast lifts	****	***	**	**	***	***	***	****
Snow	****	*****	*****	****	***	***	****	****
Extent	****	***	***	***	****	**	***	****
Expert	****	***	*****	****	****	****	***	*****
Intermediate	****	****	**	***	****	***	****	*****
Beginner	***	****	****	***	***	****	****	***
Convenience	*	****	****	****	*	****	****	****
Queues	****	*****	****	*****	****	*****	*****	***
Restaurants‡	***	*	*	**	**	*	*	**
Scenery	****	***	***	***	*****	***	***	***
Resort charm	***	**	**	**	***	**	***	***
Off-slope	*****	**	**	*	****	*	**	**

	EASTERN CANADA TREMBLANT							
Page	702							
Fast lifts	****							
Snow	****							
Extent	*							
Expert	**							
Intermediate	***							
Beginner	****							
Convenience	****							
Queues	***							
Restaurants‡	**							
Scenery	***							
Resort charm	****							
Off-slope	***							

	ANDORRA ARINSAL	PAS DE LA CASA	SOLDEU	SPAIN BAQUEIRA	NORWAY HEMSEDAL	SWEDEN ÅRE	BULGARIA BANSKO	NEW ZEALAND QUEENSTOWN
Page	109	111	113	705	711	714	717	729
Fast lifts	**	***	***	**	**	**	*****	**
Snow	****	****	****	***	****	***	***	**
Extent	*	***	***	**	*	**	*	*
Expert	*	*	*	***	**	**	**	***
Intermediate	**	***	***	****	****	****	****	***
Beginner	***	****	****	**	***	****	**	***
Convenience	***	****	***	***	**	***	**	*
Queues	***	***	***	****	****	****	***	***
Restaurants‡	*	**	**	**	*	***	***	*
Scenery	***	***	***	***	**	***	***	****
Resort charm	*	*	*	**	**	***	**	**
Off-slope	*	*	*	*	*	***	*	*****

‡ Refers to mountain restaurants only

Resort shortlists

To help you spot resorts that will suit you

To streamline the job of spotting the ideal resort for your own holiday, here are lists of the best ten or so resorts for 21 different categories. Some lists embrace European and North American resorts, but many we've confined to Europe, because the US has too many qualifying resorts (eg for beginners) or because the US does things differently, making comparisons invalid (eg for off-piste).

SOMETHING FOR EVERYONE
Resorts with everything from reassuring nursery slopes to real challenges for experts
Alpe-d'Huez, France p245
Les Arcs, France p255
Aspen, Colorado p592
Courchevel, France p288
Flaine, France p306
Mammoth, California p584
Vail, Colorado p617
Val d'Isère, France p404
Whistler, Canada p692
Winter Park, Colorado p624

INTERNATIONAL OVERSIGHTS
Resorts that deserve as much attention as the ones we go back to every year, but don't seem to get it
Alta, Utah p629
Andermatt, Switzerland p500
Bad Gastein, Austria p129
Big Sky, Montana p643
Les Contamines, France p286
Copper Mountain, Colorado p606
Laax, Switzerland p525
Monterosa Ski, Italy p452
Risoul, France p362
Telluride, Colorado p615

HIGH-MILEAGE PISTE-BASHING
Extensive intermediate slopes with big lift networks
Alpe-d'Huez, France p245
Davos/Klosters, Switzerland p510
Laax, Switzerland p523
Milky Way: Sauze d'Oulx (Italy), Montgenèvre (France) pp458/337
Paradiski, France p348
Portes du Soleil, France/Switz p359
Sella Ronda, Italy p463
Selva, Italy p470
Les Sybelles, France p384
Trois Vallées, France p402
Val d'Isère/Tignes, France pp404/393
Whistler, Canada p692

RELIABLE SNOW IN THE ALPS
Alpine resorts with good snow records or lots of snowmaking, and high or north-facing slopes
Chamonix, France p269
Cervinia, Italy p430
Courchevel, France p288
Hintertux, Austria p138
Lech/Zürs, Austria p165
Obergurgl, Austria p185
Saas-Fee, Switzerland p529
Val d'Isère/Tignes, France pp404/393
Val Thorens, France p416
Zermatt, Switzerland p563

OFF-PISTE WONDERS
Alpine resorts where, with the right guidance and equipment, you can have the time of your life
Alpe-d'Huez, France p245
Andermatt, Switzerland p500
Chamonix, France p269
Davos/Klosters, Switzerland p510
La Grave, France p315
Lech/Zürs, Austria p165
Monterosa Ski, Italy p452
St Anton, Austria p213
Val d'Isère/Tignes, France pp404/393
Verbier, Switzerland p544

DRAMATIC SCENERY
Resorts where the mountains are not just high and snowy, but spectacularly scenic too
Chamonix, France p269
Cortina, Italy p436
Courmayeur, Italy p441
Heavenly, California p579
Jungfrau resorts (Grindelwald, Mürren, Wengen), Switzerland pp517/525/558
Lake Louise, Canada p682
Megève, France p317
Saas-Fee, Switzerland p529
St Moritz, Switzerland p534
Selva, Italy p470
Zermatt, Switzerland p563

↑ Another year, another picture of Chamonix from Ian, our production manager. As he spent last season there (he says it ticks all his boxes), we had to squeeze one in. The ridge-walk down to the glacier from the Aiguille du Midi is famously the scariest part of the Vallée Blanche expedition

IAN STRATFORD

Resort shortlists

TOP TERRAIN-PARKS
Resorts with the best parks, pipes and rails for all your freestyle thrills
Avoriaz, France p265
Les Deux-Alpes, France p300
Laax, Switzerland p523
Lech, Austria p165
Livigno, Italy p446
Mammoth, California p584
Mayrhofen, Austria p175
Park City, Utah p635
Vail, Colorado p617
Whistler, Canada p692

CHOPAHOLICS
Resorts where you can quit the conventional lift network and have a day riding helicopters or cats
Aspen, Colorado p592
Fernie, Canada p675
Lech/Zürs, Austria p165
Monterosa Ski, Italy p452
Panorama, Canada p687
Verbier, Switzerland p544
Whistler, Canada p692
Zermatt, Switzerland p563

POWDER PARADISES
Resorts with the snow, the terrain and (ideally) the lack of crowds that make for powder perfection
Alta/Snowbird, Utah pp629/640
Andermatt, Switzerland p500
Big Sky, Montana p643
Big White, Canada p672
Fernie, Canada p675
La Grave, France p315
Jackson Hole, Wyoming p648
Kicking Horse, Canada p680
Monterosa Ski, Italy p452
Ste-Foy, France p378

BLACK RUNS
Resorts with steep, mogully, lift-served slopes within the safety of the piste network
Alta/Snowbird, Utah pp629/640
Andermatt, Switzerland p500
Argentière/Chamonix, France p269
Aspen, Colorado p592
Beaver Creek, Colorado p599
Courchevel, France p288
Jackson Hole, Wyoming p648
Whistler, Canada p692
Winter Park, Colorado p624
Zermatt, Switzerland p563

MOTORWAY CRUISING
Long, gentle, super-smooth pistes to bolster the frail confidence of those not long off the nursery slope
Les Arcs, France p255
Breckenridge, Colorado p601
Cervinia, Italy p430
Cortina, Italy p436
Courchevel, France p288
Megève, France p317
La Plagne, France p350
Snowmass, Colorado p610
La Thuile, Italy p483
Vail, Colorado p617

WEATHERPROOF SLOPES
Alpine resorts with snow-sure slopes if the sun shines, and trees in case it doesn't
Les Arcs, France p255
Courchevel, France p288
Courmayeur, Italy p441
Laax, Switzerland p523
Schladming, Austria p199
Selva, Italy p470
Serre-Chevalier, France p370
Sestriere, Italy p477
La Thuile, Italy p483

SPECIALLY FOR FAMILIES
Alpine resorts where you can easily find accommodation surrounded by snow, not by traffic and fumes
Les Arcs, France p255
Avoriaz, France p265
Flaine, France p306
Lech, Austria p165
Montchavin (La Plagne), France p350
Mürren, Switzerland p525
Puy-St-Vincent, France p360
Risoul, France p362
Saas-Fee, Switzerland p529
Les Sybelles, France p384
Valmorel, France p414
Wengen, Switzerland p558

peak retreats

Beat the crowds
Traditional resorts

0870 770 0408

www.peakretreats.co.uk

ABTA W5537

RESORTS FOR BEGINNERS
European resorts with gentle, snow-sure nursery slopes and easy, longer runs to progress to

BACK-DOOR RESORTS
Cute little Alpine villages linked to big, bold ski areas, giving you the best of two different worlds

SNOW-SURE BUT SIMPATICO
Alpine resorts with high-rise slopes, but low-rise, traditional-style buildings

SPECIAL MOUNTAIN RESTAURANTS
Alpine resorts where the mountain restaurants can really add an extra dimension to your holiday

VILLAGE CHARM
Resorts with traditional character that enriches your holiday – from mountain villages to mining towns

MODERN CONVENIENCE
Alpine resorts where there's plenty of slope-side accommodation to make life easy

LIVELY NIGHTLIFE
European resorts where you'll have no difficulty finding somewhere to boogie, and someone to do it with

OTHER AMUSEMENTS
Alpine resorts where those not interested in skiing or boarding can still find plenty to do

Resort shortlists

Our resort chapters

How to get the best out of them

FINDING A RESORT

The bulk of the book consists of the chapters listed on the facing page, devoted to individual major resorts, plus minor resorts that share the same lift system. Sometimes we devote a chapter to an area not dominated by one resort, in which case we use the area name (eg Les Sybelles, Monterosa).

Chapters are grouped by country: first, the five major European countries; then the US and Canada (where resorts are grouped by states or regions); then minor European countries; then Japan, and lastly countries in the southern hemisphere. Within each group, resorts are ordered alphabetically.

Short cuts to the resorts that might suit you are provided (on the pages preceding this one) by a table of comparative **star ratings** and a series of **shortlists** of resorts with particular merits.

At the back of the book is an **index** to the resort chapters, combined with a **directory** giving basic information on hundreds of other minor resorts. If the resort you are looking up is covered in a chapter devoted to a bigger resort, the page reference will take you to the start of that chapter, not to the exact page on which the minor resort is described.

There's further guidance on using our information in the chapter on 'Choosing your resort', on page 92 – designed to be helpful particularly to people with little or no experience of resorts, who may not appreciate how big the differences between one resort and another can be (ie like chalk and cheese).

READING A CHAPTER

The **cost** of visiting each resort is rated on a scale of one to six – ①②③④⑤⑥ to ①②③④⑤⑥ – reflecting the typical cost of a one-week trip based on a half-board package from the UK, plus a lift pass and an allowance for lunch in mountain restaurants. We assume two people sharing a room – even in the US, where package prices are often based on four people sharing.

Star ratings summarise our view of the resort in 12 respects, including how well it suits different standards of skier/boarder. The more stars, the better.

We give phone numbers and internet addresses of the **tourist office** (in North America, the ski lift company) and phone numbers for recommended **hotels**. We give star ratings for hotels – either official ones or ones awarded by major tour operators. The UK tour operators offering **package holidays** in each resort are listed in the margins of resort chapters.

Our **mountain maps** show the resorts' own classification of runs – so those for the US and Canada show green, blue and black runs, and no red ones. On some maps we show black diamonds to mark expert terrain without defined runs. We do not distinguish single-diamond terrain from the steeper double-diamond.

We include on the map any lifts definitely planned for construction for the coming season.

We use the following symbols to identify **fast lifts**:

⓯	fast chair-lift
⓰	gondola
⓱	'chondola' – chair/gondola
⓲	cable-car
⓳	railway/funicular

THE WORLD'S BEST WINTER SPORTS RESORTS

To find a minor resort, or if you are not sure which country you should be looking under, consult the index/directory at the back of the book, which lists all resorts alphabetically.

Our resort chapters

105

Saturday, 11:15 am

Come to ski. Come to laugh. Come to breathe.
Break your routine and come to Andorra:
you will great sun, fun and all sorts of compliments
to spend some unforgettable days.
Come to Vallnord: much more than fine snow.

www.vallnord.com

Andorra
EL PAÍS DELS PIRINEUS

VALLNORD TURISME

Andorra

Andorra is the fourth most popular winter sports destination for Brits, attracting some 80,000 package holidaymakers – well ahead of both Switzerland and North America. With all these people basically travelling to two ski areas – Grandvalira (see the chapters on Soldeu and Pas de la Casa) and Vallnord (see the chapter on Arinsal and the description of Arcalis overleaf), it's difficult to get away from fellow Brits. It's also difficult to escape traffic and building sites – Andorra has lots of both.

Andorra used to be seen primarily as a cheap and cheerful holiday destination, aimed mainly at younger singles and couples looking for a good time in the duty-free bars and clubs as well as learning to ski or snowboard. But things have changed. In recent years, some more upmarket hotels have been built (though they often resemble Spanish summer package hotels, with their self-service buffet meals). And lots of money has been pumped in to developing powerful lift systems and piste-grooming fleets that many well-known Alpine resorts would be proud of; this makes the slopes much more attractive to intermediates as well as beginners. Reporters tell us the cost of drinks as well as packages has edged up, and even Arinsal now seems to attract more families than youths. Andorra no longer competes with eastern Europe for the budget market; it costs more, and delivers much more.

One thing remains unchanged, happily: the ski schools have always been excellent, with lots of native English-speaking instructors, and standards in this key part of the Andorran recipe are holding up.

Despite a poor 2006/07 season (like much of the rest of Europe), Andorra has a relatively reliable snow record. Its situation close to both the Atlantic Ocean and the Mediterranean Sea, together with the high altitude of its resorts, mean that it usually gets substantial natural snowfalls. It has also invested heavily in snowmaking.

Both package holiday prices and prices for drinks and extras such as instruction and equipment rental are generally lower than in the Alps. Beer is reportedly no cheaper than in the UK, but large servings of spirits mean that nightlife can be lively. Some reporters find duty-free luxury goods prices not the super-bargains they had expected.

The sight of cranes – as hotels and apartments are built to keep up with demand – is still common. It is no longer true to say that the resorts resemble giant construction sites, but they all still have construction sites within them (or on the edge of them, as they expand in sprawling fashion along the roadside).

STAYING DOWN THE VALLEY

Several valley towns can be used as alternative bases to the main resorts, either to use the slopes of one ski area or to explore all three during a week.

One obviously strong candidate here is **Encamp**, which has a powerful 18-seat gondola giving a quick way into the whole of the **Grandvalira** ski

LIFT PASSES

Ski Andorra
The Ski Andorra pass
covers all Andorran
areas and allows
skiing at any single
one of them each
day. For five non-
consecutive days in
high season: €162;
for five consecutive
days in low season
€152.

Phone numbers
From abroad use the
prefix +376

TOURIST OFFICES

Ski Andorra
t 805200
skiandorra@ski
andorra.ad
www.skiandorra.ad

Arcalis
t 739600
ito.reserves@
andorra.ad
www.vallnord.com

area shared by Soldeu and Pas de la Casa. Encamp seemed to us the least attractive of the valley towns (not least because of its situation on the traffic-choked main road), but we haven't examined it closely and a couple of reporters have recommended it. It is certainly cheap.

La Massana is a more appealing town, and since 2004/05 it has been linked to the Pal-Arinsal ski area by gondola. It is also more convenient for Arcalis than Arinsal or Pal (Arcalis, Pal and Arinsal are all part of the **Vallnord** area and covered by a joint lift pass). **Ordino** is slightly nearer still to Arcalis, and pleasantly rustic, but it has no direct access to slopes.

The capital, **Andorra la Vella**, is not far down the valley from Encamp and is a more attractive base for someone wanting a more rounded holiday (though it, too, is choked by traffic and 'appalling' fumes). There are plenty of high-quality, if relatively expensive, hotels within easy walking distance of the centre, and there is also plenty of choice when it comes to dining out and finding bars and nightclubs that stay open until 4am. The clientele is mainly Andorran and Spanish. The duty-free shopping could fill a page, but probably the most interesting feature of the city is the Caldea spa at Escales-Engordany just outside the centre: indoor and outdoor pools, fountains and waterfalls, saunas, hot-tubs, Turkish baths, sunbeds, hydrotherapy, massage ... even a grapefruit bath!

OUTINGS TO ARCALIS

Arcalis is the most remote area of slopes in Andorra, tucked away at the head of a long valley, and most British visitors to Soldeu or Pas de la Casa never hear about it. But it makes a very worthwhile day trip, particularly from Arinsal and Pal. The variety of the terrain at Arcalis is greater than in most of the main resorts, the slopes are usually deserted except at weekends (when locals pour in), and the snow is usually the best you will find. It provides excellent intermediate and beginner terrain, but of all Andorra's resorts it has the most to offer experts, including lots of off-piste between the marked runs. 'A real jewel – the boarder in our group (who has visited a few Alpine resorts) was in heaven,' said a recent reporter.

There is no accommodation at the mountain, just a day lodge and a lot of car parking, but buildings are now springing up along the Vall d'Ordino leading up to it. Buses are not frequent.

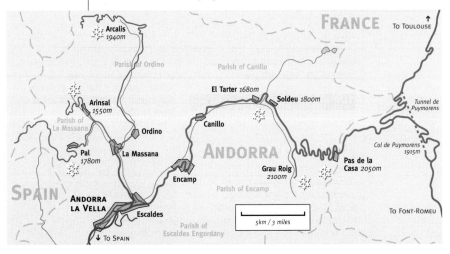

Arinsal

Cheap, lively base that suits beginners best; La Massana is better if you want to explore Arcalis (covered by the Vallnord lift pass) too

COSTS

① ② ③ ④ ⑤ ⑥

RATINGS

The slopes

Fast lifts	**
Snow	****
Extent	*
Expert	*
Intermediate	**
Beginner	***
Convenience	***
Queues	***
Mountain restaurants	*

The rest

Scenery	***
Resort charm	*
Off-slope	*

NEWS

For 2007/08 a six-pack is due to replace the old Cubil quad at Pal. In Arinsal, the blue Marrades piste back to the valley is being improved to enable it to be open more often, and there are plans for a themed children's snowpark and revamped nursery.

For 2006/07 a new snowmaking lake was built and 30 new guns were added. A new beginners' terrain-park was installed in Pal. The children's area in Pal has been extended and a new moving carpet added. And the beginners' area in Arinsal continues to be improved with a second moving carpet and piste widening.

UK PACKAGES

Airtours, Crystal, Directski.com, First Choice, Inghams, Neilson, Panorama, Ski McNeill, Ski Wild, Skitracer, Thomson

➕ Lively bars

➕ Ski school geared to British needs

➕ Cable-car link with Pal and shared Vallnord lift pass with Arcalis (see the Andorra introduction)

➕ Pretty, tree-lined slopes in Pal

➖ Very confined and bleak local slopes

➖ Runs to village need good snow to be open, and don't lead to centre

➖ Long, linear and rather dour village, with no focus

➖ Poor bus link to Arcalis

Arinsal is the most British-dominated resort in Andorra, largely because British tour operators are able to offer packages here at tempting prices. The resort attracts mainly first-time skiers and riders; reports suggest that Arinsal, like the rest of Andorra, is managing to attract more families and fewer binge drinkers.

THE RESORT

Arinsal is a long, narrow village of grey, stone-clad buildings, near the head of a steep-sided valley north of Andorra la Vella. Development in recent years has been rapid.

The gondola from the village centre is the main way to and from the slopes and staying close to it is convenient; the alternative chair-lift, 1km/0.5 miles out of town, is largely irrelevant – though you can stay next to it and ski to the door in good conditions. Or you can drive to the top of the gondola.

There is some accommodation at Pal (a bus-ride from the lift base) and in the lower town of La Massana (with a gondola up to Pal's slopes). La Massana is a better place to stay if you want to visit Arcalis (closer and with a better bus service; from Arinsal you have to change in La Massana to reach Arcalis, though some tour ops lay on weekly excursions). Buses between Arinsal and La Massana are infrequent ('and unreliable' says a 2007 reporter).

Reporters have commented on the friendliness of the locals – 'We were made to feel very welcome.'

THE MOUNTAINS

The area above Arinsal is an open, east-facing bowl. Pal, in contrast, has the most densely wooded slopes in Andorra. Most face east; those down to the link with Arinsal face north.

Slopes Arinsal's slopes consist essentially of a single, long, narrow, bowl above the upper gondola station at Comallempla, served by a network of chairs and drags, including a quad and six-pack. Almost at the top is the cable-car link to and from Pal. Pal's slopes are widely spread around the mountain, with four main lift bases, all reachable by road. The main one, La Caubella, at the opposite extreme from the Arinsal link, is the arrival point of the gondola from La Massana. The Vallnord lift pass now covers Arcalis too – see Andorra introduction. Reporters remark on the good grooming and signposting.

Terrain-parks Arinsal's big freestyle area has its own lift, a huge half-pipe, big jump, terrain-park with spines, fun-boxes, rails and quarter-pipes, boarder-cross and a chill-out area. Pal now has a beginners' park.

Snow reliability With most runs above 1950m/6,400ft, north-easterly orientation and a decent amount of snowmaking, snow is relatively assured. But 2007 was an exceptionally poor year for snow in Andorra and a January reporter found the link with Pal closed because of 'no snowmaking on a crucial blue linking run in Pal'.

Experts This isn't a great area for experts, but there are off-piste free-ride areas marked on the map in both Arinsal and Pal – the latter offering some great tree-skiing. Arcalis has more to offer.

Intermediates Arinsal offers a fair range of difficulty, but decent intermediates will want to explore the much more interesting, varied and extensive Pal and Arcalis slopes.

Beginners Around half the guests here are beginners. Arinsal and Pal both have gentle nursery slopes set apart from the main runs; they can get very crowded at peak times. There are long easy runs to progress to, as well.

↑ There's a good beginner area, but it can get crowded
DAVID MAXWELL-LEES

KEY FACTS

Resort	1470m
	4,820ft
Slopes	1550-2560m
	5,090-8,400ft
Lifts	30
Pistes	63km
	39 miles
Green	12%
Blue	38%
Red	38%
Black	12%
Snowmaking	20km
	12 miles

Phone numbers
From abroad use the prefix +376

TOURIST OFFICES

Arinsal and Pal
t 878000
palarinsal@vallnord.com
www.vallnord.com

Snowboarding It's a good place to learn. But over half the lifts are drags, and some of them are vicious. There are some tedious flat sections in Pal.
Cross-country There isn't any.
Queues Arinsal's gondola can build queues to return to the village at peak times. The cable-car link with Pal can close if the wind is high.
Mountain restaurants Mainly self-service, crowded, with snack food; a 2007 visitor says the Bella Italia at Pla de la Cot in Pal does 'tasty pizzas'. The restaurant at Comallempla is said to run a BBQ if the weather permits.
Schools and guides Over half the instructors are native English-speakers. The reports we have are nearly all positive – 'one of the best'; 'first class'. But groups can be large – 'average of 15' says a 2007 reporter. Another 2007 visitor liked his instructor's 'laid back approach', but a friend's beginner wife was 'left on the mountain to make her own way down'.
Facilities for children There are now two ski kindergartens for four- to eight-year-olds in Pal and nurseries for younger children at Pal and Arinsal.

STAYING THERE

How to go There is a wide choice of hotel and self-catering packages.
Hotels Rooms in the hotel Arinsal (835640) are not large, but it is well run, ideally placed and has a pleasant bar. The Princesa Parc (736500) is a big, glossy 4-star place close to the gondola, with a swanky spa and a bowling alley – 'good quality food; helpful, polite staff; room was palatial'. The big 4-star St Gothard (836005) is popular, except for its position a long way down the hill from the gondola. The Xalet Verdu (737140) is a smooth little 3-star. The Micolau (835052) is a characterful stone house, close to the centre, with simple rooms and a jolly, beamed restaurant. The valley run (see 'News') leads to the Crest (835866).
Self-catering There is a reasonable choice of places.
Eating out The Surf disco-pub and the Rocky Mountain do good steaks. Cisco's is a Tex-Mex place in a lovely wood and stone building. El Rusc and Micolau do good food.
Après-ski Arinsal has plenty of lively bars and discos, such as Quo Vadis ('always has the football on'), El Cau, Surf, Rocky Mountain and El Cisco's. El Derby is heaving on karaoke night. If, like us, you prefer something quieter, head for the bar of the hotel Arinsal.
Off the slopes There are lots of activities, such as dog-sledding, snowmobiling and snow-shoeing, but a recent reporter felt that family entertainment was limited in the evenings. Andorra la Vella is half an hour away by infrequent bus or inexpensive taxi.

Pic Negre
2560m/8,400ft

Pic de Cubil
2360m/7,740ft

Pla de la Cot

La Massana

La Caubella
1950m

Els Fontanals

Setúria

Coll de la Botella
2065m

Comallempla
1950m

Cota
1550m

Pal
1780m/5,840ft

Arinsal
1470m/4,820ft

SNOWPIX.COM / CHRIS GILL

Pas de la Casa

Andorra's liveliest resort – great if you like that kind of thing; we prefer to ski the extensive Grandvalira ski area from a quieter base

111

COSTS

① ② ③ ④ ⑤ ⑥

RATINGS

The slopes

Fast lifts	***
Snow	****
Extent	***
Expert	*
Intermediate	***
Beginner	****
Convenience	****
Queues	***
Mountain restaurants	**

The rest

Scenery	***
Resort charm	*
Off-slope	*

NEWS

For 2006/07 the link with France, Porte des Neiges, was developed further with a new beginner area and a freestyle rail park. The final plan is to have three chair-lifts, a gondola, 50km/31 miles of slopes with 12 runs and the largest beginner area in the Pyrenees.

More snowmaking was installed over the Grandvalira area as a whole with an extra 46 guns.

KEY FACTS

Resort	2100m
	6,890ft

Grandvalira (Soldeu/El Tarter/Pas/Grau Roig)	
Slopes	1710-2560m
	5,610-8,400ft
Lifts	64
Pistes	193km
	120 miles
Green	16%
Blue	35%
Red	29%
Black	20%
Snowmaking	40%

➕ Grandvalira area covers Soldeu too; the joint ski area rivals major resorts in the Alps for size

➕ Andorra's liveliest nightlife

➕ Attractive accommodation at Grau Roig

➖ Pas is an eyesore and the centre suffers from traffic (and fumes)

➖ Weekend crowds from France

➖ Very few woodland slopes – unpleasant in bad weather

The tour op brochures (and the few readers' reports we get) all say that Pas is Andorra's wildest party resort, and we don't doubt it. Having driven through it and skied down to it, we are quite happy to stay over the hill in Soldeu – or, for doorstep access to the Grandvalira slopes, at secluded Grau Roig.

THE RESORT

Sited right on the border between Andorra and France, Pas de la Casa owes its development as much to duty-free sales to the French as to skiing. It is a sizeable collection of dreary concrete-box-style apartment blocks and hotels, a product of the late 1960s and early 1970s. One reporter draws attention to 'loads of restaurants with plastic-covered faded images of burgers and chips'. Quite.

Most accommodation is conveniently placed near the lift base and slopes. The town centre boasts plenty of cheap shops and bars, as well as a sports centre. Reporters complain that the heavy traffic generates fumes, although attempts have been made to keep some areas traffic-free in the evenings, according to a reporter.

The resort attracts a lot of French and Spanish families, as well as Brits.

You can now drive to central Andorra via a toll tunnel which avoids the Port d'Envalira pass; you exit near Grau Roig (pronounced 'Rosh'). This is a mini-resort in an attractively wooded setting that acts as the access point for day visitors arriving by road, but it also makes a good base.

THE MOUNTAINS

The Grandvalira ski area offers an extensive 193km/120 miles of pistes – comparable to big-name Alpine resorts such as Kitzbühel and Les Deux-Alpes. With the exception of a couple of attractively wooded slopes in the central valley, the slopes above Pas are all open, and vulnerable to bad weather. Soldeu is more sheltered.

Slopes The home slopes, facing north-east, descend from a high, north–south ridge; lifts go up to it at four points. Runs on the far side of the ridge converge on Grau Roig, where there is some wooded terrain at the head of the valley. And a single lift goes on further west to the bowl of Llac del Cubill and the rest of the Grandvalira ski area. On the far side of this bowl is the arrival station of the 6km/4 mile gondola up from Encamp. In the opposite direction out of Pas, a newish six-pack is the start of expansion over the French border – on the left side of our map (and see 'News').

Terrain-parks There's a slope-style area with jumps at Grau Roig; a terrain-park (for beginners and intermediates) and a boarder-cross at Pas and rail parks at Grau Roig and over in France.

Snow reliability The combination of height and lots of snowmaking means good snow reliability and a season that often lasts until late April. But on both our visits the snow has been better in the Soldeu sector.

Experts There are few challenges on-piste – the black runs are rarely of serious steepness, and moguls are sparse. But there seem to be plenty of off-piste slopes inviting exploration – a reader recommends the bowls above Grau Roig, in particular.

Intermediates The local slopes cater for confident intermediates best, with plenty of top-to-bottom reds on the main ridge; they do rather lack variety – and can be tricky for more timid intermediates, for whom Soldeu makes a better base.

Beginners There are beginner slopes in Pas, Grau Roig and in the French sector. The Pas area is a short but inconvenient bus-ride out of town.

UK PACKAGES

Airtours, Club Pavilion, Crystal, Directski.com, First Choice, Independent Ski Links, Inghams, Lagrange, Neilson, Panorama, Ski McNeill, Skitracer, Thomson

Phone numbers
From abroad use the prefix +376

Central reservations phone number
For all resort accommodation call 801074

TOURIST OFFICE

t 871900
info@grandvalira.com
www.grandvalira.com

Progression to longer runs is easier in the Grau Roig sector.

Snowboarding Boarding is popular with the young crowd the resort attracts. Drags are usually avoidable.

Cross-country There are loops totalling 13km/8 miles below Grau Roig.

Queues Queues are rarely serious during the week. But at weekends and French school holidays some can develop, especially at Grau Roig – confirmed by a recent visitor.

Mountain restaurants There are routine places at the ridge above Pas and the top of the gondola from Encamp – 'The worst I've found,' says a recent reporter. In contrast, the Rifugi dels Llacs dels Pessons at the head of the Grau Roig bowl is a cosy, beamed table-service restaurant with excellent food – booking recommended.

Schools and guides The ski school has a high reputation – good English.

Facilities for children There are ski kindergartens at Pas and Grau Roig, and a non-ski one at the latter.

STAYING THERE

How to go There are lots of apartments and hotels and a few chalets.

Hotels Himàlaia-Pas (735 515) has a pool and is 'comfortable and recommendable', says a reporter. The Grau Roig hotel (755 556) is in a league of its own for comfort and seclusion. Beware of hotels catering for the 18-30 crowd.

Apartments The Frontera Blanca are simple, but right at the foot of the slopes.

Eating out It's not a resort for gourmets – though one reporter had 'good charcuterie and paella at the restaurant next to the Burger King', and another 'quail and foie gras' at Husky. A local recommends Cal Padri (Catalan food), KSB (good grills) and two places that were new last season: Tagliatelle (pizza and pasta) and Chez Paulo (French cuisine). A recent reader was impressed by the 'friendly and welcoming' attitude of restaurant staff in most places and the good value menu options.

Après-ski Après-ski is very lively. The Milwaukee and Underground bars are popular. The Billboard is 'by far the best club'; Amadeus, Habana, El Mexicano and Sabanah are other options.

Off the slopes You can go dog-sledding, snowmobiling and snow-shoeing, otherwise it is visiting the leisure centre, shopping, or taking a trip to Andorra la Vella for more serious shopping.

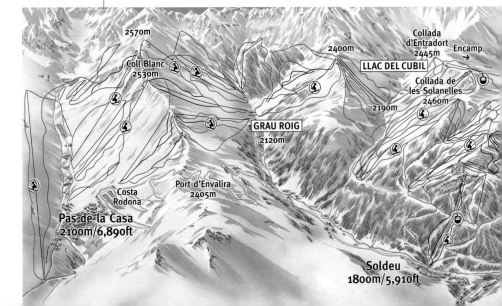

Soldeu

Our favourite place to stay in Andorra: a reasonably pleasant village, centrally placed in the impressive Grandvalira ski area

RATINGS

The slopes

Fast lifts	★★★
Snow	★★★★
Extent	★★★
Expert	★
Intermediate	★★★
Beginner	★★★★
Convenience	★★★
Queues	★★★
Mountain restaurants	★★

The rest

Scenery	★★★
Resort charm	★
Off-slope	★

NEWS

For 2006/07 a six-pack replaced the oldest chair-lift in Soldeu and runs parallel to the main gondola, making it much easier to get up the mountain in the morning. More snowmaking was installed over the Grandvalira area as a whole with the addition of 46 new guns. Soldeu's first 5-star hotel opened, with a huge new spa, Sport Wellness Mountain & Spa (spread over five floors and open to non-residents).

➕ Grandvalira area covers Pas de la Casa too; the joint ski area rivals major resorts in the Alps for size

➕ Not as rowdy a resort as it once was

➕ Excellent beginner and early intermediate terrain

➕ Ski school has excellent British-run section for English-speaking visitors

➖ Slopes can get very crowded

➖ Very little to interest experts

➖ Village is on the main road through Andorra and suffers heavy traffic

➖ Some hotels are way out of town

➖ Not much to do off the slopes

If we were planning a holiday in Andorra, it would be in Soldeu (or the isolated hotel at Grau Roig, up the road – covered in the Pas de la Casa chapter). Despite the traffic, it is the least unattractive village, and its local slopes are the most interestingly varied (though crowded). It shares with neighbouring Pas de la Casa 193km/120 miles of pistes – an area now known as Grandvalira, whose lift system includes four modern gondolas, nine six-packs and six fast quads.

THE RESORT

The village is an ever-growing ribbon of modern buildings with traditional stone cladding – on a steep hillside, lining the busy road that runs through Andorra from France to Spain. Most are hotels, apartments or bars, with the occasional shop; for serious shopping its best to go to Andorra la Vella.

The steep hillside leads down to the river, and the slopes are on the opposite side. A gondola or a new six-pack take you to the heart of the slopes at Espiolets, and a wide bridge across the river forms the end of the piste home, with elevators to take you up to the gondola. A lot of people leave their skis, boots and boards at the bottom or top of the gondola.

El Tarter, a few miles by road down the valley, and Canillo, a few miles further, offer alternative lifts into the slopes. Between all three resorts, hotels and apartments are being built along the main road and sold under the Soldeu banner – so check carefully where your proposed accommodation is. The new Grandvalira bus service (included in the area pass) runs hourly along the valley towards Andorra la Vella – you can hop on or off at different sectors, but a 2007 reporter found it 'so infrequent you have to plan your journey around a particular bus (which will often be late)'.

The terrain-park just above Riba Escorxada is great for experts and beginners alike (and for sitting around) ➔

KEY FACTS

Resort	1800m
	5,910ft

Grandvalira (Soldeu/ El Tarter/Pas/Grau Roig)	
Slopes	1710-2560m
	5,610-8,400ft
Lifts	66
Pistes	193km
	120 miles
Green	16%
Blue	35%
Red	29%
Black	20%
Snowmaking	40%

THE MOUNTAINS

The Grandvalira ski area offers an extensive 193km/120 miles of pistes – a comparable area to big-name Alpine resorts such as Kitzbühel and Les Deux-Alpes. Soldeu's main local slopes are on open mountainsides above the woods, though there are runs in the woods back to all of the lift bases.

THE SLOPES
Pleasantly varied but crowded

The gondola rises over wooded, north-facing slopes to **Espiolets**, a broad shelf that is virtually a mini-resort – the ski school is based here, and there are extensive nursery slopes. From Espiolets, a gentle run to the east

takes you to an area of long, easy runs served by a six-pack. Beyond that is an extensive area of more varied slopes, served by a quad and another six-pack, that links with the Pas de la Casa area. Going west from Espiolets takes you to the open bowl of **Riba Escorxada** and the arrival point of the gondola up from El Tarter. From here, another six-pack serves sunny slopes on Tosa dels Espiolets and a fourth goes to the high-point of Tossal de la Llosada and the link with **El Forn** above Canillo.

TERRAIN-PARKS
A good one

The terrain-park situated just above Riba Escorxada is fast gaining a reputation throughout Europe. The

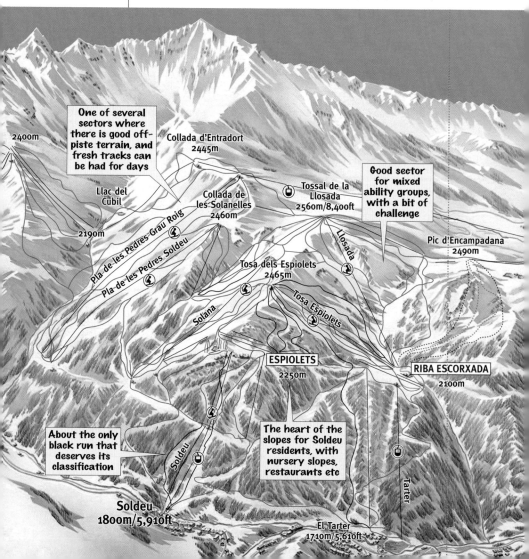

2400m

One of several sectors where there is good off-piste terrain, and fresh tracks can be had for days

Collada d'Entradort
2445m

Llac del Cubil

2190m

Collada de les Solanelles
2460m

Pla de les Pedres-Grau Roig

Pla de les Pedres Soldeu

Tossal de la Llosada
2560m/8,400ft

Good sector for mixed ability groups, with a bit of challenge

Pic d'Encampadana
2490m

Llosada

Tosa dels Espiolets
2465m

Tosa Espiolets

Solana

ESPIOLETS
2250m

RIBA ESCORXADA
2100m

About the only black run that deserves its classification

The heart of the slopes for Soldeu residents, with nursery slopes, restaurants etc

Soldeu

Tarter

Soldeu
1800m/5,910ft

El Tarter
1710m/5,610ft

triple line of kickers that ranges between 8m and 16m (26ft and 52ft) had a transfer gap added for 2006/07 and the bottom of the park is marked by an impressive hip. There is a great selection of rails including a double rainbow S-box and two wall rides. But there is fun for all levels in this little freestyle oasis. For beginners there is a series of three small jumps culminating in a 5m/16ft long medium jump and a couple of fun-boxes to slide on. In 2007 the resort acquired a pipe dragon, which means the pipe is now being shaped daily and is in better condition than it has ever been. A drag-lift services the park, but there is also a speedy quad that takes you slightly higher up the hill.

SNOW RELIABILITY
Much better than people expect
Despite its name (Soldeu means Sun God) the slopes enjoy reliable snow (though like most of Europe, 2006/07 was an exceptionally poor year for natural snow). Most slopes are north-facing, with a good natural snow record and there's snowmaking on 40 per cent of the pistes. The excellent grooming helps maintain good snow.

FOR EXPERTS
Hope for good off-piste
It's a limited area for experts, at least on-piste. The Avet black run down to Soldeu deserves its grading, but most of the other blacks would be no more than reds (or even blues) in many

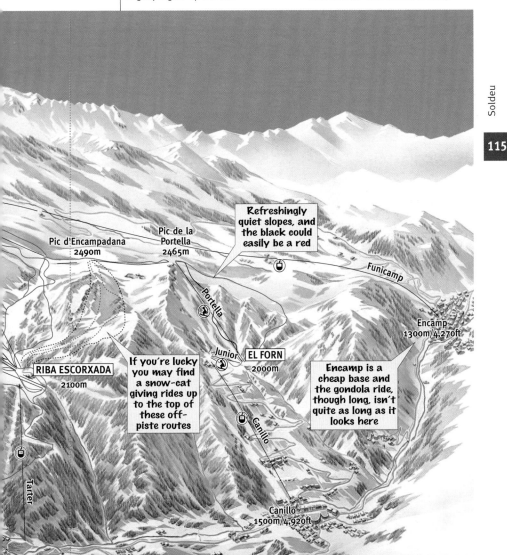

Pic d'Encampadana
2490m

Pic de la Portella
2465m

Refreshingly quiet slopes, and the black could easily be a red

Portella

Funicamp

Encamp
1300m/4,270ft

Junior   EL FORN
2000m

RIBA ESCORXADA
2100m

If you're lucky you may find a snow-cat giving rides up to the top of these off-piste routes

Encamp is a cheap base and the gondola ride, though long, isn't quite as long as it looks here

Canillo

Tarter

Canillo
1500m/4,920ft

LIFT PASSES

Grandvalira

Prices in €

Age	1-day	6-day
under 12	29	141
12 to 64	37	188
over 65	17	102

Free under 6, over 70
Beginner pass in each sector for beginners' area €22 per day

Notes
Covers all lifts in Soldeu, El Tarter, Canillo, Grau Roig and Pas de la Casa; pedestrian and local day and half-day passes available

Alternative passes
The Ski Andorra pass covers all Andorran areas and allows skiing at any single one of them each day; for five non-consecutive days in high season: €168; for five consecutive days in low season: €157.50

UK PACKAGES

Airtours, Club Pavilion, Crystal, Directski.com, First Choice, Independent Ski Links, Inghams, Neilson, Panorama, Ski McNeill, Ski Wild, Skitracer, Thomson
El Tarter Airtours, Club Pavilion, First Choice, Neilson, Panorama
Canillo Club Pavilion, Lagrange, Solo's

boarding

Soldeu has become the home of snowboarding in the Pyrenees. This is a perfect place for beginners to learn on the nice wide slopes that aren't too steep. Most of the lifts are chairs not drags – ideal for less confident snowboarders. For the more advanced, Soldeu offers some good off piste, steeper areas and the best snow-park in the Pyrenees. However, true backcountry enthusiasts should head to Arcalis, which has the steepest terrain and heli-boarding. Soldeu's snowboard shop Loaded is a real hub in the area, and the staff will give you plenty of pointers.

resorts. The blacks on Tosa dels Espiolets are indistinguishable from the neighbouring (and more direct) red and blue, for example. But there is plenty of off-piste potential – notably in the bowl above Riba Escorxada, in the Espiolets and and Solanelles areas (we had a great time there in fresh powder on our last visit), and above El Forn. And the off-piste remains untouched for days because most visitors are beginners and early intermediates. When conditions permit at weekends, a snowcat takes people up to Pic d'Encampadana, from where four off-piste routes (dotted on our map) descend to Riba Escorxada.

FOR INTERMEDIATES
Explore Grandvalira
There is plenty to amuse all but the very keenest intermediates. The area east of Espiolets is splendid for building confidence, while those who already have it will be able to explore the whole mountain. Riba Escorxada is a fine section for mixed ability groups. The Canillo/El Forn sector has an easy, little-used blue run along the ridge with excellent views all the way to Pal and Arinsal and an easy black in the valley. Many of the blues and reds have short steeper sections, preceded by a 'slow' sign and netting in the middle of the piste to slow you down.

FOR BEGINNERS
One of the best
This is an excellent place to start. The Espiolets nursery area is huge and there's a smaller area at Riba Escorxada, above El Tarter (which one reader reckons is better) – both with a moving carpet. They are relatively snow-sure, and there are numerous easy pistes to move on to (though the crowds can be off-putting). And the ski school is top-notch. The final bend on the Esquirol run to El Tarter was named 'carnage corner' by one reporter, who recommends a return to the resort by lift for the inexperienced.

FOR CROSS-COUNTRY
Er, what cross-country?
There is no cross-country in Soldeu. There is some not far away at Grau Roig (see Pas de la Casa chapter), but Andorra's serious cross-country resort is La Rabassa, in the south-west corner of the country – 15km/9 miles of loops at an altitude of 2000m/6,560ft.

QUEUES
Crowds more of a problem
Most of Grandvalira's key lifts are high-speed chairs or gondolas, though there are a lot of slow lifts too. But the system seems to be able to cope. Pressure on the gondola out of Soldeu has been eased by last season's new six-pack, but allow time for the queue-prone Cubil chair back from Grau Roig. More of a problem than queues is crowds on the blue slopes (including lots of school classes snaking along) – the reds and blacks are much quieter.

MOUNTAIN RESTAURANTS
Not a highlight
The mountain restaurants are crowded and the food generally dull (a notable exception is Rifugi dels Llacs dels Pessons – see Pas de la Casa). There is a choice of places at Espiolets, including table-service at Gall de Bosc, which was recommended by a reporter. Roc de les Bruixes at El Forn claims to be 'gastronomic' and has a 'large terrace with terrific views'. Many reporters favour descending to the valley for lunch; recommendations in 2007 include the Bruxelles hotel and Sol i Neu in Soldeu, and L'Abarset at El Tarter.

SCHOOLS AND GUIDES
One of the best for Brits
The scale of the teaching operation here is very impressive. The ski school is effectively run as two units. One deals with English-speaking clients, is led by an Englishman and has mostly native English-speaking instructors. Some 40 per cent of the pupils are

SCHOOLS

Soldeu
t 890591

Classes
15hr: €105
Private lessons
€40 for 1hr

CHILDREN

Nurseries run by ski school
Soldeu: ages 2 to 4
Grau Roig: ages 1 to 4; 2hr €17
Snow gardens run by ski school
Ages 3 to 5; five 3hr days €117

Ski school
For ages 6 to 11;
15hr: €100

GETTING THERE

Air Toulouse
196km/121 miles
(3½hr)
Rail L'Hospitalet-Près-L'Andorre (25km/16 miles); buses and taxis to Soldeu

ACTIVITIES

Indoor Thermal spas, bowling (at Pas), leisure centre (pools, hot-tub, gym)
Outdoor Helicopter rides, snowmobiling, dog-sledding, snowshoeing, paragliding, paintballing, archery

Phone numbers
From abroad use the prefix +376
Central reservations phone number
Call 801074

TOURIST OFFICE

t 890500
info@grandvalira.com
www.grandvalira.com

---

beginners and the school has devised a special 'team-teaching' scheme to cope with this volume. The school maintains its excellent reputation for teaching and friendliness: 'one of the reasons for returning to Soldeu', 'instructor was brilliant', 'everyone was very impressed, small classes of eight, English is first language, and good tuition' are typical comments.

FACILITIES FOR CHILDREN
With altitude
Children are looked after at the mid-mountain stations. There are nurseries at Espiolets, Riba Escorxada and El Forn for children from 12 months to three years old and snow gardens for three- to six-year-olds. The Mickey Snow Club (El Tarter) has Disney-themed play areas on the slopes.

STAYING THERE

HOW TO GO
Be careful where you stay
A wide range of UK tour operators offer packages here, mainly in hotels but with some apartments and chalets. Location is important – many places are a bus-ride from town.
Hotels The best hotels are of a far better standard than a decade ago.
*****Sport Hotel Hermitage (870550) Opened last season at the foot of the slopes; all bedrooms are suites with mountain views. A huge new spa is part of the hotel.
****Sport Hotel Village (870500) Right by the Hermitage. Stylish public areas – comfortable chairs and sofas, high ceilings, beams and picture windows.
****Sport (870600) Over the road from the other two Sports. Comfortable, lively bar and a popular basement disco-bar. But dull buffet-style food.
****Piolets Park (871787) Pleasant enough, with a pool. Central.
****Himàlaia (878515) Refurbished, central with sauna, steam and hot-tub.
Self-catering Most reporters are hotel-based, but apartments are available.

EATING OUT
Some atmospheric places
We enjoyed meals in two atmospheric old restored buildings: Borda del Rector (Andorran-run, and with authentic Andorran cuisine), nearer to El Tarter than Soldeu and British-run Fat Albert's (steaks, fish, burgers) in downtown Soldeu. L'Esquirol (Indian) and Pussycat have had good reports.

APRES-SKI
Lively
Après-ski is lively 'but not loutish' – mainly bars and rep-organised events (such as pub crawls with maybe 100 participants). The bar at Fat Albert's has videos shot on the mountain and often a live band. The Pussycat is a good late-night place, with changing party themes. The Piccadilly, under the Sport hotel, is popular. The Aspen and the nearby Avalanche attract a younger crowd. We liked the Villager. Expect noise from late-night revellers.

OFF THE SLOPES
Head downhill
There is the new spa in Soldeu itself. Down in Canillo is the smart Palau de Gel (see below); in Escales-Engordany, the impressive Caldea thermal spa; and in Andorra la Vella some very serious shopping opportunities.

El Tarter 1710m/5,610ft

El Tarter has grown over recent years and is rather sprawling, with no real centre. Reporters recommend two 3-star hotels, del Clos (851500) ('good food but up a steep hill') and del Tarter (802080). We have had decent reviews of the big four-star Euro Esqui (736666) half-way to Soldeu ('food adequate, rooms modern and clean'). Readers complain that the resort is 'dull at night'. The Mosquit pizzeria has been recommended.

Canillo 1500m/4,920ft

If you like the idea of deserted local slopes and don't mind riding a gondola down at the end of the day, consider Canillo, which looks an acceptably pleasant spot as you drive through it. It has the impressive Palau de Gel – an Olympic ice rink plus pool, gym and other amenities.

✗GRANDVALIRA

THE LARGEST SKI AREA IN THE PYRENEES

 Andorra

www.grandvalira.com

AT GRANDVALIRA EXCITEMENT IS GROWING

193 km. of slopes. 3 freestyle areas. 3 slalom stadiums. 450 qualified ski and snowboard instructors . 2 mickey snow club circuits. 40 food and beverage points. 2 mountain adventure centres. 6 resort accesses. Tax free shopping at 4800 stores, 10.000m^2 thermal baths. **No matter how big Grandvalira is, your emotions will always be bigger.**

Austria

Austria's holiday recipe is quite distinctive. It doesn't suit everybody, but for many holidaymakers nothing else will do; in particular, France won't do. Austria is the land of cute little villages clustered around onion-domed churches – there are no monstrous, purpose-built, apartment-block resorts of the kind that are so common in France. It's the land of friendly wooded mountains, reassuring to beginners and timid intermediates in a way that bleak snowfields and craggy peaks will never be. It's the land of friendly, welcoming people who don't find it demeaning to speak their guests' language (if it's English, at least). And it's the land of jolly, alcohol-fuelled après-ski action – in many resorts, starting in mid-afternoon with dancing in mountain restaurants and going on as long as you have the legs for it. For many visitors to Austrian resorts the partying is as important as the skiing or riding. Of course, there are exceptions to all these norms.

In general, Austria isn't the first place you'll want to consider if reliably good snow is your top priority (though there are some wonderful exceptions to this rule, including some of the world's best glacier areas – such as those at Hintertux, at Kaprun and in the Stubai valley – and high, snow-sure resorts such as Obergurgl, Obertauern and Ischgl). But most resorts are relatively low, and conditions are more likely to be problematic here than in higher places. However, Austrian resorts have made great strides in their attempts to catch up with their rivals – most have radically increased their snowmaking capacity in the last decade. In midwinter, especially, lack of snow generally coincides with low night-time temperatures, even at low altitudes, and snowmaking comes into its own. And, except for last winter, recent seasons have been bumper natural snow years for much of Austria.

It's the après-ski that strikes most first-time visitors as being Austria's unique selling point. But Austrian après-ski remains very Austrian – or perhaps German. Huge quantities of beer and schnapps are drunk, German is the predominant language, and German drinking songs are common. So is loud Europop music. People pack into mountain restaurants at the end of the day – some time before the end of the day, actually – and gyrate in their ski boots on the dance floor, on the tables, on the bar, wherever there's room. There are open-air ice bars, umbrella bars and countless transparent 'igloo' bars in which to shelter from bad weather. In many resorts the bands don't stop playing until darkness falls, when the happy punters slide off in the general direction of the village to find another watering hole. After dinner the drinking and dancing starts again – for those who take time out for dinner, that is. Of course, not all resorts conform to this image. But lots of big-name ones with the best and most extensive slopes do. St Anton, Saalbach-Hinterglemm, Ischgl, Sölden and Zell am See, for example, fit this bill.

SNOWPIX.COM / CHRIS GILL
← Big, brash restaurants on the slopes (with après-ski starting mid-afternoon) are part of the Austrian deal – this is Giggijoch, above Sölden

Carinthia (aka Kärnten) is Austria's southernmost province, on the borders with Italy and Slovenia, and it has more hours of sunshine than most other regions of the Alps. It is now easy to reach the local Klagenfurt airport by Ryanair's flights from Stansted three days a week, Thomsonfly charters from Manchester and Austrian Airlines flights via Frankfurt and Vienna.

As well as being home to several large downhill ski areas, Carinthia offers the prospect of an all-round winter holiday, with over 1000km/621 miles of cross-country trails and more than 100 frozen lakes that form natural ice rinks (one of the editors of this book has played ice golf on one of these – the Weissensee). There are also several spas, where you can relax in natural hot springs water.

Bad Kleinkirchheim (Franz Klammer's favourite ski area) is probably the Carinthian resort best known to UK skiers and boarders, and it is covered in its own chapter later in the book. It is hosting the men's slalom and giant slalom World Cup races in the 2007/08 season – on 8 and 9 December 2007.

But Carinthia's largest ski area (with 110km/68 miles of pistes and 30 lifts, including four six-packs and four quad chairs) is the Nassfeld Ski Arena. This is Carinthia's southernmost ski area and has the longest gondola (the 6km/4 mile, three-stage Millennium Express, which rises almost 1300m/4,270ft) and the longest floodlit piste (the last 2.2km/1.4 miles of the 7.6km/4.7 mile long Carnia piste) in the Alps. Most runs are red, with a few blues for beginners and a few ungroomed ski routes. There's a terrain-park, a half-pipe and an area with a quarter-pipe and jumps; and the NTC Fun Sports Park offers 11 different activities, including bikeboarding, tubing, snowbiking and snowblading – all equipment supplied. The ski area is on the border with Italy, and you can lunch in Italian huts (some of the 25 in the area).

The Hohe Tauern region includes three separate ski areas. The Heiligenblut-Grossglockner area has 55km/34 miles of pistes between 1300m/4,270ft and over 2900m/9,510ft, served by 13 lifts. The nearby Mölltal glacier is Carinthia's only glacier and offers guaranteed good snow on over 50km/31 miles of pistes rising to 3120m/10,240ft, reached by a funicular, gondola and then a fast chair. There's also the nearby Ankogel-Mallnitz area of slopes with a two-stage cable-car rising to 2635m/8,650ft and two short drags serving blue, red and black runs on the upper part of the mountain.

There are several other ski areas, including Katschberg (14 lifts, 60km/37 miles of pistes, and with a new 5.5km/3.4 mile peak-to-valley run) and Gerlitzen (14 lifts, 26km/16 miles of pistes, best suited to families, beginners and early intermediates).

All of Carinthia's ski areas are covered by the Top Ski Carinthia ski pass, which costs 175 euros for six days.

Nightlife is not limited to drinking and dancing. There are lots of floodlit toboggan runs, and UK tour operator reps organise Tirolean, bowling, fondue, karaoke and other evenings. And not all resorts are raucous. Lech and Zürs, for example, are full of rich, cool, 'beautiful' people enjoying the comfort of 4- or 5-star sophisticated hotels. And resorts such as Niederau in the Wildschönau, Westendorf and Alpbach are pretty, quiet, family resorts.

One thing that all Austrian resorts have in common is reliably comfortable accommodation – whether it's in 4- or 5-star hotels with pools, saunas and spas (which the Austrians like to call 'wellness centres'), or in great-value, family-run guest houses, of which Austria has thousands. Catered chalets and self-catering apartments are in general much less widely available (though there are one or two resorts, such as St Anton and Kitzbühel, where catered chalets are more easily come by).

One thing to beware of is Austria's strange aversion to credit cards. Reporter after reporter complains that many establishments do not accept cards – even quite upmarket hotels, as well as many ski lift companies. So check if they are accepted well in advance, and have access to plenty of cash.

Austrian resorts are now easier to get to independently using cheap flights. The standard arrival airports are Munich, Salzburg, Innsbruck and, for western resorts, Zürich. But don't overlook less well-known airports such as Klagenfurt in Carinthia and Friedrichshafen, just over the German border and handy for resorts in western Austria such as St Anton, Lech and Ischgl.

GETTING AROUND THE AUSTRIAN ALPS

Austria presents few problems for the car-borne visitor, because practically all the resorts are valley villages, which involve neither steep approach roads nor high altitude.

The dominant feature of Austria for the ski driver is the thoroughfare of the Inn valley, which runs through the Tirol from Landeck via Innsbruck to Kufstein. The motorway along it extends, with one or two breaks, westwards to the Arlberg pass and on to Switzerland. This artery is relatively reliable except in exceptionally bad conditions – the altitude is low, and the road is a vital transport link that is kept open in virtually all conditions.

The Arlberg – which divides Tirol from Vorarlberg, but which is also the watershed between Austria and Switzerland – is one of the

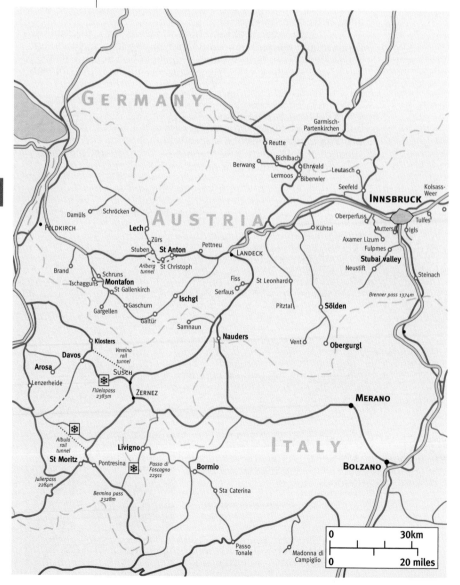

few areas where driving plans are likely to be seriously affected by snow. The east–west Arlberg pass itself has a long tunnel underneath it; this isn't cheap, and you may want to take the high road when it's clear, through Stuben, St Christoph and St Anton. The Flexen pass road to Zürs and Lech (which may be closed by avalanche risk even when the Arlberg pass is open) branches off just to the west of the Arlberg summit.

At the eastern end of the Tirol, the Gerlos pass road from Zell am Ziller over into Salzburg province can be closed. Resorts in Carinthia, such as Bad Kleinkirchheim, are usually reached by motorway, thanks to the Tauern and Katschberg tunnels. The alternative is to drive over the Radstädter Tauern pass through Obertauern, or use the car-carrying rail service from Böckstein to Mallnitz.

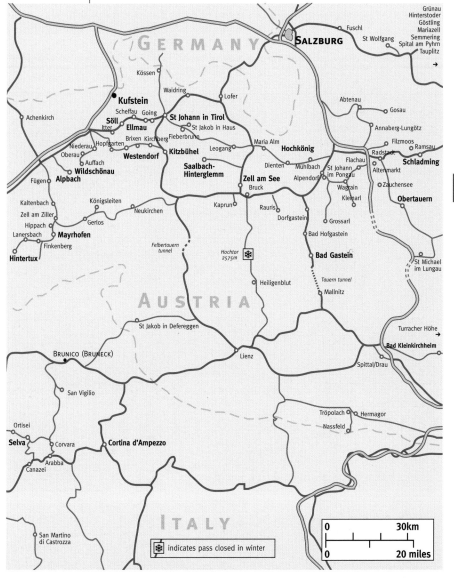

indicates pass closed in winter

Salzburgerland's Ski Amadé lift pass is one of the world's biggest in terms of the amount of terrain and number of lifts covered. What's more, with a car you really could aim to get around most of the resorts it covers – they are clustered close together, no high passes are involved in getting from one resort to another, and many areas are geared to people arriving by car, with out-of-town lifts and serious car parks. (They are also conveniently close to Salzburg airport – we have booked early cheap flights and been on the slopes before lunch time; come departure day we have skied till the end of the day, enjoyed some après-ski, had a leisurely drive to the airport and still had time to kill before our flight home.)

Some of the major resorts covered by the pass have their own chapters in the pages that follow. In the Schladming chapter we also cover the smaller linked resorts of Haus in Ennstal and Pichl, as well as Schladming's elevated outpost of Rohrmoos. Also close to Schladming is Ramsau in Dachstein, which has slopes at village level but also a lift up to the lip of the Dachstein glacier. In the Bad Gastein chapter we cover not only the resorts in the Gastein valley, but also the next-door valley of Grossarl, which is linked over the hill to Dorfgastein.

We also have a chapter on the major area of Hochkönig's Winterreich. Though largely unknown on the British market, it has an extensive network of runs linking Mühlbach, Dienten and Maria Alm.

Another big region is the the Salzburger Sportwelt. The largest linked area here is the 200km/124 mile three-valley system linking Wagrain to Flachau (home of Hermann Maier) in one direction and Alpendorf/St Johann im Pongau in the other. This area also embraces an extensive lift network linking Zauchensee, Flachauwinkl and Kleinarl, plus more modest lift systems at Filzmoos, Radstadt-Altenmarkt, Eben and Goldegg. We skied the Zauchensee and Flachauwinkl slopes for a day last winter and enjoyed it in excellent snow (Zauchensee often has the best snow in the region because of its height and north-facing slopes).

Considering the extent of the lift networks it covers (and the generally impressive efficiency of the lifts) the Ski Amadé pass is not expensive – 182 euros in high season. This is less than you'll pay for anything vaguely similar in France or Italy. Prices on the spot are not bad either – readers report prices in the mountain restaurants (which are very numerous) lower than in areas with a bigger international reputation.

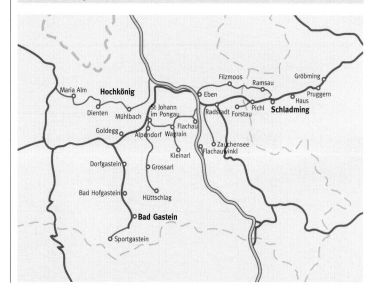

Alpbach

Small and beautiful: it's the pretty village and surroundings rather than the extent of the slopes that have attracted generations of Brits

COSTS

① ② ③ ④ ⑤ ⑥

RATINGS

The slopes

Fast lifts	**
Snow	**
Extent	*
Expert	*
Intermediate	**
Beginner	****
Convenience	**
Queues	***
Mountain restaurants	***

The rest

Scenery	***
Charm	*****
Off-slope	***

NEWS

For 2006/07 a new bar opened beside the gondola station at Inneralpbach. But the replacement lift (a quad) for the Galtenberglift drag, mentioned last year, did not materialise – no new date has been offered yet.

- ➕ Charming, traditional, relaxed village – great for young children
- ➕ Handy, central nursery slopes
- ➕ Several other worthwhile resorts within day-trip distance
- ➕ Good, varied, intermediate terrain, not without challenges, but ...

- ➖ Slopes limited in extent and variety
- ➖ Main slopes are a shuttle-bus-ride away (efficient service, though)
- ➖ Few long easy runs for beginners to progress to
- ➖ Lower slopes can suffer from poor snow, despite snowmaking help

This is an old British favourite – there is even a British ski club, the Alpbach Visitors. It is small, pretty and friendly, and inspires great loyalty in regular visitors – one who has been going since 1983 claims only junior status.

THE RESORT

Alpbach is near the head of a valley, looking south across it towards the slopes of Wiedersbergerhorn. It's an exceptionally pretty, captivating place; traditional chalets crowd around the pretty church, and the nursery slopes are only a few steps away.

The main village is the place to stay for atmosphere and après-ski, but involves using a free shuttle-bus to and from Achenwirt, a mile away, where a gondola goes up to Hornboden – though reporters find the service 'no hassle, excellent.' The backwater hamlet of Inneralpbach is much more convenient for the slopes, with its own gondola up the mountain.

The Inn valley is a few miles north, and trips east to Kitzbühel or west to Innsbruck are possible. The Hintertux and Stubaier glaciers are within reach.

THE MOUNTAIN

Alpbach's slopes, on two flanks of the Wiedersbergerhorn, are small and simple. Piste grooming is excellent.
Slopes The two gondolas take you up to open, north-facing slopes above the tree line, served by chair-lifts and drags. The runs are mostly of 200m to 400m (660ft to 1,310ft) vertical, but you can get more down the gondolas when snow is good down to valley level. Behind Gmahkopf is a short west-facing slope. A tiny separate area at Reith is on the lift pass and, says a reporter, is 'well worth a morning's visit – well groomed and deserted'. Access is by an eight-seat gondola. Night-skiing is planned for 2007/08.
Terrain-parks There's a half-pipe at the top of the Achenwirt gondola, which 'was poorly maintained and not re-shaped' during a 2006 visitor's stay.

KEY FACTS

Resort	1000m 3,280ft
Slopes	670-2025m 2,200-6,640ft
Lifts	20
Pistes	45km 28 miles
Blue	15%
Red	70%
Black	15%
Snowmaking	31km 19 miles

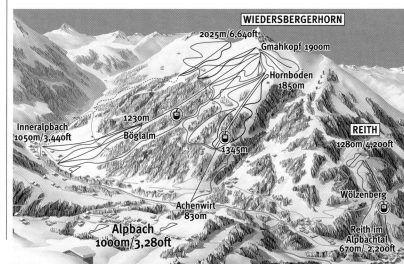

↑ Looks like a good spot to learn – gentle sunny slope, plenty of snow, no people, and a restaurant on hand: the nursery area at Reith

DAVID MAXWELL-LEES

UK PACKAGES

Alpine Answers, Crystal, Inghams, Interhome, Made to Measure

Phone numbers
From elsewhere in Austria add the prefix 05336; from abroad use the prefix +43 5336

TOURIST OFFICE

t 20094
alpbach@alpbachtal.at
www.alpbachtal.at

Snow reliability Alpbach cannot claim great snow reliability, but at least most of the Wiedersbergerhorn faces north, and two-thirds of the pistes are covered by snowmaking.

Experts Alpbach isn't ideal, but the reds and the three blacks (often groomed) are not without challenge, and runs of 1000m/3,300ft vertical are not to be sniffed at. There are a few off-piste routes to the valley, and the schools take the top classes off-piste. A 2006 reporter 'skied with a guide for three hours in untracked powder'.

Intermediates There is fine intermediate terrain; the problem is that it's limited. This resort is for practising technique on familiar slopes, not high mileage.

Beginners Beginners love the sunny nursery slopes beside the village. But the main slopes are not ideal for confidence-building: most are classified red (there are only a couple of blues).

Snowboarding There's some good free-riding terrain.

Cross-country 22km/14 miles of pretty cross-country trails rise up beyond Inneralpbach.

Queues The gondola at Inneralpbach built in 2005 seems to have relieved queues for the Achenwirt gondola.

Mountain restaurants There are several mountain restaurants – each worth a visit. One reporter recommends 'the spit-roast chicken at the Böglalm', while another enjoyed 'great food and service' at the Dauerstoa Alm.

Schools and guides We've had good reports on both main schools, Alpbach and Alpbach Aktiv; the head of the Alpbach school is qualified to teach people with disabilities (and he himself has a disability).

Facilities for children Reporters find the village very child-friendly, with good ski kindergartens; babysitters can be arranged by the tourist office.

STAYING THERE

How to go Hotels and pensions dominate in UK packages.

Hotels Of the smart 4-star places, Inghams' Alpbacherhof (5237) ('superb food and excellent service'), Alphof (5371) ('excellent, with friendly and welcoming staff') and ancient Böglerhof (5227) get most votes. The Berghof (5275) was recently recommended as 'an excellent 3-star; wholesome meals and only 20 metres from the nursery slopes'. The 3-star Post (5203) is 'better than a lot of 4-stars', says a 2007 visitor. The simpler Haus Thomas (5944), Haus Angelika (5339), and Haus Theresia (5386) have also been recommended. Pension Edelweiss (5268) is close to the nursery slopes and offers B&B and 'clean, spacious, good value apartments'.

Apartments There are quite a few to choose from now, easily bookable through the tourist office website.

Eating out The popular Post and Alphof both provide 'excellent food' according to a reporter, who also favoured the 'superb' Jakober and its non-smoking room. Wiedersbergerhorn in Inneralpbach has been recommended, as has the Rossmoos Inn for its lively Tirolean evenings, 'superb' food and the toboggan run back to the resort.

Après-ski At peak times this is typically Tirolean, with lots of noisy tea-time beer swilling in the bars of central hotels such as the Jakober and the Post. The latter has regular live music. A reporter preferred the Farmer's Pub to the Waschkuchl bar. Joe's Salett'l is new at Inneralpbach.

Off the slopes There are pretty walks and trips to Innsbruck and Salzburg. There is also an indoor swimming pool and an outdoor ice rink. The ski schools put on a 'ski show' on Wednesday evenings.

Bad Gastein

If you fancy 'taking the cure', there are few better resorts; even if you don't, you're likely to be impressed by the slopes (if not the towns)

COSTS

①②③④⑤⑥

RATINGS

The slopes

Fast lifts	**
Snow	***
Extent	****
Expert	***
Intermediate	****
Beginner	**
Convenience	**
Queues	***
Mountain restaurants	****

The rest

Scenery	***
Resort charm	***
Off-slope	****

NEWS

For 2007/08 a new red run is planned from Schlossalm to Angertal, above Bad Hofgastein. A new bridge is planned at Angertal to connect the fragmented beginner slopes there.

At Bad Gastein, snowmaking is due to be increased on both sides of Stubnerkogel.

For 2006/07 a second gondola was built above Grossarl and more snowmaking installed around the new lift.

EWAN BARR

The open slopes of Schlossalm are dotted with good restaurants – this is taken from Hofgasteinerhaus ➔

➕ Extensive, varied slopes

➕ Excellent, testing long runs for confident intermediates

➕ More reliable snow than in most low-altitude Austrian resorts

➕ Lots of good, atmospheric, traditional mountain restaurants

➕ Excellent thermal spas, but ...

➖ Main resorts are spa towns, without the usual Austrian resort ambience

➖ Bad Gastein itself has a steep, confined setting, with narrow streets

➖ Valley slopes are split into five areas and having a car is an advantage

➖ Timid intermediates and beginners are better off elsewhere

The Gastein valley is starting to attract more Brits, to judge by readers' reports. Rightly so – the slopes form one of Austria's bigger, more varied and more snow-sure areas. Steeply tiered Bad Gastein itself is a difficult place to like; we much prefer rustic Dorfgastein or spacious Bad Hofgastein – described here.

THE RESORT

Bad Gastein sits near the head of the Gastein valley. It is an old spa that has now spread widely, but still has a compact core. A bizarre mix of buildings is laid out in a cramped horseshoe, set in what is virtually a gorge. The central area is steep, and no pleasure at all to explore. Above it is a modern suburb with more of a ski-resort feel – and immediate access by gondola to the major Stubnerkogel sector of slopes. Across town, the double chair up separate Graukogel is a taxi-ride from the centre. Various ski-bus routes connect the villages and lift stations. There are trains, too. The ski-bus service is not super-efficient (although the service to Sportgastein is said to work well), and a car is a big asset here. It also allows full use of the Ski Alliance Amadé lift pass, covering over 30 resorts in the region.

THE MOUNTAIN

Most of the runs are on the open slopes above the tree line, though there are some woodland runs.
Slopes Stubnerkogel has runs in all directions from the peak, giving about 500m/1,640ft vertical on the open slopes above the tree line and rather more below it. There is night skiing once a week on the nursery slope. The much smaller Graukogel is unjustly neglected; its wooded runs are great in bad weather, and quiet at other times. The high slopes of Sportgastein, in contrast, are more exposed both to wind and sun. We cover the slopes above Bad Hofgastein and Dorfgastein later in the chapter. Piste marking is said to need improvement.
Terrain-parks There isn't one.
Snow reliability The area is higher than many Austrian rivals, and snowmaking is being increased on crucial sections.
Experts The few black runs are not severe, but many reds are long and satisfying. Graukogel has some of the most testing slopes. The other sectors have plenty of opportunities to go off-piste. Sportgastein is worth the trip – when open, the ski-route is rated 'fabulous'.
Intermediates Good for the confident, who will find long, leg-sapping runs in all the sectors in the valley. The timid are better off sticking to Schlossalm (see Bad Hofgastein, below).

KEY FACTS

Resort	1080m
	3,540ft

The Gastein valley and Grossarl areas

Slopes	840-2685m
	2,760-8,810ft
Lifts	44
Pistes	201km
	125 miles
Blue	30%
Red	58%
Black	12%
Snowmaking	
	537 guns

Bad Gastein and Bad Hofgastein only

Slopes	860-2685m
	2,820-8,810ft
Lifts	26
Pistes	121km
	75 miles

Beginners Nursery slopes are scattered and none is ideal. The main slope at Bad Gastein is simply too steep. And progression is tricky – the genuinely easy blue runs are often boring paths.
Snowboarding The valley hosts snowboard events, but doesn't seem to cater particularly well for holiday boarders. There's still a fairly high proportion of drag-lifts.
Cross-country There are 90km/56 miles of trails, but they are all low down.
Queues Recent reports vary: long January queues at Angertal (up to 30 minutes) and 5 to 10 minutes elsewhere, but no queues in March.
Mountain restaurants Atmospheric, traditional huts abound; but they can get crowded at peak periods. The 'very inviting' Jungerstube, Ahornhütte, Bergstadl and cosy Stubneralm have been recommended.
Schools and guides Reports are generally favourable ('first-class Croatian instructor', 'patient and understanding'). A 2007 visitor was 'very satisfied' with his private lesson.
Facilities for children There are facilities for all-day care and there's a 'Fun Center' for kids at the top of the Stubnerkogel gondola which was a 'great success' with a 2006 reporter's small grandchildren. There's also a snow adventure park at Angertal.

STAYING THERE

How to go British tour operators sell mainly hotel-based packages.
Hotels There are lots of smart 4- and 3-star hotels with spa facilities. The Wildbad (37610) was rated 'excellent' by a recent reporter. The Alpenblick (20620) is 'comfortable and welcoming', with a pool and spa – but well outside town. The Grüner Baum (25160) is a lovely retreat, but wildly inconvenient except for langlauf (though they do have a hotel bus).
Eating out There is a fair range of restaurants. The central Wirtshaus Jägerhäusl does excellent food in a warm, traditional atmosphere (especially upstairs). The Vier Jahreszeiten, a short drive away in Böckstein, offers big portions, 'very good value and friendly service'.
Après-ski The town feels generally subdued, but there are numerous popular bars and several discos – plus a casino ('rubbish', says a reporter). Highlights from reporters include Hirschenhutte in the Angertal, the

'boisterous' Bergfex, the 'cosy, friendly, wood-panelled' Hexenhäusl, the 'friendlier' Eden and the Weinfassl for 'dancing and drinking games'. The Silver Bullet has 'excellent live bands', but 'gets packed'. Haeggblooms is popular and has 'a great atmosphere', says a 2007 reporter. Places for a quiet late drink include the smart Bellini bar and the Ritz cocktail bar.
Off the slopes The thermal spa facilities are excellent and extensive ('best I've been to'). A 2007 visitor says the Healing Galleries at Sportgastein are worth a visit. And interesting excursions are possible.

Bad Hofgastein
860m/2,820ft
Bad Hofgastein is a sizeable, quiet spa village set where the valley is wide.

THE RESORT
Although sprawling, the village has a pleasant pedestrianised centre. The slopes are reached by a funicular to Kitzsteinalm starting a long walk or short shuttle-bus-ride away; or you can take a longer bus-ride to Angertal.

THE MOUNTAINS
Schlossalm is a broad, open bowl, with runs through patchy woods both to Bad Hofgastein and Angertal.
The slopes Schlossalm is the valley's gentlest area, with sunny open slopes classified blue and red. Another red and the mountain's first black run are planned above Angertal. The Kleine Scharte cable-car serves a serious 750m/2,460ft vertical, with a splendid long red run from Hohe Scharte to Kitzsteinalm or the valley floor.
Terrain-parks There isn't one.
Snow reliability Snowmaking is now fairly extensive, but snow-cover down to the bottom is unreliable, especially on the sunny Angertal slopes.
Experts There are no real challenges on the local pistes but there is ample opportunity to go off-piste.
Intermediates All intermediates will enjoy the Schlossalm slopes – and the more confident can go further afield.
Beginners You have to catch a bus to the nursery area at Angertal.
Snowboarding Pleasantly varied terrain, but no special facilities. Drag-lifts are dotted around every sector.
Cross-country Bad Hofgastein makes a fine base for cross-country when its lengthy valley-floor trails have snow.

Queues The queue-prone funicular and cable-car to Schlossalm can take 'the best part of an hour to get to the top' – but there are ways round both.

Mountain restaurants Well up to the high local standards are Kleine Scharte, Hamburger Skihütte and 'good value' Aeroplanstadl (its toilets are 'in the form of a pristine mock cavern').

Schools and guides One 2006 reporter was very disappointed by a three-hour private lesson.

Facilities for children See Bad Gastein.

STAYING THERE

How to go Mostly hotels.

Hotels Reporters have found the 4-star St Georg (61000), the Palace (67150), the central Salzburgerhof (62300) and the Germania (6232) excellent value. In the village centre the Osterreichischer Hof (6216) is 'well-run' and has its own 'good' spa facilities. The 3-star Rauscher (64120) is handy for the shuttle-bus and provides 'clean, spacious rooms and good food'.

Apartments Accommodation can be organised through the tourist office.

Eating out There is a good range of restaurants. Piccola Italia is 'well worth a visit'. The Wintergarten is an intimate restaurant, the Maier one of the better informal places.

Après-ski Quiet by Austrian standards. At close of play the Aeroplanstadl and central Piccolo ice bar are popular; there are several good places for cakes, among them Café Weitmoser, a historic little castle. Later on, the Glocknerkeller and the Gasteiner Discostadl are among the disco bars.

Off the slopes The Alpen Therme Gastein spa is 'huge', with several pools and a 'river' as well as saunas, steam baths etc. Other amenities include walking and ice skating.

Dorfgastein 830m/2,720ft

Dorfgastein is a rustic village further down the valley. It has its own extensive slopes, accessed by a two-stage gondola or by chair-lifts starting a little way outside the village, linked with the slopes of Grossarl in the next valley. Reporters seem to love the long and varied runs, with a good mix of open and wooded terrain amid lovely scenery – ideal for beginners and intermediates. The wide, gentle blue down to Grossarl is particularly noted. And grooming is 'excellent'. The low nursery slopes can be icy though. The resort also has the only terrain-park in the valley (skiers not allowed). Of the mountain restaurants, the table-service Wengeralm served 'the best lunch we had all week', says a 2007 reporter. The Dorf Aktiv school is said to offer 'very good' children's classes. There are a few shops, a swimming pool and some après-ski places.

Bad Gastein

131

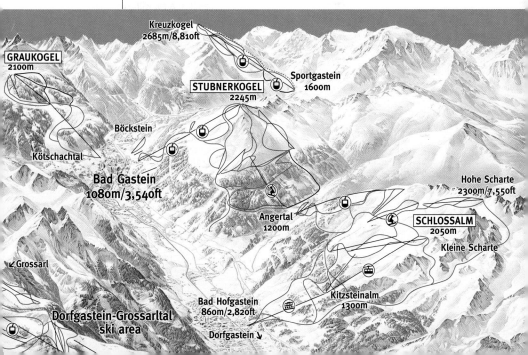

Bad Kleinkirchheim

Large resort tucked away in Carinthia, with marvellous spa facilities and a ski area best suited to intermediates

COSTS

① ② ③ ④ ⑤ ⑥

RATINGS

The slopes

Fast lifts	**
Snow	***
Extent	**
Expert	**
Intermediate	***
Beginner	**
Convenience	***
Queues	****
Mountain restaurants	***

The rest

Scenery	***
Resort charm	***
Off-slope	***

KEY FACTS

Resort	1090m
	3,580ft
Slopes	1100-2055m
	3,610-6,740ft
Lifts	26
Pistes	103km
	64 miles
Blue	17%
Red	75%
Black	8%
Snowmaking	97%

132

- ➕ Mainly intermediate slopes
- ➕ Virtually all the slopes have snowmaking
- ➕ Superb spa facilities
- ➕ Plenty to do off the slopes

- ➖ Spread-out town
- ➖ Still a lot of T-bars
- ➖ No terrain-park or half-pipe

BKK, as the locals call it, is downhill race hero Franz Klammer's favourite ski area – he learned to ski here, there's a World Cup downhill run bearing his name, and he is the proud owner of a mountain restaurant here. (What? Franz who, did you say? Oh come on! Arguably the best downhill racer ever? Innsbruck Olympics, 1976? Honestly, the young people of today ...)

Given Klammer's endorsement, it's no surprise that the resort has some serious skiing: 75 per cent of its slopes are classified red. It perhaps is a surprise that there are few real challenges for experts. So the resort suits confident intermediates best. It's a traditional spa town but, unlike many of those, has mainly easy-on-the-eye chalet-style buildings.

THE RESORT

BKK is tucked away on the edge of the Nock Mountain National Park in the province of Carinthia, in the far south-east of Austria, near the Italian and Slovenian borders. The nearest airports are Klagenfurt (around 50 minutes away) and Ljubljana (90 minutes). Salzburg is less than two hours away.

The old spa town has mainly chalet-style buildings with sloping roofs, rather than the more austere blocks of some spa resorts. But it is very spread out along the valley, and the most convenient place to stay is near one of the main lifts out. A ski-bus links all the main lift stations, and some buses also go to St Oswald, a smaller village at the far end of the shared ski area.

The spa facilities are excellent, with outdoor thermal pools (with temperatures of between 28° and 34°C), different types of sauna

KAISERBURG 2055m/6,740ft · 1905m · MAIBRUNN 1760m/5775ft · Priedröf 1965m/6,445ft · NOCKALM · Wieser Nock 1974m/6,480ft · Brunnach 1900m/6,235ft

1370m · 1025m · 1280m · St Oswald

Bad Kleinkirchheim
1090m/3,580ft

Feldkirchen ↓

NEWS

The Thermal Römerbad spa is expected to reopen in October 2007, following major renovation work. The centre will offer new saunas, an outdoor pool, a relaxation tower and a children's adventure area.

For 2006/07 snowmaking was increased along the Sonnweisenabfahrt run from Priedröf – and the ski area now has 97 per cent coverage. More snowmaking is planned for 2007/08.

BAD KLEINKIRCHHEIM TOURIST OFFICE

← The resort claims snowmaking on 97 per cent of its pistes

(including a tepidarium: a sauna with a lower temperature so you can sit there longer), steam, solarium, hot-tub, massage and therapy rooms. There are also water slides, waterfalls and massage jets in the pools. 'We found the spas superb,' says a reporter. 'They are a great way to unwind after skiing and mean there's plenty to do if the snow is limited, as it was for us.' The Thermal Römerbad has been renovated this year – see 'News'.

And for the benefit of devotees ... Franz Klammer, 1976 Olympic downhill gold medallist and winner of a record 25 World Cup Downhills, was born in Mooswald, near Bad Kleinkirchheim. His mother runs a gasthaus with his brother and sister-in-law in Fresach, about 20km/12 miles from BKK. He learned to ski at BKK, and it remains his favourite resort.

THE MOUNTAIN

BKK's shady home slopes are linked to the sunnier ones above the neighbouring village of St Oswald. Throughout, they are mainly wooded and of intermediate standard (75 per cent are classified red).

The piste map doesn't mark most of the mountain restaurants but it does mark 'Rotes Sofa' and 'Hits am Lift' – for what these are see overleaf.

There is a speed course on the Kaiserburg run open to anyone, and it is free of charge.

The lift pass covers all the resorts in Carinthia – useful for visiting other resorts if you have a car.

Slopes BKK's main home slopes are reached by lifts from two different parts of the village. A two-stage

gondola goes up to the area's high point, Kaiserburg, at one end of the ski area, where a couple of T-bars serve the highest slopes. And a fast quad chair takes you to the other end of the same mountain face at Maibrunn. Pistes go down from both peaks to the gondola mid-station and a chair takes you back to above Maibrunn.

From the same end of the village as the Maibrunn quad, successive double chair-lifts and a drag take you up the other side of the valley to the Priedröf and Nockalm slopes, which link in with St Oswald's slopes further along the valley. This area can also be accessed by a gondola midway between BKK and St Oswald, which can be reached by ski-bus. At St Oswald a gondola goes up to Brunnach, at the far end of the shared ski area.

Two quads link the Nockalm and St Oswald slopes. Apart from these quads, there are few chairs in BKK, the majority of the upper lifts being drags.

Terrain-parks There isn't one.

Snow reliability Being south of the Tauern mountain range, BKK can have completely different weather from the rest of Austria. So snow reliability can be better or worse, depending on the season. In general BKK's main home slopes are north-facing and keep their snow best. The Nockalm-St Oswald slopes are more sunny. Snowmaking additions are planned again for 2007/08, and they claim that virtually all the pistes (97 per cent) are now covered.

Experts BKK has little to keep experts interested for a week. The best and most challenging black is the Franz Klammer World Cup run, which goes from Strohsack to the gondola base.

There are two short black runs below Kaiserburg and another under the Wiesernock quad. Off-piste tours that involve some hiking can be arranged (eg to the Mallnock and Klomnock mountains from the top of the gondola from St Oswald and on Falkert mountain, which can be accessed by taxi from BKK and then a T-bar followed by a hike).

Intermediates Virtually all the slopes in both BKK and St Oswald are ideal for good intermediates as three-quarters of the slopes are classified red and many are long (up to 1000m/3,280ft vertical), wide and flattering. One of the most beautiful runs is the FIS K70 downhill run, classified red, which goes from top to bottom of the mountain away from all the lifts and through the trees in the lower section – on the extreme left-hand side of our piste map. It is almost 5km/3 miles long (and rarely groomed, says a local). There are two other long top-to-bottom red runs in this area too, as well as the Franz Klammer black. The Nockalm and St Oswald sectors also have long red runs (and T-bars to allow you to stay on the top runs), and the two quads make it easier to get between these sectors.

Beginners There are nursery slopes and drag-lifts for beginners at both BKK and St Oswald – the St Oswald ones are at the top of the Nochalm gondola and much warmer and sunnier in mid-winter, when the low BKK ones are in the shade. One reporter said: 'I had to take my kids off the BKK nursery slope because they were freezing. But they loved the sunny slope at St Oswald.' Once off the nursery slopes, there is a long blue the length of the gondola here.

Snowboarding Although the main lifts are all gondolas or chairs, there are a lot of T-bars, which less experienced boarders may not like. And there's no terrain-park or half-pipe.

Cross-country BKK takes cross-country seriously, with 54km/34 miles of tracks, some as high as 1900m/6,230ft at the top of the Nockalm.

Queues We have no reports of lift queues being much of a problem.

Mountain restaurants There are 22 mountain restaurants and huts. The most recent addition is the panoramic Nock In at the top of Brunnach above St Oswald. Franz Klammer's table-service Skibar is at the mid-station of the gondola from BKK. You might even meet the great man himself having lunch or a beer here (especially in January); he is always happy to have a chat and sign autographs.

Schools and guides There are four schools to choose from, three based in BKK and one in St Oswald. Style Check is a new twice-weekly concept, offering slope-side tips from instructors to help polish your technique (5 euros).

Facilities for children There's a non-skiing kindergarten for children from age two upwards at the foot of the gondola from BKK. First Steps takes children from two and a half, where they can learn to ski while playing.

STAYING THERE

How to go Several UK tour operators feature BKK.

Hotels Of the three 5-star hotels, the Pulverer (744) and Thermenhotel Ronacher (282) are both near the high-speed chair and nursery slope and have excellent spa facilities. The other is the St Oswald (591). There are 21 4-stars, several 3-stars and lots of gasthofs too. BKK boasts 26 hotels with swimming pools and 50 saunas.

Apartments There are lots of self-catering apartments to rent.

Eating out Being a large village with a lot of summer visitors means there are plenty of places for eating out, including a lot of hotel restaurants. The Loystub'n in the hotel Pulverer comes highly recommended by a reporter: 'A high quality, not typically Austrian meal, in very pleasant surroundings with excellent service.'

Après-ski A lot of the après-ski takes place in the hotels, but there are a few interesting bars to try. Near the BKK gondola base are several popular places: the Almstube, Viktoria Pub, Club MC 99 and the Take Five Dancing Club.

Off the slopes There are superb spa facilities, as described in the introduction. You can buy lift tickets that include the use of the thermal swimming pools. There are also some good walks, including the Spa Boulevard route at the top of the gondola from St Oswald, a tennis centre, squash courts, an outdoor ice rink, curling, snowtubing, horse-riding, horse-drawn sleigh rides and a 4km/2.5 mile floodlit toboggan run. Those with cars can also visit Villach (36km/22 miles away) for a shopping spree or carry on across the border into Italy.

Ellmau

Our favourite base on the extensive SkiWelt circuit, combining charm with reasonable convenience – just hope the snow holds up

COSTS

① ② ③ ④ ⑤ ⑥

RATINGS

The slopes

Fast lifts	**
Snow	**
Extent	****
Expert	*
Intermediate	****
Beginner	****
Convenience	***
Queues	****
Mountain restaurants	**

The rest

Scenery	***
Resort charm	***
Off-slope	***

KEY FACTS

Resort	800m
	2,620ft

Entire SkiWelt	
Slopes	620-1830m
	2,030-6,000ft
Lifts	94
Pistes	250km
	155 miles
Blue	43%
Red	48%
Black	9%
Snowmaking	180km
	112 miles

+ Pretty, friendly, extensive slopes – Austria's largest linked area

+ Excellent nursery slopes

+ Cheap by Austrian standards

+ Quiet, charming family resort – more appealing than neighbouring Söll

+ Snowmaking is now more extensive and well used; even so ...

− Low altitude can mean poor snow

− Main lift a bus-ride from village – though reachable via a drag-lift

− Upper-mountain runs are mostly short, and offer little challenge

− Limited range of nightlife

− The SkiWelt slopes can get crowded at weekends and in high season

If you like the sound of the large, undemanding SkiWelt circuit, Ellmau has a lot to recommend it as your base – quieter than Söll, but with more amenities than other neighbours such as Scheffau (covered in the Söll chapter). And Austria's largest snowmaking system makes the area less risky than it was.

THE RESORT

Ellmau sits at the north-eastern corner of the SkiWelt – an area of linked slopes that's an impressive 15km/ 9 miles across. Although sizeable, the village remains quiet, with traditional chalet-style buildings, welcoming bars and shops, and a pretty church. It has a compact centre, but accommodation is scattered – so the buses around the resort are important (and now better organised, say reporters). There is accommodation out by the funicular to the main slopes, but we prefer to stay near the heart of the village. A guest card entitles you to various discounts, including entry to the leisure centre.

THE MOUNTAIN

The SkiWelt is the largest mountain circuit in Austria, linking seven resorts. This huge area is covered by a single piste map. The completely useless map in use for some years was replaced last season by a brand new one which is much better in general, but still difficult to use in parts. Most runs are easy, and short – which means that getting around the area can take time, despite increasing numbers of fast lifts. Inconsistent piste classification has been criticised by reporters.

The SkiWelt pass also covers Westendorf, though its slopes are not linked (you take a bus from Brixen);

135

NEWS

For 2006/07 a six-pack with heated seats replaced the Tanzboden drag-lift below Hartkaiser and Brandstadl, improving the connection with Scheffau.

Ellmau's Kaiser-Park terrain-park was extended.

The SkiWelt has continued to invest in snowmaking; following last season's increase, two-thirds of the pistes are now covered – about 180km/112 miles.

LIFT PASSES

SkiWelt Wilder Kaiser-Brixental

Prices in €

Age	1-day	6-day
under 16	18	84
16 to 17	28	135
over 18	35	168

Free under 7
Senior no deals
Beginner limited pass
Notes
Covers Wilder Kaiser-Brixental area from Going to Westendorf, and the ski-bus; single ascent and part-day options
Alternative passes
Kitzbüheler Alpenskipass covers five large ski areas: Schneewinkel (St Johann), Kitzbühel, SkiWelt, Wildschönau and Alpbachtal

ON YOUR OWN?

You can team up with other skiers/boarders by turning up at 10am or 1pm at one of seven designated points in the SkiWelt; there are stickers to identify participants, and even a website forum for making prior arrangements.

from there you can also progress to the Kirchberg-Kitzbühel slopes – see the Westendorf chapter. These, along with Waidring, Fieberbrunn and St Johann, are possible day trips covered by the Kitzbüheler Alpenskipass.

Slopes The funicular railway on the edge of the village takes you up to Hartkaiser, from where a fine long red leads down to Blaiken (Scheffau's lift base station). A choice of gondolas take you up to Brandstadl. Immediately beyond Brandstadl, the slopes become rather bitty; an array of short runs and lifts link Brandstadl to Zinsberg. From Zinsberg, long, south-facing pistes lead down to Brixen. Then it's a short bus-ride to Westendorf's pleasant separate area, from which you can reach the slopes of Kirchberg and Kitzbühel, via a slope and another short bus-junction. Part-way down to Brixen you can head towards Söll, and if you go up Hohe Salve, you get access to a long, west-facing run to Hopfgarten.

Ellmau and Going share a pleasant little area of slopes on Astberg, slightly apart from the rest of the area, and well suited to the unadventurous and families. One piste leads to the funicular for access to the rest of the SkiWelt. The main Astberg chair is rather inconveniently positioned, midway between Ellmau and Going.

Terrain-parks Ellmau now has its own terrain-park, the Kaiser-Park, with newly improved boxes, rails, kickers and a chill-out zone.

Snow reliability With a low average height, and important links that get a lot of sun, the snowmaking that the SkiWelt has installed is essential; the Ellmau-Going sector now claims almost all its slopes are covered. Snowmaking can, of course, only be used when temperatures are low enough. The north-facing Eiberg area above Scheffau holds its snow well. Grooming is reported to be 'excellent' and recent reports have praised 'ace' snowmaking.

Experts There are steep plunges off the Hohe Salve summit, a ski route from Brandstadl down to Scheffau and a little mogul field between Brandstadl and Neualm, but the area isn't really suitable unless you go off-piste.

Intermediates With good snow, the SkiWelt is a paradise for those who love easy cruising. There are lots of blue runs and many of the reds deserve a blue classification ('pale blue', says one reporter). It is a big

area and you get a feeling of travelling around. The main challenge is when the snow isn't perfect – ice and slush can make even gentle lower slopes seem tricky. For timid intermediates the easy slopes of Astberg are handy.

Beginners Ellmau has an array of good nursery slopes covered by snowmaking. The main ones are at the Going end, but there are some by the road to the funicular. The Astberg chair opens up a more snow-sure plateau at altitude. The Brandstadl area has a section of short easy runs.

Snowboarding Ellmau is a good place to learn as its local slopes are easy.

Cross-country There are long, quite challenging trails (the SkiWelt area has a total of 170km/106 miles), but trails at altitude are lacking.

Queues Continued lift upgrades have greatly improved this once queue-prone area. With the exception of peak times ('10 minutes for the Aualm chair at half-term'), reporters comment on quiet and crowd-free slopes with 'few queues'. If the Hausberg chair is closed (as was the case on a 2007 reporter's two visits), you'll need to take the bus back from Hartkaiser.

Mountain restaurants The smaller places are fairly consistent in providing good-value food in pleasant surroundings. The Rübezahl above Ellmau is our favourite in the whole SkiWelt, but can be 'smoky and busy' according to a reporter. The Aualm, just below Brandstadl, is favoured, especially for its cakes and glühwein. The Jagerhütte (below Hartkaiser) is good for 'home-made strudel' and 'excellent for a drinks stop' before enjoying the 'quiet and pleasant' home-run, says another reporter. The Hartkaiser 'has vastly improved in food quality and ambiance, and even has escalators to the loos', says a 2006 visitor. The Bergkaiser has 'quick service and good food'. The hut at Neualm, halfway down to Scheffau, has been recommended, and the Kummereralm near the new Tanzboden chair is 'excellent'. The larger self-service restaurants are functional (the Jochstube at Eiberg is a pleasant exception) and suffer queues.

Schools and guides The three schools have good reputations – except that classes can be very large. Top is highly rated for children's lessons – 'All our children had a great time in different classes with Top, who made sure they

↑ Throughout the SkiWelt you are skiing on broad swathes of pasture between strips of forest

DAVID MAXWELL-LEES

137

Ellmau

Phone numbers
From elsewhere in Austria add the prefix 05358; from abroad use the prefix +43 5358

were in English-only speaking groups. It was a very busy week, but only our youngest was in the maximum class size of 12.'

Facilities for children Ellmau is an attractive resort for families, described by a regular visitor as 'so child-friendly'. Top ski school is praised (see 'Schools'). Kindergartens seem to be satisfactory and include fun ideas such as a mini train to the lifts. Kinderland has its own fun-park and play areas. But we have had no recent reports.

STAYING THERE

How to go Ellmau is essentially a hotel and pension resort, though there are apartments that can be booked locally.
Hotels The Bär (2395) is an elegant, relaxed Relais & Châteaux chalet, but twice the price of any other hotel. 'Very friendly and welcoming, wonderful food, reasonably priced house wine and a very good wellness centre,' wrote a reporter. 'Luxury without pretensions,' said another. The Hochfilzer (2501) is central, well equipped (with outdoor hot-tub) and popular with reporters (as is the simpler Pension Claudia, which it owns – use of hotel facilities allowed). Kaiserblick (2230), with good spa facilities and right by the piste, is recommended by a regular visitor, who went with six families including 12 children. A 2006 reporter rates the Kaiserhof (2022) as 'very comfortable and friendly, and had amazing food'.
Apartments There is a wide variety. The Landhof apartments continue to impress – 'spacious, immaculately clean, well equipped' – with pool, sauna and steam room. A regular reporter

rates the supermarket on the way out of town towards Going as 'excellent'.
Eating out The jolly Gasthof Lobewein is a splendid, big, central chalet, with cheerful service in countless rooms and excellent food.
Après-ski Cafes Kaiserstüberl and Bettina are good for coffee and cakes. Memory (which has internet facilities) is the early-evening riotous party pub. Pub 66 and Ötzy have regular events such as karaoke and 'erotic dancers'. The Ellermauer Alm at the Going end is 'superb fun'. Tour op reps organise events like bowling, sleigh rides, Tirolean folklore and tubing. There's an Instructors' Ball and ski displays with 'a party atmosphere' each week, and the toboggan run from the Astberg lift is recommended.
Off the slopes The KaiserBad leisure centre is good. There are many excursions available, including Salzburg and Vitipeno. Valley walks are spoiled by the busy main road. Heading up to Hartkaiser to relax on the terrace 'was a highlight for our non-skiers', writes a reporter.

Going 775m/2,540ft

Going is a tiny, attractively rustic village, ideal for families looking for a quiet time. It is well placed for the limited but quiet slopes of the Astberg and for the vast area of nursery slopes between here and Ellmau. Prices are low, but it's not an ideal base for covering the whole of the SkiWelt on the cheap unless you have a car for quick access to Scheffau and Söll. The Lanzenhof (2428) is a cosy central pension doing excellent traditional food in its woody dining rooms.

Small, unspoiled, traditional villages, high snow-sure glacier slopes and lots of other places down the valley covered by the lift pass

COSTS

① ② ③ ④ ⑤ ⑥

RATINGS

The slopes

Fast lifts	★★★
Snow	★★★★★
Extent	★★★
Expert	★★★
Intermediate	★★★
Beginner	★★
Convenience	★★
Queues	★★★
Mountain restaurants	★★

The rest

Scenery	★★★
Resort charm	★★★
Off-slope	★

NEWS

For 2006/07 snowmaking was installed on the Schwarze Pfanne ski route from Tuxer Joch to the bottom of the Hintertux lifts and more was added between Tuxer Joch and Sommerbergalm.

LIFT PASSES

Zillertaler Superskipass

Prices in €

Age	1-day	6-day
under 15	18	86
15 to 18	29	138
over 19	36	172

Free under 6
Senior no deals
Beginner no deals

Notes
1-, 2- or 3-day passes cover Hintertux glacier, Eggalm, Rastkogel and Penken areas; 4-day and over passes include all Ziller valley lifts; part-day and pedestrian passes available

138

➕ Hintertux has one of the best glaciers in the world, open summer as well as winter

➕ Lanersbach ski area linked to Mayrhofen and Finkenberg's; and several other areas are covered by the area lift pass and free buses

➕ Some excellent off-piste opportunities

➕ A choice of quiet, unspoiled, traditional villages to stay in

➖ Hintertux is a bus-ride away from the other villages

➖ Not for those who want a huge choice of shops and throbbing nightlife on their doorstep

➖ Not ideal for beginners or timid intermediates, with few easy runs to valley level

➖ Glacier can be cold and bleak in midwinter, and there are lots of T-bars and slow chairs

The Tux valley has always had its attractions, chief among them the Hintertux glacier, which arguably has the most challenging and interesting runs of any lift-served Alpine glacier. For guaranteed good snow, Hintertux is simply one of the best places to go. But the valley acquired much broader appeal in 2001 when the quieter, friendlier, non-glacial slopes above Lanersbach and its nearby twin, Vorderlanersbach, were linked by fast new lifts with those above Mayrhofen and Finkenberg. Together, they form a fair-sized circuit. With the glacier only 15 to 20 minutes away by bus, these quiet, unspoiled, traditional villages are attractive bases – for many people, more attractive than either Hintertux or Mayrhofen (covered in its own chapter). There are other areas further down the Zillertal worth a day trip to (see end of Mayrhofen chapter).

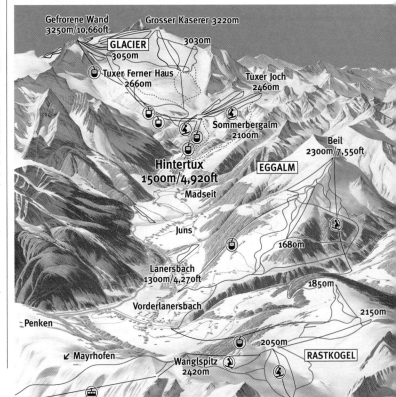

KEY FACTS

Resort	1500m
	4,920ft

Ski and Glacier World
Zillertal 3000

Slopes	630-3250m
	2,070-10,660ft
Lifts	62
Pistes	225km
	140 miles
Blue	26%
Red	60%
Black	14%
Snowmaking	93km
	58 miles

Hintertux only

Slopes	1500-3250m
	4,920-10,660ft
Lifts	21
Pistes	86km
	53 miles

For Ziller valley

Slopes	630-3250m
	2,070-10,660ft
Lifts	174
Pistes	636km
	395 miles

The Tux valley, an extension of Mayrhofen's Zillertal, has a variety of small villages, linked by regular free ski-buses. A cheap (50c) night-bus also runs until 2am. Finkenberg is the first village you come to, and Lanersbach and Vorderlanersbach are beyond it. These are small, traditional places and covered later in this chapter.

All have gondola links into the local slopes: the Finkenberg gondola goes up to the Penken slopes shared with Mayrhofen; the Vorderlanersbach one goes to Rastkogel, which is linked with the Penken slopes; and the Lanersbach one goes to Eggalm, from which you can ski to Vorderlanersbach. Hintertux is a 15-minute bus-ride from Lanersbach, at the head of the valley, a few minutes from the glacier lifts. There is also accommodation in Juns and Madseit.

There are some good rustic restaurants and bars and a few places along the valley with discos or live music. But nightlife tends to be quieter than in many bigger Austrian resorts.

The Tux valley and Mayrhofen lifts now form what is called the Ski and Glacier World Zillertal 3000. Lift passes for four days or more also cover the other resorts in the the Ziller valley (see end of Mayrhofen chapter).

Hintertux 1500m/4,920ft

THE RESORT

Tiny Hintertux is set at the end of the Tux valley. It is little more than a small collection of hotels and guest houses; there is another, smaller group of hotels near the lifts, which lie a 15-minute walk away from the village, across a car park that fills with day-visitors' cars and coaches, especially when snow is poor in lower resorts.

THE MOUNTAINS

Hintertux's slopes are fairly extensive and, for a glacier, surprisingly challenging. The glacier is one of the best in the world, with varied terrain that attracts national ski teams for summer training.

Slopes A series of three speedy gondolas takes you up from the base to the top of the glacier (vertical rise 1750m/5,740ft) in under 20 minutes. The first stage is an eight-seater up to Sommerbergalm, while the second and third stages (linked by a short slope at Tuxer Ferner Haus) have 24-person cabins. On the two lower stages there is a parallel smaller gondola which is pressed into service to meet demand at peak times. From Sommerbergalm, a fast quad chair serves the slopes

below Tuxer Joch; from the top of this sector, the excellent secluded Schwarze Pfanne ski route goes down to the base station. Between the top of the glacier and Tuxer Fernerhaus there are further chairs and drag-lifts to play on and links across to another 1000m/3,300ft-vertical chain of lifts below Grosser Kaserer on the west. Behind Gefrorene Wand is the area's one sunny piste, served by a triple chair. Descent to the valley involves a short ascent to Sommerbergalm on the way, achieved by a six-seater chair-lift.

Terrain-parks Europe's highest World Cup half-pipe is on the glacier (a popular hang-out throughout the summer), and there is a terrain-park with jumps, fun boxes and rails.

Snow reliability Snow does not come more reliable than this. Even off the glacier, the other slopes are high and face north, making for very reliable snow-cover. The runs from Tuxer Fernerhaus and Tuxer Joch down to Sommerbergalm have snowmaking, as does the Schwarze Pfanne ski route.

Experts There is more to amuse experts here than on any other glacier, with a couple of serious black runs at glacier level and steep slopes and ungroomed ski routes beneath. A lot of the off-piste is little used and one reporter said, 'We found untracked snow not far from the lifts two weeks after the last snowfall.'

Intermediates The area particularly suits good or aggressive intermediates. The long runs down from Gefrorene Wand and Kaserer are fun. And there is a pleasant, tree-lined ski route to the valley from Sommerbergalm and another from Tuxer Joch. Moderate intermediates will love the glacier.

Beginners There is a nursery slope at valley level, but the glacier isn't the ideal place to progress to.

Snowboarding There are some great off-piste opportunities, but boarders complain about the number of T-bars.

Cross-country See the Lanersbach information later in the chapter.

Queues There used to be huge queues at Hintertux when snow was poor elsewhere. Improved lifts have largely solved this problem. But the main runs can get crowded, and then it is best to head over to the quieter Kaserer lifts and runs.

Mountain restaurants The mountain restaurants tend to get very crowded and the big self-service places lack charm – 'rather soulless except for

Tuxer Joch Haus,' as one visitor said. The almost-100-year-old Spannagelhaus is another exception ('fun atmosphere,' says a recent reporter), and there are great views from the 'friendly' Gletscherhütte, at the top. The self-service at Sommerbergalm is described by a 2007 reporter as 'dull but with a pleasant terrace'.

Schools and guides There are three schools, which serve all the resorts in Tux, but we lack reports on them. The newest, Tux 3000, has special guiding, touring and race-training programmes.

Facilities for children Most of the ski schools run classes for children aged 4 to 14 and lunch is provided.

STAYING THERE

How to go Most hotels are large and comfortable and have spa facilities, but there are also more modest pensions.

Hotels Close to the lifts are the 4-star Vierjahreszeiten (8525) and Neuhintertux (8580) in which a 2007 reporter found 'a good wine list' and enjoyed the 'large pool, saunas, steam baths and modern spa'. 2007 visitors also recommend the 4-star Berghof (8585) with its 'good service and spa' and the Thermal Badhotel Kirchler (8570) for its good food and 'welcoming bar' (but it was a good 20 minute walk to the lifts, and buses were not frequent in May/June when we were there). An earlier visitor relished the 'comfort and hospitality' of the 4-star Alpenhof (8550). We have enjoyed staying in the 3-star Hintertuxerhof (8530): good food, sauna and steam room. Pensions Kössler (87490) – 3-star – and the 2-star Willeiter (87492) are in the heart of the village.

Apartments There are plenty of self-catering apartments.

Eating out Restaurants are mainly hotel-based. The Vierjahreszeiten is pleasant and informal.

Après-ski There can be a lively après-ski scene both at mid-mountain (Sommerbergalm) and at the base; the 'very lively' Hohenhaus Tenne has several different bars, the Rindererhof has a popular tea dance, and there are a couple of local bars. The cheap (50c) night-bus gets you to and from the other villages until 2am, but this is not the place for keen clubbers.

Off the slopes The spa facilities are excellent, including a thermal indoor pool, but there are many more options in Mayrhofen.

↑ Lanersbach is a delightfully unspoiled and quiet traditional village
TVB TUX-FINKENBERG

Lanersbach 1300m/4,270ft

Lanersbach and neighbouring Vorderlanersbach have long been attractive bases for exploring the resorts of the Zillertal and Tuxertal. Now that their ski areas are linked with Mayrhofen's slopes their attractions are greatly reinforced.

THE RESORT
Lanersbach is an attractive, spacious, traditional village, largely unspoiled by the busy road up to Hintertux that passes the main lift. The quiet centre near the pretty church is bypassed by the road, yet is within walking distance of the gondola up to Eggalm. It is a small and delightfully unspoiled village, but it has all you need in a resort. And prices are relatively low. Vorderlanersbach is even smaller, with a gondola up to the Rastkogel area.

THE MOUNTAINS
Slopes The slopes of Eggalm, accessed by the gondola from Lanersbach, offer a small network of pleasantly varied, intermediate pistes, usually delightfully quiet. You can descend on red or blue runs back to the village or to Vorderlanersbach, where a gondola goes up to the higher, open Rastkogel slopes; here, two fast chair-lifts – one a covered eight-seater – serve some very enjoyable long red and blue runs and link with Mayrhofen's slopes. The linking run is classified red but can get very mogulled and many people opt to ride the 150-person cable-car down; a short rope-tow cuts out the need to

hike up to the top station. The run back from Rastkogel to Eggalm is marked red but is really quite easy and is served by snowmaking. The alternative is to ride the gondola down to Vorderlanersbach (there are no pistes to the village) and catch the bus to Lanersbach.
Terrain-parks The Mayrhofen and Hintertux pipes and parks are easily accessed.
Snow reliability Snow conditions are usually good, at least in early season; by Austrian standards these are high slopes and snowmaking was increased a few seasons ago on both Eggalm and Rastkogel. But Rastkogel is basically south-facing, so snow quality can suffer.
Experts There are no pistes to challenge experts, but there is a fine off-piste route starting a short walk from the top of the Eggalm slopes and finishing at the village.
Intermediates The local slopes suit intermediates best – and you have Mayrhofen's slopes to explore too.
Beginners Both areas have nursery slopes (as do Madseit and Juns) but there are few ideal progression slopes – most of the easy runs are on the higher lifts of the Rastkogel sector.
Snowboarding The area isn't great for novices – there are drag-lifts dotted around, some in key places.
Cross-country There are 14km/9 miles of cross-country trails, alongside the Tux creek, between Madseit and Vorderlanersbach, and a 6km/4 mile skating track in Juns/Madseit.
Queues We have no reports of any

ACTIVITIES

Indoor Bowling, squash, saunas, fitness rooms and pools in hotels open to public

Outdoor Ice rink, curling, winter hiking trails, paragliding, tobogganing, cave excursions, snow-shoe tours

UK PACKAGES

Hintertux Skitracer, Snoworks, White Heat
Finkenberg Crystal

Phone numbers
From elsewhere in Austria use the prefix 05287; from abroad use the prefix +43 5287

TOURIST OFFICE

Tux-Finkenberg
t 8506
info@tux.at
www.tux.at

problems. Indeed, Eggalm can be delightfully quiet.

Mountain restaurants There's no shortage but most, though fairly rustic, are self-service with simple food; the small Lattenalm on Eggalm is a table-service exception with a terrace that has splendid views of the Tux glacier.

Schools and guides There are four schools in the valley, but we lack recent reports on them.

Facilities for children The non-ski nursery takes children aged from one to three, and most of the schools take children from four upwards. There's a new terrain-park, including a snow-tyre carousel and a bob-run, on the glacier.

STAYING THERE

How to go Both villages are essentially hotel-based resorts.

Hotels The Lanersbacherof (87256) is a good 4-star with pool, sauna, steam and hot-tub close to the lifts ('Very friendly, with good gourmet menu and great wine cellar,' says a reporter), but it is also on the main road. The cheaper 3-star Pinzger (87541) and Alpengruss (87293) are similarly situated. In Vorderlanersbach the 3-star Kirchlerhof (8560) is 'really friendly, with comfortable rooms and excellent food', says a regular visitor.

Apartments Quite a lot are available.

Eating out Restaurants are mainly hotel-based, busy, and geared to serving dinner early.

Après-ski Nightlife is generally quiet by Austrian standards, which suits us. We enjoyed the jolly Hühnerstall in Lanersbach (an old wooden building with traditional Austrian music). There is a disco or two.

Off the slopes Off-slope facilities are fairly good considering the size of the resorts. Some hotels have pools, hot-tubs and fitness rooms open to non-residents. Innsbruck and Salzburg are possible excursions.

Finkenberg 840m/2,760ft

Finkenberg is a much smaller, quieter village than Mayrhofen with a gondola into the Penken slopes the two resorts share (see the Mayrhofen chapter).

THE RESORT

Finkenberg is no more than a collection of traditional-style hotels, bars, cafes and private homes. There is a pretty central area around the church, but most of the buildings (and hotels) are spread along the busy, steep, winding main road up to Lanersbach. Beware slippery pavements. Some hotels are within walking distance of the gondola, and many of the more distant ones run their own minibuses; there is also an inefficient village minibus service.

THE MOUNTAIN

Finkenberg shares Mayrhofen's main Penken slopes.

Slopes A two-stage gondola gives direct access to the Penken slopes – and in good conditions you can ski back to the village on a ski route (though it is often closed).

Snow reliability The local slopes are not as well-endowed with snowmaking as those on Mayrhofen's side.

Experts Not much challenge, except off-piste and the Harakiri piste.

Intermediates The whole area opens up from the top of the gondola.

Beginners There's a village nursery slope, but it's a sunless spot, and good conditions are far from certain.

Snowboarding No special facilities.

Cross-country Cross-country skiers have to get a bus up to Lanersbach.

Queues We've had reports of 20-minute queues at peak times for the gondola to and from the Penken.

Mountain restaurants See the Mayrhofen chapter.

Schools and guides The Finkenberg school has a good reputation.

Facilities for children There's a non-ski nursery, and the ski nursery takes children from age four.

STAYING THERE

Hotels The Sporthotel Stock (6775), owned by the family of former downhill champion Leonard Stock, is near the gondola station, and has great spa facilities. The Eberl (62667) has been recommended ('attentive staff, excellent food – but avoid the annexe rooms'), and the Kristall (62840) was completely renovated a couple of years ago and is 150m/490ft from the gondola ('superb wellness spa'). All these are 4-stars.

Eating out Mainly in hotels, notably the Eberl.

Après-ski The main après-ski spots are the Laterndl Pub at the foot of the gondola ('jumping as the lifts close') and Finkennest ('welcoming, cosy, weird decor', but 'more civilised than the Laterndl').

Off the slopes Curling, ice-skating, swimming and good local walks.

Hochkönig

An unusual combination: small unspoiled villages and a large uncrowded ski area, virtually unknown on the British market

144

+ Traditional quiet villages

+ Plenty of uncrowded terrain

+ Friendly locals

− Little for experts except ski routes and off-piste

− Buses needed in parts, and there are some slow chairs and T-bars

The picturesque Salzburgerland villages of Maria Alm, Hintermoos, Hinterthal, Dienten and Mühlbach combine to provide a sizeable ski area, best suited to intermediates and beginners. The lift system is not completely linked, so you'll have to drive or catch the ski buses to explore it all.

THE RESORT

Maria Alm, though small, is one of the two largest villages; it's a pretty place with a splendid old church boasting the highest spire in Salzburgerland. The peaks of the Selbhorn and Schonfeldspitze provide a dramatic backdrop. Hinterthal, the next real village up the valley, is even smaller – little more than a few 4-star hotels and chalets (some owned by the rich and famous) and a couple of ski shops and bars; it has some of the best mountain views in the region. Further up the road and over a pass is Dienten, a tiny, picturesque village with a handful of traditional hotels and guest houses. Mühlbach, at the eastern end of the ski area, is a similar size to Maria Alm and, unlike the other villages which are set off the main road, sprawls along it for quite a distance. The spectacular Hochkönig (which means 'High King') massif, from which the region gets its name, overlooks the village and can be seen from many of the slopes but is not part of the ski area.

THE MOUNTAIN

There are 150km/93 miles of pistes, on a par with well-known names such as Kitzbühel and Mayrhofen.

Slopes The main slopes spread along several small mountains running east along the valley from Maria Alm to Mühlbach. Many of the runs are north-facing and have splendid views over to the high peaks opposite. Just to the west of Maria Alm is the tiny little area of Hinterreit, where the British ski team trains. Maria Alm has its own small Natrun ski area, served by what was the world's first chondola (a mix of chairs and gondola cabins). An ungroomed ski route leads off the back to the main local Aberg-Langeck mountain and an eight-seat gondola; but most people catch the bus round to Aberg (you have to catch it back, too). You also need a bus from Aberg to the rest of the main ski area, starting at Hinterthal – but you can get back from Hinterthal to Aberg along a gentle track with some flat/uphill sections. From Hinterthal you can go

SCHNEEBERG 1920m/6,300ft

Sunnhütte 1750m/5,740ft

WASTLHÖHE 1730m/5,680ft

1560m

Bischofshofen

HOCHKEIL 1785m/5,860ft

Mühlbach 855m/2810ft

Dienten 1070m/3,510ft

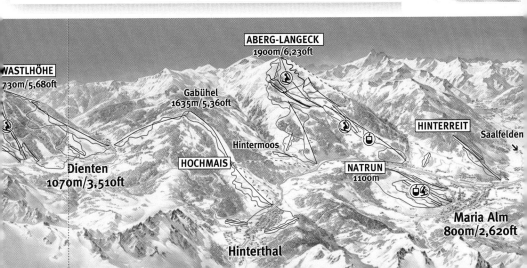

AUSTRIA

146

KEY FACTS

Resorts	800-1070m	
	2,620-3,510ft	
Slopes	800-1900m	
	2,620-6,230ft	
Lifts		37
Pistes		150km
		93 miles
Blue		35%
Red		55%
Black		10%
Snowmaking		90km
		56 miles

NEWS

The 4-star Alpine Wellness Hotel Haller in Maria Alm is adding a new guest house and outdoor swimming pool for 2007/08.

TOURIST OFFICES

region@hochkoenig.at
www.hochkoenig.at
Maria Alm
t 06584 7816
infoalm@
hochkoenig.at
Dienten
t 06461 263
info@dienten.co.at
Mühlbach
t 06467 7235
info@muehlbach.co.at

via Dienten to Mühlbach (where the gondola back up is a bus-ride from the village centre). The piste map is poor, covering the whole area in one view – it would benefit from more detail.

Terrain-parks Of the five terrain-parks, the biggest and best is on Aberg.

Snow reliability Although low altitude, the region is in a snow pocket, so tends to have good conditions for its height (there was no shortage of snow on our April 2006 visit). Some 60 per cent of the pistes have snowmaking.

Experts There are several ungroomed ski routes, the best of which is in a huge off-piste bowl behind the Aberg ridge. It is not well marked and having a guide is useful; a local says 'there are lots of ways in and it's better than Vail's back bowls'. With a guide you can explore other excellent off-piste too, such as in the trees off Aberg and on Schneeberg. There's one genuinely steep black piste on Aberg.

Intermediates The area between Hinterthal and Mühlbach is best for adventurous intermediates, with mainly challenging red runs. You really get a feeling of travelling around here. There are a few easy cruising blue runs in the centre of this area, served by fast chairs, and on Aberg.

Beginners All the villages have good nursery slopes, and the runs at the foot of the Aberg and by Hinterthal village are good progression runs.

Snowboarding Good for beginners and intermediates, but there are drag-lifts.

Cross-country There are over 40km/ 25 miles of prepared tracks.

Queues Not usually a problem.

Mountain restaurants There are 37, including some nice little huts. We liked Griessbachhütte (an isolated hut with very simple food and good views on Aberg's ski route); we also had good table-service Bauerngröstl at Tiergartenalm below Sunnhütte. A local also recommends the Tischlerhütte (Aberg), the Alm Bar (Hinterthal – good spare ribs) and Almhäusl (just above Dienten – sun deck and umbrella bar).

Schools and guides All four main villages have schools, and many instructors speak good English.

Facilities for children The kindergartens at all the main base areas take children from age two. The ski schools take them from four. Babysitting is now available by prior arrangement. The newish Schneewutzel children's park has its own lifts and playground.

STAYING THERE

How to go No big tour ops come here.

Hotels There are plenty of good hotels with spa and pool facilities. The 4-star Haller (2100) opened in Maria Alm in December 2006. The Haus Salzburg (06584 23497) in Hinterthal is a chalet-hotel run by an English couple (Carl is a ski instructor who guides his guests on the Hinterthal-Mühlbach 'safari').

Eating out The Ubergossene Alm just outside Dienten and the restaurant in the hotel Thalerhof in Maria Alm have good menus. Haus Salzburg (see Hotels) serves international rather than traditional Austrian food.

Après-ski Maria Alm is by far the most animated village. The Dengl Alm gets packed and has zither music, dancing and jolly bar staff in lederhosen. Almer Tenne has live music and a disco. Orgler Keller and Chili's are good for a quieter time. The Alm Bar in Hinterthal can be lively and opens till late, as does the Haus Salzburg bar. Saustall is a decent 'pub' in Mühlbach.

Off the slopes Maria Alm has curling, tobogganing, bowling, sleigh rides, swimming and nice walks.

UK PACKAGES

Maria Alm Elevation Holidays, Equity, Interhome, Rocketski, Tops **Hinterthal** Elevation Holidays **Hintermoos** Elevation Holidays

Innsbruck

Stay in a small, historic, cultured city and visit a different ski area every day, including one of Austria's best glacier areas

COSTS

① ② ③ ④ ⑤ ⑥

KEY FACTS

Resort	575m
	1,890ft
Slopes	800-3210m
	2,620-10,530ft
Lifts	80
Pistes	285km
	177 miles
Blue	32%
Red	49%
Black	19%
Snowmaking	200km
	125 miles

NEWS

In Innsbruck for 2007/08 a new funicular will go from the Congress station in the city centre to the cable-car that goes from Hungerburg to Seegrube – which itself was completely refurbished for 2006/07. Skiers and boarders should be able to reach the Nordpark base from the city centre in about 20 minutes.

For 2006/07, more snowmaking was installed in Oberperfuss from Stiglreith to Rangger Köpfl; Axamer Lizum received an extra 5 per cent and Mutters' pistes became 100 per cent covered by snowmaking.

Innsbruck is not a ski resort in the usual sense. It is a historic university city of around 140,000 inhabitants, with a vibrant cultural life, and is a major tourist destination in summer. The city has twice hosted the Olympic Winter Games, and is surrounded by several ski areas that share a lift pass and are accessible by efficient bus services. Among them are a glacier that is one of best in the world, the Stubaier Gletscher (see the chapter on the Stubai valley), and one of Austria's highest and most snow-sure non-glacier resorts, Kühtai (2020m/6,630ft). Lower down, the slopes above Mutters finally reopened a couple of seasons ago with three new lifts – a gondola, a fast quad and a drag.

The Inn valley is a broad, flat-bottomed trench here, but Innsbruck manages to fill it from side to side. It is a sizeable city, and as you would expect from its Olympic background, it has an excellent range of winter sports facilities, as well as a captivating car-free medieval core. It has smart, modern, shopping areas, trendy bars and restaurants, museums (including one devoted to the Olympics), concert halls, theatres, a zoo and other attractions that you might seek out on a summer holiday, but wouldn't expect to find when going skiing.

Winter diversions off the slopes include 100km/62 miles of cross-country trails (some at valley level but others appreciably above it), curling and skating at the Olympic centre, several toboggan runs totalling 100km/62 miles (the longest – above Birgitz – an impressive 11km/7 miles) and rides on a four-man bob at Igls.

Not the least of the attractions of staying in such a place is that you don't pay ski resort prices for anything.

There are hotels, inns and B&Bs of every standard and style, with 3-star and 4-star hotels forming the nucleus. Among the more distinctive hotels are the grand 5-star Europa Tyrol (59310), the ancient 4-star Goldener Adler (571111), the 4-star Grauer Bär (5924), the 3-star Weisses Kreuz (59479) in the central pedestrian zone, and the 4-star art nouveau Best Western Neue Post (59476).

As well as traditional Austrian restaurants there are several Italians, plus a smattering of more exotic alternatives, from Mexican to Japanese.

There is an impressive 1400m/4,600ft vertical of slopes on the south-facing slopes of **Nordpark-Seegrube**, reached by a new funicular from the city centre (see 'News') to the base of the access cable-car from Hungerburg on the outskirts of the city. Although there are red runs to the valley, the snow is not reliable. You go up here expecting to ski the red runs of 370m/1,210ft vertical below Seegrube, served by a chair-lift. A further stage of

147

Innsbruck's car-free medieval centre is a delightful place to wander through →

LIFT PASSES

**Innsbruck Gletscher
Skipass**

Prices in €

Age	1-day	6-day
under 15	14	99
15 to 18	23	132
19 to 59	27	165
over 60	23	132

Free under 7

Beginner no deals

Notes

Day pass is price for
Nordpark-Seegrube
area only

Alternative passes

Day passes for
individual areas;
Super-Skipass also
covers days in the
Arlberg (St Anton)
and Kitzbühel

the cable-car rises 350m/1,150ft vertical
to access the Karinne ski route, which
is said to be very steep. If you ski it
with a guide you can collect a T-shirt
and certificate to prove it.

But for visitors, if not for residents,
skiing usually means heading for the
opposite side of the Inn trench. The
runs on **Glungezer,** above Tulfes, are
on north-facing slopes. The chair-lift
from the bottom serves red and blue
runs and another chair up to the tree
line serves a red run. This in turn leads
to a drag and a chair-lift serving open
red runs from the top at 2305m/7,560ft
– almost 1400m/4,600ft above the
village.

The standard Innsbruck lift pass
covers the lifts in all the resorts dealt
with here, plus the slopes of Schlick
2000 above Fulpmes (see the Stubai
valley chapter later in the book).

Free ski-bus services run to and
from all the lift-pass-covered areas,
but only at the beginning and end of
the day. A car makes life more
convenient, especially if you are
staying outside downtown Innsbruck.

There are terrain-parks at Seegrube,
Axamer Lizum, the Stubaier Gletscher,
Kühtai and Oberperfuss.

A major road runs southwards from
Innsbruck over the Brenner pass to
Italy – opening up the possibility of
excursions to resorts in the Dolomites.

IGLS 900m/2,950ft
**Igls seems almost a suburb of
Innsbruck – the city trams run out to
the village – but it is a small resort in
its own right. Its famous downhill race
course is an excellent piste.**

The village of Igls is small and quiet,
with not much in the way of diversions
apart from the beautiful walks, an

artificial ice rink, the Olympic bob run
and the tea shops. You can stay in Igls,
and a few UK operators sell packages
there. Most hotels are small and in the
centre of the village, a bit of a walk
from the cable-car station. An exception
is the family-run 4-star Sporthotel
(377241), which occupies the prime site
between the tram and the cable-car
stations: 'Excellent facilities, good food
and nice bar,' says a reporter.

The skiing on Patscherkofel is very
limited and revolves around the
excellent, varied, long red run that
formed the men's downhill course in
1976, when Franz Klammer took ski
racing (and the Olympic gold medal) by
storm. There is a blue-run variation on
this run, but few other pistes. A cable-
car rises 1050m/3,450ft from the village
(and you can take it down if the lower
runs are poor or shut). At the top, a
chair rises a further 275m/900ft to the
summit offering wonderful views over
Innsbruck and ski routes back down.
Two fast quads and a couple of drags
serve the other slopes. There is a short
beginner lift at village level, and
another short bus-ride up the hill.
We have received mixed reports on the
grooming of the trails.

Après-ski is quiet. The resort suits
families but others might prefer to
stay in Innsbruck.

GLUNGEZER
2305m

2245m

Tulfes
920m

Hall in Tirol

Phone numbers
Calling long-distance
Add the prefix given
below for each resort;
when calling from
abroad use the
country code 43 and
omit the initial '0'.

**Innsbruck, Igls,
Mutters**
0512

Axamer Lizum
05234

Oberperfuss
05232

Kühtai
05239

AXAMER LIZUM 1580m/5,180ft
**The mountain outpost of the Inn-side
village of Axams is a simple ski station
and nothing more, but it does have
some good slopes and reliable snow
conditions – and, as a reporter says,
'You feel as if you are in a wilderness.'**
Axamer Lizum could scarcely provide a
sharper contrast to Igls. It offers much
more varied slopes and a network of
lifts, with the base station at a much
higher altitude. The slopes here hosted
all the Olympic Alpine events in 1976
except the men's downhill, and this is
the standard local venue for weekends
– hence the huge car park, which is the
most prominent feature of the 'resort'.

The main slopes are blues and reds,
almost entirely above the trees but
otherwise nicely varied, and there is
scope to 'play in gullies and bumps, as
well as true off-piste', says a reporter.
The vertical of the main east-facing
slopes above the main lift station is
700m/2,300ft and there is the
possibility (given good snow
conditions) of a 1300m/ 4,260ft
descent at the end of the day from
Pleisen to the outskirts of Axams – an
easy 6.5km/4 mile black. On the
opposite side of the valley, a chair-lift
serves a fairly easy black slope.
Beyond it are the slopes of Mutters,
which re-opened two seasons ago after

being closed since 2001; there are
plans to link the Axamer and Mutters
slopes but there is no definite
timescale for this. Snowmaking covers
75 per cent of the slopes and there is
a large restaurant with panoramic
views on Hoadl. There are two good
nursery lifts, and two ski schools.

You can stay up here – there is a 4-
star hotel, the Lizumerhof (68244) at
the lift base – 'nice rooms and decent
modern Austrian cuisine' – and a
couple of other hotels too. But there's
little in the way of après-ski apart from
a couple of bars – the Alm bar is the
most atmospheric – and you have to
eat in your hotel or go to Axams.

There is also accommodation not far
away at lower altitude in Axams –
including three 3-star hotels – and in
other nearby villages such as Götzens
(three 3-star hotels, one 3-star gasthof)
and Birgitz (two 3-star hotels).

MUTTERS 830m/2,720ft
**Almost as close to Innsbruck as Igls,
Mutters is a charming rustic village at
the foot of long slopes of 900m/2,950ft
vertical. Its slopes were closed in
2001, but were reopened two seasons
ago with three new lifts.**
The gentle slopes suit beginners and
families best. An eight-seat gondola
from the village serves a long blue run

↑ Most of the 1976 Olympic Alpine events were held at Axamer Lizum, which locals flock to at weekends

TVB INNSBRUCK

TOURIST OFFICES

Innsbruck
t 59850
office@innsbruck.info
www.innsbruck.info

Tulfes
t 78324
info@tulfes.at
www.tulfes.at

Igls
t 377101
igls@innsbruck.info
www.innsbruck.info/
igls

Axamer Lizum
t 68178
axams@innsbruck.info
www.innsbruck.info/
axams/

Mutters
t 548410
mutters@innsbruck.
info
www.tiscover.com/
mutters

Oberperfuss
t 81489
oberperfuss@
innsbruck.info
www.innsbruck.info/
oberperfuss

Kühtai
t 5222
kuehtai@
innsbruck.info
www.kuehtai.info

and an equally long toboggan run. Above that a high-speed quad takes you to the summit at 1800m/5,900ft and serves a red run. There's also a T-bar which, along with the top chair, links to a long red run down to Götzens, further along the valley.

There are plans to link the slopes with those of Axamer Lizum. But there is no timescale for this at the moment.

The five hotels in Mutters are 3- and 4-stars. There is a lively après-ski scene and great off-slope facilities including tennis courts, saunas, skating and curling.

OBERPERFUSS 815m/2,675ft

No, we hadn't heard of it, either – until the lifts on its local hill, Rangger Köpfl, were brought into the fold of the Innsbruck area lift pass.
The hill is a very limited one, with five lifts in a largely linear arrangement serving 17km/11 miles of easy-intermediate slopes – but an impressive vertical of 1200m/3,940ft. And over two-thirds of the pistes have snowmaking. The village is small but self-sufficient, with most things you need (eg pharmacy, bakery) and a big 3-star hotel, the Krone (81465). It is prettily rustic, and targets the family market with the aid of a moving carpet lift on the nursery slopes. There is night skiing and tobogganing on Tuesdays and Fridays.

KÜHTAI 2020m/6,630ft

A collection of comfortable hotels spread along a high road pass 25km/16 miles west of Innsbruck – higher than equally snow-sure Obergurgl or Obertauern, but cheaper than either.
Glaciers apart, Kühtai's altitude means it must be one of Austria's most snow-sure resorts. That is its main attraction,

given the limited nature of the village.

Six drags and three fast quad chairs serve red cruisers of 400m/1,310ft to 500m/1,640ft vertical on either side of the road, plus some token blue and black runs (which may be easier than the reds because they get less traffic). There is a good nursery slope, but no easy blues to graduate to. There's also a terrain-park with kickers and rails. And on Wednesdays and Saturdays there's night skiing. The resort attracts families during school holidays and day trippers on fine weekends – especially if lower resorts are short of snow – but it is otherwise crowd- and queue-free. There are three mountain restaurants and three ski schools.

The village is quiet in the evening, but for its size has 'a reasonable selection of bars and restaurants', says a report – practically all in hotels. The 4-star hotels include the Jagdschloss (5201) – a much-developed old hunting lodge. A recent visitor recommends the 4-star Mooshaus (5207) – 'convenient for the slopes, excellent service and delicious food'. The 3-star Elisabeth (5240) has also been recommended – 'Very friendly, excellent food.'

Reporters say that English is not spoken everywhere – and there is little resort information in English, either on paper or on the resort web site.

There are several free postbuses from Innsbruck morning and afternoon, but the journey takes over an hour.

STUBAIER GLETSCHER

The Stubaier Gletscher is one of the best glacier ski areas in the world; it is open in summer as well as in winter and is covered in more detail in the Stubai valley chapter later in the book.
The glacier is accessed by two alternative two-stage gondolas from the huge car park at Mutterberg. A third gondola from Eisgrat at 2900m/9,500 ft takes you right to the top of the slopes at over 3200m/10,500 ft.

On the glacier a variety of chair- and drag-lifts (including three six-person chairs) allow fabulous high altitude cruising on blue and red runs, which normally have excellent snow on slopes between 3200m and 2300m (10,500ft and 7,550ft). A lovely 10km/6 mile ungroomed ski route through a deserted bowl takes you down to the valley – or, if you start at the top, a descent of about 14km/9 miles and 1450m/4,760ft vertical is possible.

Ischgl

Ischgl is unique: high, snow-sure slopes, with a superb lift system, above a typically cute Austrian village with extraordinary après-ski

COSTS

① ② ③ ④ ⑤ ⑥

RATINGS

The slopes

Fast lifts	*****
Snow	****
Extent	****
Expert	***
Intermediate	****
Beginner	**
Convenience	***
Queues	****
Mountain restaurants	****

The rest

Scenery	***
Resort charm	****
Off-slope	***

NEWS

For 2007/08 the Fimbabahn gondola is to be upgraded with heated eight-seat cabins and a total capacity of 2,800 people per hour.

On the Swiss side, a new restaurant is planned at Salaas, on the way down from Greitspitz to Alp Trida Eck.

Snowmaking is due to be increased around the Greitspitz.

For 2006/07 the Alpenhaus restaurant at Idalp was rebuilt. Snowmaking was improved at Palinkopf, the Marmotte restaurant at Alp Trida was revamped, and a new red piste was added between Grivalea and Alp Bella on the Swiss side.

➕ Charming old Tirolean village, expanded in sympathetic fashion

➕ High slopes with reliable snow

➕ Lots of good intermediate runs

➕ Superb modern lift system

➕ Three other nearby resorts to try

➕ Very lively après-ski

➖ Not ideal for beginners or timid intermediates, for various reasons

➖ Few seriously steep runs

➖ Very little wooded terrain to give shelter in bad weather

➖ Eurotrash-style après-ski – eg table dancing in plush 4-star hotels – and a lot of heavy drinking

Ischgl is gradually finding a place on the UK package holiday market, and on the radar of British independent travellers. About time, too – we've been droning on about it for years. Most reporters enthusiastically endorse our view that this is one of Austria's best. The lift system is particularly impressive, topping our fast lifts league table. Unless cost is an obstacle, or you insist on lots of woodland runs with unreliable snow, put it on your Austrian shortlist.

Samnaun, over the hill and over the Swiss border, remains package-free (as well as duty-free). But it's a charming, relaxed village, and for a party including novices it makes a better base than Ischgl. Kappl, See and Galtür, in the same valley as Ischgl, are also worth considering for a quieter (and cheaper) time.

THE RESORT

Ischgl is a quite compact village tucked away on the Swiss border in the long, narrow Paznaun valley, south of St Anton; the ski area is shared with Swiss Samnaun. The wooded flanks of the valley rise steeply from the village, which gets almost no sun in early season.

The buildings are practically all in traditional chalet style, and the place has a neat, prosperous air. There's a selection of lively bars and an excellent sports centre; shops are mainly confined to winter sports. The narrow main street plus a couple of side streets are traffic-free – the village is bypassed by the valley road up to Galtür – and at the west end of the pedestrian zone is the main gondola to

the mid-mountain focus of Idalp. On the eastern fringe of the village, over a low hill, is another gondola to Idalp, and a third to Pardatschgrat, higher up. An underground moving walkway links these lifts to the main street, avoiding the trudge over the hill.

The best location, overall, is on or near the main pedestrian street. Beware of accommodation across the bypass road, a long way from the lifts.

A regional pass is available covering Galtür further up the valley and Kappl and See down the valley, described at the end of this chapter. All are worth a visit – and would make cheaper bases. There are frequent ski-buses to all of them. A car makes trips to St Anton viable. It's a very long taxi-ride from Samnaun, should you get stuck there.

THE MOUNTAINS

Ischgl is a fair-sized, relatively high, snow-sure area. Practically all the slopes are above the tree line, the main exception being the steep lower slopes above the village and a couple of short runs low in the Fimbatal.

You can leave skis and boots at Idalp and take the gondola down at the end of the day if you don't want to ski the steep valley runs with the homeward-bound crowds.

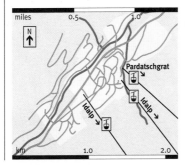

THE SLOPES
Cross-border cruising

The sunny **Idalp** plateau, reached by the 24-person Silvrettabahn and newly upgraded 8-seat Fimbabahn, is the hub of the slopes. It can be very crowded, especially at ski school meeting time, lunchtime and the end of the day. Pardatschgrat, reached by the third gondola, is about 300m/980ft higher. From Idalp, lifts radiate to a wide variety of mainly north-west- and west-facing runs. The red runs back down to Ischgl provoke regular complaints. Quite a few people ride the gondolas down. Neither is easy, conditions can be tricky, and beer-lubricated crowds don't help. The wide, quiet piste down the pretty Velilltal is much more pleasant, but doesn't entirely avoid the steep bottom part or run 1A to the Pardatschgratbahn, which should really be a black.

A short piste brings you from Idalp to the lifts serving the **Höllenkar** bowl, leading up to the area's south-western extremity and high point at **Palinkopf**. Runs from here lead down to the **Fimbatal**. On the Swiss side, the hub of activity is **Alp Trida**, surrounded by south- and east-facing runs with great views. From here a scenic red run goes down to Compatsch, where a short walk takes you to buses to Ravaisch – for the cable-car back – and Samnaun-Dorf. From Palinkopf there is a long, beautiful red run down an unspoiled valley to Samnaun-Dorf – not difficult, but excessively sunny in parts and prone to closure by avalanche risk. There is a long flat stretch at the end.

TERRAIN-PARKS
One of Europe's best

The main park above Idalp, served by the Idjochbahn, is in itself enough to

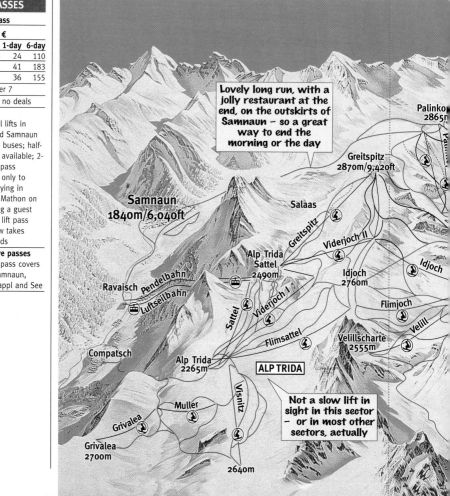

Lovely long run, with a jolly restaurant at the end, on the outskirts of Samnaun – so a great way to end the morning or the day

Not a slow lift in sight in this sector – or in most other sectors, actually

ALP TRIDA

Samnaun 1840m/6,040ft

Palinko 2865r

Greitspitz 2870m/9,420ft

Salaas

Greitspitz

Viderjoch II

Alp Trida Sattel 2490m

Idjoch 2760m

Idjoch

Viderjoch I

Flimjoch

Ravaisch Pendelbahn

Luftseilbahn

Sattel

Velill

Flimsattel

Velillscharte 2555m

Velill

Compatsch

Alp Trida 2265m

Visnitz

Muller

Grivalea

Grivalea 2700m

2640m

draw freestylers to Ischgl. It is 750m/
2,460ft long and well-shaped and
maintained. There are a host of new
rails and boxes this year, and several
good intermediate and entry-level
kickers. There is also a big pro-line
with 15-17m/50-56ft kickers and three
corner jumps. The main weakness is
that there are no fluid lines allowing
you to hit several obstacles in a row.
The pipe is well maintained. There is a
smaller pipe in the separate kids'
snowboard area. And there's another
small park on the Swiss side.

SNOW RELIABILITY
Very good
All the slopes, except the runs back to
the resort, are above 2000m/6,560ft,
and many of those on the Ischgl side
are north-west-facing. So snow
conditions are generally reliable; one
2006 reporter said, 'We've visited four

years in a row and had excellent
powder on three of them.' We also had
non-stop fresh powder during our April
2006 four-day visit. There is
snowmaking on a good proportion of
the slopes, including the descents to
Ischgl and Samnaun – more is planned
for 2007/08. Piste grooming is 'good'.

FOR EXPERTS
Not much on-piste challenge
Ischgl can't compare with St Anton for
exciting slopes, and some of the runs
marked black on the piste map would
be red elsewhere. But by general
Tirolean standards Ischgl serves
experts quite well. All the main black
areas – Greitspitz, Palinkopf and
Hollenspitze – hold snow well and
have off-piste opportunities around the
pistes; there is plenty of serious off-
piste to be found with a guide; and
powder doesn't get tracked out

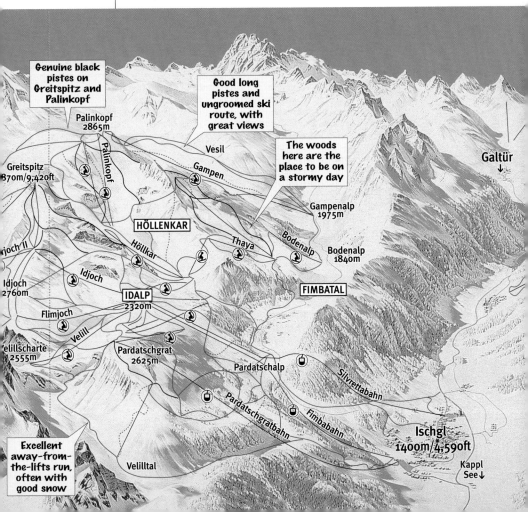

↑ High, wide slopes, generally not too challenging – but with plenty to do off-piste

ISCHGL TOURISMUS

quickly. The best steep piste is 4, from Pardatschgrat. From Greitspitz it's a long, testing descent to the village – 11km/7 miles, 1470m/4,820ft vertical. The wooded lower slopes of the Fimbatal are delightful in a storm. There are also ski routes. Ski route 39 from Palinkopf is recommended to leave you 'suitably exhausted' after the testing 1000m/3,280ft descent.

FOR INTERMEDIATES
Something for everyone
Most of the slopes are wide, forgiving and ideal for intermediates.

At the tough end of the spectrum our favourite runs are those from Palinkopf down to Gampenalp – almost 900m/2,950ft vertical and at the edge of the ski area, with great views of virgin slopes. There are also interesting and challenging black runs down the Höllspitz chair, and on Greitspitz. The reds from Pardatschgrat and Velillscharte down the beautiful Velilltal and the red from Greitspitz into Switzerland are great for quiet, high-speed cruising.

For easier motorway cruising, there is lots of choice, including those down to and around Alp Trida on the Swiss side – but on our April 2006 visit these were crowded. Timid intermediates should avoid the steep runs back to town – take the gondolas instead.

FOR BEGINNERS
Up the mountain
Beginners must buy a full lift pass and go up the mountain to Idalp, where there are good, sunny, snow-sure nursery slopes served by drags and a fast chair. The blue runs on the east side of the bowl offer pleasant progression for fast learners. Over at Alp Trida there are further easy expanses – you can return by lift.

FOR CROSS-COUNTRY
Plenty in the valley
There are 48km/30 miles of track in the valley between Ischgl, Galtür and Wirl. This tends to be shady, especially in early season, and is away from the main slopes, which makes meeting downhillers for lunch inconvenient.

QUEUES
OK once you're up the mountain
Ischgl tops our fast lift league table – 62 per cent of its lifts are fast ones. The upgrade of the Fimbabahn gondola for 2007/08 should help relieve pressure on the other two gondolas, which have nearby car/coach parks and can build serious queues. Up the mountain, more of a problem is crowds on the runs, especially the easier runs on the Swiss side, where we've found lots of people skiing too fast and too close to others.

boarding

Ischgl has long been a popular spot for snowboarders, with its long, wide, well-groomed slopes served by snowboard-friendly gondolas and high-speed chair-lifts. Although the off-piste terrain is less steep than in some other resorts, its above-the-tree-line, easily accessible nature and good snow record makes for great riding for most ability levels. Ischgl is home to one of Austria's best terrain-parks, and Silvretta Sports and Intersport Mathoy are recommended snowboard shops.

Air Innsbruck 100km/62 miles (1½hr); Zürich 300km/186 miles (3hr); Munich 300km/186 miles (3hr)

Rail Landeck (30km/19 miles); frequent buses from station

Ischgl
t 5257/5404

Classes
5 days (2hr am and pm) €158
Private lessons
€102 for 90 min; each additional person €16

Kindergarten
t 5257/5404
Run by ski school at Idalp: non-skiing children 10am to 4pm, €36 per day inc. lunch; ski-kindergarten for ages 3 to 5 €46 per 4hr day; lunch available

Ski school
Takes children from the age of 5 (5 full days €147)

MOUNTAIN RESTAURANTS
New and improving

Mountain restaurants have tended to offer quite good quality, with over half offering table-service, but inadequate capacity. But things are improving on both sides of the border. A new place is planned on the Swiss side for 2007/08 (see 'News') and Idalp now has the new Alpenhaus – with a choice of table- or self-service.

The multi-storey, glass-sided Pardorama complex at the top of Pardatschgrat opened recently – we had fabulous spicy prawns and ox fillet steak on our 2006 visit.

The Paznauner Thaya, above Bodenalp, is an attractive, rustic chalet with 'good pizza'. There is often a band playing on the terrace, or throbbing disco music. Down in Fimbatal is the Bodenalpe, a quieter, rustic table-service restaurant. The Schwarze Wand pizzeria at the top of Höllenkar is recommended by reporters, as is the Höllboden below it ('good desserts'). From Gampenalp you can be towed 5km/3 miles by snowmobile to the remote Heidelberger hütte – the way back involves 'a lot of poling, some climbs and a few gentle schusses'.

The restaurants on the Swiss side at Alp Trida are pleasant, quieter and generally recommended by reporters. At the Alp Bella, a 2006 reporter says: 'Choose the half chicken, a speciality.' The Skihaus Alp Trida serves the 'best goulash soup ever' and the Panorama Sattel (top of the Samnaun cable-car) has 'excellent food', 'splendid views'. Above the big Alp Trida self-service is the newly renovated 'smart' Marmotte (reservations needed) and Munggaloch bar ('big terrace, panoramic views').

SCHOOLS AND GUIDES
Best for late risers

The school meets up at Idalp and starts very late (10.30). In the past we've had rave reviews, but reporters said class sizes were large at around 12 people and their instructor spoke limited English. The school also organises off-piste tours.

FACILITIES FOR CHILDREN
High-altitude options

The childcare facilities are all up at Idalp – there's an enclosed learning zone and adventure garden with cartoon characters. But we have no reports of the service they provide.

HOW TO GO
Increasing choice of packages

Several British tour operators now feature Ischgl.

Hotels There is a good selection from luxurious and expensive to simple B&Bs, and no shortage of recommendations from readers.

*****Trofana Royal (600) One of Austria's most luxurious hotels, with prices to match. A celebrity chef runs the kitchen. Sumptuous spa facilities.

****Madlein (5226) Convenient, 'hip', modern hotel. Pool, sauna, steam room. Nightclub and disco.

****Elisabeth (5411) Right by the Pardatschgrat gondola, with lively après-ski. Pool, sauna and steam room.

****Solaria (5205) Near the Madlein and just as luxurious, with a 'friendly family atmosphere' and 'helpful staff'.

****Brigitte (5646) Highly recommended for 'central, but quiet location' and 'fantastic food'. Pool.

****Piz Tasna (5277) Up hill behind church: 'Quiet location, friendly, lovely views over village, excellent food.'

****Goldener Adler (5217) Central, smart, modern hotel, with 'outstanding food'. Sauna and whirlpool.

****Olympia (5432) 'Well-appointed, family-run' with 'good-sized rooms'. Bar and restaurant. Sauna and solarium.

****Jägerhof (5206) 'Jewel of a hotel,' said a reporter. Friendly, good food, large rooms. Sauna and steam.

****The Hotel (20150) Close to the Pardatschgratbahn. 'Excellent food'.

****Post (5232) Central location. Wellness centre. 'Luxurious and excellent gourmet food'.

****Christine (5346) Probably the best B&B in town. 'Huge rooms, nice views, good position near the lifts.'

****Dorfschmiede (5769) Small, central B&B with 'friendly service and a great location', says a 2006 reporter.

Apartments Some attractive apartments are available. The Golfais are conveniently placed by the Pardatschgrat gondola and have been recommended. A 2006 reporter was pleased with his apartment for four in the hotel Solaria (with use of its spa).

EATING OUT
Plenty of choice

Most of our reporters ate in their hotels. For a lighter meal such as pizza try the Nona, the Schatzi or the Trofana Alm (also 'good ribs'), which is

↑ Two of the gondola stations are on the left of the low hill that the village is built on, and the main street is on the right, with a moving underground walkway through the hill
TVB PAZNAUN-ISCHGL

ACTIVITIES

Indoor Silvretta Centre (bowling, billiards, swimming pool, sauna, solarium, massage), museums

Outdoor Ice rink, curling, sleigh rides, hiking tours, 7km/ 4 miles floodlit toboggan run

as much a bar as a restaurant, and for fondue or ribs the Kitzloch, with its galleries over the dance floor. The Allegra and Salz & Pfeffer 'pasta and pizza' have been recommended. The Grillalm and Salnerhof are popular, 'traditional Austrian fare, huge portions'. A reporter pronounces the Nudelhimmel (Hotel Solaria) his favourite – local dishes at reasonable prices. The Nevada is also recommended: 'Friendly staff, but little English is spoken.'

APRES-SKI
Very lively
Ischgl is one of the liveliest resorts in the Alps, from early afternoon on. Lots of people are still in ski boots late in the evening. Mountain restaurants such as Paznauner Thaya slide into après mode directly after lunch. When you manage to get back to the village, the obvious ports of call are Trofana Alm near the Silvrettabahn or the Schatzi bar of the hotel Elisabeth by the Pardatschgratbahn – with indoor and outdoor bars and scantily clad dancing girls. The 'tremendously lively' Niki's Stadl across the road is a great place to sing along to live Austrian hits. The Kitzloch 'rocks', with dancing on the tables in ski boots. The bar at the hotel Sonne gets crowded and has live music. The Kuhstahl under the Sporthotel Silvretta and Feuer & Eis ('expensive drinks') over the road are packed all evening. The Höllboden bar is recommended for live music. Guxa ('a cigars and cocktails type of place') and Allegra liven up after dinner, and the Golden Eagle is 'good for live bands'. The huge Trofana Arena also has live bands (and a lap dancing

club). The Coyote Ugly at the hotel Madlein – 'a lap dancing bar that just manages to avoid seediness' – has been recommended. There's a branch of the famous Pacha nightclubs, also in Ibiza and London (a bit 'tacky', says a visitor). The Living Room (hotel Grillalm) is allegedly 'more hands-on' than table dancing. And the club under the hotel Post has an ancient Roman theme.

OFF THE SLOPES
No sun but a nice pool
The village gets little sun in the middle of winter, and the resort is best suited to those keen to hit the slopes. But there's no shortage of off-slope activities. There are 24km/15 miles of well-marked and maintained walks (many at altitude), a 7km/4 mile floodlit toboggan run and a splendid sports centre. And you can browse upmarket shops, which sell Versace and Bogner. It's easy to get around the valley by bus and the Smuggler's Pass for pedestrians enables them to use specially selected lifts.

Samnaun 1840m/6,040ft

Small, quiet duty-free Samnaun is in a corner of Switzerland more easily reached from Austria. It is virtually Brit-free. There are four small components, roughly 1km/0.5 mile apart: Samnaun-Dorf, prettily set at the head of the valley is the main focus, with some swanky hotels and duty-free shops; Ravaisch, where the cable-car goes up; tiny Plan; and the hamlets of Laret and Compatsch, at the end of the main run down from the slopes. We've stayed happily on the edge of Dorf in the Waldpark B&B (8618310), and have eaten well at the Pasta in the hotel Montana (8619000). Reporters recommend the Hotel Post (8619200) ('good food but pricey') and the Stammerspitze Cafe there. The Castello hotel and spa is new in Dorf. There's a smart AlpenQuell spa-pool-fitness centre.

The Schmuggler Alm at the bottom of the long run from Palinkopf is a popular après-ski spot and 'does the best pizza in the world'.

Kappl 1260m/4,135ft

Kappl, a 15-minute bus-ride down the valley from Ischgl, is worth a visit – we had a great half-day here a couple of years back. Both the village and the slopes are family-oriented, and

Phone numbers
Calling long-distance
Add the prefix given
below for each resort;
when calling from
abroad use the
country code +43 and
omit the initial '0'
Ischgl
05444
Kappl
05445
See
05441
Galtür
05443

Samnaun
(Switzerland)
From elsewhere in
Switzerland add the
prefix 081; from
abroad use the prefix
+41 81

TOURIST OFFICES
Ischgl
t 5266
info@ischgl.com
www.ischgl.com
Samnaun
(Switzerland)
t 868 5858
info@samnaun.ch
www.samnaun.ch
Kappl
t 6243
info@kappl.at
www.kappl.at
See
t 8296
see@kappl-see.com
www.kappl-see.com
Galtür
t 8521
info@galtuer.com
www.galtuer.com

delightfully quiet compared with Ischgl. The village, with a couple of dozen hotels and guest-houses, sits on a shelf 100m/330ft above the valley floor. The Sunny Mountain area at the top of the access gondola has a big kindergarten and outside play area. There's a long floodlit toboggan run from here back to the village.

There are 40km/25 miles of sunny, largely south-facing pistes going up to 2640m/8,660ft. The slopes – served by an access gondola from the roadside and fast quads above it – offer plenty of variety, with several tough reds, including the Lattenabfahrt down a deserted valley from the top – 8km/5 miles long, 985m/3,230ft vertical, more if you go on to the valley floor. Most of the slopes are open, but the run down the gondola offers some shelter for bad-weather days. Snowmaking covers all except the highest slopes.

See 1050m/3,440ft

See, a 10-minute bus-ride further down the valley from Kappl, has 33km/20 miles of predominantly easy, largely north-facing slopes. It is worth a visit from Ischgl to get away from the crowds, if you don't mind the limited extent. It had great powder when we were there in April 2006 – excellent for making your first turns off-piste. There's a good nursery slope at the top of the access gondola, and easy runs to progress to. Piste 10 is a beautiful red run round the back of the mountain, away from all lifts, with spectacular views – a pleasant ski to start with and then a road you cruise along admiring the views. Bambini World offers childcare. There's a terrain-park and toboggan run. See is worth considering as a base for families – it's quieter and cheaper than Ischgl; but the village is not especially attractive and is rather spoiled by the main road through it. Accommodation is largely in 3-star hotels and guest houses strung along the road.

Galtür 1585m/5,200ft

Galtür is a charming, peaceful, traditional village clustered around a pretty little church, amid impressive mountain scenery at the head of the valley (and so unspoiled by through-traffic). Rebuilt and fortified after the devastating avalanche of 1999, the village is now home to the Alpinarium, featuring an exhibition centre (signs only in German), climbing wall, internet and archive room, all built within avalanche-protection structures.

Sunnier, cheaper and much quieter than Ischgl, Galtür is a good base for a quiet family holiday or mixed-ability groups – and the free buses to Ischgl are regular and quick. There are good 3- and 4-star hotels – the Almhof (8253), Flüchthorn (8202), Alpenrose (8201) and Ballunspitze (8214) have been recommended.

Galtür's own slopes (rising to 2295m/7,530ft), above a lift base at Wirl, a short bus-ride from the village, are not very challenging and can be bleak in poor weather; but the black runs are ideal for intermediates and there are fine nursery slopes. The area on the far right of the piste map, served by a slow double chair and a T-bar, has some good off-piste in a bowl and among well-spaced trees. There is a small terrain-park at the top of the Soppalift drag. The school has a high reputation and offers small classes. Kinderland has its own tow, carousel and moving carpet. Galtür has 45km/28 miles of cross-country loops, some quite testing. The cosy, wooden Wieberhimml mountain hut has waitresses in traditional costume.

Off-slope facilities are limited, but there's a sports centre with pool, tennis and squash. Night skiing and sledding are available on Wednesdays.

Kitzbühel

The extensive slopes are mostly pretty tame; the medieval town at the base, though, is something special – cute and lively

NEWS

As we go to press, we learn that the transformation of the Ehrenbachgraben lift bottleneck will be completed for 2007/08, with the installation of an eight-pack to replace the old double chair to Steinbergkogel. This follows the upgrade for last season of the triple Ehrenbachhöhe to a six-pack. A new six-pack also replaced the Haglalm T-bar at Resterhöhe. And snowmaking was increased in that sector, with more planned for 2007/08.

A new Sports Park opened last season, with ice rinks, ice hockey, curling and ice skittles, a climbing wall and a restaurant.

The Bichlalm area, which closed after operating for a couple of seasons as a purely off-piste area, has reopened its marked ski routes for snowcat skiing with the ski school.

➕ Large, attractive, varied slopes offering a sensation of travel

➕ Beautiful medieval town centre

➕ Vibrant nightlife

➕ Plenty of off-slope amenities, both for the sporty and not-so-sporty

➕ A surprisingly large amount of cheap and cheerful accommodation

➕ Excellent mountain restaurants

➕ A gondola has improved access to the high Resterhöhe slopes, for the best snow in the area, but ...

➖ Snow in the lower sectors close to Kitzbühel is often poor, especially on runs to the valley (though there's now quite a bit of snowmaking)

➖ Surprisingly little challenging terrain – though plenty of off-piste

➖ Disappointing nursery area

➖ Some crowded pistes

Kitzbühel is one of the big names of the ski world, largely thanks to its Hahnenkamm downhill race course – the most spectacular on the World Cup circuit. And there is a lot to like about the resort – particularly the beautiful, traffic-free centre, complete with cobbled streets and lovely medieval buildings. Some of these contain elegant, upscale hotels. But there is a huge amount of inexpensive accommodation which attracts low-budget visitors, many of whom are young and out to party in the resort's famous après-ski haunts.

The low altitude of the slopes is a real problem. In countless visits over a 20-year period we've encountered good snow down to the village precisely once. Our advice is to book late, when you know the conditions are good.

THE RESORT

Set at a junction of broad, pretty valleys, Kitzbühel is a large, animated town. The beautiful walled medieval centre – with quaint church, cobbled streets and attractively painted buildings – is traffic-free and a compelling place to stay. Many visitors love the sophisticated, towny ambience and swanky shops and cafes. But the resort spreads widely, and busy roads surround the old town, reducing the charm factor somewhat. Visitors used to peaceful little Austrian villages are likely to be surprised by its urban feel.

A gondola from the edge of the town goes up to the Hahnenkamm, start of the main area of slopes. Across town, close to the railway station but some way from the centre, another gondola accesses the much smaller Kitzbüheler Horn sector. The size of Kitz makes choice of location

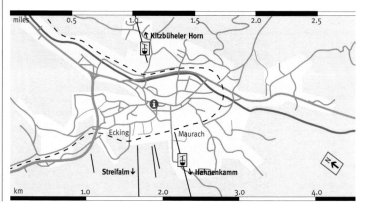

KEY FACTS

Resort	760m
	2,490ft
Slopes	800-2000m
	2,620-6,560ft
Lifts	53
Pistes	145km
	90 miles
Blue	37%
Red	43%
Black	20%
Snowmaking	65km
	40 miles

LIFT PASSES

Kitzbühel

Prices in €

Age	1-day	6-day
under 16	19	88
16 to 18	30	140
over 19	38	175

Free under 7

Senior 60+: day pass €19 on Tue only; 80+: season pass €15

Beginner seven free lifts (three in Kitzbühel)

Notes
Covers all lifts in Kitzbühel, Kirchberg, Jochberg, Pass Thurn, Mittersill/Hollersbach; 50% reduction on pool entry with passes for 2 days or more; single ascent, hourly and pedestrian tickets; family reductions

Alternative passes
Kitzbüheler Alpen-skipass covers five large ski areas – Kitzbühel, Schneewinkel (St Johann), Ski Welt, Alpbach and Wildschönau; Salzburg Super Ski Card covers 21 ski areas in the Salzburg province

Most of the mountain restaurants are considerably more charming than this →

important. Many visitors prefer to be close to the Hahnenkamm gondola. Beginners should bear in mind that the Hahnenkamm nursery slopes are often lacking in snow, and then novices are taken up the Horn. Reporters continue to say the buses around town get overcrowded and some suggest taking taxis if you don't want to walk. But the postbus service is said to be 'cheap and efficient'.

A car is useful for visiting lots of other resorts covered by the Kitzbüheler Alpenskipass – though one of those, Westendorf, is now linked by the Ki-West gondola from near Aschau.

THE MOUNTAINS

Kitzbühel's extensive slopes – shared with Kirchberg and other, smaller villages – offer a very attractive mixture of entirely open runs higher up and patchy forest lower down. Most face north-east or north-west.

THE SLOPES
Big but bitty
The slopes can be divided into several identifiable areas, most of them linked.

The **Hahnenkamm** gondola takes you (via a tedious walk along a flat piste) to the bowl of Ehrenbachgraben, a major lift bottleneck in the past but now equipped with not only a six-pack to Ehrenbachhöhe, the arrival point of lifts from Kirchberg, but also a new eight-pack to Steinbergkogel.

Beyond is the slightly lower peak of **Pengelstein**, whence several long west-facing runs go down to Skirast, where

there is a gondola back up, or Aschau. Ski buses from these points will take you to the Westendorf lifts or to Kirchberg. It reportedly takes about an hour to reach the Westendorf slopes, including the bus connection.

Pengelstein is also the start of the impressive 30-person cross-valley 3S gondola to **Wurzhöhe** above Jochberg. This peak-to-peak link has great views.

Further lifts then take you to the **Resterhöhe** sector above Pass Thurn – well worth the excursion, for better snow and fewer crowds, even though the gondola connection has made the slopes busier. There's a fine long run to Breitmoos, mid-station of the recently added gondola up from Hollersbach in the valley to the south of Pass Thurn. Runs are otherwise short, but mostly served by fast chairs.

The **Kitzbüheler Horn** gondola second stage leads to the sunny Trattalm bowl, with an alternative cable-car taking you up to the summit of the Horn, from where a fine, solitary piste leads down into the Raintal on the east side – popular with boarders apparently. There's a blue piste and two ski routes back towards town.

There's floodlit skiing on Thursday and Friday on **Gaisberg**, a small area of slopes at Kirchberg, on the other side of the road from the main ski area.

The separate **Bichlalm** area, which closed after a couple of seasons of lift-served off-piste operation, has reopened for guided snowcat skiing operated by the ski school.

The piste map is praised as 'very clear and easy to use'.

THE HAHNENKAMM DOWNHILL

Kitzbühel's Hahnenkamm Downhill race, held in mid-January each year, is the toughest as well as one of the most famous on the World Cup circuit. On the race weekend the town is packed and there is a real carnival atmosphere, with bands, people in traditional costumes and huge (and loud) cowbells everywhere. The race itself starts with a steep icy section before you hit the famous Mausfalle and Steilhang, where even Franz Klammer used to get worried. The course (now thankfully served by snow-guns) starts near the top of the Hahnenkamm gondola and drops 860m/2,820ft to finish amid the noise and celebrations right on the edge of town. Ordinary mortals can now try most of the course after the race weekend, whenever the snow is good enough – it's an unpisted red ski route mostly. We found it steep and tricky in parts, even when going slowly – it must be terrifying at race speeds of 80mph or more. The course is normally closed from the start of the season until after the race.

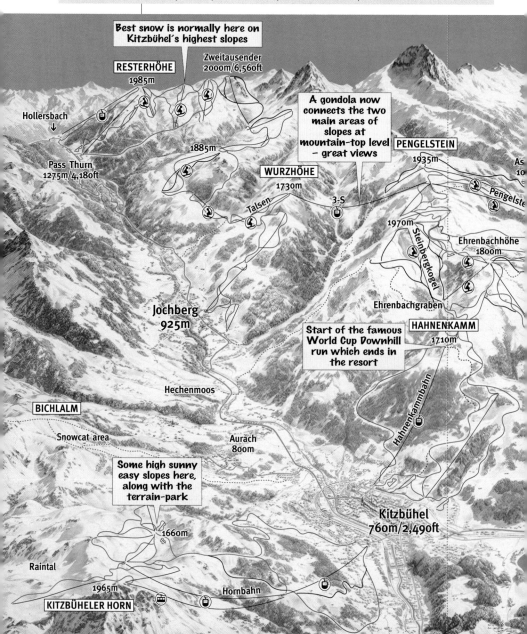

Best snow is normally here on Kitzbühel's highest slopes

RESTERHÖHE
1985m

Zweitausender
2000m/6,56oft

Hollersbach
↓

A gondola now connects the two main areas of slopes at mountain-top level – great views

PENGELSTEIN
1935m

As
10

1885m

Pass Thurn
1275m/4,18oft

WURZHÖHE
1730m

Talsen

3-S

Pengelste

1970m

Steinbergkogel

Ehrenbachhöhe
1800m

Jochberg
925m

Ehrenbachgraben

Start of the famous World Cup Downhill run which ends in the resort

HAHNENKAMM
1710m

Hechenmoos

BICHLALM

Hahnenkammbahn

Snowcat area

Aurach
800m

Some high sunny easy slopes here, along with the terrain-park

Kitzbühel
760m/2,490ft

1660m

Raintal

1965m

Hornbahn

KITZBÜHELER HORN

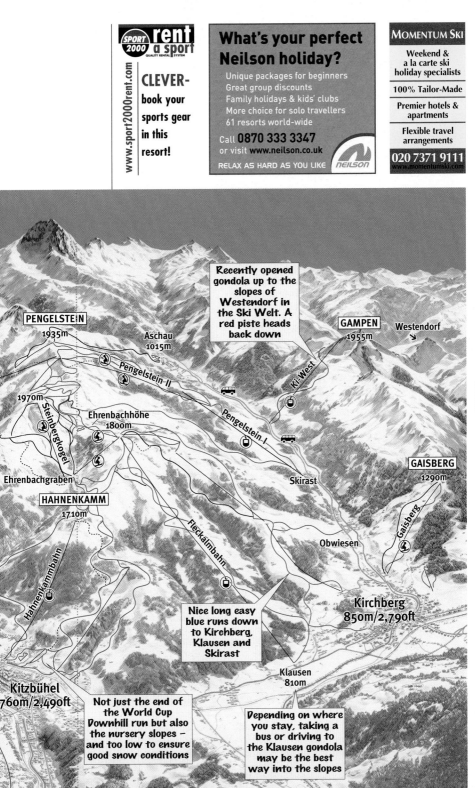

Recently opened gondola up to the slopes of Westendorf in the Ski Welt. A red piste heads back down

PENGELSTEIN
1935m

Aschau
1015m

Pengelstein-II

GAMPEN
1955m

Westendorf

Ki-West

1970m

Steinbergkogel

Ehrenbachhöhe
1800m

Pengelstein-I

GAISBERG
1290m

Ehrenbachgraben

Gaisberg

HAHNENKAMM
1710m

Skirast

Fleckalmbahn

Obwiesen

Hahnenkammbahn

Kirchberg
850m/2,790ft

Nice long easy blue runs down to Kirchberg, Klausen and Skirast

Kitzbühel
760m/2,490ft

Klausen
810m

Not just the end of the World Cup Downhill run but also the nursery slopes – and too low to ensure good snow conditions

Depending on where you stay, taking a bus or driving to the Klausen gondola may be the best way into the slopes

Kitzbühel

↑ The traffic-free medieval heart of Kitzbühel is a key part of its appeal
EDDIE BAINES

FOR EXPERTS
Plan to go off-piste
Steep slopes – pistes and off-piste terrain – are mostly concentrated around the bowl of Ehrenbachgraben. The most direct of these are challenging mogul fields ('beautifully quiet and tremendous fun to ski'). Nearby is the Streif red, the basis for the famous Hahnenkamm Downhill race (see the feature panel). When conditions allow, there is plenty of gentler off-piste potential elsewhere – some of it safely close to pistes, some requiring a guide.

FOR INTERMEDIATES
Lots of alternatives
The Hahnenkamm area is prime terrain. Good intermediates will want to do the World Cup downhill run, of course (see the feature panel). And the long blues of around 1000m/3,300ft vertical to Klausen from Ehrenbachhöhe and to Skirast from Steinbergkogel or Pengelstein are also satisfying. The east-facing Raintal run on the Horn is excellent for good intermediates.

The Wurzhöhe runs are particularly good for mixed abilities, and the short, high runs at Resterhöhe are ideal if you are more timid. There are easy reds down to Pass Thurn and Jochberg. Much of the Horn is good cruising.

FOR BEGINNERS
Not ideal
The Hahnenkamm nursery slopes are no more than adequate, and prone to poor snow conditions. The Horn has a high, sunny, nursery-like section, and quick learners will soon be cruising home from there on the long Hagstein piste. There are some easy runs to progress to if the snow is OK. But there are many more conveniently arranged places to start.

FOR CROSS-COUNTRY
Plentiful but low
There are nearly 50km/31 miles of trails scattered around, but all are at valley level and prone to lack of snow.

TERRAIN-PARKS
Take the Hornbahn
The park is on the Kitzbüheler Horn and has an intermediate table-top jump, a quarter-pipe and several small rails and boxes. The half-pipe can be OK but isn't that well maintained. There are plenty of good kicker spots in the nearby ungroomed terrain. The park in Westendorf is far bigger and better – worth the early start for park aficionados (www.boardplay.com).

SNOW RELIABILITY
More snowmaking now
The problem is that Kitzbühel's slopes have one of the lowest average heights in the Alps. To make matters worse, the Horn is also sunny. Even in an exceptionally good snow year some reporters complain of worn patches, ice and slush on the lower slopes. In a normal year, the lower slopes can be very tricky or bare at times (though the snow at the top is often OK). The expansion of snowmaking has improved matters when it's cold enough to make snow – runs down to Kitzbühel, Kirchberg, Klausen and Jochberg are covered. But many slopes still remain unprotected. If snow is poor, head for Resterhöhe, which, as well as having the best natural snow, is still improving its snowmaking.

boarding

Kitzbühel has never been known as a snowboarders' hub, but it's growing in popularity, according to a 2007 reporter. In order to attract a more freestyle-orientated clientele, a decent terrain-park has been built, complete with half-pipe, boarder-cross and speed course. There are some good off-piste runs and fun natural obstacles on the Hahnenkamm and around Pengelstein. All major lifts are gondolas and chair-lifts – the area suits beginners and intermediates well.

SCHOOLS

Rote Teufel (Red Devil)
t 62500

Jochberg
t 05355 5342

Wagstätt
t 05355 50232

Reith
t 65496

Aurach
t 65804

Classes
(Rote Teufel prices)
6 days (2hr am and pm) €150

Private lessons
€150 for 2hr; each additional person €20

CHILDREN

There is no non-ski nursery, but babysitters and nannies can be hired

Ski school
From age 3 (6 days €160 – Rote Teufel)

GETTING THERE

Air Salzburg 80km/50 miles (1½hr); Munich 160km/99 miles (2hr); Innsbruck 95km/59 miles (1½hr)

Rail Mainline station in resort. Postbus every 15min from station

UK PACKAGES

Airtours, Alpine Answers, Alpine Weekends, Corporate Ski Co, Crystal, Crystal Finest, Directski.com, Elegant Resorts, First Choice, Independent Ski Links, Inghams, Interactive Resorts, Interhome, Kuoni, Made to Measure, Momentum, Neilson, Panorama, Ski Freshtracks, Ski Line, Ski McNeill, Ski Solutions, Ski Wild, Skitracer, Snowscape, Thomson
Kirchberg Airtours, Club Pavilion, Directski.com, First Choice, Interhome, Made to Measure, Neilson, Ski McNeill, Snowscape, Thomson

QUEUES
Major improvements

Queues to get out of the town have almost been forgotten, and two major new chairs at Ehrenbachgraben – a six-pack last year and an eight-pack to Steinbergkogel this year – have solved the main problem on the mountain. The slow Maierl chairs out of Kirchberg are still tiresome. But we have had reports of queue-free weeks, and bearable queues at half-term. Both the Horn and the Hahnenkamm can have crowded pistes – though the 3S gondola link with Wurzhöhe seems to have spread the traffic across sectors.

MOUNTAIN RESTAURANTS
A highlight

There are many attractive restaurants, well marked on the piste map – 'One of the reasons we keep going back,' says one of our Kitz regulars.
Editors' choice The Seidlalm (63135), right by the lower part of the downhill course, is relatively quiet and delightfully rustic; 'Wonderful garlic soup,' says a 2006 reporter.
Worth knowing about In the Hahnenkamm sector we had a jolly meal at Berghaus Tyrol, below Ehrenbachhöhe. The Hockeckhütte has 'excellent food and atmosphere'. Melkalm 'is worth the effort of finding'. The Hochbrunn has 'very friendly' staff and 'good strudel', the Schutzhütte Steinbergkogel 'wonderful food'. The expensive Hochkitzbühel at the top of the gondola has good food, but service has been criticised. A 2007 visitor enjoyed the 'bright and modern' Ehrenbachgraben. The Kasereckhütte on the ski route to Jochberg is 'brilliant'. At Wurzhöhe, Jägerwurzhütte is recommended, as is Trattenbachalm, on the way to Resterhöhe; Hanglalm has 'the best Kaiserschmarrn', and Panoramaalm great views. On the Horn, Hornköpfl-Hütte's good food and sunny terraces still get praised despite a slight climb to reach it. Alpenhaus 'does excellent self-service meals for great prices' but can get crowded; the Gipfelhaus is quieter with 'super views and a sheltered terrace'. Gasthof Hagstein is an attractive farmhouse.

SCHOOLS AND GUIDES
Good recent reviews

The Kitzbühel Rote Teufel (Red Devils) have absorbed several other local schools (including the Total school). Reports are favourable. A 2006 visitor 'learned more than ever before' in his week with them. Another reporter 'progressed very quickly with an excellent instructor'. The other schools emphasise their small scale.

FACILITIES FOR CHILDREN
Not an ideal choice

Provided your children can take classes, you can deposit them at any of the schools. Rote Teufel takes kids from three years old – 'No complaints,' says a 2007 reporter.

STAYING THERE

HOW TO GO
Mainly hotels and pensions

Kitz is essentially a hotel resort, though a few tour operators run chalet-hotels there.
Hotels There is an enormous choice, especially of 4-star and 3-star hotels.
*****Tennerhof (63181) Luxurious former farmhouse, with renowned restaurant. Beautiful panelled rooms.
****Golfhotel Rasmushof (652520) Right on the slopes by the finish area of the Hahnenkamm race, close to centre of town. 'Excellent service from friendly staff. Book a room overlooking the slopes (a golf course in summer).'
****Schloss Lebenberg (69010) Modernised 'castle' with smart pool; inconvenient location but free shuttle-bus. Free nursery for kids aged 3-plus. Being refurbished for 2007/08.
*****Weisses Rössl (71900) Smartly traditional, exclusive 5-star aparthotel. Recently renovated. New spa facilities.
****Goldener Greif (64311) Elegant, historic inn; vaulted lobby-sitting area, panelled bar, casino.
****Jägerwirt (6981) Modern chalet with 'helpful staff and wonderful food'. Not ideally placed.
****Schwarzer Adler (6911) Traditional hotel, near centre, highly praised by a reporter: 'Great food and lovely leisure centre in basement.'
****Best Western Kaiserhof (75503) Next to the Hahnenkamm gondola. Highly recommended. 'Great spa, indoor pool and excellent food – can't fault it,' says a 2007 reporter.
****Schweizerhof (62735) Comfortable chalet right by Hahnenkamm gondola.
***Edelweiss (75252) 'Excellent food and accommodation'.
***Strasshofer (62285) 'Central, family-run, friendly, good food, good with children, quiet rooms at back.' 'Excellent value and location.'

ACTIVITIES

Indoor Aquarena Centre (pools, slides, sauna, solarium, mud baths, aerated baths, underwater massage) – discounted entry with lift pass; tennis, fitness centre, beauty centre, bridge, indoor riding school, climbing wall, bowling, museums, casino, cinema

Outdoor Ice rink (curling and skating), sleigh rides, snow-shoeing, tobogganing, ballooning, helicopter flights, paragliding, wildlife park, 65km/40 miles of cleared walking paths

Phone numbers
Kitzbühel
From elsewhere in Austria add the prefix 05356; from abroad use the prefix +43 5356
Kirchberg
From elsewhere in Austria add the prefix 05357; from abroad use the prefix +43 5357

TOURIST OFFICES

Kitzbühel
t 777
info@kitzbuehel.com
www.kitzbuehel.com
Kirchberg
t 2000
kirchberg@kitzbuehel-alpen.com
www.kirchberg.at

**Mühlbergerhof (62835) Small, friendly pension in good position.
Apartments Many of the best (and best-positioned) are attached to hotels.

EATING OUT
Something for everyone
There is a wide range of restaurants to suit all pockets, including pizzerias and fast-food outlets (even McDonald's). The Neuwirt in the Schwarzer Adler hotel is regarded as the best in town and wins awards in food guides and the Schwedenkapelle is also highly rated. Good, cheaper places include the traditional Huberbräu-Stüberl ('good Austrian food'), Chizzo, Eggerwirt and, a little out of town with great views, Hagstein, which serves big pans of communal food for groups. Goldene Gams has a wide-ranging menu and both traditional and modern dining rooms. Barrique does 'great pizza.' And the Gallo (formerly Cafe Langer) is a stylish new Italian. On Fridays and Saturdays you can dine at the top of the Hahnenkamm gondola (Hochkitzbühel). For something different take a taxi to Rosi's Sonnbergstub'n. Choose the speciality lamb or duck and expect to be serenaded by Rosi herself.

APRES-SKI
A main attraction
Nightlife is one of Kitz's great selling points. There's something for all tastes, from throbbing bars full of teenagers to quiet places, nice cafes and smart spots for fur-coat flaunting.
Immediately after the slopes close, the town is jolly without being much livelier than many other Tirolean resorts. The Streifalm bar at the foot of the slopes is popular, with 'white pine and slate, open fire, widescreen TV and Europop music', as is the Sportcafe Hölzl. Cafes Praxmair, Kortschak, Langer and Rupprechter are among the most atmospheric tea-time places for cakes and pastries. The lively Stamperl is 'classy and fun'. The Seidlalm has weekly Tirolean evenings (free). Later the American-style Highways bar and Lichtl's (with thousands of lights hanging from the ceiling) get packed. Seppi's Pub is recommended for sport on TV, pizzas and the eccentric owner. The Python and Take Five are the main discos. The Londoner Pub is a famous drinking place, well summarised by one visitor: 'Very crowded, very noisy and great fun, but the bar staff were mostly rude and arrogant.' The Fonda has been recommended for the 'younger generation'.

OFF THE SLOPES
Plenty to do
The lift pass gives a reduction for the pools in the impressive Aquarena leisure centre. There's a museum, and concerts are organised. The railway makes excursions easy (eg Salzburg).

Kirchberg 850m/2,790ft

THE RESORT
Kirchberg is a large, spread-out, lively village. There are three ways into the slopes, all a bus-ride from the village.

THE MOUNTAIN
Slopes The Maierl chair-lifts and the gondola from Klausen take you to Ehrenbachhöhe, at the heart of the Kitzbühel slopes. The gondola from Skirast meets chairs to Pengelstein which link to the gondola to Wurzhöhe. The separate small Gaisberg ski area is on the other side of the valley.
Terrain-parks Head for Kitzbühel.
Snow reliability Kirchberg suffers from the same unreliable snow as Kitzbühel.
Experts Few challenging slopes.
Intermediates The main slopes back are easy cruises when snow is good.
Beginners There's a beginner lift and area at the foot of the Gaisberg slopes.
Snowboarding Kitzbühel has the edge, with the terrain-park on the Horn.
Cross-country There are lots of trails – but they can suffer from lack of snow.
Queues There are some bottlenecks.
Mountain restaurants There are some good local huts.
Schools and guides We lack recent reports on the three schools.
Facilities for children There are non-ski and ski kindergartens.

STAYING THERE
How to go There's a wide choice of chalet-style hotels and pensions.
Hotels The 4-star Klausen (2128), close to the main gondola, and the Sporthotel Tyrol (2787), a bit out of the centre, have been recommended.
Apartments There are some available.
Eating out Mostly in hotels, but there's a pizzeria and a steak house too.
Après-ski There's a toboggan run on Gaisberg. Nightlife is very lively.
Off the slopes Some hotels have swimming pools and saunas.

Lech

If you can afford it, simply one of the best: a captivating blend of reliable snow, village charm and deeply comfortable hotels

COSTS

① ② ③ ④ ⑤ ⑥

RATINGS

The slopes

Fast lifts	****
Snow	****
Extent	****
Expert	****
Intermediate	****
Beginner	****
Convenience	***
Queues	****
Mountain restaurants	***

The rest

Scenery	***
Resort charm	****
Off-slope	***

NEWS

For 2006/07 the Trittalp and Seekopf lifts in Zürs were equipped with covers and heated seats. The Palmen Alpe became the first mountain restaurant in Austria to ban smoking (apart from at the bar).

- Picturesque Alpine village
- Sunny and usually uncrowded slopes with excellent snow record and extensive snowmaking
- Sizeable area of mainly intermediate pistes, plus good, extensive off-piste
- Easy access by bus to the slopes of St Anton and other Arlberg resorts
- Some very smart hotels, including ski-in/ski-out options at Oberlech
- More and more heated chair-lifts
- Lively après-ski scene, but ...

- Few non-hotel bars or restaurants
- Surprising shortage, for a smart resort, of seductive shopping
- Local traffic intrudes on main street of Lech (and really spoils Zürs)
- Very few challenging pistes
- Nearly all slopes are above the tree line, and unpleasant in bad weather
- Blue runs back to the village are rather steep for nervous novices
- Generally expensive
- Still a few slow, old lifts

Lech and its higher, linked neighbour Zürs are the most fashionable resorts in Austria, each able to point to a string of rich and celebrated regular visitors, and to pull in Merc-borne Germans on an unmatched scale. But, like all such 'exclusive' resorts, they aren't actually exclusive in any real sense. A holiday here is unlikely to be cheap, but it doesn't have to cost a lot more than in countless other international resorts in the Alps. We don't feel out of place here, and neither would you. We often see Lech described as 'a very chic resort' – but it has none of the flash shops of St Moritz or Cortina, for example.

The real point about these resorts is that they offer a rare and attractive combination of impressive snowfall, traditional Alpine atmosphere and excellent hotels offering a truly personal service from their family owners.

THE RESORT

Lech is an old farming village set in a high valley that spent long periods of winter cut off from the outside world until the Flexen Pass road through Zürs was constructed at the end of the 19th century. (Even now, the road can be closed for days on end after an exceptional snowfall; a road tunnel is planned, but is not imminent.)

The village is attractive, with its upmarket hotels built in traditional chalet style, its gurgling river plus bridges, its adequately impressive scenery and the high incidence of snow on the streets. But its appeal is dimmed by traffic on the main street that forms its spine (a regular complaint by reporters): although the pavements have been widened and parking is controlled, it can still get very busy, especially at weekends.

Britain is the resort's third most important market, but Brits are outnumbered 10:1 by Germans and 3:1 by Austrians.

The heart of the village is a short stretch of the main street beside the river; most of the main hotels are clustered here. Right on this street is the base station of the Rüfikopf cable-car, departure point for exploration of the Zürs slopes. A short walk away, across the river, are the Schlegelkopf chair-lifts, leading up into Lech's main area of slopes. Chalets, apartments and pensions are dotted around the valley, and the village spreads along the main street for 2km/1.5 miles. Some of the cheaper accommodation is quite a walk from the lifts.

Not far from the centre is the cable-car up to Oberlech: a small, traffic-free collection of 4-star hotels set on the

165

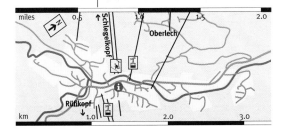

LIFT PASSES

Arlberg Ski Pass

Prices in €

Age	1-day	6-day
under 16	25	116
16 to 19	37	167
20 to 64	41	194
over 65	37	167

Free no one, but season pass only €10 if under 8 or over 75

Senior min. age for senior women is 60

Beginner points ticket

Notes
Covers all St Anton, St Christoph, Lech, Zürs and Stuben lifts, and linking bus between Rauz and Zürs; also covers Sonnenkopf (10 lifts) at Klösterle, 7km/ 4 miles west of Stuben (bus link from Stuben); single ascent, half-day and pedestrian options

mountainside, with an underground tunnel system linking the hotels and lift station – used routinely to move baggage, and by guests in bad weather. The cable-car works until 1am, allowing access to the mother resort's much livelier nightlife.

Zug is a hamlet 3km/2 miles from Lech, with a lift into the Lech-Oberlech area. The limited accommodation here is mostly bed and breakfast, with one pricey 4-star hotel.

Lech is linked by lifts and runs to higher Zürs, described at the end of this chapter. There is a free but often very crowded ski-bus service between the two resorts. Buses (also crowded) run to St Anton, St Christoph and Stuben, too, all covered by the Arlberg lift pass. For a small fee the postbus offers a less crowded alternative.

The Sonnenkopf area at Klösterle, reached by ski-bus from Stuben, is also covered – 'worth a trip' for its combination of gondola rides and woodland runs, not least in bad weather, say reporters.

THE MOUNTAINS

Practically all the slopes are treeless, the main exception being the lower runs just above the village. And practically all the slopes are quite sunny – very few are north-facing.

The toughest runs are classed as unpatrolled 'ski routes' or 'high-alpine touring runs', which are not protected against avalanche and should be skied

only with a guide. We don't have much of a problem with the latter category – in other resorts, these off-piste runs would simply not appear on the piste map at all. But the ski route concept is bad news, reducing the resort's responsibility for runs that are a key part of the area, and that should be patrolled pistes. The only ways down to Zug, for example, are ski routes; the only way to complete the Lech-Zürs-Lech circuit (the Madloch-Lech run) is a ski route; and most of the identified runs from Kriegerhorn are ski routes. To add to the confusion, these routes may be closed if avalanche conditions are dangerous; some of them are groomed after a heavy snowfall; and in practice most people ski them (often into a piste-like state) without a guide or instructor. The St Anton chapter has more on this ludicrous state of affairs.

The piste map, which attempts to cover the whole of the Arlberg region in one view, was redesigned recently, but is still unclear or misleading in places – particularly around Oberlech.

THE SLOPES
One-way traffic
The main slopes centre on **Oberlech**, 250m/820ft above Lech (just below the tree line), and can be reached from the village by chair-lifts as well as the cable-car. The wide, open pistes above Oberlech are perfect for intermediates, and there is also lots of off-piste. Zuger Hochlicht, the high point of this sector, gives stunning views.

KEY FACTS	
Resort	1450m
	4,760ft
Arlberg region	
Slopes	1305-2650m
	4,280-8,690ft
Lifts	86
Pistes	276km
	172 miles
Blue	38%
Red	51%
Black	11%
Snowmaking	58%
For Lech-Zürs only	
Slopes	1450-2450m
	4,760-8,040ft
Lifts	33
Pistes	117km
	73 miles

boarding

Lech's upper-crust image has not stood in the way of its snowboarding development. The jewel in the Arlberg crown has some of the best backcountry riding in Austria, and abundant snowfalls mean it is a popular destination for free-riders. Lech is now also host to the Nokia Snowpark tour – a prestigious stop on the freestyle calendar. A blend of impeccable piste grooming, modern chair-lifts and few drag-lifts makes for nice learning conditions; but be careful on the west-facing slopes at Zürs, which have many flat/uphill sections.

The **Rüfikopf** cable-car takes Lech residents to the west-facing slopes of Zürs. This mountainside, with its high point at **Trittkopf**, is a mix of quite challenging intermediate slopes and flat/uphill bits. On the other side of Zürs the east-facing mountainside is of a more uniform gradient. Chairs go up to **Seekopf** with intermediate runs back down. There's a chair from Zürsersee up to **Muggengrat** (the highest point of the Zürs area). This has a good blue run back under it and accesses the long, scenic, lift-free and quiet red Muggengrat Täli (beware the steep top section) with lots of nearby off-piste options back down towards Zürs; at the bottom you can take lifts up the other side or walk back through the village. Another chair from Zürsersee – slow and vulnerable to closure by wind – goes up to Madloch-Joch and the long, scenic ski route back to the fringes of Lech, completing a clockwise circuit. You can peel off part-way down and head for Zug and the slow chair-lift up to the Kriegerhorn above Oberlech, instead.

TERRAIN-PARKS
In Lech only
Just above the Schlegelkopf and visible from town lies what has become one of the best snow-parks in Austria. There are three kicker lines, separated into easy, public and pro categories, which will suit new kids on the block as well as seasoned pros. The kickers are outstanding, with well-shaped mellow transitions that are great for

Lech

167

learning on. The rails are set in lines so you can hit several in a row. A straight rail, a straight box, a rainbow, a curve box and a kink rail and double kink box combo then culminate in a wall ride. There is a good kids' park off the same run with tiny ride-on rails and little banks and jumps.

SNOW RELIABILITY
One of Austria's best
Lech and Zürs both get a lot of snow. Lech gets an average of almost 8m/26ft of snow between December and March, almost twice as much as St Anton and three times as much as Kitzbühel; but Zürs gets 50 per cent

more than Lech. The altitude is high by Austrian resort standards, and there is excellent snowmaking, helping to counter the sunny exposure of Lech and much of Zürs.

This combination, together with excellent grooming, means that the Lech-Zürs area normally has good coverage from early December until late April.

FOR EXPERTS
Off-piste is main attraction
There is only one (very short) black piste on the map, and there is no denying that for the competent skier who prefers to stick to patrolled runs

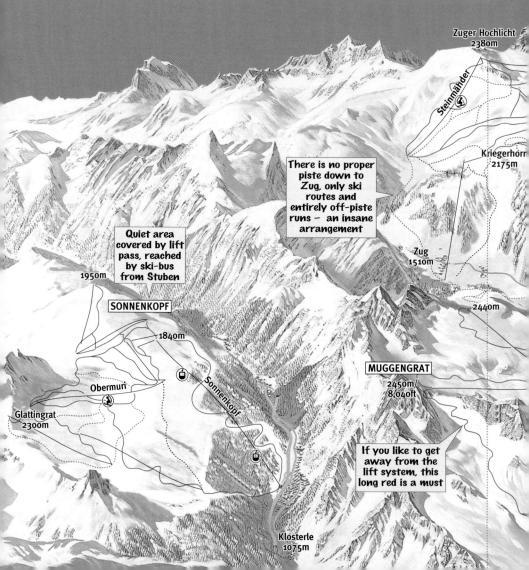

Zuger Hochlicht
2380m

Steinmähder

Kriegerhörn
2175m

There is no proper piste down to Zug, only ski routes and entirely off-piste runs – an insane arrangement

Zug
1510m

Quiet area covered by lift pass, reached by ski-bus from Stuben

1950m

2440m

SONNENKOPF

1840m

MUGGENGRAT

2450m/
8,040ft

Obermuri

Sonnenkopf

Glattingrat
2300m

If you like to get away from the lift system, this long red is a must

Klösterle
1075m

the area is very limited. There are the two types of off-piste route referred to earlier, which most people are happy to undertake without guidance. But experts will get a lot more out of the area if they do have a guide, as there is plenty of excellent off-piste other than the marked ski routes, much of it accessed by long traverses. Especially in fresh snow, it can be wonderful.

Many of the best runs start from the top of the fast Steinmähder chair, which finishes just below Zuger Hochlicht. Some routes involve a short climb to access bowls of untracked powder. From the Kriegerhorn there are shorter off-piste runs down towards

Lech and a very scenic long ski route down to Zug (followed by a slow chair and a rope tow to pull you along a flat area). Most runs, however, are south- or west-facing and can suffer from sun. At the end of the season, when the snow is deep and settled, the off-piste off the shoulder of the Wöstertäli from the top of the Rüfikopf cable-car down to Lech can be superb. There are also good runs from the top of the Trittkopf cable-car in the Zürs sector, including a tricky one down to Stuben.

Experts will also enjoy cruising some of the steeper red runs and will want to visit St Anton during the week, where there are more challenging

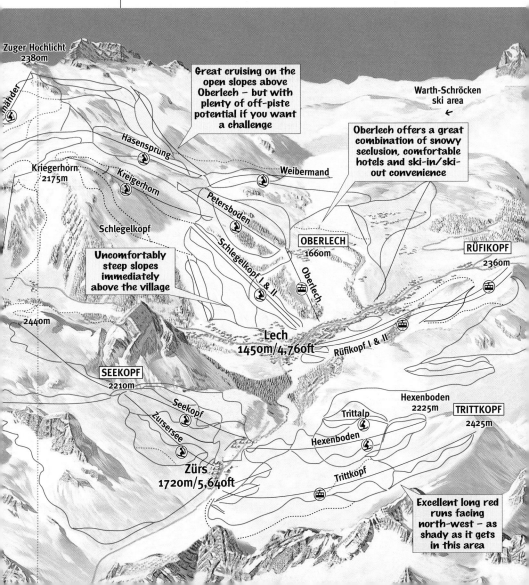

SCHOOLS

Lech
t 2355

Oberlech
t 2007

Zürs
t 2611

Omeshorn Alpincenter Lech
t 39880

Classes
(Lech prices)
6 days (2hr am and
2hr pm) €175

Private lessons
€210 for 1 day; each
additional person €16

pistes as well as more off-piste.

Heli-lifts are available to a couple of remote spots, at least on weekdays.

FOR INTERMEDIATES
Flattering variety for all
The pistes in the Oberlech area are nearly all immaculately groomed blue runs, the upper ones above the trees, the lower ones in wide swathes cut through them. It is ideal territory for leisurely cruisers not wanting surprises. And even early intermediates will be able to take on the circuit to Zürs and back, the only significant red involved being the beautiful long ski route back to Lech from the top of the Madloch chair in Zürs. It shouldn't be difficult, but because it's a ski route it is groomed only occasionally, and several readers have found it unpleasantly mogulled. 'They should make it a proper pisted run,' complained one. We couldn't agree more.

It's worth noting that the final blue-run descents to Lech (as opposed to Oberlech) are uncomfortably steep for nervous novices.

More adventurous intermediates should take the fast Steinmähder chair to just below Zuger Hochlicht and from there take the scenic red run all the way to Zug (the latter part on a ski route rather than a piste). And if you feel ready to have a stab at some off-piste for the first time, Lech is an excellent place to try it.

Zürs has many more interesting red runs, on both sides of the village. We like the north-west-facing reds from Trittkopf and the scenic Muggengrat Täli (see 'The Slopes').

FOR BEGINNERS
Easy slopes in all areas
The main nursery slopes are in Oberlech, but there is also a nice dedicated area in Lech. There are good, easy runs to progress to, both above and below Oberlech.

FOR CROSS-COUNTRY
Picturesque valley trail
A 15km/9 mile trail starts from the centre of Lech and leads through the beautiful but shady valley, along the Lech river to Zug and back. A reporter recommends the Älpele for lunch en route. In Zürs there is a 4km/2.5 mile track to the Flexen Pass and back.

QUEUES
A few complaints
The resort proudly boasts that it limits numbers on the slopes to 14,000 for a more enjoyable experience. Most reporters also stress how much quieter Lech's slopes are than St Anton's. There have been significant lift improvements in recent years: feedback is generally positive, but there are still one or two bottlenecks – the Schlegelkopf fast quad out of Lech gets very busy first thing and the crucial ('slow and cold') Madloch double chair at the top of the Zürs area generates peak-time queues on the Lech-Zürs-Lech circuit. Some readers mention the Rüfikopf cable-car to Zürs as generating queues. Reporters have also praised the care taken by attendants to help children on to lifts.

MOUNTAIN RESTAURANTS
On the up

Proper mountain restaurants are not a highlight but have improved somewhat in recent years (though reporters still complain about overcrowding). Rud-Alpe on the lower slopes above Lech is a rustic place, built using the timbers of an old hut. 'Excellent decor, food and service,' says one reporter; 'best lunch on the mountain' and 'friendly staff', enthuse others. The 'lively' Kriegeralpe, higher up, has been extended so it can open in winter as well as in summer. Rustic and charming, it is 'always full', writes a disappointed visitor; another says it has a 'limited menu, but is good for drinks'. The Schröfli Alm, just above the base of the Seekopf lift, is a pleasant chalet. The self-service Seekopf restaurant does 'quality food at decent prices' and has a good sun terrace. The cosy Palmen Alpe, above Zug, was refurbished for 2006/07, and smoking is banned in the dining area (unusual for Austria); it offers 'stunning views' and 'huge pizzas', but it gets very crowded.

Not surprisingly, lunch in Oberlech is a popular choice. There are several big sunny terraces set prettily around the piste. Quite often you'll find a live band playing outside one. Reader recommendations include the 'rustic' Ilga Stube, the lovely old Alter Goldener Berg, the Mohnenfluh, and the Petersboden hotel's round tent. But the Burgwald is 'the best', insists one reporter.

Zug is another popular low-altitude option. The Rote Wand does 'a fine lunch', and the Alpenblick is also recommended. The Klösterle is said to occupy a 'beautiful old chalet'.

SCHOOLS AND GUIDES
Excellent in parts

The ski schools of Lech, Oberlech and Zürs all have good reputations and the instructors speak good English. Group lessons are divided into no fewer than 10 ability levels. One visitor enjoyed 'the best lessons I have ever had'; another praises the 'small classes' and 'friendly instructors'. In 2005/06 the mountain guides office started a new school, Omeshorn Alpincenter – reports welcome. In peak periods, you should book instructors and guides well in advance, as many are booked every year by regular visitors.

AUSTRIA

GETTING THERE

Air Zürich 200km/ 124 miles (2½hr); Innsbruck 120km/ 75 miles (1½hr). Friedrichshafen 130km/81 miles (1½hr)

Rail Langen (17km/ 10 miles); regular buses from station, buses connect with international trains

SMART LODGINGS

Check out our feature chapters at the front of the book.

UK PACKAGES

Alpine Answers, Alpine Weekends, Corporate Ski Co, Crystal, Elegant Resorts, Erna Low, Flexiski, Independent Ski Links, Inghams, Interactive Resorts, Jeffersons, Kaluma, Made to Measure, Momentum, Oxford Ski Co, Powder Byrne, Scott Dunn, Ski Activity, Ski Expectations, Ski Freshtracks, Ski Independence, Ski Safari, Ski Solutions, Ski Weekend, Skitracer, Skiworld, Snow Finders, Total, White Roc
Oberlech Elegant Resorts, Kaluma
Zürs Alpine Answers, Corporate Ski Co, Corporate Ski Co, Crystal, Elegant Resorts, Inghams, Made to Measure, Oxford Ski Co, Powder Byrne, Scott Dunn, Ski Independence
Warth Ardmore

FACILITIES FOR CHILDREN
Oberlech's fine, but expensive

Oberlech makes an excellent choice for families who can afford it, particularly as it's so convenient for the slopes. Reporters have praised the family-friendly approach and attention paid to children using the lifts: 'Mountain staff were really polite and helpful.' The Sonnenburg and the Goldener Berg have in-house kindergartens. Children of visitors staying in Oberlech have free access to the kindergarten there, Kinderland. Reporters tell us the Oberlech school is great for children, with small classes, good English spoken and lunch offered.

STAYING THERE

HOW TO GO
Surprising variety

The accommodation ranges from luxury hotels to simple but spotless B&Bs.
Chalets There are a couple run by British tour operators, including Total's chalet-hotel with pool and sauna.
Hotels There are three 5-stars, over 30 4-stars and countless modest places.
LECH
*****Arlberg** (2134-0) Patronised by royalty and celebrities. Elegantly rustic central chalet. Pool. 'Good food and service – probably the best in Lech.'
*****Post** (2206-0) Lovely old Relais & Châteaux place on the main street; pool, sauna. 'Absolutely first class.'
****Angela** (2407) Perfect for keen skiers: in a piste-side location up the hill from the Schlegelkopf chair-lift.
****Brunnenhof** (2349) Highly recommended by a reporter: 'Food and service were excellent.'
****Elisabeth** (2330) – 'Very friendly family-run hotel with much better food than experienced in many Austrian hotels,' says a 2007 reporter.
****Haldenhof** (2444-0) Friendly and well run, with antiques and fine paintings. 'Totally brilliant – probably the best food I have had anywhere in the world,' enthuses a reporter.
****Kristiania** (2561-0) 'Outstanding decor, ambience and service – feels very homely,' says a reporter.
****Krone** (2551) One of the oldest buildings, in a prime spot by the river. 'Food and service faultless', but 'small rooms and some noise', 'superb' wellness centre with pool.
****Monzabon** (2104) 'Characterful, with friendly staff,' says a reporter. Pool and an indoor ice rink.

****Tannbergerhof** (2202) Splendidly atmospheric inn on the main street, with outdoor bar and popular disco (tea time as well as later). Pool.
***Pension Angerhof** (2418) Beautiful ancient pension, with wood panels and quaint little windows.
OBERLECH
****Burg Vital** (3140) 'Excellent – no criticism,' said a reporter.
****Burg** (22910) Sister hotel of Burg Vital – same facilities and with famous outdoor umbrella bar.
****Montana** (2460) Welcoming chalet run by the family of racer Patrick Ortlieb. 'Best hotel food ever tasted and excellent, friendly and efficient service,' says a 2007 reporter. Pool, smart wellness centre.
****Sonnenburg** (2147) Family-run chalet with a relaxed, traditional atmosphere. Good children's facilities. Pool, impressive wellness centre.
****Pension Sabine** (2718) 'Comfortable and charming with spa facilities', 'excellent food, very friendly and welcoming'. Praised again in 2007.
Apartments There are lots available to independent bookers.

EATING OUT
Mainly hotel-based

There are over 50 restaurants in Lech, but nearly all of them are in hotels. Reporter recommendations include the Krone, Ambrosius and the Post (which serves modern Austrian food). The Madlochblick has a typically Austrian restaurant, very cosy with good solid food, and Rudi's Stamperl is 'top-notch and reasonably priced'. Hûs Nr 8 is one of the best non-hotel restaurants for traditional Austrian food. Schneggarei does good pizza. The Fux does 'excellent modern/Asian food, utterly un-Austrian', and the Lecher Stube (hotel Gotthard) is 'very good value' – recommended by a 2006 visitor. The Olympia is suggested for cakes and coffee stops.

In Oberlech, hotel Montana is consistently praised and a 2007 visitor had 'the perfect' Wiener schnitzel in the hotel Sonnenburg.

In Zug, the Rote Wand is excellent for traditional Austrian food and a good night out, but is said to be 'frighteningly expensive'. Reporters recommend the 'simple and charming' Alphorn and the Gasthof Älpele (3km/ 2 miles from the road, up the valley on the cross-country route, reached by covered wagons attached to snowcats).

ACTIVITIES

Indoor Tennis, hotel
swimming pools,
saunas and fitness
centre, squash,
museum, galleries,
library, ice rink (in
hotel Monzabon)

Outdoor Cleared
walking paths, ice
rink, curling,
toboggan run (from
Oberlech), snow-
shoeing, helicopter
rides, horse-drawn
sleigh rides,
paragliding

APRES-SKI
Good but expensive

At Oberlech, the umbrella bar of the
Burg hotel is popular immediately after
the slopes close, as is the champagne
bar in hotel Montana.

Down in Lech the outdoor bars of
hotels Krone (in a lovely setting by the
river) and Tannbergerhof (where
there's an afternoon as well as a late-
night disco) are popular. Later on,
discos in the hotels Almhof-Schneider
and Krone liven up too. There are
Side Step specialises in 60s and 70s
music. The Ilga is a good place for a
drink, as is S'Pfefferkörndl.
Schneggarei's funky house music
makes a change from Austrian drinking
songs early and late. The smart,
modern Fux bar and restaurant has live
music, pop art in the toilets and a
huge wine list. Archiv is good for
cocktails and attracts a younger crowd.

Zug makes a good night out: you
can take a sleigh ride for a meal at the
Rote Wand, Klösterle or Auerhahn, and
have drinks at the 'highly
recommended' Vinothek wine bar.

After 7.30pm the free resort bus
becomes a pay-for bus called James,
which runs until 4am.

OFF THE SLOPES
At ease

Many visitors to Lech don't indulge in
sports, and the main street often
presents a parade of fur-clad strollers.
The range of shopping is surprisingly
limited – Strolz's plush emporium
(including a champagne bar) right in
the centre is the main attraction.

It's easy for pedestrians to get to
Oberlech or Zug for lunch. The village
outdoor bars make ideal posing
positions. There are various sporting
activities and 29km/18 miles of walking
paths ('well marked and popular') –
the one along the river to Zug is
'outstandingly' beautiful, and
recommended by several readers.

There is a floodlit sledging run from
Oberlech to town: 'Loved by kids and
not to be missed,' says a reporter.

Zürs 1720m/5,640ft

Some 10 minutes' drive towards St
Anton from Lech, Zürs is almost on the
Flexen Pass, with good snow virtually
guaranteed. Austria's first recognisable
ski lift was built here in 1937. But,
apart from the excellent hotels, we find
Zürs a difficult place to like. It has

Lech

173

nothing resembling a centre, few shops – and the traffic to/from Lech doesn't so much intrude as ruin the place.

The village is a fraction of the size of Lech, but matches its bigger neighbour with three 5-star hotels. We stayed at the 5-star Zürserhof (25130) and found it excellent – great service, food and spa facilities. There are eight 4-stars. Of these, the Alpenhotel Valluga (2426) is a warmly welcoming, traditional chalet in a prime position close to the Zürserseebahn; the Arlberghaus (2258) is very friendly and great for families. Reporters liked the Hirlanda (2262) for its 'excellent food and service'.

If you want to eat out, it will probably be in another hotel. The Kaminstüble (hotel Schweizerhaus) has been recommended for 'fabulous food and service', and Toni's Einkehr (hotel Flexen) is reported to be 'good value'. Nightlife is quiet. Vernissage, at the Select Alpenrose (22710), is said to be the best nightspot. There's a disco in the Edelweiss hotel (26620) and a piano bar in the Alpenhof (21910).

Many of the local Zürs instructors are booked up for private lessons for the entire season by regular clients.

Warth 1500m/4,920ft

A few kilometres up the valley from Lech is Warth – but the road is closed in winter so you have to drive there from the Bregenz area or in the opposite direction from Reutte.

Combined with Schröcken to the west, it shares 60km/37 miles of slopes served by 15 lifts, including five high-speed chairs. The runs include several blacks and ski routes as well as reds and blues, and there's a terrain-park. You can reach the Lech ski area off-piste and vice versa. The ski school organises weekly excursions to Lech, and the Warth lifts are shown on the Arlberg piste map.

The villages are small, pretty and unspoiled, and the hotels are mainly 3- and 4-stars. The 4-stars include the Walserberg (35020) – with recently renovated rooms, five-course dinners, saunas, steam room and fitness room – and the Sporthotel Steffisalp (3699) – with rooms in four different categories, a formal restaurant, the traditional Tannbergstube, and a spa area with vitality pool, sauna, steam room, solarium and beauty treatments.

AUSTRIA

174

Mayrhofen

Large, lively resort with relatively reliable snow on local slopes and access to other large areas of slopes nearby, including a glacier

COSTS

① ② ③ ④ ⑤ ⑥

RATINGS

The slopes

Fast lifts	***
Snow	***
Extent	***
Experts	**
Intermediates	***
Beginners	**
Convenience	*
Queues	*
Mountain restaurants	***

The rest

Scenery	***
Resort charm	***
Off-slope	****

NEWS

In December 2006 a 160-person cable-car opened (Austria's largest), going from Mayrhofen to the Ahorn beginner area. It starts closer to Mayrhofen than the cable-car it replaced (though it still isn't close to most accommodation).

For 2007/08 two T-bars serving beginner runs on Ahorn are due to be replaced by a fast eight-person chair.

+ Good for confident intermediates

+ Snow more reliable than usual in the Tirol, plus the snow guarantee of the Hintertux glacier nearby

+ Several nearby areas on the same lift pass (600km/370 miles of pistes) and reached by free bus or train

+ Lively après-ski – though it's easily avoided if you prefer peace

+ Excellent children's amenities

− Often long queues for the gondola to Penken – which is inconveniently sited for many visitors

− Slopes can be crowded

− Many short runs, though linked Lanersbach slopes are longer

− Few steep pistes – though they do include Austria's steepest

− No runs back to the village from Penken – the main area of slopes

Mayrhofen has long been a British favourite. Many visitors like it for its lively nightlife, but it's also an excellent family resort, with highly regarded ski schools and kindergartens and a fun pool. The liveliest of the nightlife is confined to a few places, easily avoided by families. And there are quieter alternative bases – see the end of this chapter and the Hintertux chapter.

Mayrhofen's main Penken-Horberg slopes are entirely above the tree line, with no pistes down to valley level. The upside is better-than-average snow, for the Tirol; the downside, shorter-than-average runs. The slopes near Zell am Ziller and Kaltenbach are each worth a day trip (over 150km/93 miles at each).

THE RESORT

Mayrhofen is a fairly large resort sitting in the flat-bottomed Zillertal. Most shops, bars and restaurants are on the one main, long, largely pedestrianised street, with hotels and pensions spread over a wider area. As the village has grown, architecture has been kept traditional.

Despite its reputation for lively après-ski, Mayrhofen is not dominated by lager louts. They exist, but tend to gather in a few easily avoided bars. The central hotels are mainly slightly upmarket, and overall the resort feels pleasantly civilised (though we have had a few complaints about traffic).

The main lift to Penken is set towards one end of the main street, and the new cable-car to the much smaller Ahorn sector starts 200m/660ft further along the road. The free bus service can be crowded, and it finishes early (5pm), so location is important. The original centre, around the market, tourist office and bus/railway stations, is now on the edge of things. The most convenient area is on the main street, close to the Penken gondola station.

Free buses and trains linking the Zillertal resorts mean you can easily have an enjoyably varied week visiting different areas on the Ziller valley lift pass (see the end of this chapter for the main ones) – and the excellent

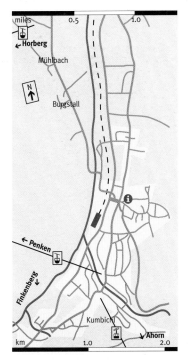

LIFT PASSES

Zillertaler Superskipass

Prices in €

Age	1-day	6-day
under 15	18	86
15 to 18	28	138
over 19	35	172

Free under 6
Senior no deals
Beginner no deals

Notes
1-, 2- or 3-day passes cover Mayrhofen areas only; 4-day and over passes include all Ziller valley lifts; part-day and pedestrian passes available

glacier up at Hintertux (which has its own chapter). If you plan to spend a lot of time there, consider staying in Lanersbach. In the past we've had reports of overcrowded buses, but a 2007 reporter found that the buses 'ran from time to time with true Teutonic efficiency, and they were able to lay on extra buses whenever needed'.

THE MOUNTAINS

Practically all Mayrhofen's slopes are above the tree line, and many are challenging reds.

THE SLOPES
Rather inconvenient

The larger of Mayrhofen's two areas of slopes is **Penken-Horberg**, accessed by the main gondola from one end of town. It is also accessible via gondolas at Hippach and Finkenberg, both a bus-ride away. You cannot get back to Mayrhofen on snow – you can catch the main gondola down, or if snow cover is good, you can descend to either Finkenberg or Hippach on unpisted ski routes (though these are often closed). The buses back from Finkenberg run at only hourly intervals.

A big cable-car links the Penken area with the **Rastkogel** slopes above Vorderlanersbach, which is in turn

linked to **Eggalm** above Lanersbach – see the Hintertux chapter. These links are a great asset, and the run to Eggalm has been more reliable since snowmaking was installed. Getting back from Rastkogel on skis means braving a red run that can be heavily mogulled, but you can avoid it by taking a rope-tow up to the top station of the cable-car and riding that down.

The smaller, gentler **Ahorn** area is good for beginners and is served by a 160-person cable-car new for 2006/07. This area also has a lovely, long red run (over 1300m/4,260ft vertical) from top to bottom of the cable-car.

TERRAIN-PARKS
Comprehensive

One of the finest parks in the Alps (sponsored by Burton Snowboards) is built beneath the Sun-Jet chair-lift on Penken – but it can get crowded. There's an easy beginner line (which also has a great mini wall ride), an intermediate line and a pro line of tabletops ranging in length between 3m/10ft and 19m/62ft, as well as a big hip jump. Every year there are more combinations of kinked, curved and flat boxes and rails for all levels. The half-pipe isn't on a par with the rest of the park; but there is a 360m/1,180ft long super-pipe in Hintertux.

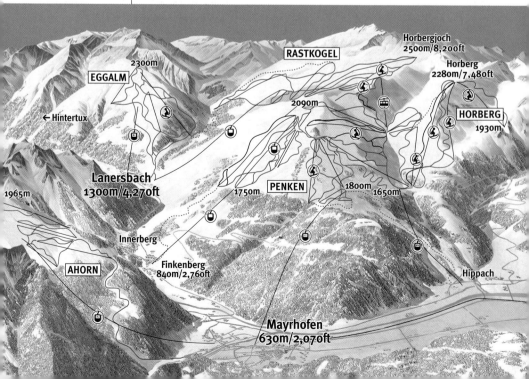

www.sport2000rent.com

Best for Rent!

boarding

Mayrhofen has long been popular with snowboarders from around the globe. And there is a large British contingent who make this town their winter home because of the extensive off-piste available. This said, however, beginners may have a hard time getting around, as the terrain tends to be relatively steep, the nursery slopes are somewhat inconvenient to get to, and the area still has quite a few drag-lifts. Intermediates and upwards, however, will relish the abundance of good red runs and easily accessible off-piste. The terrain-park is one of the best in Europe. Snowbombing, a music festival and snowboard contest, is held in April.

KEY FACTS

Resort	630m
	2,070ft

Ski and Glacier World Zillertal 3000	
Slopes	630-3250m
	2,070-10,660ft
Lifts	62
Pistes	227km
	141 miles
Blue	26%
Red	60%
Black	14%
Snowmaking	93km
	58 miles

Mayrhofen-Lanersbach only (ie excluding Hintertux glacier)	
Slopes	630-2500m
	2,070-8,200ft
Lifts	49
Pistes	157km
	98 miles

For Ziller valley	
Slopes	630-3250m
	2,070-10,660ft
Lifts	174
Pistes	636km
	395 miles

ACTIVITIES

Indoor Bowling, adventure pool, two hotel pools open to the public, massage, sauna, squash, fitness centre, indoor tennis centre, indoor riding-school, pool, billiards

Outdoor Ice rink, curling, horse sleigh rides, 45km/28 miles of paths, snow-shoeing, paragliding, tobogganing

SNOW RELIABILITY
Good by Austrian standards
Although the lifts go no higher than 2500m/8,200ft, the area is better than most Tirolean resorts for snow because the slopes are mostly above 1500m/4,920ft. Snowmaking covers the whole Ahorn area, nearly all the main slopes on Penken-Horberg and some on Rastkogel and Eggalm. And Hintertux has one of the best glaciers in the Alps.

FOR EXPERTS
Commit Harakiri
Austria's steepest piste, called Harakiri and under the Knorren chair, has a gradient of 78 per cent or 38°. It is certainly steep for a European piste; when we tried it, the run was mogul-free but rock hard except near the edges; not surprisingly, it was delightfully deserted. A recent reporter described it as 'one hell of a ride'. It does offer a worthwhile challenge for the brave but is quite short. The black run under the Schneekar chair on Horberg is a good, fast cruise when groomed, but there are few other steepish pistes. The long unpisted trail to Hippach is quite challenging but rarely has good snow because of its low altitude. There is, however, some decent off-piste to be found, such as from the top of the Horbergjoch at the top of Rastkogel – we had a great time there in fresh powder – and under the cable-car linking to Lanersbach. You can also try the other resorts covered by the valley lift pass – see the end of this chapter.

FOR INTERMEDIATES
On the tough side
Most of Mayrhofen's slopes are on the steep side of the usual intermediate range – great for confident or competent intermediates. And the Lanersbach expansion a few years ago made the area much more interesting for avid piste-bashers, with some good long runs on Rastkogel and delightfully

quiet runs on Eggalm. But many of the runs in the main Penken area are quite short. And (except on Ahorn) there are few really gentle blue runs, making the area less than ideal for nervous intermediates or near-beginners. The overcrowding on many runs can add to the intimidation factor.

If you're willing to travel, each of the main mountains covered by the Ziller valley pass is large and varied enough for an interesting day out – see the end of this chapter.

FOR BEGINNERS
Overrated: big drawbacks
Despite its reputation for teaching, Mayrhofen is not ideal for beginners. The Ahorn nursery slopes are excellent – high, extensive and sunny – but intermediate mates will want to be on Penken. The Penken nursery area is less satisfactory and there are very few easy blues to progress to.

FOR CROSS-COUNTRY
Go to Lanersbach
There is a fine 20km/12 mile trail along the valley to Zell am Ziller, plus small loops close to the village. But snow down here is not reliable. Higher Vorderlanersbach has a much more snow-sure trail.

QUEUES
Still a real problem
The Penken gondola is very oversubscribed at peak times. Reports of queues of 45 or 60 minutes at the morning peak are still common. An alternative is to take the bus to one of the other gondolas (those at Lanersbach and Vorderlanersbach are quieter than those at Finkenberg and Hippach). There can be queues for some lifts once you get up the mountain and to get down at the end of the day, too. No queues are reported for the new Ahorn cable-car, and a reader recommends using it to do the 1300m/4,26oft vertical 'lovely

Mayrhofen

177

SCHOOLS

**Die Roten Profis
(Manfred Gager)**
t 63800

Total (Max Rahm)
t 63939

Mount Everest (Peter Habeler)
t 62829

**Mayrhofen 3000
(Michael Thanner)**
t 64015

Classes
(Roten Profis prices)
6 days (2½hr am or pm) €110

Private lessons
1 day: €118 for 1 person

CHILDREN

Wuppy's Kinderland
t 63612
Ages 3mnth to 7yr;
9am to 5pm, Mon-Fri

Die Roten Profis
t 63800
From age 3; 10am-
4pm

Total
t 63939
Ages 2 to 4, 9.30-
3.30

Ski school
All run classes for
children aged 4 or 5
to 14. Lunch can be
provided (6 days
including lunch €130)

GETTING THERE

Air Salzburg
175km/109 miles
(3hr); Munich
190km/118 miles
(2½hr); Innsbruck
75km/47 miles (1hr)

Rail Local line
through to resort;
regular buses from
station

UK PACKAGES

*Club Pavilion, Crystal,
Directski.com, Equity,
First Choice,
Independent Ski Links,
Inghams, Interhome,
Neilson, Rocketski, Ski
Line, Ski McNeill, Ski
Wild, Skitracer,
Skiworld, Snowcoach,
Thomson*
Gerlos *Interhome*
Zell im Zillertal *Crystal*

swooping' red run down while waiting
for the Penken queue to subside.

MOUNTAIN RESTAURANTS
Plenty of them
Most of Penken's many mountain
restaurants are attractive and serve
good-value food, but they can get
crowded. The Schneekar restaurant at
the top of the Horberg section has
been highly recommended ('excellent
lunch', 'table-service, traditional food,
open fire, wooden beams, leather sofa,
sometimes with a jazz pianist', say
reporters). The Almstüberl at the mid-
station of the Finkenberg gondola 'was
usually quiet when others were
packed'. Schiestl's Sunnalm and
Kressbrunnalm have also been
recommended.

SCHOOLS AND GUIDES
Excellent reputation
Mayrhofen's ski schools have good
reputations, and a high proportion of
guests take lessons. We have received
many positive reports over the years,
but a few negative ones too –
including, strangely, reports of a
shortage of English-speaking instructors.
More reports would be welcome.

FACILITIES FOR CHILDREN
Good but inconvenient
Mayrhofen majors on childcare and the
facilities are excellent. But children
have to be bussed around and ferried
up and down the mountain.

STAYING THERE

HOW TO GO
Plenty of mainstream packages
There is a wide choice of hotel
holidays available from UK tour
operators, but few catered chalets.
Hotels Most of the hotels packaged by
UK tour operators are centrally located,
a walk from the Penken gondola.
★★★★★Elisabeth (6767) The only 5-star.
'Superb, excellent food and service.'
★★★★Manni's (633010) Well placed,
smartly done out; pool.
★★★★Kramerwirt (6700) Lovely hotel,
oozing character. 'Friendly and helpful
staff, good rooms, interesting food.'
★★★★Strass (6705) Right by the Penken
gondola. Lively bars, disco, fitness
centre, pool; but very big and with a
downmarket feel ('Brits in football
shirts') and rooms that lack style.
★★★★Neuhaus (6703) 'First-class
facilities,' says a reporter; good food,

but rooms above the bar are not ideal.
★★★★Rose (62229) Well placed, near
centre. Good food.
★★★★Neue Post (62131) Convenient,
family-run, on the main street – 'good
food and nice big rooms'.

EATING OUT
Wide choice
Manni's is good for pizzas ('but
expensive, especially for wine').
Wirthaus zum Griena is a 'wonderful
old wooden building with traditional
cuisine'. We had good lamb and
pepper steak at Tiroler Stuben.

APRES-SKI
Lively but not rowdy
Après-ski is a great selling point. At
close of play, the umbrella bar, at the
top of the Penken gondola, the Ice Bar
at the hotel Strass and Nicki's
Schirmbar in the Brücke hotel get
packed out. Some of the other bars in
the Strass are rocking places later on,
including the Speak Easy, with live
music; but the Sport's Arena disco is
said to be 'for the kids'. Recent visitors
have preferred the Apropos ('great
music') and Brücke's Schlüssel Alm
('still the best all-round late-night
venue'). Mo's American theme bar and
Scotland Yard remain popular with
Brits, but you might judge the latter to
be 'dated, dirty and smoky'. The Neue
Post bar and the Passage are good for
a quiet drink.

OFF THE SLOPES
Good for all
Innsbruck is easily reached by train.
There are also good walks and sports
amenities, including the swimming
pool complex – with saunas, solariums
and lots of other fun features.
Pedestrians have no trouble getting up
the mountain to meet friends for lunch.

Zillertal Arena

The Zillertal Arena was created in 2000
by linking the slopes above the village
of Gerlos to those of Zell am Ziller.
They now share 50 lifts and 160km/
99 miles of pistes (as much as the
Mayrhofen-Lanersbach area). The
slopes reach as high as 2400m/7,870ft
and suit intermediates best. You can
really get a sense of travelling around:
the area stretches for miles from west
to east beyond Gerlos to the villages
of Königsleiten and Krimml – a
distance of 37km/23 miles. As a recent

Phone numbers
From elsewhere in Austria add the prefix 05285 (Mayrhofen), 05282 (Zell), 05284 (Gerlos), 05288 (Hochfügen) and 05283 (Kaltenbach); from abroad use the prefix +43 and omit the inital '0'

TOURIST OFFICES

Mayrhofen
t 67600
info@mayrhofen.at
www.mayrhofen.at

Zillertal Arena
Zell im Zillertal
t 22810
www.zell.at
Gerlos
t 52440
www.gerlos.at

Ski Optimal
www.ski-optimal.at
Hochfügen
t 62319
Kaltenbach
t 2800

reporter said: 'Starting from Zell am Ziller, a return trip is a full day's skiing. We did the tour over two days to fit in all the other runs: Zell to Gerlos one day and Gerlos to Kriml the next.' Most runs are fairly short, the longest being down to Gerlos (4km/2.5 miles).

Zell am Ziller, the main town in the area, is a real working town rather than just a resort – it is a sprawling place, and has the oldest working brewery in the Tirol (where the strong Zillertaler beer is brewed). There are some good hotels, including the 4-star Zapfenhof (2349) on the outskirts (with pool) and the Brau (2313) in the centre. Both have sauna, steam room and jacuzzi. Of the big tour operators, Crystal features Zell. The town is a bus-ride from the gondola into the ski area (which you have to catch down as well, as there is no piste down). Après-ski centres around a few bars near the base of the gondola.

Gerlos has the big advantage of being centrally situated in the ski area, allowing you to explore in either direction each day. It is a bustling resort that straddles the road up to the Gerlos pass and is a bus-ride from the gondola that takes you into the slopes.

The home slope benefits from top-to-bottom snowmaking, and there's a good local terrain-park. Après-ski is lively and there are several good local hotels, including the 4-star Gaspingerhof (52160) with a very smart spa offering treatments as well as a gym, indoor-outdoor pool, saunas and steam room.

Ski Optimal

Ski Optimal is the name given to the linked area of slopes of the Hochzillertal-Hochfügen above the valley village of Kaltenbach. This is comparable in size with the Zillertal Arena and Mayrhofen-Lanersbach areas: it has 35 lifts, including five gondolas and several fast chairs, and 155km/96 miles of pistes going as high as 2500m/8,200ft. Again, the pistes suit intermediates best – but there is plenty of potential for off-piste, too. They are proud of their local hero and Austrian downhill star Stephan Eberharter and have named their home run (from top to bottom of the gondola from Kaltenbach) after him (it starts black near the top, turns red mid-way and has a vertical of 1200m/3,940ft).

Montafon

Extensive slopes with separate areas covered by a single lift pass – and attractive places to stay, well off the beaten package path

COSTS

① ② ③ ④ ⑤ ⑥

NEWS

For 2007/08 there may be new marked snow-shoe trails and a floodlit cross-country loop at Silvretta Nova.

Last season the NovaPark terrain-park was redesigned with features for all levels.

Snowmaking has been increased throughout the area, and the Hochjoch restaurant, above Seebliga, has been revamped. There's also a new piste to the valley at Silbertal.

The Gargellen Ski and Snowboard school now offers Sunday classes.

Also in Gargellen, 12 new chalets and 93 apartments (Landal Park) were opened.

MONTAFON TOURISMUS

Gargellen is tiny, and tucked away in a secluded side valley off the Montafon ↓

The 40km/25 mile-long Montafon valley contains no fewer than 11 resorts and five main lift systems. Packages from the UK are few, but for the independent traveller the valley is well worth a look – especially the Silvretta Nova area (linking Gaschurn and St Gallenkirch) and high, tiny, isolated Gargellen.

The Montafon is neglected by the UK travel trade. Its location in Vorarlberg, west of the Arlberg pass, makes it a bit remote from the standard Austrian charter airport of Salzburg – and the valley is said to lack the large hotels that big operators apparently need.

But it is not undiscovered by independent travellers from the UK, and we have had several positive reports on the area in recent years.

The valley runs south-east from the medieval city of Bludenz – parallel with the nearby Swiss border. The first sizeable community you come to is Vandans, linked to its Golm ski area by gondola. Next are Schruns, at the foot of Hochjoch, and Tschagguns, across the valley at the foot of Grabs. Further on are St Gallenkirch and Gaschurn, at opposite ends of the biggest area, Silvretta Nova. Up a side valley to the south of St Gallenkirch is Gargellen, close to the Swiss border – a tiny village, but not unknown in Britain.

The valley road goes on up to Partenen. You can take a cable-car from Partenen to Trominier, and then a minibus (covered by the area pass) on up to Bielerhöhe and the Silvrettasee dam, at the foot of glaciers and Piz Buin (of sunscreen fame) – the highest peak in the Vorarlberg. Bielerhöhe is a great launch pad for ski-tours, and there are high, snow-sure cross-country

trails totalling 22km/13 miles on and around the frozen lake. From here you can ski down to Galtür, near Ischgl. Some of the ski schools organise trips, with the return to Bielerhöhe by snowcat; you end the day with a long run back down to Partenen.

There are more ordinary cross-country trails along the valley, and an 11km/7 mile woodland trail at Kristberg, above Silbertal – up a side valley to the east of Schruns. Trails total over 100km/62 miles.

The shared valley lift pass covers the postbus service ('comprehensive, and not too crowded') and the Bludenz-Schruns trains, as well as the 62 lifts – so exploration of the valley does not require a car.

The top heights hereabouts are no match for the nearby Arlberg resorts; but there is plenty of skiing above the mid-mountain lift stations at around 1500m/4,920ft, and most of the slopes are not excessively sunny, so snow reliability (aided by snowmaking on quite a big scale) is reasonable. Practically all the pistes are accurately classified blue or red, but there are plentiful off-piste opportunities (including quite a few 'ski routes'). There are terrain-parks in most sectors, including the recently expanded NovaPark at Silvretta Nova.

There are 10 ski schools in the valley, operating in each of the different ski areas. And the eight ski kindergartens take kids from age three.

Tobogganing is popular, and there are several runs on the different mountains, the Silvretta Nova's 6km/4 mile floodlit run down to St Gallenkirch being the most impressive.

For those with a car, there is accommodation in various smaller villages in addition to those dealt with below. For example, a reader highly recommends the hotel Adler in St Anton im Montafon (67118) ('excellent food, large pool'), at the entrance to the valley.

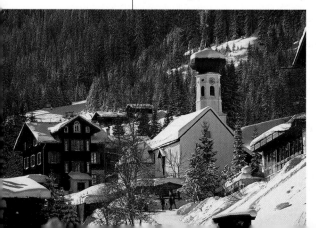

Piz Buin
3310m

Bielerhöhe

2275m/7.46oft

2150m

SCHAFBERG

Grüneck
2085m

2100m

2010m

GOLM

1720m

1850m

Gargellen
1425m/4,68oft

Hochegga
1600m

1520m

rtenen

1480m

SILVRETTA NOVA

1000m

Gaschurn
ooom/3,28oft

Gortipohl

St Gallenkirch
900m/2,95oft

Kreuzjoch
2395m/7,86oft

GRABS

Tschagguns

Vandans
655m/2510ft

2300m

Schruns
700m/2,300ft

1850m

HOCHJOCH

1335m

Silbertal 890m

Kristberg

KEY FACTS

Resorts	655-1425m
	2,150-4,680ft
Slopes	680-2395m
	2,230-7,860ft
Lifts	62
Pistes	222km
	138 miles
Blue	50%
Red	36%
Black	14%
Snowmaking	97km
	60 miles

TOURIST OFFICE

Montafon
t 722530
info@montafon.at
www.montafon.at

The tourist office is in
Schruns, so from
elsewhere in Austria
add the prefix 05556,
from abroad use the
prefix +43 5556

GARGELLEN 1425m/4,68oft
**Gargellen is a real backwater – a tiny,
friendly village tucked up a side
valley, with a small but varied piste
network on Schafberg that is blissfully
quiet.**

The eight-person gondola from the
village up to the Schafberg slopes
seems rather out of place in this tiny
collection of hotels and guest houses,
huddled in a steep-sided, narrow
valley. The runs it takes you to are
gentle, with not much to choose
between the blues and reds; but there
is lots of off-piste terrain, including five
ski routes. A special feature is the day
tour around the Madrisa – a small-
scale off-piste adventure taking you
over to Klosters in Switzerland. It
involves a 300m/98oft climb (which
can take 40 minutes, observes a
reporter), but is otherwise easy.

The altitude of the village (the
highest in the Montafon) and north-
east facing slopes make for reasonable
snow reliability. And there is
snowmaking on one of the several
pistes to the valley, which include a
couple of excellent, scenic away-from-
the-lifts runs at the extremities of the
area. With care you can ski to the door
of some hotels, including the highly
rated hotel Madrisa (6331) – 'Fantastic
food, superb staff, excellent facilities.
The hotel made the holiday,' enthuses
a 2006 visitor. Behind the hotel is a

rather steep nursery slope. There are
four pleasant mountain restaurants:
the Schafberghüsli at the top of the
gondola and two rustic huts at the tree
line – the Obwaldhütte ('very
traditional, good value') and the
Kesslhütte. The Obwaldhütte holds a
weekly après-ski party after the lifts
close, followed by a torchlit descent.
(Slide shows and bridge are more
typical evening entertainments.) The
Barga pizzeria at the foot of the
Vergalden drag can also be reached by
walkers.

SCHRUNS 700m/2,300ft
**Schruns is the most rounded resort in
the valley – a towny little place, with
the shops in its car-free centre catering
for locals and for summer tourists.**

A cable-car and gondola go up from
points outside the village into the
Hochjoch slopes. Above the trees is a
fair-sized area of easy blue runs, with
the occasional red alternative, served
by slow chairs and drags and the fast
eight-seat Seebliga chair. There are
restaurants at strategic points – the
Wormser Hütte is a climbing refuge
with 'stunning' views, while the Kapell
restaurant has a good table-service
section. Parents can leave their kids
under supervision at the huge NTC
Dreamland children's facility at the top
of the cable-car, by the skier services
building. The blue run from Kreuzjoch

↑ There are some seriously big mountain restaurants, especially in the Silvretta Nova area

MONTAFON TOURISMUS

UK PACKAGES

Gargellen *Interhome*
Schruns *Interhome*
Gaschurn *Made to Measure*

Phone numbers
From elsewhere in Austria, add the prefix 05557 (Gargellen), 05556 (Schruns), 05558 (Gaschurn); from abroad, use the prefix +43 and omit the initial '0'

TOURIST OFFICES

Gargellen
t 6303
info@gargellen.at
www.gargellen.at

Schruns
t 721660
info@schruns-tschagguns.at
www.schruns.at

Gaschurn
t 82010
info@gaschurn-partenen.com
www.gaschurn-partenen.com

back to Schruns is exceptional: about 12km/7.5 miles long and over 1600m/5,250ft vertical. Snow-guns cover the lower half of this, plus the Seebliga area.

Easily accessible across the valley are the limited slopes of Grabs, above the formless village of Tschagguns, and the more extensive area of Golm, where a gondola goes from Vandans up to a handful of chairs and drags serving easy slopes above the trees, and offering a vertical descent of over 1400m/4,590ft. A six-pack goes to the top of the area, linked via a ski tunnel to a quad on the Aussergolm slopes on the back of the hill. This serves the Diabolo black run, reputedly the steepest in the Montafon. Snow-guns cover much of the upper slopes, and the run to the valley.

As you are reminded frequently, Ernest Hemingway ensconced himself in Schruns in 1925/26, and his favourite drinking table in the hotel Taube (72384) can be admired. The Löwen (7141) and the Alpenhof Messmer (726640) are elegant, well-equipped 4-stars with big pools, the former a hub of the 'quite lively' après-ski scene.

GASCHURN / ST GALLENKIRCH
1000m/3,280ft / 900m/2,950ft
Silvretta Nova is the biggest lift and piste network in the valley. As a result, German cars fill to overflowing the huge car parks at the valley lift stations. Gaschurn is an attractive place to stay.
The two main resorts here are quite different. Whereas St Gallenkirch is strung along the main road and spoiled by traffic, Gaschurn is a pleasant village, bypassed by the valley traffic, with the wood-shingled Posthotel Rössle (8333) in the centre.

The lift network covers two parallel ridges running north-south, with most of the runs on their east- and west-facing flanks. The slopes are accessed from three points along the valley. A gondola from Gaschurn (prone to serious peak-season queues) takes you up to the east ridge, while another gondola from St Gallenkirch goes up to Valisera on the west ridge. A chair-lift to Garfrescha from a roadside station at Gortipohl, between the resorts, serves its own slopes and gives access to the central valley.

Snowmaking covers almost half the area, including down to two valley stations.

This is generally the most challenging area in the valley, with as many red as blue runs, and some nominal blacks. Most of the slopes are above the tree line, typically offering a modest 300m/980ft vertical. The Rinderhütte six-pack serves more red pistes from the top of the area. There is lots of off-piste potential, including steep (and quite dangerous) slopes down into the central valley. The map shows five 'ski routes'.

The NovaPark terrain-park, recently expanded, features a half-pipe and boarder-cross course (see www.novapark.info).

There are lots of mountain restaurants, many impressive in different ways. At the top of the east ridge, the state-of-the-art Nova Stoba has seats for over 1,500 people in various rooms catering for different markets, including splendid panelled rooms with table-service. The big terrace bar gets seriously boisterous in the afternoons. At the top of the other ridge is the splendidly woody Valisera Hüsli. A reporter recommends the strudel and glühwein at Zur Brez'n and, snow permitting, searching out the Lammhütta on run 1a down to Gaschurn: 'Basic but lovely.'

Nauders/Reschenpass

A rustic village remotely set high up on the border with Italy (and close to Switzerland) – a good base for an international tour by car

RATINGS

The slopes

Fast lifts	★★★
Snow	★★★★
Extent	★★
Expert	★★★
Intermediate	★★★★
Beginner	★★
Convenience	★★
Queues	★★★★
Mountain restaurants	★★★

The rest

Scenery	★★★
Charm	★★★★
Off-slope	★★★

NEWS

For 2006/07 at Schöneben, the Rojenbahn quad was upgraded with more covered chairs to increase capacity. Snowmaking here and at Haider Alm was improved.

At Berkastel (Nauders), there are plans to add two new runs – one blue below the Gaislochbahn and a red family piste below the Almlift drag.

➕ High-altitude slopes, by Tirolean standards – so relatively snow-sure

➕ Attractively traditional village

➕ Grand views from the top lift

➕ Day trips to various places are a possibility, but ...

➖ That's just as well – the local slopes are rather limited in extent

➖ Main Nauders lifts are a bus-ride from the village, with Schöneben and Haider Alm further away still

Nauders is in the Tirol, but only just – it's 3km/2 miles from the Swiss border, and its lifts run up to the Italian one. Nauders is the main element of the Reschenpass area, which includes two small resorts in Italy – Schöneben and Haider Alm (this bit of Italy is German-speaking). Swiss outings are possible too. All in all, an interesting departure from the Tirolean norm.

THE RESORT

Nauders is a rustic, not overly commercialised village just short of the crest of the Reschenpass to Italy – but happily bypassed by the main road. It's a quiet family resort, with chalet-style guest-houses dotted along narrow lanes (some of them one-way).

THE MOUNTAINS

Nauders' home slopes at Bergkastel start about 2km/1 mile outside the village, reached by a free shuttle-bus. The other resorts covered by the Reschenpass lift pass effectively double the terrain. An outing to Switzerland is tempting: there aren't many resorts within day-trip range of St Moritz, but this is one.
Slopes The main lift to **Bergkastel** is a powerful gondola up to the mid-

mountain meeting area (2200m/7,220ft), just above the tree line. Beyond here there are three main options: take an eight-seat chair another 400m/1,310ft up the wide slopes of Bergkastelspitz; move across to a six-pack on the next hill; or continue to another six-pack chair on Tscheyeck, surmounted by a drag to the area high-point at 2850m/9,350ft.

There are a couple of runs back to the valley – the Talabfahrt red is a beautiful, wide swathe through trees.

Schöneben is the name of a mountainside above the little village of Reschen and of the company operating lifts on it. From the valley station about 1km/0.5 miles outside Reschen a gondola goes up to a mid-mountain lift hub, just above the tree line. There are wide, gentle slopes above and below this point, served by a six-pack chair, a couple of more challenging runs served

183

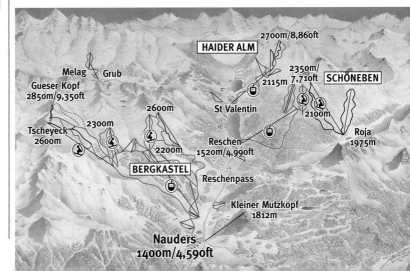

HAIDER ALM 2700m/8,860ft

2350m/7,710ft **SCHÖNEBEN**

2115m

Melag · Grub

Gueser Kopf 2850m/9,350ft

2600m · St Valentin

2100m

Tscheyeck 2600m · 2300m

2200m

Reschen 1520m/4,990ft

Roja 1975m

BERGKASTEL

Reschenpass

Kleiner Mutzkopf 1812m

Nauders 1400m/4,590ft

↑ The summit of the pass is tucked behind the trees on the right; the mountains to the right are in Italy

TVB NAUDERS / RESCHENPASS

KEY FACTS

Resort	1400m
	4,590ft
Slopes	1400-2850m
	4,590-9,350ft
Lifts	26
Pistes	111km
	69 miles
Blue	37%
Red	43%
Black	20%
Snowmaking	90km
	56 miles

Phone numbers
From elsewhere in Austria add the prefix 05473; from abroad use the prefix +43 5473

TOURIST OFFICE

t 87220
nauders@reschenpass.info
www.nauders.info
www.reschenpass.net

by two chairs beyond it (one newly upgraded), and an easy, undulating, highly enjoyable red run back to the valley, recently widened and improved.

The third area, **Haider Alm**, is named in the same fashion: Haider Alm is the tree-line focus of the lifts above the village of St Valentin. This is the most limited of the areas. But any mountain with 1200m/3,940ft vertical has to be worth a visit.

Terrain-parks There's a half-pipe and boarder-cross in Nauders, and a small park at Haider Alm.

Snow reliability The slopes are quite good for snow. The pistes of Schöneben and Haider Alm are almost entirely covered by artificial back-up, as are a good proportion of those at Nauders, most of which get a lot of afternoon sun. We've found the grooming to be immaculate.

Experts The Reschenpass area is not ideal for experts looking for a challenge, but there are satisfying runs. Die Schwarze, on Tscheyeck, just about deserves its black classification, and is designated a bumps run. The blacks at Schöneben used to be red, and properly so. There is a lot of off-piste terrain accessible from the Tscheyeck chair (including ways down to Nauders itself), and there are red-classified ski routes from the drag above it.

Intermediates Basically, all the slopes here make excellent intermediate terrain. They don't add up to a huge amount, but with three areas to play in there is no lack of variety. The long descents to the valley at Nauders and Schöneben are very satisfying.

Beginners Nauders is not ideal – the nursery slopes are some way out, beside the gondola. Most beginner

lessons take place at mid-mountain.
Snowboarding Facilities include the half-pipe on the Nauders slopes.
Cross-country There are four cross-country trails – amounting to 40km/25 miles of track in all – around Nauders itself. There are further trails accessible by car.
Queues The place seems to attract weekend crowds, but we would be surprised if lift queues were much of a problem at other times.
Mountain restaurants At Nauders there are four; Lärchenalm is the first choice – a cosy chalet with efficient table-service. At Schöneben there are three restaurants at mid-mountain, including a pleasant, woody self-service.
Schools and guides There are two ski schools at Nauders. Nauders 3000 claims new smaller classes (max six).
Facilities for children There's a learning area behind the children's restaurant at Bergkastel (classes from age three years), and a separate snow-garden. Nauderix Guest Kindergarten takes children from the age of two. Schöni's Kinderland is new at Schöneben.

STAYING THERE

How to go You're on your own here: we know of no packages.
Hotels Most of the hotels are comfortable 4-stars. The Central (872210), Naudererhof (87704), Margarete Maultasch (86101) and Tirolerhof (86111) are well-equipped possibilities in the village. Nearer the lifts are the Neue Burg (87700), and the Erika (87217). For a friendly welcome in a simpler place, you won't beat the Pension Reiterhof (87263).
Eating out Many of the eateries are hotel-based. The hotel Almhof is a popular choice, with an attractive, lively pizzeria. The Stadlwirt is recommended for more traditional food. The Gasthof Goldener Löwe is a traditional old inn.
Après-ski There are several options. The cramped, dark Traktor bar maybe has the edge on the similar Yeti. The hotel Almhof has an external round bar that is less noisy – though maybe not when the dancing girls are on display.
Off the slopes There is quite a bit to do, including long toboggan runs from Bergkastel (one is floodlit), curling lanes, tennis, ice skating, squash, bowling, swimming pool and public pools in hotels. There are 50km/31 miles of marked walks.

Obergurgl

A rare combination of extreme altitude and traditional Alpine atmosphere keeps the regulars going back, despite the drawbacks

NEWS

2007/08 will see two new eight-seat gondolas opening.

A two-stage gondola will replace the Gaisberg double chair and the two chairs above it – the double Nederlift and the long single chair to Hohe Mut. A serious upgrade if ever there was one. The ski route from Hohe Mut will be replaced by a new red run, leading across to the fast Steinmann chair; while the piste that did run down the old Nederlift will become a ski route.

The second gondola will replace the old Schermerspitz double chair at Hochgurgl.

For 2006/07, a small new restaurant, Top Mountain Star, opened at the high-point of Wurmkogel (3080m/10,100ft) – the resort's high point. The futuristic building is designed to exploit the 360-degree views up there.

➕ Glaciers apart, one of the Alps' most reliable resorts for snow – especially good for a late-season holiday

➕ Excellent area for beginners, timid intermediates and families

➕ Large areas of easy off-piste terrain

➕ Mainly queue- and crowd-free

➕ Traditional-style village with very little traffic

➕ Jolly tea-time après-ski

➖ Limited area of slopes, with no tough pistes and no terrain-park or half-pipe

➖ Exposed setting, with very few sheltered slopes for bad weather

➖ Few off-slope leisure amenities except in hotels

➖ Village is spread out and disjointed

➖ For a small Austrian resort, hotels are rather expensive

A loyal band of visitors go back every year to Obergurgl or its higher satellite Hochgurgl, booking a year in advance in recognition of the limited supply of beds. We understand the appeal of high, snow-sure, uncrowded, easy-intermediate slopes. But if we're going to a bleak, remote resort where there is not much to do but ski or board, we'd rather go somewhere with more skiing or boarding to do. Of course, most such places aren't in Austria – and perhaps that is the key to Obergurgl's appeal. It's snow-sure, and it's in Austria.

THE RESORT

Obergurgl is based on a traditional old village, set in a remote spot, the dead end of a long road up past Sölden. It is the highest parish in Austria and is usually under a blanket of snow from November until May. The surrounding slopes are bleak.

Obergurgl has no through traffic and few day visitors. The village centre is mainly traffic-free, and entirely so at night. Village atmosphere is relaxed during the day, jolly immediately after the slopes close, but rather subdued later at night; there are nightspots, but most people stay in their hotels.

Despite its small size, this is a village of widely separated parts; moving between them means long

walks, an 'excellent, prompt' shuttle-bus or taxis charging a flat rate. At the northern entrance to the resort is a cluster of hotels near the Festkogl gondola, which takes you to all the local slopes. The road then passes another group of hotels set on a little hill to the east, around the ice rink (beware steep, sometimes treacherous walks here). The village proper starts with an attractive little square with church, fountain, and the focal village hotel (Edelweiss and Gurgl). Just above are the Rosskar chair-lift and new Gaisberg gondola stations. There is an underground car park in the centre.

Hochgurgl, a gondola-ride away, is little more than a handful of hotels at the foot of its own slopes. It looks like it might be a convenience resort dedicated to skiing from the door, but in practice it isn't: from nearly all the hotels you have to negotiate roads and/or stairs to get to or from the snow. Hochgurgl is even quieter than Obergurgl at night.

In the valley is Untergurgl – linked by gondola to Hochgurgl and by regular ski-buses to Obergurgl, and worth considering as a budget base. For a day out, it's a short bus- or car-trip to Sölden, and a long car-trip to Kühtai (a high area near Innsbruck). Much closer is the tiny touring launch-pad of Vent.

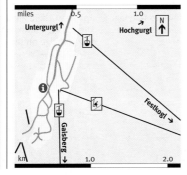

KEY FACTS	
Resort	1930m
	6,330ft
Slopes	1795-3080m
	5,890-10,100ft
Lifts	22
Pistes	110km
	68 miles
Blue	32%
Red	50%
Black	18%
Snowmaking	90km
	56 miles

LIFT PASSES

Obergurgl

Prices in €

Age	1-day	6-day
under 16	25	110
16 to 59	39	195
over 60	33	160

Free under 9

Beginner no deals

Notes

Covers lifts in Obergurgl and Hochgurgl, and local ski-bus; part-day passes available

AUSTRIA

186

THE MOUNTAINS

The gondola between Obergurgl and Hochgurgl means that the two can be thought of as forming a single area (though the gondola closes absurdly early at 4pm). Even so, the slopes are quite limited. Most of the slopes are very exposed – there are few woodland runs to head to in poor conditions. Wind and white-outs can shut the lifts and, especially in early season, severe cold can curtail enthusiasm.

The lift pass is quite expensive for the relatively small area, but the low cost upgrade to cover a day in Sölden is still available (note that this must be requested at the time of purchasing the full pass). Piste grooming is very good. Signposting is criticised again this year as 'surprisingly poor, and non-existent in places – we found ourselves inadvertently off-piste on two occasions'.

THE SLOPES
Limited cruising

Obergurgl is the smaller of the two linked areas. It is in two sections, with a link at altitude in only one direction. The gondola from the village entrance and the Rosskar fast quad chair go to the higher **Festkogl** section. This is served by two drags and a chair up to 3035m/ 9,96oft. From here you can head down to the gondola base or over to the **Gaisberg** sector, now also reached from the village via a new gondola, which goes on to the sector high point at Hohe Mut. A blue run links across from the mid-station of the new gondola to slopes served by a

slow quad and a six-pack, and a new red run will link across from the top.

There are two ski routes called 'varientenabfahrt'. The term is not explained. When we last visited these were pretty wild – ungroomed, largely unmarked, possibly unpatrolled; take care. There are 8km/5 miles of night skiing on Tuesdays ('excellent').

The slopes of **Hochgurgl** consist of high, gentle bowls, with fast lifts – chairs and two gondolas – serving the main slopes above the village, but drags serving the more testing outlying slopes. From the top stations there are spectacular views to the Dolomites. A single run leads down through the woods from Hochgurgl to Untergurgl.

TERRAIN-PARKS
Sorry, no

There used to be a terrain-park and pipes at Festkogel; these were scrapped a few years ago and there are no current plans to revive them.

SNOW RELIABILITY
Excellent

Obergurgl has high slopes and is arguably the most snow-sure of Europe's non-glacier resorts – even without its snowmaking, which was increased again recently. It has a long season by Austrian standards.

FOR EXPERTS
Not generally recommendable

There are few challenges on-piste – most of the blacks could easily be red, and where they deserve the classification it's only for short stretches (for example, at the very top

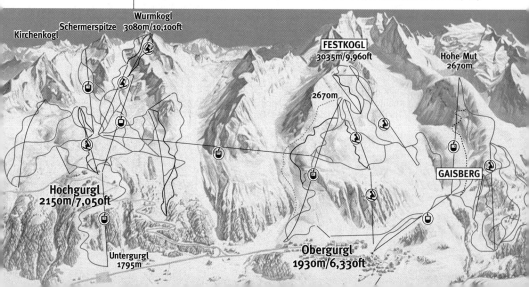

↗ There are fabulous glacier views from the terrace of the little hut at Hohe Mut
SNOWPIX.COM / CHRIS GILL

of Wurmkogl). The ski routes can offer a challenge, and there is a lot of easy off-piste to be found with a guide – the top school groups often go off-piste when conditions are right. This is a well-known area for ski touring, and we have reports of very challenging expeditions on the glaciers at the head of the valley.

FOR INTERMEDIATES
Good but limited
There is some perfect intermediate terrain here, made even better by the normally flattering snow conditions. The problem is, there's not much of it. Keen piste-bashers will quickly tire of travelling the same runs and be itching to catch the bus to Sölden, down the valley – the arrangement to upgrade a week's lift pass to include a day on Sölden's slopes is still available.

Hochgurgl has the bigger area of easy runs, and these make good cruising. For more challenging intermediate runs, head to the Vorderer Wurmkogllift, on the right as you look at the mountain. Less confident intermediates may find the woodland piste down from Hochgurgl to the bus stop at Untergurgl tricky.

The Obergurgl area has more red than blue runs but most offer no great challenge to a confident intermediate. There is some easy cruising around mid-mountain on the Festkogl. The blue run from the top of the Festkogl

gondola down to the village, via the Gaisberg sector, is one of the longest cruises in the area. And there's another long enjoyable run down the length of the gondola, with a scenic off-piste variant in the adjoining valley.

In the Gaisberg area, there are very easy runs in front of the Nederhütte and back towards the village.

FOR BEGINNERS
Fine for first-timers or improvers
The inconveniently situated Mahdstuhl nursery slope above Obergurgl is adequate for complete beginners. One reporter reckons there is 'less near-beginner terrain than you might expect', but there doesn't seem to us to be a shortage. The gentle Gaisberg run – under the new gondola out of the village – is ideal to move on to as soon as a modicum of control has been achieved. The easy slopes served by the Bruggenboden chair are also suitable.

The Hochgurgl nursery slopes are an awkward walk from the hotels, but otherwise satisfactory. And there are good blue slopes to move on to.

The quality of the snow and piste preparation make learning here easier than in most lower Austrian resorts.

CROSS-COUNTRY
Limited but snow-sure
Three small loops, one each at Obergurgl, Untergurgl and Hochgurgl,

SCHOOLS

Obergurgl
t 6305

Hochgurgl
t 6265

Classes
(Obergurgl prices)
6 days (2hr am and pm) €192

Private lessons
From €113 for 2hr;
€12 for additional person

boarding

Obergurgl is a traditional ski destination, attracting an affluent clientele. The resort is actually pretty good for snowboarding. Beginners will be pleased to find that most of the slopes can be reached without having to ride drag-lifts. And there's some good off-piste potential for more advanced riders. But the lack of any terrain features is a major drawback for most.

give just 12km/7 miles of trail. All are
relatively snow-sure and pleasantly
situated. Lessons are available.

QUEUES
Few problems
Major lift queues have been rare, and
with the new gondola up to Gaisberg
and Hohe Mut for 2007/08 should be
eliminated altogether.

MOUNTAIN RESTAURANTS
Unremarkable choice
Perhaps because the villages are so
easily accessible for lunch, mountain
huts are not a highlight, though a 2007
reporter praises 'reasonably priced
food and lots of atmosphere'.
Editors' choice We look forward to
trying the Top Mountain Star (see
below). But the jolly Nederhütte (6425)
at Gaisberg is one of the best, with
'tasty and huge portions' and
'exceptional service'. Carnivores will
relish the ribs, but the menu is
probably unique in Austria in offering
several identified vegetarian dishes.
Worth knowing about David's Skihütte
is 'very friendly', cheerful and good
value. The small hut at Hohe Mut has
fabulous glacial views from its terrace
and is popular with reporters for
'good, tasty, local dishes'. At
Hochgurgl, Wurmkoglhütte has been
replaced by the 'stunning' new glass-
walled Top Mountain Star panoramic
restaurant, run by the Top Hotel.

SCHOOLS AND GUIDES
Further good news
We continue to receive positive reports
of the Obergurgl school, with good
English spoken, a maximum of nine
per group and excellent lessons and
organisation. Reporters find the
instructors 'friendly, supportive and
professional', and classes 'a very
positive and pleasant experience' with
'excellent' English spoken. Demand for
private instruction appears to be
increasing and it is advisable to book
ahead during peak periods.

FACILITIES FOR CHILDREN
Check out your hotel
Children's ski classes start at four
years and children from age three can
join Bobo's ski-kindergarten. There's
lunchtime supervision for ski school
and kindergarten children alike. Many
hotels offer childcare of one sort or
another, and the Alpina has been
particularly recommended.

HOW TO GO
Plenty of good hotels
Most tour operators feature hotels and
pensions. Demand exceeds supply, and
for once it is true that you should
book early to avoid disappointment.
Hotels Accommodation is of high
quality: most hotels are 4-stars, and
none is less than a 3-star. Couples
have been surprised to be asked to
share tables even at 4-star hotels.
    A cheaper option is to stay down
the valley in Untergurgl, where the 4-
star Jadghof (6431) is recommended.
Some hotels don't accept credit cards.
OBERGURGL
****Edelweiss und Gurgl (6223) The
focal hotel – biggest, oldest, one of
the most appealing; on the central
square, near the main lifts. Pool and
outdoor whirlpool. 'Good marks for
food, service, comfort and location,'
says a 2007 visitor.
****Alpina de Luxe (6000) Big, smart,
excellent children's facilities. Pool.
****Bergwelt (6274) Recommended as
'very smart'. Beauty and spa facilities,
including outdoor pool.
****Hochfirst (63250) 'Superb' spa
facilities, comfortable, four or five
minutes from gondola. Ski-bus stop
right outside. Casino.
****Crystal (6454) Near the Festkogl
lift. If you don't mind the ocean-liner
appearance, it's one of the best.
****Gamper (6545) 'Excellent,' says a
reporter: 'Good food, friendly staff.' Far
end of town, past the square.
****Gotthard-Zeit (6292) 'Elegant',
spacious, comfortable, good food. Spa
facilities. Small pool. Sun terrace.
Convenient for skiing, but a 'steep walk
from the village' if you venture out.
****Jenewein (6203) 'Convenient with
attractive spa facilities,' says a reporter.
****Josl (6205) Modern, convenient –
next to the gondola. Recently
refurbished. Sauna and steam room.
Recommended by a 2007 visitor.
***Wiesental (6263) Comfortable, well
situated, good value. Terrace popular
for lunch and après-ski. 'Good food,
very friendly staff.'
***Granat-Schlössl (6363) Amusing
pseudo-castle, surprisingly affordable.
***Pension Gurgl (6533) Friendly B&B
near Festkogl lift; pizzeria; same
owners as Edelweiss und Gurgl.
***Haus Schönblick (6251) B&B with
downhill walk to main lifts. 'Very clean,
big rooms, hearty breakfast, friendly.'

↑ As you can see, Obergurgl is quite hilly, and stretches some way. In the background are the slopes of Hochgurgl

OBERGURGL TOURIST OFFICE

ACTIVITIES

Indoor Pools, saunas, whirlpools, steam baths and massage in hotels; bowling, riding, library

Outdoor Natural ice rink, curling, snow-shoe outings, winter hiking paths

Phone numbers
From elsewhere in Austria add the prefix 05256; from abroad use the prefix +43 5256

TOURIST OFFICE

t 6466
info@obergurgl.com
www.obergurgl.com

HOCHGURGL
*****Top Hotel Hochgurgl (6565)
Relais & Chateaux place – the only 5-star in the area. Luxurious, with pool.
****Angerer Alm (62410) 'Staff really friendly and helpful.' Pool.
****Riml (6261) Ski-in/ski-out location. Large rooms. 'Excellent' pool, spa. A 2007 visitor was 'very impressed'.
***Sporthotel Ideal (6290) Well situated for access to the slopes. Pool and new spa facilities.
***Laurin (6227) Well-equipped, traditional rooms, excellent food.
Apartments The Lohmann is modern and well placed for the slopes, less so for the village centre below. The 3-star Pirchhütt has apartments close to the Festkogl gondola, and the Wiesental hotel has more central ones.

EATING OUT
Wide choice, limited range
Hotel à la carte dining rooms dominate almost completely. Remember, credit cards are not widely accepted. A reporter recommends the independent and rustic Krumpn's Stadl (where staff dress in traditional clothing). The Hexenkuchl in the Jenewein receives favourable reports, serving 'good quality Austrian food'. The Romantika at the hotel Madeleine and the Belmonte are popular pizzerias. Hotels Alpina, Hochfirst ('food excellent, good

wine selection') and Gotthard-Zeit have been recommended. The Angerer Alm does 'good meals in relaxing surroundings'. The two restaurants in the Edelweiss und Gurgl are reportedly 'superb', and food at the Josl 'excellent'. The 5-star Top Hotel Hochgurgl is recommended for a 'delicious' treat. Some evenings you can eat on the hill, at Nederhütte (a fondue and live music evening, which 'rocks') and David's Skihütte – both popular snowmobile destinations.

APRES-SKI
Lively early, quiet later
Obergurgl is more animated than you might expect, at least in the early evening. Nederhütte at Gaisberg is the place for lively table dancing – 'fantastic,' says a 2006 reporter. You ski home afterwards though (or ride down on a snowmobile). All the bars at the base of the Rosskar and Gaisberg lifts are popular at close of play – the Pic-Nic is said to be lively. The Hexenkuchl at the Jenewein is also popular and a reporter enjoyed the 'excellent' and 'popular sun terrace' at the Wiesental.

Later on, the crowded Krumpn's Stadl barn is the liveliest place in town with live music on alternate nights. The Josl Keller is popular with all ages and gets busy ('lively and friendly'). The Jenewein and Edelweiss und Gurgl hotels have atmospheric bars. The Lodge is a 'smart' bar at the Hotel Bellevue. The Austria-keller disco is 'good fun' and attracts a wide age range – 6 to 60. There's a casino at the hotel Hochfirst. Reporters enjoy the Tuesday night ski school display / mountain party / night ski on Festkogl ('great night out').

Hochgurgl is very quiet at night except for Toni's Almhütte bar in the Sporthotel Olymp which has live music. There's also the African Bar disco.

OFF THE SLOPES
Very limited
There isn't much to do during the day – few shops, limited public facilities. Innsbruck is over two hours away by post-bus. Sölden (20 minutes away) has a leisure centre and shopping facilities. Pedestrians can ride gondolas to restaurants for lunch, or walk to the Gaisberg area; there are 12km/7 miles of hiking paths. The health suite at the Hochfirst is said to be open to non-residents.

Obertauern

High, snow-sure, French-style purpose-built resort on a small scale but with acceptable architecture and Austrian après-ski

COSTS

① ② ③ ④ ⑤ ⑥

RATINGS

The slopes

Fast lifts	*****
Snow	****
Extent	**
Expert	***
Intermediate	****
Beginner	****
Convenience	****
Queues	****
Mountain restaurants	****

The rest

Scenery	***
Resort charm	**
Off-slope	**

NEWS

For 2006/07 the hands-free lift pass system was introduced, and two new residences, Aparthotel Sonne and Residence Schilchegger opened in the resort.

190

- ➕ Excellent snow record
- ➕ Efficient modern lifts
- ➕ Slopes for all abilities
- ➕ Good mountain restaurants
- ➕ Lively but not intrusive après-ski
- ➕ Compact resort core, but...

- ➖ Village lacks traditional charm and spreads along the pass a long way
- ➖ Peaks are not high, so slopes are of limited vertical and extent is too small for keen piste-bashers
- ➖ Lifts and snow can suffer from exposure to high winds

Obertauern's attractions are unique. If you're looking for a change from the slush and ice of lower Austrian resorts, moving up in the world by 1000m/ 3,300ft or so could be just the ticket – French-style snow without losing that inimitable Austrian après-ski jollity.

THE RESORT

In the land of picture-postcard resorts grown out of rustic villages, Obertauern is different – a mainly modern development at the top of the Tauern pass road. Built in (high-rise) chalet style, it's not unattractive – though it's a linear affair, lacking a central focus of shops and bars. Although the core is compact, accommodation is spread widely along the road, with lifts going up either side of the road at half a dozen points. Buses run half-hourly between Untertauern and Tweng (free with lift pass), although some reporters remain unconvinced of their effectiveness as ski-buses. Taxis are available and there's ample parking.

THE MOUNTAIN

The slopes and lifts form a circuit around the village that can be travelled either way in a couple of hours. Visitors used to big areas will soon start to feel they have seen it all. Runs are short and vertical is limited – most major lifts are in the 200m to 400m (660ft to 1,310ft) range. The piste map and signposting are both poor. While pistes are numbered on the mountain, they are not on the map. Edge markers rarely reflect the piste classification – appalling.

Slopes Most pistes are on the sunny slopes to the north of the road and village: a wide basin of mostly gentle runs, some combining steepish pitches with long schusses. The slopes on the

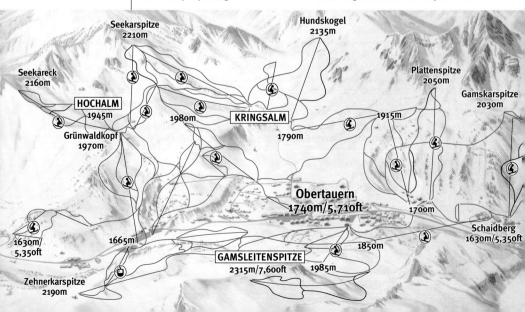

↑ The lifts and runs are of limited vertical, although most are not quite as limited as the 214m/700ft Seekareck chair at Hochalm, shown here
WENDY-JANE KING

Obertauern

KEY FACTS

Resort	1740m
	5,710ft
Slopes	1630-2315m
	5,350-7,600ft
Lifts	26
Pistes	100km
	62 miles
Blue	60%
Red	36%
Black	4%
Snowmaking	86km
	54 miles

UK PACKAGES

Alpine Answers, Inghams, Ski Wild, Snowscape, Thomson

Phone numbers
From elsewhere in Austria add the prefix 06456; from abroad use the prefix +43 6456

TOURIST OFFICE

t 7252
info@obertauern.com
www.obertauern.com

other side of the road – on Gamsleitenspitze, to the south-west – are generally quieter and have some of the steeper runs. There is floodlit skiing twice a week.

Terrain-parks The small Longplay Park is above the Almrausche hut, on the far left on our piste map.

Snow reliability The resort has exceptional snow reliability because of its altitude. But lifts can be closed by wind (which may blow snow away too). Snowmaking is said to be good, but grooming needs improvement.

Experts There are genuinely steep black pistes from the top Gamsleiten chair, but it is prone to closure. The icy race course under the Schaidbergbahn is also a challenge. Reporters recommend joining an off-piste guided group to explore the area.

Intermediates Most of the circuit is of intermediate difficulty. Stay low for easier pistes, or try the tougher runs higher up; you can't do the whole circuit without skiing reds.

Beginners Obertauern has very good nursery slopes, but they are spread around and may involve long walks to and from accommodation. The Schaidberg chair leads to a high-altitude beginners' slope and there is an easy run back home.

Snowboarding Drag-lifts are optional except for beginners. Blue Tomato is a specialist school.

Cross-country There are 17km/11 miles of trails in the heart of the resort.

Queues When nearby resorts have poor snow, non-residents arrive by the bus-load. However, the lift system is impressively efficient and lifties reportedly fill the chairs. The Grünwaldkopfbahn quad still generates long queues in the mornings – huge when we visited. The Sonnenlift double

chair can have problems at ski school time and the slow Hundskogel double is a bottleneck. Crowded pistes can be more of a problem than queues.

Mountain restaurants Mountain restaurants are numerous and good, but crowded. Treff 2000 ('excellent, good value dishes'), the 'cosy' Mankeialm, the Sonnhof ('best gröstl of the week', 'fast table-service'), Flubachalm ('traditional Austrian dishes') and Almrasch ('fine selection of main courses') are recommended. All the places at Kringsalm are praised, but a 2007 visitor rates the Almstube in the Seekarhaus as 'simply the best on the mountain – excellent fillet steak, succulent beef, professional staff'. The tiny Achenrainhutte by the Gamsleitenbahn has a 'jolly atmosphere' and the Hochalm gets 'very animated' – that is, busy.

Schools and guides There are six schools. We have good reports on Frau Holle, Willi Grillitsch, Krallinger and Koch schools.

Facilities for children Most of the schools take children.

STAYING THERE

How to go A handful of tour operators offer packages here.

Hotels Practically all accommodation is in hotels (mostly 3-star and 4-star) and guest houses. The following have been recommended: Steiner (7306) 'Smart and comfortable'; Frau Holle (7662) 'Comfortable rooms and great breakfast'; Kohlmayr (7272) 'Excellent ambiance'; Enzian (72070) 'Very good facilities'; Schütz (72040) Pool and spa; D'Glocknerin (7805) 'Lovely bar and spa facilities'.

Eating out The choices are mostly hotels and the busy après-ski bars at the foot of the lifts. The Almrasche, north of the town, is 'fantastic'.

Après-ski It's lively and varied. The Latsch'n Alm, with terrace and dancing, is good at tea time, as is the Lürzer Alm – 'full of character, lively, one of the best'. The Gruber Stadl is 'built to charm' and equally popular. Monkey's Heaven and the People bar have dancing. Other recommended places include the Taverne, the Römerbar and the 'quaint' Nanu Irish bar.

Off the slopes There's an excellent, large sports centre – no pool, though. There are marked walks up to Kringsalm. Salzburg is an easy trip.

Saalbach-Hinterglemm

Lively, noisy, traditional-style villages and extensive, varied, prettily wooded slopes; pity they are mostly so sunny

COSTS

① ② ③ ④ ⑤ ⑥

RATINGS

The slopes

Fast lifts	****
Snow	**
Extent	***
Expert	**
Intermediate	****
Beginner	***
Convenience	****
Queues	***
Mountain restaurants	****

The rest

Scenery	***
Resort charm	****
Off-slope	**

KEY FACTS

Resort	1000m
	3,280ft
Slopes	930-2095m
	3,050ft-6,870ft
Lifts	55
Pistes	200km
	124 miles
Blue	45%
Red	48%
Black	7%
Snowmaking	on all main slopes

192

+ Large, well-linked, intermediate circuit, good for mixed groups

+ Impressive lift system

+ Saalbach is a big but pleasant, affluent village, lively at night

+ Village main streets largely traffic-free

+ Lifts and pistes are conveniently close to centres of both villages

+ Atmospheric mountain restaurants

+ Large snowmaking installation

+ Sunny slopes, but ...

− Most slopes are low as well as sunny, and the snow suffers

− Limited steep terrain

− Nursery slopes in Saalbach are not ideal – sunny, and crowded in parts

− Saalbach spreads along the valley – some lodgings are far from central

− Hinterglemm sprawls along a long street with no clearly defined centre

− Both are noisy from 4pm and Saalbach can get rowdy at night

Saalbach-Hinterglemm is one of Austria's major resorts, with a claimed 200km/ 124 miles of pistes. Compared with other big names nearby, it emerges well: it has more challenging intermediate terrain and better mountain restaurants than the SkiWelt (Söll, Ellmau etc), more impressive lifts and snowmaking than Kitzbühel, and has the edge on both in terms of village altitude and ski convenience.

But – and it's a big but – most of its slopes face south and the snow suffers as a result. There is a limit to what snowmaking can achieve, especially if it is warm (as it was for much of last season). And neither Saalbach nor Hinterglemm is the place to go for a quiet time: music blasting out of bars is the norm.

THE RESORT

Saalbach and Hinterglemm are separate villages, their centres 4km/ 2.5 miles apart, which have expanded along the floor of their dead-end valley. They haven't quite merged, but they have adopted a single shared

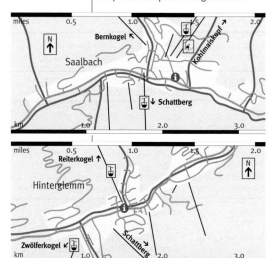

marketing identity. This doesn't mean they offer a single kind of holiday.

Saalbach is an attractive, typically Austrian village, with traditional-style (although mostly modern) buildings huddled together around a classic onion-domed church. But it is more convenient than most Austrian villages, with lifts into three sectors of the slopes starting close to the traffic-free village centre; the result is near to an ideal blend of Austrian charm with French convenience.

Saalbach has a justified reputation as a party town – but those doing the partying seem to be a strangely mixed bunch. Big-spending BMW and Mercedes drivers, staying in the smart, expensive hotels that line the main street, share the bars with teenagers (including British school kids) spending more on alcohol than on their cheap and cheerful pensions out along the road to Hinterglemm.

Hinterglemm also has lifts and runs close to the centre, and offers quick access to some of the most interesting slopes. It is a more diffuse collection of hotels and holiday homes, where prices are lower and less cash is

Saalbach is a pretty village and the black Nordabfahrt piste on the left of this photo is a great fast cruise when it has been groomed (it's north-facing too, so keeps its snow well) →

TVB SAALBACH-HINTERGLEMM

NEWS

For 2007/08 an additional reservoir is to be built to boost the capacity of the existing snowmaking network.

In 2006/07 an eight-seat gondola replaced the double chair linking Schattberg Ost and Schattberg West. And the Schönleiten six-pack with heated seats and covers replaced two drag-lifts on the slopes up to Wildenkarkogel.

flashed. The main street, lined with bars and hotels, has been relieved of through traffic, though it is not quite traffic-free.

Both villages get very noisy from mid-afternoon till the early hours, with music blasting out of bars the norm. Saalbach in particular can get very rowdy, with drunken revellers still in their ski boots long after dark. All our 2007 reporters commented on this ('quite rowdy if your hotel is on the main street', 'persistent noise from the bars', 'request a rear-facing room').

In both villages, the amount of walking depends heavily on where you stay. There is an excellent valley bus service, but it isn't perfect: it finishes early, gets very busy at peak times and doesn't get you back to hotels in central Hinterglemm, or to hotels set away from the main road. Taxis are plentiful and not expensive. The Nightliner bus runs intermittently from 7.30pm to 2am between Saalbach and Hinterglemm.

Several resorts in Salzburg province are reachable by road – including Bad Hofgastein, Kaprun and Zell am See, the last a short bus-ride away.

THE MOUNTAINS

The slopes form a 'circus' almost entirely composed of intermediate, lightly wooded slopes.

THE SLOPES
User-friendly circuit

Travelling anticlockwise, you can make a complete circuit of the valley on skis, crossing from one side to the other at Vorderglemm and Lengau – if you wish you can stick to blues almost the whole way. Going clockwise, you have to truncate the circuit because there is no lift on the south side at Vorderglemm – and there is more red-run skiing to do (and a black if you want to do the full circuit).

The lift system is very impressive, with mainly gondolas and fast chairs.

On the south-facing side, five sectors can be identified, each served by a lift from the valley – from west to east, **Hochalm, Reiterkogel, Bernkogel, Kohlmaiskopf** and **Wildenkarkogel**. The links across these south-facing slopes work well: when traversing the whole hillside you need to descend to the valley floor only once – at Saalbach, where the main street separates

Bernkogel from Kohlmaiskopf. The Wildenkarkogel sector connects via Seidl-Alm to the slopes of **Leogang**; a small, high, open area leads to a long, north-facing slope down to the base of an eight-seat gondola near Hütten, 3km/2 miles from Leogang village.

The north-facing slopes are different in character: two widely separated and steeper mountains, one split into twin peaks. An eight-seat gondola rises from Saalbach to **Schattberg Ost**, where the high, open, sunny slopes behind the peak are served by a fast quad. The slightly higher peak of **Schattberg West** is reached by gondola from Hinterglemm. And a new gondola replaced the double chair on the link

from Schattberg Ost to Schattberg West last season. The second north-facing hill is **Zwölferkogel**, served by a two-stage eight-seat gondola from Hinterglemm. A six-pack and drag-lift serve open slopes on the sunny side of the peak, and a second gondola from the valley provides a link from the south-facing Hochalm slopes.

The Hinterglemm nursery slopes are well used, and floodlit every evening.

TERRAIN-PARKS
Excellent
There's a terrain-park with half-pipe on the north-facing slopes just above Hinterglemm (floodlit and 'loved' by a recent reporter's teenagers), and

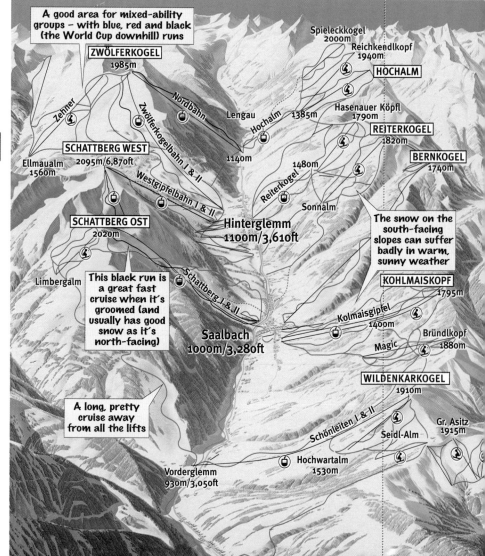

LIFT PASSES

Skicircus Saalbach Hinterglemm Leogang

Prices in €

Age	1-day	6-day
under 16	19	91
16 to 18	30	145
over 19	38	181

Free under 6

Senior no deals

Beginner points card

Notes

Covers Saalbach, Hinterglemm and Leogang, and the ski-bus; also Reiterkogel toboggan run at night; part-day passes available; supplement for swimming pool

Alternative passes

Salzburger Super Ski Card covers all lifts and pistes in Salzburgerland including Zell am See, Kaprun, Schladming and Bad Gastein

---

another below Kl. Asitz on the way to Leogang. Below Seidl-Alm there's a boarder-cross course. Several dedicated 'carving' and 'mogul' zones are dotted around the area.

SNOW RELIABILITY
A tale of two sides

Most slopes are low (below 1900m/6,235ft) and the south-facing slopes are in the majority and can suffer when the sun comes out (when we were there in early March 2007, the south-facing side just had strips of browny-white machine-made snow amid green and brown fields). The north-facing slopes keep their snow better but can get icy. The long north-facing run down to Leogang often has the best snow in the area. Piste maintenance is good (2007 reporters were impressed) and snowmaking now covers many top-to-bottom runs; but the low altitude is a problem that won't go away.

FOR EXPERTS
Little steep stuff

There are a few challenging slopes on the north-facing side. The long (4km/2.5 mile) Nordabfahrt run beneath the Schattberg Ost gondola is a genuine black – a fine fast bash first thing in the morning if it has been groomed. The Zwölferkogel Nordabfahrt at Hinterglemm is less consistent, but its classification is justified by a few short, steeper pitches. The World Cup downhill run from Zwölferkogel is interesting, as is

the 5km/3 mile Schattberg West–Hinterglemm red (and its scenic 'ski route' variant). Off-piste guides are available, but snow conditions and forest tend to limit the potential. Given good snow, however, you can have a good time (a 2007 reporter was lucky: 'We had two days of powder and saw no more than 20 other skiers off-piste – excellent').

FOR INTERMEDIATES
Paradise for most

This area is ideal for both the mileage-hungry piste-basher and the more leisurely cruiser, although one nervous third-weeker found the slopes too challenging and gave up after two days, warns a recent visitor. For those looking for more of a challenge, the most direct routes down from Hochalm, Reiterkogel, Kohlmaiskopf and Hochwartalm are good fun. The delightful blue run from Bernkogel to Saalbach gets really crowded at times.

The north-facing area has some more challenging runs, with excellent relentless reds from both Schattberg West and Zwölferkogel, and a section of relatively high, open slopes around Zwölferkogel – good for mixed-ability groups wishing to ski together, a happy reporter points out. None of the black runs is beyond an adventurous intermediate. The long, pretty cruise to Vorderglemm gets you right away from lifts – but one 2006 visitor suggests the lower section should be classified red, having witnessed 'a fair amount of distress at the end of the day'. Our

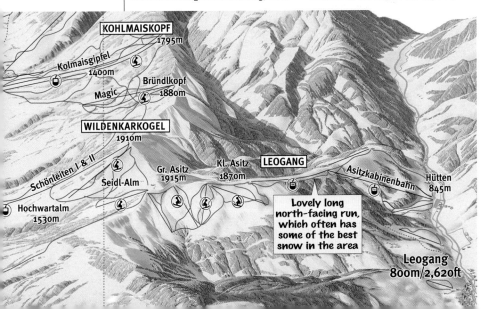

KOHLMAISKOPF 1795m

Kolmaisgipfel 1400m

Bründlkopf 1880m

Magic

WILDENKARKOGEL 1910m

Schönleiten I & II

Seidl-Alm

Gr. Asitz 1915m

Kl. Asitz 1870m

LEOGANG

Asitzkabinenbahn

Hütten 845m

Hochwartalm 1530m

Lovely long north-facing run, which often has some of the best snow in the area

Leogang 800m/2,620ft

SCHOOLS

Saalbach

Fürstauer
t 8444

Aamadel Snow Academy
t 668256

Hinterholzer
t 7607

Zink
t 0664 162 3655

Heugenhauser
t 8300

Snowboard
t 0664 345 3838

easySki
t 0699 111 80010

Hinterglemm

Hinterglemmer
t 634640

Activ
t 0676 517 1325

Classes
(Fürstauer prices)
6 days (4hr) from
€167

Private lessons
From €93 for 2hr, for
1 or 2 people; extra
person €10

CHILDREN

Several hotels have
nurseries

Ski schools
Some take children in
miniclubs from about
age 3 and can
provide lunchtime
care; from about age
4½, children can join
ski school (€142 for 6
days – Fürstauer
prices)

favourite intermediate run is the long,
off-the-main-circuit cruise on north-
facing snow down to Leogang.

FOR BEGINNERS
Best for improvers
Saalbach's two nursery slopes are right
next to the village centre. But they are
south-facing and the upper one gets a
lot of through-traffic. The lower one is
very small but the lift is free.

Alternatives are trips to the short,
easy runs at Bernkogel and Schattberg.
Hinterglemm's spacious nursery area
is separate from the main slopes and
'very good', says a recent reporter. It is
north-facing, so lacks sun in midwinter
but is more reliable for snow later on.

There are lots of easy blue runs to
move on to, especially on the south-
facing side of the valley, which 'more
than satisfied' a reporter's group.

FOR CROSS-COUNTRY
Go to Zell am See
Some 10km/6 miles of trails run beside
the road along the valley floor from
Saalbach to Vorderglemm, between
Hinterglemm and the valley end at
Lindlingalm, and there is a high trail on
the Reiterkogel. In mid-winter the
valley trails get very little sun, and are
not very exciting. The area beyond
nearby Zell am See offers more scope.

QUEUES
Only a problem in high season
Queues are a problem only in high
season, when the lifts from Saalbach
up the south-facing slopes can have
waits of up to 15 minutes at peak
times, at the end as well as the start
of the day. A mid-February visitor
found 30-minute queues for the
Schönleiten gondola up from
Vorderglemm. High-season queues can
also arise for the chair to Hasenauer
Köpfl. A March 2007 visitor found no
queues all week but did complain

about the slow Bernkogel chair-lift out
of Saalbach, which broke down twice
in the week: 'It's the poor link in an
otherwise impressive system.'

MOUNTAIN RESTAURANTS
Excellent quality and quantity
The area is liberally scattered with
around 40 attractive huts, most serving
good food. Many have pleasant rustic
interiors and a lively ambience.

On the south-facing slopes, the
Panoramaalm on Kohlmaiskopf and the
Walleggalm on Hochalm serve
particularly good food. The 'cosy'
Thurneralm close to Bründlkopf serves
'delicious BBQ ribs and glüwein'. At
the base of the Bernkogel chair, the
Bäckstättstall has 'warm and wonderful
hospitality'. The Bärnalm near the top
of the Bernkogel chair does 'good
food, good value'; the Westernstadl
lower down has a 'cowboy-themed
interior'. The Grabenhütte, tucked away
from the main piste, has 'fantastic
home-made sausages'. The rustic Alte
Schmiede at the top of the Leogang
gondola is 'still one of the very best
with great pizza' says a 2007 reporter.
Across in the Hinterglemm direction,
the Rosswaldhütte has 'excellent rösti'.

On the north-facing slopes, the
Simalalm at the base of the
Limbergalm quad chair is 'great for the
sun and the views', and the Bergstadl –
halfway down the red run from
Schattberg West – has stunning views,
good food and is 'very good value'.
Ellmaualm, at the bottom of the Zehner
lift has been praised and the
Breitfussalm, down from Zwölferkogel,
'stood out' for a 2007 visitor.

SCHOOLS AND GUIDES
Plenty of choice
With nine schools there's plenty of
choice. For the past two seasons we've
had good reports on the Aamadall
Snow Academy – in 2007 a beginner
had a week of group morning and
afternoon lessons which 'brought him
on a treat'. A boarder had 'worthwhile'
lessons with Hinterglemmer.

FACILITIES FOR CHILDREN
Hinterglemm tries harder
Saalbach doesn't go out of its way to
sell itself to families, although it does
have a ski kindergarten. Hinterglemm
has some good hotel-based nursery
facilities – the one at the Theresia is
reportedly excellent.

See what we mean about the south-facing slopes? A reader took this pic in January 2007; and they looked like this on our March 2007 visit too →

TOM BROADBENT

GETTING THERE

Air Salzburg 90km/ 56 miles (2hr); Munich 218km/135 miles (3½hr)

Rail Zell am See 19km/12 miles (40min); hourly buses

UK PACKAGES

Airtours, Alpine Answers, BoardnLodge, Club Pavilion, Crystal, Directski.com, Equity, Erna Low, First Choice, Inghams, Interactive Resorts, Interhome, Neilson, Panorama, Rocketski, Ski Expectations, Ski Independence, Ski McNeill, Ski Wild, Skitracer, Thomson, Tops

STAYING THERE

HOW TO GO
Cheerful doesn't mean cheap
Chalets We are aware of a few 'club hotels', but Saalbach isn't really a chalet resort.
Hotels There are a large number of hotels in both villages, mainly 3-star and above. Be aware that some central hotels are affected by disco noise and front rooms by all-night street noise.
SAALBACH
****Alpenhotel** (6666) Luxurious, with open-fire lounge, disco, small pool.
****Berger's Sporthotel** (6577) Lively, with a daily tea dance, disco and lap-dancing club. Small pool.
****Gartenhotel Eva** (7144) 'Small, good quality with sophisticated, simple, low calorie food,' said a reporter.
****Kendler** (62250) Position second to none, right next to the Bernkogel chair. Classy, expensive, good food.
****Kristiana** (6253) Near enough to lifts but away from night-time noise. 'Excellent food.' Sauna, steam bath.
****Panther** (6227) 'Excellent, practically ski-in, ski-out, good food.'
****Saalbacher Hof** (71110) Retains a friendly feel despite its large size; 'excellent wellness centre'; 'well above average food'.
***Haider** (6228) Best-positioned of the 3-stars, right next to the main lifts.
***Peter** (6236) 'Excellent value for main street location. Food OK.'
HINTERGLEMM
****Egger** (63220) 'I'll stay here next time, on the slopes,' says a reader.
****Theresia** (74140) Hinterglemm's top hotel, and one of the best for families. Out towards Saalbach, but

nursery slopes nearby. Pool.
****Wolf** (63460) Small but well-equipped 4-star in excellent position. 'Superb food and gala dinners.' Pool and 'excellent spa facilities'.
***Sonnblick** (6408) Convenient 3-star in a quiet location. 'Friendly service', 'excellent buffet breakfast and tasty choice at dinner,' says a recent visitor.
Haus Ameshofer (8119) 'Great value ski-in/ski-out B&B.' At Reiterkogel lift.
Apartments There's a big choice for independent travellers.

EATING OUT
Wide choice of hotel restaurants
This is essentially a half-board resort, with few non-hotel restaurants. Peter's restaurant, at the top of Saalbach's main street, is atmospheric and serves excellent meat dishes cooked on hot stones. The Wallner Pizzeria on the main street is good value. The Auwirt hotel on the outskirts of Saalbach has a good à la carte restaurant. A reader recommends the 'reindeer steaks and marvellous atmosphere' at the Berger Hochalm, '3km up the toboggan track'.

APRES-SKI
It rocks from early on
Après-ski is very lively from mid-afternoon until the early hours and can get positively wild. Most places are packed by 4pm. In Saalbach the Bäckstättstall is recommended for tea-dancing and is 'the place to start', according to one 2007 visitor. The rustic Hinterhagalm has live bands and rock music; when it closes around 6pm, the crowds slide down to Bauer's Ski-alm (an old cow shed and 'one of the liveliest and most atmospheric

ACTIVITIES

Indoor Swimming pools, sauna, massage, solarium, tennis

Outdoor Ice-rink, curling, tobogganing, sleigh rides, snow-shoeing, tubing, 40km/25 miles of cleared paths

Phone numbers
From elsewhere in Austria add the prefix 06541 (Saalbach), 06583 (Leogang); from abroad use the prefix +43 and omit the initial '0'

TOURIST OFFICES

Saalbach
t 680068
contact@saalbach.com
www.saalbach.com

Leogang
t 8234
info@saalfelden-leogang.at
www.leogang-saalfelden.at

---

après-ski bars in Austria'). The Berger's Sporthotel main bar is lively with dancing when the lifts close; and its separate Prosecco bar is 'a relaxing place to sip your G&Ts in comfort – a lot more intimate than the main bar'. The tiny Zum Turm (next door to the church) is a medieval jail that also offers 'unusual bar games' but is 'far too smoky'. The Neuhaus Taverne has live music and attracts a mature clientele. Jack-in, around halfway up the main street, has wi-fi and big screen TVs so attracts the sports fans. Bobby's Pub is cheap, often full of British school kids, has bowling and serves Guinness. King's, Arena and Castello's are clubs that liven up later on and have lap dancing adjuncts.

In Hinterglemm there are a number of ice bars, popular at close of play, including the central Gute Stube of hotel Dorfschmiede, with loud music blasting out and people spilling into the street. A wider age group enjoys the live music later on at the smart, friendly Tanzhimmel – an open, glass-fronted bar with a dance floor. The Hexenhäusl gets packed. A couple of recent reporters rate the rustic goat-themed Goasstall: 'The best and loudest bar in the area.' Bla Bla is small and smart, with reasonable prices. The Almbar has good music and some dancing.

Tour operator reps organise tobogganing, sleigh rides and bowling.

OFF THE SLOPES
Surprisingly little to do
Saalbach is not very entertaining if you're not into winter sports. There are few shops other than supermarkets and ski shops. There are some cleared paths and a 2007 visitor found the walkers' lift pass 'good value' at 50 euros, which allowed access to two lifts per day and meant their mixed group of skiers and non-skiers could easily meet for lunch. There are excursions to Salzburg.

STAYING UP THE MOUNTAIN
It's quiet
It is possible to stay up the mountain in several hotels and gasthofs – a good way of avoiding village noise and rowdiness. A 2007 reporter recommends the 2-star Sonnhof (6295) near the top of the Hochalmbahn: 'Large, newly renovated rooms, good value and instant access to the slopes for first tracks daily'.

Leogang 800m/2,620ft

A much less expensive alternative to Saalbach-Hinterglemm.

THE RESORT
Leogang is quiet, attractive and rather scattered. It's best to stay in the hamlet of Hütten, near the gondola into the main ski area.

THE MOUNTAIN
The village is linked to the eastern end of the Saalbach-Hinterglemm circuit.
Slopes A gondola from Hütten takes you into the ski area. The local slopes tend to be delightfully quiet.
Snow reliability The local slopes have some of the best snow in the region, being north- and east-facing, with snowmaking on the run home.
Experts Not much challenge locally.
Intermediates Great long blue/red run cruise home from the top of the gondola. Plus the circuit to explore.
Beginners Good nursery slopes by the village, and short runs to progress to.
Snowboarding The whole area is great for boarding and there's a terrain-park.
Cross-country The best in the area. There are 20km/12 miles of trails, plus a panoramic high-altitude trail.
Queues No local problems.
Mountain restaurants A couple of good local huts. A recent visitor recommends the Forsthofalm – 'the nicest I have ever been in'.
Schools and guides Leogang Altenberger school has a good reputation: 'Excellent service and lessons; highly recommended.'
Facilities for children There is a non-ski nursery, and children can start school at four years old.

STAYING THERE
Hotels The luxury Krallerhof (8246) has its own nursery lift, which can be used to get across to the main lift station. The 4-star Salzburger Hof (7310) is well placed, a two-minute walk from the gondola; sauna and steam.
Apartments There are quiet apartments available.
Eating out Restaurants are hotel-based. The upscale Krallerhof has excellent food and the much cheaper Gasthof Hüttwirt has a high reputation.
Après-ski The rustic old chalet Kraller Alm is very much the focal tea-time and evening rendezvous.
Off the slopes Excursions to Salzburg are possible.

Schladming

Old valley town with pleasant main square and extensive intermediate slopes on four linked mountains

COSTS

① ② ③ ④ ⑤ ⑥

RATINGS

The slopes

Fast lifts	****
Snow	****
Extent	***
Expert	**
Intermediate	****
Beginner	***
Convenience	***
Queues	****
Mountain restaurants	****

The rest

Scenery	***
Resort charm	***
Off-slope	****

NEWS

For 2007/08 a new après-ski and entertainment centre is due to open in the Planai gondola base station. It will feature restaurants, a cafe, bars and discos, on three floors. More snowmaking is planned at Planai and Hochwurzen, and some pistes may be widened.

For 2006/07 the Golden Jet gondola opened at the base of Planai West and Hochwurzen, replacing two old chair-lifts linking the two at low level. Snowmaking was increased on Hauser Kaibling.

➕ Extensive intermediate slopes in four main sectors

➕ Very sheltered slopes, among trees

➕ Lots of good mountain restaurants

➕ Appealing town with friendly people

➕ Extensive snowmaking, good grooming and shady slopes mean good piste conditions, but ...

➖ The mainly north-facing runs can be cold in early season

➖ Slopes lack variety

➖ Very little to entertain experts

➖ Nursery slopes are inconvenient if you stay in the village centre

➖ Runs to valley level are not easy

➖ Not much lively nightlife

With its four distinct mountains now all linked by lifts (and to varying degrees by pistes), Schladming offers the keen intermediate a real sense of travelling around on the snow. But you may find one slope rather like another.

The resort does not offer one of Austria's wildest après-ski scenes, but most of our reporters don't mind that and find its solid, valley-town ambience a pleasant change from the Austrian norm.

THE RESORT

The old town of Schladming has a long skiing tradition and has hosted World Cup races for many years.

The town has a pleasant, traffic-free main square, prettily lit at night, around which you'll find most of the shops, restaurants and bars (and some appealing hotels). The busy main road bypasses the town. Much of the accommodation is close to the centre. The sports centre and tennis halls are five minutes' walk from the centre.

Schladming sits at the foot of Planai, one of four mountains that are linked to form a fair-sized network. A gondola starting a few minutes' walk from the centre goes most of the way up this home mountain. From the western suburbs of Schladming there are chair-lifts towards the next mountain to the west, Hochwurzen, and a new gondola making the link back to Planai. The Hochwurzen lifts

pass through Rohrmoos, a quiet, scattered village set on an elevated slope that forms a giant nursery area – an excellent base for beginners.

To the east of Schladming is the small, attractively rustic village of Haus, where a cable-car and gondola go up to the highest of the four linked mountains, Hauser Kaibling. The fourth mountain, Reiteralm, is some way to the west, above Gleiming.

There are timetabled buses between the villages and lift bases, but they are not as frequent as reporters wished.

Apart from the main slopes we describe here, there are several other separate mountains nearby and shown on the resort's piste map – Fageralm, Galsterbergalm, Ramsau, the Dachstein glacier and Stoderzinken. The Ski Alliance Amadé lift pass also covers many other resorts. A car is useful for getting the most out of it: trips are feasible to Bad Gastein, Wagrain/ Flachau, Kleinarl and Hochkönig.

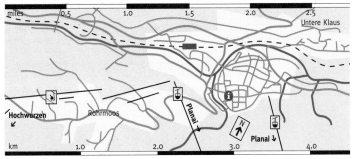

↑ Schladming was one of the first resorts to realise the importance of snowmaking, and last season was one when the resort's investment paid off
WENDY-JANE KING

THE MOUNTAINS

Most pistes are on the wooded north-facing slopes above the main valley, with some going into the side valleys higher up; there are a few open slopes above the trees.

Piste maps (you can get separate ones for each mountain) are generally 'clear and easy to use'. At the Skiline terminals at the Planai base you can get a printout showing lifts used, height gained and distance covered in the day – a neat free souvenir.

THE SLOPES
Four linked sectors – and more
Each of the sectors is quite a serious mountain, with a variety of lifts and runs to play on. **Planai** and **Hauser Kaibling** are linked at altitude via the high, wooded bowl between them. But the links with **Hochwurzen** (where you can try night skiing, boarding or tobogganing), and with **Reiteralm**, are at valley level. The link between Planai and Hochwurzen involves riding the new gondola in both directions. Getting around the whole area can take time. Some people who want to spend time on Reiteralm prefer to get the bus, or a taxi, to one of the lift bases at Pichl or Gleiming.

Several lower runs go across roads that aren't well signposted and a 2006 reporter says, 'Parents take note: there is a real danger of being hit by a car.'

There are handy ski lockers to rent at the Planai base station.

TERRAIN-PARKS
Head for Hochwurzen
There's a newish terrain-park on Hochwurzen, by the Gipfelbahn, with rails, boxes, straight- and pro-jumps – floodlit until 10pm. Reiteralm has a half-pipe and there's another park on the Dachstein glacier.

SNOW RELIABILITY
Excellent in cold weather
The northerly orientation of the slopes and good maintenance help keep the pistes in better shape than in some neighbouring resorts, and the serious snowmaking operation makes it a particularly good choice for early holidays; coverage is comprehensive, and the system is put to good use. More is planned on Planai and Hochwurzen for 2007/08. Reporters regularly complain of poor conditions on the lower slopes, notably the steep bottom part of the World Cup downhill run back to town.

Piste grooming receives mixed reviews, but was very good on our December 2006 visit despite sparse snowfalls.

FOR EXPERTS
Strictly intermediate stuff
Schladming's status as a World Cup downhill venue doesn't make it macho. The steep black finish to the Men's Downhill course and the moderate mogul runs at the top of Planai and Hauser Kaibling are the only really challenging slopes. Hauser Kaibling's off-piste is good, but limited. A 2007 reporter found some 'great' off-piste around run 5 on Reiteralm.

FOR INTERMEDIATES
Red runs rule
The area is ideal for intermediate cruising. The majority of runs are red but it's often difficult to distinguish them from many of the blues. One notable exception is the final very red section of the run below Rohrmoos, which makes it awkward for near-beginners to get to the Planai link

The open sections at the top of

boarding

Schladming is popular with boarders. Most lifts on the spread-out mountains are gondolas or chairs, with some short drags around. The area is ideal for beginners and intermediates, except when the lower slopes are icy, though there are few exciting challenges for expert boarders bar the off-piste tree runs. The Blue Tomato snowboard shop runs the 'impressive' specialist snowboard school.

KEY FACTS

Resort	745m
	2,440ft

Schladming
Ramsau/Dachstein
area

Slopes	745-2015m
	2,440-6,610ft
Lifts	81
Pistes	175km
	109 miles
Blue	29%
Red	61%
Black	10%
Snowmaking	100%

SCHOOLS

Tritscher
t 22647
Hopl (Hochwurzen-Planai)
t 61268
Blue Tomato
t 24223

Classes
(Tritscher prices)
5 days €150
Private lessons
Half day €95; each
additional person €20

Planai and Hauser Kaibling have some more challenging slopes. And the two World Cup pistes, and the red that runs parallel to the Haus downhill course to the village, are ideal for fast intermediates in good snow conditions but can get very icy and tricky.

Hauser Kaibling has a lovely meandering blue running from top to bottom, and Reiteralm has some gentle blues with good snow. Runs are well groomed, so intermediates will find the slopes generally flattering.

FOR BEGINNERS
Good slopes but poorly sited
The ski schools generally take beginners to the extensive but low-altitude Rohrmoos nursery area – fine if you are based there, a discouraging bus-ride away if you are not. Another novice area near the top of Planai is more convenient for residents of central Schladming and has better snow, but the runs are less gentle.

FOR CROSS-COUNTRY
Extensive network of trails
Given sufficient snow-cover, there are 400km/250 miles of trails in the region, and the World Championships have been held at nearby Ramsau. There are local loops along the main valley floor and between Planai and Hochwurzen.

QUEUES
Avoid peaks at Planai
Generally reporters have found few problems. The Planai gondola can have morning queues at peak-season and weekends and a New Year visitor experienced 'serious' waits for lifts on

Hochwurzen. But the new gondola into the Planai slopes from the base of Hochwurzen is an excellent development. The quiet, outlying Fageralm area is a recommended option on exceptionally busy days.

MOUNTAIN RESTAURANTS
A real highlight
There are plenty of attractive rustic restaurants in all sectors, and most get enthusiastic reports ('too many – we couldn't decide which to try', 'the best I have ever been to'). The 'quiet' Schladminger Hütte, at the top of the Planai gondola is recommended ('good pasta', 'friendly and efficient service'). Onkel Willy's Hütte has good live music and a large terrace. Schafalm offers 'excellent service, incredible food' but it gets crowded. The Holzhackerstub'n on the lower part of the World Cup run has 'high-quality freshly made food'. On Reiteralm 'you absolutely must visit' the Gasslhöh-Hütte for the 'mega huge' spare ribs. On Hauser Kaibling seek out tiny Kulmhoferhütte for a real mountain hut atmosphere, complete with fur-lined walls. Higher up, the hut off the Almlift feels wonderfully isolated, with great views and soup. The Knapplhof is full of ski-racing mementos and newly revamped Harry's Lärchenpavillion is highly recommended ('fantastic soup').

SCHOOLS AND GUIDES
Generally okay reports
We have generally had good reports: 'In five visits I have never had a bad instructor or a wasted lesson,' says a 2007 visitor. 'Excellent' is the verdict

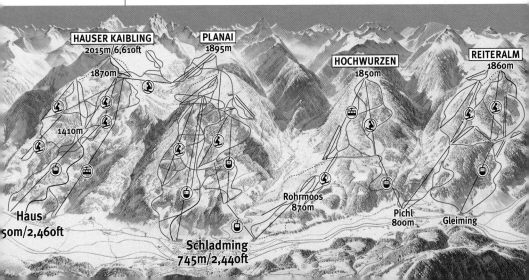

HAUSER KAIBLING
2015m/6,610ft

PLANAI
1895m

HOCHWURZEN
1850m

REITERALM
1886m

1870m

1410m

Haus
750m/2,460ft

Rohrmoos
870m

Pichl
800m

Gleiming

Schladming
745m/2,440ft

CHILDREN

Mini club
t 22647
For ages 3 and 4

Nannies
Details at tourist office

Ski school
From age 4 (€200 for 5 days including lunch – Tritscher price)

GETTING THERE

Air Salzburg 90km/ 56 miles (1½hr)

Rail Main line station in resort

UK PACKAGES

Alpine Answers, Club Pavilion, Crystal, Equity, Interhome, Rocketski, Skitracer

ACTIVITIES

Indoor Swimming pool, fitness club, tennis, sauna

Outdoor Ice skating, curling, tobogganing, sleigh rides, 50km/ 31 miles of cleared paths

Phone numbers
From elsewhere in Austria add the prefix 03687 (Schladming), 03686 (Haus); from abroad use the prefix +43 and omit the initial '0'

TOURIST OFFICES

Schladming
t 22777
urlaub@schladming.at
www.schladming.at
www.skiamade.com

Haus
t 22340
info@haus.at
www.haus.at

on private lessons with the Hopl school and another reader had a 'nice instructor who tried his best' despite poor January conditions. But the Tritscher school has been rated 'poor' for both adults' and children's classes.

FACILITIES FOR CHILDREN
Rohrmoos is the place

The extensive gentle slopes of Rohrmoos are ideal for building up youngsters' confidence. There's a Kinderland on Planai and the Top school at Pichl is praised this year for 'excellent' children's classes.

STAYING THERE

HOW TO GO
Packages mean hotels

Packaged accommodation is in hotels and pensions, but there are plenty of apartments for independent travellers.
Hotels Most of the accommodation is in modestly priced pensions but there are also a few more upmarket hotels.
****Sporthotel Royer** (200) Big, smart and comfortable, a few minutes' walk from the main Planai lift. Pool, sauna. 'Best in town.'
****Stadttor** (24525) 'Quiet, spacious and comfortable, with excellent food.' The Hogmanay gala dinner was 'a jolly event,' says a 2007 visitor.
****Almdorf-Reiteralm** (72444) New ski-in/ski-out village at Hochalm, above Pichl. Individual chalets and a hotel; restaurant, shop and spa facilities. Accessed by mountain road.
***Kirchenwirt** (22435) Just off the main square. 'Traditional atmosphere, wonderful food', 'great value for money'.
***Neue Post** (22105) Large rooms, friendly, good food, central.
***Zum Kaiserweg** (22038) Family run. Very near the new Planai West gondola. Repeatedly praised by reporters: 'Quiet location, good rooms and food.'
***Rohrmooser Schlössl** (61237) Just downhill from the new Planai West gondola. 'Really friendly', with 'excellent food and views'.
Apartments Haus Girik (22663) is close to the Planai gondola. Schütter (23230) near the new gondola is 'excellent, spacious and comfortable'.

EATING OUT
Some good places

Recommendations include the Kirchenwirt hotel ('fine home cooking'), Giovanni's (for pizza), Gasthof Brunner

('good value'), Charly's Treff ('excellent meal'), Talbachschenke ('good grills and atmosphere') and Neue Post hotel ('good but expensive'). Papa Joe's is a new grill and bar in the centre. We liked the Lasser Cafe and the Stadttor for coffee and cakes.

APRES-SKI
Explore the side streets

Some of the mountain restaurants are lively at the end of the afternoon, but down in the town there's a lack of animation. Charly's Treff (with umbrella bar) opposite the Planai gondola is the main exception. The Schladminger Hütte at the top of the gondola has live music at après-ski time on Wednesdays and the gondola stays open to bring you down. A 2007 reporter preferred the Seiterhutte Celtic Bar ('chilled atmosphere, funky music') and Tauernalm on Hochwurzen. The little Siglu has 'a good atmosphere' but quickly gets 'overcrowded and smoky'. Later on, reporters have noted the 'lack of a buzz' even though many of the central bars stay open until dawn. We liked the brewpub, Schwalbenbräu ('welcoming, good service'). The Neiderl is 'small and friendly'. Szenario is 'quite cosy, with very eclectic music choices'. The bar outside the Post hotel is recommended. Hanglbar has 'good music and a nice, friendly atmosphere'. Maria's Mexican is 'relaxing' with chilled music and margaritas. The Porta is a 'smart place with the best music and ambience'. The Sonderbar is a disco with three bars.

OFF THE SLOPES
Good for all but walkers

Non-skiers are fairly well catered for. There's a floodlit 7km/4 mile toboggan run at Hochwurzen, 'excellent' pool and an ice rink. Some mountain restaurants are easily reached on foot. The town shops and museum are worth a look. Train trips to Salzburg are easy. Buses run to the old walled town of Radstadt.

Haus 750m/2,460ft

Haus is a real village with a life of its own and its own ski schools and kindergartens. The user-friendly nursery slopes are between the village and the gondola. There's a railway station, so excursions are easy, but off-slope activities and nightlife are very limited. Hotel prices are generally lower here.

Sölden

A traditional valley town dominated by traffic and throbbing après-ski/nightlife – but with excellent slopes reaching glacial heights

FRANK HEUER

NEWS

For 2007/08 130 new snow-guns are due at Giggijoch and on slopes between the main ski area and the glaciers.

ÖTZTAL TOURISMUS / BERND RITSCHEL

Broad, open slopes at Giggijoch, with the glaciers behind ↓

➕ Excellent snow reliability, with access to two glaciers

➕ Fairly extensive network of slopes suited to adventurous intermediates

➕ Impressive lift system

➕ Very lively après-ski/nightlife, but …

➖ It can get rowdy at times

➖ Busy road through sprawling village

➖ Some central hotels are distant from the two main access lifts

➖ Inconvenient beginners' slopes

➖ English not widely spoken

Sölden deserves a close look from keen intermediates keen on Austrian après-ski – as long as you are prepared to operate mainly in German (British visitors are still few, although a couple of tour ops go there). The resort has invested massively in lifts to link its extensive glaciers to the lower slopes, and there are some seriously long runs.

THE RESORT

Despite its traditional Tirolean-style buildings and wooded valley setting, Sölden is no beauty: it is a large, traffic-filled place that sprawls along both sides of a busy main road and across the valley floor. The resort attracts a young, lively crowd – mostly Dutch and German – bent on partying.

Gondolas from opposite ends of town go up to Sölden's home slopes – the peak of Gaislachkogl and the lift junction of Giggijoch. A free shuttle-bus serves both lift stations, but a 2007 visitor complains of an inconsistent timetable and crowding. Isolated high above the town is the satellite resort of Hochsölden – a handful of 4-star hotels, and little else.

THE MOUNTAIN

Practically all the slopes you spend your days on are above the trees, though there are red runs through trees to the village. A low-cost pass for a day in nearby Obergurgl is available (when purchasing a full pass).

Slopes The two similar-sized home sectors are linked by chair-lifts (one a six-pack) out of the Rettenbachtal that separates them. Fast lifts from the Giggijoch sector lead to the Rettenbach glacier, and on to the Tiefenbach. Our repeated attempts to get to the glaciers have been thwarted by the weather; reporters repeatedly judge the link a 'long, slow trek'.

A 2007 reporter found piste marking poor, notably around the Gaislachkogl.

Terrain-parks In winter, there are two above Giggijoch: one has a half-pipe, kickers, waves, rails and a chill-out zone; the other is a kids' park. And there's a separate race course.

Snow reliability The slopes are high and mainly north-east- or south-east-facing; and there are two extensive glaciers. For 2007/08, 30 additional snow-guns are planned, which will considerably boost the extent of coverage. Grooming is generally good.

Experts None of the black pistes dotted around Sölden's map is serious, and some are silly; but you won't lack vertical – Hainbachjoch to the valley is 1400m/4,590ft. There are quite a few non-trivial reds. And there are extensive off-piste possibilities with a guide. At the top of the valley is one of the Alps' premier touring areas.

Intermediates Most of Sölden's main slopes are genuine red runs ideal for keen intermediates, and there are serious verticals to be done – almost 1700m/5,580ft from Gaislachkogl to the village. There are several easy blacks. The long, quiet red to Gaislachalm is relatively easy, and ideal for high-speed cruising. Giggijoch offers gentler gradients, but the blues here get extremely crowded. Less confident intermediates should beware the tricky red runs to town from Giggijoch and the two blacks from Rettenbachtal.

Beginners The beginners' slopes are situated inconveniently – just above the village at Innerwald – and are prone to poor snow. Near-beginners can use the blues at Giggijoch. Stay away from Hochsölden.

Snowboarding Sölden is not ideal for beginners but there's great free-riding for experienced boarders. And all drag-lifts can be avoided.

Cross-country There are a couple of uninspiring loops by the river, plus small areas at Zwieselstein and Vent.

Queues Expect big queues at the Einzeiger and Seekogl chairs on the way to and from the glacier ('half an hour wait at peak times') – taking the Rettenbachtal ski route home allows you to avoid Seekogl. The six-pack up from the Rettenbachtal has improved the link from Giggijoch to Gaislachkogl.

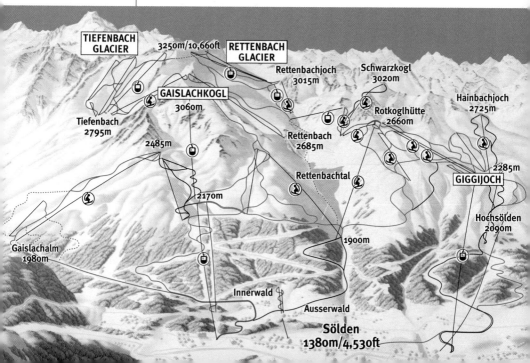

SNOWPIX.COM / CHRIS GILL

Gampealm gives a fine view up the Ötztal to the slopes of Hochgurgl ↓

Mountain restaurants The self-service places around Giggijoch can get very crowded. To escape the crowds try the places around Gaislachalm, or the big, modern Schwarzkogl on run 24. Gampealm, towards the end of piste 11, is a fine panoramic spot. Eugens Obstlerhütte below Hochsölden is a favourite – 'cosy, efficient; good food'.

Schools and guides The four schools all restrict class sizes to seven or eight. A recent reporter had a 'good' private lesson with the main school.

Facilities for children The Sölden school kindergarten takes children from the age of six months and the Yellow Power school from three years. There are special family lift pass deals.

STAYING THERE

How to go There are few UK packages.

Hotels The warmly welcoming Central (22600) is not only central but also the biggest and best in town – the only 5-star; beautiful pool. We were very happy in the Stefan (2237), right next to the Giggijoch gondola; good food. The Regina (2301) is recommended by a reporter. Several reporters have enjoyed Gasthof Grauer Bär (2564).

The Grüner-Hof B&B (2477) above town on run 7 is highly praised.

Eating out We end up in the Tavola in the hotel Rosengarten, because it doesn't take reservations, and haven't been disappointed. Recommendations from readers: Cafe Hubertus, Nudeltopf and Corso for pizza; and s'Pfandl at Ausserwald for Tirolean food.

Après-ski Sölden's après-ski is justly famous. It starts up the mountain, notably at Giggijoch, and progresses (possibly via the 'crowded' Philipp's Eisbar at Innerwald) to packed bars in and around the main street, and later to countless places with live bands and throbbing discos, often with table dancing and/or striptease. A 2007 reporter rates Snow Rock Cafe ('liveliest bar, best atmosphere'), Alibi's ('smartest bar, good live music') and the 'pleasant' Grizzly's for a quieter time – and on a quick visit to Rodelhütte to check out the 'go-go' girls found 'a surprisingly well-run operation'. There are nightly toboggan evenings – starting at Gaislachalm.

Off the slopes There's a sports centre, a swimming pool and an ice rink. Trips to Innsbruck are possible. Aqua Dome is a thermal spa centre at Längenfeld.

Sölden

SÖLL TOURIST OFFICE

Söll

The ski area is big, but the attractive village is surprisingly small and intimate. Shame it is not set right by the lifts

COSTS

① ② ③ ④ ⑤ ⑥

RATINGS

The slopes

Fast lifts	**
Snow	**
Extent	****
Expert	*
Intermediate	****
Beginner	***
Convenience	**
Queues	***
Mountain restaurants	**

The rest

Scenery	***
Resort charm	***
Off-slope	**

NEWS

For 2007/08 an additional 3km/1.5 miles of piste will be floodlit for night-skiing at Hochsöll.

For 2006/07 a six-pack with heated seats replaced the Tanzboden drag-lift between Hartkaiser and Brandstadl, improving the link with Ellmau.

The SkiWelt's snowmaking was further increased and now covers two-thirds of the pistes – 180km/112 miles.

206

- 🞦 Part of the SkiWelt, Austria's largest linked ski and snowboard area
- 🞦 Local slopes are the highest in the SkiWelt and north-facing, so they keep their snow relatively well
- 🞦 Plenty of cheap and cheerful pensions for those on a budget
- 🞦 Pretty village with lively après-ski
- 🞦 Snowmaking is now more extensive and well used; even so ...

- 🞥 Low altitude can mean poor snow
- 🞥 Long walk or inadequate bus service between the village and the lifts
- 🞥 Little to amuse experts or to challenge good intermediates
- 🞥 Not ideal for beginners, either
- 🞥 The SkiWelt slopes can get crowded at weekends and in high season – especially above Söll
- 🞥 Mostly short runs in the local sector

Söll has long been popular with British beginners and intermediates, attracting a mixture of singles looking for a fun week and families looking for a quiet time.

The resort is in fact far from ideal for beginners but, when the snow is good, Söll can be a great place for intermediates – cruising the attractive, friendly pistes of Austria's largest linked area. You now get to enjoy Austria's largest snowmaking operation too, which means that the lack of altitude is less of a problem than it was – but of course snowmaking is not a complete solution.

Many visitors are surprised by the small size of the village and the long trek out to the slopes. We'd prefer to stay near the lifts, and trek into the village in the evening. Bear in mind, also, that at this end of the SkiWelt, around the area high point of Hohe Salve, there are alternative bases that might suit you better – Itter, Hopfgarten and Brixen, dealt with at the end of this chapter.

THE RESORT

Söll is a small, pretty, friendly village, bypassed by the main valley road; you can explore it in a few minutes. New buildings are traditional in design and there's a huge church near the centre, its graveyard lit by candles. There aren't many shops.

The slopes are a bus- or taxi-ride or a 15-minute walk from the centre, the other side of a busy road with a pedestrian tunnel underneath. You can leave your equipment at the bottom of the gondola for a small charge.

There is some accommodation out near the lifts, but most is in or around the village centre and the ski-bus service is heavily criticised by reporters ('crowded', 'totally inadequate', 'we wasted 40 minutes queuing' were 2006 comments). If staying in the village, a location on the edge nearest the lifts means you can walk to the slopes. The far side of the village has the advantage that you can board the bus there before it gets too crowded. Some guest houses are literally miles from the centre and lifts, and the ski-bus does not serve every nook and cranny of this sprawling community.

THE MOUNTAINS

The SkiWelt is the largest mountain circuit in Austria, linking seven resorts. It will easily keep an early or average intermediate amused for a week. This huge area is covered by a single piste map. The completely useless map in use for some years was replaced last season by a brand new one which is much better in general, but still difficult to use in parts. Most runs are

Hochsöll is a sunny mid-mountain area, about 450m/1,480ft above the village (down in the cloud) →

DAVID MAXWELL-LEES

KEY FACTS

Resort	700m
	2,300ft

Entire SkiWelt	
Slopes	620-1830m
	2,030-6,000ft
Lifts	94
Pistes	250km
	155 miles
Blue	43%
Red	48%
Black	9%
Snowmaking	180km
	112 miles

LIFT PASSES

SkiWelt Wilder Kaiser-Brixental

Prices in €

Age	1-day	6-day
under 16	18	84
16 to 17	28	135
over 18	35	168

Free under 7
Senior no deals
Beginner limited pass

Notes
Covers Wilder Kaiser-Brixental area from Going to Westendorf, and the ski-bus; single ascent and part-day options

Alternative passes
Kitzbüheler Alpenskipass covers five large ski areas: Schneewinkel (St Johann), Kitzbühel, SkiWelt, Wildschönau and Alpbachtal

easy, and short – which means that getting around the area can take time, despite increasing numbers of fast lifts.

The SkiWelt pass also covers Westendorf, though its slopes are not linked (you take a bus from Brixen); from there you can also progress to the Kirchberg-Kitzbühel slopes – see the Westendorf chapter. These, along with Waidring, Fieberbrunn and St Johann, are possible day trips covered by the Kitzbüheler Alpenskipass.

THE SLOPES
Short run network

A gondola takes all but complete beginners up to the mid-mountain shelf of Hochsöll, where there are a couple of short lifts and connections in several directions.

These include an eight-seat gondola to the high point of Hohe Salve. From here there are stunning views and runs down to Kälbersalve, Rigi and Hopfgarten. Rigi can also be reached

by chairs and runs without going to Hohe Salve – to which it is itself linked by chairs. Rigi is also the start of runs down to Itter. From Kälbersalve you can head down south-facing runs to Brixen or up to Zinsberg and Eiberg and towards Ellmau.

A quicker way to Ellmau without taking as many south-facing slopes is by using a cable-car from Hochsöll.

We continue to receive criticism of the piste map, which is hopelessly over-ambitious in trying to show the whole area in a single view. Reporters prefer the 3D pop-up MountMap which costs 5 euros – 'An excellent investment,' says a 2006 visitor.

There's night-skiing available at Hochsöll.

TERRAIN-PARKS
You have to travel

There's none locally, but there's a park at Ellmau and a long-standing and popular park at Westendorf.

SNOW RELIABILITY
Erratic – but has artificial help

Leaving aside the generally poor 2007 season, recent winters have been great for the SkiWelt, with several reporters experiencing good fresh powder for much of their holidays. But it is not always like that, and with a low average height, and important links that get a lot of sun, the snow can suffer badly in warm weather and from precipitation falling as rain. So the

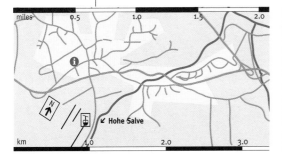

snowmaking that the SkiWelt has installed is essential. At 180km/112 miles and covering over 70 per cent of the area's pistes, it is Austria's biggest snowmaking installation. Reporters are regularly impressed by its use and efforts to maintain the pistes in times of drought. We were there one January before any major snowfalls, and snowmaking was keeping the links open well. It did not, however, stop slush and ice forming.

FOR EXPERTS
Not a lot
The two black runs from Hohe Salve towards Hochsöll and Kälbersalve and the black run alongside the Brixen gondola are the only challenging pistes. There are further blacks in Scheffau and Ellmau, but the main challenges are off-piste – from Brandstadl down to Söll, for example.

FOR INTERMEDIATES
Mainly easy runs
When blessed with good snow – not something to bank on – the SkiWelt is a paradise for early intermediates and those who love easy cruising. It is a big area and you really get a feeling of travelling around. There are lots of blue runs and many of the reds could be blue. The main challenge you may find is when the snow isn't perfect – ice and slush can make even gentle slopes seem tricky. In general the most difficult slopes are those from the mid-stations to the valleys – to Blaiken, Brixen and Söll, for example.

FOR BEGINNERS
Not ideal
The big area of nursery slopes between the main road and the gondola station is fine when snow is good – gentle, spacious, uncrowded and free from

Söll is a good place to try out boarding: slopes are gentle and there are plenty of gondolas and chairs. For competent boarders it's more limited – the slopes of the SkiWelt are tame. A reporter recommends the Scheffau school.

good skiers whizzing past. But it can get icy or slushy. In poor snow the Hochsöll area may be used. Progression to longer runs is likely to be awkward – there aren't many blue runs in this part of the SkiWelt. One is the narrow blue from Hochsöll, on which fast learners can get home when the run is not too icy.

FOR CROSS-COUNTRY
Neighbouring villages are better

Söll has 30km/19 miles of local trails but they are less interesting than the 15km/9 miles between Hopfgarten and Kelchsau or the ones around and

beyond Ellmau. There is a total of 170km/106 miles in the SkiWelt area. Lack of snow-cover can be a problem.

QUEUES
Some high-season waits

Lift upgrades have greatly improved this once queue-prone area. But the nursery drag up to the gondola at Söll remains a serious obstacle, particularly at ski school time in the mornings, and there are several bottlenecks at slow chairs around the mountain (including in the Rigi area). When snow is poor, the links between Zinsberg and Eiberg get crowded.

ZINSBERG 1675m

Very sunny slopes, with the usual worries about the effect on snow conditions

HOHE SALVE 1830m/6,000ft

Zinsberg

Filzboden

Hochbrixen 1240m

Hochbrixen

Brixen 800m

Foisching

Kälbersalve 1545m

RIGI 1530m

The highest and most testing slopes in the area, with some of the best snow

1200m

Bus link to Westendorf, which in turn links with the slopes of Kitzbühel

Westendorf 800m/2,620ft

Aualm

Hohe Salve

hsöll

Hexen

venmoos

Salvista

Salvenbahn

Hopfgarten 620m

MOUNTAIN RESTAURANTS
Good, but crowded

There are quite a few jolly little chalets scattered about, but we have had a few complaints of insufficient seating and long queues. There are three places at Hochsöll; the one called Hochsöll itself is reportedly 'excellent', but the atmospheric converted cow shed Stöckalm gets readers' vote: 'highly recommended' for 'superb spit-roasted chicken' – as elsewhere, you have to eat early or late to avoid the queues. The highly rated Hohe Salve (top of the gondola) offers a large revolving terrace and 'stunning views' – accessible to non-skiers via a moving carpet. The Stoagrub'nhütte above Hopfgarten serves 'generous and reasonably priced spaghetti'. Above Brixen the Filzalm is a good place for a quick drink on the way back from the circuit. Check out our Ellmau chapter for more recommendations in that sector of the SkiWelt.

SCHOOLS AND GUIDES
A good reputation

The Söll-Hochsöll school has a fairly good reputation. A 2007 reporter and her family enjoyed 'very good' lessons; the children 'were confidently doing red runs by the end of the week', but groups were large ('up to 12'). Another visitor 'improved immensely due to excellent instruction.'

FACILITIES FOR CHILDREN
Fast becoming a family resort

Söll has fairly wide-ranging facilities – the Söll-Hochsöll ski kindergarten, a Mini-club, which looks after children aged three to five who don't want to spend all day on the slopes, and a special kids-only drag and slope on the opposite side of the village to the main lifts. Reports welcome.

STAYING THERE

HOW TO GO
Mostly cheap, cheerful gasthofs

The major mainstream tour operators offer packages here.

Hotels There is a wide choice of simple gasthofs, pensions and B&Bs, and an adequate amount of better-quality hotel accommodation – mainly 3-star.
****Greil (5289) Attractive, but out of the centre and far from the lifts.
****Postwirt (5081) Attractive, central and traditional, with built-in stube.
****Alpenpanorama (5309) Far from

lifts but with own bus stop; wonderful views; pleasant rooms; good cakes.
***Bergland (5454) Well placed between the village and lifts.
***Tulpe (5223) Next to the lifts.
***Feldwebel (5224) Central.
***Hexenalm (5544) Next to the lifts.
***Gasthof Tenne (5282) B&B gasthof between centre and main road.
Chalets There are few catered chalets but a couple of big 'club hotels' run by British tour operators.
Apartments The central Aparthotel Schindlhaus has nice accommodation. Some of the best apartments in town are attached to the Bergland hotel, but a 2007 reporter recommends the 'ideally located' Alpin apartments ('fabulous', 'outstanding in terms of cleanliness and space').

EATING OUT
A fair choice

Some of the best restaurants are in hotels. The Greil and Postwirt ('extensive and delicious New Year buffet') are good. The Schindlhaus is said to be the best, at least if you enjoy 'rich meat' dishes. Giovanni does excellent, large pizzas, while other places worth a visit include the Dorfstub'n ('varied menu, extremely good steaks') and the Venezia.

APRES-SKI
Still some very loud bars

Söll is not as raucous as it used to be, but it's still very lively and a lot of places have live music. The Salvenstadl (Cow Shed) bar is regularly recommended by reporters ('nice atmosphere', 'the best live music'). The Whisky-Mühle is a large disco that can get a little rowdy, especially after the bars close. Buffalo's is popular and the Hotel Austria bar has 'cool music and pool tables.' Rossini is a 'lovely, modern bar,' recommended for cocktails and live music.

OFF THE SLOPES
Not bad for a small village

You could spend a happy day in the wonderfully equipped Panoramabad: taking a sauna, swimming, lounging about. There's tobogganing from the top of the gondola. The large baroque church would be the pride of many tourist towns. There are numerous coach excursions, including trips to Salzburg, Innsbruck and even Vipiteno over in Italy.

SCHOOLS

Söll-Hochsöll
t 5454

Classes
5 4-hr days: €133
Private lessons
€52 for 1hr; each additional person €25

CHILDREN

Mini-club
t 0664 4412 2773
9am–4.30, Sun to Fri;
ages 6mnth to 5
Mini-club (ski school)
t 5454
9.30–4pm, Sun to Thu; ages 3 to 5

Ski school
Takes children from 5 to 14 for 4hr daily (5 days €133)

GETTING THERE

Air Salzburg 94km/58 miles (2hr); Innsbruck 73km/45 miles (1½hr)

Rail Wörgl (13km/8 miles) or Kufstein (15km/9 miles); bus to resort

ACTIVITIES
Indoor Swimming, sauna, solarium, massage, bowling, squash
Outdoor Natural ice rink (skating, curling), sleigh rides, 3km/ 2 miles of floodlit ski and toboggan runs, walks, paragliding

Scheffau 745m/2,440ft

This is one of the most attractive of the SkiWelt villages.

THE RESORT

Scheffau is a rustic little place complete with pretty white church. It is spacious yet not sprawling, and has a definite centre 1km/0.5 miles off the busy main road (away from the slopes), which increases its charm at the cost of convenience – you can ski to the SkiWelt lifts at Blaiken (where there are several hotels) but you need a bus to get back.

THE MOUNTAIN

Scheffau is well placed for the SkiWelt's best (and most central and snow-sure) section of pistes.

Slopes Two gondolas (including an eight-seater) give rapid access directly to Brandstadl from Blaiken.

Snow reliability Eiberg is the place to go when snow is poor.

Experts The pistes above Blaiken are some of the longest and steepest in the SkiWelt.

Intermediates This is as good a base as any in the area.

Beginners The nursery slope is in the village, nowhere near other slopes, making Scheffau a poor choice for mixed-ability parties; but a reporter rates the easy blues at Brandstadl as 'excellent for beginner snowboarders'.

Cross-country See Söll and Ellmau.

Queues The second gondola has cut weekend queues at Blaiken.

Mountain restaurants See Söll, Ellmau.

Schools and guides The school is well regarded, but groups can be large. A reporter's private snowboarding lesson was 'the best I've ever had'.

Facilities for children Both the ski kindergarten and non-ski nursery have good reputations. The children's ski area and school 'Kinder-Kaiserland' is also reported to be 'very good'. And excellent progress was made by a four-year-old at Ski Esprit's nursery.

STAYING THERE

How to go Major operators offer packages here.

Hotels The best hotels – both with pool, sauna and steam room – are the 4-star Kaiser (8000) and 3-star Alpin (8556) – 'excellent food, lots of choice, spacious rooms'. Pool ('a bit cold') and sauna. The Zum Wilden Kaiser (8118) has 'a sauna and good fish dishes'.

Blaiken (8126) and Waldhof (8122) are good value gasthofs near the Blaiken gondolas. And the central Gasthof Weberbauer (8115) is said to be 'good value' and 'efficient'.

Eating out There aren't many village restaurants. Donatello is a 'good pizza place', says a visitor.

Après-ski 'Non-existent,' says one happy reporter, but another said the Red Bull had 'full-on hardcore music in a tent'. The usual rep-organised events such as bowling and tobogganing are available.

Off the slopes Walking apart, there is little to do. Tour operators organise trips to Innsbruck and Salzburg.

Hopfgarten 620m/2,030ft

Hopfgarten is an unspoiled, friendly, traditional resort off the main road.

THE RESORT

The village is a good size: small enough to be intimate, large enough to have plenty of off-slope amenities. Most hotels are within five minutes' walk of the lift to Rigi.

THE MOUNTAIN

Hopfgarten is at the western extremity of the SkiWelt.

Slopes Hopfgarten offers queue-free access to Rigi and Hohe Salve – the high point of the main SkiWelt circuit.

Terrain-parks None locally but it's a short bus ride to Westendorf.

Snow reliability The resort's great weakness is the poor snow quality on the south-west-facing home slope – especially vulnerable in late season.

Experts Experts should venture off-piste for excitement.

Intermediates When snow is good, the runs down to Hopfgarten and the nearby villages of Brixen and Itter are some of the best in the SkiWelt.

Beginners There is a beginners' slope in the village, but it is sunny as well as low; lack of snow-cover means paying for a lift pass to higher slopes. There are few easy longer runs to progress to in this part of the SkiWelt.

Snowboarding The SkiWelt is best suited to free-riding the extensive intermediate slopes.

Cross-country Hopfgarten is one of the best cross-country bases in the area. There are fine trails to Kelchsau (11km/7 miles) and Niederau (15km/ 9 miles), and the Itter-Bocking loop (15km/9 miles) starts nearby.

Phone numbers
From elsewhere in Austria add the prefix 05358 (Wilder Kaiser, Scheffau), 05333 (Söll), 05332 (Hohe Salve), 05335 (Hopfgarten, Itter), 05334 (Brixen); from abroad use the prefix +43 and omit the initial '0'

TOURIST OFFICES

WILDER KAISER
(Söll, Scheffau, Going, Ellmau)
t 505
www.wilderkaiser.info

Söll
t 5216
soell@wilderkaiser.info

Scheffau
t 7373
scheffau@wilderkaiser.info

HOHE SALVE
(Hopfgarten, Itter)
t 76007
info@hohe-salve.com
www.hohe-salve.com

Hopfgarten
t 2322
hopfgarten@hohe-salve.com

Itter
t 2670
itter@hohe-salve.com

BRIXEN
t 8433
brixen@kitzbuehel-alpen.com
www.kitzbuehel-alpen.com

SKIWELT
www.skiwelt.at

Westendorf's trails are close. But all of these trails are at valley level.

Queues We've had no reports of morning queues to leave the village since an eight-seater gondola replaced the old chair-lift a few years ago.

Mountain restaurants See Söll.

Schools and guides Partly because Hopfgarten seems to attract large numbers of Australians, English is widely spoken in the two schools.

Facilities for children Hopfgarten is a family resort, with a nursery and ski kindergarten.

STAYING THERE

How to go Cheap and cheerful gasthofs, pensions and little private B&Bs are the norm here.

Hotels The comfortable hotels Hopfgarten (3920) and Sporthotel Fuchs (2420) are both well placed for the main lift.

Eating out Most of the restaurants are hotel-based, but there are exceptions, including a Chinese and a pizzeria.

Après-ski Après-ski is generally quiet, though a lively holiday can usually be ensured if you go with Aussie-dominated Contiki Travel.

Off the slopes Off-slope amenities include swimming, riding, bowling, skating, tobogganing and paragliding. The railway makes trips to Salzburg, Innsbruck and Kitzbühel possible.

Itter 700m/2,300ft

Itter is a tiny village halfway around the mountain between Söll and Hopfgarten, with a gondola just outside the village up to Hochsöll above Söll, and so into the SkiWelt.

There's a hotel and half a dozen gasthofs and B&Bs. The school has a rental shop, and there are nursery slopes close to hand – but here are few easy longer runs to progress to in this part of the SkiWelt.

Brixen 800m/2,620ft

It may not be pretty, but Brixen has a queue-free, high-capacity gondola up to the main SkiWelt slopes.

THE RESORT

Brixen im Thale is a very scattered roadside village at the south-east edge of the main SkiWelt area, close to Westendorf (which links to Kitzbühel). The main hotels are near the railway station, a bus-ride from the lifts.

THE MOUNTAIN

Brixen is on the south side of the main SkiWelt circuit, and a short bus-ride from separate Westendorf.

Slopes The gondola takes you to Hochbrixen, where lifts diverge for Hohe Salve and Söll, or Astberg and Ellmau. There's a small area of north-facing runs, including nursery slopes, on the other side of the village. A regular visitor reported a nasty incident involving a liftie who was inside his hut and therefore failed to stop a chair-lift when her 10-year-old son slipped and fell under it, and who then threw her son at the seat of the chair. We hope this was a one-off.

Terrain-parks None locally but there's a good park nearby at Westendorf.

Snow reliability A chain of snow-guns on the main south-facing piste helps to preserve the snow as long as possible and the area continues to benefit from major investment in snowmaking.

Experts The black run alongside the Brixen gondola is one of the few challenging pistes in the area.

Intermediates When snow is good, Brixen has some of the best slopes in the SkiWelt – including some challenging ones.

Beginners The nursery slopes are secluded and shady, but meeting up with friends for lunch is a hassle – the area is a bus-ride from the village.

Snowboarding See Söll.

Cross-country In addition to valley-floor trails, a 3km/2 mile loop up the mountain at Hochbrixen provides fine views and fairly reliable snow.

Queues Lift upgrades have improved the once queue-prone area.

Mountain restaurants The Filzalm above Brixen has been recommended.

Schools and guides The ski school runs the usual group classes, and mini-groups for five to seven people.

Facilities for children There is an all-day ski kindergarten.

STAYING THERE

How to go There are plenty of hotels and pensions.

Hotels Alpenhof (88320) and Sporthotel (8191) are both 4-stars with pools.

Eating out Mainly hotel-based, but the restaurant opposite the gondola has been recommended.

Après-ski Après-ski is quiet, but livelier Westendorf is a short taxi-ride away.

Off the slopes Activities include tennis, hotel-based spa facilities and days out to Salzburg, Innsbruck and Kitzbühel.

St Anton

If what you seek is dumps, bumps, boozing and bopping, there's nowhere quite like it – and with a neat Tirolean town as a bonus

NEWS

St Anton celebrated its 70th anniversary last season with the opening of the jumbo Galzig gondola. It has replaced the first stage of the queue-prone cable-car to Galzig. The much-talked about 'ferris wheel' design allows direct access at ground level. Each cabin carries 24 people, and the hourly capacity is three times that of the old lift.

Snowmaking is to be improved for 2007/08.

+ Varied terrain for experts and adventurous intermediates – and a lot of it, once you include Lech-Zürs, a bus-ride away

+ Heavy snowfalls, backed up by a fair amount of snowmaking

+ Very lively après-ski, from mid-afternoon onward

+ Despite expansion, the resort retains some traditional charm – and the animated village centre is mainly car-free

+ Improved lift system has cut queues from the base areas, but ...

− Still some queues up the mountain

− Slopes far from ideal for beginners or timid intermediates

− Pistes can get very crowded – some of them dangerously so

− Most of the tough stuff is off-piste – including many popular runs

− Main slopes get a lot of sun, quickly affecting the snow conditions

− Resort spreads widely, with long treks from some lodgings to key lifts and bars

− Can get rowdy, with noisy drunks in the central streets in the early hours

St Anton is undeniably a big-league resort. For competent skiers and riders with an appetite for non-stop action and the stamina to keep up with it, we'd rate it even higher: it is one of the great resorts, with an après-ski scene that can be as taxing as the splendid bowls below the Valluga. The combination draws ski bums from around the world, as well as lots of regular holiday visitors.

But it won't suit everyone, as our list of ▬ points makes clear. If you are thinking of trying an Austrian change from Val d'Isère, or of taking a step up from Kitzbühel, take full account of this list.

Those going back to St Anton after a long interval may be amazed to find that the railway has disappeared – moved from the centre to the fringe of the village for the 2001 Alpine World Ski Championships. Those new to the resort may simply wonder why it has a featureless gap between the town and the lifts (where the railway track used to be).

Yet again we have to report zero progress in improving the dangerously busy piste down the Steissbachtal and on down to the village. What's needed, as we have been saying for five years, is a new piste to the village from Galzig.

THE RESORT

St Anton is at the foot of the road up to the Arlberg pass, at the eastern end of a lift network that spreads across to St Christoph and over the pass to Stuben. These two tiny villages are described at the end of the chapter.

The resort is a long, sprawling mixture of traditional and modern buildings crammed into a narrow valley. It used to be sandwiched between the busy bypass road and the mainline railway; but the railway was moved in 2000, and where there were tracks there is now a little area of parkland.

Although it is crowded and

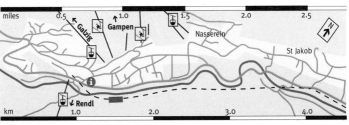

commercialised, St Anton is full of character, its traffic-free main street lined by traditional-style buildings. It is an attractively bustling place, day and night. Its shops offer little in the way of entertainment, but meet everyday needs well – self-catering reporters have observed that it has a 'wonderful Spar', for example.

The main hub of the resort is around the base stations of the lifts to Gampen (a fast quad chair) and to Galzig (a fancy jumbo gondola that reporters heap praise on: 'a mechanical miracle of engineering – very smart', 'better than a fairground ferris wheel', and 'beautifully illuminated at night'), which replaced the inadequate cable-car last season. The main street is only a short walk from these lifts, and for most purposes a location on or close to this main street is ideal.

The resort spreads down the valley, thinning out before broadening again to form the suburb of Nasserein. This backwater now has an eight-person gondola up to Gampen, and makes an appealing base for a quiet time. The nightlife action is a short bus-ride or 15-minute walk away ('quite a hike').

Staying in the suburbs of St Anton, between the centre and Nasserein, is also a more attractive idea since the Fang chair-lift, which gives access to the Nasserein gondola, was built.

On the other side of the main road a gondola goes up to the Rendl area. This is linked one-way by rope tows and a moving carpet from the end of St Anton's main street – but the return still involves a bus-ride or short walk.

St Anton spreads up the hill to the west of the centre, towards the Arlberg pass – first to Oberdorf, then Gastig, 10 minutes' walk from the centre. Further up the hill are the suburbs of Dengert and Moos – a long way out, but quite close to the slopes.

Regular buses go to Stuben, Zürs and Lech (the latter two described in the Lech chapter) and the much less well-known but worthwhile Sonnenkopf area above Klösterle. The ski-buses are free but involve a couple of changes. These buses can get crowded early and late in the day and have provoked several complaints by recent reporters. For a small fee, the post-bus offers a direct, less-crowded alternative. Minibus-style taxis can be economic if widely shared.

Serfaus, Nauders, Ischgl and Sölden are also feasible outings by car.

THE MOUNTAINS

The main slopes are essentially open: only the lower Gampen runs and the run from Rendl to the valley offer much shelter from bad weather.

St Anton vies with Val d'Isère for the title of 'resort with most underclassified slopes'. There are plenty of blue pistes that would be red in many other resorts, and plenty of reds that would be black – although, paradoxically, none of the blacks is seriously steep.

Many of the most popular steep runs marked on the piste map are classified as 'ski routes'. These have markers but they are essentially ungroomed and, more importantly, are not patrolled and are protected from avalanches only 'in the immediate vicinity of the markers'.

Clearly you should not ski such runs alone, and the piste map recommends them only for people with 'alpine experience or with a ski instructor'. In theory this puts the routes out of bounds for many holidaymakers – absurd, when these runs lie at the

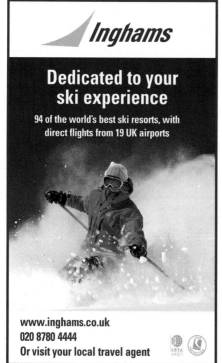

↑ St Anton's high ungroomed ski routes are a key part of its appeal to good skiers and boarders
JILL COOK

LIFT PASSES

Arlberg Ski Pass

Prices in €

Age	1-day	6-day
under 16	25	116
16 to 19	37	167
20 to 64	41	194
over 65	37	167

Free season pass €10 if under 8 or over 75

Senior min. age for senior women is 60

Beginner points ticket

Notes
Covers all St Anton, St Christoph, Lech, Zürs and Stuben lifts, and linking bus between Rauz and Zürs; also covers Sonnenkopf (10 lifts) at Klösterle, 7km/ 4 miles west of Stuben (bus link from Stuben); single ascent, half-day and pedestrian options

heart of the resort's appeal. On Rendl there is a lift serving no pistes but only a single ski route, which more or less follows the line of the lift. Why is it not a patrolled piste?

The Arlberg piste map also shows (at Stuben and Lech) lots of 'high-alpine touring runs', which are not marked on the ground at all and not protected against avalanche.

The Arlberg lift companies seem determined to present all their widely spread terrain in a single view. The map was redesigned recently, and is considerably improved – but smaller, separate maps would be better.

Reporters regularly complain of poor and limited piste grooming; many blue runs are steep enough to develop moguls when snow is soft. And in 2007 we got complaints of poor piste marking with poles too far apart to be safe in bad light. The local cable TV, showing the state of the pistes and queues, can be very useful.

THE SLOPES
Large linked area

St Anton's slopes fall into three main sectors, two of them linked.

The major sector is that beneath the local high-spot, the **Valluga**, accessed by the new jumbo gondola to Galzig, then a cable-car. The tiny top stage of the cable-car to the Valluga itself is mainly for sightseeing – you can take skis or a board up only if you have a guide to lead you down the tricky off-piste run to Zürs. The slightly lower station of Valluga Grat gives access to St Anton's famous high, sunny bowls, and to the long, beautiful red/blue run to Alpe Rauz, at the western end of St Anton's own slopes. From here there's a relatively new six-pack, the Valfagehr, to return, or you can go on to explore the rather neglected slopes of Stuben.

These high runs can also be accessed by riding the Schindlergrat triple chair, though some involve a half-hour hike – even so, this can be quicker than waiting for the cable-car, as an energetic reporter has proved.

Other runs from **Galzig** go south-west to St Christoph and east into the Steissbachtal.

Beyond this valley, with lift and piste links in both directions, is the **Kapall-Gampen** sector, reachable by chair-lift from central St Anton or gondola from Nasserein. From Gampen at mid-mountain, pistes lead back to St Anton and Nasserein. Or you can

ride a six-pack on up to Kapall to ski the treeless upper mountain.

A handful of lifts (including a fast six-pack to Gampberg) serve the west-facing runs at the top of **Rendl**, with a single north-facing piste returning to the gondola bottom station.

The slopes above **Stuben**, described at the end of the chapter, should not be overlooked.

TERRAIN-PARKS
Head for Rendl

The 200m/66oft-long park on Rendl, just below the top of the gondola, doesn't touch the park over in neighbouring Lech maintenance-wise, but it will easily keep beginners and intermediates entertained. Due to its narrow nature the park has only a

single kicker line, in the form of 3-, 6- and 12-metre tabletops and a corner jump. Around the jumps are various rails. There's a large A-frame box, a small rainbow, an A-frame rail and a flat slidebox.

SNOW RELIABILITY
Generally very good cover

If the weather is coming from the west or north-west (as it often is), the Arlberg gets it first, and as a result St Anton and its neighbours get heavy falls of snow. They often have much better conditions than other resorts of a similar height, and we've had great fresh powder here as late as mid-April. But many of the slopes face south or south-east, causing icy or heavy conditions at times. It's vital to time

Underused area of worthwhile runs, though you have to put up with slow lifts (cold ones on the front side)

Albonagrat
2400m

ALBONA

1840m

Lech / Zurs ↓

Flexen Pass

Stuben

Rauz
1620m

Excellent long red/blue down towards Stuben – over 1000m/ 3,280ft vertical

Valfagehr

Arlenmähder

GALZIG
2185m

St Christoph

St Christoph
1800m/5,910ft

Rauz is the hub of the ski-bus services – you can ski to here and catch a bus to Lech

THE VALLUGA RUNS

The off-piste runs in the huge bowl beneath the summit of the Valluga, reached by either the Schindlergrat chair or the Valluga I cable-car, are justifiably world-famous. In good snow, this whole area is an off-piste delight for experts.

Except immediately after a fresh snowfall, you can see tracks going all over the mountain. There are two main ski routes marked on the piste map – both long, steep descents that quickly get mogulled. The Schindlerkar is the first you come to and it divides into two – the Schindlerkar gully being the steeper option. For the second, wider and somewhat easier Mattun run, you traverse further at the top. Both these feed down into the Steissbachtal where there are lifts back up to Galzig and Gampen.

There are of course more adventurous ways down than the identified ski routes. The Schweinströge starts off in the same direction as the red run to Rauz, but you traverse the shoulder of the Schindler Spitze and descend a narrow gully. Perhaps the ultimate challenge is to ski off the back of the Valluga – a great adventure, according to readers who have done it. More info in our off-piste feature panel.

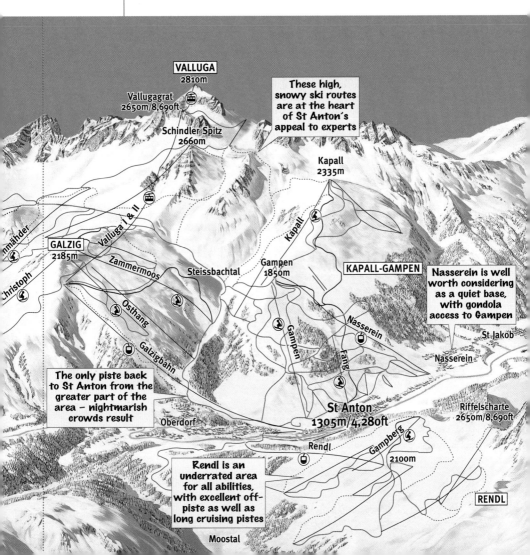

VALLUGA
2810m

Vallugagrat
2650m/8,690ft

Schindler Spitz
2666m

Kapall
2335m

These high, snowy ski routes are at the heart of St Anton's appeal to experts

GALZIG
2185m

Valluga I & II

Zammermoos

Steissbachtal

Gampen
1850m

KAPALL-GAMPEN

Nasserein is well worth considering as a quiet base, with gondola access to Gampen

Schmähder

Christoph

Osthang

Galzigbahn

Nasserein

St Jakob

Nasserein

The only piste back to St Anton from the greater part of the area – nightmarish crowds result

Gampen

Fang

Oberdorf

St Anton
1305m/4,280ft

Rendl

Gampberg

Riffelscharte
2650m/8,690ft

Rendl is an underrated area for all abilities, with excellent off-piste as well as long cruising pistes

2100m

RENDL

Moostal

descents of the steeper runs off the Valluga to get decent conditions, or you can find yourself in trouble.

The lower runs are now well equipped with snowmaking, which generally ensures the home runs remain open. As an April visitor said, 'Pistes were kept open while surrounded by green fields.'

FOR EXPERTS
One of the world's great areas
St Anton vies with Chamonix, Val d'Isère and a handful of other resorts for the affections of experts. There are countless opportunities for going off-piste, and guidance is very desirable. Read the feature panels on the Valluga runs (on the previous page) and off-piste routes (facing page).

Lower down, there are challenging runs in many directions from both Galzig and Kapall-Gampen. These lower runs can be doubly tricky if the snow has been hit by the sun.

Don't overlook the Rendl area, which has plenty of open space served by the top lifts, and several quite challenging itineraries. This is a great area for a mixed group, especially.

One of our reporters particularly liked the quieter Sonnenkopf area, down-valley from Stuben, for its excellent off-piste route to Langen. See also the Stuben section.

Each of the main sectors has its toughest piste classified as black; a couple deserve their classification, but most don't – the Fang race course from Gampen used to be red, in fact. The distinction between reds and blacks is in general a fine one.

FOR INTERMEDIATES
Some real challenges
St Anton is well suited to good, adventurous intermediates. As well as lots of testing pistes, they will be able to try the Mattun ski route and the easier of the Schindlerkar routes from Valluga Grat (see Valluga Runs feature panel). The run from Schindler Spitze to Rauz is very long (over 1000m/3,300ft vertical), varied and ideal for good (and fit) intermediates. Alternatively, turn off from this part-way down and take the Steissbachtal to the lifts back to Galzig or Gampen. The Kapall-Gampen section is also interesting, with sporty bumps among trees on the lower half. Good intermediates may enjoy the men's downhill run from the top to town.

Timid intermediates will find St Anton less to their taste. There are few easy cruising pistes; many blues get bumpy, especially just after a snowfall. The most obvious cruisers are the short blues on Galzig and the Steissbachtal (aka 'Happy Valley'). These are reasonably gentle but get uncomfortably crowded (see 'Queues'). When the Steissbachtal is closed, the only piste home from Galzig is a steepish black run. The blue from Kapall to Gampen is wide and cruisy.

boarding

Many consider St Anton as the Mecca of Austrian free-riding. Countless steep gullies and backcountry powder fields with challenging terrain form a big draw for advanced riders. The Arlberg Snowboard academy has a great reputation for showing all levels where best to apply their respective skills – whether you are a beginner on the wide-open pistes, or a more advanced rider wanting guidance through the trees or steep and deep off-piste. Rendl is an excellent mountain for free-riders and freestylers alike.

The Arlberg region is an off-piste skier's dream – renowned for its consistently high snowfall record, incredible deep powder and enormous diversity of terrain. We invited Piste to Powder Mountain Guides to give us an introduction to the possibilities. Remember you should never explore far off-piste without a guide.

Piste to Powder
Mountain Guides
St. Anton – Austria

Piste to Powder
Mountain Guides

All day guiding 9am to 5pm. Choose from four skill levels. All safety equipment provided.

t 01661 824318
00 43 664 174 6282

info@pistetopowder.com
www.pistetopowder.com

Runs from Rendl

After initial practice close to the pistes, the natural progression is to go beyond the furthest lift to access the wide rolling bowls of powder of Rossfall.

More serious routes from Rendl take you well away from all lifts. The North Face, accessed from the Gampberg six-seat chair, offers challenging terrain to the intermediate/confident off-piste skier. The Riffel chair-lifts access the imposing Hinter Rendl – a gigantic high-mountain bowl offering a huge descent down to St Anton, often in deep powder. A variant involves a climb to Rendl Scharte and a demanding descent with sections of 35° down the remote Malfontal to the village of Pettneu and a taxi back to St Anton.

Runs from Albona, above Stuben

Stuben's outstanding terrain, reached from the Albonagrat chair, is suited to the more experienced off-piste skier, as the descents are long. The open tree lines of the Langen forest, where the powder is regularly knee to waist deep, form some of the world's finest tree skiing. A 30-minute climb from Albonagrat, with skis on shoulder, opens up further outstanding terrain from Maroikopfe – either west, down undulating open slopes to Langen, or east, down steep 40° slopes to Ferwalltal, where this glorious run ends with a glass of wine at an old hunting lodge.

Runs from the Valluga

The legendary runs from the summit cable-car of the Valluga must be on the tick list of all keen and experienced off-piste skiers – the North Face, Bridge Couloir or East Couloir. Your pulse will race as you trace a steep ski line between cliff bands in the breathtaking scenery of the Pazieltal, leading down to Zürs. Here, at the top of the Madloch chair-lift and after a short hidden climb, you will be roped down into the steep Valhalla Couloir, accessing 1200m/3,940ft vertical of open slopes ending in the hamlet of Zug, close to Lech.

St Anton

219

In the under-rated Rendl area a variety of trails suitable for good and moderate intermediates criss-cross, including the long and genuinely blue Salzböden. There is a long tree-lined run (over 1000m/3,28oft vertical from the top) back to the valley gondola station. This is the best run in the area when visibility is poor, but it has some quite awkward, steep and narrow sections and gets very busy at the end of the day – early intermediates beware.

FOR BEGINNERS
Far from ideal
The best bet for beginners is to start at Nasserein, where the nursery slope is less steep than the one close to the main lifts. There are further slopes up at Gampen, and a short, gentle blue run at Rendl, served by an easy drag-lift. But there are no easy, uncrowded runs for beginners to progress to. A mixed party including novices would be better off staying in Lech or Zürs; more advanced skiers who want to explore St Anton can get on the bus.

FOR CROSS-COUNTRY
Limited interest
St Anton is not a great cross-country resort, but trails total around 35km/ 22 miles and snow conditions are usually good. There are a couple of uninspiring trails near town, another at St Jakob 3km/2 miles away, and a pretty trail through trees along the Ferwalltal to the foot of the Albona area. There is also a tiny loop at St Christoph. A couple of 2007 visitors took private cross-country lessons with the Arlberg Ski School and 'enjoyed them very much'.

QUEUES
Improvements continue, but ...
Queues are not the problem they once were, thanks to continuing lift upgrades – the latest being the replacement of the cable-car to Galzig by the gondola (see 'News'). This has reduced queueing significantly and speeded up access to Galzig.

But there are still problems up the mountain, notably the Valluga I cable-car from Galzig. In peak season,

SCHOOLS

Arlberg
t 3411
St Anton
t 3563

Classes
(Arlberg prices)
6 days (2hr am and
2hr pm) €213
Private lessons
€145 for 2hr; each
additional person €20

GUIDES

Piste to Powder
t 0664 174 6282
UK 01661 824318

CHILDREN

Kindergartens (run by ski schools)
t 3411 / 3563
From age 30mnth;
must be toilet trained

Ski schools
Both Austrian schools
take children aged
from 5 (6 days
including lunch €297)

especially when powder beckons, queues here can run into hours. Queues for the alternative Schindlergrat chair up from mid-mountain appear to have been eased by the fast Arlenmähder chair allowing access to the run to Rauz without going to the top.

The Zammermoos chair out of the Steissbachtal still generates queues (sadly, its singles line seems to be little-used). A 2007 reporter found it as quick to ski down to the new Galzig gondola as to wait in the long queues at the weekend. The Nasserein gondola is 'very efficient' and a visitor over New Year 'never encountered any queues there'.

At Rendl, the gondola gets busy when poor weather closes the lifts in the main area but one reporter was surprised to find that queues there were very 'orderly and polite'.

Perhaps more of a worry than the lift queues are the crowded pistes. Clearly the worst (at least when the top Valluga runs are open) is the Steissbachtal and the home run below it, which can be uncomfortably crowded even in January and a nightmare on a peak weekend. So acute is this problem at times that several reporters have recommended heading over to Rauz or St Christoph and getting a bus back to town rather than tangling with the Steissbachtal. There is talk of improvements last year, but nothing has appeared – and the real solution to this long-standing problem is an alternative blue run from Galzig to the village, to relieve the pressure. When heavy snow closes the top runs on the Valluga, the crowds shift to Rendl, where the home run again gets unpleasantly busy.

MOUNTAIN RESTAURANTS
Lots of options
Editors' choice It may not be a proper mountain restaurant, but we often lunch in St Christoph at the atmospheric Hospiz Alm (3625), famed for its slide down to the toilets as well as its table-service food and amazing wine cellar. Most reporters love it too ('couldn't have chosen anywhere more cheering'; 'it pleased even the fussiest eater in our group') – though a couple of recent visitors complained of 'appalling' service. But next time we visit we are resolved to stay high and try the newish Verwall Stube at Galzig (2352501) – a serious table-service

place with great views, said to be 'in a class of its own'.

Worth knowing about The Arlberg Taja is a 'jolly and welcoming' alternative to the Hospiz Alm in St Christoph. Reader recommendations on Galzig include the Ulmer Hütte near the top of the Arlenmähder chair, the big, smart self-service restaurant at Galzig itself for 'superb views and tasty food'. Lower down, the Sennhütte offers 'excellent choices'. The Rodelalm on Gampen is a 'real hut with good food at low prices and a lovely fire' and does 'great knuckles of pork'. Just above the village, the Mooserwirt serves typical Austrian food at what seems a high price, but 'the portions are absolutely massive'; the Heustadl is popular with 'good choices and efficient service'; the Krazy Kanguruh does burgers, pizzas and snacks; and Taps Bar next door does 'good goulash soup' and at the end of the 2007 season 'half of St Anton was stripped down and sunbathing there'. Over on Rendl, the self-service Rendl restaurant has great views, 'excellent salad bar and immaculate toilets', but gets very busy. Better to head down the valley run to the 'rustic and welcoming' Bifang-Alm, for regional specialities and excellent service.

SCHOOLS AND GUIDES
Mixed reports
The St Anton school and the Arlberg school are now under the same ownership but continue to operate separately. The Arlberg school generates conflicting reports: one reporter commented, 'Not enough attention was paid to putting equal standards together and groups were big.' Another complained of old-fashioned technique: 'They need to turn the clock forward.' But some reporters are very happy: a 2007 adult beginner made 'good progress' with five days of group lessons. Another reader joined a top-level guided group and was impressed with the 'superb value' and 'non-stop high mileage covered'.

We have also had mixed reports on Piste to Powder, a specialist off-piste outfit run by British guide Graham Austick. 'A good balance of guiding to instruction and a professional attitude to safety' and 'very good guiding down two very long isolated powder runs, with no tracks or other skiers' said two readers. But two reports suggest some

Air Innsbruck 100km/62 miles (1½hr); Zürich 200km/124 miles (3hr); Friedrichshafen 140km/87 miles (1½hr)

Rail Mainline station in resort

guides are better than others. One couple and their daughter, beginners to off-piste, had a 'very disappointing' experience in 2007 when they were put in a group with more experienced skiers and given no instruction. We have reports of tour ops being stopped from supplying their own ski host to show guests around the pistes unless they hire an instructor too.

FACILITIES FOR CHILDREN
Nasserein 'ideal'
The youth centre attached to the Arlberg school is excellent, and the special slopes both for toddlers (at the bottom) and bigger children (at Gampen) are well done. At Nasserein there is a moving carpet lift on the baby slope, and a reporter rates this an 'absolutely ideal' place to stay with young kids. Family specialists Esprit Ski and Mark Warner both have their own childcare facilities in chalets or chalet-hotels in the Nasserein area, and Crystal has one in the village centre.

STAYING THERE

HOW TO GO
Austria's main chalet resort
There's a wide range of places to stay, from quality hotels to cheap and cheerful pensions and apartments. Inghams features a good selection and has some chalets as well.

Chalets Plenty of catered chalets are offered by UK operators. Flexiski's Amalien Haus has a great position on the main street, and was refurbished last season. Scott Dunn has operated four luxury chalets here since last season, with access to an outdoor hot-tub, and a five-minute a drive from the main lifts. Kaluma will have a new 10-bedroom chalet for 2007/08. Total and Crystal Finest have several chalets here, and Albus is a St Anton specialist operator with chalets in Nasserein. Mark Warner has a central, child-free (except during school holidays) chalet-hotel as well as its child-friendly one in Nasserein.

Hotels There are two 5-star hotels and lots of 4- and 3-stars and B&Bs.

*****Raffl's St Antoner Hof (2910) Best in town, but its position on the bypass is less than ideal. Pool.

↑ As you can see, St Anton spreads a long way down the valley

TVB ST ANTON AM ARLBERG

ACTIVITIES

Indoor Swimming pool (also hotel pools open to the public, with sauna and massage), fitness centre, tennis, squash, museum, library

Outdoor Cleared walking paths, natural ice rink (skating, curling), sleigh rides, snow-shoeing, tobogganing, paragliding

****Alte Post** (2553) Atmospheric place on main street with lively après-ski bar.

****Banyan** (30361) New for 2007/08, an up-market B&B with 39 rooms and a fitness centre with pool.

****Brunnenhof** (2293) 'Romantic and cosy with fantastic five course dinners.' In St Jakob, beyond Nasserein – hotel minibus to lifts.

****Post** (2213) Comfortable if uninspiring at the centre of affairs, close to both lifts and nightlife.

****Schwarzer Adler** (22440) Centuries-old inn on main street. Widely varying bedrooms. 'Good service', 'lovely pool'.

****Sporthotel** (3111) Central position, varied bedrooms, good food. Pool.

***Goldenes Kreuz** (22110) A comfortable B&B hotel halfway to Nasserein, ideal for cruising home.

***Grischuna** (2304) Welcoming and family-run in peaceful position up the hill west of town; close to the slopes.

***Rendlhof** (3100) in Nasserein: 'friendly'.

Nassereinhof (3366) Close to the Nasserein gondola. Family-run with sauna and steam room. Recommended for 'good home-cooked food'.

Haus Bachseite (3866) 'Large rooms and a most welcoming host.'

Pension Alpenheim (3389) 'Basic but good breakfast, ski-in/ski-out to Nasserein lifts.'

Apartments There are plenty available, but package deals are few and far between. Reporters like the Bachmann apartments ('really excellent', 'spacious and comfortable') and the H Strolz ('well equipped'), both in Nasserein, and Haus Rali at the western end of St Anton ('very friendly, family-owned, a bargain for New Year').

EATING OUT
Mostly informal

Places such as the Trödlerstube serve big portions of traditional Austrian food. The village museum's restaurant does 'excellent' upmarket food and wine in elegant panelled rooms. Quite different in style is Ben.venuto ('excellent food', 'impeccable service'), in the Arlberg-well.com building: stark decor and eclectic menu. Scotty's and Pomodoro (pizza) are popular with reporters. The Sporthotel Steakhouse is said to be 'excellent' and the Dolce Vita does 'good meals with friendly service'. A 2007 reporter enjoyed the 'top notch curry' at the Funky Chicken and a recent reporter found 'very good set menus' at the Grossmauer Chinese. The cosy Sonnbichl is recommended for its 'superb home-cooked food'. In Nasserein, the Tenne is noted for game dishes and Robi's Rodel-Stall at the end of the toboggan run has a cosy log fire.

APRES-SKI
Throbbing till late

St Anton's bars rock from mid-afternoon until the early hours. Après-ski starts in a collection of bars on the slopes above the village. The Krazy Kanguruh is probably the most famous but the Mooserwirt has an 'infectious happy buzz' and is now the 'in' place, filling up with revellers as soon as the lunch trade finishes – reputedly dispensing more beer than any other bar in Austria. One reporter thought sending streams of waiters into the crowds, laden with trays of beers to buy 'excellent'. The Heustadl is 'the best place to boogie Tirolean style, and shouldn't be missed'. All this is followed by a slide down the piste in the dark. The bars in town are in full swing by 4pm, too. Most are lively, with loud music; sophisticates looking for a quieter time are less well provided for. One 2007 visitor found the Anton bar 'a great place to hang out and watch the world go by', and another thought the restaurant at the Museum was a 'charming and very atmospheric place for a quiet drink'. The Hazienda and, for late-night dancing, the Stanton and Piccadilly ('good live music') are popular choices. Reporters have recommended Scotty's (in Mark Warner's chalet-hotel Rosanna, with happy hour), Bar Cuba ('a good party'), Jacksy's ('a relaxed pub'), Pub 37, Bobo's, Alibi, Kandahar ('best for watching sport') and Funky Chicken. The St Antoner Hof is suggested for pre-dinner 'canapés and champagne'. In Nasserein, the Fang House and 'jolly' Sonnegg are recommended.

OFF THE SLOPES
Some improvement
St Anton is a resort for keen skiers and riders. But the fitness, swimming and skating facilities of Arlberg-well.com are impressive and highly recommended by reporters. The village is lively during the day, but has few diverting shops. Getting by bus to the other Arlberg resorts is easy, as is visiting Innsbruck by train. Some of the

better mountain huts are accessible by lift or bus. A reporter suggests using the winter walking trails to visit Pettneu and another enjoyed the walk to Verwall.

STAYING DOWN THE VALLEY
Nice and quiet
Beyond Nasserein is St Jakob. It can be reached on snow, but is dependent on the free shuttle-bus in the morning.

Stuben 1405m/4,610ft

Stuben (in Vorarlberg) is linked by lifts and pistes over the Arlberg pass to St Anton (in Tirol). There are infrequent buses from the village to Lech/Zürs, and more frequent ones from Rauz, the roadside lift station for St Anton.

Dating back to the 13th century, Stuben is a small, unspoiled village, with an old church, a few unobtrusive hotels, a school, two or three bars, a couple of banks and a few little shops. Heavy snowfalls add to the charm.

The Albona above Stuben makes a refreshingly quiet change from the busy slopes of St Anton. It has north-facing slopes that hold powder well and some wonderful, deserted off-piste

St Anton

223

Phone numbers
From elsewhere in Austria add the prefix 05446 (St Anton and St Christoph), 05582 (Stuben); from abroad use the prefix +43 and omit the initial '0'

TOURIST OFFICES

St Anton
t 22690
info@stantonamarlberg.com
www.stantonamarlberg.com

St Christoph
www.tiscover.com/st.christoph

Stuben
t 399
info@stuben.at
www.stuben.com

descents, including beautiful long runs down to Langen and to St Anton. A regular visitor recommends the small Rasthaus Ferwall for lunch at the end of the latter. Staying within the lift network, the Berghaus is repeatedly recommended, not least for 'excellent rösti' – it's 'worth booking at lunchtime'. But a reporter who visited Stuben on a Monday lunchtime was surprised to find most places closed. The slow village chair can be a cold ride but blankets are available. A quicker and warmer way to get to St Anton in the morning, if you have a car, is to drive up the road to Rauz. Stuben has sunny nursery slopes separate from the main slopes, but lack of easy runs to progress to makes it unsuitable for beginners. A covered moving carpet has improved the link between Stuben and St Anton, at Rauz, omitting the need to ride the awkward drag-lift.

Evenings are quiet, but several places have a pleasant atmosphere. The charming old Post (761) and Albona (712) are very comfortable and owned by the same family.

St Christoph 1800m/5,910ft

A small collection of smart and pricey hotels, restaurants and bars just down from the summit of the Arlberg pass. There are decent beginner slopes served by drag-lifts and a fast quad chair-lift to the heart of St Anton's slopes at Galzig, but the blue back down is not an easy run to progress to. The Hospiz Alm here is one of our favourite mountain restaurants. St Christoph is linked by bus to St Anton and to Lech and Zürs.

It's quiet at night and not the place to be if you want to experience St Anton's lively après-ski scene every night. The best hotel of all is the huge 5-star Arlberg-Hospiz (2611), with luxurious health and spa facilities – recommended by a reporter for expensive but fine gourmet dining. A more affordable but still excellent looking place is the 4-star Maiensee (21610) right on the slopes by the high-speed quad chair up to Galzig and with health and spa facilities and treatments.

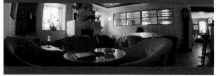

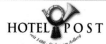

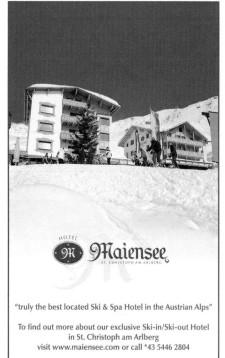

St Johann in Tirol

A traditional Tirolean resort appealing to those who want to spend as much time on jolly restaurant terraces as on the slopes

HOW IT RATES

The slopes

Fast lifts	**
Snow	**
Extent	*
Expert	*
Intermediate	***
Beginner	****
Convenience	***
Queues	****
Mountain restaurants	****

The rest

Scenery	***
Resort charm	***
Off-slope	****

NEWS

The Kitzbüheler shuttle-bus service offers transfers from Salzburg airport (from 30 euros).

KEY FACTS

Resort	650m
	2,130ft
Slopes	670-1700m
	2,200-5,580ft
Lifts	17
Pistes	60km
	37 miles
Blue	41%
Red	47%
Black	12%
Snowmaking	30km
	19 miles

+ Traditional traffic-free town centre

+ Lots of good mountain restaurants

+ Plenty of off-slope activities

+ Relatively good snow record

+ Easy to visit other resorts on the lift pass; just as well, because ...

− Local slopes very limited, with little to interest experts or keen, mileage-hungry intermediates

− Can be crowded on peak weekends, or when nearby resorts with less reliable snow are suffering

This friendly resort is an attractive place for beginners and leisurely part-timers who like to spend as much time having drinks and lunch as they do actually cruising the slopes. Keener and more proficient skiers and boarders will soon get bored unless they are prepared to visit surrounding resorts – nearby ones covered by the local pass, others by the Kitzbüheler Alpenskipass.

THE RESORT

St Johann is a sizeable valley town where life doesn't revolve entirely around skiing. Reporters emphasise the friendliness of the locals. The attractive traffic-free centre, where most of the hotels are found, is wedged between a railway track, main roads and rivers. The main access lift from the village is a gondola to the top; it's about a ten-minute walk from the centre, including a level crossing and walking beside a busy road. But there is the alternative of staying in hotels near the lift base. There is also accommodation in the hamlet of Eichenhof to the east.

The local pass covers several other resorts to the north and east; Fieberbrunn and Waidring's Steinplatte are particularly worth a visit. There's a reasonable bus service between the resorts. The Kitzbüheler Alpenskipass covers the whole region, and Kitzbühel itself is only 10 minutes by car or train.

THE MOUNTAINS

St Johann's local slopes are on the north-facing side of the Kitzbüheler Horn – the 'back' side of Kitzbühel's 'second' and smaller mountain.

Slopes From the top of the gondola a choice of north-facing pistes lead back through the trees towards town – mainly reds on the upper mountain, blues lower down. A sunnier sector of west-facing pistes lead down to another gondola at Oberndorf.

Terrain-parks There is a half-pipe at the Eichenhof lift and a jumps area above the Hochfeld chairs.

Snow reliability St Johann gets more snow than neighbouring Kitzbühel and the SkiWelt, and this, together with its largely north-facing slopes, means that it often has better conditions. It also has substantial snowmaking.

Experts There is nothing here to challenge an expert. The long black run on the piste map is really a moderate red. Off-piste is limited.

225

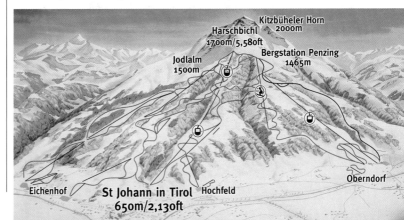

Kitzbüheler Horn 2000m
Harschbichl 1700m/5,58oft
Bergstation Penzing 1465m
Jodlalm 1500m
Eichenhof
St Johann in Tirol 650m/2,130ft
Hochfeld
Oberndorf

AUSTRIA

226

Intermediates The slopes are varied. But keen piste-bashers will ski them all in a day and are likely to want to go on to explore nearby resorts. Decent intermediates have a fairly direct-running piste between Harschbichl and town, plus the black mentioned above. There are some easier red runs on the top part of the mountain, but the best (3a and 4b) are served by slow lifts. The less adventurous can take gentle pistes from the gondola mid-station.

Beginners Most beginners rate St Johann highly, but one dissenting voice said the nursery slopes at Eichenhof are a bit steep, while those who start from Hochfeld have to ride a tricky chair once off the nursery slope.

Snowboarding It's drag-lifts or nothing on the nursery slopes.

Cross-country Given good snow, St Johann is one of the best cross-country resorts in Austria. The wide variety of trails totals 275km/171 miles.

Queues Rare except at peak times – but slow lifts is a common complaint.

Mountain restaurants With 20 or so restaurants spread over its small area, St Johann must have the highest hut density in Europe. All those tried by one reporter had 'excellent food – especially Hochfeld'. Harschbichlhütte is also recommended for 'excellent gulaschsuppe'. Our favourite is the Angerer Alm, just above the gondola mid-station, with good local food and an amazing wine cellar. Bassgeigeralm is a rustic restaurant on the Oberndorf side and the Grander Schupf at Eichenhof is also recommended.

Schools and guides The instructors of the St Johann school continue to impress reporters, but in the past we have heard of large classes and 'dreadful management and organisation'. No such problems with the Wilder Kaiser school, though, rated 'very highly' by reporters.

Facilities for children There are no nursery facilities in the resort. Bobo's, at the ski school, offers a mini-club for children under five.

STAYING THERE

How to go British tour operators concentrate on hotels, but there are numerous apartments available.

Hotels All hotels are 3- or 4-star. There are dozens of B&B pensions. The 4-star Sporthotel Austria (62507) is near the lift, with pool, sauna and steam. The Post (62230) is a 13th-century inn on the main street – 'By far the nicest,' says a regular. Visitors also recommend the Park (62226), 'very well run, very friendly, food enjoyable and plentiful'. The Fischer (62332) has a children's play area, is central, with 'friendly and helpful staff' and 'excellent' food.

Apartments There are plenty of apartments to rent.

Eating out A reporter found 'plenty of good places', including the Lange Mauer (Chinese). Villa Masianco is said to be 'lovely' and 'very good value'. The Huber-Bräu brewery serves good food but closes early. For a special meal, locals recommend the Ambiente.

Après-ski Ice bars and tea dancing greet you as you come off the slopes – Max Pub at the bottom of the main piste has 'free-flowing alcohol and blaring Europop'. In town there are lots of bars that reporters have enjoyed, including Bunny's Pub ('good alternative music'). Tour op reps organise outings, and the resort itself puts on an event most evenings.

Off the slopes There's a public pool with sauna, steam room, solarium and spa facilities, indoor tennis, ice rink, curling, tobogganing and 40km/ 25 miles of cleared walks. Easy outings by rail to Salzburg or Innsbruck.

Stubai valley

A choice of pretty little villages with their own wooded slopes, and one of the best glaciers in the world at the head of the valley

COSTS

① ② ③ ④ ⑤ ⑥

RATINGS

The slopes

Fast lifts	***
Snow	*****
Extent	***
Expert	***
Intermediate	***
Beginner	**
Convenience	**
Queues	***
Mountain restaurants	**

The rest

Scenery	****
Resort charm	****
Off-slope	***

NEWS

For 2007/08 some T-bars on the glacier are to be replaced by a fast six-pack.

For 2006/07 a terrain-park and a boarder-cross were built, the glacier's Mutterberg base station was rebuilt and a new umbrella bar opened there.

At Fulpmes (Schlick 2000), a blue run opened between the gondola mid-station and the valley. Snowmaking was added to cover the new run.

➕ High, snow-sure glacier slopes plus lower bad-weather options

➕ Quiet, pretty Tirolean villages

➖ Beginners are better off sticking to the lower slopes

➖ Not much to challenge experts

Think Austrian glaciers, and the Stubaier Gletscher should feature near the top of your list. It is the country's largest glacier ski area, and among the world's best. For a winter holiday you need non-glacial slopes as well, for the bad-weather days – and the Stubai valley has plenty at Schlick 2000 (above Fulpmes), Elfer (above the village of Neustift) and Serles (above Mieders).

The Stubai valley lies a short drive south of Innsbruck. It is a long valley (about 30km/19 miles) with countless hamlets dotted along it – and a handful of bigger villages; three have their own wooded slopes and lift systems, and are described in this chapter. Together the valley offers a sizeable 130km/81 miles of mostly intermediate terrain, all covered by the Stubai-Superski lift pass (which also covers the shuttle-bus). All the villages have impressive toboggan runs.

The **Stubaier Gletscher** offers an extensive area of runs between 3200m/10,500ft and 2300m/7,550ft accessed by two alternative two-stage gondolas from the huge car park at Mutterberg to the two mid-mountain stations of Eisgrat and Gamsgarten. A third gondola from Eisgrat takes you right to the top of the slopes.

The glacier area is broken up by rocky peaks giving more sense of variety than is normal on a glacier. Chairs (including four six-packs) and drag-lifts serve fabulous blue and red cruising runs, all of which normally have excellent snow, naturally. There is also a lovely 10km/6 mile ungroomed ski route (Wilde Grub'n) down to the valley – a run of 1450m/4,760ft vertical from the top of the glacier. And good off-piste can be found with a guide.

There aren't the challenges here that there are on the Hintertux glacier. But there are some good long runs, three blacks (one is a pretty steep mogul field) and three more ski routes. For intermediates it is splendid territory, with lots of fabulous cruising. Novices are better off learning lower down, but there is a short beginner slope at Gamsgarten.

The area is popular with snowboarders. There are lots of natural hits and kickers across the mountain, and a new terrain-park was built last season with rollers, boxes and a boarder-cross course.

There's also a 4.5km/3 mile cross-country loop.

Queues are no longer a serious problem. On a busy weekend there can be short delays at the gondola mid-station and at the Eisjoch six-pack.

At Jochdohle, Austria's highest restaurant gives stunning views but can get crowded. The Dresdnerhütte is said to be charming and uncrowded. Zur Goldenen Gams has table-service. There are two huge self-service places at Eisgrat and Gamsgarten.

There is a ski school at the glacier. Club Micky Maus is a comprehensive childcare facility at Gamsgarten. Children under ten get a free lift pass when with an adult.

Après-ski starts up the mountain in the lively snow bar at Gamsgarten.

NEUSTIFT 1000m/3,280ft
The major village closest to the glacier, 20km/12 miles away, and served by regular buses. It's an attractive, traditional Tirolean village, with limited local slopes at Elfer.
The slopes at Elfer consist of a narrow chain of runs and lifts from Elferhütte at 2080m/6,820ft down to the village. Apart from one short blue run at altitude, the pistes are all red and there's not much to entice experts, but it is a quiet place for intermediates to practise. This area is north-east-facing; there is a sunny nursery slope at village level, on the other side.

There are lots of 3- and 4-star hotels. The 4-star Tirolerhof (3278) is excellent – comfortable and relaxed with good food. It has a hire shop, and the owner is a qualified instructor and

KEY FACTS

Resort	935-1000m
	3,070-3,280ft
Slopes	935-3210m
	3,070-10,530ft
Lifts	44
Pistes	147km
	91 miles
Blue	40%
Red	31%
Black	29%
Snowmaking	some

UK PACKAGES

Neustift Ardmore, Crystal, Esprit, Interactive Resorts, Interhome, Jeffersons, Made to Measure **Fulpmes** Crystal, Lagrange

Phone numbers
From elsewhere in Austria add the prefix 05226; from abroad use the prefix +43 5226

228

TOURIST OFFICE

t 2228
info@stubai.at
www.stubai.at

AUSTRIA

guide. The central 4-star Sonnhof (2224) is also recommended. For families, the 4-star Gasteigerhof in Gasteig (2746) is suggested; it has a pool and a children's fun area.

Nightlife is focused on the Dorf, Bierfassl, Hully Gully and the Rumpl disco. Most restaurants are hotel-based. Past recommendations include Bellafonte's pizzas and the atmospheric Hoferwirt.

Neustift has quite a lot to offer off the slopes: a good leisure centre with two pools, saunas and a bowling alley.

FULPMES 935m/3,070ft
Fulpmes (with its satellite village of Telfes) sits at the foot of Schlick 2000, the most extensive of the lower ski areas. The pretty village is said to be the sunniest in the Stubaital. It attracts few British visitors.
The ski area at Schlick 2000 sits in a sheltered bowl beneath the Sennjoch. A two-stage gondola takes you to Kreuzjoch (2135m/7,000ft), from where a series of chair- and drag-lifts serve a few short, mainly north-east-facing blue and red runs and a ski route. The runs suit intermediates best, are 'rarely crowded' and have some 'genuinely testing' sections. A long blue winds its way down the valley from the Sennjoch at 2225m/7,300ft and was extended to the valley bottom with snowmaking for

2006/07. The main beginner area is beside the gondola mid-station at Froneben. There's also a children's area, Ronny's Kinderland, with moving carpets and fun features. Schlick 2000 is a good area for snowboarders, with a free-ride zone on the Sennjoch and a terrain-park lower down, at Schlickeralm. There are two schools, but English is reported to be poor.

There's a good choice of 3- and 4-star hotels, most with pools and spa facilities. The 4-star Stubaierhof (62266) is central, with a pool and a children's play room. A 2007 reporter praises the food at Café Dorfkrug.

The nearest leisure centre is in Neustift, but Fulpmes has tobogganing, sleigh rides and ice skating.

MIEDERS 980m/3,220ft
Mieders is near the entrance to the Stubai valley, 15 minutes' drive from Innsbruck. It's an unspoiled village with its own tiny area of slopes.
The slopes of Serles are limited to a couple of blues and a short red, but there are several ski routes. A gondola takes you to Kopponeck at 1680m/5,510ft, where a couple of T-bars serve the upper runs. There are a couple of mountain restaurants and 46km/29 miles of cross-country tracks above 1600m/5,250ft. The village has a small selection of hotels and guest houses.

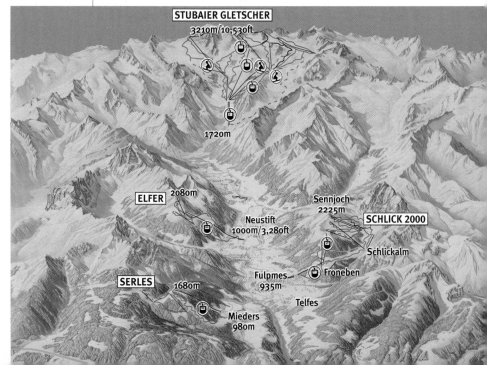

Westendorf

This cute little village now offers access to a vast amount of terrain and should start attracting a lot more keen intermediates

RATINGS

The slopes

Fast lifts	**
Snow	**
Extent	*
Expert	**
Intermediate	***
Beginner	***
Convenience	***
Queues	****
Mountain restaurants	***

The rest

Scenery	***
Resort charm	****
Off-slope	**

NEWS

For the last two seasons, Westendorf has been connected to the Kirchberg-Kitzbühel slopes, via a 4km/2.5 mile red piste down to Aschau and an eight-seat gondola back up. From Aschau, shuttle-buses run to the Pengelstein gondola at Skirast. The Kitzbüheler Alpenskipass covers the Kirchberg-Kitzbühel and Ski Welt areas.

For 2006/07 two new bars opened in the village.

- [+] Charming traditional village
- [+] Access (via short bus-rides) to the extensive SkiWelt circuit, and now to Kitzbühel's slopes
- [+] Good local beginners' slopes
- [+] Jolly if rather limited après-ski scene

- [−] Local slopes are limited in extent, and mainly of genuine red gradient
- [−] Slopes are at low altitude, and snow quality can suffer

Cute little Westendorf is worth considering as a base for keen intermediates. As well as its own small area of serious red runs, it has reasonably easy access to the extensive area of slopes shared by Kitzbühel and Kirchberg, as well as to the main SkiWelt slopes.

THE RESORT

Westendorf is a small village with a charming main street and attractive onion-domed church (it was once declared 'Europe's most beautiful village' in a floral competition). The centre is close to the nursery slopes but a five-minute walk from the main gondola outside the village.

THE MOUNTAIN

The local slopes are small, but you can get into the SkiWelt circuit easily via a bus to Brixen – and into the Kitzbühel-Kirchberg slopes by taking the red piste to Aschau and then a bus.

Slopes A two-stage gondola takes you to Talkaser, from where one main north-west-facing red run goes back to the resort (with blue options on the lower half). Short west- and east-facing pistes at the top run below the peaks of Choralpe, Fleiding and Gampen (from where the red run and gondola to Kirchberg-Kitzbühel start). A couple of red runs from Fleiding go down past the lifts to hamlets served by buses; a reporter particularly enjoyed these. The piste grooming is excellent, says a recent visitor. But the piste map is the general SkiWelt one, which doesn't deal with these slopes. There's weekly floodlit skiing.

Terrain-parks There's an excellent terrain-park with something for all levels – jumps, boxes, rails and a half-pipe (www.boardplay.com).

Snow reliability Westendorf's snow reliability is a bit better than some other SkiWelt resorts and nearly all of its pistes now have snowmaking.

Experts The slopes are among the most testing in the SkiWelt area, and we guess it's possible to have a lot of fun off-piste with a guide.

Intermediates Nearly all the local terrain is genuinely red in gradient, though we see they have reclassified

TVB WESTENDORF

The scenery is pretty rather than dramatic
→

KEY FACTS

Resort	800m
	2,620ft
Westendorf only	
Slopes	800-1960m
	2,620-6,430ft
Lifts	13
Pistes	45km
	28 miles
Blue	49%
Red	40%
Black	11%
Snowmaking	40km
	25 miles
For SkiWelt	
Slopes	620-1890m
	2,030-6,200ft
Lifts	94
Pistes	250km
	155 miles
Blue	43%
Red	48%
Black	9%
Snowmaking	180km
	112 miles

UK PACKAGES

Inghams, Thomson

Phone numbers
From elsewhere in
Austria add the prefix
05334 (Westendorf),
05358 (SkiWelt
Tourist Office); from
abroad use the prefix
+43 and omit the
initial '0'

TOURIST OFFICES

Westendorf
t 6230
info@kitzbuehel-
alpen.com
www.kitzbuehel-
alpen.com

SkiWelt
t 505
info@skiwelt.at
www.skiwelt.at

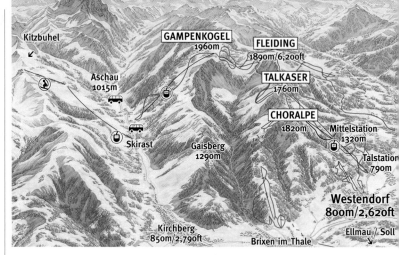

some former reds to blues. The main
SkiWelt area has lots of easier
intermediate runs but getting there
involves a bus. And it's fairly easy to
access the good mix of intermediate
runs at Kitzbühel-Kirchberg.
Beginners Extensive village nursery
slopes are Westendorf's pride and joy.
There are a couple of genuine blues to
progress to, but the reds are real reds
(as are some of the reclassified blues).
Snowboarding There are some tedious
catwalks at altitude.
Cross-country There are 30km/17 miles
of local cross-country trails along the
valley but snow-cover is erratic.
Queues Given good conditions, queues
are rare, and far less of a problem than
in the main SkiWelt area. If poor
weather closes the upper lifts, queues
can become long.
Mountain restaurants Alpenrosenhütte
is woody and warm, with good food;
reporters enjoyed the quiet, pleasant
Brechhornhaus; the Choralp (top of
gondola) gets busy but is 'reasonably
priced'; the Gassnerwirt is good but
you have to bus back to town.
Schools and guides The three ski
schools have quite good reputations,
though classes can be large. One
reporter tells of her teenager's
'excellent' private lesson with the Top
school: 'He's been skiing since he was
three, but this was a revelation.'
Others praise the Westendorf school:
'teachers very good, good value, great
prize-giving in town hall' and 'excellent
instructor, good English'.
Facilities for children Westendorf sells
itself as a family resort. The nursery
and the ski kindergarten open all day.

STAYING THERE

How to go A couple of mainstream
operators offer packages here.
Hotels There are central 4-star hotels:
the Jakobwirt (6245) and the 'excellent'
Schermer (6268) – and a dozen 3-star
ones. The 3-star Post (6202) is good
value, central and 'traditional and
charming but the half-board dinner was
bland'. Among more modest guest
houses, Haus Wetti (6348) is popular,
and away from the church bells.
Pension Ingeborg (6577) has been
recommended – next to the gondola.
Apartments The Schermerhof
apartments are of good quality.
Eating out Most of the best restaurants
are in hotels – the Schermer and
Jakobwirt are good. The Wastlhof and
Klingler have also been recommended.
Get a taxi to Berggasthof Stimlach for a
good evening out.
Après-ski Nightlife is quite lively, but
it's a small place with limited options.
The Liftstüberl, at the bottom of the
gondola, is packed at the end of the
day. The Moskito Bar has live music
and theme nights but is said by one
reporter to be 'a bit of a dive'. The
Village Pub, next to the hotel Post, is
very popular with 'good Irish craic' and
Guinness. A recent reporter enjoyed the
'good atmosphere and live music' of
In's Moment, run by a Scot. The
Mesnerkeller is now the Karat.
Off the slopes There are excursions by
rail or bus to Innsbruck and Salzburg.
Walks and sleigh rides are very pretty.
In February, the Jump and Freeze night
is recommended viewing – 'all good
fun' in a party atmosphere.

Wildschönau

Wildschönau is the dramatic-sounding name for a valley with a group of family-friendly resorts, each with small areas of slopes above

+ Traditional, family-friendly villages
+ Good nursery slopes at Niederau and Oberau
+ Jolly après-ski scene

– Three separate ski areas, linked by ski-buses
– Each area has limited slopes
– Natural snow reliability not the best (but extensive snowmaking)

Niederau, Oberau and Auffach are contrasting villages with contrasting small areas of slopes on a shared lift pass. The area best suits families and those looking for a friendly, relaxing holiday rather than hitting the slopes non-stop.

THE RESORT

Niederau has long been a favourite resort with British beginner and early intermediate skiers. It is the main resort in the Wildschönau and is quite spread out, with a cluster of restaurants and shops around the gondola station forming the nearest thing to a focal point. But few hotels are more than five minutes' walk from a main lift.

Auffach, 7km/4 miles away, is a smaller, quieter, attractive old village and has the area's highest and most extensive slopes.

On a low col between the two is **Oberau** – almost as big as Niederau and the valley's administrative and cultural centre.

The villages are unspoiled, with traditional chalet-style buildings. Roads are quiet, except on Saturdays, and the valley setting is lovely.

THE MOUNTAINS

Niederau's slopes are spread over a wooded mountainside that rises no higher than 1600m/5,250ft. The slopes at Auffach continue above the tree line.
Slopes The main lift from Niederau is an eight-person gondola to Markbachjoch. A few minutes' walk away is the alternative chair-lift, and above it is a steep drag to the high point of Lanerköpfl. Beginner runs at the bottom of the mountain are served by several short drag-lifts – a new lift and run opened this year. The whole area is very small – you can ski most of it in an hour or two. There's a sizeable 'Race 'n' Boarder Arena'; races are run here, but you can also take race-training lessons.

A reliable free bus goes to Auffach. Its sunny, east-facing area, consisting almost entirely of red runs, goes up to Schatzberg, with a vertical of 1000m/

231

A broad valley, and a tall church →

KEY FACTS

Resort	830m
	2,720ft
Slopes	830-1905m
	2,720-6,250ft
Lifts	25
Pistes	70km
	43 miles
Blue	21%
Red	62%
Black	17%
Snowmaking	27km
	17 miles

UK PACKAGES

Niederau *Airtours, Directski.com, First Choice, Inghams, Neilson, Panorama, Ski McNeill, Thomson* **Oberau** *Inghams, Interhome, Neilson*

Phone numbers
From elsewhere in Austria add the prefix 05339; from abroad use the prefix +43 5339

3,280ft. The main lift up is a two-stage gondola and two six-packs serve the top runs on open slopes – an impressive set-up. Again the area is very small – the top chairs serve verticals of under 300m/980ft.

The Kitzbüheler Alpen ski pass covers resorts in the Schneewinkel, Kitzbühel ski region, SkiWelt and Alpbachtal as well.

Terrain-parks There's a 90m/300ft half-pipe and a terrain-park with a quarter-pipe, jumps, snake, wave and fun-box served by a drag-lift on Schatzberg.

Snow reliability The low altitude means that natural snow reliability is relatively poor. But almost 40 per cent of the pistes have snowmaking, including the main runs down at both Niederau and Auffach from top to bottom. More is planned for 2007/08. And Auffach has most of its runs above mid-mountain, making for more reliable snow there than at Niederau. Grooming is good.

Experts The several black pistes are short and not severe. We skied the main black piste from the bottom of the drag-lift below Lanerköpfl to Niederau when it was well groomed and thought it great for fast carving, but of almost blue gradient for much of its length. There are a couple of ungroomed, unpatrolled ski routes at Niederau, which were bumpy and had patchy snow when we skied them. There are proper off-piste routes to be found, too – including the Gern route,

which is marked on the piste map, from the top of Schatzberg down a deserted valley to the road a little way from Auffach.

Intermediates Niederau's red runs generally merit their status but there's no blue run from top to bottom. The main black piste mentioned above is enjoyable, but the blue to reach it is just a path. Auffach has more intermediate terrain, with several short reds at the top (including a new one this year), and the long main piste from the top to the village is attractive. But all this does not add up to very much – keen intermediate piste-bashers will be able to ski it all in a day. The slopes are best suited to confident but leisurely intermediates who are happy to take it easy and have a relaxing holiday.

Beginners There are excellent nursery slopes at the top and bottom of Niederau's main slopes (including a new lift and slope this year), but the low ones don't get much sun in midwinter. Auffach has nursery slopes near the gondola mid-station. Oberau has its own nursery slopes, with a short black run above them. A problem is the lack of really easy longer runs to progress to.

Snowboarding Best for intermediates. The number of drag-lifts may deter novices.

Cross-country There are 50km/31 miles of trails along the valley, which are good when snow is abundant.

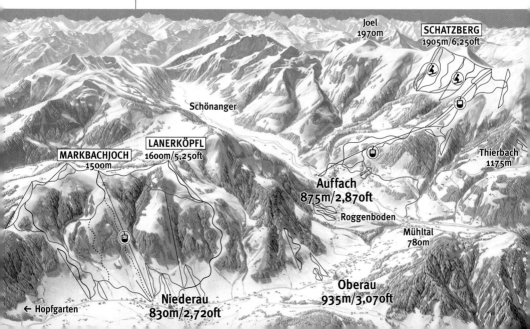

wildschönau
exciting   relaxing

Wildschönau - Tyrol
Niederau - Oberau - Auffach - Thierbach

The 70km of piste give skiers everything they are looking for, steep slopes and gentle family runs. The Wildschönau offers its guests a lift capacity that sets it aside from other resorts. With two gondolas, three chair lifts and 20 drag lifts there is no time lost by queuing and there are no overcrowded lifts.

The gentle Wildschönau hills are particularly suitable for families but there are also plenty of opportunities for experienced skiers, e.g. the FIS runs for the giant slalom and Super G and some magnificent deep-snow slopes. There is also a measured section where skiers can test their top speed. Carvers and snowboarders are welcome on all pistes and the Schatzberg mountain offers an enormous fun park with a half pipe, high jump, fun-box, snake, quarter pipe and wave ride both for fun and competition. **Our partners in Great Britain:** Thomson, Inghams, Crystal, First Choice, Neilson.

TVB WILDSCHÖNAU

There are worthwhile
red runs above
Niederau, though this
shot exaggerates the
steepness a bit ↓

Queues One reporter said: 'Very little queueing.' Another complained of queues for the Niederau gondola. We saw long queues for the beginner drag-lifts; these should have eased now that a new beginner lift is in place.

Mountain restaurants These are scarce but good, causing lunchtime queues as ski schools take a break. Many people lunch in the villages.

Schools and guides The ski schools have good reputations both for English and for teaching beginners, and a reporter raved about his beginner lessons. But classes can be large.

Facilities for children The kindergarten and nursery take kids from age two.

STAYING THERE

How to go There are a number of attractive hotels and guest houses in the three main villages – many with pools. Several major British tour operators run packages to Niederau and Oberau.

Hotels In Niederau the 4-star Sonnschein (8353) and the Austria (8188) are central recommendations. Pension Diane (8562) is close to the main lift and 'a really good place and good value,' says a 2007 visitor. (The owner is a local by birth, but spent 13 years working in Birmingham.) The Vicky, run by Thomson, has 'friendly staff, excellent food, brilliant crèche', says a reporter. The 3-star Kellerwirt (8116) in Oberau dates from 1745 and was highly recommended by a 2006 reporter ('comfort, character, excellent food'). But bear in mind that you are distant from both major areas of slopes if based here.

Eating out The restaurants at the hotels Alpenland and Wastlhof in Niederau have been recommended.

Après-ski Niederau has a nice balance of après-ski, neither too noisy for families nor too quiet for the young and lively. The Heustadl bar is popular at the end of the day. The Almbar and the Cave bar/disco ('great spot, very friendly and lively') are popular later on. The Drift-Inn at hotel Vicky has also been recommended. Cafe Treff is an internet cafe.

The other villages are quieter, once the tea-time jollity is over for the night – though Oberau claims a pub with disco music.

Off the slopes There are excellent sleigh rides, horse-riding trips and organised walks as well as the Slow Train Wildschönau – on wheels not rails – which offers varied excursions. There are a couple of local museums. Several of the Niederau hotel swimming pools are open to the public, and there's an outdoor ice rink. There's a long toboggan run at Auffach, from the mid-station of the gondola down to the bottom – a distance of 4km/2.5 miles – and there's a new guided trip on Sundays from Schatzberg to Thierbach. (Off-piste tobogganing, eh? The mind boggles.) Tobogganing is also organised twice-weekly at Oberau. Shopping excursions to Innsbruck are possible.

Zell am See

A real one-off, this: a charming lakeside town, with varied local slopes and a very worthwhile glacier option nearby at Kaprun

NEWS

For 2007/08 in Zell am See a new eight-person gondola, the TrassXpress, is planned. It will start next to the cable-car from Schmittental and end at the same place as the gondola up from Schüttdorf; this should substantially cut queues to get up the mountain. And a new six-pack with covers is due to replace the Breiteckbahn triple to the same place. On Kaprun's glacier area, a six-pack is due to replace a T-bar and there will be 4km/2.5 miles of new pistes.

For 2006/07 a six-pack with covers replaced the Almbahn double chair at Maiskogel above Kaprun, running to the top of the mountain. A new red piste was also built at the top. Two terrain-parks, the Easy Park and Central Park, were built at Kaprun's glacier area.

➕ Pretty, tree-lined slopes with great views down to the lake

➕ Lively, but not rowdy, nightlife

➕ Charming old town centre with beautiful lakeside setting

➕ Lots to do off the slopes

➕ Huge range of cross-country trails

➕ Kaprun glacier nearby

➕ Varied terrain including a couple of genuine black runs

➖ Sunny, low slopes often have poor conditions despite snowmaking, which makes the area more limited

➖ Trek to lifts from much of the accommodation, and sometimes crowded buses

➖ Less suitable for beginners than most small Austrian resorts

➖ The Kaprun glacier gets lengthy queues when it is most needed

Zell am See is not a rustic village like most of its Austrian rivals, but a lakeside summer resort town with a charming old centre. For a small area, Zell's slopes have a lot of variety and some slightly challenging terrain, but not enough to keep a keen intermediate or expert happy for long. Zell is close to Kaprun and its Kitzsteinhorn glacier; but if snow is in short supply, Zell visitors have no special claim – you have to queue for access along with visitors coming from Saalbach, Kitzbühel and other low resorts.

THE RESORT

Zell am See is a long-established, year-round resort town set between a large lake and a mountain. Its charming, traffic-free medieval centre is on a flat promontory, and the resort has grown up around this attractive core.

A gondola at the edge of town goes up the southern arm of the horseshoe-shaped mountain. You can also stay 2km/1 mile west of Zell at Schmittental, in the centre of the horseshoe, where there are two cable-cars and the new gondola (see 'News'). Another alternative is to stay 3km/2 miles south of Zell in Schüttdorf, where there is another gondola and large car park. But it is a characterless dormitory with little else going for it ('don't stay there if you want nightlife on your doorstep' says a 2007 visitor). Cross-country skiers and families wishing to use the Areitalm nursery stand to gain most from staying in Schüttdorf – and perhaps those with a car planning multiple outings to Kaprun.

Kaprun's snow-sure glacier slopes are only a few minutes by crowded buses ('best to get on at the bus station', says a reporter – getting on in Schüttdorf can be a problem) – the slopes can be crowded too, one 2007 reporter 'gave up and went back to less crowded Zell'.

Saalbach is easily reached by bus and Bad Hofgastein by train. At a push, Wagrain, Schladming and Obertauern are car-trips.

THE MOUNTAINS

Zell's horseshoe-shaped mountain has the easiest runs along the open ridges, with steeper pistes descending through woods to Schmittental.

THE SLOPES
Varied but limited
The lifts from Zell and Schüttdorf go up along the southern arm of the horseshoe mountain to the high-point at Schmittenhöhe, meeting the new gondola from Schmittental (see 'News') and a short distance from the cable-car from Schmittental. The several lifts on

KEY FACTS

Resort	755m
	2,480ft

Zell and Kaprun	
Slopes	755-3030m
	2,480-9,940ft
Lifts	56
Pistes	136km
	84 miles
Blue	42%
Red	35%
Black	23%
Snowmaking	
	94 km
	58 miles

Zell only	
Slopes	755-2000m
	2,480-6,560ft
Lifts	28
Pistes	77km
	48 miles

Kaprun only	
Slopes	785-3030m
	2,580-9,940ft
Lifts	28
Pistes	59km
	36 miles

LIFT PASSES

Europa Sportregion Kaprun–Zell am See

Prices in €

Age	1-day	6-day
under 16	19	90
16 to 18	30	143
over 19	38	179

Free under 6

Senior no deals

Beginner limited pass

Notes
Covers Zell and Kaprun; one-day price is for Schmittenhöhe (Zell) only

Alternative passes
Kitzsteinhorn only and Maiskogel only; Salzburg Super Ski Card covers a huge area round Salzburg province and is available for three days or more

the back of the hill and on the sunny slopes of the northern arm of the horseshoe are accessed via Schmittenhöhe or by riding another cable-car from Schmittental to Sonnalm.

Black runs descend from various points to Schmittental; intermediate runs go down the southern arm to Zell and Schüttdorf.

TERRAIN-PARKS
Head for the City
There's a half-pipe and the Jumping City terrain-park on Schmittenhöhe.

SNOW RELIABILITY
Good snowmaking, but lots of sun
Zell am See's slopes can be badly affected by the sun. Over 70 per cent of pistes are now covered by snow-guns, including all the runs to the valley and mostly top-to-bottom. But holidays can still be marred by slush, ice and bare patches. The Kaprun glacier is snow-sure, but oversubscribed when snow is short in the region. Grooming is good.

FOR EXPERTS
Several blacks, but still limited
Zell has more black runs than most resorts this size, but they barely deserve the classification, and don't hold out much of a challenge to experts. The blacks are usually immaculately groomed and little used – great if you like that kind of thing, especially first thing in the morning when they are completely deserted. Off-piste opportunities are limited.

FOR INTERMEDIATES
Bits and pieces for most grades
Good intermediates have a choice of fine, long runs, but this is not a place for high mileage. All blacks are usually within a confident intermediate's capability, and the red home run from Areitalm to Schüttdorf is almost equally as testing – great when conditions are good, but a struggle for many at the end of a warm day. The wide Sonnkogel runs are relatively quiet – great for carving. The timid can cruise the southern ridge blues.

Kaprun's high, snow-sure glacier runs are also ideal for intermediates not looking for too great a challenge.

FOR BEGINNERS
Two low nursery areas
There are small nursery slopes (which

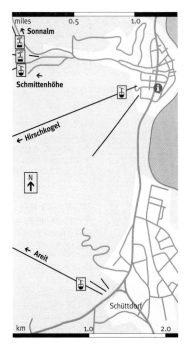

can be crowded) at Schmittental and at Schüttdorf, both covered by snow-guns. There are short, easy runs at Schmittenhöhe, Areitalm and Breiteckalm (some used by complete beginners when snow conditions are poor lower down, but it means buying a lift pass).

FOR CROSS-COUNTRY
Excellent if snow allows
The valley floor has extensive areas and at altitude there are short loops, above Zell and on the Kitzsteinhorn, making a total of 40km/24 miles, with 18km/11 miles on the Kaprun golf course.

QUEUES
Valley problems may be eased
The big problem has always been queues for the lifts out of the valley in the morning. A 2007 visitor endured a 40-minute wait for the gondola out of Schüttdorf. And reporters regularly experience lengthy waits for the Zell and Schmittental lifts too – the Sonnalm cable-car is said to be quieter than the others. These problems should be eased by the new gondola from Schmittental for 2007/08 (see 'News'). Once you are on the mountain, there aren't many problems. When snow is poor there are few daytime queues at Zell – many people

Zell am See
t 56020
Sport Alpin
t 0664 453 1417
Snowboard Academy
t 74693

Classes
(Zell prices)
5 days (2hr am and
pm) €150
Private lessons
€55 for 1 hr; €10 for
each additional
person

CHILDREN

Kinderskiwelt Areit
t 56020
From age 2; with ski
lessons for over 3s
Babysitter list
At the tourist office

Ski schools
From age 4 (5 days
€150 – Zell price)

boarding

Zell is well suited to boarders and most lifts are chairs, gondolas or cable-cars. You'll also find plenty of life in the evenings. The Kaprun glacier has powder in its wide, open bowl. But it also has a high proportion of drag-lifts – a day of this and the 'small walk' to enter the main terrain-park exhausted some reporters. Snowboard Academy is a specialist school.

are away queueing at Kaprun. The queue for the bus back from Kaprun was said by a recent reporter to be 'chaotic – a heaving mass, all scrambling and fighting to get on'.

MOUNTAIN RESTAURANTS
Plenty of little refuges
There are plenty of cosy, atmospheric huts dotted around the Zell slopes, helpfully named on the piste map. Among the best are Glocknerhaus, Kettingalm, Areitalm ('gets busy'), Breiteckalm and Blaickner's Sonnalm ('the best strudel'). Pinzgauer Hütte, in the woods behind Schmittenhöhe, is regularly recommended by reporters ('superb'); snowmobiles will tow you back to the lifts ('great fun'). The Schmiedhofalm has 'great views' and serves regional specialities ('best Tirolean pancake we've had'). The Berghotel at Schmittenhöhe is good, but expensive. Its bar with loud music is lively in the afternoons (see Après-ski). The Panorama-Pfiff gets crowded,

but 'has wonderful views and quite good food'. The Ebenbergalm just above the village has 'excellent home cooked food'.

SCHOOLS AND GUIDES
A wide choice
There is a choice of schools in both Zell am See and Kaprun. We get few reports, but a reporter had 'excellent' lessons with a 'delightful board instructor' at the main Zell school. Groups are said to be quite large. There are specialist cross-country centres at Schüttdorf and at Kaprun.

FACILITIES FOR CHILDREN
Schüttdorf's the place
We have no recent reports on the childcare provisions, but staying in Schüttdorf has the advantage of direct gondola access to the Areitalm snow-kindergarten. There's a children's adventure-park on the mountain.

Zell am See

237

That's Zell on the right with its home slopes, Schüttdorf, on the left and the Kitzsteinhorn glacier above Kaprun in the distance ➔

TVB ZELL AM SEE / TYPOSTUDIO JOSEF MARINGER

GETTING THERE

Air Salzburg 80km/ 50 miles (2hr); Munich 230km/ 143 miles (3hr)

Rail Station in resort

ACTIVITIES

Indoor Swimming, sauna, solarium, massage, fitness centre, tennis, squash, bowling, rifle range, museums, cinema, gallery, library

Outdoor Ice rink, curling, walking, tobogganing, horse-riding, plane flights, sleigh rides, paragliding

STAYING THERE

HOW TO GO
Choose charm or convenience
Lots of hotels, pensions and apartments.
Hotels A broad range of hotels (more 4- than 3-stars) and guest houses.
*****Salzburgerhof (7650) Best in town; pool. It's nearer the lake than the gondola, but has a courtesy bus.
****Tirolerhof (7720) In the old town. Pool, hot-tub, steam room. 'Very comfortable; friendly, efficient staff.'
****Eichenhof (47201) On outskirts of town, but popular and with a minibus service, great food and lake views.
****Zum Hirschen (7740) Comfortable. Easy walk to Zell gondola. Sauna, steam room, splash pool, popular bar.
****Schwebebahn (72461) Attractive, in secluded setting at Schmittental, by the cable-cars and new gondola.
****Romantikhotel (72520) Close to lake. 'Very good, really wild decor.'
****Lebzelter (7760) In pedestrian area. 'Friendly and welcoming, excellent food and good sports bar.'
***Margarete (72724) B&B at Schmittental, by the cable-cars.
***Villa Klothilde (72660) 'Family run, friendly, clean and comfortable'. On the slopes two minutes' walk from town.
Apartments Lots of options. Lederer is close to the Ebenberg lift. More central are Diana and Seilergasse.

EATING OUT
Plenty of choice
Zell has more non-hotel places than is usual in a small Austrian resort. Giuseppe's is an Italian with excellent food. Kupferkessel and Traubenstüberl both do wholesome regional dishes. There are Chinese restaurants in Zell and Schüttdorf. Car drivers can try the excellent Erlhof at Thumersbach.

APRES-SKI
Plenty for all tastes
Après-ski is lively and varied, with cafes, bars and discos aplenty. When it's sunny, Schnapps Hans ice bar outside the Berghotel, up at Schmittenhöhe, really buzzes, with 'great music, a crazy DJ and dancing on tables and on the bar'. The Diele disco bar rocks – endorsed by a recent reporter as 'the place to be' for music and videos. The Resi (formerly Crazy Daisy) on the main road has two crowded bars and still seems popular. Villa Crazy Daisy has three lively bars in a new location. Greens XL has a live band and 60s and 70s music. A 2007 reporter recommends the B17 Hangar bar ('cracking cocktails and a party buzz') and Our's Lounge ('relaxed vibe with big sofas'). The 'excellent' Viva disco allows no under 18s. Or try the smart Hirschenkeller, the cave-like Lebzelter Keller and the Sportstüberl, with nostalgic ski photos on the walls.

OFF THE SLOPES
Lots of choices
There is plenty to do in this year-round resort. The train trip to Salzburg is a must, Kitzbühel is also well worth a visit and Innsbruck is within reach. You can often walk across the frozen lake to Thumersbach, plus there are good sports facilities, a motor museum, sleigh rides, alpine flights and you can watch ice hockey. There are marked paths at Schmittenhöhe.

Phone numbers
From elsewhere in Austria add the prefix 06542 (Zell), 06547 (Kaprun), 06544 (Rauris); from abroad use the prefix +43 and omit the initial '0'

STAYING UP THE MOUNTAIN
Several options

As well as the Berghotel (72489) at the Schmittenhöhe cable-car, the Breiteckalm (73419), Blaikner's Sonnalm (73262) and Pinzgauer Hütte (53472) restaurants have rooms.

Kaprun 785m/2,580ft

Apart from providing Zell's snow guarantee, Kaprun is worth considering as a destination in its own right.

THE RESORT
Kaprun is a spacious, charming and quite lively village. The main road to the glacier bypasses it, leaving the centre pleasantly quiet.

THE MOUNTAIN
There is a small area of easy intermediate slopes on the outskirts of the village at **Maiskogel**, served by five lifts, including a cable-car and fast quad. A new six-pack with covers replaced an old double chair for 2006/07. There is also a separate nursery area. But most people will want to spend most of their time on the slopes of the nearby **Kitzsteinhorn** glacier or on Zell am See's slopes. Buses to and from both are often crowded at peak times – it's worth timing your trips carefully. The lift pass covers only one ascent of the Kitzsteinhorn access gondola per day.
Slopes A 15-person, two-stage gondola goes up to the Alpincenter and main slopes. The first-stage runs parallel to an older eight-seat gondola and the second stage parallel to a fast quad chair. The main slopes are in a big bowl above the Alpincenter, served by a cable-car, lots of T-bars and four chairs (including a new six-pack for 2007/08). The area above the top of the Alpincenter is open in summer and is particularly good for an early pre-Christmas or late post-Easter break.
Terrain-parks There are three on the Kitzsteinhorn. The main one, Gletscher Park, is open all year round.
Snow reliability Snow is nearly always good because of the glacier. And there's snowmaking too.
Queues Queues have always been a problem here. Some reports tell of 15-minute waits for the access gondola (down as well as up) and up to 10 minutes for the upper lifts. See Zell am See for comments on the buses home.
Mountain restaurants There are three

decent ones – the Gletschermühle ('awesome views, rock music, weekly specials') and Krefelderhütte near the Alpincenter, and the Häusalm near the gondola mid-station. Bella Vista at the top of the mountain has good views and is 'reasonably priced'.
Experts There's little to challenge experts except for some good off-piste; the one slightly tough piste starts at the very top.
Intermediates Pistes are mainly gentle blues and reds and make for great easy cruising. From Alpincenter there is an entertaining red run down to the gondola mid-station. This is our favourite run, though it gets crowded. There's a good unpisted ski route.
Beginners There are two nursery slopes in the village and some gentle blues on the glacier to progress to.
Snowboarding Intermediates and better will love the wide open powder bowl. Beginners may find there are too many T-bars for their liking.
Cross-country The 18km/11 miles of trails on the Kaprun golf course are good, but at altitude there is just one short loop – at the top of the glacier.
Schools and guides There are several.
Facilities for children All the schools offer children's classes and there's a kindergarten in the village.

STAYING THERE
How to go There are some catered chalets and chalet-hotels.
Hotels The 4-star Orgler (8205) and Tauernhof (8235), and 'spacious' 3-star Mitteregger (8207) are among the best.
Après-ski Nightlife is quiet, but the Baum bar is lively. The Kitsch & Bitter has 'great live music and cocktails'.
Eating out Good restaurants include the Dorfstadl, Hilberger's Beisl and Schlemmerstube.
Off the slopes There's a sports centre with outdoor rapids. A visitor enjoyed the 'rustic' bowling at the Sportsbar.

Rauris 950m/3,120ft

Rauris is a small village in a quiet, dead-end valley south-east of Zell, about 25km/16 miles by road. There are a couple of 4-star hotels, but most are 3-stars. Across the valley road from the village are nursery drag-lifts and a six-seat gondola accessing 30km/19 miles of intermediate slopes with a vertical of 1250m/4,100ft; in total 10 lifts, including a newish eight-seat gondola serving blue slopes at the top.

France

Over one-third of British skiers and snowboarders choose France for their holidays each year, almost double the number who go to Austria, the next most popular country. It's not difficult to see what attracts us to France. The country has the biggest lift and piste networks in the world; for those who like to cover as many miles in a day as possible, these are unrivalled. Most of these big areas are also at high altitude, ensuring high-quality snow for a long season. And French mountains offer a mixture of some of the toughest, wildest slopes in the Alps and some of the longest, gentlest and most convenient beginner runs.

French resort villages can't be quite so uniformly recommended; but, equally, they don't all conform to the standard image of soulless, purpose-built service stations, thrown up without concern for appearance during the boom of the 1960s and 1970s. Many resorts are based on more traditional villages, or have such places on the fringes of their slopes. Another advantage of smaller villages and less well-known resorts is that they tend to be cheaper. Some of the big-name resorts can now be very expensive – none more so than Courchevel 1850, where you can pay quite silly prices for hotel rooms, food and drink.

Towards the front of the book there is a special chapter on driving to the French Alps – still very popular, especially with people going self-catering, despite the growth of the budget airlines. The French Alps are easy to get to by car, and luxurious apartments are becoming more and more common as property developers see the market opportunities.

ANY STYLE OF RESORT YOU LIKE

The main drawback to France, hinted at above, is the monstrous architecture of some of the purpose-built resorts. But not all French resorts are hideous. Certainly, France has its fair share of Alpine eyesores, chief among them central Les Menuires, central La Plagne, Flaine, Tignes, Isola 2000 and Les Arcs. But all these places have learned from past mistakes, and newer developments there are being built in a much more attractive, traditional chalet style. The later generation of purpose-built resorts, such as Valmorel, La Rosière and La Tania, have been built in much more sympathetic style than their predecessors. The big advantages of the high, purpose-built resorts are the reliability and quality of the snow, and the amazing slope-side convenience of most of the accommodation.

If you prefer, there are genuinely old mountain villages to stay in, linked directly to the big lift networks. These are not usually as

SNOWPIX.COM / CHRIS GILL

← One high French resort (Les Deux-Alpes) seen from the slopes of another (Alpe-d'Huez)

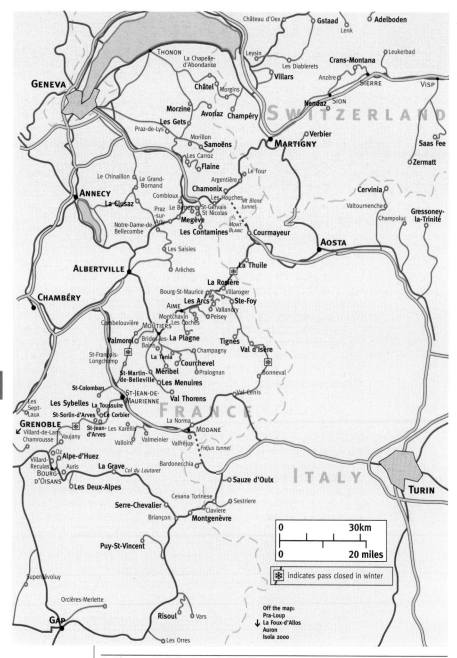

The map shows locations including:

Château d'Oex, Gstaad, Lenk, Adelboden, Leysin, THONON, La Chapelle-d'Abondance, Les Diablerets, Crans-Montana, Leukerbad, Villars, Anzère, SIERRE, VISP, GENEVA, Châtel, Morgins, Nendaz, SION, Morzine, Avoriaz, Champéry, SWITZERLAND, Les Gets, Praz-de-Lys, Verbier, Saas Fee, Morillon, Samoëns, MARTIGNY, Les Carroz, Flaine, Le Tour, Zermatt, Le Chinaillon, Le Grand-Bornand, Argentière, Chamonix, Cervinia, ANNECY, Combloux, Les Houches, Mt Blanc tunnel, Valtournenche, Gressoney-la-Trinité, La Clusaz, Praz-sur-Arly, Le Bettex, St-Gervais, St Nicolas, Champoluc, Megève, Notre-Dame-de-Bellecombe, Les Contamines, MONT BLANC, Courmayeur, AOSTA, Les Saisies, ALBERTVILLE, Arèches, La Thuile, CHAMBÉRY, La Rosière, Bourg-St-Maurice, Villaroger, Les Arcs, Ste-Foy, AIME, Vallandry, Combelouvière, Montchavin, Peisey, MOÛTIERS, Les Coches, Valmorel, Brides-les-Bains, La Plagne, Tignes, St-François-Longchamp, Champagny, Val d'Isère, La Tania, Courchevel, St-Martin-de-Belleville, Méribel, Pralognan, Bonneval, St-Colomban, Les Menuires, Les Sybelles, St-Jean-de-Maurienne, Val Thorens, Val Cenis, Les Sept-Laux, La Toussuire, Le Corbier, La Norma, St-Sorlin-d'Arves, MODANE, GRENOBLE, Villard-de-Lans, St-Jean-d'Arves, Les Karellis, Chamrousse, Vaujany, Valloire, Valmeinier, Valfréjus, Fréjus tunnel, Oz, Alpe-d'Huez, Villard-Reculas, Auris, La Grave, Bardonechia, ITALY, BOURG-D'OISANS, Les Deux-Alpes, Col du Lautaret, Sauze d'Oulx, TURIN, Cesana Torinese, Sestriere, Serre-Chevalier, Claviere, Briançon, Montgenèvre, Puy-St-Vincent, Superdévoluy, Orcières-Merlette, Risoul, Vars, GAP, Les Orres

Scale: 0 — 30km, 0 — 20 miles

✳ indicates pass closed in winter

Off the map:
Pra-Loup
↓ La Foux-d'Allos
Auron
Isola 2000

Getting around the French Alps

Pick the right gateway – Geneva, Chambéry or Grenoble – and you can hardly go wrong. The approach to Serre-Chevalier and Montgenèvre involves the 2060m/6,760ft Col du Lautaret; but the road is a major one and kept clear of snow or reopened quickly after a fall. Crossing the French-Swiss border between Chamonix and Verbier involves two closure-prone passes – the Montets and the Forclaz. When necessary, one-way traffic runs beside the tracks through the rail tunnel beneath the passes.

convenient for the slopes, but they give you a feel of being in France rather than in a winter-holiday factory. Examples include Montchavin or Champagny for La Plagne, Vaujany for Alpe-d'Huez, St-Martin-de-Belleville, Les Allues or Brides-les-Bains for the Trois Vallées, and Les Carroz, Morillon or Samoëns for Flaine. There are also old villages with their own slopes that have developed as resorts while retaining at least some of their rustic ambience – such as Serre-Chevalier and La Clusaz.

Megève deserves a special mention – an exceptionally charming little town combining rustic style with sophistication; shame about the traffic. It has now been overtaken by Courchevel 1850 as the most expensive resort in France, largely because of Courchevel's popularity not just with the Paris jet set but also with rich Russians.

And France has Alpine centres with a long mountaineering and skiing history. Chief among these is Chamonix, which sits in the shadow of Mont Blanc, Europe's highest peak, and is the centre of the most radical off-piste terrain in the Alps. Chamonix is a big, bustling town, where winter sports go on alongside tourism in general. By contrast, simple La Grave is at the foot of mountains that are almost as impressive – the highest within France.

IMPROVING APARTMENTS

One of the most welcome developments on the French resort scene
in recent years has been the availability of genuinely comfortable
and stylish apartments, in contrast to the cramped and, frankly,
primitive places that have dominated the market since the 1960s.
Our luxury apartments chapter is largely about this new generation
of French apartments, which have opened up self-catering holidays
to people who previously would not have contemplated them.

PLAT DU JOUR

France has advantages over most rival destinations in the
gastronomic stakes. While many of its mountain restaurants serve
fast food, most also do at least a plat du jour that is in a different
league from what you'll find in Austria or the US. It is generally
possible to find somewhere to get a half-decent lunch and to have it
served at your table, rather than queuing repeatedly for every
element of your meal. In the evening, most resorts have restaurants
serving good, traditional French food as well as regional specialities.
And the wine is decent and affordable.

Many French resorts (though not all) have suffered from a lack of
nightlife, but things have changed in recent years. In resorts
dominated by apartments with few international visitors, there may
still be very little going on after dinner, but places such as Méribel
are now distinctly lively in the evening.

PERFECT PISTES

France is unusual among European countries in using four grades of
piste (instead of the usual three). The very easiest runs are classified
green; except in Val d'Isère, they are reliably gentle. It's novices who
care most about choosing just the right sort of terrain to build
confidence, so this is a genuinely helpful system, which ought to be
used internationally.

AVOID THE CROWDS

French school holidays mean crowded slopes, so they are worth
avoiding if possible. The country is divided into three zones, with
three fortnight holidays staggered over a four-week period from early
February to early March – with two zones overlapping in late
February – so expect that period to be particularly busy.

SNOWPIX.COM / CHRIS GILL

One of the mistakes
the French made in
the 1960s: Le Bec
Rouge at Tignes →

Alpe-d'Huez

Impressive and sunny slopes above a hotchpotch of a purpose-built village, but with attractive alternative bases that we prefer to stay in

RATINGS

The slopes
Fast lifts	**
Snow	****
Extent	****
Expert	****
Intermediate	****
Beginner	*****
Convenience	****
Queues	****
Mountain restaurants	****

The rest
Scenery	****
Resort charm	*
Off-slope	****

NEWS

For 2007/08 90 more snow-guns are planned.

For 2006/07 a fast quad replaced the Louvets double chair to Auris-en-Oisans. And there's a new moving carpet at Les Eterlous.

The Grandes Alpes weekly lift pass now includes two days at Les Deux-Alpes.

The sports centre has new fitness rooms and there's a new 3-star hotel, with pool, in Oz-en-Oisans.

➕ Extensive, high, sunny slopes, split interestingly into various sectors

➕ Huge snowmaking installation

➕ Vast, gentle, sunny nursery slopes

➕ Efficient lift system, mostly

➕ Some surprisingly good mountain restaurants

➕ Livelier than most purpose-built resorts

➕ Pleasant alternative bases in outlying villages and satellites

➖ In late season the many south-facing runs can be icy early and slushy later

➖ Some main intermediate runs get badly overcrowded in high season

➖ Many of the tough runs are very high, and inaccessible in bad weather

➖ Practically no woodland runs to retreat to in bad weather

➖ Sprawling resort with no central focus and very little charm

There are few places to rival Alpe-d'Huez and its Massif des Grandes Rousses for extent and variety of terrain – in good wintery conditions it's one of our favourites. But as the season progresses the effects of the strong southern sun become more and more of a problem.

The village of Alpe-d'Huez has few fans, but if you don't like the sound of it, you always have the alternative of staying in rustic Vaujany, in Villard-Reculas, or in the modern ski stations of Oz-en-Oisans or Auris-en-Oisans. All are described at the end of this chapter.

THE RESORT

Alpe-d'Huez is a large, modern resort on a high, open, sunny mountainside east of Grenoble. Although developed for skiing, it has grown in a seemingly unplanned, sprawling fashion.

The resort spreads down a gentle slope in a triangular shape from the main lift station at the top corner. Access roads enter the village at the two lower corners, west and east. The nearest thing to a central focus is the main Avenue des Jeux in the middle, where you'll find the swimming pool, ice skating and some of the shops,

bars and restaurants. The buildings come in all shapes, sizes and designs (including a futuristic church which hosts weekly organ concerts). Many buildings look overdue for renovation, although some wood cladding and smartening-up can now be seen. Towards the bottom end of the triangle is the original core of the resort, with a couple of streets that have a slightly more traditional feel.

A short distance from the main body of the resort are two satellite 'quarters', both a bit of a trek from the centre but with their own lifts, and adequate local supplies of bars and restaurants. Les Bergers is at the eastern entrance to the resort; a chalet suburb is expanding this quarter uphill – convenient for skiing but even more remote from the village centre. L'Eclose is to the south of the main village.

There is also accommodation down the hill in the old village of Huez, linked by lift to the resort.

Reporters have remarked on the warm welcome from the locals, compared with other French resorts.

The bus service around the resort is free with the lift pass, and during the day there's a bucket-lift (with a piste beneath it) running through the resort to the main lifts at the top. This is

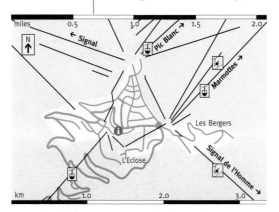

KEY FACTS

Resort	1860m
	6,100ft
Slopes	1120-3320m
	3,670-10,890ft
Lifts	84
Pistes	248km
	154 miles
Green	32%
Blue	26%
Red	28%
Black	14%
Snowmaking	
	785 guns

LIFT PASSES

Visalp

Prices in €

Age	1-day	6-day
under 16	26	137
16 to 59	37	192
over 60	26	137

Free under 5, over 72

Beginner day pass
€12

Notes
Covers all lifts in Alpe-d'Huez, Auris, Oz, Vaujany and Villard-Reculas; half-day passes; discounts for families and regular visitors; 2-day-plus passes cover sports centre, ice rink, swimming pools, concerts, two museums and shuttle service; 6-day-plus passes allow one day's skiing at one of Serre-Chevalier, Puy-St-Vincent and the Milky Way in Italy, and two days in Les Deux-Alpes

Alternative passes
Auris only, Oz-Vaujany only, Villard-Reculas only

---

handy but slow, and some people don't like jumping on and off.

Outings by road are feasible to other resorts covered on a week's lift pass, including Serre-Chevalier and Les Deux-Alpes. A helicopter does day trips to Les Deux-Alpes for a surprisingly modest fee, and a bus goes twice a week, but you need to book.

THE MOUNTAINS

Alpe-d'Huez is a big-league resort, ranking alongside giants like Val d'Isère or La Plagne for the extent and variety of its slopes. Practically all the slopes are above the tree line, and there may be precious little to do when a storm socks in; the runs around Oz are your best bet.

Reporters find the piste classification unreliable, making it a rather unnerving place for timid intermediates. You may find some reds rather tame, then find others 'steeply mogulled half-way down'.

THE SLOPES
Several well-linked areas
The slopes divide into four sectors, with good connections between them, though one reporter complained of having to pole or walk between lifts.

The biggest sector is directly above the village, on the slopes of **Pic Blanc**. The huge Grandes Rousses gondola, otherwise known as the DMC (a reference to its clever technology), goes up in two stages from the top of the village. Above it, a cable-car goes up to 3320m/10,890ft on Pic Blanc itself – the top of the small Sarenne glacier and start of the longest piste in the Alps (see the feature panel). The glacier is also reached via the Marmottes gondola, which also serves lower runs from Clocher de Macle.

The Sarenne gorge separates the main resort area from **Signal de l'Homme**. It is crossed by a down-and-up fast chair-lift from the Bergers part of the village. From the top you can take excellent north-facing slopes towards the gorge, or head south to Auris or west to tiny Chatelard.

On the other side of town from Signal de l'Homme is the small **Signal** sector, reached by drag-lifts next to the main gondola or by a couple of chairs lower down. Runs go down the other side of the hill to the old village of Villard-Reculas. One blue run back to Alpe-d'Huez is floodlit twice a week.

The generally quieter **Vaujany-Oz** sector consists largely of north-west-facing slopes, accessible from Alpe-d'Huez via good red runs. At the heart of this sector is Alpette, the mid-station of the cable-car from Vaujany. From here a disastrously sunny red goes down to Oz, a much more reliable blue goes north to the Vaujany home slopes around Montfrais, and a shady black plunges down to l'Enversin, just below Vaujany, offering an on-piste descent of 2200m/7,220ft from Pic Blanc – not the biggest vertical in the Alps, but not far short. The links back to Alpe-d'Huez are by the top cable-car from Alpette, or a gondola from Oz.

TERRAIN-PARKS
A choice
There are two parks: one for novices near the bottom of the slopes, with various jumps and rollers; and a 1.5km/1 mile advanced park near the Babars drag, with half-pipe, jumps, hips, big-air and a boarder-cross course. Teenagers can sign up for new freestyle classes with ESF. There's another terrain-park near Auris and a beginners' park above Vaujany.

SNOW RELIABILITY
Affected by the sun
Alpe-d'Huez is unique among major purpose-built resorts in the Alps in having mainly south- or south-west-facing slopes. The strong southern sun means that late-season conditions may alternate between slush and ice on most of the area, with some of the lower runs being closed altogether. There are shady slopes above Vaujany and at Signal de l'Homme. The Pic Blanc glacier is small.

In midwinter the runs are relatively snow-sure, thanks to extensive snowmaking on the main runs above Alpe-d'Huez, Vaujany and Oz. But reports suggest that neither the grooming nor the snowmaking is as enthusiastic as we would wish.

FOR EXPERTS
Plenty of blacks and off-piste
There are long and challenging pistes as well as some serious off-piste routes (see feature box).

The slope beneath the Pic Blanc cable-car, usually an impressive mogul-field, is reached by a 300m/980ft tunnel from the back side of the mountain. Despite improvements to the tunnel exit, the start of the actual

The main lift station at the top of the village is the departure point for Pic Blanc and the vast nursery slopes →
SNOWPIX.COM / CHRIS GILL

slope is often awkward. The slope is of ordinary black steepness, but can be very hard in the mornings because it gets a lot of sun. Get advice.

The long Sarenne run on the back of the Pic Blanc is described in a special feature panel. Thanks to snowmaking, we've at last been able to ski the black Fare piste to l'Enversin – a highly enjoyable long run, away from the lifts, but not steep. The Marmottes II gondola serves genuine black runs from Clocher de Macle; Balcons is steep and quiet, often with good snow; Clocher de Macle is easier but busier; don't miss the beautiful, long, lonely Combe Charbonnière. The Lièvre Blanc chair-lift serves further testing slopes – Balme, looping away from the lifts, is now classified black, and one or two reds would be classified black in many resorts.

FOR INTERMEDIATES
Fine selection of runs

Good intermediates have a fine selection of runs all over the area. In good snow conditions the variety of runs is difficult to beat. Every section has some challenging red runs to test the adventurous intermediate. The Canyon run is one of the most challenging. There are lovely long runs down to Oz and to Vaujany, with space for some serious carving. The Villard-Reculas and Signal de l'Homme sectors also have long challenging reds. Those at Signal de L'Homme are said to be quieter, which keeps their snow better. The Chamois red from the top of the gondola down to the mid-station is quite narrow, and miserable when busy and icy and/or heavily mogulled. Fearless intermediates should enjoy the super-long Sarenne black run. For

Alpe-d'Huez

247

OFF-PISTE FOR ALL STANDARDS

There are vast amounts of off-piste terrain in Alpe-d'Huez, from fairly tame to seriously adventurous. Here we pick out just a few of the many runs to be explored – always with guidance, of course.

There are lots of off-piste variants on both sides of the Sarenne run that are good for making your first turns off-piste. The Combe du Loup, a beautiful south-facing bowl with views over the Meije, has a black-run gradient at the top, and you end up on long, gentle slopes leading back to the Sarenne gorge. La Chapelle Saint Giraud, which starts at Signal de l'Homme, is another excellent itinerary for off-piste novices. Its vertical drop of 630m/2,070ft includes a series of small confidence-boosting bowls, interspersed with gentle rolling terrain.

For more experienced and adventurous off-piste skiers, the Grand Sablat is a classic which runs through a magnificently wild setting on the eastern face of the Massif des Grandes Rousses. This descent of 2000m/6,560ft vertical includes glacial terrain and some steep couloirs. You can either ski down to the village of Clavans, where you can take a pre-booked helicopter or taxi back, or traverse above Clavans back to the Sarenne Gorge. In the Signal sector, there are various classic routes down towards the village of Huez or to Villard-Reculas.

The north-facing Vaujany sector is particularly interesting for experienced off-piste enthusiasts. Route finding can be very tricky, and huge cliffs and rock bands mean this is not a place to get lost. From the top of Pic Blanc, a 40-minute hike takes you to Col de la Pyramide at 3250m/10,660ft, the starting point for the classic itinerary La Pyramide with a vertical of over 2000m/6,560ft. Once at the bottom of the long and wide Pyramide snowfield, you can link into the Vaujany pistes.

less ambitious intermediates, there are usually blue alternatives, except on the upper part of the mountain. The main Couloir blue from the top of the big gondola is a lovely run, well served by snowmaking, but it does get scarily crowded at times.

There are some great cruising runs above Vaujany; but the red runs between Vaujany and Alpe-d'Huez can be too much for early intermediates. You can travel via Oz on gondolas, if you are that keen to get around.

Early intermediates will also enjoy the gentle slopes leading back to Alpe-d'Huez from the main mountain, and the Signal sector.

FOR BEGINNERS
Good facilities

The large network of green runs immediately above the village is as good a nursery area as you will find anywhere. The six-pack installed at Les Bergers a couple of seasons ago has made that part much easier for novices. Sadly, these slopes get very crowded and carry a lot of fast through-traffic. A large area embracing half a dozen runs has been declared a low-speed zone, but the restriction is not policed and so achieves very little. All in all, with a special lift pass covering 11 lifts, Alpe-d'Huez makes a good choice.

Giant two-stage cable-car can shift the entire population of Vaujany in about 90 minutes

Excellent varied runs on the home slopes of Vaujany

Dôme des Petites Rousses 2810m

Pic Bl

Lac Blanc

2700m

Alpette-Rousses

L'Alpette 2050m

Montfrais

La Villette — Montfrais

Vaujany-Alpette

Alpette

VAUJANY/OZ

2100m

Vaujany 1250m

Station 1350m

Poutran I & II

DMC I & II

Marmottes I II & III

Oz-en-Oisans

SIGNAL 2115m

Romains

L' Enversin d'Oz 1120m

Alpe-d'Huez 1860m/ 6,100ft

Les Bergers

Televillage

Le Villarais

Above the village, what must be the world's biggest expanse of genuinely green beginner slopes

Huez

Villard-Reculas 1500m

THE LONGEST PISTE IN THE ALPS – AND IT'S BLACK?

It's no surprise that most ski runs that are seriously steep are also seriously short. The really long runs in the Alps tend to be classified blue, or red at the most. The Parsenn runs above Klosters, for example – typically 12km to 15km (7 to 9 miles) long – are manageable in your first week on skis. Even Chamonix's famous Vallée Blanche off-piste run doesn't include steepness in its attractions.

So you could be forgiven for being sceptical about the 'black' Sarenne run from the Pic Blanc: even with an impressive vertical of 2000m/6,560ft, a run 16km/10 miles in length means an average gradient of only 11 per cent – typical of a blue run. Macho-hype on the part of the lift company, presumably?

Not quite. The Sarenne is a run of two halves. The bottom half is virtually flat (boarders beware) but the top half is a genuine black if you take the direct route – a demanding and highly satisfying run (with stunning views) that any keen, competent skier will enjoy. The steep mogul-field near the top can be avoided by taking an easier option (or by using the Marmottes III gondola); and the whole run can be tackled by an adventurous intermediate. The run gets a lot of sun, so pick your time with care – there's nothing worse than a sunny run with no sun.

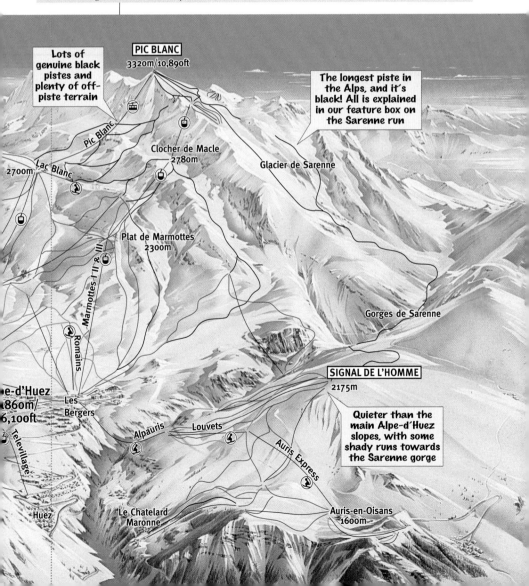

Lots of genuine black pistes and plenty of off-piste terrain

PIC BLANC
3320m/10,890ft

The longest piste in the Alps, and it's black! All is explained in our feature box on the Sarenne run

Pic Blanc

Clocher de Macle
2780m

Glacier de Sarenne

Lac Blanc

2700m

Plat de Marmottes
2300m

Marmottes I, II & III

Gorges de Sarenne

Romains

SIGNAL DE L'HOMME
2175m

e-d'Huez
1860m/
6,100ft

Les Bergers

Quieter than the main Alpe-d'Huez slopes, with some shady runs towards the Sarenne gorge

Televillage

Alpauris

Louvets

Auris Express

Huez

Le Chatelard Maronne

Auris-en-Oisans
1600m

The slopes of Signal
de l'Homme are
separated from the
village by the deep
Sarenne gorge →

FRANCE

250

SCHOOLS

ESF
t 0476 809423
International
t 0476 804277
Masterclass
t 0476 809383
Stance
t 0680 755572

Classes (ESF prices)
6 days (3hr am and
2½hr pm) €180
Private lessons
€37 for 1hr, for 1 or
2 people

GUIDES

Mountain guide office
t 0476 804255

CHILDREN

Les Crapouilloux
t 0476 113923
From age 2; 8.30-7.30
Les Intrépides
t 0476 112161
Ages 6mnth to 4yr;
8am-6.30
Les Eterlous (ESF)
t 0476 806785
Ages 2½ to 5
Tonton Mayonnaise
(International school
Ages 2½ to 3½;
10am-12 noon

Ski schools
Take children from 4
to 16 (ESF 6 days
€169)

FOR CROSS-COUNTRY
High-level and convenient
There are 50km/31 miles of trails, with
three loops of varying degrees of
difficulty, all at around 2000m/6,560ft
and consequently relatively snow-sure.

QUEUES
Generally few problems
Even in French holiday periods, the
modern lift system ensures there are
few long hold-ups. The village bucket-
lift is said to generate lengthy queues
first thing. Queues can build up for the
gondolas out of the village, but the
DMC shifts its queue quickly and the
bottom section can be avoided by
taking alternative lifts to the quieter
second stage.
   Although they may not cause
queues, there are lots of old drag-lifts
scattered around.
   Over much of the area a greater
problem than lift queues is that the
main pistes can be unbearably
crowded. We and many reporters rate
the Chamois and Couloir runs from the
top of the DMC among the most
crowded we've seen. The reds to
Vaujany and Oz are also too busy for
comfort – 'Carnage all the way,' said
one reporter of the Oz run.

MOUNTAIN RESTAURANTS
Some excellent rustic huts
Mountain restaurants are generally
good – even self-service places are
welcoming, and there are more rustic
places with table-service than is usual
in high French resorts. But the
restaurants in the more obvious
positions get over-busy.
Editors' choice Compared with some of
the places on the main pistes, the cosy
little Chalet du Lac Besson (0476
806537) is an oasis of calm – tucked
away on the cross-country loops north
of the DMC gondola mid-station (and
now with an official access piste, the
Boulevard des Lacs). Food and service
are excellent. Repeatedly endorsed by
enthusiastic reporters – 'fabulous
place', 'worth every cent'.

Worth knowing about There are a
couple of good spots low down – not
mountain restaurants as such, but very
popular targets nonetheless. The pretty
Forêt de Maronne hotel at Chatelard,
below Signal de l'Homme, is 'a
delightfully quiet suntrap', enthuses a
reporter, and has a good choice of
traditional French and international
cuisine: 'The chicken satay kept us
raving about the place all week.' The
Bergerie at Villard-Reculas has good
views and is 'highly recommended'.
   The Combe Haute, at the foot of the
Chalvet chair in the gorge towards the
end of the Sarenne run, is welcoming

boarding

The resort suits experienced boarders well – the extent and variety of the
mountains mean that there's a lot of good free-riding to be had. And, if there's
good snow, the off-piste is vast and varied and well worth checking out with a
guide. Unfortunately for beginners, the main nursery slopes are almost all
accessed by drag-lifts, but these can be avoided once a modicum of control has
been achieved. Planète Surf is the main snowboard shop.

GETTING THERE

Air Lyon 150km/ 93 miles (3hr); Geneva 220km/137 miles (4hr); Grenoble, 99km/62 miles (1½hr)

Rail Grenoble (63km/ 39 miles); daily buses from station

ACTIVITIES

Indoor Sports centre (tennis, gym, squash, aerobics, swimming, shooting range, climbing wall), sauna, cinemas, concerts, theatre, library, museum

Outdoor Ice rink, curling, cleared walking paths, snowshoeing, microlight flights, sightseeing flights, ice cave, off-road vehicle tours, hang-gliding, paragliding, ice driving school

SMART LODGINGS

Check out our feature chapters at the front of the book.

Phone numbers From abroad use the prefix +33 and omit the initial '0' of the phone number

TOURIST OFFICE

Alpe-d'Huez
t 0476 114444
info@alpedhuez.com
www.alpedhuez.com

but gets very busy. The Signal is quieter and has 'postcard views'. The 'cosy' Perce Neige, just below the Oz-Poutran gondola, 'made a great lunch' for a 2007 visitor. The Plage des Neiges at the top of the nursery slopes is one of the best places available to beginners. The Cabane du Poutat, halfway down from Plat de Marmottes, does good food but is inadequately staffed – go early. Chantebise 2100, at the DMC mid-station, gets mixed reviews this year. Reporters are also divided on the Marmottes.

The restaurants in the Oz and Vaujany sectors tend to be cheaper, but no less satisfactory. At Montfrais, the Airelles is a rustic hut, built into the rock, with a roaring log fire, atmospheric music and excellent, good-value food ('The best plat du jour I have ever eaten,' says a reporter). The Auberge de l'Alpette also gets enthusiastic reviews emphasising that it is 'really good value'. The P'Oz is also worth a visit.

SCHOOLS AND GUIDES
Contrasting reports

Reports on the ESF branches here are mixed: 'The kids progressed very well,' said one, but two others sound worrying alarms. 'Appalling,' said a reporter whose daughter was found 'sobbing after being shouted at', while another child 'was curled in a ball crying, totally ignored'. 'Don't even think about going to the ESF,' said another. Groups can be big: one reporter counted an astonishing 25 in one class. We continue to get favourable reports of Masterclass, an independent school run by British instructor Stuart Adamson: 'Solid instruction; constructive, individual attention without overloading on technical detail.' Class sizes are limited to eight. Advance booking for high season is necessary. Stance is a new school for 2007/08 – two experienced instructors specialising in teaching British clients and offering group or private lessons. The Bureau des Guides also has a good reputation.

FACILITIES FOR CHILDREN
Positive reports

Les Crapouilloux day-care centre is 'very well organised' and has been recommended, as has tour operator Crystal's childcare operation. The children's garden and nursery at Vaujany have been recommended.

STAYING THERE

HOW TO GO
Something of everything

Chalets UK tour operators run a few chalets, mostly in the recently developed area above Les Bergers; Ski à la Carte has places here and in the old part of the village. But most of the chalet accommodation is in larger chalet hotels, of which there are quite a few. We have good reports of Mark Warner's Mariandre, in the old part of the village.

Hotels There are more hotels than is usual in a high French resort, and there's a clear downmarket bias, with more 1-stars than 2- or 3-stars, and only two 4-stars.

****Royal Ours Blanc (0479 650765) Central. Luxurious, with good food. Superb fitness centre. Free (but often oversubscribed) minibus to the lifts.

****Au Chamois d'Or (0476 803132) Good facilities, modern rooms, one of the best restaurants in town and well placed for main gondola.

***Grandes Rousses (0476 803311) A visitor says, 'Great atmosphere, charming Madame, goodish food and a good guitarist.' Close to the lifts.

**Gentianes (0476 803576) Close to the Sarenne gondola in Les Bergers; a range of rooms, the best comfortable.

**Ancoli (0476 111313) Good-value chalet down the hill in Huez.

Apartments There is an enormous choice available. The Pierre et Vacances apartments near the Marmottes gondola in Les Bergers offer good facilities, but as usual in France they are too small if fully occupied. The Maison de l'Alpe close to the DMC has been recommended for its ideal location and good facilities.

EATING OUT
Good value

Alpe-d'Huez has dozens of restaurants, some of high quality; many offer good value by resort standards. The Crémaillère is recommended by a frequent visitor. Au P'tit Creux is 'fantastic; fabulous food, excellent wine list and helpful staff'. The 'outstanding' Génépi is a friendly old place with good cuisine. The Pomme de Pin is repeatedly approved. Of the pizzerias, the Origan 'served fabulous pizza and pasta'; Pinocchio 'gets very busy early', says a reporter, who also liked the 'enormous helpings' at Smithy's Tavern (Tex-Mex). The

↑ The super-long Sarenne black run gives great views of the peaks of the Ecrins national park

SNOWPIX.COM / CHRIS GILL

appealing mainly to a young crowd. The small but 'lively' Sphere bar is popular after the lifts close. O'Sharkey's (with 'comfortable leather sofas') and the Pacific (sister bar to the one in Val d'Isère) are also popular. Smithy's can get pretty rowdy late on. The live bands at the Grotte du Yéti make for 'some great nights' but a 2006 reporter said it had 'all the atmosphere of a youth club.'

The Etalon and Free Ride cafes ('relaxed, cheery atmosphere with great sports videos') are also recommended. The Zoo is great for a relaxed drink. The Sporting is 'a great bar with class bands but the highest prices in town'; this and the Igloo club liven up in peak season.

Edelweiss is recommended for its 'excellent value set menus and grills'. The Nabab (Moroccan) is recommended for 'tender slow-cooked lamb in a room decorated like a Turkish harem'. A 2007 reporter was very impressed by the friendly, helpful staff at both the Fondue en Folie and the Crêperie des Jeux.

APRES-SKI
Getting better all the time
There's a wide range of bars, some of which get fairly lively later on. There are several British-run bars in chalet hotels, mostly pretty basic and

OFF THE SLOPES
Good by high-resort standards
There is a wide range of facilities, including an indoor pool, an open-air pool (boxer-style cozzies not allowed), Olympic-size ice rink and splendid sports centre – all of this covered by the lift pass. There's also an ice-driving school and a toboggan run. You can try airboarding and snow biking on Fridays, beside the Poutran lift. Visits to the Ice Cave are highly recommended by reporters. Shops are numerous but limited in range. The helicopter excursion to Les Deux-Alpes is amusing. There are well-marked walkers' trails and there's a pedestrian lift pass. A special route map is also available. The better mountain restaurants are widely spread – some too remote for pedestrians.

Villard-Reculas

1500m/4,920ft

Villard-Reculas is a secluded village just over the hill (Signal) from Alpe-d'Huez, complete with an old church, set on a small shelf wedged between an expanse of open snowfields above and tree-filled hillsides below. A fast quad up to Signal has increased the village's popularity as a base. Its visitor beds are mainly in self-catering apartments and chalets, booked either through the tourist office or La Source – an English-run agency that also runs a comfortable catered chalet in a carefully converted stone barn. There is one 2-star hotel, the Beaux Monts (0476 804314). There is a store 'almost like a trading post' and a couple of bars and restaurants.

The local slopes have something for everyone – including a nursery slope at village level – and there is a branch of the Ecole du Ski Français.

But a reporter warns 'the place is dull at night' and 'beginners will be stuck here because the runs that link to the rest of the wonderful skiing are very undergraded'. Two near-beginners in his party were 'very put off'.

Oz-en-Oisans Station

1350m/4,430ft

The purpose-built ski station above the old village of the same name is a 'thriving small resort', says a reporter who has an apartment there. It has been built in an attractive style, with much use of wood and stone, and has a ski school, sports shops, nursery slopes, bars, restaurants, supermarket, skating rink, large underground car park and now two mid-range hotels. But another reporter complains that there is still no nightlife. Two gondolas whisk you out of the resort – one goes to Alpette above Vaujany and the other goes in two stages to the mid-station of the DMC above Alpe-d'Huez. The main run home is liberally endowed with snow-guns, but it needs to be. One clear advantage of staying here is that the slopes above Oz are about the best in the area when heavy snow is falling – and those based elsewhere may not be able to reach them.

The smart Chalet des Neiges apartments are in chalet-style buildings – about 10 apartments per chalet – with pool, sauna and restaurant. Available through Peak Retreats.

Auris-en-Oisans 1600

1600m/5,250ft

Auris-en-Oisans 1600 is another tiny ski station – a series of wood-clad, chalet-style apartment blocks with a few shops, bars and restaurants set just above the tree-line. It's a compact family resort, with a ski school, nursery and a ski kindergarten. Beneath it is the original old village of Auris, complete with attractive, traditional buildings, a church and all but one of the resort's hotels. Staying here with a car you can drive up to the lift base or make excursions to other resorts.

Unsurprisingly, evenings are quiet, with a handful of bar-restaurants to

---

Phone numbers
From abroad use the prefix +33 and omit the initial '0' of the phone number

TOURIST OFFICES

Villard-Reculas
t 0476 804569
info@villard-reculas.com
www.villard-reculas.com

Oz-en-Oisans
t 0476 807801
info@oz-en-oisans.com
www.oz-en-oisans.com

Auris-en-Oisans
t 0476 801352
info@auris.en.oisans.com
www.auris-en-oisans.com

Vaujany
t 0476 807237
info@vaujany.com
www.vaujany.com

choose from. The Beau Site (0476 800639), which looks like an apartment block, is the only hotel in the upper village. A couple of miles down the hill, the traditional Auberge de la Forêt (0476 800601) gives you a feel of 'real' rural France.

Access to the slopes of Alpe-d'Huez is no problem (but returning to Auris may prove difficult for novices – the top section of Signal de L'Homme is a bit steep). There are plenty of local slopes to explore, for which there is a special lift pass. Most runs are intermediate, though Auris is also the best of the local hamlets for beginners.

Vaujany 1250m/4,100ft

Vaujany is a quiet, small (though growing) village perched on a sunny hillside opposite its own sector of the domain. Hydroelectric riches have financed huge continuing investment in lifts and other infrastructure. A giant 160-person cable-car whisks you into the heart of the Alpe-d'Huez lift system and a two-stage gondola takes you to the local slopes at Montfrais via a mid-station below the tiny, rustic hamlet of La Villette. There are plans to double Vaujany's 2,000 visitor beds over the next two years. Small though it is, the village has identifiable sections.

As you enter the village, you come to a couple of small, simple hotels. The Rissiou is exceptionally well run by British tour operator Ski Peak: delicious food and ever-helpful staff. Ski Peak also runs comfortable, tastefully decorated catered chalets in

Vaujany and La Villette; a minibus service for guests is available.

You then come to a recently built complex around a small pedestrian square, Place Centre Village, with spacious, mid-range apartments built in traditional style (La Cascade is available through Peak Retreats). There's a good ski shop, restaurant, food shops, cafe/bar and cavernous underground car-park – and an escalator down to the nearby cable-car and gondola stations. An elevator takes you further down the hill to the superb sports centre, with pool.

An impressive enclosed escalator goes up the hillside past chalets and farm buildings to the top of the village, where sizeable apartment buildings are grouped around the Galerie Marchande – a small pedestrian shopping zone with a small supermarket, food shop, a couple of bars and a couple of restaurants. Since most of the visitor beds are up here, it is naturally the focus of evening activity.

There are no slopes leading directly to the village. But there is a 'pulse' gondola up from l'Enversin where the Fare black run finishes, or you can take a blue to the mid-station of the Montfrais gondola and ride down. Beginner children are taken to a gentle roped-off area here at the gondola mid-station and adult beginners to the nursery slope at the cable-car mid-station. There's a good self-service restaurant with sunny terrace right by the children's learning area. The ski school (adult's and children's) and nursery have been praised.

FRANCE

Les Arcs

Three first-generation purpose-built resorts plus a cute modern alternative – with an exceptional variety and extent of slopes

➕ A wide variety of pistes and easily accessed off-piste terrain

➕ Exceptional amounts of genuinely black piste skiing above Arc 2000

➕ Fast cable-car link to La Plagne

➕ Some excellent woodland runs

➕ Mainly traffic-free villages with easy slope access from most lodgings

➕ Option of staying in quiet, more traditional, lower villages

➕ Very easy rail access from UK

➕ Arc 1950 offers a rare blend of convenience and ambience, but ...

➖ Original village centres lack charm, and aren't always so convenient

➖ Few off-slope diversions

➖ Still a lot of slow old chair-lifts

➖ Very quiet in the evenings, and limited choice of bars/restaurants

➖ No green runs for novices to progress to – normally a feature of French resorts

➖ Lots of flat linking runs to annoy snowboarders

➖ Accommodation in high villages is nearly all in apartments

We've always liked Les Arcs' slopes: they offer impressive variety, including some of the longest descents in the Alps, and plenty of steep stuff. And the slick link with La Plagne puts these resorts in the same league as the Three Valleys. Keen mixed-ability groups should have Les Arcs on their shortlists.

The main villages have always put us off – fairly functional, but drab. But the new Arc 1950 mini-village is something else: a resort that's even more conveniently arranged than the others, and a lot more pleasant to inhabit.

THE RESORT

Les Arcs is made up of four modern resort units, linked by road, high above the railway terminus town of Bourg-St-Maurice. The four villages are all purpose-built and apartment-dominated, and offer doorstep access to the snow with no traffic hazards, but the original three lack Alpine charm, off-slope activities and much evening animation. There's a special feature panel on the fourth – the much more attractive Arc 1950 – later in the chapter.

Reporters repeatedly comment on the friendliness of the locals.

Arc 1600 was the first Arc. For rail travellers it is the obvious choice, with a funicular railway up from Bourg-St-Maurice. 1600 is set in the trees and has a friendly, small-scale atmosphere; and it enjoys good views along the valley and towards Mont Blanc. The central area is particularly good for families: uncrowded, compact, and set on even ground. But it is very quiet in the evening. Above the village, chair-lifts fan out over the lower slopes, leading to links to the other Arcs.

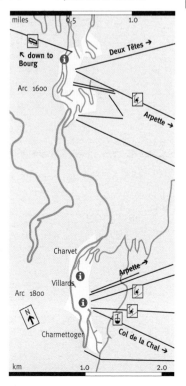

↑ The main lift departure area at Arc 1800 – Villards

NEWS

For 2007/08 a six-pack is to replace the slow Plan Bois chair-lift – a key lift on the way from Vallandry to Arc 1800.

In Arc 1950 the final buildings are due to open for 2007/08. Spa facilities, open to all, should also be finished.

For 2006/07 the Arcabulle covered six-pack opened next to the Plagnette chair to Col de la Chal, above Arc 2000. The latter now starts higher up the mountain, replacing the Bosses drag-lift. Snowmaking was increased, notably on the terrain-park at Arc 1600.

Much the largest of the villages is Arc 1800. It has three sections, though the boundaries are indistinct. Charvet and Villards are small shopping centres, mostly open-air but still managing to seem claustrophobic. Both are dominated by huge apartment blocks. More easy on the eye is Charmettoger, with smaller, wood-clad buildings nestling among trees. There are also apartments up the hillside in Le Chantel. The lifts depart from Villards – chair-lifts to mid-mountain, and the big Transarc gondola to Col de la Chal above Arc 2000.

Arc 2000 is just a few hotels, apartment blocks and the Club Med, huddled together in a bleak spot, with little to commend it but immediate access to the highest, toughest skiing. Some more upmarket apartments have been built; there is only a handful of restaurants and shops.

Just below Arc 2000 and linked to it by a short gondola, the new mini-village of Arc 1950 is due to be complete for 2007/08 – see feature panel later in this chapter.

There are lifts all around Arc 1950 and 2000, including the Varet gondola up towards the Aiguille Rouge.

At the southern end of the ski area, linked by pistes but reachable by road only by first descending to the main valley, is Peisey-Vallandry; the cable-car link with La Plagne begins here. At the northern end of the ski area is the rustic hamlet of Villaroger. These outlying bases are described at the end of the chapter.

THE MOUNTAINS

Les Arcs' terrain is notably varied; it has plenty of runs for experts and intermediates and a good mixture of high, snow-sure slopes and low-level woodland runs ideal for bad weather.

A cable-car from Plan-Peisey links to La Plagne, covered by the Paradiski passes. Even from Arc 1950 you can be at the cable-car in 20 minutes, ready for a long day at La Plagne.

Day trips by car to Val d'Isère-Tignes or the Three Valleys are possible – and if you buy a Paradiski lift pass for five days or more, we understand you'll be able to buy a 10 euro daily extension to ski Val d'Isère-Tignes or the Three Valleys too.

THE SLOPES
Well planned and varied

Arc 1600 and Arc 1800 share a west-facing mountainside laced with runs down to one or other village. At the southern end is an area of woodland runs down to Peisey-Vallandry.

From various points on the ridge above 1600 and 1800 you can head down into the wide Arc 2000 bowl. Across this bowl, lifts take you to the highest runs of the area, from the Aiguille Rouge and the Grand Col. As well as a variety of steep north-west-facing runs back to Arc 2000, the Aiguille Rouge is the start of a lovely long run (over 2000m/6,560ft vertical and 7km/4 miles long) right down to the hamlet of Villaroger. Arc 2000 has runs descending below village level, to the lift base and car park at Pré-St-Esprit, about 300m/985ft lower.

On the lower half of the Aiguille Rouge is a speed-skiing run, which is sometimes open to the public; the fee includes helmet, goggles and skis.

Piste marking is 'superb', says a 2007 reporter.

TERRAIN-PARKS
State of the art

Above Arc 1600 and below Arpette, and served by the Clair Blanc chair-lift, lies Apocalypse Parc. For years, this has been one of the most advanced parks in the Alps – on a par with Avoriaz. Snow-guns have now been installed due to recent poor snowfall, which means there will always be something built. Two kicker lines are in place for intermediate to advanced riders. This is coupled with a nice rail and box line, varied and fun for all and

LIFT PASSES

Grand Domaine Les Arcs

Prices in €

Age	1-day	6-day
under 14	31	145
14 to 59	41	193
over 60	35	164
Free under 6, over 72		
Beginner six free lifts		

Notes
Covers Les Arcs lifts; half-day pass and one-day Paradiski extension possible; free access to ice rink (1800) and pool (1600)

Paradiski Découverte

Prices in €

Age	6-day
under 14	156
14 to 59	208
over 60	177
Free under 6, over 72	
Beginner no deals	

Notes
Covers all lifts in Les Arcs areas with one day in Paradiski

Paradiski

Prices in €

Age	1-day	6-day
under 14	35	175
14 to 59	46	233
over 60	40	199
Free under 6, over 72		
Beginner no deals		

Notes
Covers all lifts in Les Arcs area and La Plagne area; family reductions

a big wall ride. Plans to mould dirt over the summer should make for an even better design for 2008. Along the far side of the park lies a 500m/1,640ft long boarder-cross course. Huge queues at peak times (eg French school holidays) are not uncommon. In addition to the main park there is a well-shaped and big half-pipe located at Arc 2000 that is floodlit until late. Its maintenance suffered this year due to the poor snowfall. There was also a small rail park above Peisey-Vallandry last season – not marked on the piste map, but recommended by a reader.

SNOW RELIABILITY
Good – plenty of high runs

A high percentage of the runs are above 2000m/6,560ft and when necessary you can stay high by using lifts that start around that altitude. Most of the slopes face roughly west, which is not ideal. Those from the Col de la Chal and the long runs down to Villaroger are north-facing, and the blacks on the Aiguille Rouge face near enough north to keep their snow well, even in spring. The limited snowmaking is being gradually extended; 80 new snow-guns were added for 2006/07, including full coverage for the terrain-park at 1600. Reporters are still finding that grooming can be 'economical'.

FOR EXPERTS
Challenges on- and off-piste

Les Arcs has a lot to offer experts – at least when the high lifts are open (the Aiguille Rouge cable-car, in particular, is often shut in bad weather).

There are a number of truly black pistes above Arc 2000, and a couple in other areas. After a narrow shelf near the top (which can be awkward), the Aiguille Rouge-Villaroger run is superb, with remarkably varying terrain throughout its vertical drop of over 2000m/6,560ft. There is also a great deal of off-piste potential. There are steep pitches on the front face of the Aiguille Rouge and secluded runs on the back side, towards Villaroger. A short climb to the Grand Col from the chair-lift of the same name gives access to several routes, including a quite serious couloir and an easier option. From Col de la Chal there is an easy route down to Pont Bodin near Nancroix. The wooded slopes above 1600 are another attractive possibility and there are open slopes beside the pistes all over the place.

FOR INTERMEDIATES
Plenty for all abilities

One strength of the area is that most main routes have easy and more difficult alternatives, making it good for mixed-ability groups. There are plenty of challenges, yet less confident intermediates are able to move around without getting too many nasty surprises. An exception is the solitary Comborcière black from Les Deux Têtes down to Pré-St-Esprit. This long mogul-field justifies its rating and can be great fun for strong intermediates. The Malgovert red, from the same point towards Arc 1600, can be equally tricky – it is narrow and often mogulled.

The woodland runs at either end of the domain, above Peisey-Vallandry and Villaroger, and the bumpy Cachette red down to 1600, are also good for better intermediates. We especially like the Peisey-Vallandry area: its well groomed, tree-lined runs have a very friendly feel and are remarkably uncrowded much of the time, allowing great fast cruising. Good intermediates can enjoy the Aiguille Rouge-Villaroger run. The lower half of the mountainside above 1600/1800 is good for mixed-ability groups, with a

Les Arcs

257

boarding

Les Arcs has always been a hotspot for snowboarders. Regis Rolland, founder of A-Snowboards (recently renamed APO), has for years been exploiting the potential of some of the most varied board-friendly terrain in Europe and has played a huge part in popularising the sport here. Les Arcs offers incredible off-piste terrain, mainly in the back bowls of Arcs 2000. Gullies, trees, natural jibs and hits, steep terrain – this place has it all. The good mix of terrain also means that there are plenty of wide-open rolling slopes for beginners, especially in Vallandry or just above Arc 1800. Be careful of the long traverses on near-flat cat-tracks and some of the blues at Arc 2000. Most of the area is serviced by fast chair-lifts and gondolas, which is an added bonus. For freestyle junkies, there is a good terrain-park; but don't stay in Peisey-Vallandry if you plan to use it.

choice of routes through the trees. The red runs down from Arpette and Col des Frettes towards 1800 are quite steep but usually well groomed.

Cautious intermediates have plenty of blue cruising terrain. Many of the runs around 2000 are rather bland and prone to overcrowding. Edelweiss is the most recent blue addition down to Arc 1950 from Col des Frettes. The blues above 1800 are attractive but also crowded. A favourite blue of ours is Renard, high above Vallandry, usually with excellent snow.

And, of course, you have the whole of La Plagne's slopes to explore if you get bored locally.

FOR BEGINNERS
1800 or Peisey-Vallandry best
There are 'ski tranquille' nursery-slope zones above each of the three main Arcs, and at mid-mountain above Peisey-Vallandry; though we and

readers haven't found them always tranquil. There is supposed to be a free lift for the use of beginners in each resort, but some are apparently free only at weekends and others may not be much practical use as a basis for learning; anyway, with only one lift to use you'll soon start paying for a points card or lift pass. In all sectors there are long, easy blue runs to move on to.

FOR CROSS-COUNTRY
Very boring locally
Short trails, mostly on roads, is all you can expect, but the pretty Nancroix valley's 40km/25 miles of pleasant trails are easily accessible by free bus.

QUEUES
Slow chairs more of a problem
Reporters have few complaints about queues, except in one or two places, though during half-term one visitor

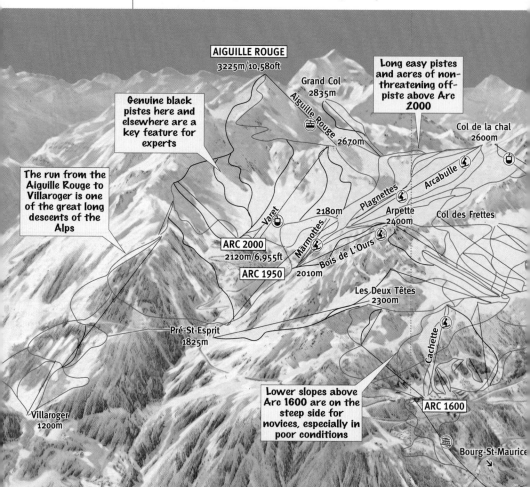

AIGUILLE ROUGE
3225m/10,58oft

Grand Col
2835m

Aiguille Rouge
2670m

Long easy pistes and acres of non-threatening off-piste above Arc 2000

Col de la chal
2600m

Genuine black pistes here and elsewhere are a key feature for experts

Plagnettes

Arcabulle

The run from the Aiguille Rouge to Villaroger is one of the great long descents of the Alps

Varet

2180m

Marmottes

Arpette
2400m

Col des Frettes

ARC 2000
2120m/6,955ft

Bois de L'Ours

ARC 1950   2010m

Les Deux Têtes
2300m

Pré-St-Esprit
1825m

Cachette

Villaroger
1200m

Lower slopes above Arc 1600 are on the steep side for novices, especially in poor conditions

ARC 1600

Bourg-St-Maurice

Arc 1600:
Garderie La Cachette
t 0479 077050
8.30 to 6pm; ages
4mnth to 11yr

Arc 1800: Les
Pommes de Pins
t 0479 042431
8.30 to 12 noon; 1.30
to 5pm; ages 3 to 6

Arc 1950: Le Cariboo
t 0479 042572
8.30 to 6.30; from
age 3

Arc 2000:
t 0479 076425
8.30 to 12 noon; 1.30
to 5pm; ages 3 to 6

Ski school
Generally take
children from age 3:
6 days (2hr am or
pm) €134 (ESF prices)

found the worst queues she had ever experienced and 'manic' pistes above 1800. A boarder complains of 'huge' peak-season queues at the Apocalypse terrain-park lift. In sunny weather, Arc 2000 attracts the crowds. The new six-pack to Col de la Chal has reduced but not eliminated queues there. The gondola to the shoulder of the Aiguille Rouge is always busy, but unique in France in having lifties ushering ones and twos into partly filled cabins – excellent. The cable-car to the top builds 'shocking' queues.

A bigger issue than queues is the time spent on slow chair-lifts, some of them very long – notably Comborcière and Mont Blanc. We're pleased to see that a six-pack is to replace the slow Plan Bois chair above Vallandry for 2007/08. We also have one report of the beginner drag-lift at Arc 2000 not opening before classes start, resulting in uphill walks ('children were crying

because it was so hard for them'). At peak periods crowded pistes can be a problem, too.

MOUNTAIN RESTAURANTS
Not much choice high-up
The proper mountain restaurants are mainly unremarkable.
Editors' choice The Chalets de l'Arc (0479 041540), just above Arc 2000 – built in traditional wood and stone – is basically the only decent restaurant above resort level. We've used it regularly since it opened, and enjoyed excellent food and service, and have multiple reports of 'fabulous' lunches – so we assume that the dreadful service we got on the terrace in March 2007 was an isolated incident. Notably good home-baked bread.
Worth knowing about Below Arc 2000, the 500-year-old Belliou la Fumée at Pré-St-Esprit is set beside a car park; but it is charmingly rustic, and judged

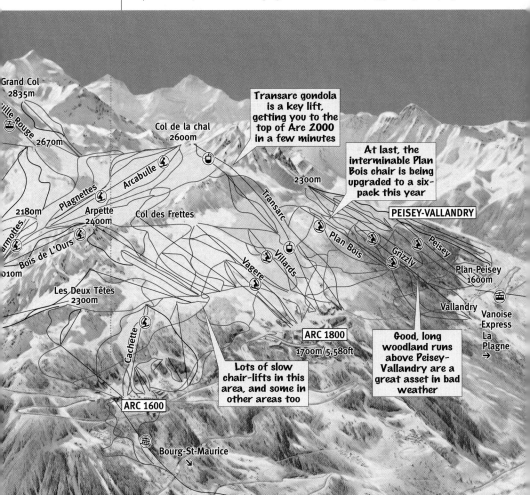

↑ The woodland runs are a great attraction
OT PEISEY

SCHOOLS

ESF Arc 1600
t 0479 074309
ESF Arc 1800
t 0479 074031
ESF Arc 2000
t 0479 074752
Arc Aventures (ESI)
t 0479 074128
Darentasia
t 0479 041681
New Generation
t 0479 010318
www.skinewgen.com
Initial-Snow
t 0612 457291
Privilege
t 0479 072338
Spirit 1950
t 0479 042572

Classes (ESF prices)
6 days (2½hr am or pm) €134
Private lessons
€37 for 1hr, for 1 or 2 people

---

the best in the resort by two 2006 reporters. At even lower altitude, the Ferme ('friendly, great place, massive portions') and Aiguille Rouge ('nice omelettes') down at Villaroger are both friendly, with good food. The Solliet above Villaroger has good views, but recently disappointed a previously happy customer with very slow service.

The Arpette, above 1800, has a 'great selection of food'. The little Blanche Murée, slightly out of the way below the Transarc mid-station, is good for a simple table-service lunch in the sun ('good salads and wine'). Above Vallandry, the Poudreuse has a 'fair choice of meals', although 'drinks at the bar are expensive – beware'. There are places in the villages, of course, some accessible on skis. Readers' recommendations include the Aiguille Grive on the fringes of 1800, the Chalet de l'Arcelle ('simply the best food and setting I have been to in the Alps') and Chez Fernand at 1600.

SCHOOL AND GUIDES
Several, including a Brit school
The ESF here is renowned for being the first in Europe to teach ski évolutif, where you start by learning parallel turns on short skis, gradually moving on to longer skis. Progress can be spectacular. But reviews are very mixed; one reporter praises 'excellent' tuition for his beginner daughter, though warns 'they will challenge and push you, which was too much for my nervous wife'. Another reader gives a scathing report of uninterested

instructors and huge classes: 'Beginners in a group of 24 – absolutely appalling. They did virtually nothing all week.' The International school (aka Arc Aventures) has impressed reporters. British school New Generation has a 'small but strong' team in Vallandry and is fast becoming popular with our readers, as in other resorts: 'Their teaching methods are tailored to the individual – you set your own objectives; brilliant,' says a 2007 reporter. 'Absolutely first rate,' says another. One reporter recommends the private lessons of Snow Escape, also in Vallandry. The Spirit school in 1950 gets good reviews all round, for small classes, English-speaking instructors and flexible private lessons ('grandma successfully learnt to ski'). Off-piste discovery days are also recommended.

FACILITIES FOR CHILDREN
Good reports
Spirit 1950 reportedly provides good care and facilities for smaller children, returning them well-fed and rested. We have received good reports on the Pommes de Pin facilities in Arc 1800. The Cariboos Club is new at Arc 1950 and takes three- to five-year-olds. Comments on children's ski classes have been favourable, too: 'Classes were crowded but teaching/childcare was good.' There is a children's area at 1800, complete with moving carpet lifts, a sledging track and a climbing wall. There are also a couple of discovery pistes, at 1800 and 1600, for children to find out about flora and fauna of the Alps.

STAYING THERE

HOW TO GO
New chalets and apartments
Most resort beds are in apartments. There is a long-established Club Med presence in Arc 2000 and there's a smarter 'village' at Peisey-Vallandry.
Chalets There are now lots of catered chalets in the Peisey-Vallandry area, and Villaroger has a couple, but there are few in the high villages. Family specialist Esprit has chalet-apartments in Arc 2000, sharing a pool.
Hotels The choice of hotels in Les Arcs is gradually widening.
***Grand Paradiso (1800) (0479 076500) Locally judged to be worth four stars rather than its actual three.
***Golf (1800) (0479 414343) An

GETTING THERE

Air Geneva 156km/ 97 miles (3½hr); Lyon 200km/124 miles (3½hr); Chambéry 127km/79 miles (2½hr)

Rail Bourg-St-Maurice; frequent buses and direct funicular to resort

SMART LODGINGS

Check out our feature chapters at the front of the book.

expensive but good 3-star, with 'great ambience around its Jazz Bar', a sauna, gym, kindergarten, covered parking. New spa and heated pool for 2007/08.
***Cachette (1600) (0479 077050) 'Very nice' but it can be 'dominated by kids', say reporters – not surprising as 1600's childcare facilities are here.
**Aiguille Rouge (2000) (0479 075707) Recently renovated. Free ski guiding.
**Mélèzes (2000) (0479 075050) Recommended by a 2007 reporter. Spa. 'Good food.'
**Beguin (1600) (0479 070292) 'Fantastic hotel, patient and friendly staff, superb food.'
Apartments The various apartment developments at Arc 1950 vary in style and space, but the general level of comfort is very high by French standards. In Arc 2000 the Chalet des Neiges and Chalet Altitude offer 'luxury' apartments. The Alpages de Chantel above Arc 1800 is typical of MGM apartments – attractive and comfortable, with pools, saunas and gyms. It is very convenient for skiing,

but a bit isolated. Erna Low's brochure has a comprehensive range of units.
   The Ruitor apartments, set among trees between Charmettoger and Villards (in Arc 1800), are reported to be 'excellent in all respects'. The Aiguille Grive apartments are reportedly spacious and convenient.

EATING OUT
Good choice in Arc 1800
In Arc 1600 and 2000 there are very few restaurants, but they include some excellent ones. Chalet de L'Arcelle in 1600 is repeatedly recommended ('worth a Michelin star'). A 2007 visitor also enjoyed meals at the Malouine and Chez Fernand. In 2000 Chez Eux gets the thumbs-up for 'excellent' Savoyard meals. 1800 has a choice of about 15 restaurants; an ad-based (so not comprehensive) guide is given away locally. The Gargantus is a decent, informal place. Readers have been satisfied by 'enormous portions' at Equipage and 'good food and great service' at the Triangle. Casa Mia is an

Les Arcs

261

Selected chalets in Les Arcs

ACTIVITIES

Indoor Squash (1800), saunas, solaria, multi-gym (1800), cinemas, concert halls, bowling (1800), billiards

Outdoor Natural skating rinks (1800/2000), tobogganing, snow-shoeing, dog-sledding, cleared paths, paragliding, snowmobiling, horse-riding, skijoring, ballooning, ice grotto

excellent all-rounder with exceptionally friendly service ('good food but expensive wine'). The Mountain Café does much more than the Tex-Mex it advertises, and copes well with big family parties. Chez les Filles is worth a visit for 'exceptional views' and 'good food'. Tantra (formerly de Bouvier) has a traditional menu. At 1950, Hemingway's Café does an 'excellent value three-course dinner', Valentino's 'good food', Chez Anne Savoyard specialities, and East does Indian etc.

APRES-SKI
Arc 1800 is the place to be
1800 is the liveliest centre. The JO bar is open until the early hours and has a friendly atmosphere with live music. The new Tantra has a lounge bar – reports please. Reporter recommendations include the friendly Red Hot Saloon for bar games and 'surprisingly good' live music, the Jungle Café for cocktails, the Jazz Bar in the Hotel Golf ('good ambience, great Mexican Bloody Mary') and Chez Boubou at Charvet. And the Gabotte in Place Miravaldi is a 'cosy upstairs bar'. The Apokalypse 'isn't terrible'. The Arpette mountain restaurant has also

been recommended – especially the 'fun, up-beat torchlit descent'.

In 1600 the Bar des Montagnes opposite (and belonging to) the hotel Cachette has games machines, pool and live bands, and can be quite lively even in low season, and a reporter has recommended the Beguin. The Abreuvoir is one reader's all-time favourite bar, with 'good live bands'.

In 2000 the Red Rock is 'good for youngsters but too crowded for grown-ups'; a reporter reckons the Tavern is 'best all round'. The Whistler's Dream, in the Chalet des Neiges, could be worth a try. At 1950, Chalet de Luigi has a bar and a nightclub, Hemingway's a bar, and the Belles Pintes is an Irish-style pub.

OFF THE SLOPES
Very poor
Les Arcs is not the place for an off-the-slopes holiday. There is very little to do, though several of the newer apartment blocks have pools; new spa facilities at Arc 1950 (open to all) are due for 2007/08. A reporter recommends bowling at 1800 and there's skating at 1800 and 2000. The cinemas have English films weekly. You

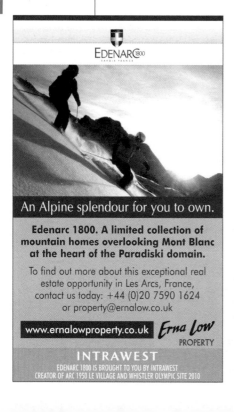

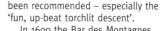

can visit the Beaufort dairy and go shopping in Bourg-St-Maurice and there are a few walks – nice ones up the Nancroix valley. There's also an ice grotto at the top of the Transarc, which pedestrians can reach.

Peisey-Vallandry

1600m/5,250ft

Plan-Peisey and Vallandry are small, still-developing ski stations above the old village of Peisey, which has a bucket-lift up to Plan-Peisey. They market themselves as Peisey-Vallandry, and the cluster of villages hereabouts is known collectively as Peisey-Nancroix. Clear as mud, eh?

The cable-car to La Plagne leaves from Plan-Peisey, which has one hotel, a few shops, bars and restaurants but no real focus other than the lift station. A fast six-seat chair takes you into the slopes. The hotel Vanoise (0479 079219) has been recommended by readers for its position, food and staff ('very welcoming, very French', with few British guests). UK operator Ski Beat has nine specially built chalets here, with 8 to 17 beds. Family specialist Esprit has an enclave of six neat chalets, each with hot-tub. For dining, reporters recommend the Cordée ('excellent, frequented by locals'), Armoise ('superb food, exceptional value menus') and Solan ('brasserie, cosy inside, large terrace'). The Flying Squirrel is British-run, has a popular happy hour, live music, 'gourmet-burgers', weekly quiz night and live sport on TV.

Reporters have enjoyed staying down the hill in the characterful old village of Peisey which dates back 1,000 years and has a fine baroque church. The other, mostly old, buildings include a few shops and a couple of bars and restaurants – a reader enjoyed the Ormelune. There are several chalets run by UK operators, including Ski Beat's Edelweiss.

Vallandry is a few hundred metres away from Plan-Peisey and linked by shuttle-bus. A fast quad takes you into the slopes. There are lots of new chalets and a small pedestrian-only square at the foot of the slopes with a small supermarket and a ski shop.

Ski Olympic's big piste-side chalet-hotel La Forêt gets a rave review this year ('Outstanding food, good rooms, fabulous views, friendly and helpful staff'). Among the other recent developments are some notable self-catering properties. The Orée des Cimes is a comfortable, traditional-style CGH development with a pool and great views.

There are several 'great' locally owned restaurants. Recommendations from reporters include the Calèche for duck, the Dahu, the Bergerie de Raphael, the Refuge ('super pizzas') and the Ourson. There is a crêperie by the Vanoise Express ('good for galettes'). Jimmy's bar is popular but

Les Arcs

WHERE NORTH AMERICA MEETS EUROPE: ARC 1950, AND NOW EDENARC 1800

The first phase of brand-new Arc 1950, just below Arc 2000, opened in December 2003; by December 2005 it was almost complete – a fully functioning mini-resort with powerful attractions. It is high and relatively snow-sure; absolutely traffic-free (cars have to go in the underground multi-storey pay-garage); very conveniently laid out, offering ski-in/ski-out lodgings; comfortable, with apartments of a standard much higher than the French norm; and it is built in a traditional, easy-on-the-eye style.

All the accommodation at present is in apartments, furnished to a high standard. The living rooms we have seen are spacious, at least by French standards, but some incorporate tiny kitchens – and the bedrooms are mostly compact. The outdoor hot-tubs and pools, saunas and steam rooms are added attractions – as are the 'animations' planned every evening, such as fireworks and live music. The apartment hotel and spa, Les Sources de Marie, is set to complete development – opening for 2007/08.

We were impressed by how established the place feels – and by how much more pleasant it is than most other purpose-built resorts in France. You can eat out in a different place each night, there is a reasonable choice of après-ski bars, and the key facilities are in place – a tiny but well stocked supermarket, a bakery, a gift shop, a crêperie, ski and board equipment shops. There is a free gondola up to Arc 2000, perched higher up the steep hillside, but we didn't feel the need to use it.

The credit for all this goes to Canadian company Intrawest, developer of Whistler and other stylish resort villages in North America. This is its first venture into Europe. Others are following: apartments in Flaine Montsoleil (see Flaine chapter) went on sale in 2006, followed early in 2007 by apartments in Edenarc 1800, a contemporary-style development on a crest above Arc 1800.

Phone numbers
From abroad use the prefix +33 and omit the initial '0' of the phone number

TOURIST OFFICES

Les Arcs
1600: 0479 077070
1800: 0479 076111
1950: 0479 071257
2000: 0479 071378
lesarcs@lesarcs.com
www.lesarcs.com

Bourg-St-Maurice
t 0479 071257

Peisey-Vallandry
t 0479 079428
info@peisey-vallandry.com
www.peisey-vallandry.com

FRANCE

SNOWPIX.COM / CHRIS GILL

Great black runs on Aiguille Rouge about Arc 2000 ↘

'noisy'. Mont Blanc Bar is a Brit hang-out and Marlu more French.

Villaroger 1200m/3,940ft

Villaroger is a charming, quiet, rustic little hamlet with three successive chair-lifts (the first two quite slow) going up to a point above Arc 2000. It has a couple of small bar-restaurants and a couple of British-run chalets, including chalet Tarentaise – a lovingly renovated old farmhouse run by Optimum Ski. All bedrooms are now en-suite and there's a sauna and massage room (complete with qualified masseuse). The chalet also has WiFi internet access. And the chef is said to be a bit of a star. Note that Villaroger is not suitable for beginners.

Les Granges 1200m/3,940ft

This hamlet at the mid-station of the funicular up from Bourg makes an interestingly rustic alternative to the bigger resorts if you want a quiet time. It's reached from 1600 by two red runs and a winding blue following a minor road. There is a good (but low and sunny) free nursery slope and kids'

snow-garden. Non-skiers have access to forest walks. No restaurants or bars, last train from Arc 1600 at 8pm (9pm weekends); taxis are reasonable if shared. UK operator Ski Adventures has three good-looking ski-in/ski-out catered chalets at attractive prices, and will ferry guests to/from Arc 1600 and Arc 1800 for après-ski.

Bourg-St-Maurice
850m/2,790ft

Bourg-St-Maurice is a real French town, with cheaper hotels and restaurants and easy access to other resorts for day trips. The funicular starts next to the TGV station and goes straight to Arc 1600 in seven minutes – but beware, the last one down is at 8pm. Reporters recommend Hostellerie du Petit-St-Bernard (0479 070432) – 'looks run-down, but is friendly with super food', and the cheap and cheerful Savoyard (0479 070403) – 'take earplugs to sell to other guests'. A 2006 reporter recommends a traditional Savoyard restaurant, the Tsablo: 'excellent', 'good value'. The new Bazoom Rider's Café incorporates a restaurant, bar, shop and art gallery.

Avoriaz 1800

The 'ski to and from the door' purpose-built resort option on the French side of the big Portes du Soleil circuit

COSTS

① ② ③ ④ ⑤ ⑥

RATINGS

The slopes

Fast lifts	★★★
Snow	★★★
Extent	★★★★★
Expert	★★★
Intermediate	★★★★
Beginner	★★★★
Convenience	★★★★★
Queues	★★★
Mountain restaurants	★★★★

The rest

Scenery	★★★
Resort charm	★★
Off-slope	★

NEWS

The triple Combe du Machon chair, serving steep black runs (and a blue back to Avoriaz) from Hauts-Forts, is to be upgraded to a fast six-pack for 2007/08. And a new terrain-park is to be built in partnership with Burton – see 'Terrain-parks'.

The great news for 2006/07 was that the old Chaux Fleurie chair (a key link from Avoriaz to Châtel and a long-standing bottleneck) was at last replaced by a six-pack. A new terrain-park, Trashers, reserved for and especially designed for 5 to 12-year-olds, opened too.

- ➕ Good position on the main Portes du Soleil circuit, giving access to very extensive, quite varied runs
- ➕ Generally has the best snow in the Portes du Soleil
- ➕ Accommodation right on the slopes
- ➕ Good children's facilities
- ➕ Snowy paths entirely free of cars are an attractive formula, but ...

- ➖ Non-traditional architecture, which some find ugly
- ➖ Much of Portes du Soleil is low for a major French area, with the risk of poor snow or bare slopes low down
- ➖ Can get very crowded at weekends
- ➖ Little to do off the slopes
- ➖ Few hotels or chalets – mostly no-frills, cramped apartments

Of the purpose-built resorts thrown up in the 1960s, Avoriaz is one of the more sympathetically designed. It is compact, its buildings (which you love or hate) are wood-clad with sloping roofs and it is truly car-free, with cars kept completely separate from its reliably snow-covered paths and pistes. And it has the highest and most snow-sure slopes of the relatively low Portes du Soleil region. It is also dramatically set above and below cliffs (floodlit at night).

THE RESORT

Avoriaz 1800 is a purpose-built, traffic-free resort perched above a dramatic, sheer rock face. From the edge of town horse-drawn sleighs or snowcats transport people and luggage from car parks to the accommodation – or you can borrow a sledge for a small deposit and transport your own. The problem of horse mess has been cut since horses now wear 'nappies' and staff on snowmobiles scoop up what escapes! Cars are left in paid-for outdoor or underground parking – choose the latter to avoid a chaotic departure if it snows. You can book space.

As our scale plan suggests, it's a compact place, with everything close to hand (turn forward to Chamonix, for a striking comparison). But the village is set on quite a slope; elevators inside the buildings (and chair-lifts outside, during the day) mean moving around is no problem except when paths are icy, but if you plan to go out much in the evening, it's worth staying near the central focus. Wherever you stay, you should be able to ski from the door.

The village is all angular, dark, wood-clad, high-rise buildings, mostly apartments. But the snow-covered paths and pistes give the place quite a friendly Alpine feel.

The evenings are not especially lively, but reporters have enjoyed 'a good ambience, both day and night',

and a 'brilliant parade in half-term week, with a fire-eating display'. Family-friendly events are laid on all season. A floodlit cliff behind the resort adds to its nocturnal charm.

You can also stay in the lower hamlets of Ardent and Les Prodains.

Avoriaz is on the main lift circuit of the Portes du Soleil – for an overview, look at our separate chapter. It has links to Châtel in one direction and Champéry (Switzerland) in the other – both covered in separate chapters. It is above the valley resort of Morzine, to which it is linked by gondola (but not by piste). The slopes of Morzine and Les Gets, on the far side of Morzine, are part of the Portes du Soleil but not on the core circuit; both are covered in their own chapters. Car trips to Flaine and Chamonix are possible.

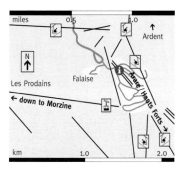

links to the even bigger open area around Les Crosets and Champoussin.

Taking a lift up through the village of Avoriaz to the ridge behind it is the way to the prettily wooded **Lindarets-Brocheaux** valley, from where lifts and runs in the Linga sector lead to Châtel.

TERRAIN-PARKS
Still leading the way

Avoriaz was one of the pioneers of snowboarding in France, and the first terrain-park to be built in the country was here in 1993. Avoriaz is still leading the way, and there will be four parks and a super-pipe for 2007/08.

The main park is Arare, next to the Bleue du Lac piste; it has its own drag-lift and is a pro-park, often used for high-profile contests. Four big kickers with red and black take-offs, big rails, a C-box, wall ride and corner jump are the order of the day.

Beginners and intermediates should head to the La Chapelle park, via the Tour or Prolays chair-lifts. This is littered with jumps of all sizes and fun little boxes. There's also a Biotop area; this isn't considered a park as such but a natural concept area situated in the trees and part of La Chapelle. Nicely constructed wooden rails are peppered amongst the trees – but the area can be inaccessible unless there's a lot of snow.

Trashers was a new addition last season and is strictly for kids. It is located by La Falaise and has several mini-jumps and ride-on boxes. For 2007/08 Avoriaz will be working with Burton to create a fourth park, in the Lindarets forest. It's called The Stash and has banked corners and jumps using the line of the mountain (check out www.thestash.com). Just above the town centre next to the Prodains lift is a good super-pipe. Avoriaz does a brilliant job of keeping the parks maintained, and as a result a lot of riders make this their winter home. Terrain-park lift passes are available at 30 euros for two days.

FRANCE

266

THE MOUNTAINS

The slopes closest to Avoriaz are bleak and treeless, but snow-sure. The main Portes du Soleil circuit is easily done by intermediates of all abilities. Going clockwise avoids two snags in Morgins – the excessively sunny lower slopes of Bec de Corbeau and the uphill walk to the next lift. The booklet-style piste map gives a reasonably clear picture of each resort along the way. The circuit breaks down at Châtel, where you need the frequent shuttle-bus.

THE SLOPES
360˚ choice

The village has lifts and pistes fanning out in all directions.

Facing the village are the slopes of **Arare-Hauts Forts** and, when snow conditions allow, there are long, steep runs down to Les Prodains.

The lifts off to the left go to the **Chavanette** sector on the Swiss border – a broad, undulating bowl. Beyond the border is the infamous Swiss Wall – a long, impressive mogul slope with a tricky start, but not the terror it is cracked up to be unless it's icy (it gets a lot of sun) or you're on a snowboard. It's no disgrace to ride the chair down – lots of people do. At the bottom of the Wall is the open terrain of Planachaux, above Champéry, with

boarding

Avoriaz is great for expert riders. As well as top parks (see 'Terrain-parks') special ungroomed snow-cross areas full of natural obstacles have been created (see 'For experts'). Check www.snowparkavoriaz.com for details. It is well worth hiring a guide here to exploit the vast quantity of good off-piste riding too. There are also plenty of wide, easy slopes, and very few drag-lifts left, making this a great resort for beginners and intermediates as well. Chalet Snowboard, the first chalet company to target snowboarders, has a couple of chalets at Les Prodains.

SCHOOLS

ESF
t 0450 740565
International (L'Ecole de Glisse)
t 0450 740218
Alpine (AASS)
t 0450 747691

Classes
(ESF prices)
6 days (2½hr am and pm) €150
Private lessons
€33 for 1hr, for 1 or 2 people

CHILDREN

Les P'tits Loups
t 0450 740038
9am to 6pm; ages 3mnth to 5yr; 6 days €189
Annie Famose Children's Village
t 0450 740446
from age 3 to 16; 6 days with meal €226

Ski schools
Take children from 4 to 12 (6 days €135)

SNOW RELIABILITY
High resort, low slopes
Although Avoriaz itself is high, its slopes don't go much higher – and some parts of the Portes du Soleil circuit are much lower. Considering their altitude, the north-facing slopes below Hauts Forts hold snow well. In general, the snow in Avoriaz is usually much better than over the border on the south-facing Swiss slopes. But when snow was sparse on our January 2005 visit we found the smooth, grassy, lower slopes of Les Gets much better than the rocky ones around Avoriaz, which need more snow cover.

During the slow start to the 2006/07 season, we had reports of disappointing piste maintenance.

FOR EXPERTS
Several challenging runs
Tough terrain is scattered about. The challenging runs down from Hauts Forts to Prodains (including a World Cup downhill) are excellent. There is a tough red and several long, truly black runs, one of which cuts through trees – useful in poor weather. Two chair-lifts serve the lower runs, which snow-guns help to keep open. The Swiss Wall at Chavanette will naturally be on your agenda, and Châtel is well worth a trip. The black runs off the Swiss side of Mossettes and Pointe de l'Au are

worth trying, and one reporter had a 'very good day' here exploring off-piste with a guide. Four 'snow-cross' runs – ungroomed but avalanche controlled and patrolled – have been introduced in the Hauts Forts, Lindarets, Chavanette and Mossettes areas. They are marked on the piste map, closed when dangerous and an excellent idea.

FOR INTERMEDIATES
Virtually the whole area
Although some sections lack variety, the Portes du Soleil is excellent for all grades of intermediates when snow is in good supply. Timid types not worried about pretty surroundings need not leave the Avoriaz sector; reporters recommend the 'wonderfully quiet' and 'scenic' blues to Prodains. Arare and Chavanette are gentle, spacious and above-the-tree-line bowls. The Lindarets area is also easy, with pretty runs through the trees, but several reporters complain about long flat sections where poling is required. Champoussin has a lot of easy runs, reached without too much difficulty via Les Crosets and Pointe de l'Au. Better intermediates have virtually the whole area at their disposal. The runs down to Pré-la-Joux and L'Essert on the way to Châtel, and those either side of Morgins, are particularly attractive – as are the long runs down to Grand-Paradis near Champéry when snow conditions allow. Brave intermediates may want to take on the Wall, but Pointe de Mossettes offers an easier route to Switzerland.

FOR BEGINNERS
Convenient and good for snow
The nursery slopes seem small in relation to the size of the resort, but are adequate because so many visitors are intermediates. The slopes are sunny, yet good for snow, and link well to longer, easy runs. The main problem can be the crowded pistes. One recent reporter complains crowds and collisions on the Plateau area made progress 'painfully slow' for novices taking classes there.

FOR CROSS-COUNTRY
Varied, with some blacks
There are 45km/28 miles of trails, a third classified as black, mainly between Avoriaz and Super-Morzine, with others around Lindarets and Montriond. But several trails are not loops, but 'out and back' routes.

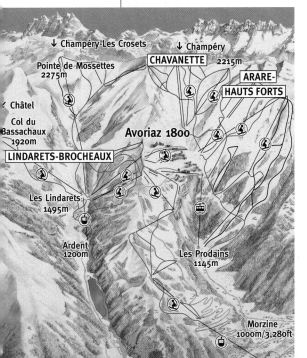

↓ Champéry-Les Crosets   ↓ Champéry

Pointe de Mossettes 2275m

CHAVANETTE 2215m

ARARE-HAUTS FORTS

Châtel

Col du Bassachaux 1920m

Avoriaz 1800

LINDARETS-BROCHEAUX

Les Lindarets 1495m

Ardent 1200m

Les Prodains 1145m

Morzine 1000m/3,280ft

GETTING THERE

Air Geneva 80km/ 50 miles (2hr); Lyon 200km/124 miles (3½hr)

Rail Cluses (42km/ 26 miles) or Thonon (45km/28 miles); bus and cable-car to resort

UK PACKAGES

Alpine Answers, Club Med, Crystal, Directski.com, Erna Low, Independent Ski Links, Interactive Resorts, Lagrange, McNab Snowboarding, Mountain Tracks, Neilson, Ski Collection, Ski France, Ski Independence, Ski Leisure Direction, Ski McNeill, Ski4you, Skifrance4less, Skiholidayextras, Skitracer, Thomson, White Roc

ACTIVITIES

Indoor Health centre 'Altiform' (sauna, gym, hot-tub), squash, ice rink, Turkish baths, cinema, yoga, bowling **Outdoor** Ice rink, dog-sledding, hot air ballooning, mountain biking on snow, ice diving, walking paths, sleigh rides, helicopter flights

Phone numbers From abroad use the prefix +33 and omit the initial '0' of the phone number

TOURIST OFFICE

t 0450 740211 info@avoriaz.com www.avoriaz.com

QUEUES
Main problems now gone

Most of the bad queues have been eliminated by new high-speed lifts. The main long-standing problem is the queue for the cable-car at Prodains. Recent visitors report few other problems. But crowds on the pistes (especially at weekends and around the village) can be bad, with care needed to avoid collisions.

MOUNTAIN RESTAURANTS
Good choice over the hill

Editors' choice The rustic chalets in the hamlet of Les Lindarets form one of the great concentrations of mountain restaurants in the Alps. The jolly Crémaillière (0450 741168) has wonderful chanterelle mushrooms and great atmosphere, but on a good day it's difficult to beat the Terrasse (0450 741617).

Worth knowing about Near the top of the gondola from Morzine, the rustic Grenouille du Marais has good food and views. The table-service Abricotine does 'excellent galettes'. Refuge des Brocheaux at Les Brocheaux and Pas de Chavanette, at the top of the Swiss Wall, have been recommended.

SCHOOLS AND GUIDES
Try AASS

The ESF has a good reputation; classes can be large, but we have a 2007 report of satisfied beginners making 'very good progress' and earlier reports of 'great instruction' and very successful private snowboard lessons. Another 2007 visitor had 'inspirational' snowboard lessons with former pro Angelique Corez-Hubert through the International school. The Avoriaz Alpine Ski School has British instructors and has been highly recommended, especially for 'quite excellent children's lessons'. A recent reporter tried both ESF and AASS for private lessons; he thought the AASS's higher price wasn't justified and criticised its 'haphazard admin system'. However, his son rated the advanced snowboard lessons as 'excellent'.

FACILITIES FOR CHILDREN
'Annie Famose delivers'

The Village des Enfants, run by ex-downhill champ Annie Famose, is a key part of the family appeal of Avoriaz. Its facilities are excellent – a chalet full of activities and special slopes complete with Disney characters.

HOW TO GO
Self-catering dominates

Alternatives to apartments are few. **Chalets** There are several available – comfortable and attractive but mainly designed for small family groups. **Hotels** There is one good hotel and a Club Med 'village'. ***Dromonts** (0450 740811) The original core of the resort, taken over and renovated by a celebrity French chef and in the *Hip Hotels* guidebook. 'Bit expensive but very nice with excellent food', said a 2007 reporter. **Apartments** Reporters say that some apartments need refurbishing, and others are typically 'cramped and basic'. But the Falaise apart-hotel, the Balcons du Soleil, Sepia and Datcha ('very basic') residences have all been recommended. The 'Shopi supermarket is far superior to the Sherpa'.

EATING OUT
Good; booking essential

There are more than 30 restaurants (though a recent reporter criticised the 'limited variety'). The hotel Dromonts has the Table du Marché restaurant ('pricey but excellent'). The Bistro and Cabane have been recommended for 'good food and value', as have the Fontaines Blanches for Savoyard food, Douchka for its 'excellent Moroccan lamb shank', Intrêts for 'pizza and pasta' and 'table-barbecues and Savoyard fare', Au Briska for a cosy night out, Falaise for 'good pizza' and Changabanga's at the bottom end of town for cheap burgers, salads and snowboard-related products.

APRES-SKI
Lively, but not much choice

A few bars have a good atmosphere, particularly in happy hour. The Yeti is busy at 4pm. The Tavaillon attracts Brits and has Sky TV and 'good draught beers', and the Fantastique is worth a visit. For late-night dancing the Choucas and the Place have bands. Going down to Morzine is possible.

OFF THE SLOPES
Not much at the resort

Those not interested in the slopes are better off in Morzine – though Avoriaz does have the Altiform Fitness Centre, with saunas and hot-tubs. Pedestrians are not allowed to ride the chair-lifts, which is a shame.

Chamonix

Traditional old mountain town with great atmosphere and towering mountains above, offering stunning views and off-piste for experts

COSTS

① ② ③ ④ ⑤ ⑥

RATINGS

The slopes
Fast lifts	***
Snow	****
Extent	***
Expert	*****
Intermediate	**
Beginner	*
Convenience	*
Queues	**
Mountain restaurants	**

The rest
Scenery	*****
Resort charm	****
Off-slope	*****

NEWS

For 2006/07, Chamonix at last got a terrain-park on one of its main areas – Les Grands Montets. And the slow Herse chair at Lognan was replaced by a six-pack, as was the Col Cornu quad from Les Vioz at Le Brévent.

A new lift pass structure was introduced, including an option to include unlimited use of the Aiguille du Midi and top Grands Montets cable-cars. But individual passes for three of Chamonix's four areas were scrapped. See 'Lift passes' for the two main options available now. An online booking system was introduced to reserve space on the top Grands Montets and Aiguille du Midi cable-cars.

The scenery here is spectacular, with jagged peaks and tumbling glaciers →

+ A lot of very tough terrain, especially off-piste

+ Amazing cable-car, for the famous Vallée Blanche (or just the views)

+ Stunning views of peaks and glaciers

+ Lots of different resorts and areas covered on Mont Blanc lift pass

+ Town steeped in Alpine traditions

+ Easy access by road, rail and air – excellent weekend destination

− Several separate mountains: mixed ability groups are likely to have to split up, and the bus service gets mixed reviews

− Pistes in each area are quite limited

− Bad weather can shut the best runs

− Still some old lifts and queues

− Few nice mountain restaurants

− Crowds and lots of road traffic

Chamonix could not be more different from the archetypal high-altitude, purpose-built French resort. Unless you are based next to one mountain and stick to it, you have to drive or take a bus each day. There is all sorts of terrain, but the resort offers more to interest the expert than anyone else, and to make the most of the area you need a mountain guide rather than a piste map. Chamonix is neither convenient nor conventional.

But it is special. The Chamonix valley cuts deeply through Europe's highest mountains and glaciers. The views are stunning and the runs are everything really tough runs should be – not only steep, but high and long. If you like your snow and scenery on the wild side, give Chamonix a try. But be warned: there are those who try it and never go home – including lots of Brits.

269

THE RESORT

Chamonix is a long-established tourist town that spreads for miles along the valley in the shadow of Mont Blanc.

On either side of the centre, just within walking distance, are lifts to two of the dozen slope areas in the valley

– the famous cable-car to the Aiguille du Midi, and a gondola to Le Brévent. Also on the fringe of the centre is the nursery slope of Les Planards. All the other lift bases involve bus-rides – the nearest being the cable-car to La Flégère at the village of Les Praz.

Chamonix is a bustling town with

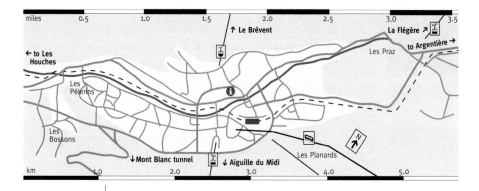

Chamonix Le Pass

Prices in €

Age	1-day	6-day
under 16	29	146
16 to 59	36	182
over 60	29	146

Free under 4

Senior half-price day passes if over 70

Beginner limited pass for beginners under 15

Notes
Covers Brévent-Flégère, Grands Montets to 2750m/ 9,020ft and Balme plus four small beginner areas; family reductions

Alternative passes
Mont-Blanc Unlimited pass covers all the above plus Les Houches, Les Grands Montets to 3300m/ 10,830ft, Aiguille du Midi cable-car, the Helbronner gondola, the Montenvers-Mer de Glace railway, the Tramway du mont-Blanc and a day in Courmayeur in Italy; Skipass Mont-Blanc covers all the lifts in the 13 resorts of the Mont Blanc area and Courmayeur in Italy

scores of hotels and restaurants, visitors all year round and a lively Saturday market. The car-free centre of town is full of atmosphere, with cobbled streets and squares, beautiful old buildings, a fast-running river, pavement cafes crowded with shoppers and tourists sipping drinks and staring at the glaciers above. Not everything is rosy: unsightly modern buildings have been built on to the periphery (especially near the Aiguille du Midi cable-car station), some of the lovely old buildings have been allowed to fall into disrepair, and at times traffic clogs the streets around the car-free centre.

Chamonix's shops deal in everything from high-tech equipment to tacky souvenirs. But reporters often comment on the number and excellence of the former, and Chamonix remains a town for mountain people rather than for poseurs. A recent reporter particularly praises Snell Sports: 'One of the best shops in the Alps for serious skiers.'

Strung out for 20km/12 miles along the Chamonix valley are several separate lift systems, some with attached villages, from Les Houches at one end to Le Tour at the other. Regular buses, free with a Chamonix guest card, link the lift stations and villages but can get very crowded and aren't always reliable (and are less frequent in April, according to a 2007 reporter). There is an evening service, but it is said to finish too early. Like many reporters, we rate a car essential. A car also means you can get easily to other resorts covered by the Mont Blanc pass, such as Megève and Les Contamines, and Courmayeur in Italy.

The obvious place to stay for the full Chamonix experience is in downtown Chamonix. If you plan to go mainly to Argentière, Le Tour or Les Houches, staying there makes sense.

Once you get over the fact that the place is hopelessly disconnected and that some of the lifts are antiquated, you come to appreciate the upside – that Chamonix has a good variety of slopes, and that each of the different areas is worth exploring. Practically all the slopes are above the tree line.

THE SLOPES
Very fragmented
The areas within the Chamonix valley – there are 11 in total – are either small, low, beginners' areas, or are much higher up, above the wooded slopes that plunge to the valley floor, reached by cable-car or gondola.

The six-seat gondola for **Le Brévent** departs a short, steep walk from the centre of town, and the cable-car above takes you to the summit. At **La Flégère**, like Le Brévent, the runs are mainly between 1900m and 2450m (6,230ft and 8,040ft), sunny and with stunning views of Mont Blanc. It is accessed by an inadequate old cable-car from Le Praz and linked by a much newer cable-car to Le Brévent (though reporters have often found the link closed by high winds).

A cable-car or chair-lift take you up to **Les Grands Montets** above Argentière. Much of the best terrain is still accessed by a further cable-car, of relatively low capacity. This costs extra – 10 euros a trip – with the Chamonix Le Pass, but unlimited use is included with the Mont Blanc Unlimited pass. You can book a slot in advance – see 'Queues' later in this chapter.

The Herse chair takes you a lot of the way up but doesn't access some of the best off-piste or the lovely Point de Vue black. The area can be very cold in early season when it gets little sun.

KEY FACTS

Resort	1035m
	3,400ft
Slopes	1035-3840m
	3,400-12,600ft
Lifts	48
Pistes	153km
	95 miles
Green	16%
Blue	36%
Red	32%
Black	16%
Snowmaking	
	125 guns

boarding

The undisputed king of free-ride resorts, Chamonix is a haven for advanced snowboarders who relish the steep and wild terrain. This means, however, that in peak season it gets crowded and fresh snow gets tracked out very quickly. The rough and rugged nature of the slopes means it is not best suited to beginners, but rather to more experienced adventurous riders, willing to try true all-mountain riding. If you do the Vallée Blanche, be warned: the usual route is flat in places. Check out former British champ Neil McNab's excellent extreme backcountry camps at www.mcnabsnowboarding.com. Most areas are equipped mainly with cable-cars, gondolas and chairs. However, there are quite a few difficult drags at Balme that cause inexperienced boarders problems – though you can avoid these if you are ready to contend with cat tracks to take you to other lifts, according to a reporter. Since last season there has been a terrain-park on Grands Montets.

Domaine de Balme above Le Tour has an area of mainly easy pistes. It is also the starting point for good off-piste runs, some of which end up over the border in Switzerland.

Les Houches is another area of slopes just outside Chamonix, covered at the end of the chapter.

There is a valley piste map and an informative little Destination Chamonix handbook, which includes all the local area piste maps, with brief descriptions of each run and assessments of suitability for different abilities (but, annoyingly, no information on lift opening and closing times).

Most of our reporters have been more impressed than they expected with the piste grooming, but not with the signposting of the runs ('virtually non-existent', 'horrendous'), or marking of edges of runs ('several reasonably experienced members of our party went off the edge of the long cat-track in Balme in near white-out conditions').

TERRAIN-PARKS
There is one at last
For years talk of a terrain-park here was sacrilege because of the excellent natural hits and off-piste terrain. However, due to popular demand, and several winters of poor snow conditions, a good park has finally been built. The experienced HO5 crew, responsible for parks in several other resorts, have taken matters into their own hands. The park is situated near Lognan on Grands Montets and you can see details at www.ho5park.com.

THE BEST OFF-PISTE SKIING IN THE WORLD?

Chamonix is renowned as an extreme sports Mecca, with arguably some of the best off-piste skiing in the world. And while thrill seekers and off-piste specialists are spoiled for choice, there is plenty for those looking for their first powder experience, too.

Les Houches and *Balme*, at opposite ends of the Chamonix Valley, are ideal for a first taste off the beaten track. The forested slopes of Les Houches are easy to navigate on bad-weather days, with gentle blue runs bringing you back to the valley. Balme's open slopes are perfect for a foray into deep snow in between the pistes, with firmer ground just a few reassuring metres away.

Snowboarders flock to *La Flégère* after a snowfall, its array of boulders and drop-offs turning it into a massive terrain-park. The open bowl of Combe Lachenal is easily accessed from the top of the Index lift, and the south-facing slopes of this ski area provide excellent spring skiing.

From the top of *Les Grands Montets* (3275m/10,740ft) skiing is mostly off-piste and on glacial terrain. The vast north-facing slope of La Face is fairly steep but with plenty of room for tracks. The steep, extensive area reached via the Point de Vue piste offers stupendous views, plus snow conditions that are often among the best in the valley. The Grands Montets also gives access to the steep Pas de Chèvre run. Skiing under the colossal granite spire of Le Dru, with views of Mont Blanc and the Vallée Blanche in the distance, is an unforgettable experience. The Couloir du Dru and the Rectiligne are also on this face, reserved for the adventurous – with some slopes of 40/45°.

These are just some of the off-piste options in the Chamonix valley, but the possibilities are endless. Together with ski-touring itineraries like the Haute Route (Chamonix to Zermatt), and heli-skiing on the Italian side of Mont Blanc and in neighbouring Switzerland, the wealth of off-piste on offer could keep you skiing for a lifetime. The Vallée Blanche is covered in a feature panel later in this chapter.

Last season it featured 16 jumps, five rails, two hips and a boardercross (which a 2007 reporter thought poor).

SNOW RELIABILITY
Good high up; poor low down

The top runs on the north-facing Grands Montets slopes above Argentière generally have good snow, and the season normally lasts well into May. The risk of finding the top lift shut because of bad weather is more of a worry. There's snowmaking on the busy Bochard piste and the run to the valley, which can now be kept open late in the season. Balme has a snowy location, a good late-season record and snowmaking on the run down to the valley at Le Tour. The largely

south-facing slopes of Brévent and Flégère suffer in warm weather, and the steep black runs to the resort are often closed. Don't be tempted to try these unless you know they are in good condition – they can be very tricky. Some of the low beginners' areas have snowmaking.

FOR EXPERTS
One of the great resorts

Chamonix is renowned for its extensive steep terrain and impressively deep snow. To get the best out of the area you really need to have a local guide. There is also lots of excellent terrain for ski-touring on skins. See the feature panel, earlier in this chapter for more on off-piste possibilities.

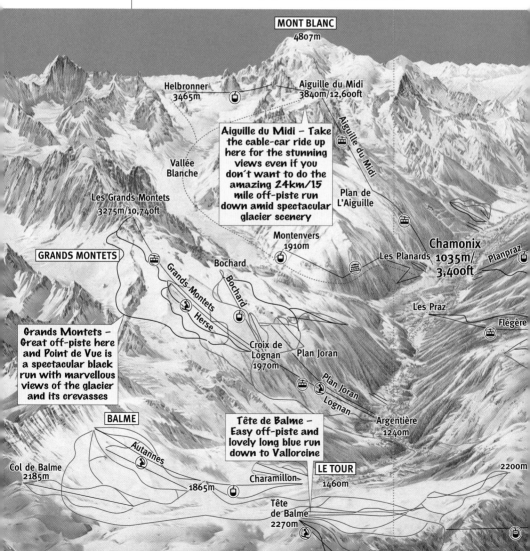

MONT BLANC
4807m

Helbronner
3465m

Aiguille du Midi
3840m/12,600ft

Aiguille du Midi

Aiguille du Midi – Take the cable-car ride up here for the stunning views even if you don't want to do the amazing 24km/15 mile off-piste run down amid spectacular glacier scenery

Vallée Blanche

Plan de L'Aiguille

Les Grands Montets
3275m/10,740ft

GRANDS MONTETS

Montenvers
1910m

Bochard

Les Planards

Chamonix
1035m/
3,400ft

Planpraz

Grands Montets

Bochard

Herse

Les Praz

Flégère

Grands Montets – Great off-piste here and Point de Vue is a spectacular black run with marvellous views of the glacier and its crevasses

Croix de Lognan
1970m

Plan Joran

Plan Joran

Lognan

Argentière
1240m

BALME

Tête de Balme – Easy off-piste and lovely long blue run down to Vallorcine

Autannes

Col de Balme
2185m

1865m

Charamillon

LE TOUR
1460m

Tête de Balme
2270m

2200m

The Grands Montets cable-car offers stunning views from the observation platform above the top station – if you've got the legs and lungs to climb the 121 steep metal steps. (But beware: it's 200 more steps down from the cable-car before you hit the snow.) The ungroomed black pistes from here – Point de Vue and Pylones – are long and exhilarating. The former sails right by some dramatic sections of glacier, with marvellous views of the crevasses.

The Bochard gondola serves a challenging red back to Lognan and a black to either Plan Joran or the chairlift below. Once over the ridge on the black, you can head off-piste down the Combe de la Pendant bowl.

At Le Brévent there's more to test experts than the piste map suggests – there are a number of variations on the runs down from the summit. Some are very steep and prone to ice. The runs in Combe de la Charlanon are quiet and include one red piste and excellent off-piste if the snow is good.

At La Flégère there are further challenging slopes – in the Combe Lachenal, crossed by the linking cable-car, say – and a tough run back to the village when the snow permits. The short drag-lift above L'Index opens up a couple of good steep runs (a red and a black) plus a good area of off-piste.

Balme boasts little tough terrain on-piste but there are off-piste routes from the high points to the village, towards Vallorcine or into Switzerland.

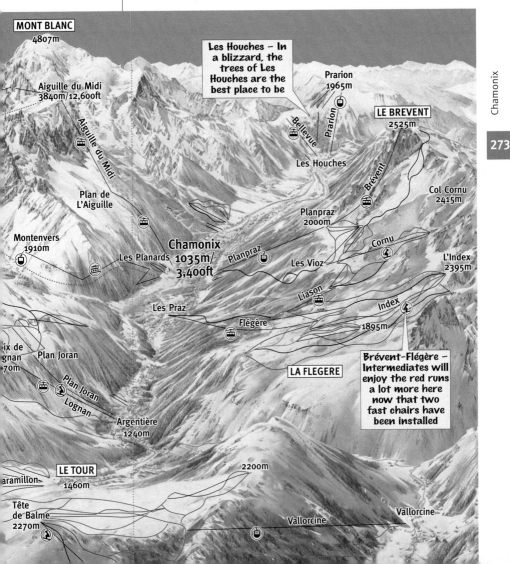

MONT BLANC 4807m

Aiguille du Midi 3840m/12,600ft

Aiguille du Midi

Plan de L'Aiguille

Montenvers 1910m

Les Planards

Chamonix 1035m/ 3,400ft

Planpraz

Les Praz

Flégère

ix de gnan 70m

Plan Joran

Plan Joran

Lognan

Argentière 1240m

LE TOUR 1460m

aramillon

Tête de Balme 2270m

Les Houches – In a blizzard, the trees of Les Houches are the best place to be

Prarion 1965m

Prarion

Bellevue

Les Houches

LE BREVENT 2525m

Brévent

Col Cornu 2415m

Planpraz 2000m

Cornu

Les Vioz

L'Index 2395m

Liason

Index

1895m

LA FLEGERE

Brévent-Flégère – Intermediates will enjoy the red runs a lot more here now that two fast chairs have been installed

2200m

Vallorcine

Vallorcine

FOR INTERMEDIATES
It's worth trying it all

For less confident intermediates, the Balme area above Le Tour is good for cruising and usually free from crowds (a 2007 reporter enjoyed 'untracked powder here well into the afternoon'). There are excellent shady runs on the north side of Tête de Balme, served by a quad. When conditions permit, you can head right down to Vallorcine and ride the gondola back up.

More adventurous intermediates will also want to try the other three main areas, though they may find the Grands Montets tough going (and crowded). The bulk of the terrain at Le Brévent and La Flégère provides a sensible mix of blue and red runs; at Le Brévent the slopes have been redesigned to achieve this.

If the snow and weather are good, join a guided group and do the Vallée Blanche (see feature panel opposite).

A day trip to Courmayeur makes an interesting change of scene, especially when the weather is bad (it can be sunny there when Chamonix's high lifts are closed by blizzards or high winds).

FOR BEGINNERS
Best to learn elsewhere

If there is snow low down, the nursery lifts at La Vormaine, Les Chosalets, Les Planards and Le Savoy are fine for first-timers, who will not be bothered by speed-merchants there. But the separation of beginners' slopes from the rest inhibits the transition to real runs, and makes lunchtime meetings of mixed groups difficult. The slopes on the south side of the valley – Les Planards, in particular – can be dark and cold in mid-winter. Le Savoy is sunny, but devoid of restaurants. Better to learn elsewhere, and come to Chamonix when you can appreciate the tough terrain.

FOR CROSS-COUNTRY
A decent network of trails

Most of the 37km/23 miles of prepared trails lie at valley level in and between Chamonix and Argentière. All the trails are shady and cold in midwinter, and they fade fast in the spring sun. Catch the bus rather than ski between the Chamonix and Argentière areas, suggests a 2007 reporter, as the link is by 'steep and difficult trails'.

QUEUES
Morning and afternoon problems

The main lifts from the valley at Chamonix and Argentière produce queues at peak times. The ancient and inadequate Flégère cable-car is worth avoiding (a recent reporter experienced queues of over an hour here) and there are often queues to come down again (as there are for the Le Brévent gondola).

The other big bottle-neck is the top cable-car on Les Grands Montets. You can book slots in advance (at the ticket office or on-line) and 'it's best to do this the day before as places tend to sell out early,' says a 2007 reporter. If you don't have a reservation, you can queue up in the 'stand by' line ('which moves quite quickly – we used it three times and it took no more than 30 minutes each time; they seem to allow no more than half the spaces to

SCHOOLS

ESF
t 0450 532257

Evolution 2
t 0450 559022

All Mountain Performance
t 0450 532833

Classes
6 half days: €172

Private lessons
€38 for 1hr, for 1 or 2 people

GUIDES

Compagnie des Guides
t 0450 530088

Chamonix Experience
t 0450 540936

be reserved,' said a 2007 reporter).

In poor weather Les Houches gets crowded and the queues for the Bellevue cable-car can then be bad. Crowded pistes are also reported to be a problem in places – most notably at Lognan on Grands Montets.

MOUNTAIN RESTAURANTS
Surprisingly dull

Editors' choice On Le Brévent the Bergerie de Planpraz (0450 530542) is the most attractive option: a wood and stone building with self- and table-service and good food; but it gets very busy. On the Grands Montets the rustic Chalet-Refuge de Lognan, off the Variante Hôtel run to the valley, and overlooking the Argentière glacier, has marvellous views and food.

Worth knowing about On Le Brévent the little Panoramic at the top enjoys amazing views over to Mont Blanc and the food is fine. There's a self-service place at La Flégère with a large terrace and excellent views. On the Grands Montets the Plan Joran serves good food and does table- (try the 'trilogie cuisine – three small dishes served on one plate' says a 2006 reporter) and self-service, but gets busy. There's also an indoor picnic area and 'good sunny terrace'. The restaurant at Lognan has been smartly renovated. At Balme at the top of the gondola from Le Tour, the Chalet de Charamillon is an adequate self-service and there's a picnic area. The Chalet-Refuge du Col de Balme – a short hike from the lifts – is charming, but the hostess there is famously grumpy.

SCHOOLS AND GUIDES
The place to try something new

The schools here are particularly strong in specialist fields – off-piste, glacier and couloir skiing, ski-touring, snowboarding and cross-country. English-speaking instructors and mountain guides are plentiful, and specialist Chamonix tour operators can arrange them in advance for guests. At the Maison de la Montagne is the main ESF office and the HQ of the Compagnie des Guides, which has taken visitors to the mountains for 150 years. Both now offer ready-made week-long 'tours' taking clients to a different mountain or resort each day. We have a good report of the ESF Ski Fun Tour, where they ski a different Mont Blanc region resort each day, transport included: 'Fantastic – we cannot speak highly enough of the guides.' A 2007 reporter also praised the ESF instructors provided by Club Med ('a witty, friendly instructor who spoke excellent English'; but 'some class sizes were large – up to 14').

THE VALLEE BLANCHE

This is a trip you do for the stunning scenery. The views of the ice, the crevasses and seracs – and the spectacular rock spires beyond – are simply mind-blowing. The run, although exceptionally long, is not steep – mostly effortless gliding down gentle slopes with only the occasional steeper, choppy section to deal with. In the right conditions, it is well within the capability of a confident, fit intermediate (but the usual route is rather flat for snowboarders). If snow is sparse ('as it can be in early season especially', warns a regular reporter), the run can be very tricky – there can be patches of sheet ice, exposed stones and rocks, and narrow snow bridges over gaping crevasses. And if fresh snow is abundant, different challenges may arise. Go in a guided group – dangerous crevasses lurk to swallow those not in the know – and check conditions before signing up. The trip is popular – on a busy day 2,500 people do it; book in advance at the Maison de la Montagne or other ski school offices. To miss the worst of the crowds go very early on a weekday, or in the afternoon if you are a good skier and can get down quickly.

The Aiguille du Midi cable-car takes you to 3840m/12,600ft. Across the bridge from the top station on the Piton Nord is the Piton Central; the view of Mont Blanc from the 3842 cafeteria (claimed to be Europe's highest restaurant) – a stair-climb higher – should not be missed, and it gives you the opportunity to adjust to the dizzying altitude. A tunnel delivers you to the infamous ridge-walk, with sheer drops on each side, down to the start of the run. Be prepared for extreme cold up here. There is (usually, but often not in early season, warns a reporter) a fixed guide-rope for you to hang on to, and many parties rope up to their guides. You may still feel envious of those nonchalantly strolling down in crampons; you may wish you'd stayed in bed.

There are variants on the classic route, of varying difficulty and danger. Lack of snow often rules out the full 24km/15 mile run down to Chamonix; a steep stairway and slow gondola link the glacier to the station at Montenvers, for the half-hour mountain railway-ride down to the town.

CHILDREN

Panda Club
t 0450 558612
Ages 3 to 12; 8.30-5pm; includes ski lessons

Babysitter list
Available from the tourist office

Ski schools
Take children aged 3 to 12 (6 days from €295 – ESF price)

UK PACKAGES

Alpine Answers, Alpine Weekends, Barrelli, Bigfoot Travel, BoardnLodge, Chalet Group, Chalet World Ski, Chamonix.uk.com, Club Med, Club Pavilion, Collineige, Corporate Ski Co, Crystal, Directski.com, Erna Low, Esprit, Flexiski, High Mountain Holidays, Independent Ski Links, Inghams, Interactive Resorts, Interhome, Jeffersons, Kuoni, Lagrange, Made to Measure, McNab Snowboarding, Momentum, Mountain Tracks, Neilson, Oxford Ski Co, Peak Retreats, Ski Activity, Ski Collection, Ski Expectations, Ski France, Ski Freshtracks, Ski Independence, Ski Leisure Direction, Ski Line, Ski McNeill, Ski Solutions, Ski Weekend, Ski Weekends, Ski4you, Skiholidayextras, Skitracer, Snow Finders, Thomson, Total, White Heat, White Roc

SMART LODGINGS

Check out our feature chapters at the front of the book.

Competition is provided by a number of smaller, independent guiding and teaching outfits. Evolution 2 'never disappoints', writes a reporter. Mark Gear, who runs All Mountain Performance, has been highly praised by a 2007 reporter. Chamonix Experience offers a full range of options, from classic itineraries and Italian heli-skiing to hidden off-piste routes and avalanche courses.

FACILITIES FOR CHILDREN
Couple of choices
The ESF's Panda Club is used by quite a few British visitors and reports have been enthusiastic. The Argentière base can be inconvenient for meeting up with children for the afternoons. Specialist family tour operator Esprit Ski has a nursery in its Sapinière chalet-hotel near the Savoy nursery slope.

STAYING THERE

HOW TO GO
Any way you like
There is all sorts of accommodation, and lots of it. The tourist office has a 'useful central booking system'. Call 0450 532333 or email reservation@chamonix.com.

Chalets Many are run by small operators that cater for this specialist market. Quality tends to be high and value for money good. Flexiski has the luxurious Bornian, built in traditional style.

Hotels A wide choice, many modestly priced, and the vast majority with fewer than 30 rooms. Bookings for a day or two are no problem – the peak season is summer. Club Med has three linked buildings near the centre and a 2007 reporter rated its all-inclusive deal 'amazing value, excellent food, highly recommended'.

****Hameau Albert 1er (0450 530509) Smart, 100-year-old chalet-style hotel with 'truly excellent' and 'reasonably

---

priced' food (two Michelin stars) but expensive rooms (especially in the farmhouse annexe). Pool.

****Auberge du Bois Prin (0450 533351) A small modern chalet with a big reputation; great views; bit of a hike into town (closer to Le Brévent).

****Mont-Blanc (0450 530564) Central, luxurious.

****Jeu de Paume (Lavancher) (0450 540376) Alpine satellite of a chic Parisian hotel: a beautifully furnished modern chalet halfway to Argentière: 'Tasteful, friendly staff ... lovely'.

****Grand Hotel des Alpes (0450 553780) Elegant, central; with pool, sauna, hot-tub. Friendly Italian staff.

****Morgane (0450 535715) Close to Aiguille de Midi cable-car; pool.

***Alpina (0450 534777) Much the biggest in town: modernist-functional place just north of centre.

***Croix-Blanche (0450 530011) Central, dates from 1793, 'rooms furnished in simple regional style'.

***Gourmets et Italy (0450 530138) Spot-on central mid-price B&B hotel.

***Labrador (Les Praz) (0450 559009) Scandinavian-style chalet close to the Flégère lift. Good restaurant.

***Prieuré (0450 532072) Mega-chalet on northern ring-road – handy for drivers, quite close to centre.

***Vallée Blanche (0450 530450) Smart, low-priced 3-star B&B hotel, handy for centre and Aiguille du Midi.

***Gustavia (0450 530031) Recently renovated with central position. 'Spacious, clean and modern rooms.'

***Hermitage (0450 531387) Central, very close to sports centre and cross-country tracks. Said to be 'modern and Savoyard-style smart'.

***Savoyarde (0450 530077) 'Reasonable and so convenient for Brévant,' says a reporter.

**Richemond (0450 530885) Traditional, with good public areas. 'Excellent; superb food,' says one reporter. 'Rather faded,' writes another.

**Arve (0450 530231) Central, by the river; small rooms. 'Good value and superb service from owners.'

**Faucigny (0450 530117) Cottage-style; in centre.

Clubhouse (0450 909656) 'Boutique hotel; rooms from a suite to bunks.'

Le Vert (0450 531358) Good value with en suite rooms for one to six people. 'Fantastic food for the price, good bar.'

Apartments Many properties in UK package brochures are in convenient but cramped blocks in Chamonix Sud.

Air Geneva 86km/
53 miles (1½hr); Lyon
226km/140 miles
(3hr)

Rail Station in resort,
on the St Gervais-Le
Fayet/Vallorcine line

Direct TGV link from
Paris on Friday
evenings and at
weekends

ACTIVITIES

Indoor Sports
complex (swimming
pool, sauna, steam
room, tennis, squash,
ice rink, fitness room,
climbing wall), Alpine
museum, library,
cinemas, bridge,
bowling

Outdoor Ice rink,
snow-shoeing,
walking paths,
tobogganing, dog-
sledding, ice-climbing,
paintballing

The Balcons du Savoy and Ginabelle
are a cut above the rest: spacious,
pool, gym, steam room etc.

EATING OUT
Plenty of quality places
The top hotels all have excellent
restaurants and there are many other
good places. The handy Resto Poche
guide gives useful information about a
selection. The Impossible is rustic but
smart and features regional dishes
('superb, one of the best meals we've
had in the Alps,' said a 2007 reporter).
We always enjoy the Atmosphère, by
the river, despite its two-sitting system
('excellent', 'cosy, trendy, friendly
efficient service' say recent reporters).
The National, next door, is also
reported to be 'very good'. The Panier
des Quatre Saisons is another favourite
('good food at reasonable prices') –
much better than its shopping-gallery
setting would suggest.

Reader recommendations include
Maison Carrier in the Albert 1er hotel
('Bustling, rustic with great value
traditional food'), Calèche ('good food,
atmosphere and service'), Monchu
(Savoyard specialities), Chaudron
('outstanding', 'excellent service')

Bergerie ('traditional' and 'fantastic'),
Casa Valerio ('fabulous pasta' and
'excellent pizza'), Pitz ('decent, not too
expensive meal'), Tigre Tigre ('English-
run curry house') and Alan Peru ('a
good noodle bar').

APRES-SKI
Lots of bars and music
Many of the bars around the
pedestrianised centre of Chamonix get
crowded at sundown – none more so
than the Choucas video bar. During the
evening, The Pub ('friendly staff and
good British/Irish beer') and Bar'd Up
are busy. The Chambre Neuf at the
Gustavia hotel remains so until late
('live music and dancing on the bar').
The Micro Brasserie is 'very good', with
live bands and DJs. No Escape is a
'funky, upmarket restaurant and lounge
bar'. Along with Privilege, it's aimed 'at
a more discerning clientele who like
their après-ski at a less frantic pace'.

The Brit-run 'small but cosy'
Dérapage has happy hours early and
mid-evening. There's a lively variety of
nightclubs and discos. The Choucas
(again) and Garage are popular. The
Cantina sometimes has live music. Bar
Terrasse has live music every night and

serves 'a good snack menu till 10pm'.

A fire in 2006 on the rue du Moulin destroyed some of Chamonix's most famous bars. Cybar, Bar du Moulin, the Queen Vic and Dick's Tea bar all suffered fire and water damage. A new bar, the Soul Food cafe ('with bags of atmosphere'), has opened on the rue du Moulin.

OFF THE SLOPES
An excellent choice
There's more off-slope activity here than in many resorts. Excursion possibilities include Annecy, Geneva, Martigny, Courmayeur and Turin. The Alpine Museum is 'very interesting as long as you speak French', the library has a selection of English language books and there's a good sports centre and pool. The Cham Gourmand pass entitles you to take the lifts to one of three mountain restaurants, where you get the 27 euros cost of the pass credited towards your meal.

Argentière 1240m/4,070ft

The old village is in a lovely setting towards the head of the valley – the Glacier d'Argentière pokes down towards it and the Aiguille du Midi and Mont Blanc still dominate the scene down the valley. There's a fair bit of modern development, but it still has a rustic appeal.

A number of the hotels are simple, inexpensive and handy for the village centre – but it's a fair hike (uphill on the way back) or a bus-ride to and from the slopes. The 3-star Grands-Montets (0450 540666) is handy for the slopes but a hike to the village. It's a large chalet-style building and 'offers the comfort and service of a 4-star' says a visitor; 'luxurious rooms and a superb pool' says another. The family-run 3-star Montana (0450 541499) provides 'lovely rooms, excellent food', the 2-star Couronne (0450 540002) is basic but 'a great value, old-fashioned French hotel', the 2-star Dahu (0450 540155) is 'excellent value'.

Restaurants and bars are informal and inexpensive; the 'wonderful setting and mouth-watering menu' at Jeu de Paume at Lavancher (see Chamonix hotels) proves the exception. The Dahu is recommended by a 2007 reporter for 'great food, good value set menus', has a 'lovely terrace' and is 'busy with locals and residents'. The Stone serves 'authentic pizzas and a few pasta

dishes' and 'is the place for a game of darts or table football'. The Office is always packed with Brits and Scandinavians and has live bands and 'terrific cooked breakfasts'. The Savoy bar is another traditional favourite – 'lively, friendly, well priced'. The 'friendly' Rencard plays reggae music and 'is a great place to relax with fine pizzas, omelettes and beer'. The Rusticana is 'laid back' with 'friendly staff, good selection of beers and decent food,' says a 2007 visitor.

Les Houches 1010m/3,310ft

Les Houches, 6km/4 miles from Chamonix, is covered by the new Mont Blanc Unlimited pass and still offers its own local pass. It's a pleasant village, sitting in the shade of the looming Mont Blanc massif. There is an old core with a pretty church, but modern developments in chalet style have spread along the road at the foot of the slopes, with the result that some of them are quite a walk from the lifts.

The wooded area above Les Houches – popular when bad weather closes other areas – is served by a queue-prone cable-car (which celebrated its 70th birthday last season) and a gondola (renovated for 2006/07). There are open, gentle runs at the top of the main lifts (including nursery slopes), long, worthwhile blues and reds back towards the village and some particularly lovely woodland runs on the back of the mountain towards St-Gervais. It is the biggest single area of pistes in the Chamonix valley and has Chamonix's World Cup Downhill course. Boarders should note that there are a few difficult drag-lifts and some flat spots to beware of.

In good weather the slopes are quiet, and the views superb from the several attractive mountain restaurants, which are cheaper than others in the valley. Recommendations include the Terrain and Vieilles Luges. Snow-cover on the lower slopes is not reliable, but there is a fair amount of snowmaking. There are still quite a few drag-lifts.

The village is quiet, but there are some pleasant bars and restaurants. Reporters like the 3-star du Bois (0450 545035): 'helpful staff, good restaurant'. There are some good apartments available, including the new MGM Hameau de Pierre Blanche ones with pool, sauna etc. Buses run to and from Chamonix all evening.

Châtel

A distinctively French base in an ideal position for exploring the huge Portes du Soleil circuit which spans the French-Swiss border

COSTS

① ② ③ ④ ⑤ ⑥

RATINGS

The slopes

Fast lifts	**
Snow	**
Extent	*****
Expert	***
Intermediate	****
Beginner	***
Convenience	**
Queues	***
Mountain restaurants	***

The rest

Scenery	****
Resort charm	***
Off-slope	**

NEWS

For 2007/08 a new terrain-park aimed at intermediates and experts, the Happy Park, will be located by the Cornebois chair-lift.

For 2006/07 the triple chair from Les Combes to the top of Linga was replaced by a six-pack. And in the Avoriaz sector, the slow Chaux Fleurie chair (a key lift from Avoriaz to Châtel) was upgraded to a six-pack. It is also now possible to book lift passes (for three days minimum) on the Châtel website.

- ➕ Very extensive, pretty, intermediate terrain – the Portes du Soleil
- ➕ Wide range of cheap and cheerful, good-value accommodation
- ➕ Pleasant, lively, French-dominated old village, still quite rustic in parts
- ➕ Local slopes are among the best in the Portes du Soleil and relatively queue-free
- ➕ Easily reached – one of the shortest drives from the Channel, and close to Geneva

- ➖ Traffic congestion can be a problem at weekends and in peak season
- ➖ Both the resort and the slopes are low for a French resort, with the resulting risk of poor snow – though snowmaking is now extensive
- ➖ Some main lifts are a bus-ride from the village centre
- ➖ Best nursery slopes are reached by bus or gondola

Châtel offers an attractive blend of qualities much like that of Morzine – another established valley village in the Portes du Soleil. Morzine is a bit more polished, Châtel (with a claimed 40 working farms) more rustic. But its key advantage is that it is part of the main Portes du Soleil (PdS) circuit. There is a gap in the circuit at Châtel, filled by buses; but this is more of an irritant to those passing through than for Châtel residents, for many of whom the excellent local bus services are part of the daily routine. At weekends it's worth trying the slopes of nearby Chapelle d'Abondance, which are pleasantly uncrowded.

THE RESORT

Châtel lies near the head of the wooded Dranse valley, at the north-eastern limit of the French-Swiss Portes du Soleil ski circuit.

It is a much expanded but still attractive old village. Modern unpretentious chalet-style hotels and apartments rub shoulders with old farms where cattle still live in winter.

Although there is a definite centre, the village sprawls along the road in from lake Geneva and the diverging roads out – up the hillside towards Morgins and along the valley towards the Linga and Pré-la-Joux lifts.

Lots of visitors take cars and the centre can get clogged with traffic – especially at weekends. Street parking is difficult but there is underground (paid-for) parking and day car parks at Linga and Pré-la-Joux (where the parking can still get very full in peak season despite the provision of new spaces). Other main French Portes du Soleil resorts are easy to reach by piste, but not by road.

The free resort bus service is approved of by most reporters. A central location gives the advantage of getting on the ski-bus to the outlying lifts before it gets very crowded, and

simplifies après-ski outings – the night bus finishes at 9.30pm. But there is accommodation near the Linga lift if first tracks are the priority.

A few kilometres down the valley is the rustic village of La Chapelle-d'Abondance (see end of chapter).

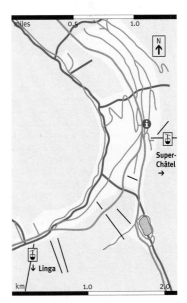

KEY FACTS

Resort	1200m
	3,940ft

Portes du Soleil

Slopes	950-2300m
	3,120-7,550ft
Lifts	209
Pistes	650km
	404 miles
Green	14%
Blue	39%
Red	37%
Black	10%
Snowmaking	
	632 guns

Châtel only

Slopes	1100-2205m
	3,610-7,230ft
Lifts	44
Pistes	83km
	52 miles
Green	30%
Blue	27%
Red	33%
Black	10%
Snowmaking	
	85 guns

THE MOUNTAINS

Châtel sits between two sectors of the main Portes du Soleil circuit, each offering a mix of open and wooded slopes, and linked by an 'excellent, practically continuous though sometimes crowded' free bus service. The circuit is easily done by intermediates of all abilities and there are sectors within it that you are likely to want to spend time exploring without doing the whole circuit more than once or twice during a week. The booklet-style piste map gives a fairly clear picture of each sector.

THE SLOPES
Two sectors to choose between
Directly above the village is **Super-Châtel** – an area of easy, open and lightly wooded slopes, accessed by a gondola or two-stage chair. From here you can embark on a clockwise Portes du Soleil circuit by heading south to the Swiss resort of Morgins, travelling via Champoussin and Champéry to cross back into France above Avoriaz. Or you can head north for the slopes straddling a different bit of the Swiss border, above **Torgon**. You can also access these slopes by chair-lifts from Petit Châtel, down the valley.

An anticlockwise circuit starts outside the village with a lift into the **Linga** sector – a gondola from Villapeyron or a choice of fast chairs from Pré-la-Joux. The fastest way to Avoriaz is via Pré-la-Joux. There is night-skiing on the Stade de Slalom run on Linga every Thursday.

TERRAIN-PARKS
A choice of two
For 2007/08 a new park for intermediates and-experts – Happy Park – is planned in the Cornebois sector. We understand that the existing Smooth Park at Super-Châtel will be redesigned to suit beginner and intermediate freestylers. La Chapelle-d'Abondance also has a 360m/1,180ft long park with half-pipe. A special park-only pass is available.

SNOW RELIABILITY
The main drawback
The main drawback of the Portes du Soleil is that it is low, so snow quality can suffer when it's warm. Châtel is at only 1200m/3,940ft and some runs home can be tricky or shut. But a lot of snowmaking has been installed at Super-Châtel and on runs down to resort level. Linga and Pré-la-Joux are mainly north-facing and generally have the best local snow. The pistes to Morgins and Lindarets, in contrast, get full sun.

FOR EXPERTS
Some challenges
The best steep runs – on- and off-piste – are in the Linga and Pré-la-Joux area. Beneath the Linga gondola and chair there's a pleasant mix of open and wooded ground, which follows the fall line fairly directly. And there's a mogul-field between Cornebois and Plaine Dranse, which has been described as 'steeper and narrower than the infamous Swiss Wall in Avoriaz'. An area under the Cornebois chair, known to the locals as Happy Valley, is also popular

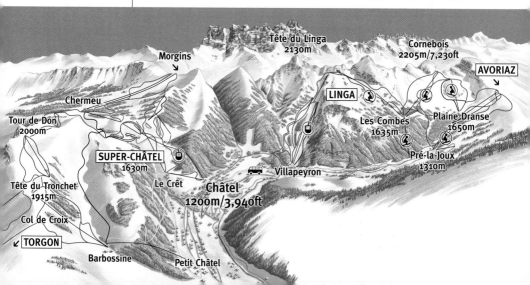

↑ There are good beginner areas and easy slopes to progress to at both Super-Châtel and Pré-la-Joux

SNOWPIX.COM / CHRIS GILL

LIFT PASSES

Portes du Soleil

Prices in €

Age	1-day	6-day
under 16	26	123
16 to 59	38	184
over 60	30	147

Free under 5

Beginner no deals

Notes

Covers lifts in all resorts; half-day pass available

Alternative pass

Châtel only (free for over-75s); private ski tows in village

(we suspect this may be turned into the Happy Park – see 'Terrain-parks'). Two pistes from the Rochassons ridge are steep and kept well groomed. On the way to Torgon from Super-Châtel, the Barbossine black run is long, steep and quite narrow and tricky at the top. There's good off-piste to be explored with a guide: on our 2007 visit we did a great run from Tête du Linga over into the next (deserted) valley of La Leiche.

FOR INTERMEDIATES
Some of the best runs in the area
When conditions are right the Portes du Soleil is an intermediates' paradise. Good intermediates need not go far from Châtel to find amusement; Linga and Plaine Dranse have some of the best red runs on the circuit. The moderately skilled can do the PdS circuit without problem, and will particularly enjoy runs around Les Lindarets and Morgins. Even timid types can do the circuit, provided they take one or two short-cuts and ride chairs down trickier bits. But some blues are said to be difficult: the 'narrow, steep and icy' route to Morgins provoked a complaint from a recent reporter, who witnessed skiers 'in tears' on its top section. The chair from Les Lindarets to Pointe de Mossettes leads to a red run into Switzerland, which is a lot easier than the 'Swiss Wall' from Chavanette and speeds up a journey round the circuit.

Expeditions to the Hauts-Forts runs above Avoriaz are worthwhile. Timid intermediates should note: the runs back to Plaine Dranse are real reds, and the Rochassons piste especially can get 'extremely busy' at the end of the day.

Don't overlook the Torgon sector, which has some excellent slopes including challenging ones.

FOR BEGINNERS
Three possible options
There are good beginners' areas at Pré-la-Joux (a bus-ride away) and at Super-Châtel (a gondola-ride). And there are nursery slopes at village level if there is snow there. Reporters have praised the Super-Châtel slopes and lifts, which 'allow the beginner to progress' and 'safely practise' on gentle gradients away from the main runs. Getting up to them is a bit of an effort, though. The home run to the village from Super-Châtel is not recommended – it is narrow, busy and steep at the end, which, coupled with often poor and icy conditions, makes it very tricky for beginners and timid intermediates. The Pré-la-Joux slopes are said to have 'less variety of slopes and quite a steep drag-lift'.

FOR CROSS-COUNTRY
Pretty, if low, trails
There are 14 pretty trails along the river and through the woods on the lower slopes of Linga, but snow-cover can be a problem. The tourist office produces good maps with suggested routes and trail times.

QUEUES
Bottlenecks have been eased
Queues have been eased throughout the Portes du Soleil circuit in recent years by the introduction of several fast chair-lifts in recent years. But queues form for the gondola to Super-Châtel when school parties gather: 'It is common to share your lift with a buzz of hyperactivity,' writes a visitor. And you can face queues to get back down again if the slope back is shut by poor snow. Reporters have also found lengthy queues at the Tour de Don and Chermeu drag-lifts at certain times of day, causing difficulties for skiers rushing back to Super-Châtel to pick up children from ski school.

MOUNTAIN RESTAURANTS
Some quite good local huts
Atmospheric chalets can be found, notably in a cluster at Plaine Dranse – the Bois Prin, Tan ô Marmottes, Vieux Chalet ('fabulous meal, low ceilinged, laden with teddies, run by a mad woman'), Chaux des Rosées and Chez Denis have been recommended. In the

SCHOOLS

ESF
t 0450 732264

International
t 0450 733192

Henri Gonon
t 0450 732304

Francis Sports
t 0450 813251

Snow Ride (Ecole de Glisse)
t 0608 337651

Classes
(ESF prices)
6 half-days (2½hr am or pm) €113

Private lessons
€34 for 1hr, for 1 or 2 people

ACTIVITIES

Indoor Bowling, cinemas, library

Outdoor Ice rink, walks, paragliding, cheese factory visits, ice-diving, skijoring, snow-shoe excursions (60km/37 miles of trails shared with Morgins – special route map available)

CHILDREN

Mouflets Garderie
t 0450 813819
Ages 3mnth to 6yr; 8am to 7pm; half-day €25

Le Village des Marmottons
t 0450 733379
Ages 3 to 6; 6 days €339 (with lunch)

Ski schools
Generally take children from age 4 or 5 (ESF 6 half-days €122)

GETTING THERE

Air Geneva 75km/ 47 miles (1½hr)

Rail Thonon les Bains (40km/25 miles)

boarding

Avoriaz is the hardcore destination in the Portes du Soleil. Châtel is not a bad place to learn or to go to as a budget option. But many lifts in the Super-Châtel sector are drags and reporters warn they can be a 'painful experience'. The Linga area has good, varied slopes and off-piste possibilities as well as more boarder-friendly chair-lifts.

Linga area the Ferme des Pistes, 'a cosy alpine barn, complete with stable-door', is said to do 'simply the best tarte aux pommes'. The Perdrix Blanche at Pré-la-Joux scarcely counts as a mountain restaurant, but is an attractive (if expensive and crowded) spot for lunch. At Super-Châtel the Portes du Soleil at the foot of the Coqs drags is much better than the big place at the top of the gondola. The Escale Blanche is worth a visit. Don't forget to check out chapters on other Portes du Soleil resorts – particularly Avoriaz.

SCHOOLS AND GUIDES
Plenty of choice
There are five ski and snowboard schools in Châtel. The International school has been recommended by reporters, including 2007 visitors who had a private lesson that was 'one of our best ever'. The ESF has also been praised, with comments such as 'very helpful and customer-focused instructors'.

FACILITIES FOR CHILDREN
Good reports
The Marmottons nursery has good facilities, including toboggans, painting, music and videos, and children are reportedly happy there. Francis Sports ski school has its own nursery area with a drag lift and chalet at Linga: 'Very organised, convenient and reasonably priced.' The ESF had a rave report from a regular visitor: 'I continue to be very impressed.' His eight-year-old grandson has always received 'sympathetic instruction from English-speaking instructors' and has made excellent progress.

STAYING THERE

HOW TO GO
A wide choice, including chalets
Although this is emphatically a French resort, packages from Britain are no problem to track down. A recent reporter praised the personal service he received from a Ski Addiction weekend visit: 'Met me at train station,

waited at hotel then took me to hire shop, guided me round slopes, nothing was too much trouble.'
Chalets A fair number of UK operators have places here, including some Châtel specialists.
Hotels Practically all the hotels are 2-stars, mostly friendly chalets, wooden or at least partly wood-clad.
★★★Macchi (0450 732412) Smart, modern chalet, with spacious, comfortable rooms and good restaurant; small pool, sauna, jacuzzi; most central of the 3-stars.
★★★Fleur de Neige (0450 732010) Welcoming chalet on edge of centre; Grive Gourmande restaurant is one of the best in town.
★★Belalp (0450 732439) Simple chalet with small rooms, but 'very good food'. The Carnotzet restaurant does good braserade.
★★Choucas (0450 732257) Recently refurbished. 'Friendly owner.' Approved of again by a recent reporter.
★★Kandahar (0450 733060) One for peace lovers: a Logis by the river, a walkable distance from the centre.
★★Lion d'Or (0450 813440) In centre, 'basic rooms, good atmosphere'.
★★Rhododendrons (0450 732404) 'Great service, friendly, comfortable, clean.'
Apartments Many of the better places are available through agencies specialising in Châtel or in self-drive holidays. The Gelinotte (out of town but near the Linga lifts and children's village) and the Erines (five minutes from the centre; can also be provided catered) look good. The Avenières is right by the Linga gondola. Châtel's supermarkets are reported to be small and over-crowded. There is a large supermarket out in the direction of Chapelle d'Abondance.

EATING OUT
Fair selection
There are an adequate number and range of restaurants. The Macchi and Fleur de Neige hotels both have pricey gastronomic restaurants (we enjoyed excellent foie gras and venison at the Macchi). We've also enjoyed the Table

The Linga slopes are mainly north-facing and generally have the best snow →

OT CHATEL / J-F VUARAND

d'Antoine restaurant (good crayfish and charming patronne) of the hotel Chalet d'Alizée.

The rustic Vieux Four does ambitious dishes alongside Savoyard specialities and is approved by readers ('good value and the best food we had all week' said a 2007 reporter). The Pierrier ('friendly, food good but not exceptional') and the Fiacre ('superb pizza and moules') are more modest, everyday restaurants. The Moroccan chef at the Hotel Soldanelles cooks a 'veritable feast'. The Refuge du Mille Pâtes does 'bargain' set menus. L'Escalier was new last season with an interestingly different menu – eg filet steak marinaded in Jack Daniels.

Out of town, the Ripaille, almost opposite the Linga gondola, is popular with the locals and highly rated by reporters, especially for its fish and the 'fantastic local Gamay wines'. The hotel Cornettes in La Chapelle-d'Abondance is worth a trip – see next column.

APRES-SKI
All down to bars
Châtel is getting livelier, especially at the weekends. The Tunnel bar is very popular with the British and has a DJ or live music every night (the caramel vodka has been recommended). The Avalanche is a very popular English-style pub with a 'good atmosphere and live music'. The Godille – close to the Super-Châtel gondola and crowded when everyone descends at close of play – has a more French feel. The 'small and cosy' Isba is the locals' choice, and shows extreme sports videos. The bar in hotel Soldanelles has been recommended. The bowling alley, the Vieille Grange du Père Crincheux, also has a good bar.

OFF THE SLOPES
Less than ideal
Those with a car can easily visit places like Geneva, Thonon and Evian. There are some pleasant walks, you can visit the cheese factory or the two cinemas, or join in daily events organised by the tourist office.

The Portes du Soleil as a whole is less than ideal for non-skiers who like to meet their more active friends for lunch: they are likely to be at some distant resort at lunchtime and very few lifts are accessible to pedestrians.

La Chapelle-d'Abondance
1010m/3,310ft

This unspoiled, rustic farming community, complete with old church and friendly locals, is 5km/3 miles along a beautiful valley from Châtel. 'A car and a bit of French are virtually essential,' says a reporter. It's had its own quiet little north-facing area of easy wooded runs for some years, but has more recently been put on the Portes du Soleil map by an outlying gondola that links it to the slopes between Torgon in Switzerland and Super-Châtel.

Nightlife is virtually non-existent – just a few quiet bars, a cinema and torchlit descents. However, we hear that a new and popular microbrewery, the Fer Rouge, opened last season, with live music.

The hotel Cornettes (0450 735024) is an amazing 2-star, run by the Trincaz family since 1894, with renovated rooms and 4-star facilities, including an indoor pool, sauna, steam room and hot-tubs. It has an atmospheric bar and an excellent restaurant (we had a brilliant dégustation of foie gras) with extremely good-value menus. Look out for showcases with puppets and dolls and eccentric touches, such as ancient doors that unexpectedly open automatically.

La Clusaz

Attractive, scenic, distinctively French all-rounder; we like it a lot – but we'd like it a lot more if it was 500 metres higher

COSTS

①②③④⑤⑥

RATINGS

The slopes

Fast lifts	**
Snow	**
Extent	***
Expert	***
Intermediate	****
Beginner	****
Convenience	***
Queues	***
Mountain restaurants	****

The rest

Scenery	***
Resort charm	****
Off-slope	***

NEWS

For 2007/08 there are plans to redevelop the Etale area. A new chondola (a mix of eight-seat gondolas and six-person chairs) will replace the old cable-car and carry over five times as many people per hour. A new quad chair will replace the old double chair to the top. And new runs back to the village will be built with snowmaking.

KEY FACTS

La Clusaz only	
Resort	1100m
	3,610ft
Slopes	1100-2470m
	3,610-8,100ft
Lifts	55
Pistes	132km
	82 miles
Green	28%
Blue	35%
Red	28%
Black	9%
Snowmaking	
	105 guns

➕ Traditional village in scenic setting

➕ Extensive, interesting slopes

➕ Very French atmosphere, good shops

➕ Very short transfer from Geneva, and easy to reach by car from UK

➕ Good, rustic mountain restaurants

➖ Snow conditions unreliable because of low altitude (by French standards)

➖ Lots of slow old chair-lifts

➖ Crowded at weekends

Few other major French resorts are based around what is still, essentially, a genuine mountain village that exudes rustic charm and Gallic atmosphere. Combine that with more than 200km/125 miles of largely intermediate slopes (if you add in nearby Le Grand-Bornand), above and below the tree line, and there's a good basis for an enjoyable, relaxed week. Snowmaking is continually increased, but of course it makes no difference if the temperatures are too high.

THE RESORT

The village is built beside a fast-flowing stream at the junction of a number of narrow wooded valleys. As it has developed into an international resort it has had to grow in a rather rambling and sprawling way, with roads running in a confusing mixture of directions. But, unlike so many French resorts, La Clusaz has retained the charm of a genuine and friendly mountain village, and the new buildings have been built in chalet style and blend in well, for the most part. Les Etages is a much smaller centre of accommodation south of the main town. You can hire a locker next to the slopes to leave skis, boards and boots for around 7.50 euros a night.

As one of the most accessible resorts from Geneva and Annecy, La Clusaz is good for short transfers, but it does get crowded, and there can be weekend traffic jams.

THE MOUNTAINS

Like the village, the slopes are rather sprawling. There are five main areas, each connected to at least one other.

Slopes Several points in La Clusaz have lifts giving access to the predominantly west- and north-west facing slopes of L'Aiguille. From here you can reach the slightly higher and shadier slopes of the La Balme area and a gondola returns you to Côte 2000 on L'Aiguille. La Balme is a splendid, varied area with good lifts.

Going the other way from L'Aiguille leads you to L'Etale via the the the Transval cable-car, which shuttles people between the two areas. L'Etale will be served by two new lifts for 2007/08 – see 'News'. From the bottom of L'Etale, you can take a piste to the village and the gondola up to the Beauregard sector, which, as the name implies, has splendid views and catches a lot of sunshine. From the top of Beauregard you can link via an easy piste and a two-way chair-lift with Manigod. From here you can move on to L'Etale.

Free buses link La Clusaz to Le Grand-Bornand, where there's another 100km/62 miles or so of largely intermediate pistes (covered by the area lift pass).

Terrain-parks The park – on the L'Aiguille – has jumps, tables, rails, boarder-cross runs and a super-pipe.

Snow reliability Most runs are west- or north-west facing and tend to keep their snow fairly well, even though most of the area is below 2000m/ 6,500ft. The best snow is on the north-west-facing slopes at La Balme. In late season, the home runs can be dependent on snowmaking.

Experts The piste map doesn't seem to have a lot to offer experts, but most sectors present off-piste variants, and there are more serious adventures to undertake. The best terrain is at La Balme – the black Vraille run, which leads to the speed-skiing slope, is seriously steep. On the opposite side of the sector, the entirely off-piste Combe de Bellachat can be reached.

The Noire run down the face of

UK PACKAGES

Alpine Answers, Aravis Alpine Retreat, Business Retreats, Classic Ski Limited, Crystal, Interhome, Karibuni, Lagrange, Last Resort, Ski France, Ski Weekend, Skiholidayextras, Skitopia, Skitracer, Skiweekender.com, Snowlife

Phone numbers
From abroad use the prefix +33 and omit the initial '0' of the phone number

TOURIST OFFICE

t 0450 326500
infos@laclusaz.com
www.laclusaz.com

Beauregard can be tricky in poor snow and is often closed. The Tétras on L'Etale is steep only at the top; the Mur Edgar bumps run on L'Aiguille is steep but short. L'Aiguille has a good off-piste run down the neglected Combe de Borderan and the long Lapiaz black piste runs down the Combe de Fernuy from Côte 2000.

Intermediates Early intermediates will delight in the gentle slopes at the top of Beauregard and over on La Croix-Fry at Manigod. L'Etale and L'Aiguille have more challenging but wide blue runs. More adventurous intermediates will prefer the steeper slopes of La Balme.

Beginners There are nursery slopes at village level, and better ones up on Beauregard and at Crêt du Merle. The Beauregard area has lovely gentle blue runs to progress to; those from Crêt du Merle are steeper, but there is a green.

Snowboarding Most of the drag-lifts are avoidable. There are some good nursery slopes, served by chair-lifts, and cruising runs to progress to. La Balme is great for good free-riders.

Cross-country The region has much better cross-country facilities than many resorts, with around 70km/43 miles of loops of varying difficulty.

Queues These aren't usually a problem, except on peak weekends or if the lower slopes are shut because of snow shortage.

Mountain restaurants A highlight: there are lots of them and most are rustic and charming, serving good food at reasonable prices. Readers repeatedly recommend the Télémark above the

chair-lift to L'Etale. The 'very attractive' Chez Arthur at Crêt du Merle has table-service behind the crowded self-service. The Relais de L'Aiguille at Crêt du Loup is also popular. The Bercail is 'good but very crowded'.

Schools and guides We have no recent reports on the schools.

Facilities for children Neither have we had recent reports on the kindergarten.

STAYING THERE

How to go La Clusaz is offered mostly by smaller operators.

Hotels Small, friendly 2- and 3-star family hotels are the mainstay of the area; luxury is not an option here. Reporters recommend the 3-star Alp'Hotel (0450 024006) – endorsed again in 2007 ('brilliant place'). The 3-star Carlina (0450 024348) is 'the best', says another reporter.

Apartments There's quite a good choice, but some are out of town.

Eating out There's a wide choice of restaurants, some a short drive away. The St Joseph at the Alp'Hotel is regarded as the best in the village. 2007 reporters recommend L'Ecuelle ('fantastic food, great ambience') and Skierie ('lovely alpine feel').

Après-ski The 'olde worlde' Caves du Paccaly has live music, the 'quaint' Pub le Salto has Sky TV and draught Guinness, and L'Ecluse nightclub has 'excellent atmosphere'.

Off the slopes There's tobogganing, an excellent aquatic centre, an ice rink and good walks.

LA BALME
2470m/8,100ft

L'AIGUILLE
2380m

Côte 2000

Col des Aravis

Crêt du Loup
1870m

L'ETALE
1960m

Lac des Confins

Les Chenons
1275m

Le Bouchet

Crêt du Merle
1525m

Les Etages

Merdassier
1500m

BEAUREGARD
1695m

MANIGOD

La Clusaz
1100m/3,610ft

La Croix-Fry
1480m

Les Contamines

A traditional French village with its own area of reliably snowy slopes and easy road access to nearby big-name resorts

COSTS

①②③④⑤⑥

RATINGS

The slopes
Fast lifts	**
Snow	****
Extent	***
Expert	***
Intermediate	****
Beginner	**
Convenience	**
Queues	***
Mountain restaurants	****

The rest
Scenery	****
Resort charm	***
Off-slope	**

NEWS

For 2006/07 a lake was built to provide water for increased snowmaking. And in the village a new restaurant/wine bar, L'O à la Bouche, opened.

- ➕ Largely unspoiled French village
- ➕ Fair-sized intermediate area
- ➕ Good snow record for its height
- ➕ Lift pass covers nearby resorts
- ➖ Not ideal for beginners
- ➖ Quiet nightlife
- ➖ Lifts a bus-ride from main village
- ➖ Can be some lengthy queues

Only a few miles from the fur coats of Megève and the ice-axes of Chamonix, Les Contamines is quite a contrast to both, with pretty wooden chalets, an impressive old church, a weekly market in the village square and prices more typical of rural France than of international resorts. Its position at the shoulder of Mont Blanc gives it an enviable snow record.

THE RESORT

The core of the village is compact, but the resort as a whole spreads widely, with chalets scattered over a 3km/2 mile stretch of the valley, and the main access lift is 1km/half a mile from the centre. There's expanding development by the lift at Le Lay but you can stay in the village centre, a shuttle-bus-ride away. Bizarrely, the local pass appears not to cover the buses. The Mont Blanc pass does cover them, plus the lifts of Chamonix and Megève (among other resorts). A car is useful.

THE MOUNTAINS

Most of the slopes are above the tree line and there are some magnificent views, though the runs down from Signal are bordered by trees (as is the run from La Ruelle down to Belleville).

Slopes From Le Lay a two-stage gondola climbs up to the slopes at Signal. Another gondola leads to the Etape mid-station from a car park a little further up the valley, with a fast

quad above it. Above these, a sizeable network of open, largely north-east-facing pistes fans out, with lifts approaching 2500m/8,200ft in two places. You can drop over the ridge at Col du Joly to south-west-facing runs down to La Ruelle, with a single red run going on down to Belleville. From Belleville, a 16-person gondola runs back up to La Ruelle, followed by a fast chair to Col du Joly.

Terrain-parks They call these X Zones. There are three in the main ski area (two near the top of the fast chair towards Aiguille Croche and the other near the Pierres Banches chair). There's a fourth area in the tiny Loyers area on the outskirts of town, which also has a 120m/390ft super-pipe.

Snow reliability Many of the shady runs on the Contamines side are above 1700m/5,580ft, and the resort has a justifiable reputation for good snow late into the season, said to be the result of proximity to Mont Blanc. There's snowmaking on the home runs from Signal down to the valley. We have several reports of snow being good here in the difficult early part of last season, with people travelling in from Chamonix and Megève daily for better snow and fewer crowds; and a regular visitor tells of 'the combination of natural and man-made snow and careful piste management' giving good conditions from December to April'.

Experts The steep western section has black runs, which are enjoyable but not terribly challenging. But there is substantial and varied off-piste terrain within the lift system and outside it – including a 'seriously steep and challenging' descent to Megève.

Intermediates Virtually all the runs are ideal for good intermediates, with a

The gondola from Le Lay takes you up here to Signal, the hub of the slopes ↓

KEY FACTS

Resort	1160m
	3,810ft

Les Contamines-Montjoie/Hauteluce	
Slopes	1160-2485m
	3,810-8,150ft
Lifts	24
Pistes	120km
	75 miles
Green	19%
Blue	21%
Red	36%
Black	24%
Snowmaking	
	260 guns

UK PACKAGES

Alpine Answers, Chalet Kiana, Classic Ski Limited, Interhome, Lagrange, Ski Expectations, Ski France, Ski Line, Skiholidayextras, Skitracer

Phone numbers
From abroad use the prefix +33 and omit the initial '0' of the phone number

TOURIST OFFICE

t 0450 470158
info@lescontamines.com
www.lescontamines.com

mix of blues and reds that one recent reporter described as 'very similar – more like purple'. Some of the best go from the gondola's top station to its mid-station and others are served by the Roselette and Bûche Croisée lifts. Given good snow, the south-facing runs down to La Ruelle are a delight. And the black runs are enjoyable for good intermediates. Timid intermediates might find sections of many blue runs too steep for comfort.

Beginners In good snow, the village nursery area is adequate for beginners. There are other areas at the mid-station and the top of the gondola. And there's a long green run from Col du Joly to La Ruelle. Beginners should take the gondola down to the village at the end of the day, as the only run down is a red one that can be icy.

Snowboarding There are quite a few drag-lifts, including four marked on the piste map as difficult, so inexperienced boarders beware. But there is excellent off-piste boarding on offer.

Cross-country There are 26km/16 miles of trails of varying difficulty. One loop is floodlit on Wednesdays.

Queues There can be 15- to 20-minute peak-period queues for the gondolas, especially if people are bussed in from other resorts with less snow. The main bottleneck at Etape, where the lower gondolas meet, has been relieved by the fast quad parallel to the second stage. More irritating on our 2007 visit was a long wait for the old Grevettaz drag-lift when it kept breaking down.

Mountain restaurants There are quite a few lovely rustic huts – not all of which are marked on the piste map. Ferme de la Ruelle is a jolly barn, and the Grange just above it does a 'great-

value plat du jour'. Roselette ('classic Savoyard cooking') and Bûche Croisée (also known as R'mize à Louis) are two cosy chalets consistently recommended by reporters, and the 'reasonably priced' Chez Gaston has great views.

Schools and guides In the past we have had mixed reports on the ESF. But 2007 beginners found it 'fun, friendly and progressive'. There's an alternative International school, and mountain guides. One recent visitor enjoyed the 'challenging off-piste' found for him by Miage Aventure. Excursions are offered, including trips to the Vallée Blanche.

Facilities for children The kindergarten, next to the central nursery slopes, takes children from age one. Children can join ski school from age four.

STAYING THERE

How to go There are some catered chalets and 11 modest hotels.

Hotels The 3-star Chemenaz (0450 470244) at Le Lay is praised: 'Comfortable, best food in the village.'

Eating out Recommendations include the Husky, Auberge du Barattet, Op Traken and, for Savoie specialities, the Savoisien and Auberge du Chalézan.

Après-ski Après-ski is quiet, but there are several bars. The Saxo near the gondola has been recommended; the Ty Breiz has live music and is 'the only lively bar', say reporters. Every Sunday there are welcome drinks with music by the village fountain.

Off the slopes There are good walks, a toboggan run, snowmobiling, dog-sledding, snow-shoeing and a natural ice rink, but St-Gervais, Megève and Chamonix have more to offer.

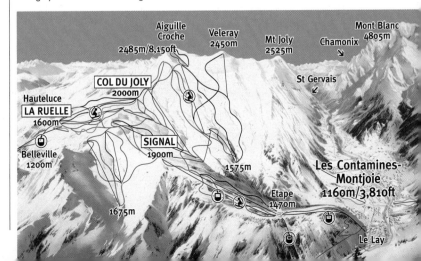

Courchevel

Four mini-resorts with completely different characters that share one of the world's best ski areas; only 1850 is famously pricey

COSTS

① ② ③ ④ ⑤ ⑥

RATINGS

The slopes
Fast lifts	****
Snow	****
Extent	*****
Expert	****
Intermediate	*****
Beginner	****
Convenience	****
Queues	****
Mountain restaurants	****

The rest
Scenery	***
Resort charm	**
Off-slope	***

NEWS

For 2007/08, 1650 will get its first 4-star hotel, the Manali, right on the piste. In 1850, the Aiglon St Roch will be renovated and reopen with 19 suites and a spa. The Byblos has changed hands and will become the Palace des Neiges for 2007/08. A new 4-star hotel, the Cheval Blanc, with spa opened for 2006/07.

Work on a new swimming pool complex has begun in 1550 with completion expected for 2009/10.

➕ Extensive, varied local terrain to suit everyone from beginners to experts – plus the rest of the Three Valleys

➕ Lots of slope-side accommodation

➕ Impressive lift system, piste maintenance and snowmaking

➕ Wooded setting is pretty, and useful in bad weather

➕ Choice of four very different villages – only 1850 is notably expensive

➕ Some great restaurants, and good après-ski by French standards

➖ Some pistes get unpleasantly crowded (but they can be avoided)

➖ Rather soulless villages, with intrusive traffic in places

➖ 1850 has some of the priciest hotels, bars and mountain restaurants in the Alps, and it's getting worse

➖ Losing a little of its French feel as more and more British – and Russian – visitors discover its attractions

➖ Little to do away from the slopes, especially during the day

Courchevel 1850 – the highest of the four components of this big resort – has long been the favourite Alpine hangout of the Paris jet set, and they have now been joined by wealthy Russians. Its top hotels and restaurants (on and off the slopes) have always been among the most expensive in the Alps, and the influx of rich Russians has pushed up prices even further.

But don't be put off: a holiday here doesn't have to cost a fortune (especially in the lower villages), the atmosphere is not generally exclusive, and Courchevel's list of ➕ points is enough to attract more and more Brits. Even so, it remains much more French than Méribel, over the hill, as well as having better snow.

The slopes are excellent: Courchevel is the most extensive and varied sector of the whole Three Valleys. Many visitors never leave this sector, which has everything from long gentle greens to steep couloirs.

Le Praz is an overgrown but still pleasant village, 1550 is quieter and good for families, 1650 has more of a village atmosphere than it seems from the road through, and the posh bits of 1850 are stylishly woody. But overall the resort is no beauty. Well, nothing's perfect.

THE RESORT

Courchevel is made up of four varied villages, generally known by numbers very loosely related to their altitudes. A road winds up from Le Praz (1300) past 1550, through 1650 to 1850. On the slopes, things work a bit differently: runs go down from 1850 to 1550 and 1300, but the slopes of 1650 form a distinct sector.

   1850 is the largest village, and the focal point of the area, with most of the smart nightlife and shops. Two gondolas go over its lower slopes towards the links with Méribel and the rest of the Three Valleys. Although the

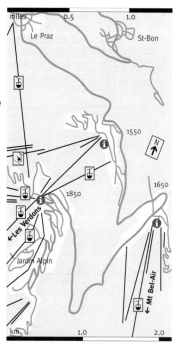

↑ Courchevel 1550 in the foreground with 1850 perched above it

KEY FACTS

Resort	1260-1850m
	4,130-6,070ft

The Three Valleys	
Slopes	1260-3230m
	4,130-10,600ft
Lifts	183
Pistes	600km
	373 miles
Green	15%
Blue	38%
Red	37%
Black	10%
Snowmaking	
	1920 guns

Courchevel/ La Tania only	
Slopes	1260-2740m
	4,130-8,990ft
Lifts	63
Pistes	150km
	93 miles
Green	22%
Blue	37%
Red	33%
Black	8%
Snowmaking	
	563 guns

approach is dreary and the centre not much better, parts are conspicuously upmarket, with some very smooth hotels on the slopes just above the village centre, and among the trees of the Jardin Alpin (a suburb served by its own gondola). There's a spreading area of smart private chalets.

You can pay through the nose to eat, drink and stay, but more affordable places are not impossible to find. Pressure on the restaurants is highest when big-spending Russians are in town – in early January and the second week in March – but we are no longer getting reports from readers unable to get a table.

1650 by contrast is 'calm and uncrowded, a world away from 1850', as a reader puts it. The main road up to 1850 cuts through but there's also an attractive old village centre, lively bars and quietly situated chalets. Its local slopes (whose main access is a gondola) are also relatively peaceful.

1550 is a quiet dormitory, a gondola or chair ride below 1850. It has the advantage of having essentially the same position as 1850, with cheaper accommodation and restaurants. But it's a long trip to 1850 by road if you want to go there in the evening.

Le Praz (or 1300) is an old village set amid woodland. It remains a pleasant spot despite expansion triggered by the 1992 Olympics – the

Olympic ski jump is a prominent legacy. Ancient gondolas go up to 1850 and towards Col de la Loze, for Méribel. It is 'excellent' for pre-skiing children. But novices face rides down from as well as up to ski school.

Efficient free buses run between and within the villages. Champagny is an easy road outing, for access to the extensive slopes of La Plagne.

THE MOUNTAINS

Although there are plenty of trees around the villages, most of the slopes are essentially open, with the notable exception of the runs down to 1550 and to Le Praz, and the valley between 1850 and 1650. These are great areas for experts when the weather closes in. Many reporters recommend buying only a Courchevel pass and then one-day extensions for the Three Valleys as necessary. If you buy a Three Valleys lift pass for five days or more, we understand you'll be able to buy a 10 euro daily extension to ski the Val d'Isère-Tignes or Paradiski areas too.

THE SLOPES
Huge variety to suit everyone
A network of lifts and pistes spreads out from 1850, which is very much the focal point of the area. The main axis is the **Verdons** gondola, leading to a second gondola to La Vizelle and a

Le Ski
the chalet specialists

COURCHEVEL
VAL D'ISÈRE AND LA TANIA

❄ 29 superbly placed chalets
❄ Genuine, friendly service
❄ Delicious food and wine
❄ Sunday flights to Chambéry

Now that Signal is equipped with two fast chairs, it's a key feature of the skiing above 1650

Vizelle is a great hill, with testing red and black pistes all around it – and, of course, lots of off-piste

Lots of easy skiing on the lower slopes above 1850, with plenty of fast lifts serving them

Méribel ↘

La Saulire
2740m/
8,990ft

Creux Noirs
2705m

La Vizelle
2660m

Col de Chanrossa
2545m

Chanrossa

CHANROSSA

Marmottes

Suisses

Saulire

Signal

Creux

Aiguilles du Fruit

SAULIRE - CREUX

Vizelle

Chapelets

Mt. Bel Air

Signal

Gravelles

Biollay

Verdons

Altiport

Pralong

Praméruel
1825m

Ariondaz

Jardin Alpin

Courchevel 185

Co

Grangettes

Courchevel 1650

Courchevel 155

Saulire
40m/
990ft

Saulire

↙ Méribel

Col de la Loze
2275m

Chenus
2245m

LOZE - PRAZ

Dou des Lanches

Excellent, testing runs in the woods, which really come into their own in bad weather

A new green run built a couple of seasons ago has made La Tania a much better place for beginners than it was

Verdons

Coqs

Chenus

Plantrey

Praz-Juget

Jardin Alpin

Courchevel 1850

Touvet

Forêt

La Tania

Grangettes

Praz

Courchevel 1550

Le Praz
1260m/4,130ft

La Tania
1350m/4,430ft

nearly parallel cable-car up to La Saulire. These high points of the **Saulire-Creux** sector give access to a wide range of terrain above Courchevel (including a number of couloirs), to Méribel and all points to Val Thorens. Next to the Verdons gondola is the Jardin Alpin gondola, which leads to runs back to 1850, and serves the higher hotels until 8pm. It also gives access via the valley of Prameruel to the Chanrossa slopes above 1650.

To the right looking up from 1850 the Chenus gondola goes towards the **Loze-Praz** sector, a second link with Méribel. Runs go back to 1850, and through the woods to La Tania (see separate chapter) and Le Praz.

There are various ways up from 1650 to the minor high-points of Bel Air and Signal, and on into the **Chanrossa** sector. From here you can link across via the valley of Prameruel to Saulire-Creux, or head for the far end of the sector, where there is another link to Saulire-Creux via the col of Chanrossa.

TERRAIN-PARKS
Something for everyone
There are four designated freestyle areas in Courchevel, all in the 1850 sector. Under the Verdons gondola are mounds and a kids' fun area. Under the Biollay chair is a small humps and bumps course. Under the Pralong chair, above the altiport, is a boarder-cross. And the main terrain-park is at Plantrey, just below 1850 on the way to Le Praz. It is accessible via the Ecureuil chair lift or the Epicea drag and is a 600m/1,970ft long park that

boarding

Despite being an upmarket resort, Courchevel has always been popular with snowboarders. There are miles of well-groomed pistes, and the lifts are in general very modern and quick with few drags. As it is very expensive, Courchevel best suits intermediates and advanced riders who can fully take advantage of this resort's resources. The big snowboard hangout in 1850 is Prends ta luge et tire toi, a combined shop/bar/internet cafe.

Courchevel's image is of up-market luxury and pampered piste skiing. But it is one of the world's best resorts for off-piste too. Manu Gaidet is a Courchevel mountain guide and a ski instructor with the Courchevel ESF. He is also one of the world's top free-riders and won the Freeride World Championship three years running. We asked him to pick out a few of the best runs.

These suggested routes are limited to the Courchevel valley. In addition, there is great off-piste in the rest of the Three Valleys. And directly from the resort you can heli-ski in Italy and Switzerland (it is banned in France). But never venture off-piste without a qualified ski instructor or mountain guide and safety equipment.

For a first experience off-piste, the Tour du Rocher de l'Ombre is great. Access is easy from the left of the Combe de la Saulire piste and you are never far from the piste. It is very quiet, the slope is very broad and easy and you get a real sense of adventure as you plan your way between the rocks. And the view of the Croix des Verdons is impressive. Keep to the left for the best snow.

Les Avals is one of my favourite routes. The easiest way to get to it is to take the Roc Merlet piste from the top of the Chanrossa chair-lift. Leave the piste on the right as soon as you can, then climb up and cross the ridge. Once you've arrived at a group of rocks (in the form of towers) descend the south side. This run is not technically difficult and is particularly beautiful in spring conditions. Another possibility from the Chanrossa chair is to traverse towards the Aiguille du Fruit. Almost anywhere along this very wide slope, you can choose your spot to start skiing down to rejoin the end of the Chanrossa black piste at the bottom. A technically more difficult run, for experienced off-piste skiers only, is Plan Mugnier. This starts with a 20-minute walk from the top of the Chanrossa chair but you are normally rewarded by very good snow because the slope you ski down faces north. Le Curé is in the Saulire area: this narrow gully starts under a towering rock and offers a steady 35° slope; it is only for expert skiers who don't mind climbing to the Doigt du Curé starting point.

The Courchevel **ESF** is the largest ski school in Europe with over 700 instructors. They can help you find the best off-piste and explore it safely. For phone numbers see the schools list. The websites of the three different branches (1550, 1650, 1850) can be accessed through www.courchevel.com.

Courchevel

293

LIFT PASSES

Three Valleys

Prices in €

Age	1-day	6-day
under 13	32	161
13 to 59	43	215
over 60	37	177

Free under 5, over 72

Beginner Special area with free lifts

Notes
Covers Courchevel, La Tania, Méribel, Val-Thorens, Les Menuires and St-Martin; family reductions; pedestrian and half-day passes

Alternative passes
Courchevel/La Tania only with One-day Three Valleys extension; Courchevel 1650 only

has a pro and intermediate kicker line, handrails and boxes. They have removed the pipe and replaced it with a new rail park, which promises to get bigger in 2007/08. Along with the usual boxes and rails there is a wall ride and rainbow box. Two shapers are on constant duty keeping the park in great shape.

SNOW RELIABILITY
Very good

The combination of Courchevel's orientation (its slopes are north- or north-east facing), its height, an abundance of snowmaking and excellent piste maintenance usually guarantees good snow down to at least the 1850 and 1650 villages. A 2007 reporter comments: 'In a difficult year for snow in the Alps, the skiing was excellent and the pistes well-groomed.' On countless visits we have found that the snow is usually much better than in neighbouring Méribel, where the slopes get more sun. The runs to Le Praz are still prone to closure in warm weather. Daily maps are available, showing which runs have been groomed overnight (normal in America but very rare in Europe).

FOR EXPERTS
Some black gems

There is plenty to interest experts, even without the rest of the Three Valleys.

The most obvious expert runs are the couloirs you can see on the right near the top of the Saulire cable-car. The three main ways down were once designated black pistes (some of the steepest in Europe), but now only the Grand Couloir remains a piste – it's the widest and easiest of the three, but you have to pick your way along the narrow, bumpy, precipitous access ridge to reach it.

There is a lot of steep terrain, on- and off-piste, on the shady slopes of La Vizelle, both towards Verdons and towards the link with 1650. Some of the reds on La Vizelle verge on black and the black M piste is surprisingly little used. If you love moguls, try the black Suisses and Chanrossa runs – and the off-piste moguls under the Chanrossa chair. For a change of scene and a test of stamina, a couple of long (700m/2,300ft vertical), genuinely steep blacks cut through the trees to Le Praz.

In good snow conditions you can ski all the way down (around

SCHOOLS

ESF in 1850
t 0479 080772

ESF in 1650
t 0479 082608

ESF in 1550
t 0479 082107

ESF Centre Pralong
t 0479 011581

Ski Academy
t 0479 081199

Supreme
t 0479 082787
(UK: 01479 810800)

New Generation
t 0479 010318
www.skinewgen.com

Magic in Motion
t 0479 010181

Oxygène
t 0479 551745

Classes
(ESF 1850 prices)
6 days (2½hr am and
pm): €272

Private lessons
€70 for 1½hr

GUIDES

Bureau des Guides
t 0479 010366

2000m/6,560ft vertical) from La Saulire to Bozel, way below Le Praz, over meadows and through trees on the final section, and catch a bus back.

There is plenty of off-piste terrain to try with a guide – see the feature panel earlier in the chapter.

FOR INTERMEDIATES
Paradise for all levels
The Three Valleys is the greatest intermediate playground in the world, but all grades of intermediates will love Courchevel's local slopes too.

Early intermediates will enjoy the gentle Pyramides and Grandes Bosses blues above 1650, and the Biollay and Pralong blues above 1850. Those of average ability can handle most red runs without difficulty. Our favourite is the long, sweeping Combe de la Saulire from top to bottom of the cable-car first thing in the morning, when it's well groomed and free of crowds; but it's a different story at the end of the day – cut up snow and very crowded. Creux, behind La Vizelle, is another splendid, long red that gets bumpy and unpleasantly crowded later on. Marmottes from the top of Vizelle is quieter and more challenging.

The Loze-Praz sector has excellent blues and reds down towards 1850 and 1550 and through the trees towards La Tania – long, rolling cruises. Over at 1650, the Chapelets and Rochers reds right at the edge of the whole Three Valleys ski area are great fun for fast cruising, although the newish six-pack serving them means they are now more heavily used.

FOR BEGINNERS
Great graduation runs
There are excellent nursery slopes above both 1650 and 1850. At the former, lessons are likely to begin on the short drags close to the village, but quick learners will soon be able to

go up the gondola. The best nursery area at 1850 is at Pralong, above the village, near the airstrip. A reporter points out that getting to it from the village isn't easy, unless you go by road. A blue path links this area with chairs to 1650, so adventurous novices can soon move further afield. The Bellecôte green run down into 1850 is an excellent, long, gentle slope – but it is used by other skiers returning to the village and does get unpleasantly crowded. It is served by the Jardin Alpin gondola, and a drag that is one of eight free beginner lifts. 1550 and Le Praz have small nursery areas, but most people go up to 1850 for its more reliable snow.

FOR CROSS-COUNTRY
Long wooded trails
Courchevel has a total of 66km/ 41 miles of trails, the most in the Three Valleys. Le Praz is the most suitable village, with trails through the woods towards 1550, 1850 and Méribel. Given enough snow, there are also loops around the village.

QUEUES
Not a problem
Even at New Year and in mid-February, when 1850 in particular positively teems with people, queues are minimal, thanks to the excellence of the lift system. However, there can be a build-up at 1850 for the gondolas and chairs, notably in 'bad weather conditions and just after ski school meeting-up time'. The Biollay chair is very popular with the ski school (which gets priority) and can be worth avoiding. Queues for the huge Saulire cable-car are rare. Many lifts have American-style singles lines, which reporters seem to like ('it allows you to jump the queue legitimately!').

↑ The centre of 1850 – the main lifts are just to the left of here

MOUNTAIN RESTAURANTS
Good but can be very expensive
Mountain restaurants are plentiful and pleasant, but it is sensible to check the prices; for table-service restaurants reservations may be needed.
Editors' choice The Bel Air (0479 080093), at the top of the gondola above 1650 has good-value simple food ('omelettes to die for'), friendly and efficient table-service, and a splendid tiered terrace; booking essential. Our other favourite in the area is the Bouc Blanc (0479 080093) just over in La Tania (see that chapter).

Worth knowing about (if only to avoid) Cap Horn, near the airstrip, is the leading lunchtime rip-off spot, according to a local who says it has a 'scarily' expensive wine list and is known as 'Moscow on Ice'. A 2007 reporter found it 'overpriced, snobbish with chaotic service'. Chalet de Pierres, on the Verdons piste is not far behind, pricewise. But it is a comfortable, smooth place built in traditional style and reporters agree it does good food: 'great unfussy mountain food and very nice staff' is a typical comment. It has a wonderful array of desserts and is easily accessible for pedestrians.

The Bergerie on the Bellecôte piste still has 'a lot of atmosphere but the prices are now quite steep'. A recent reporter found that the food at the Arc en Ciel (top of the Verdons gondola) 'lived up to our fond memories of it'. The Panoramic at the top of Saulire 'is very traditional, but not cheap'. The Chenus at the top of the gondola of that name has 'good food and fabulous views'. The Soucoupe, near here too, also has good food and views; we tried the cosy, atmospheric table-service section upstairs in 2007 and found the steaks OK but the prices for both food and wine a bit steep.

SCHOOLS AND GUIDES
Plenty of choice
Courchevel's branches of the ESF add up to the largest ski school in Europe, with over 700 instructors. Reports in 2007 vary: 'We had a private lesson every day with ESF 1650. The instructor was fantastic, joking around, and he taught us a great deal'; 'In 1850 my daughter's boyfriend had an English instructor and a great time learning quickly, but my wife had a non-English speaking grumpy old man and stayed on the nursery slopes all week.'

New Generation is a school run by top British instructors. When we joined a group lesson with them we were very impressed by their US-style of teaching: they ask the students to set their goals for the lesson on the gondola ride up and then try to help them achieve them. We nearly all opted for skiing chopped-up, off-piste snow with style, and all felt we had improved a lot by the end of the morning. We continue to receive rave reviews about this outfit: 'really great lesson – we both got a lot out of it' and 'skiing improved' were typical 2007 comments; plus 'highlight of the

Courchevel

CHILDREN

Village des Enfants (1850)
t 0479 080847
Ages from 18mnth;
9am-5pm

Les Pitchounets (1650)
t 0479 083369
Ages from 18mnth

Ski schools
Most offer lessons
from age 3 or 4 (ESF
1850 prices €255 for
6 days)

Phone numbers
From abroad use the
prefix +33 and omit
the initial '0' of the
phone number

OT COURCHEVEL JEROME
KELAGOPIAN

The piste down to
Courchevel 1650
arrives in the centre
of this photo, where
there's a gondola up
and an attractive old
village centre ➔

---

trip was skiing with New Generation. We booked some private guiding for a group of three and had a great time skiing off Chanrossa and a fabulous afternoon in the Les Avals valley'. 'Head and shoulders above any other ski school I've come across in the Alps,' said a 2006 reporter.

Supreme in 1850 (also British-run) has had mixed reviews in the past, but a 2007 reporter and two friends had a French instructor for their private lesson and 'it was probably one of if not the best lesson I have ever had'.

We hear that Ski Academy, an independent group of French instructors, is joining forces with Magic in Motion but at the time of going to press we don't have their new name. Previous reports range from 'excellent and attentive' for the former and 'good, but not outstanding' for the latter.

The Bureau des Guides runs all-day off-piste excursions. There's also an area at the foot of Les Suisses piste with at least weekly transceiver practice and avalanche rescue sessions with dogs and pisteurs (free).

FACILITIES FOR CHILDREN
Lots of chalet-based options

In the past reporters have found the ski kindergarten at 1850 over-stretched, with 19 children in a class of five to seven-year-olds. But one reader said her three-year-old daughter was happy and 'skiing on reins quite well by the end of the week'. The ESF at 1850 offers VIC (Very Important Children) lessons for English-speaking children between 6 and 12 years with a maximum of six children per group. Several tour operators run their own nurseries using British nannies and there are now rentananny agencies.

STAYING THERE

HOW TO GO
Value chalets and apartments

Huge numbers of British tour operators go to Courchevel.

Chalets There are plenty of chalets available. In 1850 several operators offer notably comfortable chalets, and a few genuinely luxurious ones.

Flexiski has the luxuriously revamped eight-bed Chinchilla, including a sauna. Kaluma and Descent both have swanky 10-bed places with all the trimmings. Among the features of Scott Dunn's flagship Aurea is a 7.5m/25ft pool in the basement. Supertravel's portfolio includes the lovely Montana with hot-tub and steam room. Although not quite in that league, Total has several properties, including a couple of neat modern places up in the Jardin Alpin and a central chalet-hotel. Mark Warner also has a central chalet-hotel. So does Crystal Finest (with childcare facilities) as well as five chalets (some of which are again aimed at families).

In 1650 Le Ski has 15 chalets from comfortable to classy, including six new ones for 2007/08 (all with hot-tub, sauna or steam room). A recent reporter found 'the food excellent and the chalet staff friendly, helpful and unassuming'. Ski Olympic has the central Les Avals chalet-hotel here plus a couple of large chalets.

Small Scottish operator Finlays has six chalets in 1550, and a couple up in 1850. Ski Power runs chalets plus the Hotel Chanrossa in 1550. Family-specialist Esprit Ski has several chalets and chalet-apartments down in Le Praz as does Ski Link (whose places are available catered, self-catered or B&B).

Air Geneva 149km/ 93 miles (3½hr); Lyon 187km/116 miles (3½hr); Chambéry 110km/68 miles (1½hr); direct flights to Courchevel altiport from London on request only (contact tourist office for details)

Rail Moûtiers (24km/ 15 miles); transfer by bus or taxi

Hotels There are nearly 50 hotels in Courchevel, mostly at 1850 – including more 4-stars than anywhere else in France except Paris – 16 at the last count, with 9 in the top '4-star luxe' category. 1650's first 4-star, the Manali, right by the piste is due to open in December 2007.

COURCHEVEL 1850

*****Airelles (0479 003838) 'Super flash and over the top. The most expensive hotel in the Alps.'

*****St Joseph (0479 081616) Like a plush country house 'with 14 fab rooms and two stunning apartments'.

*****Mélézin (0479 080133) Superbly stylish and luxurious – and in an ideal position beside the Bellecôte slope.

*****Carlina (0479 080030) Luxury piste-side pad, next to Mélézin.

*****Palace des Neiges (0479 009800) Used to be Byblos, now under new ownership. Spacious public rooms, good pool, sauna, steam complex.

****Bellecôte (0479 081019) Our favourite among the more swanky places – it offers some Alpine atmosphere as well as sheer luxury.

****Chabichou (0479 080055) Distinctive white building, right on the slopes; family-run, friendly and rustic

with very good food plus the option of a restaurant with 2 Michelin stars.

****Sivolière (0479 080833) Recently renovated, set among pines.

***Rond Point (0479 080433) Family atmosphere, central position.

***Croisette (0479 080900) Next to main lifts above the Jump bar. 'Simple and clean, staff very helpful.'

***New Solarium (0479 080201) Recently renovated, near first stop on Jardin Alpin gondola, 'sensible prices and very friendly service'.

**Courcheneige (0479 080259) On Bellecôte piste. 'A real find: lovely staff, good food.' Quiet.

COURCHEVEL 1650

*****Manali (phone number unavailable when we went to press). New for 2007/08 and promises to be the best in 1650; right by the piste just above the gondola.

***Golf (0479 009292) Rather impersonal but in a superb position on the snow next to the gondola.

***Seizena (0479 082636) Stylish and central (over road from the gondola).

COURCHEVEL 1550

***Ancolies (0479 082766) 'A real find,' said a US visitor impressed by the friendly staff and excellent food.

Le Praz

***Peupliers (1300) (0479 084147)
Smartly renovated and expanded, good restaurant – but prices now 'approach 1850 levels', we hear.

Apartments Leaving aside the swanky private chalets you can rent from local agents, the best bets are the Chalets les Montagnettes at the top end of 1650 – a choice of apartments and semi-detached chalets – and the Chalets du Forum in the heart of 1850.

EATING OUT
Pick your price

There are a lot of good, very expensive restaurants in Courchevel. A non-comprehensive pocket guide is distributed locally.

In 1850, among the best, and priciest, are the Chabichou (a recent visitor recommends the three course set menu lunch – 'absolutely fantastic'), and the Bateau Ivre – both with two Michelin stars. Other reporters praise the Chapelle ('fabulous and filling meal of lamb cooked on an open fire'). A recent reporter had a 'great meal' at the Anerie 'in a cosy and rustic setting'. A reporter liked the pizzas but not the soup at the Via Ferrata and was concerned to watch the staff smoking in the kitchen. Also mentioned by readers are the Cloche ('good atmosphere'), the Tremplin ('exemplary lamb', expensive but 'worth every penny') and the Cendrée ('a wonderful Italian', 'good value'). The Saulire (aka Chez Jacques) is a reliable spot that we have enjoyed, endorsed by a recent reporter for 'excellent service and food – a bargain by local standards'. Another recommends the Mangeoire's 'good simple food at acceptable prices, considering there is live music every night'. We've had mixed reports about the Locomotive, with railway-theme decor and a varied menu: 'Lots of character, good music, food and wine,' said one reporter; 'Very average food and service, overpriced,' said a recent visitor. The hotel Tovets is reported to have 'reasonable prices and delicious food'. A local recommends the Grand Café (underneath the hotel St Joseph) for good Asian cuisine. A visitor enjoyed the large helpings at the Tex Mex Kalico.

In 1550, the Oeil de Boeuf is good for grills. The Cortona does good-value pizza.

In 1650 the smart hotel Seizena has quickly built a good reputation for 'inventive, reasonably priced' food; and the cosy Eterlou's 'good traditional' food and 'wide range of pizzas' have led to many recommendations from readers. The Petit Savoyard ('divine fillet steak and pâté de foie gras dish') also does good French and Savoyard food, pizza and pasta.

In Le Praz, Bistrot du Praz is expensive but excellent – 'a foodie's treat'. The Ya-ca is small and 'very French'. We've had excellent meals at the hotel Peupliers (good pepper steak) but we hear that prices are on the rise.

ACTIVITIES

Indoor Ice rink, bowling, exhibitions, concerts, cinemas, language and computer courses, cookery courses, library; in hotels: health and fitness centres (swimming pools, saunas, steam-room, hot-tub, water therapy, weight-training, massage)

Outdoor Hang-gliding, helicopter flights, paragliding, flying lessons, dog-sledding, ice driving, go-karts on ice, snow-shoe excursions, snowmobile rides, climbing, ice karting, ballooning, walking on cleared paths, tobogganing

TOURIST OFFICE

t 0479 080029
info@courchevel.com
www.courchevel.com

APRES-SKI
1850 has most variety

If you want lots of nightlife, it's got to be 1850. There are some exclusive nightclubs, such as the Caves, with top Paris cabaret acts and sky-high prices. The popular Kalico ('open until 4am') has DJs and cocktails. The Bergerie has themed evenings – food, music, entertainment – but prices are high.

The 'buzzing' Jump at the foot of the main slope seems to be the place to be as the lifts close – to the point where some judge it 'very unpleasant'. The 'reasonably priced yet stylish' Equipe has free WiFi internet. Others have liked the 'cool and trendy zinc-look' S'no Limit and the Milk Pub, set underground with 'good atmosphere' and live music. The Saulire (aka Chez Jacques) and the cheap and cheerful Potinière are also popular. New for 2006/07 was the Petit Drink, specialising in wine and tapas, at the entrance to 1850 next to the new MGM apartments; affordable and popular with locals.

Piggys sounds like just the sort of place we hate: 'fur coats, pampered dogs and sky-high prices', '£9 for Guinness' and 'the world's only medieval themed French/Irish wine bar/pub/disco featuring a drawing room and library'. Mangeoire has 'an excellent piano bar (with high Piggys-style prices) and is extremely lively from about 11pm'.

Cinemas in 1850 and 1650 show English-speaking films.

One reader's 20-something kids found 'plenty to do' in 1650. The 'lively, friendly' Bubble is the hub; with satellite TV, internet access, cheap bar prices, a happy hour, some strong local beers and frequent live music, it has a largely British clientele. One 2007 reader's favourite was the Signal bar. Rocky's Bar (in chalet-hotel Avals) is popular and 'good for watching sport' but can be 'rowdy and laddish'. Remonte Pente is a tiny French bar. The Lounge Bar (formerly New Space Bar) has pool, games and live music or DJs and the local Taverne disco stays open till 4am.

In 1550 the Chanrossa bar is British-dominated, with occasional live music, the Taverne also has English owners. In Le Praz the Escorch'vel bar is 'a good, lively place'.

OFF THE SLOPES
1850 isn't bad

There are a fair number of shops in 1850, plus markets at most levels. There's an ice-driving circuit and an ice-climbing structure. Snow-shoeing among the trees is growing in popularity. A pedestrian lift pass for the gondolas and buses in Courchevel and Méribel makes it easy for non-slope users to meet up the mountain for lunch. And you can take joyrides from the altiport. A non-skier's guide to Courchevel, Méribel and La Tania is distributed by the tourist office.

Courchevel

299

Les Deux-Alpes

Sprawling resort with a long, narrow ski area that will disappoint many intermediates; popular for summer skiing and boarding

COSTS

① ② ③ ④ ⑤ ⑥

RATINGS

The slopes

Fast lifts	**
Snow	****
Extent	***
Expert	****
Intermediate	**
Beginner	***
Convenience	***
Queues	**
Mountain restaurants	**

The rest

Scenery	****
Resort charm	**
Off-slope	**

NEWS

Several central buildings are being revamped and new residences continue to open – the Balcons des Pistes and the Alba are new for 2007/08.

KEY FACTS

Resort	1650m
	5,410ft
Slopes	1300-3570m
	4,270-11,710ft
Lifts	51
Pistes	220km
	137 miles
Green	20%
Blue	40%
Red	21%
Black	19%
Snowmaking	
	214 guns

300

- ➕ High, snow-sure, varied slopes, including an extensive glacier area
- ➕ Lots of good off-piste terrain
- ➕ Excellent, sunny nursery slopes
- ➕ Stunning views of the Ecrins peaks
- ➕ Lively resort with varied nightlife
- ➕ Wide choice of affordable hotels

- ➖ Piste network modest by mega-resort standards and badly congested in places
- ➖ Home runs are either steep and icy or dangerously overcrowded – so people queue for a lift down instead
- ➖ Virtually no woodland runs
- ➖ Spread-out, traffic-choked resort
- ➖ Few appealing mountain restaurants

We have a love-hate relationship with Les Deux-Alpes. We quite like the buzz of the village – arriving here in the evening is a bit like driving into Las Vegas from the Nevada desert – and we understand the appeal of its vibrant nightlife. We love the high-Alpine feel of its main mountain, and the good snow to be found on the north-facing slopes at mid-mountain. But we're unimpressed by the limited extent of the pistes – we're very sceptical about the claimed 220km/137 miles – and we hate the congestion that results in peak season when most of the town's 35,000 visitors are crammed on to them.

THE RESORT

Les Deux-Alpes is a narrow village sitting on a high, remote col. Access is from the Grenoble-Briançon road to the north. The village is a long, sprawling collection of hotels, apartments, bars and shops, most lining the busy main street and the parallel street that completes the one-way traffic system. The resort has a lively ambience.

The village has grown haphazardly over the years, and there is a wide range of building styles, from old chalets through 1960s blocks to more

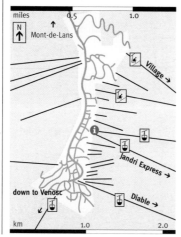

miles 0.5 1.0

N ↑ Mont-de-Lans

Village →

ⓘ

Jandri Express →

down to Venosc

Diable →

km 1.0 2.0

sympathetic recent developments. It looks better as you leave than as you arrive, because all the balconies face the southern end of the resort.

Lifts are spread fairly evenly along the village and there is no clear centre. But three sectors can be identified.

As you enter the village from the north, roads go off on the left to wind up the hill to the suburb now called Les 2 Alpes 1800 – inconvenient for shopping and nightlife, though not necessarily for skiing. Carry on and you come to the geographical centre of the resort, with the major gondola stations, popular outdoor ice rink and lots of shops and restaurants. And in due course you reach the end of the resort at Alpe de Venosc, with many of the nightspots and hotels, the most character, the fewest cars, the best shops and the Diable gondola up to the tough terrain around Tête Moute.

The free shuttle-bus service saves on some very long walks from one end of town to the other.

The six-day pass covers two days in Alpe-d'Huez and Serre-Chevalier (an hour away over the Col du Lautaret) and a day in several other resorts. Helicopter trips to Alpe-d'Huez are good value at £40 return – a 'must', says a reporter. More economical is the shuttle-bus service on Wednesdays and Thursdays.

Toura is at the heart of the high, open slopes →

LIFT PASSES

Super ski pass

Prices in €

Age	1-day	6-day
under 13	28	127
13 to 59	36	169
over 60	28	127

Free under 5, over 72

Beginner four free drag-lifts

Notes
Covers all lifts in Les Deux-Alpes; half-day and pedestrian passes; family rates; 6-day pass includes entry to swimming pool and ice rink and access to La Grave and two days in Alpe-d'Huez and one day in Serre-Chevalier, Puy-St-Vincent and the Milky Way

Alternative passes
Ski Sympa covers 21 lifts

SCHOOLS

ESF
t 0476 792121

International St-Christophe
t 0476 790421

European
t 0476 797455

Primitive Snowboard (Salomon)
t 0607 907135

Ski Privilege
t 0476 792344

Easiski
t 0682 795734

Bliss
t 0476 795676

Damien Albert
t 0476 795038

Classes
(ESF prices)
6 half days (2¾hr am or pm) €129.50

Private lessons
€34 for 1hr

GUIDES

Bureau des guides
t 0476 113629

THE MOUNTAINS

For a big resort, Les Deux-Alpes has a disappointingly small piste area, despite recent improvements. A 2006 reporter confirms our view: 'A real lack of mileage; we skied pretty much everything in a day.' The piste classification is rather inconsistent and some runs are classified differently on the map and on the mountain. The piste map is inadequate, especially for the area around Toura and Crêtes.

THE SLOPES
Long, narrow and fragmented
The western **Pied Moutet** side of Les Deux-Alpes is relatively little used. It is served by lifts from various parts of town but reaches only 2100m/6,890ft. As well as the short runs back to town, which get the morning sun, there's an attractive north-facing red run down through the trees to the small village of Bons. The only other tree-lined run in Les Deux-Alpes goes down to another low village, Mont-de-Lans.

On the broad, gentle slope east of the resort are about a dozen beginner lifts, and above it a steep slope running up to the ridge of **Les Crêtes.**

To get back to the village you have a choice of one winding green run, often very crowded, or four short black runs. These are usually mogulled (two are ungroomed), and often icy at the end of the day. Many visitors ride down.

The ridge has lifts and gentle runs along it, and behind it lies the deep, steep Combe de Thuit. Lifts span the combe to the mid-mountain station at **Toura** at the heart of the slopes. We seem to spend all our time on three key fast lifts. Above Toura, the Glaciers chair takes you up 600m/1,970ft for blue and red runs back down. Below it, the Bellecombes chair serves a range of good, high slopes. And off to the north, the Fee chair serves its own sector. The chairs going up to La Toura serve short runs and various terrain features. The middle section of the mountain, around Toura, is very narrow, and prone to crowding.

The top **Glacier du Mont de Lans** section has fine, easy runs with great views above 3200m/10,500ft, served by an underground funicular and drag-lifts. You can go from the top all the way down to Mont-de-Lans – a descent of 2270m/7,450ft vertical that we believe is the world's biggest on-piste

Les Deux-Alpes

301

boarding

Les Deux-Alpes has become a snowboard Mecca over the last few years. Its cheap and cheerful atmosphere counts for a lot – while the limited pisted slopes aren't as off-putting to boarders as to skiers. The kick-off to the French winter season begins here with a huge 'Mondial du Snowboard' event – 27-29 October in 2007. In town there are good trampoline facilities and a huge airbag to get a feeling of what air-time is all about. Although the focus is on the terrain-park, the free-riding terrain is not to be underestimated, with plenty of steep challenging terrain. Beginners will find the narrow, flat crowded areas mid-mountain and the routes down to the village intimidating. Most of the lifts on the higher slopes are chairs, and there are the specialist Primitive and new Bliss snowboard schools.

vertical. A walk (or snowcat tow) takes you to the slopes of La Grave (covered by the lift pass). There are more testing slopes off to the north, below 3200m/10,500ft, served by chairs.

TERRAIN-PARKS
A real highlight
The heavyweight terrain-park is located on the Toura run in the winter, then shifts up to the glacier in the summer and reopens mid-June (www.2alpes-snowpark.com). Easily one of the top parks in Europe, this has something for everyone (including beginners). All sizes of kickers, hips, rails and boxes will keep all levels challenged throughout the day. The highlights of this 800m/2,620ft-long park are two impeccable super-pipes and the big gap jump. There are two boarder-cross courses and a free-cross area. There are DJs playing music, a BBQ area and a snow-skate park.

SNOW RELIABILITY
Excellent on higher slopes
The snow on the higher slopes is normally very good, even in a poor winter. Above 2200m/7,220ft most of the runs are north-facing, and the top glacier section guarantees good snow. More of a concern is bad weather shutting the lifts, or extremely low

temperatures at the top. But the runs just above the village face west, so they get a lot of afternoon sun and can be slushy or icy. Snowmaking has been improved on the lower slopes – but a January visitor skiing on rocky pistes saw it used 'not once'.

FOR EXPERTS
Off-piste is the main attraction
With good snow and weather conditions, the area offers wonderful off-piste sport – see the feature panel on the facing page. There are serious routes that end well outside the lift network, with verticals of over 2000m/6,560ft. Reporters consistently recommend the renowned descent to St-Christophe (your guide will arrange transport back); one who visited in January 2006 said, 'Though the resort's slopes were hard-packed, this run offered superb powder.'

A twice-weekly Free Respect event promotes off-piste safety, with free advice and free-ride competitions.

The Super Diable chair-lift, from the top of the Diable gondola, serves a steep black piste. The Bellecombes and Fee chairs serve challenging pistes and ski routes – marked and patrolled, but not protected. If the conditions are right, an outing to the serious slopes of La Grave is a must.

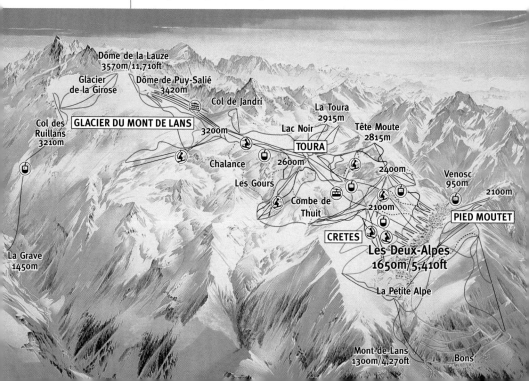

Dôme de la Lauze 3570m/11,710ft
Glacier de la Girose
Dôme de Puy-Salié 3420m
Col de Jandri
La Toura 2915m
Col des Ruillans 3210m
GLACIER DU MONT DE LANS
3200m
Lac Noir
Tête Moute 2815m
Chalance
2600m
TOURA
Les Gours
2400m
Venosc 950m
2100m
Combe de Thuit
2100m
PIED MOUTET
CRETES
Les Deux-Alpes 1650m/5,410ft
La Grave 1450m
La Petite Alpe
Mont-de-Lans 1300m/4,270ft
Bons

The off-piste routes in Les Deux-Alpes are numerous and varied in difficulty, the easiest permitting skiers even of an intermediate level to enjoy their first 'free-ride experience'. We've asked Jeremy Edwards of the European Ski and Snowboard School to share some of his favourites.

For something slightly technical, both sides off the Bellecombes red piste – 2800m-2300m (9,190ft-7,550ft) – offer a wide range of varying terrain; it's important to take care here – there are several small cliff faces. For those keen to tackle couloirs – steep, narrow slopes between rocks – this descent offers small ones that are ideal for your first attempts; they can be avoided, though.

The **European Ski and Snowboard School** does classes and guiding in small groups. Its instructors are of several nationalities, but all speak excellent English.
t 00 33 476 797455
europeanskischool@worldonline.fr
www.europeanskischool.co.uk

Traversing across the top of the black Grand Couloir piste leads to the North Rachas area, with off-piste faces that offer cold snow conditions all winter. The first large valley leads to three couloirs – one fairly broad and easy, the other two much narrower and steeper, and certainly not for the timid. Traversing further leads to a much wider descent that avoids the three couloirs.

For tree skiing it's best to head for the Vallée Blanche area, reached via the lifts on Pied Moutet. The north-east face, towards the chair-lift at Bons, offers great routes over generally deserted wooded terrain with excellent cold snow conditions.

Strong skiers will enjoy the famous Chalance run, which starts just below the glacier and descends 1000m/3,280ft vertical to the Gours run; there are several variations, mixing wide open slopes and rocky pitches. These faces are at times subject to quite a high avalanche risk because of wind slab.

Traversing above the north face of the Chalance leads to the couloir Pylone Electrique – a steep, narrow 200m/660ft-long couloir with the reward below it of an excellent wide powder field of moderate gradient. A rest on the Thuit chair-lift is a must after this adrenalin-charged descent.

These routes and many more play a large part in the off-piste free-ride courses offered by the European Ski and Snowboard School.

Les Deux-Alpes

303

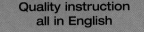

British orientated ski and snowboard school

Summer and winter

Quality instruction all in English

British instructors

Ski group courses

Adults or children Maximum 8 per group in 3-hour sessions over 5/6 days at all levels. Video analysis, progress reports, medals. Certificates for children.

Natural born skiers Whole mountain philosophy. Maximum 4 per group in 2-hour sessions over 5 days. Higher levels. Lift queue priority.

Free ride for experienced skiers. Discover Les Deux Alpes off-piste. 3 or 6 days, half or full days.

Private tuition on a 2-hourly basis, all levels. Ski, Snowboard, Telemark, Snowblades.

La Grave Guided trips to this off-piste Mecca.

Race camps Summer and winter.

Snowboard courses First go, Improving, Snow park, Free ride. Maximum 4 per group in 2-hour sessions over 3 or 6 days. Lift queue priority.

European Ski and Snowboard School, 95 Avenue de la Muzelle, 38860 Les Deux Alpes, France.
Email europeanskischool@worldonline.fr www.europeanskischool.co.uk Tel/fax 0033 476 797455

Dramatic scenery to the south of the resort →

CHILDREN

Crèche 2 Alpes 1800
t 0476 790262
Ages 6mnth to 2yr;
8.30-5.30

Bonhomme de Neige
t 0476 790677
Ages 2 to 6; 8.30-5.15 (also activity centre for ages 6 to 17)

Jardins des Neiges
t 0476 792121
Ages 4 to 6; 9.15-12 noon, 2.30-5pm; 6 mornings €135

Ski schools
Classes for ages 6 to 12 (6 mornings €111 with ESF)

FOR INTERMEDIATES
Limited cruising

Les Deux-Alpes can disappoint keen intermediates. Avid piste-bashers will cover the pistes in a couple of days. A lot of the runs are either rather tough – some of the blues could be reds – or boringly bland. The runs higher up generally have good snow, and there is some great fast cruising, especially from the glacier to Toura and on the mainly north-facing pistes served by the chair-lifts off to the sides. You can often pick gentle or steeper terrain in these bowls as you wish. The chair-lifts at the glacier serve great carving pistes. Many visitors do day-trips to Alpe-d'Huez (by helicopter).

Less confident intermediates will love the quality of the snow and the gentleness of most of the runs on the upper mountain. Their problem might lie in finding the pistes too crowded for comfort.

FOR BEGINNERS
Good slopes

The nursery slopes beside the village are spacious and gentle. The run along the ridge above them is excellent, too. The glacier also has a fine array of very easy slopes – but it's a long ride up.

FOR CROSS-COUNTRY
Needs very low-altitude snow

There are small, widely dispersed areas. La Petite Alpe, near the entrance to the village, has a couple of snow-sure but very short trails. Given good snow, Venosc, reached by a gondola down, has the only worthwhile picturesque ones. Total trail distance is 25km/16 miles. You can ski the Mont de Lans glacier with a qualified guide.

QUEUES
Can be a problem

Les Deux-Alpes has some impressive lifts, but the village is large, and queues at the morning peak can be 'diabolically' long for the Jandri Express and Diable gondolas. The eight-seat chair from the mid-station to the glacier has reduced queues for the second stage, but not eliminated them. Problems can also occur when people are bussed in because snow is in short supply elsewhere. The top lifts are prone to closure if it's windy, putting pressure on the lower lifts. We have repeated reports of queues for the gondolas back to the village when snow is poor low down.

MOUNTAIN RESTAURANTS
Still limited

There are mountain restaurants at all the major lift junctions, but they are generally unremarkable.
Editors' choice Diable au Coeur (0476 799950) is a welcome new arrival at the top of the Diable gondola – excellent food and service. On the terrace, get as far as you can from the noisy adjacent chair-lift machinery. The bigger but similarly excellent Chalet la Toura (0476 792096), in the middle of the domain, is expected to reopen in December 2007 having been devastated by fire last season.
Worth knowing about The table-service half of the Panoramic at Toura is recommended for its 'mouth-watering cuisine' – but 'it gets very crowded'. There is a small new table-service restaurant attached to the big self-service Les Glaciers at 3200m/10,500ft.

SCHOOLS AND GUIDES
We are all Europeans now

A 2006 reporter 'highly recommends' Easiski who were 'very helpful and friendly'. We have a positive report on the tuition and organisation of the European school, composed of instructors of various nationalities, all (we are assured) speaking good English. Class sizes are small – as few as four pupils if you go for their advanced classes. Bliss is a new snowboard school, featuring two-hour beginner courses.

FACILITIES FOR CHILDREN
Fine for babies

Babies from six months to two years old can be entrusted to the village nursery. The kindergarten takes kids from two to six years, and there are chalet-based alternatives run by UK tour operators. There are also four free T-bars for children at the village level and a kid's freestyle area.

peak retreats

Beat the crowds
Traditional resorts

0870 770 0408

www.peakretreats.co.uk

ABTA W5537

GETTING THERE

Air Lyon 160km/
99 miles (3½hr);
Grenoble 120km/
75 miles (2½hr);
Chambéry 126km/
78 miles (3hr);
Geneva 230km/
143 miles (4½hr)

Rail Grenoble
(70km/43 miles); four
daily buses from
station

ACTIVITIES

Indoor Swimming
pool, hot-tub, sauna,
sports centres (Club
Forme, Tanking
Center), cinemas,
games rooms,
bowling, museum,
library

Outdoor Ice rink,
snowmobiles,
paragliding, quad
bikes, snow bikes,
snow-shoeing, Kanata
(Inuit) village visit

SMART LODGINGS

Check out our feature
chapters at the front
of the book.

Phone numbers
From abroad use the
prefix +33 and omit
the initial '0' of the
phone number

TOURIST OFFICE

t 0476 792200
les2alp@les2alpes.com
www.les2alpes.com

STAYING THERE

HOW TO GO
Wide range of packages
Les Deux-Alpes has plenty of that rarity
in high-altitude French resorts,
reasonably priced hotels.

Chalets Several UK tour operators run
catered chalets; some use apartments,
but Neilson has several proper little
chalets, including the recently built
Chartreuse. Mark Warner now runs an
excellent chalet-hotel, the Bérangère –
in a slope-side position on the road up
to Les 2 Alpes 1800, at the north end
of the resort; pleasant bar/lounge, airy
dining-room; pool, sauna, steam.
Hotels There are over 30 hotels, of
which the majority are 2-star or below.
There's a Club Med 'village' here, too.
****Farandole (0476 805045) The one
four-star. At Venosc end of resort.
***Mariande (0476 805060) Highly
recommended, especially for its
'excellent' five-course dinners. At
Venosc end of resort.
***Chalet Mounier (0476 805690)
Smartly modernised. Good reputation
for food. Swimming pool and fitness
room. At Venosc end of resort.
***Souleil'or (0476 792469) Looks like
a lift station, but pleasant and
comfortable. Rooms and food reported
to be 'fantastic'. Central.
**Lutins (0476 792152) Central.
Reportedly the 'best value' and 'best
location in the resort'.
Apartments Cortina has 15 spacious
apartments at the south end, with
sauna, steam room and hot-tubs.
Alpina Lodge is central and right by
the slopes. New apartments are
expected for 2007/08 (see 'News').

EATING OUT
Plenty of choice
Chalet Mounier's P'tit Polyte restaurant
has a high reputation. The Petite
Marmite has good food and
atmosphere at reasonable prices.
Bel'Auberge does classic French and is
'quite superb'. The Patate, Cloche and
Crêpe à Gogo are also recommended.
Visitors on a budget can get a
relatively cheap meal at Bleuets bar,
the Vetrata or the Spaghetteria. One
regular visitor says that Smokey Joe
Tex-Mex is the best value in the resort.
　　The resort has contrived ways of
dining at altitude – snowmobile to the
glacier and back, eating on the way, or
at full moon ski or board back to town
after dinner (with ski patrollers).

What's your perfect Neilson holiday?
- Unique packages for beginners
- Great group discounts
- Family holidays & kids' clubs
- More choice for solo travellers
- 61 resorts world-wide

Call **0870 333 3347**
or visit **www.neilson.co.uk**

RELAX AS HARD AS YOU LIKE　**neilson**

APRES-SKI
Unsophisticated fun
Les Deux-Alpes is one of the liveliest
of French resorts, with plenty of bars,
several of which stay open until the
early hours. Smithy's Tavern is a
'massive party venue' that pulls in a
young crowd. Pub le Windsor is a
smaller, quieter place popular with
locals. Smokey Joe's is a popular
central sports bar and the Secret is a
lively venue with live music, big-screen
TV, and a wide choice of beers. Other
places mentioned in despatches
include Bar Brésilien and the 'cosy,
friendly' Bleuets. The main bar at 1800
is O'Brian's; the Tribeca has 'a lovely
ambience for grown-ups'. The
Avalanche is the main night club, at
the Venosc end of town; up at 1800,
the Opéra is recommended by locals.

OFF THE SLOPES
Limited options
The pretty valley village of Venosc is
worth a visit by gondola, and you can
take a scenic helicopter flight to Alpe-
d'Huez. There are lots of scenic walks
and a good pool. Several mountain
restaurants are accessible to
pedestrians. Snowcat tours across the
glacier provide wonderful views.

STAYING DOWN THE VALLEY
Worth considering
Close to the foot of the final ascent to
Les Deux-Alpes are two little Logis de
France hotels, near-ideal for anyone
thinking of visiting Alpe-d'Huez, La
Grave and Serre-Chevalier – the
cheerful Cassini (0476 800410) at Le
Freney and the even more appealing
Panoramique (0476 800625) at Mizoën
– approved of by a recent reporter for
'hearty food, informative Dutch hosts'
and the 'wondrous' panorama.
　　An alternative is to stay in one of
the hamlets close to the bottom of the
gondola up from Venosc.

Les Deux-Alpes

305

OT FLAINE / PHOTOZOOM

Flaine

Uncompromisingly modern, high-altitude resort sharing a big, broad area of varied slopes with more rustic alternatives

NEWS

For 2007/08 a new six-pack will go from the bottom of the resort to the middle of the main slopes above Flaine, relieving pressure on the Platières gondola. The Tourmaline blue at Grands Vans is due to be widened and the lower section of the Diamant Noir black at Les Grandes Platières redesigned. A connecting piste from Flaine Forum to Forêt may be added.

➕ Big, varied area, with plenty of terrain to suit everyone

➕ Reliable snow in the main bowl

➕ Compact, convenient, mainly car-free village, plus traditional villages on the lower fringes of the area

➕ Excellent facilities for children

➕ Scenic setting, and glorious views

➕ Very close to Geneva but ...

➖ Weekends can be busy as a result

➖ Lots of slow old chair-lifts

➖ Austere modern buildings

➖ In bad weather main Flaine bowl offers little to do, and links to outer sectors of the area may be closed

➖ Nightlife not a highlight

➖ Little to do off the slopes (in Flaine)

Flaine is best known as a convenient resort catering particularly well for families, but it has a much broader appeal than that. The Grand Massif is almost a match for Val d'Isère/Tignes in terms of extent, at least.

Flaine's family orientation is underlined by the domination of self-catering accommodation. But you open up more accommodation options by considering the outlying villages – Les Carroz, Samoëns and Morillon (the last two now covered in the separate Samoëns chapter). Not only are they more attractive, rounded places to stay in, but also they offer some sheltered woodland slopes for bad-weather days.

THE RESORT

The concrete Bauhaus-style blocks that form the core of Flaine were conceived in the sixties as 'an example of the application of the principle of shadow and light'. They look particularly shocking from the approach road – a mass of blocks nestling at the bottom of the impressive snowy bowl. From the slopes they are less obtrusive, blending into the rocky grey hillside. For us, the outdoor sculptures by Picasso, Vasarely and Dubuffet do little to improve Flaine's austere ambience.

The more recent development of Hameau-de-Flaine is built in a much more attractive chalet style – but is inconveniently situated 1km/0.5 miles from the slopes and main village, and has only one shop/bar/restaurant.

In Flaine proper, everything is close by: supermarket, sports rental shops, ski schools, main lifts out etc.

There are two parts to the main resort. The lower part, Forum, is centred on a snow-covered square with buildings on three sides, the open fourth side blending with the slopes. Flaine Forêt, up the hillside and linked by lift, has its own bars and shops, and most of the apartments.

There are children all over the place; they are catered for with play areas, and the resort is supposed to be traffic-free. In fact, roads penetrate the village and you don't have to go far to encounter traffic; but the Forum, leading to the pistes, is pretty safe.

The bus service to/from Hameau is 'excellent' but runs only to Forêt, not Forum. A car gives you the option of visiting the Portes du Soleil, Chamonix, Megève or Courmayeur in Italy.

THE MOUNTAINS

The Grand Massif is an impressive area; but the greater part of the domain lies outside the main Flaine bowl and the links can be closed by excessive wind or snow.

THE SLOPES
A big white playground

The day begins for most people at the **Grandes Platières** jumbo gondola, which speeds you in a single stage up

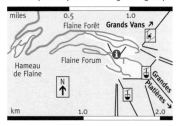

The central square of Forum leads directly on to the pistes →

KEY FACTS

Resort	1600m
	5,250ft
Grand Massif (Flaine, Les Carroz, Morillon, Samoëns, Sixt)	
Slopes	700-2480m
	2,300-8,140ft
Lifts	78
Pistes	265km
	165 miles
Green	11%
Blue	42%
Red	36%
Black	11%
Snowmaking	
	218 guns
For Flaine only	
Slopes	1600-2480m
	5,250-8,140ft
Lifts	28
Pistes	140km
	87 miles
Green	13%
Blue	37%
Red	42%
Black	8%

the north face of the Flaine bowl to the high-point of the Grand Massif, and a magnificent view of Mont Blanc. A new six-pack this season will offer an alternative, going part-way up.

Most of the runs are reds (though there are some blues curling away to skier's right, and one direct black). There are essentially four or five main ways down the barren, treeless, rolling terrain back to Flaine, or to chairs in the middle of the wilderness.

On the far right, the Cascades blue run leads away from the lift system behind the Tête Pelouse down to the outskirts of Sixt, dropping over 1700m/ 5,580ft vertical in its exceptional 14km/ 9 mile length. The gentle/flat top half is hard work, so we're not greatly concerned that the run isn't reliably open; readers seem more impressed than we are. At the end you can get buses (often crowded) to the lifts at Samoëns. Or spend some time exploring the slopes of Sixt – very quiet, with a non-trivial vertical.

On the other side of the Tête Pelouse, a broad catwalk leads to the experts-only **Gers** bowl. At the bottom, a flat trail links with the lower (more interesting) half of the Cascades run.

Back at Platières, an alternative is to head left down the long red Méphisto to the **Aujon** area – again mostly red runs but with some blues further down. The lower slopes here are used as slalom courses. This sector is also reachable by gondola or drag-lifts from below the resort.

The eight-seat Grands Vans chair, reached from Forum by means of a slow bucket-lift – reportedly not open all day – gives access to the extensive slopes of Samoëns, Morillon and Les Carroz. You come first to the wide Vernant bowl, equipped with three fast chair-lifts. Beyond here are the slopes of **Les Carroz**, **Morillon** and **Samoëns**.

Piste grooming is repeatedly commended and signing seems to have improved. But the piste map is rubbish – hopelessly ambitious in trying to cover such a big and complex area in a single view. In the middle of

the area are several distinct bowls that are simply not detectable on the map.

TERRAIN-PARKS
Cater for kids to experts
There's a big terrain-park (called the JamPark Pro – standing for Jib and Air Maniacs) in the Aujon area of Flaine. It has a quarter-pipe, tables, rails, a boarder-cross course and chill-out zone. Watch out for the 'downright dangerous' Aujon drag-lift, though, which is still as much of a challenge as the park. There's an intermediates' park under the Chariande 2 chair on the Samoëns side, with green, red and black options and a variety of rails. And there's a kids' park, JamPark Kids, with a boarder-cross run under the Esserts quad on the Morillon side.

SNOW RELIABILITY
Usually keeps its whiteness
The main part of Flaine's slopes lie on the wide north- and north-west-facing flank of the Grandes Platières, and

boarding

Flaine suits boarders quite well – there's lots of varied terrain and plenty of off-piste with interesting nooks and crannies, including woods outside the main bowl. The key lifts are now chairs or gondolas (but beware the absurdly vicious Aujon drag-lift, which serves the terrain-park). There are two other terrain-park options, including one for kids. Black Side is the local specialist shop, in the central Forum.

keep snow well. There is snowmaking on the greater part of the Aujon sector and on the nursery slopes. The runs towards Samoëns 1600 and Morillon 1100 are north-facing too, and some lower parts have snowmaking, but below here can be tricky or closed. The Les Carroz runs are west-facing and can suffer from strong afternoon sun, but a few runs have snowmaking.

FOR EXPERTS
Great fun with guidance

Flaine has some seriously challenging terrain, despite its family orientation. But much of it is off-piste and, although some of it looks like it can safely be explored without guidance, this impression is mistaken. The Flaine

bowl is riddled with rock crevasses and potholes, and should be treated with the same caution that you would use on a glacier. We are told that these hazards cause deaths most years.

All the black pistes on the map deserve their classification. The Diamant Noir, down the line of the main gondola, is tricky because of moguls, narrowness and other people, rather than great steepness; the first pitch is the steepest, with spectators applauding from the chair-lift.

To skier's left of the Diamant Noir are several short but steep off-piste routes through the crags.

The Lindars Nord chair serves a shorter slope that often has the best snow in the area, and some seriously

The long, lift-free Cascades run to Sixt, which excites some readers but not us

LES GRANDES PLATIERES
2480m/8,140ft

Tête Pelouse

Tête des Lindars

Grandes Platières

Aup de Veran

Tête de Véret
2315m

GERS
1715m

Les Grands Vans
2205m

Grands Vans

Vernant

Flaine
1600m/5,250ft

Tête des Saix
2120m

Le Lac

Vernant

Les Molliets

Sixt

1900m

Lots of slow chair-lifts above Samoëns 1600

1500m

SAMOENS
1600m

Sairon

Esserts

Samoëns Village
720m/2,360ft

Grand Massif

Saix

Good runs down the old gondola from Vercland, none down the newer one from close to Samoëns

Vercland

MORILLON
1100m

Morillon

Morillon
700m

steep gradients. Mind the chair doesn't whack you as you exit.

The Gers drag-lift, outside the main bowl, serves great expert terrain. The Styx piste is a proper black, but nearby off-piste slopes reach 45°. The main Gers bowl is a great north-facing horseshoe of about 550m/1,800ft vertical, powder or moguls top to bottom, all off-piste, ranging from steep to very steep. There are more adventurous ways in from the Grands Vans and Tête de Véret lifts.

There are further serious pistes on the top lifts above Samoëns 1600.

There are some scenic off-piste routes from which you can be retrieved by helicopter – such as the Combe des Foges, next to Gers.

FOR INTERMEDIATES
Something for everyone

Flaine is ideal for confident intermediates, with a great variety of pistes (and usually the bonus of good snow conditions, at least above Flaine itself). As a reporter puts it, 'There may not be many challenging runs, but there are very few dull ones.' The diabolically named reds that dominate the Flaine bowl tend to gain their status from short steep sections rather than overall difficulty. The relatively direct Faust is great carving territory, at least in January when it isn't cluttered. There are gentler cruises from the top of the mountain – Cristal, taking you to the Perdrix chair, or Serpentine, all the way home. The blues at Aujon are

LES GRANDES PLATIÈRES
2480m/8,140ft

Tête des Lindars

Tête Pelouse

Grandes Platières

Aup de Veran

AUJON
2035m

Tête de Véret
2315m

Grands Vans
2205m

Grands Vans

Vernant

Flaine
1600m/5,250ft

Tête des Saix
2120m

Le Lac

Vernant

Les Molliets

1900m

Kedeuze

Excellent woodland runs immediately above Les Carroz, served by a gondola – great on a bad day

LES CARROZ
1140m/3,740ft

Saïron

1500m

SAMOENS
600m

Esserts

MORILLON
1100m

Good cruising above Morillon

Morillon

Morillon
700m

SCHOOLS

ESF
t 0450 908100

International
t 0450 908441

Moniteurs indépendants
t 0450 478454

Flaine Super Ski
t 0681 061906

Flaine Ski Clinic
t 0699 862538

Freecimes
t 0664 118329

François Simond
t 0450 908097

Bruno Uyttenhove
t 0610 183082

Le Hameau Master Class
t 0450 908716

Classes (ESF prices)
6 days (3hr per day)
€125

Private lessons
€36 for 1hr, for 1 or
2 people

CHILDREN

Les P'tits Loups
t 0450 908782
Ages 6mnth to 3yr

Rabbit Club
t 0450 908100
Ages 3 to 11; 9am-
5pm; 6 days with
lunch €234

La Souris Verte
t 0450 908441
Ages from 3

**MMV Hotels Flaine
and Aujon**
t 0492 126212
Ages 18mnth to 14yr

**Cap'Vacances les
Lindars**
t 0471 508081

Ski school
For ages 3 to 11:
€105 for 6 days, 3hr
per day (ESF prices);
English-speaking
specialist private
tuition for children:
Catherine Pouppeville
(0699 862538)

excellent for confidence building, but the drag serving them is not.

The connections with the slopes outside the main bowl are classified blue but several blue-run reporters have found them tricky because of narrowness, crowds or poor snow. Once the connection has been made, however, all intermediates will enjoy the long tree-lined runs down to Les Carroz, as long as the snow is good. The Morillon slopes are also excellent intermediate terrain – the long green Marvel run to Morillon 1100 is an easy cruise with excellent signs along the way explaining the local wildlife.

Crowds on the lower slopes returning to Flaine have been a source of complaint, but the problem should be relieved to some degree by the red Aventurine piste, allowing better skiers to go left well above the village.

FOR BEGINNERS
Fairly good
There are excellent nursery slopes right by the village, served by free lifts which make a pass unnecessary until you are ready to go higher up the mountain. The area is roped off, but it is still used as a short cut back to the village by other skiers. There are no long green runs to progress to in the Flaine bowl but there are some gentle blues over on skier's right, beneath Tête Pelouse. Progress to the 'interesting and gentle blues' in the Aujon sector is not easy due to several steep drag-lifts. If you have a really nervous intermediate to deal with, it's worth driving or bussing down the access road to the green at Vernant.

CROSS-COUNTRY
Very fragmented
The Grand Massif claims 64km/40 miles of cross-country tracks but only about 17km/11 miles of that is around Flaine itself. The majority is on the valley floor and dependent on low snow. There are extensive tracks between Morillon and Les Carroz, with some tough uphill sections.

QUEUES
A few problems
Many of the trouble spots have now been eliminated and several reporters have had queue-free weeks, even in high season. But there can be problems when the resorts are full and at weekends (the area is very close to Geneva). Towards the end of the day

expect delays at the Vernant chair to get back to the Flaine bowl (an alternative is to descend to one of the lift-bases along the access road, and catch a bus) and at Les Molliets – 'horrendous' at times, partly thanks to frequent failure of the machinery or its power supply. The Aup de Veran gondola is still 'inadequate' despite upgraded cabins this year. Queues for the Grand Platières gondola should be reduced this year by the new six-pack going part-way up the same slopes.

Queues elsewhere can build up at weekends and when the lifts out of the Flaine bowl are shut due to high winds or when the weather is warm and the lower resorts have poor snow. (When this happens, the queues to go down can be worse than those to go up.)

MOUNTAIN RESTAURANTS
Back to base, or quit the bowl
In the Flaine bowl, there are few restaurants above the resort's upper outskirts. Reports suggest most are overcrowded. The Grandes Platières self-service has been recommended as 'friendly and reasonable value', though a 2007 visitor was unimpressed. The rustic Blanchot, at the bottom of the Serpentine run, has 'friendly staff' and 'excellent food'. At Forum level, across the piste from the gondola, is the welcoming Michet ('definitely worth a visit'), with very good Savoyard food and table service, and the 'rustic' Eloge. Up the slope a bit, the Cascade is self-service but with a good terrace and 'very pleasant' proprietors. Epicéa has a rustic atmosphere, a terrace and has had rave reviews. Up at Forêt level, the refurbished Bissac has a good atmosphere and 'good fare.'

Outside the Flaine bowl, we love the remote Gîte du Lac de Gers (book in advance and ring for a snowcat to tow you up from the Cascades run) – simple food but splendid isolation. The cosy and rustic Igloo above Morillon is 'friendly, with good food and service.' We had an excellent plat du jour there. The self-service Telemark in this sector gets mixed reviews. The woody Chalet les Molliets does 'outstanding food'. Cupress above Les Carroz has 'friendly table-service'.

SCHOOLS AND GUIDES
Getting better
A 2007 reporter had 'helpful' lessons with ESF: 'We advanced more than in any other resort we have been to.'

GETTING THERE
Air Geneva 90km/
56 miles (1½hr)

Rail Cluses (30km/
19 miles); regular bus
service

ACTIVITIES
Indoor Swimming
pool, sauna, solarium,
gymnasium, massage,
bowling, cinema,
climbing wall, cultural
centre with art gallery
and library

Outdoor Ice rink,
snowshoe excursions,
dog-sledding,
paragliding, helicopter
rides, quad bikes, ice-
driving

However, another reader found that classes were 'far too big – twenty in a couple of cases'. A beginner boarder enjoyed an 'excellent' week with the International school this year. The competition-oriented Super Ski has 'small classes, good instruction'.

FACILITIES FOR CHILDREN
Parents' paradise?
Flaine prides itself on being a family resort, and the number of English-speaking children around is a bonus. There are some free children's lift passes available in low season weeks. The International school offers new classes for three- to five-year-olds.

Crystal's 'well-organised and popular' hotel Le Totem has good childcare facilities for residents only.

STAYING THERE

HOW TO GO
Plenty of apartments
Accommodation is overwhelmingly in self-catering apartments.

Chalets There are few catered chalet options, but they include a couple of Scandinavian-style huts in Hameau. The 'excellent food, friendly staff, good

rooms' and childcare facilities of Crystal's Totem club-hotel continue to impress reporters.

Hotels The other hotels now seem to be called 'club' hotels, marketed by big French agencies – but also bookable through UK operator Erna Low. B&B is available at the Cascade restaurant, above the village.

Apartments The best apartments are out at Hameau – 'fabulous' says a 2006 visitor. In Flaine Forêt, the Forêt and Grand Massif apartment buildings are attractively woody.

EATING OUT
Enough choice for a week
A 2006 reporter enjoyed the 'lovely local specialities' in the 'rather cramped' pizzeria Chez Pierrot. The 'very friendly' Perdrix Noire in Forêt is recommended for 'friendly and pleasant service'. Chez Daniel offers a good range of Savoyard specialities, and is good with kids. The 'lively' Brasserie les Cîmes is recommended for 'very good local food, good prices, very friendly service'. A couple of places close to the village and described under 'Mountain restaurants' are open in the evening – the Michet

Flaine

311

Hôtel Le Bois de la Char

Your stay right on the pistes

Les Carroz-d'Arâches
40 minutes from Geneva Airport
10 minutes from highway A40

Tel: 00 33 (0) 4 50 90 06 18
E-mail: contact@hotel-boisdelachar.com
Website: www.hotel-boisdelachar.com

Photo credit: PHOTOTEM – Claude Monvoisin

and the Bissac. The Ancolie in Hameau is said to be worth the trip for its 'great food' and 'beautiful wooden chalet interior'.

APRES-SKI
Signs of life
You can eat and drink into the early hours here if you move around a bit – but you don't have much choice of venue. The White pub has a big screen TV, rock music and punters trying to get pints in before the end of happy hour – but 'not a pleasant atmosphere', says a 2007 visitor. The Flying Dutchman is 'very lively 5-7pm', very friendly, tends to wind down around 11pm'. The bar at the bowling alley has a 'family atmosphere earlier on, turns into a pub after 11pm' and is 'the only place still serving food until 3am'. The Sub is Flaine's only nightclub, but the drinks are 'very expensive' and the 'music not up to much'. The 'very French' Diamant Noir is under new management.

OFF THE SLOPES
Curse of the purpose-built
Flaine is not recommended for people who don't want to hit the slopes. But there is a great ice-driving circuit where you can take a spin (literally) in your car or theirs. Snowmobiling and dog-sledding are popular, and there's a cinema, gymnasium and swimming pool. Shopping is limited; save your souvenir shopping in the few shops in Forum for the one evening a week when there is a free hands-on display of large wooden games, enjoyed by visitors of all ages.

Les Carroz 1140m/3,740ft

This is a sprawling, sunny, traditional, family resort where life revolves around the village square with its pavement cafes and restaurants. It is a sizeable place – much bigger than Flaine, in fact – that has the lived-in feel of a real French village, with more animation than Flaine, at least in the afternoon – 'a delight', says a visitor. But a thorough recent report confirmed that the après-ski scene doesn't amount to much: the Marlow pub is popular at close of play but soon becomes quiet; Pointe Noire, next door, is cheaper and more animated; Carpe Diem is devoid of customers until the other places close. The Servages d'Armelle is praised for its 'truly outstanding dinner'.

We had a rave review of the Brit-run hotel Belles Pistes (0450 900017) – 'ideal: staff A1, food good, close to lifts'. The Bois de la Char (0450 900618) is still 'well managed, perfectly situated, excellent value'. The hotel Arbaron (0450 900267) has been commended for food and views.

Les Fermes du Soleil is an MGM development of five chalet-style buildings, with comfortable apartments and a good pool, jacuzzi and sauna.

The gondola starts a steep 300m/980ft walk up from the centre – the nursery drag is a help or you can catch the free ski-bus. It serves some excellent slopes in the woods above the village, so this is a great place on a bad-weather day.

The ski school's torchlit descent is 'not to be missed' – ending with vin chaud and live jazz in the square.

Les Gets

Friendly village with a very French feel to it and two local areas of slopes; but it's not a good base for the main Portes du Soleil circuit

COSTS

① ② ③ ④ ⑤ ⑥

RATINGS

The slopes

Fast lifts	**
Snow	**
Extent	***
Expert	***
Intermediate	****
Beginner	****
Convenience	***
Queues	***
Mountain restaurants	***

The rest

Scenery	***
Resort charm	****
Off-slope	***

Extent rating
This relates only to the Les Gets/Morzine slopes, not the whole Portes du Soleil

Piste map
The whole local area is covered by the map in the Morzine chapter

NEWS

The resort is in the middle of a programme designed to give pedestrians priority on the main street and make some areas pedestrian-only.

For 2006/07 the terrain-park on Mont Chéry doubled in length, extra features were added, and a new mountain restaurant called Grande Ourse opened at the top of it. A new bus service was introduced linking Les Gets, Morzine, St Jean-d'Aulps and Avoriaz.

Phone numbers
From abroad use the prefix +33 and omit the initial '0' of the phone number

---

+ Good-sized, varied local piste area shared with slightly lower Morzine – plus excellent, neglected Mont Chéry

+ Attractive chalet-style village, with through-traffic kept on fringes

+ Relatively short drive from the UK

+ Few queues locally

+ Part of the vast Portes du Soleil ski pass region, but ...

– To get to Avoriaz and the main Portes du Soleil circuit is a real slog, unless you drive to Ardent

– Modest altitude means there is always a risk of poor snow, though increased snowmaking has helped

– Few challenging pistes

– Too many slow, old chairs

– Weekend crowds

Les Gets is an attractive, small, family-friendly resort with a very French feel to it, partly because of local shops lining the main street selling delicious-looking food and wine. The area of slopes that it shares with Morzine offers the most extensive local slopes in the Portes du Soleil, and in some respects Les Gets is the better base for them. But if you intend to visit the main Portes du Soleil circuit a lot, it makes sense to stay closer to it.

THE RESORT

Les Gets is an attractive, sunny, much-expanded village of traditional chalet-style buildings, on the low pass leading from the A40 autoroute at Cluses to Morzine. The main road bypasses the attractive village centre, which is in the middle of a programme aimed at making it even more pedestrian-friendly. It has plenty of attractive food and other shops and restaurants lining the main street. There's also a popular outdoor ice rink, which adds to the charm. It's a good resort for families.

Although the village has a scattered appearance, most facilities are close to the main lift station – and the free 'petit train' road-train shuttle is a cute way of travelling around. The village is fairly quiet in the evenings but gets busier and livelier at weekends.

THE MOUNTAINS

Les Gets is not an ideal base for the Portes du Soleil, but its local slopes are extensive. The local pass saves a fair bit on a Portes du Soleil pass, and makes a lot of sense for many visitors. **Slopes** The main local slopes – accessed by a gondola and fast chair-lift from the nursery slopes beside the village – are shared with Morzine, and are mainly described in that chapter. On the opposite side of Les Gets is

Mont Chéry, accessed by a gondola and parallel chair. The slopes include some of the most challenging in the area, and are usually very quiet. Both sectors offer wooded and open slopes. **Snow reliability** The nursery slopes benefit from a slightly higher elevation than Morzine, but otherwise our general reservations about the lack of altitude apply. A lot more snow-guns have improved runs to the resort. The front slopes of Mont Chéry face south-east – bad news at this altitude; but grooming is good, and the other two flanks are shadier. On our January 2005 visit, when snow was sparse, we found the Les Gets pistes much better than in the higher Three Valleys resorts and Avoriaz (largely because the grassy slopes need less snow cover) and better than in neighbouring Morzine. **Terrain-parks** There's a park on the upper slopes of Mont Chéry with kickers, hip-jumps, a gap-jump, quarter-pipes and a boarder-cross. **Experts** Black runs on the flank and back of Mont Chéry chair are quite steep and often bumped. In good snow there is plenty to do off-piste, including some excellent wooded areas. **Intermediates** High-mileage piste-bashers might prefer direct access to the main Portes du Soleil circuit, but the local slopes have a lot to offer – including excellent reds on Mont Chéry. **Beginners** The village nursery slopes are convenient, and there are better,

313

↑ Coming down Les Gets' main slopes, with the slopes of Mont Chéry on the other side of the valley

OT LES GETS

KEY FACTS

Resort	1170m
	3,840ft

Portes du Soleil

Slopes	950-2300m
	3,120-7,550ft
Lifts	209
Pistes	650km
	404 miles
Green	14%
Blue	39%
Red	37%
Black	10%
Snowmaking	
	632 guns

Morzine-Les Gets only

Slopes	1000-2010m
	3,280-6,590ft
Lifts	50
Pistes	110km
	68 miles

UK PACKAGES

Alpine Answers, AmeriCan Ski, Chalet Group, Club Pavilion, Descent International, Equity, Esprit, Ferme de Montagne, First Choice, Independent Ski Links, Interactive Resorts, Lagrange, Oxford Ski Co, Peak Retreats, Rocketski, Ski Activity, Ski Expectations, Ski Famille, Ski France, Ski Hillwood, Ski Independence, Ski Weekend, Skiholidayextras, Skitracer, Snow Finders, Total

TOURIST OFFICE

t 0450 758080
lesgets@lesgets.com
www.lesgets.com

FRANCE

314

more snow-sure ones up at Chavannes, with plenty of easy runs to progress to.

Snowboarding The local slopes are good for beginners and intermediates.

Cross-country There are 18km/11 miles of good, varied loops on Mont Chéry and Les Chavannes.

Queues See the Morzine chapter for general observations. Mont Chéry is crowd-free. But there are still a lot of slow, old chairs.

Mountain restaurants See Morzine.

Schools and guides A recent reporter says Ecole International's private lessons 'brought me on'. The 'good but pricey' British Alpine Ski & Snowboard School has a branch here.

Facilities for children This is a good resort for families. As well as comprehensive resort facilities, family-specialist tour operators Esprit Ski, Ski Famille and Ski Hillwood all operate here. And the British-run Snowkidz nursery takes babies as well as infant skiers, and is reported to be 'superb – absolutely faultless'.

STAYING THERE

How to go Several tour operators have catered chalets; we've had good reports of Total's operation.

Hotels We've stayed at the Ferme de Montagne (0450 753679) and loved it (see the luxury chalets chapter – but it's as much a small hotel as a chalet). It is a beautifully renovated farmhouse with eight luxury bedrooms, gourmet food, ski guiding, sauna, outdoor hot-tub, massage therapist; right on the edge of town at La Turche. 'High standards of service, comfort and food,' said a 2007 reporter. The Crychar (0450 758050), 100m/330ft from central Les Gets at the foot of the

slopes, is one of the best 3-star hotels ('first rate, ideal location, great restaurant'). The 2-star Alpen Sports (0450 758055) is a friendly, family-run hotel ('excellent food and good value for money' but 'soundproofing and room size not good'). We've had good reports of the Nagano (0450 797146), the Marmotte (0450 758033) – 'great maître d'; large, warm pool' – and the Alpages (0450 758088) – 'friendly, good heated outdoor pool' – all 3-star.

Apartments The central Sabaudia apartments have a pool and hot-tub.

Eating out The Ferme de Montagne (see Hotels) has wonderful food, beautifully presented in a splendid renovated wooden dining room. The Tyrol and the Schuss are good for pizza, the rustic Vieux Chêne for Savoyard specialities. The Flambeau, Tanière and Tourbillon have been recommended.

Après-ski Après-ski is quiet, especially on weekdays. The Irish Pub, Canadian Bar above it, Boomerang, Copeaux and the Bush (Scottish owned and with Sky Sports) are recommended by reporters. The Igloo is a popular disco.

Off the slopes There's a well-equipped fitness centre with a pool, and an artificial ice rink. The Mechanical Music Museum is strongly recommended by a reporter (barrel organs and music boxes, for example, with guided tours in English). There's a cinema; husky rides and snow-shoeing are possible. There is a good selection of shops, and visits to Geneva, Lausanne and Montreux are feasible.

La Grave

A world apart: an unspoiled mountain village beneath high, untamed off-piste slopes, some of them extreme and very hazardous

COSTS

① ② ③ ④ ⑤ ⑥

RATINGS

The slopes

Fast lifts	★★★
Snow	★★★
Extent	★
Expert	★★★★★
Intermediate	★
Beginner	★
Convenience	★★★
Queues	★★★★
Mountain restaurants	★★

The rest

Scenery	★★★★
Resort charm	★★★
Off-slope	★

NEWS

La Grave does not change much, and that is half the charm of the place.

+ Legendary off-piste mountain

+ Usually crowd-free

+ Usually good snow conditions

+ Link to Les Deux-Alpes

+ Easy access by car to other nearby resorts

− Village spoiled by through-traffic

− Poor weather means lift closures – on average, two days per week

− Suitable for experts only, despite some easy slopes at altitude

− Nothing to do off the slopes

La Grave enjoys legendary status among experts. It's a quiet old village with around 500 visitor beds and just one serious lift – a small stop-start gondola serving a high, wild and almost entirely off-piste mountainside. The result: an exciting, usually crowd-free area. Strictly, you ought to have a guide, but in good weather many people go it alone.

THE RESORT

La Grave is a small, unspoiled mountaineering village set on a steep hillside facing the impressive glaciers of majestic La Meije. It's rather drab, and the busy road through to Briançon doesn't help. But it has a rustic feel, some welcoming hotels, friendly inhabitants and prices that are low by resort standards. The single serious lift starts just below the centre. Storms close the slopes on average two days a week – so a car is useful for access to nearby resorts.

THE MOUNTAIN

A slow two-stage 'pulse' gondola (with an extra station at a pylon halfway up the lower stage) ascends into the slopes and finishes at 3200m/10,500ft. Above that, a short walk and a drag-lift give access to a second drag serving twin blue runs on a glacier slope of about 350m/1,150ft vertical – from here (after another walk) you can ski to Les Deux-Alpes. But the reason that people come here is to explore the legendary slopes back towards La Grave. These slopes offer no defined, patrolled, avalanche-protected pistes – but there are two marked itinéraires (with several variations now indicated on the 'piste' map) of 1400m/4,590ft vertical down to the pylon lift station at 1800m/5,910ft, or all the way down to the valley – a vertical of 2150m/7,050ft.

Slopes The Chancel route is mostly of red-run gradient; the Vallons de la Meije is more challenging but not too steep. People do take these routes without a guide or avalanche protection equipment, but we couldn't possibly recommend it.

There are many more demanding runs away from the itinéraires, including couloirs that range from the straightforward to the seriously

← The setting is spectacular

KEY FACTS

Resort	1450m
	4,760ft
Slopes	1450-3550m
	4,760-11,650ft
Lifts	4
Pistes	5km
	3 miles
Green/Blue	100%

The figures relate
only to pistes;
practically all the
skiing – at least 90%
– is off-piste

| Snowmaking | none |

UK PACKAGES

*Alpine Answers,
AmeriCan Ski,
Interhome, Lagrange,
Mountain Tracks, Peak
Retreats, Ski
Freshtracks, Ski
Weekend*

Phone numbers
From abroad use the
prefix +33 and omit
the initial '0' of the
phone number

TOURIST OFFICE

t 0476 799005
ot@lagrave-lameije.com
www.lagrave-
lameije.com

hazardous, and long descents from the glacier to the valley road below the village, with return by taxi, bus, or strategically parked car. The dangers are considerable (people die here every year), and good guidance is essential. You can also descend a 'spectacular valley' southwards to St-Christophe, returning by bus and the lifts of Les Deux-Alpes.

Terrain-parks There aren't any.

Snow reliability The chances of powder snow on the high, north-facing slopes are good, but if conditions are tricky there are no pistes to fall back on apart from the three short blue runs at the top of the gondola.

Experts La Grave's uncrowded off-piste slopes have earned it cult status among hard-core skiers. Only experts should contemplate a stay here – and then only if prepared to deal with bad weather by sitting tight or struggling over the Col du Lautaret to the woods of Serre-Chevalier.

Intermediates The itinéraires get tracked into a piste-like state, and adventurous intermediates could tackle the Chancel. But the three blue runs at the top of the gondola won't keep anyone occupied for long. The valley stations of Villar d'Arène and Lautaret, around 3km/2 miles and 8km/5 miles to the east respectively, and Chazelet, 3km/2 miles to the north-west, offer very limited slopes with a handful of

intermediate and beginner runs (two new ones at Villar d'Arène).

Beginners Novices tricked into coming here can go up the valley to the beginner slopes at Le Chazelet, which has two cannons for snowmaking.

Snowboarding There are no special facilities for boarders, but advanced free-riders will be in their element on the open off-piste powder.

Cross-country There is a total of 20km/12 miles of loops in the area.

Queues Normally, there are queues only at weekends. March is reportedly the busiest month, when queues can be serious. If snow conditions back to the valley are poor, queues can build up for the gondola down from the mid and lower stations.

Mountain restaurants Surprisingly, there are three decent mountain restaurants; the jury is out on which is the best, but reporters like both the refuge on the Chancel itinéraire ('best omelette in the world') and the Haut-Dessus at the top ('great pizzas').

Schools and guides There are claimed to be 30 or so guides, offering a wide range of services through their bureau. 'Excellent,' say our 2007 reporters. See also 'Hotels' below.

Facilities for children Babysitting can be arranged through the tourist office.

STAYING THERE

How to go There are a few simple hotels.

Hotels The Edelweiss (0476 799093) is strongly recommended for its 'excellent' restaurant with 'phenomenal wine list', comfortable rooms and cosy bar. The Skiers Lodge (Hotel des Alpes) operation – all-inclusive week-long packages including guiding – is in the centre of the village (new phone number 0476 110318). A recent visitor had an 'excellent' week, advising that 'you need to get really fit beforehand'.

Apartments Bookable through the tourist office.

Eating out Most people eat in their hotels, though there are alternatives.

Après-ski The central Café des Glaciers, known to habitués as 'chez Marcel', and the bar of hotel Castillan are the standard tea-time venues. The bars of both the Edelweiss and the Skiers Lodge have live music. The Vieux Guide gets crowded later.

Off the slopes Anyone not using the slopes will find La Grave much too small and quiet.

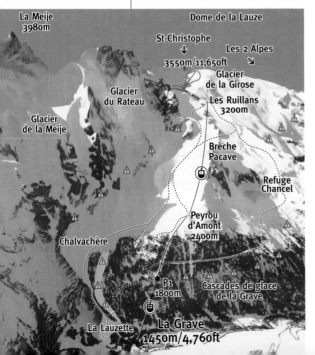

La Meije
3980m

Dome de la Lauze

St-Christophe
↓
Les 2 Alpes
3550m/11,650ft   ↘

Glacier
du Rateau

Glacier
de la Girose

Les Ruillans
3200m

Glacier
de la Meije

Brèche
Pacave

Refuge
Chancel

Peyrou
d'Amont
2400m

Chalvachère

P1
1800m

Cascades de glace
de la Grave

La Lauzette

La Grave
1450m/4,760ft

Megève

One of the traditional old winter holiday towns; best for those who enjoy relaxed cruising among splendid scenery

317

COSTS

① ② ③ ④ ⑤ ⑥

RATINGS

The slopes

Fast lifts	**
Snow	**
Extent	*****
Expert	**
Intermediate	****
Beginner	***
Convenience	**
Queues	****
Mountain restaurants	****

The rest

Scenery	*****
Resort charm	****
Off-slope	****

NEWS

For 2007/08 a six-pack is due to replace a slow chair and a drag-lift back towards Mont Joux from the St-Nicolas-de-Véroce direction. More snowmaking is planned for the main green piste on Rochebrune. And underground parking is to be built at the base of the Mont d'Arbois gondola. Several hotels are planning new or improved spa facilities.

For 2006/07 the Essartons chair on Le Jaillet above Combloux was removed. Mont Blanc Helicopters now has a base in Megève and offers airport transfers and tours of Mont Blanc. The ice rink reopened after a revamp. And there's a new bar called 'S'.

Plus points

- ➕ Extensive easy slopes
- ➕ Scenic setting, with splendid views
- ➕ Charming old village centre
- ➕ Some very smart hotels and shops
- ➕ Both gourmet and simple mountain lunches in attractive surroundings
- ➕ Excellent cross-country trails
- ➕ Great for weekends
- ➕ Great when it snows – woodland runs with no one on them
- ➕ Plenty to do off the slopes

Minus points

- ➖ With most of the slopes below 2000m/6,560ft there's a risk of poor snow – although the grassy terrain does not need a thick covering, and snowmaking has improved a lot
- ➖ Lots of slow, old lifts remain – a real irritant to mileage-hungry skiers
- ➖ Three separate mountains, only two linked (and by lift but not by piste)
- ➖ Not many challenging pistes – though there is good off-piste
- ➖ Very muted après-ski scene

Megève is the essence of rustic chic. It has a medieval heart but it was, in a way, the original purpose-built French ski resort – developed in the 1920s as an alternative to St Moritz. Although Courchevel took over as France's swankiest resort ages ago, Megève's smart hotels and chalets still attract 'beautiful people' with fur coats and fat wallets. Happily, you don't need either to enjoy the place. And it is enjoyable – the list of plus points above is as long as they come.

The risk of poor snow still makes us wary of low resorts like this. But it is true that a few inches of snow is enough to give skiable cover on the grassy slopes, and when there's fresh snow falling this is a great place to be.

The resort's managers can't do much about the altitude. What they could do, though, is drag the lift system into the 21st century. Only one in six of the area's lifts is fast, putting it close to the bottom of our fast lifts league table – presumably clocking up piste mileage is not top priority for Megève's clientele.

THE RESORT

Megève is in a lovely sunny setting and has a beautifully preserved, traditional, partly medieval centre, which is pedestrianised and comes complete with open-air ice rink, horse-drawn sleighs, cobbled streets and a fine church. Lots of smart clothing, jewellery, antique, gift and food shops add to the chic atmosphere.

The main Albertville-Chamonix road bypasses the centre, and there are expensive underground car parks. But the resort's clientele arrives mainly by car and the resulting traffic jams and fumes are a major problem. It's worst at weekends, but can be serious every afternoon in high season.

Visitors are mainly well-heeled French couples and families, who come here as much for an all-round winter holiday as for the slopes themselves. What they don't come for is après-ski action. The tea-time atmosphere is muted, and later on the nightlife is smart rather than lively.

The Chamois gondola within walking distance of central Megève gives direct access to one of the three mountains, Rochebrune. This sector can also be reached directly by a cable-car from the southern edge of town. The main

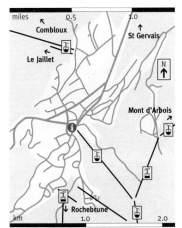

FRANCE

318

lifts for the bigger Mont d'Arbois sector start from an elevated suburb of the resort – though there is also a cable-car link from Rochebrune. The third sector, Le Jaillet, starts some way out on the north-west fringes of the town.

Staying close to one of the main lifts makes a lot of sense. Some accommodation is a long walk from the lifts, and the free bus services are a source of complaints, although a first-time visitor armed with a timetable from the tourist office tells us he found it reliable. There are several alternative bases (which offer some good-value lodging) on the fringes of the area. St-Gervais and Le Bettex above it have gondola access (St-Gervais is described at the end of this chapter). But beware slow access lifts from otherwise attractive spots such as St-Nicolas and Combloux. The most recently linked village, La Giettaz, is out on a limb but offers interesting local terrain.

The standard weekly lift pass covers Les Contamines, and the Mont Blanc pass also covers Chamonix and Courmayeur, reached through the Mont Blanc road tunnel. A car is handy for visiting these resorts.

THE MOUNTAINS

The three different mountains provide predominantly easy intermediate cruising, much of it prettily set in the woods and with some spectacular views. The wooded slopes make it a great resort to head for in poor weather. Some reporters complain that the piste grading is inconsistent. Signposting is poor, not helped by an imprecise piste map.

THE SLOPES
Pretty but low
The biggest, highest and most varied sector is **Mont d'Arbois**, accessible not only from the town but also by a gondola from La Princesse, way out to the north-east of town, with extensive free car parking. It offers some wooded slopes but is mainly open.

The slopes above the resort are sunny, but there are north-east-facing slopes to Le Bettex and on down to St-Gervais. A two-stage gondola returns you to the top. You can work your way over to Mont Joux and up to the small Mont Joly area – Megève's highest slopes. And from there you can go to the backwater village of St-Nicolas-de-Véroce (there's a splendid red run along the ridge with wonderful views of Mont Blanc); the return to Mont Joux should be speeded up for 2007/08 by the new six-pack (see 'News').

From the Mont d'Arbois lift base, the Rocharbois cable-car goes across the valley to **Rochebrune**. Alpette is the starting point for Megève's historic downhill course, now revived as an off-piste route, and narrow enough to be quite tricky. A network of gentle, wooded, north-east-facing slopes, served by drags and mainly slow chair-lifts, leads across to the high point of Côte 2000, which often has the best snow in Megève.

The third area is **Le Jaillet**, accessed by gondola from just outside the north-west edge of town, or from Combloux, linked by a series of long, gentle tree-lined runs. In the other direction is the high point of Le Christomet, which is linked to the slopes of Le Torraz, above **La Giettaz**, a

LIFT PASSES

Evasion Mont Blanc

Prices in €

Age	1-day	6-day
under 15	27	130
15 to 59	34	162
over 60	31	146

Free under 5, over 80

Beginner no deals

Notes
Covers lifts at Les Contamines as well as those of the Megève pass (see list below); family reductions

Alternative passes
Megève pass (covers Megève, Jaillet, La Giettaz, Combloux, St-Gervais and St-Nicolas); Jaillet-Combloux-Giettaz only pass; pedestrian pass; weekly Mont Blanc passes (all resorts in the Mont Blanc area plus Courmayeur in Italy)

SCHOOLS

ESF
t 0450 210097

International
t 0450 587888

Freeride
t 0450 930352

Summits
t 0450 933521

Classes (ESF prices)
5 mornings (2½hr)
€137

Private lessons
€38 for 1hr, for 1 or 2 people

GUIDES

Compagnie des Guides
t 0450 215511

boarding

Boarding doesn't really fit with Megève's traditional, rather staid, upmarket image. But free-riders will find lots of untracked off-piste powder for days after new snowfalls. It's a good place to try snowboarding for the first time, with plenty of fairly wide, quiet, gentle runs and a lot of chair-lifts and gondolas; though there are a fair number of drag-lifts, they are generally avoidable. There are no specialist snowboard schools, but all the ski schools offer boarding lessons. There's a terrain-park on Mont Joux and a smaller one above Combloux.

tiny resort half-way to La Clusaz. The slopes of Le Torraz are worth visiting, not least for the spectacular views from the summit – we found the link hard going (lots of skating and poling) when we did it in 2006; but we hear it was improved for last season.

TERRAIN-PARKS
Two, surprisingly
You wouldn't have thought there was much call for terrain-parks from Megève's clientele. But there is a 320m/1,050ft slope on Mont Joux with a half-pipe, quarter-pipe, pyramid and, apparently, some moguls. A sound system at the bottom helps to motivate the faint-hearted. And there's a small park, Snowtap, on the upper slopes above Combloux.

SNOW RELIABILITY
The area's main weakness
The problem is that the slopes are low, with very few runs above 2000m/6,560ft, and partly sunny – the Megève side of Mont d'Arbois gets the afternoon sun. So in a poor snow year, or in a warm spell, snow on the lower slopes can suffer badly.

Fortunately, the grassy slopes don't need much depth of snow. And the resort has an extensive snowmaking network (some runs are now entirely covered, including the long red Olympique run at Rochebrune) but that can't work in warm weather. There is also a high standard of piste grooming.

FOR EXPERTS
Off-piste is the main attraction
One of Megève's great advantages for expert skiers is that there is not much competition for the powder – you can often make first tracks on challenging slopes many days after a fresh dump.

The Mont Joly and Mont Joux sections offer the steepest slopes. The top chair here serves a genuinely black run, and the slightly lower Epaule chair has some steep runs back down and also accesses some good off-piste, as

well as pistes, down to St-Nicolas. The steep area beneath the second stage of the Princesse gondola can be a play area of powder runs among the trees. Cote 2000 has a small section of steep runs, including good off-piste.

The terrain under the Christomet chair can be a good spot to practise off-piste technique, given decent snow.

FOR INTERMEDIATES
Superb if the snow is good
Good intermediates will enjoy the whole area – there is so much choice it's difficult to single out any particular sectors. Keen skiers are likely to want to focus on the fast lifts, and happily several of these serve excellent terrain – the Princesse and Bettex gondolas on Mont d'Arbois, the Fontaine and Alpette chairs on Rochebrune and the Christomet chair in the Le Jaillet sector. But don't confine yourself to those – there are lots of other interesting areas, including the shady north-east-facing slopes on the back of Mont d'Arbois and Mont Joux and the front of Rochebrune, and the genuinely red/black slopes of La Giettaz.

It's a great area for the less confident. A number of comfortable runs lead down to Le Bettex and La Princesse from Mont d'Arbois, while nearby Mont Joux accesses long, problem-free runs to St-Nicolas. Alpette and Cote 2000 are also suitable.

Even the timid can get a great deal of mileage in. All main access lifts have easy routes down to them (there is now a blue down the Princesse gondola and a couple of seasons ago a 5km/3 miles long blue was built from Le Christomet to La Giettaz). There are some particularly good, long, gentle cruises between Mont Joux and Megève via Mont d'Arbois. But in all sectors you'll find long, easy blue runs.

FOR BEGINNERS
Good choice of nursery areas
There are beginner slopes at valley level, and more snow-sure ones at

Megève

altitude on each of the main mountains. There are also plenty of very easy longer green runs to progress to.

FOR CROSS-COUNTRY
An excellent area
There are 43km/27 miles of varied trails spread throughout the area. Some are at altitude (1300m-1550m/4,270ft-5,090ft), making lunchtime meetings with Alpine skiers simple.

QUEUES
Few weekday problems
Megève is relatively queue-free during the week, except at peak holiday time. But school holidays and sunny Sunday crowds can mean some delays. The Lanchettes drag between Cote 2000 and the rest of the Rochebrune slopes gets busy ('ridiculously long waits',

writes a recent visitor) – as does the cable-car linking the two mountains. Crowded pistes at Mont Joux and Mont d'Arbois can also be a problem. But out of peak season, slow lifts and breakdowns (eg of the gondola from St Gervais) provoke more complaints than queues or crowds. And on a snowy day (especially in January), the slopes can be delightfully quiet as the pampered clientele stay in bed.

MOUNTAIN RESTAURANTS
Something for all budgets
Megève has some chic, expensive, gourmet mountain huts but plenty of cheaper options too. Booking ahead is advisable for table-service places.
Editors' choice On Mont d'Arbois, the Ravière (0450 931571), tucked away in the woods near the La Croix chair, is a

Mont Joly
2525m/8,285ft
2355m

Some of Megève's steepest runs, including a genuine black run

Côte 2000

Les Contamines

L'Epaule
2110m

Alpette
1870m

Alpette
1755m

A splendid run along the ridge with spectacular views of Mont Blanc

Croix du Christ

Mont Joux
1960m

Mont Joux

Altiport

Fontaine

Caboche

ROCHEBRUN

Rochebrune

St-Nicolas-de-Véroce
1150m/3,770ft

Les Chattrix

Bettex-Arbois

Mont d'Arbois
1840m

Mt d'Arbois

Rocharbois

Megève
850m/2,790ft

Le Bettex
1380m

St Gervais-Bettex

Princesse

MONT D'ARBOIS

Jaillet

Le Chatelet

A great area to play in the trees in powder if it's snowing

La Princesse
1110m

St-Gervais
850m/2,790ft

Le Freynet

Combloux

CHILDREN

Meg'Accueil
t 0450 587784
Ages 18mnth to 12yr

Club des Piou-Piou
t 0450 589765
Ages 3 and 4

Ski schools
From age 3 or 4 (ESF
prices: 5 mornings
€100 for ages 3 and
4, €121 for ages 5 to
12)

tiny rustic hut that does a set three-course meal and where booking is essential. On Rochebrune, Alpette (0450 210369), on top of the ridge, has excellent all-round views outside, a good atmosphere inside, friendly people and good food.

Worth knowing about The Mont d'Arbois area is very well endowed with restaurants. There are two suave places popular with poseurs with small dogs and fur coats – the Club House and the Idéal 1850. The Mont d'Arbois self-service has a varied menu. Chalet des Princesses is 'beautifully located' halfway down the Princesse gondola. The Igloo, 'quiet but expensive', with wonderful views of Mont Blanc, has both self- and table-service sections. At the base of the Mont Joux lift, Chez Marie du Rosay has been

recommended. Prices are lower on the back side of the hill. The hut at the bottom of the Mont Rosset chair offers 'great food' and 'friendly staff', say recent reporters. Above St-Nicolas are several little chalets offering great charm and good food and views at modest prices.

On Rochebrune, at the foot of the Cote 2000 slopes is the popular Auberge de la Cote 2000, a former farm ('We went in for a drink and staggered out three hours and five courses later,' writes a reporter); Radaz, up the slope a little, enjoys better views but can get busy. A reporter enjoyed his Christmas Day lunch at the Super Megève. And Chalet Forestier is a 'cosy' retreat.

On Le Jaillet the Auberge du Christomet is highly rated for its 'plats du jour' and 'touches of real

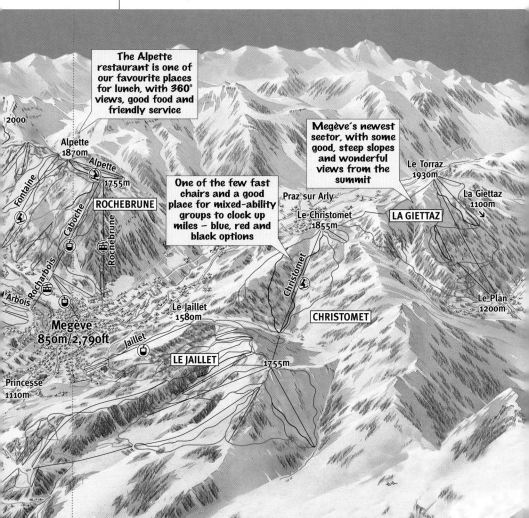

The Alpette restaurant is one of our favourite places for lunch, with 360° views, good food and friendly service

One of the few fast chairs and a good place for mixed-ability groups to clock up miles – blue, red and black options

Megève's newest sector, with some good, steep slopes and wonderful views from the summit

GETTING THERE

Air Geneva 70km/ 43 miles (1hr); Lyon 180km/112 miles (2½hr)

Rail Sallanches (12km/7 miles); regular buses from station

ACTIVITIES

Indoor Palais des Sports (tennis, ice rink, climbing wall, swimming pool, sauna, solarium, gym), beauty treatments, museum, library, cinemas, casino

Outdoor Cleared paths, snow-shoe excursions, ice rink, curling, sleigh rides, dog-sledding, ice-climbing, plane and helicopter trips

originality' about the food. It is also accessible to walkers, and gets booked out. We hear the Face au Mont Blanc at the top of the gondola does a great fixed-price buffet. A recent visitor found the Auberge de Bonjournal on the link to La Giettaz was 'well placed, well priced and excellent'.

SCHOOLS AND GUIDES
Several good options
The International school has been more popular with readers than the ESF, but we have several reports of successful private lessons with the ESF. Expeditions to the Vallée Blanche (in Chamonix) and heli-skiing (in Italy), can be arranged and mountain guides are available (we had a great morning powder skiing in the trees with Alex Périnet: 0685 428339).

FACILITIES FOR CHILDREN
Language problems
The kindergartens offer a wide range of activities. But lack of English-speaking staff could be a drawback. The slopes are family-friendly and the schools rated by reporters. There's a snow garden at Le Bettex.

STAYING THERE

HOW TO GO
Few packages
Relatively few British tour operators go to Megève, but there is an impressive range of accommodation.
Chalets A few UK tour operators offer catered chalets. For a cheap and very cheerful base, you won't do better

than Stanford's Sylvana – a creaky, unpretentious old hotel, reachable on skis, run along chalet lines.
Hotels Megève offers a range of exceptionally stylish and welcoming hotels, and there are more modest places, too.
****Mont Blanc (0450 212002) Megève's traditional leading hotel – elegant, fashionable, central.
****Chalet du Mont d'Arbois (0450 212503) Prettily decorated Relais & Châteaux hotel in a secluded position near the Mont d'Arbois gondola.
****Chalet St Georges (0450 930715) Central, very close to the gondola. Only 24 rooms, so intimate for a 4-star. 'Two very good restaurants.'
****Fer à Cheval (0450 213039) Rustic-chic at its best, with a warmly welcoming wood-and-stone interior and excellent food. Close to the centre. 'A memorable stay,' writes a reporter.
***Prairie (0450 214855) Central, 'reasonably priced' B&B. Close to the Chamois lift.
***Coin du Feu (0450 210494) 'Very well managed' chalet midway between Rochebrune and Chamois lifts.
***Coeur de Megève (0450 212530) Central, very close to the gondola. 'Excellent restaurant.'
***Ferme Duvillard (0450 211462) Smartly restored farmhouse, perfectly positioned for the slopes, at the foot of the Mont d'Arbois gondola.
***Coin du Feu (0450 210494) 'Very well managed' chalet midway between Rochebrune and Chamois lifts.
**Sévigné (0450 212309) Ten minutes from the centre, but 'really delightful –

Most people come here as much for an all-round winter holiday as for the slopes; and the traffic-free centre is a lovely place to wander around →

UK PACKAGES

Alpine Answers, AmeriCan Ski, Classic Ski Limited, Corporate Ski Co, Erna Low, Flexiski, Interhome, Kuoni, Lagrange, Made to Measure, Momentum, Oxford Ski Co, Peak Retreats, Simon Butler Skiing, Ski Barrett-Boyce, Ski Collection, Ski Expectations, Ski France, Ski Independence, Ski Leisure Direction, Ski Solutions, Ski Weekend, Skiholidayextras, Skitracer, Snow Finders, Stanford Skiing, White Roc
St Gervais AmeriCan Ski, Ardmore, Chalet Group, Club Pavilion, Erna Low, Interhome, Lagrange, Peak Retreats, Ski France, Ski Leisure Direction, Ski4you, Skifrance4less, Skiholidayextras, Snowcoach

Phone numbers
From abroad use the prefix +33 and omit the initial '0' of the phone number

TOURIST OFFICES

Megève
t 0450 212728
megeve@megeve.com
www.megeve.com

St-Gervais
t 0450 477608
welcome@st-gervais.
net
www.st-gervais.net

very quaint, excellent food'.
Apartments Chateau & Residence Megève, set on the Mont d'Arbois road overlooking the village, is a completely renovated chalet; indoor/outdoor pool, steam, sauna, restaurant.

EATING OUT
Very French
Lots of upmarket restaurants – many recommended in the gastro guides. Flocons de Sel (two Michelin stars) and the restaurants in all the best hotels are excellent but very pricey. The fashionable Cintra, also expensive, is 'great for fresh seafood'.

The Brasserie Centrale 'serves almost anything you ask for', says an impressed reporter. The Flocons de Sel is recommended for its 'excellent service'. The Prieuré is 'highly recommended – lots of atmosphere, excellent food, good value', as is the Bistrot ('great salads and pizzas'). The Delicium is also popular.

Some reporters wish there was more variety, while others say that you get this and lower prices too in the centres outside Megève ('especially in Combloux', says a recent reporter).

APRES-SKI
Strolling and jazz
Megève is a pleasant place to stroll around after the lifts close, but exciting it isn't. If there are atmospheric bars for a post-piste beer, they have eluded us. And those looking for loud disco-bars later on will also be disappointed. Our favourite place was the Club de Jazz (aka the 5 Rues) – a very popular, if rather expensive, jazz club-cum-cocktail bar, that gets some big-name musicians and opens from tea-time to late. But a change of management did not impress a recent reporter: 'It's cold, impersonal, and the pure jazz seems to have given way to more rock and roll.' The Cocoon is popular with Brits, and the Wake-Up attracts seasonaires. The casino is more slot machines than blackjack tables.

OFF THE SLOPES
Lots to do
There is a 'fantastic' sports centre with pool, a revamped outdoor ice rink, cinemas and a weekly market. Trips to Annecy and Chamonix are possible. Walks are excellent, with 50km/ 30 miles of marked paths classified for difficulty on a special map. Meeting friends on the slopes for lunch is easy.

STAYING UP THE MOUNTAIN
Several possibilities
As well as mid-mountain Le Bettex, there are hotels on Mont d'Arbois.

St-Gervais 850m/2,790ft

St-Gervais is a handsome 19th-century spa town set in a narrow river gorge, on the far side of Mont d'Arbois, with access to the slopes via a 20-person gondola from just outside the town. It's an urban but pleasant place, with interesting food shops and cosy bars, thermal baths and an Olympic skating rink. Prices are noticeably lower than in Megève. Buses are reported to be regular and convenient. Two hotels convenient for the gondola are the Liberty Mont Blanc (0450 934521), a pleasantly traditional 2-star, and the 'quite charming' 3-star Carlina (0450 934110), with a small pool and sauna. The 2-star Val d'Este (0450 936591) and its restaurant (le Serac) have been recommended – endorsed again by a 2007 reporter ('most welcoming and neat hotel we have been to in French Alps in 16 years, great restaurant').

On the opposite side of St-Gervais is a rack-and-pinion railway, which in 1904 was intended to go to the top of Mont Blanc but actually takes you to the slopes of Les Houches.

AGENCE NUTS

Les Menuires

The bargain base for the Three Valleys – with an increasing amount of stylish accommodation as well as the original dreary blocks

NEWS

For 2007/08 a new six-pack with covers from the top of the gondola from town to the top of Roc des 3 Marches is planned. This will replace the old slow Allamands chair, speed the journey to Méribel and enable pedestrians to go as far as Courchevel and back on gondolas and chairs.

For 2006/07 the resort's first 4-star hotel, the Kaya, opened in Reberty and one of Les Menuires' first buildings, Les Clarines, was demolished. MGM is building a chalet-style replacement in wood and stone to be ready for 2008/09.

A smart new leisure centre opened for 2005/06.

KEY FACTS

Resort   1800m
                    5,910ft

For other facts, see St-Martin-de-Belleville chapter

324

- ➕ Great local slopes on La Masse, and quick links with Val Thorens
- ➕ Lots of slope-side accommodation
- ➕ New, outlying parts of the resort are much more attractive than the core

- ➖ Big, dreary blocks and gloomy indoor shopping malls in centre
- ➖ Main intermediate and beginner slopes get a lot of sun
- ➖ Some lower slopes get crowded

Les Menuires is in a great position – you can get quickly from it to all parts of the Three Valleys. And its local slopes on La Masse are some of the best for good skiers: challenging, usually with good snow, and rarely used by visitors from the other valleys. Our reluctance to recommend the place has hinged around the ugliness of its original buildings, which still form its core La Croisette area. But now there are attractive satellites built in chalet style in wood and stone. Hole up there and ignore the centre and you can have a happy holiday.

THE RESORT

The original buildings that surround the main lift base, La Croisette, are among the worst examples of the thoughtless building of the 1960s/70s. But the resort is trying hard to smarten up. In outposts such as Reberty and Hameau des Marmottes, the latest additions are in stone-and-wood chalet style. These outposts have their own shops and bars – Les Bruyères is now a more-or-less self-contained resort They have also demolished a couple of the original buildings (as we advised them to nine editions ago) and are rebuilding in a more attractive style.

THE MOUNTAINS

Les Menuires is set at about the tree line, with almost entirely open slopes.
Slopes The major part of the network spreads across the broad, west-facing mountainside between Les Menuires

and St-Martin, with links to the Méribel valley at four points and to Val Thorens. A gondola and a fast chair go up from La Croisette. Lifts to La Masse, a steeper mountain, start below the village – a gondola and a chair.
Terrain-parks There's a terrain-park with slides, tables, pyramids and boarder-cross above Reberty.
Snow reliability La Masse's height and orientation ensure good snow for a long season. The west-facing slopes have lots of snowmaking but the snow lower down is often icy or slushy.
Experts The upper slopes of La Masse are virtually all of stiff red/soft black steepness – great fast cruises when groomed. There is also a huge amount of off-piste, including Vallon du Lou – a broad, sweeping route towards Val Thorens, and the ESF organises groups for exploring it (praised by a reporter).
Intermediates With good snow, you may be content with the local slopes, which are virtually all blue and red. In

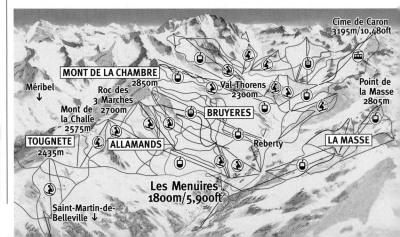

poor snow you can head up to Val Thorens on blue runs. Don't miss La Masse – the blacks are not super-steep – but beware the steep Masse drag-lift.

Beginners There are wide and gentle slopes and a special lift pass for beginners, but the snow quality on the nursery slopes is a worry and the progression slopes can be crowded.

Snowboarding There are few drags but some flattish sections of piste.

Cross-country The 28km/17 miles of prepared trails are along the valley between St-Martin and Les Menuires.

Queues Not a problem; but acute overcrowding on the slopes down to the resort centre is.

Mountain restaurants Recent visitors were 'very impressed' with the new Grand Lac, at the base of the Granges chair ('good food, friendly service, cheap'). Just above Les Menuires is the very pleasant but quite pricey Etoile. At higher altitude there are 'huge meals' and 'excellent value' at the Alpage, on the 4 Vents piste. Many people head down to the villages for lunch; you retain some sense of being on the mountain at the 'good value' Ferme, beside the piste at Reberty; the new Kaya hotel terrace near here serves excellent food; and a regular reporter recommends the 'good, reasonably priced' food at the Ours Blanc hotel.

Schools and guides The ESF has the monopoly here. We have had good reports – of the off-piste groups as well as of normal lessons.

Facilities for children Family Ski Company has its own nursery in Reberty – and sends a minder with kids going to ski school.

STAYING THERE

How to go Some big UK tour operators offer holidays here, and some chalet operators have a presence in Reberty. There is a Club Med above Reberty.

Chalets The cluster known as Reberty Village has been virtually taken over by UK chalet operators – particularly Family Ski, Ski Olympic and Ski Amis.

Hotels The two best are on the slopes at Reberty: the new Kaya (0479 414200) is the resort's only 4-star – attractively smart and modern. The top 3-star is the Ours Blanc (0479 006166).

Apartments In contrast to the blocks of the main resort, there are lots of more recent apartment developments in chalet style on the slopes. At La Sapinière are the excellent Montalys and Chalets les Montagnettes. Further up in Reberty 2000 is Les Alpages, an MGM development; and further up still the Chalets du Soleil; down the slope in Balcons des Bruyères is Les Chalets de l'Adonis; all these have pools.

Eating out Reporter recommendations include: Trattoria ('rustic French ambience'), Refuge ('reasonably priced menus'), Marmite de Géant ('excellent food, good value'). Chalet-boy night off is no problem in Reberty: the Ferme, on the spot, is 'a hot favourite for food and prices' and the smart restaurant in the hotel Kaya is a gourmet option.

Après-ski There is no shortage of bars in La Croisette, but many are in the dreadful shopping gallery. The Chalet Cafe in Les Bruyères is 'lively and welcoming'. There are discos.

Off the slopes This is a resort for keen skiers and boarders.

Les Menuires

325

Selected chalets in Les Menuires

Méribel

The enduring British favourite: a comfortable, upmarket chalet-style resort in the centre of the wonderful Three Valleys

COSTS

① ② ③ ④ ⑤ ⑥

RATINGS

The slopes

Fast lifts	****
Snow	***
Extent	*****
Expert	****
Intermediate	*****
Beginner	****
Convenience	***
Queues	****
Mountain restaurants	***

The rest

Scenery	***
Resort charm	***
Off-slope	***

NEWS

For 2006/07 a six-pack replaced the Chatelet chair serving the Plattières terrain-park, making it easier to get to Val Thorens and reducing queues for the Plattières gondola. The Plan des Mains three-part restaurant (sandwich bar, brasserie and gastronomic options) opened just above the base of the Mont Vallon gondola.

For 2007/08 a six-pack with covers is due to replace the second stage of the Tougnète gondola, and the Olympic Centre will get a new spa and fitness area.

➕ In the centre of the biggest linked lift network in the world – ideal for intermediates, great for experts, too

➕ Pleasant chalet-style architecture

➕ Impressive lift system

➕ Excellent piste maintenance and snowmaking; nevertheless ...

➖ Not the best snow in the 3V, especially on the afternoon-sun side

➖ Pistes can get very crowded

➖ Sprawling main village, with lots of accommodation far from the slopes

➖ Expensive

➖ Full of Brits (holds the record for number of UK operators, at 69)

➖ Méribel-Mottaret and Méribel-Village satellites are rather lifeless

For keen piste-bashers who like to rack up the miles but dislike tacky purpose-built resorts, Méribel is difficult to beat. The Three Valleys can keep anyone amused for a fortnight – and Méribel-Mottaret, in particular, has quick access to every part. Unlike other purpose-built resorts, Méribel has always insisted on chalet-style architecture. What more could you ask? Well, our ➖ points are mostly non-trivial, and other Three Valleys resorts have the edge in some respects. For better snow opt for Courchevel or Val Thorens. For less crowded runs, Courchevel 1650. For a smaller village, St-Martin or La Tania. For lower prices, Les Menuires. For a lower concentration of Brits, anywhere. But the other resorts have their drawbacks, too. Regular visitors love Méribel.

THE RESORT

Méribel occupies the central valley of the Three Valleys system and consists of two main resort villages.

The original resort is built on a single steepish west-facing hillside with the home piste running down beside it to the main lift stations at the valley bottom. All the buildings are wood-clad, low-rise and chalet-style, making it one of the most tastefully designed of French purpose-built resorts. A road winds up from the village centre to the Rond Point des Pistes, and goes on through woods to the outpost of the altiport (a snow-covered airstrip).

The resort was founded by a Brit, Peter Lindsay, in 1938, and has retained a strong British presence ever since – 'More like Kensington than France,' commented a reporter. It spreads widely, and although some accommodation is right on the piste, much depends on use of buses (or tour operator minibuses). There are collections of shops and restaurants at a couple of points on the road through the resort – Altitude 1600 and Plateau de Morel. The lodgings at Altiport enjoy splendid isolation in the woods, and are 'normally Brit-free'.

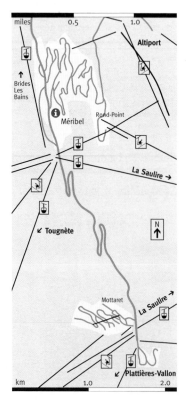

KEY FACTS

Resort	1400-1700m
	4,590-5,580ft

Three Valleys	
Slopes	1260-3230m
	4,130-10,600ft
Lifts	183
Pistes	600km
	373 miles
Green	15%
Blue	38%
Red	37%
Black	10%
Snowmaking	
	1920 guns

Méribel only	
Slopes	1400-2950m
	4,590-9,680ft
Lifts	53
Pistes	150km
	93 miles
Green	11%
Blue	47%
Red	30%
Black	12%
Snowmaking	
	650 guns

The newer satellite of Méribel-Mottaret is centrally placed in the Three Valleys ski area, offering swift access to Courchevel, Val Thorens and Les Menuires. Development started beside the piste on the east-facing slope, but the resort has spread up the opposite hillside and further up the valley. Both sides are served by lifts for pedestrians – but the gondola up the east-facing slope stops at 7.30pm and it's a long, tiring walk up.

Mottaret looks modern, despite wood cladding on its apartment blocks. Even so, it's more attractive than many other resorts built for slope-side convenience. It has far fewer shops and bars and much less après-ski than Méribel, and some visitors have found it 'lacking in atmosphere'.

The hamlet of Méribel-Village, on the road from Méribel to La Tania and Courchevel, has a chair-lift up to Altiport with a blue run back and has developed into a pleasant mini-resort. There are some luxury chalets and apartments here but little else apart

from a bread shop, small supermarket, fitness centre, bar, pizzeria and a couple of restaurants.

There are some alternative bases lower down the mountain (and price scale) – see the end of this chapter.

Local buses are free but readers complain that they are inadequate. Many UK tour operators run their own minibus services to and from the lifts. A car is mainly of use for outings to other resorts. If you buy a Three Valleys lift pass for five days or more, we understand you'll be able to buy a 10 euro daily extension to ski the Val d'Isère-Tignes or Paradiski areas too.

THE MOUNTAINS

Most of the slopes are above the tree line, but there are some sheltered runs for bad-weather days. Piste classification is not always reliable – a problem compounded by exposure of many slopes to a lot of sun. Daily maps are available showing which runs were groomed overnight.

Méribel

327

OT MERIBEL / J M GOUEDARD

The main Moon terrain-park below Tougnète; there's another, less demanding one above Mottaret →

THE SLOPES
Highly efficient lift system

The Méribel valley runs roughly north-south, and in late season you soon get into the habit of skiing one side in the morning and the other after lunch.

On the morning-sun side, a gondola (the second stage of which is due to be replaced by a fast chair for 2007/08) rises from Méribel to **Tougnète**, from where you can get down to Les Menuires or St-Martin-de-Belleville. You can also head for **Mottaret** from here. From there, a fast chair then a drag take you to another entry point for the Les Menuires runs in the next valley.

On the afternoon-sun side, gondolas leave both Méribel and Mottaret for **Saulire**. From here you can head back down towards either village or over the ridge towards Courchevel 1850.

South of Mottaret are some of the best slopes in the **Plattières-Vallon** sector. The Plattières gondola ends at another entry point to Les Menuires. To the east of this is the big stand-up gondola to the top of Mont du Vallon (wonderful views from the top). A fast quad from near this area goes south up to Mont de la Chambre, giving direct access to Val Thorens.

TERRAIN-PARKS
There's a choice

There are two parks in the area. The main Moonpark (www.moonpark.net) is accessible by the Arpasson drag-lift near the mid-mountain Tougnète gondola station. It includes a triple

Mont du Vallon
2950m/9,680ft

Mont Vallon

Great hill, both
on- and off-piste:
high, steep but
not too steep,
750m/2,460ft
vertical

PLATTIÈRES - VALLON

↙ Courchevel ↘

Plan des Mains

Mures Rouge

SAULIRE
2740m

Excessive afternoon
sun means the blue
run down to
Mottaret is often
more difficult than
you might wish

Plattières I

Better snow
here than on
most of the
afternoon-sun
side of the valley

Pas-du-Lac-I & II

1700m

BURGIN

MOTTARET

↙ Courchevel

Dent du Burgin

Ardret

Burgin I & II

Col de la Loze
2275m

Rhodos I & II

Chaudanne

1450m/4,760ft

Altiport

Méribel

A great area for
beginners and near-
beginners, with long
green runs and a
fast slow-loading
chair-lift

Altiport

Méribel-Village
1400m/4,590ft

Olympic

Brides
Les Bains
↓

kicker line for all levels with smooth take offs; and the rails here are quite advanced, as is the big spine jump. Of the two half-pipes, one is much larger than the other. There was a big improvement in maintenance last season, which bodes well for the 2007/08 park. If you head up the valley to the Plattières park above Mottaret, there is a smaller set of obstacles, just right for beginners and intermediates and worth a look by experts too.

SNOW RELIABILITY
Not the best in the Three Valleys
Méribel's slopes aren't the highest in the Three Valleys, and they mainly face east or west; the latter (the runs down from Courchevel) get the full force of the afternoon sun. So snow conditions are often better elsewhere. And grooming seems to be rather better in neighbouring Courchevel.

The lower runs have substantial snowmaking and lack of snow is rarely a problem, but ice at the start of the day or slush at the end can be. The north-west-facing slopes above Altiport generally have decent snow.

At the southern end of the valley, towards Les Menuires and Val Thorens, a lot of runs are north-facing and keep their snow well, as do the runs on Mont du Vallon.

FOR EXPERTS
Exciting choices
The size of the Three Valleys means experts are well catered for. In the

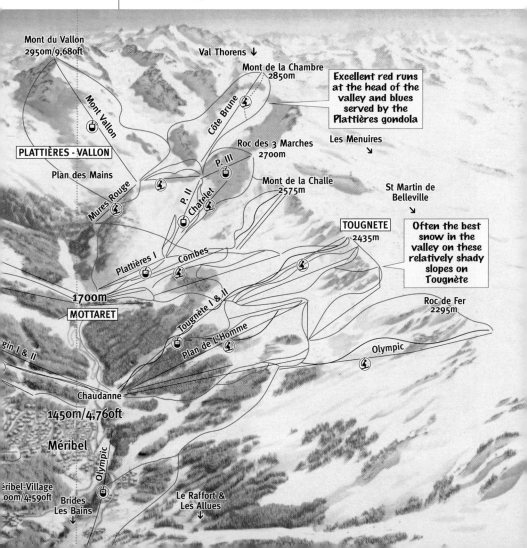

Mont du Vallon
2950m/9,68oft

Val Thorens ↓

Mont de la Chambre
2850m

Mont Vallon

Côte Brune

Excellent red runs at the head of the valley and blues served by the Plattières gondola

PLATTIÈRES - VALLON

Roc des 3 Marches
2700m

Les Menuires
↓

Plan des Mains

P. III

Mont de la Challe
2575m

St Martin de Belleville
↓

Mures Rouge

P. II

Chatelet

TOUGNETE
2435m

Often the best snow in the valley on these relatively shady slopes on Tougnète

Plattières I

Combes

1700m

Tougnète I & II

MOTTARET

Roc de Fer
2295m

Plan de L'Homme

gin I & II

Olympic

Chaudanne

1450m/4,76oft

Méribel

Olympic

éribel-Village
oom/4.59oft

Brides Les Bains
↓

Le Raffort & Les Allues
↓

Méribel valley, head for Mont du Vallon – voted 'the best skiing in the whole of the Three Valleys' by one reporter's group. The long, steep Combe Vallon run here is classified red; it's a wonderful, long, fast cruise when groomed (which it normally is), but presents plenty of challenge when mogulled. And there's a beautiful off-piste run in the next valley to the main pistes, leading back to the bottom of the gondola.

A good mogul run is down the side of the double Roc de Tougne drag-lift which leads up to Mont de la Challe. And there is a steep black run down from Tougnète back to Méribel, unrelenting most of the way.

At the north end of the valley the Face run was built for the women's downhill in the 1992 Olympics. Served by a fast quad, it's a splendid cruise when freshly groomed (with good views over town), and you can terrify yourself just by imagining what it must be like to go straight down.

Nothing on the Saulire side is as steep or as demanding as on the other side of the valley. The Mauduit red run is quite challenging, though – it used to be classified black.

Throughout the area there are good off-piste opportunities – see the feature panel later in this chapter.

FOR INTERMEDIATES
Paradise found

Méribel and the rest of the Three Valleys is a paradise for intermediates; there are few other resorts where a keen piste-basher can cover so many miles so easily. Virtually every slope in the region has a good intermediate run down it, and to describe them all would take a book in itself.

For less adventurous intermediates, the run from the second station of the Plattières gondola above Mottaret back to the first station is ideal, and used a lot by the ski school. It is a gentle, north-facing, cruising run and is generally in good condition. But below that the run can get tricky and bumpy later in the day; 'Carnage when the beginner classes went up,' said one reporter. 'People spreadeagled everywhere, with the bloodwagons overwhelmed,' said another. The run into Mottaret on the other side of the valley also gets dangerously icy and crowded. The lift company really needs to tackle both these problems as a

matter of urgency, because they spoil an otherwise ideal intermediate area.

Even early intermediates should find the runs over into the other valleys well within their capabilities, opening up further vast amounts of intermediate runs. Go to Courchevel or Val Thorens for the better snow.

Virtually all the pistes on both sides of the Méribel valley will suit more advanced intermediates. Most of the reds are on the difficult side.

FOR BEGINNERS
Strengths and weaknesses

Méribel has an excellent slope for beginners (where one of the editors of this book learned to ski many years ago). But it's out of the resort up at Altiport, which is a bit of a nuisance. There is a small nursery slope at Rond-Point, at the top of the village, which is mainly used by the children's ski school.

The Altiport area is accessible from the village by the Morel chair-lift, or by free bus. Once you have found your feet, a free drag-lift takes you halfway up a long, gentle, wide, tree-lined green run – ideal except that it can get crowded and have good skiers speeding through. Next, a longer drag takes you to the top of this run, then a chair a bit higher, then another chair higher still, on to an excellent blue usually blessed with good snow.

FOR CROSS-COUNTRY
Scenic routes

There are about 33km/21 miles in total. The main area is in the forest near Altiport and great for trying cross-country for the first time. There's also a loop around Lake Tueda, in the nature reserve at Mottaret, and for the more experienced an itinéraire from Altiport to Courchevel.

QUEUES
3V traffic a persistent problem

Huge lift investment over the years has paid off in making the area virtually queue-free most of the time, despite the vast numbers of people. Generally, if you do find a queue, there is an alternative quieter route you can take. The real problems result from the tidal flows of people between the three valleys in the morning (when the tide coincides with the start of ski school) and in the late afternoon. Reporters complain that the lift staff don't fill up the gondolas and chairs at busy times ('very frustrating'). The queue for the Plattières gondola at Mottaret has been eased by the fast Combes and new Chatelet chair (see 'News') now giving a viable alternative route. But you can still find big queues at the Côte Brune chair to Mont de la Chambre and the Plan des Mains chair (used by everyone returning from Val Thorens to avoid the ridiculously flat 'blue' Ours run that goes directly down the valley).

boarding

Méribel is a favourite for British snowboarders. The terrain is good and varied, with a lot more tree runs than in neighbouring Val Thorens. There is some very good steep free-riding that stays relatively untracked on Mont du Vallon. And there's a real wealth of red runs here for intermediates and mellow blues and greens for beginners. Most lifts are chairs or gondolas but beware some of the flat sections on the main routes to and from Val Thorens – avoid the Ours blue run down to Mottaret from Mont du Vallon, which is very hard work. Specialist shops include Board Brains (in Méribel) and Quiksilver Gotcha Surf (in Mottaret).

SAVE UP TO 45%
snowrainer.co.uk

ONLINE SKI & BOARD HIRE
COLLECT IN OVER 140 RESORTS

snowrainer.co.uk

UK PACKAGES

Airtours, Alpine Action, Alpine Answers, Belvedere Chalets, Chalet Group, Chalet World Ski, Club Med, Club Pavilion, Cooltip Mountain Holidays, Corporate Ski Co, Crystal, Crystal Finest, Descent International, Directski.com, Elegant Resorts, Erna Low, Esprit, First Choice, Flexiski, Independent Ski Links, Inghams, Inspired to Ski, Interactive Resorts, Interhome, Kaluma, Kuoni, Lagrange, Made to Measure, Mark Warner, Meriski, Momentum, Mountain Tracks, Neilson, Oxford Ski Co, Powder White, Purple Ski, Scott Dunn, Silver Ski, Ski Activity, Ski Amis, Ski Basics, Ski Beat, Ski Blanc, Ski Bon, Ski Collection, Ski Cuisine, Ski Expectations, Ski France, Ski Hame, Ski Independence, Ski Leisure Direction, Ski Line, Ski McNeill, Ski Olympic, Ski Solutions, Ski Supreme, Ski Weekend, Ski4you, Skiholidayextras, Skitracer, Skiworld, Snow Finders, Snowline, Snoworks, Supertravel, Thomson, Total, VIP, White Roc
Mottaret *Airtours, Alpine Answers, Crystal, First Choice, Neilson, Ski France, Ski Independence, Ski Line, Skiholidayextras, Skiworld, Thomson*
Brides-les-Bains *AmeriCan Ski, Crystal, Directski.com, Erna Low, First Choice, Lagrange, Peak Retreats, Ramblers, Ski France, Ski Leisure Direction, Ski McNeill, Ski Weekends, Ski4you, Skiholidayextras*

FRANCE

332

MOUNTAIN RESTAURANTS
Less than wonderful

There are lots of places on the piste map, but few that are worth singling out so there's no 'Editors' choice' here – and there aren't enough places to meet the demand, so many get very crowded (you might want to take lunch early or late). The new three-part Plan des Mains near Mont Vallon gondola sounds promising (see 'News') but a 2007 reporter found it 'pricey' and the service in the sandwich bar 'dead slow'. We continue to get good reports on the 'small and cosy' Arpasson at the mid-mountain station of the Tougnète gondola ('a variety of good-value choices'). The Chardonnet, at the mid-station of the Mottaret-Saulire gondola, has table-service and excellent food, but is expensive. The large terrace at the Rhododendrons, at the top of the Altiport drag, is also expensive but remains a popular spot. Some recent visitors found the 'ever popular' Rond Point, just below the mid-point of the Rhodos gondola 'expensive' and preferred the 'good pasta and service' as well as the views from the Darbollées, a bit lower down. The 'delightfully quaint' Crêtes, near the top of Tougnète, continues to provide 'good food and service'. Lower down, at the bottom of the Roc de Tougne drags, the Togniat has 'very good self-service food'. The pricey Altiport hotel scarcely counts as a mountain restaurant, but has a great outdoor buffet in good weather and the 'best tarts in town'. Two self-service places notable for their views are the Pierres Plates, at the top of Saulire, and the Sittelle ('good choice of cooked and cold buffet lunches') above the first section of the Plattières gondola.

SCHOOLS AND GUIDES
No shortage of instructors

The ESF is by far the biggest school, with over 450 instructors. It has a special international section with instructors speaking good English. Recent reports have been mixed. It offers useful alternatives to standard classes, such as off-piste groups, heli-skiing on the Italian border and Three Valleys tours.

Magic in Motion, the second largest school, also offers heli-skiing, couloir and extreme sessions as well as normal lessons. But again, recent reports have been mixed.

New Generation, a British school which operates in Courchevel and Méribel, continues to receive excellent reports. One reader said, 'I cannot recommend them highly enough, they were patient and kept groups small.' A recent reporter 'progressed quickly in a group of only three; the instructor explained and demonstrated techniques clearly'. A 2007 reporter heaps praise on Snow Systems for his group of three beginners: 'The instructors managed to teach us to ski while making it great fun; we will be booking them again for next year.'

FACILITIES FOR CHILDREN
Tour operators rule

We guess readers needing childcare use the facilities of chalet operators who run their own nurseries – we rarely get reports on resort facilities.

STAYING THERE

HOW TO GO
Huge choice but few bargains

Package holidays are easy to find, both with big UK tour operators and smaller Méribel specialists.
Chalets Méribel has more chalets dedicated to the British market than any other resort, and over 50 operators offering them – many, as you may have noticed, advertising their properties in these pages. What really distinguishes Méribel is the range of recently built luxury chalets. Some are perfectly positioned for the slopes, but many rely on minibuses to compensate for their inconvenient locations. Many have saunas, hot-tubs or both.

Méribel specialists include Meriski, whose portfolio includes some of our favourites; Purple Ski, with impressive places in different parts of the resort, including the lovely Iamato in Village; and Ski Blanc (see 'Staying down the valley'). At the top of the market, Ski Olympic has the Parc Alpin (which until this season was a boutique hotel) at 1600 with 12 luxurious rooms (all with plasma screen TVs), pool and sauna. Alpine Action has five smart-looking chalets, most with saunas and hot-tubs. VIP has several sumptuous looking places. Descent International has five of the best chalets. Flexiski has a new chalet – a former 19th-century farmhouse. Total has lots of chalets here and Neilson has several. Crystal Finest have two – including one with a sauna and an outdoor hot-tub.

Méribel has a lot of very good off-piste to discover, as well as the pistes that the Three Valleys is famous for. We asked Pierre-François Papet, head of Méribel's Snow Systems ski school, to pick out some of the best off-piste runs for skiers with at least some off-piste experience. Don't tackle them without guidance.

Some of the best snow is to be found on the north-facing run accessed from the 3 Vallées 2 chair-lift at Val Thorens. Ducking the rope at the top takes you into varied terrain mixing couloirs and gentle slopes, with exposures from north-east to north-west. Eventually you join the red Lac de la Chambre piste.

The run from near Roc de Fer to Le Raffort, a mid-station on the gondola from Brides-les-Bains, is an adventure with exceptional views. You ride the Olympic chair-lift, go along the ridge, then ski down a gentle bowl to finish among the trees.

The wide, west-facing slope above Altiport is enjoyable when the snow is fresh – varied terrain, from average to steep, some open some wooded, reached from the Tétras black run.

There are lots of runs suitable for more accomplished off-piste skiers. One is a descent known as The Cairn from the Mouflon piste at the top of the Plattières gondola; it starts in a fairly steep couloir and becomes wider, with a consistent pitch, until you reach the Sittelle piste.

The Roc de Tougne drag-lift accesses some challenging runs. To the right of the Lagopéde red piste is an area we call the Spot – a rather technical and steep descent to the Sittelle piste. Alternatively, a 15-minute hike brings you to the Couloir du Serail, leading to the Mouflon red piste – one of my favourites because of the vertical, the constant pitch and the quality of snow.

The Col du Fruit is a local classic, far away from the lifts and resorts. You ride the Creux Noirs chair-lift in Courchevel, then walk along the ridge for 15 minutes before descending through the national park to Lac de Tueda and the cross-country tracks ... 800m/2,620ft of flat ground from the Mottaret lifts.

Mont Vallon offers a big choice of routes and exposures – quite steep at the top but with easier slopes from the middle. The challenging northern couloir starts at the top of the Campagnol run.

Snow Systems is a ski school that operates from both Méribel and Mottaret. As well as group and private on- and off-piste lessons, they run children's lessons, snowboard lessons and instructor training.

t 0479 004022
www.snow-systems.com

Méribel

333

FRANCE

334

GETTING THERE

Air Geneva 135km/ 84 miles (3½hr); Lyon 185km/115 miles (3½hr); Chambéry 95km/59 miles (1½hr)

Rail Moûtiers (18km/11 miles); regular buses to Méribel

SMART LODGINGS

Check out our feature chapters at the front of the book.

ACTIVITIES

Indoor Parc Olympique (ice rink, swimming pool, climbing wall, karting on ice), fitness centres in hotels, bowling, library, cinemas, museum, heritage tours

Outdoor Flying lessons and excursions, snow-mobiles, snow-shoe excursions, cleared paths, paragliding

Of the few chalet-hotels, Mark Warner's Tarentaise (with a sauna and hot-tub) has a great position, right on the piste at Mottaret.

Hotels Méribel has some excellent hotels, but they're not cheap.

****Grand Coeur** (0479 086003) Our favourite almost-affordable hotel in Méribel. Just above the village centre. Welcoming, mature building with plush lounge. Magnificent food. Huge hot-tub, sauna, etc.

****Mont-Vallon** (0479 004400) The best hotel at Mottaret; good food, and excellently situated for the Three Valleys' pistes. Pool, sauna, squash, fitness room, etc.

***Altiport** (0479 005232) Smart and luxurious hotel, isolated at the foot of the Altiport lifts. Convenient for Courchevel, not for Val Thorens.

***Arolles** (0479 004040) Right on the slopes at Mottaret. 'Friendly, unpretentious, good food, highly recommended.' Pool and sauna.

***Eterlou** (0479 088900) One of three sister hotels near main lifts that share a health club. 'Great hotel, fantastic location.'

Adray Télébar (0479 086026) Welcoming piste-side chalet with pretty, rustic rooms, good food and popular sun terrace.

Roc (0479 003618) A good-value B&B hotel, in the centre, with a bar-restaurant and crêperie below.

Apartments Les Fermes de Méribel (in Méribel-Village) is a classic tasteful MGM development of six large chalets with the usual impressive pool.

EATING OUT
Fair choice

There is a reasonable selection of restaurants, from ambitious French cuisine to pizza and pasta. For the best food in town, in plush surroundings, there are top hotels – Grand Coeur ('so pleased, we ate there several times'),

Allodis and Kouisena ('traditional food at justifiably high prices'). Other recommendations from readers include: Chez Kiki – 'the best steaks'; the Taverne – 'relaxed atmosphere' but 'can be expensive'; the Tremplin – 'good pizzas'; Enfants Terribles – 'wonderful roast beef carvery', 'live music'; Refuge – 'lovely crêpes'; Grange – 'excellent food and service'; Cactus Café – 'quick service and good value'; the 'tiny' Bibi Phoque – 'good value for money' food including crêpes; Cava – for 'service, food and value'.

Alternatives include the Galette, the Fromagerie and Cro-Magnon up the hill in Morel – all popular for raclette and fondue. The Blanchot, just below Altiport, offers the choice of two dining areas, one dedicated to dishes of the region. Scott's does good American-style food.

At Les Allues, the Tsaretta will pay for a taxi to ferry you to the creations of the Australian chef. The Chaumière offers 'good value inclusive menus in pleasant, rustic surroundings'. The Chemina is another recommendation as is the Martagon at Le Raffort between Méribel and Les Allues.

APRES-SKI
Méribel rocks – loudly

Méribel's après-ski revolves around British-run places. Dick's Tea Bar is well established but is remote from the slopes. At close of play it's the piste-side Rond Point that's packed – happy hour starts around 4pm – and has live music and 'almost infamous toffee vodka'. The terrace of Jack's, near the main lift stations, remains popular.

The ring of bars around the main square do good business at tea time. The Taverne (sister to Dick's Tea Bar) gets packed. Just across the square is the Pub, with videos, pool and sometimes a band. There are a couple of alternatives to the loud pubs

Méribel

335

complained about in the past. The Poste 'serves the best vin chaud' and is a 'more French option than the bars closer to the slopes'. The Barometer has a good atmosphere and lots of leather seating.

There is late dancing at Scott's (next to the Pub) and, of course, there's Dick's Tea Bar. One reader was put off by the queues at the Pub, another liked its 'busy atmosphere'.

In Mottaret the bars at the foot of the pistes get packed at tea time – Rastro ('as good as ever' and 'good value', comment regular visitors) and Down Town are the most popular, though reporters say that Zig-Zag has lower prices. Later on the Rastro disco gets going.

Both villages have a cinema.

OFF THE SLOPES
Plenty to do
The Olympic Centre has the ice rink where the Olympic events were held in 1992, a good public swimming pool, a climbing wall and will have a new spa and fitness area for 2007/08. You can take joyrides in the little planes that operate from the altiport. There are pleasant, marked walks in the altiport area and a signposted trail through some of the hamlets down to Les Allues (you can return from there or Le Raffort in the Olympic gondola). The pedestrian's lift pass covers all the gondolas, cable-cars and buses in the Méribel and Courchevel valleys, and makes it very easy for pedestrians to meet friends for lunch.

A non-skier's guide to Courchevel,

Méribel and La Tania is distributed free by the tourist office.

STAYING DOWN THE VALLEY
Quieter, cheaper choices
For the 1992 Olympics the competitors were accommodated in **Brides-les-Bains** (600m/1,970ft), an old spa town way down in the valley, and a gondola was built linking it to Méribel. It offers a quieter, cheaper alternative to the higher resorts and has some simple hotels, adequate shops and 'plenty of good-value restaurants and friendly bars used by locals', says a reporter. Ski Weekends runs a chalet-hotel here. There is a casino, but evenings are distinctly quiet. The long gondola ride to and from Méribel (about 25 minutes) is tedious, can be cold, stops 'ridiculously early' at 5pm and arrives at a point that's a bit of a trek from the main lifts up the mountain. But in good conditions you can ski off-piste to one or other of the mid-stations at the end of the day (or in exceptional conditions down to Brides itself). Given a car, Brides makes a good base for visiting other resorts.

Some UK tour operators have places in the old village of **Les Allues**, close to a mid-station on the gondola from Brides-les-Bains. Ski Blanc has six good-looking chalets here, including three with a hot-tub. Next door to one of them is an independent British-run playgroup. There are a couple of bars – and a good-value, well-renovated hotel, the Croix Jean-Claude (0479 086105); rooms are small, though.

Montgenèvre

The snowiest part of the Milky Way circuit reaching across to Sauze d'Oulx in Italy – now with through-traffic buried in a tunnel

COSTS

① ② ③ ④ ⑤ ⑥

RATINGS

The slopes

Fast lifts	*
Snow	****
Extent	****
Expert	**
Intermediate	****
Beginner	*****
Convenience	****
Queues	****
Mountain restaurants	**

The rest

Scenery	***
Resort charm	***
Off-slope	*

NEWS

For 2006/07 a bridge across the road through the village was built so that you could ski from one sector to the other. For 2007/08, a second such link will be made near the Charmettes gondola, via a new tunnel.

A luxury hotel, le Chalet Blanc, is due to open.

In 2006/07 snowmaking was increased to cover the Souréou piste, from the top of Rocher de L'Aigle, and runs in the Gondrans sector.

And three new quads (one fast) replaced the Sagnalonga, Bercia and Gimont lifts above Cesana, improving the link with Claviere and Montgenèvre.

+ Good snow record, and local slopes largely north-facing – often the best snow in the Milky Way area

+ Plenty of intermediate cruising and good, convenient nursery slopes

+ A lot of accommodation close to the slopes, and some right on them

+ Great potential for car drivers to explore other nearby resorts

+ Few queues on weekdays, unless people are bussing in, but ...

− If nearby resorts in Italy have poor snow, queues and crowds result

− Poor base for exploring the Italian Milky Way resorts unless you have the use of a car

− Lots of slow lifts and mainly short runs in local area

− Local mountain restaurants poor

− Little to challenge experts on-piste

Montgenèvre is set on a minor pass between France and Italy, at one end of the big cross-border Milky Way network. On snow, it's a time-consuming trek from here to Sestriere and Sauze d'Oulx at the far end (you may have to ride some slow lifts down as well as up). But you can get to these worthwhile resorts much more quickly by car, which also facilitates day trips in the opposite direction to other excellent French resorts such as Serre-Chevalier. Thanks to the setting on a high pass, the local slopes shared with Claviere (in Italy, but very close) often have the best snow in the region.

The village is pleasant, and must be much more so now that traffic between France and Italy has been consigned to a 400m/1,310ft tunnel.

THE RESORT

Montgenèvre is a narrow roadside village set on a high pass only 2km/ 1 mile from the Italian border – this is an area where the euro has really simplified things. Cheap and cheerful cafes, bars and restaurants line the road running along the bottom of the nursery slopes, now happily free of through-traffic, giving an animated atmosphere sometimes missing from French resorts. And tucked away off the main road is a quite pleasant old village, complete with quaint church and friendly natives. The place gets a lot of weather – sometimes wind but also snow, which adds to the charm factor when the sun comes out.

The slopes are convenient, despite the road; most of the accommodation is less than five minutes from a lift. Some of the newer accommodation is uphill, away from the slopes – but there is a free shuttle-bus. The main lifts are gondolas from opposite ends of the village. On the village side of the col are the south-facing slopes of Le Chalvet. The more extensive north-facing slopes of Les Gondrans are across the main road, with nursery slopes at the bottom. Both sectors have piste links with Claviere, gateway to the other Italian resorts of the Milky Way – Sansicario, Sestriere and Sauze d'Oulx.

The best way to get to other resorts is by car. Serre-Chevalier and Puy-St-Vincent, with lift pass sharing arrangements, are easily reached, and well worth an outing each. Different lift pass options cater for most needs.

THE MOUNTAINS

Montgenèvre's local slopes are best suited to leisurely intermediates, with lots of easy cruising on blues and greens, both above and in the woods.

Run classification on the local area and Milky Way piste maps have

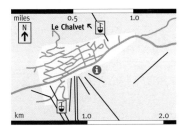

↑ The sunny village is no beauty, but pleasant enough – and more so now that main-road traffic no longer passes through
OT MONTGENEVRE

KEY FACTS

Resort	1850m
	6,070ft

Montgenèvre-Monts de la Lune (Claviere)	
Slopes	1760-2630m
	5,770-8,630ft
Lifts	35
Pistes	100km
	62 miles
Green	11%
Blue	27%
Red	42%
Black	20%
Snowmaking	35km
	22 miles

For the whole Milky Way area	
Slopes	1390-2825m
	4,560-9,270ft
Lifts	78
Pistes	400km
	249 miles
Blue	24%
Red	56%
Black	20%
Snowmaking	130km
	81 miles

differed in the past, which can be confusing – however, none of the blacks is much more than a tough red.

THE SLOPES
Nicely varied
The major north-facing **Les Gondrans** sector offers easy intermediate slopes above the mid-mountain gondola station, with more of a mix of runs lower down. It has a high-altitude link via Collet Vert (and a stiff red run) into the slopes above Claviere (**L'Aigle**). This whole area around the border is attractively broken up by rocky outcrops and woods and the scenery is quite spectacular.

The runs of the sunny sector across the road – **Le Chalvet** – are mainly on open slopes above its mid-mountain gondola station. This sector is now connected to the main area by a new red piste and bridge across the road. When conditions permit, a 'charming' long blue run from this sector goes down to Claviere, for access to Italy.

TERRAIN-PARKS
High and remote
There's a terrain-park with a half-pipe and boarder-cross near the Prarial chair and a free-ride zone higher up on the Gondrans sector, next to the Observatoire chair.

SNOW RELIABILITY
Excellent locally
Montgenèvre has a generally excellent snow record, receiving dumps from westerly storms funnelling up the valley. The high north-facing slopes naturally keep their snow better than the south-facing area. Snowmaking now covers several higher pistes as well as most of the lower slopes.

FOR EXPERTS
Limited, except for off-piste
There are very few challenging pistes locally. Many of the runs are overclassified. There is, however, ample off-piste terrain. The remote north-east-facing bowl beyond the Col de l'Alpet on the Chalvet side is superb in good snow and has black and red pistes, too. The open section between La Montanina and Sagnalonga on the Italian side is another good powder area. Those with a car should visit Sestriere for the most challenging runs. Heli-skiing can be arranged on the Italian side.

FOR INTERMEDIATES
Plenty of cruising terrain
The overclassified blacks are just right for adventurous intermediates, though none holds the interest for very long. The pleasantly narrow tree-lined runs to Claviere from Pian del Sole are steepest of the routes down in the Chalvet sector and the runs off the back of Col de l'Alpet are all fine in small doses.

Average intermediates will enjoy the red runs, though most are short. On the major sector, both the runs from Collet Vert – one into Italy and one back into France – can be great fun.

Getting to Cesana via the lovely sweeping run starting at the top of the Serra Granet quad, and heading home from Pian del Sole, is easier than the classification suggest, and can be tackled by less adventurous intermediates, who also have a wealth of cruising terrain high up at the top of

boarding

There's plenty to attract boarders to Montgenèvre. There are good local beginner slopes and long runs on varied terrain for intermediates. The only real drawback is that many of the lifts in the area are drags, and you will have to use them to get around – getting over to Sestriere and back involves lots (and some flat sections to skate along as well). There are some excellent off-piste areas for more advanced boarders and a dedicated free-ride area at Les Gondrans (now shown on the piste map). Snow Box is the local specialist shop.

the Les Anges sector. The runs down to the village are flattering cruises.

Further afield, the run down to Claviere from the top of the new Gimont quad, on the Italian side, is a beautifully gentle cruise.

FOR BEGINNERS
Good for novices and improvers
There is a fine selection of convenient nursery slopes with reliable snow at the foot of the north-facing area. Progression to longer runs could not be easier, with a very easy blue starting at Les Anges, leading on to a green and finishing at the roadside 600m/1,970ft below.

FOR CROSS-COUNTRY
Having a car widens horizons
Montgenèvre is the best of the Milky Way resorts for cross-country enthusiasts, but it's useful to have a car. The two local trails, totalling 17km/11 miles, offer quite a bit of variety, but a further 60km/37 miles of track starts in Les Alberts, 8km/5 miles away in the Clarée valley.

QUEUES
No problems most of the time
The queues here seem to be critically dependent on snow conditions elsewhere. Provided surrounding resorts have snow, the slopes are wonderfully uncrowded on weekdays, less so at weekends. If nearby Italian resorts are lacking snow, the problems start. Serious queues for the two gondolas out of the village can occur first thing in high season. Links with

Italy are gradually improving with the replacement of old lifts. Reporters praise the lift attendants.

MOUNTAIN RESTAURANTS
Head for Italy
The few mountain restaurants in the Montgenèvre sector are of the large self-service canteen variety, but 2006 reporters enjoyed the 'very friendly' Bergerie, in the Chalvet sector, for its 'wholesome, good food' and 'marvellous views'. In the Claviere sector there is a choice of atmospheric little mountain huts, such as the 'cosy' and 'friendly' Montanina Restaurant at the top of the chair lift from Sagnalonga. The two places at La Coche, above Claviere, are 'good and reasonably priced'. There are plenty of places for lunch in the village.

SCHOOLS AND GUIDES
Encouraging reports
A 2006 reporter found the ESF 'well organised, with English-speaking instructors friendly and helpful'. They found that some 'prompting' was needed to get children in the right groups, but praised the friendliness and the 'secure area with indoor and outdoor facilities' for younger children.

FACILITIES FOR CHILDREN
Hugely improved
With the intrusive main road traffic removed, Montgenèvre would now seem a fine family resort. Reports on the school's children's classes have been complimentary about both class size and spoken English.

SCHOOLS

ESF
t 0492 219046
A-Peak
t 0492 244997

Classes (ESF prices)
6 half days (2½hr)
€98
Private lessons
€32 for 1hr

CHILDREN

Les Sourires
t 0492 215250
Ages 3mnth to 6yr
Piou Piou (ESF)
t 0492 219046
Ages 3 to 5; 6 days
€230

Ski school
For ages 5 to 12
(6 half days €94)

GETTING THERE

Air Turin 98km/
61 miles (2hr);
Grenoble 145km/
90 miles (3hr); Lyon
253km/157 miles
(4½hr)

Rail Briançon (12km/
7 miles) or Oulx
(15km/9 miles); buses
available from both
five times a day

ACTIVITIES

Indoor Cinema,
exhibition hall

Outdoor Natural ice
rink, snow-shoeing,
snowmobiling,
walking, tobogganing,
heritage tours, horse-
riding

Phone numbers
From abroad use the
prefix +33 and omit
the initial '0' of the
phone number

TOURIST OFFICE

Montgenèvre
t 0492 215252
info@montgenevre.
com
www.montgenevre.com
Claviere
t 0122 878856
claviere@
montagnedoc.it
www.claviere.it

STAYING THERE

HOW TO GO
Limited choice
UK tour operators concentrate on cheap and cheerful catered chalets, though some apartments are also available and a few operators also package hotels.
Hotels There is a handful of simple places offering good value.
***Valérie (0492 219002) Central, rustic. 'Quiet and nicely French.'
***Napoléon (0492 219204) On the roadside.
*Chalet des Sports (0492 219017) Among the cheapest rooms in the Alps.
Apartments Résidences La Ferme d'Augustin are simple, ski-to-the-door apartments on the fringes of the main north-facing slopes, five minutes' walk (across the piste) from town.

EATING OUT
Cheap and cheerful
There are a dozen places to choose from. The 'pick of the bunch' is reportedly the Estable – 'a great find, full of locals'. We also have good reports of the Refuge ('excellent and extensive menu') and the Jamy – 'very good value set menu'. The 'magnificent calzone pizzas' at the 'no-frills' Italian-run Capitaine are said to be 'perfect for hungry people on a budget'. A trip to Claviere is worthwhile – reporters have testified to the excellence of the restaurants.

APRES-SKI
Mainly bars, but fun
The range is limited. The Graal is a friendly, unsophisticated place with big TVs; the Ca del Sol bar is a cosy place with open fire. The Chaberton, with pool tables, is also recommended, although a 2006 visitor found it 'pretty quiet'. The 'infamous' Blue Night disco is popular; it 'supplies half-decent

music and not too over-priced drinks till very, very late', attracting a very mixed crowd to its 'friendly and permissive atmosphere'. The Refuge, the Crepouse and the Jamy are the focal cafe-bars at tea time.

OFF THE SLOPES
Very limited
There is a weekly market and you can walk the cross-country routes, but the main diversion is a bus trip to the beautiful old town of Briançon.

STAYING UP THE MOUNTAIN
Easily arranged, recommended
The Sporthotel Sagnalonga, halfway down the piste to Cesana (on the Italian side of the border) and reached by chair-lift or snowmobile, is recommended by two reporters – 'good-value self-service meals', but 'it's in need of redecoration'. Even during February holiday weeks you get the immaculately groomed local slopes to yourself until skiers based elsewhere arrive, mid-morning. It's quiet in the evenings, but livens up considerably when Italian weekenders arrive to party. It's in some UK package programmes.

Claviere 1760m/5,770ft

Claviere is a small, traditional village, barely a mile to the east of Montgenèvre and just over the border in Italy. It's no great beauty, and the main road to Montgenèvre and Briançon that divides it in two has an obvious impact, but visitors seem to like its quiet, relaxed ambience, and are ready to go again.

The slopes of Montgenèvre are as easily reached as those on the Italian side of the border – lift upgrades have improved the links, with three new quads above Cesana this year. The weird official line is that no shared Claviere/Montgenèvre pass is sold here – you are supposed to buy day extensions for the French slopes; but a reader reports that shared passes were on sale, in 2007 at least.

Claviere's nursery slope is small and steep but usually uncrowded and snow-reliable. We have had mixed reports of its ski school – from 'lovely instructors, brilliant with the kids' to 'only average' and 'big classes'.

OT MORZINE / P JACQUES, FOC

Morzine

A large, lively, year-round resort with its own attractive slopes and linked by lift to the main Portes du Soleil circuit

COSTS

① ② ③ ④ ⑤ ⑥

RATINGS

The slopes
Fast lifts	**
Snow	**
Extent	*****
Expert	***
Intermediate	****
Beginner	***
Convenience	**
Queues	***
Mountain restaurants	***

The rest
Scenery	***
Resort charm	***
Off-slope	***

NEWS

For 2006/07 a new quad chair, the Raverettes, replaced two drag-lifts on the Nyon plateau. An outdoor ice rink opened in the square by the tourist office, and a children's sledging run opened at the bottom of Le Pléney. A new spa centre, Massages du Monde, also opened.

➕ Larger local piste area (shared with Les Gets) than other resorts in the vast Portes du Soleil area

➕ Good nightlife by French standards

➕ Quite attractive old town

➕ Few queues locally

➕ Lots of tree-lined runs

➖ Just off the Portes du Soleil circuit

➖ Bus-ride or long walk to lifts from much of the accommodation

➖ Low altitude means there is an enduring risk of poor snow

➖ Few tough pistes for experts

➖ Weekend crowds

Morzine is a long-established year-round resort, popular for its easy road access, traditional atmosphere and gentle wooded slopes, where children do not get lost and bad weather rarely causes problems. For keen piste-bashers wanting to travel the Portes du Soleil circuit regularly, the main drawback is having to take a bus and cable-car or several lifts to get to the main circuit.

Such problems can be avoided by taking a car or using a tour operator who will drive you around. The little-used Ardent gondola, a short drive from Morzine, is a particularly neat option, giving the alternative of a shorter circuit that misses out Avoriaz, where the worst crowds tend to be found.

THE RESORT

Morzine is a traditional mountain town sprawling along both sides of a river gorge. In winter, under a blanket of snow, its chalet-style buildings look charming, and in spring the village quickly takes on a spruce appearance. Morzine is a family resort, and village ambience tends to be fairly subdued – but there is plenty of après-ski action.

The centre is close to the river,

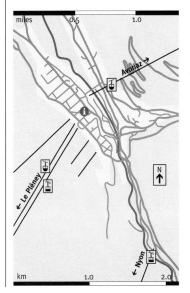

around the tourist office. Restaurants and bars line the street up to the lifts to Le Pléney, where a busy one-way street runs along the foot of the slopes. Accommodation is widely scattered, and a good multi-route bus service (including two electric buses, introduced a few of seasons ago) links all parts of the town to outlying lifts, including those for Avoriaz.

As the extensive network of bus routes and a growing number of hotel mini-buses imply, Morzine is a town where getting from A to B can be tricky. The best plan is to stay in the centre of town or near one of the gondolas. Our view that the resort suits car drivers is widely shared. But the roads are busy and the one-way system takes some getting used to.

THE MOUNTAINS

The local slopes suit intermediates well, with excellent areas for beginners and near-beginners too. Reporters have praised the system of Discovery Routes around the Portes du Soleil – choose an animal that suits your ability and follow the signs displaying it.

THE SLOPES
No need to go far afield

Morzine is not an ideal base for the Portes du Soleil main circuit but it has an extensive local area of slopes

shared with Les Gets (covered in a separate chapter).

A gondola rises from the edge of central Morzine to **Le Pléney**. (The parallel cable-car is for the hotel up there and ski school kids only, unless the gondola breaks down.) Numerous routes return to the valley, including a run down to Les Fys – a quiet junction of chairs which access **Nyon** and, in the opposite direction, the ridge separating Morzine from the Les Gets slopes. The Nyon sector has two peaks – Pointe de Nyon and Chamossière – accessible from Nyon and Le Grand Pré respectively (by slow chairs only). Nyon

can also be accessed by cable-car, situated a bus-ride from Morzine. Beyond Chamossière are two more ridges – Le Ranfoilly and La Rosta. In the valley between these two, no fewer than five chair-lifts have their base stations clustered together.

Beyond Les Gets, **Mont Chéry** is notably quiet, and well worth a visit.

Across town from the Le Pléney sector – a handy 'petit train' shuttle service runs between the two – is a gondola leading (via another couple of lifts and runs) to Avoriaz and the main Portes du Soleil circuit. You take the gondola down at the end of the day to

POINTE DE NYON
2010m/6,590ft

Chamossière
2000m

Le Ranfoilly
1850m

La Ros

Ranfoilly

Our favourite
local hut, Chez
Nannon, close
to good
challenging runs

Grains-d'O

Des Têtes

Charniaz

Nauchets

Nyon
1420m

Le Grand Pré

Les Chavannes
1485m

La
Turc

Nyon

Belvedère

Les Fys

1510m LE PLENEY

Les Gets
1170m/3,84

← Avoriaz

Pléney

Super Morzine

Morzine
1000m/3,280ft

The gondola is a link to Avoriaz
from the centre of town. But
you have to catch it down too –
there's no piste back

Lovely easy blue
run away from
all the lifts

get back to Morzine (there's no piste back). Alternatives are a bus-ride or short drive to either Les Prodains, from where you can get a (queue-prone) cable-car to Avoriaz or a chair-lift into the **Hauts Forts** slopes above it, or to Ardent, where a gondola accesses Les Lindarets for lifts towards Châtel, Avoriaz or Champéry. The tree-lined slopes at Les Lindarets are good in poor visibility and the area at the top of the gondola is a good place for mixed-ability groups to meet up. Car trips to Flaine and Chamonix are feasible. The piste map, signposting and grooming are all good.

TERRAIN-PARKS
Mont Chéry, or head for Avoriaz
Nothing locally, except a boarder-cross, aimed at children, in the Zone Enfant at the top of Les Chavannes. Try one of the four terrain-parks in Avoriaz (see Avoriaz chapter) or head to Mont Chéry (see Les Gets chapter).

SNOW RELIABILITY
Poor
Morzine has a very low average height, and it can rain here when it is snowing higher up (almost every year some reporters mention days of rain). But because you ski on grassy pastures

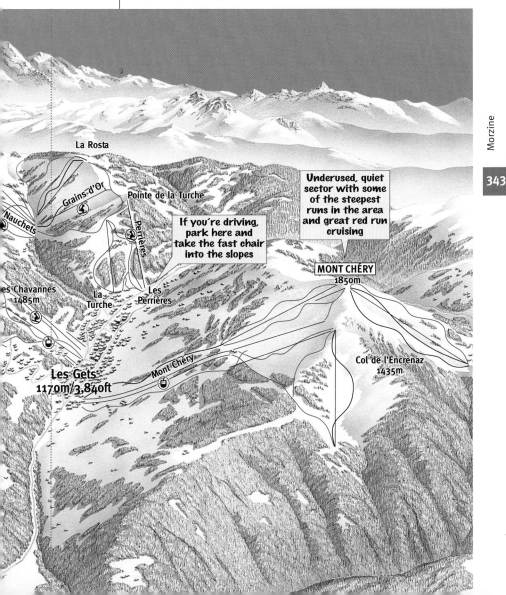

La Rosta

Grains d'Or

Nauchets

Pointe de la Turche

Perrières

If you're driving, park here and take the fast chair into the slopes

Underused, quiet sector with some of the steepest runs in the area and great red run cruising

Les Chavannes
1485m

La Turche

Les Perrières

MONT CHÉRY
1850m

Les Gets
1170m/3,840ft

Mont Chéry

Col de l'Encrenaz
1435m

FRANCE

KEY FACTS

Resort	1000m
	3,280ft

Portes du Soleil	
Slopes	950-2300m
	3,120-7,550ft
Lifts	209
Pistes	650km
	404 miles
Green	14%
Blue	39%
Red	37%
Black	10%
Snowmaking	
	632 guns

Morzine-Les Gets only	
Slopes	1000-2010m
	3,280-6,590ft
Lifts	45
Pistes	110km
	68 miles
Green	12%
Blue	35%
Red	44%
Black	9%

boarding

Morzine is very popular with boarding seasonaires because of the extensive slopes, the splendid terrain-parks in Avoriaz and the lower prices here. Chalet Snowboard, one of the first chalet companies to target snowboarders, has chalets here. And check out the new Rude Chalets, another rider-friendly operation (www.rudechalets.com). Former British champ Becci Malthouse runs the British Alpine Ski & Snowboard School. Specialist boarding shops include The Park and Misty Fly. The slopes in Morzine are great for all abilities of rider, with very few drag-lifts and flat areas. Plenty of tree-lined runs make for scenic and interesting snowboarding and the more adventurous should hire a guide to explore off-piste.

(rather than the rocky terrain of many higher resorts) you need relatively little depth of snow for satisfactory coverage. There is some snowmaking, most noticeably on runs linking Nyon and Le Pléney, and on the home runs.

FOR EXPERTS
A few possibilities
The runs down from Pointe de Nyon and Chamossière are quite challenging, as are the black runs down the back of Mont Chéry and the excellent Hauts Forts blacks at Avoriaz. There is plenty of off-piste scope; the open slopes of Chamossière offer some of the best local possibilities, and Mont Chéry at Les Gets is also worth exploring. For further off-piste ideas, see below.

FOR INTERMEDIATES
Something for everyone
Good intermediates will enjoy the challenging red and black down from Chamossière. Mont Chéry, on the other side of Les Gets, has some fine steepish runs which are usually very quiet, as everyone heads from Les Gets towards Morzine.

Those looking for something less steep have a great choice. Le Pléney has a compact network of pistes that are ideal for groups with mixed abilities: there are blue and red alternatives down to every lift.

One of the easiest cruises on Le Pléney is a great away-from-it-all, snow-gun-covered blue from the top to the valley lift station. Heading from Le

OFF-PISTE RUNS IN THE PORTES DU SOLEIL AREA

The Portes du Soleil offers a lot of great lift-served off-piste. Here is a small selection. Like all serious off-piste runs, these should only be done with a guide.

Morzine – Nyon/Chamossière area
From the Chamossière chair-lift (2000m/6,560ft), heading north brings you to two runs – one on the same north-west slope as the pistes, the other via a col down the north-east slope to the the Nyon cable-car (1020m/3,350ft) in the Vallée de La Manche – a wild area, with a great view of Mont Blanc at first.

Avoriaz area – two suggestions
From the the Fornet chair-lift (2220m/7,280ft) on the Swiss border, you head west to descend a beautiful, unspoiled bowl leading down to the village of L'Erigné (1185m/3,890ft). In powder snow you descend the west-facing slopes of the bowl; when there is spring snow, you traverse right to descend the south-facing slopes. Medium-pitch slopes, for skiers and snowboarders.

From the top of the Machon chair-lift (2275m/7,460ft) you traverse west, beneath the peaks of Les Hauts Forts, across Les Crozats de la Chaux – a steep, north-facing slope. You then turn north to descend through the forest to the cable-car station at Les Prodains (1150m/3,770ft). Testing terrain, for very good skiers. And beware that the traverse can be dangerous following a snowfall.

Châtel area
From the top of the Linga chair-lift (2040m/6,690ft), you head north-west to cross the ridge on your right at a recognisable col and then head down the La Leiche slope to the drag-lift of the same name (1550m/5,090ft). It's a north-facing slope with powder snow. This run starts in a white wilderness, taking you through trees back to civilisation. Steep slopes – for good skiers only.

Le Pléney has some good slopes for near-beginners →

LIFT PASSES

Portes du Soleil

Prices in €

Age	1-day	6-day
under 16	26	123
16 to 59	38	184
over 60	30	147

Free under 5

Beginner no deals

Notes
Covers lifts in all resorts; half-day pass available

Alternative passes
Morzine-Les Gets only

SCHOOLS

ESF
t 0450 791313
International
t 0450 790516
Snow School
t 0486 688840
BASS
t 0450 747859
(0871 7801500 UK)

Classes
(ESF prices)
6 half days (2½hr am or pm) €117
Private lessons
€35 for 1hr for 1 to 3 people

GUIDES

Mountain Office
t 0450 747223

Ranfoilly to Le Grand Pré on the blue is also a nice cruise. And the slopes down to Les Gets from Le Pléney are easy when conditions are right (the slopes face south).

The Ranfoilly and Rosta sectors have easy blacks and cruisey reds served by fast chairs.

And, of course, there is the whole of the extensive Portes du Soleil circuit to explore by going up the opposite side of the valley.

FOR BEGINNERS
Good for novices and improvers
The wide village nursery slopes are convenient, and benefit from snow-guns, though crowds are reported to be a problem. Some of the best progression runs are over at Nyon, and the slopes between Avoriaz and Morzine are also recommended. Adventurous novices also have the option of easy pistes around Le Pléney. Near-beginners can get over to Les Gets via Le Pléney, and return via Le Ranfoilly.

FOR CROSS-COUNTRY
Good variety
There are 95km/60 miles of varied cross-country trails, not all at valley level. The best section is in the pretty Vallée de la Manche beside the Nyon mountain up to the Lac de Mines d'Or, where there is a good restaurant. The Pléney-Chavannes loop is pleasant and relatively snow-sure.

QUEUES
Resort-level problems
There can be long waits at peak periods for both the gondolas out of the resort – towards Avoriaz and to Le Pléney – and for the cable-car from Les Prodains to Avoriaz. But there are chair-lift alternatives to the last two of these. The Nyon cable-car and Belvédère chair-lift (Le Pléney) are weekend bottlenecks. There can be queues for lift passes too: 'Try buying from the tourist office,' advises a 2007 reporter.

Once you are up the mountain, queues are not usually a problem in the local area.

MOUNTAIN RESTAURANTS
Some excellent huts
Editors' choice We have had several very enjoyable Savoyard lunches at the rustic Chez Nannon (0450 792115), near the top of the Troncs chair between Nyon and Chamossière – cosy inside and a nice terrace. And we look forward to trying the Pointe du Nyon (0450 791174), which reporters rave about ('we swapped our boots for slippers'; 'the food was good quality'; 'extremely well run with carpeted steps down to pristine toilets').
Worth knowing about The nice little Atray des Neiges at the foot of the d'Atray chair is good. The tiny Lhottys hut has had mixed reviews ('amazing fresh seafood', 'mediocre spaghetti Bolognese'). The Vaffieu at the top of the Folliets chair has had several recommendations ('liked the food, service, location and atmosphere'), as has the Nabor at Pléney ('the best soup I've ever tasted'). The Mouflon at the top of Rosta has 'good food but bad toilets'. The Tanière in Les Gets, at the bottom of the Chavannes chair, has been recommended for its 'varied food and lower prices'. On Mont Chéry, the new Grand Ourse is praised by a 2007 reporter for 'some of the best mountain eating in the area', and two

Morzine is a big but attractive resort →

CHILDREN

L'Outa nursery
t 0450 792600
Ages 3mnth to 6yr; 6 days €169; meals €5.50
Club des Piou-Piou
t 0450 791313
From age 3; with ESF instruction and lunch
Cheeky Monkeys
t 0450 750548
Ages from 3mnth
Jack Frosts
t 01579 384993
Ages 3mnth to 13yr

Ski school
ESF takes children from age 5: 6 half days €117

GETTING THERE

Air Geneva 75km/ 47 miles (1½hr); Lyon 195km/121 miles (3½hr)

Rail Cluses or Thonon (30km/19 miles); regular bus connections to resort

UK PACKAGES

Alpine Answers, Alpine Weekends, AmeriCan Ski, Chalet Chocolat, Chalet Company, Chalet Group, Chalet Gueret, Chalet Snowboard, Challenge Activ, Classic Ski Limited, Corporate Ski Co, Crystal, Directski.com, Erna Low, First Choice, Haig, Independent Ski Links, Inghams, Inspired to Ski, Interactive Resorts, Lagrange, Momentum, Mountain Tracks, Peak Retreats, Rude Chalets, Ski Activity, Ski Chamois, Ski Expectations, Ski Famille, Ski France, Ski Independence, Ski Line, Ski McNeill, Ski Morzine, Ski Weekend, Ski4you, Skiholidayextras, Skitracer, Snow Finders, Snowline, Thomson, Trail Alpine, White Roc

recent visitors recommend the Chanterelle on the back of the mountain ('lasagne to die for') and the rustic Ancrenaz Bar. One reporter complained that many small huts were overcrowded even midweek in January.

SCHOOLS AND GUIDES
Good reports
The British Alpine Ski & Snowboard School (BASS) is pricey but gets good reports: 'Wonderful for children – brilliant instructors but book early,' said a 2007 reporter. 'Absolutely first class,' said a recent reporter. The beginners in another's group had private lessons with 'great instructors' from the ESF (which is half the price). Another visitor and his grown-up daughter had a private lesson with 'an excellent instructor' at International: 'It was money very well spent.'

FACILITIES FOR CHILDREN
Lots of possibilities
The facilities of the Outa nursery are quite impressive, but we've received reports of poor English and low staff ratios. There is a big children's area, the Zone Enfant, in the Chavannes area. An ESF childcare centre, Club des Piou-Piou looks after children between the ages of 3 and 12 after skiing ('Our younger children were quite happy, the older ones a little bored,' says a recent visitor). The Dérêches Farm offers days learning about animals, snow-shoeing and tobogganing. 2007 reporters had mixed experiences with Cheeky Monkeys. One found the nanny to be 'brilliant', another suffered due to a shortage of nannies through illness and wouldn't recommend them. Again, Jack Frosts is highly praised. Tour operator Crystal has the fine Family Club Hotel Viking right on the slopes at Le Pléney ('impressive for families' said a 2007 reporter); and Ski Famille has good facilities.

STAYING THERE

HOW TO GO
Good-value hotels and chalets
The tour operator market concentrates on hotels and chalets. Morzinelets.com has its own half-board hotel, B&B hotel and self-catered chalets and apartments to let.
Chalets There's a wide choice, but position varies enormously and you need to check this carefully before booking. Reporters have recommended

the independently run Farmhouse (0450 790826): 'excellent service, good ski guide'; 'gourmet dinner with fine wines and invaluable minibus service to the lifts'. A 2007 snowboarder reporter praises Ride&Slide's chalets again ('beautiful chalet, outstanding food and service') and one of our assistant editors had a 'fun, laid-back week' with Rude Chalets. Snowline has some central places (most with hot-tub and/or sauna).
Hotels The handful of 3-star hotels includes some quite smart ones; and there are dozens of 2-stars and 1-stars.
***Airelles (0450 747121) Central 3-star close to Pléney lifts and Prodains and Nyon bus routes. Good pool.
***Champs Fleuris (0450 791444) Comfy 3-star next to Pléney lifts. Pool.
***Dahu (0450 759292) 3-star linked to centre by footbridge over river; good restaurant; pool. Private shuttle to lifts.
***Tremplin (0450 791231) Next to lifts; 'friendly, good food, small rooms'.
***Viking (0450 791169) is now run by Crystal. On the slopes at top of gondola. Specialises in families. Pool.
***Bergerie (0450 791369) Rustic B&B chalet, in centre. Friendly staff. Outdoor pool, sauna, massage.
**Côtes (0450 790996) Simple 2-star on the edge of town. Pool.
**Equipe (0450 791143) One of the best 2-stars; next to the Pléney lift.

ACTIVITIES

Indoor Ice rink, fitness centre, sauna, hot-tub, climbing wall, library, cinemas

Outdoor Sleigh rides, snow-shoe classes, fitness trail, helicopter flights, snowmobiles, ice-diving, ballooning, tobogganing, paragliding, cheese factory visits

Phone numbers
From abroad use the prefix +33 and omit the initial '0' of the phone number

TOURIST OFFICE

t 0450 747272
info@
morzine-avoriaz.com
www.morzine-avoriaz.com

Apartments The smart Aiglon development is new for 2007/08 with pool, sauna, steam room, hot-tub. Télémark apartments, close to the Super-Morzine gondola, and the Udrezants, by the Prodains cable-car, have been recommended. Morzinelets.com has a wide selection.

EATING OUT
A reasonable choice
The best restaurant in town is probably L'Atelier in hotel Samoyède, which offers traditional and modern cuisine – we enjoyed lobster ravioli, truffle risotto and scallops. The hotel Airelles has a fine restaurant and the hotel Dahu also has good food. The Chamade looks the part (elegant table settings) but reports are mixed. The Grange does 'excellent food, but at a price'. Locals rate the Chalet Philibert highly. The unpretentious Etale was popular with recent visitors ('excellent friendly service and a good plat du jour at lunchtime', 'our favourite'). The Pique Feu does Savoyard food at 'reasonable prices'. The Tyrolien has 'tartiflette to die for' and 'good steaks'. Clin d'Oeil has been praised.

APRES-SKI
One of the livelier French resorts
On Tuesday evenings there's a 'ski retrospective' on the slopes at Le Pléney, and on Thursdays there's a torchlit descent and floodlit skiing.

Nightlife is good by French resort standards. Bar Robinson is basic but always busy as the slopes empty. The Dixie has sport on TV, MTV, a cellar bar and some live music. Between the slopes and the centre, and all in the same building are: the Cavern, which is popular with resort staff; the Coyote for arcade games and DJ; the Boudha Café, with Asian decor. At the nearby Crepu dancing on the tables in ski boots to deafening music seems compulsory. L'Opéra and Laury's are late-night haunts.

OFF THE SLOPES
Quite good; excursions possible
There are two cinemas, an excellent ice rink, lots of pretty walks and a cheese factory you can visit. Some hotels have pools open to non-residents. 'Morzine is a shoppers' paradise,' says a recent visitor. Buses run to Thonon for more shopping, and car owners can drive to Geneva, Annecy or Montreux.

Paradiski

The newest mega-area: a single cable-car gives residents of Les Arcs more space and residents of La Plagne more challenges

KEY FACTS

Paradiski area

Slopes	1200-3250m
	3,940-10,660ft
Lifts	141
Pistes	425km
	264 miles
Green	5%
Blue	56%
Red	27%
Black	12%

348

December 2003 saw the opening of the world's largest cable-car – a double-decker holding 200 people – which swoops low across a wooded valley to link the French resorts of Les Arcs and La Plagne. The result is that the two resorts can claim a joint ski area, called Paradiski, that is one of the biggest in the world. With 425km/264 miles of pistes and 141 lifts, it beats most of the established mega-areas; only the Three Valleys and the Portes du Soleil are significantly bigger. Add in a lot of off-piste terrain and you could argue the area is bigger than either.

The cable-car, called the Vanoise Express, spans the 2km/1 mile-wide valley between Plan-Peisey (in the Les Arcs area) and a point 300m/980ft above Montchavin (in La Plagne).

The linking of these two major resorts is good news for the great British piste-basher who likes to cover as much ground as possible. For those who like a bit of a challenge, getting from your home base to both far-flung outposts of the Paradiski area – Villaroger in Les Arcs and Champagny-en-Vanoise in La Plagne – would make quite a full day.

The link is also good for experts. Those based in either resort can more easily tackle the north face of La Plagne's Bellecôte, finishing the run in Nancroix. Those based in La Plagne who are finding the piste skiing a bit tame can easily get across to Les Arcs' Aiguille Rouge.

If you want to make the most of the link it makes sense to stay near one of the cable-car stations. But once you start to study the piste maps you realise that it's easily accessible from many other bases.

On the Les Arcs side, **Plan-Peisey** and nearby **Vallandry** are in pole position. They are basically small, low-rise, modern developments, but built in a much more sympathetic style than the original Les Arcs resorts. They are quiet places to stay, but are expanding rapidly and a few UK operators have chalets there. You can also stay in the unspoiled old village of **Peisey**, 300m/980ft below and linked by bucket-lift to Plan-Peisey.

It's easy to get to the cable-car station at Plan-Peisey from the main resort parts of Les Arcs. One lift and a blue run is all it takes to get there from **Arc 1800**, which is the most attractive of the main resort units. From quieter **Arc 1600**, along the mountainside from 1800, it takes two lifts. **Arc 2000** and the stylish new **Arc 1950** development seem further away, over the ridge that separates them from 1600 and 1800; but all it takes is one fast chair to the ridge and one long blue run down the other side. Beyond and below the bowl of Arc 2000, Villaroger-Le Pré is not an ideal starting point.

On the La Plagne side, the obvious place to stay is **Montchavin**, which is below the Vanoise Express station. Montchavin is a well-restored

LIFT PASSES

Paradiski

Covers lifts in whole Paradiski area.

6-day pass €229 (over 60 €195; under 14 €172). If you buy a Paradiski lift pass for five days or more, we understand you'll be able to buy a 10 euro daily extension to ski Val d'Isère-Tignes or the Three Valleys too

Paradiski Découverte

Covers lifts in Les Arcs area or La Plagne area plus one day Paradiski extension.

6-day pass €205 (over 60 €174; under 14 €154)

traditional old village with modern additions built in traditional style. **Les Coches**, across the mountain from the station, is most easily reached with the help of a lift. It is entirely modern, but built in a traditional style. From either, one lift brings you to the cable-car.

The other parts of La Plagne are some way from the cable-car. But one long lift is all it takes to get from monolithic **Plagne-Bellecôte** up to L'Arpette, from which point it's a single long blue descent. The most attractive of the resort villages, **Belle-Plagne**, is only a short run above Plagne-Bellecôte. From the villages further across the bowl – **Plagne-Villages**, **Plagne-Soleil**, dreary **Plagne-Centre**, futuristic **Aime-la-Plagne** – you have to ride a lift to get to Plagne-Bellecôte. From **Plagne 1800**, below the bowl, add another lift. From the villages beyond the bowl – rustic, sunny **Champagny-en-Vanoise** and expanding **Montalbert** – it's going to be pretty hard work.

RIDING THE VANOISE EXPRESS

The cable-car ride from one resort to the other takes less than four minutes.

The system is designed to be able to operate in high winds, so the risk of getting stranded miles from home is low. It can shift 2,000 people an hour, and end of the day crowds don't seem to be a problem.

The lift company offers a six-day pass covering the whole Paradiski region, which is perhaps most likely to appeal to people based in the villages close to the lift, who might divide their time between the two ski areas as the mood takes them – one day here, the next there.

But it also offers a pass (Paradiski Découverte) which includes just one day's use of the Vanoise Express and the lifts in the other resort.

Alternatively, you can also buy one-day extensions to a Les Arcs or La Plagne six-day lift pass. These cost less at weekends (18 instead of 25 euros) because demand is less then.

Paradiski

349

La Plagne

Villages from the rustic to the futuristic spread over a vast area of intermediate terrain – mainly high and snow-sure

350

COSTS

① ② ③ ④ ⑤ ⑥

RATINGS

The slopes

Fast lifts	**
Snow	****
Extent	****
Expert	****
Intermediate	*****
Beginner	****
Convenience	*****
Queues	***
Mountain restaurants	****

The rest

Scenery	****
Resort charm	*
Off-slope	*

NEWS

For 2007/08 there are plans to improve the learning zones at Les Coches and Belle Plagne.

For 2006/07, a six-pack replaced the Charmettes and Bouclet drag-lifts from La Roche to Aime-la-Plagne. A new blue run was created to it. In Les Coches, the Plan Bois chair was upgraded to a six-pack and the Orgere drag removed.

- ➕ Extensive intermediate slopes, plus plentiful, excellent off-piste terrain
- ➕ Fast cable-car link with Les Arcs
- ➕ Good nursery slopes
- ➕ High and fairly snow-sure – and with some wonderful views
- ➕ Choice of convenient purpose-built resorts and attractive, traditional-style villages lower down
- ➕ Wooded runs of lower resorts are useful in poor weather

- ➖ Pistes in the main bowl don't offer much challenge – or much vertical
- ➖ Pistes get very crowded in places
- ➖ Still lots of slow old chair-lifts
- ➖ Lower villages can suffer from poor snow – sunny Champagny especially
- ➖ Unattractive architecture in some of the higher resort units
- ➖ Hardly any green runs – though some blues are very easy
- ➖ Little upscale accommodation

With 225km/140 miles of its own slopes, of which 85 per cent are blue or red, La Plagne is an intermediate's paradise. It's also a splendid resort for going off-piste, with some long descents that are often deserted and untracked compared with the classic off-piste runs of more macho resorts like Val d'Isère. The lack of on-piste challenges is an important flaw, though.

The choice of bases open to you here is unparalleled, from the monolithic blocks of Aime-la-Plagne at 2100m/6,890ft to the chalets and orchards of Montchavin at 1250m/4,100ft. If you're looking for luxury, though, look elsewhere.

THE RESORT

La Plagne consists of no fewer than 10 separate 'villages'; six are purpose-built at altitude in the main bowl, on or above the tree line and linked by road, lifts and pistes; the other four are scattered around outside the bowl. Each is a self-sufficient mini-resort.

Even the core resorts vary a lot in character. The first to be built, in the 1960s, was Plagne-Centre – still the focal point for shops and après-ski. Typical of its time, it has ugly blocks and dreary indoor 'malls' that house a reasonable selection of shops, bars and restaurants. Recent developments are more pleasing to the eye.

Lifts radiate from Centre to all sides of the bowl, the major one being the big twin-cable gondola to Grande Rochette. A cable-car goes to the even more obtrusive 'village' of Aime-la-Plagne – a group of monolithic blocks. Below these two, and a bit of a backwater ('a dormitory', says one reader), is Plagne 1800, where the buildings are small-scale and chalet-style. Access to the main bowl from here is by lifts to Aime-la-Plagne.

A little way above Plagne-Centre is Plagne-Soleil, with attractive modern chalets. This area is officially attached to Plagne-Villages, which is a rather strung-out but attractive collection of small-scale apartments and chalets in

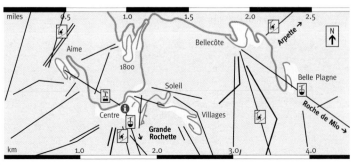

↑ Even from behind, Belle-Plagne doesn't look bad

KEY FACTS

| Resort | 1800-2100m |
| | 5,900-6,890ft |

La Plagne only

Slopes	1250-3250m
	4,100-10,660ft
Lifts	106
Pistes	225km
	140 miles
Green	7%
Blue	60%
Red	22%
Black	11%
Snowmaking	
	309 guns

Paradiski area

Slopes	1200-3250m
	3,940-10,660ft
Lifts	141
Pistes	425km
	264 miles
Green	5%
Blue	56%
Red	27%
Black	12%

traditional style, handy for the slopes and with lift link to Plagne-Centre.

The two other core resort units are a bus-ride away, on the other side of a low hill. The large apartment buildings of Plagne-Bellecôte form a wall at the foot of the slopes leading down to it. Some way above it is Belle-Plagne – as its name suggests, easy on the eye, with cars mainly parked underground. Although Belle-Plagne is convenient for skiing, reporters find its multiple levels exhausting in the evening.

Lifts from Plagne-Bellecôte lead over the lip of the bowl to the old village of Montchavin and its more modern neighbour Les Coches, at the northern extremity of the area. Beyond Grande Rochette, at the southern extremity, is rustic Champagny. Beyond Aime-la-Plagne, at the western extremity, is friendly little Montalbert. These places are described later in the chapter.

A free bus system between the core villages within the bowl runs until after midnight. Lifts between some resort units run until 1am.

A cable-car from Montchavin links to Les Arcs via Peisey-Vallandry – great if you are based reasonably close.

Day trips by car to Val d'Isère-Tignes or the Three Valleys are possible – and if you buy a Paradiski lift pass for five days or more, we understand you'll be able to buy a 10 euro daily extension to ski Val d'Isère-Tignes or the Three Valleys too.

THE MOUNTAINS

The majority of the slopes in the main bowl are above the tree line, though there are trees scattered around most of the resort centres. The slopes outside the bowl are open at the top but descend into woodland. The gondola up to the exposed glacier slopes on Bellecôte, to the west of the main bowl, is prone to closure by high winds or poor weather.

THE SLOPES
Multi-centred; can be confusing

La Plagne boasts 225km/140 miles of pistes over a wide area that can be broken down into seven distinct but interlinked sectors. From Plagne-Centre you can take a lift up to **Le Biolley**, from where you can head back to Centre, to Aime-la-Plagne or down gentle runs to **Montalbert**, from where you ride several successive lifts back up. But the main lift out of Plagne-Centre leads up to **La Grande Rochette**. From here there are good sweeping runs back down and an easier one over to Plagne-Bellecôte, or you can drop over the back into the mainly south-facing **Champagny** sector, for excellent long runs and great views over to Courchevel.

From Plagne-Bellecôte and Belle-Plagne, you can head up to **Roche de Mio**, and have the choice of a gondola, or two successive fast chairs (the first of which also accesses Champagny). From Roche de Mio, runs spread out in all directions – towards La Plagne, Champagny or **Montchavin/Les Coches.** This sector can also be reached by taking an eight-seat chair from Plagne-Bellecôte to L'Arpette.

From Roche de Mio you can also take a gondola down then up to the **Bellecôte glacier**. The top chair is normally shut in winter – but if open, it offers excellent snow and stunning views. You can descend 2000m/6,560ft vertical to Montchavin, with a not-difficult off-piste stretch in the middle.

Several reporters have complained that some runs are more difficult than their classification suggests, while others are easier. Piste names and classification seem to alter on a regular basis, too. Some also complain that the signing can be confusing. There are a lot of slow old lifts still around. The piste map marks half a dozen drag-lifts as 'difficult', and reporters say some are very much so.

La Plagne

LIFT PASSES

La Plagne

Prices in €

Age	1-day	6-day
under 14	30	144
14 to 59	40	192
over 60	34	164
Free under 6, over 72		
Beginner 12 free lifts		

Notes
Covers all lifts in La Plagne areas; individual village-area and half-day passes; Paradiski extension

Paradiski Découverte

Prices in €

Age	6-day
under 14	156
14 to 59	208
over 60	177
Free under 6, over 72	
Beginner no deals	

Notes
Covers all lifts in La Plagne areas with one day in Paradiski

Paradiski

Prices in €

Age	1-day	6-day
under 14	35	175
14 to 59	46	233
over 60	40	199
Free under 6, over 72		
Beginner no deals		

Notes
Covers all lifts in Les Arcs area and La Plagne area; family reductions

SCHOOLS

ESF
Schools in all centres.
t 0479 090668 (Belle Plagne)

Oxygène (Plagne-Centre)
t 0479 090399

El Pro (Belle-Plagne)
t 0479 091162

Reflex (Plagne 1800)
t 0613 808056

Evolution 2 (Montchavin)
t 0479 078185

Classes (ESF prices)
6 days from €167

Private lessons
From €36 for 2hr for 1-2 people

TERRAIN-PARKS
Lots of choices
There are four terrain-parks in the area. Belle-Plagne, Montchavin/Les Coches and Champagny all have decent parks; however, the Snowpark above Plagne-Centre, serviced by the Colorado chair-lift, is in a league of its own when up to scratch. With over 20 obstacles, this is a freestyle wonderland – though a 2007 reporter reckons 'it's nothing special'. There are ride-on rails and boxes for first-timers as well as huge kinked monsters, rainbows and a wall-ride to challenge the best of them. Several boxes have been replaced this year. Kicker-wise, from the smallest to the biggest jumps, it's all here. A park-only pass costs 20 euros a day.

SNOW RELIABILITY
Generally good except low down
Most of La Plagne's runs are snow-sure, being at altitudes between 2000m and 2700m (6,56oft and 8,86oft) on the largely north-facing open slopes above the purpose-built centres. The lift company is nearing the end of a five-year plan to increase snowmaking on the main runs to all the villages. The two sunny runs to Champagny are often closed. Grooming could be better.

FOR EXPERTS
A few good blacks and off-piste
There are two beautiful, long (but rarely open) black runs from Bellecôte to a lift below Col de la Chiaupe – almost 1000m/3,28oft vertical.

The long Emile Allais red run (previously black) down from above Aime-la-Plagne is little used, north-facing and very enjoyable in good snow. A new six-pack for 2006/07 has replaced the notoriously difficult drag-lift back up. The Coqs and Morbleu runs, also in the Aime-la-Plagne sector, are seriously steep.

But experts will get the best out of La Plagne if they hire a guide and explore the vast off-piste potential – which takes longer to get tracked out than in more 'macho' resorts.

Routes include numerous runs from the Bellecôte glacier to Les Bauches (a drop of over 1400m/4,59oft) and in the Biolley sector at the other end of the ski domain. For the more experienced, the north face of Bellecôte presents a splendid challenge with usually excellent snow at the top. You can descend to Peisey-Nancroix (a drop of

2000m/over 6,50oft) and then catch a taxi or free bus to the Vanoise Express cable-car. Another beautiful and out-of-the-way run starts with a climb and then goes over the Cul du Nant glacier to Champagny-le-Haut.

FOR INTERMEDIATES
Great variety
Virtually the whole of La Plagne's area is a paradise for intermediates, with blue and red runs wherever you look.

For early intermediates there are plenty of gentle blue motorway pistes in the main La Plagne bowl, and a long, interesting run from Roche de Mio back to Belle Plagne, Les Inversens (involving a tunnel). The blue runs either side of L'Arpette, on the Montchavin side of the main bowl, are glorious cruises. The easiest way over to Champagny is from the Roche de Mio-Col de Forcle area.

Better intermediates have lots of delightful long red runs to try. There are challenging red mogul pitches down from Roche de Mio to Les Bauches (a drop of 900m/2,95oft) – the first half is a fabulous varied run with lots of off-piste diversions possible; the tricky second half, Les Crozats, has reverted to black status after a period as a red.

The Champagny sector has a couple of tough reds – Kamikaze and Hara-Kiri – leading from Grande Rochette. And the long blue cruise Bozelet has one surprisingly steep section. The long, sweeping Mont de la Guerre red, with 1250m/4,10oft vertical from Les Verdons to Champagny, is also a great run in good snow (a rare thing on this sunny side of the hill).

FOR BEGINNERS
Excellent facilities
La Plagne is a good place to learn, with generally good snow and above-average facilities for beginners, especially children. Each of the main centres has nursery slopes on its doorstep. There's a free drag-lift in each resort as well. But there are no long green runs to progress to. Although a lot of the blue slopes are easy, you can't count on that; readers rate the blues in general 'quite steep' – a 2007 reporter's seven-year-old struggled. The Plan Bois area above Les Coches has good gentle slopes, served by a new six-pack. But the blue runs back into Plagne 1800 and Montchavin are difficult for novices.

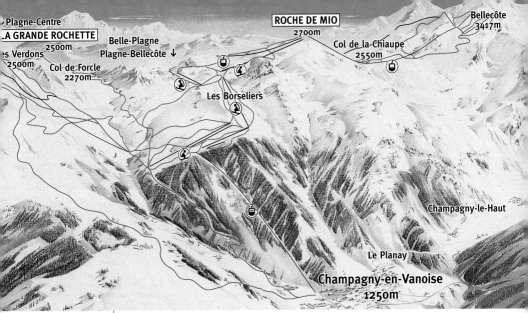

La Plagne

CHILDREN

Les P'tits Bonnets (Plagne-Centre)
t 0479 090083
Ages from 10wk

Marie Christine (Aime)
t 0479 091181
Ages 2 to 6

ESF nurseries (ages from 18 mnth or 2yr):
Aime 0479 090475
Belle 0479 090668
Bellecôte 0479 090133
Snow gardens run by ESF: ages from 3 to 5

Ski schools

Children's classes are available up to 12 or 16 depending on the village: 6 days from €157 (ESF prices)

CROSS-COUNTRY
Open and wooded trails

There are 85km/53 miles of prepared cross-country trails scattered around. The most beautiful of these are the 30km/19 miles of winding track set out in the sunny valley around Champagny-le-Haut. The north-facing areas have more wooded trails that link the various centres. It's best to have a car if you want to make the most of it all.

QUEUES
Main problems being sorted

La Plagne used to have some big bottlenecks. Recent lift upgrades have eased some of the worst problems, but even so one March visitor grew weary of the many five-minute queues when getting around the area. Reporters still complain of queues for the Roche de Mio gondola, despite its renovation, and there are still several lifts that can generate queues that you can't avoid, once you've descended to them – at Les Bauches for example, and in the Champagny sector – especially at the Verdons Sud lift, warns one reader. The gondola to the glacier is queue-prone when snow is poor lower down.

Crowds on the pistes are now as much of a problem as lift queues, particularly above Plagne-Bellecôte and Belle-Plagne in the afternoon, and at Roche de Mio – 'very crowded, quite dangerous' comments a reporter, while another advises retreating to the quieter slopes of Montalbert, Les Coches or Montchavin.

MOUNTAIN RESTAURANTS
An enormous choice

Mountain restaurants are an attraction of the area: numerous, varied and crowded only in peak periods, as many people eat in one of the resorts – particularly Champagny or Montchavin/Les Coches.

Editors' choice The recently built Chalet des Verdons Sud (0621 543924) above Champagny offers excellent, appetising food and service on a big terrace with a fine view, or in the warmly woody interior. The Rossa (0479 082803), at the top of the Champagny gondola, has friendly staff, and good, basic cooking. A great rustic place in which to hole up in poor weather is Le Sauget (0479 078351), above Montchavin. Above Montalbert, Le Forperet (0479 555127) is an old farm with 'superb views', good tartiflette and modest prices.

Worth knowing about Reader recommendations include the 'terrific' Roc des Blanchets, at the top of the Borseliers chair-lift; the cosy Au Bon Vieux Temps, just below Aime-la-Plagne; Pierre Blanches above Montchavin for 'good, simple food'; Chalet des Colosses above Plagne-Bellecôte and Chalets des Inversens at Roche de Mio ('fabulous views, good food'); the little Breton cafe at the bottom of the Quillis lift; the 'very French' Chalet du Friolin at Les Bauches; the Bergerie, with 'fantastic fireplace', above Plagne-Villages; and the 'friendly' Plein Soleil.

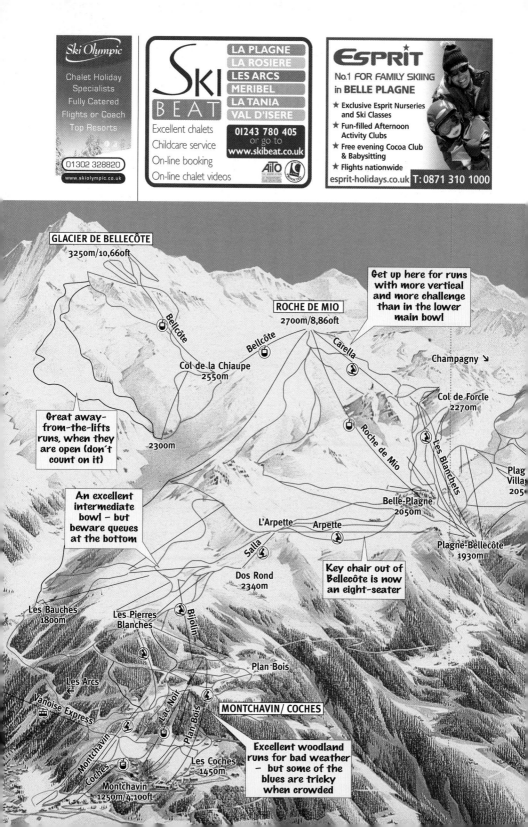

GLACIER DE BELLECÔTE
3250m/10,66oft

Bellcôte

ROCHE DE MIO
2700m/8,86oft

Bellcôte

Carella

Champagny ↘

Col de la Chiaupe
2550m

Col de Forcle
2270m

Roche de Mio

Les Blanchets

Get up here for runs
with more vertical
and more challenge
than in the lower
main bowl

2300m

Great away-
from-the-lifts
runs, when they
are open (don't
count on it)

Belle-Plagne
2050m

Plag
Villa
205

An excellent
intermediate
bowl – but
beware queues
at the bottom

L'Arpette   Arpette

Salla

Plagne-Bellecôte
1930m

Dos Rond
2340m

Key chair out of
Bellecôte is now
an eight-seater

Les Bauches
1800m

Les Pierres
Blanches

Bijolin

Plan Bois

Les Arcs

Vanoise Express

Lac Noir

Plan Bois

MONTCHAVIN/ COCHES

Montchavin

Coches

Les Coches
1450m

Montchavin
1250m/4,10oft

Excellent woodland
runs for bad weather
– but some of the
blues are tricky
when crowded

boarding

With such a huge amount of terrain, there is something for everyone in La Plagne. Expert free-riders, however, are advised to hire a guide as there is so much hidden terrain to be had off the mainly motorway-style pistes. When light gets flat hit the lower tree runs, as the open nature of the higher slopes will be a nightmare. Although this is a great place for beginners, with huge wide-open rolling pistes, be careful as there is also a lot of flat land, especially above Belle-Plagne, the tunnel in the middle of the Inversens run and the blue run linking Montchavin with Les Bauches. Make sure to get enough speed, or to avoid such areas, or you'll be doing a lot of walking. Most drag-lifts have been replaced, and others can be avoided; the more difficult ones are marked on the resort piste map.

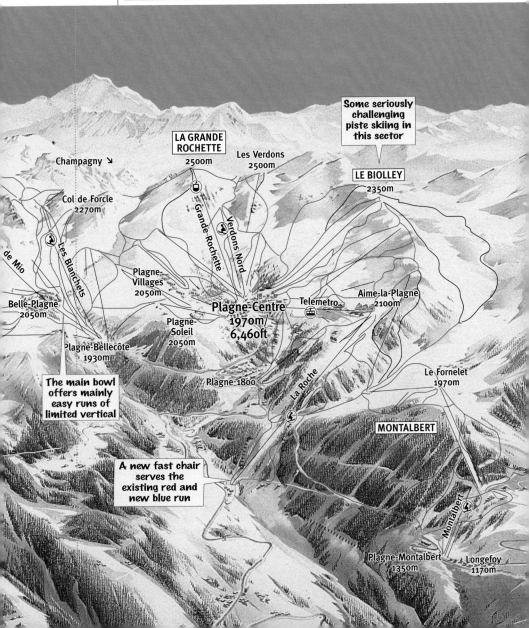

Some seriously challenging piste skiing in this sector

LA GRANDE ROCHETTE 2500m

Les Verdons 2500m

LE BIOLLEY 2350m

Champagny ↘

Col de Forcle 2270m

de Mio

Les Blanchets

Grande-Rochette

Verdons Nord

Plagne-Villages 2050m

Belle-Plagne 2050m

Plagne-Centre 1970m/ 6,460ft

Aime-la-Plagne 2100m

Telemetro

Plagne-Soleil 2050m

Plagne-Bellecôte 1930m

The main bowl offers mainly easy runs of limited vertical

Plagne 1800

La Roche

Le Fornelet 1970m

MONTALBERT

A new fast chair serves the existing red and new blue run

Montalbert

Plagne-Montalbert 1350m

Longefoy 1170m

GETTING THERE

Air Geneva 149km/ 93 miles (3½hr); Lyon 196km/122 miles (3½hr); Chambéry 92km/57 miles (2½hr)

Rail Aime (18km/ 11 miles) and Bourg-St-Maurice (35km/ 22 miles) (Eurostar service available); frequent buses from stations

SMART LODGINGS

Check out our feature chapters at the front of the book.

SNOWPIX.COM / CHRIS GILL

The main bowl is practically all above the tree line ↓

SCHOOLS AND GUIDES
Better alternatives to ESF

Each centre has its own ESF school. High-season classes can be much too large (up to 20) and good English cannot be relied upon. One youngster 'was left in floods of tears, with her confidence completely destroyed'. But reports about private lessons are generally positive, the schools in Les Coches and Montalbert have come in for praise, and one visitor had an excellent day with an ESF guide.

The alternatives to the ESF are preferable. The Oxygène school in Plagne-Centre has impressed most reporters: 'Worked very hard with us, and was very patient.' 'Superb with our children, very friendly, made everything into a game.' We have had glowing reports on the El Pro school in Belle-Plagne ('good English, asked us what we wanted to do, strong focus on technique and safety'). We have also had good reports on Evolution 2 (based in Montchavin): 'One of the most positive experiences I've had in a while, and good value.' Reflex is based in 1800 and a reporter said of a private lesson, 'The best for several years; humorous, pitched at the right level to test and enjoy.' Antenne Handicap offers private lessons for skiers with any kind of disability.

FACILITIES FOR CHILDREN
Good choice

Children are well catered for with facilities in each of the villages. The nursery at Belle-Plagne is 'excellent, with good English spoken'. Be wary, however, of ESF classes. Several UK chalet operators run childcare services.

HOW TO GO
Plenty of packages

The resort is very apartment-dominated, but there are alternatives. There are two Club Meds (both recently refurbished).

Chalets There's a large number available – the majority are fairly simple, small, and located in 1800. Ski Beat has no fewer than 16 chalets here, ranging from 6 beds to 18. For 2007/08 family specialist Esprit is opening its new flagship chalet-hotel Deux Domaines at Belle Plagne, with indoor pool and spa; it looks fab on the drawings. Mark Warner and Ski Olympic have chalet-hotels in Centre. See also our descriptions of lower villages for chalets there.

Hotels There are very few, most of 2-star or 3-star grading.

***Araucaria (0479 092020) Very modern 3-star at Plagne-Centre.

***Balcons (0479 557655) 3-star at Belle-Plagne. Pool.

***Carlina (0479 097846) Welcoming, well-run 3-star beside the piste below Belle-Plagne.

***Terra Nova (0479 557900) Big, 120-room 3-star in Plagne-Centre.

Apartments There is a huge amount of apartment accommodation; much of it is very ordinary, but there is more good accommodation being built. Chalets les Montagnettes in Belle-Plagne are spacious with good views. and the MGM/CGH Les Hauts Bois apartments in Aime-la-Plagne are highly recommended ('excellent, with a decent pool'). The 4-star Pelvoux is the newest residence in Plagne-Centre. For 2007/08, MGM/CGH is opening a new luxury development at Plagne-Soleil, Les Granges du Soleil.

EATING OUT
A surprising amount of choice

Throughout the resort there is a good range of casual restaurants including pizzerias and traditional Savoyard places serving raclette and fondue.

Reader recommendations in Plagne-Centre include the Métairie ('the most enjoyable we've encountered in the Alps'), the Vega ('pricey but friendly with excellent food'), the Maison ('easy going, relaxed place serving good pizzas until 1am'), and the Refuge ('great meal in charming, rustic atmosphere', 'very reasonable').

In Plagne-Villages, the Casa de

l'Ours is good for pizzas and steaks, the Grizzli is 'superb' for Savoyard food – 'worth visiting for the chocolate cake alone'. In Plagne 1800, the Mère-Grand (formerly Loup Garrou) has 'good food, but a short menu', the Petit Chaperon Rouge and the Mama Mia pizzeria have been praised. At Aime-la-Plagne, Au Bon Vieux Temps (see 'Mountain restaurants') is open in the evening and the Cave, buried deep in the main block, has 'exceptional' food. The smart Arlequin is 'really family-friendly' and does a 'rather special rack of lamb'.

In Plagne-Bellecôte, the Ferme and Chalet des Colosses have been recommended. In Belle-Plagne, so have Pappagone pizzeria, the Chalet Maître Kanter ('good value'), the Cloche ('good duck breast in bilberry sauce') and the Face Nord ('very friendly, lovely rabbit'). The Matafan has 'a homely feel and great pierre chaude'.

APRES-SKI
Bars, bars, bars
Though fairly quiet during low season, La Plagne has a wide range of après-ski, catering particularly for the younger crowd. Plagne-Centre has night skiing on the slalom slope.

In Belle-Plagne, the Tête Inn and the Cheyenne are the main bars. The Maître Kanter has been recommended. The No BI'm Café, with a massive TV and occasional live music, is the liveliest bar in Plagne-Centre. Plagne 1800 is fairly quiet at night – though the Mine (complete with old train and mining artefacts) is an exception: 'Get there early for a seat; quiz night and rock bands recommended.' Mama Mia's is 'fun and eccentric'. The Petit Chaperon Rouge has a new bar with 'lots of neon and plasma screens'. Plagne-Bellecôte is very limited at night, with only one real bar – Show Time Café, which is popular for

karaoke. But there is bowling, and tubing. Aime-la-Plagne is also quiet.

The Luna (Plagne-Centre), the Jet (Plagne-Bellecôte) and the Saloon (Belle-Plagne) are the main discos. There are cinemas at Aime, Bellecôte and Plagne-Centre.

OFF THE SLOPES
OK for the active
As well as the sports and fitness facilities, winter walks along marked trails are pleasant: 'There are enough walks to keep you busy for six days,' says one reporter. It's also easy to get up the mountain on the gondolas, which both have restaurants at the top. There's an ice grotto on the glacier (special pass available). The Olympic bob-sleigh run is a popular evening activity (see feature box). Excursions are limited.

Montchavin (1250m/4,100ft)
Montchavin is based on an old farming hamlet and has an attractive traffic-free centre. The cable-car link with Les Arcs starts from 300m/980ft above the village, and is reached by a fast chair. There are adequate shops, a kindergarten and a ski school. Reaching La Plagne involves a series of lifts; but the local slopes have quite a bit to offer – pretty, sheltered runs,

La Plagne

357

TRY THE OLYMPIC BOB-SLEIGH RUN – YOU CAN NOW DO IT SOLO

If the thrills of a day on the slopes aren't enough, you can round it off by having a go on the bob-sleigh run built for the 1992 Winter Olympics. The floodlit 1.5km/1 mile run has 19 bends, generating forces as high as 3g.

You can go in a driverless bob-raft (34 euros) reaching 80kph/50mph, which most people find quite exciting enough. Then there's the faster solo mono-bob (95 euros); we found this a great thrill – we had to close our eyes on the sharper bends. Fastest of all is the 'taxi-bob' (100 euros), where three of you are wedged in a real four-man bob behind the driver – advertised speed 110kph/68mph. Be sure your physical state is up to the ride; there are minimum age limits. The run is open on certain days only – book ahead. Additional insurance is available.

well endowed with snowmaking, with nursery slopes at village level and up at Plan Bois – now reached by a six-pack. The way home involves some of the trickiest blue runs we have encountered. Après-ski is quiet, but the village doesn't lack atmosphere and has a couple of nice bars, a nightclub, cinema and night skiing. The Bellecôte hotel (0479 078330) is convenient for the slopes. Esprit has a chalet with creche here.

Les Coches (1450m/4,760ft)

Les Coches is 2km/1 mile away and shares the same slopes. It is a sympathetically designed, quiet, modern mini-resort with a traffic-free centre. It has its own school and kindergarten. The Last One pub is a 'great place for a beer', with a big screen TV and live bands. The Origan (steaks and pizza), Poze (for pizza), the new Savoy'art ('stunning interior'), the Lauzes and Taverne du Monchu are recommended for eating out. There's a shuttle to the cinema in Montchavin. The 4-star Chalets de Wengen apartments are due to open there for 2007/08.

Montalbert (1350m/4,430ft)

Montalbert is a traditional but much expanded village – 'so friendly,' says a 2007 visitor – now with quicker lift access into the main area – though it's a long way from here across to the Bellecôte glacier or the Les Arcs link. The local slopes are easy and wooded

– a useful insurance against bad weather. There are 'heaps of restaurants for such a small place' and the Tourmente pub is 'great'. The Aigle Rouge (0479 555105) is a simple hotel. Ski Amis has an all-en-suite chalet with all the trimmings here. The Chalets de Montalbert and Les Granges apartments are 'simply furnished but pleasantly spacious'.

Champagny
(1250m/4,100ft)

Champagny is a charming village in a pretty, wooded setting, with its modern expansion done sensitively. It is at the opposite end of the slopes from the link to Les Arcs but well placed for an outing by taxi or car to Courchevel. Given good snow, there are lovely runs home (though not recommended for near-beginners). There are several hotels, of which the two best are both Logis de France. The Glières (0479 550552) is a rustic old hotel with varied rooms, a friendly welcome and good food. The Ancolie (0479 550500) is smarter, with modern facilities (recommended by a reporter). The Club Alpina (0479 550459) is 'consistently good for both food and rooms', says a regular visitor, and is close to the lift.

The new Alpages de Champagny is an impressive-looking chalet-style development, with a pool and sauna.

The village is quiet in the evenings, but the restaurant Poya is highly rated for a 'delightful atmosphere and excellent food at reasonable prices'.

Portes du Soleil

Low altitude, largely intermediate circuit of slopes straddling the French-Swiss border, with a variety of contrasting resorts to stay in

The Portes du Soleil vies with the Trois Vallées for the title 'World's Largest Ski Area', but its slopes are very different from those of Méribel, Courchevel, Val Thorens and neighbours. The Portes du Soleil's slopes are spread out over a large area, and not all are linked – but most are part of an extensive circuit straddling the French-Swiss border. You can travel the circuit in either direction, with a short bus-ride needed at Châtel. There are smaller areas to explore slightly off the main circuit. The runs are great for keen intermediates who like to travel long distances and through different resorts. There are few of the tightly packed networks of runs that encourage you to stay put in one area – though there are exceptions in one or two places. The area also has some nice rustic mountain restaurants, serving good food in pleasant, sunny settings.

The lifts throughout the area have been improved in recent years, with several new high-speed chair-lifts eliminating some bad bottlenecks – though there are still plenty of drags and slow chairs. But the slopes are low by French standards, with top heights in the range 2000m to 2300m (6,560ft to 7,550ft), and good snow is far from assured (though snowmaking has been expanded in recent years). When the snow is good you can have a great time racing all over the circuit. But the slopes can get very crowded, especially at weekends and in the Avoriaz area.

We have separate chapters on the major Portes du Soleil resorts. On the French side, purpose-built **Avoriaz** and the traditional old mountain village of **Châtel** are on the main circuit. (On a spur off the main circuit at Châtel – and covered briefly in that chapter – are the slopes above **Torgon** in Switzerland and **La Chapelle d'Abondance** in France.) **Morzine** and **Les Gets** are another two traditional old French mountain villages but are set off the main circuit and share their own area of local slopes.

On the Swiss side, **Champéry** is a classic, charming Swiss village – but again just off the main circuit. In the Champéry chapter we also cover briefly the other main Swiss resorts: **Morgins** (another old village) and **Champoussin** and **Les Crosets** (both purpose-built).

Puy-St-Vincent

*Underrated small modern resort with limited but varied slopes –
good for young families who haven't been spoilt by mega-resorts*

COSTS

① ② ③ ④ ⑤ ⑥

RATINGS

The slopes

Fast lifts	**
Snow	***
Extent	**
Expert	***
Intermediate	***
Beginner	***
Convenience	*****
Queues	***
Mountain restaurants	***

The rest

Scenery	****
Resort charm	**
Off-slope	*

NEWS

There are plans to install a fast chair-lift from the La Balme blue to the Lauzes drag-lifts (right side of slopes) and to add two new pistes – one from the Bois des Coqs red to La Balme, the other on the opposite side of the ski area, from the Crêtes blue down to 1400 via the Tournoux restaurant.

+ Mostly a convenient, purpose-built resort that isn't too hideous
+ Friendly locals
+ Splendid scenery
+ Some great cross-country routes
+ Good variety of slopes with challenges for all abilities, but ...

– Slopes very limited in extent
– Upper village has only apartment-based accommodation
– Queues in French holidays
– Mainly slow old lifts
– Limited après-ski/restaurants
– Not a lot to do off the slopes

Puy-St-Vincent's ski area may be limited, but when we visited we found ourselves liking it more than we expected. It offers a decent vertical and a lot of variety, including a bit of steep stuff. Provided you pick your spot with care, it makes an attractive choice for a family not hungry for piste miles.

THE RESORT

Puy-St-Vincent proper is an old mountain village. The modern resort of PSV is basically a two-part affair – the minor part, Station 1400, is just along the mountainside from PSV proper at 1400m/4,590ft; the major part, Station 1600, is a few hairpins further up (yes, at 1600m/5,250ft), consisting of long, low apartment blocks. Spreading up the hillside from here are newer developments in a more traditional style – sometimes referred to as Station 1800. Some of the accommodation is slope-side, but not all – take care if this matters. We and our reporters have found PSV friendly ('even the lift operators'), and it is understandably popular with families.

THE MOUNTAINS

Within its small area, PSV packs in a lot of variety, with runs from green to black that justify their classification.
Slopes There are gentle slopes between the two villages, but most of the runs are above 1600. A fast quad goes up to the tree line at around 2000m/6,560ft. Entertaining red runs go back down, and a green takes a less direct route. The main higher lift is a long chair to 2700m/8,860ft, serving excellent open slopes of red and genuine black steepness. Drags to either side serve further open runs here, and access splendid cruising runs that curl around the edges of the area into the woods – one linking to a blue, La Balme, all the way down to 1400. There are plans to install a fast lift

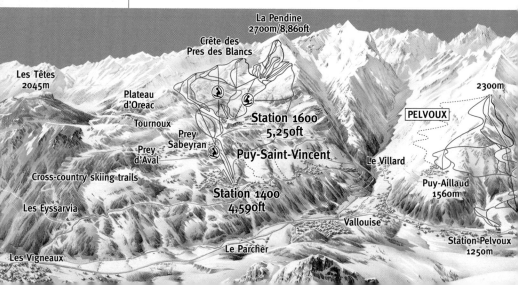

La Pendine
2700m/8,860ft

Crête des
Pres des Blancs

Les Têtes
2045m

Plateau
d'Oreac

Tournoux

Prey
Sabeyran

Prey
d'Aval

Station 1600
5,250ft

Puy-Saint-Vincent

2300m

PELVOUX

Le Villard

Puy-Aillaud
1560m

Cross-country skiing trails

Les Eyssarvia

Station 1400
4,590ft

Vallouise

Station Pelvoux
1250m

Les Vigneaux

Le Parcher

SNOWBIZZ

There are many worse-looking purpose-built resorts than this one ➔

Phone numbers
From abroad use the prefix +33 and omit the initial '0' of the phone number

from La Balme and to create another piste (shown as a short-term plan on the piste map) – but we've no news of dates yet. 1400 has a six-pack up into the main slopes. The six-day Galaxie pass covers a series of major resorts beyond Briançon. More to the point, it also covers a day's skiing above the valley hamlet of Pelvoux, 10 minutes' drive away. This area has quiet, very rewarding blue, red and black runs, and a vertical of over 1000m/3,280ft.

Terrain-parks There is a floodlit terrain-park with half-pipe at 1600.

Snow reliability The slopes face north-east and are reasonably reliable for snow. Snowmaking covers one run down to 1400 and several above 1600. Grooming is OK.

Experts The black runs are short but genuinely black, and are 'totally ungroomed, with serious moguls'. There are off-piste routes to be tackled with guidance.

Intermediates Size apart, it's a good area for those who like a challenge – but there aren't many very easy runs.

Beginners Beginners should be happy on either of the nursery slopes, and on the long green from 2000m/6,560ft.

Snowboarding Boarders are not allowed on the Rocher Noir drag-lift.

Cross-country There are 30km/19 miles of cross-country trails, including some splendid routes between 1400m and 1700m (4,590ft and 5,580ft), ranging from green to black difficulty.

Queues In a family resort like this, there are bound to be some problems in French holiday times – but with fast chairs at the lower levels these should now be confined to the upper slopes.

Mountain restaurants There is a modern but pleasantly woody place at mid-mountain, but the sunny terraces of 1600 get most of the business.

Schools and guides You have a choice of French and International ski school. British tour operator Snowbizz has now merged its school with the International school; together they claim to form the largest English-speaking children's school in the French Alps. A 2007 reporter found them 'excellent, with a very high standard'.

Facilities for children There are nurseries taking children from 18 months in 1400 and 1600, and both schools run ski kindergartens. 'A great resort for my five-year old daughter to start her skiing career,' sums up a 2007 reporter.

STAYING THERE

How to go A number of UK operators now offer accommodation here; most of it is in self-catering apartments.

Hotels There are three cheap hotels in 1400, but none in 1600.

Apartments The Gentianes apartments at 1800 are 'good-sized, very reasonably priced', with use of indoor pool. Handy for slopes but not for shops.

Eating out The Petit Chamois is 'friendly, with a good children's menu'.

Après-ski Après-ski amounts to a few bar-restaurants in each village.

Off the slopes There are 30km/19 miles of paths. Paragliding, dog-sled rides, tobogganing and outdoor skating are available. The cinema shows English-speaking films. With a car you can visit the historic town of Vallouise.

Puy-St-Vincent

361

Risoul

Modern, villagey resort with a range of accommodation in an attractive setting – and a big area of slopes shared with Vars

COSTS

① ② ③ ④ ⑤ ⑥

RATINGS

The slopes
Fast lifts	*
Snow	***
Extent	***
Expert	**
Intermediate	****
Beginner	****
Convenience	****
Queues	****
Mountain restaurants	***

The rest
Scenery	***
Resort charm	**
Off-slope	*

NEWS

For 2006/07 the terrain-parks on both sides were improved and the one at Vars moved higher up the mountain.

At Vars, a new six-pack, Sibières, replaced the Sources and Sibières drag-lifts above Les Claux. And a blue run, Serre Banet, was created above Peyrol to improve the return from Risoul.

+ One of the more attractive and convenient purpose-built resorts

+ Scenic slopes linked with Vars add up to a fair-sized area

+ High resort, reasonably snow-sure

+ Good resort for beginners, early intermediates and families

+ Plenty of good-value places to eat

– Still lots of long drag-lifts

– Not too much to challenge expert skiers and boarders

– Long airport transfers

– Little to do off the slopes

Slowly but surely the international market is waking up to the merits of the southern French Alps. Were they nearer Geneva, Risoul and its linked neighbour Vars would be as well known as Les Arcs and Flaine – the village of Risoul is more attractive than either. Brush up your school French before you go.

THE RESORT

Risoul, purpose-built in the late 1970s, is a quiet, apartment-based resort, popular with families. Set among the trees, with excellent views over the Ecrins national park, it is made up of wood-clad buildings – mostly bulky, but with some concessions to traditional style. It has a busy little main street that, surprisingly, is very far from traffic-free. But the village meets the mountain in classic French purpose-built style, with sunny restaurant terraces facing the slopes. Reporters have commented on the friendliness of the natives. The village does not offer many resort amenities. Airport transfers (usually from Turin) can take four hours.

THE MOUNTAINS

Together with neighbouring Vars, the area amounts to one of the biggest domains in the southern French Alps – marketed as the Forêt Blanche.
Slopes The slopes, mainly north-facing, spread over several minor peaks and bowls, and connect with the sunnier slopes of neighbouring Vars via the Pointe de Razis and the lower Col des Saluces. The upper slopes are open, but those back to Risoul are prettily wooded, and good for bad-weather days. Despite several recent lift upgrades, including a new six-pack at Vars, there are still too many long and steep drag-lifts. Piste grooming seems to have improved, but markings and classifications are unreliable.

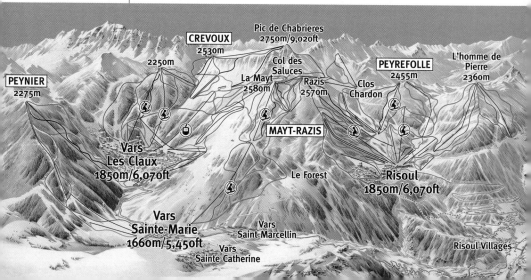

KEY FACTS

Resort	1850m
	6,070ft

The entire Forêt Blanche ski area

Slopes	1660-2750m
	5,450-9,020ft
Lifts	51
Pistes	180km
	112 miles
Green	16%
Blue	38%
Red	36%
Black	10%
Snowmaking	35 km
	22 miles

Terrain-parks There are two good terrain-parks, with half-pipes, boarder-cross, hand-rail and big air – one near the base, the other high up.

Snow reliability Risoul's slopes are all above 1850m/6,070ft and mostly north-facing, so despite its southerly position snow reliability is reasonably good. Snowmaking is fairly extensive and has been extended. Visitors recommend going over to the east-facing Vars slopes for the morning sun, and returning to Risoul in the afternoon.

Experts The pistes in general do not offer much to interest experts. However, Risoul's main top stations access a couple of steepish descents. And there are some good off-piste opportunities if you take a guide.

Intermediates The whole area is best suited to intermediates, with some good reds and blues in both sectors. Almost all Risoul's runs return to the village, making it difficult to get lost.

Beginners Risoul's local area boasts some good, convenient, nursery slopes with a free lift, and a lot of easy longer pistes to move on to: 'Pretty much perfect,' says a 2007 visitor.

Snowboarding There is a lot of good free-riding to be done throughout the area, although beginners might not like the large proportion of drag-lifts. There are weekly competitions.

Cross-country There are 45km/28 miles of cross-country trails in the whole domain. A trail through the Peyrol forest links the two resorts together.

Queues Outside French school holidays, the slopes are impressively quiet. There may be a wait to get back from Vars at the end of the day.

Mountain restaurants Most people return to the village terraces, but the mountain restaurants have increased in quantity and quality. The self-service Tetras is just 'OK'. Snack Attack, near the Forêt Blanche apartments, pleased one visitor, and the Refuge de Valbel is recommended.

Schools and guides We had a good report on the ESF last year. 'The instructors were excellent for both adults and kids – patient, with good English. Classes no bigger than eight.' There is also the Internationale school.

Facilities for children Risoul is very much a family resort. It provides an all-day nursery for children over six months. Both ski schools operate ski kindergartens, slightly above the village, reached by a child-friendly lift.

STAYING THERE

How to go Most visitors stay in self-catering apartments, but there are a few hotels and more chalets are becoming available from UK operators. Crystal's club hotel the Morgan is 'basic but perfectly adequate', although it can be 'surprisingly' noisy.

Hotels The 'value for money' Chardon Bleu (0492 460727) is right on the slopes. You can also stay overnight at the Tetras mountain refuge (0492 460983) at 2000m/6,560ft.

Apartments The Constellation Forêt Blanche apartments, although small, are said to be 'in an excellent position, well equipped and pristine'. Bételgeuse and Pégase are the recent additions.

Eating out There's plenty of choice, from pizza to good French food, and it's mostly good value – the Ecureuil is 'very friendly, with excellent food – good prices', the Chalet 'excellent'.

Après-ski Après-ski in the centre is reportedly now 'very lively' and goes on through the night, with half a dozen 'extremely friendly' bars and three

UK PACKAGES

Crystal, Interactive Resorts, Interhome, Lagrange, Neilson, Ski Collection, Ski France, Ski Independence, Ski Leisure Direction, Skiholidayextras, Skitracer, Thomson
Vars *Club Pavilion, Crystal, Equity, Erna Low, Interactive Resorts, Interhome, Lagrange, Rocketski, Ski France, Skiholidayextras, Tops*

Phone numbers
From abroad use the prefix +33 and omit the initial '0' of the phone number

TOURIST OFFICES

www.foretblanche.com
Risoul
t 0492 460260
info@risoul.com
www.risoul.com
Vars
t 0492 465131
info@otvars.com
www.vars-ski.com

clubs to move between. The best bars are, apparently, the Place ('noisy and fun') and the 'trendy' Caribbean-themed Babao. For a quieter drink, try the Chalet or the Eterlou.
Off the slopes There is little to do; excursions to Briançon are possible.

Vars 1850m/6,070ft

THE RESORT

Vars includes several small, old villages on or near the road running southwards towards the Col de Vars. But for winter visitors it mainly consists of purpose-built Vars-les-Claux, higher up the road. The resort has convenience and reasonable prices in common with Risoul, but is bigger and has far more in the way of amenities; less English is spoken though. There are a lot of block-like apartments, but Vars-les-Claux is not a complete eyesore, thanks mainly to surrounding woods. There are two centres: the original, geographical one – base of the main gondola – has most of the accommodation and shopping; Point Show is a collection of bars and shops, 10 minutes' walk away.

Vars-Ste-Marie makes a more attractive base now that fast chairs take you to the top of La Mayt, but is 'dead' in the evenings.

THE MOUNTAINS

There are slopes on both sides of the village, linked by pistes and by chair-lift at the lower end of Les Claux. Lifts also run up from both sides of Ste-Marie, lower down the mountain.
Slopes The wooded, west-facing Peynier area is the smaller sector, and reaches only 2275m/7,460ft – though there are good long descents down to Les Claux and Ste-Marie. The main slopes are in an east-facing bowl with direct links to the Risoul slopes at the top, Col du Vallon (via a recently built tunnel) and at the Col des Saluces. There's a speed-skiing course at the top (access via the ski school). Beneath it are easy runs, open at the top but descending into trees. A new six-pack has improved the connection towards Crevoux, above Les Claux.
Terrain-parks There's a newly improved terrain-park at Crevoux.
Snow reliability The main slopes get the morning sun, and are centred at around 2000m/6,560ft, so snow reliability is not as good as in Risoul, but snowmaking is widespread.

Experts There is little of challenge for experts, though the Crête de Chabrières top section accesses some off-piste, an unpisted route and a tricky couloir at Col de Crevoux. The Olympic red run from the top of La Mayt down to Ste-Marie is a respectable 920m/3,020ft vertical.
Intermediates Most of the area is fine for intermediates, with a good mixture of comfortable reds and easy blues.
Beginners There is a nursery area close to central Vars ('perfect'), with lots of 'graduation' runs throughout the area. Quick learners will be able to get over to Risoul by the end of the week.
Snowboarding There is good free-riding to be done throughout the area, although beginners might find the number of drag-lifts a problem.
Cross-country There are 25km/16 miles of trails in Vars itself. Some start at the edge of town, but those above Ste-Marie are more extensive.
Queues Queues are rare outside the French holidays, and even then Vars is not overrun as some family resorts are.
Mountain restaurants There are several in both sectors, but a lot of people head back to the villages for lunch. The Cassette, at the bottom of the Mayt chair, has 'delighted' visitors.
Schools and guides Two 2007 beginners enjoyed 'good' classes with ESF, but a lack of English speaking may be a problem.
Facilities for children The ski school runs a nursery for children from two years old. There is a ski kindergarten.

STAYING THERE

How to go There are a few small hotels, but Les Claux is dominated by apartment accommodation.
Hotels The Caribou (0492 465043) is the smartest of the hotels and has a pool. The Ecureuil (0492 465072) is an attractive, modern b&b chalet. The Vallon (0492 465472) at Ste-Marie is basic but 'highly satisfactory'.
Eating out The range of restaurants is impressive, with good-value pizzerias, crêperies and fondue places. Taverne du Torrent is 'excellent with reasonable prices' and the food at Chez Plumot 'truly haute cuisine'.
Après-ski Après-ski is animated at tea time, less so after dinner – except at weekends when the discos warm up.
Off the slopes The amenities are rather disappointing, given the size of Vars: 35km/22 miles of walking paths, a cinema and an ice rink – and that's it.

La Rosière

The sunniest slopes in the Tarentaise, but also about the snowiest; the link to La Thuile in Italy adds a vital extra dimension

COSTS

① ② ③ ④ ⑤ ⑥

RATINGS

The slopes

Fast lifts	**
Snow	***
Extent	***
Expert	**
Intermediate	***
Beginner	*****
Convenience	***
Queues	***
Mountain restaurants	*

The rest

Scenery	***
Resort charm	***
Off-slope	*

➕ Attractive, friendly, purpose-built resort with glorious views

➕ Fair-sized area of slopes shared with La Thuile in Italy

➕ Sunny home slopes

➕ Heli-skiing over the border in Italy

➕ Good nursery slope

➕ Gets big dumps of snow when storms sock in from the west, but ...

➖ Winds can close lift links with Italy

➖ Snow affected by sun in late season

➖ Lots of slow old lifts

➖ Few on-piste challenges for experts

➖ One run is much like another – though La Thuile is more varied

➖ Limited après-ski

➖ Few off-slope diversions

La Rosière is much smaller and quieter than the nearby mega-resorts such as Val d'Isère-Tignes, Les Arcs and La Plagne; and all our 2007 reporters stress the friendliness of the locals. The ski area is remarkably sunny, but gets a lot of snow; and the link with the north-facing slopes of La Thuile in Italy adds variety. All in all, the resort best suits families and groups of skiers with mixed abilities looking for a relaxed time.

THE RESORT

La Rosière has been built in attractive, traditional chalet style beside the road that zigzags its way up from Bourg-St-Maurice towards the Petit-St-Bernard pass to Italy (closed to traffic in winter – the Italian side becomes a piste). It's a quiet place with a few shops and friendly locals; don't expect lively nightlife. The most convenient accommodation is in the main village near the lifts, or in the rapidly developing alternative base of Les Eucherts, a short bus-ride to the east and served by its own fast chair.

THE MOUNTAINS

La Rosière and La Thuile in Italy share a big area of slopes, now called Espace San Bernardo. La Rosière's sunny home slopes are south-facing with great views over the valley to Les Arcs and La Plagne. The link with Italy's slopes is prone to closure because of high winds or heavy snow.

Slopes Two fast chairs at either end of the village take you into the heart of the slopes, from where a series of drags and chairs, spread across the mountain, takes you up to Col de la Traversette. From there, you can get over the ridge and to the lifts, which link with Italy at Belvédère.

Terrain-parks There's a terrain-park served by the Poletta drag lift, just above the village centre and a boarder-cross course by the Fort chair below Col de la Traversette.

Snow reliability The slopes get a lot of snow from storms pushing up the valley, but in late season the sunny orientation takes its toll.

Experts There's little to keep experts amused. The steepest terrain is on the lowest slopes, down the Marcassin black run below Les Eucherts and down the Ecudets black to the west of Le Gollet. There's also a new free-ride area just above the latter (see 'News') and some enjoyable off-piste between the pistes. And there's excellent heli-skiing from just over the Italian border

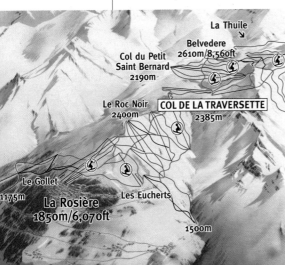

La Thuile

Belvedere
2610m/8,560ft

Col du Petit
Saint Bernard
2190m

Le Roc Noir
2400m

COL DE LA TRAVERSETTE
2385m

Le Gollet

Les Eucherts

1175m

La Rosière
1850m/6,070ft

1500m

The Les Eucherts area is developing rapidly as an alternative base to the main village centre. For 2007/08 a sports complex will open here including an ice rink and bowling alley.

For 2006/07 a new free-ride area that is avalanche controlled and patrolled opened at the west of the ski area above Le Gollet.

Alpine Answers, Chalet Group, Crystal, Erna Low, Esprit, Interactive Resorts, Interhome, Lagrange, MasterSki, A Mountain Chalet, Mountain Heaven, Ski Activity, Ski Amis, Ski Beat, Ski Collection, Ski France, Ski Leisure Direction, Ski Olympic, Ski Supreme, Ski4you, Skiholidayextras, Skitracer, Skiworld, SnowCrazy, Thomson, Vanilla Ski

FRANCE

366

(you ski or board back into France, arriving just a few miles from La Rosière – see the La Thuile chapter).
Intermediates There's a fair amount to explore if you take into account La Thuile. The main part of La Rosière's area is a broad open mountainside offering straightforward red and blue pistes. More interesting is the Fontaine Froide red, dropping 750m/2,460ft vertical through woods to the Ecudets chair, far below the village at the western end. The red beyond Col de la Traversette has good snow and views, but is narrow at the top.
Beginners There are good nursery slopes and short lifts near the main

village and near Les Eucherts.
Snowboarding Most of the lifts are chairs, making the place good for learner and early intermediate boarders. And the sunny slopes are good for gentle free-riding when the snow is soft.
Cross-country There are 5km/3 miles of trails near the altiport.
Queues Not usually a problem.
Mountain restaurants Most people have lunch in the village. Mountain recommendations include the self-service Plan du Repos for its 'friendly staff, huge pasta portions and lovely salads', the San Bernardo (on the border) and the Vieux Chalet (at the bottom of the Ecudets chair) for snacks ('very friendly service'); it is a popular poor-weather retreat.
Schools and guides There are three schools. Evolution 2 is praised for its 'small groups' and 'friendly instructors', who are good with children. And we have good 2007 reports of the ESF – 'dedicated English-only classes and a great place to learn off-piste with a guide', and 'my companion's skiing made a significant breakthrough'. Reporters also enjoyed both the open slalom race (not just for ski school participants) and the torchlit descent organised by the ESF.
Facilities for children Club des Galopins has a 'very good' snow garden, and British tour operators Esprit, Crystal and Ski Beat (see 'Chalets') all have their own childcare facilities here.

STAYING THERE

How to go A number of British tour operators now offer packages here.
Hotels There are a few 2-star hotels in the village, and more in the valley.
Chalets There is an increasing number of companies with chalets here. Ski Olympic has operated here for years

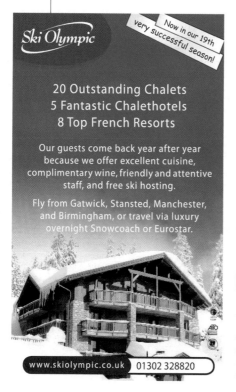

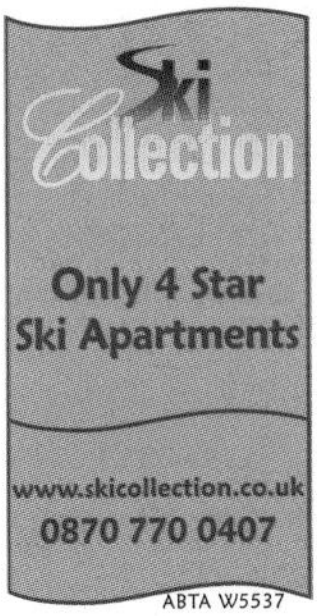

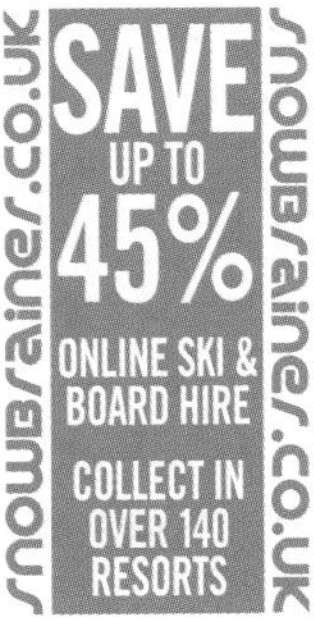

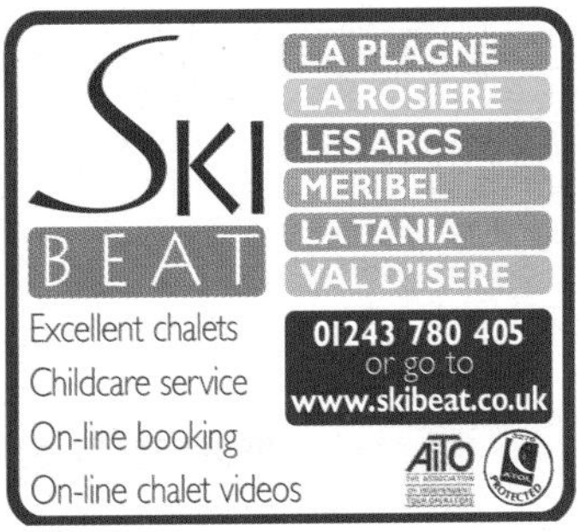

and has a chalet-hotel and four chalets (including two with access to a pool, sauna, steam and hot-tub). Ski Beat has six new places purpose-built for themselves in Les Eucherts, with childcare facilities and two shared saunas. Mountain Heaven has a splendid-looking new penthouse with a huge top-floor living room, six en-suite rooms and an outdoor hot-tub. A Mountain Chalet has one chalet, personally run by its owners. Family-specialist Esprit Ski has several chalets here and its usual comprehensive childcare facilities. Crystal and Thomson have chalets and share childcare facilities run by Crystal.

Apartments The best places are newly built at Les Eucherts. The Cîmes Blanches is a classic MGM development with attractive pool, hot-tub, sauna and steam room. The Balcons units can accommodate larger groups. Both are available through Ski Collection.

Eating out A useful pocket guide to restaurants is distributed locally. The Génépi serves 'fabulous French cuisine', says a 2007 visitor. The Turia is a rustic, smart establishment in the centre. The Marmottes is said to serve 'good salads'. We've had mixed reports on the food and service at the 'charming' Ancolie. The Relais du Petit St Bernard is popular.

Après-ski Après-ski is limited to a couple of bars in the village. 'Good live band and relaxed, no-smoking lounge upstairs at Le Petit Danois,' says a 2007 reporter.

Off the slopes There are scenic flights and walks, an indoor climbing wall and a cinema. And you can try parapenting, dog-sledding and snow-shoeing. You can visit a St Bernard dog area. Mountain restaurants are inaccessible on foot.

Staying up the mountain The Hotel San Bernardo (0165 841444), on the border and reachable only on skis, provided a memorable two-night stay for an adventurous reporter – 'simple, comfortable and peaceful', with a 'spectacular collection of grappas'.

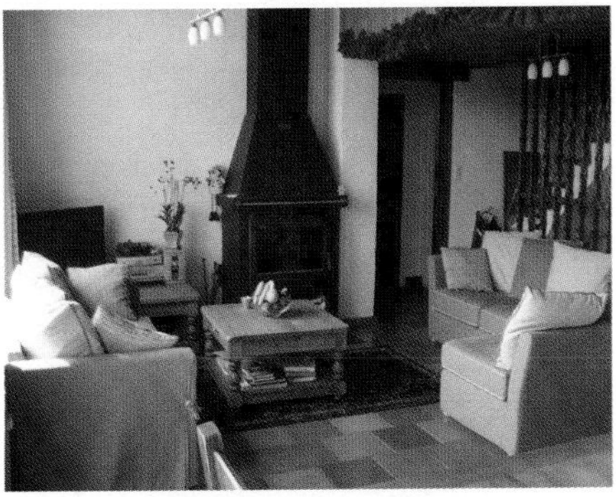

La Rosière

367

Samoëns

*Characterful but inconvenient base for the extensive and varied
Grand Massif, shared with Flaine and Les Carroz*

368

COSTS

① ② ③ ④ ⑤ ⑥

RATINGS

The slopes

Fast lifts	**
Snow	***
Extent	****
Expert	****
Intermediate	*****
Beginner	**
Convenience	*
Queues	****
Mountain restaurants	**

The rest

Scenery	****
Resort charm	****
Off-slope	***

NEWS

The Neiges et Roc hotel has new leisure facilities, including a spa and sauna. And an aquatherapy centre and spa have been built at the Table de Fifine.

KEY FACTS

Resort	720-1600m
	2,360-5,250ft

Grand Massif ski area (Samoëns and all linked resorts)	
Slopes	700-2480m
	2,300-8,140ft
Lifts	78
Pistes	265km
	165 miles
Green	11%
Blue	42%
Red	36%
Black	11%
Snowmaking	218 guns

Massif ski area (excluding Flaine)	
Slopes	700-2120m
	2,300-6,700ft
Lifts	54
Pistes	145km
	90 miles

- ➕ Lovely historic village, with traffic-free centre and weekly market
- ➕ Lift into big, varied area shared with Flaine and Les Carroz
- ➕ Glorious views from top heights
- ➕ Very close to Geneva, but ...

- ➖ Weekends can be busy as a result
- ➖ Access lift is way outside the village – yet has no return piste
- ➖ Slow lifts above mid-mountain
- ➖ Not ideal for beginners
- ➖ Surprisingly intrusive traffic

The impressive Grand Massif area is chiefly associated in Britain with high, purpose-built, apartment-dominated Flaine; but the network can also be accessed from much more attractive traditional villages – Les Carroz, Morillon and Samoëns. And the cutest of these, if not the most convenient, is Samoëns.

THE RESORT

Samoëns is a 'Monument Historique' – once a thriving centre for stonemasons, with their work much in evidence. There is a small traffic-free centre of narrow streets lined by appealing food shops, and nearby a pretty square (sadly not traffic-free) with a stone fountain, an ancient linden tree, a fine church and other medieval buildings. Also nearby is a nominally car-free area of modern development. The village as a whole retains the feel of 'real' rural France. There is a good weekly market.

The main lift is an eight-seat gondola from village level but not from the village: the lift base is a drive or a bus-ride from most accommodation. For non-beginners with a car, the slow but queue-free old gondola at Vercland is still worth considering – you can ski back to this lift, unlike the main one.

THE MOUNTAINS

Most of the skiing directly above Samoëns is on open slopes beneath Tête des Saix, from which point there are links to the next-door Morillon sector and the slightly more distant sectors of Les Carroz and Flaine (both covered in the Flaine chapter).
Slopes The two gondolas from the valley arrive at separate points on the 'hilly plateau' of Samoëns 1600. This mini-resort is also reachable by road. Tête des Saix is reached by parallel chair-lifts in two stages. These slow lifts are a real drawback: a couple of six-packs are urgently needed. From the Tête you can descend to Morillon

or Les Carroz; one more (fast) chair is needed for access to the Flaine bowl.
Terrain-parks There is a terrain-park above 1600, and another at Morillon.
Snow reliability The slopes above Samoëns face due north, so above 1600 snow is fairly reliable. There is snowmaking around 1600.
Experts The upper pistes on Tête des Saix are among the most testing in the Grand Massif, and there is lots of good off-piste in the valleys and bowls between Samoëns and Flaine.
Intermediates If you can put up with the slow lifts mentioned above, Samoëns makes a perfectly satisfactory base for all but the most timid intermediates, who might be better off in Morillon. From Tête des Saix you have a wide choice of good long runs in various directions. In good snow the valley runs to Vercland are highly enjoyable – the black is very little steeper than the red, and used less.
Beginners Beginners must buy a pass (there is a special one at about 14 euros a day) and go up to 1600. There are snow-sure, gentle slopes for absolute beginners up there – excellent when not crowded at peak times – but no long green runs to progress to. Morillon is a better bet and the nursery slopes at Sixt are 'very good.'
Snowboarding Beware drag-lifts on the nursery slopes.
Cross-country There are trails on the flat valley floor around Samoëns, and more challenging ones up the valley beyond Sixt and up at Col de Joux Plane (1700m/5,58oft).
Queues We have had reports of queues building up at 1600 for access to Tête des Saix.

PISTE MAP

Samoëns is covered on the Flaine map

Mountain restaurants There are places to eat at Samoëns 1600, but the most captivating places are above Morillon and Les Carroz – see Flaine chapter.

Schools and guides A reader last year had a 'poor' lesson with the ESF and a 'much better one' from newish 360 International. Another 2006 visitor found the ESF's private boarding instruction 'very good'.

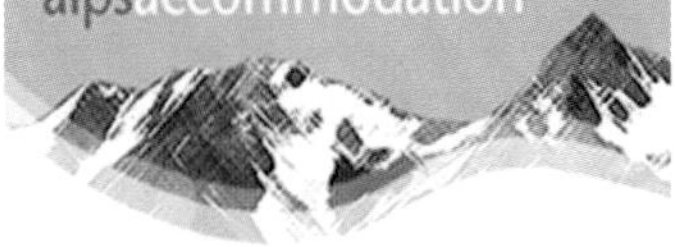

Facilities for children There is a kindergarten, and ski lessons are available. The Zig Zag school offers new multi-activity courses.

STAYING THERE

How to go A few specialist UK operators now go to Samoëns.

Hotels We and readers have enjoyed the Neige et Roc (0450 344072), a walk from the centre – 'friendly staff, excellent food, big spa area'. Avoid the annexe, though. The central Glaciers (0450 344006) is recommended.

Chalets We have glowing reports of owner-run chalets Marie Stuart and Moccand (via Alps Accommodation).

Apartments Self-catering is mostly modest, but above-average places include the Fermes de Samoëns (with pool) and Chez Michelle. Alps Accommodation has some 'great' new places near the gondola. Peak Retreats has some very appealing chalets – eg the fine Ferme de Fontany.

Eating out The Table de Fifine is a short drive from the centre, but a fine spot – beautiful wooden interior and 'good quality, imaginative menu'. The Muscade et Basilic is 'excellent, with an extensive wine list' and the Bois de Lune does 'great food'. The Louisiane has 'great' pizzas but when busy the staff will rudely turn you away.

Après-ski There are several bars – including an Irish pub, Covey's, which a 2007 reporter's teenager daughters rated 'the only place worth a visit'.

Off the slopes Samoëns offers quite a range of activities. We enjoyed a guided tour of the church one evening. Snowmobiling up at Samoëns 1600 is wilder than is usual in the Alps. There is an outdoor, covered ice rink, hosting regular hockey matches.

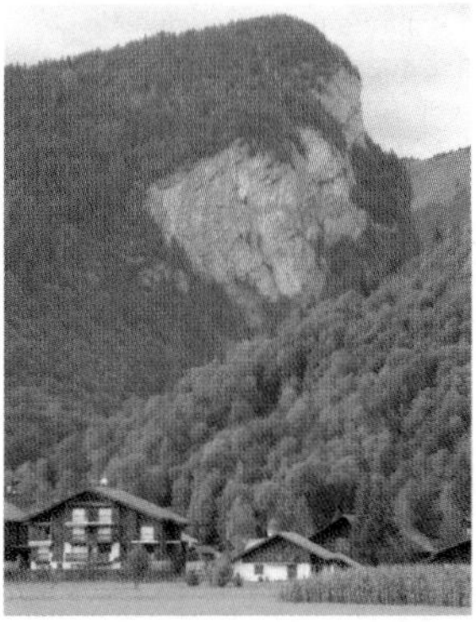

Phone numbers
From abroad use the prefix +33 and omit the initial '0' of the phone number

TOURIST OFFICE

Samoëns
t 0450 344028
infos@samoens.com
www.samoens.com

Samoëns

369

Selected apartment in Samoëns

Serre-Chevalier

Villages that are an odd mixture of ancient and modern sit beneath an extensive and varied mountain – with lots of woodland runs

370

- ➕ Big, varied mountain
- ➕ Lots of good woodland runs
- ➕ One of the few big French areas based on old villages with character
- ➕ Good-value and atmospheric old hotels, restaurants and chalets
- ➕ Generally quiet slopes, but ...

- ➖ Crowds/queues in French holidays
- ➖ Still too many slow, old lifts – including some vicious drags
- ➖ Busy road runs through the villages
- ➖ A lot of indiscriminate new building
- ➖ Limited nightlife
- ➖ Few off-slope diversions

Serre-Chevalier is one of the few French resorts offering the ambience you might look for on a summer holiday – a sort of Provence in the snow, with lots of small, family-run hotels and restaurants housed in old stone buildings (though the immediate impression is of insensitive development along the main road).

The excellent, varied slopes are split into different segments, so you get a sensation of travel. What really sets the area apart from the French norm is the quantity of sheltered woodland runs – though there are plenty of open runs, too.

Great strides are being made in bringing the lift system up to date, and upmarket accommodation is starting to appear. Who knows? Maybe Serre-Chevalier is at last going to make an impact on the international market.

THE RESORT

The resort is made up of a string of 13 villages set on a valley floor running roughly north-west to south-east, below the north-east-facing slopes of the mountain range that gives the resort its name. From the north-west – coming over the Col du Lautaret from Grenoble – the three main villages are Le Monêtier (or Serre-Che 1500), Villeneuve (1400) and Chantemerle (1350), spread over a distance of 8km/5 miles. Finally, at the extreme south-eastern end of the mountain, is Briançon (1200) – not a village but a town (the highest in France). Nine smaller villages can be identified, and some give their names to the communes: Villeneuve is in the commune of La Salle les Alpes, for example. Confusing.

Serre-Chevalier is not a smart resort,

in any sense. Although each of its parts is based on a simple old village, there is a lot of modern development, which ranges from brash to brutal, and even the older parts are roughly rustic rather than chocolate-box pretty. (A ban on corrugated iron roofs would help.) Because the resort is so spread out, the impact of cars and buses is difficult to escape, even if you're able to manage without them yourself. But when blanketed by snow the older villages and hamlets do have an unpretentious charm, and we find the place as a whole easy to like. Every year reporters stress how friendly and welcoming the local people are – hardly the norm in France.

There are few luxury hotels or notably swanky restaurants; on the other hand, there are more hotels in the modestly priced Logis de France 'club' here than in any other ski resort.

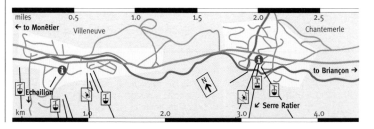

↑ Excellent beginner runs – long as well as short – at the top of the Fréjus gondola from Villeneuve

SNOWPIX.COM / CHRIS GILL

For 2007/08 a new six-pack is planned to replace the Combes 1 and 2 drag-lifts above Chantemerle, but starting much lower down at Serre-Ratier. Snowmaking will be further extended.

At Le Monêtier, a new thermal spa centre, Les Grands Bains, is due to open. A new 4-star apartment development, the Art de Vivre, is also expected.

For 2006/07 work began to improve piste signposting. Snowmaking was increased again and the terrain-park was moved higher up the mountain. The MGM apartments in Chantemerle were completed.

This is a family resort, which fills up (even more than most others) with French children in the February/March school holidays. Be warned.

The heart of the resort is **Villeneuve**, which has two gondolas and a fast quad chair going up to widely separated points at mid-mountain. The central area of new development near the lifts is brutal and charmless. But not far away is the peaceful hamlet of Le Bez, which has a third gondola, and across the valley is the old village of Villeneuve, its quiet main street lined by cosy bars, hotels and restaurants.

Not far down the valley, **Chantemerle** gives access to opposite ends of the mid-mountain plateau of Serre Ratier via a gondola and a cable-car, both with second stages above. Chantemerle has some tasteless modern buildings in the centre and along the main road. The old sector is a couple of minutes' walk from the lifts, with a lovely church and most of the small hotels, restaurants, bars and nightlife. However, a lot of accommodation is across the main road – 'Quite a long walk from the lifts,' says a weary visitor.

At the top of the valley, **Le Monêtier** has one main access lift – a fast quad chair to mid-mountain, reached from the village by bus or a 10-minute walk (downhill in the morning, uphill at the end of the day and tricky when ice is around, though you can leave your boots at the lift base). Le Monêtier is the smallest, quietest and most unspoiled of the main villages, with a Provençal feel to its narrow streets and little squares, and new building which

is mostly in sympathetic style. Sadly, the road to Grenoble, which skirts the other villages, bisects Le Monêtier; pedestrians stroll about bravely, hoping the cars will avoid them.

Briançon has a gondola from right in the town to mid-mountain and on almost to the top. The area around the lift station has a wide selection of modern shops, bars, restaurants, hotels, and a casino, but no character. In contrast, the 17th-century fortified upper quarter is a delight, with narrow cobbled streets and traditional restaurants, auberges and patisseries. Great views from the top, too. A very interesting property development in Briançon is about to be launched – see feature panel later in the chapter.

Ski-buses, covered on the free guest card and all lift passes, circulate around each village and link all the villages and lift bases along the valley. But they finish quite early, to the annoyance of some reporters (the local navettes stop soon after the lifts close, and the valley buses at approximately 7pm), and a couple of reporters have found the service inadequate; taxis aren't cheap.

A six-day area pass (or rather your receipt) covers a day in each of Les Deux-Alpes, Alpe-d'Huez, Puy-St-Vincent and the Milky Way. All of these outings are possible by bus, but are easier by car. The road from Grenoble and Lyon goes over the Col du Lautaret, which may require chains and is very occasionally closed.

Turin airport is closer than Lyon, with easier road access.

THE MOUNTAINS

Trees cover almost two-thirds of the
mountain, providing some of France's
best bad-weather terrain (we once had
a great day here when all the upper
lifts were closed by high winds). The
Serre-Chevalier massif is not notably
dramatic, but from the peaks there are
fine views of the Ecrins massif.

A new piste map was issued this
year – an improvement, but still in our
view very unsatisfactory.

Piste classification is unreliable –
many reds, in particular, could be
classified blue, but there are
occasional stiff blues, too.

THE SLOPES
Interestingly varied and pretty
Serre-Chevalier's 250km/155 miles of
pistes are spread across four main
sectors above the four main villages.
The sector above **Villeneuve** is the
most extensive, reaching back a good
way into the mountains and spreading
over four or five identifiable bowls. The
main mid-station is Fréjus. This sector
is reliably linked to the slightly smaller
Chantemerle sector well below the tree
line. The link from Chantemerle to
Briançon is over a high, exposed col
via a six-pack. The link between
Villeneuve and **Le Monêtier** is liable to
closure by high winds or avalanche
danger. Travelling from here towards
Villeneuve is a slow business – and it
involves a red run, so timid
intermediates have to use the bus.

TERRAIN-PARKS
Fully featured
Legendary French ripper Guillaume
Chastagnol and the Serre Che Brigade
have been building the freestyle
infrastructure here for several years,
trying to improve the terrain-park. This
year the park has grown and moved to
a spacious new location at the top of
the Forêt chair-lift, above Villeneuve. It
incorporates 20 different features for
all levels, including ramps, step-ups,
rails and kickers. A new boarder-cross
course has been shaped at Grand Alpe,
above Chantemerle. There's also a half-
pipe at the bottom of the Aravet
gondola in Villeneuve. There are two
boarder-cross courses, above
Chantemerle and Villeneuve.

SNOW RELIABILITY
Good – especially upper slopes
Most slopes face north or north-east

and so hold snow well, especially high
up (there are lots of lifts starting above
2000m/6,560ft). The weather pattern is
different from that of the northern Alps
and even that of Les Deux-Alpes or
Alpe-d'Huez, only a few miles to the
west. Serre-Che can get good snow
when there is a shortage elsewhere,
and vice versa. There is snowmaking
on long runs down to each village, and
it was increased above Le Monêtier
this year. More is planned for 2007/08.
Piste grooming is generally excellent.

FOR EXPERTS
Deep, not notably steep
There is plenty to amuse experts –
except those wanting extreme steeps.

The broad black runs down to
Villeneuve and Chantemerle are only
just black in steepness, but they are
fine runs with their gradient sustained
over an impressive vertical of around
800m/2,620ft. One or the other may be
closed for days on end for racing or
training. The rather neglected Tabuc
run, sweeping around the mountain
away from the lifts to Le Monêtier, has
a couple of genuinely steep pitches but
is mainly a cruise; it makes a fine end
to the day. For moguls, look higher up
the mountain to the steeper slopes
served by the two top lifts above Le
Monêtier and the three above
Villeneuve. The runs beside these lifts
– on and off-piste – form a great
playground in good snow; the slope
under the Yret chair is steep and
shady. The more roundabout Isolée
black is a reader's favourite – 'scenic
and challenging' after a rather scary
ridge start.

There are huge amounts of off-piste
terrain throughout the area – both
high-up and in the trees above
Villeneuve and Chantemerle. There are
plenty of more serious off-piste
expeditions, including: Tête de Grand
Pré to Villeneuve (a climb from
Cucumelle); off the back of L'Eychauda
to Puy-St-André (isolated, beautiful,
taxi-ride home); L'Yret to Le Monêtier
via Vallon de la Montagnolle; Tabuc
(steep at the start, very beautiful). The
experts' Mecca of La Grave is nearby.

FOR INTERMEDIATES
Ski wherever you like
Serre-Chevalier's slopes ideally suit
intermediates, who can buzz around
without worrying about nasty surprises
on the way. On the trail map red runs
far outnumber blues – but most reds

The term 'natural playground' could have quite easily been coined in Serre-Chevalier. The slopes are littered with natural obstacles that seem made for confident snowboarders. Try the Cucumelle slope and the areas around the Rocher Blanc lift at Prorel for such terrain. For beginners and intermediates the many drag-lifts can be a problem, as can the flat areas – one reporter's group stayed mostly in the Chantemerle sector, simply because they could cover a lot of ground using three major chair-lifts. Generation Snow in Chantemerle is a school that offers all sorts of courses from beginners' lessons to advanced freestyle courses.

are at the easy end of the scale and the grooming is usually good, so even nervous intermediates shouldn't have problems with them. The broad, open bowls above Grande Alpe and Fréjus offer lots of options.

There's plenty for more adventurous intermediates, though. Many runs are wide enough for a fast pace. Cucumelle on the edge of the Villeneuve sector is a beautiful long red, away from the lifts. The red runs off the little-used Aiguillette chair in the Chantemerle sector are worth seeking out – quiet, enjoyable fast cruises. Other favourites include Aya and Clos Galliard at Le Monêtier, and the wonderful long run from the top to the bottom of the gondola at Briançon (with great views of the town).

If the reds are starting to seem a bit tame, there is plenty more to progress to. Unless ice towards the bottom is a problem, the (often well-groomed) blacks on the lower mountain should be first on the agenda, and the bumpier ones higher up can be tackled if snow is good.

FOR BEGINNERS
All three areas OK
All three main villages have nursery areas (at Chantemerle the area is

small, and you generally go up to Serre Ratier or Grand Alpe – both rated as good by a beginner reporter) and there are some easy high runs to progress to. Villeneuve has excellent green runs above Fréjus. Both sectors have green paths down from mid mountain which are narrow, and not enjoyable when the runs become hard and others are speeding past. Le Monêtier's easy runs are at resort level, next to excellent nursery slopes, which beginners have recommended for 'better snow and fewer people'. But progression to long runs here isn't so easy, and the link to Villeneuve involves the red Cucumelle run.

FOR CROSS-COUNTRY
Excellent if the snow is good
There are 35km/22 miles of tracks along the valley floor, mainly following the gurgling river between Le Monêtier and Villeneuve and going on up towards the Col du Lautaret.

QUEUES
Investment at last
A range of big lifts means there are few problems getting out of the valley. But the many old, slow lifts at altitude still cause queues, as well as slowing down the whole process of exploration.

Serre-Chevalier

373

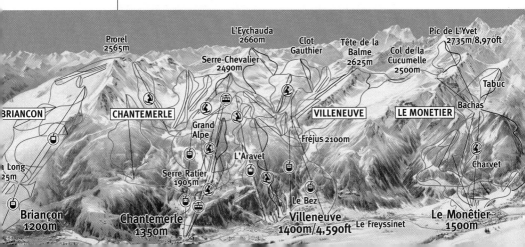

New six-packs have helped and the new one planned at Serre-Ratier for 2007/08 will help further, but more are needed. Bottlenecks include the slow and unreliable Balme chair on the way to Le Monêtier, the Fréjus chair above the Pontillas gondola and the Crète drag-lift it links with. A reader advises avoiding the Bois des Coqs drag-lifts above Chantemerle: 'vicious take-off, some horrid turns, very steep in parts'.

More than most resorts, Serre-Chevalier seems to fill up with French families in the February holidays, producing serious mid-mountain queues, especially in the central sectors – though for one 2006 visitor the queues 'were not as dreadful as we expected in the central sections'.

The lower slopes above Chantemerle, in particular, can get hideously crowded, particularly when snow conditions are poor and progress is therefore slow – head for the Aiguillette chair in these circumstances (see 'For intermediates').

SNOWPIX.COM / CHRIS GILL

The chair-lift from Le Monêtier delivers you to this mid-mountain lift junction, just on the tree line. Le Bachas is one of only two restaurants in this sector ↘

MOUNTAIN RESTAURANTS
Some good places

Mountain restaurants are quite well distributed (and, usefully, marked clearly on the piste map). Strangely, practically all the better ones are in the central sector above Villeneuve.

Editors' choice Just above the Casse du Boeuf quad, the Bivouac de la Casse (0492 248772) is an attractive chalet with both self- and table-service (inside and out). We were mightily impressed by both the food and service last season – even our rejection of a wine was handled superbly. Pi Maï (0492 248363) in the hamlet of Fréjus (so not easy to get to) is a fine retreat on a bad day, with excellent food as well as 'the best hot chocolate in the resort'.

Worth knowing about The Echaillon, just below the Bivouac, is a lofty chalet with open fire and a table-service section doing excellent food. The Fermière, just below the Fréjus chair top station, is 'basic but good value', with lengthy queues for food at times. The Bercail, at the top of the Aravet lift, is a 'good relaxed place'.

In the Chantemerle sector, the busy Soleil pleases reporters – 'good food, sun trap', 'excellent food for good

ESF In all centres
t 0492 241741

Génération Snow
(1350)
t 0492 242151

Evasion (1350)
t 0492 240241

Buissonnière (1400)
t 0492 247866

EurekaSki
t 0679 462484

Axesse (1400)
t 0662 765354

Altitude (1400)
t 0608 025182

Internationale (1500)
t 0683 67062

Classes (ESF prices)
6 half days from €91

Private lessons
From €37 for 1hr

GUIDES

Montagne Aventure
(1350)
t 0492 247440

Bureau des Guides
(1400)
t 0492 247590

Montagne à la carte
(1400)
t 0492 247320

Montagne et Ski
(1500)
t 0492 244681

CHILDREN

Les Schtroumpfs
t 0492 247095
Ages 6mnth upwards;
9am-5pm

Les Poussins
t 0492 240343
Ages 8mnth upwards;
9am-5pm

Les Eterlous
t 0492 244575
Ages 18mnth to 6yr
(6mnth to 6yr out of
school holidays);
9am-5pm

Ski school
Snow gardens for
ages 3 to 5; from age
7 children can join ski
school classes (ESF 6
half-days €93)

prices'. The Relais de Ratier is said to be 'cheaper than elsewhere' and has been praised for 'excellent fresh-cooked food'. The Grand Alpe is spacious, and also 'a bit cheaper than some of the others'.

In the Briançon sector, the 'attractive' Pra Long chalet at the gondola mid-station has good views, and food in both table- and self-service sections is 'excellent'. The little Chalet de Serre Blanc, just down from the top of Prorel, has great views and serves a 'wonderful' house speciality, says a 2007 reporter.

Above Le Monêtier the choice is between the self-service Bachas at mid-mountain ('good value – prices don't seem to have changed in three years') and the cosy, friendly Peyra Juana much lower down. Both get packed on bad-weather days.

SCHOOLS AND GUIDES
Nearly all good
EurekaSki, British-run by BASI instructors, gets consistently good reports. 'We all improved our skiing, some of us dramatically so; we cannot praise them enough,' says a 2007 visitor – returning for a fourth visit to Serre-Che 'so that we can ski with EurekaSki'. Another adds: 'The instruction was excellent; very supportive, but also progressive.' A recent reporter who took two private lessons 'learned more than I have previously in a week'. Classes with a maximum size of six range from beginner to free-ride masterclass. EurekaSki also offer special one-day Avalanche Awareness courses, including training on how to use transceivers and how to choose the safest routes off-piste, as well as some fun off-piste skiing.

We have received a number of reports on the Ecole de Ski

Buissonnière over the years – most of them full of praise ('personal and caring') but with one distressing experience of early-intermediate boarders being put with a couple of experts.

We lack recent reports of group classes with the ESF. 'Children's classes seemed to have two instructors,' observed one February 2006 reporter. But another saw 'tiny kids in groups of 12 to 13 with one instructor'. Private lessons have been praised for 'good, supportive instructors, with a sense of humour'. The Internationale school 'gave the impression of being rather more professional than the ESF', and one reporter saw 'small groups of five to six children maximum'.

We had a great morning skiing off-piste with Bertrand Collet of Axesse ski school and guiding service (which specialises in off-piste and advanced techniques).

FACILITIES FOR CHILDREN
Facilities at each village
The Ecole de Ski Buissonnière has been praised in the past, and Les Schtroumpfs in Villeneuve was in 2006: 'Brilliant, and the baby loved it.'

376

GETTING THERE

Air Turin 108km/
67 miles (1½hr);
Grenoble 92km/
57 miles (2hr); Lyon
208km/129 miles
(3hr)

Rail Briançon (6km/
4 miles); regular
buses from station

SMART LODGINGS

Check out our feature
chapters at the front
of the book.

STAYING THERE

HOW TO GO
A good choice of packages
There's a wide choice of packages from
UK tour operators.
Chalets Several operators offer chalets.
Hannibals' Marmottes is a well
renovated old farmhouse in old
Chantemerle, all en-suite. One visitor
found 'imaginative' food and a 'friendly
team' of staff at Inghams' club hotel
Lièvre Blanc. Chez Bear is a wonderful
conversion of an 18th-century
farmhouse into a luxury chalet for 10 –
remotely set above Briançon, but the
owners will ferry you around.
Hotels One of the features of this
string of little villages is the range of
attractive family-run hotels – many of
them members of Logis de France.
LE MONETIER
***Auberge de Choucas** (0492 244273)
Smart, wood-clad rooms, and
'excellent, seven-course dinners in
stone-vaulted restaurant – but
mediocre breakfast and erratic service'.
Europe (0492 244003) Simple well-
run Logis in heart of old village, with
pleasant bar and 'very good' food.
Recommended again in 2007.
Alliey (0492 244002) 'Excellent
rooms with an indoor/outdoor spa.'
Michelin-star restaurant (see 'Eating
out').
*Rif Blanc** (0492 244135) Good value,
family-run, friendly hotel. Popular bar.
Newly refurbished.
VILLENEUVE
***Christiania** (0492 247633) Civilised,
family-run hotel on main road,
crammed with ornaments.
Vieille Ferme (0492 247644) Stylish
conversion on the edge of the village.
***Cimotel** (0492 247822) Modern and
charmless, with good-sized rooms and
'excellent' food.
*Chatelas** (0492 247474) Prettily
decorated simple chalet by river.

CHANTEMERLE
***Plein Sud** (0492 241701) Modern;
pool, sauna; 'superbly run by a Brit'.
Boule de Neige (0492 240016)
Comfortable, friendly, in the old centre.
'Good food, comfortable and friendly'.
*Ricelle** (0492 240019) Charming, but
across the valley from the slopes in
Villard-Laté. Good food.
Apartments The Hameau du Rocher
Blanche, which MGM has opened by
the slopes in Chantemerle (pool, gym,
jacuzzi, sauna, steam), is a cut above
what was on offer before. A new 4-star
residence is due in Le Monêtier for
2007/08. The hotel Alliey in Le
Monêtier has apartments too.

EATING OUT
Unpretentious and traditional
In Le Monêtier, there are several good
hotel-based options. At the upper end,
the Caves de l'Alliey (hotel Alliey) has
a Michelin star, serves a 'unique' menu
and is 'well worth a meal there'; and
the Auberge du Choucas has a good
reputation. The Europe has reliable
cooking at more modest prices. The
Boîte à Fromages has been
recommended and Brasera is a 'good'
pizzeria. The Kawa and the Belote are
recommended for 'cosy atmosphere,
good staff and excellent value'.
   In Villeneuve the Swedish-run Vieille
Ferme is a 'great, stylish eating place'.
The Frog is 'better than its name
suggests'. The Marotte, a tiny stone
building with classic French cuisine in
the old part of Villeneuve, 'offers a
wide choice of very good food at very
reasonable prices'. The Refuge
specialises in fondue and raclette. And
there are good crêperies – try the
Manouille. Over in Le Bez, the Bidule is
said to have 'first-class food and
service, at good value' and is
recommended by locals. The Ours
Blanc and Passé Simple ('terrific
pizzeria') have been recommended.

PROPERTY DEVELOPMENTS IN SERRE-CHEVALIER

*Briançon is an unusual ski resort – a working town with a proud history – and now it is set to offer
some very unusual ski resort property: the Schappe. The Schappe is an impressive renovation project on
a grand scale. For 90 years, from 1842 to 1932, the building was a working silk mill; its history will
be portrayed in the museum that forms part of the renovation plans (drawn up by an Italian architect
who first studied the Schappe as part of his architectural studies).*

*Plans for the Schappe include approximately 250 apartments – from compact to grand in scale – that
have been designed to maximise the original features of the building, including the exceptionally high
vaulted ceilings and large windows. It is in a central position, close to the lift base. Apartments are
available to purchase through the leaseback scheme or via a traditional freehold acquisition. For more
information go to www.ernalowproperty.co.uk.*

In Chantemerle, the Couch'où is good value. The rustic Ricelle offers 'amazing value'.

APRES-SKI
Quiet streets and few bars
Nightlife seems to revolve around bars, scattered through the various villages, and several reporters complain that the resort is too quiet.

In Le Monêtier the British-run Alpen has a happy hour, free nibbles and welcoming staff; the bar at the hotel Rif Blanc is said to be as popular, and the Que Tal warms up later on. In Villeneuve, Loco Loco in the old village was reportedly 'the place to go, with funky music and a French atmosphere'; but a recent visitor took a dim view, reporting 'tedious music and high prices'. The Frog has 'good local beer' and the Grotte is 'very lively and enjoyable' and for 'serious fun seekers'. In Chantemerle the Kitzbühel shows sporting events on TV and 'does good pizzas'. The other Chantemerle bars to look out for are the Taverne de la Biere, the X'treme bar and the Triptyque ('popular and trendy').

In Briançon, the Auberge Mont Prorel, right by the gondola base, had live music and was full of Brits and Danes rounding off their day when we paid a tea-time visit.

OFF THE SLOPES
Try the hot baths
Serre-Chevalier doesn't hold many attractions for non-slope-users, and it's certainly not for avid shoppers, but the old town of Briançon is well worth a visit. There is a leisure complex with pools, sauna, hot-tub and steam room. Briançon also has an ice hockey team – their games make 'a good night out', says one reporter. The thermal bath in Le Monêtier has been redeveloped into a large spa complex, Les Grands Bains, and is expected to reopen for 2007/08. There is a public swimming pool and health spa near the hotel Sporting in Villeneuve. Each of the main villages has a cinema. Chantemerle and Villeneuve have ice rinks, and there is good walking on 'well-prepared trails'.

STAYING UP THE MOUNTAIN
Worth considering
Pi Maï (0492 248363) above Villeneuve (see 'Mountain restaurants') and the chalet-hotel Serre-Ratier (0492 205288) above Chantemerle have rooms.

Ste-Foy-Tarentaise

*Tasteful, modern mini-resort appealing to families and experts –
and to motorists as a base for expeditions to nearby mega-resorts*

RATINGS

The slopes

Fast lifts	**
Snow	***
Extent	*
Expert	****
Intermediate	***
Beginner	**
Convenience	***
Queues	*****
Mountain restaurants	**

The rest

Scenery	***
Resort charm	***
Off-slope	*

NEWS

For 2007/08 snowmaking is due to be increased at resort level.

Work will continue on developing the resort, with the second phase focusing on La Bataillettaz. New apartments, Le Ruitor, with pool, sauna, gym and a restaurant are due to open in October 2007.

For 2006/07, a fast six-pack was added on the upper slopes to the east of the resort's main lifts.

378

+	No crowds	−	Too quiet for many other visitors
+	Safe untracked powder within the lift system, and epic runs outside it	−	Very limited piste network
+	Cheap lift pass and good-value lodging	−	Mainly slow chair-lifts
+	Val d'Isère and Les Arcs nearby	−	Lack of good long green runs on the higher slopes
+	Quiet, good for families, but ...	−	Inadequate mountain restaurants

Ste-Foy started life in 1990 and quickly became a cult off-piste mountain. Since then, a mini-village of chalets and chalet-style apartments has grown up at the lift base, and the mountain has been made more appealing to non-experts. But the resort still constitutes a rather radical choice, making most sense for those prepared to make expeditions to the big resorts nearby, preferably by car.

THE RESORT

Ste-Foy itself is a village straddling the busy road up from Bourg-St-Maurice to Val d'Isère. Its skiing starts at Ste-Foy-Station (sometimes called Bonconseil), set 4km/2.5 miles off the main road up to Val d'Isère. Ste-Foy-Station is a complete resort in miniature, with a limited choice of bars, restaurants and ski shops, a small supermarket and now a newsagent; these are surrounded by a growing cluster of chalets and chalet-style apartment blocks, all in the traditional Savoyard style of wood and stone.

Although the place is small, it is effectively divided in two by the main chair-lift and home piste. To skier's left is the main little complex of facilities,

above the original nursery slope. To skier's right is the newer part, with the Balcons de Ste-Foy apartments plus spa, the newsagent, ESF office and smart Bergerie restaurant. It doesn't much matter which side you stay.

You can also stay down the hill in Ste-Foy village or other local hamlets; there are free buses, but they aren't very frequent. With a car you can make the most of some excellent nearby restaurants and explore other nearby resorts – Val d'Isère, Tignes, Les Arcs (via Villaroger), La Plagne and La Rosière – are all within easy reach. There is a twice-weekly bus service to Tignes. You are entitled to a day at each of these resorts for around 22 euros a time on presentation of a Ste-Foy six-day pass.

KEY FACTS

Resort		1550m
		5,090ft
Slopes		1550-2620m
		5,090-8,600ft
Lifts		5
Pistes		35km
		22 miles
Green		6%
Blue		24%
Red		47%
Black		23%
Snowmaking		Minimal

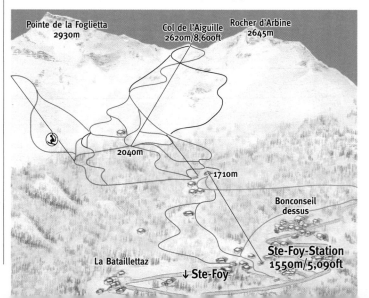

Pointe de la Foglietta
2930m

Col de l'Aiguille
2620m/8,600ft

Rocher d'Arbine
2645m

2040m

1710m

Bonconseil
dessus

La Bataillettaz

↓ Ste-Foy

**Ste-Foy-Station
1550m/5,090ft**

OT STE-FOY-TARENTAISE / A ROYER

Acres of powder below and virtually no one on the top chair-lift ↓

THE MOUNTAIN

There is an attractive mix of wooded slopes above the village and open slopes higher up.

Slopes The slow quad from the village takes you up to a tiny mid-mountain station at Plan Bois. A second goes on to the tree line, and a third to Col de l'Aiguille accesses almost 600m/1,970ft of vertical above the tree line. The two black runs from this chair form the basis of two special off-piste zones; the piste map shows these but does not explain them – we're told they are avalanche controlled. Slightly further down the hill is another such zone, less steep. The two lower chairs serve a few pleasant runs through trees and back to the base station. A six-pack opened to the east of the main area last season, and the runs out here are still developing. Most reporters have been amazed by the terrain the few lifts access: 'The map gives no indication of the variety of options available,' said one. But don't expect miles of groomed pistes.

Terrain-parks There is not an official terrain-park, but in one of the three patrolled off-piste areas mentioned

above you are encouraged to build your own features.

Snow reliability The slopes face north or west. Snow reliability is good on the former but can suffer on the latter, especially as there is snowmaking only on the run down to the resort. Snowmaking is due to increase at resort level for 2007/08, with more planned for the following season.

Experts Experts can have great fun on and between Ste-Foy's black and red runs, exploring lots of easily accessible off-piste and trees in the broad bowl, including the special zones mentioned above. The lack of crowds means you can still make fresh tracks days after a storm. There's more serious off-piste on offer too, for which you need a guide. There are wonderful runs from the top of the lifts down through deserted old villages, either to the road up to Val d'Isère or back to the base, and a splendid route from the Pointe de la Foglietta, which takes you through trees and over a stream down to the tiny village of Le Crot. The new six-pack has made this route more accessible; previously it involved a hike up to the Pointe de la Foglietta. The ESF runs group off-piste trips, with

Ste-Foy-Tarentaise

Phone numbers
From abroad use the prefix +33 and omit the initial '0' of the phone number

TOURIST OFFICE

t 0479 069519
info@saintefoy.net
www.saintefoy.net

OT STE-FOY-TARENTAISE / A ROYER

Everything is carefully designed in traditional chalet style, with lots of wood and stone finishes ↓

transport back to base. There's also a Bureau des Guides, which can arrange heli-skiing in Italy.

Intermediates Intermediates can enjoy 900m/2,950ft vertical of uncrowded reds and blues on the upper mountain, and worthwhile descents to the village when conditions are good. The red from the Col de l'Aiguille is a superb test for confident intermediates, who would also be up to the off-piste routes, especially the Monal route back to base. Anyone who doesn't fancy trying off-piste will tire of the limited runs in a day or two and be itching to get to Val d'Isère or Les Arcs.

Beginners Not the best place, but there have been improvements at the base, including a children's area near the ski school, and a moving carpet lift on the small nursery slope. After that you can progress to a long green run off the first chair and then gentle blues higher up – and the slopes are pleasantly quiet.

Snowboarding Great free-riding terrain, with lots of trees and powder between the pistes to play in, plus dedicated freestyle areas for building kickers.

Cross-country No prepared trails, but ask the tourist office about marked itinerary routes such as Planay Dessus.

Queues Except in peak season and on fresh powder days, despite all the new building and slow lifts, reporters have still failed to find queues at Ste-Foy.

Mountain restaurants There are two rustic restaurants at Plan Bois; they are tiny, and even with few people on the mountain get over-busy. Les Brevettes ('friendly and lively', 'good omelettes') has the edge over Chez Léon. In the

village, the Maison à Colonnes gets consistently good reports.

Schools and guides We've had good reports of ski school, especially for children (from age four).

Facilities for children Children under seven ski free. There is a nursery, Les P'tits Trappeurs, which takes children from age three to 11. The UK tour operator Première Neige also runs a nursery (its own guests take priority).

STAYING THERE

How to go Various small tour operators can organise chalets and hotels here.

Hotels We continue to get glowing reports of Auberge sur la Montagne (0479 069583), just above the turn-off at La Thuile. For a more French experience try the Ferme du Baptieu (0479 069752). Hotel Monal (0479 069007), in Ste-Foy village, is a basic 2-star, with a games room, bar and two restaurants.

Chalets and apartments Gîte de Ste Foy Station and Première Neige both have several chalets and apartments here, with catered and self-catered options. Première Neige has acquired the Yellowstone chalet and refurbished it to offer luxury rooms and spa facilities. Les Fermes de Ste-Foy is an impressive series of large chalets, containing 70 bright apartments, with shared private pool. 2006 reporters recommend 'great views and food' at Chalet Chevalier in the hamlet of Planay-Dessous.

Eating out In Ste-Foy-Station the central Bergerie is traditionally styled in wood and stone and does excellent food. Meals can be delivered to your apartment. The Maison à Colonnes is 'simple and good'. Chez Alison offers simple fare. In the village of Le Miroir, Chez Mérie is excellent (for lunch as well as dinner). So is the Auberge sur la Montagne. In Ste-Foy village, the Grange at the hotel Monal reportedly does 'good food'.

Après-ski Pretty quiet. Reporters enjoyed the Iceberg piano bar. The Pitchouli is the place to go for a drink later on. It has table football and sometimes plays live music. The bar of the hotel Monal can get busy, too.

Off the slopes There's not a lot to do off the slopes, but paragliding, dog-sledding and snow-shoeing are available. The excellent pool and spa at the Balcons de Ste-Foy apartments are open to non-residents for a fee.

St-Martin-de-Belleville

Explore the Three Valleys from a traditional old village – and so avoid the Méribel crowds who descend on it for lunch

COSTS

① ② ③ ④ ⑤ ⑥

RATINGS

The slopes

Fast lifts	***
Snow	***
Extent	*****
Expert	****
Intermediate	*****
Beginner	**
Convenience	***
Queues	****
Mountain restaurants	****

The rest

Scenery	***
Resort charm	****
Off-slope	*

KEY FACTS

Resort	1400m
	4,590ft

Three Valleys	
Slopes	1260-3230m
	4,130-10,600ft
Lifts	183
Pistes	600km
	373 miles
Green	15%
Blue	38%
Red	37%
Black	10%
Snowmaking	
	1920 guns

Les Menuires / St-Martin only	
Slopes	1400-2850m
	4,590-9,350ft
Lifts	38
Pistes	160km
	99 miles
Green	8%
Blue	42%
Red	40%
Black	10%
Snowmaking	
	405 guns

➕ Attractively developed traditional village with pretty church

➕ Easy access to the whole of the extensive Three Valleys network

➕ Long, easy intermediate runs on rolling local slopes

➕ Extensive snowmaking keeps local runs open in poor conditions, but ...

➖ Snow at resort level suffers from altitude, and sun in the afternoon

➖ No green runs for beginners to progress to

➖ The climb up from the lower part of the village can be taxing

➖ Limited après-ski

➖ Few off-slope diversions

St-Martin is a lived-in, unspoiled village with an old church (prettily lit at night), small square and buildings of wood and stone, a few miles down the valley from Les Menuires. As a quiet, inexpensive, attractive base for exploration of the Three Valleys as a whole, it's unbeatable.

THE RESORT

In 1950 St-Martin didn't even have running water or electricity. It remained a backwater until the 1980s, when chair-lifts were built linking it to the slopes of Méribel and Les Menuires. The old village, set on a steep slope, has been developed, of course, but the new buildings fit in well, and it remains small – you can walk around it in a few minutes. The main feature remains the lovely old 16th-century church – prettily floodlit at night. There are some good local shops and few 'touristy' ones. A regular visitor was pleased to report how 'unobtrusive' the newish gondola station is.

THE MOUNTAINS

The whole of the Three Valleys can easily be explored from here.
Slopes A gondola followed by a fast quad take you to a ridge from which you can access Méribel on one side and Les Menuires on the other.
Terrain-parks There isn't a terrain-park in the St-Martin sector, but you can get to those above Les Menuires and Méribel relatively easily.
Snow reliability The local slopes face west and get the full force of the afternoon sun, and the village is quite low. There is snowmaking from top to bottom of the main run to the village, and reporters agree that it is impressively effective at keeping the run open, but higher runs (eg Verdet) are less secure. Many people ride the gondola down if snow is poor. A recent

visitor found piste marking 'erratic' Another has said, 'In poor visibility it is quite easy to go off-piste unintentionally.

Experts Locally there are large areas of gentle and often deserted off-piste. A reader recommends the descent from Roc de Fer to the village of Béranger. Head to La Masse for steep north-facing slopes.
Intermediates The local slopes are pleasant blues and reds, mainly of interest to intermediates – including one of our favourite runs in the Three Valleys: the long, rolling, wide Jerusalem red. The Verdet blue from the top of the Méribel lifts is a

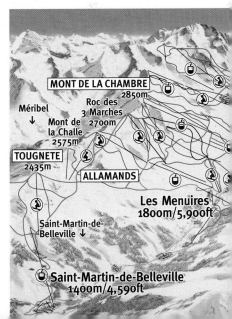

MONT DE LA CHAMBRE 2850m

Méribel
↓
Roc des 3 Marches
Mont de la Challe 2700m
2575m

TOUGNETE 2435m

ALLAMANDS

Les Menuires 1800m/5,900ft

Saint-Martin-de-Belleville ↓

🅿 **Saint-Martin-de-Belleville** 1400m/4,590ft

FRANCE

382

wonderful easy cruise with great views and is usually very quiet.

Beginners St-Martin is far from ideal – there's a small nursery slope but no long green runs to progress to.

Snowboarding There is some great local off-piste free-riding available.

Cross-country There are 28km/17 miles of trails in the Belleville valley.

Queues Queues are not usually much of a problem outside peak periods, but St-Martin's popularity as a lunch destination leads to 'often massive queues in the afternoon' for the chair to Tougnète.

Mountain restaurants There are three atmospheric old places on the run down to the village: Chardon Bleu ('good, not too expensive') and Corbeleys near the mid-mountain lift junction and the Loy, lower down ('great food and atmosphere – never disappoints'). The Grand Lac at the bottom of the Granges chair is a favourite of a 2007 reporter ('good food and friendly service at cheap prices'). St-Martin itself is a major lunch destination. For a real treat, La Bouitte in nearby St-Marcel is one of the best restaurants in the Three Valleys (see 'Eating out') – you ski to it off-piste, and the owners will ferry you to a lift afterwards.

Schools and guides A 2007 reporter went on an ESF guided group, which he highly recommends. Reports on ESF lessons are generally positive, though one reporter said the instructor was 'good at analysing faults but not so good at teaching how to improve'.

Facilities for children The Piou Piou club at the ESF takes children from age two-and-a-half from 9am to 5pm.

STAYING THERE

How to go For a small village there's a good variety of accommodation.

Hotels The Alp Hôtel (0479 089282) is at the foot of the slope by the main lift. A recent visitor was 'made to feel very welcome' by the owners of the 'charming' Saint-Martin (0479 008800), right on the slope, and the Edelweiss (0479 089667) is in the village itself. All are 3-stars. La Bouitte (0479 089677) in St-Marcel (see 'Eating out') has three lovely rooms – spacious, woody and furnished with antiques – and two suites plus an 'absolutely fabulous' new spa with various treatments open to the public.

Chalets Les Chalets de St Martin has operated here ever since the first lift was built – 'I'd recommend them,' says a recent visitor. The Alpine Club – which isn't really a club – now has two chalets and is run by a British couple. Its Ferme de Belleville is a nicely renovated 400-year-old farmhouse in the heart of the old village and its Maison de Belleville, overlooking the village, is newly built, spacious, light and airy. They run a minibus to and from the gondola. We've had good reports of their service and have enjoyed a stay and dinner at the Ferme ourselves.

Apartments The stylish new CGH/MGM development Les Chalets du Gypse is well placed beside the piste, with a smart pool. Les Chalets de St Martin has a variety of self-catered chalets and apartments.

Eating out For such a small village there is a good variety of restaurants. Readers still enjoy the Montagnard's

St-Martin's new buildings fit in well with the old village and its 16th-century church ➜

383

'very good atmosphere' and 'fabulous' Savoyard food. The Voûte was recommended again in 2007 as 'the best all-rounder' by a St-Martin regular. The Lachenal is said to do 'good mid-priced food', and the Grenier in the hotel St-Martin is 'good quality with excellent presentation', but some 2007 visitors were disappointed with both of these. La Ferme Choumette, slightly out of the village, opened last season and does 'excellent food at reasonable prices (with aromas from the goats, cows and sheep you can see through a viewing window)'.

The Etoile des Neiges is a smart, traditionally French restaurant, and a 2007 reporter was delighted to find it 'has finally changed its fixed price evening menus after five years. It was a pleasant meal in nice surroundings with good service, but the food is nowhere near the class of La Bouitte'.

La Bouitte is just up the road in the next village, St-Marcel, and boasts a

Michelin star. We have had several superb meals here and the same reporter had 'a highly original and varied meal' for Christmas lunch there. **Après-ski** The Pourquoi Pas? is cosy and lively with a roaring log fire, comfortable easy chairs and sofas, 'friendly staff' and 'a large British clientele'. Brewski's was under temporary new management last season and reporters say that standards fell as a result. You may find the Eterlou a 'much better place to gather at the end of the day', but not if you are a non-smoker apparently. The Dalhia, at the bottom of the gondola, 'makes a good rendezvous'. **Off the slopes** If you don't use the slopes, there are better places to base yourself. However, a recent visitor found the tourist office very helpful in arranging dog-sledding and cross-country skiing excursions. There are also pleasant walks, a sports hall, and musical events in the church.

Les Sybelles

Chalk-and-cheese resorts linked rather tenuously by slow lifts to form an area that's one of the biggest in the Alps

+ Extensive area of largely easy intermediate slopes and gentle, uncrowded off-piste

+ Inexpensive by French standards

+ Unusual mixture of stark, purpose-built resorts and old villages

− Lift network still painfully slow to get around, despite improvements

− Few pistes steep enough to interest adventurous intermediates

− Après-ski limited and quiet

− Mainly simple accommodation

− Few off-slope diversions

Les Sybelles is not a resort but a lift network linking a handful of little-known resorts in the Maurienne massif in the French Alps. When formed in 2003, Les Sybelles' 310km/193 miles of pistes put it straight into the big league, alongside such giants as Val d'Isère-Tignes.

Our first visit to the newly launched Les Sybelles gave us a bit of a shock; we had forgotten just how slow progress can be on a mountain with 70 slow lifts and just one fast one. Matters have since improved – four more fast chairs for 2004/05, one for 2005/06 and one more planned for this year. But Les Sybelles still languishes at the bottom of our fast-lift league table, with only one fast lift in ten. And installation of fast lifts out of the big resorts without similar improvements at altitude seems sure to create queue problems in peak season for the drag-lifts that form the links. So we still say: more six-packs, please.

The resorts are sharply contrasting in character. La Toussuire and Le Corbier are most politely described as modern, functional and downmarket, while St-Sorlin-d'Arves and St-Jean-d'Arves are largely unspoiled, traditional villages that have recently expanded tastefully and attracted some major UK tour operators.

The links between the resorts are high – mostly between 2000m and 2600m (6,560ft and 8,530ft) – so they are relatively snow-sure. They are also easily negotiated by adventurous intermediates, consisting of easy reds and tough blues (one or two of which might be better classified red). But getting from one resort to another can be slow going, because of slow lifts.

Visitors to St-Jean and St-Sorlin warn that the long road up from the valley is seriously worrying – winding, narrow in places, with precipitous drops often without barriers, all compounded by a poor surface.

LE CORBIER 1550m/5,090ft

Le Corbier is centrally placed, with direct links to St-Jean-d'Arves in one direction and La Toussuire in the other, as well as a high link to St-Sorlin.

THE RESORT

Designed in the 1960s, Le Corbier is a no-compromise functional resort. Most of its accommodation is in eight inner-city-style tower blocks – one as high as

19 storeys – with subterranean shops beneath. To our eye, it looks like a blot on the landscape. But it does accommodate its 9,000 visitors efficiently in the minimum space, and in functional terms it is hard to criticise – it is compact, family-friendly and traffic-free with all ski-in/ski-out accommodation. The apartment blocks line the foot of the slopes, and in the other direction the resort's balcony setting gives good views over the valley. It sells itself firmly as a family resort and runs a French Family Championship with teams made up of mother, father and one child. And new building is now in traditional style.

THE MOUNTAIN

Le Corbier's local ski area has 90km/56 miles of gentle pistes. Although the altitudes are modest (top height 2265m/7,430ft, resort 1550m/5,090ft), there are hardly any trees.

Slopes The Sybelles Express, a six-seat fast chair, rises over 700m/2,300ft vertical to Pte du Corbier, from where pistes and lifts go along the ridge to

KEY FACTS

Slopes	1100-2620m
	3,610-8,600ft
Lifts	71
Pistes	310km
	193 miles
Green	21%
Blue	39%
Red	35%
Black	5%
Snowmaking	
	233 guns

the hub of Les Sybelles at Pte de L'Ouillon. Runs spread across a wide, north-east-facing mountainside return to the resort, and there are links at the extremities to La Toussuire and St-Jean-d'Arves.

Terrain-park There's a park on the lower slopes just above the resort.

Snow reliability The mix of reasonable altitude and lack of crowds cutting up the pistes means the snow tends to stay in fairly good condition. The slopes get the morning sun, but there is snowmaking on all the main pistes back to the resort. The low connection from La Toussuire is a problem spot.

Experts The area lacks challenges – the one short black piste scarcely deserves a red grading. There are off-piste options in the valley between Le Corbier and La Toussuire.

Intermediates Le Corbier's gentle slopes are ideal cruising terrain, though the runs aren't very long and they rather lack variety.

Beginners There is an extensive nursery area with a moving carpet right in front of the resort, with gentle progression runs directly above.

Snowboarding The wide, open terrain is ideal for riders, as long as they don't want anything too challenging.

Cross-country There are narrow loops across the mountainside either side of the resort, one of which leads to La Toussuire and back. It's all a bit bleak.

Queues We have no reports of problems, but see introduction.

Mountain restaurants A past reporter says Le Charmun, at the foot of the Vadrouille area, 'was the restaurant of the week for us, with delicious crozets with wild mushrooms and lardons' and Chalet 2000 near the top was 'notable for its playful golden labrador as well as its welcome and food'.

Schools Our one past reporter judged the ESF 'disdainful, uncaring, very disorganised; bad tuition'.

Facilities for children The Nursery takes children from six months. A reporter praised the ski kindergarten (for age three up): 'Nice, well-equipped ski-park; good instructors.' Its location up on the pistes means a bit of a hike.

STAYING THERE

How to go There are several UK operators selling packages here.

Chalets Equity Ski runs its own chalet hotel, described by one reporter as 'clean, comfortable and very good value' and approved by others, too.

Hotels None in resort.

Apartments Nearly all the accommodation here is in apartments. There's a central reservations system.

Eating out Le Grillon, 3km/2 miles away in the Villarembert, makes a pleasant, rustic change from Le Corbier's tower blocks – and serves traditional French food.

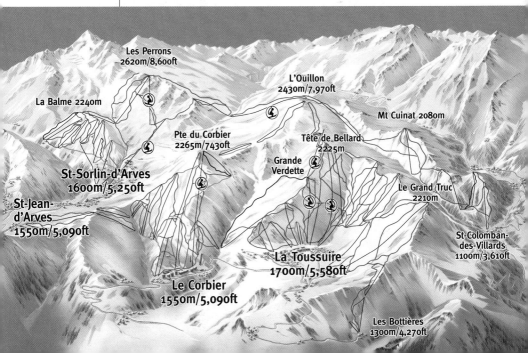

Les Perrons 2620m/8,600ft

L'Ouillon 2430m/7,970ft

La Balme 2240m

Mt Cuinat 2080m

Pte du Corbier 2265m/7430ft

Tête de Bellard 2225m

Grande Verdette

Le Grand Truc 2210m

St-Sorlin-d'Arves 1600m/5,250ft

St-Jean-d'Arves 1550m/5,090ft

St-Colomban-des-Villards 1100m/3,610ft

La Toussuire 1700m/5,580ft

Le Corbier 1550m/5,090ft

Les Bottières 1300m/4,270ft

↑ The new chalet development at La Chal above St-Jean-d'Arves looks good; but it's not a good base if you want to explore the whole Les Sybelles area

OT ST-JEAN-D'ARVES

Après ski Very quiet. The Equity Ski chalet-hotel bar is popular. Roches Blanches restaurant in the centre includes a cosy bar area with an open fire. For dancing, the Président gets busy only at peak holiday periods.

Off the slopes There's a nice natural ice rink and a fitness centre. The outdoor pool is open, and you can go snowmobiling, dog-sledding and snow-shoeing.

LA TOUSSUIRE 1700m/5,580ft
La Toussuire, along with Le Corbier, is one of the central resorts of the new network – the two have been linked at low altitude since 1986. It makes a convenient base with good local intermediate slopes and three fast lifts which give reasonably quick access to the hub of Les Sybelles at Pte de L'Ouillon.

THE RESORT
La Toussuire has grown up over many years but is predominantly modern, with a car-free and snow-covered main street lined by dreary-looking buildings dating from the 1960s and 1970s and plagued when we were there by piped music from loudspeakers. The resort has now spread widely from here, with wooden chalets as well as older hotels and small apartment blocks scattered across the mountainside.

THE MOUNTAIN
The local slopes amount to 45km/ 28 miles of pistes.

Slopes The resort sits in the pit of a wide bowl. Drags and chair-lifts (including three six-packs from 2007/08) rise just over 500m/1,640ft vertical to the high point of Tête de Ballard and the link to L'Ouillon. At one end of the bowl is the low-level link to Le Corbier and at the other the start of a long red run of 900m/2,950ft vertical to the hamlet of Les Bottières.
Terrain-park There's a boarder-cross course in the centre of the bowl.
Snow reliability With every run above 1800m/5,910ft snow-cover is fairly assured, but some of the slopes are rather exposed to the sun – particularly the low-level connection to Le Corbier.
Experts There are few challenges here, and not much space left between the pistes. The main interest is the ungroomed black Vallée Perdue run, which descends the valley separating La Toussuire from Le Corbier, away from the lifts. But it gets a lot of sun, and snow conditions can suffer. The link lifts towards L'Ouillon open up off-piste routes down this valley.
Intermediates This is ideal terrain for cruisers who don't mind mainly short runs. The longer run that goes down to Les Bottières is one of the most appealing in the whole area.
Beginners There are nice, gentle nursery slopes immediately above the centre of the village, and good, easy progression slopes.
Snowboarding There are quite a few drag-lifts in the area.
Cross-country A narrow loop goes to

Le Corbier, but it is in bleak surroundings and close to the road. There are also loops on the lower slopes of Le Grand Truc. There's 15km/9 miles in total.

Queues We have no reports of problems, but see introduction.

Mountain restaurants The Foehn at Le Marolay has been recommended for its 'friendly service', 'stunning views' and interesting interior of old photos, carvings, etc. A recent reporter says: 'The staff were even nice to our kids!' The Cigales, near the foot of the bowl, reportedly had 'good basic food and was friendly'. Another reader enjoyed the 'fantastic setting' and 'great vin chaud' of the refuge on the Bouyans blue run down to St-Colomban.

Schools A lack of English-speaking tuition can be a problem, as confirmed by a recent visitor with children. However, he also 'had a fantastic time in the ESF advanced adult class with a great bilingual teacher'.

Facilities for children The nursery accepts children from three to six. Language may be a problem.

STAYING THERE

How to go A few UK tour operators serve the resort.

Hotels There are several small 3-star and 2-star places. The 3-star Ruade (0479 830179) and Soldanelles (0479 567529) both have pools and saunas.

Apartments Les Hauts de Comborciere is new for 2007/08, with pool, sauna, steam, hot-tub. Chalet Goélia has been recommended. The Ecrins chalets are large 3-star apartments. Most others are cheap and not so cheerful.

Eating out The options are mostly inexpensive pizzerias and bar-restaurants.

Après-ski Fairly dire. There are a few bars, including the Tonneau. The Alpen Rock nightclub can get busy at peak French holiday time.

Off the slopes There's a reasonable amount to do, including snow-shoeing, snowmobiling, dog-sledding, skating on a ' very seedy' rink on the roof of a building in the main street, and hang-gliding.

ST-SORLIN-D'ARVES 1600m/5,250ft

St-Sorlin's major advantages are that it is based on a traditional village and that it has the most interesting slopes in the area for good intermediates – the slopes on Les Perrons, reached by two fast quads.

THE RESORT

St-Sorlin-d'Arves is a real, medium-sized village with a year-round life outside skiing. It's a picturesque collection of well-preserved traditional farmhouses, with a baroque church and long-established shops – fromagerie, boulangerie, crafts, etc – alongside more modern resort development. Its setting on a narrow shelf gives fine views but doesn't allow much room for expansion, so the village has grown in a ribbon-like fashion along the main road – not ideal for strolling around. Visitors have various complaints about the 'crowded and disorganised' bus services.

THE MOUNTAIN

St-Sorlin's local slopes form the biggest single sector of the linked network, with 120km/75 miles of piste. Although very much an intermediate mountain, it does offer much more variety, including some steeper options, than the rest of the area.

Slopes There are two distinct sections. The lower, gentler left side on La Balme, reached by a choice of slow chairs from the village, is crammed with lots of short, easy runs. The higher, right side on Les Perrons, reached by two successive fast six-packs, has long, sweeping, generally steeper pistes. The Vallons run off the back of Les Perrons (which forms the first part of the link to L'Ouillon and from there to the other resorts) and the runs from Petit Perron have added a lot of interest to the local skiing.

Terrain-park There is one on La Balme, accessed by a chair-lift.

Snow reliability Not bad. Les Perrons slopes are the highest in the area and the main runs back to the village are covered by snowmakers.

Experts There isn't much on-piste challenge, but Les Perrons has the best off-piste in the whole area; the slopes beneath the newish Petit Perron chair look interesting.

Intermediates The long top-to-bottom reds on both sides of Les Perrons are the best pistes in the whole area. There is only one on the back and a couple on the front, but they have the whole mountain to themselves, giving a great away-from-it-all feel. La Balme has shorter, more leisurely runs.

Beginners The nursery slope is right by the village, and there are plenty of slopes to progress to on La Balme.

Snowboarding The terrain suits

Phone numbers
From abroad use the prefix +33 and omit the initial '0' of the phone number

TOURIST OFFICES

t 0479 598800
info@les-sybelles.com
www.les-sybelles.com
La Toussuire
t 0479 830606
info@la-toussuire.com
www.la-toussuire.com
Le Corbier
t 0479 830404
info@le-corbier.com
www.le-corbier.com
St-Sorlin-d'Arves
t 0479 597177
info@saintsorlin
darves.com
www.saintsorlindarves.
com
St-Jean-d'Arves
t 0479 597330
info@saintjeandarves.
com
www.saintjeandarves.
com
**St-Colomban-des-
Villards**
t 0479 562453
villards@wanadoo.fr
www.saint-colomban.
com
Les Bottières
t 0479 832709
info@bottieres-
jarrier.com
www.bottieres-
jarrier.com

beginners and intermediates but there are a lot of drag-lifts. Freeriders will enjoy the quiet off-piste slopes.

Cross-country There's a narrow 16km/ 10 mile loop along a side valley past the foot of La Balme's Alpine area, with good views of the Aiguilles d'Arves.

Queues 'Some lifts are queue-prone in the morning,' says a 2007 reporter.

Mountain restaurants We enjoyed lunch and stunning views of the Aiguilles d'Arves on the sunny terrace of the rustic Bergerie at the top of the Plan Moulin chair at La Balme – endorsed by a 2007 visitor.

Schools A 2007 reporter whose children took ESF classes said: 'Almost no feedback from their teacher, classes a bit too big and poor English.'

Facilities for children The Petits Diables nursery accepts children from three months; a 2007 reporter said, 'It was poor; good English spoken but made no effort to be welcoming. We left after two days.' The ski kindergarten accepts kids from three-and-a-half years. Language can be a problem.

STAYING THERE

How to go Some major UK tour operators now offer holidays here.

Hotels Only two (both 2-star and both attractive chalets): the Beausoleil (0479 597142) and Balme (0479 597021).

Apartments There are scores of small properties (and the Grignotte bakery sells 'the best bread ever encountered in the Alps', says one reporter).

Eating out The choice is limited to cheap and cheerful pizzerias and raclette/fondue places. The Table de Marie, Gargoulette ('friendly, decent food, but frenetic and disorganised service'), Petit Ferme ('hearty portions of lasagne') and pizza and pasta above the Avalanche bar have been recommended.

Après-ski St-Sorlin-d'Arves is even quieter than the other major resorts. A past reporter said: 'The Avalanche bar was lively with a student-age clientele and the Godille was more frequented by locals but essentially dead. We did not think the guide's warning that there isn't much nightlife or many bars would matter to us oldies, but in practice it did.' But a 2007 reporter said there's now a 'noisy, late bar called the Yeti' and last season the new D'sybell nightclub opened.

Off the slopes There is not much to do.

Dog-sledding and snow-shoeing are options, but it's fairly tame territory.

ST-JEAN-D'ARVES 1550m/5,090ft
Although small, St-Jean-d'Arves is quite a scattered community with 'friendly locals'. The original old village, with the usual ancient church, is set across the valley from the slopes, which are at the mid-mountain hamlet of La Chal. Here, where a tasteful development of chalet-style buildings is still expanding, there are nursery slopes and the lift link to and piste back from Le Corbier.

St-Jean/La Chal is not a good base for anyone wanting to exploit the larger area – and that will include most energetic beginners as well as intermediates. The slow chair-lift towards Le Corbier 'is painful' and 'enough to make you cry every morning', say reporters. The return slopes are excessively sunny – bare and rocky when we visited; snowmaking may have improved matters, but a cure is unlikely. Usually it will be better to take the shuttle-bus to St-Sorlin to use its fast lifts.

Off-slope diversions are few – dog-sledding, cheese farm visits, snow-shoeing. Plenty of open slopes for tobogganing. Après-ski is basic, with a few bars, an Irish pub, night-tobogganing with music, and a cinema. The Marmottes and the Fontaine du Roi apartments are about the best self-catering options in the whole area – which is not saying much.

ST-COLOMBAN-DES-VILLARDS
1100m/3,610ft
St-Colomban-des-Villards is a tiny old village in the next valley to La Toussuire, only a few miles up from the Maurienne valley.

In recent years it has developed a chain of drags and chair-lifts on north- and east-facing slopes to the south of the village, with a high point at Mt Cuinat, and is now linked to L'Ouillon, at the hub of Les Sybelles. The run down is reportedly 'interesting and attractive', but the return lifts take an hour. A battery of snowmakers keeps the home slope open.

LES BOTTIERES 1300m/4,270ft
Down the mountain from La Toussuire, this tiny hamlet offers little infrastructure and extremely indirect access to the main network – it takes three lifts to get over to La Toussuire, before setting off for L'Ouillon.

JM GOUÉDARD

La Tania

A very attractive budget base for the limitless slopes of Courchevel and Méribel – and not bad looking, for a purpose-built resort

NEWS

The much-needed new green piste, Plan Fontaine – running the length of the gondola to the village – opened for 2005/06. It was improved for last winter, making it a true green all the way down.

The Farçon restaurant now has a Michelin star.

For 2007/08, a new snowmaking reservoir was built.

➕ Part of the Three Valleys – the world's biggest linked ski area

➕ Quick access to the slopes of Courchevel and Méribel

➕ Long, rolling, intermediate runs through woods back to the village

➕ New green run above the village means it's now more attractive for beginners and timid intermediates

➕ Greatly improved snowmaking

➕ Attractive, small, traffic-free village

➖ Small development with little choice of après-ski – and no doctor or pharmacy

➖ Main nursery slope is part of the blue run to the village, and gets a lot of through-traffic

➖ Some accommodation is a long walk from the centre and the main lifts

La Tania does not try to compete with its more upmarket neighbours, Courchevel and Méribel. But it has carved out its own niche as a good-value, small, quiet, family-friendly base from which to hit the slopes of both neighbouring valleys. Trips to the furthest corners of the immense Three Valleys are certainly possible, but they take a little more time than from better-placed starting points.

It is a second-generation purpose-built resort, and at 1350m/4,430ft about the lowest you'll find; its wood-clad buildings sit comfortably in a pretty woodland setting – quite a contrast to classic French ski stations like Les Menuires.

THE RESORT

La Tania is set just off the minor road linking Le Praz (Courchevel 1300) to Méribel. It has grown into a quiet, attractive, car-free collection of mainly ski-in/ski-out chalets and apartments set among the trees, most with good views. There are few shops other than food and sports shops and you can

walk around it in a couple of minutes. It does have a few bars and restaurants, but 2007 reporters weren't impressed with the après-ski.

A gondola leads up into the slopes, and there are two wonderful sweeping intermediate runs down. The nursery slope is on your doorstep, and visitors say that La Tania is 'very child friendly'. The steepness of the longer

OT LA TANIA

La Tania has an attractive collection of mainly ski-in/ski-out wood-clad chalets and apartments set among the trees ➜

KEY FACTS

Resort	1350m
	4,430ft

The Three Valleys	
Slopes	1260-3230m
	4,130-10,600ft
Lifts	183
Pistes	600km
	373 miles
Green	15%
Blue	38%
Red	37%
Black	10%
Snowmaking	
	1920 guns

Courchevel/ La Tania only	
Slopes	1260-2740m
	4,130-8,990ft
Lifts	63
Pistes	150km
	93 miles
Green	22%
Blue	37%
Red	33%
Black	8%
Snowmaking	
	563 guns

runs above the village has, until recently, been its key weakness, but the opening (in 2005/06) of the Plan Fontaine green run from Praz-Juget to the village now gives novices a long easy slope to progress to. Getting back from Courchevel still involves tackling a blue.

Free buses go to Courchevel; the hourly evening service is said to be erratic. For those with a car, Méribel is probably a bigger draw – and a lot nearer than Courchevel 1850.

THE MOUNTAINS

As well as good, though limited, local slopes, the Courchevel or the Méribel slopes are only two lifts away.

Slopes The gondola out of the village goes to Praz-Juget. From here a drag-lift takes you to Chenus and the slopes above Courchevel 1850 and a fast quad goes to the link with Méribel via Col de la Loze. An alternative way to the slopes above 1850 is to take two successive drag-lifts from the village to

Loze. From all these points, varied, interesting intermediate runs take you back into the La Tania sector.

Terrain-parks There is no local terrain-park or half-pipe, but you can get to Courchevel's four parks easily.

Snow reliability Good snow-cover down to Praz-Juget is usual all season. Snowmaking now covers the whole of the blue run back to the village; some reporters found this satisfactory, but others found the run became icy in the afternoon and preferred to ride the gondola down at times.

Experts There are no particularly testing runs directly above La Tania, but the Jean Blanc and Jockeys blacks from Loze to Le Praz are genuine challenges and there is good off-piste terrain beneath the Col de la Loze ridge and close by above Courchevel.

Intermediates There are two lovely, long, undulating intermediate runs back through the trees to La Tania – though there's little difference in gradient between the blue and the red, and timid intermediates may want to

---

Selected chalets in La Tania

use the new green. On the higher slopes you have a choice of three or four pistes. Both the red Lanches and the black Dou des Lanches are excellent and challenging.

Beginners There is a good beginner area and lift right in the village and children are well catered for. But there's a lot of through traffic on the main slope. The new green run from Praz-Juget, further improved last year, makes La Tania a lot more suitable for beginners.

Snowboarding It's easy to get around on gondolas/chairs, avoiding drags.

Cross-country There are trails at altitude with links through the woods to Méribel and Courchevel, which has an extensive 66km/41 miles of trails. To our non-specialist eye, this looks a good base.

Queues A queue can build up for the village gondola but it is quick-moving, and one of the attractions of La Tania in general is the lack of crowds.

Mountain restaurants Bouc Blanc (0479 088026), near the top of the gondola out of La Tania is our favourite: it has friendly table-service in a wood-clad dining room, good food (reliable plat du jour) and a big terrace – we've had several very satisfactory lunches there. Roc Tania, higher up at Col de la Loze, is tiny, but very pretty inside.

Schools and guides Several reporters have praised the ESF: 'Unequivocally the lessons for myself and children were excellent.' A third season skier 'really enjoyed' lessons with Magic in Motion in 2007.

Facilities for children We have had excellent reports of the two nurseries

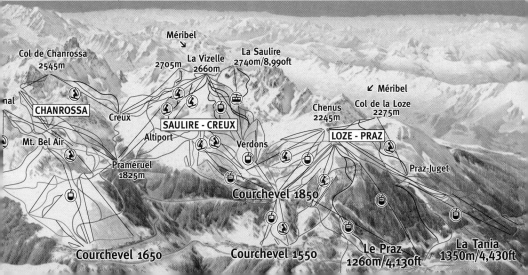

UK PACKAGES

Airtours, Alpine Action, Alpine Answers, Chalet Group, Chalet World Ski, Club Pavilion, Come-ski.com, Crystal, Directski.com, Erna Low, Hucksters, Independent Ski Links, Interactive Resorts, Lagrange, Le Ski, Neilson, Silver Ski, Ski Activity, Ski Amis, Ski Beat, Ski Deep, Ski France, Ski Independence, Ski Leisure Direction, Ski Line, Ski McNeill, Ski Power, Ski Solutions, Ski Weekends, Ski4you, Skifrance4less, Skiholidayextras, Skitracer, Snowline, Thomson

SMART LODGINGS

Check out our feature chapters at the front of the book.

Phone numbers
From abroad use the prefix +33 and omit the initial '0' of the phone number.

TOURIST OFFICE

t 0479 084040
info@latania.com
www.latania.com

run by UK tour operator Le Ski. The local Maison des Enfants kindergarten takes non-skiing children from the age of three; the Jardin des Neiges takes skiing children from the age of four. A list of babysitters is available from the tourist office.

STAYING THERE

How to go Over 30 British tour operators go here – an amazingly high number for such a small place.
Hotels The Montana (0479 088008) is a slope-side 3-star next to the gondola with a sauna and fitness club. The Télémark (0479 088032) offers simple accommodation set in the forest.
Chalets Several tour operators have selections of splendid newish ski-in/ski-out chalets with fine views, which reporters generally enjoy though we have had complaints of 'poor sound-proofing' in some. Le Ski (that we've had good reports on) has four, including a brand new one for 2007/08 and three very child-friendly ones (two of which have nurseries). Alpine Action has four swish chalets near the centre, three with outdoor hot-tubs. Ski Amis has three chalets, one aimed at families, one budget and one premium chalet with a sauna, plus some self-catering places.
Apartments There are lots of apartments – and most are more spacious and better equipped than usual in France. The Saboïa and the Christiania have been recommended. There is a deli and a bakery, as well as a small supermarket.
Eating out The Ferme de la Tania gets generally good reviews for its Savoyard fare – 'good service, good food'. The Farçon now has a Michelin star: a recent reporter says, 'We had an excellent lunch, and it did not cost a fortune.' The Ski Lodge has 'damn good chilli burgers' and 'will do a deal

for groups including all-you-can-eat-and-drink salad, chips and wine'. The Chanterelles is 'excellent' for crêpes and pizzas ('first-class meals at knockdown prices') and the Taïga does 'very good pizzas and is friendly and quite cheap'. A 2007 reporter recommends the Marmottons for 'good food and reasonable prices'. Locals praise the Bistro in the Télémark hotel.
Après-ski The Ski Lodge has long been the focal après-ski place and has live bands. But it also now has some rivals. The hotel Télémark has 'civilised live music nightly' and the Taïga 'is quite smart, with cocktails and live music', according to reporters. The hotel Montana bar is also worth trying for a quiet drink and the 'nice locals' bar' – the Arbatte – is popular as the slopes close.
Off the slopes Unless you have a car, La Tania is not the best place for someone not intending to hit the slopes – too small and limited. However, snowmobile trips, snow-shoeing, paragliding and husky dog-sledding are possibilities, and the hotel Montana has a fitness club with a swimming pool. A non-skier's guide to Courchevel, Méribel and La Tania is distributed free by the tourist office.

Tignes

Stark apartment blocks and a bleak, treeless setting are the prices you pay for the high, snow-sure slopes and great, varied terrain

COSTS

① ② ③ ④ ⑤ ⑥

RATINGS

The slopes

Fast lifts	★★★
Snow	★★★★★
Extent	★★★★★
Expert	★★★★★
Intermediate	★★★★★
Beginner	★★
Convenience	★★★★
Queues	★★★★
Mountain restaurants	★★★

The rest

Scenery	★★★
Resort charm	★★
Off-slope	★

KEY FACTS

Resort	2100m
	6,890ft

Espace Killy	
Slopes	1550-3455m
	5,090-11,340ft
Lifts	90
Pistes	300km
	186 miles
Green	15%
Blue	40%
Red	28%
Black	17%
Snowmaking	
	635 guns

Tignes only	
Slopes	1550-3455m
	5,090-11,340ft
Lifts	44
Pistes	150km
	93 miles

- ➕ Good snow guaranteed for a long season – about the best Alpine bet
- ➕ One of the best areas in the world for lift-served off-piste runs
- ➕ Huge amount of varied terrain, with swift access to Val d'Isère
- ➕ Lots of accommodation close to the slopes
- ➕ Efforts to make the resort villages more welcoming are paying off

- ➖ Resort architecture not to everyone's taste (including ours)
- ➖ Bleak, treeless setting – many lifts prone to closure by storms
- ➖ Still a few long, slow chair-lifts – though progress is being made
- ➖ You need an area pass to find long green runs
- ➖ Limited, but improving, après-ski

The appeal of Tignes is simple: good snow, spread over a wide area of varied terrain, shared with Val d'Isère. The altitude of Tignes is crucial: a forecast of 'rain up to 2000m' means 'fresh snow down to village level in Tignes'.

We prefer to stay in Val, which is a more human place. But in many ways Tignes makes the better base: appreciably higher, more convenient, surrounded by intermediate terrain, with quick access to the Grande Motte glacier. And the case gets stronger as results flow from Tignes' campaign to reinvent itself in a more cuddly form. The place is a lot less hostile to the visitor than it once was.

In the last few seasons the resort has also, at last, got around to installing some fast chairs on the western side of the Tignes bowl. But there are still a few key links that need upgrading.

THE RESORT

Tignes was created before the French discovered the benefits of making purpose-built resorts look acceptable. But things are improving, and the villages are gradually acquiring a more traditional look and feel.

Tignes-le-Lac is the hub of the resort. Some of the smaller buildings in the central part, Le Rosset, are being successfully revamped in chalet style. But the place as a whole is dreary, and the blocks overlooking the lake from the quarter called Le Bec-Rouge will remain monstrous until the day they are demolished. It's at the point where these two sub-resorts meet – a snowy pedestrian area, with valley traffic now passing through a tunnel beneath – that the lifts are concentrated: a powerful gondola towards Tovière and Val d'Isère and a fast six-pack up the western slopes. Some attractive new buildings are being added both in the centre and on the fringes, in a suburb built on the lower slopes known as Les Almes. A nursery slope separates Le Rosset from the fourth component part, the group

of apartment blocks called Le Lavachet, below which there are good fast lifts up both sides of the valley.

Val Claret (2km/1 mile up the valley, beyond the lake) was also mainly developed after Le Rosset, and is a bit more stylish. The main part of the village, Centre, is an uncompromisingly 1960s-style development on a shelf

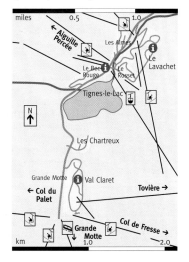

↑ Snow is what
Tignes is about:
Grande Motte, with
Grande Casse in the
background

SNOWPIX.COM / CHRIS GILL

above the valley floor. Below this, fast
chairs head up in three directions: to
the western slopes, towards Val d'Isère
and to the Grande Motte. An
underground funicular also accesses
the Grande Motte.

Beside the road along the valley to
the lifts is a ribbon of development in
traditional style, named Grande Motte
(after the peak). The two levels of Val
Claret are linked by a couple of
(unreliable) indoor elevators and stairs
and by hazardous paths.

Below the main resort villages are
two smaller places. Tignes-les-Boisses,
quietly set in the trees beside the road
up, consists of a barracks and a couple
of simple hotels. Tignes-les-Brévières is
a renovated old village at the lowest
point of the slopes – a favourite lunch
spot, and a friendly place to stay.

Location isn't crucial, as a regular
free bus service connects all the
villages until midnight – though in the
daytime the route runs along the
bottom of Val Claret, leaving residents
of Val Claret Centre with a climb.

A weekly pass may be upgraded
daily (10 euros) to cover Les Arcs, La
Plagne and the Three Valleys, all easily
reached with the aid of a car. You can
also buy your pass on the web in
advance.

The area's great weakness is that it
can become unusable in bad weather.
There are no woodland runs except
immediately above Tignes-les-Boisses
and Tignes-les-Brévières. Heavy snow
produces widespread avalanche risk
and wind closes the higher chairs.

Piste classification here is more
reliable than in Val d'Isère and
signposting is 'very clear'. But two
2007 reporters complain that lift and
piste opening information is unreliable.

THE SLOPES
High, snow-sure and varied
Tignes' biggest asset is the **Grande
Motte** – and the runs from, as well as
on, the glacier. The underground
funicular from Val Claret whizzes you
up to over 3000m/9,840ft in seven
minutes. There are blue, red and black
runs to play on up here, as well as
beautiful long runs back to the resort.

The main lifts towards Val d'Isère
are efficient: a high-capacity gondola
from Le Lac to **Tovière**, and a fast chair
with covers from Val Claret to **Col de
Fresse**. You can head back to Tignes
from either: the return from Tovière
to Tignes-le-Lac is via a steep black
run but there are easier blue runs to
Val Claret.

Going up the opposite side of the
valley takes you to a quieter area of
predominantly east-facing slopes split
into two main sectors, linked in both
directions – **Col du Palet** and **l'Aiguille
Percée**. This whole mountainside is at
last being given the fast lifts it has
needed for years – there are five so
far.

The Col des Ves chair-lift, at the
south end of the Col du Palet sector,
serves the SPOT (see 'For experts')
free-ride and freestyle learning area.
You can descend from l'Aiguille Percée
to Tignes-les-Brévières on blue, red or
black runs. There's an efficient gondola
back, but the chairs above it are old
and slow ('a quicker route back is the
bus'). A new fixed-grip quad is due to
replace the existing chair-lift between
Tignes-les-Brévières and Tignes-les-
Boisses for 2007/08, but a fast lift or
two above it would be more useful.

TERRAIN-PARKS
New but not improved
Tignes was one of the first French
resorts to build a terrain-park. This
means that the local shaping crew are

NEWS

For 2007/08 the Brévières chair-lift up to Les Boisses is to be upgraded to a fixed-grip quad.

For 2006/07 a six-pack replaced the two Palafour triple chairs towards L'Aiguille Percée. Snowmaking was increased.

The Lagon leisure centre opened in the main part of the resort, including a 25-metre pool, fun-pool with slides, spa facilities and a fitness centre.

Also last season, MGM opened the first stage of its new Nevada apartment development in Val Claret. The second stage, a 3-star hotel, is due for 2007/08.

not short of experience and know how to build a good park – although a 2007 visitor found it 'disappointing for a resort of its size'. Whether they can be bothered to keep it maintained is another story. The park is in Val Claret and is long, has several small-to-medium-sized jumps including a gap jump, a hip and several medium-sized rails. On a good day it is a lot of fun and the 120m/390ft long half-pipe is well shaped and a good size for those not comfortable with a super-pipe. It is right at the bottom of the mountain, which means if you have the energy to hike, you can ride it for free. In the summer the park doubles in size and moves up to the Grande Motte for freestyle camps. There's also a boarder-cross as part of Le SPOT (see 'For experts') and a children's park in Le Lac.

SNOW RELIABILITY
Difficult to beat
Tignes has all-year-round runs (barring brief closures in spring or autumn) on its Grande Motte glacier. And the resort height of 2100m/6,890ft generally means good snow-cover right back to base for most of the long winter season – November to May. The west-facing runs down from Col de Fresse and Tovière to Val Claret suffer from the afternoon sun, although they now have serious snowmaking. Some of the lower east-facing and south-east-facing slopes on the other side of the valley can suffer late in the season, too. Snowmaking was increased around the new six-pack this year. Grooming is 'excellent'.

FOR EXPERTS
An excellent choice
Tignes has converted six of its black runs into 'naturides', which means they are never groomed (a neat way of saving money!) but they are marked, patrolled and avalanche protected. Many of them are not especially steep (eg the Ves run – promoted from red status and renamed after the local free-ride hero Guerlain Chicherit). Perhaps the most serious challenge is the long black run from Tovière to Tignes-le-Lac, with steep, usually heavily mogulled sections (the top part, Pâquerettes, is now a naturide, but the bottom part, Trolles, is a normal black). Parts of this run get a lot of afternoon sun. Our favourite black run (still a 'normal' black) is the

Sache, from l'Aiguille Percée down a secluded valley to Tignes-les-Brévières, which can become very heavily mogulled (especially at the bottom).

But it is the off-piste possibilities that make Tignes such a draw for experts. Go with one of the off-piste groups that the schools organise and you'll have a great time. See the feature box for a few of the options.

The whole western side of the Tignes ski area has lots of off-piste possibilities. The terrain served by the slow, old Col des Ves double chair has been designated Le SPOT (Skiing the Powder of Tignes) area and has various ungroomed off-piste zones: Hardride for experts, Softride for the less experienced, and Backcountry freestyle with jumps. It is explained at length on the back of the piste map. At Chalet Freeride here you can learn to use an avalanche transceiver, practise searching for avalanche victims, read the avalanche bulletins and study maps and photos of the terrain.

Schools and guides offer the bizarre French form of heli-skiing: mountaintop drops are forbidden, but from Tovière you can ski down towards the Lac du Chevril to be retrieved by chopper.

FOR INTERMEDIATES
One of the best
For the keen intermediate piste-basher the Espace Killy is one of the top three or four areas in France, or the world.

Tignes' local slopes are ideal intermediate terrain. The red and blue runs on the Grande Motte glacier nearly always have superb snow. The glacier run from the top of the cable-car is classified red, but is wide and mostly easy on usually fabulous snow. The Leisse run down to the chair-lift is classified black and can get very mogulled but has good snow. The long red run all the way back to town is a delightful long cruise – though often crowded. The roundabout blue alternative (Génépy) is much gentler and quieter.

From Tovière, the blue 'H' run to Val Claret is an enjoyable cruise and generally well groomed. But again, it can get very crowded. There is lots to do on the other side of the valley and the runs down from l'Aiguille Percée to Tignes-les-Boisses and Tignes-les-Brévières are also scenic and fun. There are red and blue options as well as the beautiful Sache black run – adventurous intermediates shouldn't

LIFT PASSES

Espace Killy

Prices in €

Age	1-day	6-day
under 13	31	148
13 to 59	41	198
over 60	35	168

Free under 5, over 75

Beginner five free lifts

Notes
Covers Tignes and Val d'Isère; half-day and pedestrian passes; family discounts; 6-day plus passes valid for one day in the Three Valleys, Valmorel, Ste-Foy and Paradiski (La Plagne-Les Arcs), and reduced price in La Rosière

Alternative passes
Tignes-only pass available

miss it. The runs down from l'Aiguille Percée to Le Lac are gentle, wide blues – now accessed by a fast chair.

FOR BEGINNERS
Good nursery slopes, but ...
The nursery slopes of Tignes-le-Lac and Le Lavachet (which meet at the top) are excellent – convenient, snow-sure, gentle, free of through-traffic and served by a slow chair and a drag. The ones at Val Claret are less appealing: an unpleasantly steep slope within the

village served by a drag, and a less convenient slope served by the fast Bollin chair. All of these lifts are free.

Although there are some fairly easy blues on the west side of Tignes – with better access now a new six-pack is in place – for long green runs you have to go over to the Val d'Isère sector. You need an Espace Killy pass to use them, and to get back to Tignes you have a choice between the blue run from Col de Fresse (which has a tricky start) or riding the gondola down from

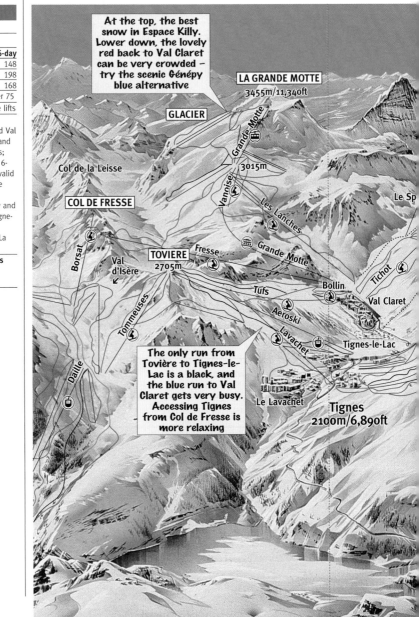

At the top, the best snow in Espace Killy. Lower down, the lovely red back to Val Claret can be very crowded – try the scenic Génépy blue alternative

LA GRANDE MOTTE
3455m/11,340ft

GLACIER

Grande-Motte

3015m

Col de la Leisse

Vanoise

Les Lanches

Le Sp

COL DE FRESSE

Borsat

Fresse

Grande-Motte

Tichot

Val d'Isère

TOVIERE
2705m

Tüfs

Bollin

Val Claret

Tommeuses

Aeroski

Lavachet

Tignes-le-Lac

Daille

The only run from Tovière to Tignes-le-Lac is a black, and the blue run to Val Claret gets very busy. Accessing Tignes from Col de Fresse is more relaxing

Le Lavachet

Tignes
2100m/6,890ft

Tovière. And in poor weather, the high Tignes valley is an intimidatingly bleak place – enough to make any wavering beginner retreat to a bar with a book.

FOR CROSS-COUNTRY
Interesting variety

The Espace Killy has 40km/25 miles of cross-country trails. There are tracks on the frozen Lac de Tignes, along the valley between Val Claret and Tignes-le-Lac, at Les Boisses and Les Brévières and up on the Grande Motte.

QUEUES
Very few

The queues here depend on snow conditions. If snow low down is poor, the Grande Motte funicular generates queues; the fast chairs in parallel with it are often quicker, despite the longer ride time. These lifts jointly shift a lot of people, with the result that the run down to Val Claret can be unpleasantly crowded. The worst queues now are for the cable-car on the glacier – half-hour waits are common. And post-

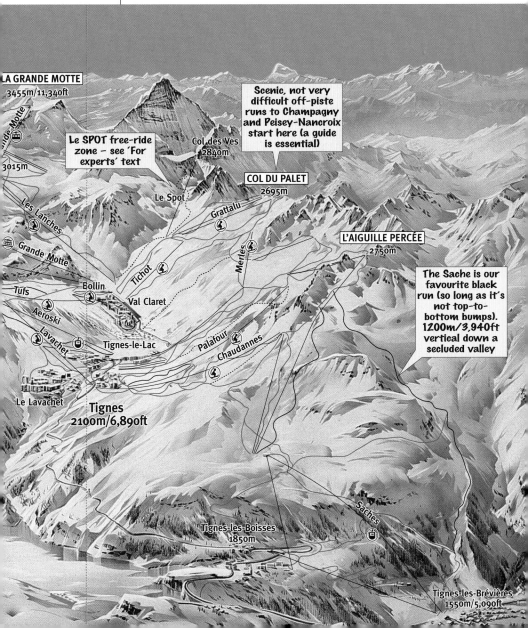

LA GRANDE MOTTE
3455m/11,340ft

3015m

Les Lanches

Grande Motte

Tufs

Aeroski

Lavachet

Le Lavachet

Tignes
2100m/6,890ft

Le SPOT free-ride zone – see 'For experts' text

Le Spot

Col des Ves
2840m

Grattalu

Merles

Tichot

Bollin

Val Claret

Tignes-le-Lac

Palafour

Chaudannes

Scenic, not very difficult off-piste runs to Champagny and Peisey-Nancroix start here (a guide is essential)

COL DU PALET
2695m

L'AIGUILLE PERCÉE
2750m

The Sache is our favourite black run (so long as it's not top-to-bottom bumps). 1200m/3,940ft vertical down a secluded valley

Saches

Tignes-les-Boisses
1850m

Tignes-les-Brévières
1550m/5,090ft

lunch queues at Les Brévières are not unknown. But reports suggest recent lift upgrades and the new hands-free system have improved matters.

Of course, if higher lifts are closed by heavy snow or high winds, the lifts on the lower slopes have big queues.

MOUNTAIN RESTAURANTS
A couple of good places
The mountain restaurants are not a highlight – a regular hazard of high, purpose-built resorts, where it's easy to go back to the village for lunch.
Editors' choice Lo Soli (0479 069863) at the top of the Chaudannes chair is a clear favourite. The terrace shares with the adjacent self-service Alpage a superb view of the Grande Motte; a 2006 reporter endorses our opinion: 'Excellent food, ambience and service; excellent gâteau d'agneau, Caesar salad and melt-in-the-mouth pot-au-feu.' The table-service bit of the Panoramic (0479 064721) at the top of the funicular competes; one regular reporter gives it the edge – 'a veritable joy – excellent rack of lamb, tiramisu'.
Worth knowing about The atmospheric chalet at the top of Tovière is 'fairly basic' but does 'very good portions'. A reporter found the 'service just OK' at the modern but pleasantly woody Chalet du Bollin – just a few metres

above Val Claret. At the top of the Tichot chair from Val Claret, the Palet 'serves good food at good prices'. The big Panoramic self-service restaurant at the top of the funicular gets crowded, but has great views from its huge terrace and 'good portions at reasonable prices'.

There are lots of easily accessible places for lunch in the resorts. One ski-to-the-door favourite of ours in Le Lac is the hotel Montana, on the left as you descend from l'Aiguille Percée. In Val Claret the Fish Tank is 'very good value'. The Taverne des Neiges has 'good food and service'. In Le Lac, the Arbina offers 'consistent high quality'.

At the extremity of the lift system, Les Brévières makes an obvious lunch stop. A short walk round the corner into the village brings you to places much cheaper than the two by the piste. Sachette, for example, is crowded with artefacts from mountain life and offers 'lots of good cheese dishes' including 'superb tartiflette'. The Etoile des Neiges 'serves great, typical Savoyard food'.

SCHOOLS AND GUIDES
Plenty of choice
There are over half-a-dozen schools, including four specialist snowboard schools, plus various independent instructors. Reporters advise that pre-booking is 'essential' at busy times like Easter. ESF gets mixed reviews: One child last year was 'admirably looked after' and the instructor showed 'great professionalism and understanding'. But a 2007 reporter calls the school 'thoroughly disorganised'. Reports on Evolution 2 are generally positive for adult tuition. Members of a 2007 reporter's group were pleased with their progress and one took private lessons with an 'encouraging and very patient

boarding

Tignes has always been a popular destination for snowboarders. Lots of easily accessible off-piste and the fact that it's cheaper than Val d'Isère are the main attractions, and quite a few top UK snowboarders make this their winter home. For those who buy the Espace Killy lift ticket, the backside of Col de Fresse in Val d'Isère is a natural playground. There are a few flat areas (avoid Génépy and Myrtilles), but the lift system relies more on chairs and gondolas than drags (though a long drag serves the boarder-cross area). There are long, wide pistes to blast down, such as Grattalu, Carline and Piste H, with acres of powder between them to play in. There are four specialist snowboard schools (Kebra, Snocool, Surf Feeling and now Alliance) and a snowboarder chalet (www.dragonlodge.com). Go to Snowpark-shop in Tignes-le-Lac for all your freestyle needs.

SCHOOLS

ESF
t 0479 063028

Evolution 2
t 0479 063576

Snocool
t 0479 400858

Kebra
t 0479 064337

333
t 0479 062088

Surf Feeling
t 0479 065363

Alliance
t 0844 484 9390

Classes (ESF prices)
6 half days: €132

Private lessons
€36 for 1hr

GUIDES

Bureau des Guides
t 0479 064276

Tetra
t 0479 419707

---

instructor'. The off-piste 'Tarentaise Tour' has also been praised ('a superb long day, with an enthusiastic guide'). But one visitor was 'very unhappy' with the children's lessons: 'The children changed level every class. At the end of one lesson, the class arrived back without our child – when asked where she was, the instructor said he simply didn't know. She returned later with another group.' The same reporter moved his children to the 333 school where 'the difference was dramatic – would highly recommend them'. BASS has 'excellent, small group clinics', and we have a glowing report of the new British-run snowboarding outfit, Alliance: 'They teach with passion and enthusiasm; by far the best week's instruction I have received.'

FACILITIES FOR CHILDREN
Mixed reports
We have had good reports on the Marmottons kindergartens – 'brilliant' says a father of a four-year-old last year – and the Spritelets ski classes arranged by Esprit Ski and Evolution 2: 'She loved her class and could snowplough by the end of the week.' But we've received a poor report for Evolution 2 this year (see Schools).

STAYING THERE

HOW TO GO
Improving range of options
All three main styles of accommodation are available through tour operators. More luxury options are appearing.
Chalets The choice of catered chalets is increasing. Total Ski and Neilson both have several smart chalets, including some with pool, hot-tub and sauna. Total Ski's Chalet Arctik is not only hip but also 'excellent, comfortable', with a pool and sauna. Family specialist Esprit has a chalet hotel and several chalets here. Ski Olympic's chalets Rosset and Madeleine have been recommended by reporters. Mark Warner has two chalet-hotels, one with an outdoor pool. Snowstar's Chalet Chardon is an exceptionally spacious apartment. Crystal's chalet-hotel Curling in Val Claret is reasonably priced and 'well operated'.
Hotels The few hotels are small and concentrated in Le Lac.
***Campanules** (0479 063436) Smartly rustic chalet in upper Le Lac, with good restaurant. One reporter was impressed enough to suggest that it deserved a 4-star rating.
***Village Montana** (0479 400144) Stylishly woody 3-star on the east-

---

A MECCA FOR OFF-PISTE SKIERS

Tignes is renowned for offering some of the best lift-served off-piste skiing in the world. There is a tremendous choice, with runs to suit all levels, from intermediate skiers to fearless free-riders and off-piste experts. Here's just a small selection. Don't go without a guide.

*For a first experience of off-piste, **Lognan** is ideal. These slopes – down the mountainside between the pistes to Le Lac and the pistes to Val Claret – are broad and not very difficult.*

*One of our favourite routes is the **Tour de Pramecou**. After a few minutes' walking at the bottom of the Grande Motte glacier, you pass around a big rock called Pramecou. There is then a multitude of possibilities, varying in difficulty – so routes can be found for skiers of different abilities.*

***Petite Balme** is a run for good skiers only – access is easy but leads to quite challenging north-facing slopes in real high-mountain terrain, far from the pistes.*

*To ski **Oreilles de Mickey** (Mickey's Ears) you start from Tovière and walk north along the ridge to the peak of Lavachet, where you get a great view of Tignes. The descent involves three long couloirs, narrow and pretty steep, which bring you back to Le Lavachet.*

*The best place to find good snow is the **Chardonnet** couloirs – they never get the sun. The route involves a 20-minute walk from the top of the Merle Blanc chair-lift.*

*The **Vallons de la Sache** is one of the most famous routes – a descent of 1200m/3,940ft vertical down a breathtaking valley in the heart of the National Park, overlooked by the magnificent Sache glacier. Starting from l'Aiguille Percée you enter a different world, high up in the mountains, far away from the ski lifts. You arrive down in Les Brévières, below the Tignes dam.*

*One of the big adventures is to go away from the Tignes ski area and all signs of civilisation, starting from the Col du Palet. From there you can head for **Champagny** (linked to La Plagne's area) or **Peisey-Nancroix** (linked to Les Arcs' area) – these are both very beautiful runs, and not too difficult.*

CHILDREN

Les Marmottons
t 0479 065167
Ages 3 to 8

Ski schools
Evolution 2 and 333 take children from age 5 and ESF takes children from age 4 (6 days €184)

GETTING THERE

Air Geneva 165km/103 miles (3½hr); Lyon 240km/ 149 miles (3½hr); Chambéry 130km/ 81 miles (2½hr)

Rail Bourg-St-Maurice (30km/19 miles); regular buses or taxi from station

SMART LODGINGS

Check out our feature chapters at the front of the book.

facing slopes above Le Lac (though a 2006 reporter says the rooms are starting to show their age), with 4-star suites section. Outdoor pool, sauna, steam, hot-tub.

***Lévanna (0479 063294) Smart 3-star in central position in Le Lac – comfortable, with a 'generous hot-tub' but a 2006 reporter found 'friendly staff but a woeful lack of them'.

***Diva (0479 067000) Biggest in town (121 rooms). On lower level of Val Claret, a short walk from lifts. 'Very comfy rooms, excellent meals.' Sauna.

**Arbina (0479 063478) Well-run place close to the lifts in Le Lac, with lunchtime terrace, crowded après-ski bar and one of the best restaurants.

**Marais (0479 064006) Prettily furnished, simple hotel in Les Boisses.

Génépy (0479 065711) Simple Dutch-run chalet in Les Brévières.

Apartments There are lots of apartments available in all price ranges. Interhome has countless options. A growing number of smart ones include the Ecrin des Neiges apartments in lower Val Claret and Residence Village Montana above Le Lac (both with pool, sauna and steam, though there's a charge for their use).

MGM has recently opened the Ferme du Val Claret at the foot of the Grande Motte funicular and the Nevada in Val Claret. In Les Brévières, the Chalets d'Hercule are a collection of good-looking individual chalets sleeping up to 16. More upmarket property is being built in Les Brévières, for sale though Erna Low – see the buying property chapter.

The Chalet Club in Val Claret is a collection of simple studios, but has a free indoor pool, sauna and in-house restaurant and bar. The supermarket at Le Lac is reported to be 'comprehensive but very expensive'.

EATING OUT
Good places scattered about

The options in Le Lavachet are rather limited, though a recent reporter enjoyed the Grenier with its 'excellent cold meats and tartiflette'. And we have a very positive report of the British-run Brasero: 'This restaurant is already establishing a good reputation in Tignes; the food was quite simply excellent. We were made to feel very welcome.' Finding anywhere with some atmosphere is difficult in Le Lac, though the food in some of the better hotels is good. The Campanules has 'exemplary service', but the food 'wasn't as memorable as on other occasions,' says a regular visitor. The Arbina continues to provide 'outstanding food, very good value and first-class service'. The Escale Blanche is almost as popular. Two visitors recommend the 'delicious food' at the 'quirky' Clin d'Oeil. Bagus Cafe's 'eclectic cuisine' is also praised. One visitor particularly highlights the Monday champagne nights at the Alpaka Lodge – 'a relaxed restaurant

OT TIGNES / M DALMASSO

Tignes-le-Lac from Tovière: Le Bec Rouge on the left, Le Rosset in the middle with Les Almes behind, and Le Lavachet on the right
→

ACTIVITIES

Indoor Wellness and fitness centres (pools, saunas, Turkish baths, hot-tub, spa and beauty treatments, weight training), multisports hall, yoga, squash, climbing wall, library, bowling, cinema, heritage centre

Outdoor Natural ice rink, dog-sledding, paragliding, helicopter rides, ice-driving, ice-diving, snowmobiling, bungee trampolining, mini-quad bikes, snow-shoeing, mountaineering, ice-climbing, skijoring

Phone numbers
From abroad use the prefix +33 and omit the initial '0' of the phone number

TOURIST OFFICE

t 0479 400440
information@tignes.net
www.tignes.net

with duck breast the star attraction'. A 2007 visitor enjoyed 'traditional food' at the Eterlou.

In Val Claret the Caveau is recommended for a special treat. The Petit Savoyard 'is friendly with efficient service'. The buffet at the Indochine has been strongly recommended by several reporters. Pepe 2000 has 'reasonable prices and helpful staff' but a reporter says the Pignatta 'slightly trumps it'. The Auberge des 3 Oursons was recommended for 'massive portions, friendly service'.

The Cordée in Les Boisses is said to offer unpretentious surroundings, great traditional French food, modest prices.

APRES-SKI
Hidden away
Reporters agree that there is plenty going on if you know where to find it. Val Claret has some early-evening atmosphere, and happy hours are popular. Reporters differ on the merits of the Crowded House and Fish Tank (both popular with Brits). Grizzly's is 'cosy and atmospheric, but you pay for the ambience'. The 'whisky lounge' in the Couloir is a 'great place to relax'.

Le Lac is a natural focus for

immediate après-ski drinks. The 'lively' Loop, with pool table, has a 'two for one' happy hour from 4 to 6pm. The bar of the hotel Arbina is our kind of spot – adequately cosy, friendly service. It's a great place to sit outside and people-watch. The Alpaka Cocktail Bar is 'hard to leave', 'a real gem later on'. Embuscade is said to be 'the only proper French bar'. The Angel has live music and TC's bar is 'very friendly, with good music'. Café de la Poste and Jack's are popular late haunts.

OFF THE SLOPES
Forget it
Despite the range of alternative activities, Tignes is a resort for those who want to use the slopes, where anyone who doesn't is liable to feel like a fish out of water. Some activities do get booked up quickly as well – a reporter said it was impossible to find a free dog-sledding slot in April. The ice skating on the lake includes a 500m/1,640ft circuit as well as a conventional rink. There's ice-driving at Les Brévières. The new Lagon leisure centre, with various pools, slides, wellness and fitness facilities, meets with readers' approval.

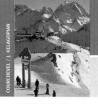

Les Trois Vallées

With the swankiest resort in the Alps at one end, and the highest at the other: the biggest lift-linked ski area in the world

Despite competing claims, notably from the Portes du Soleil, in practical terms the Three Valleys cannot be beaten for sheer quantity of lift-served terrain. There is nowhere like it for a keen skier or boarder who wants to cover as much mileage as possible while rarely taking the same run repeatedly. It has a lot to offer everyone, from beginner to expert. And its resorts offer a wide range of alternatives – not only the widely known attractions of the big-name mega-resorts but also the increasingly appreciated low-key appeal of the smaller villages.

What's more, the area undersells itself. It should actually be known as the Four Valleys because several years ago it expanded south into the Maurienne. But when you've spent millions on building a brand name why change? Three Valleys or four – whatever, the place is huge.

The runs of the Three Valleys and their resorts are dealt with in six chapters. The four major resorts are Courchevel, Méribel, Les Menuires and Val Thorens, but we also give chapters to St-Martin-de-Belleville, a small village down the valley from Les Menuires, and La Tania, a modern development between Courchevel and Méribel.

None of the resorts is cheap. **Les Menuires** has some budget accommodation but its original buildings are hard on the eye. New developments are now being built in a much more acceptable style and two of the original buildings have been demolished and are being rebuilt in a much more sympathetic style – something we suggested nine editions ago. Across the valley are some of the best (and quietest) challenging pistes in the Three Valleys on the north-facing La Masse. Down the valley from Les Menuires is **St-Martin-de-Belleville**, a charming traditional village that has been expanded sympathetically. It has

good-value accommodation and lift links into the slopes of Les Menuires and Méribel.

Up rather than down the Belleville valley from Les Menuires, at 2300m/7,550ft, **Val-Thorens** is the highest resort in the Alps, and at 3230m/10,600ft the top of its slopes is the high point of the Three Valleys. The snow in this area is almost always good, and it includes two glaciers where good snow is guaranteed. But the setting is bleak and the lifts are vulnerable to closure in bad weather. The purpose-built resort is very convenient. Visually it is not comparable to Les Menuires, thanks to the smaller-scale design and more thorough use of wood cladding.

Méribel is a two-part resort. The higher component, **Méribel-Mottaret**, is the best placed of all the resorts for getting to any part of the Three Valleys system in the shortest possible time. It's now quite a spread-out place, with some of the accommodation a long way up the hillsides – great for access to the slopes, less so for access to nightlife. **Méribel** itself is 200m/660ft lower and has long been a British favourite, especially for chalet holidays. It is the most attractive of the main

Three Valleys resorts, built in chalet style beside a long winding road up the hillside. Parts of the resort are very convenient for the slopes and the village centre; parts are very far from either. The growing hamlet of **Méribel-Village** has its own chair-lift into the system but is very isolated and quiet. You can also stay below Méribel in the valley town of **Brides-les-Bains**, or in hamlets along the route of the gondola that links it to Méribel.

Courchevel has four parts. 1850 is the most fashionable resort in France, and can be the most expensive resort in the Alps (though it doesn't have to cost a fortune to stay there). The less expensive parts – Le Praz (aka 1300), 1550 and 1650 – don't have the same choice of nightlife and restaurants. Many people rate the slopes around Courchevel the best in the Three Valleys, with runs to suit all standards.

La Tania was built for the 1992 Olympics, just off the small road linking Le Praz to Méribel. It has now grown into an attractive, car-free collection of chalets and chalet-style apartments set among the trees, and is popular with families. It has a good nursery slope and a green run and lovely long intermediate runs back.

Val d'Isère

One of the great high mega-resorts, particularly (though not only) for experts – with the bonus of a very attractive town at the base

COSTS

① ② ③ ④ ⑤ ⑥

RATINGS

The slopes

Fast lifts	****
Snow	*****
Extent	*****
Expert	*****
Intermediate	*****
Beginner	***
Convenience	***
Queues	****
Mountain restaurants	***

The rest

Scenery	***
Resort charm	***
Off-slope	**

NEWS

For 2006/07 a new fast chair was built above the Le Fornet cable-car. Piste A from Solaise was remodelled and re-named Rhônes Alpes.

Snowmaking was added to the Creux piste from Tovière towards Val d'Isère.

Two new 4-star hotels are opening.

KEY FACTS

Resort	1850m	
	6,070ft	

Entire Espace Killy area

Slopes	1550-3455m	
	5,090-11,340ft	
Lifts	90	
Pistes	300km	
	186 miles	
Green	15%	
Blue	40%	
Red	28%	
Black	17%	
Snowmaking		
	635 guns	

Val d'Isère only

Slopes	1785-3300m	
	5,860-10,830ft	
Lifts	46	
Pistes	150km	
	93 miles	

+ Huge area shared with Tignes, with lots of runs for all abilities

+ One of the great resorts for lift-served off-piste runs

+ Once the snow has fallen, high altitude of slopes keeps it good

+ Wide choice of schools, especially for off-piste lessons and guiding

+ For a high Alpine resort, the town is attractive, very lively at night, and offers a good range of restaurants

+ Wide range of package holidays – including very swanky chalets

− Some green and blue runs are too challenging, and all runs back to the village are tricky

− You're quite likely to need the bus at the start and end of the day

− Most lifts and slopes are liable to close when the weather is bad

− Nursery slopes not ideal

− Main off-piste slopes get tracked out very quickly

− At times seems more British than French – especially in low season

− Still not enough snowmaking

− Increasingly pricey

Val d'Isère is one of the world's best resorts for experts – attracted by the extent of lift-served off-piste – and for confident, mileage-hungry intermediates. You don't have to be particularly adventurous to enjoy the resort; but it would be much better for novices if the piste classifications were more reliable.

The many drawbacks listed above are mainly not serious complaints, whereas most of the plus-points weigh heavily in the balance. For a combination of seriously impressive skiing and captivating village ambience, there aren't many places we'd rather go – especially if we're looking for a luxurious chalet.

THE RESORT

Val d'Isère spreads along a remote valley, which is a dead end in winter. The road in from Bourg-St-Maurice brings you dramatically through a rocky defile to the satellite mini-resort of La Daille – a convenient but hideous slope-side apartment complex and the base of lifts into the major Bellevarde sector of the slopes. The outskirts of Val proper are dreary, but as you approach the centre the improvements put in place over the last 15 years become more evident: wood- and stone-cladding, culminating in the tasteful pedestrian-only Val Village complex. Many first-time visitors find the resort much more pleasant than they expect a high French resort to be.

Turn right at the centre and you drive under the nursery slopes and two of Val's big lifts up the mountains to a lot of new development in the suburbs of Le Joseray, Le Châtelard and Le Legettaz. Continue up the main valley instead, and you come to Le Laisinant,

a peaceful little outpost with a fast lift out of the valley, and then to Le Fornet, the fourth major lift station.

There is a lot of traffic around, but the resort is working to get cars under control and has made the centre more pedestrian-friendly.

The location of your accommodation

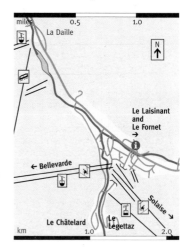

isn't crucial, unless you want to ski from the door or be close to a nursery slope. The main lift stations are linked by efficient free shuttle-buses; in peak periods you never have to wait more than a few minutes. But in the evening frequency plummets and dedicated après-skiers will want to be within walking distance of the centre. The developments up the side valley beyond the main lift station – Le Châtelard and La Legettaz – are mainly attractive, and some offer ski-in/ski-out convenience. La Daille and Le Fornet have their (quite different) attractions for those less concerned about nightlife. A car is of no great value around the resort, but simplifies outings to other resorts. A five-day lift pass may be upgraded daily (10 euros) to cover Les Arcs and La Plagne, and the Three Valleys.

Although there are wooded slopes above the village on all sectors, in practice most of the runs here are on open slopes above the tree line, and a lot of lifts can close in bad weather. Piste grooming is better than it used to be, but we continue to get complaints about the poor signing (particularly at piste junctions) and the piste classification. Many blue and some green runs are simply too steep, narrow and even bumpy; we are pleased to see that some pistes have been reclassified but more need to be.

If you plan a return visit, keep your lift pass – you may get a 'loyal customer' reduction.

The local radio carries weather reports in English as well as in French.

THE SLOPES
Vast and varied
Val d'Isère's slopes divide into three main sectors, two reachable from the village. **Bellevarde** is the mountain that is home to Val d'Isère's famous downhill course – the OK piste. You can reach Bellevarde quickly by underground funicular from La Daille or the powerful gondola from near the centre of town. From the top you can descend to the valley, play on a variety of drags and chairs at altitude or take a choice of lifts to the slopes of Tignes (see separate chapter).

Solaise is the other mountain accessible directly from the village. The Solaise fast quad takes you a few metres higher than the parallel cable-car. Once up, a short drag takes you over a plateau and down to a variety of chairs that serve this very sunny area of predominantly gentle pistes. From near the top of this area you can catch the fast Leissières chair (which climbs over a steep ridge and then drops suddenly down the other side) over to the third main area, in the valley running up to the **Col de l'Iseran**. This area can also be reached by the fast chair from Le Laisinant or by cable-car from Le Fornet. Beyond the col, you ski down to lifts on the **Glacier de Pissaillas**.

TERRAIN-PARKS
Beginners and experts welcome
Above the La Daille gondola and served by the Mont Blanc chair-lift lies a very good terrain-park (www.winterparkvaldisere.com).

Val d'Isère

405

FRANCE

406

LIFT PASSES

Espace Killy

Prices in €

Age	1-day	6-day
under 13	31	148
13 to 59	41	198
over 60	35	168

Free under 5, over 75

Beginner free lifts on nursery slopes

Notes
Covers Tignes and Val d'Isère; half-day and pedestrian passes; family discounts; 6-day plus passes valid for one day in the Three Valleys, Valmorel, Ste-Foy and Paradiski (La Plagne-Les Arcs), and reduced price in La Rosière

Alternative pass
Val d'Isère only

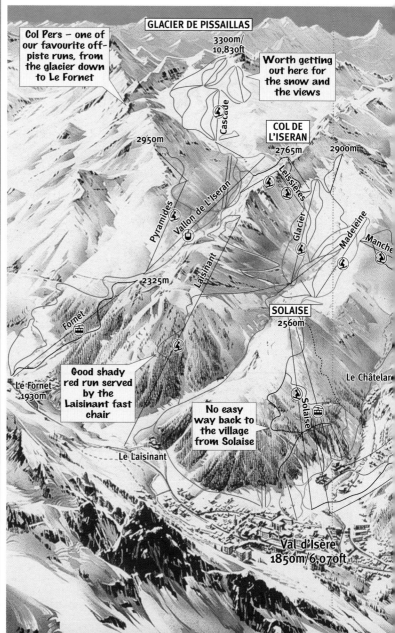

GLACIER DE PISSAILLAS

Col Pers – one of our favourite off-piste runs, from the glacier down to Le Fornet

3300m/10,830ft

Worth getting out here for the snow and the views

2950m

Cascade

COL DE L'ISERAN
2765m

2900m

Leissières

Pyramides

Vallon de L'Iseran

Glacier

Madeleine

Manche

2325m

Laisinant

SOLAISE
2560m

Le Châtelard

Fornet

Good shady red run served by the Laisinant fast chair

Le Fornet
1930m

Solaise

No easy way back to the village from Solaise

Le Laisinant

Val d'Isère
1850m/6,070ft

Good area of varied intermediate runs at altitude, with a couple of fast chairs

The blue from here is the easiest and least crowded intermediate route to Tignes

Glacier de la Grande Motte

OL DE SERAN
2765m

2900m

Leissières

Excellent runs down to the Manchet chair – though affected by sun later in the season

Lots of long, high easy runs – but also lots of slow old chair-lifts

COL DE FRESSE
2770m

Glacier

Madeleine

Manchet

Le Manchet
1940m

Borsat

Tignes

Fresse

TOVIERE
2705m

BELLEVARDE
2705m

OLAISE
2560m

Loyes

Le Châtelard

L'Olympique

Tommeuses

The world's trickiest green run – narrow in parts and crowded and mogulled at the end of the day

Solaise

Bellevarde

Funival

Daille

Val d'Isère
850m/6.070ft

The 1992 Winter Olympic men's downhill course is now a genuine black run and often mogulled from top to bottom

La Daille
1785m

Maintenance can be a bit hit or miss, but on a good day this park has a bit of everything. There are four kicker lines, with jumps ranging from 3m/10ft in the blue line to 20m/66ft in the pro line. With more and more earth-work being done during the summer to pre-shape jumps, there are now up to five jumps in a row on some of the lines, so prepare your legs. New this year was what the park shaper described as the 'mother of all hips'. A plethora of rails including flat downs, a C box, rainbow, and a range of boxes form a nice contour around the park. The boarder-cross is just outside the park and though bad snow stunted plans for a half-pipe, it is on the cards for 2008. Or head over to the Tignes pipe.

SNOW RELIABILITY
Only early season issues
In years when lower resorts have suffered, Val d'Isère has rarely been short of snow. Once a big dump of snow has fallen, the resort's height means you can almost always get back to the village. But even more important is that in each sector there are lots of lifts and runs above mid-mountain, between about 2300m and 2900m (7,550ft and 9,510ft). Many of the slopes face roughly north. And there is access to glaciers at Pissaillas or over in Tignes, although both take a while to get to. Snowmaking continues to be extended – last season to include the Creux blue piste from Tovière, with 'immediate benefit', says one visitor.

FOR EXPERTS
One of the world's best
Val d'Isère is one of the top resorts in the world for experts. The main attraction is the huge range of beautiful off-piste possibilities – see the feature panel.

There may be better resorts for really steep pistes – there are certainly lots in North America – but there is plenty on-piste to amuse the expert, despite the small number of blacks on the piste map. Many reds and blues are steep enough to get mogulled.

On Bellevarde the famous Face run is the main attraction – often mogulled from top to bottom, but not worryingly steep. Epaule is the sector's other black run – where the moguls are hit by long exposure to sun and can be slushy or rock hard (it is prone to closure for these reasons too). There are several challenging ways down from Solaise to the village: all steep, though none fearsomely so (Piste S is now classified a 'Naturide' – which means it is never groomed).

Wayne Watson of off-piste school Alpine Expérience puts a daily diary of off-piste snow conditions and runs on the web at www.alpineexperience.com.

FOR INTERMEDIATES
Quantity and quality
Val d'Isère has just as much to offer intermediates as experts. There's enough here to keep you interested for several visits – though pistes can be crowded in high-season, and the less experienced should be aware that many runs are under-classified.

In the Solaise sector is a network of gentle blue runs, ideal for building confidence. And there are a couple of beautiful runs from here through the woods to Le Laisinant – ideal in bad weather, though prone to closure in times of avalanche danger.

Most of the runs in the Col de l'Iseran sector are even easier – ideal for early and hesitant intermediates. Those marked blue at the top of the

---

THE BEST LIFT-SERVED OFF-PISTE IN THE WORLD?

Few resorts can rival the extent of lift-served off-piste skiing in Val d'Isère.

Some runs are ideal for adventurous intermediates looking to try off-piste for the first time. The Tour du Charvet goes through glorious scenery from the top of the Grand Pré chair-lift on the back of Bellevarde. For most of the way it is very gentle, with only a few steeper pitches. It ends up at the bottom of the Manchet chair up to the Solaise area. The Pays Désert is a very easy run from the top of the lift system on the Pissaillas glacier. You end up at the Pays Désert T-bar. The views are superb.

For more experienced off-piste skiers, Col Pers is one of our favourite runs. Again, it starts a traverse away from the Pissaillas glacier. You go over a pass into a big, wide, fairly gentle bowl with glorious views and endless ways down. If the snow is good, you can drop down into the Gorges de Malpasset and ski over the frozen Isère river back to the Fornet cable-car.

There are endless other off-piste options, such as Cugnai and Danaides on Solaise, Banane and the Couloir des Pisteurs on Bellevarde – and, of course, many more in Tignes.

Val d'Isère's more upmarket profile attracts a different kind of holiday boarder from Tignes; the resort is, perhaps, seen as Tignes' less hardcore cousin. But the terrain here is phenomenal and still draws a fair few boarders. The easier slopes are suitable for beginners, and there are now very few drag-lifts. There is a very good terrain-park, and there are specialist snowboard shops such as Misty Fly and Quiksilver Boardriders. Check your email and have a coffee at the snowboarder-run Powder Monkey cafe.

glacier could really be classified green.

Bellevarde has a huge variety of runs ideally suited to intermediates of all levels. From Bellevarde itself there is a choice of green, blue and red runs of varying pitch. The World Cup Downhill OK piste is a wonderful rolling cruise when groomed. The wide runs from Tovière normally give you the choice of groomed piste or moguls.

A snag for early intermediates is that runs back to the valley can be challenging. The easiest way is down to La Daille on a green run which would be classified blue or red in most resorts. It gets very crowded and mogulled by the end of the day. None of the runs from Bellevarde and Solaise back to Val itself is easy. Many early intermediates ride the lifts down.

FOR BEGINNERS
OK if you know where to go
The nursery slope right by the centre of town is 95 per cent perfect; it's just a pity that the very top is unpleasantly steep. The lifts serving it are free.

Once off the nursery slopes, you have to know where to find easy runs; many of the greens should be blue, or even red. One local instructor admits: 'We have to have green runs on the map, even if we don't have so many green slopes – otherwise beginners wouldn't come to Val d'Isère.'

A good place for your first real runs off the nursery slopes is the Madeleine green run on Solaise – served by a fast six-pack. The Col de l'Iseran runs are also gentle and wide, and not overcrowded. There is good

Val d'Isère

409

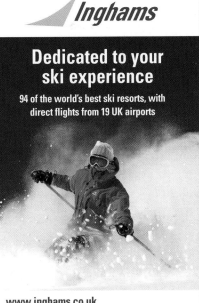

SCHOOLS

Alpine Expérience
t 0479 062881

BASS
t 0679 512405

Development Centre
t 0615 553156

ESF
t 0479 060234

Evolution 2
t 0479 411672

Misty Fly Snowboard
t 0479 400874

Mountain Masters
t 0479 060514

New Generation
t 0479 010318
www.skinewgen.com

Ogier
t 0479 061893

Oxygène
t 0479 419958

Progression
t 0621 939380

Ski Concept
t 0479 401919

Ski-lesson.com
t 0621 652944

Ski Leisure
t 0672 120140

Ski Mastery
t 0479 401768

Snow Fun
t 0479 061979

Top Ski
t 0479 061480

Val Gliss
t 0479 060072

Classes (ESF prices)
6 days (3hr am, 2½hr
pm) €219

Private lessons
€40 for 1hr

GUIDES

Mountain office
t 0479 069403

Tetra
t 0479 419707

---

progression terrain on Bellevarde, too – though getting to it can be tricky. From all sectors, it's best to take a lift back down to the valley.

FOR CROSS-COUNTRY
Limited
There are a couple of loops in each of three areas – towards La Daille, on Solaise and out past Le Laisinant. More picturesque is the one going from Le Châtelard (on the road past the main cable-car station) to the Manchet chair. But keen cross-country enthusiasts should go elsewhere.

QUEUES
Few problems
Queues to get out of the resort have been kept in check by lift upgrades and additions, recently including the big gondola to Bellevarde and the six-pack from Le Laisinant. At Solaise the slow Lac chair up to the Tête Solaise can generate queues. Crowded pistes in high season is a more common complaint than queues these days – Piste L from Solaise to Le Laisinant has been singled out this year as 'dangerously overcrowded.'

MOUNTAIN RESTAURANTS
Acceptable – at long last
It's been a long, slow business, but last year Val at last managed a three-star rating for mountain restaurants. They mainly consist of big self-service places at the top of major lifts. There are now more exceptions – but they are too few, so they are too busy, so high-season service can be poor.
Editors' choice The wood-and-stone Edelweiss (0610 287064), above Le Fornet, is our current favourite for the best food. We've had delicious duck and fish there (reporters also send us rave reviews). Worth calling in to pick a table if you can. The Fruitière (0479 060717) at the top of La Daille gondola, kitted out with stuff rescued from a dairy in the valley, crams in way too many people but handles them well. We had a good lunch here in 2007, but others have been unimpressed; more reports, please.
Worth knowing about We've always enjoyed the busy Trifollet halfway down the OK run, but we're getting reports from disappointed visitors. On the lower slopes at La Daille, and reachable on snow and by pedestrians, Tufs does good pizzas and a good-value buffet on the first floor. The

Marmottes, in the middle of the Bellevarde bowl, is an efficient self-service with a big sunny terrace and good food ('big portion of Moroccan couscous and chicken'). The small and friendly Bar de L'Ouillette, at the base of the Madeleine chair-lift, does good food at reasonable prices. La Datcha at the bottom of the Glacier Express has a small table-service section ('succulent slow-cooked lamb'). One reporter recommends the Tanière (popular with locals) set between the two chairs going up Face de Bellevarde.

Of course there are lots of places in the resort villages. When at Col de l'Iseran, one idea is to descend to the rustic Arolay ('excellent for both lunch and dinner, with a lovely terrace') at Le Fornet – also favoured by a couple of non-skiers this year. The terrace of hotel Brussel's in Val d'Isère, right by the nursery slopes, has 'good food and excellent service' and the Grand Paradis, next door, is 'an enjoyable lunch venue, very well run and efficient'.

SCHOOLS AND GUIDES
A very wide choice
There is a huge choice of schools, guides and private instructors. But as they all get busy, at peak periods it's best to book in advance. Practically all the schools run off-piste groups at various levels of competence, as well as on-piste lessons. Outside the ESF, practically all the instructors and guides speak good English, and many are native English-speakers.

New Generation, a British-run school, has a branch here. Reports are very positive: 'The morning we had was one of the highlights of our holiday – lots of fun and we learned a lot too.' 'Worth every euro,' says a 2007 reporter. The Development Centre, based in the Precision Ski shop in the heart of the village, is a group of British instructors who offer intensive clinics for all levels of skier, and have been highly praised.

Mountain Masters is a group of British and French instructors and guides, and a 2006 reporter said: 'They knew exactly how to take me over that seventh-week plateau.' Progression is a new British-run school with a maximum group size of 6 or 8.

We've heard from lots of satisfied pupils of Snow Fun ('Good value and good instructors,' said one) and Evolution 2. Reporters consistently

CHILDREN

Le Village des Enfants
t 0479 400981
Ages 3 to 13; 9am-5.30 (Sun-Thu); 9am-2pm (Fri)

Le Petit Poucet
t 0479 061397
Ages from 3; 9am-5.30

Babysitter list
Contact tourist office

Ski schools
Most offer classes for ages 5 up (ESF prices from €214 for 6 days)

GETTING THERE

Air Geneva 180km/112 miles (4hr); Lyon 220km/137 miles (4hr); Chambéry 130km/81 miles (3hr)

Rail Bourg-St-Maurice (30km/19 miles); regular buses from station

praise Bernard Chesneau of Ski Mastery. Misty Fly is a specialist snowboard school. Private lessons with BASS get a rave review from a 2007 reporter, whose nervous wife 'was skiing with competence and confidence after a few hours' lessons'.

Alpine Expérience and Top Ski specialise in guided off-piste groups – an excellent way to get off-piste safely without the cost of hiring a guide as an individual. We have had great mornings out with both. Heli-skiing trips can be arranged from over the border in Italy – heli-drops are banned in France.

FACILITIES FOR CHILDREN
Good tour op possibilities
Many people prefer to use the facilities of UK tour operators such as Mark Warner, Ski Beat or Esprit. But there's a 'children's village' for three- to eight-year-olds, with supervised indoor and outdoor activities on the village nursery slopes. A past reporter was 'very pleased' with the childcare there: 'The staff speak English, and are very organised, in particular about safety.'

STAYING THERE

HOW TO GO
Lots of choice
More British tour operators go to Val than anywhere else apart from Méribel. **Chalets** This is Planet Chalet, with properties at every level of the market. Many of the most impressive are in the side valley running south from the village – some in the elevated enclave of Les Carats. YSE is a Val d'Isère specialist, with 25 varied chalets – from swanky apartments for four or six to proper big chalets. Companies with top-end properties include VIP, Scott Dunn and Descent International. Le Ski has nine chalets, including six splendid all-en-suite places grouped together just up from the main street (with a big outdoor hot-tub) and two swanky chalets for eight nearby. Crystal Finest has three units for 10/12 (and shared wellness area) in a central new chalet. Total has a wide range, from old farmhouses to very smart apartments in Les Carats. Ski Beat has five en-suite apartments in one grand chalet. Finlays has half-a-dozen properties.

FRANCE

412

UK PACKAGES

SMART LODGINGS

Check out our feature chapters at the front of the book.

There are several chalet hotels. Mark Warner has four, including the family-friendly Cygnaski, the nightlife hot spot Moris and the central Val d'Isère with outdoor swimming pool. Total has the modern Champs Avalin at La Daille. Esprit, the family specialist, has the Ducs de Savoie near the centre.

Hotels There are about 40 to choose from, mostly 2- and 3-star, but with an increasing number of plush 4-stars; two are opening for 2007/08 – Avenue Lodge and the rebuilt Savoie.

****Barmes de L'Ours** (0479 413700) Recently built, and best in town. Good position, close to slopes and centre. The fabulous rooms are in a different style on each floor. Three restaurants. Excellent indoor pool, and spa.

****Christiania** (0479 060825) Big chalet. Chic but friendly. Pool, sauna.

****Blizzard** (0479 060207) Comfortable. Convenient. Indoor-outdoor pool and sauna. Good food.

****Aigle des Neiges** (0479 061888) Highly rated refurbished version of former Latitudes. Cool and central.

***Savoyarde** (0479 060155) Rustic decor. Leisure centre. Good food (except for vegetarians). Small rooms.

***Brussel's** (0479 060539) Excellent location, right on nursery slope, with big terrace. Sauna, steam, hot-tub.

***Grand Paradis** (0479 061173) Next to Brussel's. Good food.

***Kandahar** (0479 060239) Smart, newish building above Taverne d'Alsace on main street.

***Mercure** (0479 061293) 'The food and wine list are excellent.' 'Convenient and pleasant.'

***Sorbiers** (0479 062377) Modern but cosy B&B hotel, not far out. 'Clean, comfortable, good-sized rooms.'

***Samovar** (0479 061351) In La Daille. Traditional, with good food. 'Very friendly and helpful staff.'

Danival (0479 060065) B&B, piste-side location: 'Very reasonable'.

Apartments Among the best are Chalets de Solaise (with outdoor pool) and Alpina Lodge close to the centre, Chalets du Jardin Alpin at the foot of Solaise and Chalets du Laisinant (at Laisinant). Local agency Val d'Isère Agence (0479 067350) has a large selection of places.

There are thousands of apartments available. UK operators offer lots, but they tend to get booked up early.

EATING OUT
Plenty of good places

The 70-odd restaurants offer a wide variety of cuisines; there's a free *Guide des Tables* booklet covering 23, but many worthwhile places are missing.

The Salon de Thé Moris is recommended for tea and cakes after the lifts close. The Grande Ourse, by the nursery slope, is one place to head for a top-of-the-range meal. Another is Les Clochetons, out in the Manchet valley (they run a free minibus service) – we enjoyed the foie gras and duck. The Table de l'Ours, in the Barmes de l'Ours hotel, has a Michelin star. The hotel Aigle des Neiges restaurants are rated highly by locals.

There are plenty of pleasant mid-priced places. We always enjoy the unchanging Taverne d'Alsace. The Perdrix Blanche went through a bad spell but has now improved again. Tufs, on the snow at La Daille, is open in the evenings (see 'Mountain restaurants'). The 'impressive' Austrian-influenced menu of the Schuss restaurant in the Grand Paradis hotel has been recommended. The Barillon de la Rosée Blanche is 'completely splendid, with great steaks and home-made ice-creams'. Bar Jacques is worth a visit for 'some of the best food in town'. Chez Nano (next to Dick's Tea Bar) and Chez Paolo are praised for 'excellent' pizzas and pastas; the Corniche for being 'traditional French, very enjoyable'; Casa Scara does 'good food', though service from the welcoming family owners can be slow; the Canyon 'caters to all pockets' and is 'excellent'. The Grand Cocor has 'excellent food and choice'. The Belle Etoile is popular with locals for 'excellent French/Asian cuisine'.

APRES-SKI
Very lively
Nightlife is surprisingly energetic, given that most people have spent a hard day on the slopes. There are lots of bars, many with happy hours followed by music and dancing later on.

The Folie Douce, at the top of the La Daille gondola, has become an Austrian-style tea-time rave, with music and dancing; you can ride the gondola down. At La Daille the bar at the Samovar hotel is 'a good spot for a beer after skiing'. In downtown Val, Bananas (cosy wooden chalet with nice terrace), Café Face ('cheap beer, friendly atmosphere'), the Moris pub (live music at tea time and later) and Saloon (underneath hotel Brussel's) fill up as the slopes close; the 'friendly' Boubou, Bar Jacques and the Perdrix Blanche are popular with locals. The

Petit Danois (a good alternative to Dick's later on) is said to be better than Victor's bar. The Pacific Bar has sport on big-screen TVs. The basement Taverne d'Alsace is quiet and relaxing. But our current favourite spot for a civilised drink in welcoming surroundings is the first-floor bar of the hotel Blizzard.

Later on, the famous Dick's Tea Bar is the main disco, but it gets mixed reviews. And a new nightclub, the Doudoune, is due to open for 2007/08.

OFF THE SLOPES
A reasonable amount to do
Val is primarily a resort for those keen to get on to the slopes – though one non-skiing reporter was 'very satisfied' with the facilities. There's a swimming pool and the range of shops is better than in most high French resorts. Lunchtime meetings present problems: the easily accessible mountain restaurants are few, and your friends may prefer lunching miles away in places like Les Brévières. A 2007 reporter suggests the 'fascinating' nature walk from Le Fornet to Pont St Charles and the tourist office runs evening events once a week.

Valmorel

The purpose-built resort the French got mainly right: easy on the eye, as well as convenient; sadly, they didn't pick the ideal site

COSTS

① ② ③ ④ ⑤ ⑥

RATINGS

The slopes
Fast lifts	*
Snow	**
Extent	***
Expert	**
Intermediate	****
Beginner	*****
Convenience	*****
Queues	***
Mountain restaurants	**

The rest
Scenery	***
Resort charm	****
Off-slope	**

NEWS

For 2007/08 a quad is planned to replace the Buffle chair at St François, and a new boarder-cross is to be built.

Last season, the Madeleine chair was upgraded to a six-pack and the Mollaret chair at Longchamp to a quad.

KEY FACTS

Resort	1400m
	4,590ft

Le Grand Domaine
Slopes	1250-2550m
	4,100-8,370ft
Lifts	49
Pistes	152km
	94 miles
Green	33%
Blue	39%
Red	19%
Black	9%
Snowmaking	
	202 guns

For Domaine de Valmorel only
Slopes	1250-2405m
	4,100-7,890ft
Lifts	38
Pistes	95km
	59 miles

+ The most sympathetically designed French purpose-built, car-free resort

+ Largely slope-side accommodation

+ Extensive easy slopes linked to St-François-Longchamp give even the timid a chance to travel around

+ Beginners and children particularly well catered for

− Most pistes are easy, and of limited vertical

− Fairly low, so snow can suffer

− Still lots of slow lifts and drags, with peak-season lift queues

− Steep site, and outlying parts are very separate from the main street

− Few alternatives to self-catering

Built from scratch in the mid-1970s, Valmorel was intended to look and feel like a mountain village – or perhaps a tiny mountain town; shops and restaurants line the cute, narrow, traffic-free main street. Compared with its illustrious neighbours in the Three Valleys, the mountain feels a bit second-rate; but it really competes for French family business with cheaper resorts to the south.

THE RESORT

Valmorel is the main resort in 'Le Grand Domaine' – a ski area shared with St-François and Longchamp, across the Madeleine pass. Bourg-Morel is the heart of the resort – an intimate, traffic-free street where you'll find most of the shops and restaurants. It's pleasant and usually lively, with a distinctly family feel. Scattered here and there on the hillside are the six 'hameaux' with most of the lodgings. Hameau-du-Mottet is convenient – it is at the top of the Télébourg (the cross-village lift) with good access to the main lifts and from the return runs. All the mega-resorts of the Tarentaise are within driving distance.

THE MOUNTAINS

Variety is not lacking, and the extent is enough to provide interesting day-trips. There are still a lot drag-lifts and slow chairs, but a new six-pack has improved the link towards Longchamp.
Slopes The pistes are spread over a number of minor valleys and ridges either side of the Col de la Madeleine. The most heavily used route out of the village is the fast Altispace quad chair. From the top, a network of lifts and pistes takes you to the Col de la Madeleine and beyond that to Lauzière or the slopes of Longchamp and St-François. The Pierrafort sector has its own runs back towards the village, or you can work your way round to the

Beaudin and Madeleine sectors.
Terrain-parks The Snowzone at the top of the Crève Coeur chair has park, pipes and boarder-cross. A park-only pass is available. A second boarder-cross is planned for the Biollène chair and there's another at St François.
Snow reliability There's snowmaking on the nursery slopes and the main runs back to base, but when we visited last season it wasn't used sufficiently. The slopes are low by local standards, and quite sunny – not good news.
Experts There are a few challenging pistes; the steepest are in the Pierrafort sector; but there is good off-piste that doesn't get skied out.
Intermediates The whole area – except for the steepest black runs – is ideal, though the main home run can be quite daunting at the end of the day. We have had mixed reports about piste grooming: one report says it is 'erratic, making some red runs tricky'.
Beginners There are dedicated learning areas ('Still the best we've seen, 10/10,' according to one reporter) right by the village for both adults and children. There's a free beginner lift at Le Crey.
Snowboarding There are decent intermediate runs; but new boarders will find some of the drag-lifts tricky.
Cross-country Trails adding up to 23km/14 miles can be reached by bus.
Queues The Altispace chair out of the resort is reportedly slow to start in the morning, and both village lifts can build big queues at peak times; depending on your location, you may be able to avoid these.

Col du Mottet 2405m
Col du Gollet 1980m
PIERRAFORT
BEAUDIN 2020m
2185m
ST FRANCOIS LONGCHAMP
Crey
Les Avanchers
Valmorel 1400m
Doucy Combelouvière
MADELEINE
Lauzière 2550m
Longchamp 1650m
St François 1400m
COMBELOUVIERE

Mountain restaurants There are half a dozen or so. Banquise 2000, with a great location at Col de la Madeleine, and Prariond ('beautiful building', 'wonderful views') have been recommended. Also mentioned are the Altipiano for 'very good food and service' and the Alpage – 'very good location and good value'. Cagette is now the Arbet.

Schools and guides Recent reports have been positive for both adult and children's classes. A 2006 reporter said that his children's private lessons were 'very good', the instructor 'punctual and good'. Teaching for first-timers is a speciality of the resort.

Facilities for children Valmorel goes out of its way to cater for children. Piou-Piou club is a comprehensive childcare facility run by the ski school, and children taking ski lessons can have lunch there, too. Advance booking is essential.

STAYING THERE

How to go Self-catering packages are the norm. Ski Amis has a good-value, all en suite chalet near a lift station at Le Pré, a hamlet just down the road.
Hotels The Village Club du Soleil (0825 802805) is right on the slopes. The 'ideally located' 2-star Hotel du Bourg (0479 098666) is reportedly 'a bit faded but fit-for-purpose'.
Apartments The Athamante et Valeriane apartments have been praised.
Eating out The Petit Prince ('excellent, friendly service'), the Marmite and Ski Roc win approval from 2006 reporters.
Après-ski Immediate après-ski centres on the lively cafe-bars with terraces at the foot of the slopes; after-dark activities centre on the main street.
Off the slopes It's not a great place to hang around but there are various activities. There's a fitness centre, a cinema and a toboggan run.

Valmorel

Selected chalet in Valmorel

SKI AMIS *www.skiamis.com*   T **0207 692 0850** F **0207 692 0851**

Val Thorens

Europe's highest resort, with guaranteed good snow but also other attractions: stylish lodgings and good restaurants among them

COSTS

① ② ③ ④ ⑤ ⑥

RATINGS

The slopes

Fast lifts	****
Snow	*****
Extent	*****
Expert	****
Intermediate	*****
Beginner	****
Convenience	*****
Queues	***
Mountain restaurants	****

The rest

Scenery	***
Resort charm	**
Off-slope	**

NEWS

For 2007/08 the Cairn and Caron gondolas (from the resort to the Cîme de Caron cable-car) are due to be replaced by new eight-seat gondolas that will let you keep your skis and boards inside and that will almost double the hourly capacity (we hate to think what this will mean for the already long queues for the Cîme de Caron cable-car). The base stations will be revamped too (escalators etc).

The 4-star Fitz Roy hotel, under new ownership, has begun refurbishment work and 17 new luxury rooms are due to open this season.

For 2006/07 more snowmaking was installed and a leisure centre with eight bowling lanes, pool halls, bar and restaurant opened.

416

- ➕ Extensive local slopes to suit all abilities, and good access to the rest of the vast Three Valleys
- ➕ The highest resort in the Alps and one of the most snow-sure, with mainly north-facing slopes
- ➕ Convenient, gentle nursery slopes
- ➕ Not as much of an eyesore as most high, purpose-built resorts, with more and more smart lodgings
- ➕ Compact village with direct slope access from most accommodation

- ➖ Can be bleak in bad weather – not a tree in sight
- ➖ Parts of the village are much less attractive to walk through in the evening than to ski past in the day
- ➖ Not much to do off the slopes
- ➖ Some very crowded pistes and dangerous intersections
- ➖ Still some queues – and really serious ones for the Cîme de Caron cable-car

For the enthusiast looking for the best snow available, it's difficult to beat Val Thorens. That wonderful snow lies on some pretty wonderful slopes suitable for everyone from beginner to expert. And the village – always one of the better-designed high-altitude stations – gets more attractive as it continues to develop, and gain more smart accommodation and restaurants.

But we still prefer a cosier base elsewhere in the Three Valleys. That way, if a storm socks in, we can play in the woods; if the sun is scorching, we have the option of setting off for Val Thorens. The formula simply doesn't work the other way round. For a pre-Christmas or an April trip, though, it's the best base.

THE RESORT

Val Thorens is built high above the tree line on a sunny, west-facing mountainside at the head of its valley, surrounded by peaks, slopes and lifts. The streets are supposedly traffic-free. Most visitors' cars are banished to car parks, except on Saturday. Workers' cars still generate a fair amount of traffic, though, and Saturdays can be mayhem. A reporter recommends booking parking in advance: 'It's cheaper and you are less likely to get a far distant parking spot.'

Many buildings are designed with their 'fronts' facing the slopes, and their relatively dreary backs facing the streets. There are quite extensive shopping arcades, a fair choice of bars and restaurants, and a good sports centre.

It is a classic purpose-built resort, with lots of convenient slope-side accommodation (but some of the newer buildings are less convenient – see below). It's quite a complex little village; but it's quite compact – our scale plan is one of the smallest in these pages. At its heart is the snowy Place de Caron, where pedestrians mix with skiers and boarders. Many of the shops and restaurants are clustered here, along with the best hotels; and the sports and leisure centres are nearby.

The village is basically divided in two by a little slope (with a drag-lift) that leads down from here to the broad main nursery slope running the length of the village. The upper half of the village is centred on the Place de Péclet. A road runs across the hillside from here to the chalet-style Plein Sud area, where many of the most attractive new apartments have been built. The highest of these can be reached and left on snow only by awkward off-piste sections ('not for the faint-hearted on ice') or by road

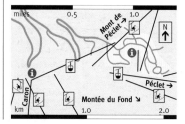

The snow quality here is difficult to beat and there is a vast amount of off-piste →

OT VAL THORENS / AGENCE
BASILE / GIL MIRANDE

KEY FACTS

Resort	2300m
	7,550ft

Three Valleys	
Slopes	1260-3230m
	4,130-10,600ft
Lifts	183
Pistes	600km
	373 miles
Green	15%
Blue	38%
Red	37%
Black	10%
Snowmaking	
	1920 guns

Val Thorens only	
Slopes	1800-3230m
	5,900-10,600ft
Lifts	29
Pistes	140km
	87 miles
Green	12%
Blue	37%
Red	40%
Black	11%
Snowmaking	
	352 guns

('frequent ski-bus, about 200m/65oft walk to piste'). The lower half of the village is more diffuse, with the Rue du Soleil winding down from the dreary bus station (visitors praise the free bus service) to the big Pierre & Vacances apartments.

Seen from the slopes, the resort is not as ugly as many of its rivals. The buildings are mainly medium-rise and wood-clad; some are distinctly stylish.

THE MOUNTAINS

The main disadvantage of Val Thorens is the lack of trees. Heavy snowfalls or high wind can shut practically all the lifts and slopes, and even if they don't close, poor visibility can be a problem. Piste marking and signposting have been criticised by reporters. If you buy a Three Valleys lift pass for five days or more we understand you'll be able to buy a 10 euro daily extension to ski the Val d'Isère-Tignes or Paradiski areas too.

THE SLOPES
High and snow-sure

The resort has a wide piste going right down the front of it, leading down to a number of different lifts. The big Péclet gondola, with 30-person cabins, rises 700m/2,300ft to the Péclet glacier, with a choice of red runs down. One links across to a wide area of intermediate runs served by lifts to cols either side

of the Pointe de Thorens. You can take red or blue runs into the 'fourth valley', the Maurienne, from one of these – the Col de Rosaël, now served by the Grand Fond 30-person gondola.

Above Orelle in the Maurienne valley two successive slow chairs go up to 3230m/10,600ft on the flanks of Pointe du Bouchet – the highest lift-served point in the Three Valleys, with stunning views. The former black run off the back of here is now off-piste because of crevasse and avalanche danger and the snow gets very windblown and icy.

The 150-person cable-car to Cîme de Caron is one of the great lifts of the Alps, rising 900m/2,950ft in no time at all. It can be reached by skiing across from mid-mountain, or by coming up on the gondola, which starts below the village. From the top there are fabulous views and a choice of red and black pistes down the front, or a black into the Maurienne.

The relatively low Boismint sector is overlooked by many visitors, but is actually a very respectable hill ('a hidden gem' says a 2007 visitor) with a total vertical of 860m/2,820ft.

Chair-lifts heading north from the resort serve sunny slopes above the village and also lead to the link to the Méribel valley. Les Menuires can be reached via these lifts; the alternative Boulevard Cumin along the valley floor is nearly flat, and can be hard work.

boarding

Val Thorens has always been popular with snowboarders as it is the highest and most snow-sure of the Three Valleys resorts, as well as having a younger and more affordable feel in comparison with Courchevel and Méribel. The terrain is rather bleak; however, there are great steep runs, gullies, and groomed pistes for all levels and forms of snowboarding. The lifts are mainly chairs and gondolas.

TERRAIN-PARKS
More than adequate

The Menhir terrain-park just above the village, served by the Deux Lacs chair-lift, has over ten obstacles that include a quarter-pipe, kicker line and hip and handrail line. There is a 110m/36oft long half-pipe that gets cut daily. The whole park is well maintained and new obstacles are often built for local competitions. Beside the bottom chair-lift towards Pointe du Bouchet in the Maurienne valley is a 1.5km/1 mile-long boarder-cross course, which will test the best of them. If neither of these are to your taste, neighbouring Les Menuires also has a good terrain-park above Reberty.

SNOW RELIABILITY
One of the best

Few resorts can rival Val Thorens for reliably good snow-cover, thanks to its altitude and generally north-facing slopes. Snowmaking covers a lot of the key pistes, including the crowded south- and west-facing runs on the way back from the Méribel valley and in the Orelle sector. But the terrain is rocky and needs a lot of snow for good coverage – we have found the higher runs patchy in recent early season visits when snow throughout the Alps has been slow to arrive.

FOR EXPERTS
Lots to do off-piste

Val Thorens' local pistes are primarily intermediate terrain; many of the

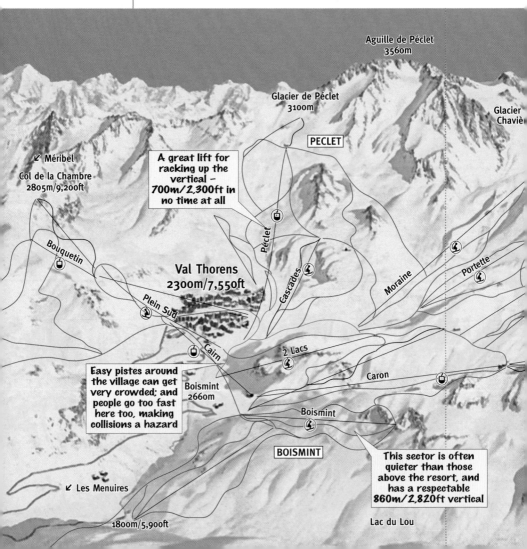

Aguille de Péclet
3560m

Glacier de Péclet
3100m

Glacier Chaviè

PECLET

Méribel
Col de la Chambre
2805m/9,200ft

A great lift for racking up the vertical – 700m/2,300ft in no time at all

Péclet

Bouquetin

Val Thorens
2300m/7,550ft

Cascades

Moraine

Portette

Plein Sud

Cairn

2 Lacs

Caron

Easy pistes around the village can get very crowded; and people go too fast here too, making collisions a hazard

Boismint
2660m

Boismint

BOISMINT

Les Menuires

This sector is often quieter than those above the resort, and has a respectable 860m/2,820ft vertical

1800m/5,900ft

Lac du Lou

blacks could easily be graded red instead. The fast Cascades chair serves a short but steep black run that quickly gets mogulled. The pistes down from the Cîme de Caron cable-car are challenging, but not seriously steep, and there's a sunny black run off the back into the fourth valley.

The red Chamois, Falaise and Variante runs from Col de Rosaël can get heavily mogulled and challenging (and a recent reporter found them 'full of out of control skiers and boarders who are not prepared for the conditions they find'). The sunny Marielle run, one of the routes from the Méribel valley, is one of the easiest blacks we've come across, but it can get crowded and be icy in the morning.

There is a huge amount of very good off-piste terrain to explore with a guide – see the special off-piste feature panel overleaf.

FOR INTERMEDIATES
Unbeatable quality and quantity
The scope for intermediates throughout the Three Valleys is enormous. It will take a keen intermediate only 90 minutes or so to get to Courchevel 1650 at the far end, if not distracted by the endless runs on the way.

The local slopes in Val Thorens are some of the best intermediate terrain in the region. Most of the pistes are easy reds and blues (the runs on the top half of the mountain are steeper than those back into the resort) and made even more enjoyable by the excellent snow.

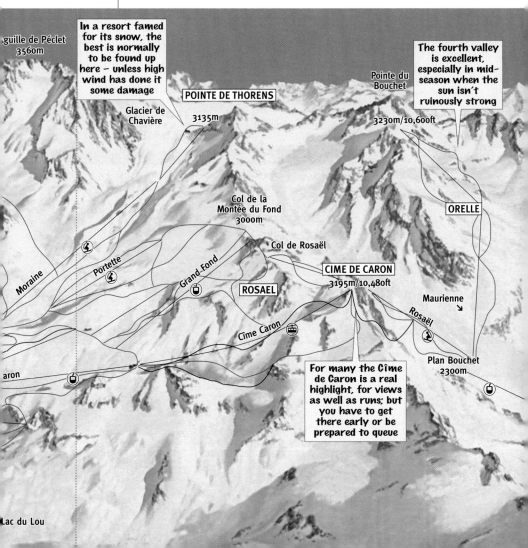

guille de Péclet
3560m

In a resort famed for its snow, the best is normally to be found up here – unless high wind has done it some damage

POINTE DE THORENS

Glacier de Chavière
3135m

Pointe du Bouchet

The fourth valley is excellent, especially in mid-season when the sun isn't ruinously strong

3230m/10,600ft

Col de la Montée du Fond
3000m

ORELLE

Col de Rosaël

CIME DE CARON
3195m/10,480ft

Moraine

Portette

Grand Fond

ROSAEL

Maurienne

Rosaël

Cime Caron

Plan Bouchet
2300m

aron

For many the Cîme de Caron is a real highlight, for views as well as runs; but you have to get there early or be prepared to queue

Lac du Lou

LIFT PASSES

Three Valleys

Prices in €

Age	1-day	6-day
under 13	32	161
13 to 59	43	215
over 60	37	177

Free under 5, over 72

Beginner day pass
€17 for five lifts

Notes
Covers Courchevel, La Tania, Méribel, Val Thorens, Les Menuires and St-Martin; family reductions; pedestrian and half-day passes

Alternative pass
Val Thorens-Orelle only with one-day Three Valleys extension available

UK PACKAGES

Airtours, Alpine Answers, Chalet World Ski, Club Med, Crystal, Directski.com, Erna Low, First Choice, Flexiski, Independent Ski Links, Inghams, Interactive Resorts, Interhome, Kuoni, Lagrange, Made to Measure, Neilson, Ski Activity, Ski Amis, Ski Collection, Ski Expectations, Ski France, Ski Freshtracks, Ski Independence, Ski Leisure Direction, Ski Line, Ski McNeill, Ski Solutions, Ski Supreme, Ski Weekend, Ski4you, Skifrance4less, Skiholidayextras, Skitracer, Skiworld, Solo's, Thomson, Total

---

The snow on the red Col run is normally some of the best around. The blue Moraine below it is gentle and popular with the schools. The Grand Fond gondola serves a good variety of red runs. The Pluviomètre from the Trois Vallées chair is a glorious varied run, away from the lifts. Adventurous intermediates shouldn't miss the Cîme de Caron runs. The black run is not intimidating – it's very wide, usually has good snow, and is a wonderful fast cruise when freshly groomed.

FOR BEGINNERS
Good late-season choice
The slopes at the foot of the resort are very gentle and provide convenient, snow-sure nursery slopes, now with moving walkway lifts. There are no long green runs to progress to, but the blues immediately above the village are easy. The resort's height and bleakness make it cold in midwinter, and intimidating in bad weather.

FOR CROSS-COUNTRY
Go to Les Menuires
There are no cross-country trails in Val Thorens. Your best bet is the 28km/17 mile link between Les Menuires and St-Martin-de-Belleville.

QUEUES
Persistent at the Cîme de Caron
Recent reports suggest that the longest queues are for the largest and most rewarding lifts, notably the Cîme de Caron cable-car. The queues move fairly quickly, but reporters warn that visits to the Cîme de Caron really need to be timed to miss the crowds – get there very early if you can. We fear that the new higher-capacity gondolas leading to the cable-car (see 'News') will make the queues even worse.

In good weather the Rosaël chair back from the fourth valley is a serious bottleneck. And when snow is in short supply elsewhere, the pressure on the Val Thorens lifts can increase markedly.

But crowded pistes and people going too quickly, especially around the village, is a bigger problem than queues. We noticed this on our 2007 visit and several reporters commented on it too; one was crashed into by an out-of-control (British) intermediate while 'standing watching the children'.

MOUNTAIN RESTAURANTS
Lots of choice
For a high, modern resort, the choice of restaurants is good.
Editors' choice We've had several good

FABULOUS OFF-PISTE IN VAL THORENS

Val Thorens offers a huge choice of off-piste. And because of the high altitude, the snow stays powdery longer here than in lower parts of the Three Valleys.

For those with little off-piste experience, the Pierre Lory Pass run is ideal. It is a very large and gentle slope, and you access the pass by doing an easy traverse on the Chavière glacier from the top of the Col chair-lift. When you arrive at Pierre Lory Pass there are breathtaking views of the Aiguilles d'Arves in the Maurienne valley, and you will be just above the glacier du Bouchet, which you then ski down, rejoining the lift system at Plan Bouchet.

For those with more off-piste under their belt already, the Lac du Lou is a famous off-piste run of 1400m/4,590ft vertical. It is easily accessible from the top of the Cîme de Caron cable-car. The many ways into this long, wide valley allow plenty of variety and opportunities for making first tracks; because many of the slopes face north or north-west it is not unusual to find good powder most of the ski season, even in late April. The views are stunning and you'll notice the quietness and vastness of the whole valley.

La Combe sans Nom on the Maurienne side in the fourth valley, also accessible from the Cîme de Caron cable-car, usually offers superb skiing and snowboard conditions. There's a choice of south-, west- and, on the far side, some east-facing slopes, which makes for excellent spring skiing conditions.

For the more adventurous there are many options, including hiking up from the Col chair-lift to a long run over the Gébroulaz glacier down to Méribel-Mottaret.

But don't even think about doing any off-piste runs without a fully qualified guide or instructor. Route finding can be difficult, there can be avalanche danger, and hidden hazards such as cliffs and crevasses lurk.

SCHOOLS

ESF
t 0479 000286
Ski Cool
t 0479 000492
Prosneige
t 0479 010700
International
t 0479 000196
Attitude
t 0479 065772

Classes (ESF prices)
6 half-days (3hr am)
€135
Private lessons
from €39 for 1hr

GUIDES

Mountain office
t 0689 292336

CHILDREN

**Nursery/mini-club
(ESF)**
t 0479 000286
Ages from 3mnth
Prosneige Kids
t 0479 010700

Ski school
The schools offer
classes for children
aged 4 or 5 and over
(ESF: 6 mornings from
€121)

GETTING THERE

Air Geneva 160km/
99 miles (3½hr); Lyon
193km/120 miles
(3½hr); Chambéry
112km/70 miles
(2½hr)

Rail Moûtiers
(37km/23 miles);
regular buses from
station

Phone numbers
From abroad use the
prefix +33 and omit
the initial '0' of the
phone number

OT VAL THORENS / B BOISSIERE

The car-free Rue du
Soleil is a pleasant
place to wander along
→

lunches at the table-service section of the Bar de la Marine (0479 000312), on the Dalles piste and accessed from the Cascades chair (good food but service can get stretched); quite big inside and a big terrace. (We're told the self-service section below does does 'outstanding homemade pizzas').

Worth knowing about The big Chalets du Thorens at the base of the Moraine chair-lift got good 2007 reports: 'lunch of the week with melt in the mouth hunks of beef', 'fab homemade waffles'. The Chalet des 2 Ours on the Blanchot run in the Boismint sector gets repeated recommendations – 'a dream; excellent quality food, large portions and reasonably priced'; 'one of the best mountain restaurants we've experienced: tasty, well-portioned far and great views'. The Moutière, near the top of the chair of the same name, is one of the more reasonably priced huts. The Chalet Chinal Donat (formerly the Plan Bouchet refuge) in the Maurienne valley is very popular and welcoming, but bar service can be slow. You can stay the night there, too. The Chalet Plein Sud, below the chair of the same name, has excellent views but a 'rather limited menu'. The Genépi, on the run of the same name, has a 'lovely open fire', 'good quality food' and 'very pleasant staff'. The Chalet des 2 Lacs is 'friendly but the waiter service was quite slow' says a 2007 reporter. If you head back to town you're sure of a good (but expensive) lunch at the Fitz Roy or Oxalys (both have slope-side terraces).

SCHOOLS AND GUIDES
A mixed bag
The ESF, has a Trois Vallées group for those who want to cover a lot of ground while receiving lessons – available by the day or the week, and can include off-piste. Two 2007 'boarder beginners were delighted with their lessons'. But the children of a recent visitor were taught in French despite 'being guaranteed that lessons would be in English'. Prosneige gets generally better reports; we had two enthusiastic reports last year from intermediates taking private lessons, and one of an absolute beginner who quit her ESF class after her first day, but who was rescued by Prosneige. Ski Cool class sizes are guaranteed not to exceed 10. They also have off-piste courses. There are several specialist guiding outfits.

FACILITIES FOR CHILDREN
Coolly efficient
Our most recent reporter on the ESF nursery found the facilities convenient and the service efficient. In spite of the fact that the staff were 'not particularly warm or friendly', by the end of the week all the children were 'comfortable' on skis. The Prosneige school takes children from age five.

STAYING THERE

HOW TO GO
Surprisingly high level of comfort
Accommodation is of a higher standard than in many purpose-built resorts – more comfortable as well as stylish.
Chalets There are catered apartments, and Total now has a real chalet sold as two units sharing a sauna.
Hotels There are plenty of hotels, and there's a Club Med, too.
****Fitz Roy (0479 000478) The sole 4-star is smart with good service and lovely rooms (17 newly refurbished). Good restaurant with flexible half-board menu. Pool. Well placed.
***Val Thorens (0479 000433) Next door to Fitz Roy. 'Good service, good food and an excellent on the slopes location.' 'Comfortable and friendly.'
***Sherpa (0479 000070) Highly recommended for atmosphere and food and 'wonderful, hard working

↑ Much of the
accommodation is
right on the slopes

SNOWPIX.COM / CHRIS GILL

SMART LODGINGS

Check out our feature
chapters at the front
of the book.

ACTIVITIES

Indoor Sports centre
(spa, sauna, fitness
room, hot-tub, tennis,
squash, swimming
pool, volleyball, table
tennis, badminton,
football), bowling,
concerts

Outdoor Paragliding,
sightseeing microlight
flights, snowmobiles,
snow-shoeing, ice-
driving, walks,
tobogganing

TOURIST OFFICE

t 0479 000808
valtho@valthorens.com
www.valthorens.com

staff'. Less-than-ideal position near the
top of the resort.
***Val Chavière (0479 000033)
Friendly, convenient, 'good food and
plenty of it'.
***Bel Horizon (0479 000477) Friendly,
family-run and popular with reporters –
'cuisine wonderful'.
Apartments Val Thorens has quite a
few above-average apartment
developments, many in the Plein Sud
area above the main village – Balcons
de Val Thorens, Chalet Altitude, Chalet
du Soleil, Chalet Val 2400 have all
been recommended; some have a
pool. On its own just above the village
is the Chalet des Neiges, with pool. At
the very bottom of the resort, the
Residence Oxalys has its own
wonderful restaurant (see 'Eating out')
as well as a large lounge, pool and
sauna. There are three Montagnettes
developments in different locations.
Reporters have also enjoyed staying in
the Temples du Soleil, Orsière and
Village Montana.

EATING OUT
Surprisingly wide range
Val Thorens has something for most
tastes and pockets. The resort's
excellent pocket guide contains a
useful restaurant section.
    Top of the range is the restaurant in
the Michelin-starred Residence Oxalys
('the highest star in Europe' the resort
likes to brag). We tried it in 2007 and
had a delicious and very inventive
meal: delightful amuse bouche,
excellent scallops, fillet of beef cooked
(but not served!) in bread, cheese and
an alcoholic chocolate dessert.
Expensive but worth it.
    The Fitz Roy (where we also had a
delicious meal) and Val Thorens hotels
do classic French food and were the
best in town before Oxalys appeared.

For something more regional, the best
bets are the 'excellent' Vieux Chalet
and the 'interesting' menu at the
Galoubet. A recent reporter says that
the Chaumière is a good, cheaper
alternative. Other recommendations by
readers include the the Auberge des
Balcons ('huge' but 'sometimes difficult
to get a table'), Cabane ('very high
quality cooking and reasonably
priced'), the Ferme de Rosalie ('good
but limited menu'), the Montana ('good
food and service'), El Gringo's ('great
for Tex-Mex food' and 'very popular so
get there early'), the Toit du Monde
('particularly good' and 'excellent value
for money') and the Joyeuse Fondue.
The Blanchot is a stylish wine bar with
a simple but varied carte. Several
pizzerias are recommended, including
the 'cosy wood-clad' Scapin and the
Grange ('good food and friendly staff').

APRES-SKI
Livelier than you'd imagine
Val Thorens is more lively at night than
most high-altitude ski-stations. The
Red Fox up at Balcons is crowded at
close of play, with karaoke. At the
opposite extreme the Sherlock in the
Temples du Soleil is 'always lively'.
The Frog and Roastbeef at the top of
the village claims to be the highest
pub in Europe and is a cheerful British
ghetto with a live band at tea time and
half-price beer while it plays. The
Friends and the Viking pub are both
lively bars on the same block. The
Underground nightclub in Place de
Péclet has an extended happy hour but
'descends into Europop' when its disco
gets going. The Malaysia cellar bar is
recommended for good live bands, and
gets very crowded after 11pm. Quieter
bars include the 'atmospheric without
being overcrowded' O'Connells and the
cosy Rhum Box Café (aka Mitch's).

OFF THE SLOPES
Forget it
There's a good sports centre with big
pool, saunas, steam room, hot-tubs,
gym etc and a new leisure centre with
bowling lanes and pool tables. Free
weekly concerts are held in the church,
there's a small cinema and twice-
weekly street markets. You can get to
some mountain restaurants by lift, and
the 360° panorama from the top of the
Cîme de Caron cable-car is not to be
missed. But it is not a good place to
choose if you're not going to hit the
slopes.

The French Pyrenees

An underrated region with decent skiing and boarding at half the price of the Alps and villages that remain distinctly French

Phone numbers
From abroad use the prefix +33 and omit the initial '0' of the phone number

TOURIST OFFICES

www.pyrenees-online.fr
Barèges
t 0562 921600
www.tourmalet.fr
www.bareges.com
La Mongie
t 0562 955071
www.tourmalet.fr
www.bagneresde
bigorre-lamongie.com
Cauterets
t 0562 925050
www.cauterets.com
Font-Romeu
t 0468 306830
www.font-romeu.fr
St-Lary-Soulan
t 0562 395081
www.saintlary.com

It took us a long time to get round to visiting the resorts of the French Pyrenees – mainly because we had the idea that they were second-rate compared with the Alps. Well, it is certainly true that they can't compete in terms of size of ski area with the mega-resorts of the Three Valleys and Paradiski. But don't dismiss them: they have considerable attractions, including price – hotels cost half as much as in the Alps, and meals and drinks are cheap.

The Pyrenees are serious mountains, with dramatic, picturesque scenery. They are also attractively French. Unlike the big plastic mega-resorts, many Pyrenean bases have a rustic, rural Gallic charm.

One of the biggest ski area – shared by **Barèges** and **La Mongie** – is called **Domaine Tourmalet**. It has 100km/62 miles of runs (69 pistes) and 43 lifts. Most are drags and slow chairs but there are three high-speed chairs. There are 20km/12 miles of cross-country.

The runs are best suited to intermediates, with good tree-lined runs above Barèges and open bowl skiing above La Mongie. The best bet for an expert is to try off-piste with a guide – one beautiful run away from all the lifts starts with a scramble through a hole in the rocks. There is a terrain-park. Rustic mountain huts are scattered around the slopes; Chez Louisette is one of the best.

Barèges is a spa village set in a narrow, steep-sided valley, which gets little sun in midwinter; the lift base is at Tournaboup, 4km/2.5 miles up the valley and served by ski-bus. It's the second oldest ski resort in France and the pioneer of skiing in the Pyrenees. Accommodation is mainly in 2-star hotels such as the Igloo, Central and Europe, which reporters recommend for good food and a friendly welcome. A 2007 reporter found the 300-year-old chalet Les Caillaux to be of a 'very high standard' and the owners offer free ski guiding. One reporter stayed in nearby Luz in the Chimes hotel, describing the food as 'divine'. The rather drab buildings and one main street of Barèges grow on you, though there's little to do in the evenings other than visit the thermal spa and a restaurant. La Mongie, on the other hand, is a modern, purpose-built resort: 'Small friendly village, great restaurants but not cheap.'

Cauterets is another spa town but a complete contrast to Barèges. It is much bigger and set in a wide, sunny valley. It is a popular summer resort, and even in March we were able to sit at a pavement cafe with a drink after dinner. A gondola takes you up to the slopes 850m/2,790ft above the town – you have to ride it down as well as up. There are only 35km/22 miles of slopes (mainly intermediate), set in a bowl that can be cold and windy.

But Cauterets' jewel is its cross-country, a long drive or bus-ride from town at Pont d'Espagne and served by a gondola. It is the start of the Pyrenees National Park and the old smugglers' route over the mountains between France and Spain. The 36km/22 miles of snow-sure cross-country tracks run up this beautiful deserted valley, beside a rushing stream and a stunning waterfall.

Font-Romeu has 21 lifts, serving 54km/34 miles of mainly easy and intermediate pistes, and is popular with families. The slopes get a lot of sun, but it has the biggest snowmaking set-up in the Pyrenees. When weekend crowds arrive both lifts and pistes can get crowded. It has 100km/62 miles of cross-country skiing. The village is a bus-ride from the slopes and hotels are mainly 2- and 3-star.

The other major Pyrenean resort is **St-Lary-Soulan**, a traditional village with houses built of stone, with a cable-car at the edge going up to the slopes, of which there are 100km/62 miles, mainly suiting intermediates. It has a terrain-park and half-pipe. There's a satellite called **St-Lary-Espiaube**, which is purpose-built and right at the heart of the slopes.

A recent reporter also visited other small resorts such as Formiguères, Eyne and Les Angles, and suggests staying down in a small valley town and visiting different resorts daily.

Italy

Italy has a lot going for it as a ski or snowboard holiday destination. It is the cheapest of the four major Alpine countries; the atmosphere is jolly; it has good food and wine; the scenery, especially in the Dolomites and Courmayeur, is simply stunning; the lift systems include some of the most modern and powerful in Europe; the snowmaking is state-of-the-art and they use it well; the grooming is top-notch; most of the slopes are ideal for beginners and intermediates.

Italian resorts vary as widely in their characteristics as they do in location – and they are spread along the full length of the Italian border, from Sauze d'Oulx to the Dolomites.

A lot of Italian runs, particularly in the north-west, seem flatteringly easy. This is partly because grooming is immaculate and partly because piste classification seems to overstate difficulty. Nowhere is this clearer than in the linked area of La Rosière in France and La Thuile – in Italy, despite the French-sounding name. Venturing from the Italian motorways to the French moguls is like moving from the shelter of the harbour to the open sea.

Many Italians based in the northern cities ski mainly at weekends, and it's very noticeable that many resorts become busy only at weekends. It's a great advantage for those of us who are there for the whole week. This pattern is especially noticeable at the chic resorts, such as Cortina, Courmayeur and Madonna, and resorts that have not yet found international fame such as the Monterosa region; it's much less pronounced in parts of the Dolomites favoured by German visitors who, like Brits, tend to go for a week.

In general, Italians don't take their skiing or boarding too seriously. A late start, long lunch and early finish are the norm – leaving the slopes delightfully quiet for the rest of us. Mountain restaurants are welcoming places almost everywhere, encouraging leisurely lunching. Pasta – even in the most modest establishment – is delicious. And eating and drinking on the mountain is still cheaper than in other Alpine resorts. But one drawback that many reporters remark upon is the primitive hole-in-the-ground toilets that are the norm in mountain restaurants (and sometimes in resorts, too). Another is the ludicrous system in many self-service places where you have to queue to pay and then queue again to order your food or drink.

One thing that Italian resorts do have to contend with is erratic snowfall. While the snow in the northern Alps tends to come from

SNOWPIX.COM / CHRIS GILL

← Welcoming mountain restaurants amid splendid scenery – a familiar Italian recipe. This is above San Cassiano, in the South Tyrol

the west, Italy's tends to come from storms arriving from the south. So it can have great conditions when other countries are suffering; or vice versa. Italian resorts have extensive snowmaking, and our observation is that they tend to use it more effectively than other Alpine countries. We have skied in Courmayeur and in the Dolomites when little natural snow has fallen, and in each case there has been excellent cruising on man-made snow.

Italy seems to be in the grip of 'legislation fever' at present, with mixed results. Italian bars and restaurants are now smoke-free, a huge improvement. And it is now compulsory for children (under 14, we understand) to wear helmets on the slopes. But many areas have also made going off-piste near their pistes illegal.

DRIVING IN THE ITALIAN ALPS

There are four main geographical groupings of Italian resorts, widely separated. Getting to some of these resorts is a very long haul, and moving from one area to another can involve very long drives (though the extensive motorway network is a great help).

The handful of resorts to the west of Turin – Bardonecchia, Sauze d'Oulx, Sestriere and neighbours in the Milky Way region – are easily reached from France via the Fréjus tunnel from Modane, or via the good road over the pass that the resort of Montgenèvre sits on.

Further north, and somewhat nearer to Turin than Milan, are the resorts of the Aosta valley – Courmayeur, Cervinia, La Thuile and the Monterosa area are the best known. These (especially Courmayeur)

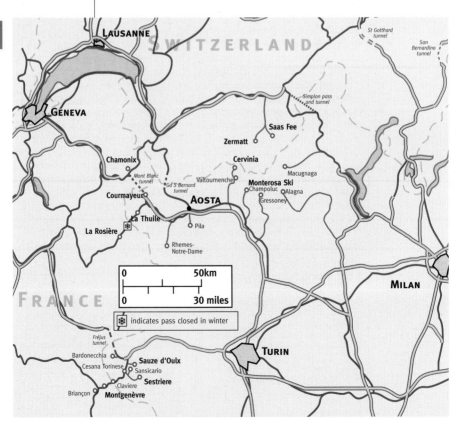

are the easiest of all Italian resorts to reach from Britain (via the Mont Blanc tunnel from Chamonix in France). The Aosta valley can also be reached from Switzerland via the Grand St Bernard tunnel. The approach is high and may require chains. The road down the Aosta valley is a major thoroughfare, but the roads up to some of the other resorts are quite long, winding and (in the case of Cervinia) high.

To the east is a string of scattered resorts, most close to the Swiss border, many in isolated and remote valleys involving long drives up from the nearest Italian cities, or high-altitude drives from Switzerland. The links between Switzerland and Italy are more clearly shown on our larger-scale Switzerland map at the beginning of that section than on the map of the Italian Alps included here. The major routes are the St Gotthard tunnel between Göschenen (near Andermatt) and Airolo – the main route between Basel and Milan – and the San Bernardino tunnel reached via Chur.

Finally, further east still are the resorts of the Dolomites. Getting there from Austria is easy, over the Brenner motorway pass from Innsbruck. But getting there from Britain is a very long drive indeed – allow at least a day and a half. We wouldn't lightly drive there and back for a week's skiing, though we routinely drive there as part of a longer tour including some Austrian resorts. It's also worth bearing in mind that once you arrive in the Dolomites, getting around the intricate network of valleys linked by narrow, winding roads can be a slow business – it's often quicker to get from village to village on skis. Impatient Italian driving can make it a bit stressful, too.

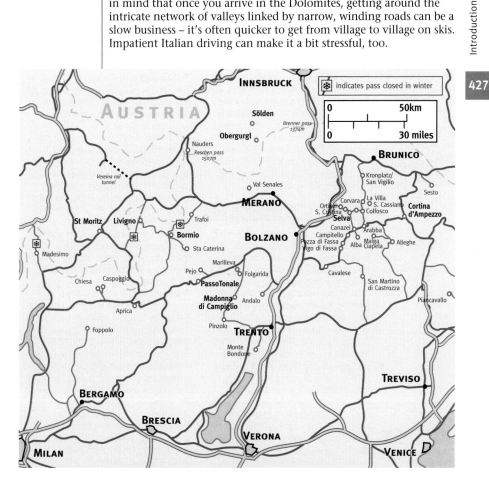

Bormio

One on its own, this: a tall, narrow mountain above a very unusual, historic town – a spa as well as a ski resort

COSTS

① ② ③ ④ ⑤ ⑥

RATINGS

The slopes

Fast lifts	★★★
Snow	★★★
Extent	★★
Expert	★
Intermediate	★★★
Beginner	★★
Convenience	★★★
Queues	★★★
Mountain restaurants	★★★★

The rest

Scenery	★★★
Resort charm	★★★★
Off-slope	★★★★

NEWS

In January 2007, the smaller of the two access gondolas (to Ciuk) closed down. As we go to press, it is not clear whether a replacement will be built.

For 2007/08 the Isolaccia chair-lift at Valdidentro will be replaced by an eight-seat gondola.

428

UK PACKAGES

Directski.com, Interhome, Ski McNeill

- ➕ Good mix of high, open pistes and woodland runs adding up to some good long descents
- ➕ Worthwhile neighbouring resorts
- ➕ Attractive medieval town centre – quite unlike any other ski resort
- ➕ Good mountain restaurants

- ➖ Slopes all of medium steepness
- ➖ Rather confined main mountain, with other areas some way distant
- ➖ Crowds on Sundays
- ➖ Lift system seems to be in decline
- ➖ Central hotels inconvenient

If you like ancient Italian towns and don't insist on a traditional Alpine resort atmosphere, you'll find the centre of Bormio very appealing – though you're unlikely to be staying right in the centre. Given the limited slopes of Bormio's own mountain, plan on taking the free bus out to the Oga-Valdidentro area and perhaps make longer outings – to Santa Caterina and maybe Livigno.

THE RESORT

Bormio, a spa since Roman times, has a splendid 17th-century town centre, with narrow, cobbled streets and grand stone facades – very colourful during the evening promenade. It is in a remote spot, close to the Swiss border; the airport transfer approaches 3hr.

The town centre is a 15-minute walk from the gondola station across the river to the south. There are reliable free shuttle-buses, but many people walk. Closer to the lifts is a suburban sprawl of hotels for skiers. Several major hotels are on Via Milano, leading out of town, which is neither convenient nor atmospheric.

THE MOUNTAINS

There's a nice mix of high, snow-sure pistes and lower wooded slopes. The main slopes are tall (vertical drop 1800m/5,900ft) and narrow. Most pistes face north-west.

Both the piste map and the piste marking need substantial improvement. The policy of opening certain lifts only at weekends has provoked complaints.

The Oga-Valdidentro area, a short bus-ride out of Bormio, shouldn't be overlooked. The open and woodland runs are very pleasant and usually empty (and have great views). Day trips to Santa Caterina (20 minutes by bus) and Livigno (90 minutes) are covered by the Alta Valtellina lift pass. A pass of two days or more entitles you to a discount rate on a one-day pass in St Moritz (three hours away).

Slopes The main access lift is an eight-seat gondola to the mid-mountain mini-resort of Bormio 2000, with a cable-car going on up to the top at over 3000m/9,840ft and a couple of fast chairs also serving the top. We await news of a replacement for the defunct gondola to Ciuk (see News).
Terrain-parks The resort has a terrain-park and super-pipe on the slopes at Bormio 2000. As well as the usual jumps and rails, there's also a separate beginner area.
Snow reliability Runs above Bormio 2000 are usually snow-sure, and there is snowmaking on the lower slopes, though this doesn't necessarily help in late March. The Valdidentro area is more reliable, and the high, shaded, north-facing slopes of Santa Caterina usually have good snow.
Experts There are a couple of short black runs in the main area, but the greatest interest lies in off-piste routes from Cima Bianca to both east and west of the piste area.
Intermediates The men's downhill course starts with a steep plunge, but otherwise is just a tough red, ideal for strong intermediates. Stella Alpina, down to 2000, is also fairly steep. Many runs are less tough – ideal for most intermediates. The longest is a superb top-to-bottom cruise. The outlying mountains are also suitable for early intermediates.
Beginners The nursery slopes at Bormio 2000 offer good snow, but there are no very easy longer pistes to move on to. Novices are better off at nearby Santa Caterina.

Phone numbers
From abroad use the prefix +39 (and do **not** omit the initial '0' of the phone number)

TOURIST OFFICE

t 0342 903300
infobormio@provincia.
so.it
www.valtellinaonline.
com

Medieval Bormio is not at all your typical ski resort town ↗
ALTA VALTELLINA

Snowboarding The terrain-park is the main attraction. The slopes are too steep for novices, and there's little to attract experienced boarders either.

Cross-country There are some trails either side of Bormio, towards Piatta and beneath Le Motte and Valdidentro, but cross-country skiers are better off at snow-sure Santa Caterina.

Queues We have no recent reports, but the gondola that replaced the cable-car from the main car park to Bormio 2000 should have dealt with any problems low down. And the fast chairs up to Cima Bianca relieve the pressure on the top cable-car. There should be few problems outside carnival week.

Mountain restaurants The mountain restaurants are generally good – 'Wonderful,' says a 2007 visitor. Even the efficient self-service at Cafe Bormio 2000 has a good choice of dishes. At the Rocca, above Ciuk, there is a welcoming chalet and a smart, modern place with table- or self-service. Cedrone, at Bormio 2000, has a good terrace and a play area for children. Several reporters recommend the very welcoming Baita de Mario, at Ciuk, as a great place for a long lunch.

Schools and guides Three schools operate from Bormio. The Nazionale school reportedly offers 'satisfactory lessons in English'.

Facilities for children The ski schools take children from the age of three from 10am to 4pm. The Contea di Bormio school at Bormio 2000 has its own snow garden and kindergarten.

STAYING THERE

How to go There are plenty of apartments, but hotels dominate the package market.

Hotels There are 40-plus hotels, mostly 2- and 3-star. The 4-star Palace (0342 903131) is the most luxurious. The Posta (0342 904753) is in the centre of the old town – rooms vary widely. The Baita dei Pini (0342 904346) is the best placed of the top hotels – on the river, between the lifts and centre. The Ambassador (0342 904625) is close to the gondola, and heartily recommended by a 2007 visitor.

Apartments The modern Cristallo apartments have been recommended.

Eating out There's a wide choice. The Kuerc and Vecchia Combo are popular. There are excellent pizzerias, including the Jap. On the outskirts at San Antonio, the Rododendri and the 'atmospheric' Al Taula ('excellent modern food') are recommended.

Après-ski The après-ski starts on the mountain at the Rocca, and at bars around the bottom lift stations. The Clem Pub, Cafe Mozart and the Aurora are popular. Shangri-Là is a friendly bar. The Sunrise is a popular disco.

Off the slopes Diversions include thermal baths and the Roman baths, riding and walks in the Stelvio National Park. Excellent sports centre, ice rink and 'superb' swimming pool. St Moritz and Livigno are popular excursions.

Staying up the mountain The modern Girasole 2000 (0342 904652), at Bormio 2000, is simple but well run by an Anglo-Italian couple; lots of events for evening entertainment.

Cervinia

Mile after mile of high-altitude, easy, snow-sure cruising above a hotchpotch of a village; best for late-season trips

COSTS

①②③④⑤⑥

RATINGS

The slopes

Fast lifts	★★★★
Snow	★★★★★
Extent	★★★
Expert	★
Intermediate	★★★★
Beginner	★★★★★
Convenience	★★★
Queues	★★★
Mountain restaurants	★★★

The rest

Scenery	★★★★
Resort charm	★★
Off-slope	★

KEY FACTS

Resort	2050m
	6,730ft

Cervinia/ Valt'nenche
Slopes	1525-3480m
	5,000-11,420ft
Lifts	24
Pistes	130km
	81 miles
Blue	30%
Red	59%
Black	11%
Snowmaking	53km
	33 miles

Cervinia/ Valt'nenche/ Zermatt combined
Slopes	1525-3820m
	5,000-12,530ft
Lifts	57
Pistes	313km
	194 miles
Blue	22%
Red	60%
Black	18%
Snowmaking	114km
	71 miles

➕ Extensive mountain with miles of long, consistently gentle runs – ideal for early intermediates and anyone wary of steep slopes or bumps

➕ High, sunny and snow-sure slopes amid impressive scenery

➕ Excellent village nursery slope

➕ Link with Zermatt in Switzerland provides even more spectacular views and good lunches

➖ Very little to interest good or aggressive intermediates and above

➖ Little to do in bad weather – almost entirely treeless, and lifts prone to closure by wind

➖ Still a few slow old lifts

➖ Steep climb to main gondola, followed by lots of steps in station

➖ Rather dreary-looking village

➖ Few off-slope amenities

If there is a better resort than Cervinia for those who like gentle cruising in spring sunshine on mile after mile of easy, snow-sure, well-groomed slopes, we have yet to find it. And then there's the easiest of Zermatt's slopes just over the Swiss border, and linked by lift and piste.

But what about the rest of us? Well, to be frank, the rest of us are better off elsewhere. In particular, those who might be harbouring thoughts about bumps or powder over in Zermatt should probably think about staying there, not here. The link between the two resorts is unreliable (especially in early season), and the best of Zermatt's slopes take a while to reach – though the journey became a lot quicker last season.

THE RESORT

Cervinia is at the head of a long valley leading off the Aosta valley on the Italian side of the Matterhorn. The old climbing village developed into a winter resort in a rather haphazard way, and it has no consistent style of architecture. It's an uncomfortable hotchpotch, neither pleasing to the eye nor as offensive as the worst of the French purpose-built resorts. The centre is pleasant, compact and traffic-free. But ugly surrounding apartment blocks and hotels make the whole place feel less friendly and welcoming than it could be.

Staying near the village centre, at the foot of the nursery slopes, has always been best for après-ski purposes. Last season this area became much better for accessing the slopes too, because of a new six-pack replacing successive slow drag-lifts from here. This cuts out the need for an awkward uphill walk to the main gondola lift.

There are also modern developments above the main village, closer to the gondola. Some hotels run their own shuttle-bus and the public bus from the Cieloalto complex, for

example, is reported to be 'efficient and well used'.

At weekends and public holidays, the resort can fill up with day trippers and weekenders from Milan and Turin. There are surprisingly few off-slope amenities, such as marked walks and spa facilities.

The slopes link to Valtournenche further down the valley (covered by the lift pass) and Zermatt in Switzerland (covered by a daily supplement, or a more expensive weekly pass).

Day trips by car are possible to Courmayeur, La Thuile and the Monterosa Ski resorts of Champoluc and Gressoney (all covered by the Aosta valley lift pass).

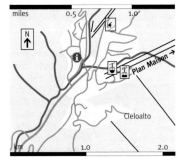

For 2007/08 there
will be more
snowmaking in
Valtournenche from
Colle Inf. Cime
Bianche to Salette.

In 2006/07 five much
needed new lifts
were built. Two chair-
lifts now go from the
bottom of the
nursery slopes in the
village, replacing four
drag-lifts: a six-pack
goes up to Plan
Torrette and meets
an existing chair-lift,
which gets you high
enough to go to Plan
Maison; and a new
quad serves the
nursery slopes. The
Pancheron two-seat
chair (right by the
Matterhorn on the
left of the ski area as
you look at the piste
map) has been
dismantled, but there
are no plans to
replace it just now.

In Valtournenche, a
six-pack and a quad
have replaced
successive drag-lifts
from Salette up to
Colle Inf. Cime
Bianche, speeding up
the journey. Another
quad has replaced a
drag on the way
down to
Valtournenche from
the top. The old
Roisette chair (the
alternative way to
get to the link with
Cervinia) has been
dismantled, so the
new chairs are now
the only way to
Cervinia. The cabins
on the gondola from
Cervinia to Plan
Maison were
replaced, increasing
its capacity.

Yup, that's Monte
Cervino (aka the
Matterhorn) that
Cervinia is named
after ➜

boarding

*The wide, gentle and always groomed slopes, generally good snow and lack of
many drag-lifts make Cervinia pretty much ideal for beginner and early
intermediate boarders. But there are some long, flat parts to beware of and there's
not much to interest better boarders – just as there's not much to interest better
skiers. Serious boarders will enjoy the terrain-park, and there's an exclusive terrain-
park pass that costs 21 euros a day; they could also try heli-boarding.*

THE MOUNTAINS

Cervinia's main slopes are high, open,
sunny and mostly west-facing. If the
weather is bad, the top lifts often close
because of high winds – and even the
lower slopes may suffer poor visibility
because of the lack of trees.

THE SLOPES
Very easy
Cervinia has the biggest, highest, most
snow-sure area of easy, well groomed
pistes we've come across, (and we're
pleased to see they have reduced their
claimed 200km of slopes to just
130km/81 miles – we never believed
the former figure). The area has Italy's
highest pistes and some of its longest
(a claimed 13km/8 miles from Plateau
Rosa to Valtournenche, interrupted
only by a new quad which replaced an
old drag-lift part-way – but see 'Snow
reliability'). Nearly all the runs are
accessible to average intermediates.
The high number of red runs on the
piste map is misleading: most of them
would be classified blue elsewhere.
There is now a handy quick-folding
piste map that covers both Cervinia's
and Zermatt's slopes fairly clearly.
    The main gondola from above the
village centre (and a parallel cable-car,
which we've rarely seen working) take
you to the mid-mountain base of **Plan
Maison**. The new six-pack from the
village nursery slopes followed by an
old, slow chair (which, perhaps
surprisingly, we have had no reports of
long queues for – more reports welcome)
now makes a viable alternative route
to Plan Maison. From Plan Maison a
further gondola goes to Laghi Cime
Bianche and then a giant cable-car
goes up to **Plateau Rosa** and one link
with Zermatt. The alternative link goes
via three successive fast quads from
Plan Maison up to a slightly lower
point on the border. Between the fast
quads and Laghi Cime Bianche, and
going all the way back to the village, is
a deep gorge that separates Cervinia's
slopes into two main sections.

Plateau Rosa is the start of the
splendid wide Ventina run. Part-way
down you can branch off left down
towards **Valtournenche**. The slopes
here are now served by three new
chair-lifts (see News) above a modern
gondola from Valtournenche – but the
final lift back to Cervinia is still a long
and tricky drag-lift.
    There is also the very small, little-
used **Cieloalto** area, served by a slow
old chair to the south of the gondola
at the bottom of the Ventina run. This
has some of Cervinia's steeper pistes
and the only trees in the area.
    Several reporters complain of poor
information and signing and others
about old decommissioned lifts being
left on the slopes giving 'an
atmosphere of shabby neglect'.

TERRAIN-PARKS
One of Italy's best
The 'Indian' terrain-park (www.
indianpark.it) by the Fomet run is one
of the best parks in Italy and is
serviced by a quick quad. Run by
Snowboard Italy's former editor, it goes

Cervinia

431

from strength to strength and 2007/08 promises further development. It has a well-maintained triple kicker line that eases you in with a 2m/6.5ft jump and culminates with a 20m/66ft monster. There are shedloads of new boxes and rails and a new wall ride and picnic table. If you are after a half-pipe, head to Zermatt, which has an equally impressive freestyle area.

SNOW RELIABILITY
Superb

The mountain is one of the highest in Europe and, despite getting a lot of afternoon sun, can usually be relied on to have good snow conditions.

The village nursery slopes, all except the top section of the Ventina run, runs under the top chair-lifts down

to Plan Maison and from Plan Maison to Plan Torrette have snowmaking. More is planned in the Valtournenche sector for 2007/08 (see News).

But the run below the top of the gondola to lower-lying Valtournenche doesn't have snowmaking – and so is prone to bare patches and closure. We've often found it closed or hard and patchy in March.

FOR EXPERTS
Forget it

This is not a resort for experts. There is little readily accessible off-piste and high winds can blow the snow off what there is (though heli-drops with guides can be arranged). There are a few black runs scattered here and there, but most of them would be classified

M. Cervino
Matterhorn
4478m

Schwarzsee
2585m

Zermatt

Trockener Steg
2940m

Theodulpass
3290m

Crowds permitting, this is a great lift for racking up some vertical

PLATEAU ROSA
3480m/11,420ft

Colle Sup.
Cime Bianche
2980m

Very easy cruising from top to bottom of the mountain (1240m/4,070ft) vertical in this sector

Laghi
Cime Bianche
2810m

Slow old chairs keep pistes around here very quiet

Bontadini

Fornet

Plan Maison

Laghi Cime Bianche

Plan Maison
2555m

Plan Torrette
2470m

Plan Maison

E Cretaz

CIELOALTO

New fast chair for 2006/07 makes this a good alternative route up the mountain and the area around the nursery slopes a better place to stay

Cretaz

Cervinia
2050m/6,730ft

SCHOOLS

Cervino
t 0166 948744

Breuil
t 0166 940960

Matterhorn-Cervinia
t 0166 949523

Valtournenche
t 0166 92515

Classes
(Cervino prices)
6 days (2hr 45min per day) €155

Private lessons
€33 for 1hr for 1 person

red elsewhere. Many reporters head over to Zermatt for more challenging slopes and have found it easier to reach them from 2006/07 – see the 'Zermatt connection' margin box. 'Left the border at 10.15am, got comfortably to the far side of Zermatt and back in Cervinia by 4pm – quick lunch though!' said one 2007 reporter.

FOR INTERMEDIATES

Miles of long, flattering runs

Virtually the whole area can be covered comfortably by average intermediates. But, as a recent reporter so aptly put it, 'Strong, aggressive intermediates will get bored quickly.' If you like wide, easy, motorway pistes, you'll love Cervinia: it has more long, flattering runs than any other resort.

The easiest slopes are on the left as you look at the mountain. From top to bottom there are gentle blue runs and almost as gentle reds in the beautiful scenery beneath the Matterhorn.

The area on the right as you look at the mountain is best for adventurous intermediates. The Ventina red is a particularly good fast cruise. You can use the cable-car to do the top part repeatedly, or go all the way down to Cervinia (8km/5 miles and over 1400m/4,600ft vertical).

The runs down towards Valtournenche are great cruises and many of the reds are more like blue gradient. The 13km/8 mile run all the way down is very satisfying, though the snow conditions on the lower part can be challenging.

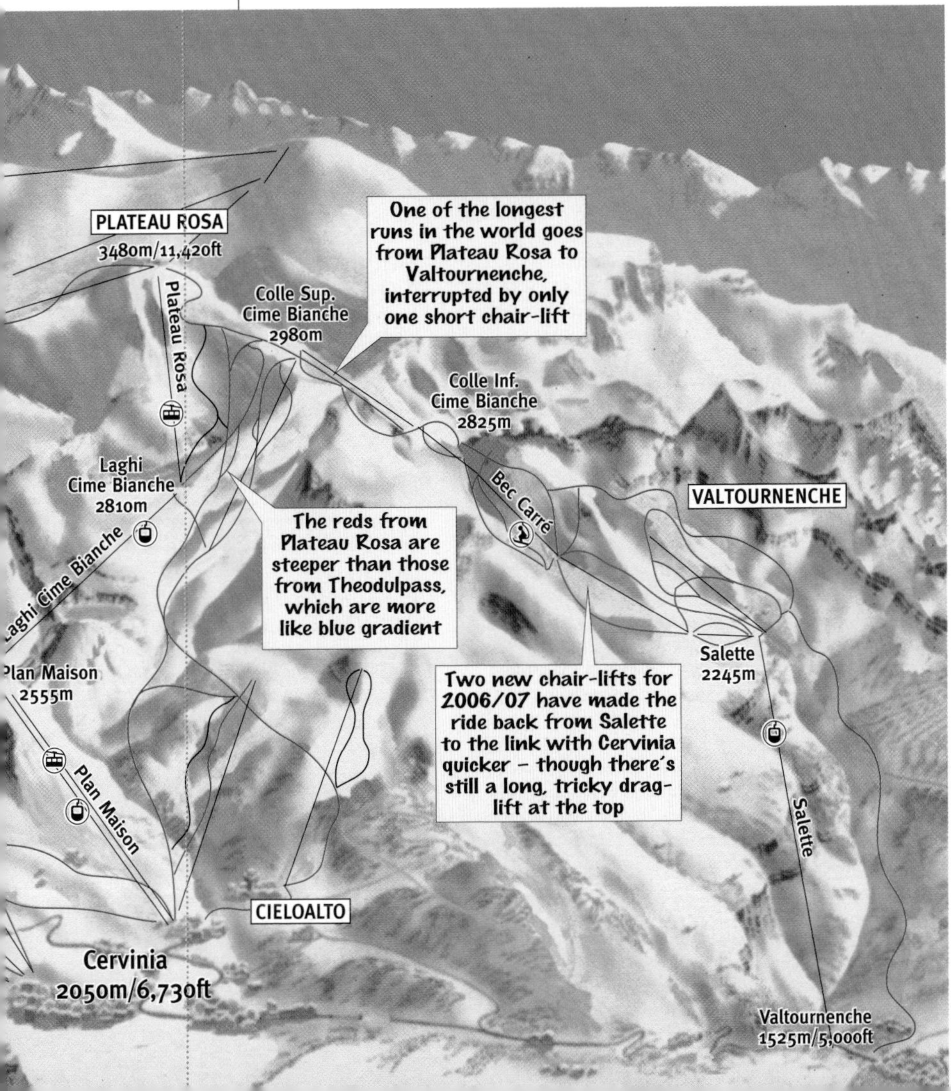

PLATEAU ROSA
3480m/11,420ft
Plateau Rosa
Colle Sup.
Cime Bianche
2980m
One of the longest runs in the world goes from Plateau Rosa to Valtournenche, interrupted by only one short chair-lift
Colle Inf.
Cime Bianche
2825m
Laghi
Cime Bianche
2810m
Laghi Cime Bianche
Bec Carré
VALTOURNENCHE
The reds from Plateau Rosa are steeper than those from Theodulpass, which are more like blue gradient
Plan Maison
2555m
Plan Maison
Salette
2245m
Two new chair-lifts for 2006/07 have made the ride back from Salette to the link with Cervinia quicker – though there's still a long, tricky drag-lift at the top
Salette
CIELOALTO
Cervinia
2050m/6,730ft
Valtournenche
1525m/5,000ft

THE ZERMATT CONNECTION

Getting to Zermatt's classic terrain on the Rothorn/Stockhorn sectors became much quicker from last season because you can now catch the new gondola from Furi to Rifelberg in the heart of the Gornergrat sector. Until then, you had to descend to the village and then get a bus or taxi to lifts on the other side of town.

Make sure you leave plenty of time for your return journey. There can be long queues for the Klein Matterhorn cable-car (a 2007 reporter writes of a 45-minute wait and crowded cabins) and for the alternative long, slow T-bars.

LIFT PASSES

Breuil-Cervinia

Prices in €

Age	1-day	6-day
under 13	24	91
13 to 64	34	182
over 65	26	137

Free under 6

Beginner limited day pass €14

Notes
Covers all lifts on the Italian side, including Valtournenche; half-day passes; daily Zermatt extension

Alternative passes
International (covers Italian side and Zermatt); Aosta Valley pass

CHILDREN

Bianca Neve
t 0166 940201
Ages 9mnth to 8yr;
9am-5pm daily

Ski school
Classes for children over 5

FOR BEGINNERS
Pretty much ideal
Complete beginners will start on the good village nursery slope (which has an excellent, long moving carpet), and should graduate quickly to the fine flat area around Plan Maison and its gentle blue runs. Fast learners will be going all the way from top to bottom of the mountain by the end of the week.

FOR CROSS-COUNTRY
Hardly any
There are two short trails – 3km/2 miles and 5km/3miles – but this is not a cross-country resort.

QUEUES
A few problems
Our 2007 reporters did not find queues a big problem. The gondola from Cervinia to Plan Maison has often generated queues at the peak morning rush. But for 2006/07 its capacity was increased by the installation of smart new cabins and this, together with the new six-pack from the nursery slopes, has eased the pressure somewhat – more reports please on queues for the gondola and the slow, old chair above the six-pack. Plan Maison can get crowded too – a 2007 reporter waited 15 minutes here. There can, of course, be queues for many lower lifts when upper lifts are shut due to wind.

MOUNTAIN RESTAURANTS
OK if you know where to go
There are some good places if you know where to go. Toilet facilities have been a traditional cause of complaints from reporters, but several have now been improved. You can, of course, head over to Zermatt for lunch.
Editors' choice The table-service section (there's self-service too) of Chalet Etoile (0166 940220), beneath the Rocce Nere chair-lift above Plan Maison. Readers love it too: 'top quality cuisine in an authentic Italian style', 'fantastic pasta, great wine list and fabulous service', 'outstanding'. The more basic table-service section of Rifugio Teodulo (0166 949400) at Theodulpass is another good option – we had excellent pasta there. Booking is recommended at both.
Worth knowing about Several readers recommend Bontadini at the top of the Fornet chair ('good value and superb view'). Other reporter tips include Tuktu at Plan Maison for the 'best UK-style toilets in the area' (plus its 'good

food and drink at reasonable prices') and the British-run Igloo, near the top of the Bardoney chair just off the Ventina piste, which serves huge burgers and again has 'a UK-style toilet'. Baita Cretaz, near the bottom of the Cretaz pistes, is good value ('the best Bombardinos').

The restaurants are cheaper and less crowded on the Valtournenche side. On the upper slopes there, the Motta does excellent food including goulaschsuppe that is 'out of this world' (and speciality hot white wine), and Lo Baracon dou Tene does a 'magnificent polenta con funghi'. Both are 'quite basic but good value'.

SCHOOLS AND GUIDES
Generally positive reports
Cervinia has three main schools, Cervino, Breuil and Matterhorn-Cervinia. The Cervino school was praised by two recent reporters, one for the beginner group lessons; the other's children 'really enjoyed their lessons in a class of six English kids'. Another reporter said the instructors at the Breuil school were 'very good'. There is a school in Valtournenche.

FACILITIES FOR CHILDREN
No recent reports
The Cervino ski school runs a ski kindergarten. And there's a babysitting and kindergarten area at Plan Maison. Another kindergarten, Bianca Neve, takes children until 10 years old. But we lack recent reports on them. The slopes, with their long gentle runs, should suit families.

STAYING THERE

HOW TO GO
Plenty of hotel packages
Most of the big operators come here, offering a wide selection of hotels, though other types of accommodation are rather thin on the ground. A 2007 visitor praises Club Med for his party of mixed abilities and ages – 'Food is amazing, room large, pool huge.'
Hotels There are almost 50 hotels, mostly 2- or 3-stars, but there are a few 4-stars. Unless they run their own minibus to the slopes, choose your location with care.
****Hermitage (0166 948998) Small, luxurious Relais et Château just out of the village on the road up to Cieloalto. Great views, pool, free bus to lifts. 'First class, good ambiance and service'.

GETTING THERE

Air Turin 118km/ 73 miles (2½hr); Geneva 220km/ 137 miles (2½hr)

Rail Châtillon (27km/17 miles); regular buses from station

UK PACKAGES

Alpine Answers, Club Med, Crystal, Elegant Resorts, First Choice, Independent Ski Links, Inghams, Interhome, Italian Safaris, Jeffersons, Kuoni, Momentum, Ski Solutions, Ski Supreme, Ski Weekend, Ski4you, Skitracer, Thomson

ACTIVITIES

Indoor Hotels with swimming pools and saunas, fitness centre, squash, bowling

Outdoor Natural ice rink, paragliding, hang-gliding, dog-sledding, hiking, mountaineering, snowmobiles, snow-shoeing, airboarding, snow-biking, snowtubing, ice climbing

Phone numbers From abroad use the prefix +39 (and do **not** omit the initial '0' of the phone number)

TOURIST OFFICE

t 0166 949136 breuil-cervinia@ montecervino.it www.montecervino.it www.cervinia.it

****Excelsior Planet** (0166 949426) Regularly recommended by reporters: 'Fantastic food and comfortable facilities,' said one visitor. Pool, spa facilities and minibus to lift. In centre, near nursery slope.

****Sertorelli Sport Hotel** (0166 949797) Excellent food, sauna and hot-tub. Ten minutes from lifts.

****Europa** (0166 948660) Family run; near centre. Pool. 'Exceptionally friendly and helpful staff, very good room.' Mixed views of the dinners.

***Astoria** (0166 949062) Right by gondola station. Family run and simple. 'Comfortable but that's all,' says a reporter.

***Mignon** (0166 949344) Central – 50 yards from the lifts. 'The best food we have ever eaten in an Italian hotel'.

***Edelweiss** (0166 949078) Four-minute walk from gondola, minibus to/from lift too. 'Cosy rooms, good bar and spa,' says a 2007 reporter.

****Marmore** (0166 949057) Friendly, family run, with 'quite good food'; on main street – an easy walk to the lifts.

****Al Piolet** (0166 949161) The flood of approval two seasons ago ('friendly' budget place, recently refurbished 'to a high standard', 'excellent – ski-in location', 'good meals') has dried up.

****Meynet** (0166 948696) Central, family hotel, recently refurbished – 100 yards from the lifts. 'Super service'.

Apartments There are many apartments, but few are available via UK tour ops. The Escargot ones in Cieloalto are 'very spacious'.

EATING OUT
Plenty to choose from

Cervinia's 50 or so restaurants allow plenty of choice. The Chamois and Matterhorn are excellent, but quite expensive. A 2007 visitor had 'very good food based on local produce' at Jour et Nuit. Casse Croute serves good pizzas. The Copa Pan has a lively atmosphere and is recommended by several reporters. The Bricole and the Nicchia have also been praised, and the Maison de Saussure does 'very good local specialities'. The Vieux Grenier at the hotel Grivola does 'an excellent pizza and is lively' and you'll find 'good pizza and pasta' at Capanna Alpina. The Pizzeria Bar Falcone and il Rustico are recommended by a recent reporter for their 'reasonably priced, excellent local food and wine'. An evening out at the Baita Cretaz mountain hut makes a change.

APRES-SKI
Disappoints many Brits

Plenty of Brits come here looking for action but find there isn't much to do except tour the bars. 'The best thing to do is take a good book,' said a recent reporter. The bar of the hotel Grivola, next to the Vieux Grenier restaurant, is attractively woody. The Copa Pan has live music and is good value. The Dragon Bar is popular with Brits and Scandinavians and has satellite TV and videos. The Ymeletrob, next door to the Punta Maquignaz hotel, is 'cosy, has live music and great canapés'. Other recommendations include Lino's, by the ice rink ('excellent pizzas and cheap beer'), the Yeti and Hostellerie des Guides (with mementos of the owner's Himalayan trips). The discos liven up at weekends.

OFF THE SLOPES
Little attraction

There is little to do for those who don't plan to hit the slopes. Village amenities include hotel pools, a fitness centre and a natural ice rink. The walks are disappointing. The mountain restaurants that are reachable by gondola or cable-car are not special.

STAYING UP THE MOUNTAIN
To beat the queues

Up at Plan Maison, Lo Stambecco (0166 949053) is a 50-room 3-star hotel ideally placed for early nights and early starts.

STAYING DOWN THE VALLEY
Great home run

Valtournenche, 9km/5.5 miles down the road, is cheaper than Cervinia. The village spreads along the busy, steep, winding road up to Cervinia.

A gondola leaves from the edge of town and new lifts (see 'News') have speeded up the journey after that. The exceptionally long run back down is a nice way to end the day – when the snow is in good condition (see 'Snow reliability'). There's a fair selection of simple hotels, of which the 3-star Bijou (0166 92109) is the best, with a leisure centre and pool. The 3-star Les Rochers (0166 92119) has been recommended by a recent visitor – 'Excellent food, and plenty of it, has a shuttle bus and is very good value.'

On the road to Cervinia, the 3-star Les Neiges d'Antan (0166 948775) was highly recommended to us during a chair-lift ride. It has a shuttle-bus.

Cortina d'Ampezzo

The scenery will take your breath away even if the slopes don't;
take your posh frocks if you want to feel part of the evening scene

COSTS

① ② ③ ④ ⑤ ⑥

RATINGS

The slopes
Fast lifts	**
Snow	***
Extent	***
Expert	**
Intermediate	***
Beginner	*****
Convenience	*
Queues	****
Mountain restaurants	****

The rest
Scenery	*****
Resort charm	****
Off-slope	*****

NEWS

For 2007/08 a new fast quad is due to replace an old double chairlift in the small Auronzo di Cadore area (33km/ 20 miles from Cortina).

For 2006/07 snowmaking was increased to cover 95 per cent of the slopes.

436

- Magnificent Dolomite scenery – a quite exceptional setting
- Marvellous nursery slopes and good long cruising runs
- Access to the vast area covered by the Dolomiti Superski pass
- Attractive, although rather towny, resort, with lots of upmarket shops
- Good off-slope facilities
- No crowds or queues

- Several separate areas spread around all sides of the resort and linked by buses
- Erratic snow record
- Expensive by Italian standards
- Gets very crowded in town and in restaurants during Italian holidays
- Very little to entertain experts
- Mobile phones and fur coats may drive you nuts

Cortina is one on its own. Sure, it has a quantity of well-maintained, enjoyable intermediate slopes, and in one or two sectors it has efficient lifts. But you shouldn't even think about a holiday here if matters like these are top of your agenda – if skiing or riding from dawn to dusk is your priority.

If, on the other hand, you like lazy days centred around indulgent lunches on sunny terraces, gazing at scenery that is just jaw-droppingly wonderful, this is the place. Dramatic pink-tinged cliffs and peaks rising vertically from the top of the slopes ring the town, giving picture-postcard views wherever you look. Every time we go back, the memory has faded and our jaws drop again.

Cortina has a regular upmarket clientele from Rome and Milan, many of whom have second homes here and enjoy the strolling, shopping, people-watching and lunching as much as the slopes. A good proportion of visitors don't go near the slopes except to drive up to a 'mountain restaurant' for lunch.

As an occasional change from serious ski resorts, we love it.

THE RESORT

Although Cortina leapt to international prominence as host of the 1956 Winter Olympics, it is not a sporty place. Most people go not for any form of exertion but for the clear mountain air, the stunning views, the shopping, the cafes and the posing potential – 70 per cent of all Italian visitors don't bother taking to the slopes. Cortina attracts the rich and famous from the big Italian cities. Fur coats and glitzy jewellery are the norm.

The resort itself is a widely spread town rather than a village, with exclusive chalets scattered around the outskirts. The centre is the traffic-free Corso Italia, full of chic designer clothes, jewellery and antique shops, art galleries and furriers – finding a ski shop can seem tricky. The cobbles and picturesque church bell tower add to the atmosphere. People quit the slopes early, and by 5pm hardly anyone is still in ski gear; the streets are packed

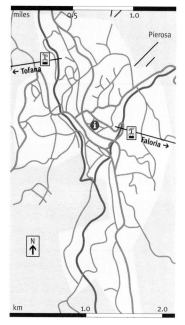

↑ Cortina's pistes can be delightfully deserted because a high proportion of the visitors just stroll and admire the views rather than take to the slopes

SNOWPIX.COM / CHRIS GILL

There is a good mixture of slopes above and below the tree line and new lifts are slowly replacing the old ones.

THE SLOPES
Inconveniently fragmented

All Cortina's smallish separate areas are a fair trek from the town centre. The largest is **Pomedes**, accessed by chair- and drag-lifts a bus-ride away. You can reach it by piste from **Tofana**, Cortina's highest area, accessed by cable-car from near the Olympic ice rink.

On the opposite side of the valley is the tiny **Mietres** area. Another two-stage cable-car from the east side of town leads to the **Faloria** area, from where you can head down to chairs that lead up into the limited but dramatic runs beneath **Cristallo**.

Other areas are reachable by road – in particular the road west over Passo Falzarego towards San Cassiano and the Sella Ronda area. (Taxis are an affordable means of access if shared.)

First is the small but spectacular Cinque Torri area. Its excellent north-facing cruising runs are accessed by a fast quad, followed by an ancient one-person chair; beyond that, a short rope tow leads to a sunny panoramic red run over the hill to Passo Giau.

Then comes the tiny Col Gallina area – north-facing, again – from where you can take a pleasant green to Cinque Torri. The cable-car from nearby Passo Falzarego up to Lagazuoi serves an excellent red run back down to the base station and accesses a longer red run down a beautiful 'hidden valley' to Armentarola on the fringe of the Alta Badia area. (For more on this run – one of our favourites – see the Sella Ronda chapter.)

Two other tiny out-of-town areas are San Vito di Cadore (11km/7 miles away) and Auronzo di Cadore (33km/20 miles) – each has just three or four lifts.

Reporters consistently praise the excellent grooming and quiet slopes but complain about other things – too many to list – related to signs, piste classification and marking, and the piste map. But most reporters judge that Cortina's other charms more than make up for the grumbles.

One way to tour the area is to use special ski itineraries, maps for which are available at the tourist and ski pass offices. 'Skitour Olympia' takes you on the 1956 Olympic downhill, GS

with people parading up and down in their evening finery, shouting and gesticulating into their mobile phones. It's all pretty flat, so easy to get around in Gucci loafers.

Unlike most of the Dolomites, Cortina is pure Italy. The Veneto region has none of the Germanic traditions of the Südtirol. And everyone is 'friendly and welcoming,' say reporters.

Surrounding the centre is a busy one-way system, reportedly less traffic-clogged than it was last time we tackled it on a weekend. The lifts to the two main areas of slopes are a fair way from the centre, and at opposite sides of town. Other lifts are bus-rides away. There's a wide range of hotels, both in the centre and scattered on the outskirts. Staying centrally is best. The local bus service is good ('very efficient and punctual'), and free to ski-pass holders. A car can be useful, especially for getting to the outlying areas and to make the most of other areas on the Dolomiti Superski pass, but a recent visitor found parking 'inadequate'. San Cassiano is a short drive to the west, with links from there to Corvara and the other Sella Ronda resorts (see the Sella Ronda chapter).

Cortina d'Ampezzo

437

KEY FACTS

Resort	1225m
	4,020ft
Slopes	1225-2930m
	4,020-9,610ft
Lifts	51
Pistes	140km
	87 miles
Blue	33%
Red	62%
Black	5%
Snowmaking	95%

boarding

Despite its upmarket chic, Cortina is a good resort for learning to board (though a recent visitor 'did not see a boarder all week'). The Socrepes nursery slopes are wide, gentle and served by a fast chair-lift. And progress on to other easy slopes is simple because you can get around in all areas using just chairs and cable-cars – though there are drags, they can be avoided. Boarderline is a specialist snowboard shop which organises instruction as well as equipment hire. There's little off-piste, but there are some nice trees and hits under the one-person chair at Cinque Torri.

ITALY

438

and slalom courses and the bob-sled run. 'Skitour Romantik View' covers the Lagazuoi-Cinque Torri area.

TERRAIN-PARKS
Not a bad one
There is a terrain-park at Faloria that has some decent kickers and rails, and a half-pipe. It's not open to skiers.

SNOW RELIABILITY
Lots of artificial help
The snowfall record is erratic – it can be good here when it's poor on the north side of the Alps, and vice versa. But 95 per cent of the pistes are now covered by snowmaking, so cover is good if it is cold enough to make snow. The run from Tofana to Pomedes involves a steep, narrow, south-facing section (with wonderful views over the town) that often has poor snow conditions and is not infrequently closed.

FOR EXPERTS
Limited
The run down from Tofana mentioned above is deservedly graded black; it goes through a gap in the rocks, and gives wonderful views of Cortina way down in the valley below. There are

short but genuinely black runs below Pomedes and Duc d'Aosta. Cortina's other major steep run goes from the top of the Cristallo area at Forcella Staunies. A chair-lift takes you to a south-facing couloir that is often shut due to avalanche danger or poor snow (tougher than it looks from below, warns a reporter).

Other than these runs there are few challenges. There are some great long red runs though, and if it snows, you'll also have very little competition for first tracks. Heli-skiing is available.

FOR INTERMEDIATES
Fragmented and not extensive
To enjoy Cortina you must like cruising in beautiful scenery, and not mind doing runs repeatedly.

The runs at the top of Tofana are short but normally have the best snow. The highest are at over 2800m/9,190ft and mainly face north. But be warned: the only way back down is by the tricky black run described above or by cable-car. The reds in the linked Pomedes area offer good cruising and some challenges.

Faloria has a string of fairly short north-facing runs – we loved the Vitelli red run, round the back away from the

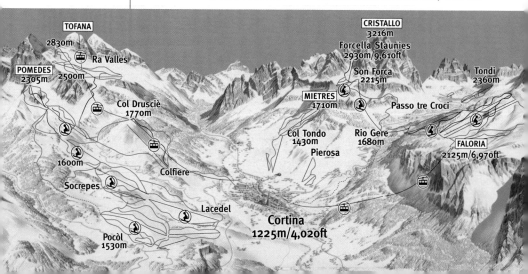

TOFANA
2830m
Ra Valles
POMEDES
2305m
2500m
Col Drusciè
1770m
1600m
Socrepes
Colfiere
Pocòl
1530m
Lacedel
Cortina
1225m/4,020ft

CRISTALLO
3216m
Forcella Staunies
2930m/9,610ft
Son Forca
2215m
MIETRES
1710m
Col Tondo
1430m
Pierosa
Rio Gere
1680m
Passo tre Croci
Tondi
2360m
FALORIA
2125m/6,970ft

lifts. And the Cristallo area has a long, easy red run served by a fast quad.

It is well worth making the trip to Cinque Torri for wonderful, deserted fast cruising on usually excellent north-facing snow ('bliss,' says a recent reporter). And do not miss the wonderful 'hidden valley' red run from the Passo Falzarego cable-car (see the Sella Ronda chapter).

FOR BEGINNERS
Wonderful nursery slopes
The Socrepes area has some of the biggest nursery slopes and best progression runs we have seen. You'll find ideal gentle terrain on the main pistes but some of the blue forest paths can be icy and intimidating.

FOR CROSS-COUNTRY
One of the best
Cortina has around 75km/47 miles of trails suitable for all standards, mainly in the Fiames area, where there is a cross-country centre and school and night skiing on a Wednesday. Trails include a 25km/16 mile itinerary following an old railway from Fiames to Cortina, and there is a special beginner area equipped with snowmaking. Passo Tre Croci offers more challenging trails, covering 10km/6 miles. A Nordic area pass is available.

QUEUES
No problem
Most Cortina holidaymakers rise late, lunch lengthily and leave the slopes early – if they get on to them at all. That means few lift queues and generally uncrowded pistes – a different world from the crowded Sella Ronda circuit. Queues can form for the cable-car to Lagazuoi, but most reporters are generally impressed. 'The

lack of queues was one of the highlights of our holiday,' said one reporter. 'No queues even on a Saturday,' said another last year (many Italian resorts are busiest at weekends). One visitor was delighted to find that the slopes got emptier in the afternoons, as the Italians left them, but that lifts stayed open as late as 5pm.

MOUNTAIN RESTAURANTS
Good, but get in early
Lunch is a major event for many Cortina visitors. At weekends you often need to book or turn up very early to be sure of a table. Many restaurants can be reached by road or lift, and fur coats arrive as early as 10am to sunbathe, admire the views and idle the time away on their mobile phones. Skiers are often in a minority.

Although prices are high in the swishest establishments, we've found plenty of reasonably priced places, serving generally excellent food. A recent visitor says they are all 'brilliant – never found a bad one'. In the Socrepes area, the Rifugio Col Taron is highly recommended and the Rifugio Pomedes is endorsed by a recent visitor. The Piè de Tofana and El Faral are also good.

At Cristallo the Rio Gere at the base of the quad chair is worth a visit, according to a recent reporter.

The restaurants at Cinque Torri – the Scoiattoli ('magnificent home-made pastas') and the Rifugio Averau ('marvellous pasta and great wine') – offer fantastic views. The Rifugio Fedare, over the back of Cinque Torri, is also recommended – 'great pasta with hare sauce'. Rifugio Lagazuoi, a short hike up from the top of the

CHILDREN

Gulliver Park
at the Pocòl ski area
t 0340 055 8399

Ski school
The schools offer all-day classes for children

UK PACKAGES

Alpine Answers,
Corporate Ski Co,
Elegant Resorts, Kuoni,
Made to Measure,
Momentum, Ski
Freshtracks, Ski
Solutions, Ski
Supreme, Ski Weekend,
Ski Yogi, Snow Finders,
White Roc

ACTIVITIES

Indoor Swimming
pool, saunas, health
spa, fitness centre,
ice stadium, curling,
museums, art gallery,
cinema

Outdoor Olympic bob
run, snowrafting
down Olympic ski
jump, snow-shoe
tours, sleigh rides,
6km/4 miles of
walking paths,
tobogganing

Phone numbers
From abroad use the
prefix +39 (and do
not omit the initial '0'
of the phone number)

TOURIST OFFICE

t 0436 866252
cortina@dolomiti.org
www.cortina.dolomiti.
org

Passo Falzarego cable-car, also has great views.

SCHOOLS AND GUIDES
Mixed reports
Of the four ski schools, we've had mixed reports of the Cortina school over the years – though we lack recent reports. The Gruppo Guide Alpine offers off-piste and touring.

FACILITIES FOR CHILDREN
Better than average
By Italian standards childcare facilities are outstanding, with all-day care arrangements for children of practically any age. However, given the small number of British visitors, you can't count on good spoken English. And the fragmented area can make travelling around with children difficult. A reporter commented how well the lift staff and instructors look after children.

STAYING THERE

HOW TO GO
Now with more packages
Hotels dominate the market but there are some catered chalets.
Hotels There's a big choice, from 5-star luxury to 1-star and 2-star pensions.
*****Miramonti (0436 4201) Spectacularly grand hotel, 2km/1 mile south of town. Pool.
*****Cristallo (0436 881111) A hike from the lifts and town centre, but there's a shuttle bus. Has a pool etc.
****Poste (0436 4271) At the heart of the town. Large rooms, some with spa baths. 'We felt very well looked after,' says a 2006 visitor.
****Ancora (0436 3261) Elegant public rooms. On the traffic-free Corso Italia.
****Victoria Parc(0436 3246) Rustic and family-run with small rooms but good food, at the Faloria end of town. Recommended by a 2006 reporter.
****Corona (0436 3251) Family run, very friendly but a 2007 reporter says 'how it qualifies for 4 stars is a mystery'. Near Tofana lift.
****Park Faloria (0436 2959) Near ski jump, splendid pool, good food.
***Olimpia (0436 3256) Comfortable B&B hotel in town, near Faloria lift.
***Menardi (0436 2400) Welcoming roadside inn, a long walk from centre and lifts.
***Villa Resy (0436 3303) Small and welcoming, just outside centre, with British owner.
***Alpes (0436 862021) On the edge

of town. 'Excellent food and service and friendly staff.' Hot tub.
**Montana (0436 862126) 'Excellent B&B. Amazing value and central location,' says a reporter.
Apartments There are some chalets and apartments – usually out of town – available for independent travellers.

EATING OUT
Huge choice
There's an enormous selection of restaurants, both in town and a little way out, doing mainly Italian food. The very smart and expensive Toulà is in a beautiful old barn, just on the edge of town. Many of the best restaurants are further out: the Michelin-starred Tivoli, the Meloncino, the Leone e Anna, the Rio Gere and the Baita Fraina. Reasonably priced central restaurants include the Cinque Torri, Croda (recommended by a recent reporter) and the Passetto for pizza and pasta.

APRES-SKI
Lively in high season
Cortina is a lively social whirl in high season, with lots of well-heeled Italians staying up very late.

The Lovat is one of several high-calorie tea-time spots. There are many good wine bars: Enoteca has 700 wines and good cheese and meats; Osteria has good wines and local ham; and Villa Sandi and P26 have been recommended. A recent reporter enjoyed drinks at the Poste ('delicious Prosecco and mandarin juice'). The liveliest bar is the Clipper, with a bob-sleigh by the door. La Suite is new this year. Discos liven up after 11pm.

OFF THE SLOPES
A classic resort
Cortina attracts lots of people who don't use the slopes. The town is attractive and the shopping 'fabulous'; as well as high fashion 'you can get anything and everything at the Co-operativa di Cortina'. Mountain restaurants are accessible by road (a car is handy). And there's plenty more to do, such as swimming and skating. There is an observatory at Col Druscè that has star-gazing tours. You can have a run (with driver!) down the Olympic bob-sleigh run and try Adrenalin Park. There's horse jumping and polo on the snow occasionally. Excursions to Venice are easy. You can visit the First World War tunnels at Lagazuoi or the memorial at Pocòl.

Courmayeur

Stunning scenery and seductive, charming village, on the opposite side of the valley from its small area of slopes

COSTS

① ② ③ ④ ⑤ ⑥

RATINGS

The slopes

Fast lifts	★★★
Snow	★★★★
Extent	★★
Expert	★★★
Intermediate	★★★★
Beginners	★★
Convenience	★
Queues	★★★
Mountain restaurants	★★★★

The rest

Scenery	★★★★
Resort charm	★★★★
Off-slope	★★★

NEWS

For 2006/07 a new gondola opened between Dolonne and Plan Checrouit. The old Pra Neyron was replaced by a six-pack, starting just below the top of the cable-car and gondola. The Checrouit gondola was also renovated.

For 2007/08 a new cinema and theatre will open in the centre of town.

The annual Swiss International City Ski Championships, in association with Momentum Ski, are held here. This season's dates are 13 to 16 March 2008.

- ➕ Charming old village, with car-free centre and stylish shops and bars
- ➕ Stunning views of Mont Blanc massif
- ➕ Day trips to Chamonix (including doing the Vallée Blanche run) possible
- ➕ Heli-skiing available
- ➕ Comprehensive snowmaking
- ➕ Some very good mountain restaurants

- ➖ Relatively small area, with mainly short runs; high-mileage piste-bashers should stay away
- ➖ Lack of nursery slopes and easy runs for beginners to progress to
- ➖ No tough pistes
- ➖ No pistes back to the village, only to Dolonne (where you catch a bus)
- ➖ Slopes very crowded on Sundays

Courmayeur is a great place for a weekend away (or a day trip to escape bad weather in Chamonix), and we always look forward to a quick visit here. (That the restaurants both on and off the mountain are excellent and the village bars among the most civilised in the skiing world are factors, we admit.) Whether it makes sense for a week's holiday is another matter. Its pistes are best suited to competent intermediates, who are likely to have an appetite for mileage that Courmayeur will arouse but not satisfy. Off-piste, there is more to do; experts who hire a guide (and the odd helicopter) can have a fine time. And with a car you can explore several other worthwhile resorts nearby.

THE RESORT

Courmayeur is a traditional old Italian mountaineering village that, despite the nearby Mont Blanc tunnel road, has retained much of its old-world feel.

The village has a charming traffic-free centre of attractive shops, cobbled streets and well-preserved buildings. An Alpine museum and a statue of a long-dead mountain rescue hero add to the historical feel.

The centre has a great atmosphere, focused around the Via Roma. As the lifts close, people pile into the many bars, some of which are very civilised. Others wander in and out of the many small shops, which include a salami specialist and a good bookshop. At weekends people-watching is part of the evening scene, when the fur coats of the Milanese and Torinese take over.

The village is quite large, and the huge cable-car to Plan Checrouit is on the southern edge. The new gondola from Dolonne to Plan Checrouit is an alternative way up. Both are bus-served, and while parking at the cable-car is very limited, there's a big new car-park at Dolonne. Drivers can also go to Entrèves, up the valley, where there is a large car park at the cable-car. Most people leave skis or boards

and boots in lockers up the mountain or at the lift base.

Buses, infrequent but timetabled, go to La Palud, just beyond Entrèves, for the Punta Helbronner-Vallée Blanche cable-car. Taxis are easily arranged for evenings out.

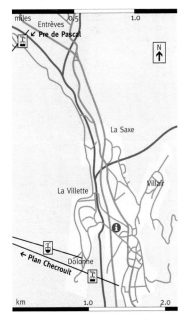

KEY FACTS

Resort		1225m
		4,020ft
Slopes	1210-2755m	
	3,970-9,040ft	
Lifts		16
Pistes		100km
		62 miles
Blue		27%
Red		62%
Black		11%
Snowmaking		
		252 guns

LIFT PASSES

Courmayeur Mont Blanc

Prices in €

Age	1-day	6-day
under 12		98
12 to 64	40	195
over 65		146

Free under 6

Beginner three free nursery lifts

Notes
Covers Val Veny and Checrouit, and the lifts on Mont Blanc up to Punta Helbronner; half-day passes; some single ascent passes; 3+ day passes allow at least one day in the Aosta valley, Flaine and on most of the Chamonix lifts

Alternative passes
Non-skier

THE MOUNTAINS

The pistes suit intermediates, but are surprisingly limited for such a well-known, large resort. They are varied in character, if not gradient. Piste marking could be improved and there are still a few old, slow chairs, although these can largely be avoided. Chamonix, La Thuile and Pila are an easy drive or bus ride and Cervinia is reachable.

THE SLOPES
Small but interestingly varied

There are two distinct sections, both almost entirely intermediate. The east-facing **Checrouit** area, accessed by the Checrouit gondola, catches morning sun, and has open, above-the-tree-line pistes. The 25-person, infrequently running Youla cable-car goes to the top of Courmayeur's pistes. There is a further tiny cable-car to Cresta d'Arp. This serves only long off-piste runs but it is no longer compulsory to have a guide with you to go up it.

Most people follow the sun over to the north-west-facing slopes towards **Val Veny** in the afternoon. These are interesting, varied and tree lined, with great views of Mont Blanc and its glaciers. There are a few alternative routes between the Checrouit and Val Veny areas, but the inadequate piste map doesn't make it easy to figure them out. The Val Veny slopes are also accessible by cable-car from Entrèves, a few miles outside Courmayeur.

A little way beyond Entrèves is La Palud, where a cable-car goes up in three stages to Punta Helbronner, at the shoulder of **Mont Blanc**. There are no pistes from the top, but you can do the famous Vallée Blanche run to Chamonix from here without the horrific ridge walk that forms the start on the Chamonix side. There are buses back from Chamonix through the Mont Blanc tunnel. Or you can tackle the tougher off-piste runs on the Italian side of Mont Blanc. None of these glacier runs should be done without a guide.

TERRAIN-PARKS
Just a boarder-cross

Like a lot of Italian resorts, Courmayeur has no terrain-park or half-pipe. However, there's now a 500m/1,640ft boarder-cross run – created a few years ago – near the top of the Plan de la Gabba high-speed chair.

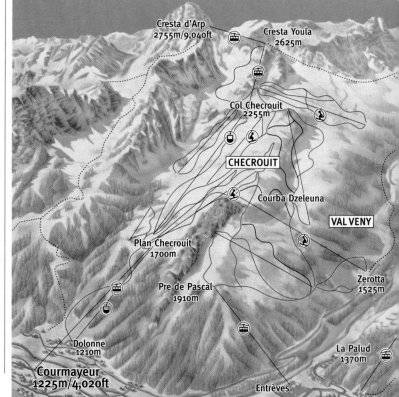

SNOW RELIABILITY
Good for most of the season

Courmayeur's slopes are not high – mostly between 1700m and 2250m (5,600ft and 7,400ft). Those above Val Veny face north or north-west, so keep their snow well, but the Plan Checrouit side is rather too sunny for comfort in late season. There is snowmaking on most main runs, so good coverage in early- and mid-season is virtually assured – we were there in a January snow drought and enjoyed decent skiing entirely on man-made snow.

FOR EXPERTS
Off-piste is the only challenge

Courmayeur has few challenging pistes. The black runs on the Val Veny side are not severe, and few moguls form elsewhere. But if you're lucky enough to find fresh powder – as we have been several times – you can have fantastic fun among the trees.

Classic off-piste runs go from Cresta d'Arp, at the top of the lift network, in three directions – a clockwise loop via Arp Vieille to Val Veny, with close-up views of the Miage glacier; east down a deserted valley to Dolonne or Pré St Didier; or south through the Youla gorge to La Thuile.

On Mont Blanc, the Vallée Blanche is not a challenge (though there are more difficult variations), but the Toula glacier route on the Italian side from Punta Helbronner to Pavillon most certainly is, often to the point of being dangerous. There are also heli-drops available, including a wonderful 20km/12 mile run from the Ruitor glacier down into France (from £150) – you ride the lifts back up from La Rosière and descend to La Thuile (a taxi-ride from Courmayeur). And you can do a day trip to Chamonix through the Mont Blanc tunnel.

FOR INTERMEDIATES
Ideal gradient but limited extent

The whole area is suitable for most intermediates, but it is small. The avid piste-basher will ski it in a day. It also lacks long, easy runs to suit the more timid.

The open Checrouit section is pretty much go-anywhere territory, but it is basically just one wide red slope. The red run to the bottom of Dolonne is now more accessible as you can catch the new gondola back (but check what the snow is like before heading down there; it was closed most of last season). Timid skiers should head up the fast six-seater Pra Neyron chair for access to the area's few blues. The Val Veny side of the mountain is basically steeper, with manageable blacks going close to the fall line and good reds and the occasional blue taking less direct routes. These runs link in with the pretty, wooded slopes heading down to Zerotta. The fast Zerotta chair dominates the Val Veny side, serving runs of varying difficulty over a decent vertical of 560m/1,800ft – including a long blue.

The Vallée Blanche, although off-piste, is easy enough for adventurous,

SCHOOLS

Monte Bianco
t 0165 842477

Courmayeur
t 0165 848254

Classes
(Monte Bianco prices)
5 days (3hr per day)
€165

Private lessons
From €33 for 1hr;
additional person €10

GUIDES

Guides Courmayeur
t 0165 842064

AIAT MONTE BIANCO

The pistes are best for intermediates who enjoy gentle cruising among glorious scenery (dominated by Mont Blanc, pictured here) ↓

---

fit intermediates to try. So is the local heli-skiing – from £125 for one drop including a guide; you are picked up on the piste so there's no wasted time.

FOR BEGINNERS
Consistently too steep
Courmayeur is not well suited to beginners. There are several nursery slopes, none ideal. The area at Plan Checrouit gets crowded, and there are few easy runs for the near-beginner to progress to. The small area served by the short Tzaly drag, just above the Entrèves cable-car top station, has decent beginner terrain, and it tends to have good snow. A regular visitor recommends the slope beside the Maison Vieille restaurant: 'great for families because mum and dad can eat, drink and keep an eye of the kids'.

FOR CROSS-COUNTRY
Beautiful trails
There are 35km/22 miles of trails. The best are the four covering 20km/12 miles at Val Ferret, served by bus. Dolonne has a couple of short trails.

QUEUES
Sunday crowds pour in
The Checrouit and Val Veny cable-cars used to suffer queues on Sundays and peak periods – down as well as up. A regular visitor tells us these are a thing of the past now that the new Dolonne gondola offers an additional way up and down (more reports welcome). The infrequent Youla cable-car may require patience – only worth it for those heading off-piste. Overcrowded slopes on Sundays, particularly down to Zerotta, can also be a problem.

MOUNTAIN RESTAURANTS
Lots – some of them very good
The area is lavishly endowed with 27 establishments ranging from rustic little huts to a large self-service place. Most huts do table-service of delicious pizza, pasta and other dishes and it is best to reserve tables in advance. But there are also snack bars selling more basic fare and relying on views and sun to fill their terraces.

Several restaurants are excellent. Chiecco, next to the drag-lift with the same name at Plan Checrouit, serves the best and most refined food with friendly service: 'the owner is passionate about her food'; 'wonderful pasta and amazing meat courses – expensive but worth it'. Maison Vieille, at the top of the chair of the same name, is a welcoming rustic place with traditional Italian food including superb home-made pastas. The pick of the Plan Checrouit places is Christiania (book a table downstairs) – 'great pizzas and a convenient meeting place', 'excellent food and service but had to wait a long time for a table', said 2007 reporters.

In Val Veny is another clutch of places worth trying. The jolly Grolla has good food and a sunny terrace with excellent views; the da Geremia (just below Grolla) is a nice snack bar with some hot food and does some 'themed' days – eg sushi or a live band; the Zerotta, at the foot of the eponymous chair, has a sunny terrace (though a recent reporter was disappointed with the food and preferred the nearby Petit Mont Blanc).

Courba Dzeleuna snack bar, just below the top of the Dzeleuna chair has wonderful views and delicious home-made myrtle grappa (but beware of the alcohol-soaked berries left in the glass). A reporter enjoyed an 'excellent lunch of charcuterie and cheese' there.

SCHOOLS AND GUIDES
Good reports
'We had the best instructor for ages – possibly ever,' said a reporter about the Monte Bianco ski school. There is a thriving guides' association ready to help you explore the area's off-piste; it has produced a helpful booklet showing the main possibilities.

FACILITIES FOR CHILDREN
Good care by Italian standards
Childcare facilities are well ahead of the Italian norm.

Air Geneva 105km/
65 miles (2hr); Turin
150km/93 miles (2hr)

Rail Pré-St-Didier
(5km/3 miles); regular
buses from station

Fun park Dolonne
9am-4.30

Ski schools
Take children from
age 5

Indoor Swimming
pool and sauna at
Pré-St-Didier (5km/
3 miles), Alpine
museum, cinema,
library, art gallery,
sports centre with
climbing wall, ice rink,
curling, fitness centre,
indoor golf, squash,
tennis

Outdoor Walking
paths in Val Ferret,
snow-shoeing,
paragliding, hang
gliding, snow-biking,
dog-sledding

Check out our feature
chapters at the front
of the book.

Phone numbers
From abroad use the
prefix +39 (and do
not omit the initial '0'
of the phone number)

t 0165 842060
info@aiat-monte-
bianco.com
www.aiat-monte-
bianco.com

HOW TO GO
Plenty of hotels
Courmayeur's long-standing popularity
ensures a wide range of packages
(including some excellent weekend
deals), mainly in hotels. Tour op
Momentum is a Courmayeur specialist
and can advise about and fix pretty
much whatever you want here. One or
two UK operators have catered chalets.
Hotels There are nearly 50 hotels,
spanning the star ratings.
****Royal e Golf** (0165 831611) Large,
grand place in centre just off Via
Roma. Outdoor pool, sauna, piano bar.
****Gran Baita** (0165 844040) Luxury
place with antique furnishings,
panoramic views and 'superb food'.
Pool. Shuttle-bus to cable-car.
****Pavillon** (0165 846120)
Comfortable 4-star near cable-car, with
a pool. Friendly staff.
***Auberge de la Maison** (0165
869811) Small, atmospheric hotel in
Entrèves; owned by the same family as
Maison de Filippo (see Eating out).
***Walser** (0165 844824) Near main
road. 'Good value hotel with exemplary
service.'
***Bouton d'Or** (0165 846729) Small,
friendly B&B near main square. 'Very
welcoming, owner ferries you to/from
lifts if you wish,' says a reporter.
***Berthod** (0165 842835) Friendly,
family-run hotel near centre.
***Grange** (0165 869733) Rustic stone-
and-wood farmhouse in Entrèves.
***Triolet** (0165 846822) 'Excellent
location near lift. Comfy, well furnished.'
***Maison Saint Jean** (0165 842880)
New, central, family-run, good.
Edelweiss (0165 841590) Friendly,
cosy, good value; close to the centre.
Scoiattolo (0165 846716) Good
rooms, good food, shame it's at the
opposite end of town to the cable-car.
Apartments The Grand Chalet is central
and has spacious apartments and
jacuzzi, steam room and sauna.

EATING OUT
Jolly Italian evenings
There is a great choice, both in
downtown Courmayeur and within taxi
range; there's a handy promotional
booklet describing many of them (in
English as well as Italian). We've been
impressed by the traditional Italian
cuisine of both Pierre Alexis and
Cadran Solaire in Courmayeur. The
Terrazza ('Best in town, wonderful local

food and great service,' says a visitor)
is a rising star. So is the Aria (with 'an
amazing wine list'). The Tunnel pizzeria
does a good job. The Mont-Fréty
('good value', 'its antipasti is a must'),
and the Vieux Pommier ('for fondue
and raclette') have been recommended
by reporters. Further afield, the touristy
but very jolly Maison de Filippo in
Entrèves is rightly famous for its fixed-
price, 36-dish feast. At La Palud the
restaurant in the hotel Dente del
Gigante is recommended by a local, as
is La Clotz in Val Ferret ('expensive but
modern refined Italian cuisine').

APRES-SKI
Stylish bar-hopping
Courmayeur has a lively evening scene
– at weekends, at least – centred on
stylish bars with comfy armchairs or
sofas to collapse into, often serving
free canapés in the early evening. Our
favourites are the Roma, the back
room of the Caffè della Posta and the
Bar delle Guide. The Cadran Solaire is
where the big money from Milan and
Turin hangs out. The Privé is excellent
for cocktails. The American Bar has
good music and a fine selection of
wines. Poppy's is recommended for
drinks and pizza. Maquis is the better
of the two night clubs in Entrèves.

OFF THE SLOPES
Lots on for non-slope users
If you're not interested in hitting the
snow you'll find the village pleasant –
parading up and down is a favourite
pastime for the many non-slope users
the resort attracts (especially at
weekends). You can go by cable-car up
to Punta Helbronner, by bus to Aosta,
or up the main cable-car to Plan
Checrouit to meet friends for lunch.
The huge sports centre is good (but no
pool). Don't miss a visit to the newly
reopened thermal baths at Pre St
Didier – with over 30 spa experiences
including saunas, waterfall and
outdoor thermal pools.

STAYING UP THE MOUNTAIN
Why would you want to?
Visiting Courmayeur and not staying in
the charming village seems perverse –
if you're that keen to get on the slopes
in the morning, this is probably the
wrong resort. But at Plan Checrouit,
the 1-star Christiania (0165 843572 –
see 'Mountain restaurants') has simple
rooms; the 3-star Baita (0165 843570)
is smarter; book way in advance.

Livigno

*Lowish prices and highish altitude – a tempting combination,
especially when you add in a quite pleasant Alpine ambience*

RATINGS

The slopes

Fast lifts	★★★
Snow	★★★★
Extent	★★
Experts	★★
Intermediates	★★★
Beginners	★★★★
Convenience	★★
Queues	★★★★
Mountain restaurants	★★★

The rest

Scenery	★★★
Resort charm	★★★
Off-slope	★★

NEWS

For 2006/07 two new
restaurants and a
couple of bars
opened.

446

+ High altitude plus snowmaking
means reliable snow

+ Large choice of beginners' slopes

+ Impressive modern lift system

+ Cheap by the standards of high
resorts, with the bonus of duty-free
shopping (eg for new equipment)

+ LIvely, friendly and quite smart
village with some Alpine atmosphere

+ Long, snow-sure cross-country trails

− No challenging pistes

− Long and gruelling transfers – 5hr
from Bergamo, less from Innsbruck

− Two widely separated slope areas

− Village is very long and straggling –
with no buses later in the evening

− Few off-slope amenities

− Bleak setting, susceptible to wind

− Nightlife can disappoint

**Livigno offers the unusual combination of a fair-sized mountain, high altitude
and fairly low prices. Despite its vaunted duty-free status, the hotels, bars and
restaurants are not much cheaper than in other Italian resorts, but shopping is –
there are countless camera and clothes shops. As a relatively snow-sure
alternative to the Pyrenees or to the smallest, cheapest resorts in Austria,
Livigno seems attractive. But don't overlook the long list of drawbacks.**

THE RESORT

Livigno is an amalgam of three villages
in a wide, remote valley near the Swiss
border – basically a string of hotels,
bars, specialist shops and
supermarkets lining a single long
street. The buildings are small in scale
and mainly traditional in style, giving
the village a pleasant atmosphere. The
original hamlet of San Antonio is the
nearest thing Livigno has to a centre,
and the best all-round location. Here,

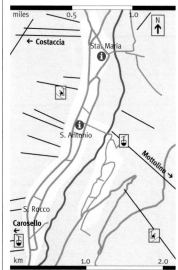

the main street and those at right
angles, linking it to the busy bypass
road, are nominally traffic-free, but
actually are not at all. The road that
skirts the centre is constantly busy,
and becomes intrusive in the hamlets
of Santa Maria, 1km/0.5 miles to the
north, and San Rocco, a bit further
away to the south (and uphill).
 Lifts along the length of the village
access the western slopes of the
valley. The main lift to the eastern
slopes is directly across the flat valley
floor from the centre.
 Depending on where you are based,
you may make heavy use of the free
bus services. They are fairly frequent,
but get overcrowded at peak times and
stop mid-evening. A 2007 visitor
comments: 'The three colour-coded
bus routes are actually simple, but not
easy to understand at first. People
often find themselves travelling in the
wrong direction.' Taxis (including
minibus taxis for groups) are an
affordable alternative.
 The Alta Valtellina lift pass covers
Bormio and Santa Caterina, an easy
drive or bus-ride (free with the lift
pass) if the high pass is open, and a
pass of two days or more entitles you
to a discount on a day in St Moritz – a
'fantastic' day out, says a reader.
 The airport transfer from Bergamo is
long. The one from Innsbruck may be
shorter, but beware travel sickness.

boarding

Livigno offers a refreshing sense of space. There really is something for everyone here, from big, wide, open and rolling motorways to natural gullies, hits, tree runs and powder. The back of Mottolino is a perfect example. As the resort stretches across such a long expanse, there is plenty of fun to be had between pistes as well as on them. Try the great yet tight tree runs sheltered from the wind between the Mottolino and Degli Amanti slopes. The terrain-park infrastructure is very good, and has a long history of hosting world-class events. Beginners be warned: practically all the smaller lower slopes are serviced by drags. But the resort still attracts good numbers of beginners, and Madness Snowboard school (see www.madnessnow.com) gets good reports (see Schools).

THE MOUNTAINS

The mainly open slopes, on either side of the valley, are more extensive than in many other budget destinations.

THE SLOPES
Widely spread
There are three sectors, two of them linked high-up and low-down.

A two-seat chair from the nursery slopes at the north end of the village takes you up to **Costaccia**, where a long fast quad chair-lift goes along the ridge towards the **Carosello** sector. The blue linking run back from Carosello to the top of Costaccia is flat in places and may involve energetic poling if the snow conditions and the wind are against you. Carosello is more usually accessed by the optimistically named Carosello 3000 gondola at San Rocco, which goes up, in two stages, to 2750m/9,020ft. Most runs return

towards the village, but there are a couple on the back of the mountain, on the west-facing slopes of Val Federia, served by a six-pack.

The ridge of **Mottolino** is reached by an efficient gondola from Teola, a tiresome walk or a short bus-ride across the valley from San Antonio. From the top, you can descend to fast quads on either side of the ridge or, if you must, take a slow antique chair up the ridge to Monte della Neve. There is the alternative of a fast quad starting a little way up the Bormio road, and linking with a six-pack above.

We don't show on our map a low-level link from the nursery drags at the bottom of Carosello to those below Costaccia; it's more of a walk than a run – not recommended for boarders.

Signposting is patchy and the piste map does not identify runs.

Night skiing is available on Thursdays.

Livigno

447

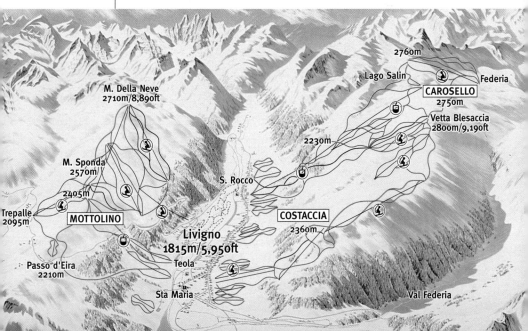

APT LIVIGNO / GIUSEPPE GHEDINA

High, wide, open
slopes are the name
of the game here ➜

TERRAIN-PARKS
Serious facilities
The main Budrider's park behind Mottolino is an awesome freestyle zone for all levels of riders. It also played host to the world-renowned Burton European Open, a six-star event on the Ticket to Ride calendar, and is still a stop on the Burton amateur tour in early December. It has three kicker lines for all levels and a hip. This is bordered by a big super-pipe, still often used as a training ground by pros. There are advanced rails that are placed in and around the jumps as well. Beyond lies the smaller Snow-park Medio with nice lines of small to intermediate kickers, good entry-level rails of varying difficulty, a mini spine and a small boarder-cross.

SNOW RELIABILITY
Very good, despite no glacier
Livigno's slopes are high (you can spend most of your time around 2500m/8,200ft), and with snow-guns on the lower slopes of Mottolino and Costaccia, the season is long. Despite the generally poor snow in Europe, January 2007 reporters were 'very pleasantly surprised' by the snow here.

FOR EXPERTS
Not recommended
The piste map shows a few black runs, but these are not particularly steep. Even the all-black terrain served by the six-pack on Monte della Neve is really no more than stiff red in gradient. There is off-piste to be done.

FOR INTERMEDIATES
Flattering slopes
Good intermediates will be able to tackle all the blacks without worry. The woodland black run from Carosello past Tea da Borch is narrow in places and can get mogulled and icy in the afternoon. Moderate intermediates have virtually the whole area at their disposal. The long run beneath the Mottolino gondola is one of the best, and there is also a long, varied, under-used blue going less directly to the valley. Leisurely types have several long cruises available; the run beneath the fast chair at the top of Costaccia is a splendid slope.

FOR BEGINNERS
Excellent but scattered slopes
A vast array of nursery slopes along the sunny lower flanks of Costaccia, and other slopes around the valley, make Livigno excellent for novices – although some of the slopes at the northern end are steep enough to cause difficulties. There are lots of longer runs to progress to.

CROSS-COUNTRY
Good snow, bleak setting
Long snow-sure trails (40km/25 miles in total) follow the valley floor, making Livigno a good choice, provided you don't mind the bleak scenery. There is a specialist school, Livigno 2000, and the resort organises major races.

QUEUES
Few problems these days
Despite reports of queues for the Costaccia chair at midday and short delays for the Carosello gondola in peak season, lift queues are not generally a problem. A bigger problem is that winds can close the upper lifts, causing crowds lower down.

MOUNTAIN RESTAURANTS
More than adequate
On Mottolino, the refuge at the top of the gondola is impressive – 'Beautiful,' says an enthusiastic 2006 visitor. The self-service section can have 'immense' queues, while the smart table-service section is 'very good, not that much dearer and much more pleasant'. The rustic restaurants at Passo d'Eira and Trepalle are good options for a quiet

CHILDREN

**Kindergarten
(run by Inverno/Estate
ski school)**
t 0342 996276
Ages 3 and over

**Miniclub Top Club
Mottolino**
t 0342 970822

M'eating Point
t 0342 997408

**Spazio Gioco
Peribimbi**
t 0342 970711
Ages 18mnth to 3yr;
8.30-1pm

Ski school
Takes children from
age 4 (6 2hr days
€97)

GETTING THERE

Air Bergamo
200km/124 miles
(5hr); Innsbruck
185km/115 miles
(5hr)

Rail Tirano (48km/
30 miles), Zernez
(Switzerland, 28km/
17 miles); regular
buses from station,
weekends only

ACTIVITIES

Indoor Saunas, fitness
rooms and swimming
pools (in hotels),
badminton, billiards,
chess, bowling,
basketball, cinema

Outdoor Cleared
paths, ice rink, snow-
shoeing, horse-riding,
ice-climbing, dog-
sledding, go-karts on
ice, snowmobiling,
paragliding

Phone numbers
From abroad use the
prefix +39 (and do
not omit the initial '0'
of the phone number)

TOURIST OFFICE

t 0342 052200
info@livigno.eu
www.livigno.it

stop – the Trela is recommended for
pizza. And there are some more
charming places lower down. The
welcoming Tea is at the base of the
same sector. Costaccia's Berghütte is
pleasantly rustic and sunny, with good
food and a great atmosphere. The self-
service place at the top of Carosello is
acceptable and Tea da Borch, in the
trees lower down, serves great food in
a Tirolean-style atmosphere.

SCHOOLS AND GUIDES
Watch out for short classes
There are several schools. English is
widely spoken, and reports are good
('good instructors with excellent
English'). Classes are short at only two
hours, but are rated as great value for
money. A 2007 visitor found the
Madness snowboard school 'good
value' with 'relatively small' groups.

FACILITIES FOR CHILDREN
Not bad for Italy
The schools run children's classes. The
Livigno Inverno-Estate school offers all-
day care and the staff speak English.

STAYING THERE

HOW TO GO
Lots of hotels, some apartments
Livigno has an enormous range of
hotels and a number of apartments.
There are some attractively priced
catered chalets from UK operators.
Hotels There is a wide choice of 2-, 3-
and 4-star places.
****Intermonti (0342 972100) Modern
with pool and other mod cons; on the
Mottolino side of the valley.
****Touring (0342 996131) 'Very
comfortable and competitively priced.'
***Bivio (0342 996137) In central
Livigno; with pool.
***Steinbock (0342 970520) Nice little
place, far from major lifts.
***Loredana (0342 996330) Modern
chalet on the Mottolino side.
***Montanina (0342 996060) Good,
central.
***Alpi (0342 996408) In San Rocco,
not far from Carosello gondola.
'Absolutely the best; exquisite food.'
***Camana Veglia (0342 996310)
Charming old wooden chalet. Popular
restaurant, well placed in Santa Maria.
***Larice (0342 996184) Stylish little
B&B well placed for Costaccia lifts.
*** Champagne (0342 996437) 'In
lovely condition and close to centre.'
**Silvestri (0342 996255) In the San

Rocco area. 'Great staff, comfortable
rooms, filling meals.'
Apartments All the big tour operators
that come here offer apartments.

EATING OUT
Still value for money
Livigno has lots of traditional,
unpretentious restaurants, many hotel-
based. Hotel Concordia has some of
the best cooking in town and the
Helvetia also has 'good value and
good quality food'. The Baita and
Astoria are recommended for 'good
food and service'. Mario's impressed a
2007 visitor with its 'great food and
service'. Bait dal Ghet and Bivio are
popular with locals, and the Rusticana
does wholesome, cheap food. Pesce
d'Oro is good for seafood and Italian
cuisine. The Bellavista is praised for its
'bustling bistro style' and 'simple tasty
food', and a 2007 visitor praised the
Mirage for 'food and atmosphere'.
Galli's, Grolla, Garden and Echo are
also recommended. Canoa and Grand
Chalet opened in 2007.

APRES-SKI
Lively, but disappoints some
The scene in Livigno is quieter than
some people expect in a duty-free
resort. Pas de la Casa it is not – to the
relief of most reporters. Also, the best
places are scattered about, so the
village lacks evening buzz. At tea time
Tea del Vidal, at the bottom of
Mottolino, gets lively, as does the
Stalet bar at the base of the Carosello
gondola and the central umbrella bar.
Nightlife gets going only after 10pm.
Galli's pub, in San Antonio, is 'a full-on
party pub'. The Kuhstall under the
Bivio hotel is an excellent cellar bar
with live music, as is the Helvetia, over
the road. The San Rocco end is
quietest, but Daphne's ('great party
atmosphere') and Marco's are popular.
The stylish Art Cafe is recommended.
Kokodi is the main disco.

OFF THE SLOPES
Look lively, or go shopping
Livigno offers a small range of outdoor
alternatives to skiing and boarding –
horse-riding among them. And a 2006
visitor 'thoroughly enjoyed' the dog-
sledding. Walks are uninspiring and
there is no sports centre or public pool
(but the pools in the hotels Helvetia
and Spöl are accessible). The duty-free
shopping may make up for this. Trips
to Bormio and St Moritz are popular.

Madonna di Campiglio

Chic, very Italian but rather spread-out resort with mainly easy intermediate local slopes amid stunning scenery

450

NEWS

For 2007/08 a new eight-seat gondola is being built from the centre of Madonna to the top of the Cinque Laghi area. There is also a project to improve the snowmaking in the Grostè area and in the terrain-park.

UK PACKAGES

Directski.com, Equity, First Choice, Inghams, Interhome, Italian Safaris, Kuoni, Rocketski, Ski McNeill, Ski Wild, Ski Yogi, Solo's

➕ Pleasant, friendly town in a pretty valley with splendid views at altitude

➕ Generally easy slopes, best for beginners and early intermediates

➖ Spread-out village and infrequent shuttle-bus service

➖ Quiet après-ski

Campiglio is a pleasant Dolomite town with an affluent, almost exclusively Italian, clientele – a bit like Cortina, though the scenery isn't in quite the same league. Folgarida and Marilleva (to which the slopes are linked) and Pinzolo (which may be linked soon) are quite different and well worth exploring by adventurous intermediates and better. They are covered in our chapter on Trentino.

THE RESORT

Campiglio is a long-established, traditional-style but largely modern town, set in a prettily wooded valley beneath the impressive Brenta Dolomites, with slopes in three linked sectors. The town spreads out along the approach roads but the centre is fairly compact: the lifts to Cinque Laghi (to the west) and to Pradalago (to the north) bracket most of the central hotels, and are about a five-minute walk apart. Five minutes outside the centre is a gondola to Monte Spinale, leading to the Grostè sector; there is another gondola to Grostè starting a short bus-ride outside the town. Beyond this lift station are the main nursery slopes at Campo Carlo Magno. The town spreads south from the centre, past a frozen lake.

Campiglio attracts an affluent Italian clientele; it has lots of smart shops. The village is busy all day, and promenading is an early evening ritual.

The free ski-bus is not frequent but some hotels run minibuses.

Passo Grostè 2505m/8,220ft

GROSTÈ

Monte Spinale 2095m

Doss del Sabion 2100m

Val d'Agola

Malga Grual

Pinzolo 770m

800m

Planned link Pinzolo - Cinque Laghi

CINQUE LAGHI 2150m

Madonna di Campiglio 1520m/4,990ft

PRADALAGO 2145m

Doss della Pesa 2155m

MONTE VIGO 2180m

Campo Carlo Magno 1860m

Monte Spolverino 2090m

1860m

1888m

Orti

Folgarida 1400m

1300m

Marilleva 1400m

Plenty of opportunity for Mr Editor Watts to engage in one of his favourite activities →

KEY FACTS

Resort	1520m
	4,990ft
Madonna, Folgarida, and Marilleva combined area	
Slopes	1300-2505m
	4,270-8,220ft
Lifts	44
Pistes	120km
	75 miles
Blue	35%
Red	50%
Black	15%
Snowmaking	77km

BEWARE THE BEGINNER DRAGS

A couple of reporters point out that the beginner drag-lifts at Campo Carlo Magno are separately owned to the main lifts and not covered by the resort pass.

italian ski specialists

it's
italiansafaris.com

+44 (0) 7930 902590
info@italiansafaris.com

Phone numbers
From abroad use the prefix +39 (and do **not** omit the initial '0' of the phone number)

TOURIST OFFICE

t 0465 447501
info@campiglio.to
www.campiglio.to

THE MOUNTAINS

The Pradalago sector is linked by lift and piste to Monte Vigo, and so to the slopes of Folgarida and Marilleva – see the Trentino chapter for more on these.
Slopes The terrain is mainly easy intermediate, both above and below the tree line. Reporters have been very impressed with the 'immaculate' grooming and piste marking.
Terrain-parks The Ursus park, at Grostè, includes boarder-cross, half- and quarter-pipes and big air jumps.
Snow reliability Although many of the runs are sunny, they are at a fair altitude, and there has been hefty investment in snowmaking. As a result, snow reliability is reasonable. Even in January 2007, when snow was in short supply, 90% of the pistes were open.
Experts Experts should plan on heading off-piste. The trees under the Genziana chair are 'a good spot for untracked snow'. But the 3-Tre race course and Canalone on Cinque Laghi and the Spinale Direttissima are steep. For other steep runs head to Marilleva.
Intermediates Grostè and Pradalago have long, easy runs, and early or timid intermediates will love them. Cinque Laghi, Campiglio's racing mountain, is a bit tougher, as are the runs at Folgarida, Marilleva and Pinzolo, which adventurous intermediates should explore (see Trentino chapter).
Beginners The nursery slopes at Campo Carlo Magno are excellent, but do involve a bus-ride. The drag-lift here is not covered by the main lift pass and you have to buy a separate day ticket when you get there. Progression to longer runs is easy.
Snowboarding The resort is popular with boarders and some major events have been held here.
Cross-country There are 22km/14 miles of pretty trails through the woods.

Queues Recent reporters have not found queuing a worry. The most serious bottleneck – access to Cinque Laghi – will doubtless be transformed by the new gondola to the top, due to open in December 2007.
Mountain restaurants Reporters like the table-service Cascina Zeledria (in the trees off blue run 7 on Pradalago). On our 2006 visit we enjoyed good local sausages at Viviani, near the top of Pradalago. Malga Montagnoli in the lower part of Grostè is a charming old (self-service) refuge – although a reporter this season found the food 'disappointing' – and Boch, higher up, has been recommended, as has Cinque Laghi ('stunning views'). Restaurants are well-marked on the piste map.
Schools and guides Language can be a problem. A 2006 visitor found the Nazionale school 'very good'; he was the only Brit in his group but managed OK as he spoke a little Italian.
Facilities for children Very limited.

STAYING THERE

How to go There is a wide choice of hotels and some self-catering.
Hotels The 4-stars Spinale (0465 441116) and Bertelli (0465 441013) are both well positioned and the Bertelli is praised for its 'excellent food'. The Savoia Palace (0465 441004) is also 4-star – 'comfortable and friendly', but the location can be noisy. The central Arnica (0465 442227) does 'super' b&b – 'very friendly owners'. The central Milano (0465 441210), Bonapace (0465 441 019) and Crozzon (0465 442222), all 3-stars, have been recommended by readers, as has the 4-star Lorenzetti (0465 441404). On our 2006 visit we enjoyed the 4-star Zeledria (0465 441010) out at Campo Carlo Magno.
Eating out There are around 20 restaurants. 'All the ones we tried were good,' says a reporter, and Belvedere, the Antico Focolare, the Roi and Stube Diana have all been recommended. Another reporter enjoyed the 'artistic dishes' at the pricey Alfiero, and Locanda degli Artisti is 'worth the expense for a special night out'. Some of the mountain huts are also open.
Après-ski Après-ski is quiet. Stube di Franz-Joseph, Bar Suisse and Cantina del Suisse are recommended. The Alpes is perhaps the smartest club.
Off the slopes Window-shopping, skating on the lake and walking are popular. There's also paragliding.

Monterosa Ski

One of Europe's best kept secrets: three unspoiled villages beneath slopes with easy pistes and uncrowded off-piste for all standards

NEWS

For 2007/08 the ancient Punta Indren cable-car in Alagna will finally be taken out of service. A new cable-car is planned from Passo Salati to service the same area (all off-piste), but this will not be ready for 2007/08 (and may not be until 2009/10). Until it is, lots of fabulous off-piste will be available only by ski-touring or heli-skiing. There may also be further lifts in the area in the more distant future.

For 2006/07 more snowmaking was put in place in the Bettaforca area. And a beginner drag-lift at Gabiet, above Gressoney La Trinité, was replaced by a triple chair.

➕ Fabulous intermediate and advanced off-piste, including heli-skiing

➕ Slopes usually very quiet weekdays

➕ Panoramic views

➕ Good snow reliability and grooming

➕ Quiet, unspoiled villages

➕ Three-valley lift/piste network gives a sensation of travel, but ...

➖ Virtually no choice of route when touring the three valleys on-piste

➖ Few challenging pistes – mainly easy cruising

➖ High winds can close links

➖ Few off-slope diversions

➖ Limited après-ski

Monterosa Ski's three resorts – Champoluc, Gressoney and Alagna – are popular with Italian weekenders, who drive up from Milan and Turin, but they are hardly heard of on the international market. As a result, they retain a friendly, small-scale, unspoiled Italian ambience that we and a growing band of readers like a lot. Strangely, few UK tour operators feature the area. But that suits us, as it makes it more likely the area will retain its unique character.

The three-valley network of lifts and pistes is anything but small-scale: Alagna and Champoluc, at opposite ends, are no less than 17km/11 miles apart – slightly further apart than Courchevel and Val-Thorens. It's around a four-hour trip by road to get from Alagna to Champoluc if you miss the last lift. But a glance at the piste map reveals that the Italian network between the two extremes is skeletal compared with the full-bodied French one. Outside the piste network, however, is a lot of great off-piste terrain, some lift-served, which has long attracted experts.

It was only three seasons ago that Alagna became accessible by piste from the top of the Gressoney lifts. Expert skiers may be inclined to regret the fact that a splendid off-piste run was sacrificed; but that's progress. They have plenty more bowls to play in – and the black Olen piste is a cracker.

THE RESORT

There is one main village in each of the area's three long valleys. Champoluc in the western valley and Gressoney in the central one are both about an hour's drive up from the Aosta valley, to the south. Alagna is even more remote, and approached from the Italian lakes, to the east.

Champoluc is a pleasant but not notably pretty place, strung out along the valley road without much ski resort ambience – the centre, where there are a couple of good hotels, is more or less devoid of bars and inviting shops. The village gondola starts from a kind of micro-resort several minutes' walk up the road. You can store boots and skis/board there overnight. The valley road continues past several new hotels towards Frachey, where there is a chair-lift into the slopes.

Gressoney La Trinité is a quiet, neat little village, with cobbled streets, wooden buildings and an old church. It is about 800m/0.5 miles from the chair-lift into the local slopes, where there are a few convenient hotels. Links with the other valleys revolve around Stafal at the head of the valley, reached by bus (five euros for a weekly pass). There is accommodation here, too. Gressoney St Jean, a bigger village, is 5km/3 miles down the valley and has its own separate slopes.

Alagna is a peaceful, rustic village with a solid church and some lovely old wooden farmhouses built in the distinctive Walser style. It bears no resemblance to a conventional ski resort. We visited on a sunny morning in March, and found the place deserted. A gondola starts from the village centre.

Trips to Cervinia, La Thuile, Courmayeur and Pila (all covered by the Aosta Valley pass) are possible by car.

THE MOUNTAINS

The slopes of Monterosa Ski are relatively extensive, and very scenic. The pistes are almost all intermediate (and well groomed), and the lifts are mainly chairs and gondolas, with few drag-lifts. The terrain is undulating and runs are long, but many lifts serve only one or two pistes.

The piste map has been improved recently and the signposting on the pistes is clear. Reporters visiting at various times have found the top lifts making the connection between valleys closed by wind, severely limiting the available terrain.

Slopes Champoluc residents reach Colle Sarezza on two successive gondolas and a quad chair. From the top a steep, narrow, bumpy run (which a lot of timid intermediates find very difficult; there are rumours that it may be being improved) is the link with the long cruising runs below Colle Bettaforca. Taking the bus to the Frachey chair avoids the tricky top run.

At Stafal a cable-car followed by a fast chair bring you back towards Champoluc, while two successive gondolas opposite take you to Passo Salati. From there, runs lead back down to Stafal and to Gressoney La Trinité and Orsia, both served by chair-lifts. Or you can head towards Alagna via the fabulous black Olen piste (which was originally classed as a red), or take a blue which only goes as far as the mid-station of the cable-car back to Passo Salati.

From Alagna a modern gondola goes to Pianalunga at mid-mountain. From here, a cable-car takes you to Passo Salati (with a pause at the mid-station). The tiny, ancient cable-car to Punta Indren from above Pianalunga will reach the end of its permitted life before the 2007/08 season. It is planned to replace it with a new cable-car from Passo Salati, serving only off-piste routes to Alagna and Gressoney (but see 'News' for the timing on this; it is rumoured that you might be allowed on this new lift only if you are wearing an avalanche transceiver).

Gressoney St Jean and Antagnod, near Champoluc, have their own small areas of slopes. The St Jean slopes have only one lift, but two reporters enjoyed half-days there. Antagnod is used by local instructors on bad-weather days and has some good off-piste terrain.

Terrain-parks Gressoney has a boarder-cross but there's no park. Big air jumps are sometimes constructed near the top of the gondola from Champoluc.

Snow reliability Generally good, thanks to altitude, extensive snowmaking and good grooming, though the last two seasons have been poor for natural snow. Reporters continue to be impressed by the snowmaking – a February 2007 visitor said: 'There was limited snow-cover, but the pistes were very well groomed and the snowmaking excellent, so on-piste skiing remained good through a week of warm sunshine. All pistes and connections were open all week.'

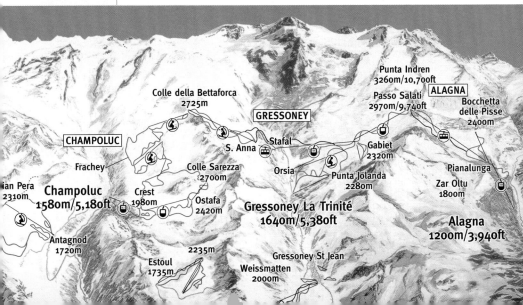

SNOWPIX.COM / CHRIS GILL

Simon (with the back pack) runs tour operator Ski 2 and has just led a group down one of the area's great off-piste runs – he's a top-qualified ski instructor, too ↘

Experts The attraction is the off-piste, with great runs from the high points of the lift system in all three valleys and some excellent heli-drops. Among the adventures we've enjoyed here was a heli-drop on Monte Rosa, skiing down to Zermatt and returning off-piste from the top of the Cervinia lifts. The lift to Punta Indren (see 'News') is important for off-piste opportunities, but a 2007 visitor discovered 'loads more off-piste in Champoluc after hiring a mountain guide, including an area of forest above Frachey that the locals keep to themselves. And the off-piste from the Rifugio Guglielmina at Passo Salati was very enjoyable.' A 2006 visitor enjoyed the tree runs in Frachey.

Intermediates For those who like to travel on easy, undemanding pistes, the area is excellent, with long cruising runs from the ridges down into the valleys ('wonderful, carefree carving'). The black Olen piste (which is more like a tough red and was graded red originally) down towards Alagna is a great blast. There isn't much on-piste challenge for more demanding intermediates, but those willing to take a guide and explore some of the gentler off-piste will have a good time.

Beginners The high nursery slopes at mid-mountain above Champoluc, served by two moving carpets, are better than the lower ones at Gressoney. But neither area has ideal gentle runs to progress to (moving on to the Del Lago run above Frachey is the best Champoluc option).

Snowboarding There's a boarder-cross at Gressoney and great free-riding.

Cross-country There are long trails around St Jean, and shorter ones up the valley; Brusson, in the Champoluc valley, has the best trails in the area.

Queues Few problems, say reporters. Usually they occur only at weekends and peak periods. The double chair to Belvedere, on the way back from Frachey/Bettaforca to Champoluc, can have long queues at the end of the day ('We waited 15 minutes,' says a 2007 reporter). She also found short waits for the gondola from Champoluc at 9.30am and for the cable-car back from Alagna as everyone headed back in the afternoon. Pistes can get crowded at weekends, but the off-piste is still delightfully quiet.

Mountain restaurants The mountain restaurants are generally simple, but there are plenty of them. The following

UK PACKAGES

Champoluc *Alpine Answers, Crystal, Interactive Resorts, Kuoni, Momentum, Mountain Tracks, Ski 2, Ski Yogi, Skitracer, Snow Finders*
Gressoney la Trinité *Alpine Answers, Crystal, Inspired to Ski, Momentum, Mountain Tracks, Ski Addiction, Ski Freshtracks, Ski Yogi, Skitracer, Snoworks*
Alagna *Alpine Answers, Italian Safaris, Mountain Tracks, Ski 2, Ski Freshtracks, Ski Weekend, Ski-Monterosa*
Gressoney St Jean *Alpine Answers, Italian Safaris*

Phone numbers
From abroad use the prefix +39 (and do **not** omit the initial '0' of the phone number)

TOURIST OFFICE

t 0125 303111
kikesly@monterosa-ski.com
www.monterosa-ski.com

have been enjoyed by reporters: the 'lively' Belvedere (one of the few mountain restaurants in the region to have a sit-down loo), the Ostafa ('excellent pasta', 'friendly staff') and the Tana del Lupo above Champoluc, the new, modern Campo Base at the top of the Frachey lift ('excellent food and views') and Stadel Soussun above Frachey ('charming, with an excellent limited menu; booking essential'). In the Gressoney valley there are recommendations for the Sitten above Stafal ('excellent specials and stunning view'), the Bedemie and Morgenrot above Orsia, the Mandria ('excellent and friendly') and the Chamois ('small but charming') at Punta Jolanda and the Del Ponte above Gabiet ('simple, good food'). Over in the Alagna valley the Alpen Stop at Pianalunga and the Baita just below have been recommended. A diversion to the right at the top of the run from Passo Salati to Alagna brings you to the ancient Rifugio Guglielmina ('fab place, great food and views').

Schools and guides We have had mixed reports on the Italian ski schools but universally good reports on the Monterosa mountain guides ('One of the best day's skiing ever,' said a 2007 reporter) and the ski school run by tour op Ski 2 ('good, friendly instructors').
Facilities for children There is a special kids' ski school and snow-park at Antagnod near Champoluc and a mini-club at Gressoney St Jean. A new tubing and adventure park opened in Gressoney St Jean for 2006/07.

STAYING THERE

How to go Surprisingly few tour operators feature the area. We've had good reports of Monterosa specialists Ski 2 ('great from pick-up to drop-off').
Hotels For a small place, Champoluc has a striking range of attractive hotels. Recent reporters liked the central Relais des Glaciers (0125 308721) – a welcoming 4-star with spa and shuttle to the gondola ('food excellent'). The central, 3-star, creaky old Castor (0125 307117) is 'an absolute gem' with 'good food and magnificent puddings'; it is managed by a British guy ('great fun') who married into the family that has owned it for generations. Our favourite luxury option is the 4-star Breithorn (0125 08734), just up the road, with beautifully furnished public areas,

beamed bedrooms and good spa facilities. 'It's a gem,' says one well-travelled reporter – 'superb service'. Food in the elegant dining room or more casual brasserie is excellent. A 2007 visitor recommends the 3-star Champoluc (0125 308088) for its 'friendly, helpful owners, an ideal family hotel'. Out beyond the lift base the 3-star California (0125 307977) is chiefly notable for the pop music themes applied to the rooms and the big saloon bar; and the 3-star Rocher (0125 308711) is 'friendly, welcoming, with good food, spa and sauna'.

At Gressoney La Trinité several reporters recommend the 4-star Jolanda Sport (0125 366140), with gym, saunas, pool; it's right by the lift. But one visitor was disappointed by the food – limited choice, especially for vegetarians. Another says of the nearby 3-star Residence (0125 366148), 'Friendliest hotel I've ever stayed at in the Alps.' The fairly new 3-star Nordend (0125 366807) has 'modern, spacious rooms and a spa – and the Monterosa guides office is in the same building'. The 3-star Dufour (0125 366139) and the 3-star Lysjoch (0125 366150) have also been mentioned. In Alagna, try the 3-star Monterosa (0163 923209) or 4-star Cristallo (0163 922822).
Eating out Both Gressoney and Champoluc have a few stand-alone restaurants; most are in hotels. In Champoluc, the Bistrot is recommended by a 2006 visitor. In Gressoney, the Walserchild pizzeria got a good review from a recent reporter, and the Capanna Carla in Stafal is 'a rustic gem serving excellent traditional fare', says a 2007 visitor.
Après-ski Après-ski is quiet. In Champoluc, the bar of the hotel Castor is cosy and popular with resort workers; the Golosone is a small, atmospheric, authentic Italian wine bar; the Galion opposite the gondola is busy as the lifts close; the West Road pub in the hotel California has karaoke some nights. At weekends, the Gram Parsons disco beneath the California gets going. Gressoney is even quieter; there's the La Pulce bar, and 'the tour-op-organised wine tasting at Hirsch Stube was excellent'. The Core underneath the Nordend hotel in Stafal was recommended in 2007 for 'cool decor and background music'.
Off the slopes There is a natural ice rink at Champoluc; otherwise there's little to amuse those not on the slopes.

Passo Tonale

Purpose-built village set on a high pass, with easy, snow-sure slopes, now linked to more challenging wooded terrain

COSTS

① ② ③ ④ ⑤ ⑥

RATINGS

The slopes
Fast lifts	****
Snow	****
Extent	**
Expert	*
Intermediate	***
Beginner	*****
Convenience	***
Queues	****
Mountain restaurants	**

The rest
Scenery	***
Resort charm	*
Off-slope	*

TRENTINO

ITALIA

NEWS

In 2006/07 a new gondola opened to connect Passo Tonale's slopes with those of Pontedilegno.

ADAMELLO SKI

A good 600m/1,970ft below Passo Tonale, the pleasant town of Pontedilegno is now linked by gondola ↓

+ Good-value, plain accommodation
+ Sunny, easy, snow-sure slopes
+ Good for beginners and early or timid intermediates
+ Link to Pontedilegno adds attractive, steeper, tree-lined runs

− Not much for experts or (except at Pontedilegno) keen intermediates
− Local slopes above the tree line and unpleasant in bad weather
− Purpose-built village straddling the pass road lacks charm

Passo Tonale offers that rare combination of a fair-sized, uncrowded, snow-sure ski area and slope-side hotels at a bargain price. Who cares if it lacks charm? It's a great place for beginners and, now that it is linked to the slopes above Pontedilegno, a more interesting destination for intermediates than it once was.

THE RESORT

Passo Tonale sits on a wide, treeless pass; it is in Trentino but right on the border with Lombardia. The village is a compact, functional affair, developed mainly for skiing and devoid of charm, with its hotels, shops, bars and restaurants spread along both sides of the busy through-road.

THE MOUNTAINS

The home slopes are entirely above the tree line, and bad weather can mean white-outs and closures. From the 2005/06 season, the Tonale slopes were linked to those of Pontedilegno, below the pass in Lombardia; these slopes are generally steeper and quieter than Passo Tonale's main area. Tonale's lift system is impressive, with seven fast chairs in the bigger of its two local areas of slopes.

Slopes Tonale's slopes are spread over two main sectors on opposite sides of the valley. The broad, south-facing area is much the larger, starts right in the village and is served by a well-laid-out mix of chairs and drags. Runs are short because of the limited vertical. The north-facing Presena area is steeper, narrower and taller. First, there is an eight-seater gondola; above that a double chair-lift; and at the top, two drag-lifts on the Presena glacier.

Pontedilegno is reached by a blue/red run through the trees (mostly wide and easy but with a short, much steeper, section). In 2006 the only way back was by bus, but in the 2007 season a gondola link opened.

Terrain-parks There's a park with jumps and a half-pipe served by the fast Valena chair at Passo Tonale.

Snow reliability Tonale is high, includes a glacier and has a lot of snowmaking, so is fairly snow-sure. But the main south-facing area gets a lot of sun, and there can be slush or ice in March and April. Pontedilegno's slopes are lower and more dependent on snowmaking, which is now claimed to cover 100 per cent of the pistes.

Experts This isn't a resort for experts. The black piste down the gondola on the Presena sector deserves its grading but is not a serious challenge. In the

Cima Presena 3015m/9,890ft — Corno Lacoscuro 3160m/10,360ft — PRESENA — Passo Paradiso 2585m — 2120m — 1905m/6,250ft — Corno d'Aola 1920m/6,300ft — Valbione 1500m — Temu — Vermiglio 1260m/4,140ft — Tonale 1885m/6,180ft — Pontedilegno 1255m/4,120ft — Passo Contrabbandieri 2575m — 2180m — 2210m — Maga Valbiolo 2245m — 2500m — 2525m

KEY FACTS

Resort	1885m
	6,180ft

Passo Tonale and Pontedilegno combined area

Slopes	1120-3015m
	3,670-9,890ft
Lifts	30
Pistes	100km
	62 miles
Blue	21%
Red	60%
Black	19%
Snowmaking	60km
	37 miles

UK PACKAGES

Airtours, Ardmore, Crystal, Directski.com, Equity, First Choice, First Choice, Inghams, Neilson, Rocketski, Ski McNeill, Ski Supreme, Ski Wild, Thomson

Phone numbers
From abroad use the prefix +39 (and do **not** omit the initial '0' of the phone number)

TOURIST OFFICE

t 0364 903838
tonale@valdisole.net
www.adamelloski.com
www.valdisole.net

right conditions there are epic off-piste runs from the glacier, including the impressive 16km/10 mile Pisgana run towards Pontedilegno (a vertical of 1650m/5,410ft). Guidance needed.
Intermediates The south-facing slopes offer gentle terrain ideal for cruising; many of these runs are graded red but are really no more than gentle blue gradient. We particularly enjoyed the 4.5 km/3 mile Alpino piste down a deserted valley to the village. The runs at the top of the glacier are short and easy and we couldn't see much difference between the reds and the black marked here. Below that the run beneath the chair is no more than a cat-track but the black beneath the gondola will be too much for timid intermediates, who should ride down. The runs at Pontedilegno are much more serious reds and deserve their grading. You could use the regional pass and visit Marilleva (free daily buses) and Madonna (free bus on Wednesdays) down the valley.
Beginners It's an excellent resort for novices. The sunny lifts on gentle slopes right by the village are ideal, and there are plenty of easy blue runs to choose from – good for 'giving lots of confidence', says a reporter.
Snowboarding The gentle slopes and ability to get around mainly on chair-lifts means the area is good for beginner and intermediate boarders.
Cross-country There are 23km/14 miles with loops at Passo Tonale and in the valley and at altitude at Pontedilegno.
Queues We have no reports of queues.
Mountain restaurants The half-dozen mountain restaurants generally meet with readers' approval. We ate at Faita, with a terrace, small ground floor area

and rustic dining room upstairs. Many people return to the resort for lunch.
Schools and guides We've heard of 'pure chaos' at ski school meeting times, but most reports are more positive: 'The instructors are not all fluent in English but we didn't find it a problem'; 'Our instructor (Presena school) was very patient, encouraging and cheerful, with excellent English.'
Facilities for children There's a kindergarten at hotel Miramonti for ages one to 12, and the ski school takes children from age four.

STAYING THERE

How to go Passo Tonale has long been popular with tour operators, but the much more traditional (and larger) village of Pontedilegno doesn't seem to have registered yet.
Hotels There are around 30 hotels, most of them in the 3-star category. Reader recommendations include the Savoia (0364 91340) – 'basic but clean, with friendly helpful staff'; Adamello (0364 903886) – 'friendly, good service, clean'; Gardenia (0364 903769) – 'modern, clean, inexpensive, food basic'. The 4-star Miramonti (0364 900501) looks to be the best (recently renovated with new pool and spa).
Apartments There are 1,400 beds in apartments, a few on the UK market.
Eating out Mainly hotel restaurants.
Après-ski Reader recommendations include the Magic Pub, El Bait and later on Heaven and the Miramonti disco.
Off the slopes If you are not intending to hit the slopes, forget Tonale. But there's snowmobiling, snow-shoeing, dog-sledding, ice skating, and the Miramonti's pool is open to the public.

Sauze d'Oulx

'Suzy does it' still, up to a point – a lively village beneath an attractive area of slopes, but with persistent drawbacks

COSTS

① ② ③ ④ ⑤ ⑥

RATINGS

The slopes
Fast lifts	***
Snow	**
Extent	****
Expert	**
Intermediate	****
Beginner	**
Convenience	**
Queues	***
Mountain restaurants	***

The rest
Scenery	***
Resort charm	**
Off-slope	*

NEWS

For 2006/07 a new fast quad chair replaced the old double accessing the slopes from Jouvenceaux. A new terrain-park was built in the Sportinia sector, and another is planned for 2007/08 – in the Clotes sector.

In 2006/07 the Via Lattea snowmaking system was expanded to cover a further 35km/22 miles, and for 2007/08 there will be 100 per cent snowmaking on the beginners' area at Sportinia. A new sports hall is also planned.

In 2006 the lift company was taken over by a local business consortium, which is said to have plans for new lifts in the pipeline.

☐ Extensive and uncrowded slopes – great intermediate cruising

☐ Linked into Milky Way network

☐ Mix of open and tree-lined runs is good for all weather conditions

☐ Entertaining nightlife

☐ Some scope for off-piste adventures

☐ One of the cheapest major resorts – and more attractive than its reputation suggests

☐ Erratic snow record – and far from comprehensive snowmaking

☐ Still lots of ancient slow lifts

☐ Crowds at weekends

☐ Getting to the French end of the Milky Way takes forever

☐ Very few challenging pistes

☐ Mornings-only classes, and the best nursery slopes are at mid-mountain

☐ Steep walks around the village, and an inadequate shuttle-bus service

Sauze is cheap, cheerful and the closest decent-sized ski area to Turin, which helps to account for its enduring popularity with impecunious Brits flying into Turin and with the city's bourgeoisie looking for weekend homes. If you were a tabloid reader in the 1980s, you couldn't fail to notice that Sauze was dominated by British youth on the binge. But these days things are much more in balance, at weekends at least. It still has lively bars and shops festooned in English signs, but sober Brits like you and us need not stay away. When we visit, we always find ourselves liking it more than we expect to – as do many reporters.

But Sauze still has a problem: investment, lack of. With its acutely unreliable natural snow, it needs the kind of comprehensive snowmaking that the Sella Ronda resorts have. Until it gets it, booking a trip well in advance is going to be a gamble. And its programme of lift upgrading needs serious acceleration.

THE RESORT

Sauze d'Oulx sits on a sloping mountain shelf facing north-west across the Valle di Susa to the mountains bordering France.

Most of the resort is modern and undistinguished, made up of block-like hotels relieved by the occasional chalet, spreading down the steep hillside from the slopes. It rather gives the impression of falling behind the times, with none of the investment in smart, woody hotels and apartments that goes on in more dynamic resorts.

The village has an attractive old core, with narrow, twisting streets and houses roofed with huge stone slabs. There is a central car-free zone, but the rest of the village can be congested morning and evening. The roads have few pavements and can become icy.

Despite the decline in lager sales, the centre is still lively at night; the late bars are usually quite full, and the handful of discos do brisk business – at the weekend, at least. Noise can be a problem in the early hours.

Out of the bustle of the centre, there are secluded apartment blocks in quiet, wooded areas and a number of good restaurants also tucked away.

Most of the hotels are reasonably central, but the lifts are less so: the Clotes chair is at the top of the village, up a short but steep hill, and the Sportinia chair is at an irritatingly long walk beyond that. Ski-buses (not covered by the lift pass) are infrequent, inadequate and absent around lunch-time. Getting to other resorts involves public buses with multiple changes in some cases. A car simplifies excursions, eg to French resorts such as Montgenèvre.

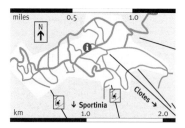

↑ An attractive mix of open and lightly wooded slopes, few of them steep

SNOWPIX.COM / CHRIS GILL

KEY FACTS

Resort	1510m
	4,950ft

Milky Way	
Slopes	1390-2825m
	4,560-9,270ft
Lifts	78
Pistes	400km
	249 miles
Blue	24%
Red	56%
Black	20%
Snowmaking	130km
	81 miles

Sauze d'Oulx-Sestriere-Sansicario	
Slopes	1390-2825m
	4,560-9,270ft
Lifts	43
Pistes	300km
	186 miles
Snowmaking	95km
	59 miles

THE MOUNTAINS

Sauze's mountains provide excellent intermediate terrain. The piste grading changes from year to year, but it doesn't matter much – many runs graded red or even black should really be blue. The higher slopes are open, the lower ones pleasantly wooded.

THE SLOPES
Big and varied enough for most
Sauze's local slopes are spread across a broad wooded bowl above the resort, ranging from west- to north-facing. The main lifts are chairs, from the top of the village up to **Clotes** and from the western fringes to **Sportinia** – a sunny mid-mountain clearing in the woods, with a ring of restaurants and hotels and a small nursery area.

The high point of the system is **Monte Fraiteve**. From here you can travel west on splendid broad, long runs to **Sansicario** – and on to a two-stage gondola near **Cesana Torinese** that links with **Claviere** and then **Montgenèvre**, in France, the far end of the Milky Way (both are reached more quickly by car).

You normally get to **Sestriere** from the lower point of Col Basset, on the shoulder of M Fraiteve – but snow cover is unreliable and in our experience you normally have to use the gondola to descend the bottom half of the mountain. In bad weather, on the other hand, the gondola is prone to closure ('closed all week', says a 2006 visitor). There is an alternative red run from M Fraiteve itself, but snow is again not reliable on this sunny slope.

As in so many Italian resorts, piste marking, direction signing and piste map design are not taken seriously.

TERRAIN-PARKS
Jump and grind
A new terrain-park in the Sportinia sector was opened for 2006/07 and another is planned for 2007/08 – in the Clotes sector. The Double Black terrain-park in the Rio Nero bowl, just below Col Basset, has been closed.

SNOW RELIABILITY
Can be poor, affecting the links
The area is notorious for erratic snowfalls, suffering droughts with worrying frequency. Another problem is that many of the slopes get a lot of afternoon sun – the links with Sestriere are very vulnerable. Snowmaking is being increased throughout the area but coverage is still far from complete – around the Sportinia nursery slopes it is said to be 'woefully inadequate'. But reporters have been impressed by the efforts to keep runs open in poor conditions ('they worked miracles') and grooming is in general 'superb'.

LIFT PASSES

La Via Lattea

Prices in €

Age	1-day	6-day
over 8	32	170

Free under 8

Senior no deals

Beginner no deals

Notes
Covers lifts in Sauze d'Oulx, Sestriere, Sansicario, Cesana and Claviere; 6-day pass allows one day in Montgenèvre and Bardonecchia; half-day passes

Alternative passes
Sauze only, Sestriere only, Cesana only

FOR EXPERTS
Head off-piste

Very few of the pistes are challenging. The best slopes are at virtually opposite ends of Sauze's local area – a short, high, north-facing run from the shoulder of M Fraiteve, and the sunny slopes below M Moncrons. There are plenty of minor off-piste opportunities within the piste network, but the highlights are long, top-to-bottom descents of up to 1300m/4,270ft vertical from M Fraiteve, ending (snow permitting) at villages dotted along the valleys. The best known of these runs is the Rio Nero, down to the road near Oulx. When snow low down is poor, some of these runs can be cut short.

FOR INTERMEDIATES
Splendid cruising terrain

The whole area is ideal for confident intermediates who want to clock up the kilometres. For the less confident, the piste map doesn't help because it picks out only the very easiest runs in blue – when actually there are many others that are manageable. The Belvedere and Moncrons sectors at the east of the area are served only by drags but offer some wonderful, uncrowded high cruising, some of it above the tree line.

The long runs down to Jouvenceaux are splendid, flattering intermediate terrain, as are those below Sportinia ('ideal for perfecting technique').

The slopes above Sansicario are also excellent – served by two fast quad chair-lifts – but the link via the shoulder of M Fraiteve can be problematic – a seriously steep double drag-lift on the way out, and the steepest pitch in the whole area on the way back. A chair-lift is needed here, to solve both problems and open up Sansicario to everyone.

At the higher levels, where the slopes are above the tree line, the terrain often allows a choice of route. Lower down are pretty runs through the woods, where the main complication can be route-finding. The mountainside is broken up by gullies, limiting the links between pistes that appear to be quite close together.

FOR BEGINNERS
There are better choices

There are signs that the resort is trying to improve life for novices but its village-level slopes are a bit on the steep side and the main nursery area is up the mountain, at Sportinia. Equally importantly, the mornings-only classes don't suit everyone. Once off the nursery slopes, the main problem is a psychological one – that most of the mountain is classified red, though the gradient is generally blue.

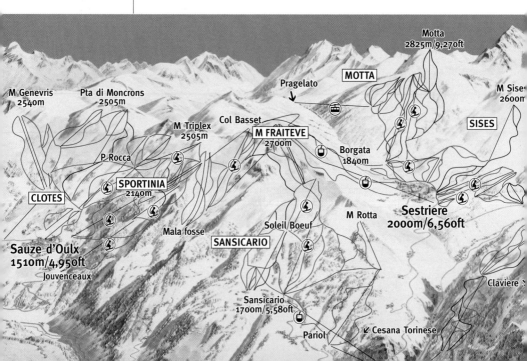

SCHOOLS

Sauze Sportinia
t 0122 850218

Sauze d'Oulx
t 0122 858084

Sauze Project
t 0122 858942

Classes
(Sauze Sportinia prices)
6 3hr days: €150

Private lessons
€32 for 1hr

GUIDES

Marco Degani
t 0335 398984

CHILDREN

La Cinciarella
t 0347 554 0245
Only available in the Christmas holiday period. Ages over 13mnth; Mon-Sat; 9am-5pm

Ski school
6 half days €150
(Sportinia prices)

GETTING THERE

Air Turin 84km/
52 miles (1½hr)

Rail Oulx (5km/
3 miles); frequent buses

UK PACKAGES

Airtours, Club Pavilion, Corporate Ski Co, Crystal, Directski.com, First Choice, Independent Ski Links, Inghams, Interhome, Neilson, Panorama, Ski High Days, Ski McNeill, Ski4you, Thomson **Sansicario** Crystal, Thomson

FOR CROSS-COUNTRY
Severely limited, even with snow
There is very little cross-country skiing, and it isn't reliable for snow.

QUEUES
Slow lifts the biggest problem
There can be irritating waits at Sportinia, especially when school classes set off, or just after lunch; otherwise the system has few bottlenecks. But there are few fast lifts – the dominance of ancient and terribly slow lifts was 'a major disappointment' for a 2006 visitor returning to the resort following a three-year gap. The quad that replaced the old double chair out of the village to Clotes is said to be 'just as slow', and still gets queues. Breakdowns of elderly lifts may be a nuisance: the old one-person chair at Col Basset is an important link, and when it fails they may resort to 'dragging skiers behind snowmobiles', says a 2006 reporter. A February 2007 visitor reports that several lifts were opened only at weekends, when the Italian crowds arrive.

MOUNTAIN RESTAURANTS
Some pleasant possibilities
Restaurants are numerous and generally pleasant, though few are particularly special. If you like a civilised table-service lunch, head for the hotel Capricorno, at Clotes. It is not cheap, and midweek in low season it can be amazingly quiet. A reader last year liked the quiet Grangia for 'good value meals'. And Bar Clotes is 'a must' for hot chocolate stops and does 'great lasagne'. Reporters also recommend the Ciao Pais, further up the hill, 'a superb rustic restaurant, ideal when the weather closes in', writes one, but 'a bit pricey', according to another. The Clot Bourget has also pleased visitors and Bar Basset at Rio Nero is 'small and friendly' with 'superb views'. Cicci's House, at the halfway point of the Jouvenceaux chair, serves 'good food and hot chocolate'. There are several places at Sportinia; Capanna Kind is a 2006 reporter's

favourite and does 'home-cooked food at very reasonable prices'. The Rocce Nere is praised yet again for 'excellent food and service'. The Marmotta on M Triplex is one reader's tip for 'drinks and service with a smile'. The Soleil Boeuf above Sansicario is 'good value, with a nice sun terrace'.

SCHOOLS AND GUIDES
Lessons variable
One reporter found his daughter enthusiastic about her lesson (in a group of eight, in low season), and another writes of 'patient instructors with good English spoken', though past reports have been mixed.

FACILITIES FOR CHILDREN
Tour operator alternatives
You might want to look at the nursery facilities offered by major UK tour operators in the chalets and chalet-hotels that they run here. All the schools take children from four years.

STAYING THERE

HOW TO GO
Packaged hotels dominate
All the major mainstream operators offer hotel packages here, but there are also a few chalets.
Hotels Simple 2-star and 3-star hotels form the core of the holiday accommodation, with a couple of 4-stars and some more basic places.
****Torre (0122 859812) Cylindrical landmark 200m/650ft below the centre. Excellent rooms, 'good food', 'plenty of choice'; mini-buses to lifts. A new health suite with pool was created for 2007.
***Gran Baita (0122 850183) Comfortable place in quiet, central backstreet, with excellent food and good rooms, some with sunset views.
***Terrazza (0122 850173) In a quiet part of town, near the Clotes chair.
**Biancaneve (0122 850160) Pleasant, with smallish rooms. Near the centre.
**Hermitage (0122 850385) Neat chalet-style hotel beside the home piste from Clotes.

boarding

Sauze has good snowboarding slopes – it's got local tree-lined slopes (with space in the trees, too), high, undulating, open terrain, and links to other resorts in the Milky Way. But although it has a fair number of chair-lifts, there are also lots of drags – a serious drawback for novice riders. There's a terrain-park in the Sportinia sector.

ACTIVITIES

Indoor Cinema, sauna, solarium, massage

Outdoor Ice rink, bobsleigh run, snowmobiling

Phone numbers
From abroad use the prefix +39 (and do **not** omit the initial '0' of the phone number)

TOURIST OFFICES

Sauze d'Oulx
t 0122 858009
sauze@montagnedoc.it
www.montagnedoc.it
www.vialattea.it

Cesana Torinese (Sansicario)
t 0122 89202
cesana@montagnedoc.it

***Des Amis** (0122 858488) Down in Jouvenceaux, but near bus stop; simple hotel run by Anglo-Italian couple.
Villa Cary (0122 850191) Recommended by a 2007 reporter as 'comfortable and welcoming' with 'excellent food for its two-star rating'.
*Stella Alpina** (0122 858731) Between main lifts. Friendly Anglo-Italian family doing 'excellent food'. Endorsed by a 2006 reporter.
Apartments Apartments and chalets available, some through UK operators.

EATING OUT
Caters for all tastes and pockets
Typical Italian banquets of five or six courses can be had in the upmarket Godfather ('excellent food') and Cantun restaurants. The Falco does a particularly good three-course 'skiers' menu'. In the old town, the Borgo and the Griglia are popular pizzerias. The Lampione does good-value Chinese, Mexican and Indian food. The Faraglioni (formerly the Pecore Nere) also gets good reviews.

APRES-SKI
Suzy does it with more dignity
Sauze's bars now impress reporters young and old. Choice is wide, with multiple happy hours.
The Assietta terrace is popular for catching the last rays of the sun at the end of the day. The New Scotch bar in the hotel Stella Alpina serves English beer and is also popular ('high standard of service'), as is the Lampione, in the old town.
After dinner, more places warm up. One of the best is the smart, atmospheric cocktail bar Moncrons, which holds regular quiz nights. But a 2006 reporter's favourite is the Gran Trun, a converted barn in the old part of town, complete with resident entertainer who 'loves you to request all the old sing-a-long songs'.

Reporters also like the 'interesting' Village Cafè with its many metal artefacts; you can eat here too ('excellent pizzas'). The Cotton Club provides good service, directors' chairs, video screen and draught cider. Max's was a favourite for a 2007 visitor ('excellent food and ski videos') along with Scatto Matto later on. Miravallino is a 'very Italian' cafe bar. Paddy McGinty's offers 'a good variety of meals including Mexican and steaks'. The 'very cosy' Derby is nice for a quiet drink and a 'civilised chill-out' and the Ghost Bar is the new place to go: it's 'lively, friendly and relaxed' and serves 'a wonderful array of burgers', according to this year's reporters. Of the discos, Clarabella (formerly Bandito) is a walk away, and popular with Italians. Schuss runs theme nights and drink promotions.

OFF THE SLOPES
Go elsewhere
Shopping is limited, there are no gondolas or cable-cars for pedestrians and there are few off-slope activities, though things are improving: you can now have a go on the Olympic bobsleigh run at Sansicario and a new sports centre is due to be completed for 2007/08. Turin or Briançon are worth a visit.

STAYING UP THE MOUNTAIN
'You pays your money ... '
In most resorts, staying up the mountain is one of the cheaper options. Here, the reverse applies. The 4-star Capricorno (0122 850273), up at Clotes, is the most attractive and expensive hotel in Sauze. It's a charming little chalet beside the piste, with only eight bedrooms.
Not quite in the same league are the places up at Sportinia – though reporters have enjoyed the isolation and ski convenience.

Sansicario 1700m/5,580ft

Sansicario is ideally placed for exploration of the whole Milky Way, being a gondola ride above Cesana and the chair-lifts for Claviere and Montgenèvre. It is a modern, purpose-built, self-contained but rather soulless little resort, mainly consisting of apartments grouped around the small shopping precinct. The 45-room Rio Envers (0122 811333) is a comfortable, expensive hotel.

Sella Ronda

Endless intermediate slopes amid spectacular Dolomite scenery, with a choice of attractive valley villages, mainly German-speaking

➕ Vast network of connected slopes – suits intermediates particularly well

➕ Stunning, unique Dolomite scenery

➕ Lots of mountain huts with good food

➕ Excellent value for money

➕ Extensive snowmaking – one of Europe's best systems, but ...

➖ They need it: natural snowfall is erratic in this southerly region

➖ Few challenges, and off-piste limited – possibly banned in places

➖ Mostly short runs with limited vertical

➖ Crowds on the Sella Ronda circuit

➖ Still some old drag-lifts

➖ Après-ski not a highlight

The Sella Ronda is an amazing circular network of lifts and pistes taking you around the Gruppo Sella – a mighty limestone massif with villages scattered around it. Among the main attractions is the simply spectacular Dolomite scenery – like something Disney might have conjured up for a theme park. But the geology that provides the visual drama also dictates the nature of the slopes. Sheer limestone cliffs rise out of gentle pasture-land, which is where you spend your time. Individual runs are short; verticals of more than 500m/1,640ft are rare, while runs of under 300m/980ft are not. And they are predominantly easy: there's scarcely a black run to be seen and very little off-piste.

But the distances you can cover on skis are huge. In overall scale, the network rivals the famed Three Valleys in France. In addition to the main Sella Ronda circuit, major lift systems lead off it at three main points along the way – Selva, covered in the chapter after this – Corvara and Arabba. These three should obviously be on your shortlist as potential destinations. But there are other villages worth considering, notably Santa Cristina and Ortisei, next to Selva, and covered in that chapter; San Cassiano, which shares with La Villa a friendly area of largely very easy slopes, just off the main circuit and linked to Corvara; and Canazei and Campitello, at the south-west corner of the circuit – in Trentino, and mainly covered in our separate chapter on that province.

This is one of the few areas where we unreservedly welcome continuous sunny weather; the snowmaking is fantastic and we really don't want clouds and snow to interfere with our lunches gazing at the views.

CHOOSING A BASE

It's important to pick the right resort. For good skiers, the best bases are Selva (covered in a separate chapter) and Arabba, a small village where classic Dolomite terrain gives way to longer, steeper slopes. Corvara and San Cassiano are better for novices, with abundant gentle slopes. Canazei has the most limited local slopes, but access to Arabba is speedy.

A vast network of slopes apparently requires a vast selection of piste maps – 12 in all, plus several variations. There are individual ones for each resort; some cover the main circuit, others do not. Reporters generally find them confusing: 'There are two maps numbered 6 for Arabba; the blue one covers the Sella Ronda, but the white does not.' To add to the confusion, the main resorts now promote additional tours, away from the main circuit. A First World War circuit of 78-100km/ 48-62 miles is one ('A macho day out for mileage-hungry intermediates,' said a 2007 reporter who spent over 7 hours on the circuit, missed the last lift and had to get a taxi back home).

The Dolomiti Superski pass covers not only the Sella Ronda resorts but dozens of others, amounting to an impressive 1220km/758 miles. We'd recommend anyone based in Corvara or San Cassiano to make a day trip to Cortina, ending the day with the famous 'hidden valley' run from Passo Falzarego – see feature panel.

THE SELLA RONDA CIRCUIT

The Sella Ronda is a unique circular tour around the Sella massif, easily managed in a day by even an early intermediate. The slopes you descend are almost all easy, and take you through Selva, Colfosco, Corvara, Arabba and Canazei (or at least the slopes above it). You can do the circuit in either direction by following very clear coloured signs. The clockwise route is slightly quicker and offers more interesting slopes. Reporters have found the anticlockwise route tends to be less crowded though. Some resort piste maps incorporate a Sella Ronda map of the usual panoramic kind; map-literate people will want the proper topographical one with contour lines, from the tourist office (not lift stations).

The runs total around 23km/14 miles and the lifts around 14km/9 miles. The lifts take a total of about two hours (plus any queuing). We've done it in just three and a half hours excluding diversions and hut stops; five or six hours is a realistic time during busy periods, when there are crowds both on the pistes and on the lifts. If possible, choose low season or a Saturday, and set out early.

Not everyone likes it. Reporters' comments include: 'It's a bit of a slog,' 'too busy and crowded' and 'over-hyped, over-sold and over-regimented'. And boarders should be aware that there are quite a few flat bits.

If you set out early, you can make more of the day by taking some diversions from the circuit. Among the most entertaining runs are the long ones down from Ciampinoi to Santa Cristina and Selva, from Dantercëpies to Selva, from the top of the Boé gondola back down to Corvara, and from the top of the Arabba gondola. Take in all those in a day doing the circuit and you'll have had a good day.

Intermediates could take time out to explore the off-the-circuit area towards San Cassiano and La Villa from Corvara. Groups of different abilities can do the circuit and arrange to meet along the way at some of the many welcoming rifugios.

ARABBA 1600m/5,250ft

Arabba, diagonally opposite Selva on the Sella Ronda circuit, is a small, quiet village appealing particularly to good skiers because of its relatively steep, shady local slopes. Off the circuit there is good skiing to be done on the Marmolada glacier.

THE RESORT

Arabba is a small, traditional-style village; it is growing fast and we are receiving more reports on it. Staying in the older part involves an uphill walk to reach the ski area, which provokes a few complaints from reporters. A new area of hotels and chalets has opened higher up, better-placed for the lifts and slopes. There's a small selection of shops, bars and restaurants, but this is not a place for lively nightlife.

THE MOUNTAIN

Arabba's local slopes cover 62km/38 miles and have some of the best natural snow and steepest pistes in the Dolomites. In various places around Arabba, reporters reckon the runs are at the steep end of their classification, and in one or two cases blues might be better classed as reds. Runs from the high point of Porto Vescovo are north-facing and longer than most in the region. The Marmolada glacier, beyond Arabba, is open most of the winter and is included on the main lift pass. It is a trip to do as much for its spectacular views as for skiing, though the red run from top to bottom is a notable 1490m/4,900ft vertical.

Slopes The two-stage DMC gondola and the cable-car beside it rise almost 900m/2,950ft vertical to the high point at Porto Vescovo (2475m/8,120ft). From here a choice of runs return to the village or you can head off around the Sella Ronda circuit, following a busy red run to Pont de Vauz. From the mid-station of the DMC, a series of chairs takes you to Passo Padon and onwards to the Marmolada glacier.

On the opposite side of the village, a fast quad gets you on the way to Burz and Passo Campolongo. You can then head directly down to Corvara and the rest of the Sella Ronda or divert right on to the quieter, gentle slopes towards San Cassiano.

Terrain-park None in Arabba. There's a half-pipe at Belvedere above Canazei.

Snow reliability Arabba offers some of the most snow-sure slopes in the Sella Ronda region. Good snow is far from assured, but snowmaking is extensive and the main runs are north-facing.

Experts Arabba has the best steep slopes of all the Sella Ronda resorts. The north-facing blacks and reds from Porto Vescovo offer genuine challenges and are great fun. Off-piste is limited – see feature panel.

Intermediates The local slopes suit adventurous intermediates best. Most are quite challenging and those on the main circuit suffer from crowds.

Beginners It is not a good choice for beginners. There is a small nursery slope near the Burz chair, but access to longer easy runs is tricky.

Snowboarding Porto Vescovo offers some decent challenge. Most of the lifts are fast chairs or gondolas.

Cross-country There is one loop at village level.

Queues New lifts have vastly improved access to and from the village and a 2007 reporter spent no more than five minutes in a queue locally (but did notice big queues elsewhere, especially on the Sella Ronda circuit). Another 2007 reporter found that an upgrade to the cable-car to Porto Vescovo has eased the queue problem at the bottom but created a bottleneck at the top. And, despite the recent upgrading of the Marmolada cable-cars, we are still getting reports of long waits at the bottom station.

Mountain restaurants Lots of choice, from rustic huts to larger places. Most are lively with good food. The Bec de Roces and Col de Burz are both suntraps (with 'amazing Bombardinos' at the latter). Cherz above Passo di Campolongo has great views of Marmolada. The Luigi Gorze at the top of the Porta Vescovo lifts has been recommended for 'excellent food' and 'stunning views', as have the 'lively' Rifugio Plan Boé, and the Fodom ('first class, good value pizza') at the bottom

Sella Ronda

There are relatively few major off-piste routes in this area, because of the nature of the mountains – gentle pasture, surmounted by cliffs. But the routes that are available are spectacular.

The cable-car from Passo Pordoi gets you up on to the Sella massif. There are fairly direct descents from here back to the pass (the very sunny Forcella) or down the Val Lasties towards Canazei. But the classic run is the Val Mesdì, a long, shady couloir on the northern side of the Gruppo Sella down to Colfosco, reached by skiing and hiking across the massif.

Marmolada, the highest peak of the Dolomites, now reached by reasonably efficient lifts from Malga Ciapela, is the other obvious launching point. It offers a range of big descents on and off the glacier.

Proguide in Arabba offers guidance on these and other routes – see www.proguide.it.

of the Lezuo Belvedere chair below Passo Pordoi and Capanna Bill, near the Marmolada lifts, on the way back to Arabba ('good food, table-service').

Schools The local Arabba school offers group and private classes. Proguide guides off-piste – see feature panel.

Facilities for children The kindergarten at the ski school takes children from two years.

STAYING THERE

How to go Several UK tour operators offer packages. New accommodation has been built at the top end of town, closer to the lifts.

Chalets There are several, including a good selection from Neilson.

Hotels Of the dozen or so hotels, several 3-stars get support from readers. The Portavescovo (0436 79139) has been described as 'excellent: wonderful food, nicely furnished rooms and a well-equipped fitness centre', but a recent reporter warns of a noisy disco every night and a chilly pool. The Malita (0436 79103) is 'comfortable with good food, at reasonable prices'. A group with experience of both reports that the Evaldo (0436 791109) is better than either – 'great food', pool and sauna. It's away from the lifts, whereas the Mesdì (0436 79119) is close to the Burz lift with 'lovely rooms, health suite and wonderful 5-course dinners'. The Garni Laura (0436 780055) B&B is also near the Burz lift and praised by a 2007 guest – 'the top floor rooms have wonderful beamed ceilings and the wellness suite is pure 5-star luxury'. The B&B hotel Royal (0436 79293) is 'a real gem' – large rooms, sauna, hot-tub and Turkish bath – but is further from the lifts. The Al Forte (0436 79329) 'has good food, and is built

around the old fort, with fascinating public rooms'. 2007 reporters praise two 4-stars: the Sporthotel (0436 79321) is 'very good value for money with good food; slightly above the lifts' and the Grifone (0436 780033) is out of town at Passo Campolongo – 'remote but food and service were superb, excellent bar and health club/pool'.

Apartments Self-catering accommodation is available.

Eating out Restaurant choice is limited. The central hotels all have busy restaurants. Reporters love Miky's Grill in the Hotel Mesdì ('best steaks in the Alps'; 'best restaurant in Arabba'). The Alpenrose hotel will send its horse-drawn sleigh to pick you up if you book a table in its Stube Ladina ('good food and surroundings'). The 7 Sass does 'delicious pizzas'. You can go up to Rifugio Plan Boé by snow-mobile on Thursdays for a 'special' 3-course dinner and dancing – 'the best meal we had'.

Après ski The après-ski is cheap but very limited – 'Still only three bars and none with any life,' says one regular who lives in hope of an improvement; 'by 5pm everything is quiet'. But the Stube bar 'has live music on Saturday and the Treina on Sunday.' There's also the 'friendly' Bar Peter. Cosy hotel bars are other options in the village. The atmospheric Rifugio Plan Boé up the mountain is good for a last drink on the pistes before heading back to the village – 'loud 70s, 80s and Europop music'. It is possible to take a taxi to nearby Corvara (6km/4 miles away) for a more animated choice.

Off the slopes Off-slope diversions are few. There's a small selection of shops, cafes, and an ice-rink. Snowmobile excursions and sleigh rides are available. Helicopter rides to the Marmolada glacier are possible.

CORVARA 1570m/5,150ft

Gentle slopes at the heart of the Sella Ronda circuit. There are plenty of hotels, restaurants, bars and sports facilities, making Corvara one of the better bases for families and novices.

THE RESORT

Corvara is the most animated village east of Selva and central to the Alta Badia region. The main shops and some hotels cluster around a small piazza, but the rest of the place sprawls along the valley floor – some accommodation is far from the lifts.

THE MOUNTAIN

Corvara is well-positioned with village lifts heading off to reasonably equidistant Selva, Arabba and San Cassiano. The local slopes are gentle and confidence-boosting.

Slopes A long gondola heads out of the village towards Boé and the clockwise Sella Ronda circuit. Two successive fast quads head in the opposite direction towards Colfosco and the anticlockwise route. The area around both lifts can get congested at peak times. A slow chair and a couple of drags take you towards the quieter area of slopes shared with San Cassiano and La Villa. A faster alternative from the other side of town is a new gondola which replaced the old chair to Col Alto for 2006/07.

Terrain-park There is a terrain-park on the Ciampai run above San Cassiano.

Snow reliability As with the rest of the Sella Ronda area, natural snowfall is erratic but snowmaking excellent.

Experts Very few of Corvara's slopes offer any real challenge and those that do are relatively short. There's hardly a black run to be seen – the one above Boé 'was red 28 years ago and is no harder now', a reporter points out. One reporter enjoyed the short black at Colfosco and there's the much longer World Cup run at La Villa. See the feature panel for off-piste runs.

Intermediates The slopes are superb for cruising and confidence-boosting and there's a vast network of interconnected slopes to explore; don't miss the Val Stella Alpina area (see Colfosco below) and the easy runs between Corvara and San Cassiano. The red underneath the Boé cable-car in Corvara is usually uncrowded and retains good snow. The adventurous can head for the steeper, wooded pistes above La Villa.

Beginners There's a nursery area and lots of easy runs to progress to.

Snowboarding Novices can make rapid progress on gentle slopes. A few awkward drag-lifts remain, but most can be avoided. There's a terrain-park above San Cassiano.

Cross-country The Alta Badia area offers 35km/22 miles of trails, including a 16km/10 mile valley loop on the way to Colfosco.

Queues New lifts have improved the area. Though we had no complaints this year, in past years reporters have had to queue for the Boé gondola at peak times, the Borest chair between Corvara and Colfosco and the T-bars in Passo Campolongo (all Sella Ronda circuit routes).

Mountain restaurants Lots of choice. A recent reporter enjoyed 'brill lasagne and hunter's platter' at the Brancia, above Col Alto.

Schools There's a local branch of the Alta Badia school – reports welcome.

Facilities for children Kinderland by the ski school takes children from age two.

STAYING THERE

How to go There is a wide choice of accommodation, but some can be a walk from the lifts.

Hotels The 4-star hotel Posta Zirm (0471 836175) has a large spa facility, and is recommended by a reporter: 'Very good food, ski-in/ski-out, comfortable rooms.' Also recommended is the pensione Villa Tony (0471 836193): 'Very reasonably priced half-board, on the main street.'

Eating out A reasonable choice. Most of the hotels have restaurants – the Stüa de Michil in the Perla has a Michelin star. See also San Cassiano.

Après ski The Posta Zirm in Corvara does a ski-boot tea dance but support may depend on tour ops organising group transport back to other villages. The hotel Tablè is recommended by reporters for its piano bar and good cakes. Other suggestions from a recent reporter are the smart bar in the Perla hotel and the 'self-consciously trendy' cocktail bar at the Marmolada.

Off the slopes There's a covered ice rink, indoor tennis courts and an outdoor artificial climbing wall.

COLFOSCO 1645m/5,400ft

Colfosco is a smaller, quieter satellite of Corvara, 2km/1 mile away. It has a fairly compact centre with a sprawl of large hotels along the road towards Passo

Gardena and Selva. It's connected to Corvara by a horizontal chair-lift. In the opposite direction, a gondola goes to Passo Gardena. There are a couple of short nursery slopes and the runs back from Passo Gardena are easy, long cruises. Immediately above the village, the Val Stella Alpina (aka Edelweisstal), off the Sella Ronda circuit, offers gentle, normally quiet pistes ideal for fast cruising. The three pleasant restaurants can get very busy. A 2007 visitor recommends the slope-side Hotel Sport (0471 836074) with its 'spacious rooms, friendly staff and excellent food'.

SAN CASSIANO 1530m/5,020ft

A quiet village with some good hotels, easy slopes away from the main Sella Ronda circuit and easy access to Passo Falzarego for the famous 'hidden valley' run.

THE RESORT

San Cassiano is a pleasant little village, set in an attractive, tree-filled valley. It is bypassed by the road to Cortina, and is working towards becoming car-free. It's a quiet, civilised resort, without much animation.

AZIENDA TURISTICA ARABBA
LIVINALLONGO

The Sella Ronda area is spectacularly beautiful and has 460km/286 miles of mainly well-groomed, intermediate slopes ↘

THE MOUNTAIN

The local slopes, shared with Corvara and La Villa, form a spur off the main Sella Ronda circuit. Access to the circuit takes time.

Slopes The gondola, a drive from the centre (many hotels run buses), rises to Piz Sorega. From the top, fast chairs form the links with Corvara and La Villa, or you can head for Pralongia and the long runs home. Most of the area has very gentle slopes, ideal for easy cruising.

Terrain-park There is a newish terrain-park at Ciampai, with boarder-cross, jumps, rails and humps.

Snow reliability The Dolomites have an erratic snowfall record, but snowmaking is excellent.

Experts Experts would be wise to stay elsewhere. There are a few steeper runs at La Villa, but not much else.

Intermediates Pretty much ideal if you love easy cruising on flattering, well-groomed runs. The red option back to town is a serious red though.

Beginners There are nursery slopes a short bus-ride away at Armentarola and at the top of the gondola – not ideal. But there are plenty of long, easy slopes to progress to.

If you like runs surrounded by spectacular scenery well away from all signs of civilisation, don't miss the easy red run from Lagazuoi, reached by cable-car from Passo Falzarego. The pass is easily accessible from Armentarola, close to San Cassiano – shared taxis run an affordable (5 euros each) shuttle service to the pass from here. There's also a bus from San Cassiano, but a recent reporter says it is 'very crowded and slow'. And buses go to the pass from Cortina.

The run is one of the most beautiful we've come across, and usually delights reporters. Views from the top of the cable-car are splendid, and the run offers isolation amid sheer, pink-tinged Dolomite peaks and frozen waterfalls. Make time to stop at the atmospheric Rifugio Scotoni near the end.

At the bottom, it's a long skate to a horse-drawn sled with ropes attached, which tows you back to Armentarola (for a couple of euros). This is more of a challenge than the run, and the risk of a pile-up if someone falls has concerned a couple of reporters. At Armentarola there is a drag-lift up to a run back to San Cassiano.

Snowboarding Endless carving on quiet pistes and there's a terrain-park.
Cross-country There's a branch of the DolomitiNordicski in Armentarola. It offers tuition and equipment hire, as well as a couple of trails.
Queues Few problems.
Mountain restaurants There are countless options. Piz Sorega gets very crowded – a reporter suggests going down to the Pic Pre, which is 'badly marked on the map and consequently quiet'. The woody Saraghes is 'friendly and popular' and the Pralongia is 'welcoming and cosy' with 'a wonderful array of pastries and strudels'. And the Punta Trieste has a collection of wooden owls and is recommended for 'excellent spaghetti'. Las Vegas is smart, modern and trendy.
Schools We have no reports.
Facilities for children The school offers the usual arrangements for children and there are several kids' parks.

STAYING THERE
How to go Tour operator Ski 2 started featuring San Cassiano last season and offers a wide range of options.
Hotels The Rosa Alpina (0471 849500) is a splendid place, coupling genuine comfort, great food and a good spa with a relaxed atmosphere. Its three restaurants include the St Hubertus, which received its second Michelin star in 2006. The Fanes (0471 849470) is a smart chalet-style place with indoor-outdoor pool and a spa. You can stay up the mountain at the modern, trendy Las Vegas restaurant (0471 840138).
Eating out As well as the Rosa Alpina's St Hubertus, two restaurants have one Michelin star in the area; one, the Siriola in the hotel Ciasa Salares, is in

Armentarola, just up the road; for the other see Corvara.
Après ski Après-ski starts up the mountain with loud music at Las Vegas. A recent reporter recommends staying late at the Utia on the home run and skiing down after dark ('the highlight of the week'). Nightlife is very limited but there's a bowling alley.
Off the slopes Walking in the pretty scenery is the main off-slope activity; swimming is the other.

LA VILLA 1435m/4,710ft
La Villa is similar to neighbouring San Cassiano in most ways – small, quiet, pretty, unspoiled. But the home pistes (served by a gondola) are challenging – a genuine red and a just-about-genuine black dropping 600m/1,970ft through woods to the village. There's a kids' snow-garden at the top. Across the village, a fast chair serves a blue slope and a link to Pedraces.

PEDRACES 1325m/4,350ft
This small roadside village has a fast quad followed by a slow double chair to Santa Croce (2043m/6,700ft). A recent reporter enjoyed a 'cheap, sunny lunch' at the Lee hut as well as the 'pleasant' run from the top. A free bus from the village now goes to Piccolino (20 mins) where you can take a gondola into the Plan de Corones/ Kronplatz ski area – well worth a day trip (see the South Tyrol chapter).

CANAZEI AND CAMPITELLO
Canazei is a sizeable village at the south-west corner of the Sella Ronda circuit. Campitello next door is smaller and quieter. Both are covered in the chapter on Trentino.

Sella Ronda

469

Selva/Val Gardena

Pleasant village amid spectacular Dolomite scenery, with the vast Sella Ronda lift network on its doorstep

NEWS

For 2007/08 the slow double Sole chair above Plan de Gralba is due to be replaced by a fast quad.

For 2006/07 fast quads replaced the Sotsaslonch drag above Plan de Gralba and the Sochers lift at Ciampinoi.

And at Alpe di Siusi, a six-pack replaced the Paradiso double chair.

More snowmaking has been installed in the Mont Seura area, and the chair-lift there has had its capacity increased.

➕ Part of the Sella Ronda region, with all the plus points we list in that chapter (immediately before this one): vast intermediate area, extensive snowmaking, stunning scenery, good mountain huts, good value for money

➕ Attractive but strung-out village in an impressive wooded setting

➕ Excellent local slopes, with big verticals by Sella Ronda standards

➕ Mix of open and wooded slopes

➕ Excellent nursery slopes, but ...

➖ All the minus points of the Sella Ronda region too: erratic natural snowfall, few challenges for advanced skiers, mostly short runs with limited vertical, crowds on Sella Ronda circuit

➖ Progression to easy long runs involves bus- or taxi- rides

➖ Bus services are frequently criticised by reporters

➖ Busy road through the village

Selva (known to 'Ski Sunday' viewers as Val Gardena – the name of the valley) is one of the main bases to consider for a visit to the unique Sella Ronda region; the Sella Ronda as a whole is now covered in a separate chapter, immediately before this one – so see that chapter too. Selva (and neighbouring Santa Cristina, which is now virtually a suburb of Selva) remains one of our favourite bases in the area, essentially because of the local slopes, including two race-courses through woods to the village that are among the most satisfying runs in the area – not least because they offer decent verticals. Beginners and near-beginners, though, are probably better off elsewhere – in Corvara, Colfosco or San Cassiano. And places such as San Cassiano and Arabba have much more of a small village feel than sprawling Selva.

THE RESORT

Selva is a long roadside village at the head of the Val Gardena, almost merging with the next village of Santa Cristina. It suffers from traffic but has traditional-style architecture and an attractive church. The valley is famed for wood carvings, which are on display (and sale) wherever you look.

The village enjoys a lovely setting under the impressive pink-tinged walls of Sassolungo and the Gruppo Sella – a fortress-like massif about 6km/ 4 miles across that lies at the hub of the Sella Ronda circuit (see separate

chapter). Despite the World Cup fame of Val Gardena, Selva is neither upmarket nor brash. It's a good-value, civilised family resort – relaxed and family-friendly once you get away from the intrusive through-road.

For many years this area was part of Austria, and it retains a Tirolean charm. German is the main language, not Italian, and many visitors are German, too. Most places have two names: Selva is also known as Wolkenstein and the Gardena valley as Gröden. We do our bit to help with Italian unity by using the Italian place names. The local language, Ladin, also survives –

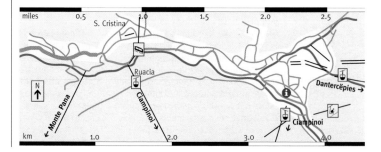

KEY FACTS

Resort	1565m
	5,130ft

The linked lift network of Val Gardena, Alta Badia, Arabba, and the Canazei and Campitello slopes of Val di Fassa

Slopes	1005-2520m
	3,300-8,270ft
Lifts	211
Pistes	460km
	286 miles
Blue	38%
Red	53%
Black	9%
Snowmaking	376km
	234 miles

Val Gardena-Alpe di Siusi only

Slopes	1005-2520m
	3,300-8,270ft
Lifts	84
Pistes	176km
	109 miles
Blue	30%
Red	60%
Black	10%
Snowmaking	150km
	93 miles

giving a third name to some places. Not surprisingly, a visitor found this confusing, 'especially on the buses'.

Ortisei, the administrative centre of Val Gardena, is described at the end of the chapter; it is not so convenient for the Sella Ronda slopes.

From the village, gondolas rise in two directions. The Ciampinoi gondola goes south from near the centre of the village to start the anticlockwise Sella Ronda route. The Dantercëpies gondola, for the clockwise Sella Ronda route, starts above the village at the top of the nursery slopes (but accessible via a central chair-lift and short run down). The most convenient position to stay is near this chair or one of the gondolas. There are local buses until early evening – five euros for a weekly card – but they generate numerous complaints from reporters about infrequency, unreliability, inadequate capacity (especially at the end of the day), poorly sited stops and lack of services to Corvara and Plan de Gralba. There's a night bus between Selva and Ortisei. Many reporters use taxis, although they are expensive unless you share. All the four-star hotels run their own free transport.

The Dolomiti Superski pass covers not only Selva and the Sella Ronda resorts but dozens of others. It's an easy road trip to Cortina – worth it for the fabulous scenery alone.

THE MOUNTAIN

Selva's own slopes cover both sides of the valley, including the quieter Seceda area above Santa Cristina and Ortisei. Practically all are ideally suited to intermediates. Most of the lifts stay open until around 5pm in high season.

The local piste map covers Selva and Alpe di Siusi (accessed from Ortisei); there are several variations, which reporters find confusing. The maps show neither names nor numbers for the runs. Piste marking and signing also provoke complaints.

THE SLOPES
High mileage piste excursions
The **Ciampinoi** gondola accesses several shady pistes, including the famous World Cup Downhill run, leading back down to Selva and Santa Cristina. In the opposite direction, runs go on to **Plan de Gralba** – and so to the rest of the anticlockwise Sella Ronda circuit.

The **Dantercëpies** gondola serves excellent runs back to Selva and accesses the clockwise Sella Ronda circuit via Corvara.

The sunny **Seceda** area is accessed by a gondola on the outskirts of Santa Cristina. This is also accessible by descending from Ciampinoi to ride a very efficient underground train across the valley. Runs descend to Santa

boarding

Selva attracts few boarders. There's little to challenge experts and off-piste opportunities are limited, but the nursery slopes are good and there are lots of gentle runs to progress to. The main lifts out of the village are all gondolas or chairs. There's a terrain-park at Alpe di Siusi and a couple of half-pipes.

Cristina or to Ortisei – a red run of about 7km/4 miles. And from Ortisei a cable-car on the other side of the valley takes you to and from **Alpe di Siusi** – a gentle elevated area of quiet, easy runs, cross-country tracks and walks. This area can also be accessed via the big gondola from the village of Siusi, to the west.

TERRAIN-PARKS
Facilities spread around
There are boarder-cross runs at Passo Sella by the Cavazes Grohmann chair and at Piz Sella by the Comici chair. And there's a half-pipe and natural pipe at Plan de Gralba. Alpe di Siusi has a terrain-park and half-pipe by the Laurin chair, and a kids' park.

Good, long blue runs for beginners to progress to – but you have to catch a bus from Selva to avoid a tricky red from Ciampinoi

Lovely long reds; the one on skier's right of the gondola used to be the Women's Downhill run

Efficient underground train links the gondolas for the Ciampinoi and Seceda sectors

Porta Vescovo 2480m

Arabba 1600m

Corvara 1570m

Sella Ronda

Cir

DANTECĖPIES
2300m

Dantercepies

Passo Pordoi

Gruppo del Sella
Sella Gruppe
3150m

Sella Ronda   Sole

Piz Seteui

PLAN DE GRALBA

Plan de Gralba
1800m

Marmolada
3340m

Canazei
1465m

PASSO SELLA
2245m

Sotsalong   Comici I

Piz Sella

Piz Sella

2255m

CIAMPINOI

Ciampinoi

Selva/Wolkenstein
1565m/5,130ft

Vallunga

Sassolungo/
Langkofel
3180m

Sochers

Saslong

Col Raiser

Col Raiser

SECEDA

SNOW RELIABILITY
Excellent when it's cold

The slopes are not high – there are few above 2200m/7,220ft and most are between 1500m and 2000m (4,920ft and 6,560ft). Natural snowfalls are erratic, but Selva's slopes, like much of the area, are well covered by snowmaking. We have enjoyed excellent pistes here in times of severe natural snow shortage and our reporters are regularly impressed – 'a revelation', 'wonderful', 'stunning', 'unbelievable coverage and quality'. Problems arise only in poor snow years if it is too warm to make snow.

FOR EXPERTS
A few good runs

Experts may find the slopes too tame; there are few challenges, essentially no moguls (the blacks all get groomed) and a low likelihood of powder. There are few major off-piste routes because of the nature of the terrain; see the off-piste panel in the Sella Ronda chapter.

The Val Gardena World Cup piste, the Saslong, is one of several steepish runs between Ciampinoi and both Selva and Santa Cristina. Unlike many World Cup pistes it is kept in racing condition for Italian team practices, but it is open to the public much of the time and makes a wonderful fast cruise

solungo/
ngkofel
180m

Ideal area for early intermediates – very gentle pistes (almost flat in places), quiet and set amid superb scenery

Punta d'Oro/Goldknopf
2210m

ALPE DI SIUSI

Paradiso

1940m

Fiè/
Völs
880m

Mont de Seura
2115m

Alpe di Siusi
Seiser Alm
2000m

Siusi/
Seis
1005m

55m

Sochers

2100m

Castel Rotto/
Kastel Ruth
1060m

Mont Seura

1665m   MONTE PANA

Saslong

Alpe di Siusi

S Cristina/
St Christina
1430m

Beautiful long run with a vertical drop of 1300m/4,270ft; not steep but quite narrow in places; wonderful views over the valley and through a very picturesque canyon

Ortisei/
St Ulrich
1235m/4,050ft

ol Raiser

The Saslong World Cup Downhill piste is a wonderful, fast, rolling cruise that's especially good in January when it's not too crowded

2280m

Furnes

SECEDA

Seceda
2520m

– it's one of our favourite runs and especially good in January, when it's not too crowded.

FOR INTERMEDIATES
Fast cruising on easy slopes

There are huge amounts of skiing to do, in several areas.

Competent intermediates will love the red and black descents from Dantercëpies and Ciampinoi to Selva.

The blue runs in the Plan de Gralba area are gentle; the red run to get there from Ciampinoi is a real obstacle – steep and crowded – but reporters find it worth the struggle. The high-altitude route back used to involve a tricky black run, but they claim to have made it wider and therefore easier (reports welcome). The quiet runs at Mont de Seura, above Monte Pana, are worth exploring.

The Alpe di Siusi above Ortisei is ideal for confidence-building – very gentle (almost flat in places), quiet, amid superb scenery with no crowds. Runs are mostly short, the main exception being the red down to Saltria from Punta d'Oro, offering 500m/1,640ft vertical.

The Seceda sector has good red and blue runs at altitude, and splendid runs to the valley – an easy blue/red back to Santa Cristina and the beautiful red Cucasattel, passing through a tight natural canyon to Ortisei.

FOR BEGINNERS
Great slopes, but ...

The village nursery slopes below the Dantercëpies gondola are excellent – spacious, convenient, and kept in good condition. There are lots of gentle, long runs to progress to, but Selva isn't the ideal base to access them. Plan de Gralba has easy blues, but you need to take a taxi to get there. Near-beginners would be better placed taking the bus to Ortisei and the cable-car to Alpe di Siusi.

FOR CROSS-COUNTRY
Beautiful trails

There are 98km/61 miles of trails, all enjoying wonderful scenery. The 12km/7 mile trail up the Vallunga-Langental valley is particularly attractive, with neck-craning views all around. Almost half the trails have the advantage of being at altitude, running between Monte Pana and across Alpe di Siusi.

SNOWPIX.COM / CHRIS GILL

You'll find cosy little huts with sun terraces like this are liberally sprinkled throughout the area ⬎

SCHOOLS

Factory Selva Gardena
t 0471 795156

2000
t 0471 773125

Classes
(Factory prices)
6 days €165
Private lessons
€35 for 1hr

GUIDES

Mountain Guides Val Gardena
t 0471 794133

CHILDREN

Casa Bimbo
(at S Cristina)
0471 793013
From 4mnth to 7yr

Ski school
For age 4 to 12:
6 days (10am to 4pm)
€285, lunch included
(Factory school price)

GETTING THERE

Air Verona 190km/
118 miles (3hr);
Bolzano 40km/
25 miles (45min);
Treviso 130km/
81 miles (2½hr)

Rail Chiusa (27km/
17 miles); Bressanone
(35km/22 miles);
Bolzano (40km/
25 miles); frequent
buses from station

UK PACKAGES

Selva Alpine Answers,
Chalet World Ski,
Crystal, Crystal Finest,
Esprit, First Choice,
Independent Ski Links,
Inghams, Interactive
Resorts, Italian Safaris,
Kuoni, Momentum,
Neilson, Ski Yogi,
Skitracer, Snow
Finders, Thomson,
Total
Ortisei Inghams,
Interhome, Italian
Safaris, Neilson

QUEUES
Now few problems
New lifts have vastly improved the area, and there are now fewer bottlenecks, especially away from the main Sella Ronda circuit. However, the Dantercëpies gondola still generates complaints from reporters ('an absolute scrum till after 10') as does the Ciampinoi gondola. The Sole chair to Piz Seteur above Plan de Gralba was queue-prone, but the queues should disappear when the old double is replaced by a fast quad for 2007/08 (see 'News').

MOUNTAIN RESTAURANTS
One of the area's highlights
There are lots of huts all over the area, and virtually all of them are lively, with helpful staff, good food, lots of character and modest prices. Reporters love them ('not a bad one all week' is a typical comment).

The Panorama is a small, cosy, rustic suntrap at the foot of the drag near the top of Dantercëpies. The 'attractive' restaurant at the bottom of the Val double chair is worth a visit, according to a recent reporter. On the way down to Plan de Gralba from Ciampinoi, the Vallongia is tucked away on a corner of the piste. In the Plan de Gralba area the top station of the cable-car does excellent pizza; the Comici is atmospheric, with a big terrace. Piz Seteur has 'superb lasagne' and is also recommended late in the day (see 'Après-ski').

In the Seceda sector there are countless options. The cosy Sangon has 'bags of atmosphere', though another reporter pronounces Baita Gamsblut her favourite: 'Super rustic hut with a good menu and a warm, friendly atmosphere.' The Seceda does 'wonderful food' although the waitresses in miniskirts or leather shorts seem to have disappeared, much to one visitor's disappointment. Other recent reporters recommend Daniel's Hütte, Curona and Sofie.

On Alpe di Siusi the rustic Sanon refuge gets a good review, particularly since 'the barman came out to serenade us with his accordion'. The Ritsch Schwaige is praised for its gulaschsuppe, apple strudel, cakes and service. The table-service restaurant at the bottom of the Monte Piz lift is also highly rated – 'good value', 'huge portions'. The Williams Hütte at the top of the Florian chair has 'superb views'.

SCHOOLS AND GUIDES
Positive reports
The Ski and Boarders Factory, run by 90s racing star Peter Runggaldier, gets favourable reports from readers ('Good tuition, excellent English,' says a recent reporter). Another praised the 'very beneficial' advanced level groups at the 2000 school. Private lessons with the Ski and Boarders Factory are said to be good value – but booking ahead is advised as it gets busy.

FACILITIES FOR CHILDREN
Good by Italian standards
There are comprehensive childcare arrangements, but German and Italian are the main languages here and English is not routinely spoken. That said, in the past we have had reports of very enjoyable lessons and of children longing to return. Casa Bimbo at Santa Cristina provides day care for toddlers. Family specialist tour operator Esprit has its own childcare facilities here.

STAYING THERE

HOW TO GO
A reasonable choice
Selva features in most major tour op brochures. Inghams, Neilson and Crystal Finest all have some of the best hotels here.

Chalets There is a fair choice of catered chalets, including some good ones with en suite bathrooms. Family specialist Esprit has chalets here, as do Total and Crystal.

Hotels There are 13 4-stars in Selva, almost 40 3-stars and numerous lesser hotels. Few of the best are well positioned.

****Gran Baita** (0471 795210) Large, luxurious sporthotel, with lots of mod cons including indoor pool. A few minutes' walk from centre and lifts. Highly recommended in 2006 ('they couldn't do enough for us').

****Granvara** (0471 795250) 'Just out of town but free hotel bus, great food and views and a spa. Recommended.'

****Aaritz** (0471 795011) Best-placed 4-star, opposite the Ciampinoi gondola, and with an open fire.

****Tyrol** (0471 774100) 'Friendly and fantastic value, handy for nursery slopes but bit of a way to Sella Ronda.'

****Oswald** (0471 771111) Near a ski bus stop and with its own free bus. 'Good rooms and fantastic food.'

***Rodella** (0471 794553) Just outside

Selva but friendly pensione, with free taxi, spa and delicious meals.'
***Linder (0471 795242) 'Friendly, family-run with good food.'
***Pralong (0471 795370) An uphill walk from the centre, but 'one of the best hotels we've visited', says a 2007 reporter.
***Solaia (0471 795104) 3-star chalet, superbly positioned for lifts and slopes.
***Wolkenstein (0471 772200) In S Cristina. Two reporters this year sing its praises – 'traditional, comfortable and friendly', 'excellent food and service'.
Villa Seceda (0471 795297) A 'friendly' B&B near the nursery slopes.
Apartments We have had excellent reports of the Villa Gardena and Isabell apartments.

EATING OUT
Plenty of good-value choices
The higher-quality restaurants are mainly hotel-based – reporters highly recommend Armin's Grill in the hotel of the same name, and the Sal Fëur in the Broi B&B. The Sun Valley Stübele does 'excellent pasta and pizza', says a 2006 visitor, as does Rino's. Another reader enjoyed 'wonderful goulash and dumplings' at Des Alpes. The Bellavista is also good for pasta, and Costabella is 'highly recommended' for Tirolean specialities.

APRES-SKI
Above average for a family resort
Nightlife is reasonably lively and informal, though the village is so scattered there is little on-street atmosphere.

La Stua is an après-ski bar on the Sella Ronda route, with live music on some nights. For an early drink we are told that the Piz Seteur bar, above Plan de Gralba, is worth a little detour from the route – 'fun, loud and a bit raunchy' (you may find scantily clad girls dancing on the bar).

For a civilised early drink try the good-value ski-school bar at the base of the Dantercëpies piste. Or the Costabella – cosy, serving good glühwein. Café Mozart on the main street is 'a great place for cakes'.

For thigh-slapping in Selva later on, the Laurinkeller has good atmosphere though it's 'quite expensive', while the popular Luislkeller is 'very German', 'lively' and 'packed', with loud music and barmaids in Tirolean garb. A 2006 reporter also enjoyed the Goalie's Irish bar with its hockey memorabilia – 'The

music was particularly suited to 30 or 40 somethings.' The bar by the Ski Factory is said to be a 'jolly place' – and noted for its flaming cocktails.

The place to go after midnight is Dali, where a mixed British and Italian crowd dances till the small hours.

OFF THE SLOPES
Good variety
There's a sports centre, snow-shoeing, lovely walks (buy a map at the tourist office for 2.50 euros) tobogganing and sleigh rides on Alpe di Siusi. One reporter enjoyed an organised bowling night ('great fun'). There is a bus to Ortisei, which is well worth a visit for its museum, large hot-spring swimming pool, shops, restaurants and lovely old buildings.

Pedestrians can reach numerous good restaurants by gondola or cable-car. There are buses to Bolzano, tour operators do trips to Cortina and Innsbruck is within reach by car.

Ortisei 1235m/4,050ft

Ortisei is an attractive, prosperous market town with a life of its own apart from tourism. It's full of lovely buildings, pretty churches and pleasant shops. The local slopes aren't on the main Sella Ronda circuit. The lift to the Seceda slopes is easily reached from the centre by a 300m/980ft-long series of underground moving walkways and escalators. The Alpe di Siusi lifts are a similar distance out and the cable-car is now accessed via a long pedestrian footbridge, an improvement over the previous steep, icy, uphill walk. The nursery area, school and kindergarten are at the foot of these slopes, and there's a fair range of family accommodation on the piste side of the road. The fine public indoor pool and ice rink are also here.

There are hotels and self-catering to suit all tastes and pockets and many good restaurants, mainly specialising in local dishes. A reporter recommends the 4-star Hotel Alpenheim (0471 796515): 'luxurious rooms', 'excellent food' but not central. Another says the 4-star Adler (0471 775000), which has a very impressive spa, is 'an excellent hotel'. Après-ski is quite jolly, and many bars keep going till late.

Sestriere

Altitude is the main attraction of this, Europe's first purpose-built resort; some would say it's the only attraction

➕ Local slopes suitable for most levels, with some tougher runs than in most neighbouring resorts

➕ Part of the extensive Milky Way area, now with improved links to Sansicario and Pragelato.

➕ Snowmaking covers all but one or two marginal slopes, but ...

➖ It needs to, given the very erratic local snowfall record

➖ The village is an eyesore, though smartened up for the 2006 Olympics

➖ For a purpose-built resort, not conveniently arranged

➖ Weekend and peak-period queues

➖ Little après-ski during the week

Sestriere was built for snow – high, with north-west-facing slopes – and it has very extensive snowmaking, too. So even if you are let down by the notoriously erratic snowfalls in this corner of Italy, you should be fairly safe here – certainly safer than in Sauze d'Oulx, over the hill. Whether this is a sensible basis for choosing to stay here is another question. When we go to Italy, we generally aim to go somewhere a bit more captivating.

THE RESORT

Sestriere was the Alps' first purpose-built resort, developed by Fiat's Giovanni Agnelli in the 1930s, though it was recently taken over by a local business consortium. It sits on a broad, sunny and windy col, and neither the site nor the village, with its large apartment blocks, looks very hospitable – though the buildings have benefited from recent investment for the 2006 Winter Olympics. This is not the most convenient of purpose-built resorts, either – some of the walks are non-trivial. The satellite of Borgata, 200m/660ft lower, is less convenient for nightlife and shops. The valley town of Pragelato is a viable alternative base now that it has a cable-car link up to Borgata.

THE MOUNTAINS

The local skiing is on shady slopes, mainly open with some woodland, facing the village. Sestriere is at one extreme of the big Franco-Italian Milky Way area.

Slopes The local slopes, served by drags and chairs, are in two main sectors: Sises, directly in front of the village, and Motta, above Borgata; Motta is more varied and bigger, with almost twice the vertical. Across the valley, gondolas go up from Borgata for Sauze d'Oulx and from a car park west of the village for Sansicario and the rest of the Milky Way. For the

return to Sestriere there are red runs down both gondolas, but they are sunny and rarely open. Signposting and the piste map are poor. There's night skiing twice a week.

Terrain-parks Sestriere now has its own park – in the Alpette area.

Snow reliability With most of the local slopes facing north-west and ranging from 1840m to 2825m (6,040ft to 9,270ft), and an 'impressive' snowmaking network, snow-cover is usually reliable, except on the runs down the gondolas mentioned above. The notoriously erratic snowfalls in the Milky Way often leave the rest of the area seriously short of snow.

Experts There is a fair amount to amuse experts – steep pistes served by the drags at the top of both sectors. There is a fair amount of off-piste, given snow. Don't count on it – or on moguls, which are erased religiously.

Intermediates Both sectors also offer plenty for confident intermediates, who can explore practically all of the Milky Way areas, conditions permitting. The runs in the Motta sector offer more of a challenge.

Beginners The terrain is good for beginners, with several nursery areas and the gentlest of easy blue runs down to Borgata. But there is a lack of easy intermediate runs to progress to.

Snowboarding Sestriere has a reasonable number of chairs, but there are also lots of drag-lifts.

Cross-country There are three loops covering a total of 10km/6 miles.

KEY FACTS

Resort	2000m
	6,560ft
Milky Way	
Slopes	1390-2825m
	4,560-9,270ft
Lifts	78
Pistes	400km
	249 miles
Blue	24%
Red	56%
Black	20%
Snowmaking	130km
	81 miles

Sestriere-Sauze d'Oulx-Sansicario	
Slopes	1390-2825m
	4,560-9,270ft
Lifts	43
Pistes	300km
	186 miles
Snowmaking	95km
	59 miles

UK PACKAGES

Alpine Answers, Club
Med, Club Pavilion,
Crystal, Equity, First
Choice, Independent
Ski Links, Inghams,
Interhome, Just Skiing,
Kuoni, Momentum,
Neilson, Rocketski, Ski
Weekend, Ski4you,
Skitracer, Thomson

PISTE MAP

Sestriere is covered
on the Sauze d'Oulx
map a few pages
back

Phone numbers
From abroad use the
prefix +39 (and do
not omit the initial '0'
of the phone number)

TOURIST OFFICE

t 0122 755444
sestriere@
montagnedoc.it
www.montagnedoc.it
www.sestriere.it
www.vialattea.it

Queues The lifts are mainly modern,
though there are still some inadequate,
'painfully slow', old ones. Queues for
the main lifts occur at the weekends
and holidays; one reporter experienced
a half-hour wait for the Cit Roc chair
up M Sises. Queues occur when poor
weather closes the gondola link to
Sauze, but the gondola to M Fraiteve –
built a couple of seasons ago – has
improved the connection with
Sansicario and the Via Lattea.
Reporters here, as in Sauze, complain
that some lifts may be kept closed
during the week, to conserve either
money or snow – with the result that
crowded pistes can also become a
problem.

Mountain restaurants The Raggio di
Sole in the Anfiteatro sector is a 'cosy
log cabin'. Reporters also recommend
the Tana della Volpe at the top of the
Banchetta chair, the Alpette ('good
portions, spectacular view') and the
busy Gargote at Garnel ('excellent hot
chocolates'). The Teit pizzeria at
Borgata has 'good choices at
reasonable prices', and the Capret is
also worth a try. But on the whole the
local restaurants are only fair. There
are better ones further afield.

Schools and guides Lack of spoken
English can be a problem, but a 2007
visitor comments that his instructor
spoke 'great' English as well as being
'brilliant and very friendly'. Another
reporter says her class included such a
mixture of abilities that it was 'totally
untesting' for her and 'far too difficult'
for her friend.

Facilities for children There are no
special facilities for children.

STAYING THERE

How to go Most accommodation is in
apartments. The complex of
apartments built for the 2006 Winter
Olympics are now an option too.

Hotels There are a dozen hotels,
mostly 3-star or 4-star. You might want
to stay near one of the gondolas. The
Shackleton Mountain Resort (0122
750773) is quite new. The Savoy
Edelweiss (0122 77040) ('charming,
excellent staff') and the Du Col (0122
76990) are central; and just out of the
village is the luxurious Principi di
Piemonte (0122 7941). Grangesises
offers an alternative base – it's 2km/1
mile from Sestriere and linked by bus.

Eating out There are plenty of options.
Try Lu Periol for home-made ravioli
and atmosphere. Tre Rubinetti is highly
recommended for 'outstanding
cooking' and an enormous wine list.
The Antica Spelonca is 'cosy with an
interesting menu'. Last Tango and the
Baita are well regarded.

Après-ski Après-ski is quiet during the
week, but the Prestige and Palace Due
are two of the many little bars that
liven up at weekends when Turin
decamps. The Pinky is one of the best
of the bars that double as eateries,
with low sofas in the classic Italian
casual-chic style, an antipasto buffet
and 'great choices of pizzas'.

Off the slopes There are some smart
shops and there's a fitness centre, an
ice rink, a sports centre and pool.
Thanks to the cable-car link from
Borgata – built a couple of years ago –
it is possible to visit the town of
Pragelato.

South Tyrol

Val Gardena is well known in the UK, thanks to 'Ski Sunday'. But this scenic region has scores of other worthwhile resorts, too

Like Trentino immediately to the south, Alto Adige/Südtirol (to use the proper name) is a region blessed with stunning Dolomite scenery and dotted with ski resorts, many of which are rather neglected by the British. Because of annual World Cup races, the large resorts best known in the UK are those of Val Gardena – notably Selva/Wolkenstein, which is on the amazing Sella Ronda lift circuit. Both Selva and the Sella Ronda are covered in their own chapters. The smaller resorts in the region run into scores. The following guide to the resorts of South Tyrol is not comprehensive; but it includes all the places that are likely to be of international interest, and more.

This is an area where place names can be very confusing. It used to be part of the Austrian Tirol, is mainly German-speaking, and draws huge numbers of German-speaking visitors. Most places have two names, and not surprisingly the German versions tend to be more widely used than the Italian. We use the name that seems most common locally, sometimes giving both when first mentioning a place.

There are two major groupings of resorts for ski pass purposes. The famously extensive Superski Dolomiti pass covers the south-east of the province, around the Sella Ronda and the Val Pusteria/Pustertal, and of course its coverage extends south into Trentino and east to include Cortina. The Ortler Skiarena covers 15 resorts in the west – Val Venosta etc. Given the small size of many resorts, it's likely that the resorts covered by these two passes will be of most interest, and we've focused on these.

SELLA RONDA RESORTS

Although the Sella Ronda gets its own chapter, it can't go without a mention here. It is a fabulously scenic area with vast amounts of easy intermediate skiing spread around the towering Gruppo Sella, spreading into Trentino. Some of its most attractive resorts fall in this region – not only Selva and its close neighbours Santa Cristina and Ortisei, but also Colfosco, Corvara, San Cassiano and La Villa.

PUSTERTAL

One of the most interesting areas is in the north-east corner of the region, the Pustertal, which leads off eastwards towards the Slovenian border from the Brenner motorway. The main town is Brunico/Bruneck, which now has lift access to one of the most compelling hills in the region, Plan de Corones/Kronplatz.

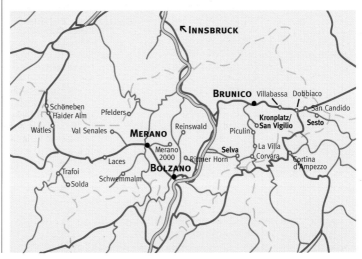

South Tyrol ...

sun-soaked

South Tyrol Information • Pfarrplatz 11 • 39100 Bozen|Bolzano • Italy
phone: +39 0471 999 999
info@suedtirol.info

Italian Alps

www.suedtirol.info

südtirol
The magic of diversity

KRONPLATZ

Kronplatz is an extraordinary dome-shaped mountain with open slopes around its bare summit, easy at the very top, tougher as you start going down – and an amazing lift system. Apparently as a result of a bizarre tax break, an astonishing 20 lifts out of 32 are gondolas, and six are fast chairs. The slopes have 100 per cent snowmaking, and it is used very well.

As well as Bruneck, several villages offer access to Kronplatz. Our favourite is San Vigilio di Marebbe, with a gondola from the village. It's a pretty village with some good 3- and 4-star hotels and a couple of lively bars.

On our 2006 visit we enjoyed two long black runs down towards Bruneck (1300m/4,270ft vertical) which were fabulously groomed in the morning.

The area best suits early-to-average intermediates willing to take on challenges – though a keen piste-basher will ski all the runs in a day or two. The red runs are serious, and many blues are quite tough. There's an easy blue under the first stage of the gondola from San Vigilio.

San Vigilio also has another area of slopes linked by a cross-village gondola to the Kronplatz and now also linked to Piccolino/Piculin in the next valley by a new black run and gondola. From there a free ski-bus runs to Pedraces, a lift base near La Villa, for access to the Sella Ronda slopes.

Just to the east of Bruneck is the area known as the **Alta Val Pusteria/Hochpustertal**. There are three small towns dotted along the valley. Westernmost is Villabassa/Niederdorf, chiefly of interest to cross-country skiers. At the watershed of the gently sloping valley, where it starts to descend towards Slovenia, is Dobbiaco/Toblach, with some short slopes on its fringes and very scenic cross-country trails. And further east is San Candido/Innichen, with a long chair-lift serving intermediate slopes.

Up an elevated side valley from here (again with scenic cross-country trails) is the main resort of this area, the village of **Sesto/Sexten** (1310m/4,300ft). This has nursery slopes all around it, and two major lifts up to higher slopes above the tree line served by chair-lifts. From Gallo Cedrone/Hahnspiel, long black and red runs of 1100m/3,610ft vertical go to the base of a gondola up from the valley.

UK PACKAGES

Kronplatz Momentum, Neilson
San Vigilio di Marebbe Italian Safaris
Dobbiaco Headwater, Ramblers, Waymark

AROUND MERANO/MERAN

Merano is an attractive town with its own modest ski resort a short drive east – **Merano 2000**. 16km/10 miles west of Merano is the valley called **Val Senales/Schnalstal**, and at the head of it an interesting resort that goes by the same names. From Maso Corto/Kurzras a cable-car rises 1200m/3,940ft to gentle glacier slopes on the Austrian border – and a 100-bed hotel, which at 3212m/10,540ft is said to be Europe's highest. (Be warned that sleeping at such altitudes may well induce altitude sickness.) There's an 8km/5 mile run to the bottom (black below the glacier) and black runs of 600m/1,970ft vertical in the lower Teufelsegg sector.

Other Ortler Skiarena resorts in this area are: Pfelders, Reinwald, Rittnerhorn and Schwemmalm.

VAL VENOSTA

If you drive west and then north from Merano you come to a clutch of resorts by the Austrian border. **Schöneben** is the name of a mountainside above Resia/Reschen and of the company operating lifts on it. A gondola goes up to a mid-mountain lift hub, just above the tree line. There are wide, gentle slopes above and below this point, served by a six-pack chair, a couple of more challenging runs served by two chairs beyond it (one newly upgraded), and an easy, undulating, highly enjoyable red run back to the valley, recently widened and improved.

A second area just down the valley is named in the same fashion: **Haider Alm** is the tree-line focus of the lifts above the village of St Valentin. It is a limited area – but any mountain with runs of 1200m/3,940ft vertical has to be worth a visit.

Tucked away in a side-valley to the south of the Val Venosta is **Solda/Sulden**, an established mountain resort in the Stelvio national park, with plenty of hotels. It has lifts radiating in three directions. A two-stage cable-car with 110-person cabins goes up to 2610m/8,565ft in the major sector, with quad chairs serving the open slopes above that reaching 3250m/10,665ft. There's an impressive 11km/7 mile red/black run from the top to the base at 1900m/6,235ft.

Other Ortler Skiarena resorts in this area are: Trafoi, Watles and Laces.

La Thuile

An unusual combination of a revitalised mining town and a modern lift-base complex; extensive, easy slopes and a link with France

COSTS

① ② ③ ④ ⑤ ⑥

RATINGS

The slopes
Fast lifts	**
Snow	****
Extent	***
Expert	**
Intermediate	****
Beginner	****
Convenience	***
Queues	****
Mountain restaurants	*

The rest
Scenery	***
Resort charm	***
Off-slope	**

NEWS

For 2006/07 a mid-station was introduced to the Chaz Dura Express chair, making it easier for beginners to access the lower blue runs and for the more experienced to repeat the top red runs. Snowmaking was also increased, with the help of a new mid-mountain reservoir.

This is the main village. The slopes are a walk or bus-ride away, across a river; there's accommodation there too →

+ Fair-sized area linked to La Rosière in France

+ Free of crowds and queues

+ Excellent beginner and easy intermediate slopes

− Most of the seriously tough pistes are low down, and most of the low, woodland runs are tough

− Winds can close lift links with France

− Not the place for lively après-ski

La Thuile deserves to be better known internationally. The slopes best suit beginners and intermediates looking for smooth cruises, but are not devoid of interest for experts, particularly if the snow conditions are good – and expeditions to La Rosière add interest. Those who try it seem to appreciate the quiet village as much as the quiet slopes.

THE RESORT

La Thuile is a resort of parts. At the foot of the lifts is the modern Planibel complex, with places to stay, a leisure centre, bars, shops and restaurants – like a French purpose-built resort, but with a distinctly Italian atmosphere. But many people find this rather soulless and prefer to stay in the old village across the river (served by a regular free bus service). Much of the old village has been restored and new buildings (and an underground car park) tastefully added. There are reasonable restaurants and bars.

The slopes link with La Rosière, over the border in France. Courmayeur is easily reached by car, and Cervinia is about an hour away.

THE MOUNTAINS

La Thuile has quite extensive slopes, with the great attraction that they are normally very uncrowded. Many runs are marked red, but deserve no more than a blue rating. The link with La Rosière adds adventure; the runs there are steeper, sunnier and bumpier – and the start of the route back is a fairly tricky red. Many reporters have found that strong winds can close the high lifts, including the link.

Slopes The lifts out of the village (a gondola and a fast chair) take you to Les Suches, with shady black runs going back down directly to the village through the trees, and reds taking a more roundabout route. From here chairs take you to Chaz Dura for access to a variety of gentle bowls facing east. You can go off westwards from here to the Petit St Bernard road or

across to a quad up to Belvedere, the launch pad for excursions to La Rosière. Below Belvedere are the slopes of Gran Testa, served by a fast and a slow chair and a drag.

Terrain-parks None in La Thuile.

Snow reliability Most of La Thuile's slopes are north- or east-facing and above 2000m/6,560ft, so the snow generally keeps well. There's also a decent amount of snowmaking, and 'grooming is immaculate'.

Experts The steep pistes down through the trees from Les Suches – the Diretta, Berthod and Muret – are serious stuff. The Fourclaz area has some genuinely black terrain and plenty of off-piste – the fast quad means you can do quick circuits in this area. A 2006 reporter was still making fresh tracks there three days after snowfall. The short black Maisonettes, by the Arnouvaz chair, is usually quiet.

KEY FACTS

Resort	1440m
	4,720ft

Espace San Bernardo
(La Rosière and La
Thuile)

Slopes	1175-2610m
	3,850-8,560ft
Lifts	37
Pistes	150km
	93 miles
Green	9%
Blue	36%
Red	40%
Black	15%
Snowmaking	
	306 guns

UK PACKAGES

Alpine Answers,
Crystal, First Choice,
Independent Ski Links,
Inghams, Interski, Just
Skiing, Neilson,
Skitracer, Thomson

Phone numbers
From abroad use the
prefix +39 (and do
not omit the initial '0'
of the phone number)

TOURIST OFFICE

t 0165 883049
info@lathuile.it
www.lathuile.it

Heli-lifts are available. The Ruitor glacier offers a 20km/12 mile run to Ste-Foy, a short taxi-ride from La Rosière and the lifts back to La Thuile.

Intermediates La Thuile has some good intermediate runs. The bowls above Les Suches have many gentle blue and red runs, ideal for cruising. There are also long reds through the trees back to the resort. A 2007 reporter enjoyed runs around the Argillien Express for 'fast turns and empty pistes'. The red runs on the other side of the top ridge, in the Fourclaz area, down towards the Petit St Bernard road, offer more challenge. The road forms the roundabout San Bernardo red to the village, taking 11km/7 miles to drop 1100m/3,610ft; 'bleak' is one view, 'boring' probably nearer the mark; avoid at all costs in fresh snow.

Beginners There are nursery slopes at village level and up at Les Suches, and long easy blues above there, including Promenade which is served by drag-lifts. You ride the gondola back down.

Snowboarding These are great slopes for learning. You need ride only chair-lifts and the gondola, and most of the slopes are easy. For the more experienced there are great tree runs, good free-riding, and some good carving runs. But there are some frustratingly flat sections too.

Cross-country La Thuile has four loops of varying difficulty on the valley floor, adding up to 17km/11 miles of track.

Queues Short queues may form at the gondola first thing, but not at the chair. Once up the hill, no problems.

Mountain restaurants New for 2006/07 was Maison Carrel on run 6 near the bottom of the Argillien Express chair, a good-value table-service place with floor to ceiling windows and 'excellent food'. The Clotze, at the foot of the Chalets chair-lift, does 'tasty table-service food at reasonable prices'. The Off Shore, above Arnouvaz, offers an 'excellent atmosphere'. The self-service Mélèze, near the top of the gondola, serves 'generous portions'. A couple of places provide an incentive to tackle the long San Bernardo home run: the Neige, is 'absolutely fabulous,' says a recent reporter – the 4-course menu is 'worth every penny'; and the Riondet serves 'good food at astonishing speed'.

Schools and guides A reporter's parents received 'patient and effective tuition' and made excellent progress. Another reader had small classes early in the season ('really good').

Facilities for children There's an 'excellent' nursery, a Miniclub and snow garden. Children over the age of five can join adult ski classes. A 2007 reporter with two small children complained that restaurants didn't serve food before 7pm.

STAYING THERE

How to go The number of tour operators going there is increasing.

Hotels The 4-star Planibel (0165 884541) is large and characterless, but recommended by a few reporters for its 'ideal location' right at the foot of the slopes and 'clean and spacious' accommodation. It has a pool, gym, sauna and steam room too. There are also a few 3-stars and some simpler places. Reporters like the 'quiet, friendly, family-run' hotel du Glacier (0165 884137), a short walk above the lifts, and Chalet Eden (0165 885050), near the gondola ('excellent value').

Apartments The Planibel apartments (in the same building as the hotel above) are spacious, by the lifts and good value.

Eating out Reader recommendations include Bricole ('excellent house pasta'), Lune for good value steaks and salads, and Rascard ('tremendous jumbo prawns'). Early on, head for Chocolat – a cafe 'not to be missed'.

Après-ski Nightlife is 'even quieter' than one reporter expected. The Bricolette bar and the neighbouring Bricole 'videodiscopub' are the liveliest bars. The Fantasia disco at the Planibel warms up well after midnight.

Off the slopes There are few shops, but the Planibel complex has a pool and there are marked walks. Pedestrians can ride up the gondola for lunch.

BELVEDERE
2610m/8,560ft

Col de
Fourclaz

Chaz Dura
2580m

COL DE LA
TRAVERSETTE
2385m
La Rosière

Arnouvaz

Les
Suches
2200m

La Thuile
1440m/4,720ft

Trentino

Not a resort, but a region with a few big resorts and a lot of smaller ones that deserve to be better known on the UK market

Trentino is a fabulously scenic region that is rather neglected by the British. It has a few large resorts, two of which (Madonna di Campiglio and Passo Tonale) are covered in their own chapters – resorts linked to the Sella Ronda (such as Canazei and Campitello, covered below) – and a lot of small ski areas that you may not have heard of. The following guide is not comprehensive; but it includes all the places that are likely to be of international interest, and more.

WESTERN TRENTINO

Madonna di Campiglio is Trentino's biggest and best-known resort – a chic place with mainly easy slopes that attracts an affluent, almost exclusively Italian clientele. It has its own chapter. Its ski area is linked to those of the much smaller resorts of Marilleva and Folgarida.

The slopes above **Marilleva** are excellent, steep, north-facing reds (with a few blues higher up the mountain), much better for adventurous intermediates than Campiglio's main Pradalago slopes. And the snow is usually the best in the area because of the largely north-facing orientation. There's also a serious black run served by a two-stage chair from the resort to Doss della Pesa (2230m/7,320ft). And there's a gondola that links to a six-

pack to Monte Vigo (2180m/7,150ft) and the links to Campiglio and Folgarida.

Marilleva itself is a modern resort consisting of several 1960s-style, ugly but functional, low-rise concrete buildings (most of them thankfully well screened by trees) built on a mid-mountain shelf at 1400m/4,590ft and reached by road or gondola from the lower part of the resort at 900m/2,950ft, on the valley floor.

The slopes down to **Folgarida** are gentler than those above Marilleva but in general somewhat more challenging than Campiglio's main slopes.

The main part of Folgarida itself is clustered around the gondola station at 1400m/4,590ft – and purpose-built in a much more traditional style than Marilleva. It feels much more upmarket, with smart hotels, a few shops and fur-

485

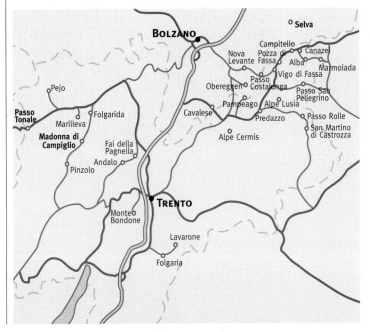

Trentino
Tread into Temptation

Promise to enjoy yourself and we promise to entice you. Sun, snow, fast pistes, slow food - stray no further for your winter thrills. The Dolomites promise you the passion of Italy on seductive slopes. Trentino - for those who can resist everything except temptation. **www.trentino.to**

Trentino Marketing - ph: S. Angelani

clad patrons. There's another area of the resort at 1300m/4,270ft by another gondola station.

The lift companies continue to discuss a development that will link the Cinque Laghi slopes of Madonna di Campiglio with those above **Pinzolo** (780m/2,560ft), currently a 20-minute drive to the south. A gondola followed by a fast chair take you to the area's high point of Doss del Sabion (2100m/6,890ft), where there are great views of the Brenta massif. The area has mainly genuinely challenging red runs, an excellent groomed black (the Competition piste) and the snow keeps in condition because most of the runs are northish facing. The Cioca and Patagonia reds are lovely steep cruises (though Cioca is steep enough to be a black in parts). Usefully, the average and maximum gradients of these and other runs are marked at the top of each (something we haven't seen elsewhere). The first two chair-lifts that are to be part of the link to Campiglio were in place when we visited in 2006 but there is no definite date for the completion of the link. When it is complete, Madonna di Campiglio, with its outlying links to Pinzolo, Marilleva and Folgarida, will be a much more attractive place for good intermediates to visit.

Pinzolo itself is not a conventional ski resort but the main town of the Val Rendena.

Passo Tonale is a short drive west of Marilleva and Folgarida – a good-value, high, snow-sure resort set on the border of Lombardia and linked to Pontedilegno over that border. Passo Tonale has its own chapter.

Just down the Val di Sole (which means Valley of Sun) is **Pejo** (1400m/4,590ft), a spa village with a narrow but tall slope area rising to 2340m/7,680ft, served by a gondola, three chair-lifts and a couple of drags.

All these areas (and the resorts described in the 'Around Trento' section below) are covered by the Superskirama Adamello-Brenta ski pass. If you have a car, it is perfectly possible to explore all these areas in a week. And a 2007 reporter recommends staying in 'a little-known gem' of a place called **Fucine**, which is not a ski resort in itself but sits in the centre of all of these resorts. He recommends the hotel Pangrazzi for its 'fantastic food' and relaxing leisure club.

AROUND TRENTO

Trento is the main town of Trentino, and its local hill – only a few minutes' drive away – is **Monte Bondone**. For a local hill it is excellent: five roadside chair-lifts serve partly wooded slopes here on Palon (2090m/6,860ft), with a longest run of 4km/2.5 miles dropping 800m/2,620ft and served by a fast quad chair. The whole of the small area is covered by snowmaking. There's a terrain-park. And great views to the Brenta Dolomites around Madonna.

To the south-east of Trento, and closer to the town of Rovereto, are the small resorts of **Folgaria** (1165m/3,820ft – not to be confused with Folgarida near Madonna) and **Lavarone**. Lavarone has a handful of lifts, but Folgaria has more than 20, serving 60km/37 miles of runs with 100 per cent snowmaking.

To the north-west are the slopes on Paganella (2125m/6,970ft) shared by **Fai della Paganella** (1000m/3,280ft) and **Andalo** (1050m/3,440ft). Andalo is a sizeable resort and pleasant enough place with a small local town feel; a couple of UK tour ops feature it. We visited for half a day in 2006 and enjoyed the small ski area very much. One new eight-seater gondola goes up from near the centre of Andalo and another leaves from a big car park nearby. Five of the other 16 lifts are fast chairs (one of these was new for 2006/07). The runs are mainly genuinely challenging reds and can be long (a maximum vertical of almost 1100m/3,610ft); most are northish-facing and so keep their snow in good condition. We especially enjoyed the Dosa Larici and La Rocca reds down to Santel (the nearest lift base to Fai). There's a beginner area near the Andalo base but only a few short blue runs (all at the top) so we don't recommend it for novices or timid intermediates.

SELLA RONDA RESORTS

Canazei and Campitello in the **Val di Fassa** are in Trentino and the slopes above them are part of the famous Sella Ronda circuit; the Marmolada glacier is also in Trentino and is reachable on skis from Arabba on the Sella Ronda circuit. See the Sella Ronda chapter for a description of the skiing. Here we cover the main Trentino resorts linked to the Sella Ronda.

Scenery like this is run of the mill in Trentino. This is the view from the top of the Andalo ski area →

Canazei is a sizeable, bustling, pretty, roadside village of narrow streets, rustic old buildings, traditional-style hotels and nice little shops, set at 1465m/4,810ft beneath the Sella Ronda's most heavily wooded section of mountains. The grand 3-star hotel Dolomiti (0462 601106) in the centre is one of the original resort hotels; the charming, chalet-style Diana (0462 601477) is five minutes from the centre.

There are numerous restaurants and the après-ski is really animated. La Stua di Ladins serves local wines and the Husky and Roxi bars are worth a visit.

Off-slope entertainment consists of beautiful walks and shopping. There's also a pool, sauna, Turkish baths and skating in neighbouring Alba.

A 12-person gondola is the only mountain access point, but it shifts the queues (which can be long) quickly.

A single piste runs back to the village but it is often closed. The local Belvedere slopes are easy and the village nursery slope is good but inconvenient, and so unlikely to be used after day one.

Campitello (1445m/4,740ft) is a pleasant, unremarkable village, smaller and quieter than next-door Canazei, and still unspoiled. It's quiet during the day, having no slopes back to the village. A reporter enjoyed a stay at the hotel Sella Ronda (0462 750525). Campitello has quite lively après-ski – the Da Giulio bar gets packed. There's an ice rink. A cable-car takes you up to the slopes: in high season this can generate 'massive queues at the beginning of the day', according to a 2007 visitor. To get home you can take the cable-car down or take the piste to Canazei and catch a bus.

OTHER TRENTINO RESORTS

Still in the Val di Fassa, close to Canazei, **Alba** has its own slopes, linked to **Pozza di Fassa** further down the valley. A reporter recommends the 4-star Gran Baita hotel (0462 764163) – 'excellent service'. Over the road from Pozza another small area of slopes is linked to **Vigo di Fassa**. Not far from the valley town of Moena is the lift system of **Alpe Lusia**, but off to the east are more extensive slopes at **Passo San Pellegrino**, linked with **Falcade** in Veneto. There is another fair-sized lift network at **Passo Costalunga**, linked with **Nova Levante** (Welschnofen) in Alto Adige.

Continuing downstream, you are now in the Val di Fiemme. Near **Predazzo** there is a lift up to the slopes shared with **Pampeago** – recommended by a 2007 visitor for its efficient lifts, wide, quiet runs and excellent restaurants – and with **Obereggen**, across the border in Alto Adige. Finally, the town of **Cavalese** has lifts up to the Alpe Cermis slopes.

To the south of the Val di Fassa/Val di Fiemme axis, a steep road over the high **Passo Rolle** – where there is a small network of drags and chairs serving easy slopes on either side of the road – leads down to the resort of **San Martino di Castrozza** (1470m/ 4,820ft). San Martino has a fabulous setting beneath a soaring wall of Dolomite cliffs and peaks – the Pale di San Martino. The village is not notably cute – there are some large, block-like buildings – but it is pleasant enough. The slopes, entirely intermediate in difficulty, are split into three sectors, only two of them linked (at altitude).

Switzerland

Switzerland is home to some of our favourite resorts. We award ★★★★★ for resort charm and for spectacular scenery to only three resorts in this book – the essentially traffic-free Swiss villages of Wengen, Mürren and Zermatt. Many other Swiss resorts are not far behind. Many resorts have impressive slopes, too – including some of the biggest, highest and toughest runs in the Alps – as well as a lot of good intermediate terrain. For fast, queue-free lift networks, Swiss resorts are not known for setting the standards – too many historic cable-cars and mountain railways for that. But the real bottlenecks are steadily disappearing. And there are compensations – the world's best mountain restaurants, for one, and pretty reliable accommodation for another.

People always seem to associate Switzerland with high prices. In the recent past, we haven't found most Swiss resorts appreciably more expensive than most French ones – though some Swiss resorts, such as Zermatt, Verbier and St Moritz, do tend to be pricey. What is clear is that what you get for your money in Switzerland is generally first class.

Many Swiss resorts have a special relationship with the British, who invented downhill skiing in its modern form in Wengen and Mürren by persuading the locals to run their mountain railways in winter, and so act as ski lifts, and by organising the first downhill races. An indication of the continuing strength of the British presence in these resorts is that Wengen has an English church.

While France is the home of the purpose-built resort, Switzerland is the home of the mountain village that has transformed itself from traditional farming community (or health retreat) into year-round holiday resort. Many of Switzerland's most famous mountain resorts

490

Two of the delights of Switzerland form a powerful combination: excellent restaurants and stunning scenery; this is St Moritz ↓

Hire from swissrent a sport for complete freedom of choice with your winter sports equipment: skis, boards or boots, we have all the top brands and models, whatever your preference, whatever your style.

So be smart and hire from swissrent a sport. All over Switzerland at 50 outlets in 35 well-known winter sports resorts. Or wherever the action is.

For more information, prices or reservations visit our website at: www.swissrent.com

Your Ski Brand :

Hire where the action is.

are as popular in the summer as in the winter, or more so. This creates places with a more lived-in feel to them and a much more stable local community. Many villages are still dominated by a handful of families lucky or shrewd enough to get involved in the early development of the area.

This has its downside as well as advantages. The ruling families are able to stifle competition and prevent newcomers from taking a slice of their action. Alternative ski schools, competing with the traditional, nationally organised school and pushing up standards, are much less common than in other Alpine countries, for example. We are only now beginning to see this grip weakened.

Switzerland means high living as well as high prices, and the swanky grand hotels of St Moritz, Gstaad, Zermatt and Davos are beyond the dreams of most ordinary holidaymakers. (St Moritz now has an amazing five 5-star hotels.) Even in more modest places, the quality of the service is generally high. The trains run like clockwork to the advertised timetable (and often they run to the top of the mountain, doubling as ski lifts). The food is almost universally of good quality and much less stodgy than in neighbouring Austria. Even the standard rustic dish of rösti is haute cuisine compared to Austrian sausages. And in Switzerland you get what you pay for: the cheapest wine, for example, is not cheap, but it is reliable.

Perhaps surprisingly for such a traditional, rather staid skiing nation, Switzerland has gone out of its way to attract snowboarders. Davos may hit the headlines mainly when it hosts huge economic conferences, but yards from the conference hall there are dudes getting big air on the Bolgen slope's training kickers. Little-known Laax claims Europe's best terrain-park.

GETTING AROUND THE SWISS ALPS

Access to practically all Swiss resorts is fairly straightforward when approaching from the north – just pick your motorway. But many of the high passes that are perfectly sensible ways to get around the country in summer are closed in winter, which can be inconvenient if you are moving around from one area to another.

There are very useful car-carrying trains in various places; they can cut out huge amounts of driving. One key link is between the Valais (Crans-Montana, Zermatt etc) and Andermatt via the Furka tunnel, and another is from Andermatt to the Grisons (Laax, Davos etc) via the Oberalp pass – closed to road traffic in winter but open to trains except after very heavy snowfalls. Another rail tunnel that's very handy is the Lötschberg, linking Kandersteg in the Bernese Oberland with Brig in the Valais. This year a new tunnel has opened in parallel – the lower, longer, faster Lötschberg Base Tunnel. But it takes only passenger and freight trains – car-carrying trains continue to use the old tunnel.

More stunning scenery – we don't need to tell you this is Zermatt – with another Swiss speciality: the mountain railway used as a ski lift ↓

St Moritz is more awkward to get to than other resorts. The main road route is over the Julier pass. This is normally kept open, but at 2285m/7,500ft it is naturally prone to heavy snowfalls that can shut it for a time. Fallbacks are car-carrying rail tunnels under the Albula pass and the Vereina tunnel from near Klosters – a relatively new option, having opened in 1999.

These car-carrying rail services are generally painless. Often you can just turn up and drive on. But carrying capacities are obviously

limited. Some services (eg Oberalp) carry only a handful of cars, and booking is vital. Others (eg Furka, Lötschberg, Vereina) are much bigger operations with much greater capacity – but that's a reflection of demand, and at peak times there may be long queues – particularly for the Furka tunnel from Andermatt, which Zürich residents use to get to the big Valais resorts. There is a car-carrying rail tunnel linking Switzerland with Italy – the Simplon. But most

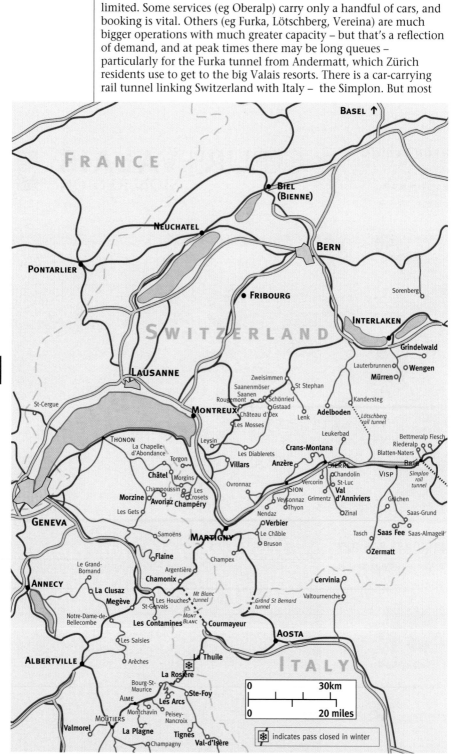

routes to Italy are kept open by means of road tunnels. See the Italy introduction for more information.

To use Swiss motorways (and it's difficult to avoid doing so if you're driving serious distances within the country) you have to buy an annual permit to stick on your windscreen (costing SF40, and valid for 14 months, from December to the end of January). They are sold at the border, and are, for all practical purposes, compulsory.

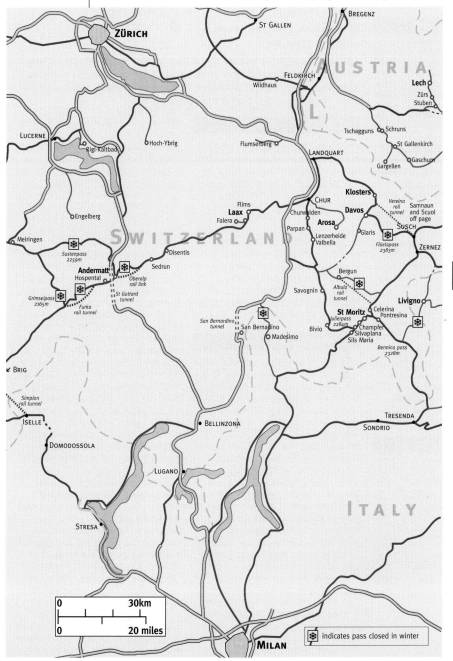

indicates pass closed in winter

Chocolate-box village with plenty to do off the snow – but also with extensive slopes including an area shared with Lenk

RATINGS

The slopes

Fast lifts	★★★
Snow	★★★
Extent	★★★
Expert	★★
Intermediate	★★★
Beginner	★★★★
Convenience	★★
Queues	★★★
Mountain restaurants	★★★

The rest

Scenery	★★★★
Resort charm	★★★★
Off-slope	★★★★

NEWS

For 2007/08 a fast quad with covers is due to replace the triple chair from Geils to Lavey, removing a major bottleneck.

For 2006/07 a covered six-pack replaced a drag-lift at Bühlberg, above Lenk, and two new blue pistes were added. Snowmaking was increased around the new lift and at Elsigenalp.

Lenk gained a new drag-lift at Betelberg.

KEY FACTS

Resort	1355m
	4,450ft
Slopes	1070-2360m
	3,510-7,740ft
Lifts	56
Pistes	185km
	115 miles
Blue	40%
Red	50%
Black	10%
Snowmaking	60%
	of main pistes

498

+ Traditional, pretty mountain village in a splendid setting

+ Good off-slope facilities

+ Extensive slopes to suit all abilities, linked to Lenk, but ...

– The slopes are fragmented and widely spread – access can involve multiple lifts or bus-rides

– Few challenges on-piste – but plenty of off-piste opportunities

Adelboden is unjustly neglected by the international market: for intermediates looking for a relaxing holiday in pretty surroundings – and perhaps spending some time doing things off the slopes – it has a lot of appeal. Surprisingly, the resort literature includes English translations.

THE RESORT

Adelboden fits the traditional image of a Swiss mountain village: old chalets with overhanging roofs line the quiet main street (cars are discouraged), and 3000m/9,840ft peaks make an impressive backdrop. The village is compact, and there are efficient buses to the outlying areas (most covered on the lift pass); the ideal location for most people is close to the main street. Adelboden is just to the west of the much better-known Jungfrau resorts (Wengen, Mürren etc). These resorts are within day-trip range, as is Gstaad to the west.

THE MOUNTAINS

Adelboden's slopes are split into five sectors spread over a wide area. One sector stretches across to the village of Lenk, with its own local slopes a bus-ride across the valley. Allow plenty of time to return from Lenk if you plan to explore there.

Slopes Village lifts access three of the sectors. A small cable-car/gondola hybrid goes up to Tschentenalp, just above the village. An even smaller one goes down to Oey (where there is a car park). From here, a proper gondola goes up to the Chuenisbärgli sector and then on (in two further stages) to more remote Silleren-Hahnenmoos. This is much the biggest sector, with long, gentle runs (and some short, sharp ones) from 2200m down to 1350m (7,220ft down to 4,430ft) – back to the village and over to Lenk.

Engstligenalp, a flat-bottomed high-altitude bowl, is reached by a cable-car 4km/2.5 miles south of the resort; Elsigenalp (another cable-car) is more

extensive, but remote; and difficult to reach by bus, say reporters.

Terrain-parks The Gran Masta Park at Hahnenmoos has jumps, big-air, rails, a boarder-cross and chill-out zone; but no half-pipe. There's a natural playground at Engstligenalp.

Snow reliability Despite unremarkable top heights, most slopes are above 1500m/4,920ft, so snow reliability is reasonable. Tschentenalp often has the best snow on its north-facing slopes. Snowmaking was increased this year and now covers over half of the main pistes. Grooming is reportedly good.

Experts There are some genuine black pistes at Geils, and a less genuine one on Chuenisbärgli. Off-piste possibilities are good and remain untracked for much longer than in more macho resorts: the Lavey and Luegli chairs in the Geils bowl access routes down to both Adelboden and Lenk (though there are protected forest areas to avoid). Engstligenalp has off-piste potential too – and is a launching point for tours around the Wildstrubel.

Intermediates All five areas deserve exploration by intermediates. At Geils there is a lot of ground to be covered – and trips across to Lenk's gentle Betelberg area (covered by the lift pass) are possible. Various timed runs are dotted around the area.

Beginners There are good nursery slopes in the village and at the foot of nearby sectors. At Geils there are glorious long, easy runs to progress to.

Snowboarding Two specialist schools offer lessons. There's a free-ride zone at Engstligenalp. The many drag-lifts are only gradually being replaced.

Cross-country There are extensive trails along the valley towards Engstligenalp with its high altitude, snow-sure circuit.

ENGSTLIGENALP 236om/7,730ft

2290m
Elsigenalp

Luegli 2140m

Metschstand 2105m

Leiterli 2000m

CHUENISBÄRGLI 1905m

ELSIGEN

Fleckli Unter Birg

Geils 1710m
Sillerenbühl 1975m

1960m

BETELBERG

Stoss 1645m

Elsigbach 1250m

Boden

Adelboden 1355m/4,450ft

Oey

Stand 2020m

Lavey 2200m

Lenk 1070m/3,510ft

TSCHENTENALP 1950m

SILLEREN-HAHNENMOOS

1135m

1540m

1645m

UK PACKAGES

Crystal, Interhome, Kuoni, Swiss Travel Service, Switzerland Travel Centre, Thomson

Phone numbers
From elsewhere in Switzerland add the prefix 033; from abroad use the prefix +41 33

TOURIST OFFICE

t 673 8080
info@adelboden.ch
www.adelboden.ch

ADELBODEN TOURIST OFFICE

The setting is as attractive as the village ↓

Queues The main access gondolas generate queues at peak times. A 2007 reporter suggests using the alternative minibus service to the main sector. A fast quad planned from Geils to Lavey for 2007/08 should greatly speed up the return from Geils to Adelboden, and over to Lenk (relieving pressure on the old Hahnenmoos gondola). The return journey from Lenk was speeded up last season with a new six-pack at Bühlberg. The main lift at Chuenisbärgli is now a quad. If snow low down is poor, queues for the Engstligenalp cable-car build up. There are some single lines, but they are little used.

Mountain restaurants Of the numerous pleasant restaurants with terraces, the Tschenten Alp is 'undoubtedly the best' with 'excellent meals', says a 2007 reporter. The Standhütte-Metsch is said to be 'small, simple, but good'. Many places have limited menus.

Schools and guides Past reports on the Adelboden ski school have been mixed – 'caring, good English', but 'mix of abilities within group'.

Facilities for children The kindergarten takes children from three to five years. There are snow gardens at Geils, Elsigen and Engstligenalp. Several hotels have childcare facilities and the resort runs a regular programme of children's events.

STAYING THERE

How to go Several UK operators go there, there is locally bookable self-catering, and some 30 pensions and hotels (mainly 3- and 4-star).

Hotels The 4-star Park Hotel Bellevue (673 8000) is expensive, but we have received good reports of its food and spa facilities. The central 3-star Adler Sporthotel (673 4141) is pretty and recommended, with a newish wellness centre. The little Bären (673 2151) is a simple but captivating wooden chalet. The Waldhaus-Huldi (673 8500) is 'very welcoming'. The Beau-Site (673 2222) has 'the best position in town'.

Eating out Possibilities are varied, and include a couple of mountain restaurants. Guests on a half-board arrangement can 'dine around' at affiliated hotels twice a week.

Après-ski The après-ski is traditional, based on bars and tea rooms – a reader recommends Hauetar and Schmid. The Arte Bar offers a bit of artistic flair and, unusually, a wide range of spirits. The Alpenrose attracts a younger crowd and the Berna-Bar disco is 'quite good'.

Off the slopes There is a fair bit to do – especially active things. There are indoor and outdoor curling and skating rinks, sleigh rides, several toboggan runs, and hiking paths. There are hotel pools open to the public. Some mountain restaurants are reachable on foot. Special lift passes are available for walkers.

Andermatt

A slow-paced, old-fashioned resort with some great steep, high terrain on- and off-piste (and the snowfall to go with it)

500

COSTS

① ② ③ ④ ⑤ ⑥

RATINGS

The slopes
Fast lifts	**
Snow	****
Extent	*
Expert	****
Intermediate	**
Beginner	*
Convenience	***
Queues	**
Mountain restaurants	*

The rest
Scenery	***
Resort charm	****
Off-slope	**

NEWS

For 2006/07 a new restaurant, Alte Apotheke, opened in the village.
And at Sedrun, a six-pack replaced drag-lifts on Cuolm Val.

There are plans to install a new chair-lift on the Gemsstock – but not until 2008/09.

KEY FACTS

Resort	1445m
	4,740ft
Slopes	1445-2965m
	4,740-9,730ft
Lifts	25
Pistes	130km
	81 miles
Blue	23%
Red	50%
Black	27%
Snowmaking	40 km
	25 miles

UK PACKAGES

Alpine Answers, Mountain Tracks, Ski Freshtracks, Ski Weekend, Switzerland Travel Centre

---

- **+** Attractive, traditional village
- **+** Excellent snow record
- **+** Some excellent steep pistes, and great off-piste terrain – plus ski-touring opportunities
- **+** Easy access from Zürich

- **−** Four separate areas of slopes are all fairly limited if you stay on-piste
- **−** Unsuitable for beginners
- **−** Limited off-slope diversions
- **−** Little English spoken
- **−** Cable-car queues at weekends

Little old Andermatt was rather left behind in the mega-resort boom of the 1960s and 1970s, but its attractions have not faded for those who like their mountains tall, steep and covered in deep powder. At first sight, it makes a tempting spot for a weekend break – but you'll be joined by the residents of Zürich, who arrive by the coachload and trainload. For a midweek break, it's superb.

THE RESORT

Andermatt is quite busy in summer and gets weekend winter business, but at other times seems deserted apart from soldiers from the local barracks. The town is quietly attractive, with wooden houses lining the dog-leg main street that runs between railway and cable-car stations, and some imposing churches. There are good road and rail links from Zürich, but in winter east-west links with the Grisons and the Valais rely on car-carrying trains. The town is big enough for reporters to appreciate the good minibus service to Gemsstock and Winterhorn.

THE MOUNTAINS

Andermatt's local skiing is split over three unlinked mountains, all limited in extent. The slopes are almost entirely above the trees. The lift pass covers Sedrun, 20 minutes away by train (included) to a tiny station just over the Oberalp pass – a good outing. The Sedrun skiing used to be an optional extra; since it is now standard, we have revised our 'Key facts'.
Slopes A two-stage cable-car from the edge of the village serves magnificent, varied slopes on the open, steep, north-facing and usually empty slopes of Gemsstock. Across town is the gentler, sunny Nätschen/Gütsch area. And a bus- or train-ride along the valley is north-facing Winterhorn (above Hospental). There is also an isolated nursery slope further along at Realp. Piste marking is slack, which is bad news in a white-out.

Terrain-parks There are facilities (park and pipe) on Gemsstock. Sedrun has a half-pipe and park at Milez (floodlit on Thursdays) and another at Valtgeva.
Snow reliability The area has a justified reputation for reliable snow. Piste grooming is generally good.
Experts It is most definitely a resort for experts. The north-facing bowl beneath the top Gemsstock cable-car is a glorious, long, steep slope (about 900m/2,950ft vertical), usually with excellent snow, down which there are countless off-piste routes, an itinerary and a piste. Outside the bowl, the Sonnenpiste is a fine open red run curling away from the lifts to the mid-station, with more off-piste opportunities. From Gurschen to the village there is a black run, not steep but often tricky. Routes outside the bowl go down the Felsental or Guspis valleys towards Hospental, or steeply into the deserted Untertal, to the east (ending in a bit of a walk). Nätschen and Winterhorn both have black pistes and off-piste opportunities, including worthwhile itinerary routes.
Intermediates Intermediates needn't be put off Gemsstock: the Sonnenpiste can be tackled (and there are special groomed sections of the piste 'for carvers'), and there is a pleasant red run and some short blues at mid-mountain. Winterhorn's modest lift system offers pistes to suit all abilities down the 1000m/3,280ft vertical, while Nätschen's sunny mountain is well worth a visit. So is Sedrun, with a good choice of red runs starting from a railway halt in a snowy wilderness and a new six-pack on the main slopes.

↑ You may be able to make out the railway snaking up the Nätschen slopes to Oberalp. The Gemsstock is out of shot to the right

ANDERMATT-GOTTHARD TOURISMUS

Phone numbers
From elsewhere in Switzerland add the prefix 041; from abroad use the prefix +41 41

Beginners The lower half of Nätschen has a good, long, easy run. But this is not a good resort for beginners.

Snowboarding The cable-car accesses some great free-ride terrain.

Cross-country There are 40km/24 miles of loops along the valley.

Queues The Gemsstock cable-car can generate morning queues in the village and at mid-mountain on fine weekends. Things take a while to get going after heavy snow. A new chairlift at Gemsstock has been talked about for several years – we are now told that it is expected for 2008/09.

Mountain restaurants They are present, but are still no more than adequate. The Gemsstockbar, at Gurschen, seems to be only a bar.

Schools and guides Bergschule Uri/ Mountain Reality, a guiding outfit run by local big wheel Alex Clapasson, is very pricey, and one reporter did not

regret hiring a guide from the Swiss ski school instead.

Facilities for children There are slopes they can handle at Nätschen, and the Swiss school does classes. There are children's parks at Realp and Sedrun.

STAYING THERE

How to go Andermatt's accommodation is in cosy 2- and 3-star hotels.

Hotels Gasthaus Sternen (887 1130) is an attractive central chalet with a cosy restaurant and bar. The lovely old 3-star Sonne (887 1226), between the centre and the lift, is welcoming and comfortable, with 'excellent service'. The neighbouring Bergidyll (887 1455) is a British favourite. Alpenhotel Schlüssel (888 7088) is 'good value', with spacious rooms.

Eating out A reporter praises the Sternen (see above) for 'generous portions, nicely cooked and very cosy surroundings'. The hotel Kronen is 'quite formal'. Tre Passi restaurant has also been mentioned in dispatches. Alte Apotheke is new this year – reports, please.

Après-ski There are several cosy bars, which come alive on Saturdays – the Spycher and the Piccadilly in particular. The Curva at the hotel Monopol is 'very pleasant'. At weekends the Gotthard disco is said to be 'lively'.

Off the slopes There's a toboggan run at Nätschen. The fitness centre at the hotel Drei König is open to the public. There are maintained footpaths.

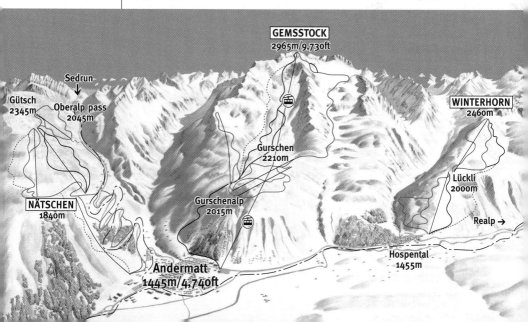

GEMSSTOCK
2965m/9,730ft

Sedrun
↓

Gütsch
2345m

Oberalp pass
2045m

WINTERHORN
2460m

Gurschen
2210m

Lückli
2000m

NÄTSCHEN
1840m

Gurschenalp
2015m

Realp →

Andermatt
1445m/4,740ft

Hospental
1455m

Attractive purpose-built resort set in a sunny position with spectacular views and a small area of intermediate slopes

COSTS

① ② ③ ④ ⑤ ⑥

NEWS

There are plans to link the Anzère ski area with adjacent Crans-Montana. When that happens it will transform the attraction of Anzère for keen piste-bashers. And a new spa is being built that might be open for the 2007/08 season. For 2006/07 a new ice rink opened in the village square and the black Masques and red Luis pistes are now 100 per cent covered by snowmaking.

KEY FACTS

Resort	1500m
	4,920ft
Slopes	1500-2,500m
	4,920-8,200ft
Lifts	11
Pistes	40km
	25 miles
Blue	12%
Red	76%
Black	12%
Snowmaking	12km
	7 miles

UK PACKAGES

Ardmore, Interhome, Lagrange

Phone numbers
From elsewhere in Switzerland add the prefix 027 (Anzère) and 0848 (Coeur du Valais); from abroad use the prefix +41 and omit the initial '0'

TOURIST OFFICES

Anzère
t 399 2800
info@anzere.ch
www.anzere.ch

Coeur du Valais
t 848 027
www.coeurduvalais.ch

➕ Attractive and family-friendly with traffic-free central square

➕ Sunny intermediate slopes good for leisurely cruising

➖ Small area of slopes

➖ Little to interest experts

This small resort set on a sunny shelf with great views over the Rhône valley is little-known on the UK market. Its position and small area of local slopes makes it good for a quiet, relaxing time and for families. It will be of more interest to keen piste-bashers when the planned link to Crans-Montana happens.

THE RESORT

Anzère is an attractive, purpose-built resort dating from 1965. It is set on a sunny plateau at 1500m/4,920ft facing south with spectacular views over the Rhône valley to the 4000m/13,120ft peaks and glaciers beyond. The heart is the traffic-free Anzère village square with shops, restaurants, terraces, a children's area and a new ice rink.

THE MOUNTAINS

The village sits at the western end of the ski area, which spreads eastwards to Les Rousses, from where the planned link to Crans-Montana will be.
Slopes From the village a gondola takes you up to Pas de Maimbre at 2360m/7,740ft. From there a series of lifts (mostly drags) serves mainly red runs leading to the high point of Le Bâte and a run down to Les Rousses.
Terrain-parks There's a park and a boardercross area.
Snow reliability The slopes are not especially high and face south, so the snow can suffer in warm weather; 30 per cent of the pistes are covered by snowmaking.
Experts There's a 5km/3 mile black run from Pas de Maimbre back to the village served top-to-bottom by snowmaking, and a 2km/1 mile mogul run, but little else to keep experts busy.
Intermediates This is primarily an intermediate resort, with 75 per cent of the runs being red. But with only 40km/25 miles of slopes, keen piste-bashers will find the extent limited.
Beginners The village nursery slope is served by a drag-lift and there are short, easy blue slopes at the top of the gondola.
Snowboarding There's a park and

boardercross and the snow soon softens in the sun – good for boarding. But there are a lot of drag-lifts for beginner boarders to cope with.
Cross-country The 5km/3 mile Go cross-country trail heads off west from the village and is ideal for beginners.
Queues No problems reported.
Mountain restaurants There are three, including one at the top of the gondola.
Schools and guides We have no reports on either the Swiss School or the rival Glycérine Sliding School.
Facilities for children This is very much a family resort, with a playground in the village square, a 200m/660ft toboggan run, and a nursery open from 8.30 to 5pm Monday to Friday. The ski school takes children from age four.

STAYING THERE

How to go A few small operators run packages here.
Lodging There are four 3-star hotels and lots of apartments.
Eating out For a small place there's a reasonable choice – from gastronomic to pizzerias.
Après-ski As well as five bars there are three discos, including the newly reopened King-Kong. And activities (especially for kids) are arranged – many in the village square.
Off the slopes There are 40km/25 miles of marked walks, 12km/7.5 miles of snow-shoe trails, a parapenting school, an ice rink and two 3km/2 mile tobogganing runs. Down in the valley, the old town of Sion is at the heart of the Coeur du Valais region of which Anzère is part, and is worth exploring. Attractions include Europe's largest navigable underground lake and walking in the Val d'Hérens, as well as trying the local Valais wines.

Arosa

A classic all-round winter resort, where walking is as much part of the scene as skiing; choose your spot with care

COSTS

① ② ③ ④ ⑤ ⑥

RATINGS

The slopes
Fast lifts	★★★
Snow	★★★
Extent	★★
Expert	★★
Intermediate	★★★
Beginner	★★★★
Convenience	★★
Queues	★★★★
Mountain restaurants	★★★

The rest
Scenery	★★★
Resort charm	★★
Off-slope	★★★★

NEWS

For 2007/08 the 5-star Tschuggen Grand Hotel is expected to open a mini-funicular, the Coaster, to transfer guests to and from the slopes.

This follows the opening of a luxury spa complex, the Bergoase, at the same hotel last season.

Snowmaking was doubled for 2006/07.

+ Classic winter sports resort ambience, with lots going on other than skiing and boarding

+ Some of the best cross-country loops in the Alps

+ Few queues

+ Choice of good nursery slopes at village or mid-mountain level

+ Relatively good snow reliability, and increasing amounts of snowmaking

+ Prettily wooded setting, complete with frozen lake, but ...

– Some very block-like buildings in main village around Obersee

– Spread-out village lacks a heart, and means some accommodation is inconveniently situated

– Slopes too limited for mileage-hungry intermediates

– Few challenging pistes for experts – though there is good off-piste

The classic image of a winter sports resort is perhaps an isolated, snow-covered Swiss village, surrounded by big, beautiful mountains, with skating on a frozen lake, horse-drawn sleighs jingling along snowy paths and people wrapped in fur coats strolling in the sun. Arosa offers exactly that. It's just a pity that many of its comfortable hotels date from that unfortunate era when wood and pitched roofs were out of fashion.

Arosa's other serious weakness is the limited extent of slopes, coupled with a remote location that more or less rules out excursions to other resorts. Roll on the long-awaited link with Lenzerheide-Valbella, which would transform the appeal of Arosa to keen intermediates, in particular.

THE RESORT

High and remote, Arosa is in a sheltered basin at the head of a beautiful wooded valley, in sharp contrast to the open slopes above it. It's a long, winding drive or splendid rail journey from Chur (both take just under an hour).

The main resort development is around Obersee – a pretty spot, centred as you might guess on a frozen lake, but spoilt by the surrounding block-like buildings. Lifts go up from here into the Weisshorn sector of the slopes. The rest of Arosa is scattered, much of it spreading up the steep road separating Obersee

AROSA TOURIST OFFICE

On the lower slopes, most of the customers in the mountain restaurants get there on foot or by sleigh ➜

503

KEY FACTS

Resort	1800m	
	5,910ft	
Slopes	1800-2655m	
	5,910-8,710ft	
Lifts	13	
Pistes	60km	
	37 miles	
Blue	27%	
Red	60%	
Black	13%	
Snowmaking	30km	
	18 miles	

from the older, prettier Inner-Arosa, where lifts from opposite extremities go up into both sectors of the slopes. Arosa is quiet; its relaxed ambience attracts an unpretentiously well-heeled clientele of families and older people. Very few of them are British.

Some accommodation is a long walk from the lifts, but there is an excellent free shuttle-bus and convenient parking.

THE MOUNTAINS

Arosa's slopes are situated in a wide, open bowl, facing north-east to south-east, with all the runs returning eventually to the village at the bottom. All the slopes are above the tree line, except those just above Obersee.

Slopes The slopes are spread widely over two main sectors. The major lift junction in the Weisshorn sector is Tschuggen (strangely un-named on the resort piste map), 500m/1,640ft away from the Mittelstation of the Weisshorn cable-car, and reachable from both Obersee and Inner-Arosa. From Mittelstation, you can take a chair to the lower peak of Brüggerhorn. The main access to the Hörnli sector is a slow gondola from Inner-Arosa. Well-used walking paths wind across the mountainsides, and great care is needed where they cross the pistes.

Piste marking is generally OK, although the blue run from the Brüggerhorn to Obersee is singled out by a recent reporter as being unclear at the top. Various night-skiing events are held once a week at Tschuggen.

Terrain-parks There is a park with jumps, rails and 150m/492ft long half-pipe.

Snow reliability The slopes are quite high, but the Weisshorn sector gets a lot of sun; the shadier Hörnli slopes hold their snow well. Grooming is good, and snowmaking on the home runs is often used. Snowmaking was doubled last season to cover 30km/18 miles of pistes.

Experts Arosa isn't an obvious target for experts, but there is plenty of gentle off-piste terrain. The resort exploits its ungroomed terrain by promoting the Brüggerhorn as its 'Free Ride Mountain', but without much enthusiasm. Two of the ski-routes it invented have become red pistes.

Intermediates This is a good area for intermediates who aren't looking for high mileage or huge challenges. The runs from Hörnli are enjoyable cruises, the black including a short steeper pitch. The Weisshorn runs are generally steeper, with some rewarding reds. The long blue to Obersee from Brüggerhorn via Prätschli is a great way to end the day, with fab views of sunlit peaks

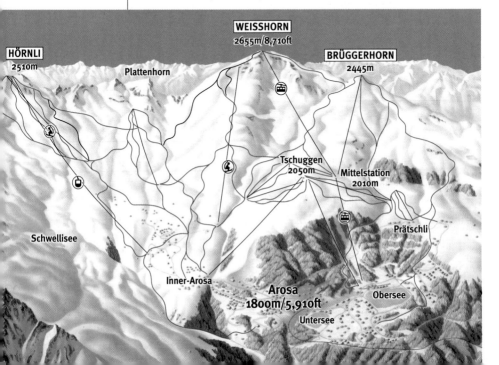

Phone numbers
From elsewhere in Switzerland add the prefix 081; from abroad use the prefix +41 81

TOURIST OFFICE

t 378 7020
arosa@arosa.ch
www.arosa.ch

from the shady piste.

Beginners The easy slopes up at Tschuggen are excellent and usually have good snow, but they get a lot of through traffic. Inner-Arosa has a quieter area for children ('nice and gentle', says a recent reporter).

Snowboarding Bananas is the specialist school and Mountain Surf Club offers two-day free-ride camps.

Cross-country Arosa's modest 26km/16 miles of loops include some of the best and most varied in the Alps.

Queues Arosa does not suffer from serious queues – even in half-term. There can be waits for the Weisshorn cable-car, though our most recent reporters have had no problems.

Mountain restaurants There's a reasonable choice, several equipped with seriously indulgent sunbeds on which you can lunch while sunbathing; Carmennahütte has row upon row of them. Tschuggenhütte has choices for all the family. Alpenblick does 'very good food' and Hörnli is a 'welcoming hut in a dramatic position'.

Schools and guides Swiss and ABC are the main schools. Class sizes can be large. There's a lot of demand for private lessons.

Facilities for children Arosa's appeal as a family resort has led to Disney endorsement, with 12 hotels and the Swiss Ski school forming the Alpine Club Mickey Mouse. A 2006 reporter was 'very pleased' with his daughter's 'excellent, friendly instructors who spoke English'. Club Mickey also includes a kindergarten, kids' restaurants and games areas.

STAYING THERE

How to go Arosa is a hotel resort, with a high proportion of 3- and 4-stars. But Snowy Pockets' catered chalet Runca is a welcome departure.

Hotels The sensitively modernised 4-star Waldhotel National (378 5555) with 'really special food' and direct access to the slopes is 'quite delightful'. The 4-star Sporthotel Valsana (378 6363) is recommended. The 5-star Tschuggen Grand (378 9999) has a spectacular new wellness centre (designed by a famous architect) with a dozen treatment rooms, two pools and so on. This season a mini-funicular will ferry guests to the slopes.

Eating out Most restaurants are hotel-based, some with a very high reputation. The Kachelofa-Stübli at the Waldhotel National is excellent. The Luna does pasta and Osteria Poltera serves Swiss dishes.

Après-ski Après-ski is quite lively. The Carmenna hotel by the ice rink has a popular piano bar. The Sitting Bull is busy and cheerful. Recommended bars include the Grischuna for grown-ups and Boomerang for kids (both with restaurants attached). The Vista (formerly Blu Club) is the place for dancing and concerts.

Off the slopes There's an indoor pool. You can get a pedestrian's lift pass, and many mountain restaurants are reachable via 60km/37 miles of cleared, marked paths shown on a special map. Sleigh rides are popular, and there are indoor and outdoor ice rinks. Shopping is limited.

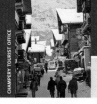

CHAMPERY TOURIST OFFICE

Champéry

Picture-postcard village that few UK tour operators feature these days, with access to the Portes du Soleil circuit

COSTS

① ② ③ ④ ⑤ ⑥

RATINGS

The slopes
Fast lifts	**
Snow	**
Extent	*****
Expert	***
Intermediate	****
Beginner	**
Convenience	*
Queues	****
Mountain restaurants	***

The rest
Scenery	****
Resort charm	****
Off-slope	***

NEWS

There are plans to modernise the lift system on the Swiss side of the Portes du Soleil, but the earliest that new lifts will appear will be for the 2008/09 season.

506

UK PACKAGES

Alpine Answers, Corporate Ski Co, Made to Measure, Piste Artiste, Ski Freedom, Ski Independence, Ski Weekend, Skitracer, White Roc
Morgins Chalet Group, Ski Morgins, Ski Rosie

+ Charmingly rustic mountain village
+ Cable-car or fast six-packs take you into the Portes du Soleil circuit
+ Quiet, relaxed – yet plenty to do off the slopes

− Local slopes suffer from the sun
− No runs back to the village – and sometimes none back to the valley
− Not good for beginners
− Not many tough slopes nearby

With good transport links and sports facilities, Champéry is great for intermediate skiers looking for a quiet time in a lovely place, especially if they have a car. Access to the Portes du Soleil circuit is not bad: Avoriaz is fairly easy to get to – and there may be fresh powder there when Champéry is suffering.

THE RESORT

Set beneath the dramatic Dents du Midi, Champéry is a village of old wooden chalets. Friendly and relaxed, it would be ideal for families if it wasn't separated from its slopes by a steep, fragmented mountainside.

Down a steepish hill, away from the main street, are the cable-car, sports centre and railway station.

THE MOUNTAINS

Once you get up to them, the local slopes are open, friendly and relaxing.
Slopes Champéry's sunny slopes are part of the big Portes du Soleil circuit, which links Avoriaz, Châtel (in France) Les Crosets, Champoussin and Morgins (see below). The village cable-car or a fast six-seat chair-lift from Grand Paradis, a short free bus-ride from Champéry, go up to Croix de Culet, above the bowl of Planachaux. If snow is good there are a couple of pistes back to Grand Paradis, with an efficient bus service back to the

village, but no pistes back to Champéry.There is night skiing on Wednesdays and Saturdays until 10pm.
Terrain-parks There is a good terrain-park at Les Crosets (which a reporter rates as the best in the area), half of which is natural. The 29 features include a half-pipe, quarter-pipes, tables, gaps, kickers and rails. The Micro Park for beginners and youngsters has rails and boxes.
Snow reliability The snow on the north-facing French side of the link with Avoriaz is usually better than on the sunnier Swiss side to the south. The local Champéry area would benefit from more snowmaking.
Experts Few local challenges and badly placed for most of the tough Portes du Soleil runs. The Swiss Wall, on the Champéry side of Chavanette, is intimidatingly long and bumpy, but not terrifyingly steep. There's scope for off-piste at Chavanette and on the broad slopes of Les Crosets and Champoussin.
Intermediates Confident intermediates have the whole Portes du Soleil at

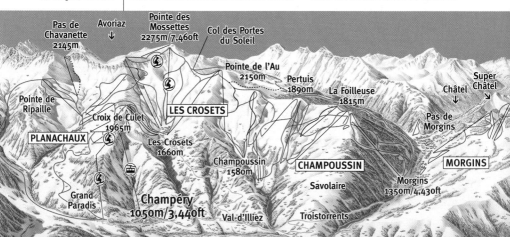

KEY FACTS

Resort	1050m
	3,440ft
Portes du Soleil	
Slopes	950-2300m
	3,120-7,550ft
Lifts	209
Pistes	650km
	404 miles
Green	14%
Blue	39%
Red	37%
Black	10%
Snowmaking	
	632 guns
Swiss side only	
Slopes	1050-2275m
	3,440-7,460ft
Lifts	35
Pistes	100km
	62 miles

Phone numbers
From elsewhere in Switzerland add the prefix 024; from abroad use the prefix +41 24

their disposal. Locally, the runs home to Grand Paradis are good when the snow conditions allow. Les Crosets is a junction of several fine runs. There are slightly tougher pistes from Mossettes and Pointe de l'Au, Champoussin's leisurely cruising, and delightful tree-lined meanders to Morgins. A highlight is the quiet, beautiful, long blue from Col des Portes du Soleil to Morgins via the 'cute' restaurant at Tovassière.

Beginners Not good. The Planachaux runs, where lessons are held, are steepish and small and some of the local blue runs are verging on red.

Snowboarding Not ideal for beginners (see above) and there are several drag-lifts (some quite steep). Good terrain-parks for experts though, and some good between-the-pistes powder areas.

Cross-country It's advertised as 10km/6 miles with 4km/2 miles floodlit every night, but it's very unreliable snow.

Queues Les Crosets is still a bottleneck at peak times. If snow is poor, end-of-the-day queues for the cable-car down are inescapable.

Mountain restaurants Chez Coquoz at Croix de Culet offers lovingly prepared food (try the lamb shank), and a knockout Valais wine list (we loved the Cornalin). Chez Gaby above Champoussin does 'marvellous rösti'. The tiny Lapisa on the way to Grand Paradis is delightfully rustic – they make cheese and smoke their own meats on site.

Schools and guides The few reports that we've had on the Swiss Ski and Snowboard school are free of criticism ('professional but friendly'). The Freeride Co and Swiss Snowsport School provide healthy competition.

Facilities for children The tourist office has a list of childminders. The Swiss ski school takes three to seven year olds.

STAYING THERE

How to go Limited packages available. Easy access for independent travellers.

Hotels Prices are low compared with smarter Swiss resorts. The Beau Séjour (479 5858) is friendly, family-run, with 'large rooms'. The National (479 1130) has 'excellent food, very friendly and helpful staff', says a 2007 reporter. The Auberge Le Paradis (479 1167) is 'charmingly rustic but noisy'.

Apartments Some are available to independent travellers. Tour op Piste Artiste has a self-catering chalet.

Eating out Mitchell's is stylish and modern and we enjoyed good Thai spring rolls, shark and reindeer there in 2007. The Café du Centre has a 'modern Asian menu in a wonderfully restored building'. The Vieux Chalet (hotel Beau Séjour) and the bistro in the hotel National have been praised. Two of the best for local specialities are just outside the village: Cantines des Rives and Auberge Le Paradis.

Après-ski Fairly quiet. But Mitchell's is popular at tea time – big sofas and a fireplace. Below the 'rather seedy' Pub, the Crevasse disco is one of the liveliest places. The Café du Centre has a micro brewery. Try the Bar des Guides in the hotel Suisse, or the Avalanche cellar nightclub.

Off the slopes Walks are pleasant and the railway allows lots of excursions. There's the Palladium (the Swiss national ice-sports centre) with indoor pool and tennis courts; plus ice climbing at Grand Paradis.

Les Crosets 1660m/5,450ft

A good base for a quiet time and slopes on the doorstep. The Télécabine hotel (479 0300) is homely, with good food.

Champoussin 1580m/5,180ft

A good family choice – no through traffic, near the slopes, no noisy late-night revellers and the comfortable Royal Alpage Club hotel (pool, gym, disco, two restaurants – 476 8300).

Morgins 1350m/4,430ft

A fairly scattered, but attractive, quiet resort with a gentle nursery slope. The hotel Reine des Alpes (477 1143) is well thought of, and there are catered chalets. The ESS ski school and village kindergarten have been recommended.

Crans-Montana

Sun-soaked slopes and stunning panoramic views above a big town base – not for those who love powder though

508

CRANS-MONTANA TOURISME

The resort is set on a broad, sunny shelf with long, panoramic views ↓

+ Large, varied piste area

+ Splendid setting and views

+ Excellent, gentle nursery slopes

+ Excellent cross-country trails

+ Very sunny slopes, but ...

− Snow badly affected by sun

− Large town (rather than village), devoid of Alpine atmosphere

− Bus- or car-rides to lifts from much of the accommodation

− Few challenges except off-piste

When conditions are right – clear skies above fresh, deep snow – Crans-Montana takes some beating: the mountains you bounce down are charmingly scenic, the mountains you gaze at are mind-blowing, and you can forgive Crans-Montana its inconvenient, linear layout and towny feel. Sadly, conditions are more often wrong. Except in the depths of winter, the strong midday sun bakes the pistes.

THE RESORT

Set on a broad shelf facing south across the Rhône valley, Crans-Montana is really two towns, their centres a mile apart and their fringes merging. Strung along a busy road, the resort's many hotels, villas, apartments and smart shops are mainly dull blocks with little traditional Alpine character. Crans is the more upmarket part, with fancy shops; it has now had a revamp to make it more pedestrian-friendly.

The resort is reached by road or by a fast funicular railway from Sierre. It depends heavily on summer conference business; hotels tend to be formal, and visitors dignified. The main gondola stations are above the main road – there is a free shuttle-bus during the day but it can get crowded and it is 'not dependable' says a 2006 reporter.

There are other gondola bases and places to stay at Les Barzettes and at Aminona. Anzère is nearby, and you can get to Zermatt, Saas-Fee and Verbier by road or rail.

THE MOUNTAINS

Crans-Montana has slopes with few challenges and no nasty surprises, and there is a pleasant mix of open and wooded slopes. The views over the Rhône valley to the peaks bordering Italy are breathtaking.

The slopes The slopes are spread over a broad mountainside, with lifts from four valley bases. Gondolas from Crans and Montana meet at Cry d'Er – an open bowl descending into patchy forest. There is free night skiing here on Fridays The next sector, focused on Les Violettes, is accessed from Les Barzettes. A new six-pack from the mid-station here up to Cry d'Er is expected for 2007/08. Above Les Violettes, a jumbo gondola goes up to the Plaine Morte glacier. The fourth sector is served by a gondola up from Aminona. Some of the runs down to the valley are narrow woodland paths, and signing is ridiculously slack.

Terrain-parks Aminona has a good park with features for all levels and a boarder-cross course.

Snow reliability The runs on the Plaine Morte glacier are limited and practically all the other slopes get a lot of direct sun. There is snowmaking on the main runs, but we have never found good snow on the runs down to the valley. A 2006 reporter tells of bare spots just 'two days after a 19-inch dump'.

For experts There are few steep pistes and the only decent moguls are on the short slopes at La Toula. There's plenty of off-piste, particularly beneath Chetseron and La Tza.

For intermediates Pistes are mostly wide, and many of the red runs don't

NEWS

For 2007/08 links between the main sectors will be improved by a six-pack to replace the Nationale chair-lift from the mid-station of the Violettes gondola to Cry d'Er. It will almost double the capacity of the existing lift. Snowmaking is also due to be improved.

For 2006/07 the Piste Nationale downhill course was remodelled and two tunnels added to improve access during competitions.

The centre of Crans was remodelled to make it more pedestrian-friendly.

UK PACKAGES

Alpine Answers, Corporate Ski Co, Directski.com, Independent Ski Links, Inghams, Interhome, Made to Measure, Momentum, Oxford Ski Co, Ski Line, Ski McNeill, Ski Solutions, Ski Weekend, Skitracer, Swiss Travel Service, Switzerland Travel Centre

Phone numbers
From elsewhere in Switzerland add the prefix 027; from abroad use the prefix +41 27

TOURIST OFFICE

t 485 0404
information@crans-montana.ch
www.crans-montana.ch

justify the grading. They tend to be uniform in difficulty from top to bottom, with few surprises. Avid piste-bashers enjoy the length of many runs, plus the fast lifts and good links that allow a lot of mileage. The 12km/8 mile run from Plaine Morte to Les Barzettes starts with top-of-the-world views and powder, and finishes among pretty woods. The Piste Nationale downhill course is a good test of technique – widened and improved in 2006/07.

For beginners There are three excellent nursery areas, including the golf course fairways which are great learning slopes.

Snowboarding Despite the resort's staid image, boarding is very popular. The Avalanche Pro is a specialist shop and school. The main lifts are chairs and gondolas, and the drag-lifts are usually avoidable.

For cross-country The 40km/25 miles of trails include a snow-sure glacier area.

Queues Investment in gondolas has helped cut queues out of the village, and a 2006 visitor found the slopes were deserted before 10.30am. The new six-pack planned for 2007/08 should improve access to Cry d'Er from the Violettes/Barzettes sector.

Mountain restaurants There are 21 mountain restaurants, usefully marked on the piste map. Above Crans, Merbé is one of the most attractive (and expensive), Chetseron has good views and Chez Erwin 'gorgeous homemade cake'. Bella-Lui, Cabane des Violettes ('good food at fairly reasonable prices') and Petit Mont-Bonvin are worth a look. Cabane Corbyre is new at Signal.

Schools and guides The Swiss schools have attracted mainly favourable comments over the years.

Facilities for children There's a snow garden and nursery above Montana, but we lack reports.

STAYING THERE

How to go There is a wide choice of hotels and apartments.

Hotels This conference resort has over 50 mainly large, comfortable, pricey hotels. Pas de l'Ours (485 9333) is our favourite – chic, attractive, wood and stone. Aïda Castel (485 4111) is also well-furnished in rustic style. Art de Vivre (formerly Beau-Site) (481 3312) has a new wellness centre.

Eating out A good variety of places, from French to Lebanese. The best is the Bistrot in the Pas de l'Ours hotel. The Chalet, Plaza, Rafaele's, and Padrino have been recommended. Tout un Art is new at the Art de Vivre and Club de la Nouvelle Rôtisserie doubles as an Indian restaurant and wine bar.

Après-ski There are tents on the hill for late-afternoon drinks, but nightlife and evening atmosphere may disappoint. The George & Dragon in Crans is one of the liveliest bars. Reporters recommend Bar 1900 and the Grange. New bars include the Baiser de la Rose and Harry's Club.

Off the slopes There are swimming pools (in hotels), two ice rinks, dog-sledding, snow-tubing, a cinema and a casino. There are also 60km/37 miles of walking. Sierre and Sion are close.

Crans-Montana

509

A grey urban sprawl at the centre of a glorious Alpine playground (for skaters and langlaufers as well as downhillers)

COSTS

① ② ③ ④ ⑤ ⑥

RATINGS

The slopes

Fast lifts	★★★
Snow	★★★★
Extent	★★★★★
Expert	★★★★
Intermediate	★★★★★
Beginner	★★
Convenience	★★
Queues	★★★
Mountain restaurants	★★★

The rest

Scenery	★★★★
Resort charm	★★
Off-slope	★★★★★

NEWS

For 2006/07 Pischa became a designated free-ride zone, with fewer lifts and less grooming. The resort launched a shuttle-bus service, the Graubünden Express, to and from Friedrichshafen airport (served by one or two budget airlines).

510

+ Very extensive slopes

+ Some superb, long, and mostly easy pistes away from the lifts, with trains to bring you back to base

+ Lots of accessible off-piste terrain, with several 'marked' itineraries

+ Good cross-country trails

+ Plenty to do off the slopes – from skating to shopping

+ Some cute mountain restaurants

– Davos is a huge, city-like place with dreary block-style buildings, plagued by traffic, lacking Alpine atmosphere and après-ski animation

– The slopes are spread over five separate areas

– Lots of T-bars, and some other inadequate lifts

– The only piste back to town from the main Parsenn area is a black run finishing on the outskirts

Davos was one of the original mega-resorts, with slopes on a scale that few resorts can better, even today. But it's a difficult resort to like. You can easily put up with slopes spread over separate mountains, some queue-prone lifts and lots of T-bars if that's the price of staying in a captivating Alpine village. But Davos is far from that.

Whether you forgive the flaws probably depends on how highly you value three plus-points: the distinctive, long runs of the Parsenn area; being able to ski different runs each day; and the off-piste potential. We value all three, and always look forward to visiting. But preferably from a base in Klosters.

THE RESORT

Davos is set in a high, broad, flat-bottomed valley, with its lifts and slopes either side. Arguably it was the very first place in the Alps to develop its slopes. The railway up the Parsenn was one of the first built for skiers (in 1931), and the first drag-lift was built on the Bolgen nursery slopes in 1934. But Davos was already a health resort; many of its luxury hotels were built as sanatoriums.

Sadly, that's just what they look like. There are still several specialist clinics and it is for these, along with its conferences and sporting facilities, that Davos has become well known. The place has the grey, neat, rectilinear feel of a Swiss city rather than the ambience of a mountain village.

It has two main centres, Dorf and Platz, about 2km/1 mile apart. Although transport is good, with buses around the town as well as the railway linking Dorf and Platz to Klosters and other villages, location is important. Easiest access to the slopes is from Dorf to the main Parsenn area, via the funicular railway; Platz is better placed for the Jakobshorn area, the big sports facilities, the smarter shopping and the evening action.

Davos shares its slopes with the famously royal resort of Klosters, which gets its own chapter.

Trips are possible by car or rail to St Moritz (the Vereina rail tunnel offers a hassle-free alternative to the snowy Flüelapass) and Arosa, and by car to Laax-Flims and Lenzerheide.

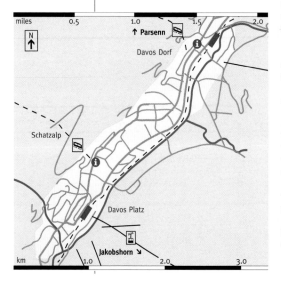

miles	0.5	1.0	1.5	2.0

N ↑

↑ Parsenn

Davos Dorf

Schatzalp

Davos Platz

Jakobshorn ↘

km	1.0	2.0	3.0

KEY FACTS

Resort	1550m
	5,090ft
Slopes	810-2845m
	2,660-9,330ft
Lifts	57
Pistes	305km
	190 miles
Blue	20%
Red	44%
Black	36%
Snowmaking	25km
	16 miles

Although the resort is reachable by train, the trip from Zürich airport involves two changes, and a reader strongly recommends the DavosExpress coach transfer service. Or you can take the new Graubünden Express service from Friedrichshafen airport.

THE MOUNTAINS

The slopes here have something for everyone, though experts and nervous intermediates need to choose their territory with care. Piste classification has been questioned by a 2007 reporter, who felt that there 'did not seem to be much difference between blue and red runs'.

THE SLOPES
Vast and varied
You could hit a different mountain around Davos nearly every day for a week, but the out-of-town areas tend to be much quieter than the ones directly accessible from the resort. Lots of reporters remark on the immaculate grooming of the slopes.

The Parsennbahn funicular from Davos Dorf ends at mid-mountain, where a choice of fast six-pack or old funicular take you on up to the major lift junction of Weissfluhjoch, at one end of the **Parsenn**. The only run back to the valley is a black to the outskirts of Dorf. At the other end of the wide, open Parsenn bowl is Gotschnagrat, reached by cable-car from the centre of Klosters. There are exceptionally long intermediate runs down to Klosters and other villages (see feature panel).

The Strelapass slopes above the hotel at Schatzalp, reached by funicular, closed some years ago.

Across the valley, **Jakobshorn** is reached by cable-car or chair-lift from Davos Platz; this is popular with snowboarders but good for skiers too. **Rinerhorn** and **Pischa** are reached by bus or (in the case of Rinerhorn) train.

Pischa became a designated free-ride area last season, with half the runs left ungroomed (and half the drag-lifts removed). Several of the runs here are now unpatrolled as well as ungroomed – a very unusual arrangement for runs going down beside a lift, and one we don't like.

Beyond the main part of Klosters, a gondola goes up from Klosters Dorf to the sunny, scenic **Madrisa** area.

There are too many T-bars for the comfort of some reporters – Rinerhorn, Pischa and Madrisa have little else. It's time Davos invested in some chairs.

Signposting is generally good, but a 2007 visitor thought the piste map 'confusing' at times. Night-skiing is available at Höhenweg on Fridays (not included on the lift pass).

TERRAIN-PARKS
Lots of choice
All four of the surrounding mountains now have functioning terrain-parks; the main one is the Sunrise park on Jakobshorn – home to the O'Neill Evolution contest. It is open as early as November, weather permitting, and is by far the best in the area. There is a good variety of jumps and rails, and a large number of boxes including a nice C-box. The park, however, is quite narrow and can feel cramped when busy. Two floodlit pipes are the training grounds for a host of Swiss professionals such as Michi Albin, and evening sessions until 9.30pm are popular with locals. For smaller crowds but a less maintained park, head to Pischa; next to the Mitteltäli lift you'll find an array of rails and kickers. If you fancy a bit of argy-bargy, drop in to one of two boarder-cross courses at Parsenn or Madrisa, 200m/660ft below the top station of the Schaffürggli lift. There is also a mini-park for beginners next to the Trainerlift in Rinerhorn.

SNOW RELIABILITY
Good, but not the best
Davos is high by Swiss standards. Its mountains go respectably high, too – though not to glacial heights. Not many of the slopes face directly south, but not many face directly north either. Snow reliability is generally good higher up but can be poor lower down – but in 2007 (considered a poor snow

year) the lower runs were reportedly functional into late March. Snow-guns cover a couple of the upper runs on the Parsenn and several on the Jakobshorn, and the home runs from the Parsenn to Davos Dorf and Klosters. Piste grooming is excellent.

FOR EXPERTS
Plenty to do, on- and off-piste
A glance at the piste map may give the misleading impression that this is an intermediate's resort – there aren't many black runs. It's also true that the few that exist are not particularly testing – and since many are on the steeper, lower, wooded slopes they are prone to closure. But they include some distinctive, satisfying descents. The Meierhofer Tälli run to Wolfgang is

a favourite – 'quite steep and exciting', said a delighted reporter who had found it closed on five previous visits. The run from Parsennhütte to Wolfgang is less challenging, and in the view of one reporter could be red.

What makes the area more interesting in principle is that there are also half a dozen off-piste itineraries – runs that are supposedly marked but not prepared or patrolled. These add up to a lot of expert terrain that in principle can be tackled without expensive guidance (though not alone, of course). But in practice it's not so: a 2007 reporter warns that descending these runs without guidance can be tricky: he found route 13 on Jakobshorn 'was simply not marked – it had no indication about what could

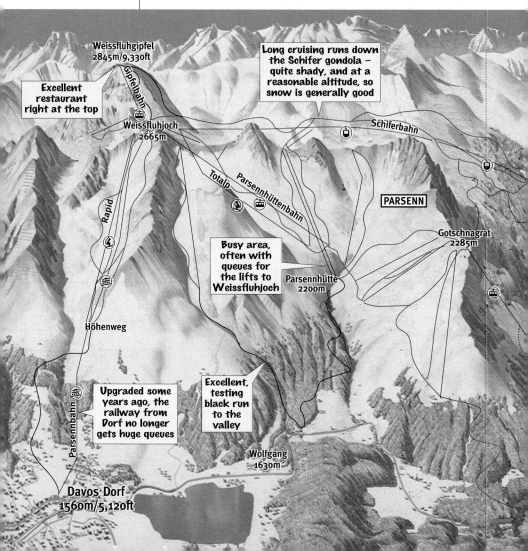

Weissfluhgipfel
2845m/9,330ft

Long cruising runs down the Schifer gondola – quite shady, and at a reasonable altitude, so snow is generally good

Excellent restaurant right at the top

Gipfelbahn

Weissfluhjoch
2665m

Schiferbahn

Totalp

Parsennhüttenbahn

PARSENN

Rapid

Gotschnagrat
2285m

Busy area, often with queues for the lifts to Weissfluhjoch

Parsennhütte
2200m

Höhenweg

Parsennbahn

Upgraded some years ago, the railway from Dorf no longer gets huge queues

Excellent, testing black run to the valley

Wolfgang
1630m

Davos Dorf
1560m/5,120ft

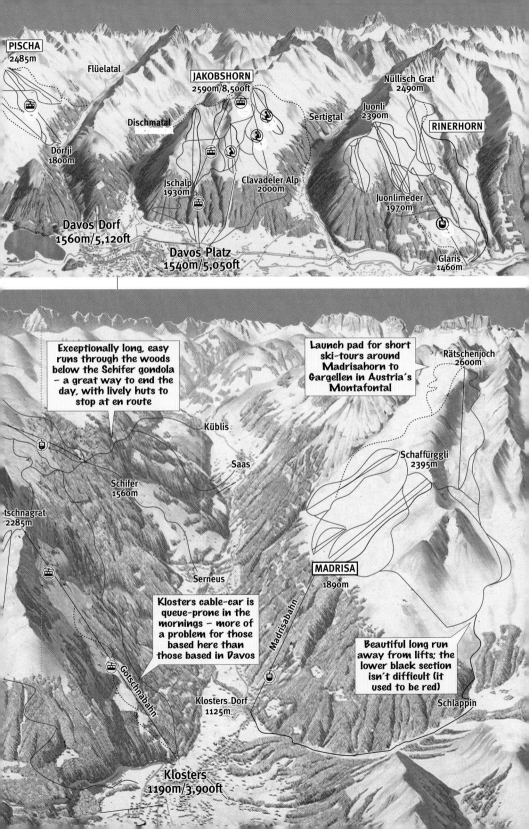

LIFT PASSES

Davos/Klosters

Prices in SF

Age	1-day	6-day
under 13	21	94
13-18	41	189
over 18	61	282

Free under 6

Senior 10% reduction on passes of 3+ days 65+ years (63+ for women); also 1- and 2-day tickets Mon to Fri

Beginner Single and return tickets on main lifts in each area

Notes Covers all Davos and Klosters areas

Alternative passes An array of passes for individual and combined areas (e.g. Parsenn/Gotschna, Jakobshorn, Pischa/Rinerhorn/Madrisa)

GETTING THERE

Air Zürich 160km/ 99 miles (2hr by car, 3hr by rail or bus)

Rail Stations in Davos Dorf and Platz

SWITZERLAND

514

---

be the main ski-route track'. This state of affairs is dangerous and disgraceful, and should be rectified without delay.

There is also excellent 'proper' off-piste terrain, for which guidance is more clearly needed. Two of the steepest routes go from Gotschnagrat down beside the infamous Gotschnawang slope – Drostobel and Chalbersäss. Reporters have also enjoyed heading away from the pistes above Serneus and Küblis. A reader also recommends the long descent from Madrisa to St Antönien, north of Küblis, not least for the 'spectacular views' along the way, returning by bus and train. And there are some short tours to be done. Arosa can be reached with a bit of help from a train or taxi, and from there you can go on to Lenzerheide, but you'll need a train back. From Madrisa you can make tours to Gargellen in Austria.

FOR INTERMEDIATES
A splendid variety of runs
For intermediates this is a great area. There are good cruising runs on all five mountains, so you would never get bored in a week. This variety of different slopes, taken together with the wonderful long runs to the Klosters valley, makes it a compelling area with a unique character.

The epic runs to Klosters and other places (described in the feature panel) pose few difficulties for a confident intermediate or even an ambitious near-beginner. Other notable away-from-the-lifts runs to the valley include one from the top of Madrisa back to Klosters Dorf via the beautiful Schlappin valley (it's an easy black – classified red until the mid-1990s).

The Jakobshorn has some genuine challenges. Rinerhorn is more of a cruise. Pischa is the gentlest of the Davos mountains; now that it has re-branded itself as free-ride territory, it should be a good spot for first attempts at skiing deep snow in safety.

FOR BEGINNERS
Platz is the more convenient
The Bolgen nursery slope beneath the Jakobshorn is adequately spacious and gentle, and a bearable walk from the centre of Platz. But Dorf-based beginners face more of a trek out to Bünda – unless staying at the hotel of the same name. There is no shortage of easy runs to progress to, spread around all the sectors. The Parsenn sector probably has the edge, with long, early intermediate runs in the main Parsenn bowl, as well as in the valleys down from Weissfluhjoch.

FOR CROSS-COUNTRY
Long, scenic valley trails
Davos is a popular spot for langlauf. It has a total of 75km/47 miles of trails running along the main valley and reaching well up into the side valleys of Sertigtal, Dischmatal and Flüelatal. There is a cross-country ski centre and special ski school on the outskirts.

QUEUES
Worst one long gone
Once the scene of some of the longest queues in the Alps, Davos has improved key lifts and now generates relatively few complaints, at least midweek ('none longer than three minutes', insists a March visitor). But there can be queues at peak times. The weekend hot spots mentioned in

SCHOOLS

Swiss Davos
t 416 2454

New Trend
t 413 2040

Top Secret
t 413 2040

inandout snowsports
t 413 0888

Wiesen
t 404 2081

Classes
(Swiss prices)
6 4hr days SF310

Private lessons
Half day SF200

CHILDREN

Kinderland Pischa
t 416 1313
Ages from 3; 11am to
4pm; SF10 per hour

Bobo Club
t 416 2454
Ages 4 to 10; 10am-
noon, 2pm-4pm; SF65
per day

Kinderhotel Muchetta
(at Wiesen)
t 410 4100
Ages from 6mnth

Babysitter list
At tourist office

Ski school
Takes ages 5 to 14 (6
days SF310)

Phone numbers
From elsewhere in
Switzerland add the
prefix 081; from
abroad use the prefix
+41 81

2007 are the cable-car out of Klosters and the Totalp chair on the mountain at Parsenn. Crowded pistes have raised concern again this year – in the Parsenn sector around Weissflühjoch especially. In contrast, the Jakobshorn is said to be 'not very busy at all'.

MOUNTAIN RESTAURANTS
Stay high or go low
The main high-altitude restaurants are dreary self-service affairs – but there are exceptions.
Editors' choice The best is the highest of all: Bruhin's at Weissfluhgipfel (417 6644) – a great place for a hang-the-cost blow-out, with table-service of excellent rustic as well as gourmet dishes, and some knockout desserts.
Worth knowing about The table-service Parsenn Weissflühjoch is also said to be 'particularly good' and the Skihütte Gruobenalp at Gotschnagrat is 'well-liked' with 'friendly table-service'. There are other compelling places lower down in the Parsenn sector. Readers praise the Höhenweg at the Parsennbahn mid-station for 'excellent pizzas' and 'quick service, even when busy'. The rustic 'schwendis' in the woods on the way down to the Klosters valley from the Parsenn still attract crowds. The Chesetta remains popular with its 'super sun terrace' and 'very cosy interior', but gave slow service, says a 2007 visitor. The Alte Conterser Schwendi is 'very friendly with good food'. These are fun places to end up as darkness falls – some sell wax torches for your final descent.
On Jakobshorn the Jatzhütte near the boarders' terrain-park is wild – with changing scenery such as mock palm

trees, parrots and pirates. We have mixed reviews of the 'small and cosy' Chalet Güggel on Jakobshorn: a 2007 reader enjoyed a 'tasty portion of cured meat with asparagus' and 'fast service', while another was less satisfied ('stodgy and uninspiring'). On Pischa, the Mäderbeiz at Flüelamäder is a friendly and spacious woody hut, cheering on a cold day. On Rinerhorn, the Hubelhütte is the best bet.

SCHOOLS AND GUIDES
Decent choice
A reporter says that 'nearly all instructors spoke English and were skilled and friendly — both my kids had a terrific time'. New Trend offers small classes (maximum of six) and Top Secret is their competing snowboard school.

FACILITIES FOR CHILDREN
Not ideal
Davos is a rather spread-out place in which to handle a family. The kids' ski school operates a special Disney-themed slope at Bolgen. A reporter tells us the nursery is 'well organised, but even good instructors sometimes slip into German'.

STAYING THERE

HOW TO GO
Hotels dominate the packages
Although most beds are in apartments, hotels dominate the UK market.
Hotels A dozen 4-stars and about 30 3-stars form the core of the hotel trade, though there are other options. You can book any hotel by calling 415 2121, or use the new online service 'Stay'.

boarding

Davos is now part of the 'top snowboard resort' alliance. In conjunction with Val d'Isère, Ischgl and Madonna di Campiglio, the resort is working toward providing top-quality facilities for sideways sliders. The mountain offers so much in terms of powder, tree runs, natural hits, cliffs and gullies for confident riders. The established boarder mountain is the Jakobshorn with its 'monster-pipes', park and boarder-cross as well as night-riding facilities and funky Jatzhütte. The terrain is vast and will keep any boarder entertained for a long time. The Pischa has a free-ride area with a large chunk of terrain left ungroomed and a new park by the Mitteltäli lift. One reporter says, 'There are no problems with crowds. The powder is amazing, and there are endless kicker-building spots with loads of windlips and cliff drops.' There are wide, mellow slopes for beginners on Parsenn; however, watch out for the flats on the long runs down to the Schifer gondola. Top Secret (www.topsecretdavos.ch) is a specialist snowboard shop and school. There are several cheap hotels geared to snowboarders, notably the 180-bed Bolgenhof near the Jakobshorn, the Snowboardhotel Bolgenschanze and the Snowboarders Palace.

The blocks of Davos have been skilfully kept out of this shot across the valley towards Dischmatal and Jakobshorn ↗

DAVOS TOURISMUS

UK PACKAGES

Alpine Answers, Alpine Weekends, Corporate Ski Co, Crystal, Crystal Finest, Descent International, Flexiski, Headwater, Independent Ski Links, Inghams, Interhome, Kuoni, Made to Measure, Momentum, Ski Freshtracks, Ski Independence, Ski Safari, Ski Solutions, Ski Weekend, SkiGower, Skitracer, Swiss Travel Service, Switzerland Travel Centre, Waymark, White Heat, White Roc

ACTIVITIES

Indoor Fitness centres, tennis, squash, swimming pools, sauna, solarium, massage, wellness centres, ice rink, cinema, casino, galleries, museums, libraries, badminton, golf-driving range, billiards, bridge

Outdoor Over 97km/ 60 miles of cleared paths, ice climbing, snow-shoe trekking, tobogganing, ice rink, curling, horse-riding, sleigh rides, paragliding

TOURIST OFFICE

Davos
t 415 2121
info@davos.ch
www.davos.ch

*****Flüela** (410 1717) The more atmospheric of the 5-star hotels, in central Dorf. Pool.

****Waldhuus** (417 9333) Convenient for langlaufers. Quiet, modern, tasteful. Pool.

****Sunstar Park** (413 1414) At far end of Davos Platz. Pool, sauna, games room. Recommended for 'excellent' food. Spa facilities.

****Meierhof** (416 8285) Close to the Parsenn funicular. 'Large rooms and good food.' Pool, sauna.

***Davoserhof** (414 9020) Our favourite. Small, old, beautifully furnished, with excellent food; well placed in Platz.

***Parsenn** (416 3232) Right opposite the Parsenn railway in Dorf. An attractive chalet marred by the big McDonald's on the ground floor.

***Panorama** (413 2373) In central Platz. Recommended by a 2006 reporter for 'excellent quality and good value' food. Piano bar.

***Hubli's Landhaus** (417 1010) 5km/ 3 miles out at Laret, towards Klosters. Quiet country inn with sophisticated, expensive food that a recent reporter describes as 'really special', and an 'attentive, friendly and helpful' owner.

Alte Post (414 9020) Traditional, cosy; in central Platz. Popular with boarders.

Ochsen (414 9020) Good-value dormitory accommodation.

EATING OUT
Wide choice, mostly in hotels

In a town this size, you need to know where to go – if you just hope to spot a suitable place to eat, you may starve. For a start, get the tourist office's pocket guidebook. The more ambitious restaurants are mostly in hotels. There are two good Chinese restaurants – the lavish Zauberberg in the Europe and the Goldener Drachen in the Bahnhof

Terminus. Good-value places include the jolly Al Ponte (pizza and steak both approved of), the Carretta (good for home-made pasta), the small and cosy Gentiana (with an upstairs stübli), and the Hotel Dischma's Röstizzeria. Excursions out of town are popular. A reporter enjoyed a fondue evening at Höhenweg, but you have to pay to ride the funicular. Schatzalp (also reached by a funicular), the Schneider and the Landhaus in Frauenkirch have also been recommended.

APRES-SKI
Lots on offer, but quiet clientele

There are plenty of bars, discos and nightclubs, and a large casino in the hotel Europe. But we're not sure how some of them make a living – Davos guests tend to want the quiet life. At tea time, mega-calories are consumed at the Weber, and the Schneider might be worth a look. The Scala (hotel Europa) has a popular outside terrace. The liveliest place in town is the rustic little Chämi bar (popular with locals); it has 'the best atmosphere later in the evening', according to a reporter. The smart Ex-Bar attracts a mixed age group. Nightclubs tend to be sophisticated, expensive and lacking atmosphere during the week. The most popular are the Cabanna and the Cava Davos (both in the hotel Europe), the Rotliechtli, and Paulaner's. Bolgenschanze and Bolgen-Plaza are popular boarder hang-outs.

OFF THE SLOPES
Great, apart from the buildings

Looks aside, Davos can be recommended for those not planning to hit the slopes. The towny resort has shops and other diversions, and transport along the valley and up on to the slopes is good – though the best of the mountain restaurants are well out of range. The sports facilities are excellent; Europe's biggest natural ice rink is supplemented by artificial rinks, both indoor and outdoor. Spectator events include speed skating as well as 'hugely popular' ice hockey – enjoyed by a reporter. And there are lots of walks on the slopes as well as around the lake and along the valleys. There's a toboggan run on Rinerhorn, floodlit twice weekly, but the best in the area is the longer run on Madrisa, at Klosters. The refurbished Eau-là-là leisure centre incorporates new pools and wellness facilities.

Grindelwald

Traditional resort in a spectacular setting – better for scenery-gazing than bashing the pistes, thanks to slow lifts and dodgy snow-cover

COSTS

① ② ③ ④ ⑤ ⑥

RATINGS

The slopes

Fast lifts	****
Snow	**
Extent	***
Expert	**
Intermediate	****
Beginner	***
Convenience	**
Queues	**
Mountain restaurants	***

The rest

Scenery	*****
Resort charm	****
Off-slope	****

NEWS

For Kleine Scheidegg in 2007/08 the Honegg drag is to be replaced with a fast six-pack, and substantial snowmaking for the upper part of the mountain is planned.

MADE *to* MEASURE SKI

Tailor-made specialists & Expert knowledge

01243 533 333
mtmhols.co.uk
ATOL 2856

➕ Dramatically set in magnificent scenery, directly beneath the towering north face of the Eiger

➕ Lots of long, gentle runs, ideal for intermediates, with links to Wengen

➕ Pleasant old village with long mountaineering history

➕ Fair amount to do off the slopes, including splendid walks

➖ Main slopes accessed by a painfully slow, queue-prone (especially at weekends) gondola or by slow trains

➖ Few challenging pistes for experts

➖ Inconvenient for visiting Mürren

➖ Snow-cover unreliable and snowmaking insufficient

➖ Village gets very little midwinter sun

For stunning views from the town and the slopes, there are few places to rival Grindelwald. The village is nowhere near as special as Mürren or Wengen, just over the hill, but staying here does give you direct access to Grindelwald's own First slopes. But you can spend ages queueing for, waiting for or sitting in the gondola or trains up into the slopes (and back down if snow is poor). (The gondola ride – the longest in Europe according to Grindelwald's literature – takes half an hour. The train to Kleine Scheidegg from Grindelwald takes about the same.) Grindelwald regulars accept all this as part of the scene.

THE RESORT

Grindelwald is set either side of a road along a narrow valley. Buildings are mainly traditional chalet style. Towering mountains rise steeply from the valley floor, and the resort and main slopes get very little sun in January.

Grindelwald can feel very jolly at times, such as during the ice-carving festival in January, when huge ice sculptures are on display along the main street. The village is livelier at night than the other Jungfrau resorts of Wengen and Mürren. There's live music in several bars and hotels, but it isn't a place for bopping until dawn.

The main lifts into the slopes shared with Wengen are at Grund, right at the bottom of the sloping village. Near the opposite end of the village, a gondola goes to the separate First area. Trains run from the centre to Grund or direct to Kleine Scheidegg, and buses link the lift stations – but these get congested at times and reporters say they are too infrequent.

The most convenient place to stay for the slopes is at Grund. But this is out of the centre and rather charmless. There's a wide range of hotels in the heart of the village, handy enough for everything else, including the First area, at the foot of which are nursery slopes, ski school and kindergarten.

Trips to other resorts are not very easy, but you can drive to Adelboden. Getting to the tougher, higher slopes of Mürren is a lengthy business unless you go to Lauterbrunnen by car.

THE MOUNTAINS

The major area of slopes is shared with Wengen and offers a mix of wooded slopes and open slopes higher up. The smaller First area is mainly open, though there are wooded runs to the village.

THE SLOPES
Broad and mainly gentle
From Grund, near the western end of town, you can get to **Männlichen** by an appallingly slow two-stage gondola or to **Kleine Scheidegg** by an equally slow cog railway. The slopes of the separate south-facing **First** area are

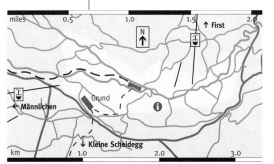

miles	0.5		1.0		1.5		2.0

↑ First

N ↑

Männlichen

Grund   ℹ

Kleine Scheidegg

km		1.0		2.0		3.0

KEY FACTS

Resort	1035m
	3,400ft

Jungfrau region	
Slopes	945-2970m
	3,100-9,740ft
Lifts	44
Pistes	213km
	132 miles
Blue	25%
Red	61%
Black	14%
Snowmaking	57km
	35 miles

First-Männlichen-Kleine-Scheidegg	
Slopes	945-2485m
	3,100-8,150ft
Lifts	28
Pistes	160km
	99 miles

LIFT PASSES

Jungfrau Top Ski Region

Prices in SF

Age	1-day	6-day
under 16	29	148
16 to 19	46	236
20 to 61	57	295
over 62	51	266

Free under 6
Beginner points card
Notes
Covers Wengen, Mürren and Grindelwald, trains between them and Grindelwald ski-bus; day pass price is for First-Kleine Scheidegg-Männlichen area only
Alternative passes
Grindelwald and Wengen only; Mürren only; non-skier pass

reached by a long, slow gondola starting a bus-ride east of the centre.

From all over the slopes there are superb views, not only of the Eiger but also of the Wetterhorn and other peaks. Piste marking is poor; several reporters found the Männlichen slopes, in particular, confusing ('marking is non-existent'). The piste map is clear, but huge.

TERRAIN-PARKS
First things first
There is a terrain-park on First with rails, boxes and jumps, a super-pipe and a boarder-cross course.

SNOW RELIABILITY
Poor
Grindelwald's low altitude and the lack of much snowmaking mean this is not a resort to book far in advance or for a late-season holiday. First is sunny, and so even less snow-sure than the main area. 2007 was a bad year for snow, and one reporter says that she didn't ski at all on her long weekend ('just a few bare runs open'); others found key runs closed and had to download at the end of the day ('virtually no snow below 1400m'). We have also had reports of 'patchy' piste grooming.

FOR EXPERTS
They are trying
The area is quite limited for experts, but there is some fine off-piste if the snow is good. Heli-trips with mountain guides are organised. The black run on First beneath the gondola back to town is quite tough, especially when the snow has suffered from the sun.

FOR INTERMEDIATES
Ideal intermediate terrain
In good snow, First makes a splendid intermediate playground, though the general lack of trees makes the area less friendly than the larger Kleine Scheidegg-Männlichen area. The runs to the valley are great fun. Nearly all the runs from Kleine Scheidegg are long blues or gentle reds. On the Männlichen there's a choice of gentle runs down to the mid-station of the gondola – and in good snow, down to the bottom. For tougher pistes, head for the top of the Lauberhorn lift and the runs to Kleine Scheidegg, or to Wixi (following the start of the downhill course). The north-facing run from Eigergletscher to Salzegg often has the best snow late in the season.

FOR BEGINNERS
Depends where you go
The Bodmi nursery slope at the bottom of First is scenic but not particularly convenient, according to a recent reporter who says, 'The chore of getting to and from it with small children was too much.' It can also suffer from the sun and its low altitude – a recent reporter said Grindelwald instructors used it despite it being icy, full of craters and spoiled by fast skiers and tobogganers racing through. A section of the Oberjoch blue run at First is a designated slow speed zone. Kleine Scheidegg has a better, higher beginner area and splendid, long runs to progress to, served by the railway.

FOR CROSS-COUNTRY
Good but shady
There are 17km/10 miles of prepared tracks. Almost all of this is on the valley floor, so it's shady in midwinter and may have poor snow later on.

QUEUES
Can be dreadful
We still receive mixed reports on queues. Waiting times for the gondola and train at Grund can be very bad in high season, especially at weekends – partly because children up to 15 can ski free on Saturday if a parent buys a day pass. Some reporters have told of half-hour waits for the gondola, which then takes a further half-hour to get to the top – a 2007 reporter experienced not only this but 'big queues to download at the end of the day', too, when the lower runs were closed.

MOUNTAIN RESTAURANTS
Wide choice
See the Wengen chapter for options around Kleine Scheidegg and down towards Wengen. Brandegg, on the railway, is recommended for 'wonderful' apple fritters and its sunny terrace; Berghaus Bort does 'very good Alpler macaroni'. The table-service restaurant at the Berggasthaus at the top of the Männlichen has splendid views, and a 2007 reporter says that 'the fillet of beef on toast was a highlight' and that the self-service section does good 'home-made hamburgers'. Other reader recommendations are the Jägerstubli, off the Rennstrecke piste, and the Berghaus Aspen, above Grund. The Spycher has a cosy indoor bar plus deckchairs and an ice-bar, which also serves sandwiches. At First, Café

boarding

Intermediates will enjoy the area most – the beginners' slopes can be bare, while experts will hanker for Mürren's steep, off-piste slopes. First is the main boarders' mountain, not only because of the terrain-park and big pipe but also because of the open free-ride terrain accessed via the top lifts. There are quite a few drags.

Genepi, at the bottom of the Oberjoch chair, is 'a must' for Flammenkuchen (thin pizza) and a good place to begin your après-ski, says a recent visitor.

SCHOOLS AND GUIDES
Mixed views

Recent reports declare the main school, Grindelwald Sports, 'very good'; spoken English is normally excellent. But one reporter had a 'wasted' first day, because abilities were not assessed before the class. However, 'the teachers (three in three days!) were excellent'. The Privat school offers off-piste guiding.

FACILITIES FOR CHILDREN
Good reputation

See above, but a past reporter who put four children through the Grindelwald mill praised caring and effective instructors. 'Faultless' was the verdict from a recent reporter, but he found the First area to be inconvenient and busy for families with small children. The First mountain restaurant runs a day nursery, which is a neat idea, and the Sunshine nursery is at the top of Männlichen.

STAYING THERE

HOW TO GO
Limited range of packages

The hotels UK tour operators offer are mainly at the upper end of the market.
Hotels There's a 5-star, a dozen 4-stars and plenty of more modest places.
*****Grand Regina (854 8600) Big and imposing; right next to the station. Nightly music in the piano bar. A 2007 reporter found it 'expensive but friendly, with good food, pool and amazing spa'. Another praised its 'excellent food and superb service'.
****Belvedere (854 5757) 100 years old, family-run, close to the station. 'Wonderful' pool. Recommended by a recent visitor on his fifth stay.
****Schweizerhof (854 5858) Chalet at west end of the centre, close to the station. Pool.
****Spinne (854 8888) Central. A reporter 'cannot praise it enough: friendly, superb food, good rooms'.
***Hirschen (854 8484) Family-run; by nursery slopes. Good food.
***Derby (854 5461) Popular, modern, next to station, with 'first-class' service, good food and great views.
***Eigerblick (854 1020) A bit away

Grindelwald

519

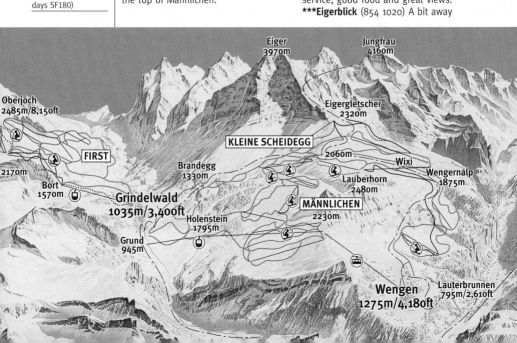

The ski area has spectacular views of these mountains: the Eiger, the Mönch and the Jungfrau →

UK PACKAGES

Alpine Answers, Corporate Ski Co, Crystal, Elegant Resorts, Independent Ski Links, Inghams, Interhome, Kuoni, Made to Measure, Momentum, Powder Byrne, Ski Freshtracks, Swiss Travel Service, Switzerland Travel Centre, Thomson, White Roc

+switzerland travel centre

Ski packages
Short breaks
Flexible dates
Tailor made
16 resorts
300 hotels
and more

Call the Swiss Specialists:

0207 420 4932
www.stc.co.uk

Atol 4013 ABTA 1432

GETTING THERE

Air Zürich 195km/ 121 miles (3hr); Bern 70km/43 miles (1½hr)

Rail Station in resort

ACTIVITIES

Indoor Sports centre (pool, sauna, steam, fitness), ice rink, bowling, curling, concerts, cinema

Outdoor 80km/ 50 miles of cleared paths, ice rink, tobogganing, snow-shoeing, climbing, snow cycling, tubing, paragliding, glacier tours, sleigh rides

Phone numbers
From elsewhere in Switzerland add 033. From abroad use the prefix +41 33.

TOURIST OFFICE

t 854 1212
touristcenter@ grindelwald.ch
www.grindelwald.com

from the station but 'great service, including free taxi'. Huge bedrooms. ***Wetterhorn** (853 1218) Cosy, simple chalet way beyond the village, with great views of the glacier.
Apartments Readers have recommended those in the Hirschen and Eiger hotels.

EATING OUT
Hotel based
There's a wide choice of good hotel restaurants. Among the more traditional places are: Bistro-Bar Memory in the Eiger; Schmitte in the Schweizerhof; Challi-Stübli in the Kreuz ('good meal and atmosphere'); and the Alte Post. The Fiescherblick's Swiss Bistro is 'brilliant but expensive'. The Kirchbühl and Oberland are good for vegetarians. Hotel Spinne has many options: Italian, Mexican, Chinese, and – for a special romantic meal – the candlelit Rôtisserie. The C&M Cafe und Mehr is 'well priced and friendly'. Onkle Tom's Hütte is recommended for pizza. The Latino does Italian home cooking.

APRES-SKI
Getting livelier
Tipirama at Kleine Scheidegg is a fun place immediately after skiing ('vibrant and welcoming'), sometimes with DJs and live bands. Pumuckl's offers a similar experience on First. For 'unforgettable' speciality coffees try the Rancher bar, says a recent reporter. The Holzer bar is also suggested as a

good drinking spot on the way down to Grund. In town, the terrace of the C&M Café und Mehr is good for coffee and cake. A handful of bars aim to keep going late. The Espresso bar in the Spinne hotel seems to be the liveliest and the Hotel Eiger has a couple of choices. From there, people head for the Mascelero club.

OFF THE SLOPES
Plenty to do, easy to get around
There are many cleared paths with magnificent views, especially around First – and there's a special (though expensive) pedestrian bus/lift pass. Many of the mountain huts are accessible to pedestrians. A trip to Jungfraujoch is spectacular (see below), and excursions by train are easy to Interlaken. There are 70km/43 miles of toboggan runs, including the world's longest (15km/9 miles) – but it's a two-and-a-half-hour uphill walk from the top of the gondola on First. There's a cinema, ice hockey and curling to watch and an excellent sports centre with pool. Helicopter flights from Männlichen are recommended.

STAYING UP THE MOUNTAIN
Several possibilities
See the Wengen chapter for details of rooms at Kleine Scheidegg. The Berghaus Bort (854 4099), at the gondola station in the middle of the First area, is an attractive alternative.

THE JOURNEY TO THE TOP OF EUROPE

From Kleine Scheidegg you can take a train through the Eiger to the highest railway station in Europe – Jungfraujoch at 3450m/11,320ft. The journey is a bit tedious – you're in a tunnel except when you stop to look out of two galleries carved into the sheer north face of the Eiger – magnificent views over to Männlichen, and then over the glacier. At the top is a big restaurant complex. There's an 'ice palace' carved out of the glacier and a viewing tower with fabulous views of the Aletsch glacier (a UNESCO World Heritage Site).

The cost is SF52 with a Jungfrau lift pass for three days or more.

Ski the extensive slopes of Davos from a traditional village base – with Davos traffic at last banished to a bypass

COSTS

① ② ③ ④ ⑤ ⑥

RATINGS

The slopes

Fast lifts	★★★
Snow	★★★★
Extent	★★★★★
Expert	★★★★
Intermediate	★★★★★
Beginner	★★★
Convenience	★★
Queues	★★
Mountain restaurants	★★★

The rest

Scenery	★★★★
Resort charm	★★★★
Off-slope	★★★★

NEWS

For 2006/07 a small hotel, the Sport-Lodge, opened in Platz, and the Bad Serneus hotel re-opened following renovations. Pischa, above Davos, was designated a free-ride mountain (see Davos chapter).

For 2007/08 the cross-country trails will be free to use.

KLOSTERS TOURIST OFFICE

There are good off-piste opportunities in all sectors ↓

- ➕ Splendid, long, intermediate runs back to the village from the Parsenn
- ➕ Lots of accessible off-piste terrain
- ➕ Some cute mountain restaurants
- ➕ Pleasant traditional village, now bypassed by the valley traffic
- ➕ Very extensive slopes, shared with Davos, but ...

- ➖ The slopes are spread over five widely separated areas
- ➖ Preponderance of T-bars is a problem for some visitors
- ➖ Queue-prone cable-car into the main Parsenn area

In a word association game, 'Klosters' might trigger 'Prince of Wales'. The resort has even named its queue-prone cable-car after him. Don't be put off: Klosters is not particularly exclusive, and it does have a lot going for it.

The relaxed, chalet-style village has always been an attractive alternative to staying in towny Davos, and has become more so since the bypass, opened for 2005/06, removed the intrusive Davos and Vereina tunnel traffic from the village. It is far from traffic-free, but pedestrians no longer go in fear of their lives.

THE RESORT

Klosters is a comfortable, quiet village with a much more appealing Alpine flavour than Davos. Klosters Platz is the main focus – a collection of upmarket, traditional-style hotels around the railway station, at the foot of the steep, wooded slopes of Gotschna. Traffic bound for Davos and the Vereina car-carrying rail tunnel, an acute problem, was removed by the opening of a bypass two years ago. The village spreads along the valley road for quite a way before fading into the countryside; there's then a second concentration of building in the even quieter village of Klosters Dorf, at the base of the gondola to Madrisa.

THE MOUNTAINS

Most of the runs are on open slopes above steeper woodland.

Slopes A cable-car from the railway station in Platz takes you to the Gotschnagrat end of the Parsenn area shared with Davos, and a gondola from Dorf takes you up to the scenic Madrisa area. There's also a little slope at Selfranga, a suburb of Platz.

Terrain-parks The Madrisa area has a boarder-cross course, and there are more options on the other mountains. The Selfranga area also has a park, which is floodlit in the evenings.

Snow reliability It's usually good higher up, but the home runs are quite low and not so reliable.

Experts The extensive off-piste possibilities are the main appeal. There are several itineraries – see Davos.

Intermediates There are excellent cruising runs in all five ski areas.

Beginners There is a slope between Dorf and Platz, plus Selfranga; but the slopes of Madrisa are more appealing.

Snowboarding Local slopes are good, but more boarders stay in Davos.

Cross-country There are 35km/22 miles of trails and lots more up at Davos; a Nordic ski school offers lessons. Trails will be free to use for 2007/08.

Queues Queues for the Gotschna cable-car can be a problem at weekends and peak times. The Madrisa gondola was upgraded for 2005/06.

521

KEY FACTS

Resort	1190m
	3,900ft
Slopes	810-2845m
	2,660-9,330ft
Lifts	57
Pistes	305km
	190 miles
Green	20%
Blue	44%
Black	36%
Snowmaking	25 km
	16 miles

UK PACKAGES

Alpine Answers, Crystal Finest, Descent International, Flexiski, Inghams, Kuoni, Made to Measure, Momentum, Oxford Ski Co, Powder Byrne, Ski Freshtracks, Ski Independence, Ski Safari, Ski Solutions, Ski Weekend, Snow Finders, Swiss Travel Service, Switzerland Travel Centre, White Heat, White Roc

Phone numbers
From elsewhere in Switzerland add 081; from abroad use the prefix +41 81

TOURIST OFFICE

t 410 2020
info@klosters.ch
www.klosters.ch

Mountain restaurants There are a number of atmospheric huts in the woods above the village – see Davos chapter. The restaurants on the Madrisa slopes are 'disappointing'.
Schools and guides There is a choice of three ski and snowboard schools. Saas receives favourable reports for 'excellent English-speaking instructors' and 'great fun' private lessons.
Facilities for children The ski schools offer 'excellent' classes for children, and the Madrisa Kids' Land takes two to six year olds.

STAYING THERE

How to go There is a wide choice of packages offered by UK tour operators.
Hotels There are some particularly attractive hotels. For most people, central Platz is the best location. Here, the smart Chesa Grischuna (422 2222) combines traditional atmosphere with modern comfort – and a lively après-ski bar. The readers' favourite is the 'wonderful' Alpina (410 2424) – 'friendly and helpful staff' and 'excellent spa facilities'. The 2-star Bündnerhof (422 1450), 400m/1,300ft from the train/lift station, provides 'extremely good value' half-board. Next door, the very cosy old Wynegg (422 1340) is a perennial British favourite. In Dorf, the Sunstar Albeina (423 2100) is not particularly convenient but is cheaper than the other 4-stars, has a good spa and is 'friendly, with good food', says a fourth-time visitor. The Sport (423 3030) is 'pleasant with good facilities', and the Sport-Lodge (422 1256) is new in Platz.

Apartments Apartments are available through local agencies.
Eating out Good restaurants abound, but a reporter comments that there is a shortage of the cheap and cheerful variety. Top of the range is the Walserhof, with two Michelin stars – 'by far the best in the area', says a 2007 visitor. Al Berto's serves 'wonderful' pizza, and the Alpina is recommended. The Casanna at Platz serves 'excellent steaks', and the Chesa Grischuna is recommended for 'fabulous venison' and good wines at moderate prices. Fellini's pizzeria is 'child-friendly'.
Après-ski In the village, the Chesa Grischuna is a focus from tea-time onwards, with its live music and its restaurant. A reporter enjoyed the music 'at a volume that allowed you to converse'. Gaudy's at the foot of the slopes is a popular stop after skiing 'if you're happy to drink in a tent', as is the lively bar at the 4-star Alpina and the warmly panelled Wynegg. The 'popular' Gotschna bar, near the base station, is 'friendly' and colourful inside. The Rossli bar is a 'nicely busy' place to watch sport on TV.
The Casa Antica is a small disco that livens up on Saturday night.
Off the slopes Klosters is an attractive base for walking and cross-country skiing, and tobogganing is popular – there is an exceptional 8.5km/5 mile run from Madrisa to Saas. A 2006 reporter recommends the return hike from Schifer ('a nice adventure'). There is a leisure centre with an ice rink, and some hotel pools are open. You can take the train to the interesting old town of Chur.

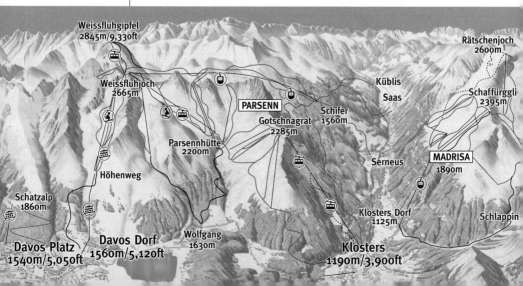

Weissfluhgipfel 2845m/9,330ft
Rätschenjoch 2600m
Weissfluhjoch 2665m
Küblis
Saas
Schaffürggli 2395m
PARSENN
Schifer 1560m
Gotschnagrat 2285m
Parsennhütte 2200m
MADRISA 1890m
Serneus
Höhenweg
Schatzalp 1860m
Klosters Dorf 1125m
Schlappin
Davos Platz 1540m/5,050ft
Davos Dorf 1560m/5,120ft
Wolfgang 1630m
Klosters 1190m/3,900ft

Pleasant, unremarkable villages – but blessed with high, wide, sunny, varied slopes that deserve to be more widely known

RATINGS

The slopes

Fast lifts	****
Snow	***
Extent	****
Expert	***
Intermediate	*****
Beginner	****
Convenience	***
Queues	****
Mountain restaurants	***

The rest

Scenery	***
Resort charm	***
Off-slope	***

KEY FACTS

Resort	1100m
	3,610ft
Altitude	1100-3020m
	3,610-9,910ft
Lifts	27
Pistes	220km
	137 miles
Blue	29%
Red	32%
Black	39%
Snowmaking	13km
	8 miles

+ Extensive, varied slopes ideal for intermediates, shared with Flims

+ Impressive lift system with few queues most of the time

– Sunny orientation can cause icy or slushy pistes and bare lower runs

– Long walks or bus-rides from some lodgings

– Weekend crowds in high season

Sorry if you have been looking under 'F': the resort formerly known as Flims has re-branded itself. The place gets the minor-resort treatment here because hardly anyone from the UK goes there, but it is clearly a major resort – with 220km/137 miles of piste, one of the biggest in Switzerland.

THE RESORT

Laax – now apparently to be called Laax Dorf – is a quiet holiday village with pleasant suburbs spreading around a lake. Just outside it is a big, busy lift base/parking/hotel complex, formerly Murschetg but now known (for skiing purposes, at least) as Laax. Clear so far? Good!

The slopes spread across to the more towny two-part resort of Flims. Flims Dorf, the main village and lift base, spreads along a busy road – but a bypass tunnel is expected to open for 2007/08. Flims Waldhaus is a leafy suburb with the smart hotels (which run courtesy buses to the lifts).

A third alternative base is Falera – a small, quiet, though much-expanded rustic village in an isolated spot at the foot of its own fast chair-lift.

THE MOUNTAINS

The villages share extensive, varied slopes beneath high, exposed peaks, with a small glacier. There are some tree-lined runs. Road-trips are possible to Lenzerheide, Klosters and Arosa.

The resort piste map shows 'free-ride routes' without explaining whether they are avalanche-protected, and patrolled. Apparently they are both.
Slopes There are powerful gondolas going into the heart of the slopes from both Flims Dorf and Laax (alongside a cable-car of exceptional length). Above mid-mountain, there is a complex web of lifts and runs. A six-pack serves the main Flims slopes below La Siala. The glacier offers limited vertical, but also accesses a superb black run away from the lifts to Alp Ruschein – 1250m/4,100ft vertical. Some chairs (eg to

523

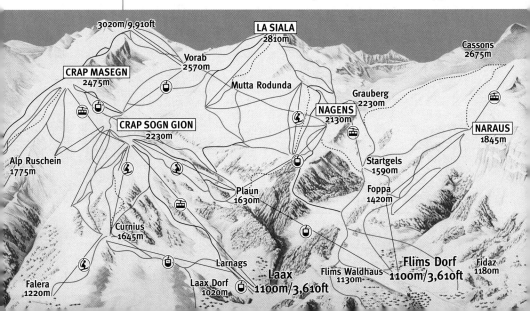

NEWS

A tunnel bypassing
Flims is due to open
in October 2007.

Construction is due
to start on a new
1,000-bed hotel
complex at Laax.

UK PACKAGES

*Alpine Answers, Snow
Finders, Switzerland
Travel Centre*
Flims *Alpine Answers,
Corporate Ski Co,
Interhome, Made to
Measure, Momentum,
Powder Byrne, Ski
Safari, Ski Weekend,
Skitracer, Swiss Travel
Service, Switzerland
Travel Centre, White
Roc*

Phone numbers
From elsewhere in
Switzerland add the
prefix 081; from
abroad use the prefix
+41 81

TOURIST OFFICE

**For Flims, Laax and
Falera**
t 920 9200
info@
flimslaaxfalera.ch
www.laax.com

Naraus) are designed for walkers – skis
are taken off. Classification of runs
often overstates difficulty.

Terrain-parks The 'very impressive'
terrain-park at Crap Sogn Gion is
claimed to be Europe's best, with
drops, jumps, rails for all levels and a
boarder-cross – plus, it seems,
Europe's largest and smallest pipes.
The competition half-pipe has walls up
to 6.7m/22ft and there's a new mini-
pipe. The park has its own drag-lift.
There's a second half-pipe on the
glacier.

Snow reliability Upper runs are fairly
snow-sure, but those back to Flims can
suffer from sun. The runs from Cassons
and the black from the glacier are both
prone to closure. Snowmaking is
limited, and not shown on the piste
map. 'Excellent' grooming.

Experts The few black pistes are not
seriously steep except in patches, but
the 'free-ride routes' add an extra
dimension and there is abundant off-
piste terrain too. In such a sunny area,
timing your runs can be crucial to
avoid rock-hard moguls.

Intermediates This is a superb area for
all intermediates. Reporters are
genuinely surprised by the extent and
length of the slopes. The bowl below
La Siala is huge and gentle. For the
more adventurous and confident, there
are plenty of reds and some blacks
worth trying. The sheltered Grauberg
valley is a favourite – long and fast.
The long black Sattel run from the
glacier is challenging only at the top.
The men's World Cup Downhill piste
from Crap Sogn Gion to Larnags is
often beautifully groomed.

Beginners There are nursery lifts up
the mountain at Crap Sogn Gion and
Nagens – shown as 'L' on the piste
map. The Foppa and Curnius areas
have good, easy runs to move on to.

Snowboarding This is a snowboard
hot-spot. The park and pipes on Crap
Sogn Gion have loud music from the
adjacent bars. Regular high-profile
competitions are held here. There's
good free-riding to be had.

Cross-country There are 60km/37 miles
of trails scattered around.

Queues Queues are generally rare, but
getting out of the villages at the
weekend can be a slow process, and
there may be long waits for the
isolated return chair at Alp Ruschein –
the only slow chair remaining (though
there are a few drags). High winds can
close the exposed upper lifts.

Mountain restaurants Sadly, only about
one-third of the 17 restaurants are now
described on the piste map. There are
some stylish modern table-service
places at altitude – Das Elephant and
Capalari. Reporters love the Alpenrose
(Startgels) by the Grauberg cable-car
('glorious views', 'excellent grills').
Tegia Curnius is newly refurbished with
panoramic windows and cosy fireplace.
Lower down are the smartly rustic
Tegia Larnags and cosy Runcahöhe
(popular with walkers as well).

Schools and guides Reporters have
'progressed very well' in group and
private lessons, and in kids' classes.

Facilities for children Children aged
three and over can be looked after at
one of three Kinderland centres. And
there is a Kids Village in the ski
school. Nannies are available.

STAYING THERE

How to go Only a handful of UK tour
operators feature Laax or Flims.

Hotels At Laax lift-base the high-tech
Riders Palace (927 9700) is a trendy
place to stay – with dorm as well as
normal rooms. The village of Laax
Dorf offers the charming little Posta
Veglia (921 4466). In Flims Waldhaus a
2006 reporter enjoyed the Adula (928
2828) ('good spa facilities'). The award-
winning Park Hotel (928 4848) has an
ultra-modern wellness centre. And in
Flims Dorf the Vorab (911 1861) is close
to the lifts and highly praised by a
2006 reporter for 'excellent food', and
the Cresta (911 3535) is 'good value
with excellent spa facilities'.

Apartments The tourist office has a
long list of available apartments.

Eating out Most restaurants are in
hotels. In Laax Dorf the Posta Veglia
does excellent food in a lovely old
stube, and in a plainer restaurant
behind. In Flims, reporters recommend
the Alpina, the Vorab and the Adula
('best gourmet restaurant in the area');
Little China (Park hotel) and Caverna
(Bellevue) have also been suggested.

Après-ski Bars at both main lift bases
get packed at close of play – the Iglu
bar is popular. Later on, the villages
are pretty quiet. In Flims Dorf, the
Legna bar is recommended as is the
'cosy' Segnes wine bar. Casa Veglia, in
Laax Dorf has live bands.

Off the slopes There's an enormous
sports centre on the edge of Flims,
with ice rink, and 60km/37 miles of
marked walks. Shopping is limited.

Mürren

The dinky, car-free mountain village where the British invented downhill ski racing; stupendous views from one epic run

➕ Tiny, charming, traditional village, with 'traffic-free' snowy paths

➕ Stupendous scenery, best enjoyed descending from the Schilthorn

➕ Good sports centre

➕ Good snow high up, even when the rest of the region is suffering

➖ Extent of local pistes very limited, no matter what your level of expertise

➖ Lower slopes can be in poor condition

➖ Quiet, limited nightlife

Mürren is one of our favourite resorts. There may be other mountain villages that are equally pretty, but none of them enjoys views like those from Mürren across the deep valley to the rock faces and glaciers of the Eiger, Mönch and Jungfrau: simply breathtaking. Then there's the Schilthorn run – 1300m/4,270ft vertical with an unrivalled combination of varied terrain and glorious views.

But our visits are normally one-day affairs; holidaymakers, we concede, are likely to want to explore the extensive intermediate slopes of Wengen and Grindelwald, across the valley. And that takes time.

It was in Mürren that the British more or less invented modern skiing. Sir Arnold Lunn organised the first ever slalom race here in 1922. Some 12 years earlier his father, Sir Henry, had persuaded the locals to open the railway in winter so that he could bring the first winter package tour here. Sir Arnold's son Peter has been a regular visitor since he first skied here in November 1916.

THE RESORT

Mürren is set on a shelf high above the valley floor, across from Wengen, and can be reached only by cable-car from Stechelberg (via Gimmelwald) or from Lauterbrunnen (via Grütschalp where you change to catch a train). You can't fail to be struck by Mürren's beauty and tranquillity. Paths and narrow lanes weave between little wooden chalets and a handful of bigger hotel buildings – all normally blanketed by snow.

A two-stage cable-car takes you up to the high slopes of Birg and the Schilthorn. Nearby lifts go to the main lower slopes, and a funicular halfway along the village accesses others.

Mürren's traffic-free status is being somewhat eroded; there are now a few delivery trucks. But it still isn't plagued by electric carts and taxis in the way that many other traditional 'traffic-free' resorts are, and reporters are generally very impressed with the place.

It's not the place to go for lively nightlife, shopping or showing off your latest gear to admiring hordes. It is the place to go if you want tranquillity and stunning views. The village is so small that location is not a concern. Nothing is more than a few minutes' walk.

KEY FACTS

| Resort | 1650m |
| | 5,410ft |

Jungfrau region	
Altitude	945-2970m
	3,100-9,740ft
Lifts	44
Pistes	213km
	132 miles
Blue	25%
Red	61%
Black	14%
Snowmaking	57km
	35 miles

Mürren-Schilthorn only	
Slopes	1650-2970m
	5,410-9,740ft
Lifts	12
Pistes	53km
	33 miles

LIFT PASSES

Jungfrau Top Ski Region

Prices in SF

Age	1-day	6-day
under 16	29	148
16 to 19	46	236
20 to 61	57	295
over 62	51	266

Free under 6

Beginner points card

Notes
Covers Wengen, Mürren and Grindelwald, trains between them and Grindelwald ski-bus; day pass price is for Mürren-Schilthorn area only

Alternative passes
Grindelwald and Wengen only; Mürren only; non-skier pass

THE MOUNTAIN

Mürren's slopes aren't extensive (53km/33 miles in total). But it has something for everyone, including a vertical of some 1300m/4,270ft. And those happy to take the time to cross the valley to Wengen-Grindelwald will find plenty of options.

THE SLOPES
Small but interesting

There are three connected areas around the village, reaching no higher than 2145m/7,040ft. The biggest is **Schiltgrat**, served by a fast quad chair behind the cable-car station. A funicular goes from the middle of the village to the nursery slope at **Allmendhubel** – from where a run and a fast chair take you to the slightly higher **Maulerhubel**. Runs go down from here to Winteregg, on the railway.

Much more interesting are the higher slopes reached by cable-car to **Birg**. Below Birg, the Engetal area now has the new Riggli quad ('A great improvement on the old T-bar,' says a regular visitor), serving short, steep, shady slopes and a new black mogul run. Two chair-lifts below this serve some snow-sure intermediate slopes. The final stage of the cable-car takes you up to the Schilthorn and its revolving restaurant, made famous by the James Bond film *On Her Majesty's Secret Service*. In good snow you can ski down to Lauterbrunnen – almost 16km/10 miles and 2175m/7,140ft. The Inferno race (see separate box) takes place over this course, snow permitting. Below Winteregg, it's all boring paths.

TERRAIN-PARKS
Affirmative

There is a terrain-park and half-pipe on the lower slopes of Schiltgrat.

SNOW RELIABILITY
Good on the upper slopes

The Jungfrau region does not have a good snow record – but Mürren always has the best snow in the area. When Wengen-Grindelwald (and Mürren's lower slopes) have problems, the Schilthorn and Engetal often have packed powder snow because of their height and orientation – north-east to east. The runs from below Engetal to Allmendhubel and parts of the lower slopes have snowmaking.

FOR EXPERTS
One wonderful piste

The run from the top of the Schilthorn starts with a steep but not terrifying slope, in the past generally mogulled but now more often groomed. It flattens into a schuss to Engetal, below Birg. Then there's a wonderful, wide run with stunning views over the valley to the Eiger, Mönch and Jungfrau. Since the chair-lifts were built here, you can play on these upper runs for as long as you like before resuming your descent. Below the lifts you hit the Kanonenrohr (gun barrel). This is a very narrow shelf with solid rock on one side and a steep drop on the other – protected by nets. After an open slope and scrappy zig-zag path, you arrive at the 'hog's back' and can descend towards the village on either side of Allmendhubel.

From Schiltgrat a short, serious mogul run – the Kandahar – descends towards the village, but experts are more likely to be interested in the off-piste runs into the Blumental – both from here (the north-facing Blumenlucke run) and from Birg (the sunnier Tschingelchrachen) – or the more adventurous runs from the Schilthorn.

FOR INTERMEDIATES
Limited, but Wengen nearby

Keen piste-bashers will want to make a few trips to the long cruising runs of Wengen-Grindelwald. The best easy cruising run in Mürren is the north-facing blue down to Winteregg. The reds on the other low slopes can get mogulled, and snow conditions can be poor. The runs served by the new Riggli chair normally have good snow, and you can choose your gradient.

boarding

Like many Swiss resorts, Mürren has a traditional image, but it is trying to move with the times and offer a more snowboard-friendly attitude – and the major lifts are cable-cars and chair-lifts. The terrain above Mürren is suitable mainly for good free-riders – it's steep, with a lot of off-piste. Intermediates will find the area tough and limited; nearby Wengen is ideal, and much better for beginners.

Competent, confident intermediates should consider tackling the Schilthorn run if snow conditions are good.

FOR BEGINNERS
Not ideal, but adequate
The nursery slopes at Allmendhubel, at the top of the funicular, are on the steep side. And there are not many easy runs to graduate to – though the blue down the Winteregg chair is easy, and a couple of blues are served by the long Gimmeln drag and the less tiring Schiltgrat chair.

FOR CROSS-COUNTRY
Forget it
There's a 12km/8 mile loop along the valley, between Stechelberg and Lauterbrunnen. But snow is unreliable at valley height.

QUEUES
Generally not a problem
Mürren doesn't get as crowded as Wengen and Grindelwald, except on sunny Sundays. There can be queues for the cable-cars to Birg and Schilthorn – usually when snow shortages bring in people from lower resorts. The top stage has only one cabin, so capacity is limited. And a visitor this year was not impressed with the lift staff's attitude when under pressure.

MOUNTAIN RESTAURANTS
Nothing outstanding
Piz Gloria revolves once an hour, displaying a fabulous 360° panorama of peaks and lakes. We don't like the ambience here, but a 2007 reporter was 'pleasantly surprised to have good food and service'; another tells of 'a very nice goulash soup' and says, 'It is incredible value for money just for the view (and cheaper than Méribel).' The Schilthornhütte, by the Engetal chair-lifts, is small and rustic, and has 'good food and friendly service', says a 2007 reporter. Lower down, the rustic Suppenalp in the Blumental is quietly set and gets no sun in January; but comments about it are good: 'cosy with excellent food', 'friendly service' and 'fantastic goulash soup and macaroni with apple sauce'. As you might expect, Sonnenberg is sunnier, and readers have enjoyed 'marvellous rösti' and speciality coffees. Gimmeln is a self-service place with a large terrace, famous for its apple cake. Winteregg does 'superb rösti' and 'the best burger east of the Rockies'. Both have little playgrounds for kids.

Mürren

527

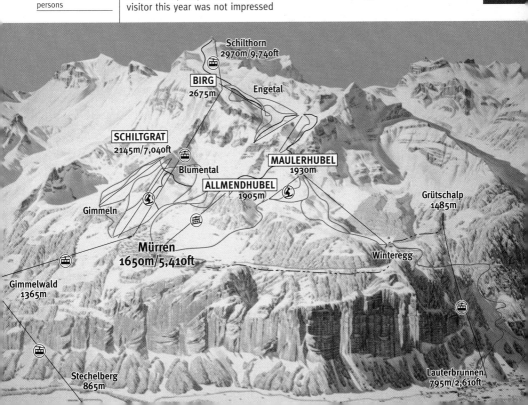

CHILDREN

Kinderhort
t 856 8686
Ages 18mnth to 5yr;
9.30-12noon; 1.30-4pm

Ski school
Takes age 5 and over
(5 2hr days SF170)

GETTING THERE

Air Zürich 195km/
121 miles (3¹/₂hr);
Bern 70km/43 miles
(1¹/₂hr)

Rail Lauterbrunnen;
transfer by mountain
railway and tram

UK PACKAGES

*Inghams, Kuoni, Made
to Measure, Ski
Freshtracks, Ski Line,
Ski Solutions, Swiss
Travel Service,
Switzerland Travel
Centre*
Lauterbrunnen *Ski
Miquel*

ACTIVITIES

Indoor Alpine Sports
Centre: swimming
pool, sauna, solarium,
steam bath, massage,
fitness room, tennis,
gymnasium, squash,
library, museum

Outdoor Ice rink,
curling, ice-climbing,
tobogganing, 12km/
7 miles cleared paths,
paragliding, snow-
shoeing

Phone numbers
From elsewhere in
Switzerland add the
prefix 033; from
abroad use the prefix
+41 33

TOURIST OFFICE

t 856 8686
info@wengen-
muerren.ch
www.wengen-
muerren.ch

THE INFERNO RACE

Every January 1,800 amateurs compete in Mürren's spectacular Inferno race. Conditions permitting, and they usually don't, the race goes from the top of the Schilthorn right down to Lauterbrunnen – a vertical drop of 2175m/7,140ft and a distance of almost 16km/10 miles, incorporating a short climb at Maulerhubel. The racers start individually at 12-second intervals; the fastest finish the course in around 15 minutes, but anything under half an hour is very respectable.

The race was started by Sir Arnold Lunn in 1928, when he and his friends climbed up to spend the night in a mountain hut and then raced down in the morning. For many years the race was organised by the British-run Kandahar Club, and there is still a strong British presence among the competitors.

SCHOOLS AND GUIDES
Declining standards?

Sadly, we received a poor review of the school last year. A regular visitor found his competent daughters of 10 and 13 placed in a group of infants – and his complaint met with a rude response.

FACILITIES FOR CHILDREN
Adequate

There is a nursery slope with a rope tow. The Kinderhort nursery takes children from 18 months old and the ski school takes children from five years old.

STAYING THERE

HOW TO GO
Mainly hotels, packaged or not

A handful of operators offer packages to Mürren.
Hotels There are fewer than a dozen hotels, ranging widely in style.
****Anfi Palace** (856 9999) Victorian pile near the station.
****Eiger** (856 5454) Plain-looking 'chalet' blocks next to the station; widely recommended; good blend of efficiency and charm; good food; pool.
***Alpenruh** (856 8800) Attractively renovated chalet next to the cable-car. 'Cuisine is second to none,' says a 2007 reporter. Sauna.
***Edelweiss** (856 5600) Block-like but friendly; praised by a 2007 visitor ('good wholesome food and excellent views').
***Jungfrau** (855 6464) Perfectly placed for families, in front of the baby slope and close to the funicular.
****Alpenblick** (855 1327) Simple, small, modern chalet near the station.
Apartments There are plenty of chalets and apartments in the village for independent travellers to rent.

EATING OUT
Mainly in hotels

The main alternative to hotels is the rustic Stägerstübli – a bar as well as a restaurant. The locals eat in the little diner at the back. The food at the Eiger hotel is good, and the Bellevue and Alpenruh have got good reports again in 2007.

APRES-SKI
Not devoid of life

The tiny Stägerstübli is cosy, and the place to meet locals. The Anfi Palace's Ballon bar is an attempt at a trendy cocktail bar; it also has a weekend disco, the Inferno. The Bliemlichäller disco in the Blumental hotel caters for kids, the Tächi disco in the Eiger for a more mixed crowd.

OFF THE SLOPES
Tranquillity but not much else

There isn't a lot to amuse people who don't hit the slopes apart from the scenery and a very good sports centre with an outdoor ice rink. Excursions to Bern and Interlaken are easy, and you can readily return to the village to meet non-skiing friends for lunch. The only problem with meeting non-skiers at the top of the cable-car is the expense of it.

STAYING DOWN THE VALLEY
A cheaper option

Lauterbrunnen is a good budget base, with a resort atmosphere and access to both Wengen and Mürren until late. We've happily stayed at the Schützen (855 2032) and Oberland (855 1241); the Silberhorn (856 2210) is highly recommended by a recent visitor for excellent food and value, and a lively bar. For more of a pub atmosphere, he recommends the bar in the Horner hotel.

Charming, car-free old village set amid spectacular scenery and snow-sure but rather less captivating slopes

COSTS

① ② ③ ④ ⑤ ⑥

RATINGS

The slopes
Fast lifts	****
Snow	*****
Extent	**
Expert	***
Intermediate	****
Beginner	*****
Convenience	***
Queues	***
Mountain restaurants	***

The rest
Scenery	****
Charm	*****
Off-slope	****

NEWS

For 2007/08 a half-hourly bus service will operate from Visp to the Saastal, linking with the new Lötschberg rail tunnel.

The limit for free children's lift-passes will be raised to age nine.

For 2006/07 a six-pack was installed at Morenia. And the Felskinn cable-car, dating from 1969, was fitted with swanky new 90-person cabins.

There are still plans to develop slopes near Britanniahütte, but no dates have been set.

➕ Spectacular setting amid high peaks and glaciers

➕ Traditional, 'traffic-free' village

➕ Most of the runs are at exceptionally high altitude and are snow-sure

➕ Good off-slope facilities – even a mountain for non-skiing activities

➖ Disappointingly small area of slopes, with mainly easy runs

➖ Still lots of T-bar drag-lifts

➖ Glacier limits off-piste exploration

➖ Much of the area is in shadow in midwinter – cold and dark

➖ Bad weather can shut the slopes

Saas-Fee is one of our favourite places – a sort of miniature Zermatt without the conspicuous consumption. And good snow is guaranteed, even late in the season: the altitude you spend most of your day at – between 2500m and 3500m (8,200ft and 11,480ft) – is unrivalled in the Alps.

But we tend to drop in here for a couple of days at a time, so the limited extent of the slopes never becomes a problem; for a week's holiday, it would. Top to bottom there is an impressive 1800m/5,900ft vertical – but there aren't many alternative ways down. Keen, mileage-hungry intermediates should look elsewhere, as should experts (except those prepared to go touring). For the rest, it's a question of priorities and expectations. Over to you.

THE RESORT

Like nearby Zermatt, Saas-Fee is a high-altitude mountain village centred on narrow streets lined by attractive old chalets and free of cars (there are car parks at the resort entrance) but not free of electric taxis and delivery vehicles. In other respects, the two resorts are a long way apart in style.

There are some very smart hotels (plus many more modest ones) and plenty of good eating and drinking places. But there's little of the glamour and greed that, for some, spoil Zermatt – and even the electric taxis here are driven at a more considerate pace. Saas-Fee still feels like a village, with its cow sheds more obviously still containing cows. The village may be chilly in January, but when the spring sun is beating down, it is a beautiful

place just to stroll around and relax in.

Depending on where you're staying and which way you want to go up the mountain, you may do more marching through the village than strolling, though. It's a long walk from one end to the other. Three major lifts start from the southern end of the village, at the foot of the slopes, and lots of the hotels and apartments (particularly cheaper ones) are 1km/0.5 miles or more away. The biggest lift, though – the Alpin Express gondola – starts from a more central location. Your hotel may run a courtesy taxi; regular taxis are not cheap – but there are now little public buses. You can store kit near the lifts, which helps.

The village centre has the school and guides office, the church and a few more shops than elsewhere, but it doesn't add up to much. On a sunny

The lunchtime trek out to (and back from) Britanniahütte is worth it if you like the atmosphere of real Alpine refuges ➔

KEY FACTS

Resort	1800m
	5,910ft
Slopes	1800-3500m
	5,910-11,480ft
Lifts	22
Pistes	100km
	62 miles
Blue	25%
Red	50%
Black	25%
Snowmaking	8km
	5 miles

day, though, the restaurant terraces by the nursery slopes at the south end of the village are a magnet, with stunning views up to the ring of 4000m/13,120ft peaks – you can see why the village is called 'The Pearl of the Alps'.

The worthwhile slopes of Saas-Almagell and Saas-Grund are not far away, and you can buy a lift pass that covers all three resorts and linking buses. Day trips by car/train to Zermatt are also possible and a day there is now covered by the six-day lift pass.

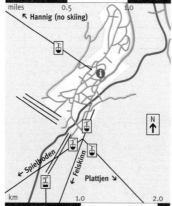

THE MOUNTAIN

The area is a strange mixture of powerful modern lifts and a lot of old-fashioned T-bars (there are only two chair-lifts). Blame the glaciers, which move too quickly for chair-lifts. Readers complain about the 'walks and climbs' involved in getting from one lift to another. Take it easy when climbing out of the top lift station: some people feel faint because of the thin air.

The upper slopes are largely gentle, while the lower mountain, below the glacier, is steeper and rockier, needing good snow-cover. There is very little shelter here in bad weather: during and after heavy snowfalls you may find yourself limited to the nursery area.

Saas-Fee is one of the leading resorts for mountaineering and ski touring, and the extended Haute Route from Chamonix via Zermatt ends here.

THE SLOPES
A glacier runs through it
There are two routes up to the main **Felskinn** area. The 30-person Alpin Express gondola, starting across the river from the main village, takes you to Felskinn via a mid-station at Morenia. The alternative is a short drag

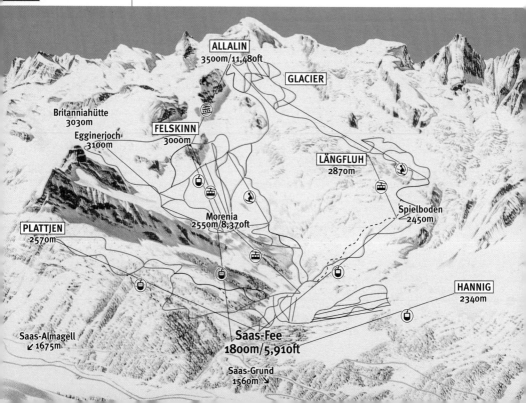

ALLALIN
3500m/11,480ft

GLACIER

Britanniahütte
3030m

FELSKINN
3000m

Egginerjoch
3100m

LÄNGFLUH
2870m

Morenia
2550m/8,370ft

Spielboden
2450m

PLATTJEN
2570m

HANNIG
2340m

Saas-Almagell
1675m

Saas-Fee
1800m/5,910ft

Saas-Grund
1560m

LIFT PASSES

Saas-Fee

Prices in SF

Age	1-day	6-day
under 16	38	190
over 16	63	317

Free under 6

Senior age 61+: pay group tariff rate

Beginner pass for village lifts only

Notes
Covers lifts in Saas-Fee only; six-day pass covers a day in Zermatt; single and return tickets available on most main lifts; also afternoon passes and family reductions

Alternative passes
Whole valley pass; separate passes for each of the other Saastal ski areas (Saas-Grund, Saas-Almagell, Saas-Balen); non-skier single fares

across the nursery slope at the south end of the village, and then the Felskinn cable-car – upgraded for 2006/07 (see News). From Felskinn, the Metro Alpin underground funicular hurtles up to **Allalin**. From below here, two drag-lifts access the high point.

Also at the south end of the village, a gondola leaves for Spielboden. This is met by a cable-car that takes you up to **Längfluh**.

Between Felskinn and Längfluh is an off-limits glacier area. A very long drag-lift from Längfluh takes you to a point where you can get down to the Felskinn area. These two sectors are served mainly by drag-lifts, and you can get down to the village from both.

Another gondola from the south end of the village goes up to Saas-Fee's smallest area, **Plattjen**.

TERRAIN-PARKS
Well developed
The 42 Crew (www.42crew.ch) are renowned for building great parks and maintaining them all year round. Although the slopes may not provide the biggest challenge for advanced riders, the big Morenia park has a plethora of kickers, rails and boxes, and a truly world-class half-pipe that will challenge anyone on a board. More technical rails and boxes have been promised for the 2007/08 season. The park can be slightly intimidating for novices, who would be better off heading to the beginner and snow-skate park in Stafelwald, near the nursery slopes. You'll find plenty of entry level jumps and rails here. In summer, a park is built on the glacier and you will often see pro riders honing their skills at the 'Laid Back' summer camp (www.laidback.ch).

SNOW RELIABILITY
Good at the highest altitudes
Most of Saas-Fee's slopes face north and many are above 2500m/8,200ft,

making this one of the most reliable resorts for snow in the Alps. The glacier is open most of the year. There has been substantial investment in snow-guns, but reports say they aren't used enough. And we have reports of poor piste grooming this year.

FOR EXPERTS
Not a lot to keep your interest
There is not much steep stuff, except on the bottom half of the mountain where the snow tends not to be as good (a short black run from Felskinn is the exception). The slopes around the top of Längfluh often provide good powder, and there are usually moguls above Spielboden. The blacks and the trees on Plattjen are worth exploring. The glacier puts limits on the local off-piste even with a guide – crevasse danger is extreme. But there are extensive touring possibilities.

FOR INTERMEDIATES
Great for gentle cruising
Saas-Fee is ideal for early intermediates and those not looking for much of a challenge. For long cruises, head for Allalin. The top of the mountain, down as far as Längfluh in one direction and as far as Morenia in the other, is ideal, with usually excellent snow. Gradients range from gentle blues to slightly steeper reds that can build up smallish bumps. For more of a challenge, head across to Längfluh.

The 1800m/5,910ft vertical descents from the top to the village are great tests of stamina – or, if you choose, an enjoyable long cruise with plenty of view stops. The lower runs have steepish, tricky sections and can have poor snow, especially if it isn't cold enough to make artificial snow – timid intermediates might prefer to take a lift down from mid-mountain.

Plattjen has a variety of runs, all of them fine for ambitious intermediates, and often under-used.

boarding

Saas-Fee has backed snowboarding from its inception and provides year-round riding at more affordable prices than neighbouring Zermatt. The terrain suits intermediates and beginners best, but while the main access lifts are gondolas, cable-cars and a funicular, nearly all the rest are T-bars. The high altitude and the glacier mean the resort is a favourite for early-season and summer riding (the British Olympic half-pipe team use Saas-Fee for off-season training). Carvers will find wide, well-groomed pistes to shred down. Half-pipe enthusiasts will love the perfect pipe next to the good terrain-park at Morenia. The Popcorn bar and shop is the favourite spot for après-snowboard beers.

532

SCHOOLS

Swiss
t 957 2348
Eskimos Snowboard
t 957 4904

Classes
5 3hr days SF186
Private lessons
SF60 for 1hr

CHILDREN

Kindertagesstätte Murmeli (Marmots Club)
t 957 4057
Ages 18mnth to 6yr;
8am-5pm, Mon to Fri;
SF76 per day
Swiss
t 957 2348
From age 4; 10am to
3.15 (half skiing, half activities)
Glückskäfer
t 079 225 8154
Evening babysitting service

Ski school
From age 4 (SF35 for
90-minute lesson);
full junior ski school
from age 5 (5 days
SF186)

FOR BEGINNERS
A great place to start
We say 'great'; our reporters say 'perfect'. There's a good, large, out-of-the-way nursery area at the edge of the village, as snow-sure as any you will find. Those ready to progress can head for the gentle blues on Felskinn just above Morenia – it's best to return by the Alpin Express. There are also gentle blues at the top of the mountain, from where you can head down to Längfluh. Again, use the lifts to return to base. A useful beginners' pass covers all the short village lifts.

FOR CROSS-COUNTRY
Good local trail and lots nearby
There is one short (6km/4 mile) pleasant trail at the edge of the village. It snakes up through the woods, providing about 150m/490ft of climb and nice views. There's more (26km/16 miles) in the Saas valley.

QUEUES
Gradual improvement?
This year's reports suggest that Saas-Fee is at last getting on top of its queuing problems. Last season's improvements were an upgrade for the Felskinn cable-car, which regularly produced long queues, and a new six-pack at Morenia, at mid-mountain. Even so, there may be irritating queues up at Längfluh and for the drag-lifts at the top of the mountain. Crowded pistes can be a problem below Morenia at the end of the day, and when bad weather closes lifts and runs higher up.

MOUNTAIN RESTAURANTS
Fair choice, but it's no Zermatt
The restaurants at the main lift stations are functional; at least the table-service one at Allalin gives changing views – see separate box.
Editors' choice If you're up for a trek (about 15 minutes each way) the Britanniahütte is special, not because of the food but because of the setting: it's a real climbing refuge, with atmosphere and great views.
Worth knowing about The best places are slightly off the beaten track: the Berghaus Plattjen (just down from Plattjen) and the cosy Gletschergrotte, halfway down from Spielboden (watch for the arrow from the piste).

The restaurant at the top of Plattjen has 'friendly service'. At Spielboden there are 'great views' of tricky slopes. At Längfluh the large terrace has

↑ Lots of broad, cruising runs up on the glacier
WENDY KING

spectacular views of huge crevasses, but the food is 'basic'. Reporters like the 'giant' Morenia for good value and a 'wide choice' – but it can get busy.

SCHOOLS AND GUIDES
Mixed reactions
It's a choice between the Swiss school and Eskimos. Reports of the Swiss school are mixed, but Eskimos receives rave reviews from all of our reporters this year: 'great success'; 'well-organised' and 'patient instructors' for both adults' and children's classes.

FACILITIES FOR CHILDREN
Good reports
The school takes children from four years old, and reports are generally positive. Last year, a reporter's daughter was 'so frustrated' by being put in much too low a group for her; but a 2007 visitor voted the school a 'great success' for his seven-year-old – with small groups even at half-term. Eskimos is highly praised: one child's instructor 'could not do enough for the group, taking them out for activities in his own time'. And the kids' fun-park proved a 'great introduction' for a 2007 reporter's toddler, with its magic carpet lift. Several hotels have an in-house kindergarten.

WORLD'S HIGHEST REVOLVING LUNCH?

If you fancy 360° views during lunch, head up to the world's highest revolving restaurant at Allalin, where you can get a different vista with starters, mains and pud. It's only the bit of floor with the tables on it that revolves; the stairs stay put (along with the windows – watch your gloves). The other two revolving cafes in the Alps are also in Switzerland – at Mürren and Leysin – and we rate the views there better. But it's an amusing novelty that most visitors enjoy, and lunch is OK too. To reserve a table next to the windows phone 957 1771.

GETTING THERE

Air Sion 70km/
43 miles (1hr);
Geneva 234km/
145 miles (3½hr);
Zürich 246km/
153 miles (4hr);
Milan 250km/
155 miles (3hr)

Rail Brig (38km/
24 miles); regular
buses from station

ACTIVITIES

Indoor Bielen leisure
centre (swimming,
hot-tub, steam bath,
whirlpool, solarium,
sauna, aerobics,
massage, tennis,
badminton, gym,
bodyforming,
aquafitness),
museums

Outdoor 30km/
19 miles of cleared
paths, horse carriage
rides, ice rink
(skating, curling,
snowbowling),
tobogganing, bob-
sleigh, snowtubing,
bob-sleigh, ice-
climbing, snow-
shoeing

Phone numbers
From elsewhere in
Switzerland add the
prefix 027; from
abroad use the prefix
+41 27

TOURIST OFFICE

t 958 1858
to@saas-fee.ch
www.saas-fee.ch

STAYING THERE

HOW TO GO
Check the location
Quite a few UK tour operators sell holidays to Saas-Fee. But there are surprisingly few chalet holidays.
Hotels There are over 50.
*****Ferienart (958 1900) Lovely relaxed place, despite 5-star status. Central, with excellent facilities (swish spa). But one reporter found some rooms not up to scratch and judged the food 'good but not exceptional'.
****Schweizerhof (958 7575) Stylish, in quiet position above the centre. 'Fantastic food, friendly staff, excellent kindergarten, wonderful service.' Pool and health facilities.
****Beau-Site (958 1560) Central, but not convenient, position. Good food. Pool. A 2006 reporter was very impressed by the staff.
***Christiania (957 3166) 'Thoroughly recommended; delivered much more than you expect,' says a visitor.
***Alphubel (958 6363) At the wrong end of town. Praised by reporters for its own 'brilliant nursery'.
***Waldesruh (958 6464) Strongly recommended by a reporter: 'Best situation for the Alpin Express.'
***Astoria (958 5500) 'Very handy for the Alpin Express, excellent, friendly,' says a reporter. Whirlpool and sauna.
***Jägerhof (957 1310) At foot of slopes. 'Service simply phenomenal.'
***Europa (958 9600) Near the Hannig gondola. Recommended in 2007 for 'exemplary' food. Wellness facilities.
**Belmont (958 1640) The most appealing of the hotels looking directly on to the nursery slopes.
Fletschhorn (957 2131) Elegant chalet in the woods, with original art and individual rooms, a trek from the village and lifts, but fabulous food.
Hohnegg (957 2268) Small rustic alternative to the Fletschhorn, in a similarly remote spot.
Apartments Most apartments featured by UK operators are at the north end of the village.

EATING OUT
Good variety
Gastronomes will want to head for the acclaimed and expensive Fletschhorn – 'The best meal I've ever had,' says a 2006 reporter. Our favourite is the rustic Bodmen, which has great food (from rösti to fillet steak). The hotel Ferienart's several restaurants include a Thai one (the Mandarin) that we have enjoyed. Boccalino is cheap and does pizzas. Don Ciccio's is 'child-friendly' and 'very good'. The rustic Alp-Hitta has 'a lot of atmosphere' and does 'reasonable' food. The Ferme is 'excellent'. Arvu Stuba, Zur Mühle, Gorge, Feeloch and the Sport-Hotel's Rôtisserie have all been recommended.

APRES-SKI
Excellent and varied
Late afternoon, Nesti's Ski-Bar, Zur Mühle and the little snow-bars near the lifts are all pretty lively, especially if the sun's shining. The Black Bull, with outdoor seating only, is reportedly still the 'in place'. Later on, Nesti's and the Alpen-Pub keep going till 1am. Popcorn is 'relaxed' and as popular as ever. The night club, Poison, offers 'legendary parties' fuelled by shots and shakers. The Metro-Bar is 'like being in a 19th-century mine shaft'. Why-Not is the place for a Guinness. The Happy bar's happy hours are popular. The Metropol Hotel – with American diner, Night-Life disco and other bars – 'livens up late'.

OFF THE SLOPES
A mountain for pedestrians
The whole of the Hannig mountain is dedicated to walking, paragliding and tobogganing, which a reporter rates as 'terrific'. It offers 'great views' of the glaciers. The splendid Bielen leisure centre boasts a 25m/82ft pool, indoor tennis courts and a sunbed area. There's the interesting Saas museum and the Bakery Museum, where kids can make bread. The Feeblitz toboggan ride beside the Alpin Express gets good reviews. If you like ice caves, don't miss the world's largest.

Ignore the stuffy, monstrous 5-star hotels: you don't need to be rolling in it to enjoy this panoramic high-altitude playground

COSTS

① ② ③ ④ ⑤ ⑥

RATINGS

The slopes

Fast lifts	****
Snow	****
Extent	*****
Expert	****
Intermediate	****
Beginner	**
Convenience	*
Queues	**
Mountain restaurants	****

The rest

Scenery	****
Resort charm	*
Off-slope	*****

NEWS

For 2007/08 the 5-star Carlton Hotel is due to re-open in all-suite form, with a new wellness centre.

For 2006/07 the Inn Lodge opened in Celerina – offering low-cost rooms and dormitories on an all-inclusive basis.

There are still plans to expand the Lagalb-Diavolezza slopes and link them properly. The first phase is scheduled for 2008/09.

➕ Wonderful panoramic scenery

➕ Off-slope activities second to none

➕ Extensive, mainly intermediate slopes

➕ High, and fairly snow-sure

➕ Good après-ski, for all tastes

➕ Good mountain restaurants, some with magnificent views

➖ A sizeable town, with little traditional Alpine character and some hideous block buildings

➖ Several unlinked mountains, and inadequate valley bus service

➖ Runs on home mountain all fairly easy and most lacking variety

➖ Expensive

St Moritz is Switzerland's most famous 'exclusive' winter resort: glitzy, expensive, fashionable and, above all, the place to be seen – a place for an all-round winter holiday, with an unrivalled array of wacky diversions such as polo, golf and cricket on snow, and countless festivals. It has long been popular with upper-crust Brits, who stay in the top hotels in order to go sledging. Well, OK: in order to descend the world-famous Cresta Run. But like all such self-consciously smart resorts, it makes a perfectly good destination for anyone.

The town of St Moritz is undeniably an eyesore. But you may find, as we do, that you can ignore the scar, and appreciate the beauty of St Moritz's spectacular setting regardless. This is one of those areas where our progress on the mountain is regularly interrupted by the need to stand and gaze.

THE RESORT

St Moritz has two distinct parts. Dorf is the fashionable main part, on a steep hillside above the lake. It has two main streets – lined with boutiques selling Rolex watches, Cartier jewellery and Hermes scarves – a few side lanes and a small main square. A funicular takes you from Dorf to the slopes of Corviglia, also reached by cable-car from Dorf's other half, the spa resort of St Moritz Bad, down beside the lake. Everything in Bad is less prestigious. Many of the buildings are block-like, and spoil otherwise superb views. There are no lifts from St Moritz itself into the second major area of slopes, Corvatsch – a bus-ride away.

In winter the lake is used for eccentric activities including horse and greyhound racing, show jumping, polo, 'ice golf' and even cricket. It also makes a superb setting for walking and cross-country skiing, which is very big in the area; the Engadine Ski Marathon is held down the valley every March – over 12,000 racers take part.

The town's clientele is typified by the results of a Cresta Run race we saw on one of our visits. In the top 30 were three lords, one count, one archduke and a baronet. But the race was won by a local Swiss guy.

For our money Bad is the better base, with the advantage that you can ski back to it from Corvatsch as well as from Corviglia. Celerina, down the

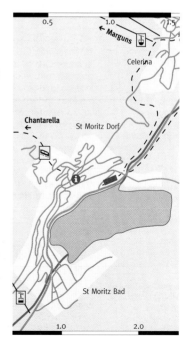

The mountain railway makes a suitably relaxed start to the day for residents of Dorf. Bad is in the distance on the right, by the lake ➜

ST MORITZ TOURIST BOARD

KEY FACTS

Resort	1770m
	5,810ft
Slopes	1730-3305m
	5,680-10,840ft
Lifts	56
Pistes	350km
	217 miles
Blue	20%
Red	70%
Black	10%
Snowmaking	70km
	43 miles

For Corviglia only

Slopes	1730-3055m
	5,680-10,020ft
Lifts	23
Pistes	158km
	98 miles

LIFT PASSES

Upper Engadine

Prices in SF

Age	1-day	6-day
under 13	24	115
13 to 17	47	227
Over 18	70	339

Free under 6

Senior no deals

Beginner no deals

Notes
Covers all lifts in Corviglia, Corvatsch, Diavolezza-Lagalb and Zuoz, and includes the Engadine bus services and certain stretches of the Rhätische Bahn railway

Alternative passes
Half-day and day passes for individual areas within Upper Engadine

valley and with a lift towards Corviglia, is the obvious alternative, and an attractively rustic one (see end of this chapter). But there are other options – 'chocolate-box-pretty' Sils Maria, for example, has immediate access to the Corvatsch slopes via Furtschellas.

There are good rail links from Zürich, but it's quicker to drive to the resort. A car is handy, too: the valley bus service (needed for access to Corvatsch) is free with the lift pass but scandalously inadequate at peak times. And a car greatly speeds up visits to the outlying mountains. Trips are possible to Davos and other resorts.

THE MOUNTAINS

There are lots of long, wide, well-groomed runs with varied terrain – practically all on open slopes above the trees. The 350km/217 miles of pistes are in three separate areas, covered on three gigantic piste maps; our maps show only the two main areas close to St Moritz. Piste signing is unhelpful: pistes are numbered on the map, but not on the ground. If the lift system irritates you, the local heli-skiing outfits will drop you at the top of the lifts. It's that kind of place.

THE SLOPES
Big but broken up
From St Moritz Dorf a two-stage railway goes up to **Corviglia**, a lift junction at the eastern end of a sunny and rather monotonous area of slopes facing east and south over the main valley. The peak of Piz Nair, reached from here by cable-car, separates these

slopes from the less sunny and more varied ones in the wide bowl above **Marguns** – and gives fabulous views across the valley to Piz Bernina. From Corviglia you can (snow permitting) head down easy paths to Dorf and Bad; you'll probably pass through Salastrains – a major focus of activity just above Dorf, with nursery slopes, restaurants and two hotels. There is a red run from Marguns to Celerina.

From Surlej, a few miles from St Moritz, a two-stage cable-car takes you to the north-facing slopes of **Corvatsch**, which reach glacial heights. From the mid-station at Murtèl you have a choice of reds to Stüvetta Giand'Alva and Alp Margun. From the latter you can work your way to **Furtschellas**, also reached by cable-car from Sils Maria. If you're lucky with the snow, you can end the day with the splendid Hahnensee run, from the northern limit of the Corvatsch lift system at Giand'Alva down to St Moritz Bad – a black-classified run that is of red difficulty for 95 per cent of its 6km/4 mile length. The run often opens at about noon, when the snow is soft. It's a five-minute walk from the end of the run to the cable-car up to Corviglia.

The third area consists of two peaks on opposite sides of the road to the Bernina pass to Italy, about 20km/ 12 miles away – Diavolezza and Lagalb. The bus takes 50 minutes. You can now ski from Diavolezza to the base of Lagalb with the aid of a short rope tow; there are plans to install two new lifts and create new runs in 2008 to form a properly linked ski area.

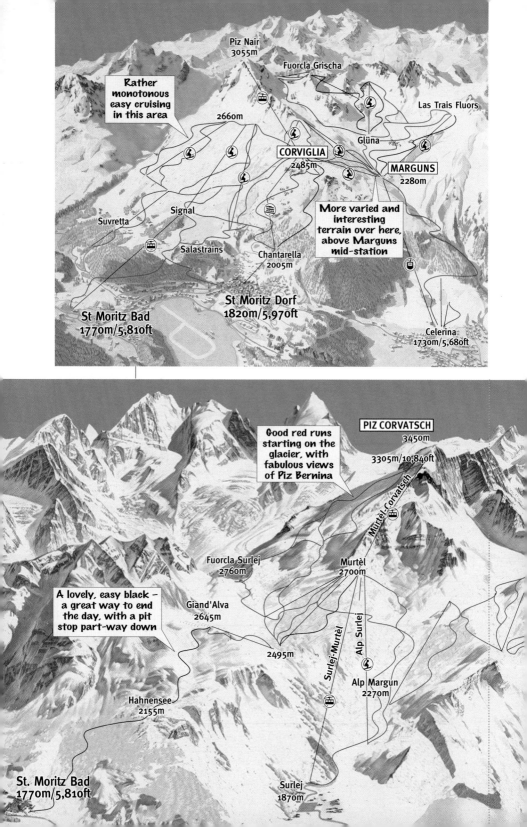

boarding

Despite the high prices and glitzy image, the terrain in St Moritz is boarder-friendly and there's a special boarder's booklet with a lot of good information. The best free-ride terrain is on Diavolezza and on Corvatsch, but be warned – there are several drag-lifts in the area. Most of the area is serviced by chairs, gondolas, cable-cars and trains; beginners will enjoy the rolling blue runs, and intermediates will relish the plethora of challenging red runs. The great thing for free-riders here is that most people tend to stay on-piste in this resort, leaving terrain untracked for days after the last snowfall. There's a very good terrain-park on Corviglia. Specialist shop Playground in Paradise will help with all your equipment needs.

Diavolezza (2980m/9,780ft) has excellent north-facing pistes of 900m/2,950ft vertical, down under its big 125-person cable-car.

Lagalb (2960m/9,710ft) is a smaller area with quite challenging slopes – west-facing, 850m/2,790ft vertical – served by an 80-person cable-car.

It's worth noting that from mid-March the Lagalb cable-car runs until 5pm and the Diavolezza one until 5.30. We thought a final sunny run from 2900m/ 9,510ft a great way to end the skiing day.

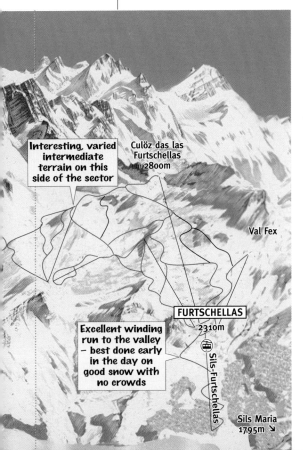

Interesting, varied intermediate terrain on this side of the sector

Culöz das las Furtschellas 2800m

Val Fex

FURTSCHELLAS 2310m

Sils-Furtschellas

Excellent winding run to the valley – best done early in the day on good snow with no crowds

Sils Maria 1795m ↘

TERRAIN-PARKS
Improved
The Mellow park on Corviglia is only two years old and is a welcome addition for freestylers in the area. Access is easier from Celerina than from St Moritz itself. The park was actually designed with female pro skiers and snowboarders and advanced riders in mind and is home to some of the biggest contests for females. There are three lines, with the hardest comprising a big 12m/39ft table jump. There are straight, kinked and rainbow rails and boxes of all sizes, and the park always has a great relaxed atmosphere to learn in. The team has worked hard this year to bring the total of jumps up to an impressive 22. In addition snow-guns allow for the park to be in place regardless of snow shortage.

SNOW RELIABILITY
Improved by good snowmaking
This corner of the Alps has a rather dry climate, but the altitude means that any precipitation is likely to be snowy. The top runs at Corvatsch are glacial and require good snow depths to be safe – a recent reporter discovered them closed during her February visit. There is snowmaking in every sector, and piste grooming is excellent.

FOR EXPERTS
Dispersed challenges
If you're looking for challenges, you're liable to find St Moritz disappointing on-piste. The few serious black runs are scattered about in different sectors, and few are genuine blacks; those at Lagalb and Diavolezza are the most challenging, and include one of the few sizeable mogul-fields – the Minor run down the Lagalb cable-car (though it's seriously steep only at the start). But there is good off-piste terrain, and it doesn't get tracked out. There is an excellent north-facing slope

UK PACKAGES

Alpine Answers, Alpine Weekends, Club Med, Corporate Ski Co, Crystal, Crystal Finest, Descent International, Elegant Resorts, Flexiski, Independent Ski Links, Inghams, Interhome, Jeffersons, Kuoni, Made to Measure, Momentum, Oxford Ski Co, Scott Dunn, Ski Independence, Ski Line, Ski Safari, Ski Solutions, Ski Weekend, SkiGower, Skitracer, Swiss Travel Service, Switzerland Travel Centre

immediately above Marguns, for example. Experts often head for the tough off-piste runs on Piz Nair or the Corvatsch summit. More serious expeditions can be undertaken – such as the Roseg valley from Corvatsch.

Out at Diavolezza, a very popular and spectacular off-piste glacier route goes off the back beneath Piz Bernina to Morteratsch. It is not difficult, but requires a bit of energy and nerve. After a gentle climb, you skirt the glacier on a narrow ledge, with crevasses waiting to gobble you up on the right. At the end of the initial 30-minute slog, a welcoming ice bar greets you. After that, it's downhill over the glacier, with splendid views. On the front of the mountain, the Gletscher chair accesses an excellent shady run down Val d'Arlas. And across at Lagalb, a route goes steeply off the back of the mountain down towards La Rosa in Val Laguné.

There are a couple of firms offering heli-drops on Fuorcla Chamuotsch, for runs back to the Engadine valley down Val Suvretta or Valletta dal Guglia.

FOR INTERMEDIATES
Good but flattering
St Moritz is great for intermediates. Most pistes on Corviglia are very well groomed, easyish reds that could well have been classified blue – ideal cruising terrain, or monotonous, depending on your requirements. The Marguns bowl is more interesting, including some easy blacks and the pleasant Val Schattain run away from the lifts. The Corvatsch-Furtschellas area is altogether more varied, interesting and challenging, as well as higher and wider. There are excellent red runs in both parts of the area, including descents to the two valley stations – particularly the Furtschellas one; do these in the morning, and return to St Moritz Bad via the lovely Hahnensee run – an easy black. Use the low-altitude way back to the Corvatsch sector from Furtschellas, to avoid a lot of tedious skating. The runs from the Corvatsch top station are genuinely red in parts, with fabulous views of Piz Bernina.

Diavolezza is mostly intermediate stuff, too. There is an easy open slope at the top, served by a fast quad, and a splendid long intermediate run back down under the lift. The link to Lagalb requires use of a black, but it is of red-run gradient. Lagalb has more

challenging pistes – basically two good reds and a genuine black.

FOR BEGINNERS
Not ideal
Beginners start up at Salastrains or Corviglia, or slightly out of town at Suvretta. Celerina has good, broad nursery slopes at village level and a child-friendly lift. Ironically, in a resort full of easy red runs, progression from the nursery slopes to longer runs is rather awkward – there are few blue runs without a difficult section.

FOR CROSS-COUNTRY
Excellent
The Engadine is one of the premier regions in the Alps for cross-country, with 180km/112 miles of trails, including floodlit loops, amid splendid scenery and with fairly reliable snow. A reporter recommends the lessons at the Langlauf Centre near the Hotel Kempinski. For cross-country, the best bases are outside St Moritz – Sils or Silvaplana, suggests one reporter.

QUEUES
Not much of a problem
St Moritz has invested heavily in new lifts, especially on Corviglia and Marguns, where there are fast chairs everywhere. New projects will add more at Diavolezza. The area as a whole has a lot of modest-sized cable-cars – both for getting up the mountain from the resort and for access to peaks from mid-mountain. Queues can result, but reporters have had good experiences lately. Happy reporters comment that many St Moritz visitors are late risers and don't ski much after lunch, leaving the slopes quiet at the start and end of the day.

MOUNTAIN RESTAURANTS
Some special places
Mountain restaurants are plentiful, and include some of the most glamorous in Europe. Prices can be high, but standards can be disappointing. We had the worst rösti in a skiing lifetime at the otherwise attractive Chamanna. The piste maps have helpful pictures and descriptions of the restaurants.

Editors' choice El Paradiso (833 4002), secluded at the extreme southern end of Corviglia, has it all: breathtaking views, a tastefully renovated, slightly trendy interior, great service and top-notch food. Fuorcla Surlej (842 6303, though we doubt they'll take a

They get up to all sorts of things on the frozen lake, overlooked by Dorf →

GETTING THERE

Air Zürich 200km/ 124 miles (3hr); Upper Engadine airport 5km/3 miles

Rail Mainline station in resort

SCHOOLS

Swiss
t 830 0101
Suvretta
t 836 3600/6161

Classes
(Swiss prices)
6 2hr days SF230
Private lessons
SF95 for 1hr

CHILDREN

Salastrains
t 830 0101
Run by Swiss school
Schweizerhof hotel
t 837 0707
From age 3; 9.30-6pm; Mon-Sat; SF45 per day for non-residents
Palazzino – in Badrutt's Palace Hotel
t 837 1000
Ages 3 to 12; 9.30am to 6pm; SF50 per day for non-residents

Ski school
Ages from 5; pick-up service and all-day care available

SMART LODGINGS

Check out our feature chapters at the front of the book.

reservation), on the Fuorcla run from the Corvatsch glacier, is a good-weather option: a refuge serving basic food very slowly, but with a view from the ramshackle terrace that is among our top three in the world.
Worth knowing about On Corviglia, the top lift station houses several restaurants run under the umbrella title of Mathis Food Affairs, including the famous Marmite. The Salastrains continues to serve 'magnificent' food. The Chasellas is also recommended, particularly for strudel. Lej de la Pêsch, behind Piz Nair, is a cosy spot, better for a snowy day than a sunny one. On the Corvatsch side, a good place for a stormy day is the rustic Alpetta, near Alp Margun – 'nice food, lovely atmosphere and a great bar' (table-service inside). On the other hand Hahnensee, on the lift-free run of the same name to Bad, is a splendid place to pause in the sun on the way home.

SCHOOLS AND GUIDES
Internal competition
There are two main schools, the St Moritz and the Suvretta (see 'Hotels'). A 2006 reporter received 'excellent' instruction from the latter. The St Moritz Experience runs heli-trips, and some hotels have their own instructors for private lessons.

FACILITIES FOR CHILDREN
Choose a hotel with a nursery
Children wanting lessons have a choice of schools. Reports suggest that classes with the Swiss school can have mixed ability levels, with better kids getting bored. There's a new kindergarten and children's restaurant at Salastrains and some hotel nurseries are now open to non-residents. Club Med has its usual good facilities.

STAYING THERE

HOW TO GO
Several packaged options
Packages are available. There is a Club Med. The tourist office can provide a list of apartments.
Hotels Over half the hotels are 4-stars and 5-stars – the highest concentration in Switzerland. We are persuaded by a reader to list one of the 5-stars, and we include another for its news value; the others – the staid but revamped Kulm, the Gothic Badrutt's Palace and the newish Kempinski – leave us cold.
*****Suvretta House (818 363636) The 5-star for skiers, in a secluded location with its own branch of the lift system. 'Splendid views, magnificent fitness centre and pool – difficult to fault, except that jackets and ties must be worn after 6pm.' Rules us out, then.
*****Carlton (836 7000) Re-opening in all-suite form in late 2007. The fact that its website has a Russian version may be all you need to know.
****Crystal (836 2626) Big 4-star in Dorf, close to the Corviglia lift.
****Schweizerhof (837 0707) 'Relaxed' hotel in central Dorf, five minutes from the Corviglia lift, with 'excellent food and very helpful staff'. Après-ski hub.
****Monopol (837 0404) Good value (for St Moritz); in centre of Dorf. Repeatedly approved by readers: 'Lovely food, delightful staff,' says a 2007 visitor. Good new spa facilities.
***Laudinella (836 0000) Our Bad favourite: refreshing, innovative place with austere decor; you can dine enjoyably in any of five different restaurants in the hotel. 'Disappointing' fitness facilities, though.
***Nolda (833 0575) One of the few chalet-style buildings, close to the cable-car in Bad.

ACTIVITIES

Indoor Swimming
pool, sauna, solarium,
golf range, tennis,
squash, museums,
fitness centre, health
spa, casino, cinema,
bowling, library

Outdoor Ice skating,
curling, polo,
sightseeing flights,
horse carriage rides,
tobogganing, hang-
gliding, bob-sleigh
rides, Cresta Run,
180km/112 miles
cleared paths, horse-
riding

Phone numbers
From elsewhere in
Switzerland add the
prefix 081; from
abroad use the prefix
+41 81

TOURIST OFFICES

St Moritz
t 837 3333
information
@stmoritz.ch
www.stmoritz.ch

Celerina
t 830 0011
info@celerina.ch
www.celerina.ch

Pontresina
t 838 8300
info@pontresina.com
www.pontresina.com

EATING OUT
Mostly chic and expensive

It's easy to spend £50 a head eating out in St Moritz – without wine – but you can eat more cheaply. We liked the excellent Italian food at the down-to-earth Cascade in Dorf and the three smooth, pricey restaurants in the Chesa Veglia – an ancient farmhouse outpost of Badrutt's hotel – though one reporter considers it a rip-off. The two top restaurants are out of town: Jöhri's Talvo at Champfèr and Bumanns Chesa Pirani in La Punt; both occupy fine old houses and are world-class for quality and price. We also liked the rustic Landhotel Meierei, by the lake.

An evening up at Muottas Muragl, between Celerina and Pontresina, offers spectacular views, a splendid sunset and an unpretentious dinner.

APRES-SKI
Caters for all ages

There's a big variety of après-skiing age groups here. The fur coat count is high – people come to St Moritz to be seen. At tea time, head for Hanselmann's – 'fabulous tea and strudels' but 'the place is a bit dull'.

Bobby's Pub attracts a young crowd, as does the loud music of the Stübli, one of three bars in the Schweizerhof ('excellent cocktails'): the others are the Mulibar, with a country and western theme and live music, and the chic Piano Bar. The Enoteca is the place to sample 'wonderful wines', according to a 2006 visitor. The Cresta, at the Steffani, is popular with the British, while the Cava below it is louder, livelier and younger. A 2007 reporter's group enjoyed 'clubbing' at the Diamond's bar and disco.

The two most popular discos are Vivai (expensive) at the Steffani, and King's at Badrutt's Palace (even more expensive; jackets and ties required). And if they don't part you from enough of your cash, try the casino.

OFF THE SLOPES
Excellent variety of pastimes

Even if you lack the bravado for the Cresta Run, there is lots to do. In midwinter the snow-covered lake provides a playground for bizarre events, but in March the lake starts to thaw. There's an annual 'gourmet festival', with chefs from all over the world. The Engadin museum is said to be 'very interesting'. And the shopping is simply 'incredible'.

There are extensive well-marked walking trails and a map is available.

Some hotels run special activities, such as a curling week. Other options are hang-gliding and indoor tennis. The public pool in Bad has closed for renovation and is unlikely to re-open before 2008. There's another pool in Pontresina. One reporter was bowled over by a train trip on the Bernina Express to Italy, with 'amazing bends and scenery; the high spot of our visit'.

STAYING UP THE MOUNTAIN
Excellent possibilities

Next door to each other at Salastrains are two chalet-style hotels, the 3-star Salastrains (833 3867), with 60 comfy beds, and the slightly simpler and much smaller Chesa Chantarella (833 3355). Great views, and no queues.

Celerina 1730m/5,680ft

At the bottom end of the Cresta Run, Celerina is unpretentious and villagey, if quiet, with good access to Corviglia. It is sizeable, with a lot of second homes, many owned by Italians (the upper part is known as Piccolo Milano). There are some appealing small hotels (reporters like Chesa Rosatsch, 837 0101) and a couple of bigger 4-stars. The Inn Lodge (834 4795) is new, with rooms and dormitories for the budget-conscious. The food at the Chesa Rosatsch attracts non-resident diners and is recommended.

THE CRESTA RUN

No trip to St Moritz is really complete without a visit to the Cresta Run. It's the last bastion of Britishness (until recently, payment had to be made in sterling) and male chauvinism (women who want to do the run need an invitation from a club member).

Any adult male can pay around £200 for five rides (helmet and lunch at the Kulm hotel included). You lie on a toboggan (aptly called a 'skeleton') and hurtle head-first down a sheet ice gully from St Moritz to Celerina. Watch out for Shuttlecock corner – that's where most of the accidents happen and the ambulances ply their trade.

COEUR DU VALAIS

Val d'Anniviers

Europe's best-kept secret: five charming unspoiled villages beneath high, snow-sure slopes with spectacular scenery

COSTS

① ② ③ ④ ⑤ ⑥

RATINGS

The slopes

Fast lifts	**
Snow	****
Extent	**
Expert	****
Intermediate	***
Beginner	***
Convenience	**
Queues	****
Mountain restaurants	**

The rest

Scenery	****
Charm	*****
Off-slope	*

NEWS

There are plans to build a gondola from the centre of Grimentz into the Zinal ski area and build a new easier slope back. There are also plans to build Grimentz's first 4-star hotel and a spa with thermal baths. But these won't be in place until 2008/09 at the earliest.

For 2006/07 Zinal's first snowmaking (6km/4 miles of it) was installed.

KEY FACTS

Resorts	1340-2000m
	4,400-6,560ft
Slopes	1340-3000m
	4,400-9,840ft
Lifts	45
Pistes	220km
	137 miles
Blue	36%
Red	52%
Black	12%
Snowmaking	24km
	15 miles

COEUR DU VALAIS

Wooden houses and narrow paths give the villages a charming old-world feel →

- ✚ Charming unspoiled villages
- ✚ Four contrasting ski areas with good uncrowded intermediate cruising
- ✚ Excellent extensive off-piste
- ✚ Reliable snow-cover

- ➖ Resorts might be too quiet for some; few shops, no nightlife
- ➖ Each area has very limited pistes
- ➖ To make the most of all the areas you really need a car

We are always looking for 'undiscovered gems'. Last winter we found one. If you like ancient, quiet, totally unspoiled mountain villages with small varied ski areas attached, get to Val d'Anniviers now. The slopes are limited in extent for keen piste-bashers, but they are delightfully uncrowded and have a good snow record. And there is fabulous off-piste to explore with a guide.

When you turn off the Rhône valley road at Sierre and head up the Val d'Anniviers (opposite Crans-Montana) you head into a time-warp. It is incredible that the ski resorts in this valley can have remained so amazingly unspoiled when they are so close to big-name resorts such as Verbier, Crans-Montana and Zermatt. The villages all have lots of old wooden houses and barns, narrow paths and lanes and few shops except ski shops and those catering for locals' needs.

The handful of reader reports we have all enthuse about its charming, old-world atmosphere and beg us not to do a full chapter on it for fear that it will be ruined by an influx of Brits.

Well, we agonised hard. But we thought we ought to let you into the secret. Our advice is to get there quickly before it has time to catch up with the 21st century. There are signs of that, with a lot of (tasteful and low-rise) new building going on – mainly aimed at providing apartments and chalets for sale as second homes.

There are four main areas of slopes, only two of which are linked (and then only one way, by a long black/itinerary run – but that is due to change, see 'News'). And if you plan to explore them all, it's best to have a car as the bus links are not great. Nearly all the slopes are above the tree line and there's a lot of skiing above 2400m/7,870ft, which usually means good snow conditions. None of the areas is huge in terms of piste mileage (we skied all Zinal's pistes in an afternoon, St Luc-Chandolin's in a day, and Grimentz's in a day). But there is good off-piste (especially in Grimentz).

ST LUC / CHANDOLIN

1650m/5,410ft / 2000m/6,560ft

These are the sunniest of the main ski resort villages and share the biggest ski area. St Luc also has the attraction of a fabulous hotel.

A funicular goes up from the edge of St Luc and a high-speed chair from the edge of Chandolin. Both are served by free ski-buses. The 75km/47 miles of slopes face south and west so get a lot of sun, and it was classic spring skiing on our visit last March – hard in the morning and softening up by noon. Apart from the one fast quad from Chandolin, there is only one other

UK PACKAGES

St Luc *Inntravel, Made to Measure*
Zinal *Interhome, Ski Freedom*
Grimentz *Alpine Answers, Mountain Tracks, Ski Freshtracks*

Phone numbers
From elsewhere in Switzerland add the prefix 0848 (for Coeur du Valais) and 027 (for everywhere else); from abroad use the prefix +41 and omit the initial '0'

TOURIST OFFICES

Val d'Anniviers
www.sierre-anniviers.ch

Grimentz
t 475 1493
info@sierre-anniviers.ch
www.grimentz.ch

St-Luc
t 475 1412
saint-luc@sierre-anniviers.ch
www.saint-luc.ch

Vercorin
t 455 5855
vercorin@sierre-anniviers.ch
www.vercorin.ch

Zinal
t 475 1370
zinal@sierre-anniviers.ch
www.zinal.ch

Chandolin
t 475 1838
chandolin@sierre-anniviers.ch
www.chandolin.ch

Coeur du Valais
t 848 848 027
www.coeurduvalais.ch

chair-lift – the other 11 lifts are drags.

The pistes suit beginners and intermediates best; there are no black runs though there are three short itinéraires and a gnarly free-ride area where competitions are held. Most of the reds and blues have a fairly similar pitch whatever the colour – best for those who like easy cruising in the sun. We loved the long red run from the high point of Bella Tola at 3000m/9,840ft away from all the lifts down to the Tipi bar in the valley, where you catch the navette back to town or the funicular – a great way to end the day. There's a good beginner area near the top of the St Luc funicular. Two good mountain restaurants are the tiny Cabane de Illhorn above Chandolin and the Cabane Bella Tola above St Luc – both with terraces with stunning views.

Both Chandolin and St Luc are fairly spread out. But St Luc has a charming compact centre with a small outdoor après-ski bar. The delightful 4-star hotel Bella Tola (475 1444) is just a few strides from here. We managed to get in for one night only, but loved it – built in 1859, it has been beautifully renovated by its current owners with a fine spa and great sunny terrace.

ZINAL 1670m/5,480ft

This small village near the head of the valley has a small area of slopes with stunning views over to a series of high peaks including the Matterhorn.

A cable-car takes you up to Sorebois at 2440m/8,000ft, the hub of the small ski area. Most of the slopes face north or east and keep their snow well. It is popular with families and there's a good beginner area near the top of the cable-car. The runs are mainly short (some only 200m/660ft or 300m/980ft vertical) but include some good reds – our favourites were those from Combe Durand at the edge of the ski area and served by a drag-lift (there's a designated free-ride area served by this drag too). The two short black runs in the main ski area are really of red steepness, but the long black run back to town can be tricky and many people ride the cable-car back down. There's also a long black run/itinéraire leading to Grimentz, which can also be tricky. And there's great off-piste in bowls between the pistes in the main ski area. Zinal has a handful of hotels, including the central modern 3-star Europe (475 4404).

GRIMENTZ 1570m/5,150ft

Grimentz has a richly deserved reputation for its extensive off-piste. And it has a small area of varied pistes above its very cute old village centre.

A gondola from the centre of the village takes you up to Bendolla at 2130m/6,990ft, where there's a good roped off beginner area. Above this are two main sectors. On the right as you look up are easy blues and reds. On the left are steeper and quieter runs including a two blacks, one of which goes from the top to almost the bottom of the mountain (1300m/4,26oft vertical) and is interestingly varied. But the real attraction for experts is the extensive off-piste. We did a great run with a guide off the back of Roc d'Orzival: a huge, ski-anywhere bowl that goes on for hundreds of turns before dropping into an area of widely spaced trees and a long run-out – we saw no one else for almost 1250m/4,100ft vertical. And there are plenty more off-piste options. The International ski school was 'highly recommended' by a 2007 reporter and her three beginner children.

The functional main restaurant near the top of the gondola is mainly self-service, with a small table-service section that serves good food. And we've had good reports of the rustic Étable du Marais. As the lifts close, Chez Florioz on the piste just above the village is the place for après-ski.

The village is spread out with a lot of new building going on. But the centre is charming – lots of tiny old barns and narrow paths. It's best to stay near the centre, close to the gondola. The 3-star Alpina (476 1616) is comfortable and the 2-star Moiry (475 1144) is recommended.

VERCORIN 1340m/4,400ft

The smallest area of slopes and not as easy to get to from the other resorts.

The pretty village of Vercorin, perched on a shelf overlooking the Rhône valley, is reached by a winding road or a cable-car from just outside Sierre. The slopes suit intermediates best.

SIERRE 560m/1840ft

Not a ski resort but the hub of the Coeur du Valais region of which the Val d'Anniviers is a part.

This small town is known as the 'city of sunshine' and is the centre of the Valais vineyards; there's a wine-growing marked walk and a museum.

Combe Durand

Corne de Sorebois
2895m

2440m

ZINAL

Zinal
1670m/5,48oft

Bella Tola
3000m

Mottec

288om

GRIMENTZ

2130m

Grimentz
157om/5,15oft

Roc d'Orzival
2855m

2770m

St-Jean

2470m

Tignousa
2180m

St-Luc
165om/5,41oft

Mt Major
2375m

Illhorn
2600m

Vissoie

ST LUC-CHANDOLIN

VERCORIN

Chandolin
2000m/6,56oft

Vercorin
134om/4,4ooft

Chalais

To
Geneva
→

Sierre
56om/1,84oft

Big, chalet-style resort that attracts powderhounds from all over the world – and big-spending night owls from Geneva

RATINGS

The slopes

Fast lifts	**
Snow	***
Extent	*****
Expert	*****
Intermediate	***
Beginner	**
Convenience	**
Queues	***
Mountain restaurants	***

The rest

Scenery	****
Resort charm	***
Off-slope	***

NEWS

For 2007/08 an eight-person gondola is planned to replace the existing one from La Tzoumaz on the back of Savoleyres. The resort also wants to replace the gondola on the Verbier side of Savoleyres, starting from a new base at the nursery slopes in Les Esserts – maybe for 2009/10.

Also next season, snowmaking is due to be increased throughout the main bowl.

For 2006/07 a six-pack with covers replaced a chair-lift and gondola from La Combe (near Les Ruinettes) to Attelas.

Snowmaking was increased around La Chaux. At Thyon, snowmaking now covers 80 per cent of the slopes.

544

➕ Extensive, challenging slopes with a lot of off-piste and long bump runs

➕ Upper slopes offer a real high-mountain feel plus great views

➕ Pleasant, animated village in a sunny, panoramic setting

➕ Lively, varied nightlife

➕ Much improved lift system, piste grooming and signposting

➖ Some overcrowded pistes and areas

➖ The 4 Valleys network is much less wonderful than it looks on paper

➖ Sunny lower slopes will always be a problem, even with snowmaking

➖ Some long walks/rides to lifts

➖ Resort's reputation means that off-piste is tracked out quickly

For experts prepared to hire a guide to explore off-piste, Verbier is one of the world's cult resorts. For vibrant nightlife, too, it is difficult to beat. With its claimed 410km/255 miles of pistes, Verbier also seems at first sight to rank alongside the French mega-networks that are so compelling for keen piste skiers. But if the Three Valleys and Paradiski are what floats your boat, you may be sorely disappointed by the 4 Valleys network, which is an inconveniently sprawling affair, with lots of tedious links to get from one end to the other. Verbier's local pistes leave a lot to be desired, too: by comparison with the slopes of somewhere like Courchevel, they are confined and crowded.

To look on the bright side, we're happy to recognise that Verbier has recently made great strides in tackling other issues that have in the past spoilt the place for the average visitor. Even its atrocious on-mountain signposting has been replaced – and linked to its piste map. At last, this is no longer a resort where we expect to get lost on the way home.

THE RESORT

Verbier is an amorphous sprawl of chalet-style buildings in an impressive setting on a wide, sunny balcony facing spectacular peaks. It's a fashionable, informal, very lively place that teems with cosmopolitan visitors. Most are younger than visitors to other big Swiss resorts.

Most of the shops and hotels (but not chalets) are set around the Place Centrale and along the sloping streets stretching both down the hill and up it to the main lift station at Médran 500m/1,640ft away. Much of the nightlife is here, too, though bars are rather scattered. These central areas get unpleasantly packed with cars at busy times, especially weekends. More chalets and apartments are built each year, with many newer properties inconveniently situated along the road to the lift base for the secondary Savoleyres area, about 1.5km/1 mile from Médran.

The Médran lift station is a walkable distance from the Place Centrale, so staying there has attractions, and there is accommodation close to the lift that is sufficiently distant from nightlife to avoid late-night noise. If nightlife is not a priority, staying somewhere near the upper (north-east) fringes of the village may mean that you can almost ski to your door – and there is a piste linking the upper nursery slopes to the one in the middle of the village. But in practice most people just get used to using the free buses, which run efficiently on several routes until 8pm.

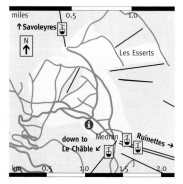

↑ The pistes on Mont-Fort offer a range of gradients from genuine black to seriously steep

WENDY-JANE KING

stay down in the valley village of Le Châble, which has a gondola up to Verbier and on into the slopes. Across the valley, Bruson is more attractive as a place to visit for a day than to stay in. These alternatives are all described at the end of the chapter.

Chamonix and Champéry are within reach by car. But a car can be a bit of a nuisance in Verbier itself. Parking is tightly controlled; your chalet or hotel may not have enough space for all guests' cars, which means a hike from the free parking at the sports centre or paying for garage space.

THE MOUNTAINS

Essentially this is high-mountain terrain. There are wooded slopes directly above the village, but the runs here are basically just a way home at the end of the day. There is more sheltered skiing in other sectors – particularly above Veysonnaz.

THE SLOPES
Very spread out
Savoleyres is the smaller area, reached by a gondola from the north-west end of the village. This area is underrated and generally underused, and plans to encourage its use by building a new access gondola from the central nursery slopes are to be welcomed. It has open, sunny slopes on the front side, and long, pleasantly wooded, shadier runs on the back. You can take a catwalk across from Savoleyres to the foot of Verbier's main slopes. These are served by lifts from Médran, at the opposite end of the village.

Two gondolas rise to **Les Ruinettes** and then a gondola and chair-lift continue on to **Les Attelas**. From Les Attelas a small cable-car goes up to Mont-Gelé, for steep off-piste runs only. Heading down instead, you can go back westwards to Les Ruinettes, south to La Chaux or north to Lac des Vaux. From Lac des Vaux chairs go back to Les Attelas and up to Chassoure, the top of a wide, steep and shady off-piste mogul field leading down to **Tortin**, with a gondola back.

The link between Les Ruinettes and La Chaux has been greatly improved by the chondola installed two years ago. The local La Chaux slopes are served by an additional slow chair-lift and are the departure point of a jumbo cable-car up to Col des Gentianes and the glacier area. A second, much smaller

Some areas have quite an infrequent service. We are told that from 7pm to 8.30 there is a special taxi service that will drop you at any of the usual bus stops for five francs per person.

Verbier is at one end of a long, strung-out series of interconnected slopes, optimistically branded the 4 Valleys and linking Verbier to Nendaz, Veysonnaz, Thyon and other resorts. These other resorts have their own pros and cons. All are appreciably cheaper places to stay than Verbier, and some are more sensible bases for those who plan to stick to pistes rather than venture off-piste – the Veysonnaz-Thyon sector, in particular, is much more intermediate-friendly than Verbier. As bases for exploration of the whole 4 Valleys, only Siviez is much of an advance on Verbier. They are much less lively in the evening. You can also cable-car then goes up to the **Mont-Fort** glacier, the high point of the 4 Valleys. From the top, a long, very steep black run leads down to very shallow reds served by drag-lifts. Below them there's another off-piste route down to Tortin; the whole north-facing run from the top to Tortin is almost 1300m/4,270ft vertical. A cable-car returns to Col des Gentianes.

Below Tortin is the gateway to the rest of the 4 Valleys, **Siviez**, where one 'ridiculously outdated' chair goes off

into the long, thin **Nendaz** sector and a fast quad heads for the **Thyon-Veysonnaz** sector, via a couple of lifts and a lot of catwalks.

Allow plenty of time to get to and from these remote corners – the taxi-rides home are expensive.

The slopes of **Bruson** are described briefly at the end of this chapter.

TERRAIN-PARKS
Expert and beginner options
The 1936 Neipark, Verbier's main

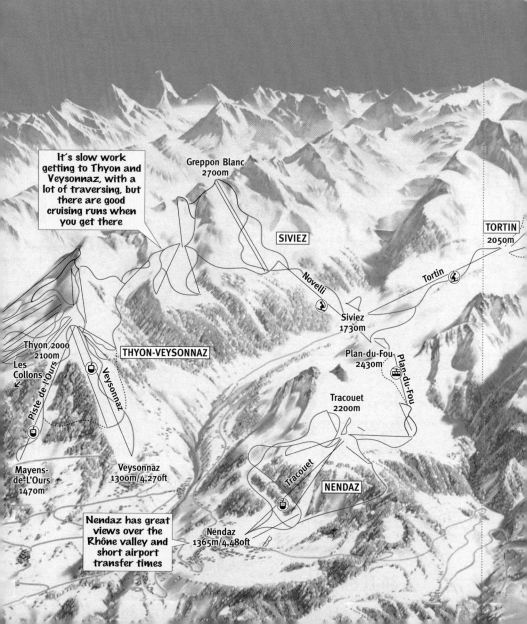

It's slow work getting to Thyon and Veysonnaz, with a lot of traversing, but there are good cruising runs when you get there

Greppon Blanc 2700m

SIVIEZ

TORTIN 2050m

Novelli

Tortin

Siviez 1730m

Thyon 2000 2100m

Les Collons

THYON-VEYSONNAZ

Veysonnaz

Piste de l'Ours

Plan-du-Fou 2430m

Plan-du-Fou

Tracouet 2200m

Mayens-de-l'Ours 1470m

Veysonnaz 1300m/4,270ft

Tracouet

NENDAZ

Nendaz has great views over the Rhône valley and short airport transfer times

Nendaz 1365m/4,48oft

freestyle area, is at La Chaux (www.neipark.ch). The park has four separate lines that they term soft, medium, hard and rail. These are made up of kickers, gap jumps, step-ups and hips. The rails are varied with boxes and rails of all types and a skate-style pyramid, which is the outstanding feature and gives the park its identity. There is a chill-out zone with deckchairs and DJs. New this year is a permanent BBQ, great for avoiding crowded restaurants. A day terrain-park

pass can be purchased, and freestyle coaching is available (check www.snowschool.ch for details). Note that helmets are mandatory. A second smaller park in Savoleyres is more geared to beginner freestylers.

SNOW RELIABILITY
Improved snowmaking

The slopes of the Mont-Fort glacier always have good snow. The runs to Tortin are normally snow-sure, too. But nearly all of this is steep, and much of

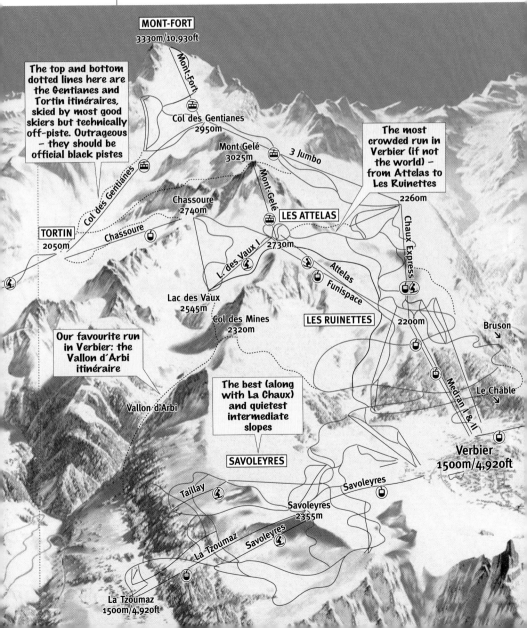

MONT-FORT
3330m/10,930ft

The top and bottom dotted lines here are the Gentianes and Tortin itinéraires, skied by most good skiers but technically off-piste. Outrageous – they should be official black pistes

Col des Gentianes
2950m

Mont-Gelé
3025m

3 Jumbo

The most crowded run in Verbier (if not the world) – from Attelas to Les Ruinettes

2260m

Chassoure
2740m

Col des Gentianes

LES ATTELAS

Chaux Express

TORTIN
2050m

Chassoure

Mont-Gelé

2730m

L. des Vaux I

Attelas
Funispace

2200m

Bruson

Lac des Vaux
2545m

Col des Mines
2320m

LES RUINETTES

Our favourite run in Verbier: the Vallon d'Arbi itinéraire

The best (along with La Chaux) and quietest intermediate slopes

Le Châble

Médran I & II

Vallon d'Arbi

Verbier
1500m/4,920ft

SAVOLEYRES

Savoleyres

Taillay

Savoleyres
2355m

Savoleyres

La Tzoumaz

Savoleyres

La Tzoumaz
1500m/4,920ft

KEY FACTS

Resort	1500m
	4,920ft

4 Valleys area	
Slopes	1500-3330m
	4,920-10,930ft
Lifts	89
Pistes	410km
	255 miles
Blue	33%
Red	41%
Black	26%
Snowmaking	50km
	31 miles

Verbier, Bruson and
Tzoumaz/Savoleyres
sectors only (covered
by Verbier pass)

Slopes	1500-3025m
	4,920-9,920ft
Lifts	40
Pistes	150km
	93 miles
Blue	33%
Red	33%
Black	34%
Snowmaking	20km
	12 miles

it is formally off-piste. Most of Verbier's main local slopes face south or west and are below 2500m/8,200ft – so they can be in poor condition at times. There is snowmaking on the main run down all the way from Attelas to Médran (though we were surprised to see it little used during our February visit); more was added at La Chaux last season and, by contrast, was well used. Further snowmaking is expected for 2007/08 as part of a long-term plan to cover 60 per cent of the pistes. The north-facing slopes of Savoleyres generally hold their snow well, and at Veysonnaz-Thyon snowmaking was increased to cover 80 per cent of the area last season. We were very impressed with its use on the runs down to Mayens-de-L'Ours and to Veysonnaz. Piste grooming is good throughout the Four Valleys, particularly at La Chaux.

FOR EXPERTS
The main attraction

Verbier has some superb tough slopes, many of them off-piste and needing a guide – see the separate feature panel on this. There are few conventional black pistes; most of the runs that might have this designation are now defined as itinéraires – which means they are 'marked, not maintained and not controlled'. But they are closed if unsafe or if snow-cover is insufficient. We'd like to see them given official black piste status, so you know clearly where you stand. The blacks that do exist are mostly indistinguishable from nearby reds. The front face of Mont-Fort is an exception: a long mogul-field, with a choice of gradient from seriously steep to intimidatingly steep. The World Cup run at Veysonnaz is a steepish, often icy red, ideal for really speeding down. The two itinéraires to Tortin are both excellent in their different ways. The one from Chassoure is just one wide, steep slope, normally a huge mogul field.

The north-facing itinéraire from Gentianes is longer, less steep, but feels much more of an adventure (keep left for quieter and shallower slopes and better snow, right for steeper moguls where the crowds go). There is an entertaining itinéraire from Greppon Blanc, at the top of the Siviez sector, into the next valley – return by bus.

FOR INTERMEDIATES
Hit Savoleyres – or Veysonnaz

Many mileage-hungry intermediates find Verbier disappointing. The intermediate slopes in the main area are concentrated between Les Attelas and the village, above and below Les Ruinettes, plus the little bowl at Lac des Vaux and the sunny slopes at La Chaux. This is all excellent and varied intermediate territory, but there isn't much of it – to put it in perspective, this whole area is no bigger than the tiny slopes of Alpbach – and it is used by the bulk of the visitors staying in one of Switzerland's largest resorts. So it is often very crowded, especially the otherwise wonderful sweeping red from Les Attelas to Les Ruinettes. Even early intermediates should taste the perfect snow on the glacier. The red run served by the T-bars is really of gentle blue steepness. And the red path from Col des Gentianes to La Chaux is not too difficult, but its high-mountain feel can be unnerving and it's no disgrace to ride the cable-car down instead.

There is excellent easy blue-run skiing at La Chaux (including a 'slow skiing' piste, though this was not policed when we were there). Thankfully, getting back from La Chaux to Les Ruinettes is now a lot easier as you can ride the chondola instead of taking a tricky red run.

Intermediates should exploit the under-used Savoleyres area. This has good intermediate pistes, usually better snow and far fewer people (especially on Sundays). It is also a

boarding

Verbier has become synonymous with extreme snowboarding and is generally seen as a free-riders' resort, with powder, cliffs, natural hits and trees all easily accessible. For years the Bec des Rosses has been the home to the Verbier extreme contest, one of the most high-profile events of the sort on the calendar. There is a lot of steep and challenging terrain to be explored with a guide, but the pistes and itinéraires will provide most riders with plenty to think about. The main area is serviced by chair-lifts and gondolas with no drags, and there is a good terrain-park at La Chaux, which improves every year. Beginners should stick to the lower blue runs and the Savoleyres area, but there are several drag-lifts there.

OFF-PISTE FOR ALL

Verbier has some of the best, most extensive and most varied off-piste in the world, and major free-ride competitions are held there every year. Here, we pick out just a few of the off-piste runs on offer.

The Col de Mines and Vallon d'Arbi itinéraires, accessible from Lac de Vaux, are relatively easy (and usually less crowded and skied out than the better-known Tortin and Gentianes itinéraires) – the former is a long, open slope back to Verbier and the latter a very beautiful run in a steep-sided valley down to La Tzoumaz and the Savoleyres lifts. Fontainay, accessible from the chondola, is an itinéraire that is great for learning how to deal with moguls, steeps or powder.

Stairway to Heaven is usually quiet and its snow is kept in good condition by the lack of crowds and its shady orientation. It starts a short ski, pole and climb from Col des Gentianes. Then you drop over the ridge into a deserted valley, and it's a long, relatively easy ski in powder down to Tortin, pretty much parallel to the popular Gentianes itinéraire.

The Mt-Gelé cable-car, when it is open, offers some of the most amazing terrain accessible anywhere by lift, with long runs down to Siviez on steep but open slopes, before a long scenic traverse and schuss along the valley. Alternatively, go down the opposite side of the mountain through the steep rock face towards Lac de Vaux , not a route for the faint of heart but a must for adrenalin junkies if conditions are good. The many couloirs accessible from Attelas can also be fantastic. There are serious adventures to be had off the back of Mont-Fort – notably down to Lac de Cleuson and eventually to Siviez.

Whenever skiing or boarding off-piste, safety equipment such as transceivers, helmets, back protection, shovels and probes should always be worn and carried, and unless you are highly experienced you should go with a guide.

good hill for mixed abilities, with variations of many runs. There is a blue run linking this sector to Médran but the way down to that link from the top of Savoleyres is not easy.

The Veysonnaz-Thyon and Nendaz sectors are worth exploring (those not willing to take on the itinéraires have to ride down to Tortin; and down from Plan du Fou to get to Nendaz). Some of the reds here might be blacks elsewhere – the one at Combatzeline is consistently steep.

FOR BEGINNERS
OK but not ideal
There are sunny nursery slopes close to the middle of the village and at Les Esserts, at the top of it. These are fine provided they have snow (they have a lot of snowmaking, which helps). For progression, there are easy blues at La Chaux (you can ride the chondola back to Les Ruinettes) and the back side of Savoleyres (from where you can ride the gondola down). Siviez has a really gentle, wide blue.

FOR CROSS-COUNTRY
Surprisingly little on offer
Verbier is limited for cross-country. There's a 4km/2.5 mile circuit in Verbier, 6km/3.5 miles at Les Ruinettes-La Chaux and 30km/19 miles down in the valley at Le Châble/Val de Bagnes.

QUEUES
Not the problem they were
Verbier's queue problems have been greatly eased by recent investment in powerful new lifts. The new chair to Attelas for 2006/07 was blissfully queue-free during our February visit and seems to have dealt with some of the pressure at the top station – but we lack sufficient reports to assess the impact on piste crowding. The cable-car from Tortin to Col des Gentianes and the Mont-Fort cable-car above it can still generate queues – but at least the low capacity of this lift means no crowds on the higher pistes. Some queues at the main village lift station at Médran can arise if Sunday visitors fill the gondola down at Le Châble, but the crowds shift quickly.

Queues can occur for outdated double chairs and for inadequate drag-lifts in the outlying 4 Valleys resorts.

Savoleyres is generally queue-free, for the moment at least.

MOUNTAIN RESTAURANTS
Could do better
There are not enough huts, which means overcrowding in high season and queues unless you book ahead. But the standard of food and service is improving.

Editors' choice In the main area, the rustic Restaurant de Clambin Chez Dany (771 2524), on the off-piste run on the southern fringe of the area, is a

Verbier's new signs: a great improvement on the ones we have struggled with for years →

WENDY-JANE KING

SCHOOLS

Swiss
t 775 3363 / 3369

Fantastique
t 771 4141

Adrenaline
t 771 7459

Altitude
t 771 6006

New Generation
t 771 1181 /
+33 479 010318

European Snowsport
t 771 6222

Powder Extreme
t 020 8675 5407 (UK)

Warren Smith Ski Academy
t 01525 374757 (UK)

Classes
(Swiss prices)
5 2½hr days SF220

Private lessons
From SF150 for 2hr
for 1 or 2 people

GUIDES

Bureau des guides
t 775 3363

Olivier Roduit
t 771 5317

CHILDREN

Schtroumpfs
t 771 6585
Ages 3mnth to 4yr;
8.30 to 5.30

Kids Club
t 775 3363
From age 3; 8.30-
5pm; 6 days SF450
including lunch

Ski school
Takes children aged 4
to 12 (5 half days
SF195)

classic cosy old chalet. It is under new management but still about the best, and gets packed – booking needed.

Worth knowing about For a choice of good spots, Savoleyres is the place to go. The rustic Marmotte does superb rösti, but the Namasté is 'the best restaurant on the mountain' (booking essential). The Sonalon, on the fringe of the village, is 'excellent, with great views', but reached off-piste, as is the nearby Marlenaz ('what a great find, hearty and well recommended').

The self-service at the top of Savoleyres has a new menu, providing 'good value' Italian and traditional dishes. The Poste hotel by the Tzoumaz chair takes some beating for value and lack of crowds.

Back in the main sector, the restaurants at Les Ruinettes – table-service upstairs – have big terraces with splendid views. The Olympique at Les Attelas is a good table-service restaurant. The Powder Spirit Bar (formerly the Attelas) does light meals. Au Mayern has 'interesting seafood choices'. Everyone loves the Cabane Mont-Fort – a proper mountain refuge off the run to La Chaux from Col des Gentianes – get there early or book a table. Chalet Carlsberg has a good position at La Combe and impressed us with fast and efficient service.

There's a choice of places at Veysonnaz-Thyon; most are clearly cheaper than in Verbier, but 'nothing special' according to a 2007 visitor.

SCHOOLS AND GUIDES
Good reports
There's no shortage of schools to choose between. The Swiss school receives a good report this year for private snowboard lessons. Adrenaline also gets good reviews for its private lessons. A 2006 reporter praised his Swiss instructor with European Snowsport. Altitude was started by top

British instructors in 2001 – though we lack reports on them. British instructor Warren Smith runs his Ski Academy here. Powder Extreme specialises in off-piste. We have skied with both Warren Smith and Powder Extreme and thought them both good. New Generation opened their first Swiss branch in the resort this year.

FACILITIES FOR CHILDREN
Wide range of options
The Swiss school's facilities in the resort are good, and the resort attracts quite a lot of families. The possibility of leaving very young babies at the Schtroumpfs nursery is valuable.

There are considerable reductions on the lift pass price for families on production of your passports.

STAYING THERE

HOW TO GO
Plenty of options
Given the size of the place there are surprisingly few apartments and pensions available, though those on a budget have inexpensive B&B options in Le Châble. Hotels are expensive in relation to their grading. If you take a sleeping bag, you can bed down at the sports centre for about £10 a night – and that includes the use of the pool.
Chalets Verbier is the chalet-party capital of Switzerland. Companies large and small have properties here. The dominant position of Verbier specialist Ski Verbier – which repeatedly gets good reports from readers – is confirmed by its recent acquisition of the superb Septième Ciel, giving the company an impressive portfolio at the top of the market. Descent still has the impressive Goodwood. If the budget is inelastic, start with Crystal Finest.
Hotels There is one 5-star hotel, five 4-star, 13 3-star and a few simpler places.
*****Chalet d'Adrien (771 6200) Relais & Chateaux. A beautifully furnished low-rise 25-room chalet, with top-notch cooking. In a peaceful setting next to the Savoleyres lift, with great views. Neat spa/gym/pool.
****Rosalp (771 6323) Relais & Chateaux. Comfortable rooms but the great attraction is the food – though Roland Pierroz has now retired. Sauna, steam, hot-tub. Good position midway between centre and Médran.
****Montpelier (771 6131) Very comfortable, but out of town (free courtesy bus). Pool.

****Vanessa** (775 2800) Central, with spacious apartments as well as rooms; 'Great food,' says a reporter.

***Rotonde** (771 6525) Much cheaper; well positioned between centre and Médran; some budget rooms.

***Verbier Lodge** (771 6666) Modern log-built place now owned by Virgin and being refurbished. Expected to re-open in December 2007.

***Poste** (771 6681) Well placed midway between centre and Médran; pool. Some rooms small. 'Friendly staff and great food.'

***Farinet** (771 6626) Central, British-owned, with a focal après-ski bar on its elevated terrace.

Apartments Few UK tour operators offer apartments, but they can be booked locally.

EATING OUT
Plenty of choice

There is a very wide range of restaurants; a pocket guide is given away locally that would be much more useful if all its advertisers gave some clues about price.

The Rosalp has for years been the best (and most expensive) in town, and among the best in Switzerland –

splash out on the seven-course menu gastronomique if you can afford it. We have had two delicious meals there. The Pinte bistro in the hotel basement is a less expensive option – worth trying. The 5-star Chalet d'Adrien also has two tempting options, with an Italian influence under the new chef at L'Appartement. The Grange is also serious about its food.

King's is one of our favourites – innovative food in a stylish, club-like setting. The King's cafe is the latest addition to the group. We've also had excellent meals in the stylish Millénium. The small, traditional Ecurie does 'excellent steaks'.

For Swiss specialities, try the Relais des Neiges, the Robinson, the Caveau, Au Mignon, Au Vieux Verbier by the Médran lifts or Esserts by the nursery slopes. The ever-popular Fer à Cheval does reasonably priced pizza and other simple dishes. Or try downstairs in the Pub Mont-Fort for 'top British gastropub food at reasonable prices'. The 'hanging meat' has to be tried at Al Capone's, out near the Savoleyres gondola – also known for its pizzas; but a 2006 reporter preferred Borsalino. Harold's Snack internet cafe

is a 'reasonable burger joint', and a 2007 visitor recommends Chez Martin for pasta.

You can be ferried by snowmobile up to Chez Dany or the Marmotte for a meal, followed by a torchlit descent.

APRES-SKI
Throbbing but expensive
It starts with a 4pm visit to the Powder Spirit Bar and its new DJ ('the liveliest place on the mountain') and moves to either the tents of 1836, halfway down from Les Ruinettes, or the Offshore Cafe at Médran, for people-watching, milk shakes and cakes. The nearby Big Ben pub is 'great and lively on a sunny afternoon'. Au Mignon at the bottom of the golf course has a popular sun deck.

Then if you're young, loud and British, it's on to the Pub Mont-Fort – there's a widescreen TV for live sport. The Nelson and Fer à Cheval are popular with locals. The Farinet has won awards for its après-ski and regularly rocks to live bands ('beer, band and bop were great'). Or you can sip sophisticated cocktails in its lounge bar next door.

After dinner the Pub Mont-Fort is again popular (the shots bar in the cellar is worth a visit). Crok No Name is a cool bar with good live bands or a DJ. Murphy's Irish bar in the Garbo hotel is popular, with a good resident DJ. King's is a quiet candlelit cellar bar with 60s decor – 'hip crowd, good music'. New Club is a sophisticated piano bar, with comfortable seating and a more discerning clientele. The Farm Club is seriously expensive – on Friday and Saturday packed with rich Swiss paying SF220 for bottles of spirits. You'll find us having a quiet nightcap in the basement Bar'Jo, across the road.

The Casbah, in the basement of the Farinet hotel, is a nightclub with a North African theme. Taratata is a friendly club that seems to be growing in popularity. The Icebox packs a big 70s party into a small, 'funky' venue ('best value, best music').

OFF THE SLOPES
No great attraction
Verbier has an excellent sports centre (with pool, saunas and hot-tubs), some nice walks and a big alpine museum, but otherwise not much to offer if you don't want to hit the slopes. Montreux is an enjoyable train excursion from Le Châble, and Martigny is worth a visit for the Roman remains and art gallery. The spa complex at Lavey-les-Bains has been highly recommended by a reporter. Various mountain restaurants are accessible to pedestrians. A walker's pass (SF40) covers most of the local lifts. Swiss Mountain Spirit offer new dog-sledding trips. There's floodlit tubing etc at Les Esserts at the weekends. The new Verbier entertainment book costs SF35 and offers worthy discounts on various shopping, dining and leisure activities.

Nendaz 1365m/4,480ft

Nendaz is a big resort with over 17,000 beds, but is little known in Britain. Although it appears to be centrally set in the 4 Valleys, getting to and from the other sectors is a slow business unless you drive/take a bus to Siviez ('To get into the Verbier skiing takes a decent skier about an hour,' said a 2006 reporter). In other respects it has attractions, relatively low prices among them. Airport transfers are quick, especially from Sion (20 minutes away).

THE RESORT
Nendaz itself is a large place with great views of the Rhône valley. Most of the resort is modern but built in traditional chalet style, and the original old village of Haute-Nendaz is still there, with its narrow streets, old houses and barns, and baroque chapel dating from 1499.

THE MOUNTAIN
Nendaz has its own area of slopes and a link to rest of the 4 Valleys via Siviez.
Slopes There's a 12-person gondola straight to the top of the local north-facing slopes at Tracouet. Here there are good, snow-sure nursery slopes plus blue and red intermediate runs.

Intermediates and better can head off down the back of Tracouet to a

The recently built Chalet Carlsberg enjoys a good position on the main slopes down to Les Ruinettes →

WENDY-JANE KING

ACTIVITIES

Indoor Sports centre (swimming pools, ice rink, curling, squash, sauna, solarium, steam bath, hot-tub), museum, gallery

Outdoor 25km/ 16 miles of cleared walking paths, hang-gliding, paragliding, snow-shoeing, dog-sledding, ice-climbing, tobogganing

cable-car that takes you to Plan du Fou at 2430m/7,970ft (if poor weather closes this link, you'll need to catch the regular bus to Siviez). From there you can go down to Siviez, on a couple of sunny, steeper runs, and the links to Verbier one way and Veysonnaz-Thyon the other. To return to Nendaz you have to negotiate an itinéraire from Plan du Fou (or take the cable-car down) followed by a black run.

Terrain-parks The two terrain-parks were recently improved.

Snow reliability Nendaz sits on a north-facing shelf so its local slopes don't get the sun that affects Verbier. Snowmaking is 'good'.

Experts Access to the tough stuff is a bit slower from here than from Verbier.

Intermediates The local slopes are quite varied, but not very extensive.

Beginners There are good nursery slopes at Tracouet.

Snowboarding The terrain is fine but

there are quite a few drag-lifts.

Cross-country There are 12km/7.5 miles of cross-country tracks.

Queues There may be queues during peak periods.

Mountain restaurants The Cabane de Balavaux under the Prarion chair has been praised for its 'excellent food'. A new bar, the Clèves, has opened at Tracouet.

Schools and guides There are four ski schools plus mountain guides.

Facilities for children The schools have a nursery area at Tracouet and there's a resort kindergarten (Le P'tit Bec).

STAYING THERE

How to go UK chalet company Ted Bentley launched a catered chalet operation here last season, and now has three properties including the newly built chalet Alice.

Hotels There are four small hotels. The Mont-Fort (288 2616) has been renovated and modernised.

Apartments There is no shortage of apartments and chalets to rent.

Eating out The Zinc restaurant of the Mont-Fort looks good and the Mont Rouge hotel restaurant, Vieux-Chalet and (out of town on the road to Siviez) the Vieux Nendaz have been recommended.

Après-ski There are plenty of bars and four discos; a 17-year-old reporter recommended the Cactus Saloon as one of the livelier spots.

Off the slopes Nendaz has 70km/ 43 miles of walks, an ice rink, fitness centre, climbing wall and squash courts.

Siviez 1730m/5,680ft

Siviez is a small huddle of buildings in an isolated spot, where the slopes of Verbier, Nendaz and Veysonnaz-Thyon meet. One of these buildings is the 2-star hotel de Siviez (288 1623). It is an ideal base from which to explore the whole 4 Valleys lift network, and the fast quad to Combatzeline has made this easier. The long and gentle blue run through the sheltered valley from Tortin is ideal beginner territory. Being set a little way down the valley from Tortin, at the foot of the steep itinerary runs from Chassoure and Mont-Fort, means it is also an excellent base for

doing the tough skiing of Verbier – you can end the day with a descent of 1600m/5,250ft vertical from Mont-Fort; no noise in the evenings; perfect.

Veysonnaz 1300m/4,270ft

Veysonnaz is a small, quiet, family resort, sunny in the afternoon, at the foot of an excellent, long red slope from the ridge above Thyon. A second excellent red regularly used for international races descends to the isolated lift base of Mayens de l'Ours, a bus-ride outside Veysonnaz.

The resort is spread widely across and down the hillside, with wide views across the Rhone valley. The original attractive old village, complete with church, is two hairpin bends below Veysonnaz Station, the lift base and the main focus of the place for the visitor. This has the essential facilities – half a dozen bars and cafes, four restaurants, a disco or two and a 'good' wellness centre with swimming pool and spa facilities. There are adequate shops.

Accommodation is mainly in apartments – substantial chalet-style buildings dotted along the road across the hillside from the lift base. There are plenty of smaller chalets, too. Of

SWITZERLAND

554

VEYSONNAZ TOURISME

Most of the lodgings at Veysonnaz are in big chalets (top left), well above the old village ↓

the two three-star hotels, the 'very comfortable' Chalet Royal (208 5644) is reportedly preferable to the Magrappé, which is the focus of noisy après-ski. There are some B&Bs.

Taking a car means you can drive to Siviez for quick access to the Verbier or Nendaz slopes, and the resort is only 15km/9 miles from the old town of Sion, which is at the heart of the Coeur du Valais region of which Veysonnaz is a part and which is well worth exploring. The link up to Thyon has been improved – it is now an eight-seat gondola – but after that progress towards Verbier is a slow business. There is, of course, a branch of the Swiss ski school, and its literature is in English as well as French and German.

There is said to be a cross-country trail along the mountainside, with panoramic views.

Thyon 2000 2100m/6,890ft

Thyon 2000 – also part of the Coeur du Valais region – is a functional, purpose-built collection of plain, medium-rise apartment blocks just above the tree line at the hub of the Thyon-Veysonnaz sector of the 4 Valleys. It has the basics of resort life – supermarket, newsagent, a couple of bar-restaurants, an indoor pool, a disco. A free shuttle-bus runs to Les Collons. There's a fair-sized terrain-park – reputedly one of Switzerland's first – and boarder-cross, 'good' children's snow-garden and a kindergarten as well as a ski school. The slopes are ideal for families and beginners, with two nursery lifts close to the accommodation. The lift network shared with Les Collons and Les Masses is elderly and slow – mainly drag-lifts, with three chair-lifts at key points. There is extensive snowmaking.

Les Collons 1800m/5,910ft

Some 300m/980ft below Thyon, at the foot of a broad, east-facing slope, Les Collons is a couple of strings of chalet-style buildings spread along two roads following the hillside, 50m/160ft vertical apart. Most accommodation is in apartments, but there are also a couple of modest hotels – including the 3-star Cambuse (281 1883) just below one of the lift bases. There's a wider range of bars, restaurants and other diversions than in Thyon. There is a short toboggan run through the woods above the village. Prepared walking trails add up to a modest 7km/4 miles. Three drag-lifts go up towards Thyon from the upper level of the resort, and a chair-lift from the lower level takes you above Thyon. A free shuttle-bus runs to Thyon.

Les Masses 1515m/4,970ft

Half-a-dozen hairpins down the mountainside from Les Collons, Les Masses is no more than a hamlet at the base of the double chair-lifts that form the southern limit of the Thyon-Veysonnaz slopes. The home run is a red. Accommodation is in apartments. There is a grocery and a restaurant.

Le Châble 820m/2,690ft

Le Châble is a busy roadside village in the valley, at the bottom of the hairpin road up to Verbier. It is linked to Verbier by a queue-free gondola that goes on (without changing cabins) to Les Ruinettes, which means access to the slopes can be just as quick as from Verbier. Le Châble is on the rail network, and is also convenient for drivers who want to visit other resorts in the Valais or further afield. And it is handy for Bruson. There are several modest hotels, of which the 2-star Giétroz (776 1184) is the pick.

Bruson 1000m/3,280ft

Bruson is a small village on a shelf just above Le Châble, and reached by a short free bus-ride. Its lifts are covered by the Verbier pass. From the village a slow chair goes up over gentle east-facing slopes dotted with chalets to Bruson les Forêts (1600m/5,250ft).

The open slopes above Bruson les Forêts are served by a quad chair up to the ridge, on the far side of which is a short drag-lift serving a tight little bowl. In addition to the intermediate pistes served by these lifts there are large areas of underused off-piste terrain, notably through woods on the front side accessed by the drag on the back. The off-piste down the back towards Orsières is good; you return by train. For years there have been plans to develop Bruson – building lifts from Le Châble and Orsières, and extending the lift network. A new Intrawest village here is at the planning stages. For now, it remains a great place to escape Verbier crowds.

Phone numbers
From elsewhere in Switzerland add the prefix 027; from abroad use the prefix +41 27

TOURIST OFFICES

Verbier
t 775 3888
info@verbier.ch
www.verbier.ch

Nendaz
t 289 5589
info@nendaz.ch
www.nendaz.ch

Siviez
www.siviez-nendaz.ch

Veysonnaz
t 207 1053
tourism
@veysonnaz.ch
www.veysonnaz.ch

Thyon 2000 / Les Collons
t 281 2727
info@thyon-region.ch
www.thyon-region.ch

Le Châble and **Bruson**
t 776 1682
bagnestourisme@verbier.ch

SNOWPIX.COM

Traditional year-round resort with local low-altitude slopes and a much needed but far-flung glacier

COSTS

① ② ③ ④ ⑤ ⑥

RATINGS

The slopes

Fast lifts	★★★
Snow	★★
Extent	★★★
Expert	★★
Intermediate	★★★
Beginner	★★★★
Convenience	★★★
Queues	★★★
Mountain restaurants	★★★

The rest

Scenery	★★★
Resort charm	★★★★
Off-slope	★★★★

NEWS

For 2006/07 a faster eight-person gondola replaced the old four-seater from the town to Roc d'Orsay.

556

➕ Pleasant, relaxing year-round resort

➕ Fairly extensive intermediate slopes linked to Les Diablerets

➕ Good nursery slopes

➕ Quite close to Geneva airport

➕ Good range of off-slope diversions

➖ Unreliable snow-cover

➖ Overcrowded mountain restaurants

➖ Short runs on the upper slopes

➖ Getting up the mountain may mean a slow, often crowded train journey or a bus-ride out to the gondola

With its mountain railway and gentle low-altitude slopes, Villars is the kind of place that has been overshadowed by modern mega-resorts. But for a relaxing and varied family holiday the attractions are clear – and the link with Les Diablerets and its glacier, now known as Glacier 3000, adds to the appeal.

THE RESORT

Villars sits on a sunny shelf, looking across the Rhône valley to the Portes du Soleil. A busy high street lined with a variety of shops gives it the air of a pleasant small town; all around are chalet-style buildings, with just a few block-like hotels.

You can travel to the centre of Villars on a picturesque cog train that goes on up to the slopes. It leaves from Bex in the valley, which is served by direct trains from Geneva airport (as

is Aigle, a bus-ride from Villars). A gondola at the other end of town is the main lift; stay nearby if you can, since shuttle-buses can be 'infrequent' and get crowded at peak times. A 2007 reporter preferred to stay near the railway. You can also stay in Gryon.

You can get a Glacier-Alpes Vaudoises pass covering Les Diablerets and Glacier 3000, plus Leysin and Les Mosses, both of which are easy jaunts by rail or road. Getting to the glacier is a long, slow business though – buses from Les Diablerets are infrequent.

Friendly intermediate terrain abounds ↗
SNOWPIX.COM / CHRIS GILL

KEY FACTS

Resort	1300m
	4,270ft

Villars, Gryon and Les Diablerets, but excluding Glacier 3000

Slopes	1115-2120m
	3,660-6,960ft
Lifts	35
Pistes	100km
	62 miles
Blue	40%
Red	50%
Black	10%
Snowmaking	10km
	6 miles

Phone numbers
From elsewhere in Switzerland add the prefix 024; from abroad use the prefix +41 24

TOURIST OFFICE

t 495 3232
information@villars.ch
www.villars.ch

THE MOUNTAINS

There's a good mix of open and wooded slopes throughout the area. Most reporters agree that the piste map and marking are poor.

Slopes The cog train goes up to the col of Bretaye, which has intermediate slopes on either side, with a maximum vertical of 300m/980ft to the col and much longer runs back to the village. To the east, open slopes (often spoilt by sun) go to La Rasse and the link to the Les Chaux sector. The upgraded gondola from town takes you to Roc d'Orsay, from where you can head for Bretaye or back to Villars. From Bretaye you can head for the long, slow, two-way chair-lift, which is the connection to Les Diablerets. The slopes on the glacier are limited, but there is a splendid red run down the Combe d'Audon back to the valley.

Terrain-parks There are parks at Les Chaux and Chaux Ronde, and a half-pipe at Les Diablerets.

Snow reliability Low altitude and sunny slopes mean snow reliability isn't good – though a modest snowfall produces good conditions on such gentle, grassy terrain. More snowmaking is badly needed.

Experts The main interest for experts is off-piste. Heli-skiing is available.

Intermediates The local slopes and Les Diablerets offer a good variety and add up to a fair amount of terrain.

Beginners Beginners will enjoy the village nursery slopes and riding the train to Bretaye. There are gentle runs here, too, but it's also very crowded.

Snowboarding There are quite a few drag-lifts, including some on the link with Les Diablerets.

Cross-country The trails up the valley past La Rasse are long and pretty, and there are more in the depression beyond Bretaye (44km/27 miles in all).

Queues Queues appear for the lifts at Bretaye mainly at weekends and peak periods, and the buses and train can get overcrowded.

Mountain restaurants They are often oversubscribed – the previously praised Col de Soud disastrously so, says a 2007 reporter. But the Golf is 'still excellent'. The Lac des Chavonnes is popular and worth the walk from Bretaye. The revamped restaurant at the top of the Roc d'Orsay gondola is also 'very good'.

Schools and guides A 2007 visitor praised 'excellent, friendly and conscientious' instructors from the Swiss school. The Villars ski school has also had good reports in the past. Riderschool is a snowboard specialist.

Facilities for children Both ski schools run children's classes, but group sizes were considered too large by a 2007 parent. There is also a non-ski nursery for children up to six.

STAYING THERE

How to go Several tour operators offer packages here. We have received glowing reports on the Club Med. If you fancy sleeping in a hi-tech tent out in the wilds, go to www.whitepod.com.

Hotels The Golf (496 3838) is popular ('spacious rooms', 'excellent restaurant'). The Eurotel Victoria (495 3131) lacks style but is near the gondola. The Bristol (496 3636) is not, but offers 'comfort, good food and service'. All are 4-star. The 3-star Alpe Fleurie (496 3070) near the railway station is 'spacious and comfortable'.

Eating out Many restaurants are hotel-based. Apart from these, the Sporting is recommended for pizza, the Vieux-Villars for local specialities and the Rôtisserie des Alpes for 'great service'.

Après-ski Charlie's, the Sporting and the Mini-Pub are popular bars. The Bowling bar can be a laugh; and El Gringo's is a disco. New venues this year include: the Warm-Up, the Marocan and the BBlounge wine bar.

Off the slopes Paragliding and hang-gliding are available, plus tennis, skating, snow-shoeing, swimming, 'excellent' walks, and trips on the train – to Lausanne, for instance.

UK PACKAGES

Alpine Answers, Club Med, Corporate Ski Co, Crystal, Inghams, Interhome, Kuoni, Lagrange, Made to Measure, Momentum, Ski Independence, Ski Line, Ski Solutions, Ski Weekend, Skitracer, Swiss Travel Service, Switzerland Travel Centre, Thomson

Villars

557

A charming old village amid stunning scenery, where life revolves around the mountain railway; the slopes, somehow, are secondary

COSTS

① ② ③ ④ ⑤ ⑥

RATINGS

The slopes

Fast lifts	****
Snow	**
Extent	***
Expert	**
Intermediate	****
Beginner	***
Convenience	***
Queues	***
Mountain restaurants	****

The rest

Scenery	*****
Charm	*****
Off-slope	****

NEWS

For 2007/08 the Honegg drag-lift (on the Grindelwald side of Kleine Scheidegg) is due to be replaced with a fast six-pack. And substantial new snowmaking for the upper part of the mountain on both sides of Kleine Scheidegg is planned.

558

➕ Some of the most spectacular scenery in the Alps

➕ Tiny, traditional, nearly traffic-free Alpine village

➕ Lots of long, gentle runs, ideal for intermediates

➕ Nursery slopes in heart of village

➕ Calm, unhurried atmosphere

➕ Good resort for families and groups that include non-skiers – easy to get around on mountain railways

➖ Limited terrain for experts and adventurous intermediates

➖ Despite some snowmaking, snow conditions are unreliable

➖ Trains to slopes from here and from Grindelwald are slow – and there are quite a few drags and slow chairs

➖ Getting to Grindelwald's First area can take hours

➖ Subdued in the evening, with little variety of nightlife

Given the charm of the village, the friendliness of the locals and the drama of the scenery, it's easy to see why many people love Wengen – including large numbers of Brits who have been going for decades. It's great for a relaxing time, for those who don't take their skiing too seriously, for families and for mixed groups of intermediates and non-skiers.

But keen piste-bashers should beware of the drawbacks: slow lifts (the only ways up from the village are a slow, infrequent cog railway or a queue-prone cable-car), poor snow reliability, inadequate snowmaking and a lack of challenging pistes are the key factors. If you're used to the modern village ambience and snow-sure networks of slopes of the Trois Vallées resorts or Val d'Isère, you'll find Wengen a huge contrast. Come here for the relaxed ambience, not for piste-bashing.

THE RESORT

Wengen is set on a shelf high above the Lauterbrunnen valley, opposite Mürren, and reached only by a cog railway, which carries on up the mountain as the main lift. Wengen was a farming community long before skiing arrived; it is still tiny, but it is dominated by sizeable hotels, mostly of Victorian origin. So it is not exactly chocolate-box pretty, but it is charming and relaxed, and almost traffic-free. The only vehicles are electric hotel taxi-trucks, which gather at the station to pick up guests, and a few ordinary, engine-driven taxis. (Why, we wonder?)

The short main street is the hub of the village. Lined with chalet-style shops and hotels, it also has the ice rink and village nursery slopes right next to it. The nursery slopes double as the venue for floodlit ski-jumping and parallel slalom races.

The views across the valley are stunning. They get even better higher up, when the famous trio of peaks comes fully into view – the Mönch (Monk) protecting the Jungfrau

(Maiden) from the Eiger (Ogre).

The main way up the mountain is to use the regular, usually punctual trains from the southern end of the street to Kleine Scheidegg (about a half-hour journey), where the slopes of Wengen meet those of Grindelwald. The cable-car is a much quicker way to the Grindelwald slopes, and starts conveniently close to the main street.

Wengen is small, so location isn't as crucial as in many other resorts. The main street is ideally placed for the station. There are hotels on the home piste, convenient for the slopes. Those who don't fancy a steepish morning climb should avoid places down the hill below the station.

You can get to Mürren by taking the train to Lauterbrunnen, then a cable-car and train to Winteregg (where you get a chair-lift up and ski down to the village) or to Mürren itself, where you have to walk though the village to the other lifts. Alternatively you can take an (infrequent) bus to Stechelberg and then a cable-car up. The Jungfrau lift pass covers all of this. Outings further afield aren't really worth the effort.

miles   0.5

Männlichen

Lauterbrunnen down to

N

Kleine Scheidegg

km   0.5

THE MOUNTAINS

Although Wengen is famous for the fearsome Lauberhorn Downhill course – the longest and one of the toughest on the World Cup circuit – its slopes are best suited to early intermediates. Most of the Downhill course is now open to the public. But the steepest section (the Hundschopf jump) can be avoided by an alternative red route. The majority of Wengen's runs are gentle blues and reds, ideal for cruising.

THE SLOPES
Picturesque playground

Most of the slopes are on the Grindelwald side of the mountain. From the railway station at Kleine Scheidegg you can head straight down to Grindelwald or work your way across the mountain with the help of a couple of lifts to the top of the Männlichen. This area is served by drags and chair-lifts, and can be reached directly from Wengen by the cable-car. There are a few runs back down towards Wengen from the top of the Lauberhorn, but there's really only one below Wengernalp.

TERRAIN-PARKS
Not right now

The nearest parks are at First and Mürren – each a fair trek. But there is talk of a new park being built near Kleine Scheidegg at some stage.

SNOW RELIABILITY
Improved snowmaking may help

Most slopes are below 2000m/6,560ft, and at Grindelwald they go down to less than 1000m/3,280ft. Very few slopes face north, and the long blue run back to the village suffers from sun and lack of altitude. So good natural snow is far from certain. Views on the snowmaking continue to improve ('very impressed – the main piste to Wengen was kept open', 'a white road in a sea of green'). We hope the planned new snowmaking higher up (see News) will make a difference.

FOR EXPERTS
Few challenges

Wengen is quite limited for experts. The only genuine black runs in the area are parts of the Lauberhorn World Cup Downhill and a couple of pistes from Eigergletscher towards Wixi including Oh God (which used to be off-piste). There are some decent off-piste runs such as White Hare from under the north face of the Eiger and more adventurous runs from the Jungfraujoch late in the season (see the Grindelwald chapter for more about going to the Jungfraujoch).

For more serious challenges it's well worth going to nearby Mürren, around an hour away.

Heli-trips with mountain guides are organised if there are enough takers.

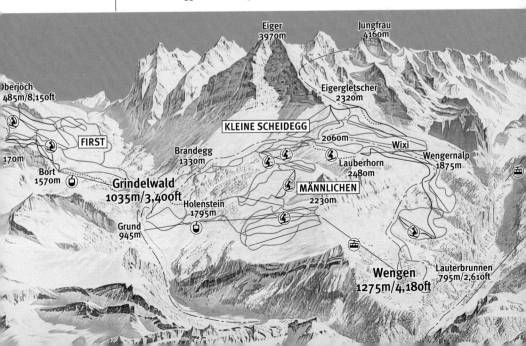

LIFT PASSES

Jungfrau Top Ski Region

Prices in SF

Age	1-day	6-day
under 16	29	148
16 to 19	46	236
20 to 61	57	295
over 62	51	266

Free under 6

Beginner points card

Notes
Covers Wengen, Mürren and Grindelwald, trains between them and Grindelwald ski-bus; day pass price is for First-Kleine Scheidegg-Männlichen area only

Alternative passes
Grindelwald and Wengen only; Mürren only; non-skier pass

FOR INTERMEDIATES
Wonderful if the snow is good

Wengen and Grindelwald share superb intermediate slopes. Nearly all are long blue or gentle red runs – see the Grindelwald chapter. The run back to Wengen is a relaxing end to the day, as long as it's not too crowded.

For tougher pistes, head for the top of the Lauberhorn lift and then the runs to Kleine Scheidegg, or to Wixi (following the start of the Downhill course). You could also try the north-facing run from Eigergletscher to Salzegg, which often has the best snow late in the season.

FOR BEGINNERS
Not ideal

There's a nursery slope in the centre of the village – it's convenient and gentle, but the snow is unreliable. There's a beginners' area at Wengernalp and another on the Grindelwald side of Kleine Scheidegg, but to get back to Wengen you either have to take the train or tackle the run down, which can be tricky, with several flat sections. There are plenty of good, long, gentle runs to progress to above Grindelwald.

FOR CROSS-COUNTRY
There is none

There's no cross-country in Wengen itself. There are 12km/7 miles of tracks down in the Lauterbrunnen valley, where the snow is unreliable.

QUEUES
Village crowds, better higher up

Both the train and the cable-car can be crowded at peak periods. It is best to avoid travelling up at the same time as the ski school. Queues up the mountain have been alleviated a lot in the last few years by the installation of fast chairs, and 2007 reporters experienced few problems. But weekend invasions can increase the crowds on the Grindelwald side, especially on a Saturday, when children up to 15 can ski free if a parent buys a day pass.

MOUNTAIN RESTAURANTS
Plenty of variety

Editors' choice The Jungfrau hotel at Wengernalp (855 1622) – where the rösti is excellent and the views of the Jungfrau from the sunny terrace are superb – is pricey but worth it; you need to book. You also get magnificent views from the narrow outside balcony of Wengen's highest restaurant Eigergletscher – get there early to grab a table. 'A fresh half pineapple with curry filling is by far the most interesting dish,' says a 2007 reporter. **Worth knowing about** The station buffet at Kleine Scheidegg gets repeated rave reviews, so it's not surprising it also gets packed – the rösti and sausage are popular ('The best food we had on the mountain,' says a visitor). A 2007 reporter recommends the nearby Bellvue hotel for 'good food and excellent service'. The Grindelwaldblick is a worthwhile trudge uphill from Kleine Scheidegg, with great food and views of the Eiger.

The Allmend, near the top of the Innerwengen chair and the train stop, is a 'great place to meet towards the end of the day' with 'friendly service' and wonderful views of the valley from the terrace. Reports on Mary's Cafe (situated at the end of the World Cup runs) are mixed: 'Very comfy, with open fires, but disappointed with the food.' For restaurants on the slopes towards Grindelwald, see that chapter.

In the village, the 'magnificent and relaxing' restaurant at the Hotel Caprice is 'strongly recommended' by a 2007 reporter ('the food is excellent, view breathtaking and the hospitality and service first-class; on our last day we got there at 1.30pm and left in the dark at 6pm') – they will even provide slippers so you don't have to wear your boots.

SCHOOLS AND GUIDES
Healthy competition

Reports on the Swiss school are generally good. One 2007 visitor found the school 'extremely understanding

boarding

Wengen is not a bad place for gentle boarding – the nursery area is not ideal, but beginners have plenty of slopes to progress to, with lots of long blue and red runs served by the train and chair-lifts. Getting from Kleine Scheidegg to Männlichen means an unavoidable drag-lift, though. And the slope back to Wengen is narrow and almost flat in places, so you may have to scoot. For the steepest slopes and best free-riding, experts will want to head for Mürren.

The main street, with the village nursery slopes and, in the centre of the pic, the cable-car station →

WENGEN-MÜRREN-LAUTERBRUNNENTAL AG

SCHOOLS

Swiss
t 855 2022

Privat
t 855 5005

Classes
(Swiss prices)
6 3hr days SF250

Private lessons
SF140 for 2hr

CHILDREN

Playhouse
t 855 1414
From 18mnth; 9am-5pm; Sun-Fri

Sunshine
t 853 0440
Ages 1mnth upwards

Babysitters
List available from tourist office

Ski school
The Swiss school takes ages 4 up
(6 3hr days SF250)

GETTING THERE

Air Zürich 195km/121 miles (3½hr); Bern 70km/43 miles (1½hr)

Rail Station in resort

---

and accommodating' when a 10-year-old in their party wanted to change to a smaller group. Another found the lessons 'excellent, well organised and friendly with the school prepared to change people from one class to another'. Yet another said, 'Several of our party had private lessons with the Privat school and would recommend it.' Guides are available for heli-trips and powder excursions.

FACILITIES FOR CHILDREN
Conveniently placed
It is an attractive and reassuring village for families. The nursery slope is in the centre. The Playhouse takes children from 18 months and the Sunshine from one month. There is a list of babysitters available at the tourist office. A recent reporter praised the children's ski school classes – 'The best so far by a mile. My four year old really enjoyed all the activities.'

The train gives easy access to higher slopes.

STAYING THERE

HOW TO GO
Wide range of hotels
Most accommodation is in hotels. There is only a handful of catered chalets (none especially luxurious). Self-catering apartments are few, too.
Hotels There are about two dozen hotels, mostly 4-star and 3-star, with a handful of simpler places.
****Beausite Park (856 5161) Reputedly the best in town. Good pool, steam and massage. But poorly situated at top of nursery slopes – a schlep up from the main street.
****Wengener Hof (856 6969) No prizes for style or convenience, but

---

recommended for peace, helpful staff and spacious, spotless rooms with good views.
****Sunstar (856 5200) Family-friendly, modern hotel on main street right opposite the cable-car. Comfortable rooms, some with good valley views; lounge has a log fire. Live music most evenings. Pool with views. Recommended by two 2007 reporters.
****Silberhorn (856 5131) Comfortable, modern and central (opposite station). Frequently praised by reporters.
****Caprice (856 0606) Small, smartly furnished chalet-style hotel just above the railway. Sauna and steam room. 'Comfortable and friendly'; 'fabulous views, excellent food'. Kindergarten.
***Belvédère (856 6868) Some way out, but we have good reports of buffet-style meals ('good for families'), spacious rooms and grand art nouveau public rooms. Endorsed by a recent reporter ('excellent value for money').
***Alpenrose (855 3216) Long-standing British favourite; eight minutes' climb to the station, which rules it out for us. Small, simple rooms, but good views; 'first-class' food; friendly staff.
***Eiger (856 0505) Very conveniently sited, right next to the station. Focal après-ski bar. Comfy modern rooms.
***Falken (856 5121) Further up the hill. Another British favourite, known affectionately as 'Fawlty Towers'. 'It's like stepping back 100 years.'
Apartments The hotel Bernerhof's decent Résidence apartments are well positioned just off the main street, and hotel facilities are available to guests.

EATING OUT
Mainly hotel-based
Most restaurants are in hotels. They offer good food and service. The Eiger

Wengen

561

ACTIVITIES

Indoor Swimming pool (in Beausite Park and Victoria Lauberhorn hotels), sauna, solarium, whirlpool, massage (in hotels), cinema (with English films), art gallery, museum

Outdoor Ice rink, curling, 50km/ 31 miles of cleared paths, tobogganing, snow-shoeing, hang-gliding, helicopter flights

UK PACKAGES

Alpine Answers, Club Med, Crystal, Independent Ski Links, Inghams, Kuoni, Made to Measure, Ski Freshtracks, Ski Line, Ski Solutions, Swiss Travel Service, Switzerland Travel Centre, Thomson

SWITZERLAND

562

Phone numbers
From elsewhere in Switzerland add the prefix 033; from abroad use the prefix +41 33

TOURIST OFFICE

t 855 1414
info@wengen.ch
www.wengen-muerren.ch

has a traditional restaurant and a stube with Swiss and French cuisine. The Bernerhof has good-value traditional dishes. The little hotel Hirschen has good steaks. There's no shortage of fondues in the village, and several bars do casual food. Da Sina does 'succulent and ample sirloin steaks' and is recommended by a couple of 2007 visitors. Cafe Gruebi has been recommended for 'the most wonderful cakes'. The Jungfrau at Wengernalp has an excellent restaurant – but you have to get back on skis or on a toboggan.

APRES-SKI
It depends on what you want

People's reactions to the après-ski scene in Wengen vary widely, according to their expectations and appetites.

If you're used to raving in Kitzbühel or Les Deux-Alpes, you'll rate Wengen dead, especially for young people. If you've heard it's dead, you may be pleasantly surprised to find that there is a handful of bars that do good business both early and late in the evening. But it is only a handful of small places. The bar at the Bumps section of the home run is a popular final-run stop-off. A 2007 reporter enjoyed the 'fun' Start Bar on the Lauberhorn – but it's a long ski down afterwards. And the Pickle-Bar (Hotel Eiger) and the tiny, 'always welcoming' Eiger Bar are popular at the end of the day. The small, traditional Tanne does 'delicious strawberry daiquiri' but can get 'crowded and smoky' and the funky Crystal, almost opposite, is lively. Sina's, a little way out by Club Med, usually has live music and karaoke. The Caprice bar has been recommended, as has Rock's with 'its three plasma screens showing Sky Sports'. There are discos and live music in some hotels (including

Tiffany's – 'full of under-18s' – in the Silberhorn). The cinema often shows English-language films.

OFF THE SLOPES
Good for a relaxing time

With its unbeatable scenery and pedestrian-friendly trains and cable-car (there's a special, though expensive, pass for pedestrians), Wengen is a superb resort for those who want a completely relaxing holiday. It's easy for mixed parties of skiers and non-skiers to meet up for lunch on the mountain, but rides on the lifts can be time-consuming. There are some lovely walks, and ice skating and curling have been popular with many 2007 reporters. Several hotels have health spas. Excursions to Interlaken and Bern are possible by train, as is the trip up to the Jungfraujoch (see the Grindelwald chapter). Helicopter flights from Männlichen are recommended.

STAYING UP THE MOUNTAIN
Great views

You can stay at two points up the mountain reached by the railway: the expensive Jungfrau hotel (855 1622) at Wengernalp – with fabulous views – and at Kleine Scheidegg, where there are rooms in the big Scheidegg Hotels (855 1212) and dormitory space above the Grindelwaldblick restaurant (855 1374) and the station buffet. The big restaurant at Männlichen has rooms.

STAYING DOWN THE VALLEY
The budget option

Staying down in Lauterbrunnen will halve your accommodation costs and give faster access to Mürren, at the price of a much longer journey time to Kleine Scheidegg when you want to ski Wengen or Grindelwald. The trains run until 11.30pm and are included in your lift pass. See the Mürren chapter for hotel recommendations.

THE BRITISH IN WENGEN

There's a very strong British presence in Wengen. Many Brits have been returning for years to the same rooms in the same hotels in the same week, and treat the resort as a sort of second home. There is an English church with weekly services, and a British-run ski club, the DHO (Downhill Only) – so named when the Brits who colonised the resort persuaded the locals to keep the summer railway running up the mountain in winter, so that they would no longer have to climb up in order to ski down again. That greatly amused the locals, who until then had regarded skiing in winter as a way to get around on snow rather than a pastime to be done for fun. The DHO is still going strong and organises regular events throughout the season.

A magical combination of nearly everything you could want from a ski resort, both on and off the slopes

NEWS

For 2007/08, the old cable-cars from Gornergrat to Hohtälli and from Hohtälli to Stockhorn will be decommissioned. A new red piste is planned from Hohtälli to Gifthittli (below Gornergrat near the top of the six-pack from Riffelberg). A drag-lift is planned from Triftji to Stockhorn. And a fast quad chair is due to replace the double from Findeln to Sunnegga; an extension of it will go from Findeln to Breitenboden (above Grunsee).

For 2006/07 an eight-seat gondola opened from Furi to Riffelberg. It has a mid-station just below Furi, which means you no longer have to go through town to get from Klein Matterhorn to the other sectors and you no longer have an uphill walk to Furi to get from the Gornergrat to the Klein Matterhorn lifts.

➕ Wonderful, high and extensive slopes in three/four varied areas

➕ Spectacular high-mountain scenery, dominated by the Matterhorn

➕ Charming, if rather sprawling, old mountain village, largely traffic-free

➕ Reliable snow at altitude

➕ World's best mountain restaurants

➕ Extensive helicopter operation

➕ Nightlife to suit most tastes

➕ Smart shops

➕ Linked to Cervinia in Italy

➖ Main lifts may be a long walk, or a crowded bus- or taxi-ride from home

➖ Beginners should go elsewhere

➖ One of Europe's priciest lift passes

➖ Some restaurants and hotels very expensive – so choose carefully

➖ Slow train up to Gornergrat annoys some people, but can be avoided

➖ Some lift queues at peak periods

➖ Annoying electric taxis detract from the car-free village ambience

➖ Walking can be treacherous on uncleared hard snow or ice

You must try Zermatt before you die. Few places can match its combination of excellent advanced and intermediate slopes, reliable snow, magnificent scenery, Alpine charm and mountain restaurants with superb food and stunning views.

Zermatt has its drawbacks – see the long list above (though one major grouse of the Klein Matterhorn sector not being properly connected to the other mountains was sorted in 2006 – see 'News'). For us, and for virtually all our reporters, these pale into insignificance compared with its attractions, which come close to matching perfectly our notion of the ideal winter resort. It's one of our favourites – and one of us regularly takes his holiday here.

THE RESORT

Zermatt started life as a traditional mountain village, developed as a mountaineering centre in the 19th century, then became a winter resort. Summer is as important as winter here.

The central part of the village is car-free. But the village doesn't have the relaxed, rustic feel of other car-free resorts, such as Wengen and Saas-Fee. Zermatt is big business, and it shows. The clientele is more overtly part of the jet set, and the electric taxis ferrying people around are more intrusive and aggressive. Most restaurants and hotels are owned by a handful of families. Many of the workers are brought in from outside the area – but that is probably one of the reasons for the increased friendliness and improved service in recent years.

The village sprawls along either side of a river, mountains rising steeply on each side. It is a mixture of chocolate-box chalets and modern buildings, most in traditional style. You arrive by rail or taxi from Täsch, where cars have

to be left for a fee. They can be left for free at more distant Visp, from where you can also get a train. The main street runs away from the station, and is lined with luxury hotels, restaurants and shops.

The resort attracts an older age group than you get in rival resorts with comparable slopes, such as Val d'Isère or St Anton, and there's not as much of the youthful vitality that you get in those resorts.

The cog railway to Gornergrat starts

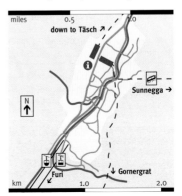

KEY FACTS

Resort		1620m
		5,310ft
Zermatt only		
Slopes		1620-3820m
		5,310-12,530ft
Lifts		33
Pistes		183km
		114 miles
Blue		25%
Red		59%
Black		16%
Snowmaking		61km
		38 miles
Zermatt-Cervinia-Valtournenche combined		
Slopes		1525-3820m
		5,000-12,530ft
Lifts		57
Pistes		313km
		194 miles
Blue		22%
Red		60%
Black		18%
Snowmaking		114km
		71 miles

from near the main station. The Sunnegga underground funicular towards Rothorn is a few minutes' walk away, but the gondola to the Glacier and Schwarzsee areas (and the link to Cervinia) is at the opposite end of the long village. Walking from the station to the Glacier lifts can take 15 to 20 minutes. And be warned: walking anywhere (especially in ski boots) can be unpleasant because of the treacherous icy paths and the electric taxis and solar-powered buses darting around. The free buses get very crowded (especially at the end of the day bringing people back from the Glacier area and in peak season). You can take an electric taxi instead (only SF6 each if you share).

Now that the new gondola from Furi to Riffelberg has opened, staying near the gondola to Furi is convenient for the slopes – 'a real boon', says a 2007 visitor. But being near the Gornergrat and Sunnegga railways, near the station end of the main street, is more convenient for most shops, bars and restaurants (as well as the other two ways up to the slopes). Some accommodation is up the steep hill across the river in Winkelmatten – you can ski back to it from all areas, and it has its own reliable bus service.

Getting up to the village from Täsch is no problem. There's a smart new station and underground car park with 2,000 spaces there (SF11 a day), and you can wheel luggage trolleys straight from the car park onto and off the trains. You are met at the other end by electric and horse-drawn taxis and hotel shuttles.

THE MOUNTAINS

Practically all of the slopes are open, above the trees – the runs served by the Sunnegga funicular are the main exception.

A single piste map (in a handy new quick-folding size) now covers both Cervinia's and Zermatt's slopes fairly clearly, ending past confusion over different names for the same point on the border. But readers complain that the prominence given to a recommended ski safari route (of either 10,000m/32,800ft or 12,000m/39,400ft vertical in a day – your choice) makes the map more difficult to use.

Some runs in all sectors and all the runs on Stockhorn were marked in yellow as 'ski runs' rather than normal pistes on the 2005/06 piste map (still handed out when we were there in March 2007). These are defined as 'protected' (from avalanches, we presume) and 'marked, but not prepared and not checked at the end of the day'. On the new map we were given in 2007, the yellow runs are now called 'freeride pistes', and there's no explanation of what this means – a really retrograde step.

On our recent visits we have been impressed by service improvements: polite and helpful lift staff; boards at the bottom of each sector indicating which lifts and pistes are open; useful announcements in several languages (including English) on the train and some cable-cars; and free tissues at most lift stations (just as in America).

THE SLOPES
Beautiful and varied

Zermatt's piste map divides the slopes into several sectors and markets some as 'paradises'. We think this is bizarre, so here we drop 'paradises' and divide the slopes into four main sectors.

The **Rothorn** sector (incorporating the lift company's Sunnegga sector) is reached by an underground funicular starting by the river, not far from the centre. A 'chondola' (chair/gondola hybrid) goes on up from the top to Blauherd, where a cable-car goes up to Rothorn itself.

From the top of this area you can make your way – via south-facing slopes served by snowmaking – to Gant in the valley between Sunnegga and the second main area, **Gornergrat**. A 125-person cable-car links Gant to Hohtälli, on the ridge above Gornergrat. A gondola makes the link back from Gant to Sunnegga. Gornergrat can be reached directly from Zermatt by cog railway trains that leave every 24 minutes and take 30 or 40 minutes to get to the top – arrive at

↑ Looking over to Italy from Klein Matterhorn. The buildings in the centre left are Plateau Rosa, and Cervinia's pistes are just the other side of the ridge

SNOWPIX.COM / CHRIS GILL

LIFT PASSES

Zermatt

Prices in SF

Age	1-day	6-day
under 16	34	168
16 to 19	58	286
20 to 64	68	336
over 65	58	286

Free under 9

Beginner no deals

Notes
Covers all lifts on the Swiss side of the border; 6-day pass covers a day in Saas-Fee; half-day passes and single-ascent tickets on some lifts also available

Alternative passes
International pass for Zermatt and Cervinia; International-Aosta for Zermatt and Cervinia plus 2 days in Val d'Aosta; Peak Pass for pedestrians

the station early to get a seat on the right-hand side and enjoy the fabulous views. It can be a long journey if you have to stand.

From Gornergrat there's a piste to Schweigmatten, just above Furi, where a gondola that was new for 2006/07 takes you up to Furi or back up to Riffelberg on the Gornergrat sector. From Furi, a cable-car to Trockener Steg and then the spectacular Klein Matterhorn cable-car take you to the top of the third and highest sector, now known as the **Glacier** area. This area gives access to Cervinia – make sure you have an appropriate pass.

From Furgg, towards the bottom of the Glacier area, a stop-start gondola goes up to the top of the small but worthwhile **Schwarzsee** area (also reached by gondola from Furi).

There are pistes back to the village from all four areas – though some of them can be closed or tricky due to poor snow conditions. They can be hazardous at the end of the day due to crowds and speeding skiers – particularly the black from Furgg.

TERRAIN-PARKS
One of Switzerland's best
Gravity Park on the Glacier area is one of Switzerland's best winter and summer parks open 365 days a year. There is a nicely integrated 120m/390ft-long super-pipe that sits next to an

array of kickers, rails, a quarter-pipe and wall-ride. All the rails were replaced for last season, and a new, small boarder-cross was built. The park is set up nicely so you can choose either a kicker or rail line, and try several hits in a row. It is a relatively short park, so you'll be doing a lot of laps (on a high-speed chair) during the day. A mini rail area at the top of the park is a perfect initiation to sliding on metal. Check www.matterhornparadise. ch for details. When we were there last season (in March) there was also a short boarder-cross at Blauherd.

SNOW RELIABILITY
Generally good
Zermatt has rocky terrain and a relatively dry climate. But it also has some of the highest slopes in Europe, and quite a lot of snowmaking.

Three of the four sectors go up to over 3000m/9,840ft, and the Glacier area has summer skiing. There are loads of runs above 2500m/8,200ft, many of which are north-facing, so guaranteeing decent snow except in freak years.

Snowmaking machines serve some of the pistes on all four areas, from about 3000m/9,840ft to under 2000m/ 6,560ft. Coverage is gradually increased each season, with 5km/ 3 miles added for 2006/07. Piste grooming is excellent.

FOR EXPERTS
Head off-piste

There is some great off-piste – see the feature box later in this chapter. But Zermatt has few challenging pistes and the three black runs marked on the piste map are not worthy of their gradings. That's one of the consequences of making their toughest regularly skied runs 'freeride pistes' (see under 'The Mountains' earlier in this chapter).

FOR INTERMEDIATES
Mile after mile of beautiful runs

Zermatt is ideal for adventurous intermediates. Many of the blue and red runs tend to be at the difficult end of their grading. There are very beautiful reds down lift-free valleys from both Gornergrat (Kelle) and Hohtälli (White Hare) to Breitenboden – we love these first thing in the morning, before anyone else is on them. From Breitenboden you can go on down to Gant, or to Riffelalp on a

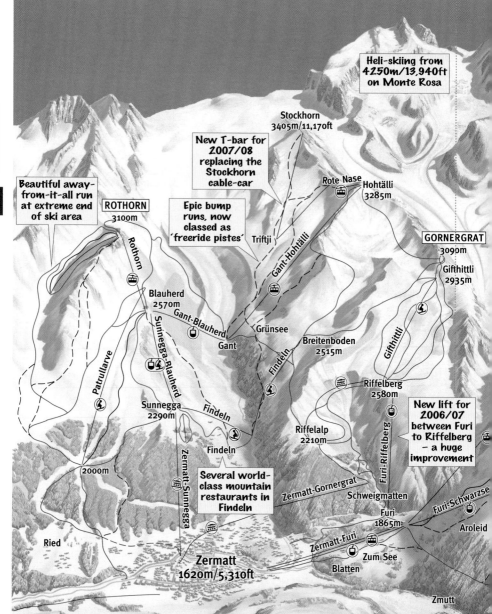

Heli-skiing from
4250m/13,940ft
on Monte Rosa

Stockhorn
3405m/11,170ft

New T-bar for
2007/08
replacing the
Stockhorn
cable-car

Rote Nase
Hohtälli
3285m

ROTHORN
3100m

Epic bump
runs, now
classed as
'freeride pistes'

Triftji

Gant-Hohtälli

GORNERGRAT
3090m

Beautiful away-
from-it-all run
at extreme end
of ski area

Rothorn

Gifthittli
2935m

Blauherd
2570m

Gant-Blauherd

Gifthittli

Sunnegga-Blauherd

Grünsee

Gant

Breitenboden
2515m

Patrullarve

Findeln

Riffelberg
2580m

Sunnegga
2290m

Findeln

New lift for
2006/07
between Furi
to Riffelberg
– a huge
improvement

Furi-Riffelberg

Riffelalp
2210m

Findeln

Zermatt-Sunnegga

2000m

Several world-
class mountain
restaurants in
Findeln

Zermatt-Gornergrat

Schweigmatten

Furi-Schwarzse

Ried

Furi
1865m

Aroleid

Zermatt-Furi

Zum See

Zermatt
1620m/5,310ft

Blatten

Zmutt

run that includes a narrow wooded path with a sheer cliff and magnificent views to the right.

On Rothorn, the 5km/3 mile Kumme run, from Rothorn itself to the bottom of the Patrullarve chair, also gets away from the lift system and has an interesting mix of straight-running and mogul pitches (though lack of snowmaking meant it was closed for much of last season). The reds and black served by the Hörnli drag at Schwarzsee are excellent. In the Glacier

sector the reds served by the fast quad chair from Furgg are long, testing and gloriously set at the foot of the Matterhorn. The Furggsattel chair from Trockener Steg serves more pistes with stunning views, notably the 1100m/3,610ft-vertical Matterhorn piste – a red that is of no more than blue gradient for much of its considerable length (it has to be graded red because of a short, much steeper pitch near the end, which has a lot of less confident intermediates struggling) –

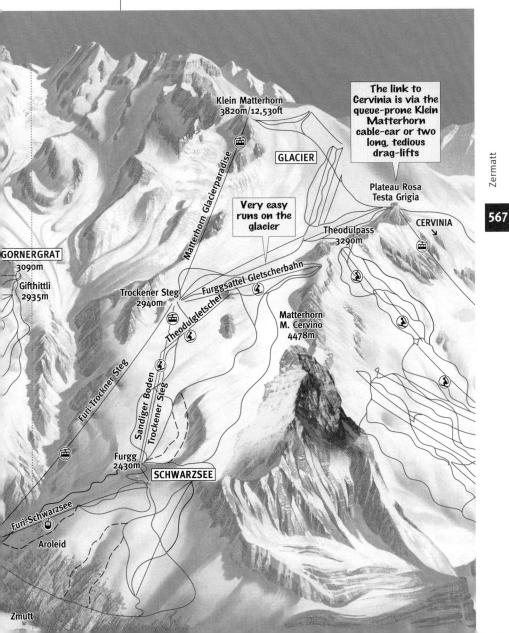

Klein Matterhorn
3820m/12,530ft

GLACIER

The link to Cervinia is via the queue-prone Klein Matterhorn cable-car or two long, tedious drag-lifts

Plateau Rosa
Testa Grigia

CERVINIA

Very easy runs on the glacier

Theodulpass
3290m

GORNERGRAT
3090m

Gifthittli
2935m

Matterhorn Glacierparadise

Furggsattel Gletscherbahn

Trockener Steg
2940m

Theodulgletscher

Matterhorn
M. Cervino
4478m

Furi-Trockner Steg

Sandiger Boden
Trockener Steg

Furgg
2430m

SCHWARZSEE

Furi-Schwarzsee

Aroleid

Zmutt

but again, the run was shut for much of last season due to lack of snowmaking.

For much less adventurous intermediates, the best runs are the blues from Blauherd on Rothorn and above Riffelberg on Gornergrat, and the runs between Klein Matterhorn and Trockener Steg. Of these, the Riffelberg area often has the best combination of good snow and easy cruising, and is popular with the school. Blauherd gets afternoon sun, but the snowmaking means that the problem is more often a foot or more of heavy snow near the bottom than bare patches.

In the Glacier sector most of the runs, though marked red on the piste map, are very flat and represent the easiest slopes Zermatt has to offer, as well as the best snow. The problem here is the possibility of bad weather because of the height – high winds, extreme cold and poor visibility can make life very unpleasant (and if you are skiing into a headwind, downhill progress can be very slow).

Even an early intermediate can make the trip to Cervinia, crossing at Theodulpass rather than taking the more challenging Ventina run from Testa Grigia/Plateau Rosa.

Beware the run from Furgg to Furi at the end of the day, because it can be chopped up, mogulled in places and very crowded (the only reason it is graded black that we can see, because it isn't very steep). A much more

OFF-PISTE RUNS FROM THE ACCESSIBLE TO THE EPIC

Zermatt offers a wide variety of off-piste runs for all levels of skier, from off-piste beginner to expert. And if the runs reached from the lift system aren't enough, heli-skiing is available (and popular).

The 'freeride pistes' (see 'The Mountains' earlier in this chapter) marked on the mountain and in yellow on the piste map (and by broken black lines on our map) open up a lot of ungroomed terrain. If you love long mogul pitches, those between Stockhorn and Triftji, are the stuff of dreams. From the top of the Stockhorn (to be served by a new T-bar for 2007/08 – see 'News') there's a steep run down to an old T-bar that serves a wide, long face that can be one vast mogul field – steep, but not extremely so. Being north-facing and lying between 3400m and 2700m (11,150ft and 8,860ft), the snow keeps in good condition long after a new snowfall. The 'freeride pistes' carry on down from the Triftji T-bar to Gant, but snow quality can deteriorate on this lower part. And be warned: this whole area does not normally open until February (and didn't until mid-March in 2007 because of lack of sufficient snow).

There are two wonderful 'freeride pistes' from Rothorn, with spectacular views of both the village and the Matterhorn. But they need good snow-cover to be really enjoyable. At Schwarzsee there are a couple of steep north-facing gullies through the woods.

Away from the marked runs, there are marvellous off-piste possibilities from the top lifts in each sector, but they aren't immediately obvious to those without local knowledge. They are also dangerous, because of rocky and glacial terrain. You can join daily ski-touring groups, but there aren't straightforward off-piste groups as there are in resorts such as Val d'Isère and Méribel; you have to hire a guide privately for a full day, so to make it economic you need to form your own group. The Ski Club of Great Britain usually hires a guide for off-piste skiing once a week – a recent reporter had 'an awesome day of powder' with them.

The fast Patrullarve chair-lift in the Rothorn sector serves some excellent terrain, between Tuftern and the National pistes, for off-piste beginners to start developing their technique. For the more accomplished, Stockhorn is a great starting point; descending towards Gant, one special run goes down 'the lost valley'; going in the other direction, there is an excellent descent to the Gornergletscher, starting with a short uphill hike and ending at Furi (but see below for a warning about the end of the glacier). In the Schwarzsee sector there are many good off-piste slopes. These include the area known as 'innru waldieni', right underneath the Matterhorn, reached from the top of the Hörnli T-bar.

Zermatt is the Alps' biggest heli-skiing centre; the helipad resembles a bus station at times, with choppers taking off every few minutes. There are only two or three main drop-off points, so you are likely to encounter other groups on the mountain. The classic run is from over 4250m/13,940ft on Monte Rosa and descends over 2300m/7,550ft vertical through wonderful glacier scenery to Furi; for most of its length it is not steep, but getting off the end of the glacier can be tricky and can involve walking along narrow rocky paths above long drops or side-stepping down steep slopes, depending on the amount of snow around (we've encountered both).

And there are lots of ski touring opportunities, too, including some among stunning glacial scenery.

boarding

Boarders in soft boots have one big advantage over skiers in Zermatt – they have much more comfortable walks to and from the lift stations! Even so, there aren't many snowboarders around. The slopes are best for experienced free-riders, because tough piste and off-piste action is what Zermatt is really about; plus there's the world-class terrain-park above Trockener Steg on the glacier. There is, however, an excellent little beginner area at Blauherd, complete with moving carpet lift, which we've seen many beginner snowboarders having lessons on. The main lifts are boarder-friendly: train, funicular, gondolas, cable-cars and fast chairs, and there aren't too many flat bits. But there are still a few T-bars. Stoked is a specialist school.

relaxed way is to use the beautifully scenic Weisse Perle run from Schwarzsee (the Stafelalp variant is even more scenic but has a short uphill section). Or you can ride the gondola from Schwarzsee.

FOR BEGINNERS
Learn elsewhere

There are many much better resorts for beginners. The best snow-sure nursery slope area here is at Blauherd – but even this can get very busy. And there are no long easy runs to progress to, except for the ones above Trockener Steg, which can be bitterly cold and windy.

FOR EVERYONE
Impressive cable-car and ice cave

If the weather is good, the Klein Matterhorn cable-car is an experience not to be missed There are stupendous views from the left side down to the glacier and its crevasses, as the car swings steeply into its hole, blasted out of the mountain at the top. When you arrive, you walk through a long tunnel, to emerge on top of the world for the highest piste in Europe. Remember to walk slowly: the air is thin and some people have altitude problems. There's a viewing platform, and substantial development is planned here. The ice grotto cut into

Rothorn, just one of many excellent mountain restaurants with spectacular views →

SNOWPIX.COM / CHRIS GILL

SCHOOLS

Swiss
t 966 2466

Stoked
t 967 7020

Summit
t 967 0001

European Snowsport
t 967 6787

Almrausch
t 9670808

Independent
t 967 7067

Prato Borni
t 967 5115

Classes (Swiss prices)
5 days (10am to 3.30
with lunch break)
SF295

Private lessons
SF160 for 2hr for 1 or
2 people

CHILDREN

Kinderparadies
t 967 7252
Ages from 3mnth

**Kinderclub Pumuckel
(Hotel Ginabelle)**
t 966 5000
Ages from 30mnth

Snowflakes (Stoked)
t 967 7020
Ages from 4; 9am-12
noon

Snowli Village (Swiss)
t 966 2466
Ages 4 to 5: SF395
for 5 days

Private babysitters
List at tourist office

Ski school
From age 6; 5 full
days incl. lunch
SF350 (Swiss prices)

the glacier is well worth a visit, with 'incredible ice carvings'.

FOR CROSS-COUNTRY
Fairly limited
There's a 4km/2.5 mile loop at Furi, 3km/2 miles of trails near the bottom of the gondola to the Glacier area and another 12km/7 miles from Täsch to Randa (don't count on good snow). There are also 'ski walking trails', best tackled as part of an organised group.

QUEUES
Main problems being solved
Zermatt has improved its lift system hugely in recent years, eliminating major bottlenecks. But a few problems remain. Both the lifts out of Gant are prone to queues at times; we've waited over 30 minutes for the cable-car in mid-morning in March and reporters tell of similar waits for the gondola. The high-speed quad from Furgg can get busy now that the Schwarzsee gondola is dumping people nearby. The Klein Matterhorn cable-car has queues much of the time. You may find there's only standing room on the Gornergrat train, which can be tiring and uncomfortable: 'Better to wait for the next one,' says a reporter. One thing we love about Zermatt is getting the 8am train with the lifties and restaurant staff. It arrives at the top just as they are dropping the rope to open the pistes, and you have the slopes to yourselves for an hour or two. A 2007 reporter complains that the queue of people waiting to get on the chondola at peak periods blocks the people trying to get out of the upper-level funicular exit at Sunnegga – resulting in people being 'violently pushed out of the way'.

Not surprisingly, the village buses

cannot handle demand at the end of the day at the foot of the slopes from the Glacier area: 'The chaos resulted in a fight over a taxi,' says a reporter.

SCHOOLS AND GUIDES
Competition paying off
The main Swiss school has a history of critical reports from readers but has allegedly improved recently.

There's a 'brilliant' Stoked snowboard school, of which we generally have good reports. A year or two back, it combined with 'The SkiSchool', and is made up of talented young instructors, some of whom are British and all of whom speak good English. One reader says they had 'a complete beginner confident on reds after three lessons', but another was disappointed by the initial 'lack of instruction' in the group classes. Group sizes are said to be small. There are now two other schools staffed mainly by Brits – Summit and European Snowsport. The wife of a 2007 reporter had 'very successful' private lessons with Summit and found them 'well organised', while beginners in another group 'progressed rapidly.

FACILITIES FOR CHILDREN
Good hotel nurseries
The Ginabelle hotel has the Kinderclub Pumuckel. The Kinderparadies, 200m/660ft from the station, takes children from three months: 'The Swiss kids in the resort go there, so it must be good,' says a recent reporter. Stoked runs Snowflakes – for children aged at least four years old – at Trockener Steg and a kindergarten for kids from three years at Schwarzsee. There's a snow garden at Riffelberg. The tourist office has a list of babysitters.

GETTING THERE

Air Geneva
244km/152 miles
(4hr by rail); Zürich
248km/154 miles
(5hr by rail); Sion
80km/50 miles (1½hr)

Rail Station in resort

STAYING THERE

HOW TO GO
A wide choice, packaged or not

Chalets Several operators have places here; many of the most comfortable are in apartment blocks. Reporters have praised Total Ski's operation here. VIP and Scott Dunn have some luxury chalets.

Hotels There are over 100 hotels, mostly comfortable and traditional-style 3-stars and 4-stars, but taking in the whole range. Inghams features a large selection (and has chalets and apartments too).

*****Mont Cervin (966 8888) Biggest in town. Elegantly traditional. Good pool and fitness centre. It has taken over hotel Nicoletta, renamed it Le Petit Cervinan and is converting it into luxury suites. Due to open December 2007.

*****Zermatterhof (966 6600) Traditional 'grand hotel' style with piano bar and pool.

*****Riffelalp Resort (966 0555) Up the mountain, pool, spa, own evening trains. 'Impeccable service, fabulous breakfasts, stunning location.'

*****Omnia (966 7171) Modern, minimalist, central, reached by a lift in a rock, smart fitness centre.

****Coeur des Alpes (966 4080) At Klein Matterhorn end of town. Smart, modern, with relaxed and friendly feel. Pool and fitness facilities visible through glass lobby floor. No restaurant.

****Alex (966 7070) Close to station. Reporters love it ('wonderful', 'amazing hospitality'). Pool. Dancing.

****Ambassador (966 2611) Peaceful position near Gornergrat station. Large pool; sauna. Some rooms 'a bit faded'. Mixed reports on the food.

****Monte Rosa (966 0333) Well-modernised original Zermatt hotel, near southern end of village – full of climbing pictures and mementos.

****Ginabelle (966 5000) Smart pair of chalets not far from Sunnegga lift; has own ski nursery as well as day care.

****Sonne (966 2066) Traditionally decorated, in quiet setting; 'superb Roman Bath complex'.

****Parkhotel Beau-Site (966 6868) Highly recommended by a recent

Zermatt

THE WORLD'S BEST MOUNTAIN RESTAURANTS

Even reporters who don't normally stop long for lunch usually succumb to temptation here. The choice of restaurants is enormous, the food usually excellent, the small hut-based places very atmospheric (some with spectacular views), the table-service friendly (if over-worked). It is impossible to list here all those worth a visit. It is best to book; check prices are within your budget when you do!

Down at Findeln below Sunnegga are several attractive, pricey, rustic restaurants. After four visits in the last two winters our current favourite – and that of many reporters – is Chez Vrony (967 2552). We've had wonderful spicy fish soup, rösti, carpaccio, calves' liver, views and service (but we've received reports of slow service, too). We've also enjoyed excellent lamb at Findlerhof (967 2588), aka Franz & Heidy's. Reporters praise Paradies (967 3451; 'good views, great rösti' and 'friendly service'), Adler (967 1058; 'prompt food, friendly service') and Enzian (967 6404; 'less busy than others').

The simple hut at Tuftern has great views from the terrace, sells good Heida wine from the highest vineyard in Europe and does a basic menu of home-made soup, cheese and cold sausage and 'wonderful apple spice cake'; you can also watch deer feeding here at the end of the afternoon. Othmar's Skihütte (967 1761), below the Patrullarve chair, has a 'good selection of fish and seafood'.

The restaurants at Fluhalp (967 2597, often with live music on the terrace) and Grünsee (967 2553) have beautiful, isolated situations, and the large terraces at Sunnegga (967 3046) and Rothorn (967 2675) have great views. The Kulmhotel (966 6400), at 3100m/10,170ft at Gornergrat, has both self- and table-service restaurants (the latter with amazing views of lift-free mountains and glaciers from the terrace). The Alphitta (967 2114) at Riffelalp has several cosy rustic rooms for bad-weather days, and we've had good pasta and rösti there.

At Furi, the Restaurant Furri (966 2777) does excellent rösti and scrumptious tarts and has a large sun terraces and cosy interior. The hotel at Schwarzsee (967 2263) is right at the foot of the Matterhorn, with staggering views and endless variations of rösti. Down the hill from here Stafelalp (967 3062) is simple, but it is good value and charmingly situated. Up above Trockener Steg, Gandegghütte (607 8868) has stunning views of the glacier. On the way back to the village below Furi, Zum See (967 2045) is a charming old hut with a reputation of being Zermatt's best – we've eaten well there, but two recent reporters were disappointed with both the food and the slow service; it is usually packed with people still eating lunch at 4.30pm. Blatten (967 2096) is 'excellent', too.

SNOWPIX.COM / CHRIS GILL

The smaller pointed peak on the right is the Klein Matterhorn, home to the highest cable-car station and piste in Europe. This photo is taken from Schwarzsee looking down to Furgg ↘

reporter. 'Faultless service with nouvelle meals of four to five courses.'

****Julen (966 7600) Charming, modern-rustic chalet over the river, with Matterhorn views from some rooms.

***Butterfly (966 4166) 'Small, friendly, as well furnished as the Alex, but much better food,' says a reporter.

***Atlanta (966 3535) No frills, but 'clean, warm, friendly and serves wholesome food'; close to centre, with Matterhorn views from some rooms.

**Alpina (967 1050) Modest but very friendly, and close to centre.

**Dufour (966 2400) B&B, fairly central. 'Only a 2-star but deserves much more, wonderful roomy bedrooms, great views.'

*Bahnhof (967 2406) Right by Gornergrat station. Cheapest place to stay in town (SF108 a night for twin room with shower, SF35 a night for a dormitory bed; with communal kitchen!)

Apartments There is a lot of apartment accommodation, but not much finds its way to the UK package market. We have enjoyed staying in the hotel Ambassador apartments (966 2611) several times (with free use of all its facilities such as a pool and a sauna), and at Apartment Scott, available

through Ski Solutions. The Vanessa complex (966 3510) and Utoring (211 7727) have been recommended by reporters. The tourist office website has apartments.

EATING OUT
Huge choice at all price levels

There are over 100 restaurants to choose from: top-quality haute cuisine, through traditional Swiss food, Chinese, Japanese and Thai to egg and chips. There is even a McDonald's.

We have enjoyed several dinners at the Pipe (tiny with interesting dishes with Asian/West Indian influence). The Schäferstube (Hotel Julen) has been recommended for 'heavenly lamb'. The Mazot is highly rated and highly priced. A 2007 visitor enjoyed the buffet at the Mirabeau hotel – 'fantastic home-made duck pie – expensive but flawless'.

Chez Heini serves excellent lamb, and the owner sings after dinner. Giuseppe's doesn't look much, but has the best Italian food in town. The Zur Alten Muhle does 'excellent steaks and venison'. Da Mario, Casa Rustica, the Swiss Chalet, the Derby, the Avenstube ('good trout'), the Old Spaghetti

ACTIVITIES

Indoor Sauna, tennis, squash, hotel swimming pools (some open to public), fitness centre, climbing wall, billiards, bowling, gallery, library, concerts, museums, cinema

Outdoor Ice rinks, curling, sleigh rides, 30km/19 miles cleared paths, snow-shoeing, tobogganing, helicopter flights, paragliding, climbing, adventure gorge, ice-climbing

UK PACKAGES

Alpine Answers, Alpine Weekends, Chalet World Ski, Corporate Ski Co, Crystal, Crystal Finest, Descent International, Elegant Resorts, Independent Ski Links, Inghams, Interactive Resorts, Interhome, Jeffersons, Kuoni, Lagrange, Made to Measure, Momentum, Mountain Tracks, Oxford Ski Co, Powder Byrne, Scott Dunn, Ski Activity, Ski Expectations, Ski Freshtracks, Ski Independence, Ski Line, Ski Solutions, Ski with Julia, Ski-Monterosa, Skitracer, Snow Finders, Supertravel, Swiss Travel Service, Switzerland Travel Centre, Thomson, Total, VIP, White Roc
Täsch Interhome

Phone numbers
From elsewhere in Switzerland add the prefix 027; from abroad use the prefix +41 27

TOURIST OFFICE

t 966 8100
info@zermatt.ch
www.zermatt.ch

Factory (in the hotel Post complex), the Stockhorn Grill ('meat grilled to perfection'), Tony's Grotta ('expensive but excellent Italian'), the Walliserhof ('good value set menu') and the Walliserkanne ('fine pizza') have all been recommended by readers.

Du Pont has good-value pasta and rösti; Grampi's, Broken, Roma and Postli do good pizzas. The Schwyzer Stübli has local specialities and live Swiss music and dancing.

Rua Thai in the basement of the hotel Abana Real has been recommended for 'excellent Thai in attractive surroundings'. Fuji in the same building is a good Japanese.

APRES-SKI
Lively and varied

There's a good mix of sophisticated and informal fun, though it helps if you have deep pockets. On the way back from the Glacier or Schwarzsee sectors there are lots of restaurants below Furi for a last drink and sunbath. Hennu Stall blasts out loud music in a very un-Zermatt-like fashion but attracts huge crowds. For a quieter time, try a cake or tart at Zum See. On the way back from Rothorn, Othmar's Skihütte has great views and organises dinners followed by tobogganing down, and the Olympia Stübli often has live music (and good food worth walking back up for in the evening, says a 2007 reporter). Near the church at Winkelmatten, the Sonnenblick is 'a great place to watch the sun set'.

Promenading the main street checking out expensive shoes and watches is a popular early-evening activity. The Papperla Pub is one of the few popular early places (it's crowded after dinner, too, and has a nightclub downstairs – 'still heaving at 3.30am', says a 2007 reporter). Elsie's bar is wood-panelled and atmospheric, and gets packed with an older crowd both early and late. The North Wall is frequented by seasonal workers.

The Vernissage is our favourite bar in town for a quiet evening drink. It is an unusual and stylish modern place, with the projection room for the cinema built into the upstairs bar and displays of art elsewhere. Heimberg was designed by the same guy and has a good cocktail bar downstairs and a restaurant above.

Later on, the hotel Post complex has something for everyone, from a quiet, comfortable bar (Papa Caesar's)

to a lively disco (Broken) and live music (Pink) and a selection of restaurants.

At Grampi's, 'watch out for the Elton John impersonator – very entertaining', says a reporter. Z'alt Hischi (in an old house, serves huge measures of spirits) and the Little Bar (crowded if there are ten people in) are good for a quiet drink. The Hexen Bar is cosy, too. The hotel Alex draws a mature clientele for eating, drinking and dancing. The Hotel Pollux has 'lively music in its bar' and 'a general party ambience'.

OFF THE SLOPES
Considerable attractions

Zermatt is an attractive place to spend time. As well as pricey jewellery and clothes shops, there are interesting places selling food, wine, books and art. It is easy (but expensive) for pedestrians to get around on the lifts and meet others for lunch (purchase the Peaks Pass), and there are some nice walks – a special map is available. The Ice Grotto at Klein Matterhorn and the new Matterhorn Museum in town are worth seeing. You can take a helicopter trip around the Matterhorn. There is a cinema, and a reader tells us the free village guided tour is 'well worth doing'. For an icy experience, visit (or stay at) the Igloo above Riffelberg.

STAYING UP THE MOUNTAIN
Comfortable seclusion

There are several hotels at altitude, of which the pick is the Riffelalp Resort at the first stop on the Gornergrat railway (see 'Hotels') – but the evening train service is a bit limited. At the top of the railway, at 3100m/10,170ft, is the Kulmhotel Gornergrat (966 6400) – an austere building but recently renovated, with good-value rooms in which you can stay just a night or two if you wish.

STAYING DOWN THE VALLEY
Attractive for drivers

In Täsch, where visitors must leave their cars, there are five 3-star hotels costing less than half the price of the equivalent in Zermatt. The Täscherhof (966 6262) – 'fine, comfortable and with a reasonably priced restaurant' – and the Walliserhof (966 3966) – 'a very good option' – have been recommended by reporters. Täsch is very quiet at night; it's just a 13-minute ride from Zermatt, with trains every 20 minutes for most of the day; the last train down is 11.20pm. Taxis can operate up to the edge of Zermatt.

Most people who give it a try find America is pretty seductive, despite the relatively small sizes of its ski areas. Key factors for us are the relatively deserted pistes, the quality of accommodation, the excellent, varied resort restaurants, the high standards of service and courtesy, and the immaculate piste grooming. Depending on the resort, you may also be struck by the cute Wild West ambience and the superb quality of the snow. And the favourable exchange rate ($2 to the pound when we went to press) is an added attraction. Of course, US skiing does have some distinct disadvantages, too. Read on.

We have organised our American chapters in regional sections – California, Colorado, Utah, Rest of the West and New England.

Most American resorts receive serious amounts of snow – typically in the region of 6m to 12m (or 250 to 500 inches, as they measure it there) in a season. And most have serious snowmaking facilities too. What's more, they use them well – laying down a base of snow early in the season, rather than patching up shortages later.

There are wide differences in quantity and quality of snowfall, both between individual resorts and between regions – we discuss some of these in our regional introductions.

Piste grooming is taken very seriously – most American resorts set standards that the best Alpine resorts are only now attempting to match. Every morning you can expect to step out on to perfect 'corduroy' pistes. But this doesn't mean that there aren't moguls – far from it. It's just that you get moguls where the resort says you can expect moguls, not everywhere. Some resorts even go so far as to groom half the width of some runs, leaving the other half mogulled.

The slopes of most American resorts are blissfully free of crowds – a key advantage that becomes more important every year as the pistes of Europe become ever more congested. If you want to ski quickly and safely with less fear of collisions, you're better off in the States. And because the slopes are mostly below the tree line, they offer good visibility in bad weather.

Most American resorts offer free guided tours of the area. Lift queues are short, partly because they are highly disciplined in civilised lanes with no pushing and shoving, and with spare seats on chair-lifts religiously filled with the aid of cheerful, conscientious attendants. Piste maps and tissues are freely available at the bottom of most lifts. Mountain 'hosts' are on hand to advise you about the best possible routes to take.

School standards are uniformly high. And facilities for children are impressive, too.

Many Europeans have the idea that American resorts don't have off-piste terrain, but this seriously misrepresents the position. It's true that resorts practically always have a boundary, and that venturing beyond it into the 'backcountry'

575

SNOWPIX.COM / CHRIS GILL

← Like most US resorts, Big Sky has lots of skiing in the trees

may be discouraged or forbidden. But within the boundary there is often very challenging terrain that is very much like off-piste terrain in an Alpine resort – and with the important advantage that it is patrolled and avalanche-controlled, so you don't need to hire a guide. We rate this as one of the great attractions of US resorts.

There are drawbacks to the US, of course. One is that many resorts have slopes that are very modest in extent compared with major Alpine areas. But many US resorts (in Colorado and California, in particular) are very close to each other – so if you are prepared to travel a bit, you won't get bored. Roads are good and car hire is cheap (but watch out for extra insurance charges). But if a storm socks in, you will need snow-chains (you'll have to buy them – we've yet to find a US rental company that will provide them) or a 4WD (our preferred option despite the extra cost).

A more serious problem is that the day is ridiculously short. The lifts often shut at 3pm or 3.30. That may explain another drawback – the dearth of decent mountain restaurants. The norm is a monster self-service refuelling station – designed to minimise time off the slopes. Small restaurants with table-service and decent food are rare.

It's also true that in many resorts the mountains are slightly monotonous, with countless similar trails cut through the forest. You don't usually get the spectacular mountain scenery and the distinctive high-mountain runs of the Alps.

The classification of pistes (or trails, to use the local term) is different from that in Europe. Red runs don't exist. The colours used are combined with shapes. Green circles correspond fairly closely to greens in Europe (that is, in France, where they are mainly found). American blue squares largely correspond to blues in Europe, but also

SNOWPIX.COM / CHRIS GILL

One of the attractions of America is the lack of people on the trails; this is Deer Valley ↘

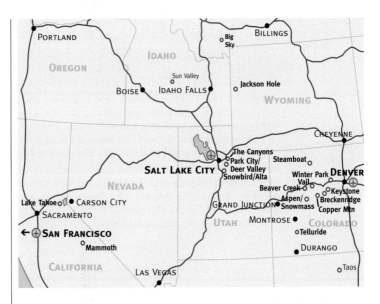

include tougher intermediate runs that would be red in the Alps; these are sometimes labelled as double-squares, although in some resorts a hybrid blue-black grading is used instead. Black diamond runs correspond to steeper European reds and easier European blacks. But then there are multiple diamonds. Double-diamond runs are seriously steep – often steeper than the steepest pistes in the Alps. A few resorts have wildly steep triple-diamonds.

It comes as a surprise to many first-timers that many chair-lifts in the States do not have safety bars; even on chairs that have them, you will find Americans curiously reluctant to use them, and if you manage to deploy the bar, you will find your companions very eager to raise it as soon as the top station is in view. They worry more about getting trapped on the chair than about falling off it. Weird.

US resort towns vary widely in style and convenience. There are old restored mining towns such as Telluride, Crested Butte and Aspen, genuine cowboy towns such as Jackson Hole, purpose-built monstrosities such as Snowbird, and even skyscraping gambling dens such as Heavenly. There is an increasing number of neat, car-free modern base villages. Two important things the resorts have in common are good-value, spacious accommodation and restaurants that are good, reasonably priced and varied in cuisine. Young people should be aware that the rigorously enforced legal age for drinking alcohol is 21; even if you are older, carry evidence of age.

In the end, your reaction to skiing and snowboarding in America may depend mainly on your reaction to America. If repeated cheerful exhortations to have a nice day wind you up – or if you like to ride chair-lifts in silence – perhaps you'd better stick to the Alps.

Crossing the pond is never going to be cheap, but the basic cost is lower than you might think: you can get February packages to California for under £600; with the £ at around $2, eating out is not expensive; and it's not difficult to find rooms with kitchenettes where you do your own catering. But lift passes, tuition and childcare are very expensive – they can be double what you would pay in the Alps. You can often save, especially on lift passes, by buying in advance through tour operators.

California/Nevada

California? It means surfing, beaches, wine, Hollywood, Disneyland and San Francisco cable-cars. Nevada means gambling. But this region also has the highest mountains in continental USA and some of America's biggest winter resorts, usually reliable for snow from November to May. What's more, winter holidays here are less expensive than you might expect.

Most visitors head for the Lake Tahoe area. Spectacularly set high in the Sierra Nevada 322km/200 miles east of San Francisco, Lake Tahoe is ringed by skiable mountains containing 14 downhill and 7 cross-country centres – the highest concentration of winter sports resorts in the USA. Then, a long way south (more often reached from LA), there is Mammoth.

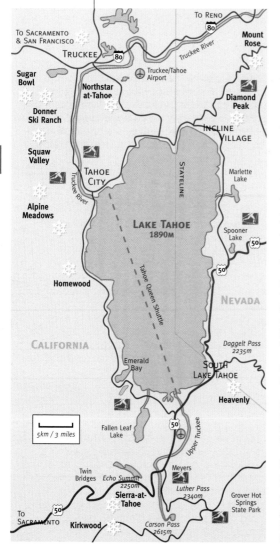

Each of the three major 'destination' resorts Heavenly and Squaw Valley in the Lake Tahoe area and Mammoth further south is covered in its own chapter immediately after this introduction page.

The other main Lake Tahoe resorts (shown on our map) each has an entry in the resort directory at the back of the book. Many are well worth visiting for a day or two, especially the four second-division resorts – Alpine Meadows, Kirkwood, Northstar and Sierra-at-Tahoe. We also enjoyed Sugar Bowl and Mount Rose. You could visit them all by car from a single base, but a two-centre holiday with some time at the north end of the lake and some at the south would be better.

Californian resorts often have the deepest snowfall in North America. Rockies powder connoisseurs are inclined to brand the snow as wet 'Sierra Cement'. The snow can be heavy – our 2006 visit was spoiled by rain. But most people find the snow just fine, especially in comparison with what you would expect in the Alps.

Resorts can get crowded with weekend visitors, but midweek the slopes are normally quiet.

In the past our main reservation has been the character of the resorts themselves; they don't have the traditional mountain-town ambience that we look for in the States.

But things are changing. At Heavenly a gondola goes up from a new car-free plaza in South Lake Tahoe. Squaw Valley and Northstar both have attractive new base villages. And a pedestrian village has opened in Mammoth – linked to the slopes by gondola.

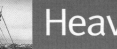
Heavenly

It's unique: fabulous lake and 'desert' views from interestingly varied slopes above a tacky lakeside casino town

COSTS

① ② ③ ④ ⑤ ⑥

RATINGS

The slopes

Fast lifts	***
Snow	****
Extent	***
Expert	***
Intermediate	****
Beginner	****
Convenience	*
Queues	****
Mountain restaurants	*

The rest

Scenery	****
Resort charm	*
Off-slope	**

KEY FACTS

Resort	1900m
	6,230ft
Slopes	2000-3060m
	6,570-10,040ft
Lifts	30
Pistes	4,800 acres
Green	20%
Blue	45%
Black	35%
Snowmaking	70%

➕ Spectacular setting, with amazing views of Lake Tahoe and Nevada

➕ Fair-sized mountain that offers a sensation of travelling around

➕ Large areas of widely spaced trees, largely on intermediate slopes – fabulous in fresh powder

➕ Some serious challenges for experts

➕ Numerous other worthwhile resorts within an hour's drive

➕ A unique nightlife scene

➕ Good snow record plus impressive snowmaking facilities

➖ South Lake Tahoe, where you stay, is a bizarre and messy place spreading along a busy highway

➖ No trail back to South Lake Tahoe

➖ Gondola very vulnerable to closure by high winds

➖ If tree-skiing is not good, or if you are not up to it, you are mainly confined to easy groomed blues

➖ If natural snow is in short supply, most of the challenging terrain is likely to be closed

➖ Very little traditional après-ski

A resort called Heavenly invites an obvious question: just how close to heaven does it take you? Physically, close enough: with a top height of 3070m/10,070ft and vertical of 1075m/3,530ft, it's the highest and biggest of the resorts set around Lake Tahoe. Metaphorically, it's not quite so close. In particular, anyone who (like us) is drawn to Heavenly partly by its exceptionally scenic setting is likely to be dismayed by the appearance and atmosphere of South Lake Tahoe.

The official line is that the place has been transformed into something like a European ski resort by the gondola between downtown and the mountain, and by the opening of a pedestrian 'village' around its base. We don't buy that. It's great to have a gondola from downtown and the 'village' is quite smart (though quiet and small). But the general feel of South Lake Tahoe isn't much affected.

THE RESORT

Heavenly is on California's border with Nevada, at the south end of Lake Tahoe. Other resorts around the lake are easily visited from a base here.

Heavenly's base-town – South Lake Tahoe – is primarily a summer resort. In this respect it is unusual, but not unique. What really sets it apart is that its economy is driven by gambling. The Stateline area at its centre is dominated by a handful of high-rise hotel-casinos located just inches on the Nevada side of the line. These brash but comfortable hotels offer good-value accommodation (subsidised by the gambling), swanky restaurants and big-name entertainers, as well as roulette wheels, craps and card games – and endless slot machines into which gambling-starved Californians feed bucketloads of quarters. It's bizarre to walk through the gambling areas in ski gear, with skis over your shoulder.

The casinos are a conspicuous part of the amazing lake views from the

SNOWPIX.COM / CHRIS GILL

There are wonderful lake views from the California side of the mountain, but it's a shame about the high-rise casinos in view too →

NEWS

For 2007/08 the slow Olympic chair on the Nevada side is due to be upgraded to a high-speed quad. Six new trails are planned – three at the top of Olympic, two in Skiways Glades and one in Powderbowl Woods – plus a skier bridge to allow skiing from the top of the gondola to the bottom of Tamarack Express. This is all part of Heavenly's Master Plan, a 10-year course of development.

Buildings close to the bottom of the gondola are due to be demolished, most likely before the start of next season, to make way for a $420 million complex to be known as The Chateau. Completion is not expected until 2009/10.

There are also plans for the North Bowl lift above Boulder Lodge on the Nevada side to be replaced by a fast quad, but this won't happen until 2008/09 or 2009/10.

lower slopes (though not from above mid-mountain). They look like a classic American downtown area, which you'd expect to be full of shops and bars. But they are actually just a cluster of high-rise blocks bisected by the seriously busy US Highway 50. The rest of the town spreads for miles along this pedestrian-hostile road – dozens of low-rise hotels and motels (some quite smart, but many rather shabby), stores, wedding chapels and so on. The general effect is less dire than it might be, thanks to the camouflage of the tall trees that blanket the area.

The new 'village', built a few years ago on the California side of the stateline right next to the base of the gondola, is an improvement, providing a downtown après-ski focus (essentially one bar) and pedestrianised area that the resort has lacked. But this could have been done much better (eg the new ice rink has a huge chiller/generator right next to it). Despite this, it is now the obvious place to stay.

Some of the casino-hotels are within five minutes' walk of the 'village' and gondola, making these an attractive choice even for those not keen on gambling and entertainment, but others are enough of a hike away to justify using the shuttle-buses. And much of the cheaper accommodation is literally miles away. If that's where you're staying, you may prefer to access the mountain from the original lift base, the refurbished California Lodge, up a heavily wooded slope 2km/1 mile out of South Lake Tahoe. That way, you'll be able to ski down at the end of the day instead of riding a lift down to the town base.

Like the town, the slopes spread across the border into Nevada – and there are two other lift bases, which can easily be reached by road, around the mountain in Nevada. There are 'adequate' free shuttle-bus services to the three out-of-town bases. A car is still handy to explore the other resorts around Lake Tahoe and to get to many

of the best restaurants, but parking can be pricey (maybe $20 a day).

There's a useful TV programme at 7.30am, *Another Heavenly Morning*, which covers weather and snow conditions. You can visit Squaw Valley by coach and return by boat across the lake. One reader recommends buying discount lift tickets from Don Cheepos.

THE MOUNTAIN

Practically all of Heavenly's slopes are cut through forest, but in many areas the forest is not dense and there is excellent tree skiing. As always in America, this 'off-piste' terrain is avalanche controlled. But it's 'patrolled' only by hollering; since collision with a tree may render you unconscious, don't ski the trees alone. Heavenly is home to famous extreme-skiing movie star Glen Plake – look out for his trademark Mohican hairstyle and you may be able to ski with him.

THE SLOPES
Interestingly complex
The gondola between downtown and the mountain is a great improvement. But it can be closed far too often if it's windy (as several reporters have found). Heavenly's mountain is complicated, and getting from A to B requires more careful navigation than is usual on American mountains (eg it's not obvious from the piste map that it's much better to take the Comet rather than the Dipper chair back from Nevada to the California side). Quite a few of the links between different sectors involve flat tracks.

There is a fairly clear division between the California side of the mountain (above South Lake Tahoe) and the Nevada side (above Boulder and Stagecoach Lodges). Near the Nevada border you can see beautiful views over Lake Tahoe in one direction and the arid Nevada 'desert' in the other.

On the California side there are four fast chairs on the upper mountain. The steep lower slopes are served by the Tram (cable-car) and Gunbarrel fast chair.

On the Nevada side, above East Peak Lodge, is an excellent intermediate area, served by two fast quad chairs, with a downhill extension served (only at weekends, warn reporters) by the Galaxy chair. From the fast Dipper chair back up, you can access the open terrain of Milky Way Bowl, leading to the seriously steep gladed runs of Mott and Killebrew canyons, served by the Mott Canyon chair. Below East Peak Lodge are runs down to Nevada's two bases, only the Stagecoach having a fast chair back up – it's successive slow chairs followed by the new Olympic quad (see News) from Boulder Lodge.

TERRAIN-PARKS
Great facilities for all standards
Heavenly has something for everyone. The Groove Terrain Park, between Groove and Patsy's chair-lifts below the top of the lifts up from California Lodge, has beginner features such as small jumps and boxes for novice park riders. Intermediates should head to Powderbowl Park on the Powderbowl run; this is a great progression area with good size jumps and basic rails. High Roller California park, near the

top of the Canyon chair, services expert riders; there are big kicker lines, and all sorts of jibs including an awesome pyramid jib-box feature and three-level box. Below this, at the top of the Powderbowl chair-lift, is a beast of a super-pipe with 7m/23ft walls. The Cascade boarder-cross can be found to the side of the Tamarack chair. High Roller Nightlife, served by the World Cup lift at the California base, is open Thursday to Saturday, 5pm-9pm.

SNOW RELIABILITY
No worries
Heavenly was one of the first resorts to invest heavily in snowmaking. The system now covers around 70 per cent of the trails and ensures that most sections are open most of the time. Last season wasn't great for natural snowfalls, but in the few years before that, California recorded some of the deepest snow-cover of any North American resort. Heavenly averages an impressive 360 inches per year.

FOR EXPERTS
Some specific challenges
The black runs under the California base lifts – including The Face and Gunbarrel (often used for mogul

SCHOOLS

Heavenly
775 586 4400

Classes
3-day (3 x 2³/₄hr) learn-to-ski package (includes equipment and pass) $340

Private lessons
$325 for 3hr

CHILDREN

Day Care Center
t 775 586 7000
Ages 6wk to 6yr; 8.30-4pm; $115 including lunch; book ahead

Ski school
For ages 4 to 13 (snowboarding 7 to 13); full day (including 5hr of teaching, equipment, pass and lunch) $155

competitions) – are seriously steep and challenging. Lots of people were struggling on the top-to-bottom icy bumps on our last two visits. Ellie's, at the top of the mountain, may offer continuous moguls too, but was groomed and a great fast cruise when we were last there. There's some really steep stuff on the Nevada side. Milky Way Bowl provides a gentle single-diamond introduction to the emphatically double-diamond terrain beyond it. The extremely steep, densely wooded Mott and Killebrew canyons have roped gateways; be warned, these are genuine double-black-diamond tree runs. The Mott Canyon chair is slow, but you may welcome the rest it affords.

Elsewhere, especially on the California side from the Sky chair, there are excellent ungroomed slopes with widely spaced trees – tremendous fun when conditions are right. Some wooded slopes are identified on the trail map, but you are not confined to those. The trail map gives a good indication of the density of trees, and the grading of nearby trails gives a good idea of steepness.

FOR INTERMEDIATES
Lots to do
Heavenly is excellent for intermediates. The California side offers a progression from the relaxed cruising of the long Ridge Run, starting right at the top of the mountain, to more challenging blues dropping off the ridge towards Sky Deck. Confident intermediates will want to spend time on the Nevada side, where there is more variety of terrain, some longer runs down to the lift bases and more carving space. There are some great top-to-bottom cruises down to Stagecoach Lodge (served by a fast chair) and Boulder Lodge (served by successive very slow chairs and then

the new Olympic quad – see 'News'). And adventurous intermediates will enjoy exploring the tree runs from the fast Sky chair on the California side (see 'For experts').

FOR BEGINNERS
An excellent place to learn
There's an excellent beginner area at the top of the gondola and others at the California base lodge and Boulder Lodge in Nevada. On the California side there are gentle green runs served by lifts at the top of the cable-car.

FOR CROSS-COUNTRY
A separate world
You can try Adventure Peak at the top of the gondola. But the serious stuff is elsewhere around the lake – notably at the Spooner Lake Cross Country Area: over 80km/50 miles of prepared trails. Organised moonlit tours are popular.

QUEUES
Gondola a problem
The gondola can have morning queues ('sometimes 20 minutes' says a recent reporter) when it can be worth taking the shuttle to the much quieter Stagecoach Lodge base. There are also queues to ride the gondola down at the end of the day. Ignore the signs telling you to set off ridiculously early to catch the gondola; it keeps going and our advice is to ski till whenever you like, then have a beer at the bar near the top of the gondola until the queue disappears. Sadly the gondola seems to close because of wind too often, when you have to catch a bus to another base to get up the mountain. We also have a report of 20-minute queues for the Sky and Canyon chairs on the California side. But 2007 reporters experienced few problems ('maximum wait was six minutes').

MOUNTAIN RESTAURANTS
Even refuelling is problematic
We have long considered the on-mountain catering grossly inadequate, especially in bad weather. We used to like the table-service Lake View Lodge at the top of the tram from California Lodge, but even that served mediocre food on our 2006 visit. East Peak Lodge was recently renovated and the menu widened. The other options consist of outdoor decks serving BBQs and pizzas (hugely unenjoyable in a blizzard, as we can testify) and grossly overcrowded cafeterias, 'I recommend

GETTING THERE

Air San Francisco 274km/170 miles (3½/hr); Reno 89km/55 miles (1¼/hr); South Lake Tahoe, 15min

UK PACKAGES

Alpine Answers, AmeriCan Ski, American Ski Classics, Crystal, Directski.com, Erna Low, Independent Ski Links, Ski Activity, Ski All America, Ski Dream, Ski Independence, Ski Line, Ski McNeill, Ski Safari, Ski Solutions, Skitracer, Skiworld, Trailfinders, United Vacations, White Mountains

ACTIVITIES

Indoor Casinos, spas, art galleries, multiplex cinema, museums

Outdoor Lake cruises, snowmobiling, sleigh rides, dog-sledding, hot springs, fishing, ice skating, factory outlet shops

Phone numbers Different area codes are used on the two sides of the stateline; for this chapter, therefore, the area code is included with each number

From distant parts of the US, add the prefix 1. From abroad, add the prefix +1

TOURIST OFFICE

t 775 586 7000
info@vailresorts.com
www.skiheavenly.com

starving, unless you're happy with crowds and stodge,' says a 2007 reporter.

SCHOOLS AND GUIDES
Mixed reports
A recent reporter joined the school for two days and was delighted to find only two in her class. However, another skier, looking for advanced tuition, found the attitude of the organisers 'terrible, really patronising'. A 2007 reporter tried the school's mountain explorer session ($75 for four hours) and found it 'well worth it to gain some local knowledge'.

FACILITIES FOR CHILDREN
Comprehensive
We lack recent feedback, but a past reporter praised the day care and ski school facilities.

STAYING THERE

HOW TO GO
Hotel or motel?
Accommodation in the South Lake Tahoe area is abundant and ranges from the huge casinos to small motels. **Chalets** UK tour operators run some good catered chalets. **Hotels** Of the main casino hotels, Harrah's (775 558 6611) and Harveys (775 558 2411) are the closest to the gondola. Rooms booked on the spot are expensive; packages are cheaper. The Block (530 544 2936) is a snowboarders' hotel – see 'Boarding'. ******Embassy Suites** (530 544 5400) Luxury suites in a modern, traditional-style building close to the gondola. *****Forest Suites** (530 541 6655) Right by the gondola, pools, hot-tubs, 'enormous rooms, very luxurious'. **Marriott's Timber Lodge** (530 542 6600) Part of the new 'village'. **Rodeway Inn** (530 541 7150) 'Basic but just what was required. About seven minutes' walk to the gondola.' **Station House Inn** (530 542 1101) Consistently recommended by reporters: 'Full cooked breakfast at no extra charge.' **Tahoe Chalet Inn** (530 544 3311) Clean, friendly, near casinos. Back rooms (away from highway) preferable. **Timber Cove Lodge** (530 541 6722) Bland but well run, with lake views from some rooms. **Apartments** Plenty of choice. We've had a rave report about The Ridge Tahoe condos near Stagecoach Lodge.

EATING OUT
Good value
The casino hotels' all-you-can-eat buffets offer fantastic value and variety ('from pizza to Chinese to roast beef' at Montbleu). They have some more ambitious 'gourmet' restaurants too – some high enough to give superb views (try the 18th floor at Harrah's and the 19th at Harveys). The sprawling resort area offers a huge variety. Reporters' suggestions include Applebee's ('still the best value meals'), Hunan Garden ('best Chinese buffet ever'), Cecile's ('excellent and reasonable'), Fresh Ketch at Tahoe Keys Marina ('wonderful fresh fish and harbour views') and Zephyr Cove Resort ('excellent, reasonable, marvellous sunset views'), The Brewery ('excellent food and a micro-brewery'), Taj Mahal ('decent Indian'), Coyote Grill ('excellent fast-food Mexican'), Freshies ('the fish tacos are out of this world') and Riva Grill ('smart and pricey marina bar/grill'). For breakfast, try the Blue Angel or 'cheap $3 breakfast' at the Lakeside Inn and Casino; or join the locals at the Driftwood Cafe.

APRES-SKI
Getting better
Things have looked up in the last few years for 4pm drinking: there's now an Austrian-style igloo bar near the top of the gondola and Fire and Ice at the foot of it (with an outdoor seating area with fires and heaters). Both get busy and form an après-ski focus. McP's was a locals' hangout but due to be razed to the ground as part of the demolition mentioned in 'News'; it may reopen elsewhere, we hear. Whiskey Dicks, on the main highway, is a 'cool' bar with live music. Later on, the casinos on the Nevada side of the stateline have shows with top-name entertainers. And you can dance and dine your way across the lake aboard a paddle steamer.

OFF THE SLOPES
Luck be a lady
If you enjoy gambling you're in the right place. If you want to get away from the bright lights, try a boat trip on Lake Tahoe, snowmobiling or a hot-air balloon ride. Pedestrians can use the cable-car or the gondola to share the lake views and at Adventure Peak, at the top of the gondola, you can go tubing, snow-biking, tobogganing and snow-shoeing.

Mammoth Mountain

A big, sprawling mountain above a car-oriented, sprawling but pleasantly woody resort, a six-hour drive from Los Angeles

COSTS

① ② ③ ④ ⑤ ⑥

RATINGS

The slopes

Fast lifts	****
Snow	****
Extent	***
Expert	****
Intermediate	****
Beginner	****
Convenience	**
Queues	****
Mountain restaurants	*

The rest

Scenery	***
Resort charm	**
Off-slope	*

NEWS

For 2007/08 the 38-year-old Chair 9 will be replaced with a six-pack, the Cloud Nine Express.

The whole Eagle Lodge base area is to be redeveloped but building won't start until spring 2008. Plans include another moving carpet and lift for the nursery slope and a new plaza, including a hotel, shops and an ice rink.

It is hoped that flights from Los Angeles to Mammoth will be re-introduced – but it won't be until December 2008.

For 2006/07 a ski school base was added at Eagle Lodge and a local history and geology centre, Top of the Sierra, opened at the Panorama Lookout Station.

- ➕ One of North America's bigger ski hills, with something for everyone
- ➕ Good mix of open Alpine-style bowls and classic American wooded slopes
- ➕ Impressive good snowfall record
- ➕ Uncrowded slopes most of the time
- ➕ Mightily impressive terrain-parks
- ➕ Good views, including more Alpine drama than usual in the US

- ➖ Mammoth Lakes is a rather straggling place with no focus, where life revolves around cars
- ➖ Most accommodation is miles from the slopes – though development is taking place at the lift bases
- ➖ Weekend crowds in high season
- ➖ Trail map and signing still poor
- ➖ Wind can be a problem

Mammoth may not be mammoth in Alpine terms – from end to end, it measures less than one-third of the size of Val d'Isère/Tignes, in area it's more like one-sixth – but it is big enough to amuse many people for a week. It can be a superb mountain for anyone who is happy in deep snow, but is equally suited to families and mixed-ability groups looking for groomed runs. The main thing it has lacked is a real village at the base.

You have to applaud the efforts of Intrawest, owner of Whistler and now of various key plots of land here, to put this right by building a new pedestrian 'village' (which we are encouraged to call The Village) on the edge of sprawling Mammoth Lakes, connected by a gondola to one of the main lift bases. If your lodgings are at The Village, no doubt its restaurants and boutiques will attract your custom. But we'd be surprised if it ever has much impact on the resort as a whole. You can't ski down to The Village, so most visitors based elsewhere (ie the majority) will ignore it. Mammoth will remain what it has always been: a resort that expects you to arrive by car, and get around by car.

THE RESORT

The mountain is set above Mammoth Lakes, a small year-round resort town that spreads over a wide area of woodland. The place is entirely geared to driving, with no discernible centre – hotels, restaurants and little shopping centres are scattered along the four-lane highway called Main Street and Old Mammoth Road, which crosses it. The buildings are generally timber-clad in traditional style – even McDonald's has been tastefully designed – and are set among trees, so although it may be short on village ambience, the place has a pleasant enough appearance – particularly when under snow.

The town meets the mountain at two lift bases, both a mile or two from most of the hotels and condos.

The major base is Canyon Lodge, with a big day lodge and four chair-lifts; there are hotels, condos and individual homes in the area below the lodge. Not far from here is Intrawest's pedestrian development,

The Village, which is linked to Canyon Lodge by a gondola.

The minor base, with a single six-pack, is Eagle Lodge (previously Little Eagle – also known as Juniper Springs, which strictly is the name of the condos built at the base) – which, if plans go ahead, will be redeveloped for the 2008/09 season.

A road runs along the north fringe of the mountain past an anonymous chair-lift base to two other major base areas: The Mill Cafe, with two fast chairs, and Main Lodge, a mini-resort with three fast access lifts and a big day lodge. You can stay here, in the Mammoth Mountain Inn; but who wants to be based four miles from the resort's 50 restaurants? Not us.

Shuttle-buses run on several colour-coded routes serving the lift bases (though they are reported to be erratic in the mornings). Night buses run via The Village until midnight. A car is useful.

The Mammoth lift pass also covers June, a small mountain half an hour's

↑ Main Park is the biggest and gnarliest of Mammoth's three award-winning terrain-parks; there are beginner and intermediate level parks too

MAMMOTH MOUNTAIN SKI AREA

KEY FACTS

Resort	2425m
	7,950ft

Mammoth only	
Slopes	2425-3370m
	7,950-11,050ft
Lifts	29
Pistes	3,500 acres
Green	25%
Blue	40%
Black	35%
Snowmaking	
	477 acres

June Mountain only	
Slopes	2290-3075m
	7,510-10,090ft
Lifts	7
Pistes	500 acres
Green	35%
Blue	45%
Black	20%
Snowmaking	none

THE MOUNTAIN

The 28 lifts access an impressive area, suitable for all abilities. The highest runs are open, the lower ones more sheltered by trees.

Finding your way around is not easy at first. Many of the chair-lifts now have names (the traditional practice was to give them numbers), but the trails are still ill-defined: the map shows trails by means of isolated symbols, not continuous lines, and signposting of runs on the mountain is sporadic. On the lower part of the mountain this is mainly an inconvenience. But higher up there are real dangers in poor visibility. The map uses six classifications, including green/blue and blue/black – a good idea, but somewhat pointless when you often end up on the wrong trail.

drive north, chiefly attractive for its astonishingly people-free slopes. See feature box, later in this chapter.

The drive up from Los Angeles takes six hours (more in poor conditions); but it is not without interest. You pass through the Santa Monica mountains close to Beverly Hills, then the San Gabriel mountains and Mojave Desert (with the world's biggest jet-plane parking lot) before reaching the Sierra Nevada range.

THE SLOPES
Interesting variety

From **Main Lodge** the two-stage Panorama gondola goes via McCoy Station right to the top. The views are great, with Nevada to the north-east and the jagged Minarets to the west. There are countless ways down the front of the mountain, which range from steep to very steep – or vertical if the wind has created a cornice, as it often does. Or you can go off the back, down to **Outpost 14**, whence chairs 14 or 13 bring you back to lower points on the ridge. The third option is to follow the ridge, which eventually brings you down to the Main Lodge area. This route brings you past an easy area served by a double chair, and a very easy area served by the Discovery fast quad.

McCoy Station can also be reached using the Stump Alley fast chair from **The Mill Cafe**, on the road up from town. The fast Gold Rush quad from here takes you into the more heavily wooded eastern half of the area. This has long, gentle runs served by lifts up from **Canyon Lodge** and **Eagle Lodge** and seriously steep stuff as well as some intermediate terrain on the subsidiary peak known as Lincoln, served by lifts 25 and 22.

TERRAIN-PARKS
Among the best

There are three award-winning parks. Main Park, situated above Main Lodge, is massive. Everything here is up to pro standard. This year saw the Boneyard Bonanza jumps added; they range from 18m to 24m/6oft to 8oft long and border the famous super-duper pipe (183m/6ooft long, with 7m/22ft walls) that looms over the car park.

For intermediate to advanced riders, South Park by the Roller Coaster fast chair is a real playground. Two tree-lined itineraries force you to choose

boarding

Mammoth has encouraged snowboarding since its early days. A huge amount has been spent on the terrain-parks, and this tends to overshadow just how good the mountain's natural terrain really is. Almost entirely serviced by fast chairs and gondolas, this is a snowboarder's heaven. There are bowls, chutes, tree runs and cliffs dotted around the mountain, and you will be hard-pressed not to find something to your liking. Take the Panorama gondola and drop into the back bowls for plenty of powder runs. There are heaps of not-so-steep and wide runs for beginners on the lower parts of the resort. The terrain-parks are about the best you will find. Wave Rave snowboard shop has a huge selection of gear.

LIFT PASSES

Mammoth Mountain

Prices in US$

Age	1-day	6-day
under 13	39	185
13 to 18	59	278
19 to 64	78	371
over 65	39	185

Free under 7, over 80

Beginner Included in price of lessons. Fixed price pass for beginner chairs only

Notes
Covers all lifts at Mammoth and June Mountains. Afternoon pass available

Alternative pass
June Mountain only

between rails or kickers. These flowing lines allow you to hit six or seven obstacles in a row – perfect. There's also a boarder-cross here.

The Family Fun Park by Canyon Lodge has a fun mini-pipe, various micro-scale rails, boxes and mini-jumps, coupled with a great atmosphere to learn in.

All the parks are groomed daily and often have original features you won't find anywhere else. The parks can get very crowded on the weekends – try neighbouring June mountain's parks for a quiet and brilliantly underrated alternative. See http://unbound. mammothmountain.com for details on Mammoth's parks and events.

SNOW RELIABILITY
A long season

Although it had a relatively poor season in 2007, Mammoth has an impressive snow record – an annual average of 385 inches, which puts it ahead of major Colorado resorts and about on a par with Jackson Hole. Mammoth is appreciably higher than other Californian resorts, and it has an ever-expanding array of snow-guns, so it enjoys a long season. The mountain faces roughly north; the relatively low and slightly sunny slopes down to Eagle Lodge are affected by warm weather before others. Strong winds are not uncommon on the upper mountain; some lifts are kept going in surprisingly breezy conditions – one reporter was blown over at the top. The snow quality can be affected by these winds, too. This is not always a bad thing – the 'wind-compacted powder' can be 'just like spring snow'.

FOR EXPERTS
Some very challenging terrain

The steep bowls that run the width of the mountain top provide wonderful opportunities for experts. There are one or two single-diamond slopes, but most are emphatically double-diamond affairs requiring a lot of bottle.

There is lots of challenging terrain lower down, too; Chair 5, Chair 22 and Broadway are often open in bad weather when the top is firmly shut, and their more sheltered slopes may in any case have the best snow. (The top of Chair 22 is higher than the very top of Heavenly, remember.) There are plenty of good slopes over the back towards Outpost 14, too. Many of the steeper trails are short by Alpine standards (typically under 400m/1,300ft vertical), but despite this we've enjoyed some great powder days here.

FOR INTERMEDIATES
Lots of great cruising

Although there are exceptions, most of the lower mountain, below the tree-line, is intermediate cruising territory. What's more, Mammoth's piste maintenance is generally good, and many slopes that might become mogulled are kept easily skiable. 'Very flattering,' says one visitor.

As you might hope, the six-point trail difficulty scale – which we haven't tried to replicate on our own small trail map – is a good guide to what you'll find on the mountain.

Some of the mountain's longest runs, blue-blacks served by chairs 9 (the new Cloud Nine Express) and 25, are ideal for good intermediates. There are also some excellent, fairly steep,

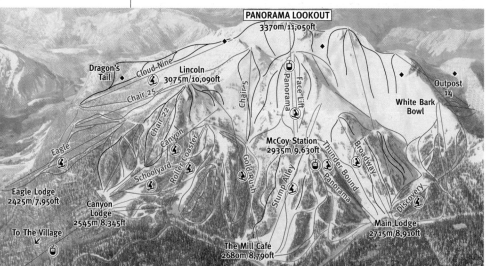

PANORAMA LOOKOUT
3370m/11,050ft

Dragon's Tail

Cloud-Nine

Lincoln
3075m/10,090ft

Chair 25

Chair 22

Chair 5

Face Lift

Panorama

Outpost 14

White Bark Bowl

Eagle

Canyon

Roller Coaster

Schoolyard

McCoy Station
2935m/9,630ft

Gold Rush

Stump Alley

Thunder Bound

Panorama

Broadway

Discovery

Eagle Lodge
2425m/7,950ft

Canyon Lodge
2545m/8,345ft

To The Village

The Mill Cafe
268om/8,790ft

Main Lodge
2715m/8,910ft

UK PACKAGES

AmeriCan Ski,
American Ski Classics,
Independent Ski Links,
Ski Activity, Ski All
America, Ski Dream,
Ski Independence, Ski
Line, Ski Safari, Ski
Solutions, Skitracer,
Skiworld, United
Vacations, Virgin
Snow, White Mountains

SCHOOLS

Mammoth Mountain
934 0745

Classes
1 3hr morning $67
Private lessons
$250 for a 2hr
afternoon lesson

CHILDREN

Small World
t 934 0646
Ages newborn to 12;
8.30-4.30

Ski school
Takes ages 4 to 12 at
a cost of $115 all day
(10am-3pm)

woodland trails down to The Mill Cafe. Most of the long runs above Eagle Lodge, and some of the shorter ones above Canyon Lodge, are easy cruises. There is a variety of terrain, including lots of gentle stuff, at the western extremity of the slopes, both on the front side and on the back side.

FOR BEGINNERS
Excellent
Chair 7 and Chair 17 (named the Schoolyard Express) at Canyon Lodge and Discovery Chair at Main Lodge serve quiet, gentle green runs – so as soon as you're off the nursery slopes you get an encouraging taste of real skiing. Excellent instruction, top-notch grooming and snow quality usually make progress speedy ('My eight-year-old son was skiing blue-black runs by the end of the week').

FOR CROSS-COUNTRY
Very popular
Two specialist centres, Tamarack and Sierra Meadows (ungroomed), provide lessons and tours. There are 30km/19 miles of trails at Tamarack, and lots of scenic ungroomed tracks, including some through the pretty Lakes Basin area: 70km/43 miles of trails in all.

QUEUES
Normally quiet slopes
During the week the lifts and slopes are usually very quiet, with few queues: 'empty', 'deserted', say reporters. And recent visitor reports only 5-10 minute waits at most in the busiest areas. But even the efficient lift system can struggle when 15,000 visitors arrive from LA on fine peak-season weekends. That's the time to try the wonderfully uncrowded June Mountain, half an hour away.

MOUNTAIN RESTAURANTS
Not a lot of choice
The only real mountain restaurants are at mid-mountain McCoy Station. This offers 'a good choice' of roasts, Italian, Asian and other dishes – but does get 'very busy'. The Parallax table-service restaurant next door does satisfying food with a calm atmosphere and a splendid view from its picture windows. The other on-mountain possibility in good weather is the primitive outdoor BBQ at Outpost 14, on the back of the hill.

Most people eat at the lift bases. Talons at Eagle Lodge has its fans. The Mill Cafe is 'pleasant' but the 'choice of food was limited', according to one visitor. The Mountainside Grill at the Mammoth Mountain Inn is also recommended. And Canyon Lodge offers Mexican, Italian, Asian and more. The Broadway Marketplace opened in 2006 in the Main Lodge for breakfast and lunch.

SCHOOLS AND GUIDES
Excellent reports
Reporters are favourably impressed by the school, which apparently contains growing numbers of Scottish instructors. A recent visitor writes of 'very sympathetic' instructors and small classes. You can encounter the general American problem that you usually get a different instructor every day. There are some special 'camps' for experts, and for women.

FACILITIES FOR CHILDREN
Family favourite
Mammoth is keen to attract families. The Woollywood school, based in the Panorama gondola station, works closely with the Small World childcare centre. We've had glowing reports; one reporter rated the facilities as 'second to none'. Canyon Kids (at Canyon Lodge) was recommended in 2006.

JUNE MOUNTAIN: THE WORLD'S QUIETEST SLOPES?

June Mountain, a scenic half-hour drive from Mammoth, is in the same ownership and covered by the lift pass. It makes a pleasant haven if Mammoth is busy. When Mammoth isn't busy, June is quite simply deserted; on a March weekday we skied run after run without seeing another person. (Because of the poor snow in 2007, June was closed from the end of January but that is unusual.)

A double chair goes up from the car park at 2290m/7,510ft over black slopes (often short of snow) to a lodge, June Meadows Chalet. A quad chair serves a gentle blue-run hill, and a double chair goes over very gentle green runs to a quad serving short but genuinely black slopes on June Mountain itself (3100m/ 10,175ft). There are three terrain-parks, two jib-parks and a super-pipe.

↑ The Village is a typically attractive car-free Intrawest development, linked by gondola to the slopes at Canyon Lodge

MAMMOTH MOUNTAIN SKI AREA

GETTING THERE

Air Los Angeles 494km/307 miles (5hr); Reno 270km/168 miles (3hr)

ACTIVITIES

Indoor Fitness centres, museum, art galleries, cinema, concerts

Outdoor Snow-shoeing, dog-sledding, snowmobiling

Phone numbers
From distant parts of the US, add the prefix 1 760; from abroad, add the prefix +1 760

TOURIST OFFICE

t 934 0745
800mammoth@
mammoth-mtn.com
www.mammoth
mountain.com

STAYING THERE

HOW TO GO
Good value packages
A good choice of hotels (none very luxurious or expensive) and condos. The condos tend to be out of town, near the lifts or on the road to them.
***Mammoth Mountain Inn** (934 2581) Way out of town at Main Lodge. 'Spacious and comfortable, perfect for access to the slopes but rather isolated'; 'Three-day special deal with lift pass and parking is good value,' says a 2007 reporter.
***Alpenhof Lodge** (934 6330) Comfortable and friendly, in central location. Shuttle-bus stop and plenty of restaurants nearby.
Quality Inn (934 5114) Good main street hotel with a big hot-tub.
Austria Hof Lodge (934 2764) Ski-out location near Canyon Lodge, recommended by a reporter, despite modest-sized rooms.
Sierra Nevada Rodeway Inn (934 2515) Central, good value, 'great spa'.
Holiday Inn (924 1234) Central location, large, comfortable rooms and 'great restaurant'. Pool.
Apartments The Juniper Springs Lodge is near lifts and town. Close to the Canyon Lodge base-station, the 1849 Condominiums are spacious and well equipped. The Mammoth Ski and Racquet Club, a 10-minute walk from the same lifts, is very comfortable. There is an 'excellent' supermarket in the Minaret Mall, with good discounts.

EATING OUT
Outstanding choice
Reporters continue to be impressed by the 50+ restaurants, varying widely in style, cost and location. Start with a copy of the local menu guide. One reporting couple had a great time dining in a different restaurant every day for a fortnight. Meshing their findings with other reports, we offer the following guidance: Slocums Grill – very good meal in wood-panelled room; Angel's – popular, good-value diner; Ocean Harvest – great atmosphere and wonderful fish; Nevados – best in town, excellent modern cooking; Chart House – excellent seafood, varied meat dishes; Alpenrose – intimate chalet-style place, good food; Matsu – small, simple, with delicious Asian food; Berger's – 'excellent giant burgers'; Old Mammoth Grill – traditional diner, 'good bar'.

Also recommended are Shogun for Japanese, Giovannis for Italian and Gomez's for Mexican food. A recent visitor says that the meal he had at the Lakefront up at Twin Lakes was 'the best ever in a ski resort'. We've had excellent dinners at Skadi and Whiskey Creek, too. A 2007 reporter says the Breakfast Club does a 'good value, tasty breakfast'. Sand Dollar Sushi (for Japanese), Lulu and the Side Door cafe are the latest additions in The Village.

APRES-SKI
Lively at weekends
The liveliest immediate après-ski spot is the Yodler, at Main Lodge – a chalet transported from Switzerland, so they say. A new bar, Tusks, has also opened at Main Lodge – apparently great for viewing the high jinks in the terrain-parks. Later on, things revolve around a handful of bars, which come to life at weekends. The Clocktower Cellar is reported to be 'best in town – lively, friendly, good music, great choice of beers'. Whiskey Creek is the liveliest (and stays open latest); it has live bands at weekends. Slocums is popular with locals and 'ideal for an after-dinner drink'. Grumpy's is a sports bar. One reporter enjoyed the venues in The Village. He says you shouldn't miss Hawaiian-style Lakanuki's with its 'bikini tree' or Dublin's Irish Pub (with Fever disco).

OFF THE SLOPES
Mainly sightseeing
There are various things to be done outdoors, including skating. You can go sightseeing by car (preferably 4WD). The town of Bishop, 40 minutes' drive south, makes an amusing day out. Factory-outlet shopping is recommended for bargains. Mono Lake is reported to be 'well worth a visit'.

Squaw Valley

Now the most compelling base in the Tahoe area – great terrain for novices and experts, above an attractive new 'village'

COSTS

① ② ③ ④ ⑤ ⑥

RATINGS

The slopes
Fast lifts	✳✳✳
Snow	✳✳✳✳
Extent	✳✳✳
Expert	✳✳✳✳
Intermediate	✳✳
Beginner	✳✳✳✳✳
Convenience	✳✳✳✳
Queues	✳✳✳✳
Mountain restaurants	✳

The rest
Scenery	✳✳✳
Resort charm	✳✳✳
Off-slope	✳

NEWS

For 2007/08 the Shirley Lake fast quad (the resort's busiest chair-lift) will be replaced by a six-pack. The Central terrain-park will be getting a new super-pipe, which will be floodlit for use in the evenings. Two educational and fun areas for kids are planned for 2007/08. One will have patrol dogs to meet kids and do demonstrations; the other will be a place where they can learn about on-mountain safety.

For 2006/07 a new children's play area opened at the Papoose Learning Area.

- ➕ Lots of challenging runs and 'off-piste' terrain of varying difficulty
- ➕ Impressive snow record
- ➕ Superb beginner slopes
- ➕ Convenient, pleasant, modern 'village' at the base

- ➖ Not for mile-hungry intermediates
- ➖ Lifts prone to closure by wind
- ➖ Adventurous skiers need guidance to really exploit the area
- ➖ Limited range of village amenities
- ➖ A bit pricey

With the construction by Intrawest of a neat little pedestrian resort at the base, Squaw is at last a proper destination. It can't rival Heavenly for nightlife or for quantity of groomed runs, but it's now our favourite base in the Tahoe area.

THE RESORT

'The Village at Squaw Valley' has been built at the base of the main lifts by Intrawest, of Whistler/Arc 1950 fame. For a built-from-scratch development it is very successful, although still very small and limited in what it offers. In classic Intrawest style, it consists of neat, linked, apartment buildings carefully arranged around traffic-free streets and squares, with a handful of restaurants and shops strategically placed. It meets the main slopes at one end, close to the cable-car.

The self-contained, luxurious conference-oriented Resort at Squaw Creek is linked into one end of the lift network by its own chair-lift.

Squaw is the major resort at the north end of Lake Tahoe, about an hour's drive from South Lake Tahoe and Heavenly. There are daily shuttle-buses, and you can go by boat.

One of Squaw's high bowls – all ski-where-you-like terrain ➔

THE MOUNTAINS

Squaw offers a lot of terrain by US standards on six linked peaks. The peaks and high bowls are treeless, but much of the terrain is lightly wooded.

Squaw has no trails marked on its mountain map (just lifts that are coloured green, blue or black) and few signs or other aids to route-finding on the ground. In some sectors, adventurous but not truly expert skiers could find themselves in real difficulty. **Slopes** There are several distinct sectors. Two impressively powerful lifts leave the village – a gondola and a big cable-car. They rise 600m/1,970ft to the twin stations of Gold Coast and High Camp (linked by the Pulse gondola). Above them is a gentle area of beginner slopes, and beyond that the three highest peaks of the area. Each has lifts of modest vertical – much the biggest is on Squaw Peak's Headwall six-pack: 535m/1,750ft.

From High Camp you can descend into a steep-sided valley from which the Silverado chair is the return. This is an area where guidance is essential.

Two peaks are accessed directly from the village. The fast quad to KT-22 gives a quick access to countless steep routes. Snow King is an excellent intermediate hill, unjustly neglected because of its slow lift access.

Squaw's cable-car runs in the evenings to serve the floodlit slopes, the Central terrain-park and pipe and the dining facilities at High Camp. **Terrain-parks** There are three impressive terrain-parks – Belmont is for kids and novices; Central Park and its planned super-pipe is great for intermediates and advanced riders and

KEY FACTS

Resort	1890m
	6,200ft
Slopes	1890-2760m
	6,200-9,050ft
Lifts	33
Pistes	4,000 acres
Green	25%
Blue	45%
Black	30%
Snowmaking	
	400 acres

UK PACKAGES

AmeriCan Ski,
American Ski Classics,
Crystal, Directski.com,
Ski Activity, Ski All
America, Ski Dream,
Ski Independence, Ski
McNeill, Ski Safari,
Skitracer, Skiworld,
United Vacations,
White Mountains

Phone numbers
From distant parts of
the US, add the prefix
1 530; from abroad,
add the prefix +1 530

TOURIST OFFICE

t 583 6985
squaw@squaw.com
www.squaw.com

is floodlit for evening use; the Ford Freestyle Park is the big pro park, with a vast array of larger jumps, boxes and rails and another super-pipe.

Snow reliability An impressive 460 inches on average, plus snowmaking.

Experts The possibilities for experts on KT-22, Squaw Peak and Granite Chief – plus the Silverado valley – are huge, with lots of steep chutes and big mogul fields; many extreme skiing and boarding movies are made here. But at first it is very difficult to identify routes that are safe – go with an instructor.

Intermediates Blue-run skiers have a choice of some lovely cruises in the Emigrant and Snow King sectors (especially the one to the Resort at Squaw Creek), and a three-mile top-to-bottom run. But there is not much more groomed cruising, so keen piste-bashers will find the area limited. There is, however, lots of steep blue and easy black terrain in which to develop deep-snow or mogul skills – particularly around the Siberia, Solitude and Granite Chief lifts.

Beginners The Papoose nursery area has a gentle slope served by a double chair-lift – a special beginner lift pass is available. There's a superb choice of easy runs to progress to at altitude.

Snowboarding This is one of the most snowboarder friendly resorts in California. The higher areas are full of steep and deep gullies, cliff drops, kicker building spots and tree runs. And the three terrain-parks are great.

Cross-country There are 18km/11 miles of groomed trails at Squaw Creek.

Queues Fast lifts now serve each sector, but there are still several old chairs, notably around Emigrant.

Mountain restaurants The mid-mountain facilities are not inspiring, except in terms of views.

Schools and guides Ski Your Pro runs adult group lessons hourly. There are specialist workshops too.

Facilities for children Squaw Kids takes children from three years. There is a children's on-slope play area at the Papoose base area (see 'News'), too.

STAYING THERE

How to go The new village has widened the choice of accommodation.

Hotels The Plumpjack Inn (800-323 7666) is our favourite – comfortable, stylish, central. The Resort at Squaw Creek (530-583-6300) offers luxury rooms, an outdoor pool and hot-tubs.

Apartments The Village has well-appointed ski-in/ski-out condos.

Eating out The Plumpjack Inn has an excellent restaurant; the Balboa Cafe, run by the same people, also has an impressive menu. More routine alternatives in The Village include the Auld Dubliner Irish pub, the Fireside (pizza/pasta), Mamsake (sushi), the High Sierra Grill (steaks etc). The Olympic House, just outside The Village, does genuine tapas. Dining up the mountain is possible at Alexander's.

Après-ski The Olympic House has several venues and the Zenbu is said to come to life later on. In The Village, the places above mostly function as bars, too: Auld Dubliner is the liveliest.

Off the slopes High Camp has an ice-rink and other activities. The Trilogy Spa offers a range of body-pampering treatments. Or you can take a paddle steamer cruise across Lake Tahoe.

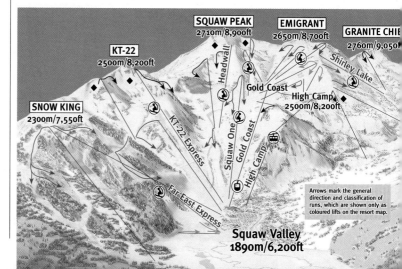

Colorado

Colorado was the first US state to market its resorts internationally and is still the most popular American destination for UK visitors. And justifiably so: it has the most alluring combination of attractive resorts, slopes to suit all abilities and excellent, reliable snow – dry enough to justify its 'champagne powder' label. It also has direct scheduled BA flights to Denver (though no longer charter flights).

Colorado has amazingly dry snow. Even when the snow melts and refreezes, the moisture seems to be magically whisked away, leaving it in soft powdery condition. Even in times of snow shortage, the artificial snow is of a quality you'll rarely find in Europe. And like most North American rivals, Colorado resorts generally have excellent, steep, ungroomed terrain that has enormous appeal to the adventurous because you don't need guidance to ski it safely.

The resorts vary enormously. If you want cute restored buildings from the mining boom days of the late 1800s, try the dinky old towns of Telluride or Crested Butte or the much bigger Aspen. Others major on convenience –

such as Aspen's modern satellite, Snowmass. Some resorts deliberately pitch themselves upmarket, with lots of glitzy, pricey hotels – such as Vail and Beaver Creek – while others are much more down to earth – such as Winter Park and Breckenridge.

There is a cluster of resorts west of Denver that can be combined in a holiday tour by car. You could visit these while staying in cheaper lodging in a valley town such as Frisco. As well as the resorts we cover in detail, you could think about quick visits to some others – notably high, steep Arapahoe Basin, up the valley from Keystone and due for big expansion for 2007/08; and snow-sure Loveland, visible from the main I70 highway from Denver.

591

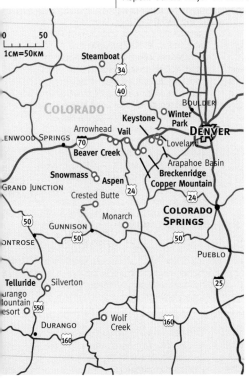

Aspen

Don't be put off by the ritzy image – with a fun, historic town and quiet, extensive slopes, this is America's best resort

COSTS

① ② ③ ④ ⑤ ⑥

RATINGS

The slopes
Fast lifts	★★★
Snow	★★★★★
Extent	★★★★
Expert	★★★★★
Intermediate	★★★★★
Beginner	★★★★★
Convenience	★★
Queues	★★★★
Mountain restaurants	★★★

The rest
Scenery	★★★
Resort charm	★★★★
Off-slope	★★★★

Our extent rating relates to the whole Aspen-Snowmass area. Aspen alone would rate ★★

592

For 2006/07 another 40 acres of advanced terrain opened in the Deep Temerity sector at Aspen Highlands.

Aspen Mountain's Silver Queen gondola got new six-person cabins.

And the list of bars and restaurants keeps growing, with several new places opening in the town last season and one new restaurant due for 2007/08.

- ➕ Notably uncrowded slopes, even by American standards
- ➕ Attractive, characterful old mining town, with lots of smart shops
- ➕ Lively, varied nightlife
- ➕ Great range of restaurants
- ➕ Excellent Snowmass just up the road

- ➖ Slopes split over three separate mountains (four if you count Snowmass, as you should), though there's efficient, free transport
- ➖ Some accommodation in Aspen town is a bus-ride from the lifts
- ➖ Expensive

Aspen is our favourite American resort. We love the town and we love the extensive and varied skiing. We admit that this affection for the skiing depends heavily on the presence of Aspen Highlands, a little way down the valley, and Snowmass, considerably further down the valley (and therefore covered in a separate chapter) – so to get to most of the slopes you have to ride a bus. That doesn't put us off, and doesn't seem to worry readers who report on the place – so it shouldn't deter you, either.

Don't be deterred by the filmstar image, either. Yes, many rich and famous guests jet in to the local airport, and for connoisseurs of cosmetic surgery the bars of Aspen's top hotels can be fascinating places. But most celebs keep a low profile; and, like all other 'glamorous' ski resorts, Aspen is actually filled by ordinary holidaymakers.

One note of reservation this year, though. When a single year sees the closure of our favourite cheap bar/restaurant (Red Onion) and our favourite spot for pool and line dancing (Shooters) and the opening of yet another impossibly fancy hotel (Hyatt), we're forced to wonder where this trend will end.

THE RESORT

In 1892 Aspen was a booming silver-mining town, with 12,000 inhabitants, six newspapers and an opera house. But Aspen's fortunes took a nosedive when the silver price plummeted in 1893, and by the 1930s the population had shrunk to 700 or so, and handsome Victorian buildings had fallen into disrepair. Development of the skiing started on a small scale in the late 1930s. The first lift was opened shortly after the Second World War, and Aspen hasn't looked back.

Now, the historic centre – with a typical American grid of streets – has been beautifully renovated to form the core of the most fashionable ski town in the Rockies. There's a huge variety of bars, restaurants, shops and art galleries – some amazingly upmarket. Spreading out from this centre, you'll find a mixture of developments, ranging from the homes of the super-rich through surprisingly modest hotels and motels to the mobile homes for the workers. Though the town is busy

with traffic, it moves slowly, and pedestrians effectively have priority in much of the central area.

Aspen is very unusual in being a cute town with a major lift close to the centre: the newly upgraded Silver Queen gondola straight to the top of Aspen Mountain is only yards from some of the top hotels, and the streets running away from the lift base are lined by the restaurants and shops that make Aspen what it is. Downtown Aspen is quite compact by American resort standards, but it spreads far enough to make the free ski-bus a necessity for many visitors staying less centrally.

The other mountains are out of town, served by efficient buses from a station near the gondola base – 'fantastic and super-frequent', says a recent reporter. A couple of miles out of town, Aspen Highlands now has some limited accommodation; 19km/ 12 miles away, Snowmass is a proper resort with great attractions as a base for families in particular, and it now gets its own chapter.

THE SLOPES
Widely dispersed

Each of the three local mountains is worth a visit – though novices should note that Aspen Mountain has no green runs. Much the most extensive mountain in the area is at Snowmass – see separate chapter.

Once you are up the gondola, a series of chairs serves the ridges of **Aspen Mountain**. In general, there are long cruising blue runs along the valley floors and short, steep blacks down from the ridges.

Buttermilk is the least challenging mountain, served by a fast quad from the fairly primitive main base lodge. The runs fan out from the top in three directions – back to the base, or down to the slow Tiehack chair, or down to the fast quad at West Buttermilk.

Aspen Highlands consists essentially of a single ridge served by three fast quad chairs, with easy and intermediate slopes along the ridge itself and steep black runs on the flanks – very steep ones at the top. And beyond the lift network is Highland Bowl, where gates give access to a splendid open bowl of entirely double-black gradient. There are free snowcat rides from the top of the lifts to the first access gate of Highland Bowl, but if these are not operating, it's a 20-minute hike. All the other gates require further hiking. The Deep Temerity triple chair accesses advanced and expert terrain below Highland Bowl and Steeplechase. The views from the upper part of Highlands are the best that Aspen has to offer – the famous Maroon Bells that appear on countless postcards.

Signposting could be better where runs merge. A 2007 reporter found piste classification 'inconsistent' between mountains. Plum TV channel offers slope information.

TERRAIN-PARKS
Some of the world's best

Aspen has a different kind of terrain-park on each of its hills. Advanced riders should head to Buttermilk's Crazy T'rain Park, currently home of the Winter X Games. The park stretches over 3km/2 miles and is said to be the longest in the world. Hit the 170m/550ft long X-games pipe or the mini panda pipe. The slope-style course includes a log rail area, big kicker sections, hip jump and box. There is also an additional separate rail-park.

↑ Highland Bowl at the top of Aspen Highlands is a magnet for experts

ASPEN / DANIEL BAYER

LIFT PASSES

Four Mountain Pass

Prices in US$

Age	1-day	6-day
under 13	52	288
13 to 17	74	420
18 to 64	82	468
over 65	74	420

Free under 7

Senior over 70: $239 for unlimited period

Beginner included in price of lessons

Notes

Covers Aspen Mountain, Aspen Highlands, Buttermilk and Snowmass, and shuttle-bus between the areas. Savings if you purchase in advance online or through certain tour operators

THE MOUNTAINS

Aspen has lots for every ability; you just have to pick the right mountain. All of them have regular, free guided tours, given by excellent amateur ambassadors. The ratio of acres to visitor beds is high, and the slopes are usually blissfully uncrowded. Most of the slopes are in the trees. Lift passes are discounted heavily for purchase in advance or through tour operators – check your options well in advance.

↓ Aspen Mountain

Aspen offers special experiences for small numbers of skiers or riders.

Fresh Tracks *The first eight skiers to sign up each day get to ride the gondola up Aspen Mountain at 8am the next morning and get first tracks on perfect corduroy or fresh powder. Free! But take your time over the descent: if you get back to the base before the normal lift opening time, you'll have to wait, like everyone else.*

Powder Tours *Spend the day finding untracked snow in 1,500 acres of backcountry beyond Aspen Mountain, with a 10-passenger heated snowcat as your personal lift. You're likely to squeeze in about 10 runs in all. You break for lunch at an old mountain cabin. Full day, $295.*

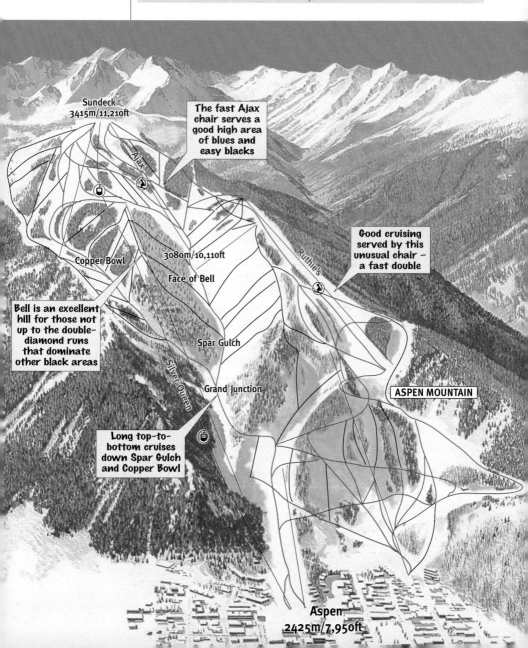

Sundeck
3415m/11,210ft

The fast Ajax chair serves a good high area of blues and easy blacks

Ajax

Good cruising served by this unusual chair – a fast double

Ruthie's

Copper Bowl

3080m/10,110ft

Face of Bell

Bell is an excellent hill for those not up to the double-diamond runs that dominate other black areas

Spar Gulch

Silver Queen

Grand Junction

ASPEN MOUNTAIN

Long top-to-bottom cruises down Spar Gulch and Copper Bowl

Aspen
2425m/7,950ft

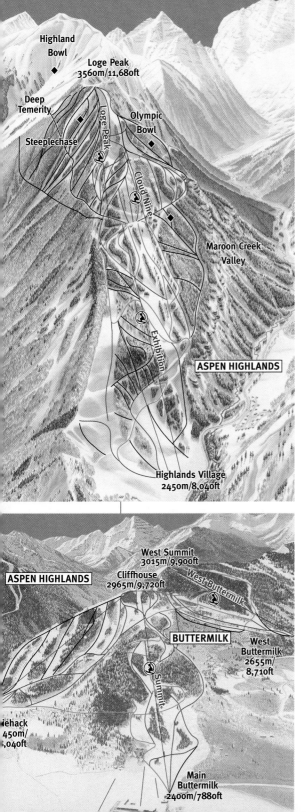

Highland
Bowl
Loge Peak
3560m/11,680ft
Deep
Temerity
Olympic
Bowl
Steeplechase
Loge Peak
Cloud Nine
Maroon Creek
Valley
Exhibition
ASPEN HIGHLANDS
Highlands Village
2450m/8,040ft

ASPEN HIGHLANDS
West Summit
3015m/9,900ft
Cliffhouse
2965m/9,720ft
West Buttermilk
BUTTERMILK
West
Buttermilk
2655m/
8,710ft
Summit
iehack
450m/
,040ft
Main
Buttermilk
2400m/7880ft

Aspen Mountain and Aspen Highlands have what they term 'natural' parks. Kickers, natural hits, a road gap and rails are dotted around the mountain, as opposed to being in designated areas, and are marked on the piste maps; so you can ride the mountain from top to bottom and do some freestyle along the way.

SNOW RELIABILITY
Rarely a problem
Aspen's mountains get an annual average of 300 inches of snow – not in the front rank, but not far behind. In addition, all areas have substantial snowmaking. Immaculate grooming adds to the quality of the pistes.

FOR EXPERTS
Buttermilk is the only soft stuff
There's plenty to choose from – all the mountains except Buttermilk offer lots of challenges.

Aspen Mountain has a formidable array of double-black-diamond runs. From the top of the gondola, Walsh's, Hyrup's and Kristi are on a lightly wooded slope and link up with Gentleman's Ridge and Jackpot to form the longest black run on the mountain. A series of steep glades drops down from Gentleman's Ridge. The central Bell ridge has less extreme single-diamonds on both its flanks, including some delightful lightly wooded areas. On the opposite side of Spar Gulch is another row of double-blacks, collectively called the Dumps, because mining waste was dumped here.

At Highlands there are challenging runs from top to bottom of the mountain. Consider joining a guided group as an introduction to the best of them. Highland Bowl, beyond the top lift, is superb in the right conditions: a big open bowl with pitches from a serious 38° to a terrifying 48° – facts you can check in the very informative Highlands Extreme Skiing Guide leaflet. Within the lift system, the Steeplechase area consists of a number of parallel natural avalanche chutes, and their elevation means the snow stays light and dry. The Deep Temerity lift has opened up more than 200 acres of double-black terrain. The Olympic Bowl area on the opposite flank of the mountain has great views of the Maroon Bells and some serious moguls. Thunderbowl chair from the base serves a nice varied area that's often underused.

KEY FACTS

Resort		2425m
		7,950ft
Aspen Mountain		
Slopes		2425-3415m
		7,950-11,210ft
Lifts		8
Pistes		673 acres
Green		0%
Blue		48%
Black		52%
Snowmaking		
		210 acres
Aspen Highlands		
Slopes		2450-3560m
		8,040-11,680ft
Lifts		5
Pistes		1,010 acres
Green		18%
Blue		30%
Black		52%
Snowmaking		
		110 acres
Buttermilk		
Slopes		2400-3015m
		7,870-9,900ft
Lifts		9
Pistes		435 acres
Green		35%
Blue		39%
Black		26%
Snowmaking		
		108 acres
Total with Snowmass		
Slopes		2400-3815m
		7,870-12,510ft
Lifts		45
Pistes		5,246 acres
Green		10%
Blue		45%
Black		45%
Snowmaking		
		613 acres

boarding

There is a huge amount of terrain to explore, which will satisfy all levels of boarder – especially when you include Snowmass (see separate chapter). For more mellow carving runs and gentle free-riding head to Buttermilk, the least testing of the mountains – but also home to the most serious terrain-park. Until April 2001 snowboarding was banned on Aspen Mountain, but now you can enjoy all of the excellent terrain here – and on Highlands, the locals' favourite. There are countless good runs, cliff drops and tree lines. The hills are free of drag-lifts, with few flat sections.

FOR INTERMEDIATES
Grooming to die for

Most intermediate runs on Highlands are concentrated above the mid-mountain Merry-Go-Round restaurant, many served by the Cloud Nine fast quad chair. But there are good slopes higher up and lower down – don't miss the vast, neglected expanses of Golden Horn, on the eastern limit of the area.

Aspen Mountain has its fair share of intermediate slopes, but they tend to be tougher than on the other mountains. Copper Bowl and Spar Gulch, running between the ridges, are great cruises early in the morning but can get crowded later. Upper Aspen Mountain, at the top of the gondola, has a dense network of well-groomed blues. The unusual Ruthie's chair – a fast double, apparently installed to rekindle the romance that quads have destroyed – serves more cruising runs.

The Main Buttermilk runs offer good, easy slopes to practise on, and can be extraordinarily quiet. And good intermediates should be able to handle the relatively easy black runs – when groomed, these are a real blast on carving skis. Buttermilk is also a great place for early experiments off-piste.

FOR BEGINNERS
Can be a great place to learn

Buttermilk is a great mountain for beginners. West Buttermilk has beautifully groomed, gentle, often deserted runs, served by a quad. The easiest slopes of all, though, are at the base of the Main Buttermilk sector – on Panda Hill. Despite its macho image, Highlands boasts the highest concentration of green runs in Aspen, served by the fast Exhibition chair.

FOR CROSS-COUNTRY
Backcountry bonanza

There are 60km/37 miles of groomed trails between Aspen and Snowmass in the Roaring Fork valley – the most extensive maintained cross-country system in the US. And the Ashcroft Ski Touring Center maintains around 35km/22 miles of trails around Ashcroft, a mining ghost town. The Pine Creek Cookhouse (925 1044) does excellent food and is accessible only by ski, snow-shoe or horse-drawn sleigh. Aspen is at one end of the famous Tenth Mountain Division Trail, heading 370km/230 miles north-east almost to Vail, with 12 huts for overnight stops.

QUEUES
Few problems

There are rarely major queues on any of the mountains. At Aspen Mountain, the gondola can have delays at peak times; although this lift has been upgraded, it seems the changes are directed at improving comfort and views, not capacity. There are alternatives to the top, but the Shadow Mountain chair is said to be 'old and slow', with an uphill walk to reach it. Aspen Highlands is almost always queue-free, even at peak times. The two lifts out of Main Buttermilk sometimes get congested.

MOUNTAIN RESTAURANTS
Good by American standards

There aren't many good spots, but they are worth seeking out.

Editors' choice At Highlands, Cloud Nine Alpine bistro (544 3063) is the nearest thing in the States to a cosy Alpine hut, with excellent food – thanks to an Austrian chef.

Worth knowing about On Aspen Mountain the Sundeck has 'one of the best self-service restaurants you'll find', with great views across to Highland Bowl. And there's a table-service area, Benedict's, offering 'wonderful food'. A 2006 reporter reckons the self-service Bonnie's is also worth a visit.

On Buttermilk the mountaintop Cliffhouse is known for its 'Mongolian Barbecue' stir-fry bar and great views.

CHILDREN

Nanny Cub Care
t 923 1227
Nanny service for ages 3 and under

Snow Cubs
t 923 0563
Ages 8wk to 3½yr

Big Burn Bears
t 923 0579
From age 3½ to 4

Grizzlies
t 923 0580
Ages 5 and 6

Powder Pandas
t 920 0935
Ages 3 to 6

All-day non-skiing nurseries
Several

Ski school
Takes ages 7 to 12, $380 for 5 days (5¾hr per day, lunch included)

There has been a lot of new development at the base of Aspen Highlands ↓

SCHOOLS AND GUIDES
Simply the best?

There's a wide variety of specialised instruction – mountain exploration groups, off-piste tours, adrenalin sessions, women's groups, and so on. Past reporters have praised the small group lessons ('the best class ever'; 'wonderful instruction'), and a 2006 visitor enjoyed 'good value' beginner classes. But another reader was unimpressed: 'Not enough mileage covered and I didn't get my video analysis as promised.' The Ski Doctor (Aspen Club and Spa) is an indoor simulator used in combination with some lessons. Lessons are said to be cheaper during Buttermilk's X-Games week (end of January).

FACILITIES FOR CHILDREN
Choice of nurseries

Past reports on the childcare arrangements have always been first class, and parents are said to regularly request the same instructor for their children. Young children are bussed to and from Buttermilk's very impressive Fort Frog. The Kids' Trail Map is a great idea. But Snowmass has clear advantages for young families.

STAYING THERE

HOW TO GO
Accommodation for all pockets

There's a mixture of hotels, inns, B&Bs, lodges and condos.

Chalets Several UK tour operators have chalets here – some very luxurious.

Hotels There are places for all budgets. Most smaller hotels provide a good après-ski cheese and wine buffet.

*****St Regis Aspen (920 3300) Opulent city-type hotel, near gondola. With a fancy spa facility.

*****Hyatt Grand Aspen (920 3204) Another grand place, opened last year near the gondola.

*****Little Nell (920 4600) Stylish, modern hotel right by the gondola, with popular bar. Fireplaces in every room, outdoor pool, hot-tub, sauna.

*****Jerome (920 1000) Step back a century: Victorian authenticity combined with modern-day luxury. Several blocks from the gondola.

****Lenado (925 6246) Smart modern B&B place with open-fire lounge, individually designed rooms.

***Hotel Aspen (925 3441) Best 'moderate' place in town, 10 minutes from lifts; comfortable, pool, hot-tubs.

UK PACKAGES

Alpine Answers, AmeriCan Ski, American Ski Classics, Chalet World Ski, Crystal, Crystal Finest, Directski.com, Erna Low, Independent Ski Links, Kuoni, Momentum, Oxford Ski Co, Ski Activity, Ski All America, Ski Dream, Ski Expectations, Ski Independence, Ski Line, Ski McNeill, Ski Safari, Ski Solutions, Skitracer, Skiworld, Supertravel, Trailfinders, United Vacations, Virgin Snow, White Mountains

SCHOOLS

Aspen
t 923 1227

Classes
Full day (5hr) $125, incl. tax

Private lessons
$390 for 3hr for up to 5 people

GETTING THERE

Air Aspen 5km/3 miles; Eagle 113km/ 70 miles (1½hr); Denver 355km/ 220 miles (4hr)

Rail Glenwood Springs (63km/39 miles)

ACTIVITIES

Indoor Club and Spa (sauna, swimming, weights, aerobics, steam, hot-tubs, ice skating); Recreation Center (pool, ice rink), galleries, cinemas, theatre

Outdoor Snow-shoeing, sleigh rides, snowmobiles, hot air ballooning

Phone numbers
From distant parts of the US, add the prefix 1 970; from abroad, add the prefix +1 970

TOURIST OFFICE

t 925 1220
intlres@skiaspen.com
www.aspensnowmass.com

↑ Aspen Mountain rises up at the edge of downtown Aspen

ASPEN / HAL WILLIAMS

***Boomerang Lodge (925 3416) Lloyd-Wright-inspired architecture, seven blocks from the centre, comfortable, pool, hot-tub.
***Mountain Lodge (925 7650) Small, friendly lodge in a quiet location.
**Mountain Chalet (925 7797) Cosy lodge five minutes from gondola. Pool, sauna and fitness room.
**Tyrolean Lodge (925 4595) On the main street; 'great, with great deals'; but no hot-tub.
Apartments The standards here are high, even in US terms. Many of the smarter developments have their own free shuttle-buses.

EATING OUT
Dining dilemma

As you'd expect, there are excellent upmarket places, but also plenty of cheaper options – and an easy way to economise in many smarter places is to choose from the bar menu.

Piñons serves innovative American food. Syzygy is a suave upstairs place with live jazz from 10pm. Pacifica Seafood Brasserie is top-notch. The basement Steak Pit is a long-established and reliable favourite ('good choice, great food and service'). The Elevation features 'original Andy Warhol artworks' and 'superb modern food'. The Hostaria and Campo de Fiori are good Italians. Cache Cache does good-value Provençal. Ute City Bar & Grill is good for local game, the Cantina serves Mexican and Jimmy's does 'excellent' steaks. Little Annie's is popular with reporters ('good meals, huge portions').

Cheaper recommendations include:

Bentley's (main courses $8 upwards), Boogie's (family-friendly diner with 'good food and service'), Paradise Bakery ('great ice cream and muffins'), Mezzaluna, Hickory House ('very good ribs') and New York Pizzas ('excellent'). Old favourite the Red Onion has now closed, but new offerings in 2007 are the Dish, the Tavern, Ruth's Chris Steakhouse and Bruno's (pizza).

APRES-SKI
Lots of options

As the lifts shut, a few bars at the bases get busy – notably Iguana's at Highlands, the Ajax Tavern in Aspen. The Bar at the Little Nell is a great place for gazing at face-lifts.

Many of the restaurants are also bars – Jimmy's (spectacular stock of tequila) and Mezzaluna, for example. The J-bar of the Jerome hotel still has a traditional feel. For pool there's Aspen Billiards adjoining the fashionable Cigar Bar, with its comfortable sofas. The Popcorn Wagon is the place for munchies after the bars close. You can get a week's membership of the famous members-only Caribou club.

OFF THE SLOPES
Silver service

Aspen has lots to offer, especially if your credit card is in good shape. There are literally dozens of art galleries, as well as the predictable clothes and jewellery shops. There are plenty of shops selling affordable stuff. Glenwood Springs is 'well worth a visit'. The best mountain restaurants are awkward for pedestrians to get to. The Aspen Recreation Center at Highlands has a huge swimming complex and an indoor ice rink. Hot-air ballooning is also recommended.

Beaver Creek

Exclusive and very pricey modern resort with quiet, varied slopes. Good for a pampered stay or a day trip from crowded Vail

COSTS

① ② ③ ④ ⑤ ⑥

RATINGS

The slopes

Fast lifts	★★★★★
Snow	★★★★★
Extent	★★
Expert	★★★★
Intermediate	★★★★
Beginner	★★★★★
Convenience	★★★★
Queues	★★★★★
Mountain restaurants	★★

The rest

Scenery	★★★
Resort charm	★★
Off-slope	★★★

NEWS

For 2007/08 a gondola is to replace a chair in the beginner area, and a new children's ski school is to open. A private dining club, Trappers Cabin, is expected to open as a table-service mountain restaurant.

A new gondola is to open from near the bus station in the town of Avon to Beaver Creek Landing, cutting the traffic up to Beaver Creek.

In 2006/07 the Stone Creek Chutes – with two double-black-diamond gladed runs – opened.

UK PACKAGES

Alpine Answers, AmeriCan Ski, American Ski Classics, Crystal Finest, Elegant Resorts, Kuoni, Ski Activity, Ski All America, Ski Dream, Ski Independence, Ski Line, Ski Safari, Ski Wild, Skitracer, Trailfinders, United Vacations, White Mountains

➕ Blissfully quiet slopes, in sharp contrast to nearby Vail

➕ Mountain has it all, from superb novice runs to daunting mogul-fields

➕ Fast chair-lifts all over the place

➕ Compact, traffic-free village centre with a smartly modern feel but ...

➖ Not much going on at night

➖ Lacks any Wild West or genuine US town atmosphere

➖ Very expensive

➖ Disappointing mountain restaurants – though a new one is expected to open up for 2007/08

Vail is upmarket and pricey. Its kid sister Beaver Creek is even more so. The two resorts share a lift pass and are efficiently linked by bus with a journey time of less than 30 minutes, so you can stay in either and ski both. If you can afford it and want a quiet pampered time choose Beaver Creek; if you prefer more choice of bars, restaurants, shops and nightlife, go for Vail.

THE RESORT

Beaver Creek, 16km/10 miles to the west of Vail, was developed in the 1980s. It is unashamedly exclusive, with a choice of top-quality hotels and condos right by the slopes. It centres on a small, smart, modern pedestrian area with escalators to the slopes, upmarket shops, an open-air ice rink and heated pavements. The choice of bars and restaurants is limited.

The lift system spreads across the mountains through Bachelor Gulch, with its Ritz-Carlton hotel, to Arrowhead, a slope-side hamlet with luxury condos, less pricey than Beaver Creek. At valley level by the town of Avon there are some free car parks for day visitors (parking in the resort is pricey and limited). There's a 'fantastic' free shuttle to the village, where you are met by hosts handing out free cookies and coffee. Or you can catch a fast chair into the slopes from Beaver Creek Landing near the car parks.

Resorts within day-trip range by car include Vail, Breckenridge and Keystone (owned by Vail Resorts and covered by multi-day lift passes), Arapahoe Basin and Copper Mountain.

THE MOUNTAINS

All the slopes are below the tree line, though there are some more open areas. Free mountain tours are held every day at 10am.

Slopes The slopes immediately above Beaver Creek divide into two sectors, each accessed by a fast quad chair – one centred on Spruce Saddle, the other Bachelor Gulch mountain (which links to Arrowhead). Between these are Grouse Mountain and Larkspur Bowl.

Terrain-parks Park 101 is a small beginners' park, Zoom Room has intermediate-level features and Moonshine has big jumps and rails, best suited to advanced riders. There's a 120m/390ft long super-pipe. Parkology is a park and pipe programme designed to offer tuition mainly to kids.

Snow reliability An impressive annual snow record (average 310 inches) plus extensive snowmaking means you can relax. Grouse Mountain can suffer from thin cover (some call it Gravel Mountain). Grooming is excellent ('never before seen eight bashers working on one slope during the day').

Experts There is quite a bit of intimidatingly steep double-diamond terrain. In the Birds of Prey and Grouse Mountain areas most runs are long, steep and mogulled from top to bottom (but watch the grooming map – when one of these is groomed it makes a great fast cruise, especially the Birds of Prey downhill race-course).

KEY FACTS

Resort	2470m
	8,100ft
Slopes	2255-3485m
	7,400-11,440ft
Lifts	16
Pistes	1805 acres
Green	19%
Blue	43%
Black	38%
Snowmaking	
	605 acres

LIFT PASSES

See Vail chapter

Central reservations
phone number
496 4500

Phone numbers
From distant parts of
the US, add the prefix
1 970; from abroad,
add the prefix +1 970

TOURIST OFFICE

t 845 9090
bcinfo@vailresorts.com
beavercreek.snow.
com

There are great steep glades on Grouse, and more opened last season in the new Stone Creek Chutes. The Talons Challenge, arranged through the ski school, is to ski 13 of the toughest runs.

Intermediates There are marvellous long, quiet, cruising blues almost everywhere you look, including top-to-bottom runs with a vertical of 1000m/ 3,280ft. The Larkspur and Strawberry Park chairs serve further cruising runs – and lead to yet more ideal terrain, served by the Bachelor Gulch and Arrowhead fast chairs.

Beginners There are excellent nursery slopes at resort level and at altitude. And there are plenty of easy longer runs to progress to.

Snowboarding Good riders will love the excellent gladed runs and perfect carving slopes. The resort is great for beginners, too, with special teaching methods and equipment that they claim will help you learn quicker.

Cross-country There's a splendid, mountain-top network of tracks at McCoy Park (over 32km/20 miles), reached via the Strawberry Park lift.

Queues We've always found the slopes deserted and virtually queue-free and so do most reporters. But two recent reporters say the Cinch chair can get busy mid-morning and the Centennial 'is prone to large queues'.

Mountain restaurants There's not much choice. Spruce Saddle at mid-mountain is the main place – a food court in a spectacular log and glass building, but a 2007 reporter found it 'incredibly busy'. Red Tail Camp is basic but does decent barbecues. If

Trappers Cabin opens to the public (see 'News') that will be a welcome table-service option.

Schools and guides We've had good reports. A 2007 visitor had a private lesson, which was 'expensive but excellent'. And a 'timid intermediate' was transformed by her group lesson into a 'daredevil'.

Facilities for children Small World Play School looks after non-skiing kids from two months to six years from 8.30 to 4.30. We've had good reports on the children's school. There are splendid adventure trails and play areas.

STAYING THERE

How to go There's a reasonable choice of packages.

Hotels Lots of upmarket places, such as the Ritz-Carlton, Inn at Beaver Creek, The Charter and Park Hyatt.

Apartments A wide choice of condos.

Eating out SaddleRidge is luxurious and packed with photos and Wild West artefacts. Toscanini, the Golden Eagle Inn, Dusty Boot, and Beaver Creek Chophouse have been recommended. You can take a sleigh ride to one of the beautiful log cabins on the slopes – Beano's, Allie's or Zach's. Or you can go to Avon by free shuttle – Masatos (Asian food) was recommended by a 2007 reporter.

Après-ski Try the Coyote Cafe, Whiskey Elk and McCoy's (live bands).

Off the slopes There are smart boutiques and galleries, an impressive ice rink, hot-air balloon rides, dog-sledding, and shows and concerts.

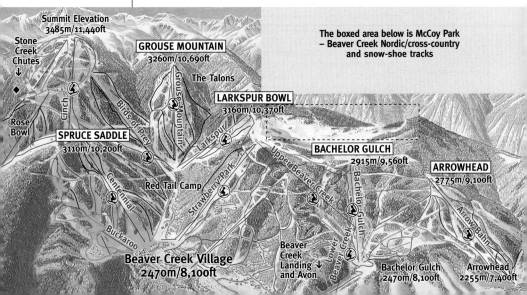

The boxed area below is McCoy Park – Beaver Creek Nordic/cross-country and snow-shoe tracks

Breckenridge

A sprawling resort with a cute 'Wild West' core, beneath a wide, varied mountain; increasing amounts of slope-side accommodation

COSTS

① ② ③ ④ ⑤ ⑥

RATINGS

The slopes

Fast lifts	****
Snow	*****
Extent	**
Expert	****
Intermediate	****
Beginner	****
Convenience	***
Queues	****
Mountain restaurants	**

The rest

Scenery	***
Resort charm	***
Off-slope	***

NEWS

For 2006/07 a new eight-seat BreckConnect gondola opened, going from the Transportation Center on the outskirts of town to the base of Peak 8 (with a mid-station at the base of Peak 7, which won't be operational until the 2008/09 season). This has greatly improved access to Peak 8 and taken the pressure off the main chairs up Peak 9. And the Snow White area opened – 150 acres of new double-black diamond terrain on Peak 8.

For 2007/08 a new fixed-grip quad is due to open in nearby Arapahoe Basin, expanding the skiable terrain by 80 per cent (adding 400 acres and 34 runs including blue and single- and double-black diamond). A new mid-mountain restaurant opened here in March 2007.

➕ Local mountains have something for all abilities – good for mixed groups

➕ Shared lift pass with nearby Keystone and Arapahoe Basin and not-so-nearby Vail and Beaver Creek

➕ Efficient lifts mean few queues

➕ Lively bars, restaurants and nightlife by US standards

➕ Some slope-side accommodation

➕ Restored Victorian mining town, with mainly sympathetic new buildings

➕ One of the nearest major resorts to Denver, so relatively short transfer

➖ Limited intermediate terrain, and few long runs

➖ Best advanced slopes can be closed by wind

➖ At 2925m/9,600ft the village is one of the highest you will encounter, with a risk of altitude sickness

➖ The 19th-century style gets a bit overblown in places, and there are some out-of-place modern buildings

➖ Lack of good-quality hotels

➖ Main Street is just that – always busy with traffic

Breckenridge is very popular with first-time visitors to Colorado, and it's not a bad introduction to the place. Some of its drawbacks are non-trivial, though. The top slopes are exceptionally high (accessed by America's highest lift), and high winds have limited our exploration more than once. Like many readers, one of us has been affected by altitude sickness, and now wouldn't think of staying in Breckenridge without first spending time in a lower resort. And intermediates more interested in mileage than challenges should plan to explore other resorts (covered by the lift pass) by car or bus.

THE RESORT

Breckenridge was founded in 1859 and became a booming gold-mining town. The old clapboard buildings have been well renovated and form the bottom part of Main Street. New shopping malls and buildings have been added in similar style – though they are obvious modern additions.

The town centre is lively in the evening, with over 100 restaurants and bars. Christmas lights and decorations remain throughout the season, giving the town a festive air. This is enhanced by a number of real winter festivals such as Ullr Fest – a carnival honouring the Norse God of Winter – and Snow Sculpture championships, which leave sculptures for weeks afterwards.

Hotels and condominiums are spread over a wide, wooded area and are linked by regular, free shuttle-buses (less frequent in the evening). If you stay in a condo and don't have a car, shopping at the local supermarket can be hard work – it is not in the centre of town. Although there is a lot of slope-side accommodation – more than any other Colorado resort, it is

claimed – there is also a fair amount that's inconveniently distant from Main Street and the lift base-stations. The planned new developments at the bases of Peaks 7 and 8 will increase the ski-in/ski-out options.

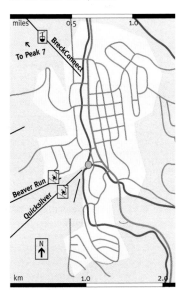

Main Street is built to blend in with Breckenridge's original 19th-century buildings ➔

VAIL RESORTS, INC / BOB WINSETT

KEY FACTS

KEY FACTS	
Resort	2925m
	9,600ft
Slopes	2925-3915m
	9,600-12,840ft
Lifts	29
Pistes	2,358 acres
Green	14%
Blue	31%
Black	55%
Snowmaking	
	565 acres

UK PACKAGES

Alpine Answers, AmeriCan Ski, American Ski Classics, Chalet World Ski, Crystal, Crystal Finest, Erna Low, Independent Ski Links, Inghams, Interactive Resorts, Ski Activity, Ski All America, Ski Dream, Ski Expectations, Ski Independence, Ski Line, Ski Safari, Ski Solutions, Ski Wild, Skitracer, Skiworld, Supertravel, Thomson, Trailfinders, United Vacations, Virgin Snow, White Mountains **Frisco** AmericanSki

THE MOUNTAINS

The slopes are mainly cut through the forest, with some open runs at the top. Breckenridge is in the same ownership as Vail, Beaver Creek and Keystone. A multi-day lift ticket covers all four resorts plus Arapahoe Basin. All of these resorts plus Copper Mountain are linked by regular buses (free except for the trips to Vail or Beaver Creek).

THE SLOPES
Small but fragmented

The grooming is excellent and the signposting very clear. There are free two-hour mountain tours at 10am daily from the base of Peaks 8 and 9. A 2007 reporter had the guide to herself one day.

There are four sectors, linked by lift and piste. Two fast chair-lifts go from the top end of town up to **Peak 9**, one accessing mainly green runs on the lower half of the hill, the other mainly blues higher up. From there you can get to **Peak 10**, which has blue and black runs served by one fast quad.

The **Peak 8** area – tough stuff at the top, easier lower down – can be reached by a fast quad from Peak 9. The base lifts of Peak 8 at the

Bergenhof can also be reached by the slow Snowflake lift from the suburbs or by the new gondola (see 'News'). Beyond here the lower slopes of **Peak 7** are served by a single six-pack.

The higher open slopes on Peaks 7 and 8 are accessed by a T-bar reachable from either base, and by the Imperial fast quad at the top of the Peak 8 lift network. The resort claims a top height of 3960m/13,000ft, but that involves a hike of 45m/148ft vertical from the Imperial chair.

TERRAIN-PARKS
Something for everyone

There are five terrain-parks and half-pipes. Freeway, one of the best in the US, is on Peak 8, with a series of great jumps, obstacles and an enormous championship half-pipe, which one reporter described as 'massive, steep, well kept and awesome'. Less intimidating is the Gold King park on Peak 9, with half-pipe, jumps and railslides designed for intermediates. Trygves, on Peak 8, has gentle jumps and an introductory pipe. And Country Boy is the latest addition – medium-sized, with jumps and rails. Eldorado is a mini-park and half-pipe on Peak 9.

boarding

Breckenridge is pretty much ideal for all standards of boarder and hosts several major US snowboarding events. Beginners have ideal nursery slopes and greens to progress to. Intermediates have great cruising runs, all served by chairs. The powder bowls at the top of Peaks 7 and 8 make great riding and can now be accessed via the Imperial quad, so you can avoid the awkward T-bar (though it is still an important lift – see 'For experts'). Boarders of all levels will enjoy the choice of five excellent terrain-parks and four half-pipes (see 'Terrain-parks'). Nearby Arapahoe Basin is another area for hardcore boarding in steep bowls and chutes (due for expansion in 2007/08 – see 'News'). Breckenridge pays homage to the early pioneers of the sport with a history of snowboarding display in the Vista Haus restaurant on Peak 8.

LIFT PASSES

**Breckenridge/
Keystone**

Prices in US$

Age	1-day	6-day
under 13	41	234
13 to 64	81	468
over 65	71	408

Free under 5

Beginner included in price of lessons

Notes

Covers Breckenridge, Keystone and Arapahoe Basin, plus 3 days (on a 6-day pass) at Vail and Beaver Creek; prices are high-season rates paid in the resort; reduced prices are available if you book in advance and to international visitors who pre-book through a UK tour operator (it is not necessary to buy a complete holiday package to obtain these prices)

SNOW RELIABILITY
Excellent

With its high altitude, Breckenridge boasts an excellent natural snow record – annual average 300 inches. That is supplemented by substantial snowmaking (used mainly early in the season to form a good base). There are a lot of east- and north-east-facing slopes, which hold snow well.

FOR EXPERTS
Lots of short but tough runs

A remarkable 55 per cent of the runs are classified black – either 'most difficult' (single-black-diamond) or 'expert' (double-black-diamond) terrain. That's a higher proportion than the famous 'macho' resorts, such as Jackson Hole, Taos and Snowbird. But most runs are quite short.

There is worthwhile terrain on all the peaks, but Peaks 7 and 8 are likely to grab your attention first. The Imperial quad rises only 285m/940ft. From this lift you can ski Imperial Bowl repeatedly, and access high terrain such as Lake Chutes that previously involved hiking. But you still have to use the T-bar if you want to do laps on the front face – such as Horseshoe and Contest bowls, where the snow is normally good.

The lightly wooded back bowls of Peak 8, beneath Chair 6 are picturesque and not too steep. Steep black mogul fields lead down to the junction with Peak 9 and Peak 9's North Slope under Chair E is very steep – we had great runs down there last

season on runs like Devil's Crotch, Hades and Inferno.

On Peak 10, at the edge of the area, is a network of interlinking steep mogul runs. To skier's left of the chair is a lovely, lightly wooded off-piste area called The Burn.

FOR INTERMEDIATES
Nice cruising, limited extent

Breckenridge has some good blue cruising runs for all intermediates. But dedicated piste-bashers are likely to find the runs short and limited in variety. Peak 9 has the easiest slopes. It is nearly all gentle, wide, blue runs at the top and almost flat, wide, green runs at the bottom. And the ski patrol is supposed to enforce slow-speed skiing in narrow and crowded areas, though a recent reader did not see much evidence of this.

Peak 10 has a number of more challenging runs classified blue-black, such as Crystal and Centennial, which make for good fast cruising. Peaks 7 and 8 both have a choice of blues on trails cut close together in the trees. Adventurous intermediates will also like to try some of the high bowl runs and more gentle gladed runs such as Ore Bucket glades on the fringe of Peak 7 and the runs beneath Chair 6 on Peak 8.

FOR BEGINNERS
Excellent

The bottom of Peak 9 has a big, virtually flat area and some good, gentle nursery slopes. There's then a

Breckenridge

603

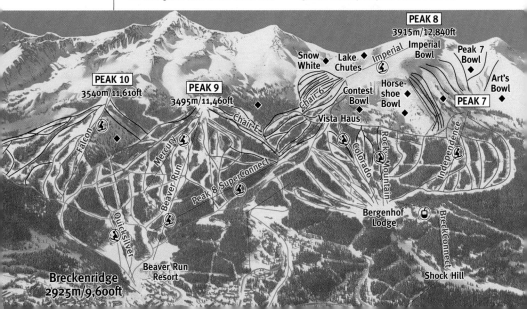

good choice of green runs to move on to. Beginners can try Peak 8 too, with another selection of green runs and a choice of trails back to town. Reporters praise the good-value beginner package which includes lessons, equipment rental and lift pass.

FOR CROSS-COUNTRY
Specialist centre in woods
There are 50km/31 miles of groomed trails in total. Breckenridge's Nordic Center is prettily set in the woods between the town and Peak 8 (served by the shuttle-bus). It has 30km/19 miles of trails and 20km/12 miles of snow-shoeing trails. A further 20km/12 miles of cross-country trails are located at the golf course.

QUEUES
Not normally a problem
Breckenridge's new gondola and nine fast chair-lifts make light work of peak-time crowds. Neither we nor our reporters have come across serious queues, apart from at exceptional times, such as President's Day weekend.

MOUNTAIN RESTAURANTS
Slow progress
Breckenridge has made some effort to improve on the standard US cafeterias: both Tenmile Station, where Peak 9 meets 10, and the Vista Haus on Peak 8 are food-court operations. But they get very busy ('a nightmare queuing and finding a table') and the food is 'uninspiring'. Border Burritos at Vista Haus serves 'huge portions'.

SCHOOLS AND GUIDES
Excellent reports
Our reporters are unanimous in their praise for the school: classes of four to eight (sometimes smaller), doing what the class, not the instructor, wants ('Superb, fantastic value for money. You can buy three days of lessons and take them whenever you want', 'friendly, first-class instruction', say recent reporters). Special clinics include women's, telemark and powder. The school's Big Mountain Experience offers guided instruction around Imperial Bowl. There is also a Burton Learn to Ride programme.

FACILITIES FOR CHILDREN
Excellent facilities
Every report on the children's school and nursery is full of plaudits. Typical comments: 'excellent, combining serious coaching with lots of fun', 'our boys loved it', 'so much more positive than ski schools in Europe'.

STAYING THERE

HOW TO GO
Lots of choice
A lot of tour operators feature Breckenridge.
Chalets Several tour operators have very comfortable chalets.
Hotels There's a decent choice except for really high-quality places.
******Great Divide Lodge** (453 5500) Owned by Vail Resorts. Prime location, vast rooms. Pool, tub, sauna.
******Lodge at Breckenridge** (453 9300) Stylish luxury spa resort set out of town among 32 acres, with great views. Private shuttle-bus. Pool, tub, steam, sauna and massage.
*****Little Mountain Lodge** (453 1969) Luxury B&B near ice rink.
******Beaver Run** (453 6000) Huge, resort complex with 520 spacious rooms. Great location, by one of the main lifts up Peak 9. Pool, hot-tubs.
******Barn on the River** (800 795 2975)

They put a lot of work into building and maintaining Breck's five terrain-parks and half-pipes; and they make a lot of snow for the pistes as well as the parks, especially early in the season to form a good base ➔

B&B on Main St. Said to do one of the best breakfasts in town. Hot-tub.
***Village** (547 5725) Central 'Good value with spacious rooms.'
Apartments There is a huge choice of condominiums, many set conveniently off the aptly named Four O'Clock run. Main Street Station (near the Quicksilver lift) and Mountain Thunder Lodge (near the new gondola and the supermarket) have been recommended at the luxury end. There are lots of houses to rent, too.

EATING OUT
Over 100 restaurants
There's a very wide range of eating places, from typical American food to fine dining. At peak times they get busy and mostly don't take bookings. The Breckenridge Dining Guide lists the full menu of most places.

We had good meals last season at the Hearthstone (upmarket food in a beautiful 100-year-old house), the Brewery (famous for its enormous portions of appetisers such as buffalo wings and splendid brewed-on-the-spot beers), Mi Casa (Mexican; great margaritas) and Mai Thai (er, Thai; basic decor and plastic cutlery but great food; cheap).

Other reader recommendations include: the sophisticated food at both Café Alpine and Relish, the Kenosha steakhouse ('specials at great prices'), Whales Tail ('great seafood and fish'), Ridge Street Seafood, Wasabi (sushi), the Blue River Bistro ('a wide selection of food at affordable prices'), Downstairs at Erics (classic American), Michael's (Italian; 'extensive menu, large portions', 'cheap'), Rasta Pasta (pasta with a Jamaican twist) and Fiesta Jalisco (Mexican).

APRES-SKI
The best in the area
There's not much tea-time animation at the lift bases but the Park Avenue Pub, just off Main Street, and the Brewery were lively as the lifts shut when we were there last season. Later on we enjoyed the Gold Pan saloon (reputedly the oldest bar west of the Mississippi). Reader recommendations for later on include Tiffany's, Liquid Lounge, Fatty's and Sherpa & Yetti's. Cecilia's serves good cocktails; Gracey O'Malley's is an Irish bar; Downstairs at Eric's is a disco sports-bar.

OFF THE SLOPES
Pleasant enough
Breckenridge is a pleasant place to wander around, with plenty of souvenir and gift shops. Silverthorne (about 30 minutes away) has excellent bargain factory outlet stores: 'Well worth a visit,' writes a reporter. A visit to Buffalo Bill's grave and museum is recommended by a recent visitor.

STAYING DOWN THE VALLEY
Good for exploring the area
Staying in Frisco makes sense for those touring around or on a tight budget. It's a small town with decent bars and restaurants. There are cheap motels, a couple of small hotels and some B&Bs. Hotel Frisco (668 5009) is 'comfortable, convenient and they remember regular guests', says a 2007 visitor whose recommendations include the Backcountry Brewery ('good micro brewed beer'), Tuscato ('good northern Italian food'), Blue Spruce Inn ('best food in town, in an old low-ceilinged cabin'), Farrellys steakhouse ('generous portions'), and Sampling ('the new hot spot – tapas-like dishes, good wines').

Copper Mountain

Great terrain with reliable snow for all ability levels, above a born-again but small and quiet Intrawest resort

COSTS

① ② ③ ④ ⑤ ⑥

RATINGS

The slopes

Fast lifts	**
Snow	*****
Extent	**
Expert	****
Intermediate	****
Beginner	****
Convenience	****
Queues	****
Mountain restaurants	*

The rest

Scenery	***
Resort charm	**
Off-slope	*

KEY FACTS

Resort	2955m
	9,700ft
Slopes	2955-3750m
	9,700-12,300ft
Lifts	22
Pistes	2,450 acres
Green	21%
Blue	25%
Black	54%
Snowmaking	
	380 acres

606

NEWS

For 2007/08 a new gladed area – with single- and double-black diamond trails – is planned above the East Village.

Three new restaurants opened for 2006/07 in The Village – Incline Bar & Grill, Copper Red Hots and CB Grille.

And the resort has built piste maps into the safety bars of some of the main lifts – a great idea because you can plan your route without getting your piste map out.

+ Convenient purpose-built resort, transformed by owners Intrawest (of Whistler fame)

+ Fair-sized mountain, with good runs for all abilities

+ Few queues on weekdays, but ...

− Can be long lift queues at weekends (avoided by Beeline Advantage pass)

− Village still limited and lacks life

− Black-diamond bowls at the top offer only limited vertical

− Risk of altitude sickness

− Mediocre mountain restaurants

Copper's slopes are some of Colorado's best, and there's a small, modern, quiet, purpose-built village at the base. But expect weekend crowds, and watch out for that altitude sickness; Copper's village is even higher than Breckenridge.

THE RESORT

Rather like the French resorts of the 1960s, Copper Mountain was originally high on convenience, low on charm. New owner, Intrawest, has done a typically thorough job with the new Village at Copper, a group of wood-and-stone-clad condo buildings with shops, restaurants and car-free walkways and squares, forming the heart of the resort, set just off the I-70 freeway from Denver. But the place still lacks much animation or charm.

There are two other bases: East Village at the foot of Copper's steeper terrain and Union Creek at the foot of the easiest runs and beginner area. Each of these is smaller and even quieter than the Village but has accommodation and restaurants. A free shuttle-bus runs between them. Keystone, Breckenridge and Arapahoe Basin are all nearby, and Vail and Winter Park a bit further.

THE MOUNTAIN

The area is medium-sized by American standards, and has great runs for all ability levels, with an attractive mix of wooded, gladed and open slopes. Guided tours are available daily at 10.30 and 1.30.

Tucker Mountain

UNION PEAK
3750m/12,300ft

COPPER PEAK
3750m/12,300ft

Copper Bowl

Union Meadows

Spaulding Bowl
3655m/11,990ft

Upper Enchanted Forest

Union Bowl

3560m/11,680ft

Excelerator

Solitude Station
3485m/11,440ft

Timberline

3300m/10,830ft

Super Bee

American Flyer

American Eagle

The Village at Copper
2955m/9,700ft

East Village

Union Creek

Cross-country and Snow-shoe Center

↑ Copper's high bowls offer some great ungroomed terrain; it's a shame it wasn't open on either of our early-season December visits

SNOWPIX.COM / CHRIS GILL

Central reservations
Call 968 2882; toll-free number (from within the US)
1 888 263 5302

Phone numbers
From distant parts of the US, add the prefix 1 970; from abroad, add the prefix +1 970

TOURIST OFFICE

t 968 2882
copper-marketing@
coppercolorado.com
www.coppercolorado.
com

Slopes The area divides into slopes below Copper Peak and below Union Peak, with fast quads towards each from the main base area. Between the two is Union Bowl. In general, as you look at the mountain the easiest runs are on the right and it gets progressively steeper the further left you go. On the back of the hill are the high Spaulding and Copper Bowls – open slopes, in contrast to the wooded lower runs.

Terrain-parks The main Catalyst park is beside the American Flyer chair and has areas for beginners, intermediates and experts, plus a super-pipe (there's a second super-pipe at the base area). At the top of the Flyer chair there's the Kidz park with a mini-pipe (open to learning adults too), and there are terrain-park zones on the High Point trail under the chair. Early season, before Catalyst opens, there's a jib park at the top of the American Eagle.

Snow reliability Height and extensive snowmaking give Copper an early opening date and excellent reliability. Snowfall averages 280 inches a year.

Experts There is a lot of good expert terrain. Spaulding and Copper bowls offer gradients ranging from moderate to seriously steep, but with limited vertical. The wooded bump runs lower down the left side of the main mountain are much longer.

Intermediates There are runs to suit everyone, from top-to-bottom greens on the right of the map through similarly long blues to challenging (usually bumpy) black runs.

Beginners The nursery slopes at Union Creek are excellent, and there are plenty of very easy green runs to graduate to.

Snowboarding There are great slopes for all abilities, plus several terrain-parks.

Cross-country There are 25km/15 miles of trails through the White River forest.

Queues On weekdays you may find no queues, but weekend visitors pour in from Denver and cause 20-minute queues. You can buy a Beeline Advantage pass to jump the queues.

Mountain restaurants Not a lot on offer. There's a food court at Solitude Station, which offers 'tasty chilli'. The T-Rex Grill has only outside seating. Or head back to base.

Schools and guides The school offers a wide variety of courses and has a fine reputation, especially for children.

Facilities for children The Belly Button childcare facility takes children from two months old and ski school takes children from age three. On the mountain, there are dedicated adventure trails and a special kids' map.

STAYING THERE

How to go A number of tour operators offer packages to Copper.

Hotels and condos There are no hotels but some condos are splendidly luxurious, with outdoor hot-tubs, etc.

Eating out The CB Grille serves the best food in town ('Colorado with Mediterranean flair'). Pizza Carlo. Endo's and JJ's Rocky Mountain Tavern ('excellent bison stew') are popular. The Imperial Palace, and Salsa Mountain Cantina have also been recommended by reporters. The Incline Bar & Grill does southwestern dishes. Sleigh rides take people out to Western-style dinners in tents.

Après-ski Après-ski is lively as the lifts close. Later on, it's much quieter. Endo's Adrenaline Cafe and JJ's Rocky Mountain Tavern (with live music) are popular. Pravda is a Russian-style vodka bar and McGillycuddy's is an Irish bar with live music. The Storm King Lounge offers cocktails, pool and sushi.

Off the slopes There's a good sports club with a huge pool, snow tubing, snowmobiling ('an absolute blast taking you up to the Continental Divide'), ice skating on the lake and regular En Fuego events (fire jugglers, street entertainment, a torchlit descent by instructors, and fireworks).

Keystone

A spread-out, quiet, modern resort with plenty of comfortable lodgings, beneath a satisfying mountain with expanding cat-skiing

COSTS

① ② ③ ④ ⑤ ⑥

RATINGS

The slopes

Fast lifts	****
Snow	*****
Extent	**
Expert	***
Intermediate	****
Beginner	****
Convenience	**
Queues	****
Mountain restaurants	***

The rest

Scenery	***
Resort charm	**
Off-slope	**

NEWS

For 2006/07 Independence Bowl was opened – 278 acres of ungroomed terrain which you hike in and out of or ride a snowcat to. The terrain-park had 30 new rails, new wall-rides and a quarter pipe.

For 2007/08 nearby Arapahoe Basin is due to get a new lift and have its terrain increased by 80 per cent – see 'News' in the Breckenridge chapter. And the Keystone Lodge spa will be renovated and expanded and the tubing hill improved and expanded.

+ Good mountain with something for everyone

+ Huge night-skiing operation

+ Other nearby resorts on lift pass

+ Luxurious condominiums

– Very scattered resort, with a lot of bussing or driving for most visitors, and no village atmosphere except in small River Run development

– Risk of altitude sickness for visitors coming straight from sea level

Keystone's slopes are impressive from many points of view, but there isn't a proper village at the foot of them. Condos are scattered over a wide area, and the nearest thing to a 'village' is the limited River Run development. We prefer to stay elsewhere and make day trips to Keystone's slopes.

THE RESORT

Keystone is a sprawling resort of condominiums spread around a partly wooded valley floor. It has no clear centre and is divided into seven 'neighborhoods'. Some are little more than groups of condos, while others have shops, restaurants and bars (though no supermarkets or liquor stores – they are on the main highway).

River Run, at the base of the main gondola, is the nearest thing to a conventional ski resort village, with condo buildings, a short main street, a square and a few restaurants, bars and shops. A second lift base area half a mile to the west, Mountain House, is much less of a village. Another mile west is Lakeside Village, which is not a village at all but a hotel and condo complex, weirdly lacking animation, beside a lake – a huge natural ice rink.

Buses ('free, efficient and friendly') link all the component parts. A regular visitor warns against late-season visits: 'From 1 April the resort pretty much closes down except for the main lifts.'

THE MOUNTAINS

By US standards Keystone offers extensive intermediate slopes and some challenging steeper stuff, recently expanded with the opening of Erickson, Bergman and Independence Bowls. The resort is owned by Vail Resorts, and the lift pass covers Vail, Beaver Creek, Breckenridge and Arapahoe Basin (a few minutes away by road and expanding for 2006/07 – see 'News'). Copper Mountain is also nearby.

Slopes Three wooded mountains form Keystone's local slopes. Lifts depart from Mountain House and River Run to the one above the resort, Dercum Mountain. Its front face has Keystone's biggest network of lifts and runs. From the top you can drop over the back down to lifts up the next hill, North Peak. Or you can ride the Outpost gondola directly to the shoulder of North Peak. Beyond North Peak is the third peak, The Outback. Keystone has the biggest floodlit skiing operation in the US, covering Dercum Mountain top to bottom up to 9pm on certain nights of the week. Finding your way around is no problem say reporters: 'big coloured banners make it easy'; 'everything is clearly marked'.

Terrain-parks The A-51 terrain-park is huge with features for all levels including a super-pipe; it has its own chair-lift and is floodlit several nights a week.

Snow reliability Snow shortage is rarely a problem, and there's one of the world's biggest snowmaking systems.

Experts Keystone has a lot of steeper, ungroomed terrain. The Windows is a 60-acre area of experts-only glade runs on Dercum Mountain's back side. From The Outback there are black runs with all sorts of challenges, route-finding being one of them; we loved the Black Forest area on our visit last season. You can hike to open and gladed runs in the North and South Bowls, Erickson Bowl, Bergman Bowl and the new Independence Bowl, or pay for snowcat access and guidance ($81 for four hours with guides from Dercum; $5 for a ride but no guide on Outback). You should have a day at Arapahoe Basin (see 'News') too.

Intermediates Keystone has lots to offer. The front face of Dercum Mountain itself is a network of

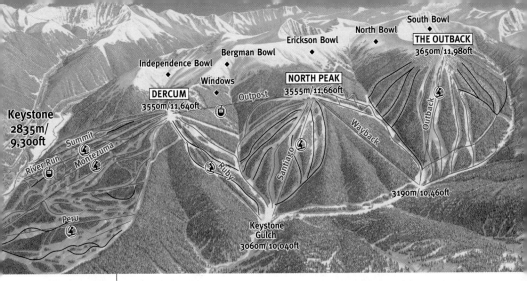

Keystone
2835m/
9,300ft

Independence Bowl
Windows
DERCUM
3550m/11,640ft

Bergman Bowl
Erickson Bowl
North Bowl
South Bowl

THE OUTBACK
3650m/11,980ft

NORTH PEAK
3555m/11,660ft

Outpost

Wayback

Outback

River Run
Summit
Montezuma
Peru
Ruby
Santiago

3190m/10,460ft

Keystone
Gulch
3060m/10,040ft

KEY FACTS

Resort	2835m 9,300ft
Slopes	2835-3650m 9,300-11,980ft
Lifts	19
Pistes	3,148 acres
Green	19%
Blue	32%
Black	49%
Snowmaking	650 acres

UK PACKAGES

Alpine Answers, AmeriCan Ski, American Ski Classics, Crystal, Erna Low, Ski All America, Ski Dream, Ski Independence, Ski Safari, Skitracer, Solo's, Thomson, United Vacations

Central reservations phone number
Call 496 4500; toll free number (from within the US) 1 877 753 9786
Phone numbers
From distant parts of the US, add the prefix 1 970; from abroad, add the prefix +1 970

TOURIST OFFICE

t 496 2316
keystoneinfo@
vailresorts.com
www.keystone.snow.
com

beautifully groomed blue and green runs through the trees. The Outback and North Peak also have easy cruising and some steeper blues. Some of the blacks are groomed, and are tremendous fun early in the day. Arapahoe Basin (see 'News') has some good cruising too.

Beginners There are good nursery slopes at the top and bottom of Dercum Mountain, and excellent long green runs to progress to.

Snowboarding Keystone is ideal for beginners and intermediates, with mainly chair-lifts and gondolas, good beginner areas and cruising runs. Expert riders will love The Outback.

Cross-country There are 16km/10 miles of groomed trails and 57km/35 miles of unprepared trails.

Queues Reporters are unanimous in their praise of quiet slopes and few queues after the morning peak.

Mountain restaurants The table-service Alpenglow Stube (North Peak) is a delightfully cosseting place (you are given slippers to replace ski boots) and one of our favourites in the US: the fixed-price lunch is a bargain at $30. The Timber Ridge Food Court next door is the best alternative. The other options are much less appealing.

Schools and guides As well as the normal lessons, there are bumps, race and various other advanced classes. One reporter enjoyed 'excellent' instruction in very small groups.

Facilities for children Excellent, with programmes tailored to specific age groups, dedicated children's teaching areas and organised kids' nights out.

Keystone

609

STAYING THERE

How to go Regular shuttles operate from Denver airport.

Hotels There isn't a great choice but they're all of a high standard.

Apartments This is condocity, with thousands to choose from including some large and luxurious ones.

Eating out Disappointing: there isn't the range of mid-market restaurants that you get in most US resorts. You can eat up the mountain at the Summit House or Alpenglow Stube.

Après-ski The Summit House has live music and caters for night skiing customers too. But this is not the resort for late-night revellers.

Off the slopes There are plenty of activities, including skating on the frozen lake, tubing and indoor tennis.

Staying down the valley You can cut costs by staying in Dillon, 10km/6 miles away, and visiting different resorts by car. A 2007 visitor says the Comfort Inn is 'a good standard but bland; restaurants and shops are good but there's no resort atmosphere'.

Snowmass

Aspen's modern satellite – with impressively varied and extensive slopes, and a cool new Base Village under construction

COSTS

① ② ③ ④ ⑤ ⑥

RATINGS

The slopes

Fast lifts	***
Snow	*****
Extent	****
Expert	*****
Intermediate	*****
Beginner	*****
Convenience	****
Queues	****
Mountain restaurants	***

The rest

Scenery	****
Resort charm	**
Off-slope	***

610

➕ Big, varied mountain with a vertical of 1340m/4,400ft – biggest in the US

➕ Aspen's three mountains also accessible by frequent free bus

➕ Uncrowded slopes

➕ Lots of slope-side lodgings

➖ Snowmass 'village' offers very limited shopping and nightlife, though things will improve as the new Base Village takes shape

➖ Diversions of Aspen town are a bus-ride away

The slopes of Snowmass are a key part of the attraction of nearby Aspen as a destination. As a base, Snowmass has mainly appealed to families wanting great green runs on their doorstep; but its appeal will broaden over the next few years as the range of restaurants and shops improves.

THE RESORT

Snowmass is a modern, purpose-built resort with most of the accommodation in low-rise buildings set alongside the gentle home slope. At the heart of these buildings is Snowmass Village Mall, with a small cluster of shops and restaurants. There are also lots of private homes set along roads that wind up into the lower slopes.

The Mall contains the essentials of resort life, but not much more. The new Base Village taking shape is a very welcome development. Aspen is some 19km/12 miles away, its Highlands and Buttermilk mountains slightly less. Efficient free bus services link the resorts and mountains. The service to Aspen town runs to 2am (small charge after 4.30pm).

THE MOUNTAIN

Snowmass is big: it has 60% of the area covered by the Aspen pass. It is almost 8km/5 miles across and has the biggest vertical in the US. Most of the slopes are in the forest; higher ones are open or only lightly wooded.

Slopes Chair-lifts and a gondola from the base go to the two extremes of the area, Elk Camp and Sam's Knob, with links higher up to the two sectors in the middle, High Alpine and Big Burn. There is also fast access from Two Creeks – much nearer to Aspen town, and with free slope-side parking.

Terrain-parks The main Pipeline park is 2.5km/1.5 miles long and incorporates a rail park, super-pipe, quarter-pipe and kicker line – all well shaped. There are separate beginner and kids' parks.

ELK CAMP 3450m/11,320ft

HIGH ALPINE 3590m Hanging Valley

The Cirque 3815m/12,510ft

BIG BURN 3610m/11,830ft

SAM'S KNOB 3240m/10,630ft

Cafe Suzanne

Ullrhof 3005m

Elk Camp

Alpine Springs

Big Burn

Sam's Knob

Gondola

Coney Glade

Village

Two Creeks

Two Creeks 2470m/8,100ft

Snowmass 2565m/8,420ft

↑ It's a big mountain with lots of slope-side lodgings

NEWS

The new Base Village continues to grow. For 2007/08 a kids' adventure centre, Treehouse Kids, is due to open. A new beginner area served by three lifts will open at the top of Elk Camp – now reached by an eight-person gondola from Base Village.

KEY FACTS

Resort	2565m
	8,420ft

Snowmass only	
Slopes	2470-3815m
	8,100-12,510ft
Lifts	23
Pistes	3,128 acres
Green	6%
Blue	50%
Black	44%
Snowmaking	
	185 acres

See Aspen chapter for statistics on other mountains – star rating for extent includes them all

Phone numbers
From distant parts of the US, add the prefix 1 970; from abroad, add the prefix +1 970

TOURIST OFFICE

t 925 1220
intlres@skiaspen.com
www.aspensnowmass.com

Snow reliability With 300 inches a year plus snowmaking, it's good.

Experts There's great terrain. Consider joining a guided group as an introduction. Our favourite area is around the Hanging Valley Wall and Glades – beautiful scenery and steep wooded slopes. The other seriously steep area is the Cirque. The Cirque drag-lift takes you well above the tree line to Aspen's highest point. From here, the Headwall is not terrifyingly steep, but there are also narrow, often rocky, chutes – Gowdy's is one of the steepest. All these runs funnel into a pretty, lightly wooded valley.

Intermediates Excellent – the best mountain in the Aspen area. All four sectors have lots to offer. Highlights include: the top slopes on Big Burn – a huge, varied, lightly wooded area, including the Powerline Glades for the adventurous; long, top-to-bottom cruises from Elk Camp and High Alpine; regularly groomed single-black runs from Sam's Knob. Long Shot is a glorious, ungroomed, 5km/3 mile run, lost in the forest, and well worth the short hike from the top of Elk Camp.

Beginners In the heart of the resort is a broad, gentle beginners' run. An even easier slope is the wide Assay Hill, at the bottom of Elk Camp. A beginner area is planned for the top of the gondola at Elk Camp for 2007/08. From Sam's Knob there are long, gentle cruises back to the resort.

Snowboarding A great mountain, whatever your boarding style.

Cross-country Excellent trails between here and Aspen – see Aspen chapter.

Queues Snowmass has so many alternative lifts and runs that you can normally avoid problems. Some long, slow chairs can be cold in midwinter. The home slope gets very crowded.

Mountain restaurants There are refuelling stops at several key points, but also some places worth seeking

out. Gwyn's High Alpine is an elegant table-service restaurant serving above-average food. The best views are from Sam's Knob, with self-service and table-service restaurants. Cafe Suzanne on Elk Camp has a French flavour and does 'exceptionally good crêpes'.

Schools and guides A recent reporter had three rewarding days, but warns that his 'off-piste' group turned out to be just a standard class, going off-piste only if everyone wanted to.

Facilities for children We lack recent reports. The Treehouse Kids' centre is due to open at Base Village this year. There are special family skiing zones.

STAYING THERE

How to go Most accommodation is self-catering.

Hotels The focal hotel is the Silvertree (923 3520) – an ocean liner parked next to the home slope and the Mall – with excellent top-floor Brothers' Grille restaurant and pools. Stonebridge Inn (923 2420) is a good-value alternative; nice restaurant, pool, hot-tub.

Apartments Tamarack Townhouses, Terrace House and Top of the Village have been recommended by reporters.

Eating out The choice is adequate. As well as the excellent Brothers' Grille and a nearby steakhouse there are Italian, Tex-Mex, Provençal and 'pan-Asian' restaurants. Butch's Lobster Bar 'is by far the best in town'.

Après-ski The Cirque next to the home slope has live bands but closes at 6pm. The restaurants have bars – the Margarita keeps 30 tequilas. The Blue Door sometimes has live music.

Off the slopes There's tubing on Assay Hill, snow-shoe trails, piste-basher rides, zip-wire rides and dog-sledding.

UK PACKAGES

Alpine Answers, AmeriCan Ski, Crystal, Ski All America, Ski Dream, Ski Independence, Ski Safari, United Vacations, White Mountains

Snowmass

611

Steamboat

The home of Champagne Powder™, with a convenient slope-side base and a working cattle-town a 10-minute bus-ride away

COSTS

①②③④⑤⑥

RATINGS

The slopes
Fast lifts	★★★
Snow	★★★★
Extent	★★★
Expert	★★★
Intermediate	★★★★
Beginner	★★★★★
Convenience	★★★
Queues	★★★★
Mountain restaurants	★★★

The rest
Scenery	★★★
Resort charm	★★
Off-slope	★★

NEWS

For 2007/08, the Christie Express six-pack will replace three chairs in the Headwall beginner area at the base. Work will also be done on the slopes of this area to make it even better for beginners and five moving carpets will be lengthened.

The complete replacement of the on-mountain signage will begin, more snowmaking is planned and so is a new walkway around the base of the hill to connect all base sectors.

For 2006/07 a fast quad replaced the Sunshine triple chair and two new green runs were built to make it easier for beginners at the top. Thunderhead and Rendezvous Saddle Lodges were renovated. The Yampa Valley regional airport has been expanded to take more flights.

612

+ Excellent easy runs

+ Famed for its gladed terrain

+ Good snow record

+ Table-service mountain restaurants

+ Plenty of high-quality slope-side lodgings at reasonable rates

+ Town has some Western character

− Town is a drive from the slopes

− Modern base 'village' is sprawling, with some eyesore buildings

− Not enough runs to amuse keen intermediates for a week

− Not a huge amount of challenging terrain − some of it is a hike away

Steamboat's mountain may not match some of its competitors for extent, but it's one of the best for powder fun among the trees. The lift-base village is no beauty; but it's best to stay there, and plan on just the occasional foray to the unremarkable 'cattle town' of Steamboat Springs. The resort was recently taken over by Intrawest (of Whistler fame) and is likely to change rapidly for the better over the next few years.

THE RESORT

The resort village is a 10-minute bus-ride from the old town of Steamboat Springs. Near the gondola there are a few shop- and restaurant-lined multi-level squares, some of which are receiving a much-needed facelift over the next few years. Some lodgings are up the sides of the piste, but the resort also sprawls across the valley.

The old town can be a bit of a disappointment. It may be a working cattle town, but the Wild West isn't much in evidence. The wide main street is lined with bars, hotels and shops in a mixture of styles, from old wooden buildings to concrete plazas. The free bus service is said by reporters to be good.

The newly expanded local airport will allow more flights and improve accessibility to the resort.

THE MOUNTAINS

Steamboat's slopes are prettily set among trees, with extensive views over rolling hills and the wide Yampa valley. The place is relatively isolated, but you could combine it with resorts west of Denver, from Winter Park to Vail.

Slopes The gondola from the base rises to the low peak of Thunderhead. Beyond it are lifts to Storm Peak and Sunshine Peak − the latter offering a broad area of blue runs now served by a fast quad. On the back of the hill is the Morningside Park area, with a slow chair back up to the high-point of Mt Werner, also accessing some of the top runs on the front side. Below these is an area served by the Pony Express fast chair. We've had complaints about signposting in the past, so we welcome the start of the installation of a new signage system. There are free daily mountain tours at 10.30am or you can ski with 1964 Olympic medallist Billy Kidd (now Steamboat's Director of Skiing) at 1pm when he's in town.

Terrain-parks There are four. The 12 acre SoBe park includes rails, jumps, a quarter-pipe and the Mavericks super-pipe. Beehive is a special park for kids. Rabbit Ears is for beginners and Sunbeam for intermediates.

Snow reliability The term Champagne Powder™ was invented here, so it's no surprise to find that, despite a relatively low altitude, Steamboat has an excellent snow record. With a 10-year annual average of 335 inches, it's not far behind the Colorado leader, Winter Park. There is snowmaking from top to bottom, too.

Experts The main attraction is the challenging terrain in the glades. A great area is on Sunshine Peak below the Sundown chair. Morningside Park and the Pony Express area also have excellent gladed runs. Three steep chutes are easily accessed via the lift back from Morningside, and a short hike gets you to the tree runs of Christmas Tree Bowl. For bumps, try the runs off Four Points. Many runs are of limited vertical; a recent reporter singles out Valley View for a longer black run to the base.

Intermediates Much of the mountain is ideal, with long cruising blue runs. Morningside Park is a great area for easy black as well as blue slopes – and 'lovely ungroomed terrain in the trees'. The Sunshine area is very gentle. Some of the black runs are regularly groomed, and 'much enjoyed' by reporters. Keen intermediates will find the mountain limited in extent, but given fresh powder it offers a great introduction to tree skiing.

Beginners There's a big nursery area at the base of the mountain, which is due for a total revamp this year to make it easier for beginners (see 'News'). Lots of easy trails offer good progression – some of the blues are quieter and more relaxing than the greens, which include many cat-tracks with steep drops at the side. The Sunshine area is particularly suited to families skiing together.

Snowboarding There's a special learning area, gentle slopes to progress to and you can get around using chair-lifts and the gondola. For experienced riders, riding the glades in fresh powder is unbeatable.

Cross-country A free shuttle takes you to 16km/10 miles of groomed tracks at the Touring Center and there is a total of 160km/100 miles of trails in the area.

Queues Queues form for the gondola first thing, but they move quickly (and can be avoided by using chairs instead – the new Christie six-pack will make that an even more attractive option from 2007/08). But we now get few other complaints.

Mountain restaurants There are food courts and table-service restaurants at Thunderhead and Rendezvous Saddle – better than the American fast-food norm, though peak-time crowds can be a problem. Both lodges were refurbished for 2006/07.

Schools and guides Reports are very positive. 'Very good in every respect, except that time was wasted as lessons were assembled and grouped,' writes a recent visitor.

Steamboat

613

Mt Werner
3220m/10,570ft
Morningside Park
Christmas Tree Bowl
Storm Peak 3160m
Sunshine Peak 3165m
Sunshine
Sundown
Four points
Rendezvous Saddle
Pony Express
Storm Peak
Thunderhead 2770m
Thunderhead
Silver Bullet
Christie Peak

Steamboat
Christie Base
Gondola base
2105m/6,900ft

↑ The 12 acre SoBe terrain-park includes jumps, rails, a quarter-pipe and the Mavericks super-pipe
STEAMBOAT / LARRY PIERCE

Facilities for children Arrangements are exceptional, winning awards from American magazines; there's even evening entertainment. Kids under 12 ski free with a parent or a grandparent buying a pass for at least five days.

STAYING THERE

How to go A fair number of UK tour operators feature Steamboat.
Chalets There are some catered chalets run by UK tour operators.
Hotels There are smart hotels at the base, including the Steamboat Grand (871 5050), and ones with more character in town. Recommendations by reporters include the Rabbit Ears Motel (879 1150) and the slope-side Ptarmigan Inn (879 1730) ('friendly, comfortable and convenient').
Apartments There are countless condos, many with good pool/hot-tub facilities, all on a free bus route. There are plenty of good places at the lift base. Antlers offers the best luxury ski-in/ski-out accommodation; Eagleridge and Canyon Creek are pretty luxurious, too. Timber Run, The Lodge, Ski Inn and the Rockies all offer good value.
Eating out There are over 70 bars and restaurants. Pick up a dining guide booklet to check out the menus. You can dine in three restaurants up the mountain. Reader recommendations at

the base area include the Tugboat Grill and Pub ('great food, good service and lively atmosphere'), Cafe Diva, La Montaña (Tex-Mex) and the 'classy but pricey' Butcher's Shop for steaks and fish. The Wired internet cafe is good for breakfast. In downtown Steamboat Springs there is quite a wide range of options. Try Antares for Asian fusion cuisine, Old West Steakhouse, or the Cottonwood Grill for its 'fabulously tasty Pacific Rim cuisine'. Reporters also recommend the 8th Street Steakhouse with its communal barbecue ('great fun, good food'). For a budget meal, head for the Double Z (pronounced 'Zee', of course).
Après-ski The base lodge area is livelier than the old town in the evening. At close of play the big Slopeside Grill is popular. The Bear River Bar has a comedy club, and the Tugboat has live music and dancing. The Old Town Pub in the town is 'great for beer and a game of pool'. There's a nightlife trail map – presumably for the ultimate bar crawl.
Off the slopes Getting to Thunderhead restaurant complex is easy for pedestrians. Visiting town is, too. The Strawberry Park Hot Springs are 'a great experience – lovely and relaxing'. Snowmobiling, ice-climbing, tubing, hot air balloons, sleigh rides and dog-sledding are also possible.

Central reservations phone number
1 800 922 2722
(toll free in the US)

Phone numbers
Calling long-distance, add the prefix 1 970; from abroad, add the prefix +1 970

TOURIST OFFICE

t 879 6111
info@steamboat.com
www.steamboat.com

Telluride

Cute old town, smart new Mountain Village, slopes to suit all.
What more could you want? More terrain, that's all

615

➕ Charming restored Victorian mining
town with a Wild West atmosphere

➕ Slopes for all, including experts

➕ Dramatic, craggy mountain scenery –
unusual for Colorado

➖ Isolated location

➖ Despite expansion, still a small
area

➖ Mountain Village a little quiet

➖ Limited mountain restaurants

**We love the old town of Telluride and always enjoy its scenic, varied slopes; but
their limited extent makes the place difficult to recommend for a holiday except in
combination with another resort – which means travelling some distance.**

THE RESORT

Telluride is an isolated resort in south-
west Colorado. It first boomed when
gold was found – and Butch Cassidy
robbed his first bank here. The town's
old red-brick and timber buildings have
been well restored, and it has more
Wild West charm than any other resort.
Shops and restaurants have gone
upmarket since its 'hippy' days of a
few years ago and a lot of celebrities
have plush holiday homes here now.
But Telluride is still friendly and small-
scale. On the slopes, Mountain Village
is a development of lavish modern
condos and hotels. A gondola links the
town and village and runs until midnight.

THE MOUNTAINS

There is something for everyone here.
Slopes Slow chairs and a gondola from
the old town access steep wooded
slopes above it and runs beyond – the
easiest leading down to Mountain
Village (which can also be reached by
staying on the gondola). There are also
steep open slopes at the very top.
Terrain-parks The huge, 10-acre Sprite
Air Garden terrain-park above Mountain
Village has a super-pipe and all the
features you could dream of. The park
off the Ute Park lift is suitable for
beginners.
Snow reliability With an average of 309
inches of snow a year and some
snowmaking, reliability is good, but
there have been some slow starts to
recent seasons; it gets a different
weather pattern from that of the main
Colorado resorts further north.
Experts The double-black bump runs
down from Giuseppe's towards town
are classic tests, and there are steep
gladed runs from all along the ridge

↑ Gorrono Ranch is the main on-mountain restaurant

SNOWPIX.COM / CHRIS GILL

COLORADO

616

between Giuseppe's and Gold Hill. The fast Gold Hill lift accesses some truly challenging terrain, from wide open steeps to narrow chutes and gnarly wooded trails. There is also hike-to backcountry terrain in Prospect Bowl that you can try with the ski school. Helitrax runs a heli-skiing operation.

Intermediates There are ideal blue cruising runs with great views from the top down to Mountain Village (including the aptly named See Forever). The Prospect Bowl lift accesses some great intermediate terrain, with dozens of rolling pitches through the trees – a very relaxing and pretty area. More challenging are some of the bumpy double-blues from the Apex and Palmyra chairs. Some of the blacks above the town get groomed – worth catching if you can. The blue Telluride Trail back to town is a narrow catwalk ('treacherous', says a reporter). But the area is small, and keen piste-bashers could get bored after a couple of days.

Beginners There are ideal runs below Mountain Village, and splendid long greens served by the Sunshine chair.

Snowboarding The lift system means it is easy to get about, and the huge terrain-park offers plenty of scope.

Cross-country The beauty of the area makes it splendid for cross-country – both in the valley and at altitude, with 30km/19 miles in total.

Queues These are rarely a problem.

Mountain restaurants Gorrono Ranch is the main on-mountain restaurant, with a new bar and terrace, live music and a BBQ. There are a couple of snack shacks higher up, with great views.

Schools and guides As well as lessons, the school offers backcountry guiding.

Facilities for children The Mountain Village Activity Center has a nursery and ski lessons can start at age three.

Telluride is tricky to get to from the UK, involving two or three flights or a long 540km/335 mile drive from Denver.

How to go Packages fly into nearby Montrose or the tiny Telluride airport (prone to closure by the weather).

Hotels In town, hotel Columbia is luxurious, as is the plush yet friendly Camel's Garden Hotel and Spa. The New Sheridan is actually old – a Main Street US classic, and comfortable, too. In Mountain Village, the Peaks Resort is due to be refurbished for 2007/08, with luxury condos, a redesigned lounge area and gourmet restaurant. Its award-winning Golden Door Spa will be for residents only. A reporter recommends the Blue Mesa Lodge and the Inn at Lost Creek.

Apartments There are plenty of luxurious-looking condos.

Eating out The Cosmopolitan in the hotel Columbia is renowned as the best in town. Other sophisticated options include the Marmotte. Flora Dora is reasonably priced and has a 'friendly atmosphere'. Honga's Lotus Petal has Asian dishes, cocktails and a huge tea menu. Allred's, at the top of the gondola, is open for gourmet dining in the evenings. In Mountain Village try 9545 at the Inn at Lost Creek. The restaurant at the Peaks Resort will reopen for 2007. Poacher's Pub and the Piazza del Villaggio are recommended for more relaxed dining.

Après-ski There's a lively bar-based après-ski scene in town. The New Sheridan has a lovely old bar dating from 1895. The Last Dollar has been recommended by locals. The Fly Me to the Moon Saloon has live music and stays open late. There's a swanky candlelit lounge called the Noir Bar attached to the Blue Point Grill. There are often concerts at the historic Sheridan Opera House. The Nugget Theater shows latest cinema releases. Mountain Village is quieter. Try Poacher's Pub or Skier's Union at the base or, for the spectacular views, Allred's at the top of the gondola.

Off the slopes There's quite a lot to do around town if you are not skiing or boarding, such as dog-sledding, horse riding, snow-shoeing, ice skating, snowmobiling and glider rides. Thrill Hill has floodlit tubing, sledding and snowbiking. A 2007 visitor recommends the 'beautiful' walk to Bear Creek.

Vail

A vast, swanky resort with some very swanky hotels at the foot of one of the biggest (but also busiest) ski areas in the States

COSTS

① ② ③ ④ ⑤ ⑥

RATINGS

The slopes

Fast lifts	****
Snow	*****
Extent	****
Expert	****
Intermediate	*****
Beginner	***
Convenience	***
Queues	**
Mountain restaurants	**

The rest

Scenery	***
Resort charm	***
Off-slope	***

NEWS

For 2007/08 the slow Highline and Sourdough chairs going up towards Two Elk are due to be replaced with high-speed quads. At the Lionshead base area, The Arrabelle at Vail Square – a hotel, restaurant and shopping complex – is set for completion. And the Children's Center at Golden Peak is being refurbished.

Plans for a $1bn project to redevelop the West Lionshead area into a resort village are in the pipeline.

+ One of the biggest areas in the US – great for confident intermediates, especially

+ The Back Bowls are big areas of treeless terrain – unusual in the US

+ Fabulous area of ungroomed, wooded slopes at Blue Sky Basin

+ Largely traffic-free resort centres, very pleasant in parts – but ...

− Resort is a vast sprawl; and a lot of redevelopment is going on

− Slopes can be crowded by American standards, with serious lift queues

− Inadequate mountain restaurants

− Blue Sky Basin and the Back Bowls may not be open in early season; warm weather can close the Bowls

− Expensive

We always enjoy skiing Vail; it's a big mountain with a decent vertical, and Blue Sky Basin has added hugely to its attractions. But it is far from being our favourite American mountain. In an American resort you expect the runs to be pretty much crowd-free; in any resort, these days, you expect 20-minute lift queues to be a thing of the past; and in such a swanky resort you expect lunch on the hill to be pleasurable. In all these respects, Vail disappoints.

At Vail's heart is the pseudo-Tirolean Vail Village, full of very expensive neo-Tirolean hotels – very nice if you can afford them, and if you can take this Disney-style approach to resort design. For our money, Vail can't compete with more distinctively American resorts based on old mining or cowboy towns. If we're going that far West, we like it to be a bit Wild.

THE RESORT

Standing in the centre of Vail Village, surrounded by chalets and bierkellers, you could be forgiven for thinking you were in the Tirol – which is what Vail's founder, Pete Seibert, intended back in the 1950s. But Vail Village is now just part of an enormous resort, mostly built in anonymous modern style, stretching for miles beside the I-70 freeway running west from Denver.

The vast village benefits from a free and efficient bus service which makes choice of location less than crucial. But the most convenient – and expensive – places to stay are in mock-Tirolean Vail Village, near the Vista Bahn fast chair,

or in functional Lionshead, near the gondola – a much less attractive area that really needs the revamp it is currently getting. The downside of all the rebuilding work that is going on is that, last season when we were there certainly, a lot of the place looked like what it was – a building site. There is a lot of accommodation further out – the cheapest tends to be across the I-70.

Beaver Creek, 16km/10 miles away, is covered by the lift pass and is easily reached by bus. A short drive (there's no bus, which surprises many reporters – and us) gets you to Breckenridge and Keystone (both owned by Vail Resorts and covered by the lift pass), and Copper Mountain.

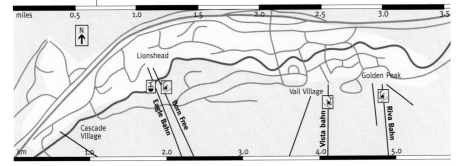

KEY FACTS

Resort	2500m
	8,200ft
Slopes	2475-3525m
	8,120-11,570ft
Lifts	34
Pistes	5,289 acres
Green	18%
Blue	29%
Black	53%
Snowmaking	
	390 acres

LIFT PASSES

Vail/Beaver Creek

Prices in US$

Age	1-day	6-day
under 13	49	270
13 to 64	81	430
over 65	71	380

Free under 5

Beginner included in price of lessons

Notes
Covers all Vail, Beaver Creek, Breckenridge and Keystone resorts, plus Arapahoe Basin; prices quoted are advance-purchase prices; further reductions for international visitors who pre-book through a UK tour operator (it is not necessary to buy a complete holiday package to obtain these prices)

THE MOUNTAINS

Vail has one of the biggest areas of slopes in the US (only recently overtaken by Big Sky/Moonlight Basin) with immaculately groomed trails and ungroomed terrain in open bowls and among the trees. You get a real sense of travelling around the mountain – something missing in many smaller American resorts. Some of the runs (especially blacks) are overclassified and some reporters have been critical of trail signposting. There are free three-hour mountain tours at 9.15am every day and tours of Blue Sky Basin starting at 10.30am.

THE SLOPES
Something for everyone
The slopes above **Vail** can be accessed via three main lifts. From right next to Vail Village, the Vista Bahn fast chair goes up to the major mid-mountain focal point, Mid-Vail; from Lionshead, the Eagle Bahn gondola goes up to the Eagle's Nest complex; and from the Golden Peak base area just to the east of Vail Village, the Riva Bahn fast chair goes up towards the Two Elk area.

The front face of the mountain is largely north-facing, with well-groomed trails cut through the trees. At altitude the mountainside divides into three bowls – Mid-Vail in the centre, with Game Creek to the south-west and Northeast Bowl to the, er, north-east. Lifts reach the ridge at three points, all giving access to the **Back Bowls** (mostly ungroomed and treeless) and through them to the **Blue Sky Basin** area (mostly ungroomed and wooded) with a satisfying 'backcountry' feel that the rest of Vail lacks.

The slopes have yellow-jacketed patrollers who stop people speeding recklessly. There's a New Technology Center where you can test equipment.

TERRAIN-PARKS
Four to fly between
There are four parks (which were all renamed with an aviation theme from 2006/07). The Flight School park is used by the ski school and is aimed at novices. It is adjacent to the big pro park, has its own entrance and is accessible by the Riva Bahn fast chair. The Sky Way park off the Wildwood Express lift out of Mid-Vail is also aimed at beginners. Intermediates should head up the Eagle Bahn gondola or Born Free chair from Lionshead to the Aviator park. Medium sized kickers and rails will prepare you to step up to the Fly Zone on Golden Peak. This park and super-pipe – again served by the Riva Bahn fast chair – are home to various high-profile events and are often in the top ten in terrain-park lists and polls. A huge triple-jump line, a quarter-pipe, and a unique log rail park are built in nice fluid lines. The pipe boasts 5.5m/18ft walls and is 130m/425ft long. Several new rails in 2007 take the total up to a whopping 40 obstacles.

SNOW RELIABILITY
Excellent, except in the Bowls
As well as an exceptional natural snow record, Vail has extensive snowmaking, normally needed only in early season. Both the Back Bowls and Blue Sky Basin usually open later in the season than the front mountain. Blue Sky is largely north-facing (and wooded) and keeps its snow well, but the Bowls are sunny, and in warm weather snow can deteriorate to the point where they are closed or a traverse is kept open to allow access to Blue Sky Basin.

FOR EXPERTS
Transformed by Blue Sky Basin
Vail's Back Bowls are vast areas, served by four chair-lifts and a short drag-lift. You can go virtually anywhere

boarding

The terrain is about as big as it comes in America. Beginners will enjoy the front side's gentle groomed pistes, ideal for honing skills and serviced by fast chair-lifts. Beware of flat areas, however, especially at the top of the Wildwood and Northwoods lifts. The back bowls will keep most riders busy for days when the snow is right. Blue Sky Basin is definitely worth checking out, with its acres of natural trails, gladed trees and cornices. There are four terrain-parks too. The Burton test centre at the New Technology Center at the top of the Mountaintop chair, will help if you have any issues with your board, or want to demo the latest gear. There are plenty of specialist shops in town, as well as good snowboard school facilities, with adult-specific courses.

Most of Vail's slopes are very well groomed, but you have to be first up the mountain to see them this deserted →
TANYA BOOTH

UK PACKAGES

Alpine Answers, AmeriCan Ski, American Ski Classics, Chalet World Ski, Crystal, Crystal Finest, Elegant Resorts, Erna Low, Independent Ski Links, Inghams, Interactive Resorts, Kuoni, Momentum, Ski Activity, Ski All America, Ski Dream, Ski Expectations, Ski Freshtracks, Ski Independence, Ski Line, Ski Safari, Ski Solutions, Ski Wild, Skitracer, Skiworld, Supertravel, Thomson, Trailfinders, United Vacations, Virgin Snow, White Mountains

you like in the half-dozen identifiable bowls, trying the gradient and terrain of your choice. There are interesting, lightly wooded areas, as well as the open slopes that dominate the area. Some 87 per cent of the runs in the Back Bowls are classified black but are not particularly steep, and they have disappointed some of our expert reporters. The snow can deteriorate rapidly in warm, sunny weather.

Blue Sky Basin has much better snow than the Back Bowls and some great adventure runs in the trees – some widely spaced, some very tight, some on relatively gentle terrain, some quite steep. All the runs funnel into the same run-out so you can't get lost.

On the front face there are some genuinely steep double-black-diamond runs, which usually have great snow; they are often mogulled but sometimes groomed to make wonderful fast cruising. The fast new Highline lift on the extreme east of the area serves three. Prima Cornice, served by the Northwoods Express, is one of the steepest on the front side.

If the snow is good, try the back-country Minturn Mile – you leave the ski area through a gate in the Game Creek area to descend a powder bowl and finish on a path by a river – ending up at the atmospheric Saloon. Go with a local guide.

FOR INTERMEDIATES
Ideal territory
The majority of Vail's front face is great intermediate territory, with easy cruising runs. Above Lionshead,

especially, there are excellent long, relatively quiet blues – Born Free and Simba both go from top to bottom. Game Creek Bowl, nearby, is excellent, too. Avanti, underneath the chair of the same name, is a nice cruiser.

As well as tackling some of the easier front-face blacks, intermediates will find plenty of interest in the Back Bowls. Some of the runs are groomed and several are classified blue, including Silk Road, which loops around the eastern edge, with wonderful views. Some of the unpisted slopes make the ideal introduction to powder skiing. Confident intermediates will also enjoy Blue Sky Basin's clearly marked blue runs and trying the easier ungroomed runs there.

FOR BEGINNERS
Good but can be crowded
There are fine nursery slopes at resort level and at altitude, and easy longer runs to progress to. But they can be rather crowded.

FOR CROSS-COUNTRY
Some of the best
Vail's cross-country areas (17km/11 miles) are at the foot of Golden Peak and at the Nordic Center on the golf course. There are also 10km/6 miles of snowshoe trails.

QUEUES
Can be bad
Vail has some of the longest lift lines we've hit in the US, especially at weekends because of the influx from Denver. Most of our reporters agree.

Vail

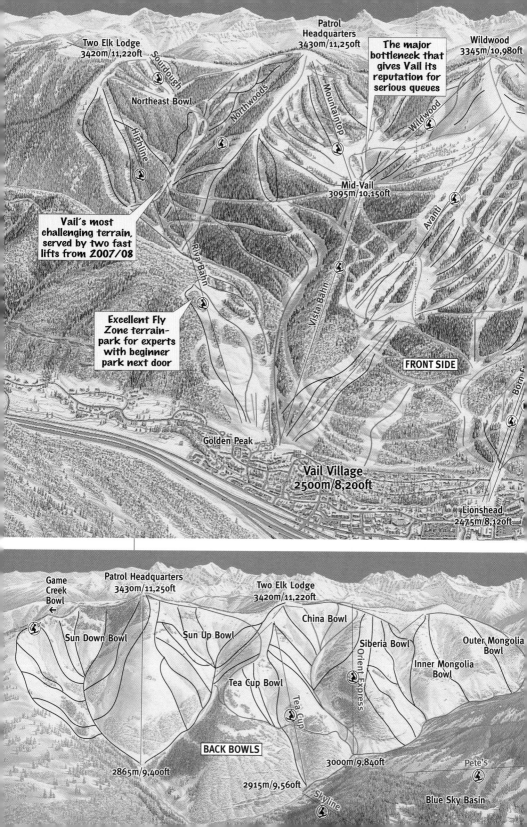

Two Elk Lodge
3420m/11,220ft

Sourdough

Northeast Bowl

Patrol
Headquarters
3430m/11,250ft

Northwoods

Mountaintop

**The major
bottleneck that
gives Vail its
reputation for
serious queues**

Wildwood
3345m/10,980ft

Wildwood

Highline

Mid-Vail
3095m/10,150ft

Avanti

**Vail's most
challenging terrain,
served by two fast
lifts from 2007/08**

Riva Bahn

Vista Bahn

**Excellent Fly
Zone terrain-
park for experts
with beginner
park next door**

Born F.

FRONT SIDE

Golden Peak

**Vail Village
2500m/8,200ft**

Lionshead
2475m/8,120ft

Game
Creek
Bowl
←

Patrol Headquarters
3430m/11,250ft

Two Elk Lodge
3420m/11,220ft

China Bowl

Sun Down Bowl

Sun Up Bowl

Siberia Bowl

Outer Mongolia
Bowl

Orient Express

Tea Cup Bowl

Inner Mongolia
Bowl

Tea Cup

BACK BOWLS

2865m/9,400ft

3000m/9,840ft

Pete's

2915m/9,56oft

Skyline

Blue Sky Basin

Patrol
eadquarters
3om/11,250ft

Wildwood
3345m/10,98oft

Pleasant, underused
bowl; you have to
ride the lift to get
back to Eagle's Nest

Game Creek Bowl

Game Creek

Mountaintop

Wildwood

Eagle's Nest
3155m/10,35oft

Mid-Vail
3095m/10,150ft

Avanti

Major complex,
with beginner
slopes, tubing and
other activities, as
well as restaurants

Pride

Vista Bahn

FRONT SIDE

Born Free

Eagle Bahn

Excellent, long,
relatively quiet
cruises down to
the Lionshead base

Vail Village
oom/8,200ft

Cascade
Village

Lionshead
2475m/8,120ft

3525m/11,57oft

Belle's Camp 3500m/11,48oft

Pete'sBowl

Earl's Bowl

Earl's

Pete's

Skyline

BLUE SKY BASIN

Orient Express

3000m/9,84oft

China Bowl

Tea Cup Bowl

2915m/9,56oft

CHILDREN

Small World Play School
t 1 800 475 4543
Ages 2mnth to 6yr;
8am to 4.30; $97 per day; reservations essential

Ski school
Ages 3 to 12 at Golden Peak and Lionshead (full day including lift pass and lunch US$139); teens $147 per day

SCHOOLS

Vail
t 1 800 475 4543

Classes
Full day (9.45-3.30)
$120

Private lessons
$625 for 1 day

GETTING THERE

Air Eagle 56km/ 35 miles (1hr); Denver 193km/ 120 miles (2½hr)

ACTIVITIES

Indoor Athletic clubs and spas, massage, ski museum

Outdoor Ice skating, fishing, tubing, snowmobiling, snow-shoe excursions, bungee trampolining, tobogganing, dog-sledding, horse-riding

Mid-Vail is a bottleneck that is difficult to avoid; 20-minute waits are common. At peak times it's possible to queue for 45 minutes here. A 2007 reporter cites the Eagle Bahn gondola as a trouble spot with 'queues of up to 20 minutes virtually all day'. But other 2007 reporters have been luckier ('only occasional' queues and 'only ten minutes maximum wait at the main lift at the bottom'). One 2007 reporter was more upset by the 'unreliability of some lifts – we were stuck on the Game Creek chair twice for up to 30 minutes at −28°C'.

MOUNTAIN RESTAURANTS
Surprisingly poor (and pricey)
As other major American resorts are gradually improving their mountain restaurants, Vail's are slipping further behind: demand is increasing to the point where the major self-service restaurants can be unpleasantly crowded from 11am to 2pm. There are not enough restaurants and those that do exist are expensive (especially the huge Two Elk, where a reporter said 'a hot dog, fries and coke cost £10'). One reporter recommends the Wildwood Smokehouse at the top of Wildwood lift – 'atmospheric, slightly different food and very good value'. 'Good barbecues,' says another. Several 2007 visitors recommend Buffalo's at the top of the Mountaintop chair for its 'light bites' and 'sandwich and soup combos'.
There's only one table-service restaurant on the hill: the Blue Moon at Eagle's Nest which was remodelled and given a new menu from 2006/07.

SCHOOLS AND GUIDES
Among the best in the world
The Vail-Beaver Creek school generates many glowing reports: 'excellent'; 'the best ski lesson I've ever had'. Class sizes are usually small: 'Never more than four in the group lesson,' says a

2007 reporter. Even the one recent critical report came from a visitor who also had a satisfactory lesson with another instructor. You can sign up for lessons on the mountain.

FACILITIES FOR CHILDREN
Excellent
The comprehensive arrangements for small children look excellent, and we've had good reports on the children's school. There are splendid children's areas with adventure trails and themed play areas. There's even a special kids' cafe area at Mid Vail. The Night Owl programme gives parents an evening off and includes supervised activities and dinner at Adventure Ridge at the top of the gondola.

STAYING THERE

HOW TO GO
Package or independent
There's a big choice of packages to Vail. It's easy to organise your own visit, with regular airport shuttles.
Chalets Several UK tour operators offer catered chalets. Many are out of the centre at East Vail or West Vail or across the busy I-70 freeway.
Hotels Vail has a fair choice of hotels, though nearly all are expensive. Check online for the best deals.
*****Vail Cascade A resort within a resort – lots of facilities and a chair-lift right outside.
*****Sonnenalp Very smart and central. Large spa and splendid piano bar-lounge.
*****Lodge at Vail Right by the Vista Bahn. Some standard rooms small. Huge buffet breakfast. Outdoor pool. 'A real treat,' writes a reporter.
****Marriot Mountain Resort Also owned by Vail Resorts, near the Eagle Bahn gondola. Impressive spa facilities.
****Manor Vail Resort At Golden Peak. Suites with sitting area, fireplace, kitchen and terrace. Hot-tub and pool. Breakfast included. 'I definitely recommend it,' says a recent visitor.
***Evergreen Lodge Between village and Lionshead. Outdoor pool, sauna and hot-tub. Sports bar. 'Excellent, value for money and spacious rooms,' says a 2007 reporter.
Apartments The Racquet Club at East Vail has lots of amenities. Mountain Haus has high-quality condos in the centre of town. And the Pitkin Creek has been recommended.

Central reservations
phone number
Call 1 800 404 3535
(toll-free from within
the US)

Phone numbers
From distant parts of
the US, add the prefix
1 970; from abroad,
add the prefix +1 970

TOURIST OFFICE

t 496 4500
vailinfo@vailresorts.
com
vail.snow.com

VAIL RESORTS, INC / JACK AFFLECK

You may love or hate
Vail Village's mock-
Tirolean architecture,
but it's only a small
part of a huge
sprawling resort (and
it's a convenient –
and expensive – place
to stay) ↓

EATING OUT
Endless choice

Whatever kind of food you want, Vail
has it – but most of it is pricey.

Fine-dining options include the
Wildflower in the Lodge, the Tour
(modern French) – recommended
highly by a reporter – and Ludwig's, in
the Sonnenalp. Other
recommendations for an Alpine
ambience are the Alpenrose and Pepi's
in the hotel Gramshammer.

For better value, we've found Blu's
'contemporary American' food
satisfactory; a reader recommends
Bagali's Italian Kitchen for pizza; Billy's
Island Grill does 'superb steaks at
moderate prices'. Bart & Yeti's is good
for local ales and no-frills, filling
American food. The Lancelot at Vail
Village (steaks and seafood) is a recent
reporter's favourite. Other reader
recommendations include May Palace
(Chinese) in West Vail, Sapphire
(seafood), Montauk (seafood), the
Bistro at the Racquet Club, Los Amigos
('decent Mexican fare', 'very family
friendly'), Russell's, the Bottega,
Vendetta's, Pazzo's ('great pizzas and
very good value for money') and Sweet
Basil at Vail Village ('good for veggies').

APRES-SKI
Fairly lively

Lionshead is said to be quiet in the
evenings; but Garfinkel's has a DJ, sun
deck and happy hour. The Red Lion in
the village centre is 'cheap and good
fun' with live music, big-screen TVs
and huge portions of food. The George
tries to be an English-style pub. Los
Amigos is lively at four o'clock. The
Tap Room in the Vista Bahn building is
a relaxed woody bar – 'good range of
wines by the glass'.

You can have a good night out at
Adventure Ridge at the top of the
gondola. As well as bars and
restaurants, there's lots to do on the
snow – though a reporter reckons the
tubing hill is no match for Keystone's.

Later on, Ski+Bar is a popular disco.
8150 is also good, with a suspended
floor that moves with the dancing; the
Semana is a snowboard hangout.

OFF THE SLOPES
A lot to do

Getting around on the free bus is easy,
and there are lots of activities to try.
The factory outlets at Silverthorne are
a must if you can't resist a bargain.

Vail

623

Winter Park

Good value, great terrain, huge snowfalls, unpretentious town and about to get a world-class village at the base

COSTS

① ② ③ ④ ⑤ ⑥

RATINGS

The slopes

Fast lifts	*******
Snow	*********
Extent	*******
Expert	********
Intermediate	********
Beginner	*********
Convenience	*******
Queues	********
Mountain restaurants	*******

The rest

Scenery	*******
Resort charm	******
Off-slope	*****

NEWS

For 2007/08 the slow Timberline double which serves Parsenn Bowl is due to be replaced by a fast six-pack, the Panoramic Express. This will cut the queues here for the highest lift-served terrain, and it will be able to run in windier conditions.

For 2006/07 the Eagle Wind triple chair was built on the back side of Parsenn Bowl. This makes the return journey to Parsenn Bowl much quicker after skiing Backside Parsenn or Vasquez Cirque. Gladed terrain and seven new trails have also been created here. Two new terrain-parks were also built – one for beginners, one for intermediates.

Intrawest's multi-million dollar plan for expanding the base area is under way – 200 condos in two new developments opened last season, plus a tubing hill.

➕ The best snowfall record of all Colorado's major resorts

➕ Superb beginner terrain and lots of groomed cruises

➕ Lots for experts, at least when conditions are right

➕ Quiet on weekdays

➕ Leading resort for teaching people with disabilities to ski and ride

➕ Largely free of inflated prices and ski-resort glitz, but ...

➖ Lacking the range of shops and restaurants you might expect

➖ Town is a bus-ride from the slopes, and strung-out along the main road

➖ 'Village' at the lift base is still very limited, and dead in the evening

➖ Trails tend to be either easy cruises or stiff mogul fields

➖ One or two slow lifts in key spots

➖ The nearest big resort to Denver, so can get crowded at weekends

Winter Park's ski area – developed for the recreation of the citizens of nearby Denver, and still owned by the city – is world class. Now there is the prospect of a world-class resort at the base, too: Intrawest (developers of resorts such as Whistler) is in the first phase of a massive expansion plan. The place looks set to be a construction site for a few years, but the end product should be good.

For the present, there's only a small 'village' at the base and most lodging, shops and restaurants are a bus-ride away downtown. If that doesn't matter to you, Winter Park is well worth considering. Some of our reporters rate it their favourite Colorado resort, partly because it makes such a refreshing change from the norm. Both the mountain and the old town have a distinct character.

THE RESORT

Winter Park started life in the 19th century and when the Rio Grande railway was built workers climbed the slopes to ski down. One of the resort's mountains, Mary Jane, is named after a legendary 'lady of pleasure', who is said to have received the land as payment for her favours.

The railway still plays an important part in Winter Park's existence, with a station right at the foot of the slopes where trains deposit Denverites every Saturday and Sunday morning; there's apparently quite an après-ski party on the homebound leg.

Most accommodation is a shuttle-bus-ride away in spacious condos scattered around either side of US highway 40, the road through the town of Winter Park. Drive into Winter Park at night, and it seems to resemble an established ski resort town, with brightly lit shops, motels, restaurants and bars – but in the daytime it's clear that the place doesn't amount to much.

In the last few years, stylish accommodation has been developed at or near the foot of the slopes, including a car-free mini-resort known as The

Village at Winter Park Resort. But as yet it's very small without many shops, bars or restaurants and very quiet at night. Confusingly, an area between the mountain and the town is known as Old Town. Shuttle-buses run between the town and the lift base, and the hotels and condos also provide shuttles. A car simplifies getting around and allows day trips to Denver or other resorts such as Copper Mountain, Breckenridge and Keystone.

The approach road is more like the Alps than Colorado, going over the Continental Divide at Berthoud Pass (3450m/11,320ft). The resort is not the highest in Colorado but it's not far off, and several reporters mention the possibility of altitude sickness.

THE MOUNTAINS

Winter Park's ski area is big by US standards, with a mix of terrain that suits all abilities – when it's all open. There are guided tours daily at 10am and 1pm, and a Fresh Tracks breakfast at 8am on Saturdays enabling you to get up the mountain before the crowds.

Mary Jane mountain (on the left) doesn't look much steeper than Winter Park mountain (on the right) here, but it has much more challenging terrain ➔

KEY FACTS

Resort	2745m
	9,000ft
Slopes	2745-3675m
	9,000-12,060ft
Lifts	25
Pistes	3,060 acres
Green	8%
Blue	36%
Black	56%
Snowmaking	
	299 acres

LIFT PASSES

Winter Park Resort

Prices in US$

Age	1-day	6-day
under 14	39	210
14 to 64	79	426
65 to 69	64	
over 70	31	
Free under 6		

Beginner included in price of lessons

Notes
Multi-day prices quoted are advance-purchase prices; one-day prices are regular season window rates; special deals for disabled skiers

UK PACKAGES

Alpine Answers, AmeriCan Ski, American Ski Classics, Crystal, Erna Low, Independent Ski Links, Interactive Resorts, Ski All America, Ski Dream, Ski Independence, Ski Safari, Ski Solutions, Skitracer, Skiworld, Supertravel, Thomson, United Vacations, Virgin Snow, White Mountains

THE SLOPES
Interestingly divided
There are five distinct, but well-linked, sectors. From the main base, a fast quad takes you to the peak of the original **Winter Park** mountain. From there, you can descend in all directions. Runs lead back towards the main base and over to the **Vasquez Ridge** area on the far right, served by the Pioneer fast quad.

You can also descend to the base of **Mary Jane** mountain, where four chairs up the front face serve tough runs; other chairs serve easier terrain on the flanks. From the top you can head up to **Parsenn Bowl** on the new Panoramic Express chair (see 'News') for intermediate terrain above and in the trees. This chair will still be exposed at the top, but the heavier chairs will be able to keep going in windier weather. From here, conditions permitting, you can skate or walk for up to half an hour to access the advanced and extreme slopes of **Vasquez Cirque**. You can now return to Parsenn Bowl by the new Eagle Wind chair (see 'News') saving a long run-out to the Pioneer lift.

TERRAIN-PARKS
Four levels for all standards
The flagship Rail Yard park, with 30 features including big jumps, a host of variously shaped rails and a super-pipe, is enough to challenge most experts. It runs down much of the front of Winter Park mountain for 1280m/ 4,200ft. Halfway down it crosses a bridge so that those on the Cranmer Cutoff green run can cross the park safely. At the bottom are the huge features of Dark Territory, open to pass holders only (you need to pay $20, sign a waiver and watch a safety video to get one). For those who prefer smaller hits, there are two parks for intermediates nearby: Dog Patch and, new for 2006/07, Dog Patch East. There's also a beginner-intermediate park, Kendrick, on the Jack Kendrick green run, plus a Starter park for beginners under Prospector Express. Check them out at www.rlyrd.com.

SNOW RELIABILITY
Among Colorado's best
Winter Park's position, close to the Continental Divide, gives it an average yearly snowfall of over 350 inches – the highest of any major Colorado resort. Snowmaking covers a lot of Winter Park mountain's runs.

FOR EXPERTS
Some hair-raising challenges
Mary Jane has some of the steepest mogul fields, chutes and hair-raising challenges in the US. On the front side is a row of long black mogul fields that are quite steep enough for most of us. There are some challenges on Winter Park mountain, too.

Some of the best terrain is open only when there is good snow and/or weather – so it's especially unreliable early in the season. The fearsome chutes of Mary Jane's back side – all steep, narrow and bordered by rocks – need a lot of snow and are accessed by a control gate. Parsenn Bowl, served by the new Panoramic six-pack, has superb blue/black gladed runs and new black-diamond gladed runs on the back side but can be closed by bad weather. Vasquez Cirque, the least reliably open area, has excellent ungroomed expert terrain but not much vertical before you hit the forest.

Winter Park

boarding
There is some great advanced and extreme boarding terrain and a high probability of fresh powder to ride. The four levels of park (see 'Terrain-parks') make Winter Park even more attractive to all levels of freestyler. The resort is also an ideal beginner and intermediate boarder area, with excellent terrain for learning. A good school provides classes for all levels, including learning to jump and ride rails.

FOR INTERMEDIATES
Choose your challenge

From pretty much wherever you are on Winter Park mountain and Vasquez Ridge you can choose a run to suit your ability. Most blue runs are well groomed every night, giving you perfect early morning cruising on the famous Colorado 'corduroy' pistes. Black runs, however, tend not to be groomed, and huge moguls form. If bumps are for you, try Mary Jane's front side. If you're learning to love them, the blue/black Sleeper enables you to dip in and out.

Parsenn Bowl has grand views and some gentle cruising pistes as well as more challenging ungroomed terrain. It's also an ideal place to try powder for the first time. But when it's actually snowing you are better off lower down, sticking to the powdery edges of tree-lined runs for better visibility.

FOR BEGINNERS
About the best we've seen

Discovery Park is a 25-acre dedicated area for beginners, reached by a high-speed quad and served by two more chairs and a tow. As well as a nursery area and longer green runs, it has an adventure trail through trees. Once out of the Park, there are easy runs back to base. And the Sorensen learning zone at the base area is good too.

FOR CROSS-COUNTRY
Lots of it

There are several different areas nearby (none actually in the resort) with generally excellent snow, totalling over 200km/125 miles of groomed trails, as well as backcountry tours.

QUEUES
Weekend crowds at the base

During the week the mountain is generally quiet. However, there may be a crowd waiting for the opening of the Zephyr Express from the main base. Queues for Parsenn Bowl should be alleviated by the new Panoramic Express for 2007/08. At weekends the Denver crowds arrive and big queues form at the base when the train gets in (though they move quickly) – 'Get up the mountain before 9am to avoid them,' says a reporter.

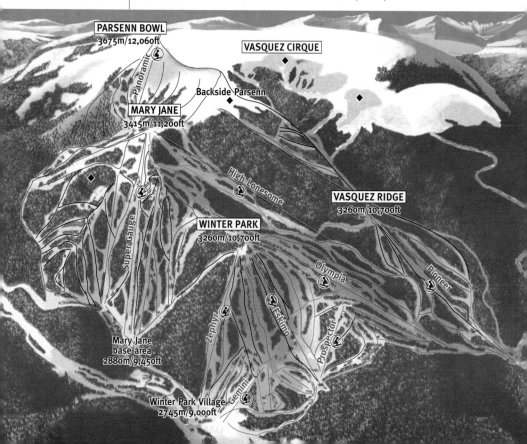

PARSENN BOWL 3675m/12,060ft

VASQUEZ CIRQUE

Panoramic

Backside Parsenn

MARY JANE 3415m/11,200ft

High Lonesome

VASQUEZ RIDGE 3260m/10,700ft

Super Gauge

WINTER PARK 3260m/10,700ft

Olympia

Pioneer

Zephyr

Eskimo

Prospector

Mary Jane base area 2880m/9,450ft

Gemini

Winter Park Village 2745m/9,000ft

SCHOOLS

Winter Park
t 1 800 729 7907

National Sports Center for the Disabled
t 726 1540
Special programme for disabled skiers and snowboarders

Classes (Winter Park prices)
Half day (2½hr) $67

Private lessons
$279 for 2hr for 1 to 3 people

CHILDREN

Child Care
t 1 800 420 8093
Ages 2mnth to 6yr; $95 per day; 8am to 4pm

Ski school
Takes ages 3 to 17 ($114 per day including lift ticket and lunch)

GETTING THERE

Air Denver 137km/ 85 miles (1½hr)

Rail Denver, Sat and Sun only; journey time 2¼hr

ACTIVITIES

Indoor Fitness clubs, hot-tubs, museum

Outdoor Dog-sledding, ice rink, snow-shoeing, sleigh rides, snowmobiling, snowcat tours, hot springs

Central reservations
Call 726 5587; toll-free number (from within the US)
1 800 729 5813

Phone numbers
From distant parts of the US, add the prefix 1 970; from abroad, add the prefix +1 970

TOURIST OFFICE

t 726 5514
wpinfo@skiwinterpark. com
www.skiwinterpark. com

MOUNTAIN RESTAURANTS
Some good facilities
The highlight is the Lodge at Sunspot, at the top of Winter Park mountain. This wood and glass building has a welcoming bar with a roaring log fire and table- and self-service sections – but it gets very busy. Lunch Rock Cafe at the top of Mary Jane does quick snacks and has a deli counter, and there is a self-service at Snoasis, by the beginner area. Otherwise, it's down to the bases. The Club Car at the base of Mary Jane offers table-service and 'a good atmosphere and more varied menu' than the American norm.

SCHOOLS AND GUIDES
Very good reports
A 2007 reporter with a school party says, 'I would like to stress how good, helpful and flexible the ski school is.' 'Three people in our group had lessons, and the improvement in all was quite startling to see,' said another recent reporter. As well as standard classes there are ideas such as Family Private (for different abilities together) and themed lessons such as bumps and women-only clinics.

FACILITIES FOR CHILDREN
Some of the best
The Children's Center at Winter Park base area houses day-care facilities and is the meeting point for children's classes, which have their own areas.

STAYING THERE

HOW TO GO
Fair choice
Several UK operators offer Winter Park.
Chalets A few are available.
Hotels There are a couple of hotel/ condo complexes with restaurants and pools near, but not in, the new Village.
***Iron Horse Resort Slope-side. 'Wonderful; ski-in/ski-out, great restaurant,' says a 2007 reporter.
***Winter Park Mountain Lodge Inconveniently positioned across the valley from the lifts; incorporates a micro-brewery; gets mixed reports.
Apartments There are a lot of comfortable condos, including the slope-side Zephyr Mountain Lodge ('fantastic, spacious, comfy, good views') and Beaver Village condos, a five-minute shuttle-bus ride ('very high standard, but the last shuttle leaves the mountain at 5.15pm'). The nearest supermarket is a drive or bus-ride away.

EATING OUT
A fair choice
The range of options is gradually improving, but still isn't a match for that in more established 'destination' resorts. Get hold of the giveaway Grand County menu guide. In town, reporters are keen on the long-established Deno's – seafood, steaks etc (also a popular après-ski bar). In the Cooper Creek Square area the New Hong Kong serves 'excellent' Chinese food says a recent reporter. Readers also recommend the Shed ('excellent steak and seafood, reasonably priced'), Carlos and Maria's for Tex-Mex, Hernando's for pizza/pasta and Untamed for steaks. Gasthaus Eichler does 'very good' German-influenced food, at slightly higher prices. Try the Crooked Creek Saloon at Fraser for atmosphere and typical American food.

APRES-SKI
If you know where to go ...
At close of play, there's action at the main lift base at the Derailer Bar ('the best and cheapest' says a report) and Doc's Roadhouse, and at the base of Mary Jane the Club Car – but reporters are disappointed at how early they close. Later on, the Shed ('excellent food') and Randi's Irish Saloon can be lively. The Crooked Creek is popular with locals and the Winter Park Pub attracts the younger crowd. Buckets is a funky sports-bar and 'the liveliest in town', says a reporter.

OFF THE SLOPES
Mainly the great outdoors
Most diversions involve getting about on snow in different ways. Several reporters are enthusiastic about the floodlit tubing at Fraser. If you like shopping, you'll want to visit Silverthorne's factory outlet stores (around 90 minutes away) – but you'll need a car to do so.

628

TOURIST OFFICE

Ski Utah
www.skiutah.com

Nowhere near as many Brits visit Utah as Colorado. But it deserves serious consideration – mainly because its marketing slogan has some basis: 'The Greatest Snow on Earth'. Some Utah resorts do get huge amounts of snow – usually light, dry powder – and if you like the steep and deep, you should at some point make the pilgrimage to Utah. Don't be put off by thinking its a 'dry' Mormon state – we've never found getting a beer or a bottle of wine a problem. But boarders beware: two of its top resorts don't allow snowboarding.

Utah's extravagant climatic claim features on many local car number plates. And, indeed, some Utah resorts do get huge dumps – over the season up to twice the amount that falls on some big-name Colorado resorts.

The biggest dumps are reserved for Snowbird and Alta (which bans boarding). Their average of 500 inches of snow a year has made them the powder capitals of the world. Park City, around 45 minutes' drive away, is the main 'destination' resort of the area, and an excellent holiday base: it has an attractive Main Street dating from the 19th century; upmarket Deer Valley (the other resort which bans boarding) is next door; and The Canyons is only a short drive away. Although only a few miles from Snowbird/Alta as the crow flies, these resorts get 'only' 300 to 350 inches of snow. There are separate chapters on these five resorts.

Other Utah resorts worth visiting include Brighton and Solitude, which are in the next valley to Alta and Snowbird. They get similar amounts of snow, but it gets tracked out less quickly because the resorts attract far fewer experts. The main claim to fame of Sundance is that it's owned by Robert Redford; it gets 320 inches of snow a year. It was unknown Snowbasin (400 inches of snow), well to the north, that hosted the Olympic downhill events in 2002. Powder Mountain (500 inches), a bit further north, is aptly named. There is more information about these resorts in the resort directory at the end of the book.

Utah is the Mormon state, which means that sale and consumption of alcohol is tightly controlled. But we've never found getting a drink a problem on our visits. Provided you're over 21 and can prove it, nether should you. If you are eating, getting alcohol with your meal is no problem. But at bars and clubs that are more dedicated to drinking (ie don't feature food but do serve spirits or beer stronger than 3.2% alcohol) membership of some kind is required. This may involve one of your party handing over $4 or more – one member can introduce numerous 'guests' – or else there'll be some old guy at the bar already organised to 'sponsor' you (sign you in) for the price of a beer. A membership lasts three weeks, but a reporter points out that the system can be very expensive if you visit different resorts most days and just want a quick beer before hitting the road. Places with tavern licences serve 3.2% beer and don't operate as clubs – but you do still need to be 21.

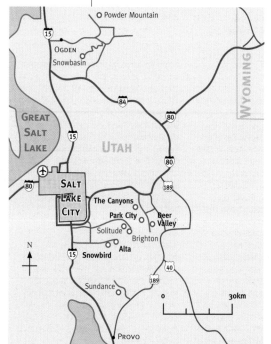

Alta

Cult powder resort linked to Snowbird but with less brutal architecture and a friendlier, old-fashioned feel

COSTS

① ② ③ ④ ⑤ ⑥

RATINGS

The slopes

Fast lifts	★★★
Snow	★★★★★
Extent	★★★
Expert	★★★★★
Intermediate	★★★
Beginner	★★★
Convenience	★★★★
Queues	★★★
Mountain restaurants	★★

The rest

Scenery	★★★
Resort charm	★★
Off-slope	★

KEY FACTS

Resort	2600m
	8,530ft

For Alta and Snowbird combined area see Snowbird

For Alta only

Slopes	2600-3200m
	8,530-10,500ft
Lifts	11
Pistes	2,200 acres
Green	25%
Blue	40%
Black	35%
Snowmaking	
	50 acres

NEWS

For 2007/08 Alta plans to follow many European resorts by introducing a hands-free lift pass system – the Alta Card. Snowbird will stick with the old barcode system, so joint passes issued in Alta will have both systems on them.

Most of Alta's slopes are lightly wooded like this; but there are lots of much steeper bowls and chutes too ➔

➕ Phenomenal snow and steep terrain mean cult status among experts (but there's great beginner terrain, too)

➕ Linked to Snowbird, making it one of the largest ski areas in the US

➕ Ski-almost-to-the-door convenience

➖ 'Resort' is no more than a scattering of lodges – not much après-ski atmosphere, and few off-slope diversions

➖ Limited groomed runs for intermediates

Alta and Snowbird are the powder capitals of the world (the snow here is as plentiful, frequent and light as it comes) and their combined area is one of the biggest in the US. Strangely, many locals we meet are still Alta or Snowbird devotees (the ski areas were separate until a few seasons ago) and never ski the other area. Madness (unless you're a boarder, in which case Snowbird is your only option – boarding is banned in Alta). On balance, we'd choose to stay in Alta – it has a friendlier feel and less brutal architecture.

THE RESORT

Alta sits at the craggy head of Little Cottonwood Canyon, 2km/1 mile beyond Snowbird and less than an hour's drive from downtown Salt Lake City. Both the resort and the approach road are prone to avalanches and closure: visitors can be confined indoors for safety. Where once there was a bustling and bawdy mining town, now there is just a strung-out handful of lodges and parking areas. Life revolves around the two separate lift base areas – Albion and Wildcat – linked by a bi-directional rope tow along the flat valley floor. There are about a dozen places to stay.

THE MOUNTAINS

Alta's slopes are lightly wooded, with some treeless slopes. Check out the Snowbird chapter for the linked slopes.

Slopes The dominant feature of Alta's terrain is the steep end of a ridge that separates the area's two basins. To the left, above Albion Base, the slopes stretch away over easy green terrain towards the blue and black runs from Point Supreme and from the top of the Sugarloaf quad (also the access lift for Snowbird). To the right, above Wildcat Base, is a more concentrated bowl with blue runs down the middle and blacks either side, now served by the fast two-stage Collins chair. The two sectors are linked at altitude, and by the flat rope tow along the valley floor.

Terrain-parks There was no park in 2007 'due to lack of demand' and there are no plans to build one for 2007/08.

Snow reliability The quantity and quality of the snow and the northerly orientation put Alta in the top rank.

Experts Even without the Snowbird link Alta had cult status among local experts, who flocked to the high ridges after a fresh snowfall. There are dozens of steep slopes and chutes.

Intermediates Adventurous intermediates who are happy to try ungroomed slopes and learn to love powder should like Alta, too. There are

UK PACKAGES

AmeriCan Ski,
Mountain Tracks, Ski
All America, Ski Dream,
Ski Independence,
Skitracer

Phone numbers
From distant parts of
the US, add the prefix
1 801; from abroad,
add the prefix +1 801

TOURIST OFFICE

t 359 1078
info@alta.com
www.alta.com

good blue bowls in both Alta and
Snowbird and not-too-tough blacks to
progress to. But if it is miles of
perfectly groomed piste you are after,
there are plenty of better resorts.

Beginners Timid intermediates and
beginners will be very happy on the
gentle lower slopes of the Albion side.
But it's hard to recommend such a
narrowly focused resort to beginners.

Snowboarding Boarding is banned (but
guided snowcat boarding is available
in nearby Grizzly Gulch).

Cross-country There's a 5km/3 mile
groomed track.

Queues The slopes are normally
uncrowded, but the fast Collins lift is
said to be increasing numbers on the
Wildcat side, with 'everybody skiing
top to bottom, making it impossible to
load at the mid-station'.

Mountain restaurants There's one in
each sector of the slopes, offering
mainly fast food. Alf's on the Albion
side 'serves great chilli in bread
bowls'. The 'nice, light and airy'
Watson Shelter on the Wildcat side has
self-service and table-service sections.
Several lodges at the base do lunch.

Schools and guides The ski school
naturally specialises in powder lessons
– though there are regular classes, too.

Facilities for children Day care for
children from six weeks is available at
the Children's Center at Albion Base.

STAYING THERE

How to go None of the hotels is
luxurious in US terms. Most get
booked up well in advance by repeat
visitors. Unusually for America, most
lodges (as they're called) operate half-
board deals, with dinner included.

Hotels The venerable Alta Lodge (742
3500) has comfortable rooms and an
atmospheric bar, and has developed a
cult following in the US by serving a
limited dinner menu at shared tables,
in two sittings, instead of enlarging its
dining room. Ingenious. Rustler Lodge
(742 2200) is more luxurious, with a
big outdoor pool, but impersonal. The
comfortable, modern and conveniently
located Goldminer's Daughter (742
2300) and the basic Peruvian Lodge
(742 3000) are cheaper. The Snowpine
Lodge (742 2000) has a sauna and is
'convenient, comfortable and friendly'
but rather 'old-fashioned'.

Eating out It is possible, but eating in
is the routine.

Après-ski This rarely goes beyond a
few drinks in one of the hotel bars and
possibly a video in your lodge. The
Goldminer's Daughter has the main
après-ski bar, with pool table etc.

Off the slopes There are few options
other than a sightseeing trip to Salt
Lake City, or the spa at Snowbird.

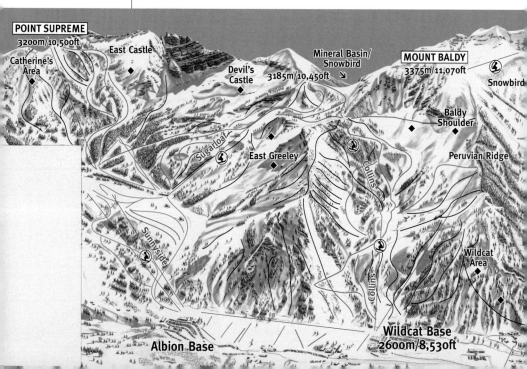

POINT SUPREME
3200m/10,500ft
Catherine's Area
East Castle
Devil's Castle
3185m/10,450ft
Mineral Basin/ Snowbird
MOUNT BALDY
3375m/11,070ft
Snowbird
Baldy Shoulder
Sugarloaf
East Greeley
Collins
Peruvian Ridge
Sunnyside
Collins
Wildcat Area
Albion Base
Wildcat Base
2600m/8,530ft

THE CANYONS / HUGHES MARTIN

The Canyons

The fourth biggest ski area in the US and still growing, with a small resort developing at the base of the slopes on the edge of Park City

631

COSTS

① ② ③ ④ ⑤ ⑥

RATINGS

The slopes
Fast lifts	★★★
Snow	★★★★
Extent	★★★
Experts	★★★★
Intermediate	★★★★
Beginner	★★
Convenience	★★★★
Queues	★★★★
Mountain restaurants	★★★

The rest
Scenery	★★★
Resort charm	★★
Off-slope	★★

KEY FACTS

Resort	2075m
	6,800ft
Slopes	2075-3045m
	6,800-9,990ft
Lifts	17
Pistes	3,700 acres
Green	14%
Blue	44%
Black	42%
Snowmaking	
	150 acres

➕ Extensive area of slopes for all abilities – and continuing to grow

➕ Modern lift system with few queues

➕ Convenient purpose-built resort village taking shape at the base

➕ Very easy access to Park City and Deer Valley ski areas

➖ Snow on the many south-facing slopes affected by sun

➖ Many runs are short

➖ Few green runs suitable for those progressing from nursery slopes

➖ Resort village limited for après-ski, dining and off-slope diversions

The Canyons has the potential to become the most extensive ski area in the US (and already claims it is the fourth biggest). It has eight linked mountains and anyone having a holiday in Park City should plan to spend some time here. Whether it makes sense to stay in the village at the base is another question.

THE RESORT

The Canyons has been transformed over the past decade or so. The area of the slopes has been doubled and a car-free village at the base now has a few shops, restaurants and bars as well as accommodation (though there's still a lot of building going on). Staying at the base is convenient, but the village isn't a very appealing place to spend time in and we would much rather stay in the centre of Park City. Regular shuttle-buses run to the resort and there is a car park below the village from which you get a cabriolet lift up to the village.

THE MOUNTAINS

The Canyons gets its name from the valleys between the eight mountains that make up the ski area.

Slopes Red Pine Lodge, at the heart of the slopes, is reached by an eight-seat gondola from the village. From here you can move in either direction across a series of ridges and valleys. Runs come off both sides of each ridge and generally face north or south. Most runs finish on the valley floors, with some long, quite flat run-outs, which make the areas feel somehow poorly linked with quite short runs. The core of the lift system either side of Red Pine Lodge consists of fast quads, but the left-hand third of the trail map has no fast lifts. Free daily mountain tours start at 10.30am and there's a new First Tracks programme (see 'News').

Terrain-parks There are six natural half-pipes across the mountain (marked on the trail map). The main terrain-park is on the Upper Respect and Lower Respect trails served by the Sunpeak Express chair and includes a

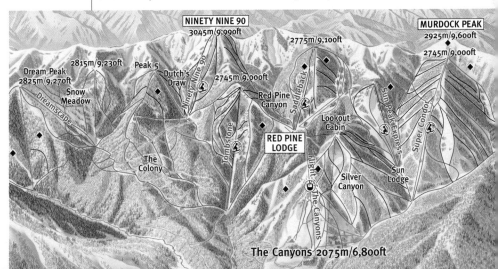

NINETY NINE 90 3045m/9,990ft
MURDOCK PEAK 2925m/9,600ft
2775m/9,100ft
2745m/9,000ft
Dream Peak 2825m/9,270ft
2815m/9,230ft
Peak 5
Dutch's Draw
2745m/9,000ft
Snow Meadow
Dreamscape
Ninety Nine 90
Red Pine Canyon
Saddleback
Sun Peak Express
Super Condor
Lookout Cabin
Tombstone
RED PINE LODGE
Flight of The Canyons
The Colony
Silver Canyon
Sun Lodge
The Canyons 2075m/6,800ft

These north-facing slopes off the ridges generally have much better snow than the south side ➔

SNOWPIX.COM / CHRIS GILL

NEWS

For 2006/07 a new quad chair opened in the north-east of the Dreamscape area, with an additional eight runs in 200 acres of intermediate and advanced terrain. A new twice-weekly Olympian First Tracks programme started, where former Olympic medallists guide skiers around the resort before it is open to the public. The Red Pine Lodge mountain restaurant was expanded, the Silverado Lodge (a 'luxury' slope-side condo-hotel) opened and extra cabins were installed on the lift from the car park to the village.

For 2007/08 glading is due to create more runs near the new Dreamcatcher quad. And new features that 'no resort has ever dared to try' are promised for the Upper Respect terrain-park.

UK PACKAGES

AmeriCan Ski, Ski All America, Ski Dream, Ski Independence, Ski Safari, Skitracer, Skiworld, United Vacations

Central reservations
Call 1 866 604 4171 (toll-free from within the US)
Phone numbers
From distant parts of the US, add the prefix 1 435; from abroad, add the prefix +1 435

TOURIST OFFICE

t 649 5400
info@thecanyons.com
www.thecanyons.com

super-pipe, jumps and rails. The beginners' park is just above here, accessed by the fast Saddleback chair.

Snow reliability Snow is not the best in Utah. The Canyons gets as much on average as Park City (350 inches) and more than Deer Valley. But the south-facing slopes suffer in late-season sun.

Experts There is steep terrain all over the mountain. We particularly liked the north-facing runs off Ninety Nine 90, with steep double-black-diamond runs plunging down through the trees to a pretty but almost flat run-out trail. There is also lots of double-diamond terrain on Murdock Peak (a 20-minute hike from the Super Condor lift). Runs off the Peak 5 chair are more sheltered.

Intermediates There are groomed blue runs for intermediates on all the main sectors except Ninety Nine 90. Some are quite short, but you can switch from valley to valley for added interest. From the Super Condor and Tombstone fast chairs there are excellent double-blue-square runs. The Dreamscape area can be blissfully quiet, and a great area for experiments off-piste. Getting back from here you ski through The Colony – a development of huge £5 million homes for the super-rich.

Beginners There are good areas with magic carpets up at Red Pine Lodge. But the run you progress to is rather short and very busy.

Snowboarding Except for the flat run-outs from many runs, it's a great area, with lots of natural hits. Canis Lupis is a mile-long, natural half-pipe with high banked walls and numerous obstacles – like riding a bob-sleigh course.

Cross-country There are prepared trails on the Park City golf course and the Homestead Resort course.

Queues The gondola can be busy at peak times. And a recent reporter complained of queues for the key Tombstone fast chair.

Mountain restaurants Satisfactory, by US standards. The recently expanded Red Pine Lodge is a large, attractive log-and-glass building with a busy cafeteria ('great soup'), a table-service restaurant and big deck. Reporters found the Sun Lodge and small Dreamscape Grill 'much quieter and more relaxing, with good soup'. The Lookout Cabin has wonderful views, and we've had excellent table-service food there.

Schools and guides As well as group and 'good' private lessons, there are special terrain-park clinics, telemark lessons, three-day women's clinics and teen clinics. Children's classes are for ages four to 14.

Facilities for children There's day care in the Grand Summit Hotel for children from six weeks to six years.

STAYING THERE

How to go Accommodation at the resort village is still fairly limited.

Hotels The luxurious Grand Summit is at the base of the gondola, and has a pool and hot-tub on the roof. Silverado Lodge opened for 2006/07.

Apartments The Sundial Lodge condos are in the resort village, with a rooftop hot-tub and plunge pool.

Eating out The Cabin restaurant, in the Grand Summit, serves eclectic US cuisine; Smokie's in the village is more casual, and Island Spice serves Jamaican food. There is a Viking yurt for 'gourmet' dining after a sleigh ride and the Red Pine Lodge does a Western barbie on Saturdays with a C&W band and dancing.

Après-ski The Cabin Lounge in the Grand Summit has live entertainment, and Smokie's is good for après-ski.

Off the slopes There's snow-shoeing, a factory outlet mall nearby and a fair bit going on in Salt Lake City and Park City.

Deer Valley

Deer Valley is top of the Ivy League of US ski resorts. It promises,
and delivers, the best ski and gastronomic experience. We love it

633

COSTS

① ② ③ ④ ⑤ ⑥

RATINGS

The slopes
Fast lifts	****
Snow	****
Extent	**
Expert	***
Intermediate	****
Beginner	****
Convenience	****
Queues	****
Mountain restaurants	****

The rest
Scenery	***
Resort charm	***
Off-slope	**

NEWS

For 2007/08, a new fast quad, the Lady Morgan Express, is planned for the Empire Canyon area. And a new 200-acre gladed area with eight new runs (ranging from beginner to expert) will be added there.

The St Regis hotel is under construction and is expected to open in December 2008.

For 2006/07 Bald Mountain got a third fast quad. And new gladed skiing was added off the Sultan Express quad.

- ➕ Immaculate piste grooming, good snow record and lots of snow-guns
- ➕ Good tree skiing
- ➕ Many fast lifts and no queues
- ➕ Good mid-mountain restaurants (and accommodation)
- ➕ Very easy access to Park City and The Canyons

- ➖ Relatively expensive
- ➖ Small area of slopes
- ➖ Mostly short runs of less than 400m/1,310ft vertical
- ➖ Deer Valley itself is quiet at night – though Park City is right next door

Deer Valley prides itself on pampering its guests, with valets to unload your skis, gourmet dining, immaculately groomed slopes, limited numbers on the mountain – and no snowboarding. But it also has some excellent slopes, with interesting terrain for all abilities, including plenty of ungroomed stuff.

The slopes of Deer Valley and Park City are separated by nothing more than a fence which, given Deer Valley's ethos, seems likely to be permanent. Any skier visiting the area should try both; for most people, Park City is the obvious base – but there are some seductive hotels here at mid-mountain Silver Lake.

THE RESORT

Just a mile from the end of Park City's Main Street, Deer Valley is unashamedly upmarket – famed for the care and attention lavished on both slopes and guests. It's very obviously aimed at people who are used to being pampered and can pay for it. But it remains surprisingly unpretentious.

There is no village as such. The lodgings – luxurious private chalets and swanky hotels – are scattered around the fringes of the slopes, with more concentrated clusters on the valley floor near the main lift base and at Silver Lake Lodge (mid-mountain but accessible by road). For ski-town animation, head for Park City, or base yourself there. There are free buses.

Gentle slopes above Silver Lake Lodge, where the plushest hotels are ➜

THE MOUNTAINS

The slopes are varied and interesting. Deer Valley's reputation for immaculate grooming is justified ('the best I have ever seen' says a 2007 reporter) but there is also a lot of exciting tree skiing – and some steep bump runs, too. There are free mountain tours for different standards (we were the only two on a black-diamond tour on our last visit and had a great time). There's a First Tracks tour at 8am.

Slopes Two fast quads take you up to Bald Eagle Mountain, just beyond which is the mid-mountain focus of Silver Lake Lodge. You can ski from here to the isolated Little Baldy Peak, served by a gondola and a quad chairlift, with mainly easy runs to serve property developments there. But the main skiing is on three linked peaks beyond Silver Lake Lodge, all served by fast quads – Bald Mountain, Flagstaff Mountain and Empire Canyon. The top of Empire is just a few metres from the runs of the Park City ski area.

Terrain-parks The TNT (Tricks 'n' Turns) park on Empire Canyon offers rails, jumps and boxes.

Snow reliability As you'd expect in Utah, snow reliability is excellent, and there's plenty of snowmaking too.

Experts Despite the image of pampered luxury there is excellent expert terrain on all three main

KEY FACTS

Resort	2195m
	7,200ft
Slopes	2000-2915m
	6,570-9,570ft
Lifts	22
Pistes	1,825 acres
Green	24%
Blue	43%
Black	33%
Snowmaking	
	500 acres

UK PACKAGES

AmeriCan Ski, American Ski Classics, Ski All America, Ski Dream, Ski Independence, Ski Safari, Skitracer

Central reservations
Call 645 6528.

Phone numbers
From distant parts of the US, add 1 435; from abroad, add the prefix +1 435

TOURIST OFFICE

t 649 1000
skierservices@
deervalley.com
www.deervalley.com

mountains, including fabulous glades, bumps, chutes and open bowls. And the snow doesn't get skied out quickly. The Ski Utah Interconnect Tour to Alta now starts here (see Park City chapter).
Intermediates There are lots of superbly groomed blue runs all over the area.
Beginners There are nursery slopes at Silver Lake Lodge as well as the base, and gentle green runs (some, like Bandana, with great views from the top) to progress to on all mountains.
Snowboarding Boarding is banned.
Cross-country There are prepared trails on the Park City and Homestead Resort golf courses and lots of scope for backcountry trips.
Queues Waiting in lift lines is not something that Deer Valley wants its guests to experience, so it limits the number of lift tickets sold. But a recent visitor found the area 'crowded compared with nearby resorts'.
Mountain restaurants There are attractive wood-and-glass self-service places at both Silver Lake and the base lodge. The grill restaurant at the Empire Canyon Lodge is consistently recommended and the tiny Deer Crest Gondola grill on Little Baldy Peak is 'great for burgers and views'. For a bit of a treat, try the Stein Eriksen Lodge (including an excellent, good value, all-you-can-eat buffet), the Goldener Hirsch, or the Royal Street Café table-service restaurant at Silver Lake Lodge.

Schools and guides The ski school is doubtless excellent and booking is essential. Telemark lessons are now available. The Mahre Training Center (run by Olympian brothers Steve and Phil) is based here.
Facilities for children Deer Valley's Children's Center gives parents complimentary pagers. The free 'early drop' system means you can leave your kids at 8.30am.

STAYING THERE

How to go A car is useful for visiting the other nearby Utah resorts, though Deer Valley, Park City and The Canyons are all linked by efficient shuttle-buses.
Hotels Stein Eriksen Lodge and the Goldener Hirsch at Silver Lake are two of the plushest hotels in any ski resort.
Apartments There are many luxury apartments and houses to rent.
Après-ski The Lounge of the Snow Park Lodge at the base area is the main après-ski venue, with live music. Then there's Main Street in Park City.
Eating out Of the gourmet restaurants, the Mariposa is the best. The Seafood Buffet is also recommended. 'Fireside Dining' evenings at the Empire Canyon Lodge are held three nights a week.
Off the slopes Park City has lots of shops, galleries etc. Salt Lake City has concerts, sights and shopping. Balloon rides and snowmobiling are popular.

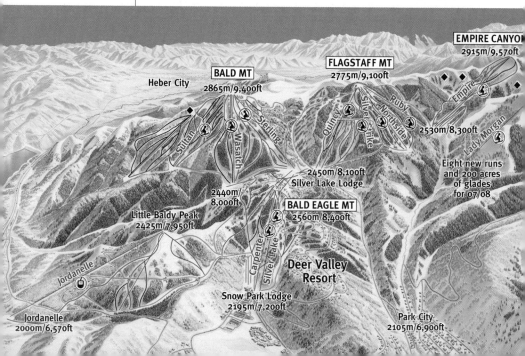

Park City

Stay near the cute and lively old Main Street and visit the three local mountains plus some further afield for a varied holiday

NEWS

From 2006/07 a new triple chair – the Silver Star – runs from Resort Base to a blue run that takes you down to the King Con fast chair. Three new intermediate trails were also created.

A new Three Resort International Pass was launched a couple of seasons ago, covering Park City, The Canyons and Deer Valley. You purchase it in advance through selected tour operators and exchange a voucher for a ticket each day. But reporters warn against buying this for the duration of your stay because you're likely to want to visit more distant ski areas too.

PARK CITY CHAMBER/VISITORS BUREAU / LATHAM JENKINS

Near the base of Park City ski area with the Eagle super-pipe that featured in the 2002 Winter Olympics →

➕ Entertaining, historic Main Street, convenient for slopes

➕ Lots of bars and restaurants make nonsense of Utah's Mormon image

➕ Well maintained slopes, with lots of snowmaking

➕ Good lift system, with four six-packs

➕ Easy to visit other resorts – Deer Valley and The Canyons (covered by area pass) are effectively suburbs

➖ Away from Main Street, town is an enormous (still expanding) sprawl – inconvenient as well as charmless

➖ The blue and black runs tend to be rather short

➖ Most lodgings involve driving or bussing to Main Street and slopes

➖ Snowfall record comes nowhere near that of Alta, Snowbird et al

➖ Lack of spectacular scenery

Park City has clear attractions, particularly if you ignore its sprawling suburbs and stay near the centre to make the most of the lively bars and restaurants in Main Street. And it's an excellent base for touring other resorts – notably next-door Deer Valley and The Canyons, both covered by the Three Resort Pass.

Deer Valley is separated from Park City's slopes by a fence between two pistes, and by separate ownership with different objectives. They could be linked by removing the fence – but it stays in place. To European eyes, all very strange. The Canyons is only a little further away, and reached by free buses.

Then there are the famously powdery resorts of Snowbird and Alta, less than an hour away by car or bus. Even the Olympic downhill slopes of Snowbasin are within easy reach if you have a car (and by special privately run buses).

THE RESORT

Park City is about 45 minutes by road from Salt Lake City. It was born with the discovery of silver in 1872. By the turn of the century the town boasted a population of 10,000, a red-light area, a Chinese quarter and 27 saloons.

Careful restoration has left the town with a splendid historic centrepiece in Main Street, now lined by a colourful selection of art galleries, boutiques, bars and restaurants, many quite smart. New buildings have been tastefully designed to blend in smoothly. But away from the centre the resort is an amorphous sprawl, still expanding. Traffic congestion can be bad, especially at weekends.

We've had reports of being hassled by real estate salespeople trying to interest people in listening to a sales pitch in return for a free lift pass (at The Canyons as well as Park City).

The slow Town chair-lift goes up to the slopes from Main Street, but the main lifts are on the fringes at Resort Base; there are lodgings out there.

Deer Valley, The Canyons and Park City are linked by 'punctual' free

KEY FACTS

Resort	2105m
	6,900ft
Slopes	2105-3050m
	6,900-10,000ft
Lifts	15
Pistes	3,300 acres
Green	17%
Blue	50%
Black	33%
Snowmaking	
	475 acres

shuttle-buses, which also go around town and run until fairly late. 'Get a map', says a 2007 reporter, 'as they are on a loop system and can be confusing at first.' A car is useful for visiting other ski areas on the good roads.

If you're not hiring a car, pick a location that's handy for Main Street and the Town chair or the free bus.

THE MOUNTAIN

Mostly the area consists of blue and black trails cut through the trees on the flanks of rounded mountain ridges, with easier runs running along the ridges and the valleys between. The more interesting terrain is in the lightly wooded bowls and ridges at the top.

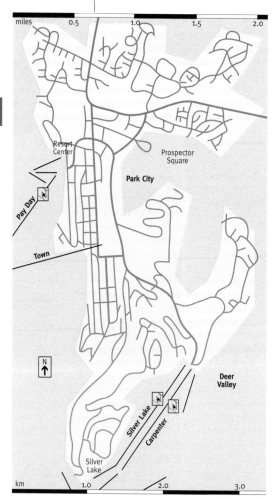

THE SLOPES
Bowls above the woods
A fast six-seat chair-lift whisks you up from Resort Base, and another beyond that up to Summit House, the main mountain restaurant.

Most of the easy and intermediate runs lie between Summit House and the base area, and spread along the sides of a series of interconnecting ridges. Virtually all the steep terrain is above Summit House in a series of ungroomed bowls, and accessed by the McConkey's six-pack and the old Jupiter double chair.

There are free, twice-daily Mountain History Tours of the slopes, looking at the area's silver mining heritage (including old mine workings). A long floodlit intermediate run and a beginner run are open until 7.30pm.

TERRAIN-PARKS
Among the best in the world
There are four terrain-parks here to suit all levels. The vast number of kickers, rails and pipes are maintained daily, and rank among the best in the world. Jonesy's park, located under the Bonanza lift, features a slew of pro-standard jumps and rails for advanced riders only. The Pick 'N' Shovel park, accessible via the Three Kings lift, is the beginner park and features six jumps and 20 rails and funboxes. The King's Crown park, on the northern slope overlooking the resort, is of intermediate standard with kickers, rails and butter boxes. The Eagle super-pipe that was used for the 2002 Winter Olympics is consistently one of the finest-shaped pipes in the world. And the Pay Day jib park, along the Pay Day run, stays open until 7.30pm with a host of lit rails and boxes.

SNOW RELIABILITY
Not quite the greatest on Earth
Utah is famous for the quality and quantity of its snow. Park City's record doesn't match those of Snowbird and Alta, but an annual average of 350 inches is still impressive, and ahead of most Colorado figures. And snowmaking covers about 15 per cent of the terrain.

FOR EXPERTS
Lots of variety
There is a lot of excellent advanced and expert terrain at the top of the lift system. It is all marked as double-diamond on the trail map, but there are many runs that deserve only a

LIFT PASSES

Park City

Prices in US$		
Age	1-day	6-day
under 13	47	240
13 to 64	77	414
over 65	47	240
Free under 7		
Beginner no deals		

Notes
Covers all lifts in Park
City Mountain Resort,
with ski-bus; 6-day
prices are advance-
purchase prices;
additional discounts if
purchased in advance
with lodging

Alternative passes
Three Resort
International Pass
covering Park City,
The Canyons and
Deer Valley available
through selected tour
operators (around
£220 for a 6 days)

boarding

It was not until 1996, when Park City won its Olympic bid, that the resort lifted its ban on snowboarding. Since then it has steamrollered ahead to attract the snowboarding community by building some of the best terrain-parks in the world. By enlisting the help and expertise of some big-name pros, namely Mark-Frank Montoya, Shaun White and Erin Comstock, Park City has created something really special, in the form of original and varied obstacles for all levels and an incredible half-pipe. And Park City has some great ungroomed terrain as well: the higher bowls offer tree-lined powder runs and great kicker-building spots. Beginners will have no trouble on the lower slopes, all serviced by fast chair-lifts. But beware: at weekends and peak season it can get very crowded, especially in the terrain-parks.

single-diamond rating – so don't be put off. We particularly like the prettily wooded McConkey's Bowl, served by a six-pack and offering a range of open pitches and gladed terrain. The old Jupiter lift accesses the highest bowls, which include some serious terrain – with narrow couloirs, cliffs and cornices – as well as easier wide-open slopes. The Jupiter bowl runs are under the chair, but there is a lot more terrain accessible by traversing and hiking – turn left for West Face, Pioneer Ridge and Puma Bowl, right for Scott's Bowl and the vast expanse of Pinecone Ridge, stretching literally for miles down the side of Thaynes Canyon.

Lower down, the side of Summit House ridge, serviced by the Thaynes and Motherlode chairs, has some little-used black runs, plus a few satisfying

trails in the trees. There's a zone of steep runs towards town from further round the ridge. And don't miss Blueslip Bowl near Summit House – so called because in the past when it was out of bounds, ski company employees caught skiing it were fired, and were given their notice on a blue slip.

Good skiers (no snowboarders, due to some long flat run-outs) should not miss the Utah Interconnect – see feature panel. For bigger budgets, Park City Powder Cats & Heli-Ski and Wasatch Powderbird Guides offer heli-skiing.

FOR INTERMEDIATES
OK for a day or two
There are blue runs served by all the main lifts, apart from Jupiter (the blue Jupiter Access is worth a go though, even if you don't ride the chair, for the

Park City

637

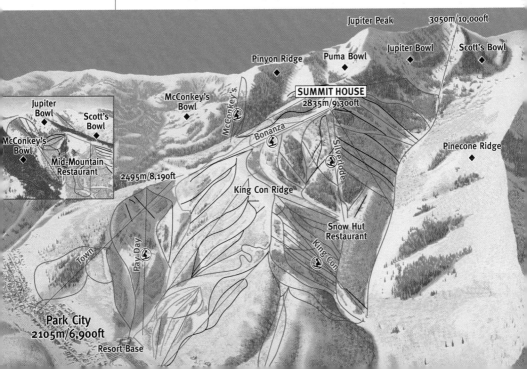

SCHOOLS

Park City
t 1 800 227 2754

Classes
1 3hr day $75
Private lessons
$120 for 1hr

CHILDREN

New Signature 3
(run by ski school)
t 1 800 227 2754
Ages 3 to 5;
$145 per day,
includes ski tuition,
lunch (max class size
is 3)

Guardian Angel
t 783 2662
Babysitting service

Ski school
The school offers
classes for ages 6 to
14, 9.30-3.30, $189
per day including
lunch (max class size
is 5)

UK PACKAGES

Alpine Answers,
AmeriCan Ski,
American Ski Classics,
Crystal, Momentum, Ski
Activity, Ski All
America, Ski Dream,
Ski Independence, Ski
Line, Ski Safari, Ski
Solutions, Skitracer,
Skiworld, Thomson,
United Vacations

sight of people coming down the chutes). The areas around the King Con high-speed quad and Silverlode high-speed six-pack have a dense network of great (but fairly short) cruising runs. There are also more difficult trails close by, for those looking for a challenge.

But there are few long, fast cruising runs – most trails are around 1 to 2km/0.5 to 1 mile, and many have long, flat run-outs. The Pioneer and McConkey's chair-lifts are off the main drag and serve some very pleasant, often quiet runs. The runs under the Town lift have great views of the town.

Intermediates will certainly want to visit The Canyons and Deer Valley for a day or two (see separate chapters).

FOR BEGINNERS
A good chance for fast progress
Novices start on short lifts and a beginners' area near the base lodge. Classes graduate up the hill quite quickly, and there's a good, gentle and wide 'easiest way down' – the three-and-a-half-mile Home Run – clearly marked all the way from Summit House. It's easy enough for most to manage after only a few lessons. The Town chair can be ridden down.

FOR CROSS-COUNTRY
Some trails; lots of backcountry
There are prepared trails on both the Park City golf course, next to the downhill area, and the Homestead Resort course, just out of town. There is lots of scope for backcountry trips.

QUEUES
Peak period crowds
Lift queues aren't normally a problem. But it can get pretty crowded (on some trails as well as the lifts) at weekends and in high season, particularly on the

Pay Day lift from Resort Base. With a pass for five days or more, the Fast Track system means you can jump the queues on four main lifts.

MOUNTAIN RESTAURANTS
Standard self-service stuff
The Mid-Mountain Lodge is a picturesque 19th-century mine building which was heaved up the mountain to its present location near the bottom of Pioneer chair. The food is standard self-service fare ('lovely clam chowder') but most reporters prefer it to the alternatives. The Summit House is cafe-style – serving chilli, pizza, soup and 'good hot chocolate'. A 2007 visitor liked the Snow Hut, a 'cosier' log building which usually has an outdoor grill. Caffé Amante is a coffee house in a yurt (tent) halfway down the Bonanza chair-lift. There are more options down at Resort Base ('a delicious salad bar and top-quality fresh fish' said a recent reporter).

SCHOOLS AND GUIDES
Good reports
A 2007 reporter's husband had a good private lesson – 'the instructor tried to take him to as much of the scarce powder as possible'. We continue to receive positive reports of snowboard group lessons: 'Excellent,' said the daughter of a recent reporter, who was given a detailed record of her achievements in a small two-day class and was riding blue runs by the end.

FACILITIES FOR CHILDREN
Well organised
There are a number of licensed carers who operate either at their own premises or at visitors' lodgings. The ski school takes children from the age of three. Book in advance.

THE UTAH INTERCONNECT

Good skiers prepared to do some hiking should consider this excellent guided backcountry tour that runs four days a week from Deer Valley to Snowbird. (Three days a week it runs from Snowbird, but only as far as Solitude.) When we did it (a few years back, starting from Park City) we got fresh tracks in knee-deep powder practically all day. After a warm-up run to weed out weak skiers, we went up the top chair, through a 'closed' gate in the area boundary and skied down a deserted, prettily wooded valley to Solitude. After taking the lifts to the top of Solitude we did a short traverse/walk, then down more virgin powder towards Brighton. After more powder runs and lunch back in Solitude, it was up the lifts and a 30-minute hike up the Highway to Heaven to north-facing, tree-lined slopes and a great little gully down into Alta. How much of Alta and Snowbird you get to ski depends on how much time is left. The price ($195) includes two guides – one leading, the other at the rear – lunch, lift tickets and transport home.

↑ Main Street is a cute place to wander up and down even when it's not this snowy

PARK CITY CHAMBER / VISITORS BUREAU / DAN CAMPBELL

GETTING THERE

Air Salt Lake City 58km/36 miles (¹/₂hr)

ACTIVITIES

Indoor Park City Racquet Club (tennis, racquetball, swimming pool, hot-tub, gym); Silver Mountain Sports Club and Spa (pools, hot-tubs, sauna, steam room, tennis, racquetball, gym); other fitness clubs, spa treatments, museum

Outdoor Ice skating, snowmobiles, dog sledding, sleigh rides, hot-air ballooning, ski jumping, alpine coaster, snow-shoeing, snowtubing, winter fly fishing

Phone numbers
From distant parts of the US, add the prefix 1 435; from abroad, add the prefix +1 435

TOURIST OFFICE

t 649 8111
info@pcski.com
www.parkcitymountain.com
www.parkcityinfo.com

STAYING THERE

HOW TO GO
Packaged independence
Park City is the busiest and most atmospheric of the Utah resorts, and a good base for visiting the others. We prefer to stay near Main Street and its bars and restaurants, but suburbs such as Kimball Junction are convenient and cheap (but soulless) if you have a car and want to try different resorts daily.
Hotels There's a wide variety, from typical chains to individual little B&Bs.
*****Park City (200 2000) Swanky all-suite place on outskirts, better placed for golf than skiing.
***Park City Peaks (649 5000) Excellent rooms, indoor-outdoor pool and 'fab hot-tub', but out of town.
***Yarrow (649 7000) Adequate, charmless base, a bearable walk from Main Street. Pool.
Silver King (649 5500) De luxe hotel/condo complex at base of the slopes, with indoor-outdoor pool.
Washington School Inn (649 3800) 'Absolutely excellent' historic inn with 'fantastic service' say reporters. In a great location near Main Street.
Best Western Landmark Inn (649 7300) At Kimball Junction. Pool.
Chateau Apres Lodge (649 9372) Close to the slopes: comfortable, faded, cheap.
1904 Imperial Inn (649 1904) Quaint B&B at the top of Main Street.
Apartments There's a big range. The Townlift studios near Main Street and Park Avenue condos are both modern and comfortable and the latter have pool and hot-tubs. Silver Cliff Village is adjacent to the slopes and has spacious units and access to the facilities of the Silver King Hotel. Blue Church Lodge is a well-converted 19th-century Mormon church with luxury condos and rooms.

EATING OUT
Lots of choice
There are over 100 restaurants. Our favourites are Wahso (Asian fusion); 350 Main (new American); and Riverhorse – in a grand, high-ceilinged first-floor room with live music. Zoom is the old Union Pacific train depot, now a trendy restaurant owned by Robert Redford (we've had mixed reports – from 'our best meal' to 'mediocre and overpriced'). Chez Betty is small and just may have the best food in town – expensive though. Other reporter recommendations include Cisero's and Grappa (Italian), Chimayo ('south-western-with-a-twist food but service too rushed'), Wasatch Brew Pub ('good steaks', 'best value'), Bandit's Grill ('good value'), Claim Jumper ('really juicy steaks, enormous desserts'), No Name Saloon ('brilliant buffalo burgers') and Butcher's Chop House ('great prime rib and steaks'). There are lots of Tex-Mex places: Zona Rosa and El Chubasco have been praised. Squatters is a new micro brewery out of town a bit ('good atmosphere and good food'). The seafood buffet at Snow Park Lodge, at Deer Valley, is 'excellent' – worth the journey.

APRES-SKI
Better than you might think
As the slopes close, Legends is the place to head for at Resort Base. Pig Pen in the ice skating plaza was recommended by a recent reporter. In Main Street, the Wasatch Brew Pub makes its own ale. The Claim Jumper, JB Mulligans, O'Shuck's and the scruffy Alamo are lively and there's usually live music and dancing at weekends. For clubs, try Harry O's and Cisero's.

OFF THE SLOPES
Should be interesting
There's a factory outlet mall at Kimball Junction. Backcountry snowmobiling, balloon flights and trips to Nevada for gambling are popular. In January there's Robert Redford's Sundance Film Festival and in February Winterfest is a 10-day celebration of the 2002 Olympics, including concerts and ice sculpture.

There are lots of shops and galleries. The museum and old jail house are worth a visit. Salt Lake City is easily reached and has some good concerts, shopping and Mormon heritage sites.

You might like to learn to ski-jump or try the Olympic bob track at the Utah Olympic Park down the road.

Park City

639

Snowbird

A powder-pig paradise linked to neighbouring Alta; with big concrete and glass base buildings that remind us of Flaine

COSTS

① ② ③ ④ ⑤ ⑥

RATINGS

The slopes
Fast lifts   ★★★
Snow   ★★★★★
Extent   ★★★
Expert   ★★★★★
Intermediate   ★★★
Beginner   ★★
Convenience ★★★★★
Queues   ★★★
Mountain
   restaurants   ★

The rest
Scenery   ★★★
Resort charm   ★
Off-slope   ★

NEWS

For 2006/07 the slow old Peruvian chair from the base was replaced by a high-speed quad that goes almost to the top of the mountain. At the top a 175m/575ft tunnel with a moving carpet provides access to Mineral Basin on the back of the mountain. This has cut queues for the cable-car and allows access to the Basin in bad weather when the cable-car is closed. The Cliff Lodge received a $6m facelift.

For 2007/08 a further 25 acres of snowmaking is planned.

UK PACKAGES

Alpine Answers, AmeriCan Ski, American Ski Classics, Ski Activity, Ski All America, Ski Dream, Ski Independence, Ski Safari, Skitracer, Skiworld, United Vacations

➕ Quantity and quality of powder snow unrivalled

➕ Link to Alta makes one of the largest ski areas in the US

➕ Fabulous ungroomed slopes, with steep and not-so-steep options

➕ Slopes-at-the-door convenience

➖ Limited groomed runs for intermediates

➖ Tiny, claustrophobic resort 'village'

➖ Stark concrete Bauhaus architecture

➖ Mainly slow chair-lifts

➖ Very quiet at night

There can be few places where nature has combined the steep with the deep better than at Snowbird and next-door Alta, and even fewer places where there are also lifts to give you access. The two resorts' combined area is one of the top powder-pig paradises in the world. So it is a shame that Snowbird's concrete, purpose-built 'base village' is so lacking in charm and ski resort ambience. Boarders are banned from Alta's slopes, so cannot take advantage of the link.

THE RESORT

Snowbird lies 40km/25 miles from Salt Lake City in Little Cottonwood Canyon – just before Alta. The setting is rugged and rather Alpine – and both the resort and (particularly) the approach road are prone to avalanches and closure: visitors are sometimes confined indoors for safety. The resort buildings are mainly block-like – but they provide ski-in/ski-out lodging.

The resort area and the slopes are spread along the road on the south side of the narrow canyon. The focal Snowbird Center (lift base/shops/restaurants) is towards the eastern, up-canyon end. All the lodgings and restaurants are within walking distance. The main cable-car station and new chair-lift are central. There are shuttle-buses, with a service to Alta.

THE MOUNTAINS

Snowbird's link with Alta forms one of the largest ski areas in the US.

Slopes The north-facing slopes rear up from the edge of the resort. Six access lifts are ranged along the valley floor, the main ones being the 125-person cable-car (the Aerial Tram) to Hidden Peak, the Peruvian Express quad (see 'News') and the Gadzoom fast quad. To the west, in Gad Valley, there are runs ranging from very tough to nice and easy. Mineral Basin, on the back of Hidden Peak, offers 500 acres of terrain for all abilities, but can be badly affected by sun. One of the two

fast quads there forms the link with Alta. The nursery slopes are floodlit three evenings a week.

Terrain-parks There are two (one for experts and one for intermediates) plus a 100m/330ft super-pipe.

Snow reliability Snowbird and Alta average 500 inches of snowfall a year – twice as much as some Colorado resorts and around 50 per cent more than the nearby Park City area. There's snowmaking in busy areas.

Experts Snowbird was created for experts; the trail map is liberally sprinkled with double-black-diamonds, and some of the gullies off the Cirque ridge – Silver Fox and Great Scott, for example – are exceptionally steep and frequently neck-deep in powder. Lower down lurk the bump runs, including Mach Schnell – a great run straight down the fall line through trees. There is wonderful ski-anywhere terrain in the bowl beneath the high Little Cloud chair, and the Gad 2 lift opens up attractive tree runs. Fantastic go-anywhere terrain under the High Baldy traverse is controlled by gates. Mineral Basin has more expert terrain. Back-country tours and heli-skiing are offered.

Intermediates The winding Chip's Run on the Cirque ridge provides the only comfortable route down from the top. For adventurous intermediates wanting to try powder skiing, the bowl below the Little Cloud lift is a must. There are some challenging runs through the trees off the Gad 2 lift and some nice long cruises in Mineral Basin. But the groomed runs don't add up to a lot.

↑ Scenery of almost Alpine character
SNOWPIX.COM / CHRIS GILL

KEY FACTS

Resort	2470m
	8,100ft

For Snowbird and Alta combined area

Slopes	2365-3350m
	7,760-11,000ft
Lifts	23
Pistes	4,700 acres
Green	25%
Blue	37%
Black	38%
Snowmaking	
	575 acres

Snowbird only

Slopes	2365-3350m
	7,760-11,000ft
Lifts	11
Pistes	2,500 acres
Green	27%
Blue	38%
Black	35%
Snowmaking	
	525 acres

Phone numbers
From distant parts of the US, add the prefix 1 801; from abroad, add the prefix +1 801

TOURIST OFFICE

t 933 2222
info@snowbird.com
www.snowbird.com

Beginners There is a nursery slope next to Cliff Lodge, and the Mountain Learning area part-way up the hill. But progression to longer runs is not easy.

Snowboarding Competent free-riders will have a wild time in Snowbird's powder (though a recent reporter complains of 'flat sticky spots where you have to walk'). Alta bans boarders.

Cross-country No prepared trails.

Queues The big problem has always been the cable-car, with queues of up to an hour at times. But the new Peruvian chair (see 'News') provides an alternative way to the top (via Mineral Basin and then the Mineral Basin Express chair) and seems to have made a big difference, say 2007 reporters. More reports welcome.

Mountain restaurants It's the Mid-Gad Lodge self-service cafeteria or back to one of the bases. A 2007 reporter recommends the table-service Forklift.

Schools and guides The ski school offers a range of lessons and clinics –

such as women-only and Big Mountain programmes. A 2007 visitor was 'highly impressed' with her private lessons.

Facilities for children The 'kids ski free' programme allows two children (six and under) to ski for free ($15 a day extra for use of the Tram) with each adult. Camp Snowbird takes children three and under.

STAYING THERE

How to go A few UK tour operators feature Snowbird.

Hotels There are several lodges, and smaller condo blocks. Cliff Lodge is a huge concrete hotel with renovated rooms, but is generally depressing; the rooftop pool and spa facilities cost $20 a day extra. The Lodge at Snowbird was recently renovated. Reporters tell of 'friendly but amateurish staff' in both places.

Eating out Cliff Lodge and Snowbird Center are the focal points. The 'fine dining' Aerie in the Cliff Lodge gets mixed reviews. Readers recommend the Steak Pit in Snowbird Center.

Après-ski Après-ski tends to be a bit muted and a 2007 visitor had a problem getting a drink at all. The Tram Club and El Chanate are lively as the slopes close. But a recent reporter complains that many places close early and 'enforce a curfew in a manner that any small dictatorship would envy' – endorsed by a 2007 visitor.

Off the slopes Apart from spas in the various lodges, there's a skating rink, ice-climbing, snowmobiling and a family tubing hill.

Snowbird

641

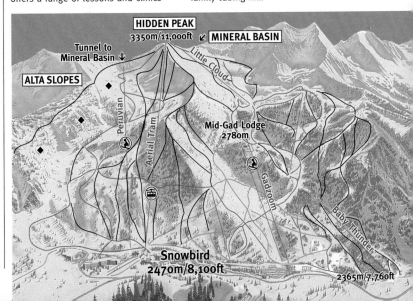

This section contains detailed chapters on just two resorts – Jackson Hole and Big Sky. Below are notes on these and various other resorts in different parts of the great Rocky Mountain chain that stretches from Montana and Idaho down through Wyoming and Colorado to New Mexico.

Sun Valley, Idaho, was America's first purpose-built resort, developed in the 1930s by the president of the Union Pacific Railway. It quickly became popular with the Hollywood movie set and has managed to retain its stylish image and ambience; it has one of our favourite luxury hotels.

Also in Idaho, as it happens, is America's latest purpose-built resort (and the first to be built since Beaver Creek) – **Tamarack**, at McCall (two hours north of Boise) on the shores of Cascade Lake, a large reservoir. The resort opened three seasons back with five lifts and now has seven, including three fast quads, serving 850 skiable acres and 855m/2,800ft vertical. Tamarack gets more snow than Sun Valley (300+ inches on average, 400+ in a good year), and it still gets a lot of sun. An American reader spent 12 days there a couple of seasons back and reported: 'Tamarack skis like a mountain that has been open 20 years or more. Great top-to-bottom fall line cruising with bowls and glades at the top of the lifts. Snowmaking on the lower runs when they need it. Even with only two major lifts in [it now has a third], it skis big. Endless backcountry either north or south from a long ridge with easy access – and the runs all end at the resort or road.' There is a super-pipe and other terrain features. There are ambitious plans for a 'lively village with three distinct plazas', now under construction. Last season, hotel rooms and condos joined the lodging options, alongside chalets, townhomes and 'cottages'.

Jackson Hole in Wyoming is a resort with an impressive snow record and equally impressive steep slopes. Jackson is the nearest there is to a town with a genuine Wild West cowboy atmosphere. A 90-minute drive (or slower excursion buses) from Jackson over the Teton pass brings you to **Grand Targhee**, which gets even more snow. The slopes are usually blissfully empty, and much easier than at Jackson. The main Fred's Mountain offers 1,500 acres and 610m/2,000ft vertical accessed from a central fast quad. One-third of smaller Peaked Mountain is accessed by a fast quad, while the rest – over 1,000 acres – is used for guided snowcat skiing.

A little way north of Jackson, just inside Montana, is **Big Sky** (not to be confused with Big Mountain, away to the north), with one of the biggest verticals in the US (1280m/4,200ft). We visited in 2006, and were very impressed – particularly by the lack of crowds. From Big Sky you might visit **Bridger Bowl**, a 90-minute drive away. It boasts broad, steep, lightly wooded slopes that offer wonderful powder descents after a fresh snowfall.

A long way south of all these resorts, **Taos** in New Mexico is the most southerly major resort in America, and because of its isolation it is largely unknown on the international market.

642

SUN VALLEY RESORT / KEVIN SYMS

Ketchum, Idaho – an old mining town that found itself in the ski business when Sun Valley was developed in the 1930s →

Big Sky

Now America's biggest linked ski area, with extraordinarily quiet slopes; unappealing modern resort village at the base, though

NEWS

For 2007/08 a triple chair-lift is planned to serve the 212 acres of Dakota Territory, which Big Sky opened on Lone Mountain last season. This will also access other runs on Lone Mountain's south face, making the tiny cable-car less of a bottleneck.

Also in 2007/08, the Village Center One building is expected to open at the base.

For 2006/07 the beginner area was improved and a new mountain restaurant, The Pinnacle, opened on the slopes of Andesite Mountain.

➕ Ski area (shared with neighbouring Moonlight Basin) is now slightly bigger than Vail, with the bonus of a big vertical by US standards

➕ By far the quietest slopes you will find in a major resort, anywhere

➕ Excellent snow record

➕ Wide range of runs for all abilities, including great expert terrain

➕ Some comfortable slope-side accommodation, but ...

➖ Many condos are spread widely away from the lift base

➖ Base area lacks charm and a village focus, though things are improving, very slowly

➖ Resort amenities are limited, with little choice of nightlife

➖ Tiny top lift accessing the most testing terrain is prone to queues

➖ Isolated location – normally needs three flights to reach it from the UK

Big Sky is renowned for its powder, steeps and big vertical. Since the resort buried the hatchet with next-door Moonlight Basin and agreed a joint lift pass, the two of them have been able to boast the biggest linked ski area in the US. They should also be boasting the world's least crowded slopes – when we visited in February 2006, we were astonished by the lack of people. In a reversal of the general Alpine formula, they've created lots of trails, and hardly any visitor beds. And there are no cities nearby to generate a weekend influx.

We have no idea how they make this arrangement work financially. We're happy to take advantage of it while it lasts – and to put up with staying in the seriously flawed resort village. But if ambling around in the evening soaking up the mountain village atmosphere is part of your holiday, forget it.

THE RESORT

Big Sky has been purpose-built at the foot of the slopes on Lone Mountain and Andesite Mountain. The main focus of development is Mountain Village, right at the lift base, with three hotels, a handful or bars and restaurants, a variety of shops and some slope-side condos.

Purpose-built it may be, but purpose-designed it was not. It is a hotchpotch of buildings in different styles (and from different eras) set vaguely around a traffic-free central plaza and bordered by car parks and service roads. The French-style underground Mountain Mall has shops and access to many of the bars and restaurants and some of the lodging. The village is emphatically not a place where you will enjoy an evening stroll.

Happily, improvements are in the pipeline. Over the next decade a new pedestrian village will take shape at the base. As part of this, a new retail, dining and accommodation building, Village Center One, is due to open at the base for 2007/08.

Some outlying condos and chalets are served by lifts to the slopes, others by free buses, but it's most convenient to stay near the main access lifts.

The resort is set amid the wide open spaces of Montana, one hour from the airport town of Bozeman, and it's a roundabout journey (normally involving three flights) to get there from the UK. Bridger Bowl ski area is an easy day trip by car.

THE MOUNTAINS

Taking Big Sky and Moonlight Basin's slopes together, they cover a big area (5,512 acres) spread over two linked mountains, with long runs for all abilities. There is a gondola, a so-called 'Tram' (see 'The slopes') and five fast quad chairs, but many of the chairs are still old triples and doubles. There are free mountain tours available at both Big Sky and Moonlight. It is cheapest to buy tickets just for the area you are staying in and to buy a Big Sky-Moonlight Interconnect ticket (substantially more expensive) only for days you intend to ski both areas.

KEY FACTS

Resort	2285m
	7,500ft
Slopes	2070-3400m
	6,800-11,150ft
Lifts	18
Pistes	3,812 acres
Green	17%
Blue	25%
Black	58%
Snowmaking	
	350 acres

Note: Big Sky and
Moonlight Basin
areas combined have
5,512 acres of slopes

LIFT PASSES

Big Sky

Prices in US$

Age	1-day	6-day
under 14	39	234
14 to 21	49	294
22 to 66	66	384
over 67	52	312
Free under 11		

Beginner first half-day
lesson includes lift
pass, then costs $25
to continue for the
rest of the day

Notes

Covers the lifts in Big
Sky. A day pass for
Moonlight alone is
$47 for adults. A joint
Big Sky-Moonlight
pass is $79 a day

THE SLOPES
Deserted terrain for all abilities

Lone Mountain provides the resort's
poster shot, with some seriously steep,
open upper slopes. From Mountain
Village a gondola and a parallel fast
quad go to mid-mountain. From there
you can get to the Lone Peak chair,
which takes you up to the Lone Peak
Tram – really two 15-person gondola
cabins, which are operated as if they
were a cable-car. This leads to the top
and fabulous 360° views (go up for the
view even if you don't fancy the runs).
A new triple chair-lift for 2007/08 is
expected to provide a second access
point to Lone's south face and its
steep bowls and glades. Lone
Mountain's lower slopes are wooded
and varied, as are those of **Andesite**

Mountain, which has less vertical, but
three of the fast lifts, including one
from Mountain Village. From various
points on Lone Mountain you can head
down to the **Moonlight Basin** slopes,
which start with a slow chair from
Moonlight Lodge. Runs from the top of
that lead to the Six Shooter fast chair
which, together with the slow Lone
Tree quad near the top, serves nearly
all Moonlight's wooded, largely easy
intermediate terrain. The Headwaters
lift at the top serves expert-only runs.

The amazing thing about the whole
area is how deserted the slopes are. In
February 2006 we often had runs to
ourselves. Between them, Big Sky and
Moonlight get an average of around
2,500 people a day on their slopes.
That means about two acres each.

Andesite has
great cruising
runs, although
the vertical
isn't huge

ANDESITE
2680m/8,800ft

Southern Comfort

Ramcharger

Thunder Wolf

Mountain
Village
2285m/
7,500ft

2070m/6,800ft
Lone Moose Meadows

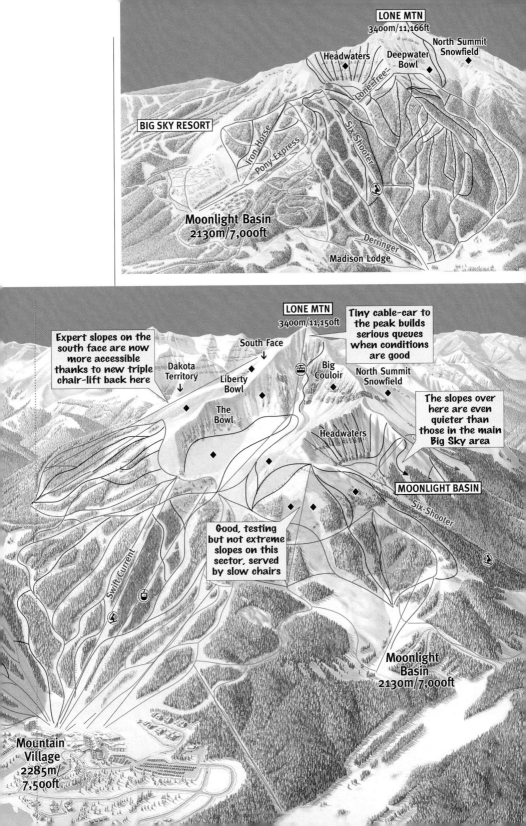

LONE MTN
3400m/11,166ft

Headwaters

Deepwater
Bowl

North Summit
Snowfield

Lone Tree

BIG SKY RESORT

Iron Horse

Pony Express

Six Shooter

Moonlight Basin
2130m/7,000ft

Derringer

Madison Lodge

LONE MTN
3400m/11,150ft

Tiny cable-car to
the peak builds
serious queues
when conditions
are good

Expert slopes on the
south face are now
more accessible
thanks to new triple
chair-lift back here

South Face

Dakota
Territory

Liberty
Bowl

Big
Couloir

North Summit
Snowfield

The Bowl

The slopes over
here are even
quieter than
those in the main
Big Sky area

Headwaters

MOONLIGHT BASIN

Six-Shooter

Good, testing
but not extreme
slopes on this
sector, served
by slow chairs

Swift Current

Moonlight
Basin
2130m/7,000ft

Mountain
Village
2285m/
7,500ft

↑ Typical Moonlight Basin lift line – this is Iron Horse chair. OK, it's early in the day, but you get the picture
SNOWPIX.COM / CHRIS GILL

TERRAIN-PARKS
Choose from three
There's a terrain-park on Andesite, with rails, boxes, slides and a half-pipe, served by the Ramcharger fast quad. Lone Mountain has a half-pipe and a beginner park. The new Zero Gravity park at Moonlight has boxes, rails, berms and small hits, accessed from the Six-Shooter chair-lift.

SNOW RELIABILITY
No worries here
Snowfall averages 400+ inches – more than most resorts in Colorado. Grooming is good, too.

FOR EXPERTS
Enough to keep you amused
All of the terrain accessed from the Tram is single- or double-black-diamond. The steepest runs are the Big Couloir on the Big Sky side and the North Summit Snowfield on the Moonlight side. For both, you are required to have a partner to ski with, an avalanche transceiver and a shovel. We'd recommend a guide, too. There are easier ways down, though – Liberty Bowl is easiest (stay left for the best snow that the prevailing wind blows in). Marx and Lenin are a little steeper. The new Dakota Territory has opened up 212 acres of glades to skier's right of Liberty Bowl – a new triple chair-lift

is planned to serve it from 2007/08. Lower down, the Lone Peak Triple, Challenger and Shedhorn chairs also serve good steep terrain. There are some excellent gladed runs, especially on Andesite. In the Moonlight sector the Headwaters is the biggest challenge – but it gets windblown and you may have to pick your way through rocks at the top. The further you hike to skier's left the steeper the couloirs. There are some good gladed runs lower down.

FOR INTERMEDIATES
Great deserted cruising
The bulk of the terrain on both mountains is of intermediate difficulty (including lots of easy blacks). The main complaint we have is that they don't seem to groom any blacks – which means that you can't hurtle down them taking advantage of the lack of people. But there is lots of excellent blue run cruising served by fast chairs and with few others on the runs – Ramcharger and Thunder Wolf on Andesite, Swift Current on Lone Mountain and Six Shooter in the Moonlight sector. Several wide, gentle bowls offer a good introduction to off-piste. And there are some good easy glade runs such as Singlejack on Moonlight and The Congo on Andesite. In general the groomed blues in Moonlight are easier than those in Big Sky, especially the ones served by the Lone Tree chair. Adventurous intermediates could try Liberty Bowl from the top of the Tram; but be prepared for a rocky, windswept traverse between wooden barriers at the top to access the run.

FOR BEGINNERS
Ideal – shame Big Sky is so far
Go to Big Sky rather than Moonlight. There's a good nursery area at the base of the Explorer chair and gondola on Lone Mountain – improved for last season. There are long, deserted greens to progress to from those lifts and from the fast Southern Comfort lift on Andesite ('Sacajewa and Deep South would give timid skiers a real sense of adventure and achievement').

boarding
The terrain suits boarders well. Advanced riders will enjoy the steeps and the glades, free-riders the terrain-parks at Big Sky and Moonlight, and beginners and intermediates the easy cruising runs served by boarder-friendly chair-lifts.

CHILDREN

Lone Peak Playhouse
t 993 2223
Ages 6mnth to 8yr;
8.30 to 4.30;
$80 per day; $122
per day incl ski
school

Ski school
Ages 7 to 14; 9.30 to
3pm; $119 per day;
ages 13 to 17, 9.30
to 3.30, $124 per day

GETTING THERE

Air Bozeman 93km/
58 miles (1hr)

UK PACKAGES

*AmeriCan Ski, Ski
Dream, Ski
Independence, Ski
Safari*

ACTIVITIES

Indoor Solace Spa
(massage, beauty
treatments), fitness
centres in hotels
Outdoor
Snowmobiles, snow-
shoeing, sleigh rides,
tubing, horse-riding,
fly-fishing, visiting
Yellowstone National
Park

Central reservations
Call 995 5000

Phone numbers
From distant parts of
the US, add the prefix
1 406; from abroad,
add the prefix +1 406

TOURIST OFFICE

Big Sky
t 995 5000
info@bigskyresort.com
www.bigskyresort.com
Moonlight Basin
t 995 7716
resort@
moonlightbasin.com
www.moonlightbasin.
com

FOR CROSS-COUNTRY
Head for the Ranch
There are 75km/47 miles of trails at
Lone Mountain Ranch, and more at
West Yellowstone.

QUEUES
Only for the Tram
The tiny Tram attracts serious queues
on busy days – up to 45 minutes, we
hear. Queues are rare otherwise. But
there are still a lot of slow lifts. And a
January 2007 reporter complains that
'the gondola did not run all week' – to
save power, he heard.

MOUNTAIN RESTAURANTS
Back to base for lunch?
Big Sky's one option is the new
Pinnacle on Andesite, with table-
service inside, a large terrace, and live
music at weekends – but little space
for drinks-only customers. In Moonlight
there's the Headwaters Grill at
Madison. Otherwise, it's back to base.

SCHOOLS AND GUIDES
Good reputation
We lack recent reports but the Big Sky
ski school has a good reputation.

FACILITIES FOR CHILDREN
Usual high US standard
Lone Peak Playhouse in the slope-side
Snowcrest Lodge takes children from
age six months to eight years and will
take them to and from ski school
('perfection', says a reporter). It also
operates on Thursday evening, and
babysitters are available with 48 hours'
notice. Children 10 years and under ski
free. Moonlight has its own care
programme and a new kids' centre.

STAYING THERE

HOW TO GO
Prepare for a long journey
Only North American specialist tour
operators offer Big Sky.
Hotels There's not much choice at the
mountain.
***Summit (995 5000) Best in town;
central, slope-side, good rooms,
outdoor hot pool with mountain views.
***Huntley Lodge (995 5000) Big Sky's
original hotel; central, part of Mountain
Mall, outdoor pool, hot-tubs, sauna.
***Rainbow Ranch (995 4132) Five
miles south of Big Sky. Luxury riverside
rooms and cabins. Recommended.
**Buck's T-4 Lodge (995 4111) Down in
the valley. Refurbished, recommended.

Apartments The good-value Stillwater
condos have been recommended,
along with Arrowhead, Beaverhead,
Snowcrest Lodge, Big Horn and, way
out of town, Powder Ridge Cabins.

EATING OUT
A fair choice for a small place
Locals' recommendations include:
Huntley Dining Room (smart restaurant,
good prime rib); The Peaks in the
Summit (formal, lots of choice); The
Cabin (local buffalo and elk); Bambu
(Asian fusion); MR Hummers (ribs,
prawns, popular with locals); Chet's
(giant burgers, sandwiches). Ten years
after it shut down Whiskey Jack's is
back in town for burgers, beers and
live music ('good food, friendly staff').
Down in the valley at Buck's T-4 we
had excellent wild boar steak and a
2007 reporter enjoyed 'very good
game in a relaxed and informal
atmosphere'. They'll fetch you from
your condo. Rainbow Ranch has been
highly recommended for 'fine dining'.
Moonlight dinners and live music are
available at a backcountry lodge.

APRES-SKI
A few places to try
Chet's bar has live music and pool. The
Carabiner in the Summit had live music
when we were there, as does the new
Whiskey Jack's. The Black Bear can be
lively, and the basement Alpine Lodge
is popular with locals.

OFF THE SLOPES
Mainly the great outdoors
There's snowmobiling, snow-shoeing,
sleigh rides, a new floodlit tubing hill,
visiting Yellowstone National Park,
treatments at the Solace Spa; the
Huntley Lodge pool etc is open to all
for a fee.

Moonlight Basin

2135m/7,000ft
There's not much at Moonlight base
except a few condos and cabins and
the impressive Moonlight Lodge –
spacious and log-built, with high
ceilings and beams. The bar at the
Lodge is lively as the slopes close, and
Timbers restaurant there gets good
reviews. But we were disappointed by
the spa, and our nearby condo was
poorly maintained. Maybe the Cowboy
Heaven Cabins are better. We had an
enjoyable dinner a drive away at what
is now the Headwaters Grill.

Jackson Hole

Touristy 'Wild West' town, big, exciting slopes and a rapidly changing base village; in some eyes, the best the US has to offer

COSTS

① ② ③ ④ ⑤ ⑥

RATINGS

The slopes
Fast lifts	**
Snow	****
Extent	***
Expert	*****
Intermediate	**
Beginner	***
Convenience	***
Queues	***
Mountain restaurants	*

The rest
Scenery	***
Resort charm	***
Off-slope	***

NEWS

The new Bridger restaurant at the top of the gondola, originally scheduled to open last season, is now expected for 2007/08.

A temporary double chair-lift, East Ridge, has been installed to access the summit of Rendezvous until a new cable-car is up and running – for 2008/09, they say. Capacity on the Bridger Gondola was increased.

648

+ Some real expert-only terrain and one of the US's biggest verticals

+ Jackson town has an entertaining Wild West ambience

+ Unspoiled, remote location with interesting wildlife

+ Excellent snow record

+ Even more snow (and empty slopes) 90 minutes away at Grand Targhee

+ Some unique off-slope diversions

+ The town is only 15 minutes from the airport, but ...

– The town is also 15 minutes from the slopes – though the lift-base Teton Village is an increasingly attractive alternative

– Intermediates wanting groomed cruises will find the area very limited, especially in fresh snow

– Low altitude and sunny orientation mean snow can deteriorate quickly

– Inadequate mountain restaurants, though a new one is due this year

– Getting there from the UK involves two or three flights

With its wooden sidewalks, country-music saloons and pool halls, tiny Jackson is a determinedly Western town, designed to amuse summer visitors to Yellowstone – great fun, if you like that kind of thing.

For those who like steep slopes smothered in deep powder or plastered with big bumps, Jackson Hole is Mecca. Like many American mountains, Jackson has steeps that you can't find in Europe except by going off-piste with a guide. What marks it out is the sheer quantity of this terrain, and the almost Alpine vertical.

Of course, there is also skiing for those afraid of the black, but intermediates wanting to build up confidence should look elsewhere. This is partly because the place gets a lot of snow, and soft, fresh snow forms bumps, even on blues.

The ancient, locally revered bottom-to-top cable-car (carrying capacity an astonishing 270 people an hour) is no more. With a replacement not expected soon, the resort has installed a temporary chair-lift to access the top slopes.

With a double-capacity cable-car imminent, three smooth, upmarket hotels at the base and a table-service restaurant about to open on the mountain, Jackson Hole is changing. Locals who think Rendezvous belongs to them will tell you the place is losing its soul, going soft, selling out. Maturing nicely, we'd say.

THE RESORT

The town of Jackson sits at the south-eastern edge of Jackson Hole – a high, flat valley surrounded by mountain ranges, in north-west Wyoming. Jackson gets many more visitors in summer than in winter, thanks to the nearby national parks. To entertain summer tourists the town strives to maintain its Wild West flavour, with traditional-style wooden buildings and sidewalks, and a couple of 'cowboy' saloons. It has lots of clothing and souvenir shops, as well as upmarket galleries appealing to second-home owners. In winter it's half-empty and accommodation prices come down. A 2006 visitor was full of praise for the friendly and helpful locals. The free

town bus is reportedly 'very efficient'.

The slopes, a 15-minute drive or $3 bus-ride ('crowded') north-east, rise abruptly from the flat valley floor. At the lift base is Teton Village, which has expanded over the last few years to become a much more attractive base, with an increased choice of bars, restaurants and hotels – some of these notably upscale. We are told the expansion is starting to attract a wider range of visitors to the slopes, including more families. Homes to rent are spread over quite an area.

A popular excursion by car or daily bus is over the Teton pass to the smaller resort of Grand Targhee, which gets even more snow (and keeps it better, with gentler, shadier slopes). See the Rest of the West introduction.

↑ Rendezvous Mountain, still equipped in this picture with the now-defunct cable-car

JACKSON HOLE RESORT

THE SLOPES
One big mountain, one small one

For the moment, pending arrival of the new cable-car, the main lift out of Teton Village is the Bridger gondola. This goes up over a broad mountainside split by gullies, and gives speedy access to the chain of three chairs accessing the upper slopes of the big mountain that makes Jackson Hole famous – **Rendezvous**. The mountain provides a 1260m/4,130ft vertical – exceptional for the US. Without the cable-car, doing top-to-bottom laps is no longer very appealing – but you can do laps on the upper slopes using just the top two chairs. Alternatively you can work your way across from the gondola to **Apres Vous** mountain, with half the vertical and mostly much gentler runs, accessed from the village by the short Teewinot and the longer Apres Vous fast quad.

Snow King is a separate area right by Jackson town. There's a good choice of short, steep slopes. Locals use it at lunch time and in the evenings (it's partly floodlit).

TERRAIN-PARKS
Getting better

There's a terrain-park by the Apres Vous chair, with jumps and rails, music and a 137m/450ft long super-pipe. Dick's Ditch is a natural pipe and there's a mini-park for novices. But you really come to Jackson for the steeps and deeps of the free-riding.

THE MOUNTAINS

Most of the slopes are below the tree line, but one of the attractions of the place is that most of the forest is not dense. Trail classifications are accurate: our own small map doesn't distinguish black from double-black-diamond runs, but the distinction matters – 'expert only' tends to mean just that. There are complimentary tours daily.

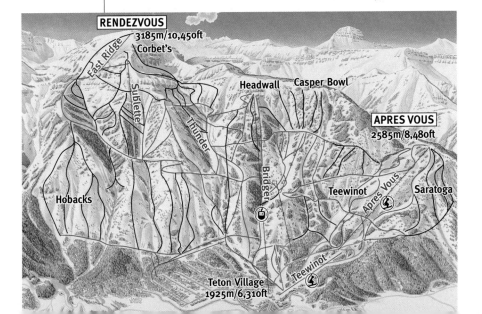

RENDEZVOUS
3185m/10,450ft
Corbet's
East Ridge
Sublette
Thunder
Headwall   Casper Bowl
APRES VOUS
2585m/8,480ft
Bridger
Hobacks
Teewinot   Apres Vous   Saratoga
Teewinot
Teton Village
1925m/6,310ft

KEY FACTS

Resort	1925m
	6,310ft

Jackson Hole	
Slopes	1925-3185m
	6,310-10,450ft
Lifts	12
Pistes	2,500 acres
Green	10%
Blue	40%
Black	50%
Snowmaking	
	160 acres

Grand Targhee	
Slopes	2440-3050m
	8,000-10,000ft
Lifts	5
Pistes	2,000 acres
(plus 1,000 acres	
served by snowcat)	
Green	5%
Blue	77%
Black	18%
Snowmaking	none

LIFT PASSES

Jackson Hole

Prices in US$

Age	1-day	6-day
under 15	36	204
15 to 21	59	330
22 to 64	72	402
over 65	36	204

Free under 6 (Eagles Rest and Teewinot lifts only)

Beginner ticket for Eagles Rest and Teewinot lifts ($10)

Notes
Covers all lifts in Jackson Hole. Half-day ticket available

Alternative passes
Grand Targhee; Snow King Mountain

boarding

Jackson Hole is a cult resort for expert snowboarders, as for skiers: the steeps, cliffs and chutes make for a lot of high-adrenalin thrills for competent free-riders. It's not a bad resort for novices, either, with the beginner slopes served by a high-speed quad chair. But intermediates not wishing to venture off the groomed runs will find the resort limited if staying more than a day or two. Two terrain-parks and a super-pipe provide the freestyle thrills. There are some good snowboard shops, including the Hole-in-the-Wall at Teton Village.

SNOW RELIABILITY
Steep lower slopes can suffer
The claimed average of 460 inches of snow is much more than most Colorado resorts claim. But the base elevation is relatively low for the Rockies, and the slopes are quite sunny – they basically face south-east. You may find the steep lower slopes, like the Hobacks, in poor shape, or even shut. Locals claim that you can expect powder roughly half the time, but even after a fall the Hobacks deteriorate quickly. Don't assume early-season conditions will be good.

FOR EXPERTS
Best for the brave
For the good skier or boarder who wants challenges without the expense of hiring a guide to go off-piste, Jackson is one of the world's best resorts – maybe even the best. Rendezvous mountain offers virtually nothing but black and very black slopes. The routes down the main Rendezvous Bowl are not particularly fearsome; but some of the alternatives are. Go down the East Ridge at least once to stare over the edge of the notorious Corbet's Couloir. It's the jump in that's special; the slope you land on is a mere 50°, they say.

Below Rendezvous Bowl, the wooded flanks of Cheyenne Bowl offer serious challenges, at the extreme end of the single-black-diamond spectrum. If instead you take the ridge run that skirts this bowl to the right, you get to the Hobacks – a huge area of open and lightly wooded slopes, gentler than those higher up, but still black.

Corbet's aside, most of the seriously steep slopes are more easily reached from the slightly lower quad chairs. From Sublette, you have direct access to the short but seriously steep Alta chutes, and to the less severe Laramie Bowl beside them. Or you can track over to Tensleep Bowl – pausing to inspect Corbet's from below – and on to the less extreme (and less chute-like) Expert Chutes, and the single-black Cirque and Headwall areas. Casper Bowl (now with named routes) – accessed through gates only – is recommended for untracked powder. The Crags terrain is an area of bowls, chutes and glades – but it involves a good half-hour hike to reach it. Thunder chair serves further steep, narrow, north-facing chutes.

Again, the lower part of the mountain here offers lightly wooded single-black-diamond slopes.

The gondola serves terrain not without interest for experts. In particular, Moran Woods is a splendid, under-utilised area. And even Apres Vous itself has an area of serious single blacks in Saratoga bowl.

The gates into the backcountry access over 3,000 acres of amazing terrain, which should be explored only with guidance. You can stay out overnight at a backcountry yurt. There are some helicopter operations.

FOR INTERMEDIATES
Exciting for some
There are great cruising runs on the front face of Apres Vous, and top-to-bottom quite gentle blues from the gondola. But they don't add up to a great deal of mileage, and you shouldn't consider Jackson unless you want to tackle the blacks. It's then important to get guidance on steepness and snow conditions. The steepest single blacks are steep, intimidating when mogulled and fearsome when hard. The daily grooming map is worth consulting.

FOR BEGINNERS
Fine, up to a point
There are good broad, gentle beginner slopes. The progression to the blue Werner run off the Apres Vous chair is gradual enough and the mid-mountain blues on the Casper Bowl chair are reached via the chairs from the beginner area. But few other runs will help build confidence.

SCHOOLS

Jackson Hole
t 739 2779

Classes
Full day (5½hr) $90
Private lessons
Half day (3hr) $310

CHILDREN

Kids' Ranch
t 739 2788
Wranglers: ages
6mnth to 2yr; 8.30-
4.30; $120 per day
Rough Riders: ages 3
to 6; 9am-3.30;
includes skiing; $120
per day
Little Rippers: ages
5-6; 9am-3.15;
includes boarding;
$185 per day

Ski school
Explorers: ages 7 to
14; 9.00-3.30; $120
per day

GETTING THERE

Air Jackson 19km/
12 miles (½hr)

JACKSON HOLE RESORT /
WADE MCKOY

The infamous Corbet's
Couloir; difficult to
see what all the fuss
is about, really ➔

FOR CROSS-COUNTRY
Lots of possibilities
There are three centres, and one at
Grand Targhee, offering varied trails.
The Spring Creek Nordic Center has
some good beginner terrain and
moonlight tours. The Nordic Center at
Teton has 20km/12 miles of trails and
organises trips into the National Parks.

QUEUES
What queues?
The defunct cable-car was famous for
its queues. But its capacity was trivial,
so it is no surprise that the substantial
increase in capacity of the Bridger
gondola has compensated for its loss –
aided by the fact that experts are now
unlikely to descend to the village
except at the end of the morning or
afternoon. We have no reports of
queues for the temporary East Ridge
chair-lift either. But the Teewinot chair,
serving the beginner area, is now said
to generate queues at peak periods –
another sign of the resort's changing
character, we wonder? Head towards
Apres Vous for quieter slopes first
thing, advises a 2007 reporter.
    One early-season visitor was very
critical of the poor information given to
visitors on the slope conditions ('we
were actively misled').

MOUNTAIN RESTAURANTS
They're building a second!
The restaurant at the base of the
Casper chair-lift does a good range of
self-service food, but gets very
crowded. The Bridger table- and self-
service restaurant is now expected to
open at the top of the gondola for
2007/08. There are simple snack bars
at four other points on the mountain.

SCHOOLS AND GUIDES
Learn to tackle the steeps
As well as the usual lessons, there are
also special types – steep and deep,
women-only, for example – on certain
dates. Backcountry guides can be hired
– Rendezvous Ski Tours is 'highly
recommended' by a reporter who
enjoyed exploring the backcountry
from Teton Pass and elsewhere.

FACILITIES FOR CHILDREN
Just fine
The area may not seem to be one
ideally suited to children, but there are
enough easy runs and the 'Kids'
Ranch' facilities are good. There are
classes catering for ages three to 17.

STAYING THERE

HOW TO GO
In town or by the mountain
Teton Village is convenient, while
Jackson has the cowboy atmosphere –
but bear in mind that some of the
town hotels are far from central.
Hotels Because winter is low season,
prices are low.
TETON VILLAGE
*****Four Seasons Resort (732 5000)
Stylish luxury, with art on the walls,
superb skier services, health club, an
exceptional outdoor pool, perfect
position just above the base.
****Teton Mountain Lodge (734 7111)
Very comfortable. Good indoor and
outdoor pool and fitness centre.
****Snake River Lodge & Spa (732
6000) Smartly welcoming and
comfortable, with fine spa facilities.
***Alpenhof (733 3242) Tirolean-style,
with varied rooms. Good food, lively
bar. Pool, sauna, hot-tub.
*Hostel x (733 3415) Basic, good
value. Recommended by a reporter.
JACKSON TOWN
****Wort (733 2190) Comfortable,
central, above the lively Silver Dollar
Bar. Hot-tub.
****Rusty Parrot Lodge (733 2000)
Stylish place with a rustic feel. Hot-tub.
'Awesome' breakfasts.

ACTIVITIES

Indoor Fitness centres, swimming, tennis, library, concerts, wildlife art and other museums

Outdoor Snowmobiles, snow-shoeing, sleigh rides, dog-sledding, hot springs, snowkite boarding

UK PACKAGES

Alpine Answers, AmeriCan Ski, American Ski Classics, Crystal, Inghams, Momentum, Mountain Tracks, Ski Activity, Ski All America, Ski Dream, Ski Freshtracks, Ski Independence, Ski Line, Ski Safari, Ski Solutions, Skitracer, Skiworld, Supertravel, Trailfinders, United Vacations

Phone numbers From distant parts of the US, add the prefix 1 307; from abroad, add the prefix +1 307

TOURIST OFFICES

Jackson Hole t 733 2292 info@jacksonhole.com www.jacksonhole.com

***Painted Porch** (733 1981) Gorgeous B&B full of antiques.

***Lodge at Jackson Hole** (739 9703) Western-style place on outskirts. Comfortable mini-suite rooms, and free breakfast. Pool, sauna, hot-tubs. Shuttle to the slopes. 'Good value,' says a 2007 visitor.

**Forty Niner Inn and Suites (733 7550) Central, good value. Recently recommended.

**Trapper Inn (733 2648) Friendly, good value, fairly central. Hot-tubs.

BETWEEN THE TWO

*****Amangani Resort (734 7333) Hedonistic luxury in isolated position way above the valley.

****Spring Creek Ranch (733 8833) Exclusive retreat; cross-country on hand. Hot-tub.

Apartments There is lots of choice around Jackson and at Teton Village.

EATING OUT
A reasonable range of options

In classic American style, Jackson offers a good range of excellent dining options. To check out menus, get hold of the local dining guide.

Most of the best bets at Teton Village are in the hotels. One reporter enjoyed 'scallops to die for' at the Alpenhof Bistro. The Vertical (Inn at Jackson Hole) is excellent, with a short, eclectic menu and a long wine list. It's rivalled by the Cascade Grillhouse and Spirits (Teton Mountain Lodge). Options at the Four Seasons include the Peak – a 'good value' casual place. The lively Mangy Moose does steaks and seafood.

In Jackson town there is more choice. The cool art-deco Cadillac Grille serves 'well-prepared fish dishes'. The Blue Lion is small and casually stylish. The 'saloons' (see 'Après-ski') do hearty meals and good steaks. The Rusty Parrot Lodge is recommended 'for a treat'. Thai Me Up does 'good value, decent food', the cute log cabin Sweetwater serves 'Greek-inspired' food, and Stone Table does 'awesome' South American dishes as well as tapas. The Snake River brew-pub – not to be confused with the excellent but expensive Snake River Grill – serves 'award winning beers and excellent pasta'. The Old Yellowstone Garage has 'superb Italian food in an elegant setting', Nani's (also Italian) is 'surprisingly inexpensive', and Rendezvous Bistro is popular with reporters and locals ('tasty meals,

excellent service'). We're told that you won't get a beer at Bubba's BBQ but they serve 'great ribs'.

Out of town, The Grill at Amangani has 'a supremely stylish setting, stunning food and prices lower than expected'. Calico is a much more modest spot – a large Italian place, popular with locals.

APRES-SKI
Amusing saloons

For immediate après-ski at Teton Village, the Mangy Moose is a big, happy, noisy place, often with live music ('a cool hangout', says a snowboarder). For a quieter time head for The Bar at the Alpenhof.

In Jackson there are two famous 'saloons'. The Million Dollar Cowboy Bar features saddles as bar stools and a stuffed grizzly bear, and is usually the liveliest place in town, with live music and dancing some nights. The Silver Dollar around the corner is less tacky and more subdued; there may be ragtime playing as you count the 2032 silver dollars inlaid into the counter. The Rancher is a huge pool-hall. The Shady Lady saloon sometimes has live music. The Virginian saloon is much quieter and a locals' hang-out: 'If you like beer, guns and ammo, you'll be in good company,' says one. For a night out of town, join the locals at the Stagecoach Inn at Wilson, especially Sundays for church: 'A real Western and blue grass swing night with music from a band that has not missed a night since 1969.'

OFF THE SLOPES
'Great' outdoor diversions

Yellowstone National Park is 100km/ 62 miles to the north. You can tour the park by snowcat or snowmobile with a guide; numbers are now restricted to reduce pollution. Some visitors really enjoy the park; we were distinctly underwhelmed. The National Elk Refuge, with the largest elk herd in the US, is next to Jackson – 'You can get really close to the elk,' says one reporter – and across the road from the National Museum of Wildlife Art. Reporters recommend both. In town there are some 40 galleries and museums and a 'good range' of shops, including a number of outlets for Western arts and crafts. Joining the Jackson Hole Ski Club ($30) is recommended – good discounts in shops, restaurants, lodgings etc.

New England

You go to Utah for the deepest snow, to Colorado for the lightest powder and swankiest resorts, to California for big mountains and low prices. You go to New England for ... well, for what? Extreme cold? Rock-hard artificial snow? Mountains too limited to be of interest beyond New Jersey? Yes and no: all of these preconceptions have some basis, but they are an incomplete and unfair picture.

Yes, it can be cold: one of our reporters recorded −27°C, with wind chill producing a perceived −73°C. Early in the season, people wear face masks to prevent frostbite. It can also be warm – another reporter had a whole week of rain that washed away the early-season snow. The thing about New England weather is that it varies – rather like ours. The locals' favourite saying is: 'If you don't like the weather in New England, wait two minutes.'

New England doesn't usually get much super-light powder or deep snow to play in. But the resorts have big snowmaking installations, designed to ensure a long season and to help the slopes to 'recover' after a thaw or a spell of rain. They were the pioneers of snowmaking technology; and 'farming' snow, as they put it, is an art form and a way of life – provided the weather is cold enough. Many of the resorts get impressive amounts of natural snow too – in some seasons.

The mountains are not huge in terms of trail mileage (the largest, Killington, is the smallest American resort to get its own chapter in these pages). But several have verticals of over 800m/2,620ft (on a par with Colorado resorts such as Keystone), and most have over 600m/1,970ft (matching Breckenridge), and are worth considering for a short stay, or even for a week if you like familiar runs. For more novelty, a two- or three-centre trip is the obvious solution. Most resorts suit snowboarders well, often having more than one terrain-park.

You won't lack challenge – most of the double-black-diamond runs are seriously steep. And you won't lack space: most Americans visit over weekends, which means deserted slopes on weekdays – except at peak holiday periods. It also means the resorts are keen to attract long-stay visitors, so UK package prices are low.

But the big weekend and day-trip trade also means that few New England resorts have developed atmospheric resort villages – just a few condos and a hotel, maybe, with places to stay further out geared to car drivers.

New England is easy to get to from Britain – a flight to Boston, then perhaps a three- or four-hour drive to your resort. And there are some pretty towns to visit, with their clapboard houses and big churches. You might also like to consider spending a day or two in Boston – one of America's most charming cities. And you could have a shopping spree at the factory outlet stores that abound in New England.

We cover two of the most popular resorts on the UK market in the chapters that follow – a long chapter on **Killington**, a short one on **Stowe**. But there are many other small areas, too, shown on the map and covered in our directory at the back of the book. Consider renting a car and visiting several resorts.

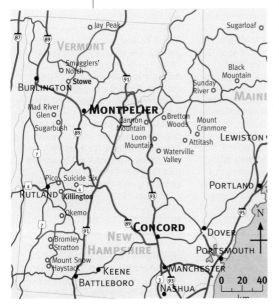

653

Killington

New England's leading resort, in most respects; good slopes, great après-ski, no village – but they're working on it, at last

COSTS

① ② ③ ④ ⑤ ⑥

RATINGS

The slopes

Fast lifts	**
Snow	***
Extent	**
Expert	***
Intermediate	***
Beginner	****
Convenience	*
Queues	****
Mountain restaurants	*

The rest

Scenery	***
Resort charm	*
Off-slope	*

NEWS

Killington was sold this year. The new owners intend to continue with plans to develop a base village in the Snowshed and Ramshead areas: work on the first stage is due to begin in 2009.

For 2006/07 the Snowshed Family Adventure Centre opened at the base – with an array of kids' activities indoors and out. And the Killington Grand opened a spa facility.

KEY FACTS

Resort	670m
	2,200ft
Slopes	355-1285m
	1,170-4,220ft
Lifts	33
Pistes	1,209 acres
Green	26%
Blue	34%
Black	40%
Snowmaking	92 km
	57 miles

➕ The biggest mountain in the east, matching some Colorado resorts

➕ Lively après-ski, with lots of bar-restaurants offering happy hours and late-night action

➕ Excellent nursery slopes

➕ Comprehensive and very effective snowmaking

➕ Good childcare, although it's not a notably child-oriented resort

➖ No resort village yet: hotels, condos and restaurants are widely spread, mostly along the five-mile access road – a car is almost a necessity

➖ Crowds on holidays and weekends

➖ New England weather – highly changeable, and can be very cold

➖ The trail network is complex, and there are lots of trail-crossings

➖ Terminally tedious for anyone who is not a skier or boarder

It's difficult to ignore Killington. It claims to have the largest mountain, largest number of quad chairs, largest grooming fleet and longest season in the eastern US, and the biggest snowmaking installation in the world. (It tries to be the first resort in the US to open, in October, but often shuts again shortly afterwards.) It also claims to have America's longest lift and longest trail (a winding 16km/10 miles) and New England's steepest mogul slope (Outer Limits – average gradient 46%). These things may matter if your choice of destination is limited to those in the eastern US. In the general scheme of things, they count for very little. Killington is a minor resort, chiefly of interest if you find yourself within driving distance at a time when conditions look good.

THE RESORT

Killington is an extraordinary resort, especially to European eyes. Most of its hotels and restaurants are spread along a five-mile approach road. The nearest thing you'll find to a focus is the occasional set of traffic lights with a cluster of shops, though there is a concentration of buildings along a two-and-a-half mile stretch of the road. The resort caters mainly for weekend visitors who drive in from the east-coast cities. The car is king; but there's also a good 'but infrequent' free day-time shuttle-bus service around the base areas and lodgings. Beyond this it costs $2.

There are lodgings around the lift base, and plans for something like a village there have been revived; the resort has new owners and we are told that development is planned to begin in 2009.

Staying near the start of the access road leaves you well placed for the gondola station on the main highway leading past the resort, and for outings to Pico, a separate little mountain in the same ownership, perhaps one day to be linked to Ramshead.

THE MOUNTAINS

Runs spread over a series of wooded peaks, all quite close together but giving the resort a basis for claiming to cover six mountains – or seven if you count Pico. An impressive number of runs and lifts are crammed into a modest area. To some extent the terrain on each sector suits a different ability level. But there are also areas where a mixed ability group would be happy, and there are easy runs from top to bottom of each peak.

Some runs of all levels are left to form bumps; there is half-and-half grooming on selected trails; and terrain features – ridges etc – are created. There are also thinned-out forest areas, not groomed or patrolled, where you pick your own line. They come in blue and single- and double-black-diamond grades. We found them great fun.

THE SLOPES
Complicated
The Killington Base area has chairs radiating to three of the six peaks – **Snowdon**, **Killington** (the high-point of the area) and **Skye** – the last also accessible by a gondola starting beside

LIFT PASSES

Killington Mountain Pass

Prices in US$

Age	1-day	6-day
under 13	47	252
13 to 18	56	306
19 to 64	72	384
over 65	47	252

Free under 6

Beginner included in price of lessons

Notes
Covers Killington and Pico ski areas; prices include sales tax; discount if you book online seven days in advance; special prices for lift pass, equipment and lessons combined

boarding

A cool resort like Killington has to take boarding seriously, and it does. There are terrain features scattered around the area, with lots of interest for all levels, and parts of the mountain have been reshaped to cut out some of the unpleasant flats on green runs. There are excellent beginner slopes, and plenty of friendly (ie slow-loading) high-speed chair-lifts – and the Perfect Turn Discovery Center caters just for beginners. Several big-name board events are held here, and the terrain-parks just get bigger and better.

US Highway 4. Novices and families head for the other main base area, which has two parts: Snowshed, at the foot of the main beginner slope, served by several parallel chairs; and Ramshead, just across the road up to Killington Base, where there's a Family Center at the foot of the entirely gentle **Ramshead** mountain.

The two remaining peaks are behind Skye Peak; they can be reached by trails from Killington and Skye, but each also has a lift base accessible by road. **Bear** is the experts' hill, served by two quad chairs from its mid-mountain base area. The sixth 'peak', **Sunrise**, is a slight blip on the mountainside, with a short triple chair up from the Sunrise Village condos. The result of all this is a complex network of runs; signposting hasn't been adequate in the past, but concentrated efforts to improve matters have paid off, says a recent reporter – 'colour coding for each mountain and trail maps located by each lift and junction'.

There are free guided tours given by 'knowledgeable, enthusiastic and entertaining' 'ambassadors'.

TERRAIN-PARKS
Lots of possibilities
There's a good choice, including early and late season parks (plus one at Pico). Bear mountain is home to the main freestyle area, with separate sections along the Wildfire, Bear Trap and Dreammaker trails. Features include a super-pipe, jumps, table-tops and an urban-style rail park. There's also a boarder-cross course with berms and rollers. All suit advanced riders best. Timberline on Ramshead has a quarter-pipe and is better suited to intermediates. Easy Street is a beginner mini-park, and kids have their own park and pipe classes. The new Snow Action Park at Snowshed offers kids the chance to jib and skate into the evenings.

SNOW RELIABILITY
Good if it's cold
Killington has a good snowfall record and a huge snowmaking system – although one reporter was surprised to find this little used during his peak season visit, despite low temperatures. But even that is no good if temperatures are too high to operate

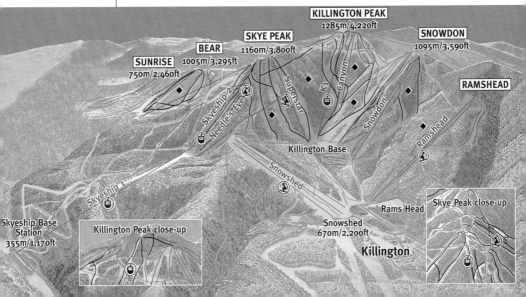

KILLINGTON PEAK
1285m/4,220ft

SKYE PEAK
1160m/3,800ft

SNOWDON
1095m/3,590ft

BEAR

SUNRISE
1005m/3,295ft

750m/2,460ft

RAMSHEAD

Skyeship 2

Needle's Eye

Superstar

K1

Canyon

Snowdon

Ramshead

Killington Base

Snowshed

Skyeship 1

Rams Head

Skye Peak close-up

Skyeship Base Station
355m/1,170ft

Killington Peak close-up

Snowshed
670m/2,200ft

Killington

SCHOOLS

Perfect Turn
t 1 800 923 9444
Learn to ski clinics
(including lift pass,
equipment and use of
Discovery Center)
1 day $89
3 days $199

Classes
One 2hr group lesson
$47
Private lessons
$100 for 1hr

CHILDREN

t 1 800 923 9444
Friendly Penguin Day Care
Ages 6wk to 6yr; $76
a day
First Tracks
Ages 2 to 3; 8.30-
4.00; $90 a day;
includes skiing
MiniStars/Lowriders
Ages 4 to 6; 8.30-
3.30; $100 a day;
includes skiing

Ski school
'Superstars' for ages
7 to 12 and
'Snowzone' for ages
13 to 18 ($89 for a
full day)

UK PACKAGES

American Ski Classics, Crystal, Directski.com, Independent Ski Links, Inghams, Ski All America, Ski Dream, Ski Independence, Ski Line, Ski McNeill, Ski Safari, Ski Solutions, Skitracer, Thomson, Trailfinders, Virgin Snow

GETTING THERE

Air Boston 251km/
156 miles (2½hr)

it. Bad weather can ruin a holiday even in mid-season. A reporter who had new powder each night on a March visit went back at the same time the following year to find people skiing in shorts and T-shirts on the few runs that were open. A February visitor told of 'everything from frostbite warnings to pouring rain'. Grooming has been reported to be poor, but the resort has recently bought additional machines, which should help.

FOR EXPERTS
Some challenges
The main areas that experts head for are Killington Peak, where there is a handful of genuine double-diamond fall-line runs under the two chair-lifts, and Bear mountain – though one reporter did not find them very challenging. Most of the slopes here are single blacks, but Outer Limits, under the main quad chair, is a double-diamond, claimed to be 'the steepest mogul slope in the east'. We suspect there are steeper runs at Stowe and Smugglers' Notch, in fact. There are two or three worthwhile blacks on Snowdon and Skye, too. The designated glades on Skye, Snowdon and Bear are also well worth seeking out.

FOR INTERMEDIATES
Limited extent
There are lots of easy cruising blue and green runs all over the slopes, except on Bear mountain, where the single blacks present a little more of a challenge for intermediates. Snowdon is a splendid area for those who like to vary their diet, although a reporter favoured the trails on Skye. There's a blue-classified gladed area on Ramshead. One reporter enjoyed an outing to Pico but complained that the blue run down was more difficult than some blacks.

FOR BEGINNERS
Splendid
The facilities for complete beginners are excellent. The Snowshed home slope is really one vast nursery slope served by three chair-lifts and a very slow drag-lift. Ramshead also has excellent gentle slopes. The ski school runs a special, purpose-built Discovery Center just for first-time skiers and boarders – they introduce you to the equipment, show you videos and provide refreshments.

FOR CROSS-COUNTRY
Two main options
Extensive loops are available at two specialist 'resorts' – Mountain Meadows, down on US Highway 4, and Mountain Top Ski Touring, just a short drive away at Chittenden.

QUEUES
Weekend crowds
Killington gets a lot of weekend and holiday business, but at other times the slopes and lifts are likely to be quiet. One holiday visitor found long lines for the Ramshead chair, the K1 gondola and the Bear Mountain chair. Overcrowded slopes are more of a problem than lift queues – the approaches to Bear lift base were singled out by a reporter.

MOUNTAIN RESTAURANTS
Bearable base lodges
The Killington Peak Lodge is the only real mountain restaurant; we lack recent reports, but we've received mixed reports in the past. There's a warming hut at Northbrook station on Skye Peak where you can get soups, and areas are provided if you wish to bring your own food. Most people use the base lodges; those at Bear, Ramshead and Snowshed have all been improved, and reporters comment on 'freshly cooked food' and 'affordable prices'. Bennedito's Bistro at the Snowshed Lodge now offers a family menu. But the K-1 lodge is said to be the liveliest of the bunch.

SCHOOLS AND GUIDES
In search of the Perfect Turn
The philosophy of the Perfect Turn school is to build on your strengths, and it seems to work for most people. Beginners start and finish their day in a dedicated building with easy chairs, coffee, videos and help with fitting equipment. Speciality clinics include mogul weekends and park classes.

FACILITIES FOR CHILDREN
Fine in practice
There is a Family Center at the Ramshead base, which takes kids from six weeks and will introduce them to skiing from age two years. Classes are reported to be small. The new Snowshed Adventure Center at the Snowshed base offers most snow-related sports you can think of, as well as indoor amusements and a family dining area at the lodge.

↑ Partying is one thing they know about at Killington

KILLINGTON RESORT

ACTIVITIES

Indoor Killington Grand Resort Hotel has massage, fitness centre, outdoor pool, hot-tub, sauna; theatre, cinemas, bowling, at Rutland; climbing wall at Snowshed base

Outdoor Ice rink, snow-shoeing, dog-sledding, snowmobile tours, tubing, sleigh rides

Central reservations phone number
Call 1 800 621 6867 (toll-free from within the US)

Phone numbers
From distant parts of the US, add the prefix 1 802; from abroad, add the prefix +1 802

TOURIST OFFICE

t 422 3333
info@killington.com
www.killington.com

STAYING THERE

HOW TO GO
Wide choices
There is a wide choice of places to stay. As well as hotels and condos, there are a few chalets.

Hotels There are a few places near the lifts, but most are a drive or bus-ride away, down Killington Road or on US4.
***Cortina Inn** (773 3333) 20 minutes away on US4, near Pico; pool, 'excellent food, poor soundproofing'.
****Grand Resort** (422 6888) Swanky resort-owned place at Snowshed, with outdoor pool and health club.
***Inn of the Six Mountains** (228 4676) Couple of miles down Killington Road; 'spacious rooms, good pool'.
North Star Lodge (422 2296) Well down Killington Road; 'good budget accommodation'.

EATING OUT
You name it
There are all sorts of restaurants spread along the Killington Road, from simple pizza or pasta through to 'fine dining' places. Many of the places in the Après-ski section serve food – be aware, though, that most bars do not allow children. The local menu guide is essential reading. Choices, the 'excellent' Grist Mill, Hemingway's, Charity's and the Cortina Inn have been recommended. Sugar and Spice is reported to serve good breakfasts, as does Ppeppers, which also has 'good burgers' and desserts.

APRES-SKI
The beast of the east
Killington has a well-deserved reputation for a vibrant après-ski scene; many of its short-stay visitors are clearly intent on making the most of their few days (or nights) here.

Although there are bars at the base lodges, keen après-skiers head down Killington Road to one of the lively places scattered along its 8km/5 mile length. From 3pm it's cheap drinks and free munchies, then in the early evening it's serious dining time, and later on the real action starts (and admission charges kick in).

The train-themed Casey's Caboose is said to have the best 'wings' in town. Charity's is another lively bar, with an interior apparently lifted from a late-19th-century Parisian brothel. The Wobbly Barn ('expensive' but 'very good' food) is a famous live-music place that claims to be one of the leading après-ski venues in the US. The Pickel Barrel caters for a younger crowd, with theme nights. The Outback complex has something for everyone, from pizzas and free massages to disco and live bands.

OFF THE SLOPES
Rent a car
If there is a less amusing resort in which to spend time off the slopes, we have yet to find it. Make sure you have a car, as well as a good book. Factory shopping at Manchester is recommended (45-minute drive).

Stowe

Classic, charming Vermont town, some miles from its small but serious – and improving – area of slopes on Mount Mansfield

COSTS

① ② ③ ④ ⑤ ⑥

RATINGS

The slopes

Fast lifts	***
Snow	***
Extent	*
Expert	***
Intermediate	****
Beginner	****
Convenience	*
Queues	****
Mountain restaurants	**

The rest

Scenery	***
Resort charm	****
Off-slope	*

KEY FACTS

Resort	475m
	1,560ft
Slopes	390-1135m
	1,280-3,720ft
Lifts	13
Pistes	485 acres
Green	16%
Blue	59%
Black	25%
Snowmaking	90%

- ➕ Cute tourist town in classic New England style
- ➕ Some good slopes for all abilities, including serious challenges
- ➕ Few queues
- ➕ Excellent cross-country trails
- ➕ Great children's facilities
- ➕ Improving base area

- ➖ Slopes a bus-ride from town
- ➖ Slopes limited in extent – though the sectors are now linked
- ➖ New England weather – highly changeable, and can be very cold
- ➖ Slow chair-lifts in main sector
- ➖ Weekend queues
- ➖ No après-ski animation

Stowe is one of New England's cutest little towns, its main street lined with dinky clapboard shops and restaurants; you could find no sharper contrast to Killington. Its mountain, 10km/6 miles away, is another New England classic: something for everyone, but not much of it. Development of the lift base area takes a big step this year with the opening of an upscale hotel there.

THE RESORT

Stowe is a picture-postcard New England town – and a popular spot for tourists year-round, with bijou shops and more 3- and 4-diamond hotels and restaurants than any other place in New England except Boston. The slopes of Mount Mansfield, Vermont's snow-capped (though mainly wooded) highest peak, are a 15-minute drive away and much of the accommodation is along the road out to it. There's a good day-time shuttle-bus service, but a car is useful.

THE MOUNTAIN

There are two main sectors, now linked by lift. Free daily mountain tours. **Slopes** The main Mansfield sector, served by a trio of chair-lifts from Mansfield base lodge, is dominated by the famous Front Four – a row of double-black-diamond runs. But there is plenty of easier stuff, too. An eight-seat gondola serves a second part of this sector. Spruce Peak has the main nursery area at the bottom. A fast quad heads up to mid-mountain, and another now serves the upper slopes.

658

Octagon Web Cafe
1135m/3,720ft

Cliff House
1110m/3,640ft

Mount Mansfield

MANSFIELD

Smugglers' Notch →

SPRUCE PEAK
1035m/3,390ft

Front Four

FourRunner

Midway Base Lodge

Gondola Base
475m/1,560ft

Mansfield Base Lodge

Spruce Base Lodge

Toll House

↑ Lots of classic New England trails, cut narrowly through the trees

STOWE MOUNTAIN RESORT

NEWS

For 2007/08 the region's first new luxury hotel in over 50 years, Stowe Mountain Lodge, is due to open at Spruce. And a new day lodge is planned.

For 2006/07 a 10-person gondola connected Spruce Peak to Mt Mansfield at base level.

UK PACKAGES

American Ski Classics, Crystal, Directski.com, Erna Low, Ski All America, Ski Dream, Ski Independence, Ski Line, Ski McNeill, Ski Safari, Skitracer, Virgin Snow, Waymark

Central reservations phone number
Call 1 877 317 8693 (toll-free from within the US); from within the UK call 0800 731 9279

Phone numbers
From distant parts of the US, add the prefix 1 802; from abroad, add the prefix +1 802

TOURIST OFFICE

t 253 3000
info@stowe.com
www.stowe.com

The old link with Smugglers' Notch, from the top of this sector, is now a backcountry route. A new gondola links the bases of Spruce Peak and Mt Mansfield. Night-skiing is offered three times a week.

Terrain-parks Stowe has three terrain-parks and a super-pipe: one is for beginners, the others are best suited to advanced users. There's also a separate early/late season rail park.

Snow reliability This is helped by snowmaking on practically all the blue (and some black) runs of the main sectors, and on all of Spruce Peak – keeping the slopes 'in great shape,' says a 2007 visitor. Grooming is reported to be 'excellent'.

Experts The 'scarily narrow' and seriously steep Front Four and their variants on the top half of the main sector present a real challenge (if they are open) – and there are others nearby. There are various gladed areas.

Intermediates The usual New England reservation applies: the terrain is limited in extent; there's also a severe shortage of ordinary black runs (as opposed to double-diamonds). The gondola link between the sectors does at least mean that you can get around all the slopes easily.

Beginners The nursery slopes at Spruce Peak are now excellent. There are also splendid long green runs to progress to in the main sector, down to Toll House base.

Snowboarding Stowe attracts many snowboarders. Beginners learn on special customised boards at the Burton Method Center on Spruce Peak. There's a snowboarder-specific resort website: www.ridestowe.com.

Cross-country There are excellent centres scattered around (including one at the musically famous Trapp Family Lodge) – 150km/93 miles of groomed and 100km/62 miles of backcountry trails form the largest network in the eastern US.

Queues The area is largely queue-free mid-week, but we've had reports of 25-minute queues at weekends – the Four Runner quad has been mentioned. Improvements at Spruce Peak should have reduced congestion there.

Mountain restaurants The renovated Cliff House, at the top of the gondola, has good views, extra seating, table-service and a new menu; it is Vermont's highest restaurant, not surprisingly. Next best is Midway Cafe near the base of the gondola, with a BBQ deck and table-service inside.

Schools and guides We lack recent reports. You can try out the latest equipment, with instruction, at the Stowe Toys Demo Centre. Semi-private lessons are available (maximum of three in a group).

Facilities for children Facilities are excellent; the nursery takes children from age three months to three years.

STAYING THERE

How to go There are hotels in and around Stowe itself and along the road to the slopes, some with Austrian or Scandinavian names and styles.

Hotels The luxury Stowe Mountain Lodge is due to open for 2007/08 at Spruce base. 1066 Ye Olde England Inne is recommended (despite the appalling name), as are Stowehof Inn, Green Mountain Inn and the 'pleasant' and welcoming Stowe Inn. The Golden Eagle has 'excellent breakfasts', pool and hot-tub. The smart Inn at the Mountain, at Toll House, offers slope-side accommodation.

Apartments There is a reasonable range of condos available for rent.

Eating out There are restaurants of every kind. The Whip in the Green Mountain Inn, Gracie's, the Shed ('good ribs') and Trattoria La Festa have all been recommended.

Après-ski Après-ski is muted – Stowe reportedly goes to bed early. The Matterhorn, Shed and Rusty Nail ('draft beers and pool') on the access road are popular. There's a good cinema.

Off the slopes Stowe is a pleasant town in which to spend time off the slopes – at least if you like shopping. The Vermont Ski Museum is 'worth a visit', says a reporter; and a trip to the Burlington shopping mall and a tour (with samples) of Ben & Jerry's ice cream factory just down the road have also been recommended. There is snowmobiling and dog-sledding.

Stowe

**More British skiers and snowboarders go to Canada than to the USA.
In many ways it combines the best that the US has to offer – good
service, a warm welcome, relatively quiet slopes, good lift systems with
lots of fast lifts, frequent dumps of snow, great grooming and a high
standard of accommodation – with more spectacular scenery and lower
prices. It also has the advantage that you can get direct flights to its
main airports without having to change planes and go through customs
part-way through your journey. There are charter flights as well as
direct Air Canada and British Airways flights.**

If Canada – well, western Canada at least – has one central attraction,
it is snow. In an average year, you can expect much better snow than
in the Alps – not only good conditions on the pistes, but frequent
fresh falls to provide the powder you dream of. And, as in the States,
there is lots of steep terrain within resort boundaries, which is
therefore avalanche protected and safely skiable without guidance.

Of course, there are good years and bad years, just as in the Alps.
After an exceptionally poor year for snow in many western resorts in
2004/05, normal service was resumed in 2005/06 and 2006/07.
Whistler (with a claimed annual average of 360 inches of snowfall)
got a bumper 470 inches and 516 inches respectively. A few seasons
ago we spent two weeks driving from Whistler to Banff, calling in at
lots of smaller resorts on the way. For eight days in the middle it did
not stop snowing. The skiing was spectacular – day after day of dry,
light powder.

So you go to Canada for the skiing or boarding, not the sunbathing.
If you prefer long lunches on sun-drenched mountain restaurant
terraces, stick to March in the Alps. If you want a good chance of
hitting powder, head for western Canada. The east is different:
expect snow and extremes of weather, much like in New England.
The main attraction of Québec for us is the French culture and
unique ambience; it also has the advantage of a shorter flight time.

If you really want untracked powder and are feeling flush, there is
nothing to beat western Canada's amazing heli-skiing and snowcat
skiing operations. The idea is that you are taken to the middle of a
deserted mountain wilderness and let loose with a guide, who takes
you down untracked slopes to another spot in the middle of
nowhere, where you are picked up and taken to the top of another
mountain for another untracked run. And so it goes on! The main

take to the skies

low cost Direct Non stop flights to Canada

Toronto & NEW Montreal

£99

prices from one way inc tax

Vancouver & Calgary

£149

prices from one way inc tax

We have the lowest prices for all the ski resorts in Canada.. call, request a brochure or go online for our full range and prices.

0107 616 9904
www.canadianaffair.com

CANADIAN *Affair*

Prices based on departures from Gatwick in November 2007. subject to availbaility and terms and conditions. Flights also available from Manchester and Glasgow - see online for details.

Whistler is the biggest resort in North America, but its slopes are split over two hills linked only at the base. However, in a couple of years' time the mountain we're looking from (Blackcomb) will be linked by a record-breaking gondola to the one we're looking at (Whistler) ➔

difference is that heli-skiing is faster paced and more expensive than cat-skiing. You can do either by the day, but the hedonistic option is to book a few days or a week in a luxury dedicated lodge, so that you step out of the door each morning straight into the chopper or snowcat. There's much more about Canadian heli-skiing in the feature at the front of the book.

But if you resist heli-skiing or snowcat heaven, you'll find a holiday in Canada can be reasonably cheap. Package prices start at under £400 for a week in Banff (no meals included). Eating and drinking have tended to be cheaper than in the US or the Alps, although the recent decline in the value of the US dollar has almost certainly reversed that comparison.

Another distinct attraction of Canada is the Canadians. They share the American service culture – 'the customer is king' – but have a sincerity in putting it into practice that our reporters appreciate. In the west you'll also find spectacular scenery (when the clouds clear) that rivals that of the Alps, and is quite unlike what you generally find in the US. You may also see an impressive range of wildlife, especially in the Rockies and the interior of British Columbia – though the days of elk roaming the back-streets of Banff are over.

Young people should be aware that laws about buying and consuming alcohol are strictly enforced. The legal age is 18 in Alberta and Québec but 19 in British Columbia; carrying your passport as evidence of age is a good idea even if you are well over the required age. People unable to prove their age may be refused entry to bars and clubs, and refused drinks in restaurants.

Another disadvantage is that, as in the US, lifts close much earlier than in Europe – as early as 3pm in some cases.

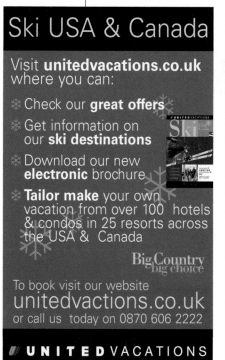

For international visitors to Canada, the main draw is the west. It has fabulous scenery, good snow and a wonderful sense of the great outdoors. The big names of Whistler, Banff and Lake Louise capture most of the British market, but there are lots of good smaller resorts that more Brits are now starting to explore. You can have a great trip by renting a car and combining two or more of these, perhaps with a couple of days on virgin powder served by helicopters or snowcats as well.

The three big resorts mentioned above and five of the smaller ones get their own write-ups in this section.

Whistler is plenty big enough to amuse you for a whole holiday, which is just as well, because it has a quite isolated position. Most visitors to Banff or Lake Louise, a half-hour drive apart, will spend time at the other resort.

Other places you might consider for a longer tour would include Silver Star and Jasper (which you can reach via the spectacular Icefields Parkway drive from Lake Louise), Apex, Red Resort and Kimberley – these have entries in the resort directory.

The big news this winter is the opening of a new resort, Revelstoke. Like Kicking Horse, it is a development of a small existing hill in heli-skiing territory, in this case Powder Springs.

This place seems set for stardom: the average annual snowfall is amazing – 500 to 700 inches – and when the main gondola is completed, the vertical will be 1830m/ 6,000ft – a new record for North America. The master plan provides for over 20 lifts over 15,000 acres – approaching Alpine mega-resorts in scale – plus 5,000 acres of cat skiing, plus heli-skiing direct from the resort centre.

Two main lifts will be open for 2007/08, and that huge vertical should be open the following year – along an extended runway at Kelowna (200km/ 125 miles away) capable of taking transatlantic jets. We can't wait.

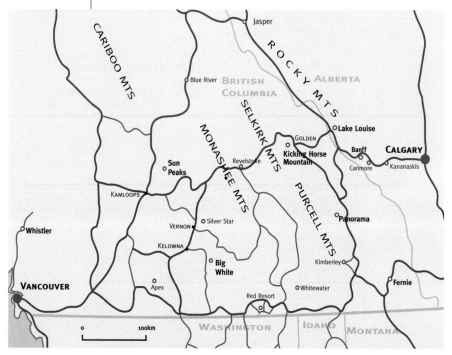

Banff

A major summer resort amid spectacular National Park scenery, with varied ski areas a bus-ride from town – including Lake Louise

COSTS

① ② ③ ④ ⑤ ⑥

RATINGS

The slopes
Fast lifts	****
Snow	****
Extent	****
Expert	****
Intermediate	****
Beginner	***
Convenience	*
Queues	****
Mountain restaurants	***

The rest
Scenery	****
Resort charm	***
Off-slope	*****

NEWS

At Sunshine, rooms at the the Sunshine Inn were renovated for 2006/07. The terrain-parks were also improved.

At Mt Norquay, the most recent improvements are to the resort's grooming fleet. Norquay also has new owners, who plan to focus future developments on families and beginners.

➕ Spectacular high-mountain scenery – quite unlike the Colorado Rockies

➕ Excellent snow and long season at Sunshine Village, the big local area

➕ Lots of touristy shops

➕ Good-value lodging because winter is the area's low season

➖ Sunshine is a 20-minute drive away, followed by a long access gondola

➖ Most lifts/runs are of limited vertical – 200/400m (660/1300ft) is typical

➖ You'll probably want to take in Lake Louise, too – a 45-minute drive

➖ Can be very cold, whether riding lifts or waiting for shuttle-buses

➖ Banff lacks ski resort atmosphere – though it's not an unattractive town

Huge numbers of British skiers and boarders go to Banff. Price has been a key factor in putting it on the map. Package costs have crept up, but most visitors are still delighted with what they find, and are keen to go back for more of Banff's distinctive combination of majestic scenery and excellent snow – plus the standard Canadian assets of people who are friendly and welcoming, and low prices for meals and other on-the-spot expenses.

We're not wild about the town of Banff, and we're distinctly unkeen on the daily commuting routine, even with a hire car – so our preferred strategy for a visit here is to stay a few nights up at Sunshine Village and then move on for a few nights at Lake Louise, which gets its own chapter.

THE RESORT

Banff is a big summer resort that happens to have some nearby ski areas. Norquay is a small area of slopes overlooking the town. Sunshine Village, reached by a long access gondola from a base station 20 minutes' drive from Banff, is a much bigger mountain; despite the name, it's not a village (it has just one small hotel at mid-mountain) – nor is it notably sunny. Most visitors buy a three-area pass that also covers Lake Louise, 45 minutes' drive away – covered by a separate chapter.

Banff is spectacularly set, with a few towering peaks on its outskirts. It has grown substantially over the years, but it still consists basically of a long main street and a small network of side roads built in grid fashion, lined with clothing and souvenir shops (aimed mainly at summer visitors) and a few ski shops. The buildings are low-rise and some are wood-clad. The town is pleasant enough, but lacks genuine charm; it's a modern tourist town, without much history in evidence.

Some of the lodgings (even on the main Banff Avenue) are quite a way from downtown. A car can be helpful here, especially in cold weather. But taxis are 'plentiful and cheap'.

Unless you stay mid-mountain at Sunshine Village (see 'Staying up the mountain'), getting to the slopes means a drive or a bus-ride. The traditional deal is that free, frequent but rather time-consuming and over-busy buses tour all the main hotels, picking up guests as they go. Note that the journey times we quote above are from when the bus leaves Banff – the total time can be longer. This scheme was in doubt, but as we go to press it has been confirmed for next season.

Buses are also arranged to the more distant major resorts of Panorama and Kicking Horse (see separate chapters) and the smaller (and closer) resort of Nakiska, and day trips for heli-skiing and boarding are offered locally. Banff Airporter does transfers to and from Calgary airport.

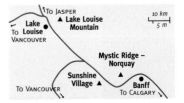

KEY FACTS

| Resort | 1380m |
| | 4,530ft |

Norquay, Sunshine
and Lake Louise,
covered by the Tri-
area pass

Slopes	1630-2730m
	5,350-8,950ft
Lifts	27
Pistes	7,748 acres
Green	23%
Blue	39%
Black	38%
Snowmaking	
	1,900 acres

Norquay only
Slopes	1630-2135m
	5,350-7,000ft
Lifts	5
Pistes	190 acres
Green	20%
Blue	36%
Black	44%
Snowmaking	85%

Sunshine only
Slopes	1660-2730m
	5,440-8,950ft
Lifts	12
Pistes	3,358 acres
Green	20%
Blue	55%
Black	25%
Snowmaking	none

THE MOUNTAINS

The Sunshine Village slopes are set on the Continental Divide – the watershed between the Pacific and the Atlantic – and as a result get a lot of snow. Most of the slopes above the village are above the tree line. Although there is a wooded sector served by the second section of the gondola, and some lightly wooded slopes higher up, in bad weather you're better off at Lake Louise. The season goes on until May.

Norquay is much smaller. But it's worth a visit, especially in bad weather or as a first-day warm-up – it has a small area of quiet wooded slopes

There are good, free mountain tours led by friendly volunteer hosts.

THE SLOPES
Lots of variety

The main slopes of **Sunshine Village** are not visible from the base station: you ride a gondola to Sunshine Village itself, with a mid-station at the base of Goat's Eye Mountain.

Goat's Eye is served by a fast quad rising 580m/1,900ft – much the most serious lift on the mountain. Although there are some blue runs, this is basically a black mountain, with some genuine double-diamonds at the extremities (including the 'backcountry' Wild West area).

Further up at Sunshine Village, lifts fan out in all directions, with short runs back from Mount Standish and longer ones from Lookout Mountain. Lookout is right on the Continental Divide. From the top here experts can pass through a gate and hike up to more 'backcountry' extreme terrain in Delirium Dive and Silver City.

Many people ride the gondola down at the end of the day. But the 2.5km/1.5 mile green run to the bottom is a pretty cruise. If you go down while the lifts are running, you can take the Jackrabbit chair to cut out a flat

section, but the run gets crowded and is much more enjoyable if you delay your descent a bit. The Canyon trail is a fun alternative for more advanced skiers and riders. Though the lower part is marked black, it's not steep – just a bit narrow and twisty in places.

The slopes at **Norquay** are served by a row of five parallel lifts and have floodlit trails on Friday nights.

TERRAIN-PARKS
Park – and ride ...

At Sunshine, the Rogers terrain-park on Lookout Mountain has some average-sized obstacles, including a wall-ride, several kickers and a host of rails and boxes – 'great fun', says a 2007 reporter. Shapers tend to add more features as the season goes on, but don't expect too much. But the park on Wawa is 'poorly maintained', according to a 2007 visitor. The bigger and more advanced park at Norquay has its own reduced Cascade park pass for avid freestylers. Gap jumps, tabletops, rails and boxes litter the park, which also boasts a good-sized half-pipe. On Friday nights from January to March the park is lit for night sessions. Then there's the superior Lake Louise park to try.

SNOW RELIABILITY
Excellent

Sunshine Village claims '100 per cent natural snow', a neat reversal of the usual snowmaking hype. In a poor snow season, some black runs can remain rocky (a 2007 visitor singles out those on Goat's Eye), but the blues are usually fine. 'Three times the snow' is another Sunshine slogan – a cryptic reference to the fact that the average snowfall here is 360 to 400 inches (depending on which figures you believe) – as good as anything in Colorado – compared with a modest 140 inches at Lake Louise and 120 inches on Norquay. But we're told the

boarding

Boarders will feel at home in Banff, and there is some excellent free-riding terrain. 'There are so many natural ledges, jumps and tree gaps to play with that the terrain-park seems almost unnecessary!' said a reporter. Delirium Dive is a controlled off-piste playground. A transceiver, probe and shovel are required to pass the start gate. Not for the faint hearted, this is steep and deep. But Sunshine also has some flat areas to beware of, where scooting or walking is required (such as the green run to the base), and the blue traverse on Goat's Eye is tedious. A trip to Lake Louise's Powder Bowls is a must for free-riders. There are specialist snowboard shops in Banff: Rude Boys, Rude Girls and Unlimited Snowboards.

Sunshine figures relate to Lookout, and that Goat's Eye gets less. At Norquay there is snowmaking on all green and blue pistes. So all in all, lack of snow is unlikely to be a problem in a normal season, and late-season snow on Sunshine is usually good (we've had great April snow there on recent visits).

FOR EXPERTS
Pure pleasure

Sunshine has plenty of open runs of genuine black steepness above the tree line on Lookout, but Goat's Eye is much more compelling. It has a great area of expert double-black-diamond trails and chutes, both above and below the tree line ('beautiful, quiet, a real adventure'). The slopes are rocky and need good cover, and the top can be windswept. But a contented reporter says that the double-diamond runs at skier's left hold their snow better than the rest of the mountain.

There are short, not-too-steep black runs on Mount Standish. One more challenging novelty here is a pitch known as the Waterfall run – because you do actually ski down over a snow-covered frozen fall. But a lot of snow is needed to cover the waterfall and prevent it reverting to ice. Also try the Shoulder on Lookout Mountain; it is sheltered, tends to accumulate powder and has been deserted whenever we've been there; access involves a long traverse that can be tricky (and was 'poorly marked' in 2007).

A popular backcountry route follows the back of the Wawa ridge, through a river valley ('great fun – tight turns in the trees of the riverbed'); a guide is essential, of course.

Real experts will want to get to grips with Delirium Dive and Silver City on Lookout Mountain's north face and the Wild West area on Goat's Eye (with some narrow chutes and rock bands) – a 2007 visitor did not see anyone on them in ten days. For all three you must have a companion, an avalanche transceiver and a shovel – and a guide is recommended. ('Book in advance' and 'rent your transceiver and shovel in Banff – you can't at Sunshine', advise disappointed reporters.) We tried Delirium in a group with the ski patrol, who provided equipment, and the scariest part was the walk in, along a narrow, icy path with a sheer drop (protected by a flimsy-looking net).

Norquay's two main lifts give only

SCHOOLS

Ski Big 3
t 760 7731

Banff-Norquay
t 760 7716

Sunshine Village
t 1 877 542 2633

Classes (Big 3 prices)
3 days guided tuition
of the three areas
C$259 incl. tax

Private lessons
Half day (3hr) C$376,
incl. tax, for up to 5
people

400m/1,310ft vertical, but both serve black slopes, and the North American chair accesses a couple of double-diamond runs that justify their grading.

Heli-skiing is available from bases outside the National Park in British Columbia – roughly two hours' drive.

FOR INTERMEDIATES
Ideal runs

Half the runs on Sunshine are classified as intermediate. Wherever you look there are blues and greens – some of the greens as enjoyable (and pretty much as steep) as the blues. We liked the World Cup Downhill run, from the top of Lookout to the Village. All three chairs on Mount Standish are excellent for building confidence, provided you choose a sensible route down. The slow Wawa chair gives access to the Wawa Bowl and Tincan Alley ('great first blues'). This area offers some shelter from bad weather.

There's a delightful wooded area under the second stage of the gondola served by Jackrabbit and Wolverine chairs. The blue runs down Goat's Eye are good cruises too, some of them with space to indulge in fast carving.

The Mystic Express quad at Norquay serves a handful of quite challenging tree-lined blues and a couple of sometimes groomed blacks.

FOR BEGINNERS
Pretty good terrain

Sunshine has a good area at the Village, served by a moving carpet. And there are great, long green runs to progress to – notably Meadow Park.

Norquay has a good small nursery area with a moving carpet and gentle greens served by the Cascade chair.

Banff is not the ideal destination for a mixed party of beginners and more experienced friends (who are likely to want to travel around more).

Goat's Eye has some great steep terrain – single- and double-black-diamond runs and an extreme zone. But it's very rocky and windswept and needs a lot of snow to be enjoyable

GOAT'S EYE
2600m/8,530ft

Deliriu Dive
◆◆

Goat's Eye

Wild West
◆◆

Wolverine

Gondola

1660m/5,440ft

2020m/6,630ft

If it's snowing hard, visibility is usually best on the easy runs in the trees around here and on the long run down to the bottom of the gondola

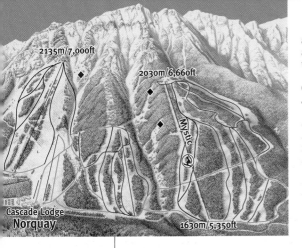

2135m/7,000ft

2030m/6,66oft

Mystic

Cascade Lodge
Norquay

1630m/5,35oft

around Lake Louise. Altogether, there are around 80km/50 miles of groomed trails within Banff National Park.

QUEUES
Sunshine can get busy
Half the visitors come for the day from cities such as Calgary – so the slopes are fairly quiet during the week. But Sunshine can get busy at weekends and public holidays; we've had reports of queues of up to 30 minutes for the gondola at Christmas and Easter, and there were big queues for Goat's Eye on our early April visit last year – though they moved quickly and there are effective singles line so you can jump the queue if in a hurry. But a 2007 visitor experienced only short queues ('no more than five minutes') during her February visit – despite school holidays. On busy weekends, we're told the trick is to arrive at the gondola by 9am.

FOR CROSS-COUNTRY
High in quality and quantity
It's a good area for cross-country. There are trails near Banff, around the Bow River, and on the Banff Springs golf course. But the best area is

---

Two of the extreme zones for which you need a companion, an avalanche transceiver and a shovel to be allowed to enter

LOOKOUT
2730m/8,95oft

Easy cruising along the Continental Divide – which helps to account for Sunshine's impressive snowfall record

Delirium
Dive

Silver City

Continental Divide

Angel

MOUNT STANDISH
2400m/7,87oft

Mount Standish

Sunshine Village
216om/7,080ft

Gondola

The Sunshine Inn is great for a couple of nights' stay. It's right on the slopes with a big outdoor hot-pool, a sauna and a good restaurant

2330m/7,64oft

GETTING THERE

Air Calgary 122km/ 76 miles (1½hr)

ACTIVITIES

Indoor Film theatre, museums, galleries, swimming pools (one with water slides), gym, squash, racquetball, weight training, bowling, hot-tub, sauna, climbing wall

Outdoor Swimming in hot springs, ice rink, sleigh rides, dog-sled rides, snowmobiles, curling, ice walks, ice fishing, helicopter tours, snow-shoeing

UK PACKAGES

Banff Airtours, Alpine Answers, AmeriCan Ski, American Ski Classics, Canadian Powder Tours, Crystal, Crystal Finest, Directski.com, Elegant Resorts, Frontier, Independent Ski Links, Inghams, Kuoni, Neilson, Ski Activity, Ski All America, Ski Dream, Ski Independence, Ski Line, Ski McNeill, Ski Safari, Ski Solutions, Skitracer, Skiworld, Supertravel, Thomson, Trailfinders, United Vacations, Virgin Snow, White Mountains **Sunshine Village** Ski Dream

CHILDREN

Tiny Tigers (Sunshine)
t 762 6560
Ages 19mnth to 6yr; 8.30-4.30

Kid's Place (Norquay)
t 760 7709
Ages 19mnth to 6yr; 9am to 4pm

Childcare Connection
t 760 4443
Childminding in guest accommodation

Ski school
Takes ages 6 to 12 (3 days C$275, incl. tax and lunch)

MOUNTAIN RESTAURANTS
Quite good

The newly renovated Sunshine Inn hotel has the best food – table-service in the Chimney Corner Lounge ('quality and service were excellent'). The Day Lodge offers three different styles of food on three floors (table-service in the top-floor Lookout Bistro, with great views). Mixed reports of the food. Mad Trapper's Saloon is a jolly Western-style place in Old Sunshine Lodge, serving good beer, but we have reports of poor food and service this year. Your only option on Goat's Eye is a functional tent-like structure at the lift base called Goat's Eye Gardens, which gets mixed reviews.

At the base of Norquay, the big, stylish, timber-framed Cascade Lodge is excellent – it has great views and a table-service restaurant upstairs as well as a self-service cafeteria.

SCHOOLS AND GUIDES
Some great ideas

Each mountain has its own school. But recognising that visitors wanting lessons won't want to be confined to just one mountain, the resorts have organised an excellent Club Ski and Club Snowboard Program – three-day courses starting on Sundays and Thursdays that take you to Sunshine, Norquay and Lake Louise on different days, offering a mixture of guiding and instruction and including free video analysis, a fun race and a group photo – and a smart dinner at the Fairmont Banff Springs. Reporters rave about it: 'absolutely brilliant', 'a great way to meet other people', 'learnt more in three days than I did in the whole week last year'. All abilities are catered for, including beginners. One reporter recommends booking a midweek group lesson: 'Normally only one or two people; I did an excellent Black Diamond class.'

FACILITIES FOR CHILDREN
Excellent

One reporter who used the facilities at Sunshine, Norquay and Lake Louise said: 'I'd recommend all three.' The school is praised: an 11-year-old experienced 'kind and friendly instructors', while his mum approved of the 'enthusiastic and motivational' tuition – but she also points out that 'enrolment can be chaotic and afternoon classes were less about learning, more about fun'.

STAYING THERE

HOW TO GO
Superb-value packages

A huge amount of accommodation is on offer; as well as hotels and self-catering, there are catered chalets.
Hotels Summer is the peak season here, with lower prices in winter (though they seem to have crept up in recent years).
*****Fairmont Banff Springs (762 2211) A late 19th-century, castle-style property, well outside town (with no shuttle-bus – you have to use taxis). It's virtually a town within itself – 2,000 beds, over 40 shops, several restaurants and bars, a nightclub and a superb spa (which costs extra).
****Rimrock (762 3356) Spectacularly set, out of town, with great views and a smart health club. Luxurious.
****Banff Park Lodge (762 4433) Best-quality, central hotel, with hot-tub, steam room and indoor pool.
****Banff Caribou Lodge (762 5887) On the main street, slightly out of town. A variety of wood-clad, individually designed rooms, sauna and hot-tub, good restaurant and bar. Repeatedly recommended by reporters.
****Banff International (762 5666) 'Central, saving walking in the evenings. Excellent, can't fault it,' said a recent reporter.
***Juniper (762 2281) At foot of Norquay and reachable on skis. Comfortable, good views, hot-tub. 'Service is outstanding and the food exceptional,' said a 2006 reporter.
**Homestead Inn (762 4471) Central, cheap, good-sized rooms, approved of by two recent reporters.
Apartments Don't expect luxury – but there are some decent options. The Banff Rocky Mountain Resort is set in the woods on the edge of town, with indoor pool and hot-tubs. Families have recommended the Douglas Fir resort ('kids loved the water-slides') – though it's 'a bit out of town'.

EATING OUT
Lots of choice

Banff boasts over 100 restaurants, from McDonald's to fine dining in the Banff Springs hotel.

We've enjoyed the designer-cool Saltlik – good game, steak and fish. Reader recommendations include Earl's (burgers and ethnic dishes, good wines/beers, very popular and lively), Magpie & Stump ('excellent', but busy

TOURIST OFFICE

Banff
t 762 4754
info@SkiBig3.com
www.SkiBig3.com
www.skibanff.com

SNOWPIX.COM / CHRIS GILL

There are sheltered
runs on Mt Standish
to retreat to if
conditions are hostile
on the open slopes of
Lookout, in the
distance ↓

Mexican, with Wild West decor),
Coyotes ('good fresh fish'), Caramba in
the Ptarmigan Inn (Mediterranean, 'well
worth the money'), the Keg ('fabulous
steaks', 'great ribs'), Wild Bill's ('the
biggest and best burgers in town',
dancing and live entertainment),
Melissa's ('good steaks', 'excellent
choice of beers', Bumpers ('big slabs
of rib', 'best steaks'), the Old Spaghetti
Factory ('great for families'), Tony
Roma's ('tasty ribs', 'fantastic value')
and Tommy's Neighbourhood Pub
('very informal atmosphere and good
food'). The Bison is a smart new place
('good food, nice atmosphere', with
live music). Evelyn's and Jump Start
('cosy and full of locals, not tourists')
are recommended cafes.

APRES-SKI
Livens up later on
Tea time après-ski is limited because
the town is a drive from the slopes.
But Mad Trapper's Saloon at the top of
the Sunshine gondola is popular
during the close-of-play happy hour
(with endless free peanuts). They also
do evenings with tobogganing, a
buffet, live music and dancing,
followed by a gondola ride down. In

town later, the two main live music
venues are the Rose & Crown and Wild
Bill's – country and western music with
line dancing. The St James's Gate Irish
pub has 'splendid Guinness'. Melissa's
and Saltlik are popular. The Elk and
Oarsman nightclub is popular. Hoodoo
Lounge attracts a young lively crowd;
Aurora is for more serious clubbing.

OFF THE SLOPES
Lots to do
Banff has lots to offer: wildlife to see,
lovely walks (including ice canyon walks
– Johnson Canyon is recommended),
and you can go snow-shoeing, dog-
sledding, skating and snowmobiling.
There are sightseeing tours and several
museums. Some reporters have been
disappointed by the natural hot
springs. Others have enjoyed evenings
in Calgary watching the ice hockey.

STAYING UP THE MOUNTAIN
Worth considering
The newly renovated Sunshine Inn
(762 6550) makes a very welcoming,
comfortable base at Sunshine Village.
Luggage is delivered while you ski.
Rooms vary in size. Big outdoor hot-
pool. Sauna. Good restaurant.

Banff

671

Big White

It's not big by Euro-resort standards, but it's certainly white. There are few places to match it if you want to learn to ski powder

➕ Great for learning to ski powder

➕ Extensive, varied slopes, quiet except at weekends and holidays

➕ Convenient, purpose-built village with high-quality, good-value condos

➕ Very friendly staff; good for families

➖ Visibility can be poor, especially on the upper mountain, because of snow, cloud or freezing fog

➖ Few off-slope diversions – and isolated without a car

➖ Limited après-ski

'It's the snow' says the Big White slogan. And as slogans go, it's spot on. If you want a good chance of skiing powder on reasonably easy slopes, put **Big White** high on the shortlist. But if you want a suntan (or lively après-ski, or extensive steep bowls and chutes), look elsewhere. Consider combining it with another BC resort such as Sun Peaks or Silver Star for variety.

THE RESORT

Big White is a rapidly growing, purpose-built resort. The village is rather piecemeal but attractive, and much accommodation is ski-in/ski-out. Reporters remark on the large number of 'friendly and happy' Aussie workers. Silver Star resort (see later in this chapter) is under the same ownership, and there are weekly day trips by bus.

THE MOUNTAINS

Much of the terrain is heavily wooded. But the trees thin out towards the summits, leading to almost open slopes in the bowls at the top. There's at least one green option from the top of each lift but the one from Gem Lake is narrow and can be tricky and busy. **Slopes** Fast chairs run from points below village level to above mid-

The resort, though small, is fairly spread out and most accommodation is ski-in/ski-out →

BIG WHITE / QUICK PICS / GAVIN CRAWFORD

NEWS

For 2006/07, the Snow Ghost Express opened, running parallel to the Ridge Rocket chair. The capacity of the Black Forest fast quad was increased by a third; and a new 135m/440ft moving carpet was installed in the Happy Valley beginner area. New boards were installed at the top of every lift to indicate which pistes are groomed.

A new 17-storey hotel and casino are being built, but they won't be ready until 2008/09.

KEY FACTS

Resort	1755m
	5,760ft
Slopes	1510-2320m
	4,950-7,610ft
Lifts	16
Pistes	2,765 acres
Green	18%
Blue	54%
Black	28%
Snowmaking	
	In terrain-park

UK PACKAGES

Alpine Answers, AmeriCan Ski, American Ski Classics, Frontier, Independent Ski Links, Ski All America, Ski Dream, Ski Independence, Ski Line, Ski Safari, Snowebb
Silver Star AmeriCan Ski, American Ski Classics, Frontier, Ski All America, Ski Dream, Ski Independence, Ski Line, Ski Safari, Snowebb

mountain, serving the main area of wooded beginner and intermediate runs above and beside the village. Slower lifts – a T-bar and four chairs – serve the higher slopes. Quite some way across the mountainside is the Gem Lake fast chair, serving a range of long top-to-bottom runs; with its 710m/2,330ft vertical, this lift is in a different league from the others. 'Snow hosts' (highly praised by reporters) run twice-daily guided ski tours.

Terrain-parks Served by a double chair and by Big White's first snowmaking, the excellent park includes a half-pipe, super-pipe, boarder-cross, rails and hits for all levels. It is floodlit at night and is highly praised by reporters.

Snow reliability Big White has a reputation for great powder; average snowfall is about 300 inches, which is similar to many Colorado resorts. At the top of the mountain the trees usually stay white all winter and are known as snow ghosts; they make visibility tricky in a white-out but are great fun to ski between on clear days.

Experts The Cliff Area at the top right of the ski area is of serious double-black-diamond pitch; the runs are short, but you can ski them repeatedly using the Cliff chair. The Sun-Rype bowl at the opposite edge of the ski area is more forgiving. There are some long blacks off the Gem Lake chair and several shorter ones off the Powder and Falcon chairs. There are glades to explore and bump runs too.

Intermediates The resort is excellent for cruisers and families, with long blues and greens all over the hill. Good intermediates will enjoy the

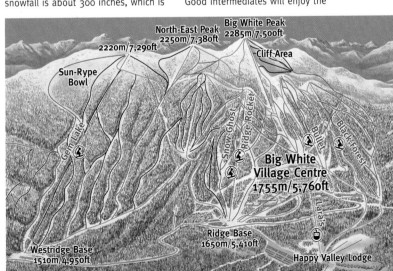

Central reservations
Call 765 8888; toll-free (within Canada)
1 800 663 1772

Phone numbers
From distant parts of Canada, add the prefix 1 250; from abroad, add +1 250

TOURIST OFFICES

Big White
t 765 3101
bigwhite@bigwhite.com
www.bigwhite.com

Silver Star
t 250 542 0224
star@skisilverstar.com
www.skisilverstar.com

easier blacks and some of the gladed runs too. In general the runs get steeper from right to left as you look at the mountain. There is marvellous easy skiing among the trees in the Black Forest area (which we loved when it was snowing) and among the snow ghosts (see above, which we loved when it was clear). Some of the blues off the Gem Lake chair are quite steep, narrow and challenging.

Beginners There's a good dedicated nursery area in the village and lots of long easy runs to progress to.

Snowboarding There's some excellent beginner and free-riding terrain with boarder-friendly lifts and few flat areas.

Cross-country Trails total 25km/16 miles.

Queues Queues are pretty rare and the new Snow Ghost Express seems to have eliminated any problems.

Mountain restaurants There aren't any – it's back to the bottom for lunch.

School and guides We receive rave reviews from reporters for both adult and children's lessons – and for the free mountain tours.

Facilities for children The excellent Kids' Centre takes children from 18 months. There are evening activities.

STAYING THERE

How to go There's an increasing range of packages to Big White including Canada specialist Frontier Ski and North America specialist AmeriCan Ski.

Hotels The White Crystal Inn receives better reports than the Inn at Big White.

Apartments Condo standards are high. We stayed at Stonebridge and loved it – big, central, well furnished, private hot-tub on the balcony. A 2007 reporter recommends the Towering Pines ('high quality, private hot-tub').

Eating out We had good meals in the Copper Kettle in the White Crystal Inn and the Kettle Valley Steakhouse at Happy Valley ('Superb food, amazing choice of wines,' says a 2007 reporter). Reporters also recommend Snowshoe Sam's ('imaginative food'), and Swiss Bear in the Chateau Big White. Frank's Chinese Laundry gets mixed reviews.

Après-ski The atmospheric Snowshoe Sam's has a DJ and live entertainment; try its trademark alcoholic gunbarrel coffee. Raakel's in the Hofbrauhaus has live music and dancing. The Snow Ghost Lounge in the White Crystal Inn has 'live music some nights and impressive malt whiskies'.

Off the slopes Happy Valley has ice skating, snowmobiling, tubing and snow-shoeing. There are two spas.

Silver Star 1610m/5,280ft

Silver Star is a small, slope-side resort with a compact car-free centre of brightly painted Victorian-style buildings with wooden sidewalks and pseudo gas lights. It's a bit Disneyesque but works well. There are several ski-in/ski-out condo-hotels, apartments and homes to let and a couple of decent restaurants, but après-ski is quiet. It is under the same ownership as Big White and easy to combine as a two-centre holiday or visit as a day trip.

There are slopes to suit everyone (but not many of them), with mainly easy intermediate cruising on the front (south) side of the mountain and mainly steep black and double-black diamond runs with big moguls on the back (north) side. Both are served by fast chairs. There are lots of flat areas, including the link with the back side, which make life difficult for boarders.

Cross-country is big; they claim 'The Best Nordic Skiing in North America'. There's a pretty ice rink on a lake and a nearby tubing hill.

Fernie

Lots of snow and lots of steeps – best explored with a guide; a choice of convenient base lodging or a drive from Fernie town

COSTS

① ② ③ ④ ⑤ ⑥

RATINGS

The slopes

Fast lifts	**
Snow	*****
Extent	***
Expert	*****
Intermediate	**
Beginner	****
Convenience	****
Queues	****
Mountain restaurants	*

The rest

Scenery	***
Resort charm	**
Off-slope	**

NEWS

For 2006/07 two new runs – a black and a blue – were built in Siberia Bowl.

The Lost Boys Cafe opened at the top of Timber Bowl. This is the resort's first sit-down on-mountain cafe; it's small and serves mainly soups and 'gourmet jacket potatoes'.

As we went to print, a press release arrived promising 'investment in mountain signage, so you can make your way around the mountain as well as a local! (Well almost)'. As you'll see overleaf, poor mountain signage is one of our major criticisms of the resort. We welcome this move ... but wait to see what they come up with.

SNOWPIX.COM / CHRIS GILL

There are a few perfectly groomed pistes, but the ungroomed steeps are what Fernie is all about →

+ Good snow record, with less chance of rain than at Whistler (and less chance of Arctic temperatures than at resorts up in the Rockies)

+ Great terrain for those who like it steep and deep, with lots for confident intermediates too

+ Snowcat operations nearby

+ Some good on-slope accommodation available, but ...

– Mountain resort is very limited

– Still too many slow, old lifts

– After a dump it can take time to make the bowls safe

– Limited groomed cruising for timid or average intermediates

– Awful trail map and on-mountain signposting – verging on dangerous

– No proper mountain restaurants

Fernie has long had cult status among Alberta and British Columbia skiers. It now attracts quite a few British visitors, and the reports we get are almost all positive. Like us, reporters are impressed by the adventurous nature of the skiing – it's mostly steep and ungroomed, with a lot of tree skiing (the sort of thing you don't experience in Europe). There's now a lot more groomed terrain than there was when we first visited, but that's not saying much – if it's groomers you want, there are plenty of better places. The resort village is convenient but small and nothing special. Fernie town, a couple of miles away, is primarily a place for locals with few of the usual tourist trappings.

THE RESORT

Fernie Alpine Resort is set a little way up the mountainside from the flat Elk Valley floor and a couple of miles from the little town of Fernie. It has grown from very little in the past few years, but there's still not much there except convenient lodging and a few restaurants, bars and small shops. It is quiet at night.

The town of Fernie is named after William Fernie – a prospector who discovered coal here and triggered a boom in the early 1900s. Much of the town was destroyed by fire in 1908, but some buildings survived. It is primarily a town for locals, not tourists. There are some lively bars, decent places to eat and good outdoor shops. It is down to earth rather than charming, and reporters' reactions to it vary: 'I liked the way it felt like real Canada and enjoyed staying in a town with some history,' said one; 'The flipside of being a real town is having

a real highway run through it,' said another. Most stress the friendliness of the locals, though not that of seasonal 'immigrant' workers.

There are buses between the town and the mountain, which run at half-hourly intervals at peak times and cost C$3 one way (they are free in the evenings and run every half an hour until 2am). Each hotel has specific pick-up times, although we have a report that the service is unreliable, and a 2007 visitor found the information on routes 'inadequate'.

Outings to Kimberley are possible; a coach does the trip every Thursday – the drive takes about 90 minutes. (there's also a helicopter option).

THE MOUNTAINS

Fernie's 2,500 acres pack in a lot of variety, from superb green terrain at the bottom to ungroomed chutes (that will be satisfyingly steep to anyone but the extreme specialist) and huge numbers of steep runs in the trees. Quite a few runs have the quality of going directly down the fall line.

THE SLOPES
Bowl after bowl
What you see when you arrive at the lift base is a trio of impressive mogul slopes towering above you. The slow Deer chair approaches the foot of these slopes, but goes no further. You get to them by traversing and hiking from the main Lizard Bowl, on the right. **Lizard Bowl** is a broad snowfield reached by a series of lifts: the slow Elk quad; the fast Great Bear quad; and finally the short Face Lift, a dreadful rope tow that has been somewhat improved by adding buttons

to the handles on the rope. It often doesn't run, because of either too little or too much snow. This is also the main way into **Cedar Bowl** and to Snake Ridge beyond it. The only lift here is the Haul Back T-bar, which brings you out. You can still traverse into the lower parts of both Lizard and Cedar Bowls when the Face Lift isn't working. There is a mini-bowl between them, served by the Boomerang chair.

The Timber Bowl fast quad chair gives access to **Siberia Bowl** and the lower part of **Timber Bowl**. But for access to the higher slopes and to **Currie Bowl** you must take the White Pass quad. A long traverse from the top gets you to the steeper slopes on the flanks of Currie (our favourite area). From there you have to go right to the bottom (unless you head over into Lizard Bowl) and it takes quite a while to get back for another go.

There are free tours in groups of different abilities, but only on blue and green runs. For the steeper, deeper stuff you need to pay (see 'Schools and guides') – we strongly recommend you do so early in your stay to help you find your way around and get the most out your holiday (see 'Why you need a guide' feature). A reporter recommends chatting to the locals: 'If you are a good skier, they will be delighted to show you the best runs.'

TERRAIN-PARKS
Up to scratch
The main Telus terrain-park is near the top of the Timber Chair, with berms, jumps, rollers, table top, large hip and box, a rail jam area and boarder-cross features. There's also an easier family park just off the Lizard Run near the base of the Great Bear quad.

KEY FACTS

Resort	1065m
	3,490ft
Slopes	1065-1925m
	3,490-6,320ft
Lifts	10
Pistes	2,504 acres
Green	30%
Blue	40%
Black	30%
Snowmaking	
	125 acres

boarding

Fernie is a fine place for good boarders (and there are a lot of local experts here). Lots of natural gullies, hits and endless off-piste opportunities – including some adrenalin-pumping tree runs and knee-deep powder bowls – will keep free-riders of all abilities grinning from ear to ear. And, as one reader commented, 'The only flat sections are at the base and coming out of Falling Star.' But there's a lot of traversing involved to get to many of the best runs. The main board shops, Board Stiff and Edge of the World, are in downtown Fernie, the latter with an indoor skate park to use while your board gets tuned. It's not a brilliant place for freestylers – the terrain-park doesn't have anything approaching a dedicated lift. And beginners and faint-hearted intermediates should stay away.

LIFT PASSES

Fernie

Prices in C$

Age	1-day	6-day
under 13	23	140
13 to 17	56	337
18 to 64	78	471
over 65	64	382

Free under 6

Beginner rental, pass and tuition deals

Notes

Prices include taxes; half-day pass available

SNOW RELIABILITY
A key part of the appeal

Fernie has an excellent snow record – with an average of 350 inches per year, better than practically all of Colorado. But the altitude is modest – rain is not unknown, and in warmer weather the lower slopes can suffer. Too much snow can be a problem, with the high bowls prone to closure – shut all week during a recent reporter's visit. Snowmaking has been increased and now covers most of the base area. Piste grooming has also been increased, and we were impressed with it on our 2007 visit.

FOR EXPERTS
Wonderful – but get a guide

The combination of heavy snowfalls and abundant steep terrain with the shelter of trees makes this a superb mountain for good skiers, so long as you know where you are going. To get the most out of the terrain we strongly recommend getting guidance early in your holiday (see feature panel).

There are about a dozen identifiable faces offering genuine black or double-black slopes, each of them with several alternative ways down. However, as one of our regular reporters says, 'Most of the single blacks are tough. With some, I don't see how you could get anything harder without falling off the mountain ... just like Jackson Hole but without the cliffs.' Even where the trail map shows trees to be sparse, expect them to be close together, and where there aren't any, expect alder bushes unless there's lots of snow.

There are backcountry routes you can take with guidance (some include an overnight camp) and snowcat operations in other nearby mountains – see feature panel. A regular reporter especially enjoyed exploring Fish Bowl, a short hike outside the resort boundary from Cedar Bowl.

FOR INTERMEDIATES
Getting better

When we first visited, only the green and blue runs on the lower mountain were groomed. But on our 2007 visit a few runs from the top were also

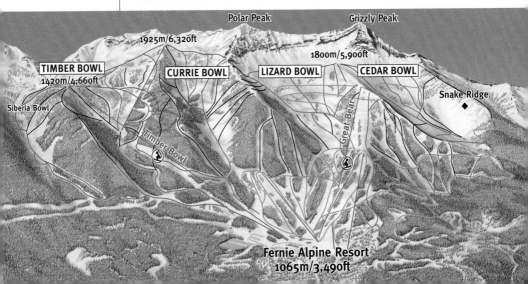

Fernie Alpine Resort
1065m/3,490ft

SCHOOLS

Fernie
t 423 4655

Classes
Half day C$87 (incl. taxes)

Private lessons
C$249 (incl. taxes) for 2hr for up to 5 people

CHILDREN

Telus Resort Kids
t 423 2430
Newborn to age 6;
8.30 to 4.30

Ski school
For ages 5 to 12
(C$109 per day, incl. taxes and lunch)

RIDE THE SNOWCATS – HELI-SKIING AT AN AFFORDABLE PRICE

Good skiers who relish off-piste should consider treating themselves to some cat skiing (where you ride snowcats instead of lifts); there are several operations in this area. Island Lake Lodge (423 3700) does three- or four-day all-inclusive packages in a cosy chalet 10km/6 miles from Fernie, amid 7,000 acres of spectacular bowls and ridges. It has 36 beds and four cats. In a day you might do eight powder runs averaging 500m/1,640ft vertical, taking in all kinds of terrain from gentle open slopes to some very Alpine adventures. You can do single days on a standby basis; we managed this once and loved it, but our second attempt failed. A 2006 visitor picked up a late-season bargain with Powder Cowboy (422 8754). It has two cats accessing 6,000 acres, 60km/37 miles from Fernie. 'Absolutely superb; best day's skiing we have ever had.' Fernie Wilderness Adventures (423 6704) has three cats, and recent reports have been positive.

groomed, including some great blue cruisers down Lizard Bowl. But it doesn't add up to much, and if you are not happy to try some of the easier ungroomed terrain in the bowls and glades, we'd recommend you go elsewhere. For the adventurous willing to give the powder a go, though, Fernie should be on your shortlist.

FOR BEGINNERS
Excellent
There's a good nursery area served by two lifts (a moving carpet and a drag), and the lower mountain served by the Deer and Elk chairs has lots of wide, smooth trails to gain confidence on. But the green runs from the top of the mountain are usually cat-tracks, which nonetheless have tough parts to them.

FOR CROSS-COUNTRY
Some possibilities
There are 14km/9 miles of trails marked out in the forest adjacent to the resort. In the Fernie area as a whole there are around 50km/31 miles of tracks (including some on the fairways of the Fernie golf course).

QUEUES
Not usually a problem
Unless there are weekend crowds from Calgary, or heavy snow keeps part of the mountain closed, queues are rare. The slopes are delightfully quiet, too. But people do complain about the slow chair-lifts, and about frequent stoppages on one or two.

MOUNTAIN RESTAURANTS
One small sit-down place
Lost Boys Cafe opened last season – a small place with good views at the top of the Timber Express chair-lift. It has a very limited menu – mainly soups and baked potatoes with fillings. Bear's

Den at the top of the Elk chair is an open-air fast-food kiosk. Most people head back to base for lunch. The ancient Day Lodge is a no-frills place serving salads and burgers ('friendly with good service'), Snow Creek is handy for the nursery slopes and Kelseys is popular for burgers, soups and the like. On Sundays you can try the brunch at the Lizard Creek ('you won't eat for the rest of the day').

SCHOOLS AND GUIDES
Highly praised
Reporters praise the school, which seems to achieve rapid progress – no doubt partly because groups are often very small. A recent reporter enjoyed 'excellent lessons, which took us from powder novices to bump and tree skiing in three hours'. We've also had good reports of the Steep and Deep camps and private lessons. Steep and Deep is a two-day programme (C$249) where you get technique tips while exploring Fernie's steep terrain – a great way to learn how to find your way around the mountain. There is also a Mountain Guide programme (C$99 a day) where you are guided around the groomed and ungroomed runs but not given any coaching. 'First Tracks' (C$169) gets you up the mountain at 8am for two hours – a 2007 reporter was delighted with this: 'He took us to an untracked bowl and invited us to rip it up!'

FACILITIES FOR CHILDREN
Good day care centre
There's a day care centre in the Cornerstone Lodge, which a reporter found 'very well run'. There are also 'Kids' Activity Nights' for children aged six to 12. And there's a Wilderness Adventure Park where kids ski past cut-outs of bears and wolves.

← There's a bit more to the slope-side village than this, but not a huge amount
SNOWPIX.COM / CHRIS GILL

EATING OUT
Steadily improving
At the base, the Lizard Creek Lodge has been recommended for 'good-sized portions and the Okanagan red wines'. Gabriella's does cheap and cheerful Italian, and lots of readers have enjoyed it. Kelsey's (part of a chain) serves standard steaks, burgers, soups etc. The Slope Side Coffee and Deli in the Cornerstone Lodge has been recommended.

In the town of Fernie, there are quite a few options, which may be a key factor in deciding where to stay. Reporter recommendations include the pricey Old Elevator (a converted grain store with 'good grills and pasta'), Jamochas (a coffee house that does meals), Curry Bowl (various Asian styles and 'a beer menu with 60 brews'), Mojo Rising (Cajun food) in the Royal hotel, Rip'n Richard's Eatery (south-western food and a lively atmosphere), the Corner Pocket in the Grand Central Hotel ('terrific bison, venison and steaks'), Yamagoya ('good sushi') and Sawai Thai ('out of town a bit but the best value around; very popular'). El Guapo, in the Edge of the World board shop, does 'cheap and tasty' Mexican.

APRES-SKI
Have a beer
The Griz bar has a sun deck and is quite lively when the lifts close – it sometimes has live bands. During the week, the resort bars are pretty quiet later on. In town, the bars of the Royal hotel are popular with locals. Other recommendations are the Park Place Lodge Pub ('service, prices and atmosphere were excellent') and the bar in the Grand Central hotel ('all the patrollers go there').

The resort offers BBQ at Bear's Den on Fridays, with a torchlit descent.

OFF THE SLOPES
Get out and about
There is a walking tour of historic Fernie and a 'mountain heritage snow-shoe tour'. The old railroad station is now the Art Station. You could take in an ice-hockey game. There's a pool at the Aquatic Centre and a bowling alley in town. But the main diversion is the great outdoors.

Fernie

679

GETTING THERE
Air Calgary 322km/200 miles (3½hr)

ACTIVITIES
Indoor Museum, galleries, Aquatic Centre, bowling, fitness centre, ice skating, cinema, curling

Outdoor Sleigh rides, snowmobiling, dog-sledding, snow-shoe excursions, walking

Central reservations phone number
Call 1 800 258 7669 (toll-free from within Canada)

Phone numbers
From distant parts of Canada, add the prefix 1 250; from abroad, add the prefix +1 250

TOURIST OFFICE
t 423 4655
info@skifernie.com
www.skifernie.com

STAYING THERE

HOW TO GO
More packages
Fernie is increasingly easy to find in tour operator brochures.

Chalets Some UK tour operators run chalets. Beavertail Lodge at the resort is run along chalet lines and has received several rave reviews: 'The best chalet I have ever stayed in; food equal to a Michelin-starred restaurant.' Canadian Powder Tours has a chalet in town and includes in the price guiding by the owners: 'Food excellent. I am a novice off-piste but had a brilliant time.'

Hotels and condos There's a wide choice, some impressively comfortable.
AT THE RESORT
****Lizard Creek Lodge** Best ski-in/ski-out condo hotel. Spa, outdoor pool and hot-tub. A 2007 reporter found the staff 'extremely friendly and helpful'.
****Snow Creek Lodge** Similar to the Lizard Creek Lodge. 'Lovely slope-side position. Absolutely no complaints.'
***Wolf's Den Mountain Lodge** 'Simple but comfortable,' say reporters. Indoor hot-tub, small gym. At base of slope.
Cornerstone Lodge Condo hotel – 'very clean, modern and well equipped'.
Griz Inn Sport Hotel Condo-hotel with good facilities. Pool.
Timberline Lodges Very comfortable condos a shuttle-ride from the lifts.
Alpine Lodge B&B praised by a reporter.
IN OR TOWARDS TOWN
****Best Western Fernie Mountain Lodge** Next to golf course near town. Recommended by reporters. Pool, hot-tub, fitness room. But a 30-minute bus-ride to the slopes.

Kicking Horse

Canada's newest resort: only a few lifts, but great powder at the top, and an already impressive fledgling village at the base

COSTS

① ② ③ ④ ⑤ ⑥

RATINGS

The slopes
Fast lifts	**
Snow	****
Extent	***
Expert	****
Intermediate	***
Beginner	***
Convenience	****
Queues	*****
Mountain restaurants	**

The rest
Scenery	***
Resort charm	**
Off-slope	*

➕ Great terrain for experts and some for adventurous intermediates

➕ Big vertical served by a fast lift

➕ Splendid mountain-top restaurant

➖ Resort village still in early stages

➖ Gondola has no mid-station, so you may have to ski crud lower down

➖ Few groomed intermediate runs

In 2000/01 Whitetooth, a tiny locals' hill with lifts only on the lower slopes, was transformed by a new gondola rising 1150m/3,770ft to access high, powder-filled bowls. In 2002 came a new quad chair-lift serving more high slopes. Now, with a choice of lodgings forming a mountain village at the lift base, Kicking Horse is a proper little resort. If you can't arrange to include a stay here in your plans, it makes a good day trip from Banff or Lake Louise.

THE RESORT

Eight miles from the logging town of Golden, Kicking Horse is planned for completion by 2010. The first phase of a resort village at the lift base now has six lodges, a few restaurants and bars, a ski shop and a general store. Daily buses run from Banff and Lake Louise – C$75 including a lift pass.

Golden is a spread-out place beside the transcontinental highway. It has no real charm or centre; we prefer to stay at the mountain, though we don't dispute the view of a 2007 visitor that there is 'more fun' to be had in the bars of Golden.

THE MOUNTAINS

The lower two-thirds of the hill are wooded, with trails cut in the usual style. The upper third is a mix of open and lightly wooded slopes, with scores of ways down through the bowls, chutes and trees.

Slopes The eight-seat gondola to Eagle's Eye takes you to the top in one stage of 1150m/3,770ft vertical. This serves two bowls and CPR Ridge that separates them. If you want to stay high, you can repeat-ride the slow chair to the slightly higher peak of Blue Heaven. But most of the high slopes lead you below this chair, and with no mid-station on the gondola you have to make the full descent – and the snow conditions on the lower slopes may be poor. Two chair-lifts from near the base serve the lower runs that formed the original ski area. There are free mountain tours, and First Tracks is a new deal that gets you breakfast at the mountain top and access to the slopes as soon as they open (extra cost; Saturdays only).

Terrain-park There's a small park on the lower slopes.

Snow reliability An average of 275 inches of snow a year is not enough to put the resort in the top flight, but not far off. The top part of the mountain usually has light, dry powder; the lower part may have crud and thin cover.

Experts It's advanced skiers and riders who will get the most out of the area.

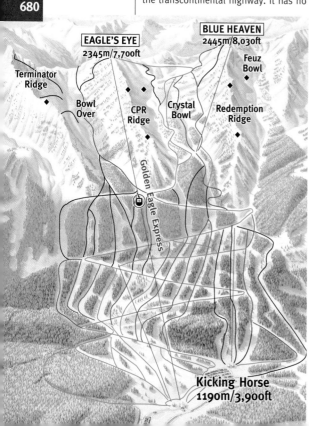

EAGLE'S EYE
2345m/7,700ft

BLUE HEAVEN
2445m/8,030ft

Feuz Bowl

Terminator Ridge

Bowl Over

CPR Ridge

Crystal Bowl

Redemption Ridge

Golden Eagle Express

Kicking Horse
1190m/3,900ft

↑ Mountaineer and Glacier lodges couldn't be much closer to the gondola base station

NEWS

For 2007/08 one run on the lower slopes is to get snow-guns. And the terrain-park will be improved.

KEY FACTS

Resort	1190m 3,900ft
Slopes	1190-2445m 3,900-8,030ft
Lifts	5
Pistes	2,750 acres
Green	20%
Blue	20%
Black	60%
Snowmaking	Some

UK PACKAGES

Alpine Answers, AmeriCan Ski, Canadian Powder Tours, Crystal, Frontier, Neilson, Ski All America, Ski Dream, Ski Freshtracks, Ski Independence, Ski Safari, Skitracer, Skiworld

Central reservations
Call 439 5424

Phone numbers
From distant parts of Canada, add the prefix 1 250; from abroad, add the prefix +1 250

TOURIST OFFICE

t 439 5424
guestservices@kicking horseresort.com
www.kickinghorse resort.com

From CPR Ridge, drop off to skier's right through trees or to skier's left through chutes – there are endless options. If it's open, you can also hike to Terminator Ridge (often closed due to avalanche danger). The chair to Blue Heaven opens up easier ski-anywhere terrain back into Crystal Bowl, and access to the wide Feuz Bowl, via treeless chutes ranging from fairly steep to seriously so. The lower half of the mountain has short but serious black runs cut through the woods, some with serious moguls – they are rarely groomed. There is also heli-skiing nearby.

Intermediates Adventurous intermediates will have a fine time learning to play in the powder from Blue Heaven down to Crystal Bowl. Most of it is open, but you can head off into trees if you want to. There is very little groomed cruising – though the resort claims to be increasing it, and there is a top-to-bottom 10km/6 mile winding green run. Timid intermediates, go elsewhere.

Beginners We can't imagine why a UK-based beginner would come here, but the beginner slopes are fine.

Snowboarding Free-riders will love this powder paradise.

Cross-country There are 25km/16 miles of trails at Dawn Mountain and a 5km/3 mile loop on the golf course.

Queues We have no reports of serious queues, although the gondola 'can get busy' at peak times.

Mountain restaurants The Eagle's Eye at the top of the gondola is Canada's best mountain restaurant – table-service of excellent food in stylish log-cabin surroundings with splendid views. A yurt (tent) in Crystal Bowl serves snacks.

Schools and guides Two reporters booked group lessons, and each was the only pupil: 'excellent' was the verdict from both. Another joined a

free mountain tour and again was the only one. Yet another took an avalanche safety course that 'was worth every penny; truly memorable'.

Facilities for children The school teaches children from the age of three.

STAYING THERE

How to go Assuming you want to be at the mountain (not in Golden), you have a choice of smart but relatively impersonal condo-style places on the slopes, or three more captivating places (each with about 10 rooms) a short walk away – described below.

Hotels The log-built Vagabond Lodge, run by the amiable owners, features a fabulous first-floor living room, comfortable, traditional-style rooms, a steam room and an outdoor hot-tub. Copper Horse Lodge has spacious but more austere rooms in modern styles; outdoor hot-tub. Our favourite is Highland Lodge – rooms warmly done out with hardwood furniture from India, a welcoming sitting room and a cosy, woody bar; outdoor hot-tubs.

Apartments The Whispering Pines town homes were 'the most luxurious ski lodgings we've had', said a reporter.

Eating out The bar in Highland Lodge does modern Canadian cooking with a Scottish flavour. Corks in Copper Horse Lodge does excellent 'mountain bistro dining'. Kuma is a sushi bar. Eagle's Eye at the top of the gondola opens some nights. Extreme Peaks is a big restaurant in Glacier Lodge. In Golden, Kicking Horse Grill and the out-of-town Cedar House are highly rated.

Après-ski The liveliest place as the lifts close is reportedly The Local Hero with its deck, blazing outdoor fireplace and music. In Golden the Mad Trapper and Golden Taps are lively bars.

Off the slopes There is snowmobiling, snow-shoeing, ice-climbing, dog-sledding and a new tubing park.

Stunning views and the biggest ski area in the Banff region, with some good places to stay but no real village

682

➕ Spectacular high-mountain scenery – the best of any North American resort

➕ Slopes are the largest in the Canadian Rockies

➕ Snowy slopes of Sunshine Village within reach (see Banff chapter)

➕ Lots of wildlife around the valley

➕ Good value for money

➖ Local slopes are a short drive away from the 'village', Banff areas further

➖ Snowfall modest by local standards

➖ Can be very cold and the chair-lifts have no covers, but the Grizzly Express gondola is warmer

➖ 'Village' is just a few hotels and shops, fairly quiet in the evening

If you care more for scenery than for après-ski action, Lake Louise is worth considering for a holiday. We've seen a few spectacular mountain views, and the view from the Fairmont Chateau Lake Louise hotel of the Victoria Glacier across the frozen Lake Louise is as spectacular as they come; it is simply stunning.

Even if you prefer the more animated base of Banff, you'll want to make expeditions to Lake Louise during your holiday. It can't compete with Sunshine Village for quantity of snow, but it's a big and interesting mountain. And from the slopes you get a distant version of that stunning view.

THE RESORT

Although it's a small place, Lake Louise is a resort of parts. First, there's the lake itself, in a spectacular setting beneath the Victoria Glacier. Tom Wilson, who discovered it in 1882, declared, 'As God is my judge, I never in all my exploration have seen such a matchless scene.' Neither have we. And it can be appreciated from many of the rooms of the vast Fairmont Chateau Lake Louise hotel on the shore. Then there's Lake Louise 'village' – a collection of a few hotels, condos, petrol station, liquor store and shops, a couple of miles away on a road junction. Finally, a mile or two across the valley, there's the lift base station. A car helps, especially in cold weather. Buses to the Lake Louise ski area run every half hour, but a lot less frequently to the Banff areas of Sunshine and Norquay. Bus trips to the more distant resorts of Panorama and Kicking Horse and the small resorts of

Nakiska and Fortress are possible. Day-trip heli-skiing can also be arranged. Banff Airporter do transfers from and to Calgary airport.

THE MOUNTAINS

The Lake Louise ski area is big by North American standards, with a mixture of high, open slopes, low trails cut through forest and gladed slopes between the two. Reporters are usually full of praise for the free guided tours given by volunteers. There has been some criticism of inconsistent piste grading and lots about cold lifts with no covers.

THE SLOPES
A wide variety
From the base area you have a choice of a fast quad to mid-mountain, followed by a six-pack to the top centre of the Front Side (also called the South Face), or the gondola direct to a slightly lower point on the right side of the Front Side. From both, as elsewhere, there's a choice of green, blue or black runs (good for a group of mixed abilities who want to keep meeting up). In poor visibility, the gondola is a better option, as the tree line goes almost to the top there. Or stay on the lower part of the mountain using the chairs. From mid-mountain

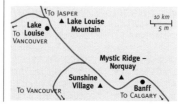

KEY FACTS

Resort	1645m
	5,400ft

Sunshine, Norquay and Lake Louise, covered by the Tri-area pass

Slopes	1630-2730m
	5,350-8,950ft
Lifts	27
Pistes	7,748 acres
Green	23%
Blue	39%
Black	38%
Snowmaking	
	1,900 acres

Lake Louise only

Slopes	1645-2635m
	5,400-8,650ft
Lifts	9
Pistes	4,200 acres
Green	25%
Blue	45%
Black	30%
Snowmaking	40%

on the left, the long Summit drag-lift takes you to the high-point of the area, at the shoulder of Mount Whitehorn – there's a stunning view of peaks and glaciers, including Canada's Matterhorn lookalike, Mount Assiniboine.

From here or the top chair you can go over the ridge and into Lake Louise's almost treeless **Powder Bowls** (previously the Back Bowls) – open, predominantly north-facing and mainly steep. From the top of the gondola, the Ptarmigan area is more wooded.

From low down in the bowls you can take the Paradise lift back to the top again or continue lower to the separate **Larch** area, served by a fast quad chair. With a lift-served vertical of 375m/1,230ft it's not huge, but it has pretty wooded runs of all grades. From the bottom you can return to the top

of the main mountain via the Ptarmigan chair or take a long green path back to the main base area. Grooming is 'good'.

TERRAIN-PARKS
Huge and varied

The Telus park under the Glacier lift has been divided into three separate areas to cover all levels. The beginner line has small roller-style jumps, which will ease you into being comfortable in the air. There are also several small ride-on boxes and rails to get the feeling for sliding on steel. Use the bottom entrance of the park and stick to the left. Intermediates and experts have a choice of several excellent fluid lines and can enter the park from both entrances, but will want to stay to the right. Three kickers lead to a 7m/24ft

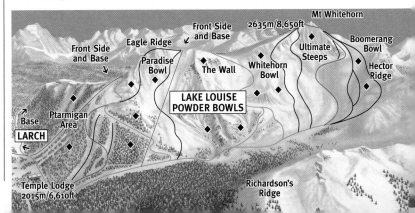

LIFT PASSES

Tri-area lift pass

Prices in C$

Age	1-day	6-day
under 13	23	216
13 to 17	56	407
18 to 64	78	458
over 65	64	407
Free under 6		

Beginner lift, lesson and rental package

Notes
Day pass is for Lake louise only; 3-day-plus pass covers all lifts and transport between Banff, Lake Louise, Norquay and Sunshine Village; prices include tax

SCHOOLS

Ski Big 3
t 760 7731

Lake Louise
t 522 1333

Classes (Big 3 prices)
3 days guided tuition of the three areas C$259 incl. tax

Private lessons
Half day (3hr) C$376, incl. tax, for up to 5 people

boarding

Lake Louise is a great mountain for free-riders, with all the challenging terrain in the bowls and glades. The two sides of the mountain mean there is ample space at this sometimes very crowded resort. Get up early and head to the Powder Bowls first thing for some epic fun. Ask a local or hire a guide to get the best out of the bowls, as there is often great terrain only a short hike away. Beginners will have fun on the Front Side's blue and green runs. But there's a T-bar at the base area and beware of the vicious Summit button-lift (top left looking at the trail map). Also avoid the long, flat green run through the woods from Larch back to base. For those less into free-riding there are three terrain-parks to suit all levels.

quarter-pipe and a 12m/40ft down rail. The park will then test all aspects of your riding with a host of boxes, rails, more kickers and a wall ride with 15 new features this year. Shoot out the bottom and jump on the Glacier lift for another loop.

SNOW RELIABILITY
Usually OK
Lake Louise gets around 140 inches a year on the Front Side, which by the standards of western Canada is not a lot, and nowhere near as much as Sunshine Village down the road (see Banff chapter). But it is usually enough, and there is snowmaking on 40 per cent of the pistes. The north-facing Powder Bowls and Larch hold the snow pretty well.

FOR EXPERTS
Widespread pleasure
There are plenty of steep slopes. On the Front Side, as well as a score of marked black-diamond trails in and above the trees, there is the alluring West Bowl, reached from the Summit drag – a wide open expanse of snow outside the area boundary. Because this is National Park territory, you can in theory go anywhere. But outside the boundaries there are no patrols and, of course, no avalanche control. A guide is essential. 'You get a real feel of being in the middle of nowhere. The return through thick woods is great fun,' says a reporter.

Inside the boundaries, going over to the Powder Bowls opens up countless black mogul/powder runs. From the Summit drag, you can drop into The Ultimate Steeps (if it is open), directly behind the peak. The runs here gave our fearless Aussie editor what she called 'some of the most exciting in-bounds skiing in North America' – a row of extreme chutes, almost 1km/0.5 miles long. You can also access lots of much tamer, wide open Powder

Bowl slopes that take you right away from all signs of lifts.

The Top of the World six-pack takes you to the very popular Paradise Bowl/Eagle Ridge/East Bowl area, also served by its own triple chair on the back side – there are endless variants here, ranging from the comfortably steep single diamonds to very challenging double diamonds. The seriously steep slope served by the Ptarmigan quad chair has great gladed terrain and is a good place to beat the crowds and find good snow. The Larch area has some steep double-diamond stuff in the trees, and open snowfields at the top for those with the energy to hike up ('needs good snow cover though,' says a reporter). Heli-skiing is available outside the National Park.

FOR INTERMEDIATES
Some good cruising
Almost half the runs are classified as intermediate. But from the top of the Front Side the blue runs down are little more than paths in places, and there are very few blues or greens in the Powder Bowls. Once you get part way down the Front Side the blues are much more interesting. And when groomed, the Men's and Ladies' Downhill black runs are great fast cruises on the lower half of the mountain. Juniper is a wonderful cruising run in the same area. Meadowlark is a beautiful tree-lined run to the base area – to find it from the Grizzly Express gondola, first follow Eagle Meadows. The Larch area has some short but ideal intermediate runs – and reporters have enjoyed the natural lumps and bumps of the aptly named blue, Rock Garden ('never had so much fun; really away from it all'). The adventurous should also try the blue-classified Boomerang, which starts with a short side-step up from the top of the Summit drag, and some of the ungroomed Powder Bowls terrain.

↑ You can just make out the Fairmont Chateau hotel at the foot of the grand peaks across the valley from the lift base station

SNOWPIX.COM / CHRIS GILL

FOR BEGINNERS
Excellent terrain

Louise has a good nursery area near the base, which has attracted praise, served by a short T-bar, which has not. You progress to the gentle, wide Wiwaxy, Pinecone Way and the slightly more difficult Deer Run or Eagle Meadows (all designated 'slow skiing zones'). There are even green slow-skiing zones round the Powder Bowls and in the Larch area – worth trying for the views, though some do contain slightly steep pitches ('our beginner was very nervous trying the Saddleback Bowl'). A past reporter lost confidence by tackling these, and found that people still skied fast in the slow areas and that they were quite crowded.

FOR CROSS-COUNTRY
High in quality and quantity

It's a very good area for cross-country, with around 80km/50 miles of groomed trails in the National Park – plenty of scenic stops needed. There are excellent trails in the local area and on Lake Louise itself. And Emerald Lake Lodge 40km/25 miles away has some lovely trails and has been recommended as a place to stay for a peaceful time.

QUEUES
Not unknown

Half of the area's visitors come for the day from nearby cities such as Calgary – so it can have queues at weekends and public holidays ('ten minutes', says a 2007 visitor), especially for the slow chairs on the back of the mountain. Most shift quickly, say reporters.

MOUNTAIN RESTAURANTS
Good base facilities

There's not much choice up the mountain. Temple Lodge, near the bottom of Larch and the Ptarmigan chair, is built in rustic style with a big terrace, but can get crowded. Its restaurant, Sawyer's Nook, is the only table-service option on the mountain, and it continues to receive praise from reporters; reserve a table. Whitehorn Lodge, at mid-mountain on the Front Side, is a cafeteria with fine views across to Lake Louise from its balcony.

Most people eat at the base, where there are big-scale facilities. The Lodge of the Ten Peaks is a hugely impressive, spacious, airy, modern, log-built affair with various eating, drinking and lounging options, including the Great Bear Room self-service (which is described as having 'Interactive Lunch Stations'). The neighbouring Whiskeyjack building has another self-service. The Kokanee Kabin has BBQ food.

SCHOOLS AND GUIDES
Generally good reports

We get good reports. 'The best teaching we've encountered' is how a reporter described his 'bumps' lesson at Lake Louise. Another reporter enjoyed the lessons, but said she could not get afternoon-only classes. And her five-year-old daughter did not like being put in classes with eight- to ten-year-olds. See the Banff chapter for details on the excellent three-day, three-mountain Club Ski and Club Snowboard Program.

FACILITIES FOR CHILDREN
Varying reports

A reporter who used Lake Louise, Sunshine and Norquay facilities said: 'I'd recommend all three and advise booking in advance at Lake Louise.' The Minute Maid Wilderness Adventure Park is a children's discovery and learning area at the bottom of the gondola.

The Larch area is mainly cruising, but don't underestimate the double-diamond blacks in those gladed areas →

SNOWPIX.COM / CHRIS GILL

GETTING THERE

Air Calgary 177km/110 miles (2hr)

ACTIVITIES

Indoor Mainly hotel-based pools, saunas and hot-tubs, bowling, cinema, museums

Outdoor Ice rinks, walking, swimming in hot springs, sleigh rides, dog-sled rides, snow-shoeing

UK PACKAGES

Alpine Answers, AmeriCan Ski, Crystal, Crystal Finest, Directski.com, Elegant Resorts, Frontier, Independent Ski Links, Inghams, Neilson, Ski Activity, Ski All America, Ski Dream, Ski Independence, Ski Line, Ski McNeill, Ski Safari, Skitracer, Skiworld, Supertravel, Thomson, Trailfinders, United Vacations, Virgin Snow, White Mountains

Phone numbers
From distant parts of Canada, add the prefix 1 403; from abroad, add the prefix +1 403

TOURIST OFFICE

t 522 3555
info@skilouise.com
www.skilouise.com
www.SkiBig3.com

STAYING THERE

HOW TO GO
Good value accommodation
Hotels Summer is the peak season here. Prices are much lower in winter.
*****Fairmont Chateau Lake Louise (522 3511) Grand monster with 500 rooms in fantastic setting with stunning glacier views over frozen Lake Louise; shops, pool, hot-tub, sauna.
****Post (522 3989) Small, relaxed, comfortable Relais & Châteaux place in the village, with excellent restaurant (huge wine list), pool, hot-tub, steam room. Avoid rooms on railway side.
***Lake Louise Inn (522 3791) Cheaper option in the village, with pool, hot-tub and sauna. 'Comfortable rooms'; 'good food'; 'staff helpful'.
***Deer Lodge (522 3747) Charming old hotel next to the Chateau, good restaurant, roof-top hot-tub.
Apartments Some is available but local shopping is limited. The Baker Creek Chalets (522 3761) were highly recommended by reporters on their honeymoon ('really romantic').

EATING OUT
Limited choice
The Post hotel's restaurant has repeatedly impressed us with its ambitious food and excellent service. The Fairview Dining Room at the Chateau is also top notch. The Outpost Pub (part of the Post) does inexpensive, 'good' pub food. The Station restaurant is in an atmospheric old station building ('delicious food, good range for vegetarians').

APRES-SKI
Lively at tea time, quiet later
There are several options at the bottom of the slopes. The Lodge of the Ten Peaks has lovely surroundings, an open fire and a relaxed atmosphere. The Kokanee Kabin has live music on spring weekend afternoons, outdoor fire and new terrace. The Powderkeg was refurbished last season. On Monday and Friday there's live music and dancing and a buffet dinner at the mid-mountain Whitehorn Lodge. You ski or ride there as the lifts close, and the evening ends with a torchlit descent. It is hugely popular with British visitors.

Later on, things are fairly quiet. But the Glacier Saloon, in Chateau Lake Louise, with traditional Wild West decor, often has live music until late. Explorer's Lounge, in the Lake Louise Inn, has entertainment. The Post's Outpost Pub is worth a look.

OFF THE SLOPES
Beautiful scenery
Lake Louise makes a lovely, peaceful place to stay for someone who does not intend to hit the slopes. The lake itself makes a stunning setting for walks, snow-shoeing, cross-country skiing and ice skating. You can go on ice canyon walks, sleigh rides, dog-sledding, snowmobiling, sightseeing tours and visit natural hot springs.

For a more lively day or for shopping you can visit Banff.

Lake Louise is near one end of the Columbia Icefields Parkway, a three-hour drive to Jasper through National Parks, amid stunningly beautiful scenery of high peaks and glaciers – one of the world's most beautiful drives.

STAYING UP THE MOUNTAIN
Try ski touring
Skoki Lodge (522 3555) is 11km/ 7 miles on skis from Temple Lodge. Built in the 1930s, it sleeps 22 in the lodge and cabins and allegedly has 'gourmet food'. Reports welcome.

Panorama

*A purpose-built Intrawest resort with an unusual mountain –
not many lifts, but a sizeable area and an impressive vertical*

COSTS

① ② ③ ④ ⑤ ⑥

RATINGS

The slopes

Fast lifts	★★★
Snow	★★★
Extent	★★
Expert	★★★★
Intermediate	★★★
Beginner	★★★★
Convenience	★★★★
Queues	★★★★★
Mountain restaurants	★

The rest

Scenery	★★★
Resort charm	★★
Off-slope	★

NEWS

For 2006/07 Elkhorn Cabin at mid-mountain started opening to the public for lunch. For 2007/08 snowmaking will be increased.

- ➕ Car-free village with some slope-side accommodation, plus a lower part
- ➕ Fair-sized ski area with big vertical
- ➕ Runs are usually deserted
- ➖ Not many easy cruising runs
- ➖ Snowfall record not impressive by high local standards
- ➖ Quiet, even lifeless village

Panorama's vertical of 1220m/4,000ft is one of the biggest in North America, and it has some excellent terrain for experts and adventurous intermediates. It's good for beginners, too. But timid intermediates may find themselves confined to the rather limited lower mountain.

THE RESORT

Panorama is a small, quiet, purpose-built resort above the lakeside town of Invermere in eastern British Columbia, about two hours' scenic drive south-west of Banff. Accommodation is concentrated mainly in two car-free areas. There are attractive lodges with a hot-pool complex and a skating rink at the foot of the main slopes; with ski-in/ski-out convenience, this is the best place to stay. But a lot of lodging is in a 'lower village' that lacks character or life. This is linked to the 'upper village' and the slopes by a bucket lift that runs until 10pm. The resort runs day trips to Lake Louise and Kicking Horse (given a demand).

THE MOUNTAIN

The slopes basically follow three ridges, joined at top and bottom. Almost all of the terrain is wooded. Free tours of the mountain are available twice daily. Night-skiing is offered Thursday to Sunday.

Slopes From the upper village, a fast quad goes over gentle slopes to mid-mountain, and above it another fast quad serves both intermediate and expert slopes. Then a slow quad takes you to the summit. From here there are long blue and black runs down various ridges and two serious expert areas. The trail map is twice the size it needs to be, but is clear. Helpful hand-written boards at the lifts show trail conditions.

Terrain-parks There are two: the main Showzone terrain-park, with table tops, spines, rails, fun-boxes and a half-pipe, and the new 1km/0.5 mile long park on Powder Trail with hits, jumps and rails.

Snow reliability Annual snowfall is low by local standards – less than half the Fernie figure. But snowmaking covers 40% of trails, and grooming is 'excellent', say reporters.

Experts There are genuine black runs scattered all over the mountain, and some expert-only areas. At the very top of the mountain and accessed through a gate is the Extreme Dream Zone – seriously steep trails with cliffs and tight trees. Off the back of the summit is the Taynton Bowl area. We skied this last season and loved it – open areas, lightly and more densely forested areas, very few people. It is marked double-black diamond, but it really isn't worryingly steep. Locals say that hiking over to the far runs can be worth it for fresh tracks. Great views, too. The long, shallow ski out is an enjoyable fast cruise. And the vertical of 1220m/4,000ft is one of the greatest

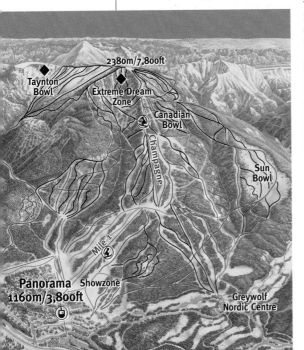

2380m/7,800ft

◆ Taynton Bowl

Extreme Dream Zone

Canadian Bowl

Champagne

Sun Bowl

Mile 1

Panorama Showzone
1160m/3,800ft

Greywolf Nordic Centre

↑ The 'upper village' with the nursery slopes and the hot-pools. The mountain you ski on is out of sight to the left

SNOWPIX.COM / CHRIS GILL

KEY FACTS

Resort	1160m
	3,800ft
Slopes	1160-2380m
	3,800-7,810ft
Lifts	9
Pistes	2,847 acres
Green	20%
Blue	55%
Black	25%
Snowmaking	40%

UK PACKAGES

AmeriCan Ski, Ardmore, Frontier, Inghams, Ski All America, Ski Dream, Ski Independence, Ski Safari

Central reservations
Call 341 4203

Phone numbers
From distant parts of Canada, add the prefix 1 250; from abroad, add +1 250

TOURIST OFFICE

t 341 4203
paninfo@intrawest.com
www.skipanorama.com

in North America. There's local heli-skiing, too (see 'Intermediates').

Intermediates For adventurous intermediates the terrain is excellent – there are easy blacks all over the mountain, some of them regularly groomed. The black View of 1000 Peaks has fabulous views but can be a bit tricky in parts. Both this and the blue run from the top are long for North America (up to 3.5km/2 miles). Sun Bowl is a good introduction to a powder bowl and Millennium (black running into blue) is a great roller-coaster. But the less confident may find all this uncomfortably challenging. The blues in the centre of the area are gentler but they don't add up to a lot. RK Heli-Skiing is based in the village and specialises in one-day sessions for first-time heli-skiers – 'Excellent: skiing was astounding,' said a 2007 reporter.

Beginners There are a couple of nursery lifts and a moving carpet serving a quiet and gentle nursery area. Then there are good, longer runs to progress to served by the Mile 1 quad.

Snowboarding There is good steep terrain and tree runs for expert free-riders. The main lifts are all chairs, and beginners have several good long green runs to practise on.

Cross-country There are 20km/12 miles of trails starting from the Nordic Centre.

Queues We get no reports of queues, but the Sunbird triple chair is said to be prone to breakdowns.

Mountain restaurants Reserve a table at Elkhorn Cabin, a tiny, charming old mountain hut (complete with roaring log fire) that many European resorts would be proud of. They serve a C$16.90 two-course lunch – go for the delicious Quebec Meat Pie followed by Maple Syrup ice cream. The Ski Tip Lodge at the base is also excellent, but gets busy. The clubhouse at the Nordic Centre is quieter – 'good soups'.

Schools and guides We have mainly had glowing reports of the ski school. 'My daughter has had excellent boarding lessons on each of our three visits,' says a 2007 repeat visitor. 'Progressed quickly' and 'massive leap in skiing' are typical comments. There's an Extreme Makeover clinic.

Facilities for children Wee Wascals is the childcare centre, taking children from 18 months. Snowbirds is for three- to four-year-olds, and the Adventure Club caters for kids from five to 14. Kids' themed nights are arranged some evenings. Evening babysitters are also available.

STAYING THERE

How to go The better places are the newer ones in the upper village.

Hotels Earl Grey Lodge is a smart, central, six-bedroom, log-built place.

Apartments Panorama Springs is right on the slopes with a big outdoor hot-pool and sauna facility. We stayed at the 1000 Peaks Summit last season and thought it very comfortable and spacious. The 1000 Peaks Lodge is similar. The grocery store is inadequate, so stock up in Invermere.

Eating out Options are limited but improving. Earl Grey Lodge has established itself at the top of the market with excellent fixed menus. The Wildfire Grill, the Heli Plex restaurant ('great views, marvellous steaks') and the Great Hall (pasta and pizza) are recommended by reporters. The ski school organises BBQs at the Elkhorn Cabin (see 'Mountain restaurants'), followed by a torchlit descent. There's a horse-drawn wagon ride followed by chilli around a campfire. A shuttle-bus goes once a night to and from restaurants in Invermere. 2007 reporters recommend Angus McToogle's, Portabellas and Strands there and Gerry's Gelatis (ice creams).

Après-ski This revolves around the Crazy Horse Saloon in the Pine Inn, which sometimes has live music, and the Jackpine pub in the Horsethief Lodge. Ski Tip Lodge is popular as the lifts close. The Earl Grey Lodge has 'upmarket après-ski cocktails/sushi'.

Off the slopes The hot-pool facility, with thermal baths, a swimming pool, slides and sauna, is excellent, but it gets rather taken over by kids. There is snowmobiling, ice-fishing, snow-shoeing and skating. The Wolf Education Centre and Bavin Glassworks ('quirky handmade glass jewellery') are worth visiting.

Sun Peaks

Attractive, car-free village at the foot of BC's second-biggest ski area; with varied slopes including some unusual easy groomed gladed runs

COSTS

① ② ③ ④ ⑤ ⑥

RATINGS

The slopes

Fast lifts	✱✱✱
Snow	✱✱✱✱
Extent	✱✱✱
Expert	✱✱✱
Intermediate	✱✱✱✱
Beginner	✱✱✱✱
Convenience	✱✱✱✱
Queues	✱✱✱✱✱
Mountain restaurants	✱

The rest

Scenery	✱✱✱
Resort charm	✱✱✱
Off-slope	✱✱

➕ Some great terrain for all standards

➕ Excellent glades for intermediates up

➕ Slopes very quiet during the week

➕ Attractive, traffic-free, slope-side village – with some smart shops

➕ Good for families

➖ Village may be too small and quiet for some tastes

➖ Snow on some of the lower steep terrain can suffer from the sun

➖ Although the second largest ski area in BC, it's not big by Alpine standards

Sun Peaks has sprung from the drawing board since the mid-1990s and we have been increasingly impressed on each of three successive visits. It now has an almost complete small village and a fair amount of varied terrain. Former Olympic Giant Slalom champion Nancy Greene and husband Al Raine, who were instrumental in developing Whistler, have made Sun Peaks their home and live in the Cahilty Lodge. Nancy is Director of Skiing and skis with guests daily. We suggest combining it with, say, Silver Star or Big White on a multi-centre trip.

THE RESORT

Until 1993 Sun Peaks was known as Tod Mountain, a local hill for the residents of nearby Kamloops. Since then the company that bought it has overseen the development of a small, attractive resort village with low-rise pastel-coloured buildings with a vaguely Tirolean feeling to them.

The traffic-free main street is lined with accommodation, restaurants and shops including a smart art gallery, a great chocolate shop and a good coffee bar. It's a pleasant place to stroll around and very family-friendly.

689

NEWS

For 2007/08 there are plans to expand the terrain-park features for beginners and intermediates. The Delta Residence, a suite hotel in the heart of the village, is due to open, together with a larger grocery store inside.

For 2006/07 the new fixed-grip Elevation quad chair on Mt Tod opened. This takes you from mid-mountain to the top of the Sunburst Express, allowing you to ski green, blue, black and gladed runs repeatedly without returning to the lower slopes. Four new blue runs were created on Orient Ridge (mainly to access homes in the East Village area). A new ski-in/ski-out Umbrella cafe near the base of Mt Morrisey also opened. And a new Kids Ranch animated theme park with fun features designed for kids three to 12 years old was been created at the top of the beginner area.

THE MOUNTAINS

With almost 3,700 acres of skiable terrain, Sun Peaks is the second biggest ski area in British Columbia (Whistler is the biggest). There are free guided tours twice a day (9.15am and 1pm) and at 11am and 1.30pm you can ski for free with former Olympic champion and Canada's Female Athlete of the 20th Century Nancy Greene when she's in town (don't miss it – she is great fun!). At the top of all main lifts there is a board with grooming conditions of the pistes in that area.

Slopes There are three distinct sectors, each served by a high-speed quad.

One goes from the centre of the village to mid-mountain on Sun Peaks' original ski hill, Mt Tod. This has mainly black runs but there are easier blues and greens. A tiny snowcat offers day-long backcountry skiing here, but runs are very short (100–130m/ 328–426ft vertical), and lots of slopes had been tracked by snowmobilers when we did it. Many of Mt Tod's steepest runs are served only by the slow Burfield quad (there's a mid-station to allow you to ski the top runs only) – these runs are 'even quieter than the rest', says a recent reporter.

Also reached from the village centre, the Sundance area has mainly blue and green cruising runs. Both Sundance and Tod have some great gladed areas (12 of them marked on the trail map) to play in.

Mt Morrisey is reached by a long green run from the top of Sundance and has a delightful network of easy blue runs with trees left uncut in the trails, effectively making them groomed glade runs that even early intermediates can try.

Terrain-parks The park on Sundance has an advanced section with table-tops, rails and fun-boxes, plus intermediate and beginner sections that are being expanded for 2007/08. There was no half-pipe last season, and the resort says it doesn't plan to build one for 2007/08 either.

Snow reliability Sun Peaks gets an average snowfall of 220 inches a year; not in the top league but better than some. The snow can suffer on the lower part of Mt Tod's south-facing slopes, especially later in the season.

Experts Mt Tod has most of the steep terrain, though some of the blacks on Mt Morrisey (such as Static Cling) are long mogul runs, too. You can ski lots of good steep and gladed runs without descending to the bottom of Mt Tod by riding the Burfield quad from its mid-station, the Crystal chair and the new Elevation chairs. You could also try the backcountry snowcat operation.

Intermediates This is great terrain for early intermediates, with the easy and charming groomed glades of Mt Morrisey, lovely swooping blues on Sundance and the long 5 Mile run from Mt Tod. More adventurous intermediates can also tackle the

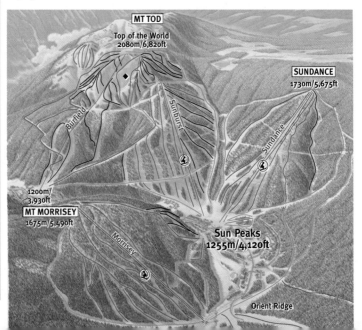

↑ The main part of Sun Peaks village is in the centre here, with private homes in the distance at the foot of Mt Morrisey going up to the right

easier glades (such as Cahilty) and blacks (such as Peek-A-Boo).

Beginners There are nursery slopes right in the village centre, with long easy greens to progress to.

Snowboarding Boarders can explore the whole mountain. But beware the flat greens to and from Mt Morrisey.

Cross-country 40km/25 miles of trails.

Queues Weekdays are usually very quiet; it's only at peak weekends that you might find short queues ('six or seven minutes', says a recent reporter).

Mountain restaurants The Sunburst Lodge is the only option but has 'well-priced fare with a good choice', says a 2007 reporter; its cinnamon buns are highly recommended. The new Umbrella Cafe at the Morrisey base serves hot soup and sandwiches and 'has the best toilets on the mountain'.

Schools and guides A 2007 reporter chose private lessons and 'found the instruction second to none and worth every cent'. In 2006 a reporter had a 'fantastic instructor' and was the only person in a group lesson. Her kids 'were happy', too, but her husband found that his lesson (with five others) was 'more like a guided tour'.

Facilities for children The playschool takes kids from age 18 months and the ski school from three years.

STAYING THERE

How to go There's a lot of self-catering accommodation as well as hotels.

Hotels Nancy Greene's Cahilty Lodge is a friendly and comfortable ski-in/ski-out base and you get the chance to ski with her and husband Al Raine (former Canadian ski team coach) at 9am most days – 'Great fun skiing with Nancy and Al, good rooms, a very welcoming hotel,' says a reporter. The ski-in/ski-out Delta Sun Peaks Resort (outdoor pool and hot-tub) in the village centre is 'luxurious with lovely rooms and facilities' with 'well-priced food'.

Eating out For a small resort, there's a good choice of restaurants, including Thai, Italian and, of course, North American. Macker's Bistro is popular, and we had great Thai-style sea bass there. Powder Hounds (good steaks), Servus (more sophisticated food) and Bella Italia have been recommended.

Après-ski Bottoms, Masa's and Macker's are the main après-ski bars. At weekends MackDaddy's nightclub in The Delta can get lively. There are fondue evenings with torchlit descents, winter bonfires and tobogganing.

Off the slopes There's skating, tubing, snowmobiling, dog-sledding, snow-shoeing and sleigh rides.

North America's biggest mountain, with terrain to suit every standard and a big, purpose-built, largely car-free village

COSTS

① ② ③ ④ ⑤ ⑥

RATINGS

The slopes

Fast lifts	★★★★
Snow	★★★★
Extent	★★★★
Expert	★★★★★
Intermediate	★★★★★
Beginner	★★★
Convenience	★★★★
Queues	★★★
Mountain restaurants	★★

The rest

Scenery	★★★
Resort charm	★★★
Off-slope	★★

NEWS

The big news is that Whistler's two mountains are soon to be united: a 28-person gondola is planned to connect the two areas for 2008/09. Peak to Peak will run between the mid-stations at Whistler's Roundhouse Lodge and the Rendezvous Lodge on Blackcomb. The lift will span 4.4km/2.7 miles between the two mountains, with a capacity of over 2,000 people per hour in each direction.

For 2007/08 the Village Gondola is expected to be upgraded and a new hotel, Nita Lake Lodge, is due to open at Creekside.

For 2006/07 the Symphony Express quad opened near the top of Whistler Mountain, serving new glades and runs. Snowmaking was also increased.

692

➕ North America's biggest, both in area and vertical (1610m/5,280ft)

➕ Good slopes for most abilities, with an unrivalled combination of high open bowls and woodland trails

➕ Good snow record

➕ Almost Alpine scenery

➕ Attractive modern village at the foot of the slopes, with car-free central areas, and some lively après-ski

➕ Good range of restaurants and bars (though not enough of them)

➖ Proximity to the ocean means a lot of cloudy weather, and snow on the mountain can mean rain lower down

➖ Two separate mountains for now – but with a gondola connection promised for two years' time.

➖ Whistler is now attracting so many people that lift queues and crowded runs can be a problem – a really serious one at weekends

➖ Mountain restaurants are mostly functional (and overcrowded)

Whistler is unlike any other resort in North America. In some respects – the scale, the scenery, the crowds – it is more like an Alpine resort. But it follows the North American pattern in offering excellent snow, and a lot of woodland runs as well as the high bowls and glaciers that evoke the Alps.

All things considered, the mountain is about the best that North America has to offer, and for us a visit here is always a highlight of the season. But we'll admit that we are generally lucky with the weather, and haven't had to put up with much rain at resort level – a real hazard.

Whistler will host many events during the 2010 Winter Olympics. In preparation, the resort has made huge investments in infrastructure and base area facilities; but it is the project to connect its two mountains with a record-breaking gondola for 2008/09 that is making the current headlines (see 'News').

THE RESORT

Whistler Village sits at the foot of its two mountains, Whistler and Blackcomb, a scenic 115km/70 mile drive from Vancouver on Canada's west coast. Whistler started as a locals' ski area in 1966 with a few ramshackle buildings in what is now the revamped Whistler Creek (aka Creekside). Whistler Village, a 10-minute bus-ride away, developed in the late 1970s. More development spread around the base of Blackcomb Mountain in the 1980s; this area, a 10-minute walk from central Whistler, is now known simply as Upper Village.

The village centres are all traffic-free. The architecture is varied and, for a purpose-built resort, quite tasteful – but it is all a bit urban, with lots of blocks approaching 10 storeys high. There are also lots of chalet-style apartments on the hillsides.

Whistler Village has most of the bars, restaurants and shops, and two gondolas (one to each mountain). A pedestrian bridge over an access road links the main centre to newer Whistler North, further from the lifts, making a huge car-free area of streets lined with shops, condos and restaurants. Upper Village is much smaller and quieter.

Creekside has been revamped and expanded and it will play an important role in the Olympics, with many of the Alpine events finishing above here.

There is a free bus between central Whistler and Upper Village but it can be just as quick to walk. Some lodging is a long way from the centre and means taking (inexpensive) buses or taxis. Some hotels have free buses, which will pick you up as well as take you to restaurants and nightlife.

The most convenient place to stay is Whistler Village, as you can access either mountain by gondola (though some reporters find the central area around Village Square noisy in the early hours). Creekside is quieter and though convenient for Whistler Mountain, is less so for Blackcomb.

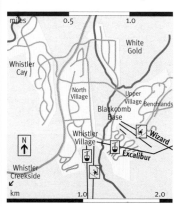

↑ From Whistler's Symphony and Harmony areas you get a clear view of the 7th Heaven area on Blackcomb

SNOWPIX.COM / CHRIS GILL

KEY FACTS

Resort	675m
	2,210ft
Altitude	650-2285m
	2,140-7,490ft
Lifts	38
Pistes	8,171 acres
Green	18%
Blue	55%
Black	27%
Snowmaking	
	565 acres

THE MOUNTAINS

Whistler and Blackcomb together form the biggest area of slopes, with the longest runs, in North America.

Many reporters enthuse about the mountain host service and the 'go

slow' patrol – some find the latter 'over zealous', but crowded slopes, especially on the runs home, mean they're often needed.

But reporters also comment on the early closing times for lifts (3pm until end-January, 3.30 in February and 4pm thereafter). Upper lifts may close earlier. Grooming 'could be better', says a 2007 visitor. Another reader remarked that piste marking needed improvement.

THE SLOPES
The best in North America

Whistler Mountain is accessed from Whistler Village by a two-stage, 10-person gondola that rises over 1100m/3,610ft to Roundhouse Lodge at mid-mountain. There is an alternative of two fast quads, which don't go so high but avoid queues for the gondola (if they are running – see 'Queues').

Runs back down through the trees fan out from the gondola – cruises to the Emerald and Big Red fast chairs, longer runs to the gondola mid-station.

From Roundhouse you can see the jewel in Whistler's crown – magnificent above-the-tree-line bowls, served by the fast Peak and Harmony quads. The bowl beyond Harmony is now served by the Symphony fast quad. The bowls are mostly go-anywhere terrain for experts but there are groomed trails, so anyone can appreciate the views.

A six-person gondola from Creekside also accesses Whistler Mountain.

Access to **Blackcomb** from Whistler Village is by an eight-seat gondola, followed by a fast quad. From the base of Blackcomb you take two consecutive fast quads up to the main Rendezvous restaurant. From the arrival points you can go left for great cruising terrain and the Glacier Express quad up to the Horstman Glacier area, or right for steeper slopes, the terrain-park or the 7th Heaven chair. The 1610m/5,280ft vertical from the top of 7th Heaven to the base is the largest in North America (and big even by Alpine standards). Or you can go into the glacier area. A T-bar from the Horstman Glacier brings you (with a short hike) to the Blackcomb Glacier in the next valley – away from all lifts.

Fresh Tracks is a deal that allows you to ride up Whistler Mountain (at extra cost) from 7.30am, have a buffet breakfast and get to the slopes as they open – very popular with many reporters. Free guided tours of each mountain are offered at 11.30am.

One of our favourite runs is behind the mountain away from all the lifts on the Blackcomb glacier – over 1000m/3,280ft vertical to the Excelerator chair

BLACKCOMB

Lovely sunny cruising above and among the trees

The Nintendo terrain-park is one of North America's best – with a Highest Level section that you can enter only if you wear a helmet and sign a waiver

Blackcomb Glacier

Horstman Hut 2285m/7,490ft

Flute Bow

7th Heaven

Horstman Glacier

Rendezvous Lodge 1860

Crystal Hut

Glacier

Jersey Cream 1645m

Solar Coaster

Glacier Creek

Excelerator

Great blue and green cruising, but beginners should beware of some steeper sections on the greens

1130m

Wizard

Excalibur

Blackcomb Base

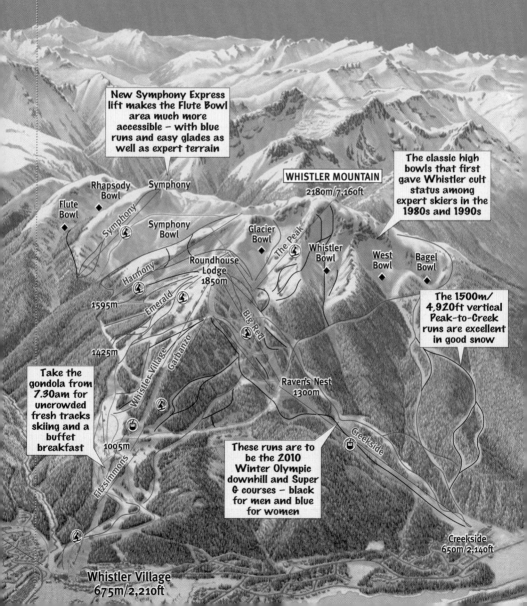

New Symphony Express lift makes the Flute Bowl area much more accessible – with blue runs and easy glades as well as expert terrain

The classic high bowls that first gave Whistler cult status among expert skiers in the 1980s and 1990s

WHISTLER MOUNTAIN
2218m/7,16oft

Rhapsody Bowl

Symphony

Flute Bowl

Symphony

Symphony Bowl

Glacier Bowl

The Peak

Whistler Bowl

West Bowl

Bagel Bowl

Harmony

Roundhouse Lodge 1850m

Emerald

1595m

Big Red

The 1500m/ 4,920ft vertical Peak-to-Creek runs are excellent in good snow

1425m

Garbanzo

Whistler Village

Raven's Nest 1300m

Take the gondola from 7.30am for uncrowded fresh tracks skiing and a buffet breakfast

1005m

Creekside

Fitzsimmons

These runs are to be the 2010 Winter Olympic downhill and Super G courses – black for men and blue for women

Creekside 650m/2,140ft

Whistler Village 675m/2,210ft

LIFT PASSES

Whistler/Blackcomb

Prices in C$

Age	1-day	6-day
under 13	47	229
13 to 18	75	394
19 to 64	86	464
over 65	75	394

Free under 7

Beginner lift, lesson and rental deal

Notes
Covers Whistler and Blackcomb mountains; prices include sales tax

TERRAIN-PARKS
For high-fliers and mere mortals

'The best parks I've come across,' says a 2007 reporter. There's a good rating system based on size (S, M, L, XL). Novices should begin in the Terrain Garden in Blackcomb. It features small rails and rollers to get a feel for airtime and improve your control. For the S-M line hit the Habitat park by the Emerald chair on Whistler Mountain. Initiate yourself on a host of rails, boxes, medium kickers and a hip. The M-L Nintendo park is huge, but is usually the busiest and is by the Catskinner chair-lift on Blackcomb. Step-up jumps, hips, tabletops, rails, boxes: this park will suit most intermediate to advanced riders. Pros and very confident freestylers should hit the Highest Level Park (part of the Nintendo park). The fact that you need to sign a waiver, wear a helmet and buy a special pass indicates the size of the obstacles here. The super-pipe in Blackcomb is over 137m/450ft long with 5m/16.5ft high walls, and it is shaped daily. From Thursday to Saturday in the evening the super-pipe and a mini-jib park are open near the Magic Chair on Blackcomb; the same pass will get you into both. There is also a boarder-cross track visible from the Solar Coaster Chair next to the super-pipe ('lots of fast, flowing corners; excellently groomed').

SNOW RELIABILITY
Excellent at altitude

Snow conditions at the top are usually excellent – the place gets around 360 inches of snow a year, on average. After the exceptionally poor season in 2005, when it was plagued by high temperatures and rain, Whistler has had two big years, recording its second largest snowfall ever in 2007 – 516 inches. Because the resort is low and close to the Pacific, the bottom slopes can be wet, icy or unskiable – leading people to 'download' from the mid-stations, especially in late season.

FOR EXPERTS
Few can rival it

Whistler Mountain's bowls are enough to keep experts happy for weeks. Each has endless variations, with chutes and gullies of varied steepness and width. The biggest challenges are around Flute, Glacier, Whistler and West Bowls, with runs such as The Cirque and Doom & Gloom – though you can literally go anywhere in these high, wide areas. The new Symphony quad makes Flute Bowl, on the area boundary, much more accessible.

Blackcomb's slopes are not as extensive as Whistler's, but some are more challenging.

If you're feeling brave, go in the opposite direction and drop into the extremely steep chutes down towards Glacier Creek, including the infamous 41° Couloir Extreme, which can have moguls the size of elephants at the top. Or try the also serious, but less frequented, steep bowls reached by hiking up Spanky's Ladder, after taking the Glacier Express lift.

Both mountains have challenging trails through trees. The Peak to Creek area offers another 400 acres below Whistler's West Bowl to Creekside.

If all this isn't enough, there's also out-of-bounds backcountry guiding (see Schools and guides), cat-skiing and local heli-skiing available by the day – a 2007 reporter used Coast Range and praised 'top-quality guides and superb skiing'.

FOR INTERMEDIATES
Ideal and extensive terrain

Both mountains are an intermediate's paradise. In good weather, good intermediates will enjoy the easier slopes in the high bowls.

boarding

Whistler has world-class terrain-parks as well as epic terrain for free-riders: bowls with great powder and awesome steeps, steep gullies, tree runs, and shedloads of natural hits, wind lips and cliffs. Get up early if you fancy cutting first tracks, however. There are mellow groomed runs ideal for beginners, too, and the lifts are generally snowboard-friendly; there are T-bars on the glacier, but they're not vicious and any discomfort is worth it for the powder. The resort is fast gaining as big a reputation for its summer snowboarding facilities and camps on the glacier as for its winter snowboarding. The resort's specialist school will teach riders how to ride piste, pipe, park and powder according to your level. Specialist snowboard shops include Showcase and Katmandu Boards.

a series of efficient fast chairs to bring you back up to the top of the gondola. It's a cruiser's paradise – especially the aptly named Ego Bowl. A great long run is the fabulous Dave Murray Downhill all the way from mid-mountain to the finish at Creekside. Although it will be the Olympic men's downhill course and is classed black, it's a wonderful fast and varied cruise when it has been groomed. There is also the groomed blue Peak to Creek run to try if snow is good enough.

FOR BEGINNERS
OK if the sun shines

Whistler has excellent nursery slopes by the mid-station of the gondola, as does Blackcomb, down at the base area. Both have facilities higher up too.

The map has a guide to easy runs, and slow zones are marked. On Whistler, after progressing from the nursery slopes, there are some gentle first runs from the top of the gondola. Their downside is other people speeding past. You can return by various chairs or continue to the base area on greens.

On Blackcomb, Green Line runs from the top of the mountain to the bottom. The top part is particularly gentle, with some steeper pitches lower down.

In general, greens can be trickier than in many North American resorts – steeper, busier and on the lower mountain in less good condition. 'Our tentative beginner found it hard to move around with confidence because of the varying steepness of green runs,' says a reporter.

Another serious reservation is – you guessed – the weather. Beginners don't get a lot out of heavy snowfalls, and might be put off by rain and unpredictable conditions.

FOR CROSS-COUNTRY
Picturesque but low

There are over 32km/20 miles of cross-country tracks around Lost Lake, starting by the river, on the path between Whistler and Blackcomb. But it is low altitude here, so conditions can be unreliable. There's a specialist school, Cross-Country Connection (905 0071) offering lessons, tours and rental. Keen cross-country merchants can catch the train to better areas.

QUEUES
An ever-increasing problem

Whistler has become a victim of its

One of our favourite intermediate runs is down the Blackcomb Glacier, from the top of the mountain to the bottom of the Excelerator chair over 1000m/3,280ft below. This 5km/3 mile run, away from all lifts, starts with a two-minute walk up from the top of the Showcase T-bar. Don't be put off by the sign that says 'Experts only'. You drop over the ridge into a wide bowl; traverse the slope to get to gentler gradients – descend too soon and you'll get a shock in the very steep double-diamond Blowhole.

You are guaranteed good snow on the Horstman Glacier too, and typically gentle runs. The blue runs served by the 7th Heaven chair are 'heavenly on a sunny day', as a reporter put it. Lower down there are lots of perfect cruising runs through the trees – ideal when the weather is bad.

On Whistler Mountain, the ridges and bowls served by the Harmony and Symphony quads have lots to offer – not only groomers, but excellent terrain for experiments off-piste. The Saddle run from the top of the Harmony Express lift is a favourite with many of our reporters, though it can get busy. The blue Highway 86 path, which skirts West Bowl from the top of the Peak chair, has beautiful views over a steep valley and across to the rather phallic Black Tusk mountain. The green Burnt Stew Trail also has great views, but is reportedly much busier now.

Lower down the mountain there is a vast choice of groomed blue runs, with

SCHOOLS

**Whistler and
Blackcomb**
t 904 7060

Classes
3 days Ski Esprit
C$349 (incl. taxes)
Private lessons
Half day (3hr) from
C$317

GUIDES

Whistler Guides
t 904 7060

CHILDREN

Whistler Kids
t 1 866 218 9690
Ages 3mnth to 4yr;
from 8am; non-skiing;
C$105 per day (incl.
taxes)

Ski school
Offers Adventure
Camps for ages 3 to
12 and Teen Ski
programmes for ages
13 to 17 (from C$453
incl. taxes for 4 days
for 5 to 6 year olds)

own success. Even with 17 fast lifts – more than any other resort in North America – the mountains are queue-prone, especially at weekends when people pour in from Vancouver ('horrendous'). There are displays of waiting times at different lifts, which readers generally find useful.

Some reporters have signed up with the ski school just to get lift priority. Others have visited Vancouver at the weekend to avoid the crowds.

The routes out of Whistler Village in the morning can be busy. Creekside is less of a problem. Some of the chairs higher up also produce long queues; the Harmony quad, especially, is no longer up to the job (even the singles line can take ages). And we had a report of a 45-minute wait for The Peak chair on an early-January Sunday. We have several reports of lift closures – a March 2007 visitor noted the Peak Chair open 'only once during eleven days'. Another reader found the Fitzsimmons and Garbanzo quads 'rarely open', despite queues for the gondola. Visiting outside peak season may not help – we found some lifts, including the gondola to Blackcomb, were kept closed in an early-December visit. Crowds on the slopes, especially the runs home, can be annoying too.

MOUNTAIN RESTAURANTS
Overcrowded

The main restaurants sell decent, good-value food but are charmless self-service stops with long queues. They're huge, but not huge enough. 'Seat-seekers' are employed to find spaces, but success is not guaranteed. You may have to resort to eating about 11am, or just surviving on breakfast.

Blackcomb has the Rendezvous, mainly a big (850-seat) self-service place but also home to Christine's, a table-service restaurant that is the best on either mountain. Glacier Creek Lodge, at the bottom of the Glacier Express, is a better self-service place. But even this (1,496 seats) gets incredibly crowded. Whistler has the massive (1,740-seat) Roundhouse Lodge; Steeps Grill is its unremarkable table-service refuge.

Reporters generally prefer the smaller places – but they're still packed unless you time it right, and may be closed early and late season. On Blackcomb, Crystal Hut (great waffles, say reporters) and Horstman Hut are tiny, with great views.

On Whistler, Raven's Nest, at the top of the Creekside gondola, is a small and friendly deli/cafe. The Chic Pea near the top of the Garbanzo chair-lift – 'funky and rustic' but 'noisy' – does pizza and barbecue. Harmony Hut, at the top of the Harmony chair, specialises in stews and cider. You can of course descend to the base – the table-service Dusty's at Whistler Creek has been recommended.

SCHOOLS AND GUIDES
A great formula

Ski Esprit and Ride Guides programmes run for three or four days and combine instruction with showing you around the mountains – with the same instructor daily. Many of our reporters have joined these groups (usually small), and all reports are glowing: 'Big improvement in confidence and skill' is typical. A 2007 reporter comments on 'small, personalised and attentive' instruction at the Whistler school. There are various specialist clinics and snowboard classes.

Extremely Canadian specialises in guiding and coaching adventurous advanced intermediates upwards in Whistler's steep and deep terrain. A lot of its coaches compete in free-ride and skier-cross competitions. We have been with them a few times and they really are great. As a reporter said, 'You end up skiing places that other people don't even know about – we were very impressed.' They run two-day clinics three times a week.

Backcountry day trips or overnight touring are available with the Whistler Alpine Guides Bureau.

FACILITIES FOR CHILDREN
Impressive

Blackcomb's base area has a slow-moving magic chair to get children part-way up the mountain. Whistler's gondola mid-station has a splendid kids-only area. A reporter found the staff 'friendly and instilled confidence'. Classes are said to be 'very flexible'.

The Children's Adventure Park on Blackcomb features a Magic Castle, terrain features and 'colourful characters'. A 2006 reporter was enthusiastic about 'climb and dine', where children can spend a few fun hours at the Great Wall climbing centre (see 'Off the slopes'), including a meal, while parents go out to eat.

Air Vancouver
115km/71 miles (2hr)

Alpine Answers, AmeriCan Ski, American Ski Classics, Chalet World Ski, Cold Comforts Lodging, Crystal, Crystal Finest, Directski.com, Elegant Resorts, Erna Low, Friendship Travel, Frontier, Independent Ski Links, Inghams, Interactive Resorts, Kaluma, Kuoni, Mark Warner, Momentum, Momentum, Neilson, Ski Activity, Ski All America, Ski Dream, Ski Expectations, Ski Freshtracks, Ski Independence, Ski Line, Ski McNeill, Ski Miquel, Ski Safari, Ski Solutions, Ski Wild, Skitracer, Skiworld, Solo's, Supertravel, Thomson, Trailfinders, United Vacations, Virgin Snow, White Mountains

STAYING THERE

HOW TO GO
High quality packages
A lot of British tour operators go to Whistler and some run catered chalets. If you want to arrange your own trip, Holiday Whistler make it easy to book accommodation.

Hotels There is a wide range, including a lot of top-end places.

*****Fairmont Chateau Whistler (938 8000) Well run, luxurious, at the foot of Blackcomb. Recommended in 2007. Excellent spa with pools and tubs. The Gold floor is expensive and cosseting.

*****Westin Resort & Spa (905 5000) Luxury all-suite hotel at the foot of Whistler mountain next to the lifts, with pools and hot-tubs.

*****Four Seasons (935 3400) Luxury hotel five minutes from Blackcomb base, but with ski valet service at the base. Unremarkable public areas but good food. Good fitness/spa facilities.

*****Pan Pacific Mountainside (905 2999) Luxury, all-suite, at Whistler Village base. Pool/sauna/hot-tub.

****Crystal Lodge (932 2221) 'Comfortable, friendly, convenient', in Whistler Village. Pool/sauna/hot-tub.

****Sundial Boutique (932 2321) One and two bedroom suites. 'Great for groups and families, excellent location in Whistler Village.' Hot-tubs.

***Lost Lake Lodge (932 2882) 'Excellent' place: studios and suites, out by the golf course. Pool/hot-tub.

***Glacier Lodge (932 2882) In Upper Village. 'Big rooms, quiet area, recommended.' Pool/hot-tub.

Apartments There are plenty of spacious, comfortable condominiums in both chalet and hotel-style blocks.

EATING OUT
High quality and plenty of choice
Reporters are enthusiastic about the range, quality and value of places to eat, but we and they find Whistler simply doesn't have enough restaurant seats to meet demand. You have to book well ahead, even to eat in bars, or queue for some cheaper places that won't take bookings for small groups. There's a dining guide booklet, but it's not comprehensive and it doesn't give prices, so is of limited use.

At the top of the market, Il Caminetto di Umberto in Whistler Village has classy Italian cuisine ('excellent food, worth the price'). The

Whistler

699

Skiing holidays à la carte
Luxury chalets, ski-in/ski-out, hot tubs, log fires...

Holiday
Whistler

Call us on 001-604-7327477
or visit **www.holidaywhistler.com**

↑ Upper Village at the Blackcomb lift base is a small, quiet satellite of Whistler proper, but includes some big, upscale hotels – on the right here is the Fairmont Chateau Whistler

SNOWPIX.COM / CHRIS GILL

ACTIVITIES

Indoor Sports arena (ice rink, pool, hot-tubs), museum, art galleries, tennis, spa and health clubs, library, cinemas, climbing wall

Outdoor Flightseeing, snow-shoeing, snowmobiling, sno-limo (chauffeur-driven motorised sled), skating on frozen lake, walking, fishing, dog-sledding, sleigh rides, ice climbing, bungee jumping, treetrek, ziplining

Phone numbers
From distant parts of Canada, add the prefix 1 604; from abroad, add the prefix +1 604

TOURIST OFFICE

t 932 3928 or
1 800 9447 8537
wbres@intrawest.com
www.whistler-blackcomb.com
www.mywhistler.com

Rimrock Cafe at Whistler Creek serves 'outstanding seafood and game' and Araxi (Pacific) is repeatedly praised ('superb', 'excellent service').

Good mid-market Whistler Village places include the Keg ('great value' steak and seafood), Teppan (Japanese), Mongolie (Asian) and Kypriaki Norte ('excellent duck'). Reporters also suggest the Bocca (Italian: 'excellent home-made pasta', 'inexpensive'), the Bearfoot Bistro (European: 'the best gourmet restaurant, with a stellar wine list', 'bar is out of this world') and Sushi Village ('impressive quality for quite a simple place'). A 2007 visitor rates 21 Steps and suggests you may get a table here when everywhere else is busy.

In Village North: the good-value Brewhouse (steaks, burgers, beef ribs) has good microbrews and a lively atmosphere, Caramba has 'good Mediterranean food at reasonable prices'. Hy's Steakhouse has 'melt in your mouth' steaks. Sushi-Ya and Quattro (Italian) are good.

In Upper Village, options are limited. Thai One On is 'excellent', and Monk's Grill has 'good steaks and service'.

There are plenty of budget places, including the après-ski bars below. The Old Spaghetti Factory in Whistler Village has been recommended for pasta. Morgan's at Creekside (organic specialities) has a cosy fireplace and blues music.

APRES-SKI
Something for most tastes
Whistler is very lively. Popular at Whistler are the Longhorn ('lively, good music and local beer'), with a huge terrace, the Brewhouse ('excellent atmosphere'), the Garibaldi Lift Company ('the tables are full by 3pm') and The Dubh Linn Gate Irish pub. Tapley's seems 'the nearest thing to a locals' bar'. Merlin's is the focus at Blackcomb base ('great', with live music on Fridays) though readers also recommend the Monk's Grill. Dusty's is the place at Creekside – good beer, loud music.

Later on, Buffalo Bill's is lively and loud and the Amsterdam Cafe is 'a favourite'. Tommy Africa's, Maxx Fish, the Savage Beagle, Garfinkel's and Moe Joe's are the main clubs. Try the Mallard bar in Chateau Whistler and the Crystal Lounge for a quieter time.

OFF THE SLOPES
Not ideal
Whistler is a long way to go if you don't intend to hit the slopes. Meadow Park Sports Centre has a full range of fitness facilities. There are also several luxurious spas. Reporters have recommended walks around the lake, the Great Wall Underground climbing centre (recently expanded) and a shop where you can paint your own pottery. There's an eight-screen cinema in Whistler Village. And Ziptrek Ecotours offers 'adrenaline tours' on ziplines and suspension bridges through the forest between Whistler and Blackcomb mountains. You can also do ATV/snowmobile trips and dog-sledding. Excursions to Squamish (famous for its eagles) are easy, as are day trips to Vancouver. The Fire and Ice show (Sundays) is recommended.

Eastern Canada

For us the main attraction of skiing or riding in eastern Canada is the French culture and language that are predominant in the province of Québec. It really feels like a different country from the rest of Canada – as, indeed, many of its residents want it to become. It is relatively easy to get to – only a six-hour flight from the UK, compared with a 10-hour flight for western Canada.

Tremblant is the main destination resort and is one of the cutest purpose-built resorts we've seen (though it is now in danger of being spoiled by expansion). The other main base is Québec city, which dates from the 17th century and is full of atmosphere and Canadian history. Slopes of the main resorts are small, both in extent and in vertical drop, and the weather can be perishingly cold in early and midwinter. But at least this means that the extensive snowmaking systems, common to all the resorts, can be effective for a long season. Be prepared for variable snow conditions, and don't go expecting light, dry powder – if that's what you want, head west.

There are lots of ski and snowboard areas in Ontario – Canada's most populated province – but most of them are tiny and cater just for locals. For people heading on holiday for a week or more, eastern Canada really means the province of Québec. The province and its capital, Québec city, are heavily dominated by the French culture and language. Notices, menus, trail maps and so on are usually printed in both French and English. Many ski area workers are bilingual or just French-speaking. And French cuisine abounds. The Frenchness of it is one of the big attractions for us.

The weather is very variable, rather like New England's – but it can get even colder. Hence the snow, though pretty much guaranteed by snowmaking, can vary enormously in quality. When we were there one April, we were slush skiing in Tremblant one day and rattling along on a rock-hard surface in Mont-Ste-Anne the next. One reporter who visited Mont-Ste-Anne, Stoneham and Le Massif in late January experienced mild temperatures and several perfect blue-sky days.

The main destination resort is **Tremblant** (covered in the next chapter), about 90 minutes' drive from Montreal. The other main place to stay for easy access to several ski resorts is **Québec city**. Old Québec, at the city's heart, is North America's only walled city and is a World Heritage site. Within the city walls are narrow, winding streets and 17th- and 18th-century houses. It is situated right on the banks of the St Lawrence river. In January/February there is a famous two-week carnival, with an ice castle, snow sculptures, dog-sled and canoe races, parades and balls. But most of the winter is low season, with good-value rooms available in big hotels.

There are several ski and snowboard areas close to Québec city. The biggest and most varied is **Mont-Ste-Anne**, 30 minutes from Québec and with some accommodation of its own. It extends to only 450 acres – easily skied in a day by a good skier. A gondola takes you to the top, and slopes lead down the front (south) and back (north) sides. The views from the front over the ice floes of the St Lawrence river are spectacular.

Stoneham is the closest resort to Québec city, around 20 minutes away. It also has its own small village with accommodation and an impressive base lodge. It is a small area, with 325 acres of terrain spread across three linked peaks. But it is very sheltered in a sunny setting protected from wind. It suits families well, with mainly intermediate and beginner terrain.

Le Massif is around an hour away from Québec city and is a cult area with locals. It is in a UNESCO World Biosphere Reserve and is just metres from the St Lawrence river. The views of the ice floes are stunning, and you feel you are heading straight down into them when you are on the pretty, tree-lined trails. The area of slopes, though small, has the largest vertical in the east – 770m/2,530ft.

INTRAWEST

Tremblant

Cute, purpose-built, traffic-free village with a real French Canadian feel, at the foot of a very small area of slopes

COSTS

① ② ③ ④ ⑤ ⑥

RATINGS

The slopes
Fast lifts	****
Snow	****
Extent	*
Expert	**
Intermediate	***
Beginner	****
Convenience	****
Queues	***
Mountain restaurants	**

The rest
Scenery	***
Resort charm	****
Off-slope	***

702

➕ Charming, purpose-built core village
➕ Good snow reliability with extensive artificial back-up
➕ Some good runs for all abilities

➖ Very limited area for piste-bashers
➖ Can be perishingly cold in midwinter
➖ Weekend queues and overcrowding
➖ Lots of new building planned

Tremblant is eastern Canada's main destination resort and attracts quite a lot of Brits. But for keen piste-bashers the limited slopes don't really match the appeal of the cute and lively little core village, built in traditional style and with typical thoroughness by Intrawest.

THE RESORT

Tremblant has been transformed from a locals' hill to being eastern Canada's leading destination ski resort. Intrawest (which also owns Whistler and several other North American resorts) developed a purpose-built village in the style of old Québec. Buildings in vibrant colours line narrow, cobbled, traffic-free streets and squares, and it has a very French feel to it. Recent expansion on the edge is not so cute. There's a regular, free ski-bus and a local town service for C$1.

THE MOUNTAIN

In its small area, Tremblant has a good variety of pleasantly wooded terrain.
Slopes A heated gondola takes you to the top, from where there are good views over the village and a 14km/9 mile lake on the so-called South Side, and over National Park wilderness on the North Side (which is really north-east facing and gets the morning sun). A high-speed quad brings you back and there are two other chairs to play on. The slow Edge lift accesses another summit, serving mainly expert terrain. On the South Side (really south-west facing and so good for the afternoon sun) you can go right back to town on blue or green runs, or use two high-speed quads to explore the top and bottom halves. The Versant Soleil area is more directly south-facing and has one top-to-bottom blue run, all the rest being black runs and tree runs. Free mountain tours go twice daily.
Terrain-parks The excellent 18-acre Advanced terrain-park, a super-pipe and a Progression park for beginners are on the top half of the North Side. A third park on the South Side is for intermediates. The school offers freestyle classes.
Snow reliability Canada's east coast doesn't get as much snow as the west, but around 75 per cent of the trails are

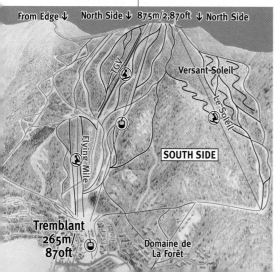

From Edge ↓   North Side ↓ 875m/2,870ft ↓ North Side

TGV

Versant-Soleil

Le Soleil

Flying Mile

SOUTH SIDE

Domaine de La Forêt

Tremblant
265m/
870ft

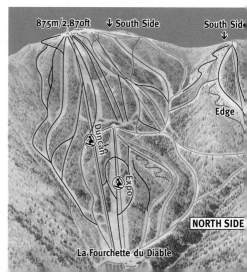

875m/2,870ft   ↓ South Side   South Side ↓

Duncan

Edge

Expo

La Fourchette du Diable

NORTH SIDE

NEWS

For 2006/07 more snow-guns were installed, rails were added to the terrain-park, and helicopter charters were started.

KEY FACTS

Resort	265m
	870ft
Slopes	230-875m
	750-2,870ft
Lifts	13
Pistes	620 acres
Green	17%
Blue	33%
Black	50%
Snowmaking	75%

UK PACKAGES

Alpine Answers, American Ski Classics, Crystal, Elegant Resorts, Erna Low, Frontier, Inghams, Kuoni, Neilson, Ski Activity, Ski All America, Ski Dream, Ski Independence, Ski Safari, Ski Solutions, Ski Wild, Skitracer, Skiworld, Thomson, Trailfinders, United Vacations, Virgin Snow

Central reservations phone number
Call 1 514 876 7273

Phone numbers
From distant parts of Canada, add the prefix 1 819; from abroad, add the prefix +1 819

TOURIST OFFICE

t 1 514 876 7273
info_tremblant@intrawest.com
www.tremblant.ca

The summit that splits the South and the North Sides →

TREMBLANT RESORT

covered by snowmaking. Grooming is excellent.

Experts Half the runs are classified as suitable for advanced skiers and riders. But we found many of the blacks did not deserve their grading. There are steep, top-to-bottom bump runs on the North Side and great gladed tree runs off the Edge lift. The Versant Soleil area has more black runs and some tough runs in the trees. However, the gladed runs really need decent snow, preferably fresh, to be much fun.

Intermediates Both North and South Sides have good cruising, and we found the North Side less crowded. There are blue-classified runs in the trees as well as on groomed trails.

Beginners The 2-acre beginner area is excellent, and there are long, easy, top-to-bottom green runs to progress to.

Snowboarding The slopes are good for beginners, but better boarders can't count on fresh natural snow to play in. A specialist shop, Adrénaline, runs a Burton learn-to-ride programme. And there are good terrain-parks.

Cross-country There are around 65km/40 miles of trails, some at the top of the mountain, with great views.

Queues At weekends there can be queues, but they tend to move quickly. We found crowds on the main run back to the village more of a problem.

Mountain restaurants The main Grand Manitou restaurant has good views and decent food, but can get crowded. Many people go back to town for lunch.

Schools and guides Reporters praise the school: 'good instructors and both children made progress', 'excellent – a 4-year-old was skiing greens in a week'.

Facilities for children The Kidz Club offers day care from age 1 to 6 years, until 4.30pm. There's a children's adventure area on the Nansen trail.

STAYING THERE

How to go There's no shortage of packages from the UK.

Hotels and condos The luxurious Fairmont Tremblant and the condos in the Place St Bernard, the Tour des Voyagers and the Chouette have been recommended by readers. But the nearest supermarket is a car- or bus-ride away, and there can be long waits between buses.

Eating out Try the Forge, Ya'ooo Pizza Bar, Shack, Casey's and the Loup Garou at the Fairmont. Fat Mardi's (steaks and seafood) has a kids' menu and live jazz music Friday and Saturday evenings. Plus Minus, Spag & Co and Windigo were recommended by a recent reporter.

Après-ski Octobar Rock is popular with British visitors, the Forge is good as the slopes close, and the Shack brews its own beer. There is often live music and a good atmosphere in the main square.

Off the slopes The Aquaclub La Source pool complex resembles a lake set in a forest, but reporters complain it's pricey (C$14.50 for three hours). For adults only, the 'excellent' Spa Scandinavie offers sauna, steam room, outdoor hot-tubs and waterfalls. You can also go hiking, ice-climbing, horse-riding, ice skating, snow-shoeing, tubing, snowmobiling and dog-sledding. You can also visit Montreal ('highly recommended'), and you can take a helicopter charter with a scenic stop on top of a mountain.

Spain

These days it's dangerous to generalise about Spanish resorts – which is why we don't provide the lists of ➕ and ➖ points that we do for other second-division countries. There are now some well-equipped Pyrenean resorts with fine, snow-sure slopes that compare favourably with mid-sized places in the Alps. Two resorts are certainly not downmarket – Sierra Nevada and Baqueira-Beret (see next chapter) are both frequented by the King of Spain. Winter sports are becoming more popular with the prosperous Spanish themselves, and as a result many of the smaller resorts are continually improving.

The general ambience of Spanish resorts is attractive – with eating, posing and partying taken seriously.

Sierra Nevada (2100m/6,890ft) is in the extreme south of Spain, near Granada (a must-see, and much quieter than in summer), with views from the top to the Atlas mountains in Morocco.

The hub of the resort is Pradollano, a stylish modern development with shops and a few restaurants and bars set around traffic-free open spaces.

Most of the accommodation is in older, less smart buildings set along a road winding up the steep hillside. A two-stage chair-lift also goes up the hillside, with red runs back down to the main lift stations at Pradollano. Choose your location with care.

From Pradollano an old four-person gondola and a newer 14-person one go up to Borreguiles, at the heart of the 87km/54 miles of slopes. Here there are excellent nursery slopes, and lifts going up to the broad upper slopes beneath the peak of Veleta, where there is also a terrain park. There are three identifiable sectors, well linked, with a good range of intermediate and easy runs. It is not a big area, and there is not a lot for experts.

Queues can develop at Pradollano and higher up there are quite a lot of slow old lifts that cause queues at peak times. The chair up the village slope gets the biggest queues of all. Most chairs have singles lines, though. The home run can get crowded.

Sierra Nevada can have good snow years when the Alps has bad, and vice versa. Most slopes face north-west, but some get the afternoon sun. And when the wind blows, as it does, the slopes close; there are no trees.

There is a group of worthwhile resorts in the western Pyrenees, between Pau and Huesca.

Formigal is only the third-largest ski area in the Spanish Pyrenees (106km/66 miles of runs) but is a favourite with experts for its 28 black runs (though many of them could be red). For 2007/08 a couple of new free-ride areas are planned, along with heli- and snowcat skiing and boarding. The village, of solidly built apartment blocks, is on the east side of the Tena valley, while all the slopes are on the west side, spreading over a series of side-valleys with north- and south-facing treeless slopes served by 22 lifts. So ski-in/ski-out this is not. The whole thing is really set up for motorists, who can park at one of four lift bases. Sextas, the first and the nearest to the village, was fully renovated for 2006/07, with a smart if unatmospheric reception building and eight-seat chair. Although the top station is only 2250m/7,380ft, Formigal has a justified reputation for wind. If it gets too bad you can slip down to **Panticosa**, about 10km/6 miles away and under the same ownership. It has also seen some modernisation, and the 34km/21 miles of runs offer something for everybody in a slightly more protected environment. Thermal baths and two new 4-star hotels are planned for 2007/08.

Candanchu and nearby **Astún**, with almost 80km/50 miles of pistes between them, are popular on the Spanish market. They offer a wide range of lodging set in some of the Pyrenees' most stunning scenery. Both resorts have some tough runs.

The other main group of Spanish resorts is just east of Andorra. The 50km/31 miles of runs at **La Molina** are linked to those of **Masella**, over the mountain, via a gondola and six-pack. The whole area, called Alp 2500, now offers 113km/70 miles of slopes.

Baqueira-Beret

Spain's leading winter resort, with high, extensive, north-facing slopes; for Spanish animation, though, stay down the valley

RATINGS

The slopes

Fast lifts	**
Snow	***
Extent	**
Expert	***
Intermediate	****
Beginner	**
Convenience	***
Queues	****
Mountain restaurants	**

The rest

Scenery	***
Resort charm	**
Off-slope	*

UK PACKAGES

Inghams, Ski Miquel

The original high-rise blocks of Baqueira in the valley, with more recent tasteful development above ↓

- ➕ Compact modern resort
- ➕ Reasonable snow reliability
- ➕ Some good off-piste potential
- ➕ Lots of good intermediate slopes
- ➕ Friendly, helpful locals

- ➖ Drab blocks dominate the main village, which lacks atmosphere
- ➖ Resort is not cleverly laid out, and traffic intrudes
- ➖ Still lots of old, slow lifts

Baqueira is in a different league from other resorts in the Spanish Pyrenees – a smart, family-oriented resort with a wide area of slopes that gives a real feeling of travel. It attracts an almost entirely Spanish clientele (which regularly includes their royal family), so don't count on English being spoken.

THE RESORT

Baqueira was purpose-built in the 1960s and has its fair share of drab, high-rise blocks; these are clustered below the road that runs through to the high pass of Port de la Bonaigua, while the main lift base is just above it. But up the steep hill from the main base are some newer, smaller-scale stone-clad developments. At the very top is an alternative chair-lift into the slopes. The most convenient base is close to the main lifts, but the village is small enough for location not to be too much of an issue. There is a lot of accommodation spread down the valley, and a big car park with road-train shuttle up to the lift base.

THE MOUNTAINS

There is an extensive area of long, mainly intermediate runs, practically all of them on open, treeless slopes and facing roughly west.

Slopes The slopes are split into three distinct but well-connected areas – Baqueira, Beret and Bonaigua. From the base station at Baqueira, a fast quad, which you ride with skis off, and a new parallel gondola take you up to the nursery slopes at 1800m/5,910ft. Fast chairs go up to Cap de Baqueira. From here there is a wide variety of long runs, served by chairs and drags – including a long black down to Orri. From several points you can descend into the Bonaigua sector, leading over to the summit of the Bonaigua pass. You can ride a chair from the pass to get to an expanding area of slopes descending to the east of the pass and served by a fast quad.

From the opposite extremity of the Baqueira sector at Orri a triple chair takes you off to the Beret sector, where a series of more-or-less parallel chairs serve mainly blue and red runs. A fast quad from Beret accesses a fourth sector at Blanhiblar, with red and blue pistes and an itinerary. All main lift bases are accessible by road.

Terrain-parks There's a terrain-park with half-pipe in the Bonaigua area.

Snow reliability Most of the slopes are above 1800m/5,910ft and there is extensive snowmaking, but afternoon sun is a problem in spring. We've had mixed reports of the grooming.

Experts Experts will find few on-piste challenges, but there are extensive off-piste opportunities all over the area. And there are four ungroomed itinerary

NEWS

For 2006/07 the road to Baqueira was improved. There is a new beginners' area at the top of the cable-car with several moving carpets and a tow. A new green run has been built and the Bonaigua cafe has been enlarged and has a restaurant.

KEY FACTS

Resort	1500m
	4,920ft
Slopes	1500-2510m
	4,920-8,230ft
Lifts	33
Pistes	104 km
	65 miles
Green	7%
Blue	51%
Red	34%
Black	8%
Snowmaking	
	549 guns

Phone numbers
From abroad use the prefix +34

TOURIST OFFICE

t 973 639010
viajes@baqueira.es
www.baqueira.es

SPAIN

706

runs including the steep and narrow Escornacrabes, from the top of Cap de Baqueira. Cheap heli-lifts are available.

Intermediates It's excellent, with lots of good long runs such as the 4km/2 mile blue from Tuc deth Dossau and some classic reds such as Muntanyó down to Port de la Bonaigua and Mirador above town. Less daring intermediates will enjoy the Beret and Bonaigua areas best.

Beginners There are good nursery runs above Baqueira, recently improved. Some of the longer blues can be a bit tough. Beret has an excellent nursery slope and gentler blues.

Snowboarding The main nursery slopes are served by a drag-lift and moving carpets. Experienced free-riders have plenty of chair-served off-piste.

Cross-country There are 7km/4 miles of trails between Orri and Beret.

Queues Weekdays are quiet and weekend queues seem to have been removed by the newish gondola. The Blanhiblar sector is always quiet.

Mountain restaurants All run by the lift company, the huts are said to be 'lacking in number and variety, and very smoky'. Another reader recommends the self-service places at Beret, and the table-service place at 1800m. You can also get table-service at Cap del Port (at the Bonaigua pass), at Baqueira 2200 and at Beret.

Schools and guides A 2007 reporter 'highly recommends' the new Baqueira British Ski School (four British instructors) – which offers a cheaper rate for guiding only.

Facilities for children The kindergarten takes very young children but lack of spoken English is a problem. Ski school classes start from age four and there are snow gardens in each sector.

STAYING THERE

How to go There is a reasonable choice of hotels and apartments locally. Ski Miquel has a catered chalet.

Hotels In the main village the 4-star Montarto (973 639001) has a pool and 'wonderful food' and the 5-star Rafael La Pleta (973 645550), just above the village has 'spacious rooms, wonderful service', says a 2007 reporter. The Parador (973 640801) down the valley in Arties and the 2-star Husa Vielha (973 640275) in Vielha, 15km/9 miles away, have been recommended.

Eating out The more interesting restaurants are down the valley in Salardu, Arties and Vielha. Reporters have enjoyed the local tapas bars.

Après-ski There are pubs and discos down the valley. Pacha, in the main village, gets going late.

Off the slopes Pool and spa facilities are available in some hotels. Vielha has a sports centre and ice rink.

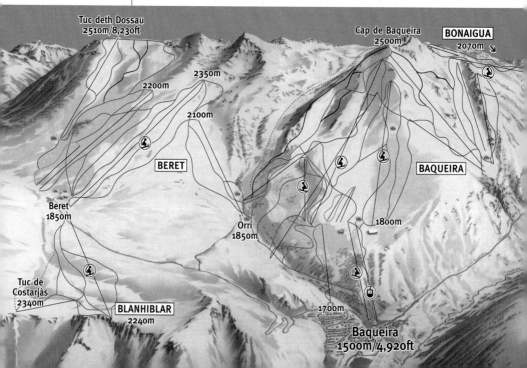

Finland

COSTS

①②③④ ⑤ ⑥

NEWS

Ylläs plans to install Finland's second gondola (the first is in Levi) for 2007/08. The new lift is expected to run from the Iso-Ylläs (Ylläsjärvi) base up to Ylläskammi and forms part of a major expansion project for the area.

Two new pistes were added last season, and for 2007/08 there are plans for a new quad, more snowmaking and more runs in the Ylläs-Ski sector (Äkäslompolo). The mountain restaurants are also expected to get a revamp – two new ones are planned.

Sport Resort Ylläs is a new complex being built at Iso-Ylläs. When complete it will offer 5,000 beds in a mix of chalet and hotel lodgings.

Work has started at Ruka on the construction of a new pedestrian village at the foot of the slopes, with all cars banished to an underground garage. The development will provide 'high-class' apartments, shops and at least one restaurant. The project is called Ruka Village 2009, from which you can deduce the planned completion date.

+ Peace, quiet and Lapp charm
+ Ideal terrain for cross-country and gentle downhilling
+ Reliable late snow
+ Jolly outings

– Cold
– Small ski areas
– Quite expensive
– Uninspiring food

For skiers with no appetite for the hustle and hassle of Alpine resorts in high season – perhaps especially for families – escape to the white silence of Lapland may be an attractive alternative. Finland has the lion's share of Lapland and has successfully marketed it, not only for day-trip visits to Santa but also for ski holidays to resorts with limited downhill slopes but limitless cross-country. Of the resorts covered here, only Ruka and Iso-Syöte are south of the Arctic Circle.

The Arctic landscape of flat and gently rolling forest punctuated by many lakes and the occasional treeless hill is a paradise for cross-country skiing. Weather permitting, it also offers good beginner and intermediate downhilling, albeit on a small scale.

The resorts usually open a few runs in late November. For two months in midwinter the sun does not rise – at least, not at ground level. Most areas have floodlit runs. The mountains do not open fully until mid-February, when a normal skiing day is possible and Finnish schools have holidays that usually coincide with ours – a busy time. Finland comes into its own at the end of the season, with friendlier temperatures and long daylight hours. Understandably, Easter is extremely popular, and the slopes are crowded.

Conditions are usually hard-packed powder or fresh snow from the start of the season to the end (early May).

The temperature can be extremely variable, yo-yoing between zero and minus 30°C several times in a week. Fine days are the coldest, but the best for skiing: it may be 10 to 15 degrees warmer on the slopes than at valley level. 'Mild' days of cloud and wind are worse, and face masks are sold.

The staple Finnish lift is the T-bar. Ruka has some chairs, and Levi and Ylläs each have a gondola. Pistes are wide and well maintained, with good nursery slopes. The Finns are great boarders and consider their terrain-parks far superior to those in the Alps; super-pipes are increasingly common.

None of the areas has significant vertical by alpine standards, and in some cases it is seriously limited.

There is no need for mountain restaurants – you are never far from the base, with its self-service restaurant. The ski areas also have shelters or 'kotas' – log-built teepees with an open fire and a smoke hole – where you can eat a snack .

Ski school is good, with English widely spoken. All ski areas have indoor playrooms for small children, but they may be closed at weekends.

Excursions are common – husky-sledding, snowmobile safaris, a reindeer sleigh ride and tea with the Lapp drivers in their tent. 'The whole experience is wonderful,' says a typically enthusiastic participant.

Hotels are self-contained resorts, large and practical rather than stylish, typically with a shop, a cafe, a bar with dance floor, and a pool and sauna with outdoor cooling-off area. Hotel supper is typically served no later than seven, sometimes followed by a children's disco or dancing to a live band. Finns usually prefer to stay in cabins, and tour operators offer the compromise of staying in a cabin but taking half-board at a nearby hotel. Cabins vary, but are

UK PACKAGES

Ylläs *Crystal, First Choice, Inghams, Inntravel, Neilson, Waymark*
Levi *Crystal, First Choice, Inghams, Neilson*
Ruka *Crystal, Inghams, Kuoni, Thomson*
Pyhä *Crystal*
Iso-Syöte *Crystal, Thomson*

Phone numbers
From abroad use the prefix +358 and omit the initial '0' of the phone number

TOURIST OFFICES

Levi
www.levi.fi

Ylläs
www.yllas.fi

Ruka
www.ruka.fi

Pyhä
www.pyha.fi

Iso-Syöte
www.isosyote.fi

mostly well equipped, with a sauna and drying cupboard as standard.

The main resorts are Levi and Ylläs, respectively 17km/10 miles north and 50km/31 miles west of Kittilä, which has direct charter flights from Britain.

Ylläs mountain has two gateways, both 4km/2 miles from the mountain. The minor one is Ylläsjärvi, the major one Äkäslompolo – a traditional lakeside Lapp settlement. Cross-country skiing makes sense of a resort such as Äkäslompolo, which has 320km/200 miles of trails, transforming it from awkward sprawl to doorstep ski resort of limitless scope. From the lift base trails fan out around the mountain, across the frozen lake and away through the endless forest.

Ylläs is the largest downhill ski area, with 463m/1,520ft vertical. Lifts and pistes on two broad flanks of the mountain give plenty of scope for novices. Second- and third-week skiers will rapidly conquer the benign black runs. Ylläs has a welcoming mountain-top restaurant – the highest in the country at 718m/2,360ft. There are major expansion plans, including the country's second gondola (see 'News').

The Hillankukka log cabins at Äkäslompolo are exceptionally good, but the 10-minute walk to and from meals at the Äkäs hotel (016 553000) is not to be underestimated. A reporter praises the hotel itself – 'beautiful hotel, excellent hydrotherapy pool'.

Levi is a purpose-built village of hotels and cabins at the foot of its slopes: 44 runs served by 27 lifts, including 22 red and three black slopes. It claims Finland's biggest terrain-park. Our most recent reporter loved the resort. Levi has 230km/143 miles of cross-country trails. Its biggest hotel, Levitunturi (016 646301), was rated 'great' by a recent reporter, with 'excellent' facilities – pool, tennis, and a children's centre. Of the 30 or so restaurants, readers recommend the Steak House, Myllyn Aija, Arran and the White Reindeer; and of the bars, Panimo (a microbrewery) and Crazy Reindeer (karaoke).

Ruka lies 80km/50 miles south of the Arctic Circle, close to Kuusamo airport and the Russian border, in a region known for abundant and enduring snow. The ski area, on two sides of a single low hill (Ruka East and Ruka West), has a mixture of open and forest terrain, 19 lifts (including one six-pack and four other chairs),

and 20km/12 miles of pistes, most covered by floodlighting and snowmaking. There are runs of all colours, but none is steep. A 2006 reporter rates it 'excellent for beginners and intermediates looking for a relaxed atmosphere and blissfully uncrowded slopes'. But be warned: the vertical is a very modest 200m/660ft. There are of course terrain-parks.

Our reporter was very happy with the ski school, despite having to join a class below his standard.

The cross-country scope is vast: they advertise 500km/310 miles, of which 40km/25 miles are floodlit.

The atmosphere at the resort and on the slopes is upbeat – with live music in the Wunderbar and sun terraces outside the Piste, very popular in spring. Hotels include the Rantasipi Rukahovi (08 85910), only 50m/160ft from the slopes, and the Royal Ruka (08 868 6000), the resort's flagship property. The best accommodation is in cabins. Most of it requires use of the ski-bus. Good restaurants include Riipinen, which offers capercaillie, bear and boar, Vanha Karhu, and Kalakeidas – an intimate little place doing 'a range of traditional Finnish food'. There's lots to do off the slopes.

Pyhä, 150km/93 miles north-east of Rovaniemi, has seven lifts (including two chairs) and 10 runs on a mountain, much of which is a National Park. The vertical is only 280m/920ft and there is no steep terrain, but it has good off-piste. The best powder runs are on both sides of a long T-bar on the north slope. The Hotel Pyhätunturi (016 856111) is at mid-mountain.

Iso-Syöte, 150km/93 miles south of the Arctic Circle and 140km/87 miles from Oulu airport, is Finland's southernmost fell region – but it receives the most snow in the country. Catering mainly for families, it suits beginners and intermediates since, of its 12 pistes (covering 20km/12 miles), there are only two black runs. However, there is a free-ride area among the trees. The runs are short, with the longest 1200m/3940ft and a maximum vertical of less than 200m/660 feet. Seven runs are floodlit at night. There's a terrain-park, a snow-tubing area and a sledging hill. Cross-country is big here, with 120km/75 miles of trails. Accommodation is mainly hotels and cabins, including the Iso-Syöte hotel (0201 476400) at the top of the slopes (pool, sauna).

Norway

COSTS

① ② ③ ④ ⑤ ⑥

NEWS

At Geilo, snowmaking is due to be increased for 2007/08 and the terrain-parks are being upgraded. Last season the Dr Holms hotel was revamped, including new spa facilities.

In Trysil, for 2006/07 a six-pack with heated seats opened in the Fageråsen area and the slope beside it was widened. A kids' Minipark was added and two more restaurants opened.

In Hafjell an eight-seat gondola opened last season, beginning a series of improvements planned for the area.

Voss gained a fast quad in 2006/07 and Oppdal installed a chair-lift to serve a new blue piste.

➕ One of the best places in Europe for serious cross-country skiing

➕ The home of telemark – plenty of opportunities to learn and practise

➕ Complete freedom from the glitz and ill-mannered lift queues of the Alps

➕ Impressive snowboard parks

➕ Usually reliable snow conditions throughout a long season

➖ Very limited downhill areas

➖ Very basic mountain restaurants

➖ Booze is prohibitively taxed

➖ Unremarkable resort scenery

➖ Après-ski that is either deadly dull or irritatingly rowdy

➖ Short daylight hours in midwinter

➖ Highly changeable weather

➖ Limited off-slope activities

Norway and its resorts are very different from the Alps, or indeed the Rockies. Some people find the place very much to their taste. For downhillers who dislike the usual ski-resort trappings and prefer a simpler approach to winter holidays, it could be just the place. For families with young children, in particular, the drawbacks are less pronounced than for others; you'll have no trouble finding junk food to please the kids – the mountain restaurants serve little else.

Speaking for ourselves, any one of the first three ➖ points we've listed above would probably be enough to put us off. Combine these in a single destination – then add in the other non-trivial negative points – and you can count us out.

There is a traditional friendship between Norway and Britain, and English is widely spoken.

For the Norwegians and Swedes, skiing is a weekend rather than a special holiday activity, and not an occasion for extravagance. So at lunchtime they tend to haul sandwiches out of their backpacks as we might while walking the Pennine Way, and in the evening they cook in their apartments. Don't expect a tempting choice of restaurants.

The Norwegians have a problem with alcohol. Walk into an après-ski bar at 5pm on a Saturday and you may find young men already inebriated – not merry, but incoherent. And this is despite – or, some say, because of – prohibitively high taxes on booze. Restaurant prices for wine are ludicrous, and shop prices may be irrelevant – Hemsedal has no liquor store. Our one attempt at self-catering there was an unusually sober affair as a result. Other prices are generally not high by Alpine standards.

Cross-country skiing comes as naturally to Norwegians as walking; and even if you're not very keen, the fact that cross-country is normal, and not a wimp's alternative to 'real' skiing, gives Norway a special appeal. Here, cross-country is both a way of

getting about the valleys and a way of exploring the hills. What distinguishes Norway for the keen cross-country skier is the network of long trails across the gentle uplands, with refuges along the way where backpackers can pause for refreshment or stay overnight.

More and more Norwegians are taking to telemarking, and snowboarding is very popular – local youths fill the impressive terrain-parks at weekends.

For downhill skiing, the country isn't nearly so attractive. Despite the fact that it is able to hold downhill races, Norway's Alpine areas are of limited appeal. The most rewarding resort is **Hemsedal**, covered in the next chapter.

Just 20 minutes from the centre of Oslo on an extension of the

UK PACKAGES

Lillehammer *Crystal, Directski.com, Ski McNeill*
Geilo *Crystal, Headwater, Inntravel, Neilson, Waymark*
Beitostølen *Neilson*
Voss *Ardmore, Crystal, Inghams*

Phone numbers
From abroad use the prefix +47

TOURIST OFFICES

Tryvann
www.tryvann.no
Lillehammer
www.lillehammerturist.no
Geilo
www.geilo.no
Beitostølen
www.beitostolen.com
Oppdal
www.oppdal.com
Trysil
www.trysil.com
Voss
www.skiinfo.no/voss/

underground system is **Tryvann** (150m/490ft), a small area popular with the locals. The train arrives near the top station (525m/1720ft) on Holmenkollen. The main slopes – with a vertical of 380m/1,250ft – are served by two drags and two chairs, one of them fast. Two drags serve a separate nursery slope. There's a good terrain-park and a half-pipe. The whole area has snowmaking and can offer good conditions even when downtown Oslo has no snow in the streets. The slopes are floodlit until 10pm most evenings – and are busier then than in the day. A new day lodge is expected for 2007/08.

The site of the 1994 Olympics, the little lakeside town of **Lillehammer**, is not actually a downhill resort at all. The Olympic slalom events were held 15km/9 miles north at Hafjell (230m/750ft). This is a worthwhile little area with a vertical of 830m/2,720ft, 12 lifts (including a new eight-person gondola) and 33km/21 miles of pistes. The downhill and super-G races went to Kvitfjell, about 35km/22 miles further north, developed specially for the purpose. It's steeper but smaller – 18km/11 miles of pistes.

Norway's other internationally known resort is **Geilo** (800m/2,620ft). This is a small, quiet, unspoiled community on the railway line from Bergen, on the coast, to Oslo. It provides all the basics of a resort – a handful of cafes and shops around the railway station, a dozen hotels more widely spread around the wide valley, children's facilities and a sports centre.

Geilo is a superb cross-country resort. As the Bergen-Oslo railway runs through the town it is possible to go for long tours and return by train.

Geilo is very limited for downhillers, but it does claim to have Scandinavia's only super-pipe. The 32km/20 miles of piste are spread over two small hills – one, Geilolia, a bus-ride away from Geilo, with a good, informal hotel, a restaurant at its foot and a pizzeria on the mountain. This area was extended recently by a six-pack link to the family beginners' zone. None of the runs is really difficult. The terrain-park there was upgraded for this year and there are plans to revamp the Fugleleiken one for 2007/08.

Clearly the best hotel, and one of the attractions of staying in Geilo, is the Dr Holms Hotel (call central reservations on 320 95940) – smartly white-painted outside, beautifully furnished and spacious inside, with new spa facilities and revamped bar/cafe. This is the centre for après-ski, but prices are steep. The resort is quiet at the end of the day, but the main hotels provide live entertainment.

On the edge of the beautiful Jotunheimen National Park, about 225km/140 miles north-west of Oslo, lies the small resort of **Beitostølen** (750m/2,460ft). The 18 slopes are best suited to beginners and early intermediates. Confident intermediates and experts will find more of a challenge at the Alpine Centre, 6km/4 miles away, where they will find blacks, moguls and off-piste. There are 150km/93 miles of cross-country, some in the national park.

A long way north of the other resorts is **Oppdal** (550m/1,800ft), with more downhill runs than any of its rivals (55km/34 miles). The total vertical is 790m/2,590ft, but this is misleading – most runs are short. A new chair-lift and blue run were added this year.

There are slightly more extensive slopes at **Trysil** (460m/1,510ft), off to the east, on the border with Sweden, and the runs are longer (up to 4km/2 miles and 685m/2,250ft vertical). Well suited to families, it has a fast lift to the nursery area and gentle runs to progress to. A new six-pack with heated seats has replaced several drag-lifts, and the children's area has been improved. A reporter loved the 'long blue runs' and recommends the ski school. The runs here are all around the conical Trysilfjellet, some way from Trysil itself – though there is some accommodation at the hill. A connecting lift now serves accommodation at Fageråsen and there's a new shuttle-bus service at Høyfjellssenter.

In complete contrast to all of these resorts is **Voss** (50m/160ft), a sizeable lakeside town quite close to the sea, which is 'friendly, child friendly and has high standards of accommodation'. A cable-car links the town to the slopes on Hangur and Slettafjell, with a total of 40km/25 miles of 'impeccably maintained' pistes and 'no queues'. A fast quad was added this year. The ski school is reportedly 'brilliant', with small classes. And there are 11km/7 miles of cross-country trails. There are plenty of excursion possibilities, in particular the spectacular Flåm railway.

Hemsedal

The best place for Alpine skiing in Norway (though we prefer the Alps) with the slopes an awkward distance from Hemsedal village

COSTS

① ② ③ ④ ⑤ ⑥

RATINGS

The slopes
Fast lifts	**
Snow	****
Extent	*
Expert	**
Intermediate	****
Beginner	***
Convenience	**
Queues	****
Mountain restaurants	*

The rest
Scenery	**
Resort charm	**
Off-slope	*

NEWS

A new skier services centre is planned beside the children's area, including 40 apartments, rental shop, restaurant, kindergarten and parking – due for completion in December 2008.

For 2007/08 snowmaking is due to be increased along two more runs and further floodlights added for night-skiing. The Fjellet and Hollvin restaurants are to be revamped.

For 2006/07 a new drag-lift and slope opened in the children's area.

＋ Impressive snow reliability because of northerly location

＋ Increasing amounts of convenient slope-side accommodation

＋ Extensive cross-country trails compared to the Alps

＋ Some quite challenging slopes, and mountains with a slightly Alpine feel

－ Not much of a village

－ Limited slopes

－ Exposed upper mountain prone to closure because of bad weather

－ Weekend queues

－ One abysmal mountain restaurant

－ No liquor store for miles

－ Après-ski limited during the week and rowdy at weekends

Hemsedal's craggy terrain is reminiscent of a small-but-serious Alpine resort. Most people not resident in Scandinavia would be better advised to go for the real thing, but if you like the sound of Norway, Hemsedal is the place for downhill skiing. Go after the February school holidays, if possible.

THE RESORT

Hemsedal is both an unspoiled valley and a village, also referred to as Trøym and Sentrum ('Centre'), which is little more than a couple of apartment/hotel buildings, a few shops, a garage, a bank and a couple of cash-points that are usually empty by evening. Note the absence of a liquor store. There has been talk of a lift from Trøym to the slopes, but for now the lift base is a mile or two away, across the valley.

There are self-catering apartments and houses beside the slopes (more seem to open each year) in the Skarsnuten area, which is linked to the main network by its own lift and red piste – and in a pleasantly woody separate cluster a walkable distance down the hill from the lifts.

A ski-bus links these points and others, but a 2006 visitor says it is 'busy, irregular and not suitable for a child's buggy'. The place is geared to weekenders arriving by car or coach.

THE MOUNTAINS

Hemsedal's slopes pack a lot of variety into a small space. They are shaded in midwinter, and can be very cold.
Slopes With four fast chairs to play on, you can pack a lot of runs into the day. And there's night skiing until 9pm, Tuesdays to Fridays. The lift pass also covers smaller Solheisen, up the valley. For a small supplement you can ski at Geilo, an hour away.

Terrain-parks There are two terrain-parks ('absolutely fantastic'). The main one has sections for advanced and expert jibbers, a half- and two quarter-pipes plus a big jump, rails and boxes. The beginner park was recently upgraded and also has a half- and quarter-pipe, jumps, rails and tabletops.
Snow reliability The combination of latitude, altitude and orientation makes for impressive snow reliability. There's extensive snowmaking – increasing again for 2007/08.
Experts There is quite a bit to amuse experts – several black pistes of 450m/1,48oft vertical served by a fast eight-seat chair (or the adjacent 'very steep and very bumpy' T-bar) from the base (a couple left as a mogul slope) – and wide areas of gentler off-piste terrain served by drags above the tree line.
Intermediates Mileage-hungry piste-bashers will find Hemsedal's runs very limited. There are quite a few red and blue runs to play on, but the difference in difficulty is slight.
Beginners There's a gentle nursery area for absolute beginners. And there are splendid long green runs – but they get a lot of traffic, some of it irresponsibly fast. Some long blues and reds also suit near-beginners.
Snowboarding There is plenty of free-riding terrain, and some pistes are suitable for carving. The parks are popular and there's a boarder-cross.
Cross-country By Alpine standards there is lots to do – 130km/81 miles of

KEY FACTS

Resort	650m
	2,130ft
Slopes	670-1450m
	2,200-4,760ft
Lifts	22
Pistes	43km
	27 miles
Green	41%
Blue	25%
Red	18%
Black	16%
Snowmaking	18km
	11 miles

Here, as elsewhere in
Norway, terrain-parks
are big news ➔

HEMSEDAL TOURIST OFFICE

UK PACKAGES

Crystal, Neilson

Phone numbers
From abroad use the
prefix +47

TOURIST OFFICE

t 320 55030
info@hemsedal.com
www.hemsedal.com

Facilities for children The facilities at
the lift base are good, with day care
for children over three months. But a
2006 reporter complains that 'you
can't book in advance and parents are
expected to check on their children
hourly and provide all snacks and
meals'. The kids' nursery slopes keep
growing (another lift and slope were
added last season) and classes are
now available for four-year-olds.

STAYING THERE

How to go Most of the accommodation
is in apartments, varying widely in
convenience. Catered chalets are
available through certain UK operators.
Hotels The best hotel is the recently
refurbished Skogstad (320 55000) in
central Hemsedal – comfortable, but
noisy at weekends. Other hotels along
the valley are used by UK tour
operators. The hotel Skarsnuten (320
61700), on the mountain, is stylishly
modern (with no smoking).
Apartments The Alpin apartments, a
walk from the lift base, are satisfactory
if you don't fill all the beds. The
adjacent Tinden ones are quite smart.
Eating out The Oxen restaurant and bar
and Peppe's pizza were recommended
last season.
Après-ski It's minimal in the week,
rowdy at weekends and holidays.
Off the slopes Diversions include dog-
sledding, tobogganing and
snowmobiling. The hotel Skogstad
pool is open to the public.

prepared trails in the valley and forest
and (later in the season) 80km/50
miles at altitude. There is a special trail
map. Most of the trails are a few miles
down the valley at the Gravset centre
and 12km/7 miles of them are floodlit.
Queues Hemsedal is only a three-hour
drive from Oslo, the capital. Good
weekend weather fills the car parks,
leading to queues for the main access
lifts. But during the week it is quiet.
The upper lifts are very exposed, and
are easily closed by bad weather,
producing crowds lower down.
Mountain restaurants There is one
functional self-service mountain
restaurant doing dreary fast food, plus
two or three kiosks with benches.
Schools and guides Our most recent
reporter was greatly impressed: 'Lots
of one-to-one, very encouraging.'

Totten
1450m/4,760ft

Tinden
1350m

Røgjin
1325m

Fjellet
1125m

940m

Skarsnuten

Veslestølen

670m/2,200ft

Hemsedal
Skisenter

Fjellandsby

Hemsedal
640m/2,100ft

Sweden

COSTS

① ② ③ ④ ⑤ ⑥

NEWS

For 2007/08 in the Sälen area a new eight-seat chair will replace a quad, a new blue run will be built and more snowmaking is planned.

Björkliden is discontinuing the cat-skiing it offered for 2006/07, but more guided off-piste touring and heli-skiing is planned for this season.

- ➕ Snow-sure from December to May
- ➕ Unspoiled, beautiful landscape
- ➕ Uncrowded pistes and lifts
- ➕ Vibrant (but regimented) après-ski
- ➕ Excellent cross-country and good range of non-skiing activities

- ➖ Limited challenging downhill terrain
- ➖ Small areas by Alpine standards
- ➖ Lacks the dramatic peaks and vistas of the Alps
- ➖ Short days during the early season

Sweden's landscape of forests and lakes and miles of unspoiled wilderness is entirely different from the Alps' grandeur and traffic-choked roads. Standards of accommodation, food and service are good and the people welcoming, lively and friendly. There are plenty of off-slope activities, but most of the downhill areas are limited in size and challenge. Sweden is likely to appeal most to those who want an all-round winter holiday in a different environment and culture.

Holidaying in Sweden is a completely different experience, culturally as well as physically, from a holiday in the Alps. The language is generally incomprehensible to us and, although virtually everyone speaks good English, the menus and signs are often written only in Swedish. The food is delightful, especially if you like fish and venison. And resorts are very family-friendly.

Sweden is significantly cheaper than neighbouring Norway, but reporters still complain that beer is £5 a pint, wine £15 a bottle and traditional Swedish restaurants very expensive.

One myth about Swedish skiing is that it is dark. It is true that the days are very short in December and early January. But from early February the lifts generally work from 9am to 4.30 and by March it is light until 8.30pm. Most resorts have some floodlit pistes.

On the downside, downhill slopes are generally limited in both challenge and extent and the lift systems tend to be dominated by T-bars. But there is lots of cross-country and backcountry skiing. Snowboarding is also popular, with parks and pipes in most resorts.

Après-ski is taken very seriously – with live bands from mid- to late-afternoon. But it stops suddenly, dinner is served and then the nightlife starts. There is plenty to do off the slopes: snowmobile safaris, ice fishing, dog-sled rides, ice-climbing, and saunas galore. You can also visit a local Sami village.

The main resort is **Åre** (see separate chapter). **Sälen** is Scandinavia's largest winter sports area – and is made up of four separate sets of slopes totalling

144km/89 miles of piste. Most slopes are very gentle, suiting beginners and early or timid intermediates best. Lindvalen and Högfjället are vaguely linked by a lift and a long cross-country slog. But you need the unreliable bus service to the others.

Vemdalen has two main areas of slopes 18km/11 miles apart by road and linked by buses. A joint lift pass serves both, there are no queues in either and T-bars dominate. **Björnrike** is great for families, beginners and early intermediates, with nine lifts and 15km/9 miles of mainly gentle pistes. There is a hotel right on the slopes, built in modern style. **Vemdalsskalet** has more advanced intermediate terrain, nine lifts, 20km/12 miles of pistes (with night-skiing on some runs) and a terrain-park. The ski school is 'decent', says a 2007 reporter. The Högfjällshotell at the base is large, dates from 1936 and prides itself on its lively après-ski with live entertainment.

Riksgränsen, above the Arctic Circle, is an area of jagged mountain peaks and narrow fjords. The season starts in mid-February and ends in June – when you can ski under the midnight sun. There are only six lifts and 21km/13 miles of piste. But there is some good off-piste and midnight heli-skiing.

Björkliden, also above the Arctic Circle, is famous for its subterranean skiing inside Scandinavia's largest cave system. You need to go with a guide.

Ramundberget is a small, quiet, ski-in/ski-out family resort. It gets lots of snow and has 22km/14 miles of mainly easy or intermediate pistes.

UK PACKAGES

Ramundberget *Waymark*
Vemdalen *Neilson*

TOURIST OFFICES

www.visit-sweden.com
Sälen
www.skistar.com
Vemdalen (Björnrike, Vemdalsskalet)
www.skistar.com
Riksgränsen
www.riksgransen.nu
Björkliden
www.bjorkliden.com
Ramundberget
www.ramundberget.se

Åre

Sweden's best slopes, strung out along a frozen lake above a small but charming town and with lots of non-skiing activities to try

COSTS

① ② ③ ④ ⑤ ⑥

RATINGS

The slopes

Fast lifts	**
Snow	***
Extent	**
Expert	**
Intermediate	****
Beginner	****
Convenience	***
Queues	****
Mountain restaurants	***

The rest

Scenery	***
Resort charm	***
Off-slope	***

NEWS

For 2006/07 the Olympia fast chair was replaced by a new 'chondola' with eight-seat chairs and eight-seat gondolas. At Rödkullen a large warming hut and 14 toilets were built. The Rödhake kids' run there was extended and widened, and a 70m/230ft moving carpet installed.

Three new restaurants opened in the main square.

714

+ Cute little town centre
+ Good snow reliability
+ Good intermediate and beginner runs
+ Extensive cross-country trails
+ Excellent children's facilities
+ Lively après-ski scene
+ Lots of off-slope diversions

− Lots of T-bars
− Exposed upper mountain prone to closure because of bad weather
− High winds detrimental to snow conditions
− Few expert challenges
− High season and weekend queues

Åre has the biggest area of linked slopes in Sweden and some of its most challenging terrain. But it suits beginners, intermediates and families best. It has a dinky little town centre and a long area of slopes set along a frozen lake.

THE RESORT

Åre is a small town made up of old, pretty, coloured wooden buildings and some larger modern additions. When we were there the main square had a roaring open fire to warm up by. As well as accommodation in town, there is lots spread out along the valley, with a concentration in the Duved area. All the slopes and accommodation are set on the shore of a huge, long lake, frozen in the winter months.

THE MOUNTAINS

The terrain is mainly beginner and intermediate tree-lined slopes, with a couple of windswept bowls above.
Slopes There are two main areas (linked by an efficient ski-bus). The largest is accessed by a funicular from the centre of town or by a six-pack or cable-car a short climb above it. This takes you to the hub of a network of

runs and (mainly) T-bars that stretches for 10km/6 miles from end to end. The cable-car is often shut because it goes to the top of the above-the-tree-line slopes (known as the 'high zone'), which often suffers from howling gales. A gondola also accesses the high zone from a different point. You can get back on-piste right into the town square. A separate area of slopes is above Duved and served by a high-speed chair. There are several floodlit slopes, each open on a different night. A reporter who had suffered altitude problems in the Alps particularly liked the low altitude of the slopes.
Terrain-parks There's a boarder-cross course, a half-pipe and a big terrain-park, plus two parks for novices.
Snow reliability Snow reliability is good from November to May. But high winds can blow fresh snow away. They also mean that artificial snow is often made wet so that it doesn't blow away and it compacts to a hard, icy surface.

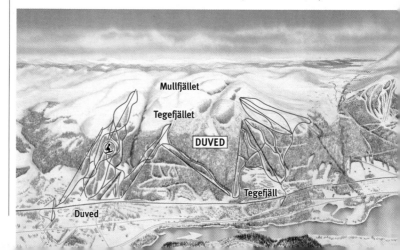

KEY FACTS

Resort	380m
	1,250ft
Slopes	380-1275m
	1,250-4,180ft
Lifts	40
Pistes	97km
	60 miles
Green	12%
Blue	39%
Red	43%
Black	6%
Snowmaking	
	23 pistes

UK PACKAGES

Neilson

Central reservations
phone number
For all resort
accommodation call
17700

Phone numbers
From elsewhere in
Sweden add the
prefix 0647.
From abroad use the
prefix +46 647

TOURIST OFFICE

t 13350
info@areresort.se
www.skistar.com

Experts Experts will find Åre's slopes limited, especially if the 'high zone' is closed. If it is open, there is a lot of off-piste available, including an 8km/ 5 mile run over the back, accessed by a snowcat service in high season. On the main lower area the steepest (and iciest when we were there) pistes are in the Olympia area. There are also steep black and red runs back to town. **Intermediates** The slopes are ideal for most intermediates, with pretty blue runs through the trees. Because they tend to be more sheltered, the blue runs also often have the best snow. You can get a real sense of travelling from hill to hill on the main area.
Beginners There are good facilities, both on the main area and at Duved.
Snowboarding There's good varied terrain for boarders, plus three terrain-parks (see above). But there are a lot of drag-lifts (31 out of a total of 40).
Cross-country There's an amazing 300km/185 miles of cross-country trails, both on prepared tracks and unprepared trails marked with red crosses. Some trails are floodlit.
Queues In high season there can be ('orderly and polite') queues for some lifts, especially in the central area immediately above Åre.
Mountain restaurants There are some good ones. Our favourite was the rustic Buustamons, tucked away in the woods near Rödkulleomradret.
Schools and guides The ski school has a good reputation and a recent reporter was impressed with his private lesson.
Facilities for children There are special children's areas and under eight-year-olds get free lift passes if wearing helmets. There's a kindergarten that takes children from the age of two.

STAYING THERE

How to go Neilson is the only UK tour operator to offer packages to Åre.
Hotels The best central hotel is the charming old Åregarden. The renovated slope-side Tott has good spa facilities and views, and 'friendly and efficient staff'. The Holiday Club (with bowling, a games room and its own childcare facilities) by the lake and the Renen in Duved ('well organised with good meals') are popular with families.
Apartments There are plenty of cabins and apartments; reporters have recommended the ones at Åre Fjällby.
Eating out The Bistro is good and there are plenty of alternatives.
Après-ski Après-ski is lively. The Tott and Diplomat are packed from 3pm and have live bands. Later on, the Country Club and Bygget also have live bands and there are plenty of bars for a quiet drink. Reporters recommended the concerts held in igloos by the 'awe inspiring' Tannforsen frozen waterfall .
Off the slopes Lots to do, including dog- or reindeer-sled rides, skating, curling, ice fishing, tobogganing, ice-driving, ice-climbing, snowmobiling (with amazing views) and paragliding.

Åre

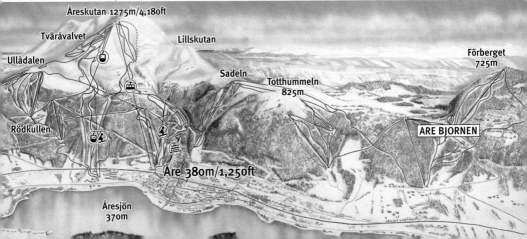

Bulgaria

716

Bulgaria has traditionally attracted beginners and early intermediates looking for a jolly time on a tight budget. Standards have been low. But Bansko's arrival on the international scene has raised the bar for Bulgarian resorts (see separate chapter), and perhaps things are improving in general.

A reporter who went to Borovets over New Year 2007 provides our latest dispatch from the front: 'Skis: old and well used. Ski school: easily arranged, no shortage of English speakers. Hotels: modern, clean, over-heated. Staff: mostly operating scams to relieve you of cash. Food: in the hotel and resort restaurants, good standard stuff; on the mountain, rubbish. Bars: all a bit quiet. Bulgarians: mainly miserable. Conclusion: you get what you pay for – and next time we will be paying a lot more to get a lot more.'

Pamporovo is strictly for beginners and very unadventurous intermediates, with mostly easy runs. Others are likely to find the limited area of short runs inadequate, despite recent expansion.

There are plans to build links to the slopes of nearby Mechi Chal in an ambitious project known as 'Perelik'; this would result in a linked area of some 80km/50 miles of pistes.

The slopes are pretty and sheltered, with pistes starting at a high point of 1925m/6,320ft and cutting through pine forest. The ski schools are repeatedly praised – instructors are patient, enthusiastic and speak good English, and class sizes are usually quite small. The main hotels are in a purpose-built village in an attractively wooded setting slightly away from the slopes – there is a shuttle-bus. The hotel Pamporovo gets the best reports, but the food is reportedly 'very poor'. The 5-star Orlovetz opened a couple of seasons ago. There is a handful of lively bars and discos.

Borovets has more to offer intermediates. The resort is a collection of large, modern hotels in a beautiful wooded setting, with bars, restaurants and shops housed within them. There is a small selection of quirkier bars, shops and eating places.

A long gondola rises over 1000m/ 3,280ft to reach both the small, high, easy slopes of Markoudjika and the longer, steepish Yastrebets pistes. The runs are best for good intermediates. There are no challenges for experts. The slopes are not ideal for novices; nursery slopes are overcrowded, and the step from the Markoudjika blue runs to testing reds is a big one.

Our New Year visitor met disastrously long queues for the gondola and other lifts, partly explained by other lift closures.

Grooming is erratic. The gondola is said to be prone to closure by wind.

Instructors are generally praised by reporters, but classes can be large.

Most reporters stay at the Rila or the Samokov hotels – both huge but with 'good, clean rooms'. The Lion is recommended this year. One reader ate out at Katy's Steak Pub. There are lively bars catering well an '18-30' type crowd – Buzz is said to be the best. Tour operator reps organise pub crawls, folklore evenings etc. Excursions to the Rila monastery or Sofia by coach are interesting.

UK PACKAGES

Pamporovo Airtours, Balkan Holidays, Crystal, Directski.com, First Choice, Inghams, Panorama, Ski Balkantours, Ski McNeill, Thomson
Borovets Airtours, Balkan Holidays, Crystal, Directski.com, First Choice, Inghams, Neilson, Panorama, Ski Balkantours, Ski McNeill, Thomson

TOURIST OFFICES

Pamporovo
www.pamporovo.net
Borovets
www.borovets-bg.com

Bansko

Small area of beginner and intermediate slopes served by a modern lift system above a rapidly growing resort town and base

COSTS

① ② ③ ④ ⑤ ⑥

RATINGS

The slopes

Fast lifts	*****
Snow	***
Extent	*
Expert	**
Intermediate	****
Beginner	**
Convenience	**
Queues	***
Mountain restaurants	***

The rest

Scenery	***
Resort charm	**
Off-slope	*

KEY FACTS

Resort	935m
	3,070ft
Slopes	935-2560m
	3,070-8.400ft
Lifts	23
Pistes	65km
	40 miles
Blue	35%
Red	40%
Black	25%
Snowmaking	45 guns

UK PACKAGES

Balkan Holidays, Crystal, Directski.com, First Choice, Inghams, Neilson, Ski Balkantours, Ski McNeill, Thomson

BANSKO SKI AREA

You're seeing most of the main mountain in this one shot ↓

- ➕ Bulgaria's best mountain
- ➕ Lots of fast lifts on the mountain
- ➕ Picturesque town at the base
- ➕ Smart new or renovated hotels
- ➕ Low prices
- ➕ Friendly, helpful locals
- ➕ Cheap and very cheerful traditional restaurants all over the town, but ...
- ➖ You may find you want to eat out in those restaurants even if you've bought a half-board package
- ➖ Long gondola-ride up to the main lift base – and big peak queues
- ➖ Limited slopes by Alpine standards
- ➖ Long airport transfers on poor roads
- ➖ Few off-slope diversions

Bansko completed its first season in full operation in 2004/05 and has shown what eastern Europe can offer the skiing world, given proper investment – more than £20 million spent on smart lifts, snowmaking and even a hands-free pass system. Readers are impressed: 'Bansko for us next year,' says one of several highly satisfied reporters – in sharp contrast to reports on the rest of Bulgaria. But the bed-base is expanding rapidly (many apartments are being sold to Brits) and the access gondola no longer seems able to cope with demand.

THE RESORT

Bansko, set on a flat valley floor circled by spectacular peaks, looks like a giant goods yard on the outskirts – more of an industrial town than a tourist destination. But around the central square the town has a quiet and charming heart, with architecture straight out of Disney's *Beauty And The Beast*. There are few outward signs of commercial tourism here except for hotels, which nestle between homes, shops, restaurants and churches. But a new hub with apartments, hotels and retail centre is developing rapidly near the gondola base; it's a fair walk from the centre and 'a shuttle-bus would be a good idea,' says one visitor.

For visitors, life in the town revolves around the dozens of mehanas (traditional inns) selling traditional Bulgarian food very cheaply and providing entertainment in the shape of live traditional music. There are lots of little shops, well stocked.

THE MOUNTAINS

Until 2003/04, the drag-lifts and pistes in the Pirin National Park were accessible only by army jeeps and minibuses up a tortuous 12km/7 mile road. Now an eight-seater gondola ferries skiers to the main lift base at Bunderishka. There is a blue piste back to the town, with snowmaking.
Slopes From Bunderishka two successive fast quad chairs take you up mainly north-facing slopes to the high point of the area. From there you can ski down reds or blues to Shiligarnika, or a red followed by a black (called Alberto Tomba, after the famous Italian racer who opened the revamped ski area) to Bunderishka. There are also a few slopes near the

NEWS

For 2007/08 a fast quad is planned to replace the drag-lift below the mid-station. The two red runs here will get snowmaking. And a ring road is being built to ease traffic congestion in the centre.

Work has also begun to construct a new shopping centre at the base of the gondola, including a restaurant and casino – due to be finished for 2008/09.

Snowmaking was increased last season and an ice rink opened.

TOURIST OFFICE

www.banskoski.com

mid-station of the gondola – a new quad and red piste are planned here for 2007/08 (see 'News').

Terrain-parks There's no half-pipe, but there's meant to be a terrain-park near the top.

Snow reliability A claimed 75 per cent of the pistes are covered by snowmaking. Together with good grooming (by Bulgarian standards) and north-facing slopes, this means more reliable snow than the Bulgarian norm.

Experts There are no challenging pistes – the one black ought to be red – but there is some good tree skiing.

Intermediates Good medium-to-difficult reds come straight down the face from the top, and varied blues go round to skier's right. All in all, there are four or five ways down the 900m/2,950ft vertical of the main area.

Beginners The nursery slopes near the top of the gondola are good, with little through traffic. There are blue runs served by drag-lifts at the top of the mountain and the long ski road back from top to bottom of the gondola is gentle and easy if the snow is good.

Snowboarding Varied, but limited. A 2007 visitor 'had great fun' in his

second week on a snowboard. There are some good off-piste routes to be explored with a guide.

Queues One reporter complains of waiting 'hours' for the gondola – clearly a problem at peak times. A second gondola has been talked about, but no dates given yet. Alongside all the chairs there are still some old drag-lifts, which can break down.

Mountain restaurants A fair sprinkling, including some modern ones with outdoor bars. The char-grills they serve are 'delicious and cheap'. The Platoto near the top is our reporters' favourite.

Schools and guides The main Ulen school gets good reports, but one visitor said her children could 'wander freely out of lessons' and were grouped with much younger children. A 2007 reporter was 'very impressed' with the small Pirin 2000 school – 'very good and flexible tuition'.

Facilities for children There's a kindergarten, with rope tows, moving carpet, carousel and satellite TV.

STAYING THERE

How to go Several UK operators feature Bansko.

Hotels There is a growing cluster of newish hotels around the gondola station, including the swanky but traditional-style Kempinski Grand Arena, with 'excellent facilities' and 'efficient' bus transfer to Sofia airport; the more modern Perun and the 'spacious' Lion. Refurbished places include the 'excellent' Pirin, near the town square and the 'wonderful' Strazhite, near the gondola. All these hotels have pools and some spa/fitness facilities. Most central hotels run a shuttle-bus service to the gondola.

Eating out Reporters enthuse about the town's scores of authentic mehanas with roaring fires, attentive waiters, real Bulgarian food and good wine.

Après-ski There are lively bars at the gondola base and new ones keep opening. The Lion pub, B4 and Amigos are popular with reporters, as is the bowling alley at the hotel Strazhite. The nightclub Amnesia is 'good' on some nights, 'empty' on others.

Off the slopes Excursions to the Rila monastery and trips across the border into Greece are possible. The spa at the Grand Arena got a rave review and there's a new ice rink.

TODORKA
2745m/9,000ft

2560m/8,400ft

Shiligarnika
1725m

Bunderishka
1635m

Chalin Valog
1465m

Bansko
935m/3,070ft

Romania

COSTS
①②③④⑤⑥

+ Cheap packages, and extremely low prices on the spot

+ Interesting excursions and friendly local people

+ Good tuition, enthusiastic instructors

− Primitive facilities – especially mountain restaurants and toilets

− Uninspiring food

− Very limited slopes – of no interest to anyone other than novices

Romania sells mainly on price. On-the-spot prices, in particular, are very low. Provided you don't have unreasonably high expectations, you'll probably come back from Poiana Brasov content. It allows complete beginners to try a ski holiday at the absolute minimum cost, and to have a jolly time in the evenings without adding substantially to that cost.

We haven't had any readers' reports on Romania for years. If you go, or indeed if you have been recently, please do let us have your views.

Romania's main resort – and now the only one featuring regularly in UK package programmes – is **Poiana Brasov** (1030m/3,380ft). It is a short drive above the city of Brasov in the Carpathian mountains, about 120km/ 75 miles (on alarmingly rough, slow roads) north-west of the capital and arrival airport, Bucharest.

Poiana Brasov is purpose-built, but not designed for convenience: the hotels are scattered about a pretty, wooded plateau, served by regular buses and cheap taxis. The place has the air of a spacious holiday camp, but one that incorporates some serious-sized hotels – some right by the lifts.

The slopes are extremely limited – approximately 12km/7 miles of pistes in total. They consist of decent intermediate tree-lined runs of about 750m/2,460ft vertical, roughly following the line of the main cable-car and gondola, plus an open nursery area at the top. There are also some nursery lifts at village level, which are used when snow permits. There's a terrain-park and half-pipe. Night skiing

is also available. The resort gets weekend crowds from Brasov and Bucharest, and queues can result, but during the week there are few problems.

A key part of the resort's appeal is the friendly and effective teaching.

Hotel standards are higher than you might expect. The linked Bradul (0268 407330) and Sport (0268 407330) hotels are handy for the lower nursery slopes and for one of the cable-cars, and look smart after refurbishment. Guests in both have use of the Sport's sauna/hot-tub/fitness room. The resort's first five-star, the Heraldic Club, opened recently.

Après-ski revolves around the hotel bars, night clubs and discos – supplemented by carnivorous outings to rustic barns with gypsy music. With cheap beer and very cheap spirits on tap, things can be quite lively. Off-slope facilities are limited; there is a good-sized pool, and bowling. Outings to the bars and restaurants of Brasov are recommended. An excursion to nearby Bran Castle (Count Dracula's home) is also popular.

UK PACKAGES

Poiana Brasov *Airtours, Balkan Holidays, Inghams, Neilson, Ski Balkantours, Solo's, Thomson*

Phone numbers
From abroad use the prefix +40 and omit the initial '0' of the phone number

TOURIST OFFICE

www.poiana-brasov.com

Slovenia

➕ Good value for money

➕ Beautiful scenery

➕ Good beginners' slopes and lessons

➖ Limited, easy slopes on the whole

➖ Mainly slow, antiquated lifts

➖ Uninspiring food, but improving

Slovenia offers good value for money 'on the sunny side of the Alps'. The main resorts are popular with economy-minded British and Dutch visitors and with visitors from neighbouring Italy and Austria, giving quite a cosmopolitan feel.

Slovenia is a small country bordering Italy to the west and Austria to the north. The first state to break away from Yugoslavia, Slovenia managed to escape the turmoil that engulfed the Balkans. There is a positive feel to the resorts – along with a warm and hospitable welcome. Prices are low: our latest reporters say drinks are under £1.

The main resorts are within two-and-a-half hours' bus-ride of the capital, Ljubljana. The ski areas are small, but with improving lift systems and few queues. Ski schools are of a high standard and cheap, reputedly with good English. Hotel star ratings tend to be a trifle generous, but standards of service and hygiene are high.

In addition to the resorts covered here, there are one or two described briefly in our directory at the back of the book – notably Kanin, on the border with Italy.

Kranjska Gora (810m/2,660ft) is the best-known resort, a pretty village not far from the Austrian and the Italian borders and dominated by the majestic Julian Alps. The Lek, Kompas and Larix hotels – with pools – are the best placed for slope-side convenience. A reporter enjoyed varied food and 'amazing breakfasts' at the Larix.

There are 30km/19 miles of mainly intermediate slopes, rising up to 1570m/5,150ft. Challenges are largely confined to the World Cup slalom run. Snow reliability is not good, despite snowmaking and a northerly exposure. The lift system is rather antiquated (14 of the 19 lifts are T-bars), but at least queues are rare, except at New Year and on local holidays. And there are plans for two new lifts to replace old ones for 2007/08. A terrain-park may also be built. There are 40km/25 miles of cross-country trails. Although it is family orientated, there is a selection of bars and discos.

Vogel (1535m/5,040ft), in the beautiful **Bohinj** basin, has the best slopes and conditions in the area. The 18km/11 miles of slopes are reached by a cable-car up from the valley. There's a collection of small hotels and restaurants at the base. Pistes of varying difficulty run from the high point at 1800m/5,910ft back into a central bowl with a small beginner area. When conditions permit, there is a long run to the bottom cable-car station. Two new quads are due for 2007/08. For a change of scene, **Kobla**, with 23km/14 miles of wooded runs, is a short bus-ride away.

Bled, with its beautiful lake and fairly lively nightlife, is an attractive base. Its local slopes are very limited, but free buses run to Vogel (about 20km/12 miles) and Kobla (a bit nearer).

Slovenia's second city, **Maribor** (265m/870ft), in the north-east, is 6km/4 miles from its local slopes – the biggest ski area in the country, with 64km/40 miles of runs, 36km/22 miles of cross-country and 21 lifts. The area lift pass now covers Kranjska Gora. There are several atmospheric old inns serving good, Hungarian-influenced food. A swimming pool opened at the Bolfenk apartments this year.

Scotland

NEWS

All five Scottish centres continue to operate despite the erratic snowfall of recent years.

At the Lecht, a new moving carpet was installed and family day passes introduced for 2006/07.

We are told that plans for Cairngorm may eventually involve the removal of the Coire na Ciste chair-lifts, effectively reducing the size of the ski area and limiting access to some of the mountain's steepest terrain.

FURTHER INFORMATION

The VisitScotland organisation runs an excellent website at: ski.visitscotland.com

t 0845 22 55 121
info@visitscotland.com

- Easy to get to from northern Britain
- It is possible to experience perfect snow and stirring skiing
- Decent, cheap accommodation and good-value packages are on offer
- Mid-week it's rarely crowded
- Extensive ski-touring possibilities
- Lots to do off the slopes

- Weather is extremely changeable and sometimes vicious
- Snowfall is erratic, to say the least, and pistes can be closed through lack of snow
- Slopes are limited; runs mainly short
- Queueing can be a problem
- Little ski village ambience and few memorable mountain restaurants

Conditions in Scotland are unpredictable, to say the least. If you live nearby and can go at short notice when things look good, the several ski areas are a tremendous asset. But booking a holiday here as a replacement for your usual week in the Alps is just too risky.

For novices who are really keen to learn, Scotland could make sense, especially if you live nearby. You can book instruction via one of the excellent outdoor centres, many of which also provide accommodation and a wide range of other activities. The ski schools at the resorts themselves are also very good.

Most of the slopes in most of the areas fall around the intermediate level. But all apart from The Lecht offer one or two tough or very tough slopes.

Snowboarding is popular and most of the resorts have some special terrain features, but maintaining these facilities in good nick is problematic. The natural terrain is good for free-riding when the conditions are right.

Cairngorm is the best-known resort, with 16 lifts and 37km/23 miles of runs. Aviemore is the main centre (with a shuttle-bus to the slopes), but you can stay in other villages in the Spey valley. The slopes are accessed by a funicular from the main car park up to Ptarmigan at 1100m/3,610ft.

Nevis Range opened in 1989 and is the highest Scottish resort. It has 11 lifts in addition to the long six-seat gondola accessing the slopes, and 35km/22 miles of runs on the north-facing slopes of Aonach Mor – Britain's eighth-highest peak. There are many B&Bs and hotels in and around Fort William, 10 minutes away by shuttle.

Glenshee boasts 21 lifts and 40km/25 miles of runs, spread out over three minor parallel valleys. Glenshee remains primarily a venue for day-trippers, though there are hotels, hostels and B&Bs in the area.

Glencoe's more limited slopes (seven lifts, 20km/12 miles of runs) lie just east of moody Glen Coe itself. You have to ride a double chair-lift and a button lift to get to the main slopes, including the nursery area. The isolated Kings House Hotel is 2km/1 mile away.

The Lecht is largely a novices' area, with 15 lifts and 20km/12 miles of runs on the gentle slopes beside a high road pass, with a series of parallel lifts and runs above the car parks. With a maximum vertical of only 200m/66oft, runs are short. There's extensive snowmaking. And there's a newish day lodge at the base. The village of Tomintoul is 10km/6 miles away.

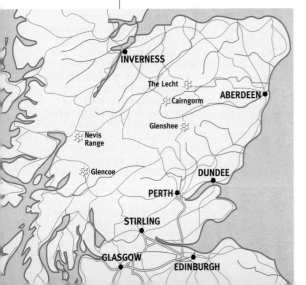

Japan

+ Reliable deep powder snow in Hokkaido resorts, lift-served
+ Exotic atmosphere, fabulous food
+ Polite and gracious locals
+ Extremely inexpensive alcohol
+ Night skiing is the norm, allowing a long ski day if you want one

- The language barrier
- It's a long way – around 6,000 miles and you have to change planes
- Lack of off-slope diversions
- Snowfall can go on for weeks in Hokkaido resorts

Although it is roughly the same size as the British Isles, Japan has hundreds of ski resorts. This season, several UK tour operators are featuring Japanese resorts, going to resorts on the northern island of Hokkaido that have developed something like cult status with keen skiers and riders from Australia, in particular. The reason? Snow – huge and reliable falls of powder snow.

In these remote parts of Japan, hardly anything is written in English and no English-language media are available. Going independently sounds like hard work; but presumably going with a tour operator is not.

You fly in to Sapporo (about two hours by bus from Rusutsu and a bit longer to Niseko or Furano), via Tokyo or Osaka. As you are travelling such a great distance you might want to combine your skiing with a stay in Tokyo or Kyoto.

Niseko is made up of three areas of slopes – Grand Hirafu (Hirafu and Hanazono), Annupuri and Higashiyama – with a total of 38 lifts covered by a single pass. The three are linked, but not as efficiently as you might wish. There are modern lifts, but also some old single chairs on upper slopes.

The most popular and most easily accessible area, Grand Hirafu, is open from 8.30am to 8.30pm, thanks to what is one of the world's largest – and most heavily used – night skiing operations.

Niseko has a well-deserved reputation for powder snow, which falls almost constantly from December to the end of February. Skiing waist-deep powder is an everyday occurrence. Clearly, this will suit some holiday skiers and not others. Niseko does offer groomed runs, but you can get those closer to home, and get a tan while you ski them. The snow does stop sometimes, and when it does the powder gets tracked out quickly. But it's usually not too long before another snowstorm marches in across the Sea of Japan from Siberia, and the powder returns. The terrain is not steep, disappointing some experts.

The lack of sun has not proved a deterrent to Australians, who now

← There are lots of resorts on the main island of Honshu; only the better-known ones are shown on our map. But the best snow is on Hokkaido

↑ No, the skiing doesn't take place on the volcano; the 500-room hotel Prince is at the foot of Niseko's Higashiyama slopes

TRAVELPLAN AUSTRALIA

UK PACKAGES

Niseko *Crystal, Inghams, Ski Dream, Ski Independence, Ski Safari*
Rusutsu *Crystal, Inghams, Ski Independence, Ski Safari*
Furano *Ski Independence, Ski Safari*

More information
To really get to grips with the resorts on offer in Japan, spend some time delving into this site: www.snowjapan.com

TOURIST OFFICES

Niseko
www.niseko.ne.jp
Hirafu
0136 22 0109
www.grand-hirafu.jp
Higashiyama
0136 44 1111
www.niseko-higashiyama.co.jp
Annupuri
0136 58 2080
www.niseko.ne.jp/annupuri

Rusutsu
0136 46 3331
www.rusutsu.co.jp

Furano
www.furano-kankou.com/english

come in their thousands (and, it must be said, are not an entirely welcome presence). For them, guaranteed powder and reasonable costs are an unbeatable combination. For UK-based travellers, the cost is higher: between around £1,000 and £1,900 for a week.

There are several modern ski-in/ski-out hotels (but little else) at the bases. Or you can stay in the atmospheric little town of Hirafu where, in the last few years, impressive modern apartments have gone up beside traditional pensions and lodges, raising accommodation standards well above the norm for the simple country town. The lift bases are well serviced by shuttle-buses.

While there isn't a lot to do outside of ski, eat and drink in Hirafu, the Australian influx means that the little town makes up for its lack of sophistication with a vibrant nightlife and plenty of variety in the way of bars, restaurants and tiny underground-style clubs. There are now a few very upmarket restaurants in town and several chic bars. And an igloo-style Ice Bar is dug out of a snowdrift each year, complete with icicles on the roof and a real bar selling all manner of cocktails.

Rusutsu is about an hour from Niseko, and makes a viable day trip from the larger resort; or you could combine the two in a two-centre holiday. The slopes, over three interlinked mountains, are more limited, but offer slightly more challenge. And for 2007/08 they are

opening up more terrain and tree-skiing between the pistes. The snow here can be as good as in Niseko, and it doesn't get tracked out so quickly.

The pivotal, self-contained Rusutsu Resort Hotel complex offers a wide choice of good restaurants plus all sorts of other facilities – bars, shopping mall, swimming and wave pool, spas.

One of the main alternatives to these two on Hokkaido is **Furano** – one of the more famous resorts within Japan, capable of hosting World Cup events and offering a tad more vertical than Niseko, at 950m/3,120ft over two linked sectors. It is five to six hours from Niseko and Rusutsu, so not within day-trip range but OK for a two-centre holiday. This is a resort where you can either stick to the relatively easy trails or join a guided group to explore off-piste, including the lift-served but ungroomed Asahidake mountain. You can stay either at the base of the slopes or in the town, a bus-ride away.

The largest ski area in Japan is on the main island of Honshu: **Shiga Kogen**, comprising 21 interlinked resorts and a huge diversity of terrain covered by one lift ticket. It was the site of several major events in the 1998 Winter Olympics.

Hakuba is also handy to reach by train if you find yourself in Tokyo and don't have time for the trip to Hokkaido. It is a group of 10 resorts accessing more than 200 runs amid the rugged peaks of Japan's 'Alps'.

THE ONSEN EXPERIENCE

Onsen are complexes of hot baths to soak in, showers and communal volcanic thermal pools; they are a key part of Japanese culture and a major part of après-ski. All onsen are basically set up in the same way: men and women shower and bathe in their separate areas. Then, if they wish, they can congregate to soak and drink beer in a communal thermal pool, which more often than not will be outside and surrounded by snow.

- ➕ Offers skiing and boarding during the European summer
- ➕ Some of the resorts offer upmarket slope-side accommodation
- ➕ Snowcat skiing offered in a couple of resorts

- ➖ It's a long way from Britain
- ➖ Mountains rather low and slopes rather limited by Alpine standards
- ➖ Day lift passes are very expensive – up to £40 per day

Even more than New Zealand, Australia offers resorts that are basically of local interest, but which might amuse people with other reasons to travel there – catching up with those long-lost relatives, say.

The major resorts are concentrated in the populous south-east corner of the country, between Sydney and Melbourne, with the largest in New South Wales (NSW) – in the National Park centred on Australia's highest mountain, Mt Kosciusko (2230m/ 7,320ft), about six hours' drive south of Sydney. It costs A$27 a day just to enter the Kosciusko National Park. Skiing has been going on here since the early 1900s – as it has in the next-door state of Victoria.

The season generally runs from early June to mid-October. In the last few years there have been major dumps in early July or even June, but August and September remain the most reliable months.

Thredbo, established in 1957, is a sophisticated, upmarket Alpine-style village in NSW. It hosted the only World Cup race event held in Australia, thanks to a vertical of 670m/2,200ft.

Thredbo is rather like a small French purpose-built resort – user-friendly, and mostly made up of modern apartments, many new luxury ski-in/ski-out chalets and lodges run by clubs. There are many upmarket chalets for rent, too. Originally Thredbo had an Austrian flavour but this has now given way to lively, modern, casual-elegant bars and restaurants, increasing numbers of very smart architect-designed apartments and a pedestrian mall with good shopping and sculptures. It's a steep place, with stiff climbs to get around from one part to another. Road access is easy.

The slopes, prettily wooded with gum trees, rise up across the valley from the village, served by a regular shuttle-bus through the resort. Snowmaking has greatly improved

reliability on the sometimes problematic lower slopes, and when the big falls arrive conditions can be as good as anywhere. But temperatures are rarely low enough for powder to last for more than a few hours. The runs are many and varied. The dozen lifts include three fast quad chairs, and the trails include Australia's highest (2037m/6,680ft) and longest (6km/4 miles). While the blacks are not steep – except for one called Funnelweb, after Australia's most poisonous spider – on the higher lifts there are off-piste variants, including a beautiful guided backcountry tour to Dead Horse Gap, with transport back to the resort provided. Thredbo's slopes are now dotted with terrain features.

There is an attractive pedestrian mall with good shopping and some high-class restaurants both on and off the mountain. There is also an impressive sports training complex open to the public, with an Olympic-size pool. The 700m/2,300ft public bob-sleigh track is popular.

On the other side of the mountain range is the large **Perisher Blue** resort complex, with a pass covering 50 lifts and six base stations – more than anywhere else in Australia – but a vertical of less than 400m/1,310ft. The main area is Perisher/Smiggins, where lifts and runs – practically all easy or intermediate – range over three lightly wooded sectors. The resort is reachable by road, or by the Skitube, a rack railway that tunnels up from Bullocks Flat and goes on to the second area, **Blue Cow/Guthega**, where the slopes offer more challenges.

Perisher Blue is doing its best to catch up with Thredbo by upgrading hotels and building more facilities. The resort is very spread out and has no central focus except for one cavernous base facility full of shops and eateries, and while a sophisticated pedestrian village has been widely talked about, the project has stalled. Perisher has more ski-in/ski-out accommodation than Thredbo, although it does appeal more to the masses, with its shopping-mall-style village centre filled with every manner of shop, bar and fast food restaurant. Its main advantage over Thredbo is its snow, thanks to its position further within the mountain ranges and its higher altitude. There is a super-sized terrain-park at Blue Cow.

Many on a budget choose to stay in the lakeside town of Jindabyne, a half-hour drive from both Thredbo and Perisher, with a lively youth-oriented nightlife scene. There are also some upmarket chalets along the Alpine Way leading to Thredbo.

From Perisher, a snowcat can take you on an 8km/5 mile ride to the isolated chalets of Australia's highest resort, **Charlotte Pass** (1760m/5,770ft), with five lifts but only 200m/66oft vertical. People visit the Pass more for its charm and Alpine beauty than for the skiing although it is very popular with families and beginners – the entire ski field can be seen from most of the lodges, and it is virtually impossible to get lost. The major hotel is the historic and turreted Kosciusko Chalet, a good spot for romantic weekends. Mt Kosciusko is easily reached on cross-country skis.

If you want to learn to ski among the gum trees at the most affordable price, **Selwyn Snowfields** is the place. It has 12 lifts, snowtubing and tobogganing and is about an hour from Cooma, near Jindabyne.

In Victoria, resorts are not as high as in NSW but many have good snow. **Mount Hotham** has a justified reputation for good snow and bills itself 'the powder capital of Australia'. An airport 20 minutes' drive from the slopes makes it the most accessible resort in Australia, with nine 85-minute flights a week from Sydney alone and two from Melbourne. To attract the professional Sydney crowd, there are concierges at the airport to arrange everything during your stay, and some of Australia's most exclusive hotels are now being constructed. The resort's 13 lifts serve a complete range of runs, with plenty of variety. The longest run is 2.5km/1.5 miles and there is more

consistently steep terrain here than at any other area in Australia. A snowcat service tows skiers out to nearby backcountry slopes and the resort has introduced snowkiting lessons. The village is built along the top of a ridge, with the slopes below it. The focus of the village is Mount Hotham Central, with apartments, shops, a few good restaurants and now the new White Mountain Spa. Hotham Heights Chalets is a nest of upscale architect-designed multi-storey buildings. You can also stay 15 minutes' drive away at Dinner Plain – stunning architect-designed chalets set prettily among gum trees. There are also a number of restaurants and bars here, and cross-country trails.

A six-minute A$99 return helicopter ride takes you to another resort nearby (and covered by the same lift pass), **Falls Creek**. Falls Creek is the most Alpine of Australia's resorts, completely snow-bound in winter (there are snowcats from the car park). There are 18 lifts, though the area is smaller than Mount Hotham's and the runs are mostly intermediate. There are extensive terrain-park features. Falls Creek has also built a lavish spa to rival Mt Hotham's, called the Huski and added a number of funky architect-designed lodges.

For some, the big attraction at Falls Creek is being able to access Australia's steepest skiing on the adjacent **Mt McKay** – 365m/1,200ft vertical of true black-diamond terrain. Guided snowcat trips take place twice a day. It's well worth the trip.

The other Victorian resort of note is the isolated peak of **Mt Buller**. Only a two-hour drive from Melbourne, this place is a magnet for old money, which has financed a proper sophisticated resort village with a luxury hotel, a pampering spa, Australia's highest cinema complex and even a university campus. Draped around the mountain are 25 lifts – the largest network in Victoria, including 13 chair-lifts. There's a hefty resort entry fee of A$30 and then A$6 to park overnight.

Mt Buffalo is worth visiting, mainly to stay in the historic Mt Buffalo Chalet, with its dramatic views over the craggy Victorian Alps. The Chalet, done up in true 1930s style, offers gourmet dining and is improving under new ownership. The slopes, a short drive away, are in an Alpine basin surrounded by boulders, with five lifts almost purely for beginners.

TOURIST OFFICES

Thredbo
www.thredbo.com.au
Perisher Blue
(for Perisher, Smiggins, Blue Cow, Guthega)
www.perisherblue. com.au
Charlotte Pass
www.charlottepass. com.au
Selwyn Snowfields
www.selwynsnow.com. au
Mount Hotham
www.mthotham. com.au
Falls Creek
(for Falls Creek and Mt McKay)
www.fallscreek.com. au
Mt Buller
www.mtbuller.com.au
Mt Buffalo
www.mtbuffalochalet. com.au

New Zealand

➕ For Europeans, more interesting than summer skiing on glaciers

➕ Huge areas of off-piste terrain accessible by helicopter

➕ Some spectacular scenery, as seen in *The Lord of the Rings* movies

➖ Limited on-mountain restaurants – though these are being upgraded

➖ Half-hour-plus drives from accommodation up to the ski areas

➖ Highly changeable weather

➖ No trees

The number of keen Kiwi skiers and boarders kicking around the Alps gives a clue that there must be some decent slopes back home – and indeed there are. The networks of lifts and runs are rather limited. But the heli-skiing around the Mt Cook region on the South Island is definitely worth writing home about. For Europeans already spending a lot to travel to New Zealand, the extra cost of a day or two's heli-drops around the Methven area is well worthwhile.

There are resorts on both North Island and South Island. The main concentration on South Island is around the scenic lakeside resort of Queenstown – see next chapter.

As in the northern hemisphere, the season doesn't really get under way until midwinter – mid or late June; it runs until some time in October. Mount Hutt aims to open first, in mid-May, and disputes the longest-season title with Whakapapa, generally open until mid-November and again in December for Christmas skiing.

Skiing at almost every New Zealand ski resort involves at least a half-hour drive from a nearby town – usually below the snowline – to the ski field itself. Coach transfers from the hotels and towns to the ski fields are generally well organised. The ski field will have a base lodge, usually with a restaurant and a cafeteria, equipment rental and one or two shops, as well as the main lifts. The only on-snow accommodation is in smart apartments at Cardrona on the South Island, and some private lodges at the base of Whakapapa on the North Island.

In what follows, we describe the most prominent resorts (apart from Queenstown and its mountains), but there are other possibilities.

Any of the major resorts is worth a day or two of your time if you're in the area and the conditions are right. But if your credit card is also in good condition, don't miss the heli-skiing; even if you're no expert off-piste, with powder skis it's a doddle, and tremendously satisfying.

Methven Heliski or Wilderness Heliski (03 302 8108) offer the longest and most spectacular runs. Both are operated by the same company, Alpine Guides (based at Mt Cook), but fly to different regions. The cost for about five runs averaging 1000m/3,280ft vertical each is around NZ$825. There are several other companies operating on South Island. Harris Mountain Heliskiing (03 442 6722), operating out of Queenstown and Wanaka, caters mainly for the large Japanese market, and the three-run days are generally very easy skiing, with long waits between lifts. New two seasons ago was Alpine Heliski (03 441 2300), based in Queenstown, started by a breakaway group from the major Queenstown operation, Southern Lakes Heli-Ski (03 442 6222). Alpine's prices start at NZ$729 for three runs; Southern offers 2, 4, 6 and 8 run packages ranging from NZ$645 to NZ$995 or NZ$1250 for a private charter. Both these companies are more amenable than Harris Mts to exciting skiing. Try to leave the arrangements loose, to cope with the changeable weather.

An alternative adventure is to fly by plane to ski down the Tasman Glacier. For two gentle 10km/6 mile schusses down the length of the glacier the cost is high – about NZ$725 for the day. The main draw is the immense grandeur of the place, along with the flights over stunning blue ice floes. If you're a good skier, you will find the Clarke Glacier eight-run day out of Queenstown more satisfying, though

KEY FACTS

Whakapapa

Altitude	1630-2300m
	5,350-7,550ft
Lifts	14
Pistes	1050 hectares
	2,590 acres
Blue	25%
Red	50%
Black	25%
Snowmaking	some

Mount Hutt

Altitude	1405-2085m
	4,610-6,840ft
Lifts	9
Pistes	365 hectares
	900 acres
Green	25%
Blue	50%
Black	25%
Snowmaking	
	42 hectares
	104 acres

Treble Cone

Altitude	1200-1960m
	3,940-6,430ft
Lifts	5
Pistes	550 hectares
	1,360 acres
Green	10%
Blue	45%
Black	45%
Snowmaking	
	50 hectares
	125 acres

Cardrona

Altitude	1670-1895m
	5,480-6,220ft
Lifts	7
Pistes	320 hectares
	791 acres
Green	25%
Blue	55%
Black	20%
Snowmaking	none

Snow Park

Altitude	1530m
	5,020ft
Lifts	1
Snowmaking	100%
Notes	2 super-pipes; 1 quarter-pipe; more than 40 rails, hits and jumps. Progressions Park for novices new last season. 1000-rider limit on hill

priced at $NZ995. There is an extensive range of ski touring on offer through Alpine Guides (03 302 8108) as well, from NZ$2595 for two people.

Snowboarding is very popular in New Zealand, and most of the major resorts have special terrain-parks.

New Zealand's biggest resorts are on the slopes of the active volcano Mt Ruapehu, which has occasionally erupted in recent years, leaving the slopes black with volcanic ash. Mt Ruapehu is within four hours' drive of both Auckland and Wellington.

The two ski fields, Whakapapa (pronounced Fukapapa) and Turoa, are in the same ownership and are in the middle of a NZ$30 million upgrade. Both fields offer exciting skiing and wide open slopes on a larger scale than found on the South Island.

Whakapapa, New Zealand's largest ski field, is located on the north-facing slopes, with a vertical of 670m/2,200ft served by 14 lifts including one fast quad. Current plans include two new fast lifts for the 2008 season. Terrain is typified by large, wide open cruisers plus challenging off-piste. Next to the base lodge is an extensive beginners' area, Happy Valley, with half-a-dozen rope tows, a chair-lift and snowmaking that allows this particular section to open early in the season. The resort's lifts and runs range across craggy terrain made especially interesting because of the twists, turns and drops of the solidified lava on which it sits. There is a mix of deep gullies, superb natural half-pipes for snowboarders and narrow chutes. There is a handful of mountain restaurants.

Accommodation is mostly 6km/ 4 miles away at Whakapapa village, and the best middle-of-the-road property is a motel named the Skotel. There is on-snow accommodation at the base. A complete anomaly in this area of rustic lodges is the Chateau, a hotel in the grand style of the 1920s, with high ceilings, sweeping drapes over picture windows and marble floors. In recent years it has undergone major renovations and extensions and is highly recommended as the place to stay if skiing Whakapapa.

Worth knowing about is the hike to Mt Ruapehu's fizzing Crater Lake. Ask a ski patrol for directions or, better, talk them into taking you on a guided trip. This involves about a half-hour (500m/ 1,640ft) hike up from the top of the highest T-bar, and then a long traverse across a large flat tundra-like area. A few lefts and rights and you are staring into the mouth of a volcano. Awesome views and neighbouring volcanos give this area an other-worldly feel.

Turoa is a fraction smaller than Whakapapa, but with an impressive 722m/2,370ft vertical – the biggest in Australasia. The longest run is 4km/ 2.5 miles. A new six-pack made its debut in 2007. There's plenty of off-piste scope away from the gentle intermediate runs, plus the chance to ski on the Mangaehuehu Glacier. Accommodation is 20 minutes away in the funky and lively town of Ohakune.

The South Island has 15 ski areas, including five club fields. **Mt Hutt**, an hour west of Christchurch in the

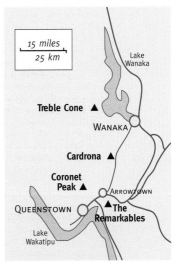

Phone numbers
From abroad use the prefix +64 and omit the initial '0' of the phone number

TOURIST OFFICES

Whakapapa
t 07 892 3738
info@mtruapehu.com
www.mtruapehu.com

Mount Hutt
t 03 302 8811
service@mthutt.co.nz
www.nzski.com

Treble Cone
t 03 443 7443
info@treblecone.com
www.treblecone.co.nz

Cardrona
t 03 443 7341
info@cardrona.com
www.cardrona.com

Snow Park
t 03 443 9991
info@snowparknz.com
www.snowparknz.com

Waiorau Snow Farm
t 03 443 0300
info@snowfarmnz.com
www.snowfarmnz.com

northern part of the island, has a 670m/2,200ft vertical and some of the country's most impressive, consistently steep, wide-open terrain – all within view of the Pacific Ocean. On a clear day you can even see the sandy beaches in the distance beyond the patchwork Canterbury plains – in fact it often snows on the beaches here. The lift system is half the size of Whakapapa's but recently it was totally upgraded and rearranged. The main area is an open bowl with gentle terrain in the centre and the steeper terrain up higher, ringing the ski field.

Mt Hutt has an impressive modern base lodge, including a spacious, welcoming cafe and brasserie with a glorious outdoor terrace, plus a well-stocked rental shop.

Mt Hutt Heliskiing operated by the Alpine Guides team (03 302 8401) offers three runs in the Mt Hutt backcountry for NZ$465, or one 800m/2,620ft vertical run on a peak just behind Mt Hutt for NZ$155, with extra runs for NZ$90. The helicopter departs from the heli-pad right in the car park – just book in at the heli-hut or take the NZ$79 per person one-way heli-taxi to the ski field.

There is no accommodation on-mountain – most people stay in the little town of **Methven**, where there are several comfortable up-market B&Bs as well as motels. The very British South Island capital of Christchurch, 90 minutes away, is also an option.

About six hours' drive south of Christchurch is the quiet lakeside town of Wanaka, which is also 90 minutes from Queenstown, and there are two resorts accessible from here.

Treble Cone, 20km/12 miles from Wanaka, has more advanced slopes than any other NZ ski area, plus the advantage of a better lift system. In area, the ski field comes second only to the North Island fields. Three new runs were added in 2006. There are backcountry ski tours, the only ones out of a resort in NZ, offering powder runs in Treble's back bowls. Back on the ski field, there are two well-maintained intermediate trails, one 3.5km/2 miles, the other 2km/1.2 miles. Both on the main flank and off to the side in Saddle Basin there are long natural half-pipes which are great fun when snow is good, as well as smooth, wide runs for cruising. Treble Cone is reached by a long and winding dirt track that adds to the excitement,

although the new owners are planning to install a gondola from the valley floor for the 2008 season. The ski field offers stunning views across Lake Wanaka, with snowcapped Alpine-style peaks in the distance. There's a cosmopolitan cafe at the lift base; an enormous sun deck sharing that view was added in 2004. The food here is generally quite good.

Cardrona, 34km/21 miles from Wanaka, is famous for its dry snow and is popular with families due to its superior childcare and teaching facilities. The terrain is noted for its well-groomed, flattering cruisers. But there are some serious if short chutes, and the middle basin, Arcadia, hosts the New Zealand Extreme Skiing Championships. The total vertical is a modest 390m/1,280ft. Millions have been poured into the resort by its family owners over the past few years, resulting in a large base area focused around an odd clock tower. Cardrona is unique in that it has a 1.2km/0.75 mile long terrain-park – the largest in the Southern Hemisphere, with four half-pipes – and right beside it a park for intermediates/beginners.

There's a bar and brasserie-style restaurant, a new ski-in/ski-out noodle bar with sun deck overlooking the nursery slopes, large rental facility and a licensed childcare centre, plus 15 modern apartments at the base. Learners are looked after well, with three moving carpets.

Snow Park – a dedicated terrain-park across the valley from Cardrona – is really making waves and attracting the cream of international free-ride skiers and snowboarders. Snow Park is in its fifth season and provides two super pipes, a quarter pipe, big kickers and more than 40 rails, hits and jumps all serviced by one fast quad. A proper restaurant, the Woolshed, and bar have now been built, along with budget ski-in/ski-out accommodation sleeping up to 44 people, and four luxury four-bedroom apartments with LCD TVs, decks and barbecues.

Nearby, at a height of 1500m/ 4,920ft, is New Zealand's only cross-country ski area, the **Waiorau Snow Farm**, a beautiful place with 55km/ 34 miles of what the owners claim are the best-prepared trails in the world. There are classic and skating lanes on all trails, designed for all levels. Accommodation is in the older-style Snow Farm Alpine Lodge.

Queenstown

A lively lakeside year-round resort, famous for its adrenalin-rush activities and well placed for a range of South Island resorts

RATINGS

The slopes

Fast lifts	**
Snow	**
Extent	*
Experts	***
Intermediates	***
Beginners	***
Convenience	*
Queues	***
Mountain restaurants	*

The rest

Scenery	****
Resort charm	**
Off-slope	*****

➕ For Europeans, more interesting than summer skiing on glaciers

➕ Huge heli-skiing areas

➕ Lots to do off the slopes, especially for adrenalin junkies

➕ Lively town, with good restaurants

➕ Grand views locally, and the spectacular 'fjord' country nearby

➖ Slopes (in two separate areas locally) are a drive from town

➖ Limited lift-served slopes

➖ Highly changeable weather

➖ No trees, so skiing in bad weather is virtually impossible

If you want a single destination in New Zealand – as opposed to visiting a few different mountains on your travels – Queenstown is probably it, especially if you can cope with the cost of a few heli-drops. Although the resorts of North Island are impressive, the Southern Alps are, in the end, more compelling – and their resorts are free of volcanic interruptions.

From Queenstown you have a choice of the two local ski areas – Coronet Peak and The Remarkables – plus the option of an outing to Cardrona and Treble Cone, perhaps with a few nights in the up and coming lakeside town of Wanaka. There are direct flights to Queenstown from Sydney, Brisbane and Melbourne.

THE RESORT

Queenstown is a winter-and-summer resort on the shore of Lake Wakatipu. (There is a map of the area in the introductory chapter on New Zealand.) Although the setting is splendid, with views to the peaks of the aptly named Remarkables range beyond the lake, the town itself is no great beauty – it has grown up to meet tourists' needs, and has a very commercial feel. Shopping is good, of course, as are the many wineries and cheese factories that are well worth a visit.

In recent years much effort has been put into smartening up the town, with such additions as the classy Steamer Wharf; the many new lakeside luxury apartments and hotels include the boutique Spire Hotel and the Sofitel Queenstown. It has a lively, relaxed feel, and makes a satisfactory base, with more than 160 licensed bars and cafes, some good restaurants, and lots of touristy clothes shops. There are no fewer than 173 activity operators in town; it's the base for every kind of adventure activity, offering bungee jumping, jet boating, river surfing and horse-trekking.

There are four lift-served mountains – all small by Alpine standards – that you can get to from Queenstown. The two described here – Coronet Peak and The Remarkables – are close by (about a 30-minute drive). The others – Treble Cone and Cardrona – are at least 90 minutes away, near Wanaka – a much quieter town in another beautiful lakeside setting with accommodation. See the New Zealand introduction.

THE MOUNTAINS

At each base area you'll find a mini-resort – a ski school, a ski rental shop, a functional self-service restaurant, but no accommodation except at Cardrona.

All the areas have something for all abilities of skier or boarder, with off-piste opportunities as well as prepared and patrolled trails. They use the American green/blue/black convention for run classification. New last season were the Burton Learn To Ride systems at both The Remarkables and Coronet Peak, designed to turn beginners into life-time skiers and riders.

THE SLOPES
Not the height of convenience
The Remarkables, true to their name, are a dramatic range of craggy peaks visible across the lake from some parts of Queenstown. The slopes are tucked in a bowl right behind the largest visible peak, a 45-minute drive from town. This resort is fine for families and beginners (though there is limited

KEY FACTS

Resort	310m
	1,020ft

The Remarkables

Slopes	1580-1945m
	5,180-6,380ft
Lifts	5
Pistes	220 hectares
	545 acres
Green	30%
Blue	40%
Black	30%
Snowmaking	
	25 acres

Coronet Peak

Slopes	1230-1650m
	4,040-5,410ft
Lifts	6
Pistes	280 hectares
	690 acres
Green	25%
Blue	45%
Black	30%
Snowmaking	
	200 acres

boarding

Boarding is popular in New Zealand, and although the two mountains close to Queenstown don't seem to have quite such a hold on the boarding market as Cardrona (see New Zealand introduction), they have everything you need, including equipment and tuition. You needn't go anywhere near a drag-lift, and there are no flats to worry about except on the lowest green at The Remarkables and a few lower dips to watch in the Rocky Gully area of Coronet.

extreme skiing for experts), with the emphasis on taking it easy and enjoying entertainment on the restaurant's sun decks during the week. Children under 10 ski for free at The Remarkables. Top-notch terrain-parks here, competing with Coronet Peak, have brought a younger vibe to the mountain in recent years.

Two chairs go up from the base, a fast quad serving easy runs and the Sugar Bowl chair, which accesses mainly long, easy runs plus a couple of black chutes. The terrain-parks have transformed the resort and attracted a whole new market of jibbers. The Shadow Basin chair leads to steeper terrain, including three hike-accessed, expert-only chutes that drop down to Lake Alta, and the Homeward Run – a broad, fairly gentle, unprepared slope down to the resort access road, where a shuttle-truck takes you back to the base.

Coronet Peak, about 25 minutes' drive from Queenstown, is a far more satisfying resort, especially for intermediates and above. There is some seriously steep terrain in the back bowls for experts. Again, there are three main chair-lifts, including a

fast quad that accesses practically all the runs, and new in the 2005 season was a six-seater that opened up more terrain and improved the resort dramatically. A novice trail was added a few seasons ago to appeal to beginner skiers and boarders. The main mountainside is a pleasantly varied intermediate slope, full of highly enjoyable rolling terrain that snowboarders adore, though it steepens near the bottom. A fourth lift, a T-bar, serves another intermediate area to one side. There are also drags for beginners. Last season the beginners' area was enlarged and separated from the main slopes. There's night skiing at weekends. A couple of seasons ago the resort added 30 new guns on the 1.8km/ 1.1 mile main trail.

TERRAIN-PARKS
The Remarkables rules

Coronet Peak has two half-pipes but The Remarkables recently became a competitor in the park market with its spectacular mountain-top super-pipe plus two enormous 30m/100ft wide terrain-parks, one for beginners and the other for intermediates/advanced.

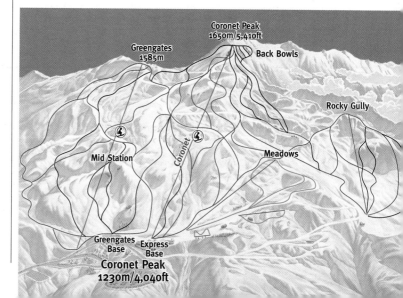

Coronet Peak
1650m/5,410ft

Greengates
1585m

Back Bowls

Rocky Gully

Mid Station

Coronet

Meadows

Greengates Base

Express Base

Coronet Peak
1230m/4,040ft

Cardrona is a bit of a drive away from Queenstown, and is described in the New Zealand introduction chapter ➔

CARDRONA

SNOW RELIABILITY
Good overall, but unpredictable

The New Zealand weather is highly variable, so it's difficult to be confident about snow conditions – though the mountains certainly get oodles of snow. The South Island resorts are at the same sort of latitude as the Alps, but are much more influenced by the ocean; fortunately, their ocean is a lot colder than ours. Coronet tends to receive sleet and/or rain even when it's snowing in The Remarkables. But Coronet Peak has snowmaking on practically all its intermediate terrain.

FOR EXPERTS
Challenges exist

Both areas have quite a choice of genuinely black slopes. Coronet's Back Bowls is a seriously steep experts-only area, and there are other black slopes scattered around the mountain. The main enjoyment comes from venturing off-piste all over the place. The Remarkables' Shadow Basin chair serves some excellent (if short) slopes. And The Remarkables' hike-up expert chutes are truly world-class.

FOR INTERMEDIATES
Fine, within limits

There's some very enjoyable intermediate skiing in both areas – appreciably more at Coronet, where there are also easy blacks to go on to. But remember: these are very small areas by Alpine standards.

FOR BEGINNERS
Excellent

There are gentle slopes at both areas, served by rope tows, and longer green runs served by chairs. And many other diversions if you decide it's a drag.

FOR CROSS-COUNTRY
Limited

There is a short loop around a lake in the middle of The Remarkables area, but the only serious cross-country area is the Waiorau Snow Farm, near Cardrona (see New Zealand intro).

QUEUES
It depends

Coronet and The Remarkables can suffer a little from high-season crowds – there are certainly enough beds locally to lead to queues at peak times. But these aren't normally a major worry.

MOUNTAIN RESTAURANTS
Er, what mountain restaurants?

Both areas have a simple cafeteria at the base, and Coronet has a brasserie facing the slopes, but nothing up the mountain. The Remarkables cafeteria has a big sunny deck, most days with entertainment – and is regularly visited by the local parrots (keas).

SCHOOLS AND GUIDES
All the usual classes

The schools are well organised, with a wide range of options, including 'guaranteed' beginner classes.

FACILITIES FOR CHILDREN
Look good

Childcare looked okay to us. At both resorts there is a nursery for children aged from two to five years old. Coronet Peak has a Skiwiland Club for children aged four to six. The Remarkables has Skiwiland for four and five year olds. There's also a wide range of kids' activities on offer each day. The Queenstown nursery can take younger children all day.

STAYING THERE

HOW TO GO
Sheer luxury?
There are lots of big, luxury hotels – all either new or refurbished – built to meet the big summer demand. **Hotels** Some hotels are quite some way from central Queenstown – inconvenient for après-ski unless there's a shuttle-bus. In town they range from the very simple to the glossily pretentious Millennium (03 441 8888), the new five-star Sofitel (03 450 0045) and The Spire (03 441 0004) – a chic new spot. Two of the best and most reasonable places to stay are the Heritage Hotel (03 442 4988) or the Mercure Grand Hotel St Moritz (03 442 4990). Azur is a luxury lodge with swanky rooms overlooking the lake.

EATING OUT
Lots of choice
We're told there are now over 160 bars and restaurants – a quite astonishing figure. Restaurants include Chinese, Italian, Malaysian, Japanese – you name it, Queenstown has it. The Boardwalk in the Steamer Wharf complex overlooking the lake is the place to go for seafood, especially the Wai. Breakfast at Joe's Garage is a must. You might see the famous actor Sam Neil, who's a local. A dining experience with a difference is the Bath House, located in a 1911 Victorian bath house right on the lake shore. Solero Vino has delicious Mediterranean food and a rustic bar. The best upmarket bars are Bardeaux, Barmuda and Dux de Lux, an excellent brew-pub with a range of tasty beers, housed in a stone cottage. The Halo restaurant is the newest in town and serves up delicious organic meals with vegan options. Opposite Halo is the new Destination Organic, which sells organic fruit and veg. The Bunker does excellent local cuisine such as Bluff oysters and lamb. Gantley's, in a historic home a little way out of town, is a classic restaurant with the most expensive wine list in the area. At the other end of the scale, pizza-lovers crowd into The Cow, a cosy barn-like place where you sit on logs around a fire waiting for tables or takeaways. Lone Star offers satisfying American-style food.

APRES-SKI
Lively little town
Queenstown has a good range of bars and clubs that stay open late, with disco or live music. Winnebagos is very lively and has a roof that slides back to the night sky to allow the hot and sweaty dance floor a blast of fresh air and even fresh snow. There's a small upmarket casino in the plush Steamer Wharf, and Skycity Casino in the mall. The Steamer Wharf also contains Minus Five, an ice bar, and The Boiler Room for 80s music. There's good duty-free shopping in the mall complex opposite.

OFF THE SLOPES
Scare yourself silly
There are lots of scary things to do – see the feature box below. To the west is the spectacularly scenic 'fjord country', and you can go on independent or guided walks. The sightseeing flights by plane or helicopter are to be preferred to the slow bus-ride – weather permitting. A marvellous thing to do is to take the Skyline gondola 400m/1,310ft above Queenstown for the great view; try a spin down the public go-cart track, too. Cruise the lake on an historic steamship or go wine tasting. Arrowtown is interesting for a quick visit – it's a cute, touristy old mining town where you can kit yourself out to go panning for gold. The Winter Festival, in early July, is an annual 'action-packed week of mayhem'.

GET THAT ADRENALIN RUSH

The streets of Queenstown are lined by no fewer than 173 activity operators offering various artificial thrills. We've sampled just a few.

AJ Hackett's bungee jump at Kawarau Bridge is where this crazy activity got off the ground, as it were. The Shotover Jet Boat experience is less demanding – whizzing along the rocky river in a boat that can get along in very shallow water, passing very close to cliffs and trees. Fly By Wire involves swinging through a canyon on a cable propelled by a fan engine on your rear. The whitewater rafting takes you over some exciting rapids. One route even passes through a tunnel excavated in the gold-mining days.

Phone numbers
From abroad use the prefix +64 and omit the initial '0' of the phone number

TOURIST OFFICE

The Remarkables and Coronet Peak
t 03 442 4640
snowcentre@nzski.com
www.nzski.com

Argentina

+ Varied terrain and excellent off-piste
+ Favourable exchange rate means cheap local prices

− Remote and inaccessible, even from Buenos Aires
− Very little English spoken

Argentina's two main resorts are of sharply contrasting character and a long way apart physically as well. Go to San Carlos de Bariloche for the cultural experience and the intermediate piste skiing, and go to Las Leñas for the best and most extensive off-piste terrain in the southern hemisphere. We combined Las Leñas with Chilean resorts on our 2006 visit – something we'd recommend.

Argentina lies on the eastern, rain-shadowed side of the Andes, a recipe for dry, light powder at high altitudes throughout a season that lasts from June to October.

The premier resort is **Las Leñas**, built by Frenchmen in the 1980s when pyramid architecture ruled. It dominates a white wilderness, miles from civilisation; the nearest major airport is Mendoza 400km/250 miles away (Malargue is much nearer but has few scheduled flights).

But be warned: gales and blizzards can close most of the resort down for days, especially during late July and early August. Mid-August to mid-September is the best time to visit.

A dozen lifts serve a few groomed slopes, and freestylers can rip it up in the terrain-park and half-pipe. But the real attraction is for experts: an antiquated double chair called El Marte opens up 270° of ski-anywhere off-piste terrain (plus a couple of pistes) – from gentle slopes suiting powder novices to couloirs and cliffs for the brave. But before you are allowed to venture into the great off-piste, you have to stop at a mountain-top hut where a local asks you to enter your name and passport number, and sign a document in Spanish releasing the resort from all responsibility for you. He then sticks a coloured tag, valid for a week, on your clothing, which allows you to venture where you like.

But venture not without a guide. We saw snowboarders precariously perched on top of 100m/330ft cliffs and skiers riding under dodgy-looking cornices. The place is vast and you need to know where you are going. Our recommendation would be to book a week with the Whistler-based ski school Extremely Canadian, which

specialises in steep and deep terrain and runs trips to Las Leñas every year (see www.extremelycanadian.com). We went with them in 2006 and had a great time. There's a good cat-skiing operation, too.

The smartest hotel is the 5-star Pisces, with a pool, hot-tub, sauna and gym. Escorpio is a 4-star option. There are a few bars and clubs, and a casino.

San Carlos de Bariloche has almost nothing in common with Las Leñas, except that it is Argentina's only other international winter sports option. Founded in 1903 by Swiss and German immigrants, it is a substantial resort town with a cheerful lifestyle, and is still influenced by the Swiss-German culture. The smart Llao Llao Resort and Spa, on a bluff above the lake, has a pool, sauna and fitness centre. The Edelweiss offers top-quality facilities in the town centre.

The slopes are at Gran Catedral, 20 minutes by shuttle-bus. They are well below the tree line, and good-quality snow cannot be guaranteed. The runs, which are cut through the forest, face east as protection from the prevailing westerlies and suit intermediates best, though there is some good off-piste. There's a terrain-park and half-pipe. It's best to avoid August, which is the Argentinian society choice and therefore prone to long queues.

Cerro Castor, the most southerly city in the world, is a remote outpost just 195m/640ft above sea level. The Beagle Strait off Tierra del Fuego is famously windy, but winter is the calmest period and conditions are often surprisingly good. It has a small ski area with 19 runs but a vertical drop of 770m/2,530ft. The British team trained here in the run-up to the Turin Winter Olympics.

733

Chile

+ One of the most varied options for the European summer
+ The Andes are spectacular
+ Good snow records
+ Good local food and wine

- It's a long way from Britain
- By Alpine standards, the ski areas are small and resorts lack character
- Little English spoken outside hotels
- Nightlife is limited

If you want to carry on skiing or boarding in our summer, Chile is a good choice. It's a long way to go (it took us 36 hours from leaving home to arriving at our first hotel on our 2006 visit) and the ski areas are small; but if you combine visits to at least two resorts with, say, a tour of Chile's wine areas or a visit to the Atacama desert, it can make a varied and compelling holiday.

KEY FACTS

Valle Nevado/La Parva/El Colorado

Slopes	2430-3670m
	7.970-12,040ft
Lifts	43
Pistes	113km
	70 miles
Green	14%
Blue	30%
Red	42%
Black	14%

Portillo

Slopes	2560-3320m
	8,400-10,890ft
Lifts	13
Pistes	1200 acres
Green	10%
Blue	35%
Red	35%
Black	20%

Termas de Chillán

Slopes	1600-2700m
	5,250-8,860ft
Lifts	13
Pistes	46km
	29 miles
Green	22%
Blue	41%
Red	31%
Black	6%

Lying in the path of the prevailing winds off the Pacific, the Chilean Andes are ideally located to catch all the snow that's going, resulting in truly dramatic falls in good years. In such a long narrow country, conditions vary considerably from north to south. In general, the season starts in mid-June and finishes in early October (mid-July to mid-September is the best time to visit). The ski areas are small in comparison with big Alpine resorts (a keen piste-basher could ski all the pistes in an area in a day) but there's a lot of off-piste available. Adventurous skiers and boarders should sign on for the well-run heli-ski operations, both for the spectacular flights over 5000m/16,400ft peaks and the remote powder fields. We'd recommend visiting two or three ski areas as you are travelling so far.

Valle Nevado (just 60km/37 miles from Santiago), La Parva and El Colorado form the biggest area of linked pistes and are known as the Tres Valles (Chile's equivalent of the Three Valleys). **La Parva** is condoville for the capital's elite, a collection of apartments occupied mostly at weekends, while **El Colorado** offers a scattering of accommodation around a shabby base station. Both are linked to **Valle Nevado**, a high-rise, wood-clad tourist development in the mode of Les Arcs, not surprisingly as it was designed by the Chilean architect Eduardo Stern after he'd worked in France and on the Les Arcs project. The best hotel is called Valle Nevado and has the best restaurant, the Fourchette d'Or which serves delicious international food and excellent breakfasts. Puerta del Sol is the mid-

market option (with an Italian restaurant) and 3 Puntas (with a buffet of typical Chilean dishes) the budget choice. All three offer half-board packages and you can generally eat dinner at a restaurant in a different hotel if you like. There is a small communal outdoor pool, a few shops, hotel bars and a nightclub.

Valle Nevado is ski-in/ski-out and has a network of well-groomed, mainly intermediate pistes served by 11 lifts including the Andes Express (South America's only high-speed chair).

Portillo, 164km/102 miles from Santiago, consists of little more than the startlingly bright yellow Hotel Portillo, set beside the potholed main road from Chile to Argentina. It was built in the 1940s and owned and run by the Chilean government until they sold it to two Americans in 1962. It is now run by Henry Purcell (the nephew of one of the Americans) and his son Michael (aka Miguel). Service is impeccable, with 550 staff (mostly long-serving – the head waiter has been there over 40 years) serving a maximum of 450 guests. The traditional public rooms are handsomely furnished with polished wood and leather. And there's a huge outdoor hot pool to relax in after coming off the slopes.

The hotel and a lake in front of it stand between two unconnected areas. Turn right for the El Plateau double chair to Tio Bob's, the only mountain restaurant. Then drop into the rocky jaws of Garganta, the challenging black run back to base, or sweep down the friendly blue. The Laguna quad chair, on the other side of the hotel, accesses the Juncalillo piste, the longest

in the resort. But to stick to the groomers – and there are few of them (you could ski them all in a couple of hours) – is to miss the point. Portillo has radical terrain on both sides of the mountain, but the first challenge is the unique Va et Vient slingshot lifts. Skiers ride on linked buttons, four or five abreast, blasting upwards at high speed to a treacherously steep landing point. From the top of Roca Jack, the longest of the three slingshots, a high traverse, leads to a series of chutes. When the lake is frozen, skiers can take the steep powder slopes down to the shore and skate back to the hotel. To get the most out of the area you need a guide (and you need to be prepared to hike from the top of the lifts). Good off-piste skiers should consider going on former World Freeskiing Champion, Chris Davenport's, Ski with the Superstars week here – see www.steepskiing.com.

Termas de Chillán is Chile's leading ski and spa resort, in a forested setting and with a small network of lifts under twin volcanoes, which provide the thermal water and mud for the spa. You can ski all day and then enjoy a relaxing soak and a spa treatment to get rid of the aches and pains. It is around 80km/50 miles from the railway station at Chillán, a small town four hours by train to the south of Santiago (or you can fly to Concepción 195km/121 miles away).

There are three contrasting hotels. The ski-in/ski-out 5-star Gran is the best and is home to the main spa and a new casino and conference centre. It has 120 rooms and two restaurants. The nearby 3-star, Pirigallo has a thermal pool and a spa, log fires, a restaurant, a pub and a games room. The cosier, chalet-style Pirimahuida is

10 minutes drive down the valley in Las Trancas. And there are slope-side apartment buildings, a shop and a rustic Club Haus restaurant.

The top of the El Tata T-bar at 2700m/8,860ft is the starting point for the wonderful, away-from-all-the-lifts top-to-bottom of the mountain Golf Alto run – at 13km/8 miles long and with a vertical drop of 1100m/3,610 feet it is South America's longest piste. It is rolling, undulating and interestingly varied with some narrow sections and some where you need to schuss to get up the incline beyond. As well as 33 largely intermediate pistes (which we skied in three hours or so), there is off-piste (best in September, when there is spring snow normally). For freestylers, there's a terrain-park with half- and quarter-pipes, jumps and a fun-box. As well as downhill skiing there is cross-country, snowmobiling and dog-sledding.

Like Termas de Chillán, **Pucón**, on the eastern shore of Lake Villarrica, was developed as a summer resort. The present lift system was installed between 1988 and 1990 and serves limited terrain for all standards. The climb up to the crater, which requires skins and crampons, takes between two and four hours from the top of the lifts, but it's worth it for the awesome close-up of molten lava. The Gran Hotel Pucón, built in 1934 on the lake shore, is the best place to stay.

Cerro Mirador is Chile's most southerly snow-zone, located 8km/ 5 miles outside Punta Arenas in the Magellanes National Reserve. It has wooded runs and dramatic views over the Magellan Straits. But it is tiny, with just 11 pistes accessed by a double chair and a T-bar. There is no on-mountain accommodation.

REFERENCE SECTION

A classified listing of the names, numbers and addresses you are likely to need.

Most people still prefer the convenience of a package holiday, which is what most of the companies listed are set up to provide. But note that we've also included some operators that offer accommodation without travel arrangements.

TOUR OPERATOR DIRECTORY

This is a list of all the UK-based companies we know of that offer ski holidays – mainly but not exclusively package holidays including travel as well as accommodation. Lists of which operators go where are given in the Resort directory / Index right at the back of the book.

360 Sun and Ski
Family holidays in Les Carroz
Tel 0870 068 3180
info@360sunandski.com
www.360sunandski.co.uk

Airtours
Mainstream operator
Tel 0871 664 7940
pretravelservices@airtours.co.uk
www.airtoursski.co.uk

Albus Travel
St Anton specialist
Tel 01449 711952
info@albustravel.com
www.albustravel.com

Alpine Action
Chalets in Les Trois Vallées
Tel 01273 597940
sales@alpineaction.co.uk
www.alpineaction.co.uk

Alpine Answers
Tailor-made holidays
Tel 020 8871 4656
select@alpineanswers.co.uk
www.alpineanswers.co.uk

Alpine Club
St-Martin-de-Belleville chalets
Tel 01273 690830
info@thealpineclub.co.uk
www.thealpineclub.co.uk

Alpine Events
Corporate ski specialist
Tel 0207 622 2265
info@offsiteevents.co.uk
www.alpineevents.co.uk

Alpine Weekends
Weekends in the Alps
Tel 020 8944 9762
info@alpineweekends.com
www.alpineweekends.com

Alps Accommodation
... in Samoens and Les Carroz
Tel 0033 (0)6 88 65 50 70
whereto@alpsaccommodation.com
www.alpsaccommodation.com

Alpsholiday
Apartments in Serre-Chevalier
Tel +33 492 204426
info@alpsholiday.com
www.alpsholiday.com

Altitude Holidays
Chalet in Le Grand Massif
Tel 0870 870 7669
info@altitudeholidays.com
www.altitudeholidays.com

AmeriCan Ski
North America specialist plus undiscovered gems in France
Tel 01892 511894
ian@awwt.com
www.awwt.co.uk

American Ski Classics
Holidays in N America
Tel 0870 242 0623
sales@holidayworld.ltd.uk
www.americanskiclassics.com

Aravis Alpine Retreat
Renovated Alpine farmhouse in St Jean-de-Sixt (La Clusaz)
Tel 020 82 82 16 50
info@aravis-retreat.com
www.aravis-retreat.com

Ardmore Educational Travel Ltd
Group and schools holidays
Tel 01628 826699
info@theardmoregroup.com
www.theardmoregroup.com

Balkan Holidays
Holidays in Bulgaria, Slovenia, Romania and Serbia
Tel 0845 130 1114
res@balkanholidays.co.uk
www.balkanholidays.co.uk

Barrelli Ski
Chalets in Champagny, Chamonix and Les Houches
Tel 0870 220 1500
chalets@barrelliski.co.uk
www.barrelliski.co.uk

Belvedere Chalets
Méribel and Verbier specialists
Tel 01264 738 257
info@belvedereproperties.net
www.belvedereproperties.net

Bigfoot Travel
Holidays in Chamonix
Tel 0870 300 5874
sales@bigfoot-travel.co.uk
www.bigfoot-chamonix.com

BoardnLodge.com Ltd
Holidays in Europe
Tel 020 7419 0722
bookings@boardnlodge.com
www.boardnlodge.com

Borderline
Specialist in Barèges
Tel +33 562 926895
info@borderlinehols.com
www.borderlinehols.com

Business Retreats Limited
Business retreat in St Jean-de-Sixt (La Clusaz)
Tel 020 82 82 16 50
info@business-retreats.co.uk
www.business-retreats.co.uk

Canadian Powder Tours Chalet Holidays
Chalets in Western Canada
Tel +1 250 423 3019
cdnpowder@elkvalley.net
www.canadianpowdertours.com

Canterbury Travel
Holidays in Finland
Tel 01923 457017
reservations@laplandmagic.com
www.laplandmagic.com

Chalet Bezière
Chalet in Samoëns
Tel +33 450 905181
grant@chaletbeziere.com
www.chaletbeziere.com

Chalet Chocolat
Chalet in Morzine
Tel 01872 580814
sales@skiretreatmorzine.com
www.skiretreatmorzine.com

The Chalet Company
Catered chalets in Morzine
Tel 0871 717 4208 /
+33 450 79 68 40
moran@thechaletco.com
www.thechaletco.com

The Chalet Group
Chalets in Europe and Canada
katie@chaletgroup.com
www.chaletgroup.com

Chalet Gueret
Luxury chalet in Morzine
Tel 01884 256542
info@chaletgueret.com
www.chaletgueret.com

Chalet Kiana
Chalet in Les Contamines
Tel +33 450 915518
info@chaletkiana.com
www.chaletkiana.com

Chalet Number One
Chalet in Ste-Foy
Tel +33 479 069533
info@chaletnumberone.co.uk
www.chn1.co.uk

Les Chalets de St Martin
Catered and self-catered chalets in St-Martin
Tel +33 479 089177
les.chalets@virgin.net
www.leschalets.co.uk

Chalet Snowboard
Holidays in Morzine
Tel 020 8133 4180
info@chaletsnowboard.co.uk
www.chaletsnowboard.co.uk

Chalet World Ski
Chalets in big-name resorts
Tel 01743 231199
sales@chaletworldski.co.uk
www.chaletworldski.co.uk

Challenge Activ
Chalets/apartments in Morzine
Tel 0871 717 4113
info@challenge-activ.com
www.challenge-activ.com

Chamonix Backcountry
Backcountry skiing in the Chamonix Valley
Tel 01274 530 313
s@mcnab.co.uk
www.chamonixbackcountry.com

Chamonix.uk.com
Apartments in Chamonix
Tel 01224 641559
sales@chamonix.uk.com
www.chamonix.uk.com

Le Chardon Mountain Lodges
Upmarket chalets in Val d'Isère
Tel 0845 092 0350
sales@lechardonvaldisere.com
www.lechardonvaldisere.com

Chez Michelle
Chalet in Samoens
Tel 01372 456463
www.chezmichelle.co.uk

Chill Chalet
Accommodation in Paradiski
Tel 07931 967861
chris@chillchalet.com
www.chillchalet.com

Classic Ski Limited
Holidays for 'mature' skiers/beginners
Tel 01590 623400
info@classicski.co.uk
www.classicski.co.uk

Club Europe Schools Skiing
Schools trips to Europe
Tel 0800 496 4996
travel@club-europe.co.uk
www.club-europe.co.uk

Club Med
All-inclusive 'ski villages'
Tel 0845 3676767
admin.uk@clubmed.com
www.clubmed.co.uk

Club Pavilion / Concept
Budget holidays and weekends
Tel 0870 241 0427
info@conceptholidays.co.uk
www.conceptholidays.co.uk

Cold Comforts Lodging
Whistler specialist
Tel 0800 881 8429
info@cold-comforts.com
www.cold-comforts.com

Collineige
Chamonix valley specialist
Tel 01276 24262
sales@collineige.com
www.collineige.com

Come-ski.com
Chalets in La Tania
Tel 01621 891768
info@come-ski.com
www.come-ski.com

Connick Ski
Chalet in Châtel
Tel +33 450 732212
nick@connickski.com
www.connickski.com

Contiki Holidays
Coach holidays for 18-35
Tel 020 8290 6422
www.contiki.com

Cooltip Mountain Holidays
Chalets in Méribel
Tel 01964 563563
ski@cooltip.com
www.cooltip.com

The Corporate Ski Company
Corporate specialists
Tel 020 8542 8555
ski@vantagepoint.co.uk
www.thecorporateskicompany.co.uk

Crystal
Major mainstream operator
Tel 0870 160 6040
skires@crystalholidays.co.uk
www.crystalski.co.uk

Crystal Finest
Holidays to Europe and North America
Tel 020 8939 0842
info@crystalfinest.co.uk
www.crystalfinest.co.uk

Descent International
Luxury chalets in France and Switzerland
Tel 020 7384 3854
sales@descent.co.uk
www.descent.co.uk

Directski.com
Holidays in Europe/N America
Tel 0800 587 0945
sales@directski.com
www.directski.com

Elegant Resorts
Luxury ski holidays
Tel 01244 897333
enquiries@elegantresorts.co.uk
www.elegantresorts.co.uk

Elevation Holidays
Holidays in the Austrian Alps
Tel 0845 644 3578
info@elevationholidays.com
www.elevationholidays.com

Equity Ski
All-in holidays
Tel 01273 622111
sales@equity.co.uk
www.equityski.co.uk

Erna Low
Hotel/self-catering holidays in the Alps and North America
Tel 0845 863 0525
info@ernalow.co.uk
www.ernalow.co.uk

Esprit Ski
Families specialist in Europe
Tel 01252 618300
www.esprit-holidays.co.uk

The Family Ski Company
Family holidays in France
Tel 01684 540333
enquiries@familyski.co.uk
www.familyski.co.uk

Ferme de Montagne
Luxury chalet hotel in Les Gets
Tel +33 450 753679
enquiries@fermedemontagne.
com
www.fermedemontagne.com

Finlays
*Catered chalets and short
breaks in France/Switzerland*
Tel 01573 226611
info@finlayski.com
www.finlayski.com

First Choice Holidays
Major mainstream operator
Tel 0871 664 0130
sales@fcski.co.uk
www.firstchoice.co.uk/ski

Flexiski
*Weekends and corporate
events in Europe*
Tel 01273 244667
reservations@flexiski.com
www.flexiski.com

Friendship Travel
Holidays for singles 25-60
Tel 028 9446 2211
sales@friendshiptravel.com
www.friendshiptravel.com

Frontier Ski
Holidays in Canada and Alaska
Tel 020 8776 8709
ski@frontier-travel.co.uk
www.frontier-ski.co.uk

Haig Ski
Chalet near Morzine
Tel +33 450 811947
sales@haigski.com
www.haigski.com

Hannibals
Holidays in Serre-Chevalier
Tel 01233 813105
sales@hannibals.co.uk
www.hannibals.co.uk

Headwater Holidays
Cross-country skiing holidays
Tel 01606 720199
info@headwater.com
www.headwater.com

High Mountain Holidays
Holidays in Les Praz
Tel 01993 775540
info@highmountain.co.uk
www.highmountain.co.uk

Hucksters
Lodges in the French Alps
Tel 01208 821100
info@huckterslodge.com
www.huckterslodge.com

Independent Ski Links
*Tailor-made holidays in Europe
and N America*
Tel 01964 533905
info@ski-links.com
www.ski-links.com

Inghams
Major mainstream operator
Tel 020 8780 4433
reservations@inghams.co.uk
www.inghams.co.uk

Inntravel
Cross-country skiing holidays
Tel 01653 617909
winter@inntravel.co.uk
www.inntravel.co.uk

Inspired to Ski
Holidays with tuition in France
Tel 0208 877 5775
sally@inspiredtoski.com
www.inspiredtoski.com

Interactive Resorts
Catered chalets worldwide
Tel 020 3080 0202
info@interactiveresorts.co.uk
www.interactiveresorts.co.uk

Interhome
Apartments/chalets in Europe
Tel 020 8891 1294
info@interhome.co.uk
www.interhome.co.uk

Interski
Group holidays in Italy
Tel 01623 456333
email@interski.co.uk
www.interski.co.uk

Italian Safaris
Italian ski specialists
Tel +39 347 348 5757 /
07930 902590
info@italiansafaris.com
www.italiansafaris.com

James Orr Heli-ski
Heli-skiing in Canada
Tel 01799 516964
james.orr@btinternet.com
www.heliski.co.uk

Jeffersons Private Jet Holidays
Holidays by private jet
Tel 0870 850 8181
info@jeffersons.com
www.jeffersons.com

Just Skiing
Courmayeur specialist
Tel 01202 479988
holidays@justskiing.co.uk
www.justskiing.co.uk

Just Slovenia
Accommodation in Slovenia
Tel 01373 814230
justslovenia@planos.co.uk
www.justslovenia.co.uk

Kaluma Ski
Holidays in the Alps
Tel 0870 442 8044
enquiries@kalumatravel.co.uk
www.kalumatravel.co.uk

Karibuni
Chalet holidays in La Clusaz
Tel 01202 661865
info@karibuni.co.uk
www.karibuni.co.uk

Kuoni
Holidays to Europe/N America
Tel 01306 747000
holidays@kuoni.co.uk
www.kuoni.co.uk

Lagrange Holidays
Ski holidays in Europe
Tel 020 7371 6111
info@lagrange-holidays.co.uk
www.lagrange-holidays.co.uk

The Last Resort
St Jean-de-Sixt accommodation
Tel 0800 652 3977
info@lastresort.info
www.lastresort.info

Le Ski
*Chalets in Courchevel, Val
d'Isère and La Tania*
Tel 01484 548996
mail@leski.com
www.leski.com

Made to Measure Holidays
Tailor-made holidays
Tel 01243 533333
sales@mtmhols.co.uk
www.mtmhols.co.uk

Mark Warner
*Chalet-hotel holidays in big-
name resorts*
Tel 0871 208 5116
sales@markwarner.co.uk
www.markwarner.co.uk

MasterSki
Christian holidays
Tel 020 8942 9442
sales@mastersun.co.uk
www.masterski.co.uk

McNab Snowboarding
Snowboarding holidays
Tel 0141 416 3828
info@mcnabsnowboarding.com
www.mcnabsnowboarding.com

Meriski
Chalet specialist in Méribel
Tel 01285 648510
sales@meriski.co.uk
www.meriski.co.uk

MGS Ski Limited
Apartments in Val Cenis
Tel 01799 525984
skimajor@aol.com
www.mgsski.com

Momentum Ski
*Tailor-made and ski weekend
specialists*
Tel 020 7371 9111
sales@momentumski.com
www.momentumski.com

Moswin Tours
German programme
Tel 08700 625040
germany@moswin.com
www.moswin.com

Mountain Beds
Tailor-made holidays
Tel 020 7924 2650
info@mountainbeds.com
www.mountainbeds.com

A Mountain Chalet
Chalet in La Rosière
Tel +33 479 065738
amountainchalet@wanadoo.fr
www.amountainchalet.co.uk

Mountain Heaven
*Apartments in La Plagne and
catered chalet in La Rosière*
Tel 0151 625 1921
info@mountainheaven.co.uk
www.mountainheaven.co.uk

Mountainsun Ltd
Chalets in Europe
Tel 07941 196517
mail@mountainsunltd.com
www.mountainsunltd.com

Mountain Tracks
Off-piste courses, ski touring
Tel 020 8877 5773
info@mountaintracks.co.uk
www.mountaintracks.co.uk

Neilson
Major mainstream operator
Tel 0870 333 3347
sales@neilson.com
www.neilson.co.uk

Nick Ski
Catered chalet in La Tania
Tel +33 673 436769
nick@nickskithreevalleys.co.uk
www.nickskithreevalleys.co.uk

Optimum Ski
*Chalet in Villaroger, part of Les
Arcs ski area*
Tel 0131 208 1154
info@optimumski.com
www.optimumski.com

The Oxford Ski Company
Holidays in Europe/N America
Tel 0870 787 1785
info@oxfordski.com
www.oxfordski.com

Panorama Holidays
Budget holidays in Europe
Tel 0871 664 7984
panorama@phg.co.uk
www.panoramaski.co.uk

Peak Leisure
Chalets/ski safaris in France
Tel 0870 760 5610
info@peak-leisure.co.uk
www.peak-leisure.co.uk

Peak Retreats
Holidays to traditional French Alps resorts
Tel 0870 770 0408
bonjour@peakretreats.co.uk
www.peakretreats.co.uk

Peak Ski
Chalets in Verbier
Tel 01442 832629
peakski@which.net
www.peakski.co.uk

PGL Ski Europe
School group specialist
Tel 0870 143 0143
ski@pgl.co.uk
www.pgl.co.uk

PGL Travel
Holidays for teenagers
Tel 08700 507507
holidays@pgl.co.uk
www.pgl.co.uk

Piste Artiste Ltd
Self-catered chalets in Champéry
reserve@pisteartiste.com
www.pisteartiste.com

Powder Bound
Chalet in Serre-Chevalier
Tel 0845 838 1216
reservations@
  powderbound.co.uk
www.powderbound.co.uk

Powder Byrne
Hotels in Europe
Tel 020 8246 5300
enquiries@powderbyrne.co.uk
www.powderbyrne.com

Powder Skiing in North America Limited
Heli-skiing holidays in Canada
Tel 020 7736 8191
info@psna.co.uk
www.canadianmountain
  holidays.com

Powder White
Chalets in France/Switzerland
Tel 020 8355 8836
info@powderwhite.co.uk
www.powderwhite.com

Première Neige
Catered and self-catered holidays in Ste-Foy
Tel 0870 383 1000
snow@premiere-neige.com
www.premiere-neige.com

Purple Ski
Chalet holidays in Méribel
Tel 01885 488799
michael@purpleski.com
www.purpleski.com

Pyrenees Ski Experience
Holidays in the Pyrenees
Tel +33 468 041879
info@pyrenees-ski-
  experience.com
www.pyrenees-ski-
  experience.com

Ramblers Holidays
Mostly cross-country holidays
Tel 01707 331133
info@ramblersholidays.co.uk
www.ramblersholidays.co.uk

Rocketski.com
All-in holidays online
Tel 01273 810777
info@rocketski.com
www.rocketski.com

Rude Chalets
Holidays in Morzine
Tel 0870 068 7030
info@rudechalets.com
www.rudechalets.com

Scott Dunn Latin America
Holidays to South America
Tel 020 8682 5030
latin@scottdunn.com
www.scottdunn.com

Scott Dunn Ski
Luxury ski holidays
Tel 020 8682 5050
ski@scottdunn.com
www.scottdunn.com

Silver Ski
Chalet holidays in France
Tel 01622 735544
karen@silverski.co.uk
www.silverski.co.uk

Simon Butler Skiing
Holidays + tuition in Megève
Tel 0870 873 0001
info@simonbutlerskiing.co.uk
www.simonbutlerskiing.co.uk

Ski 2
Monterosa specialists
Tel 01962 713330
info@ski-2.com
www.ski-2.com

Ski Activity
Holidays in big-name resorts
Tel 0870 626 0701
sales@skiactivity.com
www.skiactivity.com

Ski Addiction
Chalets and hotels in Châtel and Monterosa Ski
Tel 01580 819354
sales@skiaddiction.co.uk
www.skiaddiction.co.uk

Ski Adventures
Chalet holidays in Paradiski
Tel +33 385 546515
info@skiadventures.co.uk
www.skiadventures.co.uk

Ski à la Carte
Luxury chalets in Alpe-d'Huez
Tel 020 8542 5559
info@skialacarte.co.uk
www.skialacarte.co.uk

Ski All America
N and S American holidays
Tel 08701 676 676
sales@skiallamerica.com
www.skiallamerica.com

Skialot
Chalet in Châtel
Tel 0780 156 9264
stuey@skialot.com
www.skialot.com

Ski Amis
Catered chalet and self-catered holidays in the French Alps
Tel 020 7692 0850
info@skiamis.com
www.skiamis.com

Ski Balkantours
Holidays in Eastern Europe
Tel 028 9024 6795
info@balkan.co.uk
www.balkan.co.uk

Ski Barrett-Boyce
Chalet in Megève with tuition
Tel 01737 831184
info@skibb.com
www.skibb.com

Ski Basics
Chalets in Méribel
Tel 01225 444143
info@skibasics.co.uk
www.skibasics.co.uk

Ski Beat
Chalets in the French Alps
Tel 01243 780405
Ski@skibeat.co.uk
www.skibeat.co.uk

Ski Blanc
Chalet holidays in Méribel
Tel 020 8502 9082
info@skiblanc.co.uk
www.skiblanc.co.uk

SkiBound
Schools division of First Choice
Tel 0870 754 3477
sales@skibound.co.uk
www.skibound.co.uk

Ski Chamois
Holidays in Morzine
Tel 01302 369006
sales@skichamois.co.uk
www.skichamois.co.uk

Ski Collection
French self-catering 4-star
apartment specialist
Tel 0870 770 0407
reservations
@skicollection.co.uk
www.skicollection.co.uk

Ski Cuisine
Chalets in Méribel
Tel 01702 589543
info@skicuisine.co.uk
www.skicuisine.co.uk

Ski-Dazzle
Chalets in Les Trois Vallées
Tel +33 479 001725
info@ski-dazzle.com
www.ski-dazzle.com

Ski Deep
Chalets in La Tania/Le Praz
Tel 01483 722706 /
+33 479 081905
ferg@skideep.net
www.skideep.net

Ski Dream
Major N American operator
Tel 0870 350 7547
holidays@skidream.com
www.skidream.com

Ski Etoile
Chalets/hotels in Montgenèvre
Tel 01952 253252
info@skietoile.co.uk
www.skietoile.co.uk

Ski Expectations
Chalets and hotels in Europe,
the USA and Canada
Tel 01799 531888
ski.expectations@virgin.net
www.skiexpectations.com

Ski Famille
Family holidays in Les Gets
and Morzine
Tel 0845 644 3764
info@skifamille.co.uk
www.skifamille.co.uk

Ski4you
Accommodation in Europe
Tel 0870 192 1621
enquiries@ski4you.co.uk
www.ski4you.co.uk

Ski France
Holidays to France
Tel 0870 787 3402
ski@skifrance.co.uk
www.skifrance.co.uk

Skifrance4less
Apartments/chalets in France
Tel 01724 290660
info@skifrance4less.com
www.skifrance4less.com

Ski Freedom
Chalets in Switzerland
Tel +41 788 810978
info@skifreedom.com
www.skifreedom.com

Ski Freshtracks
Holidays for Ski Club of GB
Tel 0845 458 0784
holidays@skifreshtracks.co.uk
www.skifreshtracks.co.uk

SkiGower
School trips to Switzerland
Tel 01527 851410
peter@gowertours.com
www.gowertours.com

Ski Hame
Catered chalets in Méribel
Tel 01875 320157
powderpigs@skihame.co.uk
www.skihame.co.uk

Ski High Days
Holidays in Italy and France
Tel 0117 955 1814
sales@high-days.co.uk
www.skihighdays.com

Ski Hillwood
Family holidays in Europe
Tel 01923 290700
sales@hillwood-holidays.co.uk
www.hillwood-holidays.co.uk

Ski Hiver
Chalets in Peisey (Paradiski)
Tel 01329 847788
skihiver@wanadoo.fr
www.skihiver.co.uk

Skiholidayextras.com
Accommodation in France
Tel 0870 251 0009
admin@skiholidayextras.com
www.skiholidayextras.com

Ski Independence
USA, Canada, Japan, France,
Switzerland and Austria
Tel 0845 310 3030
ski@ski-i.com
www.ski-i.com

Ski La Cote
Holidays in Portes du Soleil
Tel 01482 668357
adrian@ski-la-cote.karoo.co.uk
www.ski-la-cote.karoo.net

Ski Leisure Direction
Hotels/self-catering in France
Tel 0870 442 9842
ski@leisuredirection.co.uk
www.leisuredirection.co.uk

Ski Line
Chalets in Europe/N America
Tel 020 8313 3999
angus@skiline.co.uk
www.skiline.co.uk

Ski Link
Courchevel specialist
Tel 0871 218 0174
info@ski-link.com
www.ski-link.co.uk

Ski Magic
Chalets in Courchevel/La Tania
Tel 0151 6772317
sales@skimagic.co.uk
www.skimagic.co.uk

Ski McNeill
Packages + tailor-made trips
Tel 02890 666699
skiholidays@skimcneill.com
www.skimcneill.com

Ski Miquel
Small but eclectic programme
Tel 01457 821200
ski@miquelhols.co.uk
www.miquelhols.co.uk

Ski-Monterosa Ltd
Monterosa (Alagna) specialist
Tel 0151 353 2317
richard@ski-monterosa.com
www.ski-monterosa.com

Ski Morgins Holidays
Chalet holidays in Morgins
Tel 01568 770681
info@skimorgins.com
www.skimorgins.com

Ski Morzine
Accommodation in Morzine
Tel 0845 370 1104
info@skimorzine.com
www.skimorzine.com

Ski Olympic
Chalet holidays in France
Tel 01302 328820
info@skiolympic.com
www.skiolympic.com

Ski Peak
Specialist in Vaujany
Tel 01428 608070
info@skipeak.com
www.skipeak.com

SkiPlan Travel Service
Schools programme
Tel 01273 622111
sales@sts-skiplan.co.uk
www.skiplan.co.uk

Ski Power
Chalets in La Tania and
Courchevel 1650
Tel 01737 306029
info@skipower.co.uk
www.skipower.co.uk

Ski Rosie
Chalet in Morgins and self-
catered apartments in Châtel
Tel +33 450 813100
rosie@skirosie.com
www.skirosie.com

Ski Safari
Canada/US specialist
Tel 01273 224060
info@skisafari.com
www.skisafari.com

Ski Solutions
Tailor-made holidays
Tel 020 7471 7777
alc@skisolutions.com
www.skisolutions.com

Ski Supreme
Holidays to France and Italy
Tel 01355 260547
info@skisupreme.co.uk
www.skisupreme.co.uk

Skitopia
Holidays to the French Alps
Tel 01872 272767
info@skitopia.com
www.skitopia.com

Skitracer
Holidays in Europe/N America
Tel 0870 420 5782
info@skitracer.com
www.skitracer.com

Ski-Val
Holidays in France and Austria
Tel 0870 746 3030
reservations@skival.co.uk
www.skival.co.uk

Ski Verbier
Specialists in Verbier
Tel 020 7385 8050
info@skiverbier.com
www.skiverbier.com

Ski Weekend
Weekend and 10-day holidays
Tel 01392 878353
sales@skiweekend.com
www.skiweekend.com

Skiweekender.com
Ski weekends in La Clusaz
Tel 01202 661865
info@skiweekender.com
www.skiweekender.com

Ski Weekends & Board Breaks
3- and 6-day trips to France
Tel 0870 4423400
sales@skiweekends.com
www.skiweekends.com

Ski Wild
Austria specialist
Tel 0870 746 9668
info@llgroup.co.uk
www.skiwild.co.uk

Ski with Julia
Hotels/chalets in Verbier
Tel 01386 584478
julia@skijulia.co.uk
www.skijulia.co.uk

Skiworld
European/N American trips
Tel 0870 241 6723
sales@skiworld.ltd.uk
www.skiworld.ltd.uk

Ski Yogi
Hotels/catered chalets in Italy
Tel 01799 531886
ski.expectations@virgin.net
www.skiexpectations.com

Sloping Off
Schools holidays
Tel 01273 648200
info@sloping-off.co.uk
www.sloping-off.co.uk

Snowbizz
Family ski specialist in Puy-St-Vincent
Tel 01778 341455
wendy@snowbizz.co.uk
www.snowbizz.co.uk

Snowcoach
Holidays to Austria and France
Tel 01727 866177
info@snowcoach.co.uk
www.snowcoach.co.uk

SnowCrazy
Chalets in La Rosière and La Plagne
Tel 01342 302910
gosnowcrazy@aol.com
www.snowcrazy.co.uk

Snowebb
Catered chalets in Big White, Sun Peaks and Silver Star
Tel 020 8123 5861
office@snowebb.com
www.snowebb.com

Snow Finders
Holidays to Europe
Tel 01858 466888
sales@snowfinders.com
www.snowfinders.com

Snowfocus
Chalet in Châtel
Tel 01392 479555
action@snowfocus.com
www.snowfocus.com

Snowlife
Catered chalet in La Clusaz
Tel 01534 863630
info@snowlife.co.uk
www.snowlife.co.uk

Snowline
Catered chalets in France
Tel 08701 123118
ski@snowline.co.uk
www.snowline.co.uk

Snow Monkey Chalets
Chalets in Paradiski
Tel +33 677 018625
enquiries@
  snowmonkeychalets.co.uk
www.snowmonkeychalets.co.uk

Snoworks
Holidays with tuition
Tel 08701 225549
philsmith@snoworks.co.uk
www.snoworks.co.uk

Snowscape
Flexible trips to Austria
Tel 08453 708570
skiandboard@snowscape.co.uk
www.snowscape.co.uk

Snowstar Holidays
Tignes specialist
Tel 0870 068 6611
info@snowstar.co.uk
www.snowstar.co.uk

SnowYourWay.com
Holidays in Valfréjus
Tel 0870 760 6448
info@snowyourway.com
www.snowyourway.com

Snowy Pockets
Chalet holidays in Arosa
Tel 01707 251696
info@snowypockets.com
www.snowypockets.com

Solo's
Singles' holidays
Tel 08700 720700
travel@solosholidays.co.uk
www.solosholidays.co.uk

La Source
Chalet/other accommodation in Villard-Reculas (Alpe-d'Huez)
Tel 01707 655988
lasourcefrance@aol.com
www.lasource.info

Stanford Skiing
Megève specialist
Tel 01603 477471
info@stanfordskiing.co.uk
www.stanfordskiing.co.uk

St Anton Ski Company
Hotels and chalets in St Anton
Tel +43 676 495 3438
jonathanstanton@mac.com
www.theoldhouse.at

Supertravel
Holidays in Europe/N America
Tel 020 7962 9933
ski@lotusgroup.co.uk
www.supertravel.co.uk

Susie Ward Alpine Holidays
Flexible holidays to Châtel
Tel 01872 553055
susie@susieward.com
www.susieward.com

Swiss Travel Service
Hotels in Switzerland
Tel 0870 191 7170
gholmes@bcttravelgroup.co.uk
www.swisstravel.co.uk

Switzerland Travel Centre
Specialists in Swiss resorts
Tel 020 7420 4900
sales@stc.co.uk
www.stc.co.uk

Ted Bentley Chalet Holidays
Luxury chalets in Nendaz
Tel 01934 820854
info@tedbentley.co.uk
www.tedbentley.co.uk

TheWhiteChalet.com
Chalet in Argentière
Tel 01274 530 313
s@mcnab.co.uk
www.chamonixbackcountry.com

Thomson Ski
Major mainstream operator
Tel 0870 606 1470
info@thomson-ski.com
www.thomson-ski.com

Tops Ski Chalets/Club Hotels
Holidays in France/ Austria
Tel 0870 240 1133
sales@topstravel.co.uk
www.topstravel.co.uk

Total
Chalet holidays in Europe
Tel 08701 633633
www.skitotal.com

Trail Alpine
Chalet in Morzine
Tel 0870 750 6560
info@trailalpine.co.uk
www.trailalpine.co.uk

Trailfinders
North American programme
Tel 0845 050 5900
www.trailfinders.com

UCPA
Budget trips to France
contact@kika.ucpa.com
www.ucpa.com/en

United Vacations
US and Canada programme
Tel 0870 606 1006
info@unitedvacations.com
www.unitedvacations.co.uk

Val d'Isère A La Carte
Specialists in Val d'Isère
Tel 01481 236800
info@skivaldisere.co.uk
www.skivaldisere.co.uk

Vanilla Ski
Chalet in Seez
Tel 01932 860696
sam@vanillaski.com
www.vanillaski.com

VIP
French and Swiss chalets
Tel 08701 123119
ski@vip-chalets.com
www.vip-chalets.com

Virgin Snow
Holidays to America
Tel 0871 222 8972
customerrelations
  @virginholidays.co.uk
www.virgin.com/Holidays

Waymark Holidays
Cross-country skiing holidays
Tel 0870 950 9800
enquiries
  @waymarkholidays.com
www.waymarkholidays.com

Weekends in Val d'Isère
... not just in Val d'Isère
Tel 020 8944 9762
info@alpineweekends.com
www.alpineweekends.com

White Heat Skiing
Holidays with off-piste tuition
Tel 020 7193 4793
info@whiteheatski.biz
www.whiteheatski.biz

White Mountains
Ski holidays in North America
Tel 0871 222 6006
sales@white-mountains.co.uk
www.white-mountains.co.uk

White Roc
Weekends/tailor-made holidays
Tel 020 7792 1188
ski@whiteroc.co.uk
www.whiteroc.co.uk

YSE
Holidays in Val d'Isère
Tel 0845 122 1414
sales@yseski.co.uk
www.yseski.co.uk

SKI BUSINESS DIRECTORY

This is a list of companies and organisations providing goods and services you might find helpful in organising a holiday, grouped under a dozen headings. Tour operators are listed separately, in the previous section, starting on page 736.

AIRLINES

Air Canada
Tel 0871 220 1111
www.aircanada.ca

Air France
Tel 0870 142 4343
www.airfrance.com/uk

Air New Zealand
Tel 0800 028 4149
www.airnewzealand.com

Alitalia
Tel 0870 544 8259
www.alitalia.co.uk

American Airlines
Tel 08457 789789
www.aa.com

Austrian Airlines
Tel 0870 124 2625
www.austrianairlines.co.uk

Bmibaby
Tel 0871 224 0224
www.bmibaby.com

British Airways
Tel 0870 850 9850
www.britishairways.com

Continental Airlines
Tel 0845 607 6760
www.continental.com

Delta Airlines
Tel 0845 600 0950
www.delta.com

EasyJet
Tel 0871 244 2366
www.easyjet.com

Flybe
Tel 0871 522 6100
www.flybe.com

Jet2.com
Tel 0871 226 1737
www.jet2.com

KLM
Tel 08705 074074
www.klmuk.co.uk

Lufthansa
Tel 0870 837 7747
www.lufthansa.com

Qantas
Tel 0845 774 7767
www.qantas.com.au

Ryanair
Tel 0871 246 0000
www.ryanair.com

Swiss International Air Lines
Tel 0845 601 0956
www.swiss.com

Thomsonfly
Tel 0870 190 0737
www.thomsonfly.com

United Airlines
Tel 0845 844 4777
www.unitedairlines.co.uk

Virgin Atlantic Airways
Tel 0870 380 2007
www.virgin-atlantic.com

Zoom Airlines
Tel 0870 240 0055
www.flyzoom.com

AIRPORTS

Aberdeen
Tel 0870 040 0006
www.baa.co.uk

Belfast
Tel 028 9448 4848
www.bial.co.uk

Birmingham
Tel 08707 335511
www.bhx.co.uk

Bournemouth
Tel 01202 364000
www.flybournemouth.com

Bristol
Tel 0870 121 2747
www.bristolairport.co.uk

Cardiff
Tel 01446 711111
www.cial.co.uk

Dublin
Tel +353 1 814 1111
www.dublin-airport.com

Durham Tees Valley
Tel 08712 242426
www.durhamteesvalleyairport.
com

Edinburght
Tel 0870 040 0007
www.baa.co.uk

Exeter
Tel 01392 367433
www.exeter-airport.co.uk

Glasgow
Tel 0870 040 0008
www.baa.co.uk

Leeds Bradford
Tel 0113 250 9696
www.lbia.co.uk

London Gatwick
Tel 0870 000 2468
www.baa.com

London Heathrow
Tel 0870 000 0123
www.baa.co.uk

London Luton
Tel 01582 405100
www.london-luton.com

London Stansted
Tel 0870 000 0303
www.baa.co.uk

Manchester
Tel 0161 489 3000
www.manchesterairport.co.uk

Newcastle
Tel 0870 122 1488
www.newcastleairport.com

Nottingham East Midlands
Tel 0871 919 9000
www.eastmidlandsairport.com

Southampton
Tel 0870 040 0009
www.baa.co.uk

AIRPORT TRANSFERS

Airport Transfer Service
Tel +33 450 536397
www.a-t-s.net

AlpineCab
Tel 00 33 450 731938
www.alpinecab.com

Alp Line
Tel +33 450 743842
www.alp-line.com

Bensbus.co.uk
www.bensbus.co.uk

Cham Van
Tel +33 632 240394
www.cham-van.com

Flytransfer
Tel 01224 641559
www.flytransfer.com

Geneva Airport Transfers
Tel +33 619 423752
www.geneva-airport-
transfers.com

Mountain Express
Tel +33 619 172600
www.mountainexpress.co.uk

Skihoppa.com
Tel +33 632 240394
www.skihoppa.com

Terravision
Tel +39 0645 441345
www.lowcostcoach.com

Threevalleetransfers
Tel 01782 644420
www.3vt.co.uk

Whitetracks
Tel 0779 664 0841
www.whitetracks.co.uk

BREAKDOWN INSURANCE

AA Five Star Europe
Tel 0800 085 2840
www.theAA.com

Autohome
Tel 0800 371 280
www.autohome.co.uk

Direct Line Rescue
Tel 0845 246 8702
www.directline.com/rescue

Europ Assistance
Tel 0870 737 5720
www.europ-assistance.co.uk

Green Flag Motoring Assistance
Tel 0845 246 1557
www.greenflag.com

Mondial Assistance UK
Tel 0208 681 2525
www.mondial-assistance.co.uk

RAC Travel Services
Tel 0800 015 6000
www.rac.co.uk

CAR HIRE

Alamo Rent A Car
Tel 0870 400 4562
www.alamo.co.uk

Avis Rent A Car
Tel 0844 581 0147
www.avis.co.uk

Budget Car and Van Rental
Tel 0353 9066 27711
www.budget-uk.com

Europcar UK
Tel 0845 758 5375
www.europcar.co.uk

Hertz UK Ltd
Tel 08708 448844
www.hertz.co.uk

Holiday Autos International Ltd
Tel 0870 400 4461
www.holidayautos.co.uk

Suncars
Tel 0870 500 5566
www.suncars.co.uk

CAR WINTER EQUIPMENT

Brindley Chains Ltd
Snowchains
Tel 01925 825555
www.brindley-chains.co.uk

GT Towing Ltd
Ski boxes and snowchains
Tel 01707 262526
www.gttowing.co.uk

Latchmere Motor Spares
Snowchains, roof bars, ski clamps, boxes
Tel 020 7223 5490
www.latchmeremotorspares.com

Motor Traveller / Carbox
Racks, boxes, snowchains
Tel 01753 833442
www.carbox.co.uk

The Roof Box Company
Tel 01539 621884
www.roofbox.co.uk

RUD Chains Ltd
Snowchains
Tel 01227 276611
www.rud.co.uk

skidrive.co.uk
Roof systems, boxes, snowchains
Tel 01223 323488
www.skidrive.co.uk

Snowchains Ltd
Boxes, roof bars, ski racks, snowchains
Tel 01732 884408
www.snowchains.co.uk

Spikes Spider
Tel 01706 819365
www.spikesspider.com

Thule Ltd
Tel 01275 340404
www.thule.co.uk

CROSS-CHANNEL TRAVEL

Brittany Ferries
Portsmouth-Caen
Tel 0870 9076 103
www.brittanyferries.co.uk

Eurotunnel
Folkestone-Calais/Coquelles via the Channel Tunnel
Tel 08705 35 35 35
www.eurotunnel.com

LD Line
Portsmouth-Le Havre
www.ldline.co.uk

Norfolkline
Dover-Dunkerque
Tel 0870 870 1020
www.norfolkline.com

P&O Ferries
Dover-Calais; Portsmouth-Le Havre; Hull Rotterdam Zeebrugge
Tel 08705 980 333
www.poferries.com

SeaFrance
Dover-Calais
Tel 08705 711 711
www.seafrance.com

SpeedFerries
Dover-Boulogne
Tel 0870 220 0570
www.speedferries.com

Stena Line
Harwich-Hook of Holland
Tel 08705 707070
www.stenaline.co.uk

DRY SKI SLOPES

SOUTH-WEST ENGLAND

Avon Ski Centre
Lyncombe Lodge, Churchill
Tel 01934 852335
info@highaction.co.uk
www.highaction.co.uk

Dorset Snowsport Centre
Warmwell, Dorchester
Tel 01305 853245
enquiries@dorsetsnowsportcentre.co.uk
www.dorsetsnowsportcentre.co.uk

Exeter and District Ski Club
Clifton Hill Sports Ground, Belmont Road, Exeter
Tel 01392 211422

John Nike Leisuresport – Plymouth
Plymouth Ski Centre, Alpine Park, Marsh Mills, Plymouth
Tel 01752 600220
www.jnll.co.uk

Snowtrax
Matchams Lane, Hurn, Christchurch
Tel 01202 499155
info@snowtrax.eu
www.snowtrax.eu

Torquay Alpine Ski Club
Barton Hall, Kingskerswell Road, Torquay
Tel 01803 313350
info@skitorquay.co.uk
www.skitorquay.co.uk

Yeovil Alpine Village
Addlewell Lane, Nine Springs, Yeovil
Tel 01935 421702
info@yeovilski.co.uk
www.yeovilalpinevillage.co.uk

SOUTH-EAST ENGLAND

Alpine Snowsports Aldershot
Gallwey Road, Aldershot
Tel 01252 325889
info@alpinesnowsports.co.uk
www.alpinesnowsports.co.uk

Bowles Outdoor Centre
Sandhill Lane, Eridge Green, Tunbridge Wells
Tel 01892 665665
admin@bowles.ac
www.bowles.ac

Bromley Ski Centre
Sandy Lane, St Paul's Cray, Orpington
Tel 01689 876812
management@bromleyski.co.uk
www.c-v-s.co.uk/bromleyski/

Calshot Activities Centre
Calshot Spit, Fawley, Southampton
Tel 023 8089 2077
calshot.ac@hants.gov.uk
www.hants.gov.uk/calshot

Christ's College Ski Club
Larch Avenue, Guildford
Tel 01483 504988
www.ccski.co.uk

Diggerland Snow Park
Medway Valley Leisure Park, Roman Way, Strood
Tel 08700 344437
www.thesnowpark.co.uk

Folkestone Sports Centre
Radnor Park Avenue, Folkestone
Tel 01303 850333
www.folkestonesports.ndo.co.uk/swimski.html

John Nike Leisuresport – Bracknell
Bracknell Ski Centre, Amen Corner, Bracknell
Tel 01344 789000
www.jnll.co.uk

John Nike Leisuresport – Chatham
Alpine Park, Capstone Road, Gillingham
Tel 01634 827979
www.jnll.co.uk

Knockhatch Ski Centre
Hailsham Bypass, Hailsham
Tel 01323 843344
knockhatch@aol.com
www.ski-knockhatch.com

Sandown Ski Centre
More Lane, Esher
Tel 01372 467132
ski@sandownsports.co.uk
www.sandownsports.co.uk

Southampton Alpine Centre
The Sports Centre, Bassett, Southampton
Tel 023 8079 0970
info@southampton-alpine-centre.co.uk
www.southampton-alpine-centre.co.uk

MIDDLE ENGLAND

The Ackers
Golden Hillock Road, Small Heath, Birmingham
Tel 0121 772 5111

Bassingbourn Ski Centre
Royston
Tel 01462 618091
booking@skibass.org
www.skibass.org

Gloucester Ski Centre
Matson Lane, Robinswood Hill, Gloucester
Tel 01452 874842
www.gloucesterski.com

John Nike Leisuresport – Swadlincote
Hill Street, Swadlincote
Tel 01283 217200
www.jnll.co.uk

Kidsgrove Ski Centre
Bathpool Park, Kidsgrove, Stoke-on-Trent
Tel 01782 784908
info@ski-kidsgrove.co.uk
www.ski-kidsgrove.co.uk

Stoke Ski Centre
Festival Park, Stoke-on-Trent
Tel 01782 204159
wilsonpb@postmaster.co.uk
www.stokeskicentre.co.uk

Tallington Ski Centre
Leisure Park, Barholm Road, Tallington, Stamford
Tel 01778 347000
info@tallington.com
www.tallington.com

Tamworth Snowdome
River Drive, Tamworth
Tel 08705 000011
info@snowdome.co.uk
www.snowdome.co.uk

Telford Ski Centre
Court Street, Madeley, Telford
Tel 01952 382688
madeleyskicentre@telford.gov.
uk

xXscape Milton Keynes
602 Marlborough Gate,
Central Milton Keynes
Tel 0871 200 3220
enquiriesmk@xscape.co.uk
www.xscape.co.uk

EASTERN ENGLAND

Brentwood Park Ski Centre
Little Warley, Brentwood
Tel 01277 211994
info@brentwoodskicentre.co.uk
www.brentwoodskicentre.co.uk

Gosling Ski Centre
Stanborough Road, Welwyn
Garden City
Tel 01707 331056
www.goslingsports.co.uk
www.goslingsports.co.uk

Hemel Ski Centre
St Albans Hill, Hemel
Hempstead
Tel 01442 241321
communicate@hemel-ski.co.uk
www.hemel-ski.co.uk

Norfolk Ski Club
Whitlingham Lane, Trowse,
Norwich
Tel 01603 662781
info@norfolkskiclub.co.uk
www.norfolkskiclub.com

Suffolk Ski Centre
Bourne Hill, Wherstead,
Ipswich
Tel 01473 602347
info@suffolkskicentre.co.uk
www.suffolkskicentre.co.uk

NORTHERN ENGLAND

Alston Training Centre
High Plains Lodge, Alston
Tel 01434 381886
alstontraining@btconnect.com
www.alstontraining.com

Halifax Ski Centre
Ploughcroft Lane, Halifax
Tel 01422 340760
skislope@ridehalifax.co.uk
www.ridehalifax.co.uk

Kendal Ski Club
Canal Head North, Kendal
Tel 0845 6345 173
sec@kendalski.co.uk
www.kendalski.co.uk

Pendle Ski Club
Clitheroe Road, Sabden,
Clitheroe
Tel 01200 425222
info@pendleskiclub.org.uk
www.pendleskiclub.org.uk

Runcorn Ski Centre
Town Park, Palace Fields,
Runcorn
Tel 01928 701965
info@runcornskicentre.co.uk
www.runcornskicentre.co.uk

Sheffield Ski Village
Vale Road, Parkwood Springs,
Sheffield
Tel 0114 276 9459
ask@sheffieldskivillage.co.uk
www.sheffieldskivillage.co.uk

Ski Rossendale
Haslingden Old Road,
Rawtenstall, Rossendale
Tel 01706 226457
ski-rossendale@rltrust.co.uk
www.ski-rossendale.co.uk

Whickham Thorns Centre
Market Lane, Dunston
Tel 0191 433 5767
whickhamthorns@leisure.
gateshead.gov.uk

Xscape Castleford
Colorado Way,
Glasshoughton, Castleford
Tel 0871 200 3221
enquiriescastleford@xscape.
co.uk
www.xscape.co.uk

WALES

Cardiff Ski Centre
198 Fairwater Rd, Cardiff
Tel 029 2056 1793
info@skicardiff.com
www.skicardiff.com

Dan-yr-Ogof Ski Slopes
Glyn Tawe, Abercraf
Tel 01639 730284
www.showcaves.co.uk

**John Nike Leisuresport –
Llandudno**
Wyddfyd Road, Great Orme,
Llandudno
Tel 01492 874707
www.jnll.co.uk

Plas y Brenin
Capel Curig, Conwy
Tel 01690 720214
info@pyb.co.uk
www.pyb.co.uk

Pontypool Ski Centre
Pontypool Leisure Park,
Pontypool
Tel 01495 756955

Ski Pembrey
Pembrey Country Park,
Pembrey, Llanelli
Tel 01554 834443

SCOTLAND

Alford Ski Centre
Greystone Road, Alford
Tel 01975 563024
keith.morris@aberdeenshire.
gov.uk
www.aberdeenshire.gov.uk/
recreation

Ancrum Outdoor Centre
10 Ancrum Road, Dundee
Tel 01382 435911
ancrum.centre@dundeecity.
gov.uk
www.ancrum.com

Bearsden Ski & Board
Stockiemuir Road, Bearsden,
Glasgow
Tel 0141 943 1500
info@skibearsden.co.uk
www.skibearsden.co.uk

Firpark Ski Centre
Tillicoultry, Clackmannanshire
Tel 01259 751772
www.clacksweb.org.uk/culture/
sport/

Glasgow Ski Centre
Bellahouston Park, 16
Dumbreck Road, Glasgow
Tel 0141 427 4991
info@ski-glasgow.org
www.ski-glasgow.org

Glenmore Lodge
Scottish National Sports
Centre, Aviemore
Tel 01479 861256
enquiries@glenmorelodge.org.
uk
www.glenmorelodge.org.uk

Loch Insh Ski Centre
Kincraig, Kingussie
Tel 01540 651272
office@lochinsh.com
www.lochinsh.com

Midlothian Snowsports Centre
Hillend, near Edinburgh
Tel 0131 445 4433
ski@midlothian.gov.uk
ski.midlothian.gov.uk

Polmonthill Ski Centre
Polmont Farm, Polmont,
Falkirk
Tel 01324 503835

Xscape Braehead
Kings Inch Road, Braehead,
Renfrew
Tel 0871 200 3222
enquiriesbraehead@xscape.co.
uk
www.xscape.co.uk

NORTHERN IRELAND

Craigavon Golf and Ski Centre
Turmoyra Lane, Silverwood,
Lurgan, Co Armagh
Tel 028 3832 6606
golf.ski@craigavon.gov.uk
www.craigavon.gov.uk

INSURANCE COMPANIES

Atlas Insurance
Tel 0870 811 1700
www.atlasdirect.net

Best Ski Insurance
Tel 0870 458 2985
www.best-ski-insurance.co.uk

CGNU
Tel 0808 101 4991
www.norwichunion.co.uk

Direct Line Travel Insurance
Tel 0845 246 8704
www.directline.com/travel

Direct Travel Insurance
Tel 0845 605 2500
www.direct-travel.co.uk

P J Hayman & Company
Tel 0845 230 0631
www.pjhayman.com

Preferential
Tel 0870 428 4399
www.preferential.co.uk

Primary Insurance Group
Tel 0870 220 0634
www.primaryinsurance.co.uk

ski-insurance.co.uk
Tel 0870 755 6101
www.ski-insurance.co.uk

Skicoverdirect
www.skicoverdirect.co.uk

Skisure.com
Tel 0845 222 0020
www.skisure.com

**Snowcard Insurance Services
Ltd**
Tel 01327 262805
www.snowcard.co.uk

Sportscover Direct Ltd
Tel 0845 120 6400
www.sportscover.co.uk

Travelcover.co.uk
Tel 0845 450 0610
www.travelcover.co.uk

Worldwide Travel Insurance
Tel 0870 112 8100
www.worldwideinsure.com

NATIONAL TOURIST OFFICES

Andorran Embassy
Tel 020 8874 4806
andorra.embassyuk
@btopenworld.com

Argentine Embassy
Tel 0800 999 5000
info@turismo.gov.ar
www.turismo.gov.ar

Australia Tourism
Tel 020 7438 4601
www.australia.com

Austrian National Tourist Office
Tel 0845 101 1818
holiday@austria.info
www.austria.info/uk

Canadian Tourism Commission
Tel 0870 380 0070
visitcanada@dial.pipex.com
www.travelcanada.ca

Chile – Consulate General
Tel 020 7580 6392
embachile@embachile.co.uk
www.echileuk.demon.co.uk

Finnish Tourist Board
Tel 020 7365 2512
finlandinfo.lon@mek.fi
www.visitfinland.com/uk

French Government Tourist Office
Tel 09068 244123
info.uk@franceguide.com
www.franceguide.com

German National Tourist Office
Tel 020 7317 0908
gntolon@d-z-t.com
www.germany-tourism.co.uk

Italian State Tourist Office
Tel 020 7408 1254
italy@italiantouristboard.co.uk
www.italiantouristboard.co.uk

Japan National Tourist Organisation
Tel 020 7734 9638
info@jnto.co.uk
www.seejapan.co.uk

Norwegian Tourist Board
Tel 020 7389 8800
london@invanor.no
www.visitnorway.com

Romanian Tourist Office
Tel 020 7224 3692
romaniatravel@btconnect.com
www.romaniatourism.com

Scottish Tourist Board
ski.visitscotland.com

Slovenian Embassy
Tel 020 7222 5400
vlo@gov.si
www.slovenia-tourism.si

Spanish Tourist Office
Tel 020 7486 8077
info.londres@tourspain.es
www.tourspain.co.uk

Swedish Travel and Tourism
Tel 020 7108 6168
uk@visitsweden.com
www.visit-sweden.com

Switzerland Tourism
Tel 00800 100 200 30
info.uk@myswitzerland.com
www.MySwitzerland.com

Tourism New Zealand
Tel 0906 601 3601
www.newzealand.com

Visit USA Association
Tel 0870 777 2213
www.visitusa.org.uk

RAILWAYS

Deutsche Bahn AG
Tel 0870 243 5363
sales@bahn.co.uk
www.deutsche-bahn.co.uk

Eurostar
Tel 08705 186 186
new.comments@eurostar.co.uk
www.eurostar.com

Rail Europe
Tel 08708 371 371
reservations@raileurope.co.uk
www.raileurope.co.uk

Swiss Federal Railways
Tel 00800 100 200 30
info.uk@switzerland.com
www.rail.ch

RETAILERS

SOUTH-WEST ENGLAND

Devon Ski Centre
Oak Place, Newton Abbot
Tel 01626 351278
www.devonski.co.uk/
www.skisuk.com

Mission Adventure Ltd
1 Bank Lane, Brixham
Tel 0870 1430 689
www.missionadventure.co.uk

Noahs Ark
London Road, Chalford, Stroud
Tel 01453 884738
www.noahsark.co.uk

Skate and Ski
104 High Street, Staple Hill, Bristol
Tel 0117 970 1356

Snow & Rock
Units 1-3 Shield Retail Centre, Link Road, Filton, Bristol
Tel 0117 914 3000
www.snowandrock.com

Snow Togs
6 St Michaels Road, Bournemouth
Tel 01202 557690
www.skishops.co.uk

Snowtrax
Matchams Lane, Hurn, Christchurch
Tel 01202 499155
www.snowtrax.eu

Team Ski
37 High East Street, Dorchester
Tel 01305 268035
www.teamski.co.uk

Westsports
Market House, Marlborough Rd, Old Town, Swindon
Tel 01793 532588
www.skishops.com

SOUTH-EAST ENGLAND

Alpine Room
71-73 Main Road, Danbury
Tel 01245 223563
www.alpineroom.co.uk

Captains Cabin Sevenoaks
113-115 St John's Hill, Sevenoaks
Tel 01732 464463
www.theski-shop.co.uk

Edge2Edge
Unit 10, Oakwood Industrial Park, Gatwick Road, Crawley
Tel 01293 649300
www.edge2edge.co.uk

Finches Ski and Sports
25-29 Perry Vale, Forest Hill, London
Tel 020 8699 6768
www.finches-ski.com

John Pollock
67 High Street, Barnet
Tel 020 8440 3994
www.johnpollock.co.uk

John Pollock
157 High Road, Loughton
Tel 020 8508 6626
www.johnpollock.co.uk

Mountain High
41 Reading Road, Pangbourne
Tel 0118 984 1851
www.mountainhigh.co.uk

Outdoor Life
3 High Street, Old Town, Eastbourne
Tel 01323 725372

Ski Bartlett
1-2 Rosslyn Parade, Uxbridge Road, Hillingdon
Tel 020 8848 0040
www.skibartlett.com

Snow & Rock
54-55 Market St, Brighton
Tel 01273 827660
www.snowandrock.com

Snow & Rock
99 Fordwater Road, Chertsey
Tel 01932 566886
www.snowandrock.com

Snow & Rock
188 Kensington High Street, London
Tel 020 7937 0872
www.snowandrock.com

Snow & Rock
4 Mercer Street, Covent
Garden, London
Tel 020 7420 1444
www.snowandrock.com

Snow & Rock
150 Holborn, Corner of Grays
Inn Road, London
Tel 020 7831 6900
www.snowandrock.com

Snow & Rock
Sporting Club, 38-42 King's
Road, London
Tel 020 7589 5418
www.snowandrock.com

Snow & Rock
47-51 King William Street,
London
Tel 020 7256 3940
www.snowandrock.com

Snow & Rock
The Boardwalk, Port Solent,
Portsmouth
Tel 023 9220 5388
www.snowandrock.co.uk

Snow & Rock
Unit 1 Davidson Way, Rom
Valley Way, Romford
Tel 01708 436400
www.snowandrock.com

Snow Togs
431 Millbrook Road,
Southampton
Tel 023 8077 3925
www.skishops.co.uk

MIDDLE ENGLAND

Active Outdoor & Ski
77 Castle Quay, Banbury
Tel 01295 273700
www.aosbanbury.com

Beans
86 Sheep Street, Bicester
Tel 01869 246451
www.beansonline.co.uk

BestBuys
Nene Court, 27-31 The
Embankment, Wellingborough
Tel 01933 272699
www.best-buys.co.uk

Lockwoods Ski Shop
125-129 Rugby Road,
Leamington Spa
Tel 01926 339388
www.lockwoods.com

Mountain High
Tower Court, Hornes Lane,
Princes Risborough
Tel 01844 274260
www.mountainhigh.co.uk

Noahs Ark
London Road, Chalford,
Stroud
Tel 01453 884738
www.noahsark.co.uk

Snow & Rock
14 Priory Queensway,
Birmingham
Tel 0121 236 8280
www.snowandrock.com

EASTERN ENGLAND

Revolutionz
21 Lower Goat Lane, Norwich
Tel 01603 629313
www.revolutionz.co.uk

Snow & Rock
Hemel Ski Centre, St Albans
Hill, Hemel Hempstead,
Hertfordshire
Tel 01422 235305
www.snowandrock.com

SnowFit
2 Cucumber Lane, Brundall,
Norwich
Tel 01603 716655
www.snowfit.co.uk

NORTHERN ENGLAND

Freetime Climb + Ski
1-2 Market Street, Carlisle
Tel 01228 598210
www.freetime1.co.uk

Glide & Slide
5/7 Station Road, Otley
Tel 01943 461136
www.glideslide.co.uk

**Severn Sports Mountain
Adventures**
80 Town Street, Armley,
Leeds
Tel 0113 279 1618
www.severnsports.co.uk

**Severn Sports Mountain
Adventures**
5-7 Church Lane, Crossgates,
Leeds
Tel 0113 264 3847
www.severnsports.co.uk

Snow & Rock
Metro Park West, Gibside
Way, Gateshead
Tel 0191 493 3680
www.snowandrock.com

Snow & Rock
Princess Parkway, Princess
Park, Didsbury, Manchester
Tel 0161 448 4444
www.snowandrock.com

Snow & Rock
Ski Centre, Vale Road,
Parkwood Springs, Sheffield
Tel 0114 275 1700
www.snowandrock.com

Snow & Rock
Unit 1 Eastham Point, New
Chester Road, Eastham, Wirral
Tel 0151 328 5500
www.snowandrock.com

SCOTLAND

Craigdon Mountain Sports
5 St Andrew's St, Aberdeen
Tel 01224 624333
www.craigdonmountainsports.
com

Craigdon Mountain Sports
Advertising House, Burghmuir
Circle, Inverurie
Tel 01467 624900
www.craigdonmountainsports.
com

Craigdon Mountain Sports
25-29 Kinnoull Street, Perth
Tel 01738 831006
www.craigdonmountainsports.
com

NORTHERN IRELAND

Macski
140 Lisburn Road, Belfast
Tel 028 9066 5525
www.macski.com

REPUBLIC OF IRELAND

The Great Outdoors
Chatham Street, Dublin 2
Tel 00 353 1 679 4293
www.greatoutdoors.ie

SKI EMPLOYMENT

Bunac / Gap Canada
Tel 020 7251 3472
enquiries@bunac.org.uk
www.bunac.org

Free Radicals
Tel 07968 183848
enquiries@freeradicals.co.uk
www.freeradicals.co.uk

Just Jobs 4 Students
Tel 020 7000 9994
www.justjobs4students.co.uk

Natives
Tel 08700 463377
info@natives.co.uk
www.natives.co.uk

Season Workers
Tel 01383 851166
info@seasonworkers.com
www.seasonworkers.com

Ski Connection
amanda@skiconnection.co.uk
www.skiconnection.co.uk

Voovs.com
Tel 01707 396511
info@voovs.com
www.voovs.co.uk

SKI/BOARDING ORGANISATIONS

British Association of Snowsport Instructors (BASI)
Tel 01479 861717
www.basi.org.uk

British Ski Club for the Disabled
www.bscd.org.uk

Disability Snowsport UK
Tel 01479 861272
info@uphillskiclub.co.uk
www.disabilitysnowsport.org.uk

Ski Club of Great Britain
Tel 020 8410 2000
skiers@skiclub.co.uk
www.skiclub.co.uk

Snowboard Club UK (SCUK)
Tel 01273 620877
www.snowboardclub.co.uk

Snowsport England
Tel 0121 501 2314
admin@englishski.org
www.snowsportengland.org.uk

Snowsport Scotland
Tel 0131 445 4151
info@snowsportscotland.org
www.snsc.demon.co.uk

Snowsport Wales
Tel 029 2056 1904
admin.snowsportwales@virgin.net
www.snowsportwales.net

SnowsportGB
Tel 0131 445 7676
info@snowsportgb.com
www.snowsportgb.com

SKI TRAVEL AGENTS

Alpine Answers
Tel 020 8871 4656
ski@alpineanswers.co.uk
www.alpineanswers.co.uk

Catered Ski Chalets
Tel 020 3080 0202
info@catered-ski-chalets.co.uk
www.catered-ski-chalets.co.uk

Iglu.com
Tel 020 8542 6658
enquiries@iglu.com
www.iglu.com

Independent Ski Links
Tel 01964 533905
info@ski-links.com
www.ski-links.com

Kwik Ski
Tel 0800 655 6506
ski@kwiktravel.co.uk
www.kwiktravel.com

Simply Alpine
Tel 023 9279 8901
enquiries@simply-alpine.co.uk
www.simply-alpine.co.uk

Ski & Surf
Tel 0208 731 2111
janm@skisurf.com
www.skisurf.com

Ski-direct.co.uk
Tel 08700 171935
email@ski-direct.co.uk
www.ski-direct.co.uk

Ski Expectations
Tel 01799 531888
ski.expectations@virgin.net
www.skiexpectations.com

Ski Line
Tel 020 8313 3999
angus@skiline.co.uk
www.skiline.co.uk

Ski McNeill
Tel 0870 600 1359
skiholidays@skimcneill.com
www.skimcneill.com

Ski Solutions
A La Carte department:
020 7471 7777
Tel 020 7471 7700
www.skisolutions.com

Ski Tracer
Tel 0870 420 5782
info@skitracer.com
www.skitracer.com

Ski Travel Centre
Tel 0141 649 9696
snow@skitravelcentre.com
www.ski-travel-centre.co.uk

Skis and Tees
Tel 0870 240 7416
enquiries@skisandtees.co.uk
www.skisandtees.co.uk

Snow Finders
Tel 01858 466888
sales@snowfinders.com
www.snowfinders.com

Snow Hounds
Tel 01243 788487
sales@snowhounds.co.uk
www.snowhounds.co.uk

Snow-Line
Tel 0871 222 6000
sales@snow-line.co.uk
www.snow-line.co.uk

WorldSki
Tel 0870 428 8706
info@worldski.co.uk
www.worldski.co.uk

This is an index to the resort chapters in the book; you'll find page references for about 400 resorts that are described in those chapters. But you'll also find brief descriptions here of another 700 resorts, most of them smaller than those we've covered in full.

Key

⛷ *Lifts*
⛷ *Pistes*

49 Degrees North USA
Inland area with best snow in Washington State, including 120-acre bowl reserved for powder weekends.
1195m; slopes 1195–1760m
⛷5 ⛷ 780 acres

Abetone Italy
Resort in the exposed Appennines, less than two hours from Florence and Pisa.
1390m; slopes 1390–1900m
⛷25 ⛷ 50km

Abtenau Austria
Sizeable village in Dachstein-West region near Salzburg, on large plain ideal for cross-country.
710m; slopes 710–1260m
⛷6 ⛷ 10km

Achenkirch Austria
Unspoiled, low-altitude Tirolean village close to Niederau and Alpbach. Beautiful setting overlooking a lake.
930m; slopes 930–1800m
⛷7 ⛷ 25km

Adelboden 498

Les Aillons-Margériaz France
Traditional village near Chambéry. Nicely sheltered.
1000m; slopes 1000–1900m
⛷20 ⛷ 40km

Alagna 452
Small resort on the western fringe of Monterosa Ski area.

Alba 485
Trentino village with a small, quiet area.

Albiez-Montrond France
Authentic old French village in Maurienne valley with panoramic views. Own easy slopes and close to other ski areas.
1500m; slopes 1500–2200m
⛷13 ⛷ 67 hectares

Alleghe Italy
Dolomite village near Cortina in a pretty lakeside setting close to numerous areas.
980m
⛷24 ⛷ 80km

Les Allues 326
Rustic village on the road up to Méribel.

Alpbach 127

Alpe-d'Huez 245

Alpe-du-Grand-Serre France
Tiny resort near Alpe-d'Huez and Les Deux-Alpes. Good for bad-weather days.
1370m; slopes 1370–2185m
⛷19 ⛷ 55km

Alpendorf Austria
Outpost of St Johann im Pongau, at one end of an extensive three-valley lift network linking via Wagrain to Flachau – all part of the Salzburger Sportwelt area.
850m; slopes 800–2185m
⛷64 ⛷ 200km

Alpenglow USA
Alaskan ski resort.
762m; slopes 2500–3900m
⛷4 ⛷ 320 acres

Alpine Meadows USA
Squaw Valley's next-door neighbour. Lightly wooded terrain, with runs best for intermediate cruisers, but a modest total vertical. Impressive snow record and long season. There's no resort in the European sense of the word, but lots of lodgings close by in lakeside Tahoe City.
2085m; slopes 2085–2635m
⛷13 ⛷ 2400 acres

Alps Resort South Korea
Korea's most northerly, snow-reliable resort, about five hours from Seoul. ⛷5

Alta 629

Alta Badia 463

Altenmarkt Austria
Unspoiled village, well placed just off the Salzburg-Villach autobahn for numerous resorts including snow-sure Obertauern and those in the Salzburger Sportwelt. 'Splendid nursery slopes,' says a 2006 visitor
855m; slopes 855–2130m
⛷23 ⛷ 150km

Alto Campoo Spain
Barren, desolate place with undistinguished slopes, but with magnificent wilderness views.
1650m; slopes 1650–2170m ⛷11

Alt St Johann Switzerland
Old cross-country village with Alpine slopes connecting into Unterwasser area near Liechtenstein.
900m; slopes 900–2260m
⛷19 ⛷ 60km

Alyeska USA
Alaskan area 60km/37 miles from Anchorage, with luxury hotel currently (2007) undergoing extensive renovation. Also in 2007 $4.5 million was spent on mountain upgrades, including the extension of its snowmaking system.
75m; slopes 75–1200m
⛷9 ⛷ 785 acres

Aminona 508
Purpose-built resort in the Crans-Montana network.

Andalo 485
Trentino village not far from Madonna.

Andermatt 500

Andorra la Vella 106

Angel Fire USA
Intermediate area near Taos, New Mexico. Height usually ensures good snow.
2620m; slopes 2620–3255m
⛷5 ⛷ 455 acres

Les Angles France
Attractive resort with one of the best ski areas in the Pyrenees. Pretty, tree lined, mostly easy skiing. New quad, blue run and beginner area in 2006/07.
1600m; slopes 1600–2400m
⛷18 ⛷ 40km

Ankogel 120

Annaberg-Lungötz Austria
Peaceful village in a pretty setting, sharing a sizeable area with Gosau. Close to Filzmoos.
775m; slopes 775–1620m
⛷33 ⛷ 65km

Annupuri 722
One of the three interlinked ski areas of Niseko.

Anthony Lakes USA
Ski resort in Oregon, 482km/300 miles east of Portland.
slopes 2165–2435m
⛷2 ⛷ 23 trails

Anzère 502

Aosta Italy
Historic working valley town with a gondola up to the mountain resort of Pila.
1800m; slopes 1550–2750m
⛷14 ⛷ 70km

Apex Canada
Small, friendly, rather isolated modern village. Well worth stopping off here for a night or two on a tour of western BC resorts. We recommend the friendly Sheeprock Lodge B&B –

great rooms with big wooden beds. Varied terrain that suits confident intermediates best, but also excellent beginner slopes.
1575m; slopes 1575–2180m
⛷4 ⛷ 1112 acres

Aprica Italy
Ugly, straggling village between Lake Como and the Brenta Dolomites, with bland slopes and limited facilities.
1180m; slopes 1180–2310m
⛷24 ⛷ 40km

Arabba 463

Aragnouet-Piau France
Purpose-built mid-mountain satellite of St-Lary, best suited to families, beginners and early intermediates.
1850m; slopes 1420–2500m
⛷18 ⛷ 80km

Arapahoe Basin USA
Small, exceptionally high day-skiing area near Keystone with excellent snowfall record and very long season. Good mix of open and wooded runs of every standard served by slow chair-lifts, plus serious steeps reached by hiking. There will be 400 acres of new terrain in Montezuma Bowl for 2007/08.
3285m; slopes 3285–3800m
⛷7 ⛷ 900 acres

Arcalis 106

Les Arcs 255

Ardent 265
Quiet hamlet with quick access to Avoriaz.

Åre 714

Arêches-Beaufort France
Secluded little village 25km/16 miles from Albertville, with mostly intermediate terrain on two areas 3km/2 miles apart. The slopes of both Les Saisies and Les Contamines are less than 25km/16 miles away.
1080m; slopes 1080–2300m
⛷15 ⛷ 50km

Argentière 269
Village beneath Chamonix's Grands Montets.

Arinsal 109

Arnoldstein/Dreiländereck Austria
One of several little areas overlooking the town of Villach.
680m; slopes 680–1455m
⛷7 ⛷ 10km

Arolla Switzerland
Tiny village in pretty riverside setting south of Sion. Main attraction is heli-skiing. Wonderful descents from 3800m/12,470ft. 'Good for a day,' says a recent reporter.
2000m; slopes 2000–2890m
6 47km

Arosa 503

Arrowhead 599
Slope-side hamlet next to Beaver Creek.

Artesina Italy
Purpose-built Piedmont resort south of Turin, lacking character and atmosphere. Part of Mondolé ski area with Prato Nevoso.
1300m; slopes 1320–2100m
25 90km

Ascutney Mountain USA
Family resort in Vermont 60km/37 miles from Killington, 200km/124 miles from Boston.
6 200 acres

Asiago Italy
Sizeable resort close to Verona, but at low altitude and with limited vertical.
1000m; slopes 1000–1380m 17

Aspen 592

Attitash USA
One of the biggest ski areas in eastern US. Uncrowded slopes. Lodging in nearby North Conway, and other New Hampshire areas close by.
slopes 180–715m
12 280 acres

Auffach 231

Auris-en-Oisans 245
Quiet hamlet linked to Alpe-d'Huez.

Auron France
Pleasant, family-oriented and recently redeveloped village with varied, sheltered, intermediate slopes; a stark contrast to nearby Isola 2000. Good choice of mountain restaurants.
1600m; slopes 1150–2450m
21 135km

Auronzo di Cadore Italy
Sizeable village that's a cheaper base for visiting Cortina. Its own slopes are of negligible interest.
865m; slopes 865–1585m
5 7km

Aussois France
One of many rustic working villages near Modane in the Maurienne valley.
1500m; slopes 1500–2750m
11 55km

Autrans France
Major cross-country village, close to Grenoble. Two limited areas of downhill slopes, including a new blue run.
1050m; slopes 1050–1710m
16 19km

Avon USA
Small town only a couple of miles from Beaver Creek. Inexpensive base from which to ski Beaver Creek, Vail and Breckenridge.

Avoriaz 1800 265

Axamer Lizum 147

Axams 147
Quiet village in Innsbruck area.

Ax-les-Thermes France
Sizeable spa village near Font-Romeu and Andorra. Gondola access to the ski area above Bonascre. Mostly fast chair-lifts, serving an expanding area of intermediate slopes.
1400m; slopes 1400–2400m
19 75km

Bad Gastein 129

Badger Pass USA
Base for 350 miles of superb backcountry touring in Yosemite National Park. Spectacular views.
2195m; slopes 2195–2435m
5 90 acres

Bad Hofgastein 129
Relaxed and spacious spa resort in the Gastein Valley.

Bad Kleinkirchheim 132

Banff 665

Bansko 717

Baqueira-Beret 705

Barboleuse 556
Quiet base for skiing the Villars slopes.

Bardonecchia Italy
Traditional market-town near the Italian/French border; two separate areas of slopes add up to a big area, mainly easy area. Mostly intermediate terrain, but still a lot of drag-lifts.
1310m; slopes 1290–2750m
21 100km

Barèges 423

Bariloche 733

Les Barzettes 508
Smaller base along the road from Crans-Montana.

Bayrischzell Germany
Bavarian resort south of Munich and close to Austrian border.
800m; slopes 1090–1563m
25 40km

Bear Mountain USA
Southern California's main area, in the beautiful San Bernardino National Forest region. Full snowmaking.
slopes 2170–2685m
12 195 acres

Bears Town South Korea
Modern resort with runs cut out of thick forest. Biggest resort near Seoul (only an hour's drive), so it can get very crowded. English-language website at www.bearstown.com. 9

Bear Valley USA
Resort in northern California, between Lake Tahoe and Yosemite.
2010m; slopes 2010–2590m
10 1280 acres

Beaulard Italy
Little place just off the road between Sauze d'Oulx and Bardonecchia.
1215m; slopes 1215–2120m
6 20km

Beaver Creek 599

Beaver Mountain USA
Small Utah area north of Salt Lake City, too far from Park City for a day trip.
2195m; slopes 2195–2680m
3 525 acres

Beitostølen 709

Belleayre Mountain USA
State-owned resort near Albany, New York State. Cheap prices but old lifts and short runs.
775m; slopes 775–1015m
7 170 acres

Bellwald Switzerland
Traditional Rhône valley resort near Fiesch, Riederalp and Bettmeralp. Part of the Goms Valley region.
1600m; slopes 1600–2560m
5 31km

Ben Lomond Australia
Small intermediate/beginner area in Ben Lomond National Park, Tasmania, 260km/162 miles from Hobart.
1450m; slopes 1460–1570m
6 14 hectares

Berchtesgaden Germany
Pleasant old town close to Salzburg, known for its Nordic skiing but with several little Alpine areas nearby. *550m*

Bergün Switzerland
Traditional, quiet, unspoiled, virtually traffic-free little family resort on the rail route between Davos and St Moritz. 5km/3 mile toboggan run.
1375m; slopes 1400–2550m
5 23km

Berkshire East USA
Resort in Massachusetts, southern New England, near the Mohawk Trail.
165m; slopes 165–525m
5 200 acres

Berthoud Pass 624
Powder heaven on the drive to Winter Park.

Berwang Austria
Unspoiled village nestling in a spacious valley, close to Lermoos.
1335m; slopes 1335–1740m
12 40km

Bessans France
Old cross-country village near Modane. Well placed for touring Maurienne valley resorts such as Val Cenis. The two lifts now serve a new beginner area at the bottom station for 2006/07.
1710m; slopes 1740–2200m
2 3km

Besse France
Charming old village built out of lava, with purpose-built slope-side satellite Super-Besse. Beautiful extinct-volcano scenery.
1050m; slopes 1300–1850m
22 45km

Bethel USA
Pleasant, historic town very close to Sunday River, Maine. Attractive alternative to staying in the slope-side resort.

Le Bettex 317
Small base above St-Gervais, with links to Megève.

Bettmeralp Switzerland
Central village of the sizeable Aletsch area near Brig, high above the Rhône valley, amid spectacular glacial scenery. Reached by cable-cars from the valley.
1955m; slopes 1900–2870m
35 99km

Beuil-les-Launes France
Alpes-Maritimes resort closest to Nice. Medieval village which shares area with Valberg.
1450m; slopes 1400–2100m
26 90km

Bezau Austria
Virtually no slopes of its own, but the main village lies in low Bregenzerwald region north-west of Lech.
650m; slopes 1210–1650m 2

Biberwier Austria
Limited little village with a small area of its own. Best as a quiet base from which to access the Zugspitz area.
1000m; slopes 1000–1790m
6 8km

Bichlbach Austria
Smallest of the Zugspitz villages with very limited slopes of its own. Suitable as an unspoiled base for visiting the rest of the area.
1070m; slopes 1070–1620m
3 7km

Bielmonte Italy
Popular with day trippers from Milan. Worthwhile on a bad-weather day.
1200m; slopes 1200–1620m
13 20km

Big Powderhorn USA
Area with the most 'resort' facilities in south Lake Superior region – and the highest lift capacity too. The area suffers from winds.
370m; slopes 370–560m
10 250 acres

Big Sky 643

Big White 672

Bischofshofen Austria
Working town and mountain resort near St Johann im Pongau, with very limited local runs and the main slopes starting nearby at Muhlbach (Hochkönig area).
545m; slopes 545–1000m
⬆1 ⬆2km

Bivio Switzerland
Quiet village near St Moritz and Savognin, with easy slopes opened up by a few lifts.
1770m; slopes 1780–2560m
⬆4 ⬆40km

Bizau Austria
One of two main areas in the low Bregenzerwald region north-west of Lech.
680m; slopes 680–1700m
⬆6 ⬆24km

Björkliden 713

Björnrike 713

Blackcomb 692
Smaller and quieter than neighbouring Whistler.

Black Mountain USA
New Hampshire area with lodging in nearby Jackson.
⬆4 ⬆143 acres

Blatten Switzerland
Mountainside hamlet above Naters, beside the Rhône near Brig. Small but tall Belalp ski area, with larger Aletsch area nearby. New six-pack for 2006/07.
1320m; slopes 1320–3100m
⬆9 ⬆60km

Bled 720

Blue Cow 724

Blue Mountain Canada
Largest area in Ontario, with glorious views of Lake Huron. High-capacity lift system and 100% snowmaking.
230m; slopes 230–450m
⬆15 ⬆275 acres

Blue River Canada
Base of world-famous Mike Wiegele heli-ski operation in Cariboo and Monashee mountains.

Bluewood USA
Particularly remote area even by American north-west standards. Worth a visit if you're in Walla Walla.
1355m; slopes 1355–1725m
⬆3 ⬆530 acres

Bogus Basin USA
Sizeable area overlooking Idaho's attractive, interesting capital, Boise.
1760m; slopes 1760–2310m
⬆8 ⬆2600 acres

Bohinj 720

Bois-d'Amont France
One of four resorts that make up Les Rousses area in Jura region.
1050m; slopes 1120–1680m
⬆40 ⬆40km

Boi Taull Spain
A typical Pyrenean resort set high above the Boi Valley, close to the stunning Aigues Tortes National Park. Good intermediate terrain.
slopes 2020–2750m
⬆16 ⬆43km

Bolognola Italy
Tiny area in Macerata region near the Adriatic Riviera.
1070m; slopes 1070–1845m
⬆7 ⬆5km

Bolton Valley USA
Resort near Stowe with mostly intermediate slopes.
465m; slopes 465–960m
⬆6 ⬆155 acres

Bonneval-sur-Arc France
Unspoiled, remote old village in the Haute Maurienne valley with many of its slopes at high altitude. Pass to neighbouring Val d'Isère is closed in winter.
1800m; slopes 1800–3000m
⬆11 ⬆25km

Bons 300
Rustic, unspoiled old hamlet linked to Les Deux-Alpes' skiing.

Boreal USA
Closest area to north Lake Tahoe town, Truckee. Limited slopes, best for novices.
2195m; slopes 2195–2375m
⬆9 ⬆380 acres

Bormio 428

Borovets 716

Bosco Chiesanuova Italy
Weekend day trippers' place near Verona. A long drive from any other resort.
1105m; slopes 1105–1805m
⬆18 ⬆20km

Bosco Gurin Switzerland
Highest ski area in Ticino. The only German speaking village in the Italian canton.
1500m; slopes 1500–2400m
⬆6 ⬆30km

Les Bottieres 384

La Bourboule France
Spa and cross-country village with the Alpine slopes of Le Mont-Dore nearby. Spectacular extinct-volcano scenery.
850m; slopes 1050–1850m
⬆41 ⬆80km

Bourg-d'Oisans France
Pleasant valley town on main Grenoble-Briançon road. Cheap base for visits to Alpe-d'Huez and Les Deux-Alpes.

Bourg-St-Maurice 255
French valley town with a funicular to Les Arcs.

Bovec Slovenia
Town near the small area of Kanin on the Italian border.

Boyne Highlands USA
Area with impressive, high-capacity lift system for weekend Detroit crowds. Fierce winds off Lake Michigan.
225m; slopes 225–390m
⬆10 ⬆240 acres

Boyne Mountain USA
Resort popular with weekend Detroit crowds. Not as windy as sister resort Boyne Highlands.
190m; slopes 190–340m
⬆12 ⬆115 acres

Bozel France
Small town that, in good snow conditions, you can ski down to off-piste from Courchevel. Also near road to Champagny-en-Vanoise (which has a gondola up to the La Plagne ski area).
860m

Bramans France
Old cross-country village near Modane. Well placed for touring numerous nearby resorts such as Val Cenis and Valloire.
1230m
⬆1 ⬆3km

Bramberg Austria
Village near Pass Thurn (Kitzbühel area). Shares odd area with Neukirchen – the only valley lift is in Neukirchen.
820m; slopes 820–900m ⬆2

Brand Austria
Family resort with small, low area, but a full-scale overhaul of its lift system for 2007/08 means it will be linked to Burserburg ski area via a high altitude cable car across a dividing valley.
1050m; slopes 1050–1920m
⬆13 ⬆50km

Les Brasses France
Collective name for six traditional hamlets with some of the closest slopes to Geneva, but best known for cross-country.
900m; slopes 900–1600m
⬆14 ⬆50km

Braunwald Switzerland
Sunny but limited area, a funicular ride above Linthal, Liechtenstein. New combi-mix lift for 2006/07.
1300m; slopes 1300–1905m
⬆8 ⬆32km

Breckenridge 601

Brentonico Italy
Little resort just off Verona-Trento motorway.
1160m; slopes 1160–1520m ⬆16

La Bresse France
Largest resort in the northerly Vosges mountains near Strasbourg. Three separate downhill areas (with a lot of snowmaking), but also extensive ski de fond and lots of other activities.
900m; slopes 900–1350m
⬆26 ⬆62km

Bretton Woods USA
Area with best snowfall record in New Hampshire, and one of several small resorts scattered along the Interstate 93 highway. Mostly easy slopes. Attractive base lodge, good views. Plans incude a new pedestrian village.
480m; slopes 480–940m
⬆9 ⬆435 acres

Briançon 370
Part of the Grand Serre Chevalier region, but with own ski area.

Brian Head USA
Utah area south of Salt Lake City, too far from Park City for a day trip.
2925m; slopes 2925–3445m
⬆10 ⬆500 acres

Brides-les-Bains 326
Quiet spa town in valley below Méribel.

Bridger Bowl 642

Brigels-Andiast Switzerland
In the same valley as Laax/Flims. Access from two sunny villages. Mostly red runs.
1300m; slopes 1100–2415m
⬆7 ⬆75km

Brighton USA
At the end of Big Cottonwood Canyon, and better all-round area than neighbour Solitude. Seems bigger than acreage implies, with challenging runs and superb powder areas.
2670m; slopes 2665–3200m
⬆15 ⬆2250 acres

Brixen 206
Grossraum village that shares slopes with Söll and Ellmau.

Brodie Mountain USA
Largest Massachusetts area. 100% snowmaking and mostly easy slopes.
440m; slopes 440–820m
⬆6 ⬆250 acres

Bromley USA
New York City weekend retreat, reputedly the warmest place to ski in chilly Vermont.
595m; slopes 595–1000m
⬆9 ⬆300 acres

Bromont Canada
Purpose-built resort an hour east of Montreal, with one of the best small areas in eastern Canada, popular for its night skiing.
slopes 405–575m
⬆6 ⬆135 acres

Bruck am Grossglockner Austria
Low beginners' resort, but could suit intermediates looking for a small, quiet base from which to visit nearby Zell am See.
760m

Brundage Mountain USA
Remote, uncrowded Idaho area with glorious views across the lake towards Hell's Canyon. Mostly intermediate slopes. Also has a snowcat operation.
1760m; slopes 1760–2320m
⬆5 ⬆1300 acres

Brunico/Bruneck Italy
Town with gondola link into the Plan de Corones/Kronplatz area.

Bruson 544
Relaxing respite from Verbier's crowds.

Les Bugnenets-Savagnieres
Switzerland
Very small area in the Jura
mountains, north of Neuchatel.
Short runs served by drag lifts.
Valid with the Valais Ski Card.
slopes 1090–1440m
⛟7 ⛷ 30km

Burke Mountain
USA
Uncrowded, isolated family
resort in Vermont with mostly
intermediate slopes. Great views
from the top.
385m; slopes 385–995m
⛟4 ⛷ 130 acres

Bürserberg
Austria
Undistinguished valley town that
is due to be linked to Brand via
a high altitude cable car across
a dividing valley for 2007/08.
900m; slopes 1035–1850m
⛟13 ⛷ 50km

Cairngorm
721
Caldirola
Italy
Genoese weekend day tripper
spot in a remote region off the
motorway to Turin.
1010m; slopes 1010–1460m
⛟3 ⛷ 5km

Cambre-d'Aze
France
Quiet ski area in the Pyrenees
with few British visitors. Good
beginner and intermediate
terrain. Forms part of the Neiges
Catalan (10 resorts on one pass).
1640m; slopes 1640–2400m
⛟17 ⛷ 35km

Camigliatello
Italy
Tiny area on the foot of the
Italian 'boot' near Cosenza.
Weekend/day trip spot.
1270m; slopes 1270–1750m
⛟4 ⛷ 6km

Campitello
485
Linked to the Sella Ronda, with
quick connections to the
interesting Arabba section.

Campitello Matese
Italy
The only slopes near Naples.
Surprisingly large area when
snowcover is complete.
Weekend crowds.
1440m; slopes 1440–2100m
⛟8 ⛷ 40km

Campo di Giove
Italy
Highest slopes in L'Aquila region
east of Rome.
1070m
⛟6 ⛷ 23km

Campodolcino
Italy
Valley town with new funicular
up to the fringe of Madesimo.
1070m; slopes 1545–2880m
⛟6 ⛷ 8km

Campo Felice
Italy
Easiest resort to reach from
Rome, off Aquila motorway. One
of the better lift systems in the
vicinity.
1410m; slopes 1520–2065m
⛟14 ⛷ 40km

Campo Imperatore
Italy
One of the best of many little
areas east of Rome.
1980m
⛟8 ⛷ 20km

Canazei
485
Sizeable and lively rustic village
in the Sella Ronda's most
heavily wooded section of
mountain.

Candanchu/Astún
704

Canillo
113
Small, quiet town linked to
Soldeu.

Canmore
Canada
Old frontier town on the way to
Nakiska/Fortress, well placed for
touring the region and an
attractive alternative to staying
in Banff.

Cannon
USA
One of several small New
Hampshire resorts scattered
along the Interstate 93 highway;
a ski area and nothing more.
High, steep mountain by eastern
standards.
605m; slopes 605–1260m
⛟9 ⛷ 165 acres

The Canyons
631
Cardrona
726
Les Carroz-d'Arâches
306
An attractive, spacious village
on the road up to Flaine.

Caspoggio
Italy
Attractive, unspoiled village
north-east of Lake Como, with
easy slopes (and more at nearby
Chiesa).
1100m; slopes 1100–2155m
⛟8 ⛷ 22km

Castelrotto
Italy
Picturesque village west of Sella
Ronda circuit with small sunny
Alpine area and good cross-
country trails.
1060m

Castel S Angelo
Italy
Tiny area in Macerata region
near Adriatic Riviera.
805m
⛟4 ⛷ 2km

Castle Mountain
Canada
Remote resort south of Calgary.
Good proportion of intermediate
and advanced terrain. New area
on Haig Ridge planned to
provide more beginner and
intermediate terrain, says a
2006 visitor.
1410m; slopes 1410–2270m
⛟5 ⛷ 250 acres

Cauterets
423
Cavalese
485
Unspoiled medieval town in Val
di Fiemme.

Caviahue
Argentina
Mountain village at the foot of
the Copahue Volcano, 357km/
222 miles from Neuquén City.
1645m; slopes 1645–2045m
⛟8 ⛷ 37km

The Cedars
Lebanon
The largest of Lebanon's ski
areas, 130km/80 miles inland
from Beirut. Good, open slopes
with a surprisingly long season.
1850m; slopes 2100–2700m ⛷5

Ceillac
France
Tight cluster of rustic old
buildings near Serre-Chevalier.
Not far from the highest village
in Europe, St-Veran.
1600m; slopes 1600–2450m
⛟7 ⛷ 25km

Celerina
534
Quiet village with links to St
Moritz's slopes.

Cerkno
Slovenia
Modern, family resort 50km/31
miles from Ljubljana. Lifts
include four fast chairs.
1935m; slopes 1935–1290m
⛟8 ⛷ 70 hectares

Cerler
Spain
Very limited, purpose-built resort
with a compact ski area similar
to that of nearby Andorra's
Arinsal.
1500m; slopes 1500–2630m
⛟19 ⛷ 71km

Le Cernix
France
Hamlet near Megève where Les
Saisies' slopes link to those of
Crest-Voland. Uncrowded retreat.
1250m; slopes 1150–1950m
⛟45 ⛷ 80km

Cerrato Lago
Italy
Very limited area near the
coastal town of La Spezia.
1270m; slopes 1270–1890m
⛟5 ⛷ 3km

Cerro Bayo
Argentina
Limited area amid stunning
scenery 10km/6 miles from La
Angostura, and 90km/56 miles
from San Carlos de Bariloche.
slopes 1050–1780m
⛟11 ⛷ 200 hectares

Cerro Castor
733
Cerro Catedral (Bariloche)
733
Cerro Mirador
734
Cervinia
430
Cesana Torinese
337
Italian village in the Milky Way.

Le Châble
544
Small village below Verbier.

Chacaltaya
Bolivia
Highest lift-served ski area in
the world and the only ski area
in Bolivia. Reached by four-
wheel drive vehicle from La Paz
30km/19 miles away. Only open
in summer (too cold in winter).
5190m; slopes 5220–5420m
⛟1 ⛷ 2km

Chaillol
France
Cross-country base on the edge
of the beautiful Ecrins National
Park, near Gap. Small Alpine
area, lots of snowmakers.
1600m; slopes 450–2000m ⛟10

Chamois
Italy
Small area above Buisson, a few
miles down the road from
Valtournenche (near Cervinia).
1815m; slopes 1815–2270m
⛟9 ⛷ 20km

Chamonix
269
Champagny-en-Vanoise
350
Charming village linking to the
La Plagne network.

Champéry
506
Champex-Lac
Switzerland
Lakeside hamlet tucked away in
the trees above Orsières. A nice
quiet, unspoiled base from
which to visit Verbier's area.
1470m; slopes 1470–2220m
⛟4 ⛷ 25km

Champfér
534
Lakeside hamlet between St
Moritz and Silvaplana.

Champoluc
452
Unspoiled village at one end of
the Monterosa Ski area.

Champorcher
Italy
Small village south of Aosta
valley with tall but narrow ski
area, mostly red runs on open
slopes, with one black through
the trees to the lift base.
1430m; slopes 1430–2500m
⛟5 ⛷ 21km

Champoussin
506
Quiet mountainside village in
the Champéry area.

Chamrousse
France
Functional family resort near
Grenoble, with good, sheltered
slopes. Chair-lifts and a cable-
car from three bases (1650, 1700
and 1750) serve largely beginner
and intermediate slopes.
1650m; slopes 1400–2255m
⛟24 ⛷ 92km

Chandolin
541
Chantemerle
370
Valley village with direct access
to Serre-Chevalier's slopes.

Chapa Verde
Chile
60km/37 miles north-east of
Rancagua and 145km/90 miles
from Santiago.
1200m; slopes 1200–2500m
⛟4 ⛷ 1200 hectares

Chapelco
Argentina
Small ski area 19km/12 miles
from sizeable town of San
Martin de Los Andes.
Accommodation in hotels 11km/
7 miles from the slopes.
slopes 1250–1980m
⛟10 ⛷ 140 hectares

La Chapelle-d'Abondance
279
Unspoiled village 5km/3 miles
down the valley from Châtel.

Charlotte Pass
724
Château d'Oex
Switzerland
Pleasant French-speaking valley
town sharing a lift-pass with
neighbouring, but unconnected,
Gstaad. Good rail links to other
sectors. Low slopes (top height
1630m/5,350ft). Famous for its
Alpine Balloon festival.
960m; slopes 890–3000m
⛟63 ⛷ 250km

Châtel
279
Le Chatelard
France
Small resort in remote Parc des
Bauges between Lake Annecy
and Chambéry.

Durango Mountain Resort USA
Mountain formerly known as Purgatory, with good slopes accessed by a long six-pack (the main base is still known as Purgatory). Durango itself, a half hour away, is a fun western town with an historic main street.
2680m; slopes 2680–3300m
🎿 11 ⛷ 1200 acres

Eaglecrest USA
Close to famous Yukon gold rush town Skagway. Family resort famous for its ski school.
365m; slopes 365–790m
🎿 3 ⛷ 640 acres

Eben im Pongau Austria
Part of Salzburger Sportwelt Amadé area that includes nearby St Johann, Wagrain, Flachau and Zauchensee. Village spoiled by the autobahn passing through it.
855m; slopes 855–2185m
🎿 100 ⛷ 350km

Ehrwald Austria
Friendly, relaxed, pretty village with several nicely varied areas, notably the Zugspitz glacier. Poor bus services, so a car is desirable.
1000m; slopes 1000–3000m
🎿 11 ⛷ 45km

El Colorado/Farellones 734
Area connected to the Valle Nevado ski area.

Eldora Mountain USA
Day visitor resort with varied terrain (including plenty of steep stuff) close to Denver Boulder (45min by regular scheduled bus). All forest trails, but with some good glade areas. Crowded at weekends, and all the chairs are slow.
2795m; slopes 2805–3230m
🎿 12 ⛷ 680 acres

Elk Meadows USA
Area south of Salt Lake City, more than a day trip from Park City.
2775m; slopes 2745–3170m
🎿 6 ⛷ 1400 acres

Ellmau 135

Elm Switzerland
One hour from Zürich, at the head of a quiet, isolated, valley. Good choice of runs including a long black to the valley.
1000m; slopes 1000–2105m
🎿 6 ⛷ 40km

Encamp 106

Enego Italy
Limited weekend day trippers' area near Vicenza and Trento.
1300m; slopes 1300–1445m
🎿 7 ⛷ 30km

Engelberg Switzerland
Popular, traditional resort close to Lucerne. Fragmented but varied slopes, with a snow-sure glacier and one of the biggest verticals in the Alps. The main slopes rise almost 2000m/ 6,560ft above the town by three successive lifts, the top one rotating 360° on the way.

Weekend queues can be long. The famous Laub descent attracts experts; there are few easy slopes. Mountain restaurants are plentiful and good-value. Wide choice of accommodation, but eating out is mostly hotel-based.
1050m; slopes 1050–3020m
🎿 24 ⛷ 82km

Entrèves 441
Hotels at the base of the lift up to Courmayeur's slopes.

Escaldes Andorra
Central valley town, effectively part of Andorra la Vella.

Etna Italy
Scenic, uncrowded, short-season area on the volcano's flank, 20 minutes from Nickolossi.
1800m; slopes 1800–2350m
⛷ 5km

Evolène Switzerland
Charming rustic village with own little area in unspoiled, attractive setting south of Sion.
1370m; slopes 1405–2680m
🎿 7 ⛷ 42km

Faak am See Austria
Limited area, one of five overlooking town of Villach.
560m; slopes 560–800m
🎿 1 ⛷ 2km

Fai della Paganella 485
Trentino village that shares its slopes with Andalo.

Fairmont Hot Springs Canada
Major luxury spa complex ideal for a relaxing holiday with some gentle skiing thrown in.
🎿 2 ⛷ 60 acres

Faistenau Austria
Cross-country area close to Salzburg and St Wolfgang. Limited Alpine slopes.
785m; slopes 785–1000m
🎿 5 ⛷ 3km

Falcade 485
Trentino village south of the Sella Ronda.

Falera 523
Small village with access to ski area shared by Flims and Laax.

Le Falgoux France
One of the most beautiful old villages in France, set in the very scenic Volcano National Park. Several ski areas nearby.
930m; slopes 930–1350m

Falkertsee Austria
Base area rather than a village, with bleak, open slopes in contrast to nearby Badkleinkirchheim.
1690m; slopes 1690–2385m
🎿 5 ⛷ 15km

Falls Creek 724

La Feclaz France
One of several little resorts in the remote Parc des Bauges. Popular cross-country ski base.
1165m

Fernie 675

Fieberbrunn Austria
Friendly old traditional village, an inconvenient distance from its small but attractive ski area. Newly opened gondola for 2006/07 has increased off-piste potential.
800m; slopes 835–2020m
🎿 11 ⛷ 35m

Fiesch Switzerland
Traditional Rhône valley resort close to Brig, with a lift up to Fiescheralp (2220m/7,280ft) at one end of the beautiful Aletsch area extending across the mountainside via Bettmeralp to Riederalp.
1050m; slopes 1900–2900m
🎿 36 ⛷ 100km

Fiescheralp Switzerland
Mountain outpost of Fiesch, down in the Rhône valley. At one end of the beautiful Aletsch area extending across the mountainside via Bettmeralp to Riederalp.
2220m; slopes 1900–2870m
🎿 36 ⛷ 99km

Filzmoos Austria
Charming, unspoiled, friendly village with leisurely slopes that are ideal for novices. Good snow record for its height. 'Quiet pistes', 'superb piste preparation' and 'splendid nursery slopes', say reporters. A 2007 visitor recommends the hotel Dachstein.
1055m; slopes 1055–1645m
🎿 12 ⛷ 32km

Finkenberg 138
Village between Mayrhofen and Hintertux.

Fiss Austria
Nicely compact, quiet, traditional village sharing an extensive, sunny area with bigger Serfaus.
1435m; slopes 1200–2700m
🎿 42 ⛷ 160km

Flachau Austria
Quiet, spacious village in a pretty setting at one end of an extensive three-valley lift network linking via Wagrain to Alpendorf. Flachauwinkl, up the valley, is at the centre of another similarly extensive lift system. All these resorts are covered by the Salzburger Sportwelt area. A 2005 visitor comments on the lack of clear signposting.
925m; slopes 800–2185m
🎿 64 ⛷ 200km

Flachauwinkl Austria
Tiny ski station beside Tauern autobahn, at the centre of an extensive lift network linking Kleinarl to Zauchensee. Flachau, down the valley, is at one end of a similarly extensive lift system. All these resorts are covered by the Salzburger Sportwelt ski pass that our figures relate to.
930m; slopes 800–2185m
🎿 59 ⛷ 200km

Flaine 306

Flims 523
Long-established resort sharing a huge area with Laax.

Flumet France
Surprisingly large traditional village, the main place from which to ski the sizeable Val d'Arly ski area, now linked through to Les Saisies/Crest Voland. Close to better-known Megève.
1000m; slopes 1000–2070m
🎿 84 ⛷ 175km

Flumserberg Switzerland
Collective name for the villages sharing a varied area an hour south-east of Zürich. Part of the wider Heidiland region. Mostly red and black runs, served by good network fast lifts.
425m; slopes 1220–2220m
🎿 16 ⛷ 65km

Folgaria 485
Largest of several resorts east of Trento. Old lift system.

Folgarida 485
Small Trentino village, with links to Madonna di Campiglio.

Foncine-le-Haut France
Major cross-country village in the Jura Mountains, with extensive trails.

Fonni Gennaragentu Italy
Sardinia's only 'ski area' – and it's tiny.
🎿 1 ⛷ 5km

Font-Romeu 423

Foppolo Italy
Relatively unattractive but user-friendly village, a short transfer from Bergamo.
1510m; slopes 1610–2160m
🎿 9 ⛷ 47km

Forca Canapine Italy
Limited area near the Adriatic and Ascoli Piceno. Popular with weekend day trippers.
1450m; slopes 1450–1690m
🎿 11 ⛷ 20km

Formazza Italy
Cross-country base with some downhill slopes.
1280m; slopes 1275–1755m
⛷ 8km

Formigal 704

Formigueres France
Small downhill and cross-country area in the Neiges Catalanes. There are 110km/ 68 miles of cross-country trails.
slopes 1700–2350m
🎿 8 ⛷ 19km

Le Fornet 404
Hamlet 3km/2 miles down the valley from Val d'Isère.

Forstau Austria
Secluded hamlet above Radstadt-Schladming road. Very limited area with old lifts, but nice and quiet.
930m; slopes 930–1885m
🎿 7 ⛷ 14km

Gstaad Switzerland
An attractive, traditional village, with four separate areas of easy and intermediate low-altitude skiing. Snow-cover can be unreliable except on the Glacier des Diablerets, 15km/9 miles away, but there are adequate nursery slopes and good runs to progress to. A new run for 2006/07 connects Rinderberg to Lengebrand. Bus and train travel may account for more time lost than lift queues. Mountain restaurants are plentiful. There's a wide choice of hotel and chalet accommodation.
1050m; slopes 950–3000m
⛟ 62 ⛷ 250km

Gunstock USA
One of the New Hampshire resorts closest to Boston, popular with families. Primarily easy slopes. Gorgeous Lake Winnisquam views.
275m; slopes 275–700m
⛟ 8 ⛷ 220 acres

Guthega 724

Guzet France
A charming cluster of chalets set among a pine forest at Guzet 1400. Three main sectors offer slopes for all levels.
1400m; slopes 1100–2100m
⛟ 14 ⛷ 40km

Hafjell Norway
Main ski area for Lillehammer.
⛟ 12 ⛷ 33km

Haider Alm 183
Area in the Val Venosta in the South Tyrol close to Nauders.

Hakuba Happo One 722
European-style resort four hours from Tokyo.

Harper Mountain Canada
Small, family-friendly resort in Kamloops, British Columbia.
1100m; slopes 1100–1525m
⛟ 3 ⛷ 400 acres

Harrachov Czech Republic
Closest resort to Prague, with enough terrain to justify a day trip. No beginner area.
650m; slopes 650–1020m
⛟ 15 ⛷ 8 runs

Hasliberg Switzerland
Four rustic hamlets on a sunny plateau overlooking Meiringen and Lake Brienz. Two of them are the bottom stations of a varied intermediate area.
1050m; slopes 600–2430m
⛟ 18 ⛷ 55km

Haukelifjell Norway

Haus 199
Village next to Schladming.

Haystack USA
Minor satellite of Mount Snow, in Vermont, but with a bit more steep skiing.
580m; slopes 580–1095m
⛟ 26 ⛷ 540 acres

Heavenly 579

Hebalm Austria
One of many small areas in Austria's easternmost ski region near Slovenian border. No major resorts in vicinity.
1350m; slopes 1350–1400m
⛟ 6 ⛷ 11km

Heiligenblut 120

Hemlock Resort Canada
Area 89km/55 miles east of Vancouver towards Sun Peaks. Mostly intermediate terrain and with snowfall of 600 inches a year. Lodging is available at the base area.
1000m; slopes 1000–1375m
⛟ 4 ⛷ 350 acres

Hemsedal 711

Heremence Switzerland
Quiet, traditional village in unspoiled attractive setting south of Sion. Verbier's slopes are accessed a few minutes' drive away at Les Masses.
1250m

Hermagor Austria
Main village base for the Nassfeld ski area in Carinthia.
600m; slopes 610–2000m
⛟ 30 ⛷ 100km

Higashiyama 722
One of the three interlinked ski areas of Niseko.

Hintermoos 144
Village in the Hochkönig area.

Hintersee Austria
Easy slopes very close to Salzburg. Several long top-to-bottom runs and lifts means the size of the area is greatly reduced if the snowline is high.
745m; slopes 750–1470m
⛟ 9 ⛷ 40km

Hinterstoder Austria
Quiet, unspoiled traditional village, 80km/50 miles east of Salzburg, with a good snow record for its height.
600m; slopes 600–1860m
⛟ 10 ⛷ 35km

Hinterthal 144
Village in the Hochkönig area.

Hintertux/Tux valley 138

Hippach 175
Hamlet near a crowd-free lift into Mayrhofen's main area.

Hochfügen 175
This is the Ski Optimal area above Kaltenbach, not far from Mayrhofen.

Hochgurgl 185
Quiet village with connection to Obergurgl's slopes.

Hochkönig 144

Hochpillberg Austria
Peaceful, virtually traffic-free hamlet with fabulous views towards Innsbruck and a lift into varied terrain above Schwaz.
1300m; slopes 1300–2100m
⛟ 5 ⛷ 10km

Hochsölden 203
Satellite above Sölden.

Hoch-Ybrig Switzerland
Purpose-built complex only 64km/40 miles south-east of Zürich, with facilities for families.
1050m; slopes 1050–1830m
⛟ 10 ⛷ 40km

Hohuanshan Taiwan
Limited ski area with short season in high, wild, inaccessible Miitaku mountains. Also known as Mt Hehuan.
3275m ⛟ 1

Holiday Valley USA
Family resort in New York state, an hour south-east of Buffalo.
slopes 485–685m
⛟ 12 ⛷ 270 acres

Hollersbach Austria
Hamlet near Mittersill, over Pass Thurn from Kitzbühel.
805m; slopes 805–1000m
⛟ 2 ⛷ 5km

Homewood USA
Uncrowded area with unsurpassed Lake Tahoe views, near Tahoe City. Most sheltered slopes in the vicinity so a good choice in bad weather.
1900m; slopes 1900–2400m
⛟ 7 ⛷ 1260 acres

Hoodoo Ski Bowl USA
Typical Oregon area with sizeable but short runs. Snow record isn't as good as its competitors near Portland. Two new quads installed in 2002/03.
1420m; slopes 1420–1740m
⛟ 5 ⛷ 800 acres

Hopfgarten 206
Small chalet village with lift link into the Ski Welt area.

Horseshoe Resort Canada
Toronto region resort with high-capacity lift system and 100% snowmaking. The second mountain – The Heights – is open to members only.
310m; slopes 310–405m
⛟ 7 ⛷ 60 acres

Hospental 500
Small village connected to Andermatt by road and rail.

Les Houches 269
Varied, tree-lined area at the entrance to the Chamonix valley.

Hovden Norway
Big, modern luxury lakeside hotel in wilderness midway between Oslo and Bergen. Cross-country venue with some Alpine slopes.
820m; slopes 820–1175m
⛟ 5 ⛷ 14km

La Hoya Argentina
Small uncrowded resort 15km/9 miles from Esquel.
slopes 1350–2150m
⛟ 6 ⛷ 22km

Huez 245
Charming old hamlet on the road up to Alpe-d'Huez.

Hunter Mountain USA
Popular New Yorkers' area so it gets very crowded at weekends.
485m; slopes 485–975m
⛟ 14 ⛷ 230 acres

Hüttschlag Austria
Hamlet in a dead-end valley with lifts into the Gastein area at nearby Grossarl.
1020m; slopes 1020–1220m ⛟ 1

Hyundai Sungwoo Resort South Korea
Modern high-rise resort, 140km/87 miles from Seoul. Own English-language web site at www.hdsungwoo.co.kr. ⛟ 9

Idre Fjäll Sweden
Collective name for four areas 490km/305 miles north-west of Stockholm.
slopes 590–890m ⛟ 30 ⛷ 28km

Igls 147

Iizuna Japan
Tiny area 2.5 hours from Tokyo. ⛟ 6

Incline Village USA
Large village on northern edge of Lake Tahoe – it is a reasonable stop-off if you are touring.

Indianhead USA
South Lake Superior area with the most snowfall in the region. Winds are a problem.
395m; slopes 395–585m
⛟ 12 ⛷ 195 acres

Inneralpbach 127
Small satellite of Alpbach.

Innerarosa 503
The prettiest part of Arosa.

Innichen 479
Small resort in the South Tyrol. San Candido is its German name.

Innsbruck 147

Interlaken 558
Lakeside resort near Wengen, Grindelwald and Mürren.

Ischgl 151

Ishiuchi Maruyama-Gala-Yuzawa Kogen Japan
Three resorts with a shared lift pass 90 minutes from Tokyo by bullet train and offering the largest ski area in the central Honshu region.
255m; slopes 255–920m ⛟ 52

Isola 2000 France
Small purpose-built family resort 90km/56 miles from Nice, with a compact ski area and an improving range of amenities. High slopes, mostly above the tree line. Some excellent beginner slopes near the base.
2000m; slopes 1840–2610m
⛟ 24 ⛷ 120km

Iso Syöte 707

Itter 206
Next to Söll.

Jackson USA
Classic New England village, and a major cross-country base. A lovely place from which to ski New Hampshire's Alpine areas.

Jackson Hole 648

Jasná Slovakia
Largest area in the Low Tatras
mountains, linked to Chopok,
which has an additional 11 lifts
covering 11 km/7 miles.
slopes 1240–2005m
🚡 13 🎿 21km

Jasper Canada
Friendly railroad town, best as a
two-centre holiday with Lake
Louise or Banff. Limited for keen
piste-bashers, but excellent for
beginners. Most accommodation
is out of town and the local
slopes are a 30-minute drive.
'Great skiing, no queues and a
lot of fun in the gladed bowl,'
says a 2007 visitor.
1065m; slopes 1065–2610m
🚡 9 🎿 1675 acres

Jay Peak USA
Vermont resort near Canadian
border with best snowfall record
in the east. Tree-lined
intermediate/advanced slopes –
as many classified black as blue.
New hike-in/out terrain opened
up in West bowl.
550m; slopes 550–1205m
🚡 8 🎿 385 acres

Jochberg 158
Straggling village, 8km/5 miles
from Kitzbühel.

La Joue-du-Loup France
Slightly stylish little purpose-
built ski-in/ski-out family resort
a few km north-west of Gap.
Shares a fair-sized intermediate
area with Superdévoluy.
1500m; slopes 1500–2510m
🚡 32 🎿 100km

Jouvenceaux 458
Less boisterous base from which
to ski Sauze d'Oulx's terrain.

Jukkasjärvi Sweden
Centuries-old cross-country
resort with unique ice hotel
rebuilt every December.

June Mountain USA
Small area a half-hour drive
from Mammoth and in same
ownership. Empty slopes except
on peak weekends.
2300m; slopes 2300–3090m
🚡 8 🎿 500 acres

Juns 138
Small village between
Lanersbach and Hintertux.

Kals am Grossglockner Austria
Village in a remote valley north
of Lienz.
1325m; slopes 1325–2305m
🚡 7 🎿 28km

Kaltenbach 175
One of the larger, quieter
Zillertal areas.

Kananaskis Canada
Small area near Calgary, nicely
set in woods, with slopes at
Nakiska and Fortress Mountain.
slopes 1525–2465m
🚡 12 🎿 605 acres

Kandersteg Switzerland
Good cross-country base set
amid beautiful scenery near
Interlaken. Easy, but limited,
slopes. Popular with families.
1175m; slopes 1175–1900m
🚡 7 🎿 14km

Kanin Slovenia
Small area near Bovec, 17km/
11 miles from the Italian border,
with plans to link with Sella
Nevea. The slopes are Slovenia's
highest. A 2007 visitor was
impressed with the quality of
the area and particularly enjoyed
its 'massive' area of off-piste.
980m; slopes 1600–2300m
🚡 6 🎿 15km

Kappl 151
Small village down the valley
from Ischgl.

Kaprun 235
Village near Zell am See.

Les Karellis France
Resort with slopes that are more
scenic, challenging and snow-
sure than those of better-known
Valloire, nearby.
1600m; slopes 1600–2550m
🚡 19 🎿 60km

Kastelruth Italy
German name for Castelrotto.

Kasurila Finland
Siilinjarvi ski area popular with
boarders. 🚡 5

Katschberg 120

Keystone 608

Kicking Horse 680

Killington 654

Kimberley Canada
New mountain village at the foot
of limited slopes a few miles
from the Bavarian/mock Tudor
resort, and in a beautiful setting
2 hours from Banff.
1230m; slopes 1230–1980m
🚡 5 🎿 1800 acres

Kirchberg 158
Lively town close to Kitzbühel,

Kirchdorf 225
Attractive village a bus-ride from
St Johann in Tirol.

Kirkwood USA
Collection of condos near Lake
Tahoe with varied skiing,
including some of the toughest
in the region. The wooded
slopes cover three main bowls,
mostly served by slow chair-lifts.
2375m; slopes 2375–2985m
🚡 12 🎿 2300 acres

Kitzbühel 158

Kleinarl Austria
Secluded traditional village up a
pretty side valley from Wagrain,
at one end of a three-valley lift
network linking it to Zauchensee
– all part of the Salzburger
Sportwelt ski pass area that our
figures relate to.
1015m; slopes 800–2185m
🚡 59 🎿 200km

Klippitztörl Austria
One of many little areas in
Austria's easternmost ski region
near Slovenian border. 'Great
little area with pretty tree-lined
runs,' says a 2007 visitor.
1550m; slopes 1460–1820m
🚡 6 🎿 25km

Klösterle Austria
Valley village at the base of the
Sonnenkopf ski area a few km
west of the Arlberg pass – and
covered by the Arlberg ski pass.
1100m; slopes 1100–2300m
🚡 10 🎿 39km

Klosters 521

Kobla 720

Kolsass-Weer Austria
Pair of Inn-side villages with
low, inconvenient slopes.
555m; slopes 555–1010m
🚡 3 🎿 14km

Königsleiten Austria
Quiet, high resort sharing fairly
snow-sure area with Gerlos, now
also linked to Zell im Zillertal to
form a fair-sized area. 'Two
excellent blacks for high-speed
carving runs', enthuses a 2006
reporter.
1600m; slopes 1245–2300m
🚡 55 🎿 155km

Kopaonik Serbia
Modern, sympathetically
designed family resort in a
pretty setting.
1770m; slopes 1110–2015m
🚡 21 🎿 57km

Koralpe Austria
Largest and steepest of many
gentle little areas in Austria's
easternmost ski region near
Slovenian border.
1550m; slopes 1550–2050m
🚡 10 🎿 25km

Kössen Austria
Village near St Johann in Tirol
with low, scattered and limited
local slopes.
600m; slopes 600–1700m
🚡 9 🎿 25km

Kötschach-Mauthen Austria
One of many little areas near
Hermagor in eastern Austria,
close to the Italian border.
710m; slopes 710–1300m
🚡 4 🎿 7km

Kranjska Gora 720

Krimml Austria
Sunny area, high enough to
have good snow usually. Shares
regional pass with Wildkogel
resorts (Neukirchen).
1075m; slopes 1640–2040m
🚡 9 🎿 33km

Krispl-Gaissau Austria
Easy slopes very close to
Salzburg. Several long top-to-
bottom lifts mean the size of
area is greatly reduced if the
snow line is high.
925m; slopes 750–1570m
🚡 11 🎿 40km

Kronplatz 479

Krvavec Slovenia
Slopes spread across Kalska
mountain. Lifts include a new
gondola.
1450m; slopes 1450–1970m
🚡 11 🎿 24km

Kühtai 147

Kusatsu Kokusai Japan
Attractive spa village with hot
springs, three hours from
Tokyo. 🚡 13

Laax 523

Le Lac Blanc France
Mini-resort in the northerly
Vosges mountains near
Strasbourg. Extensive ski de
fond trails.
830m; slopes 830–1235m
🚡 9 🎿 14km

Laces Italy
Village in the Val Venosta in the
South Tyrol covered by the
Ortler Skiarena pass.

Lachtal Austria
Second largest ski resort in the
styrian region north-east of
Salzburg.
1600m; slopes 1600–2100m
🚡 8 🎿 29km

Ladis Austria
Smaller alternative to Serfaus
and Fiss, with lifts that connect
into the same varied ski area.
1200m; slopes 1200–2540m
🚡 42 🎿 160km

Lagunillas Chile
83km/52 miles south-east of
Santiago. 🎿 494 acres

Le Laisinant 404
Hamlet a short bus-ride down
the valley from Val d'Isère.

Lake Louise 682

Lake Tahoe USA
Collection of 14 ski areas
spectacularly set on California-
Nevada border – Heavenly and
Squaw Valley best known in
Britain.

Lamoura France
One of four villages that makes
up the Les Rousses area in the
Jura.
1120m; slopes 1120–1680m
🚡 40 🎿 40km

Landeck-Zams Austria
Small ski area in the Tirol region
816m; slopes 816–2210m
🚡 7 🎿 22km

Lanersbach 138
Attractive village near Hintertux.

Lans-en-Vercors France
Village close to Villard-de-Lans
and 30km/19 miles from
Grenoble. Highest slopes in the
region; few snowmakers.
1020m; slopes 1400–1805m
🚡 16 🎿 24km

Lanslebourg France
One of the villages that makes
up Val Cenis.

Lanslevillard France
One of the villages that makes
up Val Cenis.

Marble Mountain   Canada
Tiny area in the Humber Valley on the island of Newfoundland, near the charming town of Corner Brook and Gros Morne National Park. Good snow record by east coast standards. Splendid base lodge, and some slope-side lodging. Blomidon Cat Skiing operates nearby.
85m; slopes 10–545m
🚡 5 🚠 175 acres

Les Marecottes   Switzerland
Small area near Martigny. Valid with the Valais Ski Card.
1100m; slopes 1775–2200m
🚡 5 🚠 25km

Maria Alm   144
Charming village at one end of the Hochkönig area.

Mariapfarr   Austria
Village at the heart of one of the longest, most snow-reliable cross-country networks in Europe. Sizeable Mauterndorf-St Michael Alpine area and Obertauern area are nearby.
1120m
🚡 5 🚠 30km

Mariazell   Austria
Traditional Styria village with an impressive basilica. Limited slopes.
870m; slopes 870–1265m
🚡 5 🚠 11km

Maribor   720

Marilleva   485
Small Trentino resort linked with Madonna di Campiglio.

Le Markstein   France
Long-standing small resort in the northerly Vosges mountains near Strasbourg, which has hosted World Cup slalom races. Extensive ski de fond trails.
slopes 770–1270m 🚡 10

Masella   Spain
Pyrenean village linked with slopes of La Molina to form the Alp 2500 area.
1600m; slopes 1600–2535m
🚡 20 🚠 100km

La Massana   106

Le Massif   701

Matrei in Osttirol   Austria
Large market village south of Felbertauern tunnel. Mostly high slopes.
1000m; slopes 1000–2400m
🚡 7 🚠 33km

Maurienne Valley   France
A great curving trench with over 20 winter resorts, ranging from pleasant old valley villages to convenience resorts purpose-built in the 1960s.

Mauterndorf   Austria
Village near Obertauern with tremendous snow record.
1120m; slopes 1075–2360m
🚡 10 🚠 35km

Maverick Mountain   USA
Montana resort with plenty of terrain accessed by few lifts. Cowboy Winter Games venue – rodeo one day, ski races the next.
2155m; slopes 2155–2800m
🚡 2 🚠 500 acres

Mayens de Riddes   544
Tiny hamlet linked via La Tzoumaz to the Verbier network.

Mayens-de-Sion   544
Tranquil hamlet that is part of the Verbier area.

Mayrhofen   175

Méaudre   France
Small resort near Grenoble with good snowmaking to make up for its low altitude.
1000m; slopes 1000–1600m
🚡 10 🚠 18km

Megève   317

Meiringen   Switzerland
Varied terrain, a good outing from the nearby Jungfrau resorts or Interlaken. Particularly suitable for beginners. High-speed gondola to the slopes.
600m; slopes 600–2435m
🚡 22 🚠 80km

Melchsee-Frutt   Switzerland
Limited, but high and snow-sure bowl above a car-free village. Family-friendly.
1920m; slopes 1080–2255m
🚡 11 🚠 32km

Les Menuires   324

Merano 2000   479

Méribel   326

Métabief-Mont-d'Or   France
Twin villages in the Jura region, not far from Geneva.
900m; slopes 880–1460m
🚡 22 🚠 42km

Methven   726
Nearest town/accommodation to Mt Hutt.

Mieders   227

Mijoux   France
Pretty wooded slopes between Dijon and Geneva. Lélex nearby.
1000m; slopes 900–1680m
🚡 29 🚠 50km

Mission Ridge   USA
Area in dry region that gets higher-quality snow than other Seattle resorts but less of it. Good intermediate slopes.
1390m; slopes 1390–2065m
🚡 6 🚠 300 acres

Misurina   Italy
Tiny village near Cortina. A cheap alternative base.
1755m; slopes 1755–1900m
🚡 4 🚠 13km

Mittersill   Austria
Valley-junction village south of Pass Thurn. About to gain prominence following construction in 2005 of a gondola from Hollersbach up to the Resterhöhe sector above Pass Thurn.
790m; slopes 1265–1895m
🚡 15 🚠 25km

Moena   Italy
Large village between Cavalese and Sella Ronda resorts, ideally located for touring the Dolomites area.
1180m; slopes 1180–2515m
🚡 24 🚠 35km

La Molina   704

Mölltal Glacier   120

Molveno   Italy
Lakeside village on edge of Dolomites, with a couple of lifts – but mostly used as a base to ski nearby Andalo.

Monarch   USA
Wonderfully uncrowded area, a day trip from Crested Butte. Great powder. Good for all but experts.
3290m; slopes 3290–3645m
🚡 5 🚠 800 acres

Monesi   Italy
Southernmost of the resorts south of Turin. Close to Monaco and Nice.
1310m; slopes 1310–2180m
🚡 5 🚠 38km

Le Monêtier   370
Quiet little village with access to Serre-Chevalier's slopes.

La Mongie   423

Montafon   180

Montalbert   350
Traditional village with direct access to the La Plagne network.

Mont Blanc   Canada
Small locals' hill near Tremblant, with only 300m/980ft of vertical and no resemblance to the Franco-Italian item.
🚡 7 🚠 36km

Montchavin   350
Attractive village on the fringe of La Plagne.

Mont-de-Lans   300
Low village near Les Deux-Alpes.

Le Mont-Dore   France
Attractive traditional small town, the largest resort in the stunningly beautiful volcanic Auvergne region near Clermont-Ferrand.
1050m; slopes 1350–1850m
🚡 18 🚠 42km

Monte Bondone   485
Trento's local hill.

Monte Campione   Italy
Tiny purpose-built resort, spread thinly over four mountainsides. 80% snowmaking helps to offset the low altitude.
1100m; slopes 1200–2010m
🚡 16 🚠 80km

Monte Livata   Italy
Closest resort to Rome, popular with weekenders.
1430m; slopes 1430–1750m
🚡 8 🚠 8km

Monte Piselli   Italy
Tiny area with the highest slopes of the many little resorts east of Rome.
2100m; slopes 2100–2690m
🚡 3 🚠 5km

Monte Pora   Italy
Tiny resort near Lake d'Iseo and Bergamo. Several other little areas nearby.
1350m; slopes 1350–1880m
🚡 11 🚠 30km

Monterosa Ski   452

Mont Gabriel   Canada
Montreal area with runs on four sides of the mountain, though the south-facing sides rarely open. Two short but renowned double-black-diamond bump runs. 🚡 9

Montgenèvre   337

Mont Glen   Canada
Least crowded of the Montreal areas, so a good weekend choice.
680m; slopes 680–1035m
🚡 4 🚠 110 acres

Mont Grand Fonds   Canada
Small area sufficiently far from Québec not to get overrun at weekends.
400m; slopes 400–735m 🚡 4

Mont Habitant   Canada
Very limited area in the Montreal region but with a good base lodge. 🚡 3

Mont Olympia   Canada
Small, two-mountain area near Montreal, one mostly novice terrain, the other best suited to experts. 🚡 6

Mont Orford   Canada
Cold, windswept lone peak (no resort), worth a trip from nearby Montreal on a fine day.
slopes 305–855m
🚡 8 🚠 180 acres

Mont-Ste-Anne   701

Mont-St-Sauveur   Canada
Perhaps the prettiest resort in Canada, popular with Montreal (60km/37 miles) day trippers and wealthy condo owners.

Mont Sutton   Canada
Varied area with some of the best glade skiing in eastern Canada, including some for novices. Quaint Sutton village nearby.
🚡 9 🚠 175 acres

Moonlight Basin   643
Quiet area of slopes linked to Big Sky, Montana.

Morgins   506
Chalet resort indirectly linked to Champéry.

Morillon   France
Valley village with a gondola link up to its purpose-built satellite and the Flaine network.
700 – 1100m
slopes 1100–1800m 🚡 7

Morin Heights   Canada
Area in the Montreal region with 100% snowmaking. Attractive base lodge. 🚡 6

Morzine 341

Les Mosses Switzerland
Peaceful resort and area, best
for a day trip from Villars or Les
Diablerets. Mainly reds and
blues served only by drag-lifts.
1500m; slopes 1500–2200m
🚡 *13* 🎿 *40km*

Mottaret 326
Purpose-built but reasonably
attractive component of Méribel.

Mottarone Italy
Closest slopes to Lake Maggiore.
No village – just a base area.
1200m; slopes 1200–1490m
🎿 *25km*

Les Moulins Switzerland
Village down the road from
Château d'Oex with its own low
area of slopes, part of the big
Gstaad lift-pass area.
890m; slopes 890–3000m
🚡 *67* 🎿 *250km*

Mount Abram USA
Small, pretty, tree-lined area in
Maine, renowned for its
immaculately groomed easy
runs.
295m; slopes 295–610m
🚡 *5* 🎿 *170 acres*

Mountain High USA
Best snowfall record and highest
lift capacity in Los Angeles
vicinity – plus 95% snowmaking.
Mostly intermediate cruising.
2010m; slopes 2010–2500m
🚡 *12* 🎿 *200 acres*

Mount Ashland USA
Arty town in Oregon renowned
for Shakespeare. Mountain
includes glaciated bowl rimmed
with steeps. Best for experts.
1935m; slopes 1935–2285m
🚡 *4* 🎿 *200 acres*

Mount Bachelor USA
Extinct volcano in Oregon
offering deserted runs on every
side served by many fast chairs.
Gets a lot of rain. You have to
stay in Bend, 40km/25 miles
away.
1740m; slopes 1740–2765m
🚡 *13* 🎿 *3680 acres*

Mount Baker USA
Almost on the coast near
Seattle, yet one of the top
resorts for snow (averages 600
inches a year). Plenty of
challenging slopes. Known for
spectacular avalanches.
1115m; slopes 1115–1540m
🚡 *9* 🎿 *1000 acres*

Mount Baldy Canada
Tiny area, but a worthwhile
excursion from Big White. Gets
ultra light snow – great glades/
powder chutes. A new lift and
ten new runs expected for
2006/07.
slopes 1705–2150m
🚡 *2* 🎿 *150 acres*

Mount Baldy USA
Some of the longest and
steepest runs in California. Only
an hour's drive from Los Angeles
so a day trip is feasible, but
20% snowmaking and
antiquated lifts are major
drawbacks.
1980m; slopes 1980–2620m
🚡 *4* 🎿 *400 acres*

Mount Baw Baw Australia
Small but entertaining
intermediate area in attractive
woodland, with great views.
Closest area to Melbourne
(150km/93 miles).
1450m; slopes 1450–1560m
🚡 *7* 🎿 *35 hectares*

Mount Buffalo 724

Mount Buller 724

Mount Dobson New Zealand
Mostly intermediate slopes in a
wide, treeless basin near Mt
Cook, with good snow-cover.
Accommodation in Fairlie, 40
minutes away.
1610m; slopes 1610–2010m
🚡 *3* 🎿 *990 acres*

Mount Falakro Greece
Area two hours' drive from
Salonica in northern Greece;
almost as big as Parnassos,
uncrowded and with good
views.
1720m 🚡 *2*

Mount Hood Meadows USA
One of several sizeable areas
amid magnificent Oregon
scenery. Impressive snowfall
record but snow tends to be
wet, and weather damp.
1375m; slopes 1375–2535m
🚡 *12* 🎿 *2150 acres*

Mount Hood Ski Bowl USA
Sizeable area set amid
magnificent Oregon scenery.
Weather can be damp.
1095m; slopes 1095–1540m
🚡 *9* 🎿 *960 acres*

Mount Hotham 724

Mount Hutt 726

Mount Lemmon USA
Southernmost area in North
America, close to famous Old
West town Tombstone, Arizona.
Reasonable snowfall.
2500m; slopes 2500–2790m
🚡 *3* 🎿 *70 acres*

Mount McKay 724

Mount Pilio Greece
Pleasant slopes cut out of dense
forest, only 15km/9 miles from
the holiday resort of Portaria
above town of Volos. 'Very small
and disorganised,' says a
reporter.
1500m 🚡 *3*

Mount Rose USA
Only 35km/22 miles from Reno.
Relatively high, with good
slopes of its own and well
placed for trips to other Tahoe
resorts.
2520m; slopes 2410–2955m
🚡 *6* 🎿 *1200 acres*

Mount Shasta Ski Park USA
Californian resort 483km/
300 miles north of San
Francisco.
🚡 *4* 🎿 *425 acres*

Mount Snow USA
Minor peak with a fair amount
of accommodation around the
base, and reputedly excellent
terrain-parks.
580m; slopes 580–1095m
🚡 *19* 🎿 *590 acres*

Mount Spokane USA
Little intermediate area outside
Spokane (Washington State).
1160m; slopes 1160–1795m
🚡 *5* 🎿 *350 acres*

Mount St Louis / Moonstone
Canada
Premier area in Toronto region,
spread over three peaks. Very
high-capacity lift system and
100% snowmaking.
🚡 *13* 🎿 *175*

Mount Sunapee USA
Area in New Hampshire closest
to Boston; primarily
intermediate terrain.
375m; slopes 375–835m
🚡 *10* 🎿 *230 acres*

Mount Vermio Greece
Oldest ski base in Greece. Two
areas in central Macedonia
60km/37 miles from
Thessaloniki. Barren but
interesting slopes.
slopes 1420–2000m 🚡 *4*

Mount Washington Resort
Canada
Scenic area on Vancouver Island
with lodging in the base village.
Impressive snowfall record but
rain is a problem.
1110m; slopes 1110–1590m
🚡 *6* 🎿 *970 acres*

Mount Waterman USA
Small Los Angeles area where
children ski free. The lack of
much snowmaking is a
drawback.
2135m; slopes 2135–2440m
🚡 *3* 🎿 *210 acres*

Mühlbach 144
Village in the Hochkönig area.

Mühltal Austria
Small village halfway between
Niederau and Auffach in the
Wildschönau. No local skiing of
its own.
780m; slopes 830–1900m
🚡 *29* 🎿 *42km*

Muhr Austria
Village by Katschberg tunnel
well placed for visiting St
Michael, Badkleinkircheim,
Flachau and Obertauern.
1110m

Muju Resort South Korea
Largest area in Korea and with a
fair amount of lodging. Though
it is the furthest resort from
Seoul (four hours south) it is
still overcrowded. 🚡 *14*

Mürren 525

Mutters 147

Myoko Suginohara Kokusai
Japan
A series of small resorts two or
three hours from Tokyo, which
together make up an area of
extensive slopes with longer,
wider runs than normal for
Japan. 🚡 *15*

Naeba Japan
Fashionable resort with lots of
accommodation two hours north
of Tokyo. Crowded slopes.
900m; slopes 900–1800m 🚡 *28*

Nakiska Canada
Small area of wooded runs
between Banff and Calgary, with
emphasis on downhill speed.
Unreliable snow, but state-of-
the-art snowmaking and
pancake-flat grooming.
1524m; slopes 1525–2215m
🚡 *4* 🎿 *230 acres*

Nasserein 213
Quiet suburb of St Anton.

Nassfeld Ski Arena 120

Nauders/Reschenpass 183

Nax Switzerland
Quiet, sunny village in a balcony
setting overlooking the Rhône
valley. Own little area and only
a short drive from Veysonnaz.
Handful of red and blue runs.
1300m 🚡 *6*

Nendaz 544
Quiet alternative to Verbier.

Neukirchen Austria
Quiet, pretty beginners' resort
with a fairly snow-sure plateau
at the top of its mountain.
855m; slopes 855–2150m
🚡 *14* 🎿 *35km*

Neustift 227

Nevegal Italy
Weekend place near Belluno,
south of Cortina.
1030m; slopes 1030–1650m
🚡 *14* 🎿 *30km*

Nevis Range 721

Niederau 231

Niederdorf 479
Cross-country village in the
South Tyrol. Villabassa is its
German name.

Niseko 722

Nockberge Innerkrems Austria
Area just south of Katschberg
tunnel.
1500m; slopes 1500–2300m
🚡 *10* 🎿 *33km*

Nordseter Norway
Cluster of hotels in deep forest
north of Lillehammer. Best for
cross-country.
850m; slopes 1000–1090m
🚡 *2* 🎿 *2km*

Norefjell Norway
Norway's toughest run, a very
steep 600m/1,970ft drop.
120km/75 miles north-west of
Oslo.
185m; slopes 185–1185m
🚡 *10* 🎿 *23km*

Pebble Creek USA
Small area on Utah-Jackson Hole route. Blend of open and wooded slopes.
1920m; slopes 1920–2530m
3 *600 acres*

Pec Pod Snezku
                Czech Republic
Collection of hamlets spread along the valley road leading to the main lifts and the very limited ski area.
770m; slopes 710–1190m
5 *12km*

Pedraces 463
Roadside village linked via La Villa to the Alta Badia and Sella Ronda.

Peisey 255
Small village linked to Les Arcs.

Peisey-Vallandry 255
Group of small villages linked to Les Arcs and the Paradiski area.

Pejo 485
Trentino resort near Madonna.

Penitentes Argentina
Inaugurated in 1979, 180km/ 112 miles from Mendoza. Accommodation at the base.
10 *300 hectares*

Perelik Bulgaria
New development aiming to link Pamporovo with Mechi Chal. Construction of the first lodgings is planned for 2007, but it's not clear when the 12 lifts and 28km/17 miles of pistes will be open.

Perisher/Smiggins 724

Pescasseroli Italy
One of numerous areas east of Rome in L'Aquila region.
1250m; slopes 1250–1945m
6 *25km*

Pescocostanzo Italy
One of numerous areas east of Rome in L'Aquila region.
1395m; slopes 1395–1900m
4 *25km*

Pettneu 213
Beginners' resort with an irregular bus link to nearby St Anton.

Petzen Austria
One of many little areas in Austria's easternmost ski region near the Slovenian border.
600m; slopes 600–1700m
5 *16km*

Peyragudes-Peyresourde
                France
Small Pyrenean resort with its ski area starting high above.
1000m; slopes 1600–2400m
15 *37km*

Pfelders Italy
Resort near Merano in the South Tyrol covered by the Ortler Skiarena pass.

Pfunds Austria
Picturesque valley village with no slopes but quick access to several resorts in Switzerland and Italy, as well as Austria.
970m

Phoenix Park South Korea
Golf complex with 12 trails in winter. Two hours (140km/ 87 miles) from Seoul.
slopes 650–1050m *8*

Piancavallo Italy
Uninspiring yet curiously trendy purpose-built village, an easy drive from Venice. 'Not for piste-bashers and experts, but highly suitable for beginners and intermediates,' says a recent reporter.
1270m; slopes 1270–1830m
17 *45km*

Piani delle Betulle Italy
One of several little areas near the east coast of Lake Como.
730m; slopes 730–1850m
6 *10km*

Piani di Artavaggio Italy
Small base complex rather than a village. One of several little areas near Lake Como.
875m; slopes 875–1875m
7 *15km*

Piani di Bobbio Italy
Largest of several tiny resorts above Lake Como.
770m; slopes 770–1855m
10 *20km*

Piani di Erna Italy
Small base development – no village. One of several little areas above Lake Como.
600m; slopes 600–1635m
5 *9km*

Piau-Engaly France
User-friendly St-Lary satellite in one of the best Pyrenean areas.
1850m; slopes 1700–2500m
20 *40km*

Piazzatorre Italy
One of many little areas in the Bergamo region.
870m; slopes 870–2000m
5 *25km*

Pichl 199
In Dachstein-Tauern region, close to Schladming.

Pico 654
Low-key little family area (no resort) close to Killington.

Piesendorf Austria
Cheaper, quiet place to stay when visiting Zell am See.
780m
3 *3km*

Pievepelago Italy
Much the smallest and most limited of the Appennine ski resorts. Less than 2 hours from Florence and Pisa.
1115m; slopes 1115–1410m
7 *8km*

Pila Italy
Purpose-built mountain resort linked by gondola to the historic valley town of Aosta. Varied, snow-sure terrain. Uncrowded slopes, good for beginners. A 2007 visitor says: 'If you like small and friendly with flattering pistes, Pila is for you.'
1800m; slopes 1550–2750m
14 *70km*

Pinzolo 485
Trentino resort near Madonna.

Pisoderi Greece
The longest run in Greece (over 2km/1 mile), in an unspoiled setting 18km/11 miles from the town of Florina in the north.
1650m *5*

Pitztal Austria
Long valley with good glacier area at its head, accessed by underground funicular.
1250m; slopes 880–3440m
19 *87km*

Pla-d'Adet France
Limited purpose-built complex at the foot of the St-Lary ski area (the original village is further down the mountain).
1680m; slopes 1420–2450m
32 *80km*

La Plagne 350

Plan de Korones 479

Plan-Peisey 255
Small development with link to Les Arcs.

Plose Italy
Varied area with the longest run (9km/6 miles) in the South Tyrol. Part of the Dolomiti Superski region.
560m; slopes 1065–2500m
11 *40km*

Poiana Brasov 719

Pomerelle USA
Small area in Idaho on the Utah-Sun Valley route.
2430m; slopes 2430–2735m
3 *300 acres*

Pontechianale Italy
Highest, largest area in a remote region south-west of Turin.
1600m; slopes 1600–2760m
8 *30km*

Ponte di Legno Italy
Attractive sheltered alternative to bleak, ugly neighbour Passo Tonale. Linked by piste and bus.
1255m; slopes 1255–1920m
5 *15km*

Pontresina Switzerland
Small, sedate sunny village linked to nearby St Moritz by road, with extensive cross-country trails. One long run on its own hill, Languard, has a cheaper base than St Moritz.
1805m
56 *350km*

Port-Ainé Spain
Small but high intermediate area in the Spanish Pyrenees near Andorra. Lifts include a six-pack; eponymous 3-star hotel at base.
1975m; slopes 1650–2440m
8 *44km*

Port del Comte Spain
High resort in the forested region of Lleida, north-west of Barcelona. The slopes spread across three linked sectors: El Sucre; El Hostal and El Estivella.
slopes 1730–2110m
15 *40km*

Porté Puymorens France
Little-known Pyrenean area close to Pas de la Casa in Andorra. Plans to link the two are now moving forward with the opening in 2005 of the first lift on the French side of Pas de la Casa.
slopes 1600–2600m
13 *45km*

Porter Heights New Zealand
Closest skiing to Christchurch (one hour). Open, sunny bowl offering mostly intermediate skiing – with back bowls for powder.
1340m; slopes 1340–1950m
5 *200 acres*

Portes du Soleil 359

Portillo 734

Powderhorn USA
Area in west Colorado perched on the world's highest flat-top mountain, Grand Mesa. Sensational views. Day trip from Aspen.
2490m; slopes 2490–2975m
4 *300 acres*

Powder King Canada
Remote resort in British Columbia, between Prince George and Dawson City. As its name suggests, it has great powder. Plenty of lodging.
880m; slopes 880–1520m
3 *160 acres*

Powder Mountain USA
Sizeable Utah area, a feasible day out from Park City, renowned for bowls of fluffy virgin powder. Snowcat operation too. Limited base area, but you can also stay in Ogden, 32km/20 miles away.
2100m; slopes 2100–2740m
7 *5500 acres*

Pozza di Fassa 485
Pretty Trentino village with its own slopes.

Pragelato Italy
Inexpensive base, linked by cable-car to Sestriere.
1535m; slopes 1535–2700m
6 *50km*

Prägraten am Grossvenediger
                Austria
Traditional mountaineering/ski touring village in lovely setting south of Felbertauern tunnel. The Alpine ski slopes of Matrei are nearby.
1310m; slopes 1310–1490m
3 *30km*

Prali Italy
Tiny resort east of Sestriere – a worthwhile half-day trip.
1450m; slopes 1450–2500m
7 *25km*

Pralognan-la-Vanoise France
Unspoiled traditional village overlooked by spectacular peaks. Champagny (La Plagne) and Courchevel are close by.
1410m; slopes 1410–2355m
14 *30km*

Pra-Loup France
Convenient, purpose-built resort
with an extensive intermediate
area linked to La Foux-d'Allos.
1500m; slopes 1500–2600m
⛷ 32 ⛷ 83km

Prati di Tivo Italy
Weekend day trip place east of
Rome and near the town of
Teramo. A sizeable resort by
southern Italy standards.
1450m; slopes 1450–1800m
⛷ 6 ⛷ 16km

Prato Nevoso Italy
Purpose-built resort with rather
bland slopes. Part of Mondolé
ski area with Artesina.
1500m; slopes 1500–1950m
⛷ 25 ⛷ 90km

Prato Selva Italy
Tiny base development (no
village) east of Rome near
Teramo. Weekend day trip place.
1370m; slopes 1370–1800m
⛷ 4 ⛷ 10km

Le Praz 288
The lowest and most attractive
of the Courchevel resorts.

Les Praz 269
Quiet hamlet near Chamonix.

Praz-de-Lys France
Little-known snow-pocket area
near Lake Geneva that can have
good snow when nearby resorts
(eg La Clusaz) do not.
1500m; slopes 1200–2000m
⛷ 23 ⛷ 60km

Praz-sur-Arly France
Traditional village in a pretty,
wooded setting just down the
road from Megève. Newly linked
slopes to Notre Dame de
Bellecombe and beyond to Crest
Voland/Les Saises, to form the
Espace Diamant.
1035m; slopes 1035–2070m
⛷ 84 ⛷ 175km

Le Pré 255
Hamlet with lifts up to Arc 2000.

Predazzo 485
Small, quiet place in Trentino
near Sella Ronda resorts.

Premanon France
One of four resorts that make
up Les Rousses area in the Jura.
1050m; slopes 1120–1680m ⛷ 40

La Presolana Italy
Large summer resort near
Bergamo.
1250m; slopes 1250–1650m
⛷ 6 ⛷ 15km

Pucón 734

Puigmal France
Resort in the French Pyrenees.
1830m; slopes 1830–2700m
⛷ 12 ⛷ 34km

Puy-St-Vincent 360

Pyhä 707

Pyrenees, French 423

Pyrenees 2000 France
Tiny resort built in a pleasing
manner. Shares a pretty area of
short runs with Font-Romeu.
2000m; slopes 1750–2250m
⛷ 32 ⛷ 52km

Québec City 701

Queenstown 729

Radium Hot Springs Canada
Summer resort offering an
alternative to the purpose-built
slope-side resort of Panorama.
slopes 975–2155m
⛷ 8 ⛷ 300 acres

Radstadt Austria
Interesting, unspoiled medieval
town near Schladming that has
its own small area, with the
Salzburger Sportwelt slopes
accessed from nearby
Zauchensee or Flachau.
855m; slopes 855–2185m
⛷ 100 ⛷ 350km

Ragged Mountain USA
Family-owned ski area in New
Hampshire.
⛷ 9 ⛷ 200 acres

Rainbow New Zealand
Northernmost ski area on South
Island. Wide, treeless area, best
for beginners and intermediates.
Accommodation at St Arnaud.
1440m; slopes 1440–1760m
⛷ 5 ⛷ 865 acres

Ramsau am Dachstein Austria
Charming village overlooked by
the Dachstein glacier. Renowned
for cross-country, it also has
Alpine slopes locally, on the
glacier and at Schladming.
1200m; slopes 1100–2700m
⛷ 18 ⛷ 30km

Ramundberget 713

Rauris 235
Old roadside village close to
Kaprun and Zell am See.

Ravascletto Italy
Resort in a pretty wooded
setting near Austrian border,
with most of its terrain high
above on an open plateau.
920m; slopes 920–1735m
⛷ 12 ⛷ 40km

Reallon France
Traditional-style village, with
splendid views from above Lac
de Serre-Ponçon.
1560m; slopes 1560–2115m
⛷ 6 ⛷ 20km

Red Lodge USA
Picturesque Old West Montana
town. Ideal for a combined trip
with Big Sky or Jackson Hole.
1800m; slopes 2155–2860m
⛷ 8 ⛷ 1600 acres

Red Mountain Resort Canada
Area renowned for its steep and
deep powder, eight hours east
of Vancouver, 3km/2 miles from
Rossland, a sleepy and charming
old mining town. New quad and
100 acres of additional beginner
terrain for 2007/08.
1185m; slopes 1185–2075m
⛷ 6 ⛷ 1685 acres

Red River USA
New Mexico western town –
complete with stetsons and
saloons – with intermediate
slopes above.
2665m; slopes 2665–3155m
⛷ 7 ⛷ 290 acres

Reichenfels Austria
One of many small areas in
Austria's easternmost ski region
near the Slovenian border.
810m; slopes 810–1400m

Reinwald Italy
Resort near Merano in the South
Tyrol covered by the Ortler
Skiarena pass.

Reit im Winkl Germany
Southern Bavarian resort,
straddling the German-Austrian
border. Winklmoos ski area is
best suited to intermediates.
750m; slopes 750–1800m
⛷ 7 ⛷ 40km

The Remarkables 729
Three bleak basins 45 minutes
from Queenstown.

Rencurel-les-Coulumes France
One of seven little resorts just
west of Grenoble. Unspoiled,
inexpensive place to tour.
Villard-de-Lans is the main
resort.

Reschenpass 183

Rettenberg Germany
Small resort near Austrian
border.
750m; slopes 820–1650m
⛷ 15 ⛷ 40km

Reutte Austria
500-year-old market town with
many traditional hotels, and rail
links to nearby Lermoos.
855m; slopes 855–1900m
⛷ 9 ⛷ 19km

Revelstoke 664
New resort for 2007/08, which
will have North America's
longest vertical when completed.

Rhêmes-Notre-Dame Italy
Unspoiled village in a
beautiful Rhêmes valley, south
of Aosta. Courmayeur and La
Thuile within reach.
2 ⛷ 5km

Riederalp Switzerland
Pretty, vehicle-free village
perched high above the Rhône
valley amid the glorious scenery
of the Aletsch area. Access by
cable-car or gondola from the
valley village of Mörel near Brig.
1900m; slopes 1900–2870m
⛷ 36 ⛷ 99km

Rigi-Kaltbad Switzerland
Resort on a mountain rising out
of Lake Lucerne, with superb all-
round views, accessed by the
world's first mountain railroad.
1440m; slopes 1195–1795m
⛷ 7 ⛷ 9km

Riihivuori Finland
Small area with 'base' at the top
of the mountain. 20km/12 miles
south of the city of
Jyväskylä. ⛷ 5

Riksgränsen 713

Riscone Italy
Dolomite village sharing a pretty
area with San Vigilio. Good
snowmaking. Short easy runs.
1200m; slopes 1200–2275m
⛷ 35 ⛷ 40km

Risoul 362

Rittner Horn Italy
Resort near Merano in the South
Tyrol covered by the Ortler
Skiarena pass.

Rivisondoli Italy
Sizeable mountain retreat east
of Rome, with one of the better
lift systems in the vicinity.
1350m; slopes 1350–2050m
⛷ 7 ⛷ 16km

Roccaraso Italy
Largest of the resorts east of
Rome – at least when snow-
cover is complete.
1280m; slopes 1280–2200m
⛷ 12 ⛷ 56km

Rohrmoos 199
Set in the Dachstein-Tauern
region, next to Schladming.

La Rosière 365

Rossland Canada
Remote little town 5km/3 miles
from cult powder paradise Red
Mountain.

Rougemont Switzerland
Cute rustic hamlet just over the
French/German language border
near Gstaad, with worthwhile
local slopes and links to
Gstaad's Eggli sector.
991m; slopes 890–3000m
⛷ 62 ⛷ 250km

Les Rousses France
Group of four villages – Les
Rousses, Premanon, Lamoura
and Bois d'Amont – in the Jura
mountains, 50km/31 miles from
Geneva airport.
1120m; slopes 1120–1680m
⛷ 40 ⛷ 40km

Ruka 707

Russbach Austria
Secluded village tucked up a
side valley and linked into the
Gosau-Annaberg-Lungotz area.
The slopes are spread over a
wide area.
815m; slopes 780–1620m
⛷ 33 ⛷ 65km

Rusutsu 722

Saalbach-Hinterglemm 192

Saalfelden Austria
Town ideally placed for touring
eastern Tirol. Extensive lift
networks of Maria-Alm and
Saalbach are nearby.
745m; slopes 745–1550m
⛷ 3 ⛷ 3km

Saanen Switzerland
Cheaper and more convenient
alternative to staying in Gstaad
– but much less going on.
slopes 950–3000m
⛷ 62 ⛷ 250km

Saanenmöser Switzerland
Small village with rail/road links
to Gstaad. Scenic and quiet local
slopes, with good mountain
restaurants (Horneggli and
Kübelialp are recent
recommendations).
1270m; slopes 1270–3000m
⛷ 67 ⛷ 250km

Saas-Almagell   Switzerland
Compact village up the valley from Saas-Grund, with good cross-country trails and walks, and a limited Alpine area.
1670m; slopes 1670–2400m
⛷ 8 ⛷ 12km

Saas-Fee   **529**

Saas-Grund   Switzerland
Sprawling valley village below Saas-Fee, with a separate, small but high Alpine area.
1560m; slopes 1560–3200m
⛷ 7 ⛷ 35km

Saddleback   USA
Small area between Maine's premier resorts. High slopes by local standards.
695m; slopes 695–1255m
⛷ 5 ⛷ 100 acres

Sahoro   Japan
Ugly, purpose-built complex on snowy northern Hokkaido island, with a limited area.
400m; slopes 400–1100m
⛷ 9 ⛷ 15km

Les Saisies   France
Traditional-style cross-country venue, surrounded by varied four-mountain Alpine slopes. Now part of Espace Diamant. Easy runs, but some lift queues at peak times.
1650m; slopes 1035–2070m
⛷ 84 ⛷ 175km

Sälen   **713**

Salt Lake City   USA
Underrated base from which to ski Utah. 30 minutes from Park City, Deer Valley, The Canyons, Snowbird, Alta, Snowbasin. Cheaper and livelier than the resorts.

Salzburg-Stadt   Austria
A single, long challenging run off the back of Salzburg's local mountain, accessed by a spectacular lift-ride from a suburb of Grodig.
425m

Samedan   Switzerland
Valley town, just down the road from St Moritz. A run heads back to base from Corviglia-Marguns.
1720m; slopes 1740–2570m
⛷ 56 ⛷ 350km

Samnaun   **151**
Shares large ski area with Ischgl.

Samoëns   **368**

San Bernardino   Switzerland
Pretty resort south of the road tunnel, close to Madesimo.
1625m; slopes 1600–2525m
⛷ 8 ⛷ 35km

San Candido   **479**
Small resort in the South Tyrol. Innichen is its German name.

San Carlos de Bariloche   **733**

San Cassiano   **463**
Village linked to the Sella Ronda.

Sandia Peak   USA
The world's longest lift ride ascends from Albuquerque. Mostly gentle slopes.
slopes 2645–3165m
⛷ 7 ⛷ 100 acres

San Grée di Viola   Italy
Easternmost of resorts south of Turin, surprisingly close to the Italian border.
1100m; slopes 1100–1800m
⛷ 30km

San Martin de los Andes   Argentina
Sizeable town, 19 km/12 miles from the Chapelco ski area.

San Martino di Castrozza   **485**
Trentino village south of Val di Fassa.

Sansicario   **458**
Small, stylish resort in the Milky Way near Sauze d'Oulx.

San Simone   Italy
Tiny development north of Bergamo, close to unappealing Foppolo area.
2000m; slopes 1105–2300m
⛷ 9 ⛷ 45km

Santa Caterina   Italy
Pretty, user-friendly village near Bormio, with a snow-sure novice and intermediate area.
1740m; slopes 1740–2725m
⛷ 8 ⛷ 25km

Santa Cristina   **470**
Quiet village on the periphery of the Sella Ronda.

Santa Fe   USA
One of America's most attractive and interesting towns. Varied slopes – glades, bowls, cruiser pistes, desert views. Great excursion from Taos.
3145m; slopes 3145–3645m
⛷ 6 ⛷ 660 acres

Santa Maria Maggiore   Italy
Resort south of the Simplon Pass from the Rhône valley, and near Lake Maggiore.
820m; slopes 820–1890m
⛷ 5 ⛷ 10km

San Vigilio di Marebbe/ Kronplatz   **479**

San Vito di Cadore   Italy
Sizeable, alternative place to stay for Cortina. Negligible local slopes, though.
1010m; slopes 1010–1380m
⛷ 9 ⛷ 12km

Sappada   Italy
Isolated resort close to the Austrian border below Lienz.
1215m; slopes 1215–2050m
⛷ 17 ⛷ 21km

Sappee   Finland
Resort within easy reach of Helsinki, popular with boarders and telemarkers. Lake views. ⛷ 7

Sarnano   Italy
Main resort in the Macerata region near Adriatic Riviera. Valley village with ski slopes accessed by lift.
540m
⛷ 9 ⛷ 11km

Le Sauze   France
Fine area near Barcelonnette, sadly remote from airports.
1400m; slopes 1400–2440m
⛷ 23 ⛷ 65km

Sauze d'Oulx   **458**

Savognin   Switzerland
Pretty village with a good mid-sized area; a good base for the nearby resorts of St Moritz, Davos/Klosters and Laax.
1200m; slopes 1200–2715m
⛷ 10 ⛷ 80km

Scheffau   **206**
Rustic village not far from Söll.

Schia   Italy
Very limited area of short runs – the only ski area near Parma. No village.
1245m; slopes 1245–1415m
⛷ 7 ⛷ 15km

Schilpario   Italy
One of many little areas near Bergamo.
1125m; slopes 1125–1635m
⛷ 5 ⛷ 15km

Schladming   **199**

Schnalstal   **479**
Val Senales ski area, in the Dolomites near Merano.

Schöneben   **183**
Area in the Val Venosta in the South Tyrol close to Nauders.

Schönried   Switzerland
A cheaper and quieter resort alternative to staying in Gstaad.
1230m; slopes 890–3000m
⛷ 67 ⛷ 250km

Schoppernau   Austria
A scattered farming community, one of two main areas in Bregenzerwald north-west of Lech.
860m; slopes 860–2060m
⛷ 8 ⛷ 39km

Schröcken   **165**
Bregenzerwald area village near Lech.

Schruns   **180**
Pleasant town at the heart of the Montafon region.

Schüttdorf   **235**
Ordinary dormitory satellite of Zell am See.

Schwarzach im Pongau   Austria
Riverside village with rail links. There are limited slopes at Goldegg; Wagrain (Salzburger Sportwelt) and Grossarl (Gastein valley) are also nearby.
600m

Schwaz   Austria
Valley town beside the Inn with a lift into varied terrain shared with the village of Pill and its mountain outpost, Hochpillberg.
540m; slopes 540–2030m
⛷ 6 ⛷ 10km

Schweitzer   USA
Excellent small family resort in the Rockies, near Spokane (Washington state), but long journey from UK a drawback. Low altitude but snow-sure.
1215m; slopes 1215–1945m
⛷ 6 ⛷ 2350 acres

Schwemmalm   Italy
Resort near Merano in the South Tyrol covered by the Ortler Skiarena pass.

Scopello   Italy
Low area close to the Aosta valley, worth considering for a day trip in bad weather.
slopes 690–1700m
⛷ 6 ⛷ 35km

Scuol   Switzerland
Year-round spa resort close to Austria and Italy, with an impressive range of terrain.
1250m; slopes 1250–2800m
⛷ 15 ⛷ 80km

Searchmont Resort   Canada
Ontario area with modern lift system and 95% snowmaking. Fine Lake Superior views.
275m; slopes 275–485m
⛷ 4 ⛷ 65 acres

Sedrun   Switzerland
Charming, unspoiled old village on the Glacier Express rail route close to Andermatt. Fine terrain amid glorious scenery; covered on Gotthard Oberalp lift-pass.
1450m; slopes 1150–2350m
⛷ 9 ⛷ 50km

Seefeld   Austria
A smart, all-round winter holiday resort in a pretty setting, with superb cross-country trails and off-slope activities, and a couple of small, separate areas of downhill slopes. Innsbruck is not far away.
1200m; slopes 1200–2100m
⛷ 25 ⛷ 45km

See im Paznaun   **151**
Small family-friendly area in the Paznaun Valley, near Ischgl.

Le Seignus-d'Allos   France
Close to La Foux-d'Allos (which shares large area with Pra-Loup) and has its own little area, too.
1400m; slopes 1400–2425m
⛷ 13 ⛷ 47km

Seis   Italy
German name for Siusi.

Sella Nevea   Italy
Limited but developing resort in a beautiful setting on the Slovenian border (there are plans to link to Kanin). Summer glacier nearby.
1140m; slopes 1190–1800m
⛷ 11 ⛷ 8km

Sella Ronda   **463**

Selva/Val Gardena   **470**

Selvino   Italy
Closest resort to Bergamo.
960m; slopes 960–1400m
⛷ 9 ⛷ 20km

Spital am Pyhrn Austria
Small village near Hinterstoder
in Upper Austria, a bus-ride from
its limited intermediate slopes at
Wurzeralm.
650m; slopes 810–1870m
⬆ 8 ⬈ 14km

Spittal an der Drau Austria
Historic Carinthian town with a
limited area starting a lift-ride
above it. A good day trip from
Bad Kleinkirchheim or from
Slovenia.
555m; slopes 1650–2140m
⬆ 12 ⬈ 27km

Spitzingsee Germany
Beautiful small lake (and village)
an hour from Munich.
⬆ 18 ⬈ 25km

Splugen Reinwald Switzerland
Small intermediate area south of
Chur.
1455m; slopes 1455–2215m
⬆ 7 ⬈ 30km

Sportgastein 129
Mountain village in the
Badgastein valley.

Squaw Valley 589

Stafal 452
Tiny, isolated village, with good
access to the Monterosa Ski
area.

St Andra Austria
Valley-junction village ideally
placed for one of the longest,
most snow-sure cross-country
networks in Europe. Close to the
Tauern pass and to St Michael.
1045m

St Anton 213

Starhill Resort South Korea
Purpose-built resort formerly
called Cheonmasan, 30km/
19 miles north-east of Seoul. ⬆ 8

Stari Vrh Slovenia
About 30 minutes from Ljubljana
airport. A reader who lives there
says: 'Runs range from a never-
groomed black and three
interesting reds to a winding
blue virtually from top to
bottom.' New heated six-pack
for 2006/07.
slopes 580–1200m
⬆ 4 ⬈ 12km

St Cergue Switzerland
Limited resort in the Jura
mountains, less than an hour
from Geneva and good for
families with young children.
1045m; slopes 1045–1700m
⬆ 7 ⬈ 20km

St Christoph 213
Small village on Arlberg pass
above St Anton.

St-Colomban-des-Villards 384

Steamboat 612

Ste-Foy-Tarentaise 378

Steinach Austria
Pleasant village in picturesque
surroundings, just off the
autobahn near the Brenner Pass.
An easy outing from Innsbruck.
1050m; slopes 1050–2205m
⬆ 6 ⬈ 15km

Stevens Pass USA
A day trip from Seattle, and
accommodation 60km/37 miles
away in Bavarian-style town
Leavenworth. Low snowfall and
no snowmakers. Mostly
intermediate slopes,
1235m; slopes 1235–1785m
⬆ 14 ⬈ 1125 acres

St-François-Longchamp 414
Sunny, gentle slopes linked to
Valmorel.

St Gallenkirch 180
Small village in the Montafon
valley.

St-Gervais 317
Small village sharing its ski area
with Megève and Chamonix.

St Jakob in Defereggen
Austria
Unspoiled traditional village in a
pretty, sunny valley close to
Lienz and Heiligenblut, and with
a good proportion of high-
altitude slopes.
1400m; slopes 1400–2520m
⬆ 9 ⬈ 34km

St Jakob in Haus Austria
Snowy village with its own
slopes. Fieberbrunn, Waidring
and St Johann are nearby.
855m; slopes 855–1500m
⬆ 8 ⬈ 16km

St-Jean-d'Arves 384

St Jean d'Aulps France
Small village in Portes du Soleil
area, not part of main circuit but
with its own interesting slopes
consisting of two small areas –
Domaine Chèvrerie and Domaine
Grande Terche.

St-Jean-de-Sixt France
Traditional hamlet, a cheap base
for La Clusaz and Le Grand-
Bornand (3km/2 miles to both).
960m

St-Jean-Montclar France
Small village at the foot of
thickly forested slopes. Good
day out from nearby Pra-Loup.
1300m; slopes 1300–2500m
⬆ 18 ⬈ 12km

St Johann im Pongau Austria
Bustling, lively working town
with its own small area. An
extensive three-valley lift
network starts 4km/2 miles away
at Alpendorf, linking via Wagrain
to Flachau – all part of the
Salzburger Sportwelt ski pass
area.
650m; slopes 800–2285m
⬆ 64 ⬈ 200km

St Johann in Tirol 225

St Lary Espiaube 423

St-Lary-Soulan 423

St Leonhard in Pitztal Austria
Village beneath a fine glacier in
the Oetz area, accessed by
underground funicular.
1250m; slopes 1735–3440m
⬆ 12 ⬈ 40km

St Luc 541

St Margarethen Austria
Valley village near Styria/
Carinthia border, sharing slopes
with higher Katschberg.
1065m; slopes 1075–2210m
⬆ 14 ⬈ 70km

St Martin bei Lofer Austria
Traditional cross-country village
in a lovely setting beneath the
impressive Loferer Steinberge
massif. Alpine slopes at Lofer.
635m

St-Martin-de-Belleville 381

St Martin in Tennengebirge
Austria
Highest village in the Dachstein-
West region near Salzburg. It
has limited slopes of its own but
nearby Annaberg has an
interesting area.
1000m; slopes 1000–1350m
⬆ 5 ⬈ 4km

St-Maurice-sur-Moselle France
One of several areas near
Strasbourg. No snowmakers.
550m; slopes 900–1250m
⬆ 8 ⬈ 24km

St Michael im Lungau Austria
Quiet, unspoiled village in the
Tauern pass snowpocket with an
uncrowded but disjointed
intermediate area. Close to
Obertauern and Wagrain.
1075m; slopes 1075–2360m
⬆ 25 ⬈ 105km

St Moritz 534

St-Nicolas-de-Véroce 317
Small hamlet in the Megève
network.

St-Nicolas-la-Chapelle France
Small village close to larger
Flumet, in the Val d'Arly.
1000m; slopes 1000–1600m
⬆ 10 ⬈ 40km

St-Nizier-du-Moucherotte
France
Unspoiled, inexpensive resort
just west of Grenoble with no
lifts of its own. Villard-de-Lans is
the main resort.

Stoneham 701

Stoos Switzerland
Small, unspoiled village an hour
from Zürich. Overcrowded at
weekends. Magnificent views of
Lake Lucerne.
1300m; slopes 570–1920m ⬆ 9

Storlien Sweden
Small family resort amid
magnificent wilderness scenery.
One hour from Trondheim, 30
minutes from Åre.
600m; slopes 600–790m
⬆ 7 ⬈ 16km

Stowe 658

St-Pierre-de-Chartreuse France
Locals' weekend place near
Grenoble. Unreliable snow.
900m; slopes 900–1800m
⬆ 14 ⬈ 35km

Stratton USA
Smart, purpose-built, car-free
village at foot of fair-sized
mountain in Vermont, with
efficient lifts and spread-out
accommodation.
570m; slopes 570–1180m
⬆ 14 ⬈ 660 acres

Strobl Austria
Close to St Wolfgang in a
beautiful lakeside setting. There
are slopes at nearby St Gilgen
and Postalm.
545m; slopes 545–1510m
⬆ 8 ⬈ 12km

St-Sorlin-d'Arves 384

St Stephan Switzerland
Unspoiled old farming village at
the foot of the largest sector of
slopes in the area around
Gstaad. Upgraded chair-lift and
new run for 2006/07.
995m; slopes 950–3000m
⬆ 67 ⬈ 250km

Stubai valley 227

Stuben 213
Small, unspoiled village linked
to St Anton.

St Veit im Pongau Austria
Spa resort with limited slopes at
Goldegg; Wagrain (Salzburger
Sportwelt) and Grossarl (Gastein
valley) are nearby.
765m

St-Veran France
Said to be the highest 'real'
village in Europe, and full of
charm. Close to Serre-Chevalier
and the Milky Way. Snow-
reliable cross-country skiing.
2040m; slopes 2040–2800m
⬆ 15 ⬈ 30km

St Wolfgang Austria
Charming lakeside resort near
Salzburg, some way from any
slopes, best for a relaxing winter
holiday with one or two days on
the slopes.
540m; slopes 665–1350m
⬆ 9 ⬈ 17km

Sugar Bowl USA
Exposed area north of Lake
Tahoe with highest snowfall in
California, best for experts.
Lodging in Truckee but Squaw
Valley nearby.
2100m; slopes 2100–2555m
⬆ 8 ⬈ 1500 acres

Sugarbush USA
Dynamic resort in upper
Vermont, with two mountains
linked by fast chair, and
something resembling a village
at the foot of one of them. Good
range of runs, including some
real challenges.
480m; slopes 450–1245m
⬆ 16 ⬈ 508 acres

Sugarloaf USA
Developing Maine resort, five
hours from Boston, with the
Eastern US's best open terrain.
430m; slopes 405–1290m
⬆ 15 ⬈ 1410 acres

Sulden 479
Small resort in the South Tyrol. Solda is its Italian name.

Summit at Snoqualmie USA
Four areas – Summit East, Summit Central, Summit West and Alpental – with interlinked lifts. Damp weather and wet snow are major drawbacks.
slopes 915–1645m
⛷ 24 ⛷ 2000 acres

Sun Alpina Japan
Collective name for three ski areas four hours away from Tokyo. ⛷ 20

Sundance USA
Robert Redford-owned, tastefully designed family resort set amid trees in snow-sure Utah, with a fair amount of mostly intermediate terrain.
1860m; slopes 1860–2515m
⛷ 4 ⛷ 450 acres

Sunday River USA
One of the more attractive resorts in the East, four hours from Boston, best for intermediate cruisers.
245m; slopes 245–955m
⛷ 18 ⛷ 663 acres

Sunlight Mountain Resort USA
Quiet area near Glenwood Springs. Varied terrain with fine glades and terrain park. Works well as a half-day ski, half-day sightseeing trip from Aspen or Vail.
2405m; slopes 2405–3015m
⛷ 4 ⛷ 460 acres

Sun Peaks 689

Sunrise Park USA
Arizona's largest area, operated by Apaches. Slopes are spread over three mountains; best for novices and leisurely intermediates.
2805m; slopes 2805–3500m
⛷ 12 ⛷ 800 acres

Sunshine Village 665
One-hotel mountain station in Banff's ski area.

Sun Valley 642

Suomu Finland
A lodge (no village) right on the Arctic Circle with a few slopes but mostly a ski-touring place.
140m; slopes 140–410m ⛷ 3

Superbagnères France
Little more than a particularly French-dominated Club Med; best for a low-cost, low-effort family trip to the Pyrenees. Said to have good off-piste if the snow is good.
1880m; slopes 1440–2260m
⛷ 16 ⛷ 35km

Super-Besse France
Purpose-built resort amid spectacular extinct-volcano scenery. Shares area with Mont-Dore. Limited village.
1350m; slopes 1300–1850m
⛷ 22 ⛷ 45km

Superdévoluy France
Purpose-built but friendly family resort, with huge tower blocks, a few km north-west of Gap, with a sizeable intermediate area shared with La Joue-du-Loup. 'Some reasonable restaurants,' says a 2007 visitor.
1500m; slopes 1500–2510m
⛷ 29 ⛷ 100km

Super Espot Spain
Small area on the eastern edge of the Aigües Tortes National Park, close to the valley town of Sort.
slopes 1500–2430m
⛷ 10 ⛷ 28km

Supermolina Spain
Dreary, purpose-built satellite of Pyrenean resort of La Molina, with a reasonable sized area of its own and linked to the slopes of Masella to form an area called Alp 2500.
1700m; slopes 1600–2535m
⛷ 29 ⛷ 100km

Les Sybelles 384

Tahko Finland
Largest resort in southern Finland. Plenty of intermediate slopes in an attractive, wooded, frozen-lake setting. ⛷ 9

Tahoe City USA
Small lakeside accommodation base for visiting nearby Alpine Meadows and Squaw Valley.

Talisman Mountain Resort Canada
One of the best areas in the Toronto region, but with a relatively low lift capacity. 100% snowmaking.
235m; slopes 235–420m ⛷ 8

Tamarack 642

Tamsweg Austria
Large cross-country village with rail links in snowy region close to Tauern Pass and St Michael.
1025m

La Tania 389

Taos USA
Small Alpine-style development, 20 miles from Taos town, with compact ski area of cult status with experts.
2805m; slopes 2805–3600m
⛷ 12 ⛷ 1294 acres

Tärnaby-Hemavan Sweden
Twin resorts in north Sweden, offering downhill, cross-country and heliskiing. Own airport.
slopes 465–1135m
⛷ 13 ⛷ 44km

El Tarter 113
Relatively quiet, convenient alternative to Soldeu.

Tarvisio Italy
Interesting, animated old town bordering Austria and Slovenia. A major cross-country base with fairly limited Alpine slopes.
750m; slopes 750–1860m
⛷ 12 ⛷ 15km

Täsch 563
The final road base on the way to car-free Zermatt.

Tauplitz Austria
Traditional village at the foot of an interestingly varied area north of Schladming.
900m; slopes 900–2000m
⛷ 19 ⛷ 40km

Telluride 615

Temù Italy
Sheltered hamlet near Passo Tonale. Worth a visit in bad weather.
1155m; slopes 1155–1955m
⛷ 4 ⛷ 5km

Tengendai Japan
Tiny area three hours by train and bus from Tokyo. One of Japan's best snow records, including occasional powder. ⛷ 5

Termas de Chillán 734

Termignon France
Traditional rustic village 6km/ 4 miles down the Maurienne valley from Lanslebourg and the slopes of Val Cenis, to which a link is planned. The local slopes are limited and served by slow lifts, but have the advantage of being extremely quiet.
1300m; slopes 1300–2500m
⛷ 6 ⛷ 35km

Terminillo Italy
Purpose-built resort 100km/ 62 miles from Rome with a worthwhile area when its lower runs have snow cover.
1500m; slopes 1500–2210m
⛷ 15 ⛷ 40km

Thollon-les-Mémises France
Attractive base for a relaxed holiday. Own little area and close to Portes du Soleil.
1000m; slopes 1600–2000m
⛷ 19 ⛷ 50km

Thredbo 724

La Thuile 483

Thyon 2000 544
Mid-mountain resort above Veysonnaz in the Verbier ski area.

Tignes 393

Timberline (Palmer Snowfield) USA
East of Portland, Oregon, and the only lift-served summer skiing in the US: winter snow is maintained by spreading vast amounts of salt to harden it.
slopes 1830–2600m
⛷ 6 ⛷ 2500 acres

Toblach 479
Small resort in the South Tyrol. Dobbiaco is its Italian name.

Togari Japan
One of several areas close to the 1998 Olympic site. Nagano, 2.5 hours from Tokyo. ⛷ 10

Torgnon Italy
Small village off the road up to Cervinia, good for bad-weather days. Some good cross-country loops.
1500m; slopes 1500–1965m
⛷ 7 ⛷ 6km

Torgon Switzerland
Old village in a pretty wooded setting, with a connection to the Portes du Soleil. Still some steep drag-lifts.
1150m; slopes 975–2275m
⛷ 209 ⛷ 650km

Le Tour 269
Charming, unspoiled hamlet at the head of the Chamonix valley.

La Toussuire 384

Trafoi Italy
Quiet, traditional village in the Val Venosta in the South Tyrol, covered by the Ortler Skiarena pass.
1570m; slopes 1570–2550m
⛷ 6 ⛷ 10km

Treble Cone 726

Tremblant 702

Trentino 485

Les Trois Vallées 402

Troodos Cyprus
Ski area on Mt Olympus, a 70-minute drive from Nicosia. Pretty, wooded slopes and fine views.
⛷ 4 ⛷ 5km

Tröpolach Austria
Small village at base of access gondola for Nassfeld ski area.
610m; slopes 610–2195m
⛷ 30 ⛷ 100km

Trysil 709

Tryvann 709

Tschagguns 180
Village in the Montafon valley.

Tsugaike Kogen Japan
Sizeable resort four hours from Tokyo, three hours from Osaka. Helicopter service to the top station.
800m; slopes 800–1700m ⛷ 28

Tulfes 147

Turoa 726

Turracherhöhe Austria
Tiny, unspoiled resort with varied intermediate slopes above and below it. A good outing from Bad Kleinkirchheim.
1765m; slopes 1400–2200m
⛷ 11 ⛷ 30km

Tyax Mountain Lake Resort Canada
Heli-skiing operation in the Chilcotin mountains – transfers from Whistler or Vancouver.

Uludag Turkey
Surprisingly suave, laid-back, well-equipped, purpose-built resort south of Istanbul.
1750m; slopes 1750–2322m
⛷ 14 ⛷ 15km

Unken Austria
Traditional village with the closest slopes to Salzburg.
565m; slopes 1000–1500m
⛷ 4 ⛷ 8km

Untergurgl 185
Valley-floor alternative to staying in Hochgurgl or Obergurgl.

Unternberg Austria
Riverside village with trail connecting into one of the longest, most snow-sure cross-country networks in Europe. St Margarethen downhill slopes close by.
1030m

Unterwasser-Toggenburg Switzerland
Old but not especially attractive resort 90 minutes from Zürich. Fabulous lake and mountain views. The more challenging half of the area shared with Wildhaus.
910m; slopes 900–2260m
⛷ 19 ⛷ 60km

Uttendorf-Weiss-See Austria
Astute alternative to crowded Kaprun when the snow line is high.
805m; slopes 1485–2600m
⛷ 9 ⛷ 18km

Vail 617

Valbella Switzerland
Convenient but ordinary village sharing large intermediate Lenzerheide area.
1540m; slopes 1230–2865m
⛷ 37 ⛷ 155km

Valberg France
Large Alpes-Maritimes resort (bigger than better-known Isola 2000) close to Nice.
1650m; slopes 1430–2100m
⛷ 26 ⛷ 90km

Val Cenis France
Two pleasant villages in the Haute Maurienne, over the Iseran pass (closed in winter) from Val d'Isère. Mostly north-facing runs; wooded lower down. Something for all levels, including excellent beginner slopes at Lanslevillard.
1400m; slopes 1400–2800m
⛷ 20 ⛷ 80km

Val d'Anniviers 541

Val di Fassa 485
Valley area of Campitello and Canazei – part of the Sella Ronda circuit.

Val d'Illiez Switzerland
Peaceful, unspoiled village a few minutes below Champoussin. Open-air thermal baths. Good views of impressive Dents du Midi.
950m
⛷ 209 ⛷ 650km

Val d'Isère 404

Val Ferret Switzerland
Old climbing village near Martigny, with spectacular views. Own tiny area.
1600m
⛷ 3 ⛷ 20km

Valfrejus France
A small, quiet and unusual modern resort in the Maurienne valley – built in the woods, with most of the slopes higher up above the tree line. Some genuine bumpy blacks and natural terrain-park. There are two hotels and a choice of restaurants.
1550m; slopes 1550–2740m
⛷ 13 ⛷ 65km

Val Gardena 470
Valley area of Selva, Ortisei and Santa Cristina – part of the Sella Ronda circuit.

Vallandry 255
Family-friendly satellite of Les Arcs. For package holidays see Peisey-Vallandry.

Valle Nevado 734

Valloire France
Old village above the Maurienne valley, with a fair-sized area of mainly intermediate skiing spread over three sectors, shared with Valmeinier. Snow on most of the slopes is affected by the sun, but there is a lot of snowmaking. A 2007 visitor reports 'mixed results' with the ESF. A new quad is planned at Valmeinier for 2007/08.
1430m; slopes 1430–2595m
⛷ 34 ⛷ 150km

Vallter 2000 Spain
Small resort on the far eastern fringes of the Pyrenees, close to the Costa Brava.
slopes 1950–2535m
⛷ 8 ⛷ 420 acres

Valmeinier France
Old mountain village with a modern purpose-built satellite where most people stay. Shares with Valloire the most extensive slopes in the Maurienne region, spreading widely over three mostly sunny sectors. New quad planned for 2007/08.
1500-1800m;
slopes 1430–2595m
⛷ 34 ⛷ 150km

Valmorel 414

Val Senales 479
Valley near Merano in the South Tyrol.

Val Thorens 416

Valtournenche 430
Cheaper alternative to Cervinia.

Vandans 180
Sizeable working village in the Montafon area.

Vars 362
Large, convenient purpose-built resort linked to Risoul.

Vasilitsa Greece
Resort in northern Greece, in the Pindos range, offering 'very good intermediate skiing', according to reports.
1750m ⛷ 2

Vaujany 245
Tiny village in the heart of the Alpe-d'Huez ski area.

Vegas Resort USA
Area formerly known as Lee Canyon, cut from forest only 50 minutes' drive from Las Vegas. Height and snowmaking gives fairly reliable snow. Night skiing.
2590m; slopes 2590–2840m
⛷ 3 ⛷ 200 acres

Velka-Race Slovakia
600m; slopes 600–1050m
⛷ 4 ⛷ 15km

Vemdalen 713

Vemdalsskalet 713

Venosc France
Captivating tiny village of cobbled streets, ancient church and craft shops.

Vent Austria
High, remote Oztal village known mainly as a touring base, with just enough lift-served skiing to warrant a day trip from nearby Obergurgl.
1900m; slopes 1900–2680m
⛷ 4 ⛷ 15km

Ventron France
Small village near La Bresse in the northerly Vosges mountains near Strasbourg, with more ski de fond than downhill terrain.
630m; slopes 900–1110m
⛷ 8 ⛷ 15km

Verbier 544

Vercorin 541

Verditz Austria
One of several small, mostly mountain-top areas overlooking the town of Villach.
675m; slopes 675–2165m
⛷ 5 ⛷ 17km

Vex Switzerland
Major village in unspoiled, attractive setting south of Sion. Verbier slopes accessed nearby at Mayens-de-l'Ours.
900m

Veysonnaz 544
Little, old village within Verbier's Four Valleys network.

Vichères-Liddes Switzerland
Limited area near to Martigny. Part of the Grand St Bernard region, including Val Ferret and Champex-Lac. Valid with the Valais ski Card.
1350m; slopes 1350–2270m
⛷ 4 ⛷ 15km

Vic-sur-Cère France
Charming village with fine architecture, beneath Super-Lioran ski area. Beautiful extinct-volcano scenery.
680m; slopes 1250–1850m
⛷ 24 ⛷ 60km

Viehhofen Austria
Cheaper place to stay when visiting Saalbach; 3km/2 miles from the Schönleiten gondola, and there is a run back to the village from the Asitz section.
860m ⛷ 1

Vigo di Fassa 485
Best base for the Fassa valley.

La Villa 463
Quiet Sella Ronda village.

Villabassa 479
Cross-country village in the South Tyrol. Niederdorf is its German name.

Villach-Dobratsch Austria
One of several small, mostly mountain-top areas overlooking the town of Villach.
900m; slopes 980–2165m
⛷ 8 ⛷ 15km

Villar-d'Arêne France
Tiny area on the main road between La Grave and Serre-Chevalier. Empty, immaculately groomed, short easy runs, plus a couple of hotels.
1650m

Villard-de-Lans France
Unspoiled, lively, traditional village west of Grenoble. Snow-sure, thanks to snowmaking.
1050m; slopes 1160–2170m
⛷ 29 ⛷ 130km

Villard-Reculas 245
Rustic village on periphery of Alpe-d'Huez ski area.

Villaroger 255
Rustic hamlet with direct links up to Arc 2000.

Villars 556

Vipiteno Italy
Bargain-shopping town close to Brenner Pass.
960m; slopes 960–2100m
⛷ 12 ⛷ 25km

Virgen Austria
Traditional village in a beautiful valley south of the Felbertauern tunnel. Slopes at Matrei.
1200m

Vitosha Bulgaria
Limited area of slopes and a few widely scattered hotels, 22km/ 14 miles from Sofia, leading to crowds at weekends. The slopes are north-facing and have a decent snow record.
1810m; slopes 1515–2290m
⛷ 8 ⛷ 29km

Vogel 720

Vorderlanersbach 138
Village with access to Mayrhofen's ski area.

Voss 709

Vuokatti Finland
Small mountain in a remarkable setting, surrounded on three sides by lots of little lakes. Good activity base. ⛷ 8

Wagrain Austria
Traditional village at the heart of the intermediate three-valley lift system linking Flachau and Alpendorf – all it part of the huge Salzburger Sportwelt Amadé lift-pass area that our figures relate to. New six-pack planned for 2007/08.
850m; slopes 850–2190m
⛷ 64 ⛷ 200km

Waidring Austria
Quiet valley village north of
Kitzbühel, with nursery slopes
on the doorstep and a powerful
gondola (with big car parks) on
the outskirts going up to
Steinplatte – an area of mainly
gentle open slopes which is also
accessible from Germany.
Impressive lift system with two
six-packs and four quads, but
still prone to weekend queues.
Slopes face north, and there is
extensive snowmaking.
780m; slopes 1230–1860m
🚠 8· 🎿 25km

Waiorau Snow Farm 726

Wald im Pinzgau Austria
Cross-country village surrounded
by Alpine areas – Gerlos, Krimml
and Neukirchen – and with Pass
Thurn also nearby.
885m
🚠 55 🎿 155km

Wanaka 726

Warth 165
Bregenzerwald area village near
Lech.

Waterville Valley USA
Popular New Hampshire area
with spread-out village built in
pleasing wooden low-rise style.
There are a couple of genuine
double-black-diamond mogul
fields, but most of the slopes
are intermediate.
600m; slopes 600–1215m
🚠 12 🎿 255 acres

Watles Italy
Village in the Val Venosta in the
South Tyrol covered by the
Ortler Skiarena pass.

Weinebene Austria
One of many gentle little areas
in Austria's easternmost ski
region near the Slovenian
border. No major resorts in the
vicinity.
1560m; slopes 1560–1835m
🚠 5 🎿 12km

Weissbach bei Lofer Austria
Traditional resort between Lofer
and Saalfelden. It has no slopes
of its own, but it's well placed
for touring the Tirol. Kitzbühel,
Saalbach, St Johann and Zell am
See are nearby.
665m

Weissensee Naggeralm
Austria
Little area in eastern Austria and
the location of Europe's largest
frozen lake, which is used for all
kinds of ice sports, including
ice-golf.
930m; slopes 930–1400m
🚠 5 🎿 6km

Weisspriach Austria
Hamlet on snowy pass near
Obertauern that shares its area
with Mauterndorf and St
Michael.
1115m; slopes 1115–2050m
🚠 5 🎿 30km

Wengen 558

Wentworth Canada
Long-established Nova Scotia
area with largest accessible
acreage in the Maritime
Provinces. Harsh climate ensures
good snow-cover despite low
altitude.
55m; slopes 55–300m
🚠 6 🎿 150 acres

Werfen Austria
Traditional village spoiled by the
Tauern autobahn, which runs
between it and the slopes. Good
touring to the Dachstein West
region.
620m

Werfenweng Austria
Hamlet with the advantage over
the main village of Werfen of
being away from the autobahn
and close to the slopes. Best for
novices.
1000m; slopes 1000–1835m
🚠 10 🎿 25km

Westendorf 229

Whakapapa 726

Whistler 692

Whitecap Mountains Resort
USA
Largest, snowiest area in
Wisconsin, close enough to Lake
Superior and Minneapolis to
ensure winds and weekend
crowds.
435m; slopes 435–555m
🚠 7 🎿 500 acres

Whiteface Mountain USA
Varied area in New York State
15km/10 miles from attractive
lakeside resort of Lake Placid.
93% snowmaking ensures good
snowcover. Plenty to do off the
slopes.
365m; slopes 365–1345m
🚠 10 🎿 211 acres

Whitefish Mountain Resort
USA
Resort formerly known as Big
Mountain, renamed to match the
nearby town. Impressive ski area
close to Canadian border and to
Montana's Glacier National Park.
Good snow and low prices. Lots
of redevelopment taking place.
Plans for 2007/08 include
another fast quad.
1370m; slopes 1370–2135m
🚠 12 🎿 3000 acres

White Pass Village USA
Closest area to Mt St Helens.
Remote and uncrowded with a
good snowfall record. Mostly
intermediate cruising.
1370m; slopes 1370–1825m
🚠 6 🎿 635 acres

Whitewater Canada
Renowned for powder (40% off-
piste), food ('Excellent day
lodge,' says a 2006 reporter)
and weekend party atmosphere.
Accommodation in the historic
town of Nelson or a great day
out from nearby Red Resort.
1640m; slopes 1640–2040m 🚠 3

Wildcat Mountain USA
New Hampshire area infamous
for bad weather, but one of the
best areas on a nice day.
Lodging in nearby Jackson and
North Conway.
slopes 600–1250m
🚠 4 🎿 225 acres

Wildhaus Switzerland
Undeveloped farming community
in stunning scenery near
Liechtenstein; popular with
families and serious
snowboarders. Shares its slopes
with Unterwasser.
1100m; slopes 1100–2260m
🚠 19 🎿 60km

Wildschönau 231

Willamette Pass USA
US speed skiing training base in
national forest near beautiful
Crater Lake, Oregon. Small but
varied slopes popular with
weekenders.
1560m; slopes 1560–2035m
🚠 7 🎿 550 acres

Williams USA
Tiny area above the main place
to stay for the Grand Canyon.
slopes 2010–2270m
🚠 2 🎿 50 acres

Windischgarsten Austria
Large working village in Upper
Austria with cross-country trails
around and downhill slopes at
nearby Hinterstoder and Spital
am Pyrhn.
600m

Winter Park 624

Wolf Creek USA
Remote area on a pass of the
same name, with 'the most
snow in Colorado' – 465 inches
a year. One-third of the terrain is
standard American trails through
the trees; two-thirds is
'wilderness', served by a single
lift. Great stop en route between
Taos and Telluride. Stay in
Pagosa Springs to the west, or
South Fork to the east.
3140m; slopes 3140–3630m
🚠 6 🎿 1600 acres

Wolf Mountain USA
Utah cross-country area close to
Salt Lake City. Powder Mountain
and Snowbasin are nearby
Alpine areas.
slopes 🚠 3 🎿 100 acres

Xonrupt France
Cross-country venue only 3km/
2 miles from nearest Alpine
slopes at Gérardmer.
715m

Yangji Resort South Korea
Modern resort an hour (60km/
37 miles) south of Seoul, with
runs cut out of dense forest.
Gets very crowded. 🚠 6

Ylläs 707

Yong Pyong Resort
South Korea
The first of South Korea's dozen
recently developed resorts, also
known as Dragon Valley.
200km/125 miles east of Seoul,
close to the east coast. Self-
contained purpose-built resort
village is centred on 200-room
Dragon Valley Hotel. Modern
lifts serve a small, mainly
wooded slope area, with
snowmaking on all its runs.
Daily night skiing. English web
site at www.yongpyong.co.kr.
750m; slopes 750–1460m
🚠 15 🎿 20km

Zakopane Poland
An interesting old town
100km/62 miles south of Kraków
on the Slovakian border. Mostly
intermediate slopes. In 2007 it
was reported to be renovating
its 70-year-old cable-car.
830m; slopes 1000–1960m
🚠 20 🎿 10km

Zao Japan
Big area with unpredictable
weather, four hours from Tokyo
by train. Known for 'chouoh' –
pines frozen into weird shapes.
Hot springs.
780m; slopes 780–1660m 🚠 42

Zauchensee Austria
Purpose-built resort isolated at
the head of its valley, at one
end of big three-valley lift
network linking it via
Flachauwinkl to Kleinarl – all
part of the Salzburger Sportwelt
ski pass area that our figures
relate to. 'Good intermediate
terrain and the lift system works
pretty efficiently,' comments a
2007 visitor.
855m; slopes 800–2185m
🚠 59 🎿 200km

Zell am See 235

Zell im Zillertal 175
Sprawling valley town with
slopes on two mountains.

Zermatt 563

Zillertal Austria
Valley of ten ski resorts, of
which the most well known is
Mayrhofen.

Zinal 541

Zug 165
Tiny village with Lech's toughest
skiing on its doorstep.

Zürs 165
High, smart but soulless village
on road to Lech.

Zweisimmen Switzerland
Limited but inexpensive base for
slopes around Gstaad, with its
own delightful little easy area
too.
965m; slopes 950–3000m
🚠 67 🎿 250km